ADMINISTRATIVE LAW

ADMINISTRATIVE LAW

BY
THE LATE

SIR WILLIAM WADE
QC, LLD, LittD (Hon), FBA

*An Honorary Bencher of Lincoln's Inn, Formerly Master of Gonville and Caius College,
Cambridge, Rouse Ball Professor of English Law in the University of Cambridge and
Professor of English Law in the University of Oxford*

AND

CHRISTOPHER FORSYTH
BSC, LLB (Natal), LLB, PhD (CANTAB)

*An Academic Bencher of the Inner Temple, Quondam Director of the Centre for Public
Law, Professor of Public Law and Private International Law, University of Cambridge
Extraordinary Professor of Law, University of Stellenbosch, Fellow of Robinson College
Member of 4–5 Gray's Inn Square*

Eleventh Edition

BY

CHRISTOPHER FORSYTH

OXFORD
UNIVERSITY PRESS

OXFORD
UNIVERSITY PRESS

Great Clarendon Street, Oxford, OX2 6DP,
United Kingdom

Oxford University Press is a department of the University of Oxford.
It furthers the University's objective of excellence in research, scholarship,
and education by publishing worldwide. Oxford is a registered trade mark of
Oxford University Press in the UK and in certain other countries

© Sir William Wade and Christopher Forsyth 2014

The moral rights of the authors have been asserted

Eighth edition 2000
Ninth edition 2004
Tenth edition 2009

Impression: 1

Public sector information reproduced under Open Government Licence v1.0
(http://www.nationalarchives.gov.uk/doc/open-government-licence/open-government-licence.htm)

Crown Copyright material reproduced with the permission of the
Controller, HMSO (under the terms of the Click Use licence)

Published in the United States of America by Oxford University Press
198 Madison Avenue, New York, NY 10016, United States of America

British Library Cataloguing in Publication Data
Data available

Library of Congress Control Number: 2014936310

ISBN 978-0-19-968370-3

Printed in Italy by
L.E.G.O. S.p.A.—Lavis TN

Links to third party websites are provided by Oxford in good faith and
for information only. Oxford disclaims any responsibility for the materials
contained in any third party website referenced in this work.

CONTENTS

PART III EUROPEAN INFLUENCES

PART IV POWERS AND JURISDICTION

PART V DISCRETIONARY POWER

PART VI NATURAL JUSTICE

PART VII REMEDIES AND LIABILITY

PART VIII ADMINISTRATIVE LEGISLATION AND ADJUDICATION

PREFACE

This is the third edition of this book to be published since the death of Sir William Wade in March 2004. The structure and style of the book, I hope, remain the same so that it is truly a fitting memorial to its senior author. But meeting the standard set by Sir William has become steadily more difficult. As the law becomes more complex the clarity that characterised earlier editions becomes elusive. And the electronic age, as well as the growth in the number of applications for judicial review, means that the student of administrative law is in constant danger of being overwhelmed by a deluge of decisions accessible immediately at the click of a mouse. Today's textbook writer can present only a snapshot of a moving target with inevitably some details out of focus.

In these circumstances the importance of principle and conceptual analysis becomes more important. Adherence to fundamental principle in the analysis and assessment of cases is necessary in order to impose order upon the 'wilderness of single instances' that otherwise threatens. And that order is essential to the great and abiding task of administrative law: the imposition of the rule of law onto the exercise of public power. Even a comprehensive account of the law can, in the absence of principle, readily lapse into superficiality.

Sir William in a letter to Lord Cooke of Thornton (written as long ago as 12 March 1988) wrote of the academic wanting 'everything clear and sharp and logical and in accordance with principle' with the judge, on the other hand, being resistant to being driven 'into a corner by ruthless logic and . . . compelled to decide contrary to what he wants'. While Sir William recognised that the judge's was 'a sound instinct for the administration of justice', he concluded: 'I am by my cloth obliged to protest when blurring becomes woolly thinking and blasphemy against basics.'

The distinction between the academic and judge may be noted in the distinct tendency in the Supreme Court to make decisions based upon pragmatism and practicality rather than principle. Thus the decision that the Upper Tribunal was only in certain circumstances subject to judicial review (discussed below at 222–4) was based not on a principled development of the law of jurisdiction but on a pragmatic desire to impose judicial review only when it was 'rational and proportionate' to do so. As worthy as this outcome may be, the court's path to it has sown uncertainty and conceptual confusion. A further example is the treatment by the Supreme Court of the distinction between law and fact as malleable. So the court can manipulate that distinction for pragmatic reasons (discussed below at 216–17) on grounds that have nothing to do with any conceptual difference between law and fact. Once more this approach sows uncertainty and forces the judge to decide cases on an artificial basis. These are bold decisions whose full impact remains to be determined. The Supreme Court's law-making powers, it is submitted, should be interstitial and incremental. It should develop the law within the constraints imposed by the fundamental principles of our subject.

A word should be added here about the Lord Chancellor's current programme to reform the application for judicial review (discussed at 567–8, 595 and Appendix 3). Some of the proposals for reform are to be welcomed (for instance, the creation of a Planning Court in the High Court and the extension of the 'leapfrogging' appeals procedure) but the general focus of the proposals is to restrict access to the Administrative Court to those claimants bringing applications for some ulterior or unjustified purpose. The trouble with this is that often the claimant with a well-founded claim is deterred (by a restriction of the availability of legal aid or a hostile costs regime) from making that claim as much as the claimant with an ill-founded claim. Moreover, there is an important public interest in ensuring compliance with the principles of good administration in decision making. This interest is served by subjecting decision making to judicial scrutiny even where the claimant has an ulterior motive. There is little awareness of these considerations in the proposed changes nor, it seems, does the evidence support many of the proposed changes. The final outcome of this reform process remains to be seen. Not all of the changes made may be beneficial. But judicial review is robust; apocalyptic predictions should be treated with caution.

Finally, I add a heartfelt word of thanks to my many students and colleagues who have probed and stimulated my thoughts about administrative law in the years since the last edition. But I owe particular thanks to those who have helped directly with particular parts of the task of writing this edition. They are Dr Alistair Price, Dr Mark Elliott, Catherine Maclay and Chintan Chandrachud. But in particular I want to thank Tom Pascoe who, as my research assistant, laboured mightily on this edition and developed a preternatural capacity to anticipate the changes which I thought should be incorporated into this edition. I thank them all most sincerely. I would like to thank also the team from OUP who nursed this mammoth text through the press. They are: Carol Barber, Suzy Armitage, Jeremy Langworthy and Carolyn Fox.

CFF

29 April 2014

Cambridge

TABLE OF STATUTES

A chronological list can be found on page xxxiv

TABLE OF STATUTES

A chronological list can be found on page xxxiv

TABLE OF EUROPEAN LEGISLATION AND INTERNATIONAL CONVENTIONS, DIRECTIVES AND TREATIES

CHRONOLOGICAL LIST OF STATUTES

For page references, see alphabetical table

1215	Magna Carta		1883	Municipal Corporations Act
1461	Statute 1 Edw. IV, c....1		1886	Local Government Act
1531	Statute of Sewers		1887–1945	British Settlements Acts
1539	Statute of Proclamations		1888	Local Government Act
1571	Statute		1889	Arbitration Act
1601	Poor Relief Act		1890–1913	Foreign Jurisdiction Acts
1660	Statute 12 Charles II, c....23		1892	Foreign Marriage Act
1679	Habeas Corpus Act		1893	Public Authorities Protection Act
1688	Bill of Rights		1893	Rules Publication Act
1700	Act of Settlement		1894	Local Government Act
1706	Act of Union		1899	Local Government Act
1707	Act of Union		1899	London Government Act
1742	Justices Jurisdiction Act		1908	Old Age Pensions Act
1751	Constables Protection Act		1908	Smallholdings and Allotments Act
1780	Constitution of Massachusetts (U.S.A.)		1911	National Insurance Act
			1911	Official Secrets Act
1800–1961	Crown Private Estates Acts		1911	Parliament Act
1816	Habeas Corpus Act		1911–39	Official Secrets Acts
1832	Reform Act		1920	Census Act
1834	Poor Law Act		1920	Emergency Powers Act
1835	Highway Act		1920	Government of Ireland Act
1835	Municipal Corporations Act		1921	Tribunals of Inquiry (Evidence) Act
1842	Defence Act			
1843	Scientific Societies Act		1923	Universities of Oxford and Cambridge Act
1845	Lands Clauses Act			
1845	Lands Clauses Consolidation Act		1925	Housing Act
1848	Summary Jurisdiction Act		1925	Land Registration Act
1848	Treason Act		1927	Audit (Local Authorities) Act
1849	Quarter Sessions Act		1930	Housing Act
1850	Court of Chancery, England, Act		1930	Land Drainage Act
1851	Evidence Act		1931	National Economy Act
1852	Court of Chancery Procedure Act		1931	Statute of Westminster
1857	Burial Act		1932	Wheat Act
1857	Summary Jurisdiction Act		1933	Administration of Justice (Miscellaneous Provisions) Act
1860	Petitions of Right Act			
1861	Offences Against the Person Act		1933	Local Government Act
1862	Habeas Corpus Act		1934	Betting and Lotteries Act
1868	Promissory Oaths Act		1936	Public Health Act
1873–75	Judicature Acts		1936	Tithe Act
1875	Public Health Act		1937	Local Government Superannuation Act
1881	Fugitive Offenders Act			
1882	Municipal Corporations Act		1938	Administration of Justice (Miscellaneous Provisions) Act

TABLE OF CASES

Principal references are shown in **bold** type

PART I

INTRODUCTION

1

INTRODUCTION

GOVERNMENT, LAW, AND JUSTICE

THE ADMINISTRATIVE STATE

'Until August 1914,' it has been said, 'a sensible law-abiding Englishman could pass through life and hardly notice the existence of the state, beyond the post office and the policeman.'[1] This worthy person could not, however, claim to be a very observant citizen. For by 1914 there were already abundant signs of the profound change in the conception of government which was to mark the twentieth century and which was to continue into the twenty-first century. The state schoolteacher, the national insurance officer, the job centre, the sanitary and factory inspectors, and, as the twentieth century progressed, the executive agency and the official regulator (complete with unattractive acronym), with their necessary companion the tax collector, were among the outward and visible signs of this change. The modern administrative state was taking shape, reflecting the feeling that it was the duty of government to provide remedies for social and economic evils of many kinds. This feeling was the natural consequence of the great constitutional reforms of the nineteenth century. The enfranchised population could now make its wants known, and through the ballot box it had acquired the power to make the political system respond.

The advent of the welfare state might be dated from the National Insurance Act 1911. But long before 1911 Parliament had imposed controls and regulations by such statutes as the Factories Acts, the Public Health Acts, and the railway legislation.[2] By 1854 there were already sixteen central government inspectorates.[3] The period 1865–1900 had been called 'the period of collectivism'[4] because of the outburst of regulatory legislation and the tendency to entrust more and more power to the state.[5] The author of that remark would have been hard put to it to find words for the period since the Second World War, which is as different from his own as his own was different from that of the Stuart kings. As his generation came to recognise the need for the administrative state, they had also to devise more efficient machinery. The Northcote-Trevelyan Report (1854) on the civil service was one milestone; another was the opening of the civil service to competitive examination in 1870. The modern ministerial department was taking shape and the doctrine of ministerial responsibility was crystallising, with its correlative principles of civil service anonymity and detachment from politics. Thus were laid the foundations of the vast and powerful bureaucracy which is the principal instrument of administration

---

[1] A. J. P. Taylor, *English History, 1914–1945*, 1.

[2] For the growth of the central government's powers and machinery in the nineteenth century see Holdsworth, *History of English Law*, xiv. 90–204.   [3] Parris, *Constitutional Bureaucracy*, 200.

[4] Dicey, *Law and Opinion in England in the Nineteenth Century*, 64.

[5] In 1888 Maitland wrote (*Constitutional History of England*, 1955 reprint, 501): 'We are becoming a much governed nation, governed by all manners of councils and boards and officers, central and local, high and low, exercising the powers which have been committed to them by modern statutes.'

today. Scarcely less striking has been the expansion of the sphere of local government, extending to education, town and country planning, and a great many other services and controls. The devolution of power has now been carried to new levels with the grant of substantial law-making powers to Scotland and Wales.

If the state is to care for its citizens from the cradle to the grave, to protect their environment, to educate them at all stages, to provide them with employment, training, houses, medical services, pensions, and, in the last resort, food, clothing, and shelter, it needs a huge administrative apparatus. Relatively little can be done merely by passing Acts of Parliament. There are far too many problems of detail, and far too many matters that cannot be decided in advance. No one may erect a building without planning permission, but no system of general rules can prescribe for every case. There must be discretionary power. If discretionary power is to be tolerable, it must be kept under two kinds of control: political control through Parliament, and legal control through the courts. Equally there must be control over the boundaries of legal power, as to which there is normally no discretion. If a water authority may levy sewerage rates only upon properties connected to public sewers, there must be means of preventing it from rating unsewered properties unlawfully.[6] The legal aspects of all such matters are the concern of administrative law.

ADMINISTRATIVE LAW

A first approximation to a definition of administrative law is to say that it is the law relating to the control of governmental power. This, at any rate, is the heart of the subject, as viewed by most lawyers. The governmental power in question is not that of Parliament: Parliament as the legislature is sovereign and, subject to one apparent exception,[7] is beyond legal control. The powers of all other public authorities are subordinated to the law, just as much in the case of the Crown and ministers as in the case of local authorities and other public bodies. All such subordinate powers have two inherent characteristics. First, they are all subject to legal limitations; there is no such thing as absolute or unfettered administrative power. Secondly, and consequentially, it is always possible for any power to be abused. Even where Parliament enacts that a minister may make such order as he thinks fit for a certain purpose, the court may still invalidate the order if it infringes one of the many judge-made rules. And the court will invalidate it, a fortiori, if it infringes the limits that Parliament itself has ordained.

The primary purpose of administrative law, therefore, is to keep the powers of government within their legal bounds, so as to protect the citizen against their abuse. The powerful engines of authority must be prevented from running amok. 'Abuse', it should be made clear, carries no necessary innuendo of malice or bad faith. Government departments may misunderstand their legal position as easily as may other people, and the law which they have to administer is frequently complex and uncertain. Abuse in this broad sense is therefore inevitable, and it is all the more necessary that the law should provide means to check it. It is a common occurrence that a minister's order is set aside by the court as unlawful, that a compulsory purchase order has to be quashed or that the decision of a planning authority is declared to be irregular and void. The courts are constantly occupied with cases of this kind which are nothing more than the practical application of the rule of law, meaning that the government must have legal warrant for what it does and that if it acts unlawfully the citizen has an effective legal remedy.

---

[6] See *Daymond* v. *Plymouth City Council* [1976] AC 609; below, p. 726.
[7] European Community law; below, p. 162.

As well as power there is duty. It is also the concern of administrative law to see that public authorities can be compelled to perform their duties if they make default. HM Revenue & Customs may have a duty to repay tax, a licensing authority may have a duty to grant a licence, the Home Secretary may have a duty to admit an immigrant. The law provides compulsory remedies for such situations, thus dealing with the negative as well as the positive side of maladministration.

FUNCTION DISTINGUISHED FROM STRUCTURE

As a second approximation to a definition, administrative law may be said to be the body of general principles which govern the exercise of powers and duties by public authorities. This is only one part of the mass of law to which public authorities are subject. All the detailed law about their composition and structure, though clearly related to administrative law, lies beyond the scope of the subject. So it is not necessary to investigate how local councillors are elected or what are the qualifications for service on various tribunals. Nor is it necessary to enumerate all the powers which governmental authorities possess. A great deal must be taken for granted in order to clear the field.

What has to be isolated is the law about the *manner* in which public authorities must exercise their functions, distinguishing function from structure and looking always for general principles. If it appears that the law requires that a man should be given a fair hearing before his house can be pulled down, or before his trading licence can be revoked, and before he can be dismissed from a public office, a general principle of administrative law can be observed. If likewise a variety of ministers and local authorities are required by law to exercise their various statutory powers reasonably and only upon relevant grounds, there too is a general principle. Although this book supplies some limited particulars about the structure of public authorities and about some of their more notable powers, this is done primarily for the sake of background information. The essence of administrative law lies in judge-made doctrines which apply right across the board and which therefore set legal standards of conduct for public authorities generally.

There are, however, some areas in which more attention must be paid to structure. This is particularly the case with special tribunals and statutory inquiries, and to some extent also with delegated legislation. They stand apart for the reason that the problems which need discussion relate as much to the organisation of the machinery for dispensing justice, and in the case of delegated legislation to the machinery of government, as to the role of the courts of law.

'RED LIGHTS' AND 'GREEN LIGHTS'

This book's conception of administrative law has been said to typify a 'red light' theory of the subject, aimed mostly at curbing governmental power, as contrasted with 'green light theory' whose advocates favour 'realist and functionalist jurisprudence' designed to make administration easier and better.[8]

> What one person sees as control of arbitrary power may, however, be experienced by another as a brake on progress. While red light theory looks to the model of the balanced constitution, green light theory finds the 'model of government' more congenial.

---

[8] Harlow and Rawlings, *Law and Administration*, 3rd edn, 31.

Where red light theorists favour judicial control of executive power, green light theorists are inclined to pin their hopes on the political process.[9]

The path of progress by green light, it is said, is through improved ministerial responsibility, more effective consultation, decentralisation of power, a reduced role for the judiciary (therefore rejecting human rights legislation), freedom of information and other reforms to be sought by political means.[10] But these objectives, whether or not desirable, are of a different order from those of this book, and there is no easy 'red or green' contrast between them. This book is concerned with the present realities of legislative, executive and judicial power and aims to analyse them in a way helpful to lawyers. There is an 'amber' element in that some subjects, such as devolution of power and freedom of information, are common ground between both approaches. But the purposes of the legal and the political approaches are so different that they cannot usefully be presented as a neat contrast of alternatives. 'Chalk or cheese' would be a better metaphor than 'red or green'.

ALLIANCE OF LAW AND ADMINISTRATION

It is a mistake to suppose that a developed system of administrative law is necessarily antagonistic to efficient government. Intensive administration will be more tolerable to the citizen, and the government's path will be smoother, where the law can enforce high standards of legality, reasonableness and fairness. Nor should it be supposed that the continuous intervention by the courts, which is now so conspicuous, means that the standard of administration is low. This was well observed by Sir John Donaldson MR:[11]

> Notwithstanding that the courts have for centuries exercised a limited supervisory jurisdiction by means of the prerogative writs, the wider remedy of judicial review and the evolution of what is, in effect, a specialist administrative or public law court is a post-war development. This development has created a new relationship between the courts and those who derive their authority from the public law, one of partnership based on a common aim, namely the maintenance of the highest standards of public administration.
>
> With very few exceptions, all public authorities conscientiously seek to discharge their duties strictly in accordance with public law and in general they succeed. But it must be recognised that complete success by all authorities at all times is a quite unattainable goal. Errors will occur despite the best of endeavours. The courts, for their part, must and do respect the fact that it is not for them to intervene in the administrative field, unless there is a reason to inquire whether a particular authority has been successful in its endeavours. The courts must and do recognise that, where errors have, or are alleged to have, occurred, it by no means follows that the authority is to be criticised. In proceedings for judicial review, the applicant no doubt has an axe to grind. This should not be true of the authority.

Provided that the judges observe the proper boundaries of their office, administrative law and administrative power should be friends and not enemies. The contribution that the law can and should make is creative rather than destructive.

The connecting thread which runs throughout is the quest for administrative justice. At every point the question is, how can the profession of the law contribute to the improvement of the technique of government? It is because all the various topics offer scope for this missionary spirit that they form a harmonious whole. Subject as it is to the

---

[9] Ibid.   [10] See (1979) 42 *MLR* 1, [1985] *PL* 564, [2000] *MLR* 159 (J. A. G. Griffith).
[11] *R* v. *Lancashire CC ex p Huddleston* [1986] 2 All ER 941 at 945.

vast empires of executive power that have been created, the public must be able to rely on the law to ensure that all this power may be used in a way conformable to its ideas of fair dealing and good administration. As liberty is subtracted, justice must be added. The more power the government wields, the more sensitive is public opinion to any kind of abuse or unfairness. Taken together, the work of judiciary and legislature amounts to an extensive system of protection. It has its weaknesses, but it also has great strengths.

PUBLIC LAW AND POLITICAL THEORY

It would be natural to suppose that there must be intimate connections between constitutional and administrative law and political theory. The nature of democracy, governmental power, the position of the Crown—these and many such subjects have foundations which are first and foremost political and only secondarily legal. Yet legal exposition and analysis normally inhabits a world of its own, paying due respect indeed to history but little or none to theories of government. Despite some brave attempts which have been made from the legal side,[12] most students of public law feel no need to explore the theory which forms its background; or, if they do, they find little illumination.

Yet it is possible to claim that 'the nature and content of constitutional and administrative law can only be properly understood against the background of political theory which a society actually espouses, or against such a background which a particular commentator believes that a society ought to espouse'.[13] This is of course true in the sense that every lawyer will carry his own ideas of the political and social environment in which he works, and the better he understands it, the better will be his service to the community. But that need not involve political theory in the abstract. Legal antipathy to political theory is likely to be motivated by instinctive belief in the virtue of objectivity in law, the belief that law should be kept as distinct as possible from politics, and that there is positive merit in keeping a gulf between them. A judge or an advocate may be a conservative, a socialist or a Marxist, but he will be a good judge or advocate only if his understanding of the law is unaffected by his political theory; and the same may be true of a textbook writer.

The most obvious opportunities for theory lie on the plane of constitutional law. Does the law provide a coherent conception of the state? Is it, or should it be, based on liberalism, corporatism, pluralism, or other such principles? What are its implications as to the nature of law and justice? More pragmatically, should there be a separation of powers, and if so how far? Is a sovereign parliament a good institution? Is it right for Parliament to be dominated by the government? Ought there to be a second chamber? The leading works on constitutional law, however, pay virtually no attention to such questions, nor can it be said that their authors' understanding of the law is noticeably impaired. The gulf between the legal rules and principles which they expound, on the one hand, and political ideology on the other, is clear and fundamental, and the existence of that gulf is taken for granted.

---

[12] Notably the books by P. P. Craig, *Public Law and Democracy in the United Kingdom and in the United States of America*; T. R. S. Allan, *Law, Liberty, and Justice*; M. Loughlin, *Public Law and Political Theory*; and articles by Sir John Laws, [1995] *PL* 72, [1996] *PL* 622 and Sir Stephen Sedley, (1994) 110 *LQR* 270, [1995] *PL* 386; Paul Craig and Richard Rawlings (eds.), *Law and Administration in Europe: Essays in Honour of Carol Harlow* (2003); 'Theory and Values in Public Law' [2005] *PL* 48 (M. Loughlin). See also Harlow and Rawlings, *Law and Administration*, 3rd edn, ch. 1, for discussion and references. See, further, Craig, 'Political Constitutionalism and Judicial Review' in Forsyth, Elliott, Jhaveri and Scully-Hill (eds.), *Effective Judicial Review: A Cornerstone of Good Governance* (2010), 19–42, and Adam Tomkins, *Our Republican Constitution* (2005). [13] Craig, *Public Law and Democracy*, 1.

On the plane of administrative law the openings for political theory are even fewer. Where the emphasis falls, as it does in this book, upon the central body of legal rules which regulate the use of governmental power, the focus is narrower. Those rules are based upon elementary concepts of legality, reasonableness and fairness which are self-evident in their own right and are even further detached from politics than are the principles of constitutional law. Although their natural home is in a liberal democracy, there is no necessary reason why they should not be observed under any regime, even if illiberal or undemocratic. The central part of administrative law, as presented in this book, has a neutrality which is lacking in constitutional law. Constitutional law and administrative law are subjects which interlock closely and overlap extensively. The rule of law, for instance, is a basic concept which runs through them both and which offers scope for political theory as well as for the discussion of its practical features which will be found below. But other such universals are not easily found in the field of administrative law, and the lack of them limits the assistance which political theory can provide.

CHARACTERISTICS OF THE LAW

THE ANGLO-AMERICAN SYSTEM

The British system of administrative law, which is followed throughout the English-speaking world, has some salient characteristics, which mark it off sharply from the administrative law of other European countries. Although in the United States of America it has naturally followed its own line of evolution, it is recognisably the same system.[14] This is true also of Scotland, although it must never be forgotten that Scots law may differ materially from English.[15]

The outstanding characteristic of the Anglo-American system is that the ordinary courts, and not special administrative courts, decide cases involving the validity of governmental action. The ordinary law of the land, as modified by Acts of Parliament, applies to ministers, local authorities, and other agencies of government, and the ordinary courts dispense it. This is part of the traditional concept of the rule of law, as explained in the next chapter. This has both advantages and disadvantages. The advantages are that the citizen can turn to courts of high standing in the public esteem, whose independence is beyond question; that highly efficient remedies are available; that there are none of the demarcation problems of division of jurisdictions; and that the government is seen to be subject to the ordinary law of the land. Its disadvantages are that many judges are not expert in administrative law: that neglect of the subject in the past has seriously weakened it at times; and that its principles have sometimes been submerged in the mass of miscellaneous law which the ordinary courts administer. These disadvantages have recently become less menacing as the judiciary has become both more specialised and more determined to find remedies for any kind of governmental abuse.

---

[14] The British and American systems are compared in Schwartz and Wade, *Legal Control of Government*.

[15] For the Scots system see Mitchell, *Constitutional Law*, 2nd edn, pt 3; Scottish Law Commission's Memorandum No. 14 (1971, A. W. Bradley); *The Laws of Scotland* (Stair Memorial Encyclopaedia), i (A. W. Bradley).

THE CONTINENTAL SYSTEM

In France, Italy, Germany and many other countries there is a separate system of administrative courts which deal with administrative cases exclusively. As a natural consequence, administrative law develops on its own independent lines, and is not enmeshed with ordinary private law as it is in the Anglo-American system. In France droit administratif is a highly specialised science, administered by the judicial wing of the Conseil d'État, which is staffed by judges of great professional expertise, and by a network of local tribunals of first instance.[16] Courts of this kind, whose work is confined to administrative law, may have a clearer view of the developments needed to keep pace with the powers of the state than have courts which are maids of all work. Certainly the Conseil d'État has shown itself more aware of the demands of justice in respect of financial compensation,[17] in contrast to the English reluctance—as Lord Wilberforce has observed.[18] But the French system is not without its disadvantages. Its remedies are narrow in scope and not always effective, and the division of jurisdictions between civil and administrative courts is the subject of technical rules which can cause much difficulty.

Although the structure of the courts is so different, many of the cases that come before the Conseil d'État are easily recognisable as the counterparts of familiar English situations. Review of administrative findings of fact and determinations of law, abuse of discretion, ultra vires—all of these and many other English rubrics can be illustrated from the administrative law of France. There is also the similarity that both English and French systems are contained in case law rather than in any statutory code. French authorities are by no means out of place when precedents are being sought for guidance on some novel issue.

EUROPEAN UNION LAW

The European Communities, now the European Union, of which Britain became a member in 1973, have their own legal system, which has been vigorously developed by the European Court of Justice in Luxembourg in accordance with a series of treaties (Rome (1957) to Lisbon (2009)) and the legislation made under them by the Community authorities. It is a condition of membership, fulfilled in Britain by the European Communities Act 1972,[19] that Community law takes precedence over national law, and many rules of Community law have direct effect in the Member States, so that they must be applied and enforced by national courts. A brief general account of this system will be found below.[20] Community law contains its own administrative law, under which the Court of Justice can annul unlawful acts of the Community authorities and award compensation against them. The Court's constitution and powers are modelled on those of the French Conseil d'État. The subordination of all the law of the Member States to Community law as declared by the Court makes the Court an extremely powerful tribunal.

The impact on British administrative law, which came slowly at first, has now made itself felt dramatically. Community law has revolutionised one of the fundamentals of constitutional law, as explained later, by demanding that an Act of our sovereign Parliament must be 'disapplied' by a British court if held to be in conflict with Community law;[21] and ministerial regulations have been invalidated by judgments given in Luxembourg.[22]

---

[16] See Brown and Bell, *French Administrative Law*, 5th edn.   [17] As noted below, p. 285.
[18] In *Hoffmann–La Roche & Co v. Secretary of State for Trade and Industry* [1975] AC 295 at 358, contrasting 'more developed legal systems'.   [19] s. 2. See below, p. 162.
[20] See p. 156.
[21] Below, p. 163.   [22] As in the *Bourgoin* case, below, p. 663.

Wide categories of government liability, enforceable in British courts, have been created similarly, as will later be explained.[23] The incoming tide, as Lord Denning once described it,[24] may percolate into any creek or backwater of our law, which will then be submerged by its superior power.

EUROPEAN HUMAN RIGHTS

Another European system which our law is now absorbing is that of the European Convention on Human Rights and Fundamental Freedoms, to which Britain acceded as one of the founder members in 1950 but to which it gave domestic legal force only in 2000. During the intervening half-century the government accepted the obligations of the Convention as interpreted by the European Court of Human Rights in Strasbourg but refused to make them enforceable in British courts. That anomaly was ended by the Human Rights Act 1998 which came into force in 2000. As explained later,[25] that Act provides that the decisions and practice of the European Court are to be followed by British courts in enforcing the human rights set out in the Convention and incorporated in the Act. Here therefore is another non-indigenous source of law, which is both fundamental and far-reaching.

HISTORICAL DEVELOPMENT

Administrative law in England has a long history, but the subject in its modern form did not begin to emerge until the second half of the seventeenth century. A number of its basic rules can be dated back to that period, and some, such as the principles of natural justice, are still older. In earlier times the justices of the peace, who were used as all-purpose administrative authorities, were superintended by the judges of assize, who on their circuits conveyed instructions from the Crown, dealt with defaults and malpractices, and reported back to London on the affairs of the country. Under the Tudor monarchy this system was tightened up under the authority of the Privy Council and of the provincial Councils in the North and in Wales.[26] This was a long step towards the centralisation of power in a state of the modern type. The Privy Council's superintendence was exercised through the Star Chamber, which could punish those who disobeyed the justices of the peace, and reprove or replace the justices themselves. But the powers of the state were not often challenged at the administrative level. A freeman of a borough might resist unlawful expulsion by obtaining a writ of mandamus ('a mandatory order' in modern parlance)[27] and a writ of certiorari (now 'a quashing order') might lie against the Commissioners of Sewers if they usurped authority.[28] But it was on the constitutional rather than on the administrative plane, and notably on the battlefields of the civil war, that the issues between the Crown and its subjects were fought out.

After the abolition of the Star Chamber in 1642, and the destruction of most of the Privy Council's executive power by the Revolution of 1688, a new situation arose. The old machinery of central political control had been broken, and nothing was put in its place. Instead, the Court of King's Bench stepped into the breach and there began the era of the control of administration through the courts of law. The King's Bench made its writs of

---

[23] Below, p. 662.   [24] *Bulmer (HP) Ltd* v. *J Bollinger SA* [1974] Ch 401 at 418.
[25] Below, p. 135.   [26] Holdsworth, *History of English Law*, iv. 71.
[27] As in *Bagg's Case* (1616) 11 Co Rep 93; below, p. 406.
[28] As in *Hetley* v. *Boyer* (1614) Cro Jac 336; *Smith's Case* (1670) 1 Vent 66; below, p. 293.

mandamus, certiorari, and prohibition (now 'a prohibiting order'), as well as its ordinary remedy of damages, available to anyone who wished to dispute the legality of administrative acts of the justices and of such other authorities as there were. The political dangers of doing so had ceased to exist, and the field was clear for the development of administrative law. At first the justices had many administrative functions, but in the course of the nineteenth century most of these were transferred to elected local authorities. All through this time the courts were steadily extending the doctrine of ultra vires and the principles of judicial review. These rules were applied without distinction to all the new statutory authorities, such as county councils, boards of works, school boards and commissioners, just as they had been to the justices of the peace. As the administrative state began to emerge later in the nineteenth century, exactly the same rules were applied to central government departments. This is the same body of law which is still being developed today. The history of many of the detailed doctrines, such as the rules for review of jurisdictional questions, the principles of natural justice, and the scope of certiorari, will be seen in the treatment of them later in this book.

Administrative law, as it now exists, has therefore a continuous history from the later part of the seventeenth century. The eighteenth century was the period par excellence of the rule of law,[29] and it provided highly congenial conditions in which the foundations of judicial control could be consolidated. It is remarkable how little fundamental alteration has proved necessary in the law laid down two centuries ago in a different age. The spread of the tree still increases and it throws out new branches, but its roots remain where they have been for centuries.

TWENTIETH-CENTURY FAILINGS

Up to about the end of the nineteenth century administrative law kept pace with the expanding powers of the state. But in the twentieth century it began to fall behind. The courts showed signs of losing confidence in their constitutional function and they hesitated to develop new rules in step with the mass of new regulatory legislation. In 1914 the House of Lords missed an important opportunity to apply the principles of natural justice to statutory inquiries,[30] a new form of administrative procedure which ought to have been made to conform to the ordinary man's sense of fairness, for example by allowing him to know the reasons for the minister's decision and to see the inspector's report on which the decision was based. Not until 1958 were these mistakes corrected. Meanwhile the executive took full advantage of the weak judicial policy, and inevitably there were loud complaints about bureaucracy. Eminent lawyers, including a Lord Chief Justice, published books under such titles as *The New Despotism*[31] and *Bureaucracy Triumphant*.[32] At the same time, Parliament was losing its control over ministers, so making it all the more obvious that the law was failing in its task of enforcing standards of fairness in the exercise of governmental powers.

The report of the Committee on Ministers' Powers of 1932[33] was intended to appease the complaints about bureaucracy. It covered ministerial powers of delegated legislation and of judicial or quasi-judicial decision.[34] Although the Committee made some sound criticisms of the system of public inquiries which had come into use and recommendations for fairer and more impartial administrative procedures, these proved unacceptable

---

[29] See below, p. 90.   [30] *Local Government Board* v. *Arlidge* [1915] AC 120; below, p. 412.
[31] By Lord Hewart CJ (1929).   [32] By Sir Carleton Allen (1931).   [33] Cmd 4060 (1932).
[34] See below, p. 31.

to the strongly entrenched administration.[35] In most respects it was little more than an academic exercise. It did not discuss the scope of judicial control, and although it called for the vigilant observance of the principles of natural justice, it did not consider how widely they should be applied.

Discontent with administrative procedures therefore continued to accumulate. The practical reforms that were needed for tribunals and inquiries were not made until 1958, when the Report of the Committee on Administrative Tribunals and Enquiries (the Franks Committee)[36] led to the Tribunals and Inquiries Act 1958 and to a programme of procedural improvements, all to be supervised by a new body, the Council on Tribunals. The story of these reforms is told in later chapters.[37] They were of great importance in administrative law, but they were in no way due to the work of the courts.

THE RELAPSE AND THE REVIVAL

During and after the Second World War a deep gloom settled upon administrative law, which reduced it to the lowest ebb at which it had stood for centuries. The courts and the legal profession seemed to have forgotten the achievements of their predecessors and they showed little stomach for continuing their centuries-old work of imposing law upon government. It was understandable that executive power was paramount in wartime, but it was hard to understand why, in the flood of new powers and jurisdictions that came with the welfare state, administrative law should not have been vigorously revived, just when the need for it was greatest.

Instead, the subject relapsed into an impotent condition, marked by neglect of principles and literal verbal interpretation of the blank-cheque powers which Parliament showered upon ministers. The leading cases made a dreary catalogue of abdication and error. Eminent judges said that the common law must be given a death certificate, having lost the power to control the executive;[38] that certiorari was not available against an administrative act;[39] that there was no such thing in Britain as droit administratif;[40] and that there was no developed system of administrative law.[41] The following are some of the aberrations of what might be called 'the great depression':

The court's power to quash for error on the face of the record was denied.[42]

The principles of natural justice were held not to apply to the cancellation of a licence depriving a man of his livelihood.[43]

Statutory phrases like 'if the minister is satisfied' were held to confer unfettered and uncontrollable discretion.[44]

Statutory restrictions on legal remedies were literally interpreted, contrary to long-settled principles.[45]

The Crown was allowed unrestricted 'Crown privilege' so as to suppress evidence needed by litigants.[46]

---

[35] 'Few reports have assembled so much wisdom whilst proving so completely useless... its recommendations are forgotten, even by lawyers and administrators, and in no important respect did the report influence, much less delay, the onrush of administrative power, and the supersession of the ordinary forms of law which is taking place to-day.' Professor G. W. Keeton in *The Nineteenth Century and After* (1949), 230.

[36] Cmnd 218 (1957). The Act of 1958 has been replaced by the Tribunals and Inquiries Acts 1971 and 1992.

[37] Below, pp. 762, 794.   [38] Lord Devlin in 8 *Current Legal Problems* (1956), 14.

[39] Lord MacDermott, *Protection from Power under English Law* (1957), 88.   [40] Below, p. 18.

[41] Lord Reid in *Ridge v. Baldwin* [1964] AC 40 at 72, quoted below, p. 416.   [42] Below, p. 225.

[43] Below, p. 414.   [44] Below, p. 357.   [45] Below, p. 625.   [46] Below, p. 711.

It was not even as if these were matters of first impression where the court had to consider questions of legal policy. Plentiful materials, in some cases going back for centuries, were available in the law, but they were ignored.

Fortunately, in the 1960s the judicial mood completely changed. It began to be understood how much ground had been lost and what damage had been done to the only defences against abuse of power which still remained. Already in the 1950s the courts had reinstated judicial review for error on the face of the record;[47] and there had been the statutory and administrative reforms of tribunal and inquiry procedures,[48] which helped to give a lead. Soon the courts began to send out a stream of decisions which reinvigorated administrative law and re-established continuity with the past. The principles of natural justice were given their proper application, providing a broad foundation for a kind of code of administrative due process.[49] The notion of unfettered administrative discretion was totally rejected.[50] Restrictions on remedies were brushed aside where there was excess of jurisdiction, in accordance with 200 years of precedent;[51] and the law was widened so as to make an excess of jurisdiction out of almost every error.[52] The citadel of Crown privilege was overturned and unjustifiable claims were disallowed.[53] In all these matters the rules for the protection of the citizen had been repudiated by the courts. All were now reactivated. Lord Reid's remark of 1963 that 'we do not have a developed system of administrative law' was countered in 1971 by Lord Denning's, that 'it may truly now be said that we have a developed system of administrative law'.[54] Both Lord Reid and Lord Denning had made conspicuous contributions to its development, but they had done so more by steering the law back onto its old course than by making new deviations.

In retrospect it can be seen that the turning-point of the judicial attitude came in 1963 with the decision of the House of Lords which revived the principles of natural justice.[55] From then on a new mood pervaded the courts. It was given still further impetus by a group of striking decisions in 1968–9, one of which, Lord Diplock said,[56]

> made possible the rapid development in England of a rational and comprehensive system of administrative law on the foundation of the concept of ultra vires.

Since then the judges have shown no reluctance to reformulate principles and consolidate their gains. They have pressed on with what Lord Diplock in a case of 1981 described as[57]

> that progress towards a comprehensive system of administrative law that I regard as having been the greatest achievement of the English courts in my judicial lifetime.

So conspicuous has that progress been that he said in the same case that judicial statements on matters of public law if made before 1950 were likely to be a misleading guide to what the law is today.

A DEVELOPED SYSTEM?

Had the materials not been neglected, a developed system could have been recognised long beforehand. In 1888 Maitland had percipiently remarked:[58]

[47] Below, p. 224. [48] Below, p. 800. [49] Below, p. 375. [50] Below, p. 295.
[51] Below, p. 612. [52] Below, p. 219. [53] Below, p. 713.
[54] *Breen* v. *Amalgamated Engineering Union* [1971] 2 QB 175 at 189.
[55] *Ridge* v. *Baldwin* (above).
[56] In the *Racal* case (below, p. 220), referring to the *Anisminic* case (below, p. 219).
[57] In the *Inland Revenue Commissioner's Case* (below, p. 586). See likewise Lord Diplock's remarks in *O'Reilly* v. *Mackman* [1983] 2 AC 237 at 279 and in *Mahon* v. *Air New Zealand* [1984] AC 808 at 816.
[58] *Constitutional History of England* (1955 reprint), 505.

If you take up a modern volume of the reports of the Queen's Bench Division, you will find that about half the cases reported have to do with rules of administrative law; I mean such matters as local rating, the powers of local boards, the granting of licences for various trades and professions, the Public Health Acts, the Education Acts, and so forth.

And he added a caution against neglecting these matters, since otherwise a false and antiquated notion of the constitution would be formed. But his advice was not taken. No systematic treatises were published.[59] The decisions on housing, education, rating, and so on were looked upon merely as technicalities arising on some isolated statute, and not as sources of general rules. Tennyson's description of the law as a 'wilderness of single instances'[60] exactly fitted the profession's attitude. So far from undertaking systematic study, generations of lawyers were being brought up to believe, as Dicey had supposedly maintained, that administrative law was repugnant to the British constitution.[61] This belief was misconceived, as explained below,[62] but it blighted the study of the law in what should have been a formative period. Even Lord Hewart, despite his protests in *The New Despotism* and elsewhere against bureaucracy and its devices for evading judicial control, referred disparagingly to 'what is called, in Continental jargon, "administrative law" '.[63]

Whether a developed system or not, administrative law is a highly insecure science so long as it is subject to such extreme vacillations in judicial policy as have taken place since the Second World War. One of the arguments for a written constitution and a new Bill of Rights is that they should give the judiciary more confidence in their constitutional position and more determination to resist misuse of governmental power, even in the face of the most sweeping legislation. At the present time the courts are vigorously asserting their powers, now augmented by the Human Rights Act 1998, and there seems to be no danger of another judicial relapse.

---

[59] Port, *Administrative Law*, appeared in 1929. But there was no full-scale treatment of judicial review until Professor de Smith's pioneering work, *Judicial Review of Administrative Action*, was first published in 1959. The treatment in *Halsbury's Laws of England* was fragmentary and inadequate until a title on Administrative Law, by Professor de Smith and others, appeared in the 4th edn, 1973.

[60] 'Aylmer's Field', line 441.

[61] In 1915 Dicey published a short article on the *Rice* and *Arlidge* cases (below, pp. 408–9) entitled 'The Development of Administrative Law in England', 31 *LQR* 495. But this did not remove the misconceptions which he had caused.   [62] Below, p. 18.

[63] *Not Without Prejudice*, 96.

2

CONSTITUTIONAL FOUNDATIONS OF THE POWERS OF THE COURTS

THE RULE OF LAW

LEGALITY AND DISCRETIONARY POWER

The British constitution is founded on the rule of law,[1] and administrative law is the area where this principle is to be seen in its most active operation. The rule of law has a number of different meanings and corollaries. Its primary meaning is that everything must be done according to law. Applied to the powers of government, this requires that every government authority which does some act which would otherwise be a wrong (such as taking a man's land), or which infringes a man's liberty (as by refusing him planning permission), must be able to justify its action as authorised by law—and in nearly every case this will mean authorised directly or indirectly by Act of Parliament. Every act of governmental power, i.e. every act which affects the legal rights, duties or liberties of any person, must be shown to have a strictly legal pedigree. The affected person may always resort to the courts of law, and if the legal pedigree is not found to be perfectly in order the court will invalidate the act, which he can then safely disregard.

That is the principle of legality. But the rule of law demands something more, since otherwise it would be satisfied by giving the government unrestricted discretionary powers, so that everything that they did was within the law. *Quod principi placuit legis habet vigorem* (the sovereign's will has the force of law) is a perfectly legal principle, but it expresses rule by arbitrary power rather than rule according to ascertainable law. The secondary meaning of the rule of law, therefore, is that government should be conducted within a framework of recognised rules and principles which restrict discretionary power. Coke spoke in picturesque language of 'the golden and straight metwand' of law, as opposed to 'the uncertain and crooked cord of discretion'.[2] Many of the rules of administrative law are rules for restricting the wide powers which Acts of Parliament confer very freely on ministers and other authorities. Thus the Home Secretary has a nominally unlimited power to revoke any television licence and a local planning authority may make planning

---

[1] The classic exposition is that of Dicey, *The Law of the Constitution*, ch. 4. And see the valuable modern account in [2007] *CLJ* 67 (Lord Bingham) delivering the Sir David Williams lecture. Lord Bingham subsequently expanded his lecture into an important book, *The Rule of Law* (2010). The principle is recognised, if not affirmed, in the statute book. The Constitutional Reform Act 2005, s. 1, provides that the Act 'does not adversely affect (a) the existing constitutional principle of the rule of law, or (b) the Lord Chancellor's existing constitutional role in relation to that principle'. For a different view see Allan, *The Sovereignty of Law: Freedom, Constitution and the Common Law* (2013), ch. 3.   [2] 4 Inst. 41.

permission subject to such conditions as it thinks fit, but the courts will not allow these powers to be used in ways which Parliament is not thought to have intended.[3] An essential part of the rule of law, accordingly, is a system of rules for preventing the abuse of discretionary power. Intensive government of the modern kind cannot be carried on without a great deal of discretionary power. And the rule of law requires that the courts should prevent the abuse of such powers. For this purpose the courts have performed many notable exploits, reading between the lines of the statutes and developing general doctrines for keeping executive power within proper guidelines, both as to substance and as to procedure.[4] All this is the exemplification of the rule of law to which 'the principles of judicial review' have been said by Lord Bingham to 'give effect'.[5]

The principle of legality is a clear-cut concept, but the restrictions to be put upon discretionary power are a matter of degree. Faced with the fact that Parliament freely confers discretionary powers with little regard to the dangers of abuse, the courts must attempt to strike a balance between the needs of fair and efficient administration and the need to protect the citizen against oppressive government. Here they must rely on their own judgement, sensing what is required by the interplay of forces in the constitution. The fact that this involves questions of degree has sometimes led critics to disparage the rule of law, treating it as a merely political phenomenon which reflects one particular philosophy of government.[6] But this is true only in the sense that every system of law must have its own standards for judging questions of abuse of discretionary power. As will be seen throughout this book, the rules of law which our own system has devised for this purpose are objective and non-political, based on the judicial instinct for justice, and capable of being applied impartially to any kind of legislation irrespective of its political content. Without these rules all kinds of abuses would be possible and the rule of law would be replaced by the rule of arbitrary power. Their existence is therefore essential to the rule of law, and they themselves are principles of law, not politics.

JUDICIAL INDEPENDENCE

A third meaning of the rule of law, though it is a corollary of the first meaning, is that disputes as to the legality of acts of government are to be decided by judges who are independent of the executive. It is in this sense, and in this sense only, that 'the British constitution, though largely unwritten, is firmly based upon the separation of powers'.[7] In the unwritten constitution it is venerated as a principle of policy rather than of law, though it is now reinforced by the developing law of human rights. The written constitutions of independent Commonwealth countries, on the other hand, have their foundations in legislation from which legal rights can flow. The separation of judicial from executive power 'is implicit in the very structure of a constitution on the Westminster model', so that,

[3] See below, pp. 301 and 345 respectively.

[4] See especially Chapters 11, 14. For an example see *R (Anufrijeva)* v. *Home Secretary* [2003] UKHL 36, [2004] 1 AC 604 (implied duty to communicate decision found). See [2004] *PL* 246 (Jowell).

[5] *R (Corner House Research)* v. *The Serious Fraud Office* [2008] UKHL 60, [2009] 1 AC 756, para. 41 and see *R (Alconbury Developments Ltd)* v. *Secretary of State for the Environment, Transport and the Regions* [2001] UKHL 23, [2003] 2 AC 295, para. 73 (Lord Hoffmann).

[6] The best-known criticism is that of Sir I. Jennings, *The Law and the Constitution*, 5th edn, 42–62, attacking Dicey's exposition (above). An effective reply was made by Sir W. Holdsworth in (1939) 55 *LQR* at 586 and in his *History of English Law*, xiv. 202.

[7] *Duport Steel* v. *Sirs* [1990] 1 WLR 142 at 157 (Lord Diplock). For discussion of the proper role of the judiciary see Lord Hoffmann's lecture *Separation of Powers* [2002] *JR* 137. Cf. [2003] *JR* 12 (M. Chamberlain).

for example, the judiciary and not the government must control the length of prisoners' detention as a matter of law.[8]

In Britain, as in the principal countries of the Commonwealth and in the United States of America, disputes between citizen and government are adjudicated by the ordinary courts of law. Although many disputes are dealt with by specialised tribunals, these are themselves subject to control by the ordinary courts[9] and so the rule of law is preserved. In countries such as France, Italy and Germany, on the other hand, there are separate administrative courts organised in a separate hierarchy—though it does not follow that they are less independent of the government. The right to carry a dispute with the government before the ordinary courts, manned by judges of the highest independence, is an important element in the Anglo-American concept of the rule of law.

FAIRNESS

A fourth meaning is that the law should be even-handed between government and citizen. Clearly the law cannot be the same for both, since every government must necessarily have many special powers. What the rule of law requires is that the government should not enjoy unnecessary privileges or exemptions from ordinary law. There remain examples of such privileges and exemptions in the modern law. The Crown is exempt from obeying Acts of Parliament unless they contain some positive indication to the contrary effect.[10] And it was 'a black day for the rule of law' when the High Court held that the law was unenforceable against ministers and civil servants.[11] In principle all public authorities should be subject to all normal legal duties and liabilities which are not inconsistent with their governmental functions.

In addition to its central principles the rule of law has a large periphery of controversial aspects. In so far as dictatorial government confers arbitrary power on some autocrat or legislature it can be claimed that there can be no real rule of law without representative democracy.[12] Wide claims have also been made for other areas of political theory, even to the point of asserting that the rule of law demands beneficial social and economic services and conditions.[13] Personal independence, also, is claimed to be included, as expressed in 'the principle of minimal interference'.[14] A contrast has been made between 'formal' and 'substantive' versions of the rule of law, the former being sometimes not much more than the principle of legality and the latter insisting on wider range and positive content.[15] But this ought not to be seen as a dilemma, since the rule of law necessarily has both formal and substantive features. As a legal principle its value is greatest if it is not stretched beyond the core of basic doctrine centred upon legality, regularity and fairness, always with emphasis on the rejection of arbitrary power. It is in this sense that it is most often referred to by judges, for instance, in Lord Steyn's statement that

---

[8] *Director of Public Prosecutions of Jamaica* v. *Mollison* [2003] 2 WLR 1160. See also *Hinds* v. *The Queen* [1977] AC 195; *Pinder* v. *The Queen* [2003] 1 AC 620. A striking example is *Liyanage* v. *The Queen* [1967] 1 AC 259 (retrospective criminal legislation enacted to convict particular prisoners of acts of rebellion held an unlawful usurpation of judicial power).   [9] Below, p. 762.

[10] Below, p. 706.

[11] For this temporary lapse see below, p. 704.

[12] For comment see Craig, *Public Law and Democracy*, ch. 2; Allan, *Law, Liberty and Justice*, ch. 2; Harden and Lewis, *The Noble Lie: The British Constitution and the Rule of Law*; Jowell in Jowell and Oliver, *The Changing Constitution*, 5th edn, 90; Allan in (1988) 8 *OJLS* 266 and (1999) 115 *LQR* 221.

[13] As in the resolution of the International Commission of Jurists, Delhi, 1959, cited in Allan (as above), 20.   [14] See [1996] *PL* 630 (Sir John Laws).

[15] For a survey of opinions and a balanced analysis see [1997] *PL* 467 (P. Craig).

> Unless there is the clearest provision to the contrary, Parliament must be presumed not to legislate contrary to the rule of law. And the rule of law enforces minimum standards of fairness, both substantive and procedural.[16]

Most lawyers would agree that it is these central elements of the rule of law, lying outside the areas of controversy, which are the most genuine and valuable.

Quixotic though it is to hope that 'it may be a government of laws and not of men',[17] the rule of law remains none the less a vital necessity to fair and proper government. The enormous growth in the powers of the state makes it all the more necessary to preserve it. In one sense, the whole of this book is devoted to explaining how that is being done.

FALLACIOUS COMPARISONS

Although the concept of the rule of law might be called the mainspring of administrative law, Dicey's famous formulation of it in *The Law of the Constitution*[18] cast a prolonged blight over administrative law in Britain. At the root of this paradox was a verbal misunderstanding. Dicey maintained that 'administrative law' was utterly foreign to our constitution, that it was incompatible with the rule of law, with the common law, and with constitutional liberty as we understand it. But Dicey's 'administrative law' was a translation of the French droit administratif, and it was this, rather than any British conception, that Dicey denounced. He regarded it as a prime virtue of the rule of law that all cases came before the ordinary courts, and that the same general rules applied to an action against a government official as applied to an action against a private individual. Under the French system, with its special administrative courts, actions against officials or the state are in many cases subject to a separate system of judicature. What Dicey meant by 'administrative law' was a special system of courts for administrative cases. Even in Dicey's generation this was an unusual sense of the expression. But once that sense is appreciated, the paradox disappears.

Dicey's denunciation of the French system was based on his mistaken conclusion that the administrative courts of France, culminating in the Conseil d'État, must exist for the purpose of giving to officials 'a whole body of special rights, privileges, or prerogatives as against private citizens',[19] so as to make them a law unto themselves. It has long been realised that this picture was wrong, but it has become a traditional caricature.

The reality is that the French Conseil d'État is widely admired[20] and has served as a model for other countries, as well as for the Court of Justice of the European Communities. Undoubtedly the French administrative courts have succeeded in imposing a genuinely judicial control upon the executive and in raising the standard of administration. They are impartial and objective courts of law in the fullest sense. Both countries can claim advantages for their methods. In Britain the standing of the courts is high, and few would wish to see them abandon their historic function of protecting the subject against unlawful acts of government. But no one should suppose that administrative courts necessarily weaken the rule of law.

---

[16] *R v. Home Secretary ex p Pierson* [1998] AC 539 at 591. For this case, which involved a retrospective penalty, see below, p. 377. See also *Boddington v. British Transport Police* [1999] 2 AC 143 at 161, 173 (Lord Irvine LC and Lord Steyn); *R v. Home Secretary ex p Stafford* [1998] 1 WLR 503 at 518 (Lord Bingham CJ). See to like effect Lord Griffiths in *R v. Horseferry Road Magistrates' Court ex p Bennett* [1994] 1 AC 42 at 62.

[17] Constitution of Massachusetts (1780), Pt I, Art. 30.　　[18] Ch. 4, first published in 1885.

[19] *The Law of the Constitution*, 10th edn, 336.

[20] See Brown and Bell, *French Administrative Law*, 5th edn, for a good general account in English.

THE SOVEREIGNTY OF PARLIAMENT

LEGISLATIVE SOVEREIGNTY

The sovereignty of Parliament is a peculiar feature of the British constitution which exerts a constant and powerful influence.[21] In particular, it is an ever-present threat to the position of the courts; and it naturally inclines the judges towards caution in their attitude to the executive, since Parliament is effectively under the executive's control. It is also responsible for the prominence in administrative law of the doctrine of ultra vires, as will shortly appear.

The sovereign legal power in the United Kingdom lies in the Queen in Parliament, acting by Act of Parliament. An Act of Parliament generally requires the assent of the Queen, the House of Lords, and the House of Commons, and the assent of each House is given upon a simple majority of the votes of members present. But exceptionally an Act of Parliament may be enacted under the special procedure provided by the Parliament Acts 1911 and 1949 in which the assent of the House of Lords is not required.[22] The power of an Act of the sovereign Parliament, howsoever enacted, is boundless.[23]

Under the traditional rules, any previous Act of Parliament can always be repealed by a later Act. Acts of the most fundamental kind, such as the Habeas Corpus Act 1679, the Bill of Rights 1688, the Act of Settlement 1700, the Statute of Westminster 1931, the European Communities Act 1972 and the Human Rights Act 1998 are just as easy to repeal, legally speaking, as is the Antarctic Treaty Act 1967. No special majorities or procedure are needed. The ordinary, everyday form of Act of Parliament is sovereign, and can effect any legal consequences whatsoever.

In accordance with general principle the repeal of an Act may be express or, where there is a conflict between two Acts, implied, the later Act repealing the earlier Act to the extent necessary to resolve the conflict. But the courts are naturally reluctant to see fundamental Acts repealed and the rights embodied in them set at naught unless it is clear that repeal was Parliament's intention. Lord Hoffmann made it clear that fundamental rights are not at the mercy of an inadvertent or unthinking Parliament when he said in a dictum that has become canonical:[24]

---

[21] Here also Dicey's is the classic exposition: *The Law of the Constitution*, ch. 1. For valuable discussion see de Smith and Brazier, *Constitutional and Administrative Law*, 8th edn, ch. 4. Goldsworthy, *The Sovereignty of Parliament* (1999) is the outstanding modern account. See also Young, *Parliamentary Sovereignty and the Human Rights Act* (2009).

[22] Section 2 of the 1911 Act (as amended by the 1949 Act) provides that where a 'public Bill' (excluding a money Bill or a Bill to extend the life of Parliament), having been passed by the Commons in two successive sessions, is rejected in the House of Lords in both those sessions, it may be presented to Her Majesty for assent provided at least one year has elapsed between the two occasions on which it was passed by the Commons. For discussion see Forsyth, (2011) 9 *International Journal of Constitutional Law* 132 and Ekins, (2007) 123 *LQR* 91.

[23] *Jackson v. A-G* [2005] UKHL 56, [2006] 1 AC 262. Their Lordships made it clear that, contrary to the view expressed in several scholarly works (see Hood Phillips, *Constitutional and Administrative* Law, 8th edn, 80 and [1954] *CLJ* at 263 and [1955] *CLJ* at 193 (Wade); Wade, *Constitutional Fundamentals*, 27 and earlier editions of this book), such legislation was not delegated legislation (and as such invalid when beyond the power delegated). Section 2(1) of the Parliament Act 1911, which provides that no Act passed under the Parliament Acts can prolong the life of Parliament beyond 5 years, remains effective. For commentary on *Jackson* see [2006] *PL* 539 (McHarg); (2006) *CLJ* 1 (Elliott); (2007) *LQR* 91 (Ekins); [2006] *PL* 562 (Jowell); [2007] *PL* 187 (Young). Note particularly Lord Cooke's spirited criticism of *Jackson* (2006) *LQR* 224.

[24] *R v. Home Secretary ex p Simms* [2000] 2 AC 115 at 131. See *Ahmed* v. *HM Treasury* [2010] UKSC 2, para. 61 (Lord Hope). See below, p. 738 for discussion of the influential suggestion that 'constitutional Acts' (such as those just mentioned) may only be repealed by express words.

Parliamentary sovereignty means that Parliament can, if it chooses, legislate contrary to fundamental principles of human rights. The Human Rights Act 1998 will not detract from this power. The constraints upon its exercise by Parliament are ultimately political, not legal. But the principle of legality means that Parliament must squarely confront what it is doing and accept the political cost. Fundamental rights cannot be overridden by general or ambiguous words. This is because there is too great a risk that the full implications of their unqualified meaning may have passed unnoticed in the democratic process. In the absence of express language or necessary implication to the contrary, the courts therefore presume that even the most general words were intended to be subject to the basic rights of the individual.

This legal paramountcy can be exercised only by an Act of the sovereign Parliament. The two Houses of Parliament by themselves dispose of no such power, either jointly or severally. A resolution of either House, or of both Houses, has no legislative or legal effect whatever unless an Act of Parliament so provides.[25] There are many cases where some administrative order or regulation is required by statute to be approved by resolutions of the Houses.[26] But this procedure in no way protects the order or regulation from being condemned by the court, under the doctrine of ultra vires, if it is not strictly in accordance with the Act.[27] Whether the challenge is made before[28] or after[29] the Houses have given their approval is immaterial.

The devolution of legislative power to Scotland, Wales, and Northern Ireland, though of great importance constitutionally, has not altered the essentials of parliamentary sovereignty. Acts of the Scottish Parliament receive the royal assent, but their authority derives entirely from the Scotland Act 1998 of the United Kingdom Parliament, which expressly preserves that Parliament's power to make laws for Scotland and imposes other limits.[30] The framework of the Northern Ireland Act 1998 is broadly the same. The Government of Wales Act 1998 conferred only powers of secondary legislation on the Welsh Assembly, and while the Government of Wales Act 2006 enhances the legislative powers of the Assembly, there is no challenge to the supremacy of Parliament. A more detailed account of the devolution legislation is reserved for Chapter 4.

LACK OF CONSTITUTIONAL PROTECTION

One consequence of parliamentary sovereignty is that this country has no constitutional guarantees. In other countries there is normally a written constitution, embodied in a formal document, and protected, as a kind of fundamental law, against amendment by simple majorities in the legislature. In Britain, however, we have never made a fresh start with a new constitution, although in the seventeenth century the courts bowed to several revolutionary changes of sovereign. Not only do we have no constitutional guarantees: we cannot, according to classical doctrine, create them.[31] Since an ordinary Act of Parliament

---

[25] *Stockdale v. Hansard* (1839) 9 Ad & E 1.   [26] Below, p. 323.   [27] See below, pp. 323, 737.

[28] As in *R v. Electricity Commissioners ex p London Electricity Joint Committee Co (1920) Ltd* [1924] 1 KB 171; *R v. HM Treasury ex p Smedley* [1985] QB 657.

[29] As in *Hoffmann–La Roche & Co v. Secretary of State for Trade and Industry* [1975] AC 295 at 354, 365, 372; *Laker Airways Ltd v. Dept of Trade* [1977] QB 643; and see *R v. Secretary of State for the Environment ex p Nottinghamshire CC* [1986] AC 240, explained below, p. 321.

[30] s. 28. The limitation on the power of the Scottish Parliament will be discussed below at pp. 104–5.

[31] In 1977 the House of Lords was advised by a Select Committee including Lord Wilberforce, Lord Diplock and Lord Scarman that this was impossible under the constitution: HL 176, May 1978. But even within the traditional rules entrenchment could be achieved by putting the judges under oath to uphold the constitution (or Bill of Rights) as supreme law: see Wade, *Constitutional Fundamentals*, 30–50.

can repeal any law whatever, it is impossible for Parliament to render any statute unrepealable, or repealable only in some special way. If two Acts of Parliament conflict, the later Act must prevail and the earlier Act must be repealed by implication to the extent of the conflict—but subject to one important qualification which has been propounded in the Divisional Court in an influential judgment.[32] Parliament cannot bind its successors. Parliament cannot, therefore, modify or destroy its own continuing sovereignty, for the courts will always obey its latest commands. This situation could, indeed, be changed by a revolution of some kind, 'revolution' here meaning a legal discontinuity, a fundamental change which defies the existing rules of law but is accepted by the courts—as when James II was succeeded by William and Mary in 1688.

THE SUPREMACY OF EU LAW: A LEGAL REVOLUTION?

Just such a revolution has perhaps resulted from Britain's accession to the European Communities. The European Communities Act 1972 laid down that Community law should prevail over British law, including 'any enactment passed or to be passed'.[33] By those last four words Parliament attempted to bind its successors and to subordinate all future legislation to Community law. And the attempt has succeeded. When the Merchant Shipping Act 1988, by imposing restrictions on Spanish fishing vessels, proved to be contrary to Community law, the House of Lords found no difficulty in holding that the Act must give way. Lord Bridge explained that it had been obvious from the beginning that Community membership demanded just such a limitation of Parliament's sovereignty, that Parliament's acceptance of that limitation had been 'entirely voluntary' and that 'there is nothing in any way novel in according supremacy to rules of Community law'.[34] But for a court thus to 'disapply' an Act of Parliament, and to grant an injunction forbidding a minister from obeying it, was a revolutionary change.[35] The hallowed rule that Parliament cannot bind its successors had to yield to political necessity and constitutional law had to adjust itself to realities, just as it did in 1688. Since the House made no

---

[32] By Laws LJ in *Thoburn* v. *Sunderland CC* (below) where he held that fundamental constitutional statutes (in this case the European Communities Act 1972) were repealable only by express words and not by mere implication.

[33] Act of 1972, s. 2(4). Section 2 has been amended by the Legislative and Regulatory Reform Act 2006 so that treaty obligations may be implemented 'by order, rules, regulations or scheme' and not just regulations (s. 27). And a reference in an Act to a community instrument includes that instrument as subsequently amended or extended (s. 25).

[34] *R* v. *Secretary of State for Transport ex p Factortame Ltd (No 2)* [1990] 1 AC 603. Only one speech (that of Lord Bridge) dealt with sovereignty. Labour legislation was similarly disapplied in *R* v. *Secretary of State for Employment ex p Equal Opportunities Commission* [1995] 1 AC 1, for which see below, p. 163 where further cases are referred to. See Appendix 3.

[35] That the change was truly revolutionary is disputed by Sir John Laws in [1995] *PL* 72 at 89, on the ground that sovereignty is preserved by Parliament's undoubted ability to repeal the Act of 1972 and take Britain out of the EU; and by T. R. S. Allan in (1997) *LQR* 443, on the ground that the change was within the existing law of statutory interpretation, properly understood. The difficulty with the former objection is that Parliament has for the time being effectively bound its successors, thus restricting their power. That is certainly revolutionary for the time being; what might happen later is another matter. The difficulty with the latter objection is that the supposed law had not previously been evident. For a balanced and helpful discussion see (1991) 11 *YBEL* 22 (Craig), and for support of Allan's position see Murray Hunt, *Using Human Rights Law in English Courts*, 79. But in *Fleming (t/a Bodycraft)* v. *HM Revenue and Customs* [2008] UKHL 2 in para. 25 Lord Walker said: 'Only in the most formal sense . . . can disapplication be described as a process of construction.'

mention of the hallowed rule it must be doubtful whether it is still in existence.[36] Nothing similar to the feat of the 1972 Act has since been attempted and the extent of Parliament's power to bind itself in this way is unclear. But the exercise of the power to bind its successors is in any event not irrevocable. Parliament retains the power to repeal section 2(4) of the 1972 Act, demonstrating in the final analysis its continuing supremacy.[37]

ARE THERE LIMITS ON THE POWER OF PARLIAMENT?

There is much dissatisfaction with undiluted parliamentary power, since the control of legislation has effectively passed into the hands of the executive. Parliament's independent control has been progressively weakened by the party system and it is called upon to pass many more Acts in each session than it can scrutinise properly. Dicey extolled judge-made law as a better protection for the liberty of the citizen than constitutional guarantees. But it is now understood that a written constitution which is respected, as it is for example in the United States, provides valuable safeguards which in Britain have been lacking. On the other hand, effective safeguards for many basic rights were obtained when Britain became a founding member of the European Convention on Human Rights and Fundamental Freedoms of 1950, and when she acceded to the European Communities in 1973.[38] And now the substance of the European Convention has been incorporated into our law by the Human Rights Act 1998. Care has been taken, however, to respect the sovereignty of Parliament, so that the new human rights are given no special constitutional status and Parliament is not legally restrained from amending or repealing them.[39]

But are there, nonetheless, limits on the power of Parliament? Several distinguished judges have indeed suggested extra-judicially that constitutional fundamentals such as the rule of law, judicial independence and judicial review may be beyond the power of Parliament to abolish.[40] And in a leading decision of the House of Lords there have been *obiter dicta* to like effect.[41] Lord Steyn, for instance, said that if an Act purported to abolish judicial review the courts would have to 'consider whether [judicial review] is a constitutional fundamental which even a sovereign Parliament acting at the behest of a complaisant House of Commons cannot abolish'.[42] Even these tentative remarks have provoked several effective responses,[43] including one from Lord Bingham,[44] defending

---

[36] The rule is emphatically restated by Laws LJ in *Thoburn* v. *Sunderland City Council* [2003] 1 QB 151, although without comment on its conflict with the speech of Lord Bridge (above) which is also restated.

[37] See Lord Bingham's Commemoration Oration, see below, n. 44.

[38] For the effect of these international obligations in administrative law see below, ch. 6.

[39] See below, p. 137.

[40] For such suggestions made by Lord Woolf MR, Laws and Sedley LJJ and by Lord Cooke of Thorndon, and for the riposte of Lord Irvine QC (as he then was) ('judicial supremacism' prompted by 'extra-judicial romanticism') see [1996] *PL* 59 at 75 and below, p. 31. For further discussion see (2003) 23 *OJLS* 435 (Poole) and Adam Tomkins, *Our Republican Constitution* (2003), ch. 1. For another view see Allan, *The Sovereignty of Law*, chs. 4 and 5 (sophisticated justification for limits on supremacy).

[41] *R (Jackson)* v. *A-G* [2005] UKHL 56, [2006] 1 AC 262.

[42] Para. 102. Baroness Hale said that the courts 'might even reject' legislation of this kind (para. 159). See also Lord Hope (para. 120). Lord Hope in *AXA General Insurance Ltd and ors* v. *Lord Advocate and ors* [2011] UKSC 46, para. 51 reiterated his view that where one party dominates Parliament a government may seek to abolish judicial review or similar; thus the 'rule of law requires that the judges must retain the power to insist that legislation of that extreme kind is not law which the courts will recognise'.

[43] See (2007) 123 *LQR* 91 (Ekins) and (2005) 3 *New Zealand Journal of Public and International Law* 7–37 (Goldsworthy).

[44] 'The Rule of Law and the Sovereignty of Parliament' being the Commemoration Oration 2007 at King's College London. It is published in Lord Bingham, *The Rule of Law* (2010); the quoted passage is at 167. The oration is also published in (2008) 19 *King's Law Journal* 223.

the orthodox view. Such theoretical justification as exists for these assertions of judicial power over the legislature rest on the proposition that the doctrine of parliamentary sovereignty was created by the judges developing the common law and so the judges can abolish it.[45] But as Lord Bingham remarks, 'the principle of parliamentary sovereignty has been recognised as fundamental in this country not because the judges invented it but because it has for centuries been accepted as such by judges and others officially concerned in the operation of our constitutional system. The judges did not by themselves establish the principle and they cannot, by themselves, change it.'[46] Its vigour depends not only upon the judges' loyalty to it but upon its acceptance by the relevant officials in all the branches of government. As Lord Millett said in another case 'the doctrine of Parliamentary supremacy is [not] sacrosanct, but...any change in a fundamental constitutional principle should be the consequence of deliberate legislative action and not judicial activism, however well meaning.'[47]

As we have already seen judges will rightly strain to interpret legislation in a way that is consistent with the rule of law.[48] But, when the will of Parliament is clear, even if inconsistent with the principles of the rule of law, the judges must bow to that will.[49] 'What is at stake [here] is the location of the ultimate decision-making authority—the right to the "final word" in a legal system.'[50]

Generally any conflict between judiciary and legislature can be avoided by sensible construction of the relevant statute since, on the whole, Parliament will intend to comply with the rule of law. But if the judiciary, frustrated by the failings of the elected legislature, were to assert a power to hold Acts of Parliament invalid it would be stepping from law into politics and the outcome of its efforts impossible to predict.

THE POSITION OF THE JUDGES

Parliamentary sovereignty, as it now exists, profoundly affects the position of the judges. They are not the appointed guardians of constitutional rights, with power to declare statutes unconstitutional, like the Supreme Court of the United States. Subject only to the overriding law of the European Union, they can only obey the latest expression of the will of Parliament. Nor is their own jurisdiction sacrosanct. If they fly too high, Parliament may clip their wings. They entirely lack the impregnable constitutional status of their American counterparts. Nevertheless they have built up for themselves a position which is a good deal stronger than constitutional theory by itself might suggest. Feeling their way, case by case, they define their powers for themselves. In doing so they draw upon strong traditions of long standing and upon their own prestige, and with these resources they can do much. Some of their bold decisions discussed in this book, particularly those of recent years, show that they need not be deterred by the weakness of their constitutional status. Even under the British system of undiluted sovereignty, the last word on any question of law rests with the courts.

---

[45] See also Jowell ([2006] *PL* 562) who considers that 'the preconditions of any constitutional democracy, properly so-called, is respect for certain rights that neither the executive nor the legislature, representative as it may be, should be able to deny with impunity' and on this hypothesis Parliament's power to intrude upon such fundamental rights is limited.

[46] At p. 22, relying on H. L. A. Hart, *The Concept of Law* 1st edn (1961), chs. 5–6.

[47] *Ghaidan* v. *Godin-Mendoza* [2004] UKHL 30, para. 57.   [48] Above p. 19.

[49] Contra T. R. S. Allan, (2004) 63 *CLJ* 527 and Allan, *The Sovereignty of Law* (above). For a contrast see R. Ekins, (2006) 31 *Australian Journal of Legal Philosophy* 95.

[50] Goldsworthy, *The Sovereignty of Parliament: History and Philosophy* (1999) at 3.

MINISTERIAL RESPONSIBILITY

One aspect of the supremacy of Parliament is that ministers are responsible to it, both individually and collectively, through the Cabinet. Parliament is the body before which ministers are called to account, and without the confidence of which they cannot continue. But here again the theory is far from the reality. The party system means in practice that, in anything but the last resort, the government controls Parliament. This is especially evident in the process of legislation. Bills are drafted by government departments and are often driven through Parliament by the party whips and with inadequate time for many of their clauses to be properly considered. Many matters of importance in administrative law, such as restrictions on legal remedies and the proliferation of statutory tribunals, are enacted without comment in either House and without attention to their legal consequences. Ministerial responsibility fails in practice to control legislation effectively; most statutes being enacted in almost exactly the form on which the government decided in advance.

The traditional methods of calling ministers to account for errors in administration are parliamentary questions, debates on the adjournment, and occasional debates such as those on Supply days in the House of Commons. But by these relatively cumbersome processes Parliament cannot possibly control the ordinary run of daily governmental acts except by taking up occasional cases which have political appeal. Administrative justice demands some regular, efficient and non-political machinery for investigating individual complaints against governmental action of all kinds, including the action of subordinate officials.

The deficiencies of ministerial responsibility as a system of protection against administrative wrongdoing led an eminent judge to say bitterly, as long ago as 1910,[51]

> If ministerial responsibility were more than the mere shadow of a name, the matter would be less important, but as it is, the Courts are the only defence of the liberty of the subject against departmental aggression.

Dicey expressed similar views in 1915, criticising judicial reliance on 'so-called ministerial responsibility'.[52] And in 1981 Lord Diplock said:[53]

> It is not, in my view, a sufficient answer to say that judicial review of the actions of officers or departments of central government is unnecessary because they are accountable to Parliament for the way in which they carry out their functions. They are accountable to Parliament for what they do so far as regards efficiency and policy, and of that Parliament is the only judge; they are responsible to a court of justice for the lawfulness of what they do, and of that the court is the only judge.

A constitutional improvement was introduced in 1967 in the person of the Parliamentary Commissioner for Administration. His method of investigating complaints against administration has all the advantages which the parliamentary process lacks: it is impartial, non-political and it can penetrate behind the screen which ministerial responsibility otherwise interposes between Parliament and government departments.

The high degree of detachment and anonymity in which the civil service works is largely a consequence of the principle of ministerial responsibility. Where civil servants

---

[51] *Dyson v. A-G* [1911] 1 KB 410 at 424 (Farwell LJ). The 'departmental aggression' was an unjustified demand for information by the Commissioners of Inland Revenue.   [52] (1915) 31 *LQR* 148 at 152.

[53] *R v. Inland Revenue Commissioners ex p National Federation of Self-Employed and Small Businesses Ltd* [1982] AC 617.

carry out the minister's orders, or act in accordance with his policy, it is for him and not for them to take any blame. He also takes responsibility for ordinary administrative mistakes or miscarriages.

GOVERNMENT SUBJECT TO LAW

ORDINARY LAW AND PREROGATIVE REMEDIES

It is now necessary to explain in general terms some of the elements of judicial control, the details of which occupy so much of this book. The rules which govern disputes involving the government and public authorities come before the ordinary courts, and the courts so far as possible apply 'ordinary law', treating public authorities as if they were private individuals with normal legal duties and liabilities, except so far as modified by statute. Thus a local authority or a public corporation is legally liable for the negligence of its employees in exactly the same way as any other employer. Ministers as such, though acting ministers of the Crown, have none of the Crown's prerogatives or immunities in law, and are in principle in the same position as private individuals.[54] The great majority of proceedings by and against public authorities, therefore, can be adjudicated without making any distinction between private and official capacities.

Nevertheless there are many administrative wrongs that the ordinary law cannot reach. Public authorities may often act unlawfully without rendering themselves liable in trespass, nuisance, and so forth. If an application for a licence is wrongly refused, or if a licence is wrongly revoked, or if a claim to national insurance benefit is wrongly rejected, there will usually be no remedy in private law.[55] It is true that almost any kind of wrong can be brought before the court by an action for a declaration, in which the court can declare the claimant's rights. But this remedy has only recently come to the fore. Long before it did so, the courts had developed the nucleus of a system of public law out of the special 'prerogative' remedies of certiorari, prohibition and mandamus, together also with habeas corpus.[56] These remedies are still of the greatest importance for the purpose of compelling ministers, tribunals and other governmental bodies to act lawfully and to perform their duties. They cover the area where the remedies of private law are weak or ineffective. This in no way alters the fact that legality is enforced through the ordinary courts, applying principles of ordinary law.

These prerogative remedies are so called because they were originally used by the Crown and by the royal courts for the purpose of preventing inferior tribunals and other bodies from meddling in matters that did not concern them. They were designed to enforce order in the complex network of jurisdictions, both central and local, which was a feature of the legal system. Certiorari would issue from the Court of King's Bench to quash a decision, for example of justices of the peace, which was outside their jurisdiction or patently contrary to law. Prohibition would prevent them from proceeding in any matter outside their jurisdiction. Mandamus would command them to carry out their legal duties, if they were in default. Habeas corpus would release any person wrongfully detained. But it was private individuals who usually called the attention of the court to these wrongs, and in time the prerogative remedies ceased to be a royal monopoly and

---

[54] Below, p. 35.   [55] Below, p. 668.
[56] Below, p. 501. As explained at p. 501 the names of these ancient remedies, save for habeas corpus, have been changed.

became available to any subject. Nevertheless the Crown remained the nominal plaintiff and the remedies retained their character of remedies devised for upholding public order rather than private right. This character, as will be seen later, makes them especially valuable for correcting administrative illegalities which do not directly injure any particular person, for example a failure by a cinema licensing authority to prevent the exhibition of indecent films.[57]

The High Court is the source of all these remedies. Formerly the prerogative remedies were sought through the Crown Court Office of that court but now they come under the Administrative Court, which itself is part of the High Court Queen's Bench Division, and is basically an administrative arrangement only which does not infringe the principle that public law is enforced by the ordinary courts.

REVIEW, LEGALITY AND DISCRETION

The system of judicial review is radically different from the system of appeals.[58] When hearing an appeal the court is concerned with the merits of a decision: is it correct? When subjecting some administrative act or order to judicial review, the court is concerned with its legality: is it within the limits of the powers granted? On an appeal the question is 'right or wrong?' On review the question is 'lawful or unlawful?'[59]

Rights of appeal are always statutory.[60] Judicial review, on the other hand, is the exercise of the court's inherent power to determine whether action is lawful or not and to award suitable relief. For this no statutory authority is necessary: the court is simply performing its ordinary functions in order to enforce the law. The basis of judicial review, therefore, is common law. This remains true even though nearly all cases in administrative law arise under some Act of Parliament.

Judicial review is thus a fundamental mechanism for keeping public authorities within due bounds and for upholding the rule of law. Instead of substituting its own decision for that of some other body, as happens when on appeal, the court on review is concerned only with the question whether the act or order under attack should be allowed to stand or not. If the Home Secretary revokes a television licence unlawfully, the court may simply declare that the revocation is null and void.[61] Should the case be one involving breach of duty rather than excess of power, the question will be whether the public authority should be ordered to make good a default. Refusal to issue a television licence to someone entitled to have one would be remedied by an order of the court requiring the issue of the licence. If administrative action is in excess of power (ultra vires), the court has only to quash it or declare it unlawful (these are in effect the same thing) and then no one need pay any attention to it. The minister or tribunal or other authority has in law done nothing, and must make a fresh decision.

Judicial control, therefore, primarily means review, and is based on a fundamental principle, inherent throughout the legal system, that powers can be validly exercised only within their true limits. The doctrines by which those limits are ascertained and enforced form the very marrow of administrative law. But there are many situations in which the courts interpret Acts of Parliament as authorising only action which is reasonable or

---

[57] Below, p. 344.

[58] Sometimes the courts use 'review' in the opposite sense to make the same contrast, describing judicial review as 'supervision' and the appellate function as 'review'. See *R* v. *Nat Bell Liquors* [1922] 2 AC 128 at 156; *Anisminic Ltd* v. *Foreign Compensation Commission* [1969] 2 AC 147 at 195.

[59] The difference is shown by the rule that the existence of a right of appeal does not normally prejudice the right to review: below, p. 600.   [60] Below, p. 771.

[61] See below, p. 247.

which has some particular purpose, so that its merits determine its legality. Sometimes the Act itself will expressly limit the power in this way, but even if it does not it is common for the court to infer that some limitation is intended. The judges have been deeply drawn into this area, so that their own opinion of the reasonableness or motives of some government action may be the factor which determines whether or not it is to be condemned on judicial review. The further the courts are drawn into passing judgment on the merits of the actions of public authorities, the more they are exposed to the charge that they are exceeding their constitutional function. But today this accusation deters them much less than formerly, particularly now that Parliament has in the Human Rights Act 1998 licensed more intrusive review by the courts.[62]

It is a cardinal axiom that every power has legal limits. If the court finds that the power has been exercised oppressively or unreasonably, or if there has been some procedural failing, such as not allowing a person affected to put forward his case, the act may be condemned as unlawful. Although lawyers appearing for government departments have often argued that some Act confers unfettered discretion on a minister, they are guilty of constitutional blasphemy. Unfettered discretion cannot exist where the rule of law reigns. The same truth can be expressed by saying that all power is capable of abuse, and that the power to prevent abuse is the acid test of effective judicial review.

THE DOCTRINE OF ULTRA VIRES

THE CENTRAL PRINCIPLE

The simple proposition that a public authority may not act outside its powers (ultra vires) might fitly be called the central principle of administrative law.[63] 'The juristic basis of judicial review is the doctrine of ultra vires.'[64] To a large extent the courts have developed the subject by extending and refining this principle, which has many ramifications and which in some of its aspects attains a high degree of artificiality.

Where the empowering Act lays down limits expressly, their application is merely an exercise in construing the statutory language and applying it to the facts. Thus if land may be taken by compulsory purchase provided that it is not part of a park, the court must determine in case of dispute whether the land is part of a park and decide accordingly.[65] If the Act says 'provided that in the opinion of the minister it is not a park', the question is not so simple. Reading the language literally, the court would be confined to ascertaining that the minister in fact held the opinion required. But then the minister might make an order for the acquisition of land in Hyde Park, certifying his opinion that it was not part of a park. It is essential to invalidate any malpractice of this kind, and therefore the court will hold the order to be ultra vires if the minister acted in bad faith or unreasonably or on no proper evidence.[66] Results such as these are attained by the art of statutory construction. It is presumed that Parliament did not intend to authorise abuses, and that certain safeguards against abuse must be implied in the Act. These are

---

[62] See below, p. 171.

[63] Approved in terms in *Boddington* v. *British Transport Police* [1999] 2 AC 143 at 171 (Lord Steyn). Cf. (2002) 7 *EHRLR* 723 at 725 (Lord Steyn), but without consideration of the constitutional questions. The question is considered further below, pp. 29–30.

[64] *Boddington* v. *British Transport Police*, at 164 (Lord Browne-Wilkinson), affirming his view in *R* v. *Hull University Visitor ex p Page* [1993] AC 682 at 701.   [65] For this case see below, p. 211.

[66] See below, pp. 227, 293, 354.

matters of general principle, embodied in the rules of law which govern the interpretation of statutes. Parliament is not expected to incorporate them expressly in every Act that is passed. They may be taken for granted as part of the implied conditions to which every Act is subject and which the courts extract by reading between the lines. Any violation of them, therefore, renders the offending action ultra vires.

As with substance, so with procedure. One of the law's notable achievements has been the development of the principles of natural justice, one of which is the right to be given a fair hearing before being penalised in any way. These principles are similarly based upon implied statutory conditions: it is assumed that Parliament, when conferring power, intends that power to be used fairly and with due consideration of rights and interests adversely affected. In effect, Parliament legislates against a background of judge-made rules of interpretation. The judges have constructed a kind of code of good administrative practice, taking Parliament's authority for granted. Even where sophisticated reasoning makes them appear to be frustrating Parliament's intentions they still claim, paradoxically, to be respecting them.[67]

An act which is for any reason in excess of power (ultra vires) is often described as being 'outside jurisdiction'. 'Jurisdiction', in this context, means simply 'power', though sometimes it bears the slightly narrower sense of 'power to decide', e.g. as applied to statutory tribunals. It is a word to which the courts have given different meanings in different contexts, and with which they have created a certain amount of confusion. But this cannot be explained intelligibly except in the particular contexts where difficulties have been made. Nor should the difficulties be exaggerated. For general purposes 'jurisdiction' may be translated as 'power' with no risk of inaccuracy.

Any administrative act or order which is ultra vires or outside jurisdiction is void in law, i.e. deprived of legal effect. If it is not within the powers given by the Act, it has no legal leg to stand on. The situation is then as if nothing had happened, and the unlawful act or decision may be replaced by a lawful one.

NECESSARY ARTIFICIALITIES

The technique by which the courts have extended the judicial control of powers is that of stretching the doctrine of ultra vires. As already observed, they can readily find implied limitations in Acts of Parliament, as they do when they hold that the exercise of a statutory power to revoke a licence is void unless done in accordance with the principles of natural justice. For this purpose they have only one weapon, the doctrine of ultra vires.[68] This is because they have no constitutional right to interfere with action which is within the powers granted (intra vires): if it is within jurisdiction, and therefore authorised by Parliament, the court has no right to treat it as unlawful.

Having no written constitution on which he can fall back, the judge must in every case be able to demonstrate that he is carrying out the will of Parliament as expressed in the statute conferring the power. He is on safe ground only where he can show that the offending act is outside the power. The only way in which he can do this, in the absence of an express provision, is by finding an implied term or condition in the Act, violation of which then entails the condemnation of ultra vires.

Into this bed of Procrustes, accordingly, must be fitted not only the more obvious cases of inconsistency with statute, such as failure to follow expressly prescribed procedure,

---

[67] The *Anisminic* case (below, p. 612) is an outstanding example.
[68] Formerly there was an exception in the case of error on the face of the record, explained below.

irregular delegation, and breach of jurisdictional conditions: but also the more sophisticated types of malpractice, such as unreasonableness, irrelevant considerations,
improper motives, breach of natural justice and, more recently, mere error of law. If an
Act empowers a minister to act as he thinks fit in some matter, the court will read into the
Act conditions requiring him to act within the bounds of reasonableness, to take account
of relevant but not of irrelevant considerations, to conform to the implicit policy of the
Act, and to give a fair hearing to anyone prejudicially affected. These are examples of the
many grounds on which the court will invalidate improper action. Somehow they must
be forced into the mould of the ultra vires doctrine, for unless that can be done the court
will be powerless.

'JURISDICTION'

It is at this point that artificiality becomes a problem. From time to time the judicial
mind rebels against the misuse of language which is seemingly involved in saying that, for
example, a minister who acts on wrong considerations or without giving someone a fair
hearing is acting outside his jurisdiction. It is tempting to call this, in words which will
be quoted later,[69] 'a wrong exercise of a jurisdiction which he has, and not a usurpation of
a jurisdiction which he has not'. Sometimes, therefore, judges have said that errors such
as improper motives or breach of natural justice do not involve excess of jurisdiction.[70]
But then they forgot that, if this were correct, they would have no title to condemn them.
Every administrative act is either intra vires or ultra vires; and the court can condemn it
only if it is ultra vires. Even now there are sometimes signs of judicial unfamiliarity with
the 'basic English' of administrative law. Relatively seldom do the courts feel it necessary
to expound the analysis of ultra vires in its more subtle applications. But the House of
Lords has done so in several important modern decisions, which put the matter beyond
doubt. In *Ridge* v. *Baldwin*,[71] a leading case on natural justice, the House held that the
dismissal of a chief constable, being vitiated by failure to give him a fair hearing, was void,
and from that it follows inexorably that it was outside jurisdiction, i.e. ultra vires.[72] In the
Anisminic case,[73] one of the high-water marks of judicial control, the House similarly held
that a tribunal's decision was a nullity if it misunderstood the law and so took account of
wrong factors. The connection between these various elements was clearly expressed in
the same case by Lord Pearce:[74]

> Lack of jurisdiction may arise in many ways. There may be an absence of those formali-
> ties or things which are conditions precedent to the tribunal having any jurisdiction
> to embark on an inquiry. Or the tribunal may at the end make an order that it has no

---

[69] Below, p. 217.
[70] As in *R* v. *Secretary of State for the Environment ex p Ostler* [1977] QB 122 (below, p. 623); but in *The
Discipline of Law*, 108, Lord Denning MR recanted these 'unguarded statements'. Another example is *R*
v. *Home Secretary ex p Cheblak* [1991] 1 WLR 890 at 894 (decision flawed by procedural error etc. said to be
'within the powers of the person taking it').
[71] [1964] AC 40; below, p. 415. A statement by the Privy Council that this was not the decision of the
majority is erroneous: below, p. 420.
[72] Expressly confirmed by the Privy Council (Lord Diplock) in *A-G* v. *Ryan* [1980] AC 718 at 730.
[73] *Anisminic Ltd* v. *Foreign Compensation Commission* [1969] 2 AC 147; below, p. 612; see similarly
O'Reilly v. *Mackman* [1983] 2 AC 237 at 278.
[74] At 195. Lord Reid at 171 in substance says the same thing, but he gives an unusually narrow meaning
to 'jurisdiction', thus holding that a decision can be a nullity without being in excess of jurisdiction. In the
normal sense of these words, this is a contradiction in terms: see below, p. 217.

jurisdiction to make. Or in the intervening stage, while engaged on a proper inquiry, the tribunal may depart from the rules of natural justice; or it may ask itself the wrong questions; or it may take into account matters which it was not directed to take into account. Thereby it would step outside its jurisdiction. It would turn its inquiry into something not directed by Parliament and fail to make the inquiry which Parliament did direct. Any of these things would cause its purported decision to be a nullity.

In 1992, and again in 1998, the House of Lords strongly confirmed this analysis, holding that any error of law rendered a tribunal's decision ultra vires.[75] History testifies, in fact, that the courts have long been using it consistently,[76] for example when awarding damages for trespass when a public authority demolished a building under an order which was void for violation of natural justice.[77] If the order is void, it cannot be within jurisdiction; for if it is within jurisdiction, it must be valid.

CRITICISMS OF THE ULTRA VIRES DOCTRINE

Sceptical comments on this long-established doctrine have been made by critics who justly observe that the restraints implied into Acts of Parliament have in reality been largely created by the judges on their own initiative and owe little to any perceptible Parliamentary intention. Eminent judges, writing extra-judicially, have described the doctrine as a 'fairy-tale'[78] and a 'fig-leaf'[79] serving to provide a facade of constitutional decency, with lip-service to the sovereign Parliament, while being out of touch with reality. The reality, it is argued, is that the judges are fulfilling the duties of their constitutional position, acting in their own right independently of Parliament, adjusting the balance of forces in the constitution, and asserting their title to promote fairness and justice in government under the rule of law.[80] These critics find the foundations of judicial review in the common law as developed by the judges rather than in the doctrine of ultra vires. Yet in their decisions the judges are firm upholders of the classical doctrine, based upon assumed Parliamentary approval,[81] since they rightly regard this as the sheet-anchor of

[75] *R* v. *Hull University Visitor ex p Page* [1993] AC 682; *Boddington* v. *British Transport Police* [1999] 2 AC 143.

[76] See e.g. *Short* v. *Poole Cpn* [1926] Ch 66, a much-cited case, where Warrington LJ observes (at 90) that no public body can have statutory authority to act in bad faith or on irrelevant grounds, and any such act is unauthorised and ultra vires. Similarly in *R* v. *North ex p Oakey* [1927] 1 KB 491 at 503, 505.

[77] *Cooper* v. *Wandsworth Board of Works* (1863) 14 CBNS 180; below, p. 408.

[78] See [1995] *PL* 65 (Lord Woolf MR). For Lord Irvine's support of the classical doctrine see [1999] EHRLR 350 at 368.

[79] See Sir John Laws in Supperstone and Goudie (eds.), *Judicial Review*, 1st edn, at 67; 2nd edn, 4.15; [1995] *PL* at 79. For a reply to these criticisms and comment on the technical problems of abandoning the traditional doctrine see (1996) 55 *CLJ* 122 (Forsyth). For Sir John Laws's response see *Judicial Review* (as above), 3rd edn, 4.13. For further valuable discussion see [1999] *CLJ* 129 (M. Elliott); Forsyth (ed.), *Judicial Review and the Constitution* (2000) with contributions by Elliott (269, 341), Forsyth (393), Craig (373) and Jowell (327); and Elliott, *The Constitutional Foundations of Judicial Review* (2001). See also [1999] *PL* 428 and 448; (2002) 61 *CLJ* 87 (Allan); [2003] *PL* 286 (Forsyth and Elliott); and Allan, *The Sovereignty of Law*, above, ch. 6.

[80] For a balanced discussion see (1998) 57 *CLJ* 63 (Craig).

[81] This is the modified ultra vires doctrine advanced by Forsyth and Elliott in the writings cited in the last note but one. It is consistent with the well-established approach to the interpretation of statutes granting a discretionary power. See, for instance, *R* v. *Home Secretary ex p Pierson* [1998] AC 539 where Lord Steyn said in this context: 'Parliament does not legislate in a vacuum. Parliament legislates for a European liberal democracy founded on the principles and traditions of the common law. And the courts may approach legislation on this initial assumption.' And in the same case Lord Browne-Wilkinson said: 'A power conferred by Parliament in general terms is not to be taken to authorise the doing of acts by the donee of the power which adversely affect the legal rights of the citizen or the basic principles on which the law of the United Kingdom

their constitutional authority.[82] While they remain of that mind, rival doctrines, even if plausible, must remain in the realm of theory. Those who would abandon the doctrine of ultra vires inevitably founder on the principle of Parliamentary supremacy. If, for instance, the maker of an administrative decision complies with all the requirements for validity, express or implied, laid down in the relevant statute, the common law cannot add any additional requirement (or remove or amend an existing requirement) without challenging the power of Parliament to specify the requirements of validity. The powers of the judges, moreover, have been greatly increased by the development of administrative law, and are now increased again by the Human Rights Act 1998. If they are seen to be staking claims to constitutional autonomy (criticised by Lord Irvine as 'judicial supremacism' prompted by 'extrajudicial romanticism')[83] they may be all the more exposed to attack as being unelected, unaccountable, devoid of democratic legitimacy, and no longer 'the weakest and least dangerous department of government'.[84]

There is, nevertheless, 'an inescapable tension between, on one hand, the traditional doctrine of ultra vires and its foundation in legislative supremacy and, on the other, the contemporary recognition of a range of common law rights conceived as basic components of a liberal, democratic legal order'.[85]

LEGISLATIVE, ADMINISTRATIVE, JUDICIAL AND QUASI-JUDICIAL FUNCTIONS

Administrative law needs consistent working definitions of the three primary constitutional functions, legislative, administrative and judicial; and also of the hybrid 'quasi-judicial' function which has a part of its own to play. But the reader must be warned that the courts themselves are addicted to distinctions which are more superficial and more confusing than those discussed here, and which by no means always help to clarity.

The one distinction which would seem to be workable is that between judicial and administrative functions. A judicial decision is made according to rules. An administrative decision is made according to administrative policy. A judge attempts to find what is the correct solution according to legal rules and principles. An administrator attempts to find what is the most expedient and desirable solution in the public interest. It is true, of course, that many decisions of the courts can be said to be made on grounds of legal policy and that the courts sometimes have to choose between alternative solutions with little else than the public interest to guide them. There will always be grey areas. Nevertheless the mental exercises of judge and administrator are fundamentally different. The judge's approach is objective, guided by his idea of the law. The administrator's approach is empirical, guided by expediency. Under this analysis, based on the nature of the functions, many so-called administrative tribunals, such as social security and employment tribunals, have judicial rather than administrative functions, since their sole task is to find facts and apply law objectively.

is based unless the statute conferring the power makes it clear that such was the intention of Parliament.' The modified ultra vires doctrine thus holds that the courts should, unless a contrary intention appears, assume that Parliament intended the powers granted to be exercised in accordance with the principles of the rule of law. In imposing good administrative standards on decision-makers judges are acting in accordance with this assumption.

[82] See above, p. 22.   [83] In a lecture published in [1996] *PL* 59 (see at 77).

[84] The words of Alexander Hamilton (The Federalist, No. 78) and the title of Lord Steyn's article in [1997] *PL* 84.   [85] T. R. S. Allan in Forsyth and Hare (eds.), *The Golden Metwand*, 15 at 35.

A quasi-judicial function is an administrative function which the law requires to be exercised in some respects as if it were judicial. A typical example is a minister deciding whether or not to confirm a compulsory purchase order or to allow a planning appeal after a public inquiry. The decision itself is administrative, dictated by policy and expediency. But the procedure is subject to the principles of natural justice, which require the minister to act fairly towards the objectors and not (for example) to take fresh evidence without disclosing it to them.[86] A quasi-judicial decision is therefore an administrative decision which is subject to some measure of judicial procedure. Since nowadays the great majority of administrative decisions which affect the rights or legal position of individuals are subject to the principles of natural justice in any case, the term quasi-judicial is now little used. It will however recur in Chapter 15, with comment on erratic judicial opinions.

In 1932 the Committee on Ministers' Powers formulated contrasting definitions of judicial and quasi-judicial decisions.[87] The important difference was that a judicial decision 'disposes of the whole matter by a finding upon the facts in dispute and an application of the law of the land to the facts so found', whereas in an administrative decision this is replaced by 'administrative action, the character of which is determined by the minister's free choice'.

To distinguish cleanly between legislative and administrative functions, on the other hand, is, as the Committee said, 'difficult in theory and impossible in practice'. They are easy enough to distinguish at the extremities of the spectrum: an Act of Parliament is legislative and a deportation order is administrative. But in between is a wide area where either label could be used according to taste, for example where ministers make orders or regulations affecting large numbers of people. This is further explained at the outset of Chapter 22.

---

[86] As explained by Lord Hoffmann in *R (Alconbury Developments Ltd)* v. *Secretary of State for the Environment, Transport and the Regions* [2001] 2 WLR 1389 at 1402.   [87] Cmd 4060 (1932), 73.

PART II

AUTHORITIES AND FUNCTIONS

3

THE CENTRAL GOVERNMENT

INTRODUCTION

This chapter aims to supply miscellaneous information about public authorities of various kinds and their legal status. An exhaustive account of the structure and functions of government belongs to constitutional rather that to administrative law. But some of the more prominent features of the system are here sketched, so as to illustrate the machinery by which executive power is conferred and exercised, and so as to fill in the administrative background to situations which will be analysed in later chapters. Taking first the central government, we may start at the apex of the pyramid with the Crown and ministers. The legal nature of the Crown itself is explained in a later chapter.[1]

THE CROWN AND MINISTERS

ALLOCATION OF POWERS

'The Crown' means the Queen, whether in her official or her personal capacity. The Crown's legal powers, whether prerogative or statutory, must be exercised by the sovereign personally as a matter of law, e.g. by Order in Council or letters patent or royal warrant. In practice these powers are controlled by ministers, since convention requires that the Crown should act as its ministers advise. The one case where the Crown may have to act of its own volition is in the appointment of a Prime Minister, the initial act of impetus which sets the machinery of cabinet government in motion; but even that is normally governed by convention.

The Crown itself, however, has relatively few important legal powers, except in the capacity of employer.[2] In almost all other areas administrative powers are statutory, and it has long been the practice for Parliament to confer them upon the proper minister in his own name.[3] The Act will say 'the minister may make regulations' or 'the minister may appoint' or 'the minister may approve'. The minister will of course be acting as a minister of the Crown and on behalf of the Crown. But his powers and duties under the Act will in law be his alone. This is of great legal and constitutional importance, since the minister as such has none of the Crown's prerogatives and immunities.[4] His unlawful actions may be invalidated, or he may be compelled to perform his duties, by remedies which do not lie against the Crown; and judgments may be enforced against him or his department in ways which are impossible in the case of the Crown itself. If on the other hand the Act had

---

[1] See below, p. 689. See generally Sunkin and Payne (eds.), *The Nature of the Crown*.
[2] See below, p. 48.
[3] Maitland, *Constitutional History*, 417, traced this practice from about the time of the Reform Bill of 1832.   [4] See below, p. 693.

conferred the powers upon the Crown, as by saying 'Her Majesty may (etc.)', the Crown's immunity would prevent control by the courts, at least in theory.[5] The settled practice of conferring powers upon designated ministers therefore greatly assists the operation of legal remedies. The minister is treated in law as an ordinary person, with no special privileges. He is liable to compulsory remedies, such as injunctions, and he may be made liable for contempt of court. This is the essence of the rule of law.

Fundamental as these principles are, they have not escaped being called into question, either inadvertently[6] or intentionally, by judges with heretical constitutional ideas. A case of 1993,[7] in which the Home Secretary was found guilty of contempt of court, assumed exceptional importance when the judge of first instance and a dissenting judge in the Court of Appeal held that the courts had no coercive power over ministers and other Crown officers, but that their relationship could only be one of trust. The Court of Appeal by a majority and the House of Lords unanimously rejected these propositions, and Lord Templeman said:

> For the purpose of enforcing the law against all persons and institutions, including ministers in their official capacity and their personal capacity, the courts are armed with coercive powers exercisable in proceedings for contempt of court...the argument that there is no power to enforce the law by injunction or contempt proceedings against a minister in his official capacity would, if upheld, establish the proposition that the executive obey the law as a matter of grace and not as a matter of necessity, a proposition which would reverse the result of the Civil War.

Lord Woolf then supplied the detailed analysis for confirming the traditional powers of the courts.

Powers are frequently conferred upon 'the Secretary of State' without naming his department, and they are then exercisable by any Secretary of State,[8] though only the appropriate one will normally act. The most powerful of all ministers, the Prime Minister, has in law less power than his colleagues due to the curious practice of not mentioning him or her in the statute book. But this practice is waning and in recent statutes the Prime Minister is given both powers and duties.[9]

The titles and functions of ministers and their departments are constantly being changed under schemes of reorganisation, normally effected under the Ministers of the

---

[5] In practice the courts may be able to grant remedies against the responsible minister, as explained below, p. 486.

[6] Statements in *Town Investments Ltd* v. *Department of the Environment* [1978] AC 359 to the effect that ministerial executive acts are acts done by 'the Crown' (Lord Diplock) and that a minister is incorporated with the Crown and 'an aspect or member of the Crown' (Lord Simon) are, as legal propositions, radically misconceived and ignore constitutional principles, as explained below, p. 689. The case decided by a majority, reversing a unanimous Court of Appeal, that a lease granted to a minister made the Crown the tenant. If it is to stand at all, it should be confined to property transactions: see *M* v. *Home Office* [1994] AC 377, distinguishing correctly between the Crown and its officers. *Town Investments* was quoted but not applied in *Linden* v. *Department of Health and Social Security* [1986] 1 WLR 164, holding that a lease to the Secretary of State made him and not the Crown the tenant, in *Pearce* v. *Secretary of State for Defence* [1988] 2 WLR 144, affirmed [1988] AC 755 and in *British Medical Association* v. *Greater Glasgow Health Board* [1989] AC 1211.

[7] *M* v. *Home Office* [1994] AC 377, discussed below, p. 705 where an inconsistency as to the ultimate power of enforcement is noted. *M* was applied in *R (Lamari)* v. *Home Secretary* [2012] EWHC 1895 (finding of contempt made against Home Secretary (non-compliance with undertaking to release immigrant from detention)).   [8] Interpretation Act 1978, 1st Sched.

[9] e.g. Parliamentary Commissioner Act 1967, s. 8; Regulation of Investigatory Powers Act 2000, s. 57; Constitutional Reform Act 2005, s. 2; Fixed Term Parliaments Act 2011, s. 1(5); Justice and Security Act 2013, ss. 1 and 2.

Crown Act 1975.[10] Orders in Council may be made under this Act both for the transfer of functions from one department to another and for the dissolution of departments no longer required. If it merely transfers functions the order need only be laid before Parliament and is then subject to annulment if either House so resolves; but if it dissolves an existing department, the order may not be made until each House has presented an address to the Crown in its favour.[11]

These orders often confer corporate personality on a newly created department, so that it can hold property, make contracts etc. in its own name and not merely as agent for the Crown. The usual, but not invariable, form is to make the minister a corporation sole, so that he and his successors have continuous corporate personality. The reorganisation of departments can reach beyond the nuts and bolts of efficient administration and raise constitutional issues. When in 2007 the Department of Constitutional Affairs (previously the Lord Chancellor's Department) was renamed the Ministry of Justice and given responsibility for criminal justice policy (including prisons and probation), concerns were expressed by the Lord Chief Justice and others that the new responsibilities would adversely affect the funding and independence of the court service. The change was the subject of an adverse report by the Constitutional Affairs Committee.[12]

EXECUTIVE AGENCIES

An important and far-reaching change in the organisation of government was made with the creation of numerous executive agencies (colloquially known as 'Next Steps' agencies). These agencies were established following a civil service report to the Prime Minister, entitled 'Improving Management in Government: The Next Steps',[13] and are designed to deliver improved public services to both the citizen and other government departments. They have no role to play in the development of policy. Executive agencies are established on a semi-autonomous basis with a professional manager, usually recruited from outside the civil service, as chief executive. Executive agencies do not, however, have a separate legal existence from their parent departments, and their personnel remain in law servants of the Crown.

These agencies are designed to deliver public services more efficiently by concentrating on value for money and running their 'businesses' on profit and loss lines.[14] They operate under framework documents—essentially agreements between the chief executive and the responsible minister—which specify how the performance of the agency is to be measured.[15] Under the Government Trading Act 1990 executive agencies are sometimes

---

[10] The Secretary of State for the Environment was shown as possessing powers under 65 different heads: *Index to the Statutes, 1235–1990*, 777. He is, of course, assisted by several non-cabinet ministers, though none of them is invested with legal powers.   [11] s. 5.

[12] 'The creation of the Ministry of Justice' (HC 466; 26 July 2007). And see the discussion at p. 773 on the abolition of the Administrative Justice and Tribunals Council.

[13] HMSO, 1988. An extensive literature exists on executive agencies. See James, *The Executive Agency Revolution in Whitehall* (2003). And see Jenkins and Gold, 'Unfinished Business: Where Next for Executive Agencies?' at <http://www.instituteforgovernment.org.uk/sites/default/files/publications/Unfinished%20 Business.pdf>.

[14] Oliver, *Government in the United Kingdom: The Search for Accountability, Effectiveness and Citizenship* (1991), 65. The Civil Service (Management Functions) Act 1992 allows management functions, including pay and conditions of service, to be delegated to the chief executive; and this is usually done.

[15] But, since agencies have no corporate identity, these agreements cannot be legally enforced; the autonomy of the agency subsists only in public law. See Freedland, [1994] *PL* 86, 89 and Harden, *The Contracting State* (1992), 46.

financed on a trading fund basis and are not subject to the normal parliamentary supply procedures. The Royal Mint, the Vehicle Inspectorate (now the Vehicle Operator Service Agency), the Civil Service College, Companies House, the government property lawyers, the National Weights and Measures Laboratory (now the National Measurement Office), the Employment Service, the Benefits Agency, and the Prisons Service *inter alia* have been established as executive agencies. There are now more than 100 executive agencies. This reform, which was adumbrated by the Fulton Report,[16] has generally been welcomed.[17] It rests on an undeniable distinction between the managerial functions of government in the provision of services of all kinds, and the development and implementation of policy by government departments. The government considers that the executive agency should be the 'default delivery option' for public services 'where there is a need to deliver public functions within central government but with a degree of operational independence and autonomy from ministers'.[18]

However, doubts have been expressed over the weakening of parliamentary scrutiny and the normal rules of accountability over the public service functions of government.[19] The dismissal in October 1995 of the chief executive of the Prisons Service (Derek Lewis) by the then Home Secretary (Michael Howard) following several high profile escapes from custody illustrated this vividly. The Home Secretary did not accept responsibility to Parliament for 'operational matters' (such as, he said, the escapes); he was only responsible for 'policy' and no failure of policy was shown.[20] The upshot was that there was no effective accountability to Parliament for the failings of the Prisons Service.[21]

THE CONTRACTUALISATION OF GOVERNMENT

Another important change in administrative style is the widespread privatisation of activities previously undertaken by the state and the introduction of some form of competition wherever possible.[22] These developments rest on the perception that the state delivers many services and performs many functions inefficiently. The private sector, driven by competition, can often perform these functions and deliver these services more effectively. The public, or the public's representative, is given a choice and will choose the best service. The state's role in these areas is thus limited to deciding how the discipline

[16] *Report of the Committee on the Civil Service*, Cmnd 3638 (1968), para. 190. See G. Drewry [1988] *PL* 505, 506.   [17] Oliver (as above), 66, pointing out that the report is cross-party.

[18] HM Government Response to the Administration Select Committee Report 'Smaller Government: Shrinking the Quango State' (March 2011) para. [102] at <http://www.official-documents.gov. uk/document/cm80/8044/8044.pdf>.

[19] Drewry (as above), 512–13; Drewry [1990] *PL* 322 at 325–8; and P. Giddings (ed.), *Parliamentary Accountability: A Study of Parliament and Executive Agencies* (Macmillan, 1995).

[20] This justification depends on the chief executive enjoying operational autonomy in fact. But the dismissed chief executive showed significant interference by the minister in operational matters; and secured a substantial settlement for the premature termination of his appointment: *The Times*, 17 October 1995; Bradley and Ewing, *Constitutional and Administrative Law*, 14th edn (2007), 287.

[21] HC Deb. col. 31 (16 October 1995); HC Deb. col. 519 (19 October 1995). See the discussion in Bradley and Ewing (as above), 284–5. The government has rejected the proposal of the Treasury and Civil Service Select Committee that agency chief executives should be directly accountable to select committees. Cm. 2748 (1995) (emphatically reaffirmed after the 1997 change of government: Cm. 4000 (1998)).

[22] For accounts see Harden, *The Contracting State* (1992); Freedland, [1994] *PL* 86 and Sunkin and Payne (eds.), *The Nature of the Crown*, ch. 5 (M. Freedland). This is part of a wider development termed 'New Public Management'. See Harlow and Rawlings, *Law and Administration*, 2nd edn (1997), 128, 150 and Osborne and Gaebler, *Reinventing Government* (1992). And see, Vincent-Jones, *The New Public Contracting* (2006); [2007] *PL* 40 (Auby); and Davies, *The Public Law of Government Contracts* (2008), ch. 1.

of the market is to be brought to bear and to providing the private sector with the opportunity to provide those services and functions. 'The state steers, it does not row' is the celebrated metaphor that captures this change.[23]

Private law concepts, primarily contract, have inevitably been prominent in this development.[24] Typically the government chooses a private contractor to deliver the service and enters into a contract with that person. Considerable changes in administrative law are implied by such changes. Services that were previously delivered by a government department or other public body (subject to judicial review) are now delivered by a private body under a contract to which the ordinary recipient of the service is usually not a party. The effect of such 'contracting out' arrangements on the reach of the Human Rights Act 1998 is discussed elsewhere.[25]

The forms by which these changes are achieved vary greatly. The privatisation of previously public utilities (telecommunications, electricity supply, gas supply etc.) is one form. And since these utilities are often powerful players in the relevant market their regulation is vital.[26] The private finance initiative is another. Here private bodies contract with public bodies to build, maintain and manage facilities (such as schools or hospitals) to be used by the public body in return for a fixed payment out of its current income. The benefits of such arrangements are the efficiency of the private sector being brought to the management of the facility as well as large capital sums being raised by the private body, but dedicated to a public use, without impacting upon the public finances. On the other hand, paying regularly out of current income over a long period may turn out to be more expensive than outright purchase.

Another form, adumbrated above, is direct 'contracting out' where a government body simply contracts with a private party for the provision of some benefit. This is not novel in the sense that every time a government department buys a paper clip, uses the services of a consultant or makes use of a private transport service it 'contracts out'. And it has been doing such things for centuries. But Part II of the Deregulation and Contracting Out Act 1994 sets up a mechanism whereby certain functions of ministers and officials may be delegated to private contractors. Although a veneer of accountability is maintained by deeming that the acts of the contractor 'shall be treated for all purposes as done... [by the minister or official]' these provisions have attracted much criticism.[27] Other forms include the establishment of NHS Trusts as suppliers of services to health authorities.

The impact of these developments on administrative law is a matter of some debate.[28] Most applications for judicial review arise from governmental activities—such as the administration of immigration controls, and maintenance of prisons—largely untouched by the changes described. Indeed, judicial control of regulators may offer new vistas for judicial review.[29] There will doubtless be fresh challenges to administrative law but classic principles, flexibility and judicial ingenuity will ensure that the shift of some previously public power into private hands will not leave the citizen unprotected.[30]

---

[23] Osborne and Gaebler cited in Harlow and Rawlings (as above), 131.
[24] For 'government by contract' see further below, p. 674.   [25] Below, p. 147.
[26] See below, p. 116.   [27] Freedland, [1995] PL 21.
[28] See generally, Taggart (ed.), *The Province of Administrative Law* (1997), and in particular the contributions by Taggart, Hunt and Aronson.   [29] See below, p. 123.
[30] See Oliver in Taggart (as above), 217, finding common values in private and public law. They will prove important in this task.

THE CIVIL SERVICE

GENERAL ASPECTS

The civil service comprises all the permanent and non-political offices and employments held under the Crown, with the exception of the armed forces. All these officers and employees form the permanent administrative staff of the central government. The legal test of a civil servant is that he should be in the non-military service of the Crown, i.e. there must be a legal relationship of master and servant. This test excludes the great majority of public corporations. The legal nature of Crown service is investigated in a later section. Meanwhile some broader features may be indicated here.[31]

The grand total of civil servants, if all clerical and industrial employees are included, is about 444,000.[32] But the number of those who occupy positions of any constitutional importance and who have authority to take decisions is very much smaller, probably less than 10,000. Perhaps half this number are the true governors of the great administrative machine, formerly known as the administrative class, below whom there used formerly to be the executive class. This system of classes was criticised as over-rigid by the Fulton Committee in 1968[33] and was thereupon abolished by the government, since when it has not been so easy to estimate the precise size of the more important classes within the civil service. In addition there are great numbers in the clerical and industrial grades employed in work which is similar to other civilian work outside the service of the Crown. Employees of the Post Office are not civil servants.[34]

The powers of the central government are normally conferred upon ministers themselves, as already explained, and are exercised by their departments in the ministers' names. Powers are, however, conferred directly upon civil servants who have adjudicatory functions such as social security officers and inspectors of taxes and the Commissioners of Customs and Excise. Part II of the Deregulation and Contracting Out Act 1994, however, permits many functions of ministers or office holders to be exercised by other persons—even non-civil servants such as private contractors.[35]

MACHINERY OF CONTROL

Apart from the period 1968–81 the general control of the civil service has been the responsibility of the Treasury. The legal sanction behind the government's powers of control over the civil service is nothing more than the Crown's power to dismiss its servants at pleasure, so that the Crown can prescribe or vary their conditions of employment as it wishes.[36]

---

[31] For general information and history see the Fulton Report (below); Holdsworth, *History of English Law*, xiv. 106–40; Parris, *Constitutional Bureaucracy*. The word 'bureaucracy' came into use in the 1830s. In 1838 Lord Palmerston had to explain it to the young Queen Victoria: Carr, *Concerning English Administrative Law*, 1. See further, Hennessy, *Whitehall*. See [2006] *PL* 653 (Sandberg) for criticism of the definition of the service.

[32] There was significant growth after the 1997 change of government and a decline in numbers since 2004 with a further decline under the Coalition Government. For the latest figures see <http://www.civilservice. gov.uk/about/facts/statistics>.

[33] *Report of the Committee on the Civil Service*, Cmnd 3638 (1968), para. 215. The Report will be referred to as the Fulton Report. For the government's decision to abolish the former classes see 767 HC Deb. col. 456 (26 June 1968). [34] See below, p. 114.

[35] See below, p. 675; [1995] *PL* 21 at 23–6 (Freedland).

[36] *Council of Civil Service Unions* v. *Minister for the Civil Service* [1985] AC 374 at 409 (Lord Diplock). For this passage see Appendix 1.

For centuries the civil service was regulated under Orders in Council which had no statutory basis and were held by the courts to be made under the royal prerogative.[37] But Part 1 of the the Constitutional Reform and Governance Act 2010 replaces these arrangements and places the management of the civil service on a statutory basis.[38] The purpose of these reforms is said to be to ensure 'that the Civil Service is not left vulnerable to change at the whim of the Government of the day without proper parliamentary debate and scrutiny'.[39]

A civil servant of at least two years' standing threatened with dismissal or premature retirement can appeal to the Civil Service Appeal Board[40] and will have the benefit of the statutory law about unfair dismissal and other matters, as explained later.

RECRUITMENT AND CHARACTER

The ideals of the modern civil service were proclaimed in the Northcote-Trevelyn Report of 1853.[41] In the future entry was to be by competitive examination[42] instead of patronage; and promotion was based on merit. The Civil Service Commission, an independent body established in 1855,[43] was set up to achieve this and it has been very successful. The approval of the Commission is required for the appointment of the most senior civil servants but most are appointed by their departments according to the principles set out in a Recruitment Code.[44] Although it was feared at the time that the stress on examinations would create a civil service consisting of 'statesmen in disguise', in fact the service has been noted for its combination of executive ability with political neutrality. Concern that these traditional values were being eroded led to the adoption of the Civil Service Code which underlines the core values of the service, integrity, honesty, objectivity and impartiality.[45] The Code requires civil servants to act according to law. They have access to the commissioners if asked to do something improper.[46]

Apart from ministers who come and go with the tides of politics, government departments consist almost wholly of permanent career officials. Ministers, however, have increasingly felt a need for advice of a politically sympathetic kind and have brought numbers of personal or 'special' advisers with them into their departments. They are usually appointed to temporary civil service posts and they leave the department when the minister goes. The detachment of civil servants from the political battle is an important element in preserving the stability of the state notwithstanding regular changes of government.[47] One consequence

---

[37] But note the alternative basis suggested by Lord Diplock (ibid.), namely a special rule of constitutional law.   [38] Act of 2010, s. 3(1).

[39] See the Green Paper 'The Governance of Britain' Cm. 7170 (July 2007), para. 44.

[40] See [1972] PL 149; R v. Civil Service Appeal Board ex p Bruce [1988] ICR 649; R v. Civil Service Appeal Board ex p Cunningham [1991] 4 All ER 310. For matters affecting national security see Security Procedures in the Public Service, Cmnd 1681 (1962); [1963] PL 51 (M. R. Joelson).

[41] Reprinted in the Fulton Report (Cmnd 3638 (1968), Appendix B).

[42] The current practice is to supplement school and university examinations with special examinations and interviews.

[43] It is now on a statutory footing: Constitutional Reform and Governance Act 2010, s. 2(1).

[44] Turpin and Tomkins, British Government and the Constitution, 7th edn (2011), 440. The appointment functions of the Commission are now to be found in the 2010 Act, ss. 11–14.

[45] The current code is available at <http://resources.civilservice.gov.uk/wp-content/uploads/2011/09/civil-service-code-2010.pdf>. The Constitutional Reform and Governance Act 2010, s. 5(1) requires the Minister for the Civil Service to publish a Code. Statute now requires the Code to have certain minimum requirements (2010 Act, s. 7) and in particular the Code must require that 'civil servants…carry out their duties (a) with integrity and honesty, and (b) with objectivity and impartiality' (s. 7(4)).

[46] Act of 2010, s. 9.

[47] There are stringent (non-statutory) restrictions on the political activities of civil servants, particularly in the higher grades and, by statute, civil servants cannot be MPs (House of Commons Disqualification Act

of this detachment is that ministers should take responsibility in Parliament for what happens in their departments and that the civil servants involved should generally remain anonymous.[48] But public inquiries when something has gone wrong sometimes identify the officials responsible[49] and Permanent Secretaries (and sometimes more junior civil servants) give evidence to the Select Committees.[50] This loss of anonymity should be treated with caution for it tends to undermine the necessary detachment from the public arena of politics. The suicide in 2003 of Dr David Kelly, the arms control inspector, after he had been questioned before the Foreign Affairs Committee on his role in preparing the dossier containing inaccurate information on Iraq's possession of weapons of mass destruction and his relationships with journalists underlines the need for caution.[51]

The original 'philosophy of the amateur' that was much criticised by the Fulton Report of 1968, has been abandoned; and professionalism now pervades the service. It is noteworthy, though, how few lawyers are employed in the civil service, outside the Ministry of Justice. And they are employed as technicians—as legal advisers or as draftsmen—rather than to assist in the development of policy. A distinctly legal voice in the administration is seldom heard. This can sometimes lead to a certain antagonism between the legal and official mentalities. A harbinger of changing attitudes may be the publication of the booklet, 'The Judge Over Your Shoulder',[52] by the Cabinet Office. It is designed to alert civil servants to 'danger areas' where their decisions might expose a minister to challenge in the courts. And it certainly tends to improve the quality of decisions.

OFFICIAL SECRECY

A counterpart of the virtues of impartiality and anonymity is the occupational vice of secrecy, of which the civil service is continually accused despite the vast number of informative publications which it issues. The official reluctance to allow the public to see departmental papers was buttressed by the Official Secrets Acts 1911–39, which were a serious impediment to openness in government.[53] The principal Act of 1911 was a hasty piece of catch-all legislation which passed through the House of Commons in one day without debate at the time of the Agadir crisis. Section 2 (now repealed) was absurdly broad in scope, rendering criminal all unauthorised disclosure of information from official sources, regardless of whether the public interest demanded secrecy or not.[54] Prosecutions required the consent of the Attorney-General, and it was only by

1975). These restrictions do not infringe the European Convention on Human Rights (*Ahmed* v. *UK* (2000) 29 EHRR 1 (similar restrictions on local authority employees upheld)).

[48] But see above, p. 37 dealing with executive agencies.

[49] See the *Inquiry into the Export of Defence Equipment and Dual Use Goods to Iraq and Related Prosecutions, 1995–6*, HC 115 (The Scott Report).

[50] The guidance on the appearance of civil servants before select committees used to be called the 'Osmotherley Rules'. But the name seems to have been dropped. The current rules are to be found at <http://www.gov.uk/government/uploads/system/uploads/attachment_data/file/61192/guide-deptal-evidence-and-response-to-select-committees.pdf>. Since it is the minister who is accountable, the official appears on behalf of the minister and subject to his direction. But if a named official is requested by the committee, there is a presumption that he will appear.

[51] Discussed in Bradley and Ewing, as above, 288.

[52] To be found at <http://www.tsol.gov.uk/Publications/Scheme_Publications/judge.pdf>.

[53] For their history and defects see David Williams, *Not in the Public Interest*.

[54] The Franks Committee (as below) at p. 112 epitomised the primary provision as making it an offence 'for a Crown servant or government contractor to make an unauthorised disclosure of information which he has learnt in the course of his job'. It also covered communication of information obtained in contravention of the Act or entrusted in confidence by an official, including the police.

executive control that the law was rendered tolerable. An indiscriminate law of this kind is a breeding-ground of abuse.

Continuous complaint about this oppressive law, and the difficulty of obtaining convictions under it,[55] led to a committee of inquiry in 1972, the Franks Committee, which condemned the main provision of the Act of 1911 and recommended less indiscriminate legislation.[56] Although the government received the Committee's report favourably,[57] the proposed legislation, based on the report, foundered in the House of Commons in 1979 amid confusion and controversy.[58] Eight years later, following the *Spycatcher* saga,[59] the government once more proposed reform, and the Official Secrets Act 1989 was enacted. The 1989 Act repeals the notorious section 2 of the 1911 Act and decriminalises much that was previously criminal. However, in other respects it remains restrictive.

First, the Act makes it a criminal offence for a person who is, or has been, a member of the security or intelligence services to disclose any information obtained by virtue of his position.[60] Crown servants or government contractors—who are not also members of the security or intelligence services—also commit an offence if they disclose information relating to security or intelligence matters, but that disclosure must in addition be 'damaging'.[61]

Second, although the Act abandons the 'catch-all' approach of section 2 of the 1911 Act, it creates broad categories of protected information whose disclosure is generally a criminal offence. Apart from the security or intelligence information already mentioned, these categories are defence,[62] international relations[63] and law enforcement.[64] Disclosure without lawful authority of defence information and information about international relations must be 'damaging'[65] before an offence is committed, but this is not so with information relating to law enforcement.[66] Furthermore, a person—not a Crown

---

[55] In 1986 the House of Commons Select Committee on the Treasury and Civil Service reported that s. 2 was now unenforceable (7th Report, HC 1985–6, No. 92-1). For the government's comments see Cmnd 9841.

[56] Departmental Committee on Section 2 of the Official Secrets Act 1911 (chairman, Lord Franks), Cmnd 5104 (1972).

[57] See Cmnd 7285 (White Paper, 1978); *Disclosure of Official Information: A Report on Overseas Practice* (HMSO, 1979). [58] The details are given in the 6th edn of this book at p. 59.

[59] This tale is too notorious to need a detailed account here. In brief, the Attorney-General sought injunctions prohibiting newspapers from publishing extracts from P. M. Wright's *Spycatcher* which contained confidential information about the security services. Although the book had already been published elsewhere, interim injunctions were obtained: *A-G* v. *Guardian Newspapers Ltd* [1987] 1 WLR 1248. Final injunctions, however, were refused by the House of Lords: *A-G* v. *Guardian Newspapers Ltd (No 2)* [1990] 1 AC 109. Once the material was in the public domain, it was futile to attempt to restrain further publication.

[60] s. 1(1) and (2). The provisions of s. 1 can be extended to non-members of the security and intelligence services by written notification from a minister of the Crown (s. 1(1)(b), (6), (7) and (8)). It is a defence to a charge under s. 1 to show the defendant did not know and had no reasonable cause to believe that the information related to security or intelligence matters (s. 1(5)).

[61] s. 1(3). A disclosure of information will be 'damaging' if it causes actual damage to the work of the security and intelligence services or if it is likely to have that effect or if the information falls into a class of information likely to have that effect (s. 1(4)). [62] s. 2.

[63] s. 3. [64] s. 4.

[65] The precise meaning of 'damaging' depends on the context. For defence information it relates to damage, or likely damage, to the capability of the armed forces of the Crown or which leads to loss of life or injury to members of the armed forces or serious damage to their equipment or installations or which endangers the UK's interests abroad or seriously obstructs the promotion and protection of those interests or which endangers British citizens abroad (s. 2(2)). For information relating to international relations 'damaging' relates to damage, or likely damage, to UK interests abroad or seriously obstructs the promotion and protection of those interests or which endangers British citizens abroad (s. 3(2)). As before, there is a defence where the defendant did not know and had no reasonable cause to believe that the information was protected or that its disclosure would be damaging (s. 2(3), s. 3(4)). [66] s. 4.

servant or government contractor—who comes into possession of information disclosed in breach of the Act commits an offence if he makes a further 'damaging' disclosure of that information and he had reasonable cause to believe (or know) that the disclosure would be damaging.[67]

The 1989 Act has been much criticised.[68] There is no public interest defence—so the civil servant who makes an unauthorised disclosure in order to reveal serious wrongdoing is as guilty as one who acts in the interests of a foreign power.[69] The Act has been seen as designed to render convictions for unauthorised disclosure easier to obtain rather than to facilitate the flow of information from government to citizen.[70] Moreover, the civil law of confidence and breach of contract remains in place: unauthorised disclosure of official information, whether or not that disclosure is an offence under the Act, will often be liable to be forbidden by injunction.[71]

THE PROTECTION OF PERSONAL INFORMATION

In the modern world, information about individuals is held by many bodies, private and public, and there is a clear need to regulate the processing of such information as well as the use and disclosure of it. This is achieved in the main[72] by the Data Protection Act 1998.[73] Unlike its predecessor, the Data Protection Act 1984, the Act of 1998 defines 'data' widely. Thus automatically processed information (such as that held on a computer) as well as information which is held in other forms in a way that specific information relating to a particular individual is readily accessible[74]—for instance a card index or files held under individuals' names—is covered by the Act. Subject to a range of qualifications and exemptions individuals have a right of access to personal data about themselves;[75] and where the personal information held is shown to be inaccurate the court may order rectification or erasure of the offending material.[76] An individual who suffers damage as a result of a breach of the Act by a data controller may recover damages from the controller.[77]

---

[67] s. 5(2) and (3).

[68] See e.g. S. Palmer, 'Tightening Secrecy Law: The Official Secrets Act 1989' [1990] PL 243.

[69] Confirmed in R v. Shayler [2003] 1 AC 247 (HL) which also held that the 1989 Act did not breach Art. 10 (freedom of expression) of the European Convention (restrictions justified under Art. 10(2)).

[70] Palmer (as above), 256.

[71] But not if the information was no longer confidential. A claim for profits made by breach of contract may lie (A-G v. Blake [1998] 2 WLR 805). The current contractual arrangements (under which an officer in the employ of the Crown must seek clearance for any publication) have been several times enforced by injunction to restrain special forces soldiers from publishing without clearance (R v. A-G [2003] UKPC 22 (not duress to be required to sign contract on pain of return to unit) and Ministry of Defence v. Griffin [2008] EWHC 1542 (clearance procedure to be followed even where disclosure sought to reveal wrongdoing). The decision to refuse clearance may be subject to judicial review (R, para. 36).

[72] See also the Protection of Freedoms Act 2012 which regulates the treatment of personal information in specific areas (the retention and destruction of DNA, fingerprint and other evidence (Part 1, Chapter 1); the processing of biometric data of school children (Part 1, Chapter 2); and the regulation of surveillance cameras (Part 2).

[73] This Act implements Council Directive 95/46 ([1995] OJ L281/31). Article 1 of the Directive imposes a duty upon Member States to protect the 'fundamental rights and freedoms of natural persons and, in particular, their right to privacy with respect to the processing of personal data'. The Act, however, does not use the language of fundamental rights. The Law Commission has announced that it will investigate the perceived problems experienced by public bodies applying the Data Protection Act 1998: <http://lawcommission. justice.gov.uk/areas/data-sharing.htm>.   [74] s. 1(1).

[75] ss. 7–12.   [76] s. 14.   [77] s. 13.

The Act establishes the necessary administrative machinery to ensure that the 'data protection principles' are observed by data processors.[78] These principles, which are both detailed and complex lay down, very broadly,[79] that processing should not take place without the consent of the individual who is the subject of the data, or pursuant to the processor's legal obligations, or to protect the interests of the data subject or where it is necessary for the administration of justice or other central government function.[80] Processing is also lawful where it is pursuant to the 'legitimate interests' of the processor provided that it is not prejudicial to the data subject's 'rights, freedoms or legitimate interests'.[81] More onerous restrictions apply where 'sensitive personal data' are being processed.[82] Subject to some qualifications, processors may not process personal data unless they are registered with the Information Commissioner.[83] There are many exemptions from particular provisions of the Act in order to protect national security, to prevent crime, to assess or collect tax and related purposes.[84] The exemptions allowing processing for journalistic, literary and artistic purposes and for the purpose of research may be noted.[85] The Act binds the Crown.[86]

The Information Commissioner polices the 'data protection principles'[87] and if satisfied that they are being breached may issue an 'enforcement notice' requiring the data processor to take remedial action.[88] It is a criminal offence to breach an 'enforcement notice'.[89] But there is a right of appeal to the Information Tribunal[90] and a further appeal to the High Court on a point of law.[91]

THE INTERCEPTION OF COMMUNICATIONS

Legislation now provides protection for the communication of messages both by post and by telecommunication systems. After many years of controversy, the legislation was prompted by litigation which established that telephone-tapping was not a tort at common law[92] but was a violation of the European Convention on Human Rights (ECHR) unless legally restricted by precise and justifiable rules.[93] The Interception of Communications Act 1985 first gave the Home Secretary restricted powers to issue interception warrants, constituted a tribunal to deal with complaints and with power to award compensation and a commissioner to review the working of the Act. That Act, however, was overtaken by advances in technology and it failed to provide adequately for human rights. It is now replaced by Part One of the Regulation of Investigatory Powers Act 2000, which in part follows the scheme of the earlier Act but makes wider provision,

---

[78] s. 4(4).   [79] No more than a rough outline now follows.   [80] 2nd Sched.
[81] 2nd Sched., para. 6(1).
[82] 3rd Sched. This is data relating to race, ethnic origin, political opinions, religious or similar beliefs, health, sexual life, membership of a trade union and criminal proceedings against the individual (para. 2).
[83] s. 17.   [84] Pt IV.   [85] ss. 32–3.   [86] s. 63.
[87] And to this end he publishes a 'data sharing code' (Act of 1998, s. 52A).
[88] s. 40. The Commissioner also has powers, on the request of any person affected by processing of data in breach of the Act, to require the data processors to provide the information necessary to assess whether there has been a breach (ss. 42–3), but this is restricted where the journalistic, literary and artistic purposes exemption is engaged (s. 44).   [89] s. 47(1).
[90] s. 48. The tribunal is established under s. 6(3) and (4). The chairman and deputy chairman are appointed by the Lord Chancellor (powers now exercised by the Secretary of State for Constitutional Affairs: SI 2003 No. 1887) and the other members, who must be legally qualified, are appointed by the Home Secretary to represent the interests of data controllers and data subjects.   [91] s. 49.
[92] *Malone* v. *Metropolitan Police Commissioner* [1979] Ch 344; *Malone* v. *UK* [1985] 7 EHRR 14.
[93] *Malone* v. *UK* [1985] 7 EHRR 14 (Art. 8 of the Human Rights Convention infringed).

covering both public and private telecommunications systems. Interception is a crime but the Home Secretary has power by warrant to authorise it.[94] The Home Secretary must believe that a warrant is necessary in the interests of national security, for the prevention or detection of serious crime, for safeguarding the economic well-being of the country or for giving effect to international crime-prevention arrangements. The Act provides more elaborately for interception warrants and for who may apply for them, including chief officers concerned with defence, intelligence and public security. Interception without warrant is also provided for in some cases, for instance, where there is the consent of both parties (or the consent of one party where directed surveillance has been authorised (see later) or in accordance with any business practice authorised under rules made by the Home Secretary).[95] The Tribunal and the Commissioner are the subject of new provisions. The President of the Tribunal and the Commissioner are senior judges. Even so, and notwithstanding that the Tribunal is to be 'the only appropriate Tribunal' for human rights claims, judicial review is not wholly excluded.[96]

New areas brought under control by the Act are 'directed surveillance', 'intrusive surveillance' and 'covert human intelligence sources'. An example of this last class would be a police officer working under cover. The jurisdiction of the tribunal is extended accordingly and there are 'surveillance commissioners' who are the same as the commissioners appointed under the Police Act 1997 to monitor searches of property, being holders or former holders of high judicial office. There are also powers to compel the decrypting of encrypted information. In a controversial development some local authorities have undertaken 'directed surveillance' (which may involve interception of communications without a warrant where one party consents) for petty matters (disputes over rubbish collection, fly-tipping and dog fouling).[97] The use of these powers to investigate whether the parents of a child had lied about their place of residence on a school application form has been held to be a breach of Article 8 of the European Convention by the Investigatory Powers Tribunal.[98]

FREEDOM OF INFORMATION

The growing recognition that 'open government is part of effective democracy'[99] led first to a Code of Practice on Access to Government Information[100] and then after the change of government in 1997, to the Freedom of Information Act 2000.[101] The Act was preceded by a White Paper[102] which proposed a somewhat more far-reaching reform. Nonetheless, it is clear that an important change in the culture of government is under way. Instead

---

[94] s. 1 (criminal offence) and s. 7 (Home Secretary's powers).   [95] ss. 3 and 4.

[96] s. 65(2)(a) and R (A) v. B [2008] EWHC 1512. Section 67(8) precludes challenge in a court of a decision of the Tribunal 'including decisions as to...jurisdiction' but this ouster is only applicable to proceedings pursuant to s. 65(2)(a) and (b) (s. 67(9)) (para. 5).

[97] 'Council Spy Cases Hit 1,000 a Month', Daily Telegraph, 14 April 2008.

[98] Paton v. Poole BC, IPT/09/01/C (29 July 2010).

[99] From the Open Government White Paper.

[100] Implemented in terms of the Open Government White Paper, Cm. 2290 (1993), which concluded that a statutory freedom of information regime was not necessary. See [1993] PL 557 (Birkinshaw).

[101] See The Law of Freedom of Information (2003) (Macdonald and Jones). There is similar but separate legislation in Scotland (Freedom of Information (Scotland) Act 2002).

[102] Your Right to Know: The Government's Proposals for a Freedom of Information Act, Cm. 3818 (1997). For comment see Palmer, 'Freedom of Information—Principles and Problems' in Constitutional Reform in the United Kingdom: Practice and Principles (Centre for Public Law, 1998), 147–56 and [1998] PL 176 (Birkinshaw).

of keeping matters secret as a matter of course, government and other public bodies will need to justify a failure to disclose relevant information upon request. The relationship between citizen and state is being significantly altered.

The crucial provision of the Act is section 1(1) which provides that 'any person making a request for information to a public authority is entitled—(a) to be informed in writing by the public authority whether it holds information of the description specified in the request, and (b) if that is the case, to have that information communicated to him.' A lengthy schedule to the Act specifies the public authorities involved. They include central government departments (but not the Security Service, the Secret Intelligence Service and GCHQ), the Armed Forces of the Crown (but not the special forces), the NHS, local authorities, state-funded schools, colleges of further education, universities in receipt of financial support from the state (as well as their colleges) and the police (including police authorities).[103] The public authority must comply promptly with any request for information and in any event within twenty working days.[104] All public authorities must publish a 'publication scheme' setting out the manner in which it intends to make information public and whether a fee is payable.[105] If reasonably practicable the applicant is entitled to inspect the document itself, not just a copy or summary.[106]

The general duty to provide information is subject to widespread exemptions.[107] The public authority may refuse a request for information where the cost of complying would be excessive[108] or where a vexatious or repeated request is made.[109] Other exemptions— too numerous to list comprehensively here—include information that is accessible to the public by other means[110] or which is intended for publication in the future.[111] Unqualified exemptions exist for information supplied by security services,[112] national security[113] and information relating to the development or formulation of government policy, communications between ministers as well as Cabinet minutes, the advice of Law Officers and the operation of ministerial private offices.[114] But the exemptions in regard to defence,[115] international relations,[116] inter-administration relations within the United Kingdom,[117] economic matters,[118] law enforcement[119] and other information held by government departments and other public authorities[120] are qualified. The qualification is generally that disclosure would 'prejudice' the relevant interest. For instance, such 'other [governmental] information' need not be disclosed if, in the reasonable opinion of the 'qualified person', the disclosure would 'prejudice' the collective responsibility of ministers, 'inhibit' free and frank deliberation or 'would otherwise prejudice or would be likely to prejudice, the effective conduct of public affairs'.[121] In the White Paper a less restrictive test of 'substantial harm' was proposed in this and other areas.

---

[103] s. 3 (1) and 1st Sched. The schedule may be amended by order: s. 5.

[104] s. 10. But where a fee is payable (under s. 9) time runs from the payment of the fee (s. 10(2)).

[105] s. 19. The Commissioner must approve the scheme (s. 19(1)(a)) and he may publish model schemes (s. 20).   [106] s. 11.

[107] The wide exemptions are none the less not a breach of the right under Art. 10 of the European Convention to receive information: *Sugar* v. *BBC* [2012] UKSC 4, [2012] 1 WLR 439, paras. 94–8 (Lord Brown).

[108] s. 12. For this exemption to apply the cost of complying with the request must exceed a limit set by the Secretary of State.   [109] s. 14.

[110] s. 21.   [111] s. 22.

[112] s. 23. A minister's certificate to that effect is conclusive (s. 23(2)) but there is an appeal to the Tribunal (s. 60).

[113] s. 24. A minister's certificate to the effect that the information concerned falls within the exemption is conclusive (s. 24(3)) but there is an appeal to the Tribunal (s. 60).   [114] s. 35.

[115] s. 26.   [116] s. 27.   [117] s. 28.

[118] s. 29.   [119] s. 31.   [120] s. 36.   [121] s. 36(2).

There are further exemptions concerning communications with Her Majesty,[122] endangering health and safety,[123] personal information,[124] information provided in confidence,[125] legal professional privilege,[126] cases where disclosure would be prejudicial to commercial interests[127] and where disclosure is prohibited under another enactment or a community obligation.[128] The minister can add exemptions by order.[129] Where information is exempt the public authority is generally not obliged to confirm or deny that it holds the information requested.[130]

The machinery necessary to administer the duty to disclose is set up by the Act. The Secretary of State issues a code of practice to guide public authorities as to good practice in regard to the general right of access set out in Part 1 of the Act[131] and the Secretary of State for Constitutional Affairs issues a code of practice in regard to the keeping, management and destruction of records.[132] The Information Commissioner has general functions with regard to the encouragement of good practice and reports to Parliament.[133] In particular, individuals may complain to the commissioner where they consider that a request for information has not been dealt with properly; if after investigation the Commissioner considers that there has been failure to comply with Part 1 of the Act he may issue an 'enforcement notice'.[134] Failure to comply with such a notice is considered a contempt of court.[135] There is an appeal to the Information Tribunal from the decisions of the Commissioner,[136] and a further appeal on a point of law to the High Court.[137] There is also a much-criticised 'ministerial override'. Where a Cabinet minister (or law officer) issues an appropriate certificate the relevant decision or enforcement notice 'shall cease to have effect'.[138]

THE LAW OF CROWN SERVICE

NATURE OF CROWN SERVICE

Crown service is one of the most curious departments of public law. In most other democratic countries the position and rights of state employees form an important branch of administrative law, and the tenure of posts in the civil service gives rise to many questions for the courts, whether they be ordinary courts of law or special administrative courts. In England the position is different. The civil service, despite its great size and importance, is largely staffed and regulated under arrangements which are legally anomalous. It has generally been held that at common law civil servants of the Crown, and military servants also, have no legal right to their salaries and no legal protection against wrongful

---

[122] s. 37 (includes communications about honours). This exemption does not cover the Prince of Wales's communications with ministers (*Evans* v. *Information Commissioner* [2012] UKUT 313).

[123] s. 38.

[124] s. 40 (information exempt if disclosure would breach the 'data protection principles' explained above, p. 61).

[125] s. 41.   [126] s. 42.   [127] s. 43.   [128] s. 44.   [129] ss. 4, 5.

[130] s. 17.   [131] s. 45.

[132] s. 46. Lord Chancellor's powers transferred to Secretary of State by SI 2003 No. 1887.

[133] ss. 18, 47–9. The Information Commissioner was previously the Data Protection Commissioner.

[134] ss. 50–2.

[135] s. 54. The Commissioner certifies to the High Court that there has been a failure to comply and the court then deals with the matter 'as if [the public authority] had committed a contempt of court'.

[136] s. 57.   [137] s. 59.

[138] Act of 2000, s. 53(2). Discussed in *R (Evans)* v. *A.-G.* [2013] EWHC 1960 (certificate overriding order to reveal correspondence between the Prince of Wales and ministers upheld (after intense judicial review)).

dismissal. Although recently the picture has changed substantially, the law has long regarded the civil service as if it still consisted of a handful of secretaries working behind the scenes in a royal palace. Although it has lost its domestic character in every other respect, it is still in a primitive state of legal evolution.

Another paradox is that in practice the situation is just the opposite of what these legal rules would suggest. Crown service, though legally the most precarious employment, is in reality the most secure. This is merely convention, but in the civil service the convention is deeply ingrained, so that there are probably better grounds for complaining that civil servants are excessively protected than for criticising their defencelessness in law.[139] Even when a public inquiry reveals serious failings in the conduct of civil servants, they are rarely dismissed.[140]

Crown servants of all ranks are in law the servants of the Crown and not of one another.[141] A civil servant therefore has no contractual rights against his department, his minister or any superior officer. Whoever engages him acts merely as the Crown's agent, and his contract of employment[142] is directly between himself (as servant) and the Crown. Any remedy must therefore be sought against the Crown alone.[143]

TENURE: NO PROTECTION AT COMMON LAW

The best-known decision on the legal insecurity of civil service tenure concerned the dismissal of a consular agent in Nigeria. He had been engaged for a term (as he said) of three years certain, but was prematurely dismissed. He sued the Crown by petition of right, but the Court of Appeal refused him relief,[144] holding that it 'is not competent for the Crown to tie its hands by such a contract [with a civil servant]'.

The basis of the rule that Crown servants are dismissible at pleasure, therefore, is the principle that the public interest requires that the government should be able to disembarrass itself of any employee at any moment. All the emphasis was on public policy. There was no suggestion that the rule had any connection with the royal prerogative.[145]

The rule so laid down was followed in later decisions.[146] Yet the reasons put forward for this policy will not really bear examination. Any employer can always dismiss a

---

[139] The Fulton Committee found it hard to believe that the rate of dismissals for misconduct and inefficiency should not have been higher: Cmnd 3638 (1968), para. 123.

[140] There were no dismissals of civil servants in the Crichel Down affair of 1954 (see p. 920) or the 'Arms to Iraq' affair (see p. 852). The government has settled actions brought for abuse of public office without disciplining the senior civil servants concerned (The Times, 9 December 1999).

[141] Bainbridge v. Postmaster-General [1906] 1 KB 178; Secretary of State for the Environment v. Hooper [1981] RTR 169.   [142] Civil servants' contracts of employment are discussed below, p. 52.

[143] Even where a statutory authority administers a public service (e.g. the National Health Service) on behalf of a minister, those employed in that service are servants of the Crown. See Wood v. Leeds Area Health Authority [1974] ICR 535, applying Pfizer Corporation v. Ministry of Health [1965] AC 512. See also Marshall v. Southampton Health Authority [1986] QB 401 at 414 (European Court of Justice, opinion of Sir Gordon Slynn).

[144] Dunn v. The Queen [1896] 1 QB 116; similarly Hales v. The King (1918) 34 TLR 589; Denning v. Secretary of State for India (1920) 37 TLR 138. But see Cameron v. Lord Advocate 1952 SC 165, distinguishing Dunn's case where it was alleged that a promised post in Nigeria was never provided at all. See also Hogg, Liability of the Crown, 2nd edn, 175; (1975) 34 CLJ 253 (G. Nettheim). Dunn's claim against the officer who engaged him for breach of warranty of authority (see below, p. 700) also failed: Dunn v. Macdonald [1897] 1 QB 401.

[145] It is ascribed to the prerogative in R v. Civil Service Appeal Board ex p Bruce [1988] ICR 649, but presumably in the loose sense noted below, p. 180.

[146] e.g. Rodwell v. Thomas [1944] KB 596; Riordan v. War Office [1959] 1 WLR 1046, affirmed [1961] 1 WLR 210.

servant: the only question is whether, if he does so, he should pay damages for breach of contract.[147] No master can be compelled to employ a servant, any more than a servant can be compelled to serve a master. The argument that the Crown could not otherwise relieve the public of an undesirable servant therefore falls to the ground. It may be said that the Crown should not be put in the dilemma of ignoring the public interest or else committing a breach of contract—for a breach of contract, despite Mr Justice Holmes's famous theory to the contrary,[148] is a wrongful act. But to that it can be answered that it is of even greater importance that engagements expressly entered into should at least be honoured in the breach, if not in the observance. The Crown should be an honest man, and if driven to break its contract ought to pay damages, as it does for breach of other contracts. Yet the latest decision has confirmed that civil servants can be dismissed at will.[149]

In the armed forces the lack of any legal remedy for wrongful dismissal has been made clear in a parallel line of decisions which are, if anything, more categorical than those dealing with civil servants.[150] The military cases tend to the conclusion that this type of Crown service is not contractual at all.[151] This was flatly stated by Lord Esher MR in 1890:[152]

> The law is as clear as it can be... that all engagements between those in the military service of the Crown and the Crown are voluntary only on the part of the Crown and give no occasion for an action in respect of any alleged contract... The courts of law have nothing to do with such a matter.

REMUNERATION: CONFUSION AT COMMON LAW

The judicial reluctance to give even a money judgment against the Crown on a contract of service led to a decision in 1943 that a Crown employee has not even a contractual right to arrears of pay.[153] The wife of an Indian civil servant, who had made default in payments of alimony, attempted to attach arrears of pay due to her husband. It was held that since the husband could not sue for the pay, it was not legally due to him and so not attachable by his creditors.[154]

In decisions such as these, as in the cases on dismissal, the courts seemed determined to reduce the contractual element in Crown service almost to vanishing point, tending to the conclusion that it was not contractual at all.[155] But these views are no longer correct.

---

[147] See below, p. 465.

[148] Holmes held that a contract was a promise to perform or to pay damages at the promisor's option: *The Common Law*, 301.

[149] *R* v. *Lord Chancellor's Department ex p Nangle*, discussed below, pp. 51 and 574. Civil servants' contracts, however, assert that 'because of the constitutional position of the Crown, [civil servants] cannot demand a period of notice as of right when [their] employment is terminated'. For criticism see [1995] *PL* 224 (M. Freedland).

[150] *Re Tufnell* (1876) 3 Ch D 164; *Grant* v. *Secretary of State for India* (1877) 2 CPD 445; *De Dohse* v. *R* (unreported, House of Lords), cited in *Dunn* v. *The Queen* (above).

[151] For the modern position in regard to civil servants see p. 52 below.

[152] *Mitchell* v. *R* [1896] 1 QB 121, note. Confirmed in *Quinn* v. *MOD* [1997] EWCA Civ 2865 (no intention to contract shown).

[153] *Lucas* v. *Lucas* [1943] P 68. See similarly *High Commissioner for India* v. *Lall* (1948) LR 75 1A 225 (Privy Council); but contrast *Picton* v. *Cullen* [1900] 2 IR 612. As to military pay see *Gibson* v. *East India Co* (1839) 5 Bing NC 262; *Mitchell* v. *R* (above).

[154] Following the Scots case of *Mulvenna* v. *The Admiralty* 1926 SC 842 (dockyard telephone attendant's contract of service with Crown held subject to implied condition that the right to a salary was not legally enforceable).   [155] *Inland Revenue Commissioners* v. *Hambrook* [1956] 2 QB 641 at 654.

The Privy Council, after hints that a wrongfully dismissed civil servant might have a contractual remedy,[156] has held that the law of Ceylon allowed a civil servant to sue the Crown for increments of salary.[157] Closer to home a Divisional Court has held[158] that there is no constitutional bar to a contract of employment between a civil servant and the Crown, and more positively in a later case,[159] that civil servants do, after all, have contracts of employment with the Crown.[160] However, since the court also made it clear that civil servants could still be dismissed at will, this finding does little more than give the civil servant the right to sue for arrears of pay.

In these cases it was the Crown that sought to establish the existence of contracts,[161] because, if civil servants' appointments were contractual, the courts would, as explained later,[162] deny them recourse to judicial review. This can be disadvantageous for civil servants.[163] For instance, judicial review will no longer be available to the civil servant when his conditions of employment are changed. Of course, contractual consent to such changes will now be required. But this provides only illusory protection, since the civil servant can be dismissed at will if he does not consent. Only in the anomalous world of Crown employment could the establishment of hitherto non-existent legal rights for employees foreshadow a reduction in the actual protection of their employment. Indeed the government has, in the interests of decentralisation of managerial responsibility within the civil service (including executive agencies), adopted the policy of regularising its contractual relations with senior civil servants,[164] and has published a draft model contract.[165] These changes seem unlikely to enhance the legal protection of civil servants although they may render management more effective.

---

[156] *Shenton* v. *Smith* [1895] AC 229; *Reilly* v. *The King* [1934] AC 176. See also *Robertson* v. *Minister of Pensions* [1949] 1 KB 227 at 231; *Terrell* v. *Secretary of State for the Colonies* [1953] 2 QB 482 at 498 (below, p. 53).

[157] *Kodeeswaran* v. *A-G of Ceylon* [1970] AC 1111 at 1123. The Court of Appeal of New South Wales did the same in *Suttling* v. *Director General of Education* [1985] 3 NSWLR 427 (2-year appointment held binding and arrears of salary awarded). The House of Lords has allowed a Crown servant to recover arrears of pay by petition of right but without consideration of the legal difficulties: *Sutton* v. *A-G* (1923) 39 TLR 294.

[158] *R* v. *Civil Service Appeal Board ex p Bruce* [1988] 3 All ER 686 (affirmed on different grounds in the Court of Appeal: [1989] 2 All ER 907); followed in *British Telecommunications plc* v. *Royal Mail Group Ltd* [2010] EWHC 8 (civil servants appointed by the Postmaster General had contracts of employment).

[159] *R* v. *Lord Chancellor's Department ex p Nangle* [1992] 1 All ER 897 (civil servant accused of sexual harassment; after internal disciplinary procedures, transferred and denied increment in salary; held, since he had a contract of employment with the Crown, he could not challenge the fairness of the disciplinary procedures by way of judicial review). In Hong Kong civil servants have long been held to have contracts with the Crown (*Lam Yuk-Ming* v. *A-G* [1980] HKLR 815 (CA)).

[160] The difference between these cases turns on whether the parties had contractual intention. Para. 14 of the Civil Service Pay and Conditions of Service Code said that 'a civil servant does not have a contract of employment enforceable in the courts'. In *ex p Bruce* May LJ held that this showed that the parties did not intend to contract; but in *ex p Nangle* Stuart-Smith LJ disagreed: the parties had the intention to create legal relations and that was enough, notwithstanding para. 14.

[161] The Crown's attitude to this question has not been consistent. Barely a year before *ex p Nangle* the Crown had, in order to defend an action brought by a civil servant, asserted, in *McClaren* v. *Home Office* [1990] IRLR 338, that civil servants did not have contracts of employment.   [162] See p. 539.

[163] See [1991] *PL* 485; (1991) 107 *LQR* 298 (S. Fredman and G. Morris).

[164] See Cm. 2627 (1995). See [1995] *PL* 224 (M. Freedland).

[165] Available at <http://www.civilservice.gov.uk/about/resources/employment-practice/conditions-of-service>.

STATUTORY REGULATION OF CROWN EMPLOYMENT

The Crown, as the largest employer of labour in the country, could not remain unaffected by the far-reaching laws on employment, labour relations and social security enacted in recent years. These statutes may be said without exaggeration to have transformed the legal character of Crown service, changing it from a relationship which was almost ignored by the law into one in which the employee has many legal rights and in which the relationship is in some important ways minutely regulated by legal rules. But these rights are generally enforceable through specialised tribunals rather than through the ordinary courts.

The most radical alteration of the position of the Crown's employees at common law is that which brings them within the provisions against unfair dismissal first enacted in 1971 and now contained in the Employment Rights Act 1996.[166] But there are many other occasions on which civil servants may claim the benefit of the law on social security and non-discrimination.

THE JUDICIARY

Judges may be regarded as servants of the Crown in the sense that they are 'Her Majesty's judges', holding offices granted by the Crown and bound by oath well and truly to serve the sovereign in those offices.[167] On the other hand it is axiomatic that judges are independent: the Crown has no legal right to give them instructions,[168] and one of the strongest constitutional conventions makes it improper for any sort of influence to be brought to bear upon them by the executive.[169] They do not therefore satisfy the test of the relationship of master and servant at common law, which is that the master must have power to control the servant. Consequently, as explained, the Crown bears no liability for acts of the judiciary, and the judiciary themselves have an extensive immunity.[170]

In a constitutional sense it is nevertheless evident that the judges in administering justice supply one of the most important services of the Crown. In this context judges and others performing judicial functions may well fall within the meaning of 'servants of the Crown' or of similar expressions.[171] They were treated as 'persons in His Majesty's service' under the National Economy Act 1931.[172]

It is a cardinal principle that the superior judges, unlike others in the service of the Crown, should enjoy security of tenure. In the case of the judges of the High Court and the Court of Appeal their tenure is protected by the Senior Courts Act 1981,[173] replacing the Act of Settlement 1700, under which they hold office 'during good behaviour subject to a power of removal by Her Majesty on an address presented to Her by both Houses of Parliament'. The judges of the Supreme Court are protected in similar terms by the Constitutional Reform Act 2005.[174] Only once has a judge been removed on an address

---

[166] Pt X, not applying to the police, who are also excluded from some other benefits (s. 200).

[167] Promissory Oaths Act 1868, s. 4; Senior Courts Act 1981, s. 10(4); Courts and Legal Services Act 1990, s. 76.   [168] Below, p. 697.

[169] For a remarkable ministerial attempt to influence the High Court to release the imprisoned Poplar councillors (below, p. 614) see [1962] PL 62 (B. Keith-Lucas). The Constitutional Reform Act 2005 (see below, p. 63) establishes a statutory duty on ministers to 'uphold the continued independence of the judiciary' (s. 3(1)).   [170] Below, p. 670. See A. Olowofoyeku, *Suing Judges: A Study of Judicial Immunity* (1993).

[171] *Ranaweera* v. *Ramachandran* [1970] AC 962 at 972 (Lord Diplock, dissenting); *R* v. *Barrett* [1976] 1 WLR 946 (registrar of births 'serving under the Crown').   [172] See below, p. 697.

[173] s. 11(3). Although the Crown Court is a senior court (s. 1), circuit judges and recorders, who are judges of the Crown Court, are not senior court judges (s. 151(4)).   [174] s. 33.

from both Houses.[175] All holders of judicial office, if appointed after 1993, are subject to a retirement age of 70.[176] Appointments below High Court level may be extended on an annual basis until 75.[177] Judges will need to be appointed before they reach 50, if they are to qualify for a full pension at 70.[178]

The lower ranks of the judiciary, on the other hand, have scarcely more legal protection against dismissal than have other holders of office under the Crown. Circuit judges, county court judges, recorders and magistrates are by statute subject to removal by the Lord Chancellor for incapacity or misbehaviour.[179] Nor is there any legal principle to safeguard the tenure of judges in the absence of statute.[180]

The tenure of the judiciary of all ranks, however, is as firmly protected in practice as it could be by positive law. Any undue interference with it would raise a political storm. Fearless judicial impartiality is the indispensable basis of the rule of law, and has been respected as a constitutional principle since the revolution of 1688 put an end to the abuses of the Stuart kings.

CONSTITUTIONAL REFORM ACT 2005

This measure, enacted in curious circumstances—an ill thought-out attempt to abolish the office of Lord Chancellor[181]—affirms the independence of the judiciary and places ministers under a duty to uphold that independence[182] but does much else too. The office of Lord Chancellor is shorn of its judicial functions;[183] his administrative functions have for the most part been transferred to the Secretary of State for Justice.[184] His place as head of the judiciary is taken by the Lord Chief Justice.[185]

A Supreme Court of the United Kingdom is established and takes over the judicial functions of the House of Lords and those of the Privy Council in regard to devolution.[186] It commenced operation in October 2009.

A Judicial Appointments Commission is established.[187] It has fourteen members (appointed by Her Majesty on the recommendation of the Lord Chancellor) and a lay chairman.[188] It is directed to make its recommendations on merit[189] (having regard to

---

[175] Sir Jonah Barrington, an Irish judge (removed in 1830).

[176] Judicial Pensions and Retirement Act 1993, s. 26. Judges of the High Court, Court of Appeal and House of Lords appointed before 1993 must retire at 75 (Judicial Pensions Act 1959, s. 2 and Act of 1993, s. 26(11)). [177] Act of 1993, s. 26(4), (5), (6).

[178] Judicial Pensions and Retirement Act 1993, Pt 1.

[179] Courts Act 1971, ss. 17, 21; justices of the peace are removable from the commission of the peace on the order of the Lord Chancellor, under prerogative power except in certain statutory cases, e.g. under Justices of the Peace Act 1949, s. 1. [180] *Terrell* v. *Secretary of State for the Colonies* [1953] 2 QB 482.

[181] For discussion of the circumstances of enactment see [2005] *PL* 806; [2006] *PL* 35 (Lord Windlesham). And see *Constitutional Reform: Reforming the Office of Lord Chancellor* (DCA, 2003) (published after the abolition of the office had been announced). See also (2002) 118 *LQR* 382 (Lord Steyn).

[182] Act of 2005, s. 3. See [2008] *PL* 470 (Bradley).

[183] Turpin and Tompkins, as above, p. 117. See Act of 2005, s. 24 (Lord Chancellor not a member of the Supreme Court).

[184] Prior to the Act of 2005 orders transferring functions were made under the Ministers of the Crown Act 1975 (see above, p. 41). Special provision is now made in the Act (ss. 15, 19 and 20 (functions not transferable) and Sched. 4). See SI 2006 No. 1016 for a current order.

[185] Act of 2005, s. 7. The LCJ has the power to lay written representations about the judiciary before Parliament (s. 5). [186] Act of 2005, s. 40(4) and Sched. 9.

[187] See Pt 4, Ch. 2 of the Act of 2005.

[188] Act of 2005, s. 61 and Sched. 12 as amended by the Crime and Courts Act 2013, Sched. 13 (Pt 3). Five of the Commissioners are judges (at least one a Lord Justice), there are five lay members, two professional members, a magistrate and a tribunal member. [189] Act of 2005, s. 63. See Appendix 3.

'advice on selection' from the Lord Chancellor);[190] it has regard to 'the need to encourage diversity'.[191] The general pattern being that a recommendation is made to the Lord
Chancellor by a JAC panel (whose composition varies with the seniority of the appointment (and includes senior judges in the most senior appointments)).[192] If the Lord
Chancellor accepts the recommendation, depending on the rank of judge, he then makes
the appointment or passes the recommendation to the Prime Minister for him to advise
Her Majesty to make the appointment.[193] Achieving a more diverse judiciary (i.e. a better balance of gender, ethnicity and social origin) was a major aim of this legislation.[194]
But remedying these imbalances may require structural changes in society and the legal
system extending beyond reform of appointments.[195]

SOME GOVERNMENTAL FUNCTIONS

The modern administrative state has many functions and the performance of those
functions requires an administrative machine of immense complexity. Each part of that
machine is created and moulded by rules of administrative law. But it is not practicable
to set out all those rules here. Only a sketch may be provided of some of the functions of
more importance to administrative law. However, this is far from a comprehensive guide.
In particular there are some areas, for instance, planning, where the subject is so specialised and complicated that only the briefest account can be given.

THE COMPULSORY PURCHASE OF LAND

It has long been possible for land to be compulsorily purchased for public purposes and
many government departments, local authorities and public corporations have such
powers.[196] All these powers, however, are under central government control for every
purchase must be confirmed by a minister. The procedures determining whether the
land may be taken and requiring notice etc., to be given to interested parties, are generally found in the Acquisition of Land Act 1981 while the assessment of compensation is
determined under the Compulsory Purchase Act 1965. In order to enable the acquiring
authority to obtain safe title to the land the validity of a compulsory purchase order may
only be challenged within six weeks of the date on which notice of confirmation of the
order is published.[197]

---

[190] Act of 2005, s. 65.   [191] Act of 2005, s. 64.

[192] Act of 2005, ss. 25–30 (Supreme Court) and Pt 4, Ch. 2 (other appointments).

[193] The Lord Chancellor generally has an option either to appoint (or notify for appointment), reject or
order reconsideration by the panel. See s. 29 (Supreme Court), and Pt 4, Ch. 2 (several sections).

[194] See *A New Way of Appointing Judges* (2003), CP 10/03, para. 28 (cited in Bradley and Ewing, as above,
p. 386).

[195] The Crime and Courts Act 2013, Sched. 13 provides that the JAC may 'where two persons are of
equal merit, [prefer] one of them over the other for the purpose of increasing diversity within (a) the group
of persons who hold offices for which there is selection' (para. 10); and see similarly para. 9 (Supreme
Court).

[196] For detailed accounts see Brand (ed.), *Encyclopedia of Compulsory Purchase* (1960–99) and Roots
et al., *The Law of Compulsory Purchase*, 2nd edn (2011). For historical and comparative discussion see M.
Taggart, 'Expropriation and Public Purpose' in Forsyth and Hare (eds.), *The Golden Metwand*, 91–112. See
also below, p. 682.   [197] Act of 1981, ss. 23–5. See below, p. 620.

TOWN AND COUNTRY PLANNING

One of the most prominent twentieth-century developments in administrative law has been the control exercised over the 'development' of land.[198] 'Development' is very widely defined to include both the carrying out of any building, engineering or mining operations on the land and the making of any material change in the use to which the land or buildings are put.[199] The basic rule of planning law is that permission must be sought from the local planning authority (usually a local authority) before any development takes place.[200] The decision whether to grant such permission is made against the background of a development plan (largely drawn up by the planning authority and confirmed by the Secretary of State), the planning policy of the Secretary of State (as made known by circulars, White Papers and planning guidance notes (PPGs)) and EC Council Directive No. 85/337 (which requires in certain cases that environmental impact assessments are made and taken into account).[201] Permission, if granted, is usually made subject to various conditions.[202]

There is no right of appeal against the grant of planning permission. But against refusal of permission there is a right of appeal to the Secretary of State;[203] and in certain circumstances there is a further right of appeal to the High Court on a question of law. The validity of many planning decisions, like the compulsory purchase decisions just mentioned, can only be challenged in the High Court by way of a special statutory species of judicial review.[204] The challenge must be made within six weeks of the contested decision and only on the grounds that it 'is not within the powers of this Act' or other statutory provisions.[205] The courts, however, retain their jurisdiction to grant ordinary applications for judicial review where this is not excluded—for instance, where the grant of planning permission contains conditions which are ultra vires.[206]

A breach of planning control is not generally a criminal offence but the planning authority may issue an enforcement notice requiring that the breach be remedied,[207] e.g. the demolition of a building erected without permission. A failure to heed the enforcement

---

[198] The modern system of planning law was inaugurated by the Town and Country Planning Act 1947. The primary statute is now the Town and Country Planning Act 1990. See Sir D. Heap, *An Outline of Planning Law*, 11th edn (1996); Moore, *A Practical Approach to Planning Law*, 12th edn (2002); and Grant (ed.), *Encyclopedia of Planning: Law and Practice* (1960–2008). [199] Act of 1990, s. 55.

[200] The Planning Act 2008 establishes an Infrastructure Planning Commission will be established with the task of granting permission for major infrastructural projects (including nuclear power stations) avoiding major public inquiries. There is no appeal to the Secretary of State from the Commission's decision, but the Commission is bound by national policies.

[201] Act of 1990, s. 70(2). And for the special weight given to the development plan, see s. 54A.

[202] Act of 1990, s. 70(1); but the conditions must fairly and reasonably relate to the proposed development. See below, p. 407.

[203] Act of 1990, s. 79(2). This usually involves an informal hearing (or an appeal on written representations) before an inspector. Increasingly, the decision is taken by the inspector himself under delegated powers from the minister (s. 79(1)). Each year a small number of particularly sensitive or important planning appeals are decided by the Secretary of State himself, after an inquiry conducted by an inspector who recommends to the minister. This procedure, including the right of appeal to the court on a point of law, was held not to breach Art. 6(1) of the European Convention on Human Rights: *R (Alconbury Developments Ltd) v. Secretary of State for the Environment, Transport and the Regions* [2001] UKHL 23, [2003] 2 AC 295 (HL). Discussed below, pp. 381–3. Under the Planning Act 2008 the appeal in minor developments is to local councillors, not to inspectors. [204] Act of 1990, s. 288. Below, p. 619.

[205] But the 'powers of this Act' include the classic grounds of judicial review: see below, p. 624.

[206] *R v. Hillingdon LBC ex p Royco Homes Ltd* [1974] QB 720. See below, p. 345.

[207] Act of 1990, s. 172(1).

notice within the set time is an offence and substantial fines can then be imposed.[208] The breach may be remedied by the planning authority at the owner's expense. There are other forms of enforcement of which the 'stop order' is the most drastic. It requires that the activity specified in an enforcement notice should cease before the enforcement notice itself would take effect (usually twenty-eight days).[209]

THE NATIONAL HEALTH SERVICE

The National Health Service, and the connected welfare services, provided on both a national and local basis, are a vital area of public administration. However, although on occasion the health service does generate important administrative law cases, particularly where difficult decisions about the allocation of limited resources have to be taken,[210] on the whole the most important issues arise in the context of tribunals[211] or before the National Health Service Commissioner.[212]

The basic structure of the health service is set out in the National Health Service Act 2006 as amended by the Health and Social Care Act 2012 which retains the basic structure of regional health authorities and family practitioner health authorities set up in the earlier legislation (since 1946). The 1990 Act also sets up NHS Trusts as the providers of health services to the health authorities who acquire the services on behalf of individuals resident within their areas. A further step has been taken with the Health and Social Care (Community Health and Standards) Act 2003,[213] which enables NHS Trusts, if supported by the Secretary of State, to apply to the Independent Regulator of NHS Foundation Trusts for 'foundation status'. This transforms them into independent not-for-profit organisations with considerable autonomy.

SOCIAL SECURITY

The operations of the welfare state are naturally much to the fore in administrative law.[214] Benefits are distributed to very large numbers of people under legislation, both primary and secondary, of formidable complexity. Many of the problems that arise, however, are dealt with by tribunals discussed elsewhere.[215] The welfare state provides both benefits in kind and in cash. The cash benefits may be divided into those which are financed, at least in part, from contributions by the beneficiaries (such as jobseeker's allowance, sickness and industrial injury benefit) and non-contributory benefits (such as certain pensions, child benefit and income support). The non-contributory benefits themselves are divided into those that are means tested ('income-related' in current jargon) and those which are not. The principal statutes are today the Social Security Contributions and Benefits Act 1992, the Social Security Administration Act 1992, the Jobseeker's Act 1995 and the Welfare Reform Acts 2007–12. The usual pattern is that decisions are taken by adjudication officers but a disappointed claimant has a right of appeal to a unified appeal tribunal.[216]

---

[208] s. 179. But there is an appeal to the Secretary of State against an enforcement notice (s. 174(1)) and one ground of appeal is that planning permission ought to have been granted (s. 174(2)).

[209] Act of 1990, s. 183(1)–(5A).

[210] R v. Cambridge Health Authority ex p B [1995] 1 WLR 898 (CA) and below, p. 329.

[211] See below, p. 762.   [212] See below, p. 85.

[213] Now replaced by the National Health Service Act 2006, s. 33.

[214] For a detailed account see Calvert (ed.), Encyclopedia of Social Security Law (1960–99).

[215] See below, p. 762.   [216] See below, p. 771.

But not all benefits follow this pattern. With the social fund, for example, the decisions of the social fund officers are subject to internal review but no other appeal.[217] With housing benefit—paid to tenants on low incomes—decisions are taken by local authorities and there is no appeal, but rudimentary provision is made for internal review.[218] Local authorities are also under a duty to 'secure accommodation' for the homeless—broadly those in priority need who are not intentionally homeless.[219] An applicant has had a right of appeal (after an internal review) to the county court on a point of law.[220]

PRISONS

Prisoners have in recent years been conspicuous litigants in judicial review proceedings[221] and have enjoyed many successes.[222] In addition the European Court of Human Rights has brought about notable improvements in prison administration and discipline in fulfilment of its maxim that justice cannot stop at the prison gate.[223] The Human Rights Act 1998 now underpins and strengthens these developments.

In a departmental reorganisation in 2008 discussed earlier[224] prisons are no longer the responsibility of the Home Secretary, but now fall under the Secretary of State for Justice. The primary statute is the Prison Act 1952. Under that Act, as amended, the Secretary of State makes the Prison Rules[225] which make provision for many aspects of prison life including privileges, remission of sentence, religion, medical attention, work, education, correspondence, discipline and numerous other matters. The purpose of the training and treatment of convicted prisoners is expressly stated to be to encourage and assist them to lead a good and useful life. The Prison Rules are supplemented by Prison Service Orders and by Prison Service Instructions (which take the place of the previous system of Standing Orders and circular instructions).[226] It is undisputed that 'a convicted prisoner, in spite of his imprisonment, retains all civil rights which are not taken away expressly or by necessary implication'.[227]

---

[217] Social Security Administration Act 1992, ss. 64–6.

[218] Social Security Administration Act 1992, ss. 63, 134–5.

[219] Housing Act 1996, s. 195 replacing similar legislation in force since 1977.

[220] Act of 1996, s. 204. 'Point of law' includes the full range of issues that could be raised on judicial review: *Begum (Nipa)* v. *Tower Hamlet LBC* [2000] 1 WLR 306 (CA). This procedure was held not to breach Art. 6(1) of the European Convention on Human Rights: *Runa Begum* v. *Tower Hamlets LBC* [2003] UKHL 55, [2003] 2 AC 430 (HL), discussed below, p. 382.

[221] For the detail see Livingstone, Owen and MacDonald, *Prison Law*, 4th edn (2008).

[222] Though legal aid to prisoners is being restricted. See below, p. 564 and at <http://www.independent. co.uk/news/uk/politics/no-legal-aid-for-prisoners-says-chris-grayling-8799084.html>.

[223] For instance, *Golder* v. *UK* (1975) Series A, No. 18 (strict censorship of prisoner's correspondence successfully challenged; right to correspond with legal advisers, Members of Parliament and others established); *Weeks* v. *UK* (1987) Series A, No. 114 confirmed in *Thynne, Wilson and Gunnell* v. *UK* (1990) Series A, No. 190 (although independent, Parole Board's role in release of 'discretionary' lifers was only advisory; this was insufficient protection of the right to have lawfulness of detention determined by a court; Criminal Justice Act 1991, s. 35, imposing duty on Home Secretary to follow recommendation, enacted to secure this); *Vinter* v. *UK* (App. No. 66069/09, 9 July 2013) (sentence of life imprisonment without periodical reviews incompatible with Art. 3); *James* v. *UK* (2013) 56 EHRR 12 (unavailability of rehabilitative courses for IPP (imprisonment for public protection) prisoners incompatible with Art. 5); and *Hirst* v. *UK (No 2)* (2006) 42 EHRR 41 (automatic disenfranchisement for all prisoners incompatible with Art. 3, Protocol 1; discussed below, at pp. 58 and 153).   [224] See above, p. 37.

[225] SI 1999 No. 728 and regularly amended, usually annually, since. See [1981] *PL* 228 (G. Zellick).

[226] These have no express statutory authority but provide in great detail for innumerable aspects of daily life in prison.

[227] *Raymond* v. *Honey* [1983] AC 1 at 10; *R* v. *Home Secretary ex p Leech (No 2)* [1994] QB 198 at 209. Prisoners may not vote for or be elected to Parliament under the Representation of the People Acts 1981

Breaches of the rules, however, do not give rise to a claim for breach of statutory duty.[228] But Prison Rules will be declared ultra vires where, for instance, they intrude upon the prisoner's fundamental right of access to the courts[229] and Prison Service Orders will be read as subject to fundamental civil liberties.[230] The right of access to the courts naturally includes the right to consult a solicitor,[231] and any attempt by the prison authorities to impede it may be treated as contempt of court.[232] Even operational or managerial decisions affecting prisoners are subject to judicial review.[233]

PRISON DISCIPLINE

Any disciplinary penalty imposed upon a prisoner must be authorised by the Prison Act or by the Rules. The Rules provide that minor disciplinary offences are dealt with by the prison governor,[234] who can impose a variety of punishments (known as awards), such as cellular confinement for up to twenty-one days, stoppage of privileges or earnings for up to eighty-four days.[235] More serious charges, such as attempted escape or assault on a prison officer, are dealt with by the courts.[236] Governor's awards are subject to judicial

and 1983 respectively. See [2002] *PL* 524 (H. Lardy). The Strasbourg Court has held that this blanket ban is incompatible with Art. 3 of the First Protocol of the European Convention: *Hirst* v. *UK (No 2)* (2006) 42 EHRR 41.

[228] *Hague* v. *Deputy Governor of Parkhurst Prison* [1992] 1 AC 58 (prisoners in lawful custody have no action for false imprisonment, even if held in intolerable conditions or otherwise in breach of the rules). See also *R (Munjaz)* v. *Mersey Care NHS Trust* [2003] EWCA 1036, [2003] 3 WLR 1505 (seclusion of lawfully detained mental patient capable of breaching Art. 3 and Art. 8 of the ECHR). See also *Iqbal* v. *Prison Officers Association* [2009] EWCA Civ 1312, [2010] QB 732 (trade union that called strike of prison officers not liable for false imprisonment of prisoners consequently confined to their cells).

[229] *ex p Leech* (as above, p. 57) (over-broad power permitting governor to read prisoner's correspondence (including pre-litigation correspondence with solicitor) declared ultra vires so far as it related to correspondence with solicitor). See further *Weeks* (above, p. 57) and *Campbell* v. *UK* (1992) Series A, No. 233-A (only in exceptional circumstances could correspondence with lawyers be read). See *R (Daly)* v. *Secretary of State for the Home Department* [2001] UKHL 26, [2001] 2 AC 532 (policy requiring absence of prisoner from cell when legally privileged correspondence examined (but not read) held unlawful as disproportionate intrusion on prisoner's rights). See below, p. 733.

[230] *R* v. *Home Secretary ex p Simms* [2000] AC 115 (HL) (journalists visiting prisoners required by Standing Order to sign undertakings not to use information obtained for professional purposes; SO interpreted as subject to fundamental civil liberties and thus not justifying indiscriminate ban on interviews with journalists since this would infringe the right to seek access to justice).

[231] *R* v. *Home Secretary ex p Anderson* [1984] QB 778 (Standing Order that required prisoner to make internal complaint simultaneously with approach to lawyer to discuss civil claim set aside).

[232] *Raymond* v. *Honey* (as above) (governor's temporary stopping of application to court held contempt but no penalty imposed).

[233] *R* v. *Deputy Governor of Parkhurst Prison ex p Hague* [1992] 1 AC 58.

[234] r. 44 ensures that elementary fairness is applicable to disciplinary charges before the governor (notice of charge, 'full opportunity' to hear case against him and present his own case).

[235] r. 55. Some 95 per cent of offences are dealt with by governors. But a disciplinary charge before the governor might be sufficiently grave (e.g. 'extra days' awarded) to engage Art. 6 of the European Convention on Human Rights; and in these cases legal representation before the governor was required: *Ezeh* v. *UK* (2004) 39 EHRR 1. Decisions on segregation or cellular confinement do not engage Art. 6 because there is no 'civil right' to associate with others: *R (King)* v. *Secretary of State for Justice* [2012] EWCA Civ 376. Serious offences are now referred to an adjudicator who can add days to the sentence (Prison (Amendment) Rules 2002 (SI 2002 No. 2116)). In *Tangney* v. *Governor of HMP Elmley and Home Secretary* [2005] EWCA Civ 1009 it was held that 'lifers' were not entitled to representation in such matters since they cannot have additional days imposed. There is a right to legal representation for hearing before an adjudicator: r. 54(3). The findings of an adjudicator will, on request, be reviewed by a Senior District Judge: r. 55B.

[236] The system whereby Boards of Prison Visitors exercised disciplinary powers in more serious cases was often criticised (since they lacked independence and legal expertise) and was ended in 1992 (SI 1992 No. 514).

review.[237] But there is also a non-statutory system of internal appeals.[238] After appealing to an area manager, the prisoner may take his grievance to an independent Prisons Ombudsman who may review both procedure and merits. The Ombudsman's decisions, however, are not binding on the Home Office.[239]

EARLY RELEASE OF PRISONERS

The Criminal Justice Act 2003,[240] governs the early release of prisoners. In the most straightforward case a prisoner sentenced by the judge to a determinate term of imprisonment will serve half that term before the Secretary of State is required to release him on licence.[241] Prisoners serving less than twelve months are released unconditionally.[242] The Secretary of State may recall a prisoner released on licence (for instance, when he breaches a licence condition). The prisoner will then serve the remainder of his sentence unless his release is ordered by the Parole Board to which the Secretary of State may refer the case.[243] With life prisoners, whether serving a mandatory life sentence (for murder) or a discretionary life sentence, the procedure is now the following: the trial judge sets the prisoner's tariff period, i.e. the period considered by the trial judge as appropriate punishment taking into account the seriousness of the offence.[244] On the expiry of the tariff period the Parole Board may direct the release of the prisoner on licence if 'satisfied that it is no longer necessary for the protection of the public that the prisoner should be confined.'[245] The Parole Board may also direct the release of prisoners imprisoned for public protection as well as those serving an extended sentence.[246]

When established in 1967 the Parole Board was little more than an advisory committee advising the Home Secretary on the early release of prisoners on licence. But developing judicial policy, at the domestic as well at the European level, strongly favours imposing judicial standards of independence and impartiality upon the decisions of the Parole Board. In the result the Parole Board has been transformed into an independent public body having a vital task in assessing the risk that offenders pose to the public.[247] Since the

---

[237] *R* v. *Deputy Governor of Parkhurst Prison ex p Leech* [1988] 1 AC 533 (HL) overruling *R* v. *Deputy Governor of Camphill Prison ex p King* [1985] QB 735. See below, p. 533.

[238] r. 61 (Home Secretary may quash any finding of guilt by governor and remit or reduce punishment).

[239] See Livingstone, Owen and MacDonald (as above). The Prisons Ombudsman also investigates all prison suicides. See <http://www.ppo.gov.uk>.

[240] Pt 12, Ch. 6, ss. 237–68 (fixed term sentences) and Ch. 7, ss. 269–77 (life sentences). It has been amended by the Criminal Justice and Immigration Act 2008 and the Legal Aid, Sentencing and Punishment of Offenders Act 2012. [241] s. 244.

[242] s. 243A.

[243] s. 254. But note that under the Criminal Justice and Immigration Act 2008, ss. 24–32 prisoners recalled on licence will now often be automatically released after 28 days (without consideration by the Board). The release of those serving extended sentences who have served half their sentence will generally be automatic rather than at the discretion of the Parole Board. See Padfield, 'Parole and Early Release: the Criminal Justice and Immigration Act 2008 Changes in Context' [2009] *Criminal Law Review* 166.

[244] Crime (Sentences) Act 1997, s. 28 as amended by the 2003 Act. With a mandatory life sentence the court may order that the early release provisions are not to apply (s. 269(4)). This is a 'whole life tariff' upheld in *R* v. *Home Secretary ex p Hindley* [2002] 2 WLR 730. And see *R* v. *Bieber* [2008] EWCA Crim holding that *Kafkaris* v. *Cyprus* (App. No. 21906/04, 12 February 2008) did not outlaw 'whole life tariff'. But see now *Vinter* v. *UK* (App. No. 66069/09) (whole life sentence with no possibility of review or release incompatible with Art. 3).

[245] Crimes (Sentences) Act 1997, s. 28(6); Act of 2003, s. 275. See *R (Sturnham)* v. *Parole Board* [2013] UKSC 47. [246] s. 247.

[247] These reforms were often spurred by adverse decisions of the Human Rights Court (*Thynne, Wilson and Gunnell* v. *UK* (1990) Series A, No. 190 and *Stafford* v. *UK* (2002) 35 EHRR 32) and the making of declarations of incompatibility (*R (Anderson)* v. *Home Secretary* [2002] UKHL 46, [2003] 1 AC 837). But a small number of long-term determinate prisoners continue to be held under the Criminal Justice Act 1991, s. 35

decisions of the Board now determine the length of time a prisoner actually serves[248] it has been held that Article 5 (right to liberty and security) and in particular the procedural guarantees of Article 5(4) are applicable to many of the decisions of the Board.[249] The fairness of the decisions of the Parole Board fall to be closely scrutinised as will be observed in several parts of this book.[250]

The Board retains links with the Secretary of State which undermines perceptions and, perhaps, the reality of its independence and impartiality. In mid-2008 the Court of Appeal held that the Board lacks the attributes of a 'court' as required by Article 5(4) where the lawfulness of detention is determined.[251] This decision was based upon several factors including the Ministry of Justice's 'sponsorship' (including funding) of the Board and the Secretary of State's continued role in making appointments to the Board.[252]

IMMIGRATION

Immigration cases are a prominent and important feature of administrative law, and in particular they are the part of the subject where the remedy of habeas corpus plays its most conspicuous part.[253] At common law the Crown has the prerogative power to refuse an alien admission to the realm[254] but the subject is now largely statutory. The relevant law (primarily—but not exclusively—the Immigration Act 1971; the Immigration and Asylum Act 1999;[255] the Nationality, Immigration and Asylum Act 2002; the Asylum and Immigration (Treatment of Claimants, etc.) Act 2004; the Immigration, Asylum and Nationality Act 2006; and subordinate legislation made under these Acts) confers wide discretionary powers upon the Home Secretary,[256] backed up by powers of detention and deportation; and the consequences for individuals may be extremely severe.

which provides that where the prisoner 'has served one-half of his sentence, the Secretary of State may, if recommended to do so by the Board, release him on licence'. In *R (Black)* v. *Secretary of State for Justice* [2009] UKHL 1 the House of Lords held (Lord Phillips dissenting) that this arrangement was not incompatible with Art. 5(4) which it did not apply to the early release of determinate sentence prisoners (although it did apply to the original decision to imprison). Judicial review of the Secretary of State's decision would ensure that the decision to release was not arbitrary.

[248] The Secretary of State is now generally bound to follow the directions of the Board in regard to release (1991 Act, s. 28(5)).

[249] *Brooke's* case, below, para. 18. And see the discussion by Elliott in Padfield (ed.), *Who to Release?: Parole, Fairness and Criminal Justice* (2007), 43 at 49. And see *R (Giles)* v. *Parole Board* [2003] UKHL 42, [2004] 1 AC 1 (longer than commensurate sentence not a breach of Art. 4(5)).

[250] See below, p. 436 (oral hearings) and pp. 178, 433 (implied power to adopt special advocate procedure).

[251] *R (Brooke)* v. *The Parole Board* [2008] EWCA Civ 29, para. 78.

[252] Paras. 77–81. On the Secretary of State's power to give directions to the Board (Criminal Justice Act 1991, s. 32(6)) see para. 82 and *R (Girling)* v. *Home Secretary* [2006] EWCA Civ 1779, [2007] 2 WLR 782. See further *R (D'Cunha)* v. *Parole Board* [2011] EWHC 128.

[253] Ian Macdonald QC and Ronan Toal, *Macdonald's Immigration Law and Practice*, 8th edn (2010).

[254] *Musgrave* v. *Chun Teeong Toy* [1891] AC 472; *R* v. *Immigration Appeal Tribunal ex p Secretary of State* [1990] 1 WLR 1126. This prerogative power is preserved by the Act of 1971, s. 33(5). In reliance upon this power the Secretary of State grants 'exceptional leave to remain' to persons who do not qualify for such leave under the immigration rules. See [1992] *PL* 300 (C. Vincenzi). See also [1985] *PL* 93 (C. Vincenzi) for discussion of whether there was a prerogative power to expel friendly aliens.

[255] This Act implements the White Paper, *Faster, Firmer and Fairer—A Modern Approach to Immigration and Asylum*, Cm. 4018 (1998).

[256] The Home Secretary, for instance, may direct exclusion of particular individuals because of anticipated threats to public order: *R (Farrakhan)* v. *Home Secretary* [2002] QB 1391 (wide margin of discretion extended to minister; leader of 'Nation of Islam' excluded). Contrast *R (Naik)* v. *Secretary of State for the Home Department* [2011] EWCA Civ 1546, [2012] Imm AR 381. Carnwath LJ said: 'the modern law is not fully reflected in *Farrakhan*... [while] great weight will be given to the assessment of the responsible

The Act of 1971 (as amended by the British Nationality Act 1981) grants the right of abode in the United Kingdom exclusively to British citizens. In broad terms British citizenship is acquired by birth in the UK to parents at least one of whom is already a citizen or settled in the UK, or by birth outside the UK to parents at least one of whom is a British citizen.[257] Special provision is made for those who acquired rights of abode before 1981, others from within the British Isles (i.e. the Irish) and nationals of EU Member States who have overriding rights under the Treaty of Rome.[258]

To all others immigration officers may refuse admission to enter or grant it permanently or temporarily or subject to any conditions.[259] Detailed guidance as to the exercise of this discretion is found in the Immigration Rules.[260] These specifically provide that they are to be applied without regard to a person's race, colour or religion and 'in compliance with the provisions of the Human Rights Act 1988'.[261]

The rules are an elaborate code, covering leave to remain and also leave to enter as well as variations to such leave and deportation. The most prominent feature of the rules is the 'points-based system'[262] in which the applicant for leave to enter has to score a requisite number of points by fulfilling a range of requirements. The requirements are determined by the 'tier' through which the application is made. Tier 1 is for highly skilled workers (including entrepreneurs), Tier 2 is for skilled workers with the offer of a job from a sponsor, Tier 3 is to for low-skilled workers meeting a temporary labour shortage (but it has never been used), Tier 4 is for students (with the offer of a place from a sponsoring institution) and Tier 5 is for temporary workers. The requirements vary between tiers and may include educational qualifications, availability of funds, anticipated salary, ability in the English language etc. The rules are of formidable complexity and this account is no more than a sketch.

Those seeking asylum must show well-founded fear[263] of being persecuted[264] for reasons of race, religion, nationality, membership of a particular social group[265] or political

---

Minister...where rights under Article 10 are engaged, [the court will judge whether the] measure taken was proportionate to the legitimate aims pursued' (para. 48).

[257] British Nationality Act 1981, s. 1.   [258] See *Van Duyn* v. *Home Office* [1975] Ch 358.

[259] Act of 1971, s. 3.

[260] The current rules are in HC 395 (1994). The rules, updated, are found at <http://www.ukba.homeoffice.gov.uk/policyandlaw/immigrationlaw/immigrationrules/>. The rules 'are not subordinate legislation but detailed statements by a minister of the Crown as to how the Crown proposes to exercise its executive power to control immigration': *Odelola* v. *Home Secretary* [2009] UKHL 25, para. 6 (Lord Hope) (similarly, *R (BAPIO Action Ltd)* v. *Home Secretary* [2007] EWCA Civ 1139, para. 28). But this status does not mean that the rules may not be subject to judicial review on the usual public law grounds (*BAPIO*, para. 32). They create legal rights in that an immigrant can appeal against an immigration decision on the grounds that it is not in accord with the rules (Nationality, Immigration and Asylum Act 2002, s. 84(1)). Notwithstanding their unusual status the power to make the rules derives from the 1971 Act and not the prerogative (*R (Munir)* v. *Home Secretary* [2012] UKSC 32, para. 26 (Lord Dyson)). But a concessionary policy did not form part of the rules and was not required to be laid before Parliament (Act of 1971, s. 3(2)) (*Munir*, para 45). But the specification of the skills level to be attainted to qualify under the Point Based System did form part of the rules and had to be laid before Parliament (*R (Alvi)* v. *Home Secretary* [2012] UKSC 33). For further valuable discussion of the status of immigration rules see *R (Pankina)* v. *Home Secretary* [2010] EWCA Civ 719 (Sedley LJ).   [261] r. 2.

[262] Immigration Rules, Pt 6A.

[263] The fear must exist throughout the country of origin. Thus where there is a safe area to which the asylum-seeker might reasonably relocate, asylum may be denied: *AE* v. *Home Secretary* [2003] EWCA Civ 1032, [2004] 2 WLR 123 (CA). Cf. *R (Rashid)* v. *Home Secretary* [2005] EWCA Civ 744 discussed below, p. 319.

[264] This includes persecution by 'non-state agents' where the state is unable or unwilling to intervene: *R* v. *Home Secretary ex p Adan* [2001] 2 AC 477 (HL); *Nouue* v. *Home Secretary* [2001] INLR 526 (CA). See *Karanakarau* v. *Home Secretary* [2003] 3 All ER 449 (CA) for the approach to proof of this issue. But applicant must show in addition to persecution by non-state actor that receiving country did not provide reasonable level of protection against such threat (*R (Bagdanavicius)* v. *Home Secretary* [2005] UKHL 38, [2005] 2 WLR 1359 (HL)).

[265] See *Islam* v. *Home Secretary* [1999] 2 WLR 1015 (HL) (Pakistani women suspected of adultery comprised 'a particular social group'). Cf. *Ouanes* v. *Home Secretary* [1998] 1 WLR 218 (Algerian midwives

opinion. But asylum-seekers who arrive in the United Kingdom from 'a safe third country' may be removed to that country for investigation of their claim.[266] A procedure exists whereby particular countries may be designated by the Home Secretary as 'safe third countries' in which 'in general there was no serious risk of persecution'. Applicants from these countries may then be removed under an expedited procedure and with attenuated rights of appeal.[267]

DEPORTATION AND REMOVAL

Aliens and Commonwealth citizens (without the right of abode) are subject to deportation after recommendation by a court on conviction.[268] In addition the Home Secretary may order deportation of such persons when he considers that deportation would be 'conducive to the public good'.[269]

Far more numerous are the persons who are not deported but are administratively removed.[270] These are: illegal entrants, i.e. those who enter or seek to enter in breach of the law;[271] overstayers (i.e. those who remain in the UK after expiry of their leave); those in breach of a condition attached to leave (such as a condition against taking employment); and those who are members of the family of a person in the just mentioned categories. They can be removed by immigration officers without deportation orders, and may be detained pending a decision and then removed.[272] They are also liable to fine and imprisonment. Carriers who bring in passengers without proper documents or clandestine entrants may be fined and made to bear the expense of their return.[273]

RIGHTS OF APPEAL IN IMMIGRATION, DEPORTATION AND ASYLUM CASES

Rights of appeal in immigration and asylum cases have been the subject of frequent legislation and are prone to change. At present a person may appeal against an immigration or asylum decision made by an immigration officer to the Immigration and Asylum

---

giving controversial contraceptive advice not 'a particular social group'). Members of a family involved in a feud are not 'a particular social group' (*Skenderaj* v. *Home Secretary* [2002] 4 All ER 553; neither are returning nationals (*R* v. *Evans (Fabian)* [2013] EWCA Crim 125, [2013] 1 Cr App R 34, para. 28). But gay men do constitute a 'particular social group' because of their shared characteristic (i.e. their sexual orientation): *HJ (Iran)* v. *Secretary of State for the Home Department* [2010] UKSC 31, [2011] 1 AC 596 (paras. 10, 42). Compulsory military service is not a Convention reason (*Fadli* v. *Home Secretary* [2001] Imm AR 392 (CA)).

[266] The Asylum and Immigration (Treatment of Claimants) Act 2004, Sched. 3, Pt 2 (Dublin Convention states) and Pt 3 (other states). Where a third country does not apply the Convention in a way consistent with its true meaning (e.g. as not applying to persecution by 'non-state agents') that country is not a 'safe' third country (*ex p Adan*). And see *R (Thangarasa)* v. *Home Secretary* [2002] UKHL 36, [2003] 1 AC 920.

[267] The rights of appeal are found in the Asylum and Immigration (Treatment of Claimants) Act 2004, Sched. 3, para. 5 (Dublin Convention states) and para. 10 (other states). Although the designation must be approved by both Houses of Parliament, the court may still review it on the grounds of illegality, procedural impropriety and unreasonableness (*R (Javed)* v. *Home Secretary* [2001] 3 WLR 323 (CA) (designation of Pakistan found irrational). Designation as a safe third country was successfully challenged in *R (JB (Jamaica))* v. *Home Secretary* [2013] EWCA Civ 666 (irrational to designate where general risk of persecution of homosexuals shown; Black and Pill LJJ; Moore-Bix LJ dissenting).

[268] Act of 1971, s. 3(5). More generally, see Dubinsky, *Foreign National Prisoners* (2012).

[269] Act of 1971, s. 3(6)(b).

[270] Deportation orders were formerly much more widely used. See Act of 1999, s. 8.

[271] Act of 1971, s. 33. This includes entry by deception.   [272] Act of 1971, 2nd Sched.

[273] Pt II (ss. 32–43) of the Act of 1999 contains the current provisions. See also the 2002 Act, s. 88.

Chamber of the First-tier Tribunal.[274] From the First-tier Tribunal there is a further appeal (with permission) to the Immigration and Asylum Chamber of the Upper Tribunal on the ground that 'there was an error of law in the decision'.[275] An appeal (with permission) lies to the Court of Appeal from a decision of the Upper Tribunal on 'any point of law' arising from the decision.[276] These appeal provisions were supplemented by judicial review which is available when no appeal or no further appeal lies.[277]

It should not be supposed from this account that that there is a general right of appeal by disappointed immigrants or asylum-seekers against the decisions of the immigration officers, the First-tier Tribunal or the Upper Tribunal.[278] The right of appeal is hedged about with many restrictions. Some of these may be set out here.[279]

The only possible grounds of appeal for immigration decisions are set out in section 84(1) of the 2002 Act. These include that the decision should not be in breach of discrimination law or the Human Rights Act 1998 or the Community Treaties as well as that 'the decision is not in accordance with immigration rules', that 'the decision is otherwise not in accordance with the law' and that 'the person taking the decision should have exercised differently a discretion conferred by immigration rules'. The only ground of appeal for asylum decisions is that 'removal of the appellant from the United Kingdom would breach the United Kingdom's obligations under the Refugee Convention'.[280] Appeals may be determined without an oral hearing.[281]

Under the Act of 2002 if, in a human rights or asylum case, the Home Secretary certifies that the appeal relates to a 'clearly unfounded claim', the appeal may only be brought from outside the UK.[282] Thus applicants may be promptly removed prior to any appeal. But there is no right of appeal to the First-tier Tribunal where the ground of the decision is that 'his deportation is conducive to the public good in the interests of national security or of the relations between the United Kingdom and any other country or for other reasons of a political nature'.[283] An asylum-seeker's right of appeal is removed where the decision

---

[274] Act of 2002, ss. 82 and 83. Appeals previously heard by the Asylum and Immigration Tribunal have been transferred to the Immigration and Asylum Chamber of the First-tier Tribunal (Transfer of Functions, etc. Order (SI 2010/21, reg. 2(1)).

[275] Tribunals, Courts and Enforcement Act 2007, s. 11(1) and (2).

[276] Act of 2007, s. 13(1) and (2). Asylum and Immigration Tribunal (Procedure) Rules 2005, SI 2005/230, r. 26 (as amended). Applications for permission to appeal are made in writing (r. 24(1) and must be made within 5 days if the applicant is within the UK (r. 24(2)) and 28 days otherwise (r. 24(3)).

[277] By a Practice Direction made by the LCJ on the 21 August 2013, as from 1 November 2013 most applications for judicial review (including applications for permission) concerning immigration decisions (or decisions regarding leave to enter made outside the immigration rules) shall be heard in the Upper Tribunal. Applications for judicial review that challenge the validity of primary or secondary legislation concerning the lawfulness of detention or a challenge to a decision concerning inclusion on the register of licensed sponsors are excluded. This direction is made under powers in the Tribunals, Courts and Enforcement Act 2007, s. 18 and the Constitutional Reform Act 2005, Sched. 2, Pt 1. For the judicial review jurisdiction of the Upper Tribunal see below, pp. 772–3.

[278] But note R (Cart) v. Upper Tribunal [2011] UKSC 28, [2012] 1 AC 663 (judicial review available in limited circumstances against Upper Tribunal decision to refuse permission to appeal). See below, p. 222 for discussion.

[279] Further restrictions to rights of appeal are found in the Immigration, Asylum and Nationality Act 2006, ss. 1–14.   [280] Act of 2002, s. 84(3).

[281] Asylum and Immigration Tribunal (Procedure) Rules 2005, SI 2005/230, r. 15.

[282] Act of 2002, s. 115. In R (L) v. Home Secretary [2003] EWCA Civ 25, [2003] 1 WLR 1230 (CA) the 'fast track' procedure for dealing with such cases was upheld as giving sufficient opportunity to establish that the claim was not 'clearly unfounded'. See [2003] PL 260 and [2003] PL 479 (R. Thomas).

[283] Act of 2002, s. 97A, which provides for a right of appeal to the Special Immigration Appeals Commission established under the Special Immigration Appeals Commission Act 1997. This Commission, headed by a person who has held or holds high judicial office, takes the place of the non-statutory body of

is taken on grounds of national security.[284] Where a claim for asylum is made after an application for leave or the variation of leave or an order directing removal is made, the right of appeal is also lost.[285] Special provision is made for the welfare support of destitute asylum-seekers (and their dependants). This is intended to be provided predominantly in kind.[286] Applications for asylum must be made 'as soon as reasonably practicable' or else welfare support will be denied.[287] But a refusal to provide welfare support may violate Article 3 of the Convention.[288]

EXTRADITION OF FUGITIVE OFFENDERS

Extradition is the surrender by one country to another of some person charged with or convicted of serious crime.[289] Extradition is less prominent in administrative law than are immigration and deportation, since the legislation and the case law are concerned more with courts of law than with administrative authorities. Nevertheless some of the decisions are relevant to general principles of judicial review and most of them illustrate the remedy of habeas corpus.

The law is now dominated by the Extradition Act 2003,[290] which replaces the previous consolidating statute, the Extradition Act 1989, and the Backing of Warrants (Republic of Ireland) Act 1965.

In the first place the 2003 Act, Part 1,[291] creates a fast track extradition arrangement between EU Member States, known as the 'European Arrest Warrant'.[292] Under this procedure the EAW, which must be in the prescribed form specifying the judicial authority[293] issuing the warrant, details of the alleged offence (including possible sentence) as well as particulars of the person to be arrested, is sent to the Serious Organised Crime Agency (the Crown Office in Scotland)[294] for certification as authentic and then execution. In other words, diplomatic channels are not used at all. Upon arrest the suspect is brought before a judge within forty-eight hours. This initial hearing is simply to confirm that the person named in the warrant is the person who has been arrested.[295] If the suspect does

'three wise men' who advised the Home Secretary in the past. This procedure did not survive scrutiny by the European Human Rights Court in *Chahal* v. *UK* (1997) 23 EHHR 413. There is a further appeal to the Court of Appeal on a point of law. See *Home Secretary* v. *Rehman (Consolidated Appeals)* [2003] 1 AC 153 (national security threatened not only by acts directed against the UK, but also by acts against other (friendly) countries; whether deportation 'conducive to the public good' 'prima facie a matter for the executive discretion').

[284] Act of 2002, s. 97 (so certified by the Home Secretary). But the appellants may go to the Special Immigration Appeals Commission (Act of 1997, s. 2). [285] Act of 2002, s. 92(4).

[286] Act of 1999, ss. 4, 95–101. The Act of 2002, Pt 2, makes provision for 'accommodation centres' for asylum-seekers pending determination of their claims.

[287] 2002 Act, s. 55. See *R (Q)* v. *Home Secretary* [2003] EWCA Civ 364 holding that regard should be had to the asylum-seeker's state of mind (and information) in assessing whether they had claimed in time.

[288] *R (Limbuela)* v. *Secretary of State for the Home Department* [2004] EWHC 219.

[289] See Nicholls, Montgomery and Knowles, *The Law of Extradition and Mutual Assistance* (2013) and the Baker Report, 'A Review of the United Kingdom's Extradition Arrangements' (2011) (<http://www.gov.uk/government/uploads/system/uploads/attachment_data/file/117673/extradition-review.pdf>).

[290] As amended and supplemented by the Police and Justice Act 2006, Sched. 13, given effect by s. 42.

[291] ss. 1–68A.

[292] This was initiated by an EU Council Framework Decision of 13 June 2002 adopted pursuant to Title VI of the Treaty on European Union (2002/584/JHA) Official Journal 18.7.2002 L 190/1. There is nothing in the 2003 Act, however, that prevents the extension of this procedure to non-EU Member States. It cannot be extended to states which retain the death penalty (s. 1(3)).

[293] Which in the circumstances includes a public prosecutor: *Assange* v. *Swedish Prosecution Authority* [2012] UKSC 22, paras. 14, 54–7. [294] These are the designated authorities in terms of s. 2(9).

[295] s. 7(3).

not consent to extradition an 'extradition hearing' takes place within twenty-one days. But this hearing does not assess the strength of the case against the suspect; it is simply concerned with whether there are any of the specified 'bars to surrender'. The most prominent 'bars to surrender' include whether the offence is one to which the procedure applies;[296] whether the accused will be subject to double jeopardy if extradited; whether the purpose of the prosecution is to persecute the accused on the grounds of his or her race, religion, nationality, political opinions, gender or sexual orientation or to prejudice the trial on any of these grounds; and whether there has been delay that would render the surrender unjust[297] or oppressive[298] or if the accused was at the relevant time below the age of criminal responsibility or if their medical or physical condition makes it unjust or oppressive to extradite him or her.[299] If there is no 'bar to surrender' the judge must order the extradition but there are provisions for appeal.

In the second place, the 2003 Act makes provision for extradition to countries which have been designated under Part 2. Most countries have been designated under this part.[300] But the request for extradition is made through diplomatic channels. The Home Secretary must refer the request to the appropriate judge if it complies as to matters of form.[301] The judge may issue an arrest warrant but he must have reasonable grounds for believing that the offence is an extraditable offence and there is evidence against the suspect that 'would justify the issue of a warrant for the arrest of a person accused of the offence within the judge's jurisdiction'.[302] Thereafter an extradition hearing takes place. The judge may refuse to order extradition if there is insufficient evidence 'to make a case requiring an answer by the person if the proceedings were the summary trial of an information against him'.[303] There must also not be a specified bar to extradition.[304] These are not dissimilar to those mentioned above.[305] There is

---

[296] See ss. 64, 65 for the offences to which the procedure applies. Any offence punishable by 3 years qualifies, even if it is not an offence under the law of any part of the UK. But 'all the conduct' complained of need not have occurred in the country seeking extradition; it is enough if some of it did (*Office of the King's Prosecutor, Brussels* v. *Cando Armas* [2005] UKHL 67, [2006] 2 AC 1 (Lord Bingham, para. 17)). Note that under s. 19B of the Act (as inserted by the Police and Justice Act 2006, Sched. 13, para. 4) extradition is barred on grounds of forum if it appears that '(a) a significant part of the conduct alleged to constitute the extradition offence is conduct in the United Kingdom, and (b) in view of that and all the other circumstances, it would not be in the interests of justice for the person to be tried for the offence in the requesting territory'. This section is not in force at the time of writing (late 2013).

[297] See *Kociukow* v. *District Court of Bialystok* [2006] EWHC 56 (unjust to extradite 6 years after alleged offence).

[298] The absence of explicit consideration of proportionality has attracted adverse comment: *Assange* above, para. 90.

[299] See 2003 Act, ss. 11–25. For consideration of medical conditions see *R (McKinnon)* v. *Home Secretary* [2009] EWHC 2021 (Asperger's syndrome insufficiently severe). But the Home Secretary subsequently blocked the extradition on 'human rights' grounds: <http://www.bbc.co.uk/news/uk-19957138>.

[300] The list stretches from Albania to Zimbabwe. The list includes Commonwealth countries, British Overseas Territories and Hong Kong (but not China). See SI 2003 No. 3334.

[301] s. 70. If there is a competing request from another Part 2 territory, the Home Secretary may choose between them: s. 126.   [302] s. 71(3)(a).

[303] s. 84(1). The judge has an implied power to protect the integrity of the process where the prosecution is an abuse (*Bermingham*, para. 97 (abuse not found)) approved *McKinnon* v. *The United States of America* [2008] UKHL 59, para. 8 (Lord Brown). Where abuse found power extends to a permanent stay of the proceedings and the discharge of the accused. But plea bargain negotiations (including threats that accused would not be able to serve sentence in home country) did not amount to an abuse (*McKinnon*). See also *R (Government of the USA)* v. *Bow Street Magistrates' Court* [2006] EWHC 2256, [2007] 1 WLR 1157, paras. 82–3 (no power to order requesting state to disclose relevant documents; but power to control and investigate abuse).   [304] These are set out in s. 79.

[305] The same rule as in *Cando Armas*, as above, applies—the conduct need not take place wholly in the extraditing state (*R (Bermingham)* v. *Director, Serious Fraud Office* [2006] EWHC 200 (Admin), [2007] 2

a right of appeal from the judge to the High Court.[306] Crucially, however, the final decision rests with the Home Secretary; and he may refuse to order extradition on several grounds.[307] At all stages the extradition must be compatible with the accused's rights under the Human Rights Act 1998.[308]

The Act allows for the requirement of evidence before arrest to be eased for countries designated by the Home Secretary to simply a requirement of information.[309] This has allowed the UK to negotiate an extradition treaty with the USA (ratified September 2006)[310] in which there is no consideration of the evidence against the accused before extradition.[311] Several other countries have been designated in the same way, opening the way to similar treaties.[312]

Habeas corpus may be granted to an accused person held in breach of a provision of the 2003 Act.[313]

COUNTERTERRORISM

The events of 11 September 2001 and their aftermath led inevitably to the enactment of extraordinary measures to counter the threat of terrorism. Countering such threats is a core function of government; and special legislation to counter terrorism has long been a feature of British law, mostly through the creation of special criminal offences.[314] But several of the post-2001 measures provide for action to be taken against suspects through the exercise of executive discretion and so engage the principles of administrative law. The first of these was the ill fated Part 4 of the Anti-terrorism, Crime and Security Act 2001, enacted in the immediate aftermath of the outrage. It provided for the indefinite detention without trial of non-nationals 'if the Home Secretary believed that their presence in the United Kingdom was a risk to national security and he suspected that they were terrorists who, for the time being, could not be deported because of fears for their safety or other practical considerations'.[315] There was a right of appeal to the Special Immigration

---

WLR 635). Note that under the s. 83A of the Act (as inserted by the Police and Justice Act 2006, Sched. 13, para. 5) extradition is barred on grounds of forum if it appears that '(a) a significant part of the conduct alleged to constitute the extradition offence is conduct in the United Kingdom, and (b) in view of that and all the other circumstances, it would not be in the interests of justice for the person to be tried for the offence in the requesting territory.' But s. 83A has not been brought into force.

[306] s. 103.

[307] s. 93. The grounds include that the accused may be subject to the death penalty or tried for an offence other than that for which he is being extradited.   [308] s. 87.

[309] s. 71(4) and a similar rule applies at the extradition hearing: s. 84(7).

[310] 31 March 2003. But it will still be necessary to submit evidence of guilt when the UK seeks extradition of an alleged offender from the USA.

[311] These provisions naturally proved controversial and have provoked a legislative response (on an amendment moved in the House of Lords). The Police and Justice Act 2006, s. 43(1) provides that in the statutory instrument designating the countries in respect of which only information is required (SI 2003 No. 3334) 'the entry for the United States of America is omitted'. However, this provision is only to be brought into force in certain circumstances notably when both Houses pass a resolution to that effect (s. 43(2)–(6)).

[312] SI 2003 No. 3334, reg. 3.

[313] *Nikonovs* v. *HM Prison Brixton* [2005] EWHC Admin 2405 (para. 18) (notwithstanding ouster in s. 34; discussed below, pp. 504, 613) affirmed in *Hilali* v. *Governor of Whitemoor Prison* [2008] UKHL 3 [2008] 1 AC 805, para. 21.

[314] For accounts see Bradley and Ewing, as above, pp. 578–602; Fenwick, *Civil Liberties and Human Rights*, 6th edn (2013). The core statute is the Terrorism Act 2000 (as amended by the Protection of Freedoms Act 2012). See also [2008] *PL* 234 (Poole).

[315] From the headnote to the official report crisply summarising the convoluted statute. The reason why such persons could not be deported was because they faced persecution in the country to which they would be sent.

SOME GOVERNMENTAL FUNCTIONS

Appeals Commission.[316] Some 11 persons were detained under these provisions but, as explained elsewhere,[317] the House of Lords made a declaration of incompatibility in respect of section 23 (which made specific provision for the detention of such persons). Since this provision did not extend to the British citizens who posed a similar threat but only to the non-nationals, it could not be said to pass the test of being 'strictly required by the exigencies of the situation'. 'If it is not necessary to lock up the nationals' said Baroness Hale, 'it cannot be necessary to lock up the foreigners'.[318]

Part 4 of the 2001 Act had thus to be abandoned and its place was taken by the 'control orders regime' established by the Prevention of Terrorism Act 2005. The 2005 Act empowered the Home Secretary to make a 'control order' against any individual.[319] A control order specified and imposed a range of obligations upon the controlee. These were very various but generally specified the individual's residence, imposed a curfew requirement and restricted his communications with others. It was a criminal offence to contravene any obligation.[320] The Home Secretary could only make a control order 'if [she] (a) [had] reasonable grounds for suspecting that the individual was... involved in terrorism-related activity; and (b) considered that it is necessary, [to protect]... the public from a risk of terrorism, to make a control order imposing obligations on that individual'.[321]

The making of a control order was subject to automatic judicial supervision before the High Court with the 'function of the court [being] to consider whether the Secretary of State's decision that there are grounds to make that order is obviously flawed'.[322] Since some of the evidence placed before the Special Immigration Appeals Commission (SIAC) was likely to come from intelligence sources which the authorities are reluctant to reveal to the controlled person, provision is made for 'special advocates' to be appointed to whom that evidence may be dealt with by them in the absence of the controlled person.[323]

Control orders themselves proved controversial[324] and they have now been replaced by Terrorism Prevention and Investigation Measures ('TPIMs').[325] A TPIM may be imposed by the Home Secretary when she 'reasonably believes that the individual is, or has been, involved in terrorism-related activity' and she 'reasonably considers that it is necessary, for purposes connected with protecting members of the public from a risk of terrorism, for terrorism prevention and investigation measures to be imposed on the individual'.[326] As before, the TPIM may only be imposed with the permission of the court unless the Home Secretary considers that the matter is urgent;[327] the court determines whether the TPIM is 'obviously flawed'.[328] There is once more provision made for 'special advocates' and closed hearings to deal with intelligence material.[329] If the court grants permission for a TPIM, it must set a date for a 'review hearing', which the individual who is the subject

---

[316] Described above, p. 63 n. 283.   [317] Below, p. 145.

[318] A v. Home Secretary [2004] UKHL 56, para. 231.

[319] Provisions exist (ss. 4–6 of the 2005 Act) for a court to make a 'derogating' control order, i.e. an order that does involve a breach of Art. 5. But thus far such orders have not been made. They would require a derogation from Art. 5 under Art. 14 of the Convention.   [320] Act of 2005, s. 9.(1).

[321] Act of 2005, s. 2.

[322] Act of 2005, s. 3(2). Previously the court was the Special Immigrations Appeal Commission but see Act of 2011, s. 30(1).   [323] The 'special advocate' procedure is discussed below, p. 433.

[324] For an account see the 10th edition of this book, pp. 72–3.

[325] These changes being effected by the Terrorism Prevention and Investigation Measures Act 2011. This followed a Command Paper presented to Parliament by the Home Secretary in January 2011: 'Review of Counter-Terrorism and Security Powers: Review Findings and Recommendations' (Cm. 8004). The Paper is available at <http://www.gov.uk/government/uploads/system/uploads/attachment_data/file/97972/review-findings-and-rec.pdf>.   [326] Act of 2011, s. 3(1), (3).

[327] Act of 2011, s. 3(5).   [328] Act of 2011, s. 6(3)(a)   [329] Below, p. 433.

of the TPIM is allowed to attend.[330] At this hearing the court will apply the 'ordinary principles of judicial review'.[331] A TPIM may remain in force for up to two years.[332]

The powers of the Secretary of State are somewhat weaker under the TPIM regime than they were under the Control Order regime. In particular there is no longer the power to 'relocate' the subject, curfews have been renamed 'overnight residence measures' and the subject is now entitled to access to a fixed-line telephone and the internet in their home.[333]

COMPLAINTS AGAINST ADMINISTRATION

NON-LEGAL REMEDIES

Much of this book is devoted to explaining the legal remedies which may be invoked against governmental action which is irregular or improper. But there are other, non-legal remedies which are also important. The picture cannot be seen in true perspective without some knowledge of them.

The administration of so many services and controls under the vast bureaucratic machinery of the central government inevitably causes many grievances and complaints. If something illegal is done, administrative law can supply a remedy, though the procedure of the courts is too formal and expensive to suit many complainants. But justified grievances may equally well arise from action which is legal, or at any rate not clearly illegal, when a government department has acted inconsiderately or unfairly or where it has misled the complainant or delayed his case excessively or treated him badly. Sometimes a statutory tribunal will be able to help him both cheaply and informally. But there is a large residue of grievances which fit into none of the regular legal moulds, but are nonetheless real. A humane system of government must provide some way of assuaging them, both for the sake of justice and because accumulating discontent is a serious clog on administrative efficiency in a democratic country. The aggrieved citizen's classical constitutional remedy of complaining to his Member of Parliament and getting him to put a parliamentary question to a minister is quite inadequate for this purpose.[334]

The primary necessity is the impartial investigation of complaints. It has always been possible for the government to commission a special inquiry, but this is far too ponderous and expensive a process for the ordinary run of grievances. What every form of government needs is some regular and smooth-running mechanism for feeding back the reactions of its disgruntled customers, after impartial assessment, and for correcting whatever may have gone wrong. Nothing of this kind existed in our system before the establishment of the Parliamentary Commissioner for Administration (or ombudsman) in 1967, except in very limited spheres. Yet it is a fundamental need in every system.[335] This was why the device of the ombudsman suddenly attained immense popularity, sweeping round the democratic world and taking root in Britain and in many other countries, as well

---

[330] Act of 2011, s. 8.   [331] Act of 2011, s. 9(2).   [332] Act of 2011, s. 5.
[333] Act of 2011, Pt 1 and Sched. 1. See [2012] *Crim LR* 421 (Walker and Horne) (review of the differences between the two regimes).   [334] Already noted above, p. 24.
[335] The need for an ombudsman is not obviated by a system of separate administrative courts of the French type, and ombudsmen, under an appropriate local name, are often established in such systems.

as inspiring a vast literature.[336] Ombudsmen have since been established for the health service (1973), for local government (1974) and for many other areas of national life.[337]

There is a Public Service Ombudsman for Wales who may investigate the Welsh Assembly itself as well as other Welsh public bodies.[338] The Scottish Parliament is under a duty to make provision for the investigation of maladministration reported to its members[339] and has duly established an ombudsman.[340] A European ombudsman charged with the investigation of complaints against the institutions of the European Communities is established under the Treaty of Maastricht.[341]

THE OMBUDSMAN: TRIBUNE OF THE PEOPLE

Ombudsman is a Scandinavian word meaning officer or commissioner. In its special sense it means a commissioner who has the duty of investigating and reporting to Parliament on citizens' complaints against the government. An ombudsman requires no legal powers except powers of inquiry. In particular, he is in no sense a court of appeal and he cannot alter or reverse any government decision. His effectiveness derives entirely from his power to focus public and parliamentary attention upon citizens' grievances. But publicity based on impartial inquiry is a powerful lever. Where a complaint is found to be justified, an ombudsman can often persuade a government department to modify a decision or pay compensation in cases where the complainant unaided would get no satisfaction. For the department knows that a public report will be made and that it will be unable to conceal the facts from Parliament and the press. The department is not bound to accept the recommendations of the ombudsman. But the Secretary of State may only reject her

[336] A few references are: for Britain: Gregory and Hutchesson, *The Parliamentary Ombudsman*; Stacey, *The British Ombudsman*; Wheare, *Maladministration and its Remedies*, ch. 5; Seneviratne, *Ombudsmen in the Public Sector*; for other countries: Gellhorn, *Ombudsmen and Others*; Gellhorn, *When Americans Complain*; Rowat, *The Ombudsman Plan*; Rowat (ed.), *The Ombudsman, Citizen's Defender*; *Il Difensore Civico* (Turin, 1974); D. W. Williams, *Maladministration, Remedies for Injustice*; [1958] *PL* 236 (Stephan Hurwitz); [1959] *PL* 115 (I. M. Pedersen); [1968] *JSPTL* 101 (Sir Edmund Compton, the first Parliamentary Commissioner); [1980] *CLJ* 304 (A. W. Bradley); (1990) 53 *MLR* 745 (G. Drewry and C. Marlow); [1992] *PL* 353 (A. W. Bradley); [1993] *PL* 221 (W. K. Reid, a sometime Parliamentary Commissioner responding to suggestions that the office is insufficiently known to the public); [1996] *PL* 384 (Sir C. Clothier, a sometime PC, discussing fact-finding by the Commissioner); [2008] *PL* 1 (Abrahams (the current Ombudsman)). See also *The Parliamentary Ombudsman: Withstanding the Test of Time* (HC 421), March 2007 published to mark the 40th Anniversary of the Parliamentary Commissioner and containing much useful information. Further literature is referred to below.

[337] Discussed below, p. 85 (Health Service Commissioner), p. 117 (Local Commissioners for Administration) and p. 87 (list of other ombudsmen). See [2006] *PL* 84 (Elliott) and [2011] *PL* 20 (Buck, Kirkham and Thompson) for discussion of reform proposals.

[338] Government of Wales Act 1998, s. 111 and 9th Sched. (But now see the 2005 Act (below) Sched. 1). After a period in which the offices of Health Service Commissioner for Wales and the Local Commissioner for Administration in Wales were held by the Ombudsman for the Welsh Administration these three offices have been unified by the Public Services Ombudsman (Wales) Act 2005. The Social Housing Ombudsman for Wales is also integrated with the others. See discussion of the plans [2003] *PL* 656 (M. Seneviratne). The first year in which the unification took effect is 2006 (see *Annual Report 2006/07* of the Public Service Ombudsman for Wales). [339] Scotland Act 1998, s. 91.

[340] Scottish Public Services Ombudsman Act 2002.

[341] Art. 195 (ex 138E) of the Treaty of Rome, now Art. 228 TFEU. Complaints are made directly to the ombudsman who is appointed by the European Parliament. The Ombudsman can (and does) act on his own initiative. See *The European Ombudsman*, HL paper 18 (1997–8). The relevant provision is now Art. 228 TFEU. The most recent EU Committee paper on the European Ombudsman is the Twenty-Second Report (February 2006, HL 117). For up-to-date statistics see the European Ombudsman's 2012 Annual Report at <http://www.ombudsman.europa.eu/activities/annualreports.faces>.

findings of fact 'on cogent reasons'[342] and a decision to reject a finding may itself be subject to judicial review (and quashed if shown to be irrational).[343]

The essence of the ombudsman's technique is to receive the complaint informally, to enter the government department, to speak to the officials and read the files, and to find out exactly who did what and why. No formal procedure is involved at any stage, nor is any legal sanction in question.

As his name implies, the ombudsman first appeared in Scandinavia. Sweden has had the institution, in a somewhat special form, for over a century and a half. But it was as established in Denmark after 1954 that it suddenly captured the attention of other countries, largely as a result of the missionary spirit of the first Danish ombudsman.[344]

MINISTERIAL RESPONSIBILITY UNDERMINED?

The main opposition to a British ombudsman was founded on the sacred principle of ministerial responsibility.[345] It was argued that it was fundamental to the constitution that, since the minister was responsible to Parliament for all that was done in his department and officials did not bear public responsibility, it would be wrong for an ombudsman to go behind the minister's back and pry into the workings of his department. But the truth was that some of the supposed corollaries of ministerial responsibility had become an abuse, sheltering mistakes and injustices and making it impossible for complainants and their Members of Parliament to find out what had really happened. As one Member of Parliament complained,[346] 'ministerial responsibility is a cloak for a lot of murkiness, muddle and slipshoddery within the departments'.[347] Nor was the principle as inviolable as the critics supposed. The Comptroller and Auditor-General had acted as a kind of financial ombudsman since 1866, reporting to the House of Commons on wasteful government expenditure with the aid of several hundred inspectors working permanently in the departments and 'engaged in an internal and continuous, and to a large extent preventive, check on maladministration'.[348] Experience soon showed that his investigations, so far from conflicting with ministerial responsibility, helped it to work better by enabling both Parliament and ministers to correct faults in administration which would

---

[342] R (Bradley) v. Department of Work and Pensions [2008] EWCA Civ 36, para. 72 (Sir John Chadwick) departing from the court at first instance ([2007] EWHC 242 (Bean J), para. 58) holding that the ombudsman's finding of fact could not be rejected unless they were quashed on judicial review. The minister had to be free to give a full account to Parliament. The position may be different in other contexts (R v. Home Secretary ex p Danaei [1997] EWCA Civ 2704 and the Eastleigh BC case, as below). In R (Gallagher) v. Basildon DC [2010] EWHC 2824 it was held that the 'cogent reasons' rule did not apply to findings of fact by the Local Government Ombudsman (paras. 28–30). In R (Equitable Members Action Group) v. HM Treasury [2009] EWHC 2495 (Admin), the 'cogent reasons' test was applied to the findings of the Parliamentary Commissioner. Noted (2010) 69 CLJ 1 (Elliott).

[343] Bradley, para. 95 (irrational for the Secretary of State to reject a finding of the ombudsman that 'official information—about the security that members of final salary occupational pension schemes could expect from the MFR [Minimum Funding Requirement]...was sometimes inaccurate, often incomplete and therefore potentially misleading, and that this constituted maladministration).

[344] Professor Stephan Hurwitz, whose visits to Britain aroused great interest and to whom a number of complaints were sent by hopeful Britons.

[345] For an illuminating discussion of the misconceptions surrounding ministerial responsibility in this context see Sir K. Wheare, Maladministration and its Remedies, ch. 3.

[346] 806 HC Deb. col. 648 (12 November 1970, Mr F. Willey).

[347] Quoted by Wheare (as above), 95.

[348] Wheare (as above), 110. Significantly, the first British ombudsman was a former Comptroller and Auditor-General.

otherwise never have been brought to light.[349] Experience has now shown that minister and ombudsman operate for the most part on different levels and with general constitutional compatibility. Indeed, a minister has said that the Parliamentary Commissioner system 'works extremely well [but] not always comfortably for the Government'.[350]

THE ACT OF 1967

The Parliamentary Commissioner Act 1967 established an ombudsman for the United Kingdom under the title of Parliamentary Commissioner for Administration.[351] The first thing to emphasise is the word 'Parliamentary'. The Commissioner may receive complaints only through members of the House of Commons,[352] and not, as in many other countries, from the public directly. He must report the result of his investigation to the member through whom the complaint came.[353] On his functions generally he reports to the two Houses of Parliament, and in particular he appears before the House of Commons Public Administration Select Committee, which frequently examines both him and officials of the department which he criticises.[354] His case reports, issued quarterly, and his annual and special reports, together with the reports of the Select Committee, are the main sources of information about his work. The annual reports[355] contain catalogues of injustices remedied, briefly summarised. In the quarterly reports selected cases are reported in full detail, but anonymously, although the government department involved is necessarily indicated. The Select Committee has also begun to issue thematic reports, such as *Maladministration and Redress*,[356] which when accepted and implemented by government can improve the quality of administration. The Parliamentary Commissioner herself has published a report, the *Principles of Good Administration*, to mark the fortieth Anniversary of the office. The principles distil what has been learned over that period of time.[357]

The Parliamentary Commissioner is thus in effect an agency of Parliament, helping to remedy grievances and check administrative errors and abuses. But, like the Comptroller and Auditor-General, he is appointed by the government despite the parliamentary character of the office;[358] and, like a High Court judge, he holds office during good behaviour,

---

[349] As ministers now acknowledge: see 109 HC Deb. 1056 (4 February 1987).

[350] Mr Francis Maude MP, Financial Secretary to the Treasury, in evidence to the Select Committee on the Parliamentary Commissioner (see Second Report, HC 1991–2, No. 158, p. 1).

[351] As explained below, p. 86, this office is generally held concurrently with that of the Heath Service Commissioner and is thus often referred to as the 'Parliamentary and Health Service Ombudsman' (see e.g. <http://www.ombudsman.org.uk/>).   [352] s. 5(1)(a).

[353] s. 10. A copy must go to the government department concerned.

[354] The government contended that ministerial responsibility required that the Select Committee should examine only heads of departments and such officials as they wished to accompany them, but the Committee asserted their right to examine subordinate officers: Second Report, Session 1967–68, HC 350, para. 24.

[355] Indexed at <http://www.ombudsman.org.uk/about-us/publications/annual-reports>.

[356] HC 112 (1994–5). This encourages the early admission of error by departments as well as prompt financial compensation where this is quantifiable and appropriate. The government's generally positive response is in HC 316 (1994–5) and see *Annual Report 1997–98*, p. 9, commending 'speedier and more effective redress'.

[357] The six principles of good administration are: 'getting it right', 'being customer focused', 'being open and accountable', 'acting fairly and proportionately', 'putting things right' and 'seeking continuous improvement'.

[358] Nominally by the Crown: s. 1. But the practice is to consult the Chairman of the Select Committee before appointment: Cmnd 6764 (1977). The Act of 1987 (below), s. 6, allows an acting Commissioner to be appointed to fill a temporary vacancy. For a recent pre-appointment consultation with the Public Administration Select Committee see Ninth Report, Session 2010–12, HC-1220I.

i.e. permanently, to the retiring age.[359] The first three commissioners were appointed from the civil service, and, unlike most of the world's ombudsmen, none of them had legal training. The current Commissioner, Dame Julie Mellor, is not a lawyer. The Commissioner charges no fees to complainants but is one of the services of the welfare state.

MATTERS INCLUDED AND EXCLUDED

The Act of 1967 gave the Parliamentary Commissioner jurisdiction only over the central government, and only over the departments listed in a schedule.[360] The Parliamentary and Health Service Commissioners Act 1987 extended the schedule of departments from less than fifty to more than a hundred. In addition a large number of non-departmental public bodies[361] including the British Library, the Arts Council, the Equal Opportunities Commission, the Commission for Racial Equality, the Research Councils, Industrial Training Boards and the Nature Conservancy Council.[362] And in 2005 sixty new bodies came under the jurisdiction of the Parliamentary Commissioner.[363]

The list of departments may be amended by Order in Council and thus it is kept up to date as changes take place.[364] But the Act of 1987 restricts additions to bodies which are government departments or which act on behalf of the Crown, or official bodies financed as to half at least by Parliament or statutory fees or charges and wholly or partly appointed by the Crown or a government department; nor may bodies be added which are involved in education or non-industrial training, professional qualifications and conduct, or the investigation of complaints. The government's purpose, as explained to Parliament, is to confine the list to bodies 'subject to some degree of ultimate ministerial accountability to Parliament, in that they are dependent for their financing and continuing existence on government policy'.[365] The establishment of executive agencies[366] and the 'contracting out' of some government services has not affected the Commissioner's jurisdiction, since he may investigate any action taken by 'or on behalf of' a body subject to his jurisdiction.[367]

An important point is that the Act of 1967, unlike the corresponding New Zealand Act, expressly includes ministers along with their departments.[368] The Parliamentary Commissioner may therefore investigate and criticise decisions taken by ministers personally.

[359] s. 1. This contrasts with many other countries which favour short-term appointments. Provision for his removal on grounds of ill health is made by the Parliamentary and Health Service Commissioners Act 1987, s. 2.   [360] s. 4 and 2nd Sched., now replaced by the Act of 1987.

[361] Colloquially known as quangos (quasi-autonomous non-governmental organisations).

[362] There are special Commissioners for the National Health Service and for Local Administration (as explained below).

[363] *Parliamentary and Health Service Ombudsman. Annual Report 2004–05: A Year of Progress*, HC 348, p. 5. And the Commissioner lost jurisdiction when complaints over access to government information were transferred to the Information Commissioner. For the latest position see the Parliamentary Commissioner Order 2013 (SI 2013/238), Art. 2.

[364] s. 4(2) as amended by the Act of 1987. The administrative actions of court staff fall within the Commissioner's jurisdiction: Courts and Legal Services Act 1990, s. 110. By an order made under s. 4(2), the jurisdiction of the Parliamentary Commissioner has been extended to a wide range of non-departmental public bodies as diverse as the British Museum, the Apple and Pear Research Council and the Higher Education Funding Council (SI 1999 No. 277).   [365] 109 HC Deb. 1057 (4 February 1987).

[366] See above, p. 37.

[367] Act of 1967, s. 5(1) and see the Commissioner's *Annual Report*, 1992, HC 1992–3, No. 569, p. 2.

[368] s. 4(8)(a).

A number of matters are excluded by the Act of 1967 and so are not subject to the Commissioner's investigation.[369] These are set out in a schedule which may be summarised as follows:

Action affecting foreign affairs.

Action taken outside the United Kingdom (except action by consular officers).[370]

Action taken in connection with territory overseas.

Extradition and fugitive offenders.

Investigation of crime.

Protection of state security (including passport matters).

Legal proceedings before any court of law in the United Kingdom or any international court or tribunal, and all disciplinary proceedings in the armed forces.

The prerogative of mercy and the reference of questions to certain courts.

The hospital service (Clinical Commissioning Groups).

Contractual and commercial transactions, other than the acquisition of land compulsorily or by agreement and the disposal of surplus land so acquired.

All personnel matters (including pay, discipline, removal) in the civil service and the armed forces, or where the government has power to take or determine or approve action.[371]

The grant by the Crown of honours, awards, privileges, or charters.

Action taken by the administrative staff of a court or tribunal on the direction or on the authority, express or implied, of a judge or a member of the tribunal.

Two controversial items in the list of exclusions are personnel administration in the civil service and contractual and commercial transactions. The Select Committee has made repeated attempts to bring these into the Parliamentary Commissioner's jurisdiction, since he receives a flow of complaints about them, but so far without success.[372] The list of exclusions may also be criticised in other respects, e.g. as regards passports.[373]

But a Cabinet Office 'Review of Public Sector Ombudsman'[374] foreshadows significant changes including the abolition of the MP filter—it can 'no longer', said the review, 'be sustained in the era of joined-up government'—and the extension of the Commissioner's jurisdiction to contractual matters.[375] The Review also recommended a collegiate Commission that would comprise all, or most, of the public sector ombudsmen including the Parliamentary Commissioner, the Health Service and Local Government Commissioners.

---

[369] s. 5(3) and 3rd Sched. The notes to the 2nd Sched. also make various exclusions.

[370] Parliamentary Commissioner (Consular Complaints) Act 1981, replacing SI 1979 No. 915.

[371] e.g. where the Home Secretary refuses approval of appointment of a chief constable.

[372] The inclusion of commercial and contractual matters was recommended by the Royal Commission on Standards of Conduct in Public Life, Cmnd 6524 (1976) and by the Commissioner himself: *Annual Report for 1983*, para. 9.

[373] See *Our Fettered Ombudsman* (JUSTICE, 1977), ch. 14; Commissioner's *Annual Report for 1978*, para. 13.

[374] Published on 13 April 2000 and followed by an undated Consultation Paper in June of that year. Discussed [2000] *PL* 582 (M. Seneviratne).

[375] Note also the Law Commission Report 'Public Service Ombudsmen', Law Com. No. 329 (2011).

MALADMINISTRATION: DISCRETIONARY DECISIONS AND RULES

The key provision of the Act of 1967[376] is that the Commissioner may investigate action taken 'in the exercise of administrative functions' by or on behalf of any of the scheduled central government departments where

(a) a written complaint is duly made to a member of the House of Commons by a member of the public[377] who claims to have sustained injustice in consequence of maladministration in connection with the action so taken and

(b) the complaint is referred to the Commissioner, with the consent of the person who made it, by a member of that House with a request to conduct an investigation thereon.

Maladministration was a new term in the law, though not in the language.[378] The Act does not explain or define it, as is perhaps natural since it requires only that the complainant should *claim* that maladministration has occurred. Parliament was told that the word would cover 'bias, neglect, inattention, delay, incompetence, ineptitude, arbitrariness and so on', and that 'it would be a long and interesting list'.[379] The effect of all this is that the Ombudsman has 'very considerable discretion as to what he investigates and how he investigates'.[380]

It is necessary, of course, that the complainant should have 'sustained injustice'; and the courts have held that the Commissioner should not report adversely unless that is so.[381] But the test of bias to found a finding of maladministration is less onerous than that required to found judicial review.[382] And the Commissioner must investigate the complaint made not some other complaint that, perhaps, ought to have been made. And if he strays from the complaint made, the courts will set him right.[383]

Furthermore, the Act 'declares' that the Commissioner is not authorised to 'question the merits of a decision taken without maladministration by a government department or other authority in the exercise of a discretion vested in that department or authority'.[384] There is thus a distinction between a decision tainted by maladministration, which the Commissioner may question, and an unmeritorious decision, reached without maladministration, which he may not. The Commissioner's role is to identify and criticise maladministration; he does not provide an appeal on the merits against an unfavourable decision. The Ombudsman is also not required to determine questions of law.[385]

---

[376] s. 5(1).   [377] Not a very apt term, since it includes a corporation: s. 6(1).

[378] It has been in use at least since 1644: *OED*.

[379] 734 HC Deb. col. 51 (18 October 1966). In ombudsman circles this became known as the 'Crossman catalogue'. But clearly it is open-ended, as stated by Lord Denning MR in *R* v. *Local Commissioner for Administration ex p Bradford MCC* [1979] QB 287.

[380] *R (Sharma)* v. *Parliamentary and Health Service Ombudsman* [2011] EWHC 2609, para 8.

[381] *R* v. *Local Commissioner for Administration ex p Eastleigh BC* [1988] QB 855. 'Injustice' includes that 'sense of outrage aroused by unfair or incompetent administration even where the complainant has suffered no actual loss': *R* v. *Parliamentary Commissioner for Administration ex p Balchin (No 2)* (2000) 2 LGLR 87. Discussed [2000] *PL* 201 (P. Giddings).

[382] *R* v. *Local Commissioner for Local Government for North and North East England ex p Liverpool City Council* [2001] 1 All ER 462. This must be so since otherwise there would be a legal remedy. See below, p. 76.

[383] *R (Cavanagh)* v. *Health Service Commissioner for England* [2005] EWCA Civ 1578 (Commissioner reported that claimant misdiagnosed, a matter in respect of which no complaint was made). The Ombudsman cannot 'expand the ambit of a complaint beyond what it contains' (para. 16, Sedley LJ).

[384] s. 12(3), 'drafted by the formidable pen of the Lord Chancellor himself' (Sir E. Compton, [1968] *JSPTL* at 110).

[385] *R (Mencap)* v. *Parliamentary and Health Service Ombudsman* [2011] EWHC 3351, paras. 32–6 following *R* v. *Local Commissioner for Administration in North East England ex p Liverpool City Council* [2001]

In the past, after criticism by the Select Committee,[386] the Commissioner was willing to criticise decisions that were simply bad on their merits.[387] However, several dicta have indicated that the courts will intervene to stop a Commissioner who interferes with the merits in the absence of maladministration[388] and the practice of the Commissioner has changed: mere disagreement will not be the basis of criticism.[389] The distinction is drawn in the decided cases between the *manner* in which the decision is reached and implemented (which is the concern of the Commissioner) and the *merits* of the decision (which should be eschewed by the Commissioner).[390]

The manner in which a decision is reached or implemented can cover so many aspects of the decision that its merits, as a distinct concept, disappear. The Commissioner, for instance, regularly criticises the weight attached to particular circumstances in making the decision;[391] but criticism of the merits can, practically always, be presented as criticism of the weight attached to some consideration or circumstance. In New Zealand the ombudsman is expressly empowered to report on any decision which was unreasonable, unjust, based on mistake, or merely 'wrong'.[392] The Commissioner should enjoy a similar power: bad decisions are bad administration and bad administration is maladministration.

Along with the 'bad decision' goes the 'bad rule'. The Commissioner was at first unwilling to criticise departmental rules and regulations,[393] so that what was maladministration if done once apparently ceased to be so if done repeatedly under a rule. Here again the Select Committee induced him to change his mind.[394] After some initial confusion with the fallacy that statutory regulations, because they are legislative, do not involve administrative action,[395] the Select Committee concluded that statutory instruments and other statutory orders should fall within the Commissioner's field, at least as regards their effect and the action taken to review them.[396] Although the Commissioner seldom criticises non-statutory policy guidance given by ministers to decision-makers, he does criticise such procedural guidance where it is unfair.[397]

---

1 All ER 462, para. 46; *Maxwell v. The Office for the Independent Adjudicator for Higher Education* [2011] EWCA Civ 1236, paras. 33–4.

[386] HC 1967–8, No. 350, para. 14.

[387] e.g. where the Customs and Excise refused a discretionary refund of gaming licence duty 'on grounds which do not stand up to examination', the Commissioner obtained a refund of £22,500 for the complainant company (*Annual Report for 1970*, HC 261, 36).

[388] *R v. Local Commissioner for Administration ex p Eastleigh BC*, above.

[389] See e.g. *The Barlow Clowes Affair*, HC 1989–90, No. 76, introduction, para. 6.

[390] *R v. Local Commissioner for Administration ex p Bradford MCC* [1979] QB 287 at 311, 314, 318; *R v. Local Commissioner for Administration ex p Eastleigh BC* (above), at 863. Note though that in *R v. Local Commissioner for Administration ex p Croydon LBC* [1989] 1 All ER 1033, Woolf LJ (at 1043) did not commit himself on this question.

[391] As was seen in the Barlow Clowes case (third area of maladministration), discussed below, p. 79.

[392] Parliamentary Commissioner (Ombudsman) Act 1962 (NZ), s. 19. See (1971) 4 NZULR 361 (K. J. Keith).   [393] HC 6, 1967–8, para. 36.

[394] HC 350, 1967–8, para. 16; HC 9, 1968–9; HC 129, 1968–9, para. 17. For an example of criticism of a bad rule, see *Annual Report for 1979*, para. 55.

[395] The Attorney-General so contended in the case of statutory instruments but not in the case of other statutory orders: see HC 385, 1968–9, para. 10.

[396] HC 385, 1968–9, para. 11, suggesting however a wider jurisdiction in the case of statutory orders other than statutory instruments.   [397] [1987] *PL* 570 (A. Mowbray).

CASES WHERE THERE ARE LEGAL REMEDIES

An ombudsman is not a substitute for the ordinary courts and tribunals. Consequently the Act of 1967 provides that the Commissioner shall not investigate cases where the person aggrieved has or had a remedy in any court of law, or a right of appeal, reference or review in any statutory or prerogative tribunal.[398] But there is a significant proviso: the Commissioner may nevertheless investigate the complaint if he is satisfied that in the particular circumstances it is not reasonable to expect the remedy or right to be, or to have been, invoked.[399] This proviso means that the line of demarcation between the Commissioner and the legal system is not a rigid one, and that much technicality and inconvenience can be eliminated by the Commissioner using his discretion.[400] It may frequently happen that there is a possibility of a legal remedy but that the law is doubtful; in such cases the Commissioner may decide that it is not reasonable to insist on recourse to the law.[401] Where there is clearly a case for a court or tribunal, on the other hand, he will refuse to act.[402] It is not easy to tell from the Commissioner's reports how often he has made use of the proviso.[403] But it seems probable that, with or without doing so, he has investigated many cases where there would have been legal remedies.[404]

An example of a case where the Commissioner found maladministration, but the law later provided a remedy, is that of the revocation of television licences in 1975.[405] The Home Office had threatened to revoke the licences of members of the public who had taken them out before their current licences expired, in order to renew them, as they were legally entitled to do, before a large increase of fee came into force. Many complaints were made to the Commissioner and, after full investigation, he found the Home Office seriously to blame for not giving the public proper warning, for inefficiency and lack of foresight, and for insufficient frankness with the public. But he felt, illogically,[406] that he could not criticise them for acting as their lawyers had advised was legal, and he therefore refrained from asking them to reconsider their threat to revoke some 36,000 licences.

---

[398] s. 5(2).

[399] In 'A Debt of Honour' The ex gratia scheme for British groups interned by the Japanese during the Second World War (HC 324, 2006) the Ombudsman discussed the 'alternative remedy' rule. The Ombudsman said that in considering 'reasonableness' she would consider the 'emotional and financial cost of litigation'; she would also take into account her superior fact-finding powers and resources. Available at <http://www.ombudsman.org.uk/__data/assets/pdf_file/0017/1097/A-Debt-of-Honour.pdf>.

[400] Previous three sentences cited with apparent approval in In the Matter of an Application by JR55 [2012] NIQB 108, para. 9 (Treacy J).

[401] e.g. Annual Report for 1968, p. 19 (complaint against Customs and Excise investigated where legal remedy possible but doubtful). Legal proceedings need merely be appropriate rather than bound to succeed before the Commissioner may decline to investigate: R v. Commissioner for Local Administration ex p Croydon LBC [1989] 1 All ER 1033. See [1988] PL 608 (M. Jones). But see R v. Local Commissioner for Administration in North and North East England ex p Liverpool City Council [2001] 1 All ER 462 (Commissioner's powers 'to compel both disclosure of documents, and the giving of assistance to the investigation' meant that the commissioner was more likely to 'to get to the bottom of a prima facie case of maladministration' than a judicial review brought by the complainants). For fact-finding in judicial review see below, p. 230.

[402] e.g. Annual Report for 1968, p. 148 (complaint of minister's dismissal of appeal against enforcement notice: right of appeal to High Court). In the Barlow Clowes case the Commissioner warned investors that he could not deal with their complaints if they brought their own legal actions (The Times, 13 July 1988). And see [1991] PL 408, 422 (R. Gregory and G. Drewry); R v. Commissioner for Local Administration ex p H [1999] ELR 314 (judicial review held an appropriate remedy, justifying a refusal to investigate by Commissioner, where maladministration continuing).

[403] Examples are given in (1971) 34 MLR 377 (D. Foulkes).

[404] See e.g. below, p. 809, n. 96; also HC 573, 1970–1, para. 13 (Select Committee).

[405] HC 680, 1974–5 (special report).   [406] Most acts of maladministration are legal.

But shortly afterwards the Court of Appeal held that the Home Secretary's threat to use his power of revocation for this purpose was wholly unlawful, being an abuse of a power given to him for other purposes.[407] It then became clear that the complainants had a legal remedy from the start. The Commissioner, had he known this, might not have thought fit to invoke the proviso, since the situation was eminently one for a test case in a court of law.[408]

A certain overlap between the Commissioner and the legal system must be accepted as inevitable, and this, though untidy, is doubtless in the public interest.[409] The Commissioner provides a service which is free from both the expense and the uncertainty of the law. Although, unlike courts and tribunals, he has no decisive power, he has facilities for investigation and access to evidence which are not available to litigants. His probing into the television licence case revealed serious maladministration which it was salutary to bring to light. An ombudsman is a valuable adjunct to any system of administrative law, however comprehensive and efficient.

MISLEADING STATEMENTS AND ADVICE

A common form of maladministration is the giving of wrong information or advice by officials dealing with the public. The Commissioner has investigated many cases where the complainant had thus been misled and suffered loss, and in many of them he has persuaded the department to make compensation in money. This is a particularly interesting branch of his activities, since one of the defects of the law, as will appear later,[410] is that it has failed to develop remedies in similar situations. Although occasionally there may be a right of action for negligent misstatement, or under the developing doctrine of legitimate expectation, the Commissioner's policy seems once again to be to disregard any possible legal remedy.

The following are some examples of such cases. Where the Customs and Excise department wrongly advised a company that its product would not be liable to purchase tax, and exaction of the tax drove the company into liquidation, the department agreed to pay £6,000 in compensation.[411] In the Barlow Clowes case, discussed later, a novel point arose. Did the misleading advice have to be given to the complainant? The Department of Trade and Industry had incorrectly advised the Barlow Clowes partnership in 1985 that they did not require a licence to carry on their business. The Commissioner found that this was maladministration notwithstanding that the misleading statement was not made to a complainant.[412] All the compensation payments were technically made ex

---

[407] *Congreve v. Home Office* [1976] QB 629; see below, p. 301. The Home Office refunded the fees paid under threat of revocation.

[408] A similar example is the case concerning compensation for farmers whose poultry was slaughtered in the scare over salmonella enteritidis in eggs in 1989 (Fourth Report 1992–93, HC 1992–3, No. 519). The Commissioner commented that the compensation scheme was arbitrary, based on improper considerations and fell short of the government's legal obligations. Substantial additional payments were made. See also the Select Committee's view of the scheme (HC 1992–3, No. 593).

[409] See [1980] *CLJ* 304 at 320 (A. W. Bradley) for comment on this question. The Law Commission recommends ('Public Service Ombudsmen' (2011) (Law Com. No. 329), paras. 3.23–3.49) that the 'alternative remedy' rule under s. 5 should be repealed and replaced with a general discretion exercised by the Ombudsman. This would 'give complainants greater freedom of choice over the institution, and related procedure, for administrative redress they can use': para. 3.40).   [410] Below, p. 284.

[411] *Annual Report for 1973*, HC 106, 7. For other examples, see *Annual Report for 1979*, para. 55 (misleading advice from 'jobcentre': £990 recovered); Select Cases 1981, ii. 32 (misleading advice about pension: £500 compensation paid): *Annual Report for 1986*, p. 7 (tax cases).

[412] *Barlow Clowes Affair*, para. 3.9; [1991] *PL* 192 at 428–9 (R. Gregory and G. Drewry).

gratia, on the assumption that there was no legal liability but that injustice and loss were suffered because of misleading official advice. It is probably a safe guess that without the Commissioner's intervention none of them would have been made. An example of misleading statements in respect of which compensation has not, at the time of writing, been paid concerns the Department of Work and Pensions.[413] The Ombudsman[414] had found *inter alia* that the Department had issued a leaflet stating that 'The Pensions Act [1995] introduces a new rule aimed at making *sure* that salary related schemes have enough money in them to meet the pension rights of their members' (emphasis added). But at the same time the Department was seeking actuarial advice on the basis that it was only necessary to ensure that there was an 'even chance' that the schemes would be able to meet their obligations.

As distinct from positive advice, a mere failure to warn may have a similar effect. Objections to many proposed orders affecting land, such as compulsory purchase orders, must be heard by a representative of the minister either at a public local inquiry or at a less formal hearing.[415]

UNJUSTIFIED DELAY

Unjustified delay is a well-recognised and common species of maladministration, either as a major or a contributory ground.[416] A husband who applied in April 1984 for entry clearance for his wife to join him in the United Kingdom had, despite many enquiries, to wait until May 1988 before it was granted. The Commissioner found that there had been unacceptable delay and the Home Office apologised and made an ex gratia payment of £1,000.[417] In another case, after administrative confusion between two counsel with similar names, a barrister did not receive the fees that were due to him from the Legal Aid Board. For eighteen months he received no satisfactory response to his letters requesting payment and when payment was eventually made, it was sent to the wrong address. The Commissioner found that there had been serious delay. The Legal Aid Board apologised and paid interest on the main bill as well as a further £60 compensation for the fruitless correspondence.[418] And in the Barlow Clowes case, discussed in the next section, one of the species of maladministration found by the Commissioner was a delay from early July 1987 (when the Department of Trade was alerted to the Stock Exchange's doubts about the firm) until 13 October 1987 (when a recommendation was made to the minister that the firm should be investigated).[419] In an investigation into alleged maladministration in the UK Border Agency the Ombudsman found lengthy delays in determining immigration and asylum applications. She commented that 'the Agency's failure to resolve applications within reasonable timescales can have serious implications for the individuals concerned, and for society in general'.[420]

---

[413] August 2008.

[414] In her report, *Trusting in the pensions promise* (2006). But the Department does not accept the recommendations of the Ombudsman's report. See below, for discussion of the litigation about this case.

[415] See below, p. 794.   [416] See [1997] *PL* 159 (McMurtrie).

[417] Selected Cases 1992, HC 1992–3, No. 11, ii. 2, 22–31.

[418] Selected Cases 1993, HC 1992–3, No. 400, i. 3, 34–6.

[419] *First Report, 1989–90, The Barlow Clowes Affair*, HC 1989–90, No. 76, paras. 6.53–6.61.

[420] 'Fast and Fair? A Report by the Parliamentary Ombudsman on the UK Border Agency' (HC 329, 2010) at p. 16. The Report is available at <http://www.ombudsman.org.uk/__data/assets/pdf_file/0016/673/UKBA-2010-02-09.pdf>.

The importance of minimising delay should not be underestimated. Whether the subsequent decision is favourable to the applicant or not, the applicant will have been subjected to unnecessary frustration and stress; and small grievances will have grown into large ones.

THE BARLOW CLOWES AFFAIR

The Parliamentary Commissioner's success in securing some £150m. compensation to those who had lost money in the Barlow Clowes affair has been his most spectacular single achievement thus far,[421] and deserves to be separately considered.

Barlow Clowes was a brokerage business selling gilt-based investments under a 'bond washing' scheme which transmuted highly taxed income into lowly taxed capital. When the tax loophole was closed in 1985, funds were diverted from the UK firm to associated firms in Gibraltar and Jersey and were put into highly speculative investments and high living for the fund managers, and interest was paid out of capital. Eventually the firms' liabilities greatly exceeded their assets and many investors lost their life savings. The Department of Trade and Industry, which was responsible for the regulation of the financial services industry,[422] was accused of having persistently disregarded evidence of serious malpractices and having known for several years that the UK firm was trading without the necessary licence, but only in late 1987 did they appoint statutory inspectors.[423] Calls for compensation from the government fell upon deaf ears.[424] But then the Parliamentary Commissioner, in response to a reference from Mr Alf Morris MP (the first of 159 MPs to refer cases to him), took up the case.

The Commissioner identified five areas in which there had been significant maladministration by the DTI.[425] First, the DTI had given erroneous advice to Barlow Clowes in 1975 that the firm did not need a DTI licence. Secondly, the DTI ought to have realised in 1984 that there was a separate Barlow Clowes partnership established in Jersey (which contradicted several of the representations made by the UK firm). This should have alerted the DTI that something untoward was happening. Thirdly, when alerted the DTI eventually decided to grant a retrospective licence in 1985; that decision had been taken 'maladministratively' in that too much regard was paid to the fact that such a licence would shield the DTI from criticism and too little to whether the grant of such a licence would be in the interests of the investors. Fourthly, the DTI, concerned that the capital of the fund was being eroded, had sought reassurances from accountants but these reassurances were too narrow to be satisfactory. Fifthly, there had been several months' delay in acting after warnings that all was not well from the Stock Exchange.

However, the important question was whether the maladministration identified had caused the losses to the investors. The Commissioner concluded that this was the case particularly in regard to the Jersey partnership. Had the significance of this been appreciated the Barlow Clowes operations would have been brought to a halt before most of the

---

[421] *The Barlow Clowes Affair* (as above). The affair is extensively discussed in [1991] PL 192, 408 (R. Gregory and G. Drewry).

[422] Gregory and Drewry (as above), 194–6, set out the regulatory framework and the criticisms of it.

[423] Under the Financial Services Act 1986, s. 106.

[424] The independent inquiry set up by the government (the Le Quesne Inquiry) restricted itself to the facts rather than fault and the government decided that it provided no grounds for concluding that compensation should be paid (HL Deb. 500, cols. 1255–69 (20 October 1988): Gregory and Drewry (as above), 196–200.

[425] *The Barlow Clowes Affair*, paras. 3.9, 4.89, 4.99, 4.108, 6.53, 8.1 and Gregory and Drewry (as above), 206–14.

losses were incurred. Hence he recommended that compensation should be paid. The response of the government to the report is discussed later.[426]

THE EQUITABLE LIFE AFFAIR

This high-profile affair may yet turn out to be an even greater triumph for the Ombudsman. It deserves to be sketched here.[427] The Equitable Life Assurance Society was founded in 1762 and is the 'oldest surviving mutual life assurance company in the world'. The difficulties into which the company fell arose from a judgment of the House of Lords declaring that the society's differential terminal bonus policy was unlawful.[428] As a result the society closed to new business in the 2000 and cuts were imposed upon with profits policy holders. Complaints were made to the Parliamentary Commissioner alleging maladministration in the regulation of the society either under the Insurance Companies Act 1982 (prudential regulation (i.e. ensuring the financial soundness of the society) and the Financial Services Act 1986 (conduct of business regulation (e.g. sales and marketing of insurance products)) and it was only in respect of the former that the Ombudsman had jurisdiction. The department responsible for prudential regulation was at various times the Treasury and the Department of Trade and Industry (or it predecessors) and for a time the Financial Services Authority (under contract from the Treasury). Fifteen lead complaints (out of 898 complaints referred by MPs) were investigated by the Ombudsman. The general complaint made was that 'the public bodies responsible for the prudential regulation of insurance companies failed for considerably longer than a decade properly to exercise their regulatory functions in respect of the Equitable Life Assurance Society and were therefore guilty of maladministration.'

After an extensive and far-reaching investigation the Ombudsman made some ten detailed findings of fact. They cannot all be dealt with here but a taste may be provided. The first finding of fact was that the regulators failed to act when the same person was appointed Society Approved Actuary and Chief Executive of the Society. The second finding of fact was that the Government Actuary, 'in providing advice to the prudential regulators, failed to satisfy themselves that the way in which the Society had determined its liabilities and had sought to demonstrate that it had sufficient assets to cover those liabilities accorded with the requirements of the applicable Regulations', with the result that regulators could not satisfy themselves as to the solvency of the society. The third finding of fact was that although the Government Actuary identified the terminal bonus policy while scrutinising the society's annual returns it 'failed to inform the prudential regulators, as [it] should have done, of that introduction or to raise the matter with the Society.'

---

[426] Below, p. 83.

[427] The Ombudsman report is *Equitable Life: A Decade of Regulatory Failure*, HC 815 (18 July 2008). It is in five parts and the fifth part consists in a guide to the main report and summary of findings and recommendations from which the quotations in the following paragraphs come. The full report exceeds 2,800 pages in length. The Ombudsman has since published a further report setting out further recommendations: 'Injustice Unremedied: The Government's Response to Equitable Life' (HC 435, 2009), available at <http://www.ombudsman.org.uk/__data/assets/pdf_file/0010/640/PHSO-0058-web-version.pdf>.

[428] *Equitable Life Assurance Society v. Hyman* [2002] 1 AC 408. This was the heart of the society's difficulty. It had entered into policies which provided guaranteed annuity rates on retirement of the policy holder (thus the size of the policy holder's pension would not depend upon the market annuity rate at their retirement). But when market rates fell below the guaranteed rate the cost to the society of fulfilling its obligations under these policies rose steeply. The society's response to introduce its differential terminal bonus policy under which policy holders who took their benefit as a guaranteed rate annuity were given a reduced rate of bonus. When this policy was shown to be unlawful the insolvency of the society became plain.

In the light of these three findings and the seven other findings not dealt with here (in which the Ombudsman found the regulators or the Government Actuary's conduct fell below that which would reasonably be expected of them) the Ombudsman assessed whether 'those acts or omissions were so unreasonable, or fell so far short of acceptable standards of good administration, as to constitute maladministration.' She in fact made ten determinations of maladministration—one against the DTI, four against the Government Actuary, and five against the FSA. Findings of injustice and causation readily followed (although the then government did not accept all the findings).[429]

There are more than one million Equitable Life policy holders who might make claims for compensation and the cost of providing that compensation will be about £4 billion.[430] Government policy changed after the 2010 General Election and the Equitable Life (Payments) Act 2010 was enacted. It authorises the Treasury to make payments to policy holders out of money provided by Parliament; a complex scheme to that end has been set up.[431] Disputes continue over the amount of compensation and eligibility. But after a delay of many years and a change of government the policy holders harmed by maladministration have received some compensation.

COMPLAINTS, INVESTIGATIONS, REPORTS

A complaint to the Commissioner may be made by any 'member of the public'[432]—an expression wide enough to include prisoners and immigrants, two classes who have both had success with various complaints.[433] Every complaint must be made through a member of the House of Commons, but the member need not be the complainant's own member, and a peer must likewise complain through an MP.

It has often been suggested that complainants should have direct access to the Commissioner, particularly since this is allowed in the case of the Health Service and Local Commissioners and in Scotland. The expectation that MPs would weed out ineligible complaints has not been fulfilled. Instead of rejecting every complaint made to him directly, however, the Commissioner now offers to forward suitable cases to the appropriate MP, so that the MP may then refer back to him. Opinion is now moving against the MP 'filter'; the Public Administration Select Committee,[434] the Commissioner[435] and the Law Commission[436] all favour a change.

The complainant may be an individual or a body corporate, provided it is not a local authority, public service body, nationalised industry, or a body which is appointed or financed by the government.[437] The complaint must be made by the person actually aggrieved, except that a suitable representative may make it after his death.[438] He need

[429] See the 2009 Report (above) paras. 14–22. The government's response (rejecting some recommendations) was declared unlawful in part because it lacked 'cogency': R (Equitable Members Action Group) v. HM Treasury [2009] EWHC 2495, para. 97. See above, p. 70 for the discussion of the 'cogent reasons' rule.

[430] Daily Telegraph, 18 July 2008.

[431] See <http://webarchive.nationalarchives.gov.uk/20130129110402/http://www.hm-treasury.gov.uk/d/equitable_life_payments_scheme_main_doc_160511.pdf>.

[432] Parliamentary Commissioner Act 1967, s. 5(1).

[433] See e.g. Annual Reports for 1979, HC 402, para. 35; for 1983, HC 322, para. 51; for 1984, paras. 33, 34; for 1986, HC 248, paras. 50, 51.   [434] Fourth Report, Session 2009–10 HC 107, paras. 2–6.

[435] <http://www.ombudsman.org.uk/__data/assets/pdf_file/0009/13599/16129-Direct-Access.pdf>.

[436] 'Public Service Ombudsmen' (Law Com. No. 329, 2011), paras. 3.89–3.103, available at <http://lawcommission.justice.gov.uk/docs/lc329_ombudsmen.pdf>, and favouring a 'dual track' with the individual choosing to proceed through his MP or direct to the Commissioner.   [437] s. 6(1).

[438] s. 6(2).

not be a British subject or a parliamentary elector, provided that he was resident in the United Kingdom or else present there when the impugned action was taken.[439] A British subject resident abroad may complain about consular matters, provided that he has the right of abode in the United Kingdom.[440]

The complaint must be made to the MP not later than twelve months from the day on which the person aggrieved first had notice of the matters alleged. But the Commissioner may dispense with this time limit if he considers it proper on account of special circumstances.[441]

The Commissioner has complete discretion in deciding whether to hold or pursue an investigation.[442] There is therefore no legal means of compelling him to act if he declines to do so.[443] It is also for him to determine whether a complaint is duly made.[444] But these powers do not allow him to extend his jurisdiction, e.g. by receiving complaints directly from members of the public, or by investigating authorities not permitted by the Act, or by acting on his own initiative.[445] Moreover, the Commissioner is subject to judicial review although the courts are reluctant to intervene given the subjective nature of his discretion.[446] But, in one case, the Commissioner's failure to consider 'a potentially decisive element' in deciding that there had been no maladministration meant that that decision had to be reconsidered.[447] That reconsidered decision was also quashed for the failure of the Commissioner to give adequate reasons for not finding maladministration.[448]

An investigation must be private, and the head of the department and any other official complained of must be given an opportunity to comment. In other respects the Commissioner may determine his own procedure.[449] He will normally examine both the department's files and the officials personally. He may make contact with the complainant directly, sometimes by sending one of his staff to interview him in his home. He may call for information and documents from anyone, including ministers and officials, save only where they relate to the Cabinet.[450] For obtaining evidence he has all the compulsory powers of the High Court, including the power to administer oaths, and he can call upon the High Court to deal with obstruction or contempt.[451] No minister can veto his investigations. No plea of secrecy or Crown privilege can be put in his way,[452] for he is himself subject to the Official Secrets Acts.[453] But he can be prevented from disclosing

[439] s. 6(4).

[440] Parliamentary Commissioner (Consular Complaints) Act 1981. And see 1967 Act, s. 6(2).

[441] s. 6(3).   [442] s. 5(5).

[443] Re Fletcher's Application [1970] 2 All ER 527 (leave to apply for mandamus refused).

[444] s. 5(5).

[445] He has regretted this last restriction, which does not apply elsewhere in the world: Annual Report for 1983, para. 8.

[446] R v. Parliamentary Commissioner for Administration ex p Dyer [1994] 1 WLR 621. And see R (M) v. Commissioner for Local Administration [2006] EWHC 2847 which confirms that the reluctance to review extends to the decision whether to investigate. See also R (Sharma) v. Parliamentary and Health Service Ombudsman [2011] EWHC 2609 at para. 9. Cf. the Parliamentary Commissioner for Standards, below, p. 538.

[447] R v. Parliamentary Commissioner for Administration ex p Balchin [1998] 1 PLR 1; principle applied in Argyll and Bute Council v. Scottish Public Services Ombudsman [2007] CSOH 168, 2008 SC 155 (Ombudman's decision quashed for error of law).

[448] R v. Parliamentary Commissioner for Administration ex p Balchin (No 2) (2000) 2 LGLR 87 (planning blight case; Commissioner failed to investigate the state of knowledge of officials at the time they did not draw county council's attention to alternative method of compensating owners).   [449] s. 7.

[450] s. 8(4). A certificate issued by The Secretary of State of the Cabinet with the approval of the Prime Minister is conclusive. Such a certificate was issued in the Court Line case: HC 498, 1974–5, para. 9.

[451] ss. 8, 9.   [452] s. 8(3).   [453] s. 11.

secret information in his reports, if a minister certifies that this would be contrary to the public interest; and this may be certified for any class of documents and information generally as well as in particular cases.[454] Information obtained in the Commissioner's investigations may not be disclosed except in his reports and certain legal and consultative proceedings.[455]

Reports on investigations must be made by the Commissioner both to the Member of Parliament through whom the complaint came and also to the head of the government department and any of his officials who were complained against.[456] The Commissioner must also make a general report annually, to be laid before each House of Parliament; and he may make other reports from time to time, and in particular special reports where there has been a failure to remedy injustice caused by maladministration.[457] His present practice is to make quarterly reports containing selected case histories, often in full detail but always without naming complainants or officials, and to make annual reports with general comments and statistics. He has made a number of independent reports on important cases.[458] His reports are in general no less detailed and elaborate than the judgments of courts of law, and in some cases more so.

REMEDIES AND EFFECTIVENESS

The Commissioner's reports show that he has been able to remedy a great many cases of injustice where, almost certainly, no remedy would otherwise have been obtained.[459] In general he has found that government departments are willing to pay compensation or otherwise make reasonable amends when he has exposed maladministration, though in some cases he has had to press hard for it. In 1972 the Select Committee observed with satisfaction that 'Government departments are very ready to accept the views of the Commissioner and to afford a remedy for injustice'.[460] A share of the credit is due to the Select Committee itself, which has kept up a steady pressure on the departments. Another influential factor is the department's knowledge that every case of maladministration will be reported to an MP. Even when the government does not accept the Commissioner's finding it sometimes pays compensation. In the Barlow Clowes case[461] the government did not accept the reasoning in the Commissioner's report, and published a lengthy document explaining why.[462] Nonetheless, 'in the exceptional circumstances of the case and out of respect for the office of Parliamentary Commissioner',[463] the government, while stressing that the case was not to be treated as a precedent, paid out £150m. Doubtless the political pressure from the many MPs with constituents who had lost money in the scandal fortified the government's respect for the Commissioner. These results seem to

---

[454] s. 11(3).

[455] s. 11(2) as amended by Act of 1987, s. 4, allowing disclosure to Health Service Commissioners and vice versa. [456] s. 10.

[457] s. 10(3). For the occasion of the first such special report see *Annual Report for 1978*, para. 56.

[458] War Pensions (HC 587, 1970–1); Television Licences (above, p. 76); Barlow Clowes (above, p. 79).

[459] The suggestion by the Select Committee ((Fourth Report, Session 2009–10, HC 107, para. 11) that the Ombudsman should be able to require Parliament to debate when the government is failing to remedy injustice found by the Ombudsman has been rejected. See: <http://www.publications.parliament.uk/pa/cm200910/cmselect/cmpubadm/471/471.pdf>. [460] HC 334 (1971–2), para. 33.

[461] HC 1989–90, No. 76, discussed above.

[462] *Observations of the Government on the Report of the Parliamentary Commissioner for Administration* (HC 1989–90, No. 99); for discussion see [1991] *PL* 408 (R. Gregory and G. Drewry).

[463] HC Deb. 164, cols. 201–11 (19 December 1989; statement by Mr Nicholas Ridley MP).

justify the verdict that the Commissioner 'has been remarkably effective'.[464] A notable improvement in administrative justice has been achieved.

In addition, a number of general reforms have resulted from the exposure of bad practices, as the Commissioner now reports annually.[465] As the result of a special report criticising the Department of Health and Social Security for not duly back-dating an officer's disability pension, some £12,000 was paid out in over forty other cases and over thirty were reviewed.[466] A class of war pensioners was compensated after investigation of an exceptionally bad case where the Commissioner found that disabled officers had been deliberately and deceitfully refused part of their entitlement.[467] After this the Civil Service Department undertook a wide review of practices which might infringe the rights of individuals.[468] The Commissioner has played a prominent part in drawing attention to the administrative standards of the Child Support Agency (CSA). A sorry catalogue of error, delay and incompetence has been revealed by his special reports on the topic,[469] and his Annual Report keeps track of whether promised improvements have been implemented.[470] CSA cases continue to generate a disproportionate amount of the Commissioner's work.[471] The shortcomings of the CSA range from simple delay in dealing with cases (often coupled with failure to reply to letters) to dangerous errors (informing a violent ex-spouse of wife's current address). In this intimate and personal area many errors can cause serious harm, e.g. an erroneous allegation that a partner is the parent of a child by someone else. As all the reports make plain, there remains ample scope for the CSA to improve, although it is now more ready to make amends.[472] Although the situation has improved, child support cases continue to generate a significant part of the Commissioner's workload.[473]

But the tax credits system whereby people previously in receipt of benefit from the Department of Social Security now receive credits through the tax system administered by HM Revenue and Customs has been dogged by many errors and now also generates a disproportionate amount of the Commissioner's case load. The Commissioner reported first in 2004 that the Child and Working Tax Credits system 'had been marred by significant technical problems which had led first to delays in payments, and then created other problems when the Revenue tried to remedy the situation'.[474] This was followed by a special report 'Tax Credits—Putting Things Right'.[475] Delay and overpayment are particularly pernicious forms of maladministration in this context. Many of those in receipt of tax credits have very limited means so the benefit is needed immediately and any overpayment is spent immediately, making recovery of overpayments difficult or impossible and often unjust. But the Commissioner reported in 2007 that tax credit cases were still a 'significant proportion' of the workload and that a further special report was planned.[476] Another

---

[464] Wheare, *Maladministration and its Remedies*, 125.

[465] A first list was given in his *Annual Report for 1972* (HC 72), para. 19.

[466] HC 587 (1970–1) (special report); HC 334 (1971–2), para. 28 (Select Committee). And see *Annual Reports for 1974*, HC 126, para. 20; *for 1975*, HC 141, para. 28; HC 454 (1974–5), para. 28 (Select Committee).

[467] HC 312 (1977–8).   [468] *Annual Report for 1979*, para. 14.

[469] HC 135 (1994–5), HC 20 (1995–6).

[470] See e.g. *Annual Report 1995*, HC 296 (1995–6), 3–4; *Annual Report 1996*, HC 386 (1996–7), 2; and *Annual Report 1997–98*, HC 845 (1997–8), ch. 3.   [471] *Annual Report 1997–98*, 19.

[472] Ibid., 23–5.

[473] The *Annual Report 2006–07* reveals that 174 child support cases were dealt with in the year and that claimants had a success rate of 78 per cent.   [474] *Annual Report 2003–04*.

[475] 2004–05, HC 124, discussed (including role of special reports) [2005] *PL* 740 (Kirkham).

[476] *Annual Report* for 2006–07, p. 22. A total of 174 such cases had been reported on during the year and claimants had had a 78 per cent success rate.

example was the Commissioner's report on the administrative failures of the UK Border Agency (UKBA).[477] In acknowledgement of the shortcomings revealed by the report, the Home Secretary dissolved the UKBA. The Agency was 're-centralised' to the Home Office, and significant investment in IT infrastructure was announced.[478]

The Commissioner has not always had success, and from time to time he has reported that a department has refused to make amends.[479] Most of the cases concern the Inland Revenue and Customs and Excise, since in the sphere of taxation the administrative mind is particularly stubborn.

Difficulty has also been experienced in securing redress for the injustice caused by the widespread 'blight' that affected many properties in Kent through the uncertainty extending over many years of the route of the Channel Tunnel Rail Link. The existing compensation schemes did not apply to many affected and the Commissioner[480] (and the Select Committee)[481] concluded that the Department of Transport had been guilty of maladministration in failing to consider the effect of their policy (which had generated the uncertainty); the DOT had a responsibility to consider whether some redress should be made available to those severely affected. The government's initial response was that there could be no compensation for 'generalised blight', but a compensation scheme was announced in 1996 which was implemented by the incoming government in 1997.[482] Once more the Commissioner and the Select Committee have seen their recommendations substantially implemented.

Although the head of the Inland Revenue testified that the Commissioner's investigations were 'gradually sapping morale and having a very bad effect indeed', the Select Committee found that they were not causing as much dislocation as had been feared.[483] In the long run the Commissioner should prove to be an ally of the civil service, since so many of his reports justify the department rather than the complainant. But even where they do not, the reports generally lead to improvements. Moreover, on the recommendation of the Select Committee a booklet *The Ombudsman in Your Files* has been prepared by the Cabinet Office and circulated through the civil service. It contains much useful advice which will ensure less maladministration and fewer complaints to the Commissioner.

THE HEALTH SERVICE COMMISSIONERS

When the National Health Service was brought wholly under the central government by the National Health Service Reorganisation Act 1973, there was no longer any reason for excluding it from the system for investigating complaints. But separate provision was made in that Act which, while generally on the model of the Parliamentary Commissioner Act 1967, contained some important differences. The legislation was consolidated in the Health Service Commissioners Act 1993.[484]

---

[477] (2010 HC 329); see <http://www.ombudsman.org.uk/__data/assets/pdf_file/0016/673/UKBA-2010-02-09.pdf>.

[478] See Hansard, HC Deb., 26 March 2013, col. 1500, available at <http://www.theyworkforyou.com/debates/?id=2013-03-26b.1500.0>.

[479] See e.g. *Annual Reports for 1974*, HC 126, paras. 25, 35; *for 1978*, HC 205, para. 56. And see the Commissioner's disappointment at Parliament's response to the Equitable Life affair ('Injustice Unremedied: The Government's Response on Equitable Life' (HC 435, 2009) at <http://www.ombudsman.org.uk/__data/assets/pdf_file/0010/640/PHSO-0058-web-version.pdf>.

[480] HC 193 (1994–5); [1996] *PL* 31 (R. James and D. Longley).   [481] HC 270 (1994–5).

[482] HC 819 (1994–5).   [483] HC 334 (1971–2), para. 13 (the quotation is from p. 37).

[484] As amended by the Health Service Commissioners (Amendment) Acts 1996 and 2000 (allowing investigation of GPs since retired). For discussion see [1999] *PL* 200 (P. Giddings).

The Act of 1973 constituted the new and separate offices of Health Service Commissioner for England and Health Service Commissioner for Wales. For Scotland there was separate but similar legislation.[485] In fact the practice was to appoint the Parliamentary Commissioner for Administration to all three of the new health service offices (for England, Wales and Scotland), so that there was a single administration for health service complaints along with others. In law, however, his functions were distinct, and he made separate reports on health service complaints in his capacity as Health Service Commissioner for all three countries.[486] In Scotland, however, these functions now belong to the Scottish Public Services Ombudsman under legislation of the Scottish Parliament.[487]

The powers of holding investigations and making reports conferred upon the Health Service Commissioner are in general the same as those of the Parliamentary Commissioner. His reports on investigations must be sent to the complainant, any MP who assisted in making the complaint, the person complained of and the health service bodies involved.[488] His annual and special reports are made to Parliament.[489] The same Select Committee of the House of Commons examines the work of the Commissioner in all his various capacities. However, the complainant has direct access to the Commissioner and need not make his complaint through an MP.[490] Furthermore, a relative or other suitable person may complain on behalf of a person who has died or is unable to act for himself,[491] and a health service authority may itself refer to the Commissioner a complaint made to it about some matter within its own responsibility, so as to obtain an independent investigation.[492]

A number of matters are excluded from the Commissioner's powers of investigation.[493] These are the following:

Employment, pay, discipline or other personnel matters.

Contractual or commercial transactions, except when made for providing services for patients.

Matters subject to inquiry under the Act.[494]

There is also a saving clause to exclude cases where there is a legal remedy, subject to the same power to make exceptions as under the Parliamentary Commissioner Act 1967.[495] Subject to these limitations, the Commissioner may investigate any failure in the services provided by the various health service authorities listed in the Act, or any other action taken by them or on their behalf.[496] The complaint must allege 'injustice or hardship in

---

[485] National Health Service (Scotland) Act 1972.

[486] But for Wales he has now been placed on a separate statutory basis (with reporting responsibilities to the Welsh Assembly) (Government of Wales Act 1998, s. 112, 10th Sched.). See below, p. 110.

[487] Scottish Public Services Ombudsman Act 2002, s. 11.   [488] s. 14(1).

[489] s. 10(4) of the Act of 1996. Prior to this amendment these reports went to the Secretary of State who laid them before both Houses of Parliament.   [490] s. 9.

[491] s. 9(3).   [492] s. 10.

[493] s. 7. Previously, questions of 'clinical judgment' and actions taken by doctors, dentists and others which were the responsibility of family health service authorities were excluded. The Act of 1996, ss. 1, 2 and 6, removed these restrictions.   [494] i.e. where an inquiry is held under s. 84 of the Act of 1977.

[495] The Health Service Commissioners Act 1993, s. 4 provides that the Commissioner 'shall not conduct an investigation' where the person aggrieved has or had a legal remedy 'unless the Commissioner is satisfied that in the particular circumstances it is not reasonable to expect that person to resort or have resorted to it'. See R (Mencap) v. The Parliamentary and Health Service Ombudsman [2011] EWHC 3351 para. 30: 'Particular circumstances need not be unique to an individual or family.... [They] include the unwillingness of individuals to litigate, their inability to do so, their wish to have their complaint determined in all its aspects, and not having monetary compensation at the forefront of their mind.'

[496] ss. 2, 3(1)(b).

consequence of a failure in a service provided by a health service body...or in consequence of maladministration connected with any other action taken by...such a body'.[497]

The Health Service Commissioner's reports follow much the same pattern as the Parliamentary Commissioner's. Generally speaking the results are similar. In the year 1997–8 he received 2,660 complaints of which 1,990 were rejected directly[498] and a further 348 cases were rejected with advice to the relevant NHS body or agreement by it to take remedial action. Only 4 per cent of complaints were fully investigated and over 90 per cent of these were upheld in whole or in part.[499] The largest groups of complaints concerned nurses, medical staff and the handling of complaints by health authorities. In many such cases the complaint is of inconsiderate or rude behaviour, and an adequate remedy is an apology. The health service appears to generate a large volume of complaints about matters which are difficult to remedy, such as long waiting lists, postponement of operations, and inadequate nursing care.

Every health authority is required to ensure that all its hospitals have a regular complaints procedure in accordance with directions given by the Secretary of State, but no right of appeal or review conferred by that procedure can prevent an investigation by the Health Service Commissioner.[500]

SPREAD OF THE OMBUDSMAN PRINCIPLE

One of the many proofs of the success of the ombudsman principle is its continual extension into new areas.[501] Having been instituted in Britain for the central government, it has now been extended to the national health service and local government. Every year there are new extensions of the principle in other countries. Few indeed are the constitutional innovations for which such widespread success can be claimed.

The principle has spread outside the sphere of government into that of business and finance. Voluntary ombudsman systems have been established successfully in the insurance and banking industries. There is a Financial Services Ombudsman with a wide jurisdiction over persons 'authorised' to provide regulated financial services.[502] A Legal Services Ombudsman ensures that the professional bodies that exercise disciplinary functions over the various forms of legal professional (including licensed conveyancers) deal with complaints about misconduct properly.[503] Prisoners have recourse to a non-statutory Independent Complaints Adjudicator.[504] There is an independent Housing

---

[497] s. 3(i).

[498] Mostly because the internal complaints procedure was not exhausted or insufficient evidence of maladministration was provided.

[499] *Annual Report 1997–98*, HC 811 (1997–8). Separate statistics for parliamentary and health service investigations are no longer collected.　　　　　　　　　　　[500] Hospital Complaints Procedure Act 1985.

[501] There is a list of the ombudsmen in the United Kingdom at <http://www.ombudsmanassociation.org/association-members-by-country.php?area=1>.

[502] Financial Services and Markets Act 2000, Pt XVI and 17th Sched. Section 228(2) provides that 'A complaint is to be determined by reference to what is, in the opinion of the ombudsman, fair and reasonable in all the circumstances of the case.' There is both a compulsory and a voluntary jurisdiction; and the Ombudsman has power to make enforceable awards in the former case (subject to a limit of £100,000). See [2001] *PL* 308 (R. Nobles); [2002] *PL* 640 (R. James and P. Morris). See *R (IFG)* v. *Financial Ombudsman Service and Jenkins* [2005] EWHC 1153.

[503] Legal Services Act 2007, Pt 6 and 2nd Sched.

[504] See [1993] *PL* 314, 323–6 (R. Morgan). He is often referred to as the 'Prisons Ombudsman' but the Select Committee considers this title 'most inappropriate' since he is not wholly independent and a dissatisfied complainant has further recourse to the Parliamentary Ombudsman (HC 380 (1995–6), para. 61). But the government has declined to change the name (HC 367 (1996–7)).

Ombudsman.[505] The so-called Pensions Ombudsman, who has power to determine as well as to investigate complaints of maladministration in occupational or personal pension schemes, is in reality a statutory tribunal. His awards are legally enforceable and are subject to a right of appeal to the High Court on a point of law.[506]

As this last example makes plain several of these more recently created 'ombudsmen' are strictly speaking not ombudsmen in the sense generally used in this chapter. They often have the power to give directions rather than simply make recommendations; and they are often concerned with the resolution of private disputes (with judicial review being used as an appeal against an ombudsman's award) rather than with holding government to account for maladministration. They might more properly be termed adjudicators or tribunals. But a cavil over a name should not divert attention from their success and usefulness.

---

[505] Housing Act 1996, s. 51 and 2nd Sched.   [506] Pension Schemes Act 1993, Pt 10.

4

LOCAL AND DEVOLVED
GOVERNMENT

LOCAL ADMINISTRATION

Local authorities are organised in a hierarchy of geographical units by counties, districts and parishes, with special arrangements for London.[1] Nearly all local authorities are directly elected by the inhabitants of their areas, but there are also certain bodies such as joint fire service authorities which cut across county and district boundaries and have constitutions of their own. All local authorities work in more or less close conjunction with the central government, and they generally enjoy less autonomy than the bare legal framework would suggest. The social services and controls which in the aggregate make up the welfare state are administered partly centrally and partly locally. National insurance, income support, and the national health service are the province of the central government, whereas housing, public health and sanitation, welfare services for the handicapped, provision of accommodation for those in need, and the care of children are entrusted to local authorities. The provision of schools is another local responsibility, though subject to detailed central control. An efficient working partnership between central and local governments is therefore essential. In law, however, local authorities have their own independent existence and their own legal duties and liabilities. They are not part of the services of the Crown and they have no special privileges or immunities at common law.

HISTORICAL BACKGROUND

From the late fifteenth century onwards local government was in the hands of the justices of the peace, who replaced the obsolete medieval system of county and hundred courts supervised by the sheriff.[2] There were also commissioners created by statute for special purposes, such as the commissioners of sewers, empowered to make land drainage schemes, build sea-walls and levy rates, and there were the commissioners of customs created by the royal prerogative.

---

[1] The primary sources for local government law in England and Wales are the Local Government Acts 1972 and 1974 and the Local Government Finance Act 1988; but there are many other less important statutes; the Localism Act 2011 may be mentioned specifically. The government's current policy is set out in a White Paper ('Open Public Services', Cm. 8145 (2011)). General works are Cross and Bailey, *Local Government Law*, 9th edn (1996); *Cross on Principles of Local Government Law*, 3rd edn (2004) by Bailey; Loughlin, *Local Government in the Modern State* (1986); and Elias and Goudie (eds.), *Local Government Law* (1998). For history see Holdsworth, *History of English Law*, x. 126; xiv. 204; Redlich and Hirst, *Local Government in England*.

[2] Holdsworth, *History of English Law*, iv. 134.

In the Tudor period the justices were given many new statutory powers which they exercised in their quarter sessions along with their judicial powers. They controlled the upkeep of roads and bridges, the licensing of alehouses, the poor law, the building of gaols, the levying of rates and so many other matters that they were in effect general purpose local authorities. Originally they were under the control of the Crown through the Council and the Star Chamber, but after the Revolution of 1688 they were free from political control. Then began the golden age of the justices, 'the uncrowned kings of every county', who could be called to account only by cumbersome legal process through the Court of King's Bench and the writs of certiorari, prohibition and mandamus. They governed 'in a spirit of autocratic dilettantism'[3] under a 'rule of law' of almost theoretical perfection (but without democracy).

The reign of the county justices did not really close until the Local Government Act 1888. But long before that there had been a proliferation of statutory authorities such as the Poor Law Commissioners (1834), highway boards, boards of health, burial boards and so forth, creating a dense governmental jungle.

In addition there were the boroughs. Boroughs were corporations created by royal charter obtained (and commonly purchased) from the Crown. For a sufficient sum they could obtain grants of commercial and jurisdictional privileges, and representation in Parliament; and having corporate personality they could accumulate and administer their own property. A privilege which they often obtained was the power to elect their own magistrates, thus escaping from the rule of the county justices. Reform finally arrived with the Municipal Corporations Act 1835 and was completed by the Municipal Corporations Acts 1882 and 1883 and by the Local Government Act 1888.

Before this last Act there was only one municipal corporation in London: the ancient City, a corporation by prescription, confined within its own small enclave and with its medieval guild-based constitution untouched by the reforming statutes. The chief executive body, the Court of Common Council, acquired in 1888 the functions of a London borough council. The remainder of London, a vastly greater area, was administered by a medley of authorities, ultimately replaced by the London County Council and the London Borough Councils under the Local Government Act 1886 and the London Government Act 1899 respectively.

THE GENESIS OF THE MODERN SYSTEM

The watershed between the old and the new systems of local government may be said to be the two Local Government Acts of 1888 and 1894. These Acts carried forward the policy of entrusting administrative functions to elected 'general purpose' authorities; and they established the 'two-tier' system which is still the basis of much local government organisation today. The Act of 1888 established an elected county council for each county and transferred to it the administrative powers of the justices in quarter sessions. But the large cities[4] were made separate county boroughs. The Act of 1894 divided the counties, but not the county boroughs, into urban and rural districts and for each it established an elected urban or rural district council. A greatly simplified structure of authorities thus emerged, keeping pace also with the extension of democracy. The law was consolidated

---

[3] Redlich and Hirst, *History of Local Government*, i. 102.

[4] 'City' has no legal meaning distinct from 'borough'. Some boroughs traditionally claim the title of city and others have obtained it by royal letters patent. It has no significance except as a title of honour, like 'lord mayor'. See Local Government Act 1972, s. 245(10).

and codified in a massive statute, the Local Government Act 1933, which stood as the basic enactment until the Local Government Act 1972.

THE LOCAL GOVERNMENT ACT 1972

The new regime of local authorities was established by the Local Government Act 1972. This Act not only provided for the new system of areas and authorities: it replaced the massive Act of 1933 which contained the general law regulating local authorities' elections, proceedings, powers, functions, and finance. It is an equally massive Act, with thirty schedules. It is further supplemented by the Local Government Act 1974, dealing mainly with finance, rating, and the new machinery for complaints against local authorities.[5] Financial matters are dealt with in the Local Government Finance Act 1988.

Boroughs were abolished by the Act of 1972,[6] but the Act also contained a detailed plan for preserving borough titles, ceremonials, privileges and property, together with the rights of freemen of boroughs, since these were often a stimulus to local spirit. A new district council might petition the Crown for a charter conferring 'the status of a borough', entitling it to appoint 'officers of dignity' and preserving other privileges.[7] Scotland does not come within the Act of 1972.[8]

In England the Act established six metropolitan counties, divided into thirty-six metropolitan districts, and thirty-nine non-metropolitan counties divided into 296 districts.[9] In Wales it established eight counties (non-metropolitan) divided into thirty-seven districts. The metropolitan counties, however, were abolished in 1986. The districts within them are defined by the Act of 1972. The non-metropolitan counties are fewer and larger than the old counties. The districts within the English counties are defined only by order.[10] Those in the Welsh counties are defined in the Act.[11]

The former English rural parishes continue to exist as parishes.[12] Wales has a new system of 'communities' covering the whole country.[13]

EXTENSION OF UNITARY AUTHORITIES

Since 1992 further reform has taken place as policy shifted away from two-tier government in the non-metropolitan counties and towards powerful unitary authorities combining the functions of district and county councils. Thus some of the unpopular counties (Avon, Humberside and Cleveland) created by the 1972 reorganisation have been abolished and their constituent parts have become unitary authorities. Many large urban areas (such as Peterborough, York and Milton Keynes) have been carved out of the counties of which they used to form part and established as unitary authorities. In 2009 unitary authorities were established in Cornwall, Durham, Northumberland, Cheshire West, Chester and Cheshire East.

---

[5] See below, p. 100 for an account of this machinery (the Local Government Commissioners for Administration).   [6] s. 1(9)–(11).

[7] ss. 245, 246. Special arrangements were made for appointing 'officers of dignity' where the former borough became a mere parish (s. 246(3)).

[8] Scotland is divided into 32 single-tier authorities: Local Government (Scotland) Act 1994.

[9] 1st Sched.   [10] SI 1972 No. 2039.   [11] Act of 1972, 4th Sched., Pt II.

[12] Act of 1972, s. 1(6).

[13] Act of 1972, s. 20(4). See now the Local Government (Wales) Act 1994 (there are now 22 unitary authorities).

Part 1 of the Local Government and Public Involvement in Health Act 2007 provides the mechanism whereby two-tier government may be reorganised into single-tier government and also so that the boundaries between authorities may be altered. The Secretary of State was empowered to direct authorities to make proposals for the establishment of single tier but the direction can only be made prior to the 25 January 2008,[14] thereafter he may only invite proposals.[15] But in a change of policy—adopted in order to save reorganisation costs—the creation of unitary authorities was brought to an end by the Local Government Act 2010 which provided in section 1 'no further relevant order may be made under…[the relevant section] of the 2007 Act'.

LONDON GOVERNMENT

The overhaul of local government in London took place under the London Government Act 1963. The Act replaced the London County Council, created in 1888,[16] and the metropolitan borough councils, created in 1899,[17] by the Greater London Council and thirty-two London borough councils,[18] taking in a much larger area. The City of London, with its ancient constitution intact, forms in effect an additional London borough. London therefore continued under a two-tier system, the London boroughs corresponding generally to the metropolitan districts elsewhere, until the abolition of the Greater London Council in 1986.

Two-tier government, however, was re-established in London in 1999. The people of London approved in a referendum[19] the new government's plans for a Greater London Authority consisting of a directly elected mayor and a separately elected London Assembly. There are twenty-five members of the assembly. Fourteen are elected from 'assembly constituencies' and eleven from London as a whole.[20] The mayor and assembly are elected on the same day every fourth year.[21]

The Authority's purpose is to promote economic and social development and to improve the environment in London; it has power 'to do anything which the Mayor considers will further [this] purpose'.[22] But the Authority may not incur expenditure in regard to education, social services or health services where the London borough councils or other public bodies are competent to act.[23] The major areas in which the Authority may act include transport strategy, development, municipal waste, air quality, ambient noise and culture.[24] In these areas the mayor, after consultation, will develop and implement strategies.[25] The Assembly reviews the mayor's exercise of his powers,[26] and the authority raises money by issuing a precept.[27]

---

[14] Act of 2007, ss. 2 and 3.

[15] When the Secretary of State made his decision on whether Exeter and Norwich should be unitary authorities on a different basis from that on which he had consulted, his decision was found to be unlawful (*Devon County Council* v. *Secretary of State for Communities and Local Government* [2010] EWHC 1456).

[16] Local Government Act 1888.   [17] London Government Act 1899.

[18] The GLC was incorporated but the London borough councils are not: the corporation was the whole body of burgesses, i.e. electors: London Government Act 1963, s. 1(2), (3).

[19] Held in terms of the Greater London (Referendum) Act 1998.

[20] Greater London Authority Act 1999, s. 2.   [21] s. 3(2).

[22] s. 30. And see the enhancement of powers in regard to housing and regeneration in the Localism Act 2011, s. 187.   [23] s. 31(1). And money may not be raised as incidental to the authority's functions.

[24] The Greater London Authority Act 2007 added new competences including: health equality (see s. 30(5)(aa) of the 1999 Act (as amended)) and mitigation of climate change (s. 30(5)(c) of the 1999 Act).

[25] ss. 41 and 42. But generally the mayor can only exercise a function jointly with the assembly (s. 35).

[26] s. 59(1).   [27] s. 82 and Pt III, generally.

ALLOCATION OF FUNCTIONS

The principal functions of local government are parcelled out among the main authorities by a long series of provisions of the Act of 1972, which were necessary to adapt the empowering enactments to the new hierarchy of authorities.[28] Only in the case of the former rural parishes was no reallocation required; their functions are inherited directly by the successor parishes in England and by the communities in Wales.[29]

Subject to a certain amount of overlap, and subject also to special arrangements flowing from the extensive powers of cooperation and delegation given by the Act, the allocation of the most important functions in non-metropolitan areas is as shown in Table 4.1. Licensing powers are numerous and miscellaneous.[30] Among many other matters district councils license theatres, cinemas, pawnbrokers, moneylenders, riding establishments, dogs, and dealers in game as well as public houses.

OPERATIONS AND PROCEEDINGS

Despite its power to make byelaws, mentioned later, a council is an executive rather than a legislative body. It exercises its powers directly in its own name, taking decisions by majority vote of those present at a meeting of the council.[31] But among these powers is a very extensive power of delegation, so that the council need not decide everything itself. Under the Act of 1972 a local authority may 'arrange for the discharge of any of

Table 4.1 Allocation of functions in non-metropolitan areas

County council	District council	Parish or community council or meeting
Education	Housing	Footpaths
Town and country planning and development (S)	Town and country planning and development (S)	Allotments
Social services (S)	Public health and sanitary services	Bus shelters
Food and drugs (S)		Recreation grounds
Roads (mostly)	Food and drugs (S)	Village greens
Refuse disposal	Minor urban roads	Burial grounds
Libraries	Refuse collection	Parking places for motor cycles and bicycles
Highways	Entertainments	Car-sharing schemes
Traffic	Recreation (S)	Grants for bus services
Public transport	Coast protection	Taxi fare concessions
Recreation (S)	Local licensing	Traffic calming
Fire service		Crime prevention

S = shared or divided service.

[28] Pt IX.   [29] See s. 179(4).

[30] On licensing see Hart, *Local Government*, 9th edn, ch. 28; Street, *Justice in the Welfare State*, ch. 4. The Local Government (Miscellaneous Provisions) Act 1982 gave new powers over public entertainments, sex establishments, street trading, take-away food shops, acupuncture, tattooing and other things and the Public Entertainments Licences (Drug Misuse) Act 1997 gave power to revoke or refuse to renew entertainment licences after receiving a report from the chief constable regarding the supply or use of controlled drugs at or near the premises. The Licensing Act 2003 removed the ancient power of Justices of the Peace to license the sale of alcohol and vests that power—along with the licensing of certain entertainments—in the relevant local authorities as 'licensing authorities'.   [31] Act of 1972, 12th Sched., para. 39.

their functions' by a committee, a sub-committee or an officer of the authority, or by any other local authority.[32] The policy of the Act of 1972 is to give councils greater freedom to organise their business in the most efficient way,[33] though naturally committees[34] are still used a great deal.

The public, including the press, have a right to attend meetings of local authorities and also meetings of their committees and sub-committees. In addition they are entitled to inspect agenda, minutes, reports, background papers and other documents.[35] These rights are restricted where the business involves confidential information of certain kinds, such as information made confidential by government departments or by law, and personal information about employees, tenants, and children in care; negotiations about contracts, labour relations, and legal proceedings are also protected, among other matters.[36] The authorities concerned include police and fire authorities and various other joint boards and committees.

There are criminal penalties for members of local authorities who take part in business in which they have a pecuniary interest which they fail to disclose.[37] But the Secretary of State has a dispensing power where the number of members disqualified is inconveniently large or dispensation is in the interests of the inhabitants.[38] The effect of interest or bias on the validity of an authority's decision is explained in Chapter 13.

CABINETS AND DIRECTLY ELECTED MAYORS

The Local Government Act 2000, Part 1A[39] reorganised the structure of the executive within local authorities in England. Under this scheme a local authority must operate (a) 'executive arrangements' or (b) 'committee system' or (c) any other arrangements prescribed by the Secretary of State.[40] An 'executive arrangement' involves the executive of the local authority being structured as a directly elected mayor and two or more councillors appointed by the mayor (known as 'a mayor and cabinet executive') or a councillor elected as leader by the authority and two or more councilors appointed by the leader (known in each case as 'a leader and cabinet executive').[41] In each case, the authority must establish one or more 'overview and scrutiny committees' (consisting of councillors not on the executive).[42] There is a presumption that, subject to contrary regulations made by the Secretary of State, the executive may discharge all the functions of the local authority.[43] A 'committee system' means the well-known traditional system in which decisions are taken either by the council itself or by committees of the council.[44] The local authority must hold a referendum if it proposes to change from one governance structure to another.[45]

---

[32] s. 101. These powers have now been somewhat restricted by the Localism Act 2011, discussed below at pp. 86, 96.

[33] As recommended by the Committee on the Management of Local Government, 1967, HMSO (chairman, Sir John Maud), and in The New Local Authorities: Management and Structure, 1972, HMSO (chairman, M. A. Bains).

[34] 'Committee' in this context means a body of more than one person: R v. Secretary of State for the Environment ex p Hillingdon LBC [1986] 1 WLR 192, affirmed [1986] 1 WLR 807.

[35] Public Bodies (Admission to Meetings) Act 1960, as extended by Local Government Act 1972, s. 100 and Local Government (Access to Information) Act 1985.

[36] See the Local Authorities (Executive Arrangements) (Meetings and Access to Information) Regulations 2012 (SI 2012/2089).   [37] Localism Act 2011, ss. 31 and 34.

[38] Localism Act 2011, s. 33.

[39] Inserted by the Localism Act 2011, s. 21 and Sched. 2.   [40] Act of 2000, s. 9B.

[41] Act of 2000, s. 9C.   [42] Act of 2000, s. 9F.   [43] Act of 2000, s. 9DA.

[44] This system is set out in Pt VI of the Local government Act 1972; see also the Act of 2000, s. 9D.

[45] Act of 2000, s. 9M.

There are currently (as at July 2013) fifteen directly elected mayors in England, apart from the mayor of London established under different legislation.[46]

This reform shifted decision-making away from the multifarious committees which had grown up through the years. The whole council naturally retains its original function of approving the budget. These reforms were intended both to clarify and strengthen decision-making as well as to strengthen the scrutiny of decisions.

FINANCE: REVENUE

The problems of the finance of local government are intensely political as well as economic.[47] The political problems are centred round the fact that the revenue which local authorities can provide for themselves is quite unequal to their vastly extended functions. Consequently they depend upon central government grants, and inevitably the grants are subject to conditions. Local independence is therefore undermined by central control, to the point where some local authority services might rather be regarded as agency services for the central government, and confusion arises over where responsibility and initiative really reside. Political tension is all the greater when the central government and local authorities are controlled by opposed political parties.

The revenue which local authorities raise for themselves consists partly of miscellaneous receipts such as rents, fees and charges for services. But, in addition, local authorities have long had limited powers of taxation. Those powers, however, were in a state of flux and the subject of acute political controversy[48] for many years prior to 1992. The ancient, and much criticised, rates,[49] levied on the assessed annual value of the occupation of land and buildings, were replaced in 1988 by the community charge,[50] a 'poll tax' on individuals and not based on property. This proved to be even more unpopular and was in its turn replaced in 1992 by the council tax, levied on dwellings according to their value.[51] Rates continue to be levied on non-domestic landed property under a uniform national system controlled by the Secretary of State. Today the non-domestic rate and the council tax are the primary sources of locally raised tax revenue for local authorities.[52] In addition local authorities are in receipt of large subsidies from the central government by way of revenue support grant as explained later.

The collection of the council tax is in the hands of the district councils (or in London the borough councils) which are known as 'billing authorities'. An appeal lies to the local valuation tribunal against the decision of the billing authority that a particular dwelling is chargeable, or that the person aggrieved is the person liable or that the calculation of the amount due is erroneous.[53] The Secretary of State may, however, restrict the grounds of appeal.[54]

[46] See <http://www.parliament.uk/briefing-papers/SN05000>. As the relatively small number of mayors indicates, this proposal has not proved as popular as the government intended.

[47] For detailed discussion of local government finance see the Lyons Report (London 2007) especially Pt III, available at <http://www.webarchive.org.uk/wayback/archive/20070329120000/http://www.lyonsinquiry.org.uk/index8a20.html>.   [48] That frequently spilt over into the courts; see below, p. 99.

[49] Rates date from the Poor Relief Act 1601. They were considered by many to bear unfairly upon single occupiers of large properties.

[50] Imposed by Local Government Finance Act 1988. Although the community charge was subject to various exemptions and rebates, it was unpopular because it was not progressive—a dustman paid as much as a duke. It was also very difficult to collect.   [51] By the Local Government Finance Act 1992.

[52] But the Local Government Finance Act 1988, Sched. 7B (inserted by the Local Government Finance Act 2012) requires that billing authorities pay a specified portion of non-domestic receipts into a central fund.   [53] Act of 1992, s. 16.

[54] s. 16(3).

The billing authorities collect the tax not only on their own behalf but also on behalf of various precepting authorities, primarily the county and parish councils, but including bodies which cover several local authority areas (such as the London Fire and Civil Defence Authority or police authorities).[55] Neither the precepting authorities nor the billing authorities have an unfettered discretion to set either precept or council tax; complicated calculations which may be judicially reviewed[56] are set out in the statute and have to be completed by both authorities.[57]

The central government has long had a power to limit,[58] or 'cap', the level of the council tax imposed by the billing authorities or the precept issued by precepting authorities.[59] In England the current arrangement—following the Localism Act 2011—is that billing authorities are required to hold a referendum if the authority calculates that a proposed increase in council tax rates is 'excessive'. The calculation will be carried out against criteria prescribed by the Secretary of State.[60]

Since 1929 there has been a system of 'block grants' from central funds in aid of expenditure generally. The amount of grant was adjusted by various systems of weighting according to the population and resources of each area. The current system for determining the 'revenue support grant' is to be found in the Local Government Finance Act 1988.[61] The Act grants power to the Secretary of State, after consulting various authorities, to lay a revenue support grant report before the House of Commons. After approval by the House of Commons, the Secretary of State pays the amount approved to each authority.

Most of the capital expenditure of local authorities is financed by borrowing, often by issuing loan stock or by borrowing from the Public Works Loan Board.[62]

FINANCE: EXPENDITURE

Local councils are now statutory authorities, with the sole exception of the City of London, and they therefore have power to spend money only for such purposes as are authorised by Parliament.[63] But these purposes include what is reasonably incidental,[64] and the Act of 1972 expresses this principle in apparently generous terms: it covers anything 'which is calculated to facilitate, or is conducive or incidental to, the discharge of any of their functions'.[65] But a power is not incidental simply because it is convenient, desirable or profitable. Thus speculative interest rate swap transactions which were beyond the local authorities' ordinary

---

[55] s. 39.

[56] They may not be challenged in collateral proceedings but only by way of judicial review (s. 66(1)(c)).

[57] ss. 31A–37 (billing authorities), ss. 42A–51 (precepting authorities).

[58] The central government also had power to 'cap' the rates and the community charge. High-spending local authorities challenged the exercise of these powers in judicial review proceedings. These are discussed below, pp. 340–1.

[59] The previous provisions are in the Local Government Finance Act 1992, Ch. IVA (ss. 52A–Z, inserted by the Local Government Act 1999, s. 23(1) and 1st Sched. These provisions still apply in Wales. Parish and community councils are not liable to be limited (ss. 39, 52A).

[60] See the 1992 Act, Pt IVZA, s. 52ZB, inserted by the Localism Act 2011.

[61] Act of 1988, ss. 76–88.

[62] Local Government Act 2003, s. 1 now vouchsafes local government borrowing powers.

[63] Formerly boroughs founded by charter could claim the wider powers of chartered bodies: see below, p. 181. Under the Act of 1972 all local authorities are statutory (ss. 1(10), 20(6)) and have no powers other than those conferred by statute: *Hazell* v. *Hammersmith and Fulham LBC* [1992] 2 AC 1. But the Localism Act 2011, s. 1 confers the power 'to do anything which individuals may generally do'. This power is subject to limitations (s. 2(2) and (3), s. 4(1)).

[64] Below, p. 177.   [65] s. 111.

borrowing powers were not saved.[66] And a council could not guarantee the borrowings of a company set up by the council to construct a leisure pool when the council lacked the power to borrow itself for that purpose.[67]

Local authorities are partly freed from the ultra vires doctrine by the Local Government Act 2000, section 2 which grants them power 'to do anything' (including incurring expenditure) which the council considers likely to promote the economic, social or environmental well being of its area or its residents.[68] While this measure does not oblige the authority to do anything it does mean that the authority has the power to fulfil expectations that would otherwise be unprotected.[69]

Uncertainty over whether private finance schemes[70] were within the powers of local authorities led to the Local Government (Contracts) Act 1997. This provides that every local authority has a general power to contract with a provider of assets or services[71] 'for the purposes of, or in connection with, the discharge of [any statutory] function by the local authority'.[72]

The principles which require local authorities, like other public bodies, to spend money reasonably and with due regard to the interests of their council tax payers are explained later.[73] Many examples of the restraints imposed upon them by administrative law will be found throughout this book. The courts have invalidated excessive wages,[74] excessive rent subsidies[75] and free travel schemes.[76] But some of the decisions were given when the authorities' statutory powers were narrower than they are now.

THE AUDIT SYSTEM

Audit of local authority accounts has a special importance in administrative law, since it is one of the mechanisms of judicial review.[77] It is also of special interest since it has occasionally shown how a recalcitrant local authority may be able to defy the central government with impunity. The law has, however, been radically altered by the Local Government Act 2000, which has greatly relaxed the previous regime. Before that Act the audit system was the means whereby improper expenditure could not only be brought to light but also charged personally to the councillors or others responsible. The certainty

---

[66] *Hazell* v. *Hammersmith and Fulham LBC*, above. Such transactions are also void in Scotland: *Morgan Guaranty Trust Co* v. *Lothian Regional Council*, The Times, 30 November 1993. See below, p. 676 for whether the money paid is recoverable. [67] *Crédit Suisse* v. *Allerdale BC* [1997] QB 306. See below, p. 676.

[68] As proposed in a White Paper, *Modern Local Government* (Cm. 4014 (1998)). The power does not extend to overcoming 'any prohibition, restriction or limitation on their powers which is contained in any enactment (whenever passed or made)' (s. 3(1)). This power has been extended to parish councils (Local Government and Public Involvement in Health Act 2007, s. 77).

[69] *R (Theophilus)* v. *London Borough of Lewisham* [2002] EWHC 1371 (student support); *R (J)* v. *London Borough of Enfield* [2002] EWHC 432 (accommodation). [70] See, below, p. 676.

[71] And to contract with a financier who provides funding for the provision contract.

[72] s. 1. See below, p. 676 for discussion particularly of the authority's power to certify that it has power to enter into the contract in question. [73] Below, p. 336.

[74] See below, p. 340. This is the case of *Roberts* v. *Hopwood* [1925] AC 578, a classic example of the working of the former district audit system. See also *Asher* v. *Secretary of State for the Environment* [1974] Ch 208; *Lloyd* v. *McMahon* [1987] AC 625 and *Gibb* v. *Maidstone and Tunbridge Wells NHS Trust* [2009] EWHC 862 (excessive compensation package for NHS trust chief executive ultra vires). Contrast *Pickwell* v. *Camden LBC* [1983] QB 962. [75] *Taylor* v. *Munrow* [1960] 1 WLR 151; below, p. 340.

[76] *Prescott* v. *Birmingham Cpn* [1955] Ch 210; below, p. 341.

[77] At the time of writing a Bill is before Parliament (Local Audit and Accountability Bill 2013–14) to abolish the Audit Commission here described and replace it with suitably qualified local auditors. Later developments will be noted in Appendix 3.

that irregularities would be exposed and charged in the audit was often a more effective deterrent than the vague responsibility of councillors to their constituents. Every councillor and official was thus made conscious of his personal liability.

From 1844 to 1982 the central figure in this system was the district auditor, an official of the Department of the Environment (as it became) who was thus, in effect, a central government inspector.[78] In 1982 the corps of auditors was detached from the Department and put under the Audit Commission, a statutory body appointed by the Secretary of State and substantially controlled by him since he could give it binding directions.[79] The Commission's chief officer was the Controller of Audit, and auditors might be either officers of the Commission or independent accountants. The Commission had to maintain a code of practice which had to be approved by each House of Parliament.

All accounts of a local authority and its committees, and certain other bodies had to be audited annually in accordance with the Act of 1998.[80] The commission, and likewise the Secretary of State, could also direct an extraordinary audit at the request of an elector or at their own motion.[81]

The accounts were open to inspection and any local government elector for the area (or his representative) could appear before the auditor and object to any item.[82] If it appeared to the auditor that an item was contrary to law, the auditor might apply to the court for a declaration accordingly; and the court might also order that any person responsible should repay the cost of it personally unless the item was 'sanctioned' by the Secretary of State or the person in question could persuade the court that he had acted reasonably or in the belief that the expenditure was lawful; and the court had to take account of personal means.[83] Under the pre-1972 system the auditor had a mandatory duty to disallow unlawful expenditure and to surcharge those responsible, subject to appeal to the court or the Secretary of State.[84]

This system of personal liability and surcharges was abolished by the Local Government Act 2000 and replaced by a system of 'advisory notices' to be issued by the auditor.[85] Items of account may be challenged as before, but so in addition may any decision, course of action or proposed action which seems likely to lead to unlawful expenditure. The advisory notice must specify which of these categories is concerned and it must be followed by a statement of the auditor's reasons within seven days. It must require that before taking action the recipient shall give the auditor not more than twenty-one days' notice of the intended action.

The effect of an advisory notice is that the decision, course of action or expenditure becomes unlawful until the council has reconsidered the matter and the above-mentioned period of notice has expired. From then on the auditor has the same powers as previously to apply to the court for judicial review and the body or person concerned may appeal likewise. The court may order rectification of the accounts or award the usual remedies of judicial review for prohibiting unlawful action or quashing an unlawful decision.

Under the former system of surcharges the audit sometimes provided a battleground for acute political strife, when councillors deliberately disobeyed the law and

---

[78] Local Government Act 1972, s. 156, allowing alternatively choice of an auditor approved by the Secretary of State.

[79] Audit Commission Act 1998, replacing Pt III of the Local Government Finance Act 1992. For the Secretary of State's power to give directions, see s. 1(5) and 1st Sched., para. 3.

[80] s. 2 and 2nd Sched.   [81] s. 25.

[82] s. 16. But see now the requirement for a written complaint (Local Government and Public Involvement in Health Act 2007, s. 161).   [83] s. 17.

[84] s. 18. See the notable case of *Porter* v. *Magill* [2002] 2 AC 357.   [85] ss. 90–1.

were surcharged with the financial consequences of their misdeeds. On two occasions Parliament intervened by legislation to relieve them of personal liability for surcharges. These were occasions when political rebellion succeeded.

BYELAWS

The Act of 1972 confers a wide power upon district and London borough councils 'to make byelaws[86] for the good rule and government of the whole or any part of the district or borough, as the case may be, and for the prevention and suppression of nuisances therein'.[87] This general power is not enjoyed by other authorities, but many statutes have conferred byelaw-making powers for particular purposes such as public health, housing and highways.[88] Furthermore, the general power given by the Act of 1972 may not be invoked where there is byelaw-making power under some other enactment.[89] It is therefore a residuary power.

Byelaws made under the Act of 1972 require confirmation by the Secretary of State,[90] and byelaws made under other Acts normally require ministerial confirmation.[91] They are therefore under firm central control. Confirming ministers issue model byelaws which local authorities will be expected to follow. Whether made under the Act of 1972 or otherwise, byelaws must be made under the authority's common seal and must be advertised and open to inspection for a month before the application for confirmation.[92] Unless some other Act authorises larger fines, the maximum penalty for infringement is a fine of £50 plus £5 per day for continuing offences.[93] Byelaws may now also be enforced by way of fixed penalty notice.[94]

The law as to the validity of byelaws under the ultra vires doctrine is explained in the chapter on delegated legislation.

CENTRAL INFLUENCE AND CONTROL

After what has been said it is needless to emphasise that local government is subjected to central government in numerous and important ways.[95] The Act of 1972 and other Acts conferring powers are shot through with restrictive provisions giving powers of

---

[86] This is the statutory spelling, but 'by-law' is common, as in by-election, by-product etc., 'by' meaning secondary. The original derivation may be from 'byr', meaning village or town, or from 'by', meaning town.

[87] s. 235.

[88] Public Health Act 1936 (e.g. ss. 61, 81, 104); Housing Act 1985, s. 23; Highways Act 1980, s. 186.

[89] s. 235(3).

[90] ss. 235(2), 236(7). Note the special arrangements for Wales (by Act of the Assembly) in the Local Government Byelaws (Wales) Act 2012 (confirmation not required in all cases); arrangements upheld A-G v. National Assembly for Wales Commission [2012] UKSC 53.   [91] See Act of 1972, s. 236(1), (7).

[92] s. 236(4), (5).   [93] s. 237.

[94] s. 237A. The default amount of a fixed penalty is £75 (s. 237B).

[95] See the Report of the Communities and Local Government Committee 'The Balance of Power: Central and Local Government' (2008–9) HC-33I (<http://www.publications.parliament.uk/pa/cm200809/cmselect/cmcomloc/33/33i.pdf>) proposing a statutory footing for the relationship between central and local government (para. 134). This was favoured by the Political and Constitutional Reform Committee, 'Prospects for Codifying the Relationship between Central and Local Government' (2012–13) HC-656-I (<http://www.publications.parliament.uk/pa/cm201213/cmselect/cmpolcon/656/656.pdf>) but rejected by the government (<http://www.official-documents.gov.uk/document/cm86/8623/8623.pdf>). The Lyons Report (2007) identifies both 'hard' and 'soft' central controls as a major impediment to effective local government, paras. 3.5–24. And see 'Open Public Services: White Paper', Cm. 8145 (2011) at para. 1.13 proposing decentralisation. See [2013] PL 702 (Himsworth) and (2009) 68 CLJ 436 (Bailey and Elliott).

yea or nay to the Secretary of State and ministers. The Local Government Finance Acts 1982–92 have given the central government a stranglehold on local authority revenue and expenditure.[96]

Despite the lip-service paid to the need for financial independence, and the policy of reducing the number of earmarked grants, it is through financial administration that the central government's control makes itself most felt. The 'appropriate minister' may make regulations for prescribing standards and general requirements in relation to any function of a local authority.[97] With these powers in the background the central government is in a strong position to make its wishes felt in innumerable ways. It can exercise tight control over capital expenditure, both through the power to withhold loan sanction and by restricting aggregate expenditure. It has control over the remaining earmarked grants.[98] It may make regulations as to all the details of accounts and audit.[99] In both great matters and small it maintains a powerful financial grip.

Behind this powerful battery of weapons lies the ultimate sanction, the default power. This enables the minister, if he considers that the local authority is failing to perform some function as it should, to make a legally enforceable order directing it what to do.[100]

Default powers are of importance in administrative law because the courts sometimes regard them as a substitute for other remedies, as will be explained in due course.[101]

COMPLAINTS AGAINST LOCAL GOVERNMENT

THE LOCAL GOVERNMENT COMMISSIONERS

In 1974 the ombudsman system[102] was extended to complaints against local authorities by the Local Government Act 1974.[103] Special arrangements were made for Scotland and Wales.[104] The Parliamentary Commissioner is a member of both Commissions and the other commissioners are appointed by the Crown and hold office during good behaviour until the retiring age.[105] The Local Commissioners investigate complaints made in writing directly[106] by members of the public against any local authority (including its committees, members and officers). The complainant, who must allege that he or she has sustained injustice through maladministration, must also specify the action in connection with which the maladministration is alleged.[107] The following matters are, however, excluded from the Local Commissioners' remit: legal proceedings, investigation or prevention of crime, contractual and commercial transactions, personnel matters, educational matters and the provision of social housing.[108]

---

[96] But see above, p. 96 for local authorities' power to increase council tax by holding a local referendum.

[97] Local Government Act 1974, s. 5(2).

[98] e.g. housing grants may be made subject to any conditions: Housing Act 1985, 15th Sched., Pt II.

[99] Local Government Act 1999, s. 23.

[100] Local Government Act 1999, s. 15(6). See *R* v. *Secretary of State for the Environment ex p Norwich CC* [1982] QB 808.   [101] See below, p. 629.

[102] See above, p. 71 (central government ombudsman).

[103] Amendments were made by the Local Government Act 1988, 3rd Sched.

[104] There is separate legislation for Scotland (the Scottish Public Service Ombudsman Act 2002) and for Wales (Public Services Ombudsman (Wales) Act 2005, Sched. 4).

[105] s. 23. The Welsh Administration Ombudsman is a member of the Welsh Commission (Government of Wales Act 1998, 12th Sched., para. 11.)

[106] There is no requirement akin to the filter of complaints to the Parliamentary Commissioner through MPs.   [107] s. 26B. of the 1974 Act. A complaint may now be made electronically: s. 34(1A).

[108] s. 26(8) and 5th Sched. The Commissioners have frequently asked for wider powers.

Provisions similar to those in the Act of 1967 exclude cases where there is a remedy before a tribunal or court of law.[109] And the Commissioner should not question the merits of decisions taken without maladministration.[110] Local Commissioners have powers similar to those of the Parliamentary Commissioner to carry out their investigations[111] and there are similar provisions in regard to disclosure.[112] The report must be sent to the complainant, the local authority and the councillor (if any) who originally referred it.[113] There are special arrangements for publicising the report and re-publicising it if the authority's response is unsatisfactory. In order to encourage recalcitrant authorities to make amends for maladministration, the Commissioner may require an authority, at its own expense, to publish the details of the action recommended by the Commissioner and the reasons why the authority has failed to comply.[114]

Each commissioner makes an annual report to a representative body of local authorities who then publish the joint report (in England entitled *The Local Government Ombudsman*). The Local Commissioners have been successful in obtaining satisfaction for many complainants and in remedying injustice. They deal with many more complaints than does the Parliamentary Commissioner.

Local authorities have now been given power to pay compensation, or provide some other benefit, to any person who has been, or may have been, adversely affected by any exercise of their functions which in their opinion amounts, or may amount, to maladministration.[115]

POLICE

INDEPENDENT LOCAL POLICE FORCES

An outstanding fact about the British police is that they are not under the direct control of the central government: they are organised into local forces headed by a chief constable (or commissioner in the case of the Metropolitan Police). In the past the local forces were maintained by police authorities[116] but in 2013 their place was taken by directly elected local police and crime commissioners (PCCs).[117] The police and crime commissioners have a duty to maintain an 'efficient and effective' force and to hold the chief constable to account for the exercise of his functions.[118] For each force area there is a Police and Crime

---

[109] s. 26(6). There is a similar proviso to allow the Commissioner to accept complaints where there would be legal remedies.   [110] s. 34(3).

[111] s. 30. This extends to privileged, confidential files relating to adoption since adoption was within the Commissioner's jurisdiction: *Re a Subpoena issued by the Commissioner for Local Administration* (1996) 8 Admin LR 577.   [112] s. 29(1).

[113] s. 30(1), (3).   [114] s. 31(2D), (2E) and (2F).   [115] Local Government Act 2000, s. 92.

[116] These were bodies corporate independent of the elected local authorities. Their typical membership of 17 comprised 9 local councillors appointed by the councils within the force area, and 8 independent members appointed by the other members of the authority from a shortlist drawn up by a selection panel on which the Home Secretary is usually represented. They elected their own chairman. They appointed, disciplined and might dismiss the chief constable, deputy chief constable and assistant chief constables. See generally the Police Act of 1996. Police authorities were abolished by the Police Reform and Social Responsibility Act 2011, s. 1(9).

[117] Police and Crime Commissioners are created for each force area by the 2011 Act, s. 1(1) which further provides that they are corporations sole (s. 1(2)). For their election see s. 50. Special arrangements apply to London; instead there is a 'Mayor's Office for Policing and Crime', which for the time being is occupied by the London Mayor (s. 3).

[118] Act of 2011, s. 1(6) and (7). The PCCs have powers similar to those of the police authorities to appoint, suspend, dismiss or require the resignation of a chief constable. PCCs themselves, although elected, 'may'

Panel established by the local authority[119] which scrutinises and reviews the PCC's decisions and reports on the draft police and crime plan.[120] The change to police and crime commissioners was made to increase local democratic accountability and to reduce central bureaucratic accountability.[121]

The modern police system, which replaced the inefficient system of constables inherited from the Middle Ages, was devised in the golden age of political liberty in the nineteenth century and this continues to be reflected in the absence of control by the central or local government as well as local organisation of the police.[122]

Recent decades saw growing central government influence over local policing. But the Police Reform and Social Responsibility Act 2011, as already remarked, was enacted to reduce central bureaucratic accountability marked a change of direction. Under the new arrangements the Home Secretary issues a 'strategic policing' document which identifies 'national threats' and the capabilities required to address them.[123] The Home Secretary also gives guidance as to the matters to be addressed in the local police and crime plans.[124] The Home Secretary also issues a 'policing protocol' to encourage a good working relationship between PCCs and the Panels.[125]

Finance supplies another potent instrument of central influence; for many years the bulk of a police authority's income has come by way of central grant, with most of the rest coming by way of a precept paid by the local council tax payers.[126] More power left the local forces with the establishment in 2005 of the Serious and Organised Crime Agency (SOCA) to prevent and detect serious and organised crime.[127] But SOCA's place was taken by the National Crime Agency (NCA) in 2013.[128] The NCA has both crime reduction and intelligence gathering duties and to these ends extensive powers.[129] Significantly, the Director General of the NCA (who is appointed by the Home Secretary)[130] 'may direct' chief officers of police to perform appropriate tasks in furtherance of the NCA's functions.[131] This is a plain reduction in the autonomy of the chief officers and a step towards a national force.

Despite all the regulatory and financial powers of the central and local authorities, the responsibility for deciding whether, for example, the police shall arrest some particular person or investigate a particular offence rests upon the police and no one else. This is an important facet of the constitution, and a prime safeguard against the evils of a police state.

---

be suspended by the Police and Crime Panels if charged with an offence that carries a maximum term of imprisonment exceeding 2 years (s. 30(1)).

[119] Act of 2011, s. 28(1)) and see Sched. 6, para. 3. The Panel for the Metropolis is a committee of the London Assembly (s. 32).   [120] Act of 2011, s. 28(2) and (6).

[121] 'Policing in the 21st Century: Reconnecting Police and the People', Cm. 7925 (2010).

[122] After the Bichard report (*The Bichard Inquiry Report*, HC 653 (2004)) the government favoured the amalgamation of smaller forces into larger 'strategic forces' with greater capability and capacity. But there was much local resistance (especially from areas where the precept (see below) would be higher but the service more remote) and the estimated cost of amalgamations was expensive.

[123] Act of 1996, s. 37A.   [124] Act of 2011, s. 7.

[125] Act of 2011, s. 79. The current protocol is at <https://www.gov.uk/government/uploads/system/uploads/attachment_data/file/117474/policing-protocol-order.pdf>.

[126] Local Government Finance Act 1992, s. 39.

[127] Established by the Serious and Organised Crime and Police Act 2005, s. 1.

[128] Crime and Courts Act 2013, Pt 1.   [129] Act of 2013, ss. 2–4.

[130] Act of 2013, Sched. 1, Pt 11. The Home Secretary may also call upon the Director General to resign or retire (ibid.).

[131] Act of 2013, s. 5(5). Section 5(6) restricts the circumstances in which a direction may be issued.

THE LEGAL STATUS AND RESPONSIBILITY
OF POLICE OFFICERS

In their ordinary daily acts and decisions the police are as independent of the local police commissioner as they are of the central government: a police officer holds a public position, that of peace officer, in which he owes obedience to no executive power outside the police force. Thus, for example, in the leading English case, where the police had by mistake arrested the wrong man on a criminal charge, an action for damages against the local police authority met with no success because the police, in making the arrest, were acting on their own authority not that of the authority.[132] It is equally fallacious to suppose that police officers are servants of the Crown.[133] They do, indeed, hold office under the Crown and when appointed they swear that they will well and truly serve the sovereign in the office of constable. But this does not make them servants of the Crown; and the Crown is not liable for any wrongdoing by the police.[134]

This independence of constables means that there is no vicarious liability by their employer for their misdeeds. But special statutory provision ensures that chief constables are liable for their subordinate police constables, so that the victims of wrongdoing are not left with no effective remedy: damages and costs being paid out of the police fund.[135]

THE INDEPENDENCE OF CHIEF CONSTABLES

The authorities quoted apply with special force to the chief constable since he has command over his force but no one has command over him.[136] Lord Denning cited them with approval when he said:[137]

> I hold it to be the duty of the Commissioner of Police of the Metropolis, as it is of every chief constable, to enforce the law of the land. He must take steps so as to post his men that crimes may be detected; and that honest citizens can go about their affairs in peace.... But in all these things he is not the servant of anyone save the law itself. No minister of the Crown can tell him that he must, or must not, keep observation on this place or that...Nor can the police authority tell him so. The responsibility for law enforcement lies on him. He is answerable to the law and to the law alone.

But the chief constable is answerable to the law and should he fail to enforce the law—for instance, by adopting a policy not to enforce the law at all in certain circumstances—the law will intervene. In an application of these principles the House of Lords has upheld the decision of the chief constable to restrict the policing of a port area to two days a week, notwithstanding daily and violent protests obstructing trade in the area.[138] The courts, it was said, would 'respect the margin of appreciation or discretion which a chief constable has'.[139]

---

[132] *Fisher* v. *Oldham Corporation* [1930] 2 KB 364. Confirmed in regard to Ministry of Defence Police: *R (Mousa)* v. *Secretary of State for Defence* [2013] EWHC 1412, para. 74 (Silber J).

[133] *A-G for New South Wales* v. *Perpetual Trustee Co Ltd* [1955] AC 457 at 480.

[134] *Lewis* v. *Cattle* [1938] 2 KB 454.   [135] Police Act 1996, s. 88.

[136] Although note that under the Police Reform and Social Responsibility Act 2011, s. 2(5) the chief constable must exercise his 'power of direction and control...in such a way as is reasonable to assist the relevant police and crime commissioner to exercise the commissioner's functions'.

[137] *R* v. *Metropolitan Police Commissioners ex p Blackburn* [1968] QB 118 at 135 approved (Lord Hoffmann) and *R* v. *Chief Constable of Sussex ex p International Trader's Ferry Ltd* [1999] 2 AC 418 discussed below, p. 331.   [138] *International Trader's Ferry Ltd*, above. Discussed more fully below, p. 331.

[139] *International Trader's Ferry Ltd*, at p. 90 (Lord Slynn). On the European law aspects of this case, see below, p. 331, n. 304.

Judicial review may be granted against chief constables for procedural failings in disciplinary matters,[140] but only exceptionally in the employment or operational field.[141]

COMPLAINTS AND DISCIPLINE

The police are a disciplined force and have always been in charge of their own discipline, including the investigation of complaints. But this makes them judges in their own cause, with the result that many complainants are unsatisfied. For many years the Police Complaints Authority supervised the investigation of serious complaints (and others referred to them by the police authorities or the chief constable). Its place has now been taken by the Independent Police Complaints Commission, established by Part 2 of the Police Reform Act 2002. This new organisation may itself investigate complaints made about the police—without the police being involved at all. To this end it has the powers of search and seizure necessary to enable it to carry out a proper investigation. Most investigation of complaints will still be undertaken by police officers, however, but in addition to supervision of an investigation by officers, the Commission will be able now to conduct a managed investigation in which it has powers to direct the police team that conducts the actual investigation.

DEVOLUTION—SCOTLAND AND WALES

Aspirations to self-government in Scotland and Wales, and a growing sense of their national identities, have brought about a new constitutional settlement and a radical redistribution of power.[142] The Scotland Acts 1998–2012[143] and the Government of Wales Acts 1998–2006[144] have created the Scottish Parliament and the Welsh Assembly, with ministerial and administrative systems to match. The Scottish Parliament (the first such body since 1707) has been endowed with powers of primary legislation, in the sense that it can itself choose the subjects of its enactments, whereas the Welsh Assembly has more limited powers as explained later. Technically speaking, all such Scottish and Welsh legislation is delegated under the Acts of 1998 or later Acts,[145] and there has been no transfer

[140] R (O'Leary) v. The Chief Constable of Merseyside [2001] EWHC 57 (failure to disclose prejudicial report).

[141] R (Morgan) v. Chief Constable of South Wales [2001] EWHC 262 (removal from list of those ready for promotion) and R (Tucker) v. Director General of National Crime Squad [2003] EWCA Civ. 2, [2003] ICR 599 (cancellation of secondment to NCS). But Tucker was doubted in Manning v. Ramjohn [2011] UKPC 20, para. 34 (Lord Brown).

[142] More drastic changes may occur. If the independence referendum to be held in Scotland in September 2014 secures a majority of votes, Scotland will become an independent state.

[143] The Scotland Act 2012 followed the recommendations of the Calman Commission on Devolution (<http://www.commissiononscottishdevolution.org.uk/uploads/2009-06-12-csd-final-report-2009fbookmarked.pdf>). It makes many miscellaneous changes to the 1998 Act but in particular empowers the Parliament to set a 'Scottish rate of income tax' (Act of 1998, s. 80C inserted by Act of 2012, s. 25). But this is not yet in force (no order under s. 25(5) made). The Act, s. 12, also changes the name of the executive from the 'Scottish Executive' to the 'Scottish Government'.

[144] As explained below, p. 110, the 2006 Act enhanced the legislative powers of the Assembly but in a complex way shifting from a form of secondary legislation ('measures') to primary legislation ('Acts').

[145] But, in recognition of the 'depth and width of the experience of its elected members and the mandate that has been given to them by the electorate' Acts of the Scottish Parliament are not subject to judicial review 'on the grounds of irrationality, unreasonableness or arbitrariness' (AXA General Insurance Ltd and ors, below, para. 52).

of Parliamentary sovereignty.[146] Parliament could at any time repeal or amend these Acts without special formality and they do not therefore constitute a federal system. The full power of the Westminster Parliament to make laws for Scotland[147] and Wales[148] is expressly reserved.

Proposals for devolution have a long history, but the chain of recent events began with the Royal Commission on the Constitution (1969–73), which suggested various options, by no means unanimously.[149] Devolution statutes for both countries were enacted in 1978, but, after failing to attract sufficient support in referendums, were duly repealed. Twenty years later, in a more favourable atmosphere, devolution was once again proposed as part of the government's scheme of constitutional reform, and this time the referendum votes were positive, though only marginally in Wales. The two constituent Acts were passed in 1998 and the two new legislatures were inaugurated in 1999. The Government of Wales Act 2006[150] made far reaching changes to the devolution arrangements for Wales and is discussed later.

These Acts are basic constitutional instruments and a full account of them belongs to constitutional law. But they form essential background for administrative law and there is a wide overlap, especially in the area of dispute resolution. There are likely to be many legalistic contests about the division of powers and much of the material of judicial review, as discussed in this book, will be relevant:[151] The Supreme Court resolves disputes over devolution matters, playing the role of a constitutional court. A brief account of the new legal machinery, which now follows, is therefore necessary.

Devolution to Northern Ireland is omitted from this account. The Northern Ireland Act 1998, brought into force in 1999, follows the pattern of the Scotland Act 1998 by empowering the Northern Ireland Assembly to pass Acts in any field not specifically excepted or reserved. The Assembly's competence includes health and social services, education, finance (but not taxation), agriculture, environment and economic development. The administration consists of the first minister and other ministers, and there is a committee system resembling that for Wales. There are special provisions for power-sharing and for giving effect to the Belfast Agreement of 1998.[152]

SCOTLAND

THE SCOTTISH PARLIAMENT AND EXECUTIVE

The Scottish Parliament consists of a single chamber of 129 members, elected partly (seventy-three) by simple majority vote and partly (fifty-six) by proportional representation under the additional member system. Electors have two votes, one in each category. A Parliament is to last for four years, but in two cases it must be dissolved earlier: first, if

---

[146] Confirmed *AXA General Insurance Ltd and ors* v. *Lord Advocate and ors* [2011] UKSC 46, para. 46 (Lord Hope).   [147] Scotland Act 1998, s. 28(7).
[148] Government of Wales Act 2006, ss. 93(5) and 107(5).   [149] Cmnd 5460 (1973).
[150] Enacted following a White Paper, *Better Governance for Wales*, Cm. 6582 (2005), itself following the Report of the Richard Commission (commissioned by the Welsh Assembly) (Report of the 21 March 2004 to be found at <http://image.guardian.co.uk/sys-files/Politics/documents/2004/03/31/richard_commission.pdf>.
[151] For a survey of provisions and interpretative possibilities, see [1999] *PL* 274 (P. Craig and M. Walters). For a prominent example see *Axa General Insurance Ltd* v. *HM Advocate*, above.
[152] Cm. 3883 (1998). See B. Hadfield in *Constitutional Reform in the United Kingdom* (Cambridge Centre for Public Law, 1998), ch. 5 and in [1998] *PL* 599. And see Northern Ireland (St Andrews Agreement) Act 2006, especially s. 8 (compulsory power-sharing between the two largest parties).

two-thirds of the total membership so resolve; and secondly, if Parliament fails to nominate one of its members as First Minister within the statutory period of (basically) twenty-eight days.[153] Peers are eligible for membership. One member is appointed the Presiding Officer, taking the place of Speaker. Standing orders regulate procedure, the committee system, and so forth. The Presiding Officer and at least four members form a corporate body holding property and providing services on behalf of Parliament.[154]

The Scottish Government consists of the First Minister, nominated by the Parliament but appointed by the Queen, together with such ministers as he may appoint (and whom he may remove) and the two law officers, the Lord Advocate and the Solicitor General for Scotland.[155] Ministerial appointments must be approved both by Parliament and by the Queen. Ministers hold office at Her Majesty's pleasure[156] and exercise their functions on her behalf.[157] They must resign, as also must the two law officers, if the Parliament resolves that the Scottish Government no longer enjoys its confidence.

A new law officer, the Advocate General for Scotland, has come into being, not created by the Act but endowed with certain powers under it.[158] He or she is a minister of the Crown and advises the central government on Scottish constitutional and legal affairs, particularly in cases where the division of powers is in question. The Advocate General therefore stands outside the Scottish Parliament and Executive, being Westminster's agent and watchdog, replacing for those purposes the former Scottish law officers, who are now Scottish ministers.

LEGISLATIVE POWERS

Acts of the Scottish Parliament become law when they receive the royal assent and their validity is not affected by any invalidity in the parliamentary proceedings.[159] Their scope is however severely restricted by the limits which the Act sets to their competence. By contrast with the abortive Act of 1978, which devolved only specified powers leaving the remainder with the central government, the Act of 1998 devolves legislative power generally, subject to specific reservations. Specific powers are also granted, notably the tax-varying power, under which the Parliament may increase or reduce the basic rate of income tax by not more than 3 per cent.[160] Despite the massive list of reservations (see later) there is a wide area of competence remaining to the Parliament, including education, health, economic development, environment, local government, law, housing, planning, agriculture, forestry, police, fire services, heritage and tourism.

The limits to the powers of the Parliament must be found in the lengthy and intricate catalogue of the 'protected provisions' and 'reserved matters' which are beyond its competence, most of which are contained in the fourth and fifth schedules. It is important to note, however, that those schedules may be modified, as may be considered necessary or expedient, by Order in Council, so that the central government may at any time and in any way adjust them to meet difficulties such as conflicts of competence.[161] This power may prove to be a valuable safety-valve.

An Act of the Scottish Parliament 'is not law so far as any provision of the Act is outside the legislative competence of the Parliament'.[162] An element of ultra vires, therefore, will

---

[153] Scotland Act 1998, s. 3. The Scottish Parliament is subject to the jurisdiction of the courts like other statutory bodies: *Whalley* v. *Watson*, 2000 SLT 475.   [154] s. 21 as amended by the 2012 Act.
[155] ss. 46–8.   [156] s. 47(3).   [157] s. 52(2).   [158] s. 87.   [159] s. 28.
[160] The 2012 Act, s. 25(4) and (5) provides that this restriction may be removed by Treasury Order (but this has not yet been done (October 2013). There is also a new power to levy tax on transactions involving interests in land: s. 80I of the 1998 Act, inserted by the 2012 Act.   [161] s. 30.
[162] s. 29. And see Weintrobe, below.

invalidate the offending provision but not the whole Act. Moreover, a doubtful provision is to be read 'as narrowly as is required for it to be within competence if such a reading is possible',[163] and problems caused by ultra vires Acts may be remediable by subordinate legislation or by reconsideration in the Parliament.[164]

Legislation incompatible with Convention [sc. human] rights or with Community law is outside the Parliament's competence.[165] The fourth schedule of the Act prevents the Parliament from modifying certain legislation, including the provisions for freedom of trade in the Acts of Union of 1706 and 1707, the Human Rights Act 1998, the Scotland Act 1998 itself and provisions about judicial salaries and the Advocate General. The fifth schedule contains the long list of 'reserved matters' which are beyond the Parliament's competence so far as its legislation 'relates' to them, thus giving them wide effect. This schedule occupies more than twenty pages in the printed statute and only a selective description of its first two parts can be given here.[166]

Part I (general reservations) includes the Crown, the royal prerogative, the Union with Scotland, 'any office in the Scottish Administration', the superior Scottish courts, the civil service, foreign affairs and defence. Part II (specific reservations) includes, under numerous heads and sub-heads, financial policy and services, taxation (other than local taxes),[167] data protection, immigration, nationality and extradition, national security, official secrets and terrorism, emergency powers; consumer protection, telecommunications, postal services; electricity, oil and gas, nuclear energy; road, rail, marine and air transport; social security schemes and pensions; regulation of professions (architects, health professions and auditors); employment, industrial relations, health and safety, medicines; broadcasting; judicial remuneration; equal opportunities. Some of these items are described in general terms. Others are minutely defined by reference to sections or subsections of specified Acts. Many are accompanied by exceptions or qualifications. It is a formidable list and a likely source of much contention.

As we have seen, Parliament in Westminster retains the power to legislate for Scotland even over devolved matters.[168] One of the surprising aspects of the devolution settlement is the frequency with which Parliament has legislated for Scotland on devolved matters. Such legislation of course secures uniform law on the matter in question over the whole UK which may be considered necessary or at least desirable. A convention has been created, the Sewel Convention,[169] to the effect that 'Westminster will not normally legislate with regard to devolved matters in Scotland without the consent of the Scottish Parliament'. In practice this means that a so called 'Sewel motion' is passed in the Scottish

[163] s. 101. But the court in considering human rights issues will use its powers under s. 3 of the Human Rights Act 1998 (see below, p. 142) in preference to its s. 101 power: S v. L [2012] UKSC 30, para. 17 relying on DS v. HM Advocate [2007] UKPC D1, paras. 23–4.   [164] ss. 107, 34.
[165] s. 29(2). See Petition of Trevor Adams [2002] SCCR 881 (unsuccessful challenge to validity of the Protection of Wild Mammals (Scotland) Act 2002 on human rights grounds) and Salvesen v. Riddell [2013] UKSC 22, 2013 SLT 863 (retrospective provision concerning agricultural landlords' power to terminate tenancies incompatible with Art. 1 of Protocol 1). See the discussion in [2005] PL 3 (Weintrobe) pointing out that in Scotland, unlike England, Parliament (the Scottish Parliament) does not have the 'last word' on human rights questions.
[166] But note now Sched. 5, para. 54 (power to hold independence referendum).
[167] But see now the Scotland Act 2012, s. 25 (Scottish rate of income tax), s. 28 (taxes on transactions involving interests in land) and s. 30 (tax on disposals to landfill).   [168] Act of 1998, s. 28(7).
[169] Based on an undertaking by a minister (Lord Sewel) in the House of Lords while the Bill was being enacted (HL Deb vol. 592, col. 791, 21 July 1998) subsequently incorporated into a Memorandum of Understanding between the UK government and the devolved administrations (see Turpin and Tomkins, 242). The convention echoes the arrangements whereby, prior to the Statute of Westminster 1931 the UK government undertook not to legislate for the Dominions without their consent.

Parliament before Westminster legislates. A total of 131 'Sewel motions' have been passed since 1999.[170]

EXECUTIVE FUNCTIONS

The Act makes a general transfer of functions to Scottish ministers in respect of the Crown's prerogative and executive functions and of ministerial powers conferred by pre-devolution statutes, 'so far as they are exercisable within devolved competence'.[171] These will often be powers of making subordinate legislation, with varying arrangements for laying before Parliament etc. The seventh schedule to the Act specifies eleven varieties of procedure and the powers of the Act to which they are to apply, requiring in some cases approval by the Westminster Parliament and in others by the Scottish Parliament, and in others by both. The power to modify the fourth and fifth schedules by Order in Council, for example, requires positive resolutions of both Parliaments. There is also a list of 'shared powers' which may be exercised by a minister of the Crown as well as by a Scottish minister.[172] Additional powers may be transferred by Order in Council.[173]

The central government has a power of veto over proposed action of the Scottish Parliament or of the Scottish Government[174] which the Secretary of State reasonably believes would be incompatible with international obligations, including presumably the Human Rights Convention and European Union law; and there is a corresponding power to compel necessary action to be taken.[175] In these cases the order is subject to annulment by either House of the Westminster Parliament.

As in the case of the Parliament, already mentioned, members of the Scottish Government have no power to act in any way so far as the act is incompatible with Convention rights (i.e. statutory human rights) or with Community law.[176] The Convention rights set out in the Human Rights Act 1998, like the rules of Community law, operate as jurisdictional barriers: any legislation or executive action under devolved power which infringes them is ultra vires. Criminal trials were invalidated for this reason because they were held before temporary sheriffs whose tenure was at the pleasure of the executive and who were therefore not independent under Article 6.[177]

Even though, as already mentioned, Scottish ministers 'hold office at Her Majesty's pleasure' and their statutory functions 'are exercisable on behalf of Her Majesty', it seems that they are not 'Ministers of the Crown' within the meaning of the Act, since many of its provisions make a contrast between them.[178] This question is important for purposes of subordinate legislation, since where the Act provides, as it often does, for subordinate legislation without saying who is to make it, it may be made only by Order in Council or by a Minister of the Crown, i.e. by the central government.[179]

---

[170] For a list of the relevant Acts see <http://www.scotland.gov.uk/About/Government/Sewel>; and for the statistics see <http://www.scottish.parliament.uk/parliamentarybusiness/Bills/19023.aspx>.

[171] s. 53. Lord Rogers has said that this provision means that 'the Scottish Ministers are now to be in the same position as the Secretary of State before devolution' (*Beggs* v. *Scottish Ministers* [2007] UKHL 3, para. 32).

[172] s. 56.   [173] s. 63.

[174] Previously the Scottish Executive but renamed by the Act of 2012, s. 12.

[175] s. 58. Note *Friend* v. *Lord Advocate* [2007] UKHL 53, para. 9 pointing out that this provision does 'not limit the legislative competence of the Scottish Parliament in a way that can be decided upon by a court'.

[176] s. 57(2).   [177] *Millar* v. *Dickson* [2002] 1 WLR 1615 (PC).

[178] See s. 52(6) (Lord Advocate 'ceases to be a Minister of the Crown'); s. 112(5) ('a Minister of the Crown or a member of the Scottish Government') and likewise ss. 53(1), 60(1), 108(1). The lack of a definition is a defect of the Act.   [179] s. 112.

The Scottish Parliament is required by the Act to make provision (as it has since done)[180] for the investigation of complaints of maladministration by or on behalf of Scottish ministers or other office-holders in the Scottish administration and the arrangements may be extended to certain other bodies.[181] A Scottish Parliamentary Commissioner for Administration has been appointed, being the same person as the English Parliamentary Commissioner.

The appointment of judges of the Court of Session and sheriffs is a matter for the First Minister, whose recommendation, after prescribed consultations, is passed via the Prime Minister to the Queen. Judges of the Court of Session are removable by the Queen on a resolution of the Parliament after a motion by the First Minister, and only if a tribunal constituted by the First Minister and chaired by a member of the Judicial Committee of the Privy Council has so recommended on account of inability, neglect of duty or misbehaviour.

DISPUTED COMPETENCE AND 'DEVOLUTION ISSUES'

The potential competence or otherwise of a Bill, or any provision in it, may be referred to the Supreme Court by the Advocate General, the Lord Advocate or the Attorney-General within four weeks from the passing of the Bill, and meanwhile it may not be presented for the royal assent.[182] The question whether any legislation or function is, or would be, within competence is a 'devolution issue' governed by the detailed provisions of the sixth schedule. If the issue arises in proceedings in Scotland, proceedings for its determination may be instituted by the Advocate General or the Lord Advocate, to whom intimation of the issue must be given. A court or tribunal may refer a devolution issue to the Court of Session (if civil) and the Court of Justiciary (if criminal) and from their decision an appeal lies (with leave) to the Judicial Committee. Proceedings for the determination of an issue arising in England or Wales may be instituted by the Attorney General and the court or tribunal must give notice of it to him and the Lord Advocate. The issue may then be referred to the High Court or the Court of Appeal as the Act prescribes, with a right of appeal (with leave) to the Supreme Court. There are corresponding provisions for Northern Ireland.

A court or tribunal which finds an excess of competence in Scottish legislation, whether primary or subordinate, is empowered to make an order 'removing or limiting any retrospective effect of the decision' or 'suspending the effect of the decision for any period and on any conditions to allow the defect to be corrected'.[183] The first limb of this clause is designed to mitigate the problems of the doctrine of retrospectivity discussed later in this book, under which situations accepted as legal in the past may be reopened if the law under which they were determined is later held to have been wrong. It may not prove easy to exercise this new discretion. The second limb of the clause makes way for the power already mentioned which allows excesses of competence to be remedied by subordinate legislation.

Executive or administrative action by Scottish ministers can likewise raise a devolution issue if it is alleged to be beyond devolved competence or incompatible with any of the Convention rights or with Community law. Every human rights claim against the Scottish Government may thus raise a devolution issue. So where, as related above, the precarious tenure of temporary sheriffs was held to violate article 6 of the Convention,

---

[180] The Scottish Public Services Ombudsman Act 2002, s. 11. [181] s. 91. [182] s. 33.
[183] s. 102.

the Judicial Committee held on a devolution issue that by continuing prosecutions before them the Lord Advocate was infringing the Convention rights of the defendants and acting unlawfully.[184] The Judicial Committee has, however, rejected a number of other claims alleged to raise devolution issues but where no breach of Convention rights was shown.[185]

WALES

THE WELSH ASSEMBLY AND ADMINISTRATION

Devolved power in Wales is exercised by the Welsh Assembly created by the Government of Wales Act 1998 and entitled the National Assembly for Wales. The Assembly consists of sixty members, elected partly (forty) by simple majority vote and partly (twenty) by proportional representation under the additional member system, using party lists. Electors have two votes, one for a candidate and one for a party. The life of the Assembly is four years. It is a body corporate and exercises its functions on behalf of the Crown.[186]

The structure of government—sometimes called 'executive devolution'—in Wales established by the 1998 Act was significantly changed by the Government of Wales Act 2006. The 2006 Act abandons the rather curious arrangement in which the executive (the Assembly First Secretary and the other Secretaries) was not distinct from the legislature. The original Assembly simply took over in large measure the functions of the Secretary of State for Wales.

Under the 2006 Act the structure of government is much closer to that of the traditional Westminster model. The executive, called the Welsh Assembly Government (WAG), is established as separate from but accountable to the Assembly.[187] It is headed by a First Minister followed by other ministers (together known as the 'Welsh Ministers') and Deputy Ministers all of whom must be members of the Assembly.[188] There is also the Counsel General, who is appointed by the First Minister, and is also a member of the WAG. The First Minister is appointed by Her Majesty on the nomination of the Assembly and holds office during her pleasure.[189] He appoints 'with the approval of Her Majesty' the other ministers who must resign if the Assembly passes a vote of no confidence.[190] Provision is made for the transfer of functions to the WAG by Order in Council[191] and the WAG now exercises most of the functions previously exercised by the Welsh Assembly.[192]

In addition the 2006 Act sets up mechanisms whereby the legislative powers of the Assembly are enhanced.[193] The Assembly was given power to enact 'Measures' provided such a measure lay within its competence.[194] Part 1 of schedule 5 of the 2006 Act lists various 'matters' which lie within the competence of the Assembly provided they take effect only 'in relation to Wales'.[195] There is no power to legislate contrary to human

---

[184] *Miller* v. *Dickson* [2002] 1 WLR 1615 (PC), holding also that the defendants had not waived their rights by not objecting earlier.

[185] See e.g. *Brown* v. *Stott* [2001] 2 WLR 817; *Montgomery* v. *HM Advocate* [2001] 2 WLR 779.

[186] s. 1. An important and controversial change made by the 2006 Act (s. 7) was to restrict candidates from standing for election in a constituency and being on a party list.   [187] Act of 2006, s. 45.

[188] s. 46.   [189] s. 47.

[190] s. 48. There may be only 12 Welsh Ministers (including Deputy Ministers) but not including the First Minister and Counsel General (s. 51).   [191] s. 58.

[192] Turpin and Tomkins, as above, 225. And see ss. 56–86.

[193] Broadly, the Assembly previously had the powers of the Secretary of State to make delegated legislation for Wales transferred to it.   [194] ss. 93 and 94, especially s. 94(2).

[195] s. 94(2) and (4). In addition a Measure may be enacted to enforce another provision or if it is incidental to such a provision (s. 94(5)). The fields listed in Part 1 are: agriculture, fisheries, forestry and rural

rights or Community law[196] or to an Act of Parliament intended to apply to Wales.[197] Furthermore, schedule 5, Part 2 contains restrictions on competence, listing Acts which cannot be amended and limiting the power to enact serious criminal offences as well as other matters. With the approval of both Houses of Parliament and the Assembly, Orders in Council (known as Legislative Competence Orders) may be made adding matters to schedule 5.

But a mechanism was also set up in the Act of 2006 to enable the making of 'Acts of the Assembly'. These powers were only to become effective following a referendum.[198] The referendum was duly held[199] in March 2011 and these provisions have now been brought into force.[200] The competence of the Assembly to make Acts is set out in Schedule 7[201] where the subjects on which it will be able to make primary legislation are listed. This is unlike the position in Scotland where powers are expressly reserved to Westminster and all other powers are devolved.[202]

DISPUTED COMPETENCE AND 'DEVOLUTION ISSUES'

The 1998 Act provides for the resolution of 'devolution issues' in a manner like that already described for Scotland.[203] Any question whether a function, or any proposed action, of the Assembly is within its powers, and any question of default of duty on its part, may be determined in proceedings brought by the Attorney-General.[204] Any such question arising in the course of litigation may be referred by the court or tribunal, after notice to the Attorney-General and the Assembly, to the appropriate superior court, with a right of appeal to the Supreme Court.[205] There is the same provision as in the case of Scotland, noted above, for allowing a court or tribunal to regulate the retrospective effect of its decision.[206]

---

development, ancient monuments and historic buildings, culture, economic development, education and training, environment, fire and rescue services and promotion of fire safety, food, health and health services, highways and transport, housing, local government, National Assembly for Wales, public administration, social welfare, sport and recreation, tourism, town and country planning, water and flood defence and Welsh language.

[196] s. 94(6).   [197] s. 93(5).   [198] s. 103.

[199] Following an agreement between the Welsh Labour Party and Plaid Cymru ('One Wales: A Progressive Agenda for the Government of Wales' (2007) (see <http://wales.gov.uk/strategy/strategies/onewales/one-walese.pdf?lang=en>).

[200] The 'Assembly Act' provisions of the 2006 Act were brought into force on 5 May 2011: Government of Wales Act 2006 (Commencement of Assembly Act Provisions, Transitional and Saving Provisions and Modifications) Order 2011 (SI 2011/1011).

[201] The schedule lists some 20 'subjects' on which the Assembly may make Acts, each subject to specific and general exceptions. The list is: Agriculture, forestry, animals, plants and rural development; Ancient monuments and historic buildings; Culture; Economic development; Education and training; Environment; Fire and rescue services and fire safety; Food; Health and health services; Highways and transport; Housing; Local government; National Assembly for Wales; Public administration; Social welfare; Sport and recreation; Tourism; Town and country planning; Water and flood defence; and the Welsh language.

[202] This is justified by the government on the necessity to preserve the unity of the English and Welsh legal systems. See Turpin and Tomkins, 228 and see [2004] *PL* 78 (Jones and Williams).

[203] s. 109 and 9th Sched.   [204] 9th Sched., para. 4.

[205] For instance, *A-G* v. *National Assembly for Wales Commission* [2012] UKSC 53.   [206] s. 153.

5

PUBLIC CORPORATIONS, PRIVATISATION AND REGULATION

PUBLIC CORPORATIONS

THE USES OF CORPORATE PERSONALITY

Throughout the government system it has often been found convenient to confer corporate personality on a particular body that performs public functions.[1] But there is no set pattern. Sometimes central government departments (such as the Department of the Environment) are incorporated by making the Secretary of State a corporation sole[2]— thus the department can own property and contract in its own name. But other departments are not incorporated (such as the Foreign Office). All local authorities, however, have separate legal personality;[3] and may be seen as a particular form of public corporation. As explained above, executive agencies do not have separate legal personality and are not part of this discussion.[4]

Particular use has been made since the nineteenth century of public corporations, set up at arm's length from central government, to carry out specific administrative functions which needed to be 'taken out of politics'. The Poor Law Commissioners established in 1834 may serve as an early example while the Civil Aviation Authority,[5] the Independent Television Commission[6] and the Radio Authority.[7] Health authorities and NHS Trusts are public corporations. The membership of such bodies is as varied as their functions. Sometimes members are elected, sometimes they are nominated (by the appropriate minister) and sometimes a mixture of election and nomination is adopted.[8]

There is no need here to catalogue the numerous different types of public corporation, many of which have too little in common to illustrate any legal principle.[9] Whenever Parliament is willing to grant a sufficient measure of autonomy, the public corporation is

---

[1] Bradley and Ewing, *Constitutional and Administrative Law*, 15th edn (2011), ch. 14.
[2] The corporation is composed of the minister and his successors in office. Above, p. 37.
[3] Above, p. 89.   [4] Above, p. 37.   [5] Civil Aviation Act 1971.
[6] Broadcasting Act 1990, s. 1 and 1st Sched., para. 1.
[7] Broadcasting Act 1990, s. 83 and 8th Sched., para. 1.
[8] Under the Public Appointments Order in Council 1995 such appointments should be made 'on merit'. There is a Commissioner for Public Appointments to whom complaints may be made and who publishes a Code of Practice for Ministerial Appointments to Public Bodies and an Annual Report. The Commissioner's jurisdiction is limited to the bodies listed in an annex to the Order in Council. The Code is available at <http://publicappointmentscommissioner.independent.gov.uk/the-code-of-practice/>.
[9] For a synoptic (and selective) account which attempts a classification see Garner, *Administrative Law*, 8th edn, 347–54.

commonly employed. It has a legal existence of its own, and can be given statutory functions which can operate outside the normal organisation of the service of the Crown. It offers scope for many kinds of governmental experiment, under which central control, local control, particular expertise and independence can be blended in the desired proportions.

After 1945 corporations were much used as the vehicle for the nationalisation of industry with legislation vesting the assets of the industry in a corporate body, such as the National Coal Board. An alternative technique—adopted in the case of the nationalisation of steel—was for the government compulsorily to acquire the shares in the relevant commercial companies and to vest those shares in a public corporation—or, in some cases (e.g. the Bank of England), simply to hold those shares itself. There was normally provision for the minister to give 'directions of a general character' to the corporation, to appoint its chairmen and members and to control its borrowing. Ministers thus had a great deal of power, formal and informal, over the affairs of a nationalised industry. The theory that they would give only general directions and refrain from interference in day-to-day management was falsified by their frequent interference behind the scenes. Nationalised industries did thus not enjoy sufficient independence for them to adopt consistent long-term policies.

DEGREES OF CONTROL

Corporations which form part of the administrative structure of social services (such as health authorities) are subject to ministerial directions in all respects.

On the other hand there are corporations which enjoy a very substantial degree of autonomy. The British Broadcasting Corporation, first constituted by royal charter in 1926 and at present chartered until 2016,[10] operates under a statutory licence granted by the Home Secretary under the Wireless Telegraphy Act 1949. The licence contains numerous restrictive conditions, both technical and political. In particular, it may be required to transmit government announcements; and it may be required by the Home Secretary to refrain from transmitting any specified matter or class of matter. The corporation is given standing directions forbidding it to give its own comments on current affairs and restricting party political broadcasts. From 1988 to 1996 restrictions were imposed on the publication of the words of members and supporters of certain terrorist organisations.[11] Similarly the Office of Communications[12] may be required by the Home Secretary to transmit or refrain from transmitting particular items, and is subject to direction as to various matters;[13] but otherwise it is independent.

There is a wide range of other public corporations of a governmental character, mostly with regulatory functions, which operate independently. These include the Civil Aviation Authority,[14] the Health and Safety Executive[15] and the Gambling Commission,[16] which all have licensing and controlling powers. An Office of Communications (OFCOM) has been established as a unified regulator for broadcasting and telecommunications.[17]

---

[10] The most recent charter renewal replaced the BBC Governors with the BBC Trust (as well as making other changes). The members of the trust are appointed by the Crown, like the Governors before them.
[11] These restrictions were challenged but upheld in *R* v. *Home Secretary ex p Brind* [1991] 1 AC 696; below, pp. 315, 321 and 335. [12] Established under the Office of Communications Act, s. 1.
[13] Communications Act 2003, s. 5(2), (3). [14] Civil Aviation Acts 1971, 1980.
[15] Health and Safety at Work etc. Act 1974. [16] Gambling Act 2005.
[17] Office of Communications Act 2002, s. 1. OFCOM's substantial powers have been transferred to it under the Communications Act 2003, s. 2. This was proposed in a White Paper (Cm. 5010, 12 December 2000).

OFCOM has very wide powers to set conditions for the provision of telecommunications services and to license independent broadcasters.[18] The National Lottery Commission is similarly independent; it licenses the lottery operator.[19] The public corporations responsible for the regulation of the privatised utilities, financial services and commerce are discussed later.[20]

THE POST OFFICE

The Post Office has a special position, having been a government department in the full sense until turned into a public corporation by the Post Office Act 1969. Here, in contrast with the nationalised industries, the device of a public corporation was employed to increase rather than reduce the independence of a major industry. In order further to enhance its commercial freedom and to lead to increased competitiveness and efficiency, the Post Office has now become a public limited company. All its shares are owned by the Crown but the Postal Services Act 2011 authorises the sale of shares to the public, subject to various restrictions.[21] The Post Office now operates as an ordinary commercial company under the control of its Board of Directors and is accountable to its shareholders. It no longer enjoys a formal statutory monopoly on the carriage of letters. Indeed, any person may carry letters provided they notify OFCOM of their intention and comply with its regulatory conditions.[22] Those conditions relate primarily to the provision of a universal service and OFCOM is under a duty to regulate so as to achieve this end.[23] The universal postal service comprises several minimum requirements including a requirement that letters be delivered six days a week.[24]

The Secretary of State retains the power to give directions to the Commission in the interests of national security or in the interests of encouraging or maintaining the United Kingdom's relations with other countries.[25]

The Post Office (or any other provider of a universal postal service) is immune from liability in tort for what happens to anything in the post.[26] This immunity extends to any of its officers, servants, agents or sub-contractors.[27]

This is a breach of the principle that a public official is personally liable for wrongful injury.[28] A person who delivers a parcel to the Post Office and sees it damaged or destroyed before his eyes has, it seems, no civil remedy—though criminal proceedings will lie, and even carelessness is a statutory offence in such a case.[29] There is, however, a scheme of limited liability for the loss of inland registered packets.[30] It is surprising that the wide immunity of Post Office employees is still tolerated.

---

[18] 2003 Act, Pt 3, Ch. 2.

[19] National Lottery Act 1998, s. 1. There are also the independent distribution bodies that distribute the money raised; they are subject to general directions by the Secretary of State (e.g. s. 13 (duty to draw up strategic plans on Secretary of State's direction)).   [20] Below, p. 121.

[21] Pt 1, particularly ss. 1, 2 and 3.   [22] Act of 2011, s. 28.   [23] Act of 2011, s. 29

[24] Act of 2011, s. 30.

[25] Act of 2000, s. 101. The Secretary of State also has power to ensure compliance with the European Postal Service Directive: s. 102.   [26] Act of 2000, s. 90(1).

[27] Act of 2000, s. 90(2). *American Express Co* v. *British Airways Board* [1983] 1 WLR 701 (airport authority claimed immunity as a sub-contractor when travellers cheques stolen by its employee; breach of bailment (not a tort) covered by immunity).   [28] Below, p. 693.

[29] Act of 2000, ss. 83 and 84. See also *Gouriet* v. *Union of Post Office Workers* [1978] AC 435 (offence of detaining or delaying postal packet).

[30] Act of 2000, ss. 89, 91. The action has to be brought within 12 months (instead of the usual 6 years) and does not extend to overseas packets even if lost or damaged locally. See *Royal Mail Group plc* v. *Consumer Council for Postal Services* [2007] EWCA Civ 167.

LEGAL STATUS AND LIABILITY

Public corporations are as subject to the ordinary law, e.g. as to corporate powers, taxation and liability in tort as are other corporate bodies, unless they enjoy some statutory exemption. Contracts made outside their powers are null and void.[31] Public corporations do not generally enjoy any of the immunities of the Crown. 'In the eye of the law, the corporation is its own master and is answerable as fully as any other person or corporation. It is not the Crown and has none of the immunities or privileges of the Crown. Its servants are not civil servants, and its property is not Crown property.'[32] Thus the British Transport Commission in ejecting a tenant was unable to rely upon the Crown's immunity from legislation protecting tenants.[33] The NHS, however, enjoys the Crown's right to use patents.[34] Its other immunities have been largely removed by the National Health Service and Community Care Act 1990.

Public corporations have no direct responsibility to Parliament.

RELEVANCE IN ADMINISTRATIVE LAW

The actions of public corporations are judicially reviewable in the same way as those of other bodies, where they have powers of a public law character.[35] Thus the Independent Television Commission's licensing decisions are subject to judicial review,[36] and a decision of British Coal, before privatisation, to close certain coal mines was successfully challenged.[37] On the other hand, the decision of a public corporation to dismiss an employee is no more subject to judicial review than a similar decision by a private corporation.[38] The modern law of judicial review is, in this regard, guided by function rather than form.

THE MECHANISMS OF PRIVATISATION AND NATIONALISATION

As adumbrated, since 1980 practically all of the previously nationalised industries have been privatised. The usual statutory pattern was to provide that on an appointed day the assets of the public corporation should vest in a successor company nominated by the Secretary of State.[39] This company was to take the form of a normal commercial company limited by shares. In the first instance the shares would all be held by the government, but they would proceed to sell part or all of them to private investors. The government might or might not then retain a majority shareholding and might or might not take special powers to appoint directors.[40] But it would have no power to give directions, control

---

[31] The clearest examples are from the field of local government. See below, p. 676.

[32] Per Denning LJ in Tamlin v. Hannaford [1950] 1 KB 18.

[33] Tamlin v. Hannaford (ibid.). And see British Broadcasting Corporation v. Johns [1965] Ch 32.

[34] Pfizer Corporation v. Minister of Health [1965] AC 512.   [35] See below, p. 512.

[36] R v. Independent Television Commission ex p TSW Ltd, The Times, 30 March 1992, [1996] EMLR 291 (application unsuccessful). See [1992] PL 372 (T. Jones).

[37] R v. British Coal Cpn ex p Vardy [1993] ICR 720; contrast R v. National Coal Board ex p National Union of Mineworkers [1986] ICR 791.

[38] R v. East Berkshire Health Authority ex p Walsh [1985] QB 152 (below, p. 536).

[39] This was the model adopted in the privatisation of British Petroleum.

[40] Although there were many differences of detail this was the basic mechanism adopted for most privatisations. But, particularly in the case of the utilities, the nationalised industry was first re-organised before sale on either a regional or functional basis into several enterprises.

capital investment etc., otherwise than as a shareholder under normal company law. Where the concern to be privatised was already an ordinary company, all that was necessary was to authorise the government to put part or all of its shareholding on the market.[41]

The constitutions of the new companies frequently provided that the government retains a special share (commonly known as the 'golden share') which gives it paramount rights, e.g. to appoint directors and outvote all others. The purpose is to protect the independence of the company so that it may not, for example, come under foreign control. Golden shares, however, restrict the free movement of capital contrary to Article 56 EC and are struck down by the ECJ unless justified on public policy or security grounds.[42]

The technique of nationalisation was revived during the financial crisis of 2008. An Act of Parliament[43] was rapidly passed permitting the transfer by Order of shares (or other property) in any 'authorised UK deposit taker' to the Treasury or the Treasury's nominee (or even a private body).[44] These powers were only exercisable where it appeared to the Treasury that such action was desirable to protect the stability of the financial system or to protect the public interest.[45] A compensation scheme must be set up.[46]

REGULATION

THE CHANGING NATURE OF REGULATION

Privatisation necessitated radical changes in the technique of regulation. The bane of the nationalised industries had been ministerial interference, often politically motivated, which frustrated the operation of market forces.[47] Shareholder control, in so far as it worked at all, would work to maximise profits rather than to protect the consumer. The solution found was to establish independent regulators armed with strong statutory powers and given the statutory duty of safeguarding consumers' interests and preventing the abuse of monopoly.[48] Control by government command (or, more often, by surreptitious pressure) was replaced by independent regulation. This was a new constitutional

---

[41] The government's shares in Cable & Wireless, British Petroleum, Jaguar Motors and Rolls-Royce were all sold in this way.

[42] Case C-98/01 *Commission* v. *UK* (13 May 2003) (golden share in British Airports Authority held a breach). For discussion see (2002) 3 *German Law Journal* No. 8 (Adolff).

[43] The Banking (Special Provisions) Act 2008 whose place was soon taken by the more sophisticated and complicated 'special resolution regime' established under the Banking Act 2009.

[44] s 2. Under the 2009 Act, s. 1, a wider range of mechanisms exists whereby the shares (or other assets) in the affected bank many transferred to a private-sector purchaser, a 'bridge bank' or into temporary public ownership.

[45] Ibid. Where public money had been loaned to the deposit taker it may be in the public interest to take over the bank even where there is no threat to stability.

[46] s. 5. But the compensation is based on the assumption that no financial assistance was available to the deposit taker from the Bank of England or the Treasury or that it had been withdrawn (s. 5(4)).

[47] See above, p. 24.

[48] For a general account and comment see Prosser, *Law and the Regulators* (1997). See also [1995] *PL* 94 (J. M. Black) for discussion on types of rules and regulatory policy and [1998] *PL* 77 (J. M. Black) for the formation of rules through discussion between regulator and the regulated. For comment on regulatory procedures and decisions see Ogus, *Regulation, Legal Forms and Economic Theory*. See also Graham and Smith (eds.), *Competition, Regulation and the New Economy* (2004). Note particularly in the abundant literature Faure and Stephen, *Essays in the Law and Economics of Regulation*; Moran, *The British Regulatory State: High Modernism and Hyper-innovation* (2007); and [2007] *PL* 58 (Black) ('Tensions in the Regulatory State').

experiment, being a sharp departure from the principle of ministerial responsibility.[49] It poses important issues of public policy.[50]

One recent development has been the imposition of statutory duties on regulators exercising specified regulatory functions[51] to 'have regard to' the principle that 'regulatory activities should be carried out in a way which is transparent, accountable, proportionate and consistent' and that such activities 'should be targeted only at cases in which action is needed'.[52] In addition a minister may after consultation issue a 'code of practice' to which regard must be had by the regulator.[53] The impact of these obligations is not yet clear.[54]

The regulatory machinery might take various forms. Since 1948 the Monopolies Commission, now replaced by the Competition Commission, had had powers of investigation over monopolies and restrictive practices, as noted later. When the denationalised industries were privatised a new pattern emerged for the control of utilities such as telecommunications, gas, electricity and water. For each industry there was established a government-appointed but otherwise independent regulator who could grant, revoke and modify their statutory licences and penalise infringements. Sometimes there was non-statutory regulation, as in the case of the Takeover Panel of the Stock Exchange, which could enforce its rulings by excluding an offending trader from the market.[55] Nor were these the only forms of regulation. The only common element throughout was the sharply reduced role of government policy, once the regulatory regime was established. Regulation was to be done by regulators, not by ministers, although ministers had important powers over the conditions within which regulation was done (such as the number of telecommunications licences to be granted) and in some cases were empowered to give directions or guidance.[56] Sometimes, also, ministers were given important reserve powers.[57]

The regulators have been given social as well as economic duties. In the case of gas, for example, the first of the listed duties of the Secretary of State and the Director is to protect the interests of consumers and they are required also to take account, in particular, of the interests of the chronically sick, the disabled and pensioners.[58] In granting licences the Director is prohibited from including discriminatory conditions of certain kinds, and he must impose standard conditions to the same effect on licensees. Disconnections are controlled and have been reduced, as also in the case of electricity. The regulator's general duty to promote efficiency and economy in the industry is therefore qualified substantially by his social obligations.

---

[49] 'On one view, to the classical question "quis custodiet ipsos custodes?"—who regulates the regulator?—the truthful answer is "no one"' (Harlow and Rawlings, *Law and Administration*, 2nd edn, 329; passage not in 3rd edn).

[50] See the Sixth Report of the House of Lords' Select Committee on the Constitution, *The Regulatory State: Ensuring its Accountability* (May 2004, HL 68).

[51] The functions are specified by the minister by Order (s. 24 of the 2006 Act (below)). But he may not specify a function that is the responsibility of the devolved administrations (s. 24(3)) or one entrusted to the regulators of the public utilities (including postal services) (s. 24(5)).

[52] Legislative and Regulatory Reform Act 2006, s. 21.

[53] s. 22. This is the Regulator's Compliance Code: Statutory Code of Practice for Regulators available at <http://www.berr.gov.uk/files/file45019.pdf>.

[54] See also the Regulatory Enforcement and Sanctions Act 2008 which creates a 'Local Better Regulation Office' (Pt 1). This office provides guidance to local authorities to ensure the effective and targeted exercise of regulatory functions in a way that does not give rise to unnecessary burdens and conforms to the principles of transparency, accountability, proportionality and consistency (s. 5). The Act also provides for civil sanctions for regulatory offences.   [55] See below, p. 540.

[56] See below, p. 123.   [57] As in the Electricity Act 1989, ss. 11, 12, 34.

[58] Gas Acts, 1986, s. 4, 1995, s. 1. See Prosser (as above), 106.

SOME REGULATORY MECHANISMS

THE REGULATION OF COMMERCE

For many years[59] there has been statutory law regulating competition in trade in the UK and this is a specialised area of law in its own right. The bulk of the relevant law is now to be found in the Competition Act 1998 which is designed to ensure that UK competition law is consistent with European Community law.[60] The 1998 Act deals in the main with trade practices as explained later. The Enterprise Act 2002[61] establishes the current control regime for mergers and inquiries into monopolies (the latter now called 'market investigations').

Subject to exemptions, both particular and general, agreements between undertakings (i.e. companies, partnerships, or individuals), decisions by associations of undertakings and concerted practices which affect trade within the UK and have as their object or effect the prevention, restriction or distortion of competition within the UK are prohibited (Chapter One prohibitions)[62] and void.[63] The fixing of prices, the limitation of supply, the sharing of markets (or sources of supply), discrimination against trading parties and making contracts conditional upon conditions unconnected to the subject of the contract are all prohibited.[64] These prohibitions are intended to mirror Article 81 of the Treaty of Rome (now Article 101 of TFEU).

In a similar way, the abuse of a dominant position in a market which may affect trade in the UK is also prohibited (Chapter Two prohibitions).[65] Such abuse includes, but is not limited to, the imposition of unfair prices or other trading conditions, the limitation of production, or markets, or technical developments to the detriment of the consumer as well as discrimination against trading parties and making contracts conditional upon conditions unconnected to the subject of the contract.[66] These prohibitions are intended to mirror Article 86 (now 82) of the Treaty of Rome.

Of particular importance to administrative law is the procedure for enforcement of these prohibitions.[67] The Office of Fair Trading (OFT) has power to investigate if there are reasonable grounds for suspicion that there has been an infringement of either Chapter One or Chapter Two.[68] If he concludes that there has been an infringement he may issue directions to bring

---

[59] There has been relevant statutory law governing competition and restrictive trade practices since the Monopolies and Restrictive Trade Practices (Inquiry and Control) Act 1948.

[60] Arts. 81 and 82 EC Treaty. And the 1998 Act, s. 60, creates an obligation to secure consistency as far as compatible with Pt 1 of the Act with EU law.

[61] Replacing the regime established in the Fair Trading Act 1973. For discussion of the Act, see (2004) 67 *MLR* 273–88 (Cosmo Graham). For discussion of policy in this area, see Graham and Smith, as above.

[62] Act of 1998, s. 2. Section 3 providing that this prohibition does not apply to the bodies and agreements listed in three schedules (two of which can be amended by the Secretary of State). Individual exemption may be granted by the Director-General of Fair Trading (s. 4). Block exemptions may be issued by the Secretary of State (s. 6).   [63] s. 2(4).

[64] s. 2(2). Decisions prior to the Act of 1998 were *Garden Cottage Foods Ltd* v. *Milk Marketing Board* [1984] AC 130 and *An Bord Bainne Co-operative Ltd* v. *Milk Marketing Board* [1984] 2 *CMLR* 584 for which see below, p. 572.

[65] s. 18. Once more provision is made for exclusion from the reach of s. 18 by schedule (generally liable to be altered by the Secretary of State): s. 19.   [66] s. 18(2).

[67] In addition to enforcement by the OFT, enforcement by private law action is possible. This seems to have been the government's intention (HL Deb., vol. 582, col. 1148, 30 October 1997) but the Act does not directly grant such a right to individuals and the existence of a statutory enforcement procedure may preclude this. See [1998] 7 *ECLR* 443 (Kon and Maxwell). But a private law action was brought in *Attheraces Ltd* v. *The British Horseracing Board Ltd* [2007] EWCA Civ 38. For discussion of the private law action under EU law, see *Crehan* v. *Courage Ltd* [1999] EWCA Civ 1501, paras. 18–35.

[68] s. 25. The OFT may require the production of documents or information from 'any person' (s. 26(1) and may enter premises under a warrant without notice (s. 28) or without a warrant but with notice (s. 27)). See

the infringement to an end,[69] and he may impose penalties.[70] If a person fails without reasonable excuse to comply, the OFT may apply to the court for an order requiring the default to be made good.[71] The OFT may also give guidance whether particular agreements or conduct are infringements;[72] and he may take interim measures before he has completed an investigation where there would otherwise be irreparable damage to a particular person or groups.[73]

Any decision of the OFT in respect of an agreement, or in respect of some person's conduct, may be appealed to the Competition Appeal Tribunal (CAT).[74] Moreover, third parties may appeal to the Competition Appeal Tribunal.[75] There is a further right of appeal, with leave, to the Court of Appeal on a point of law or on any penalty.[76]

There are other mechanisms of enforcement. Some offending agreements (for instance, that fix prices or which share markets) are breaches of the criminal law.[77] And once an infringement (of Chapter One or Two or the relevant EU law) has been established third parties and consumers may be able to seek damages before the CAT.[78]

As adumbrated the Enterprise Act 2002 establishes a new control regime governing the approval of mergers and market investigations (previously monopoly inquiries).[79] The broad test of 'public interest' used in the past has been replaced by much narrower tests. The Office of Fair Trading may make a reference to the Competition Commission when it concludes, following a market investigation, that there are 'reasonable grounds' for suspecting that a feature of a market 'prevents, restricts or distorts competition'.[80] And proposed mergers are assessed by a test of whether they may expect to result in 'substantial lessening of competition'.[81]

In the past a report preceded by an investigation by the Competition Commission following a reference by the Office of Fair Trading went to the appropriate minister who had wide powers to remedy the deficiencies found.[82] Under the 2002 Act, save in a small number of 'public interest' cases,[83] ministers are no longer involved. The Competition Commission itself decides on the appropriate action and has powers to that end.[84] Its decision, however, as well as the original decision to make a reference is subject to appeal to the Competition Appeal Tribunal[85] which, however, applies judicial review principles.[86]

R (Cityhook Ltd) v. Office of Fair Trading [2009] EWHC 57 (administrative priority a relevant consideration when deciding to close an investigation).

[69] ss. 32 and 33.   [70] ss. 36–8.   [71] s. 34.

[72] s. 12. Where the OFT has given guidance that a particular agreement does not infringe Chapter One, then no further action will be taken and no penalty imposed unless there has been a material change of circumstances (or like development) (s. 16).   [73] s. 35.

[74] See Enterprise Act 2002, ss. 12, 21 and Sched. 5 read with ss. 46 and 47 of the 1998 Act. If the OFT has decided not to proceed in a particular matter, then there is no right of appeal; but in accordance with general principle there may be a remedy by way of judicial review. See Cityhook Ltd v. Office of Fair Trading [2007] CAT 18 for discussion of the boundaries of the right of appeal.

[75] s. 47 of the 1998 Act, read with Sched. 5 of the Act.   [76] s. 49.   [77] Act of 2002, Pt 6.

[78] Act of 1998 (as amended by the Act), ss. 47A (third parties) and 47B (consumers).

[79] Discussed [2003] JR 41 (Rayment).   [80] Act of 2002, s. 131(1).

[81] Act of 2002, s. 22. In addition there must be a 'relevant merger situation' which requires in broad terms that 'two or more enterprises have ceased to be distinct enterprises' and the 'turnover in the United Kingdom of the enterprise being taken over exceeds £70 million' (s. 23). Similar rules apply where the merger is simply anticipated (s. 33).   [82] See the discussion in the 8th edn at 151.

[83] Act of 2002, Pt 3, Ch. 2, ss. 45–55 (mergers). The minister's power is a default power—to act when the matter would not otherwise reach the Competition Commission. See also Ch. 3 dealing with special public interest cases (government contractors involved). There are similar powers for market investigations (Pt 4, Ch. 2).

[84] Act of 2002, Sched. 8. The normal method in the case of mergers is to seek an undertaking that an enterprise divest itself of certain assets etc. But if undertakings are not given orders may be made. The OFT has the duty of enforcing the orders made (s. 162).

[85] For the structure of the Tribunal see Act of 2002, Pt 2 and Sched. 4.

[86] Act of 2002, s. 179 (market investigations), s. 120(4) (mergers).

There is a further appeal on a point of law to the Court of Appeal.[87] Although many applications for judicial review have been made against the Competition Commission or its predecessor, few have been successful.[88] Although the principles of judicial review applicable remain the same the courts show understandable reluctance to intervene in questions of economic and competition policy, especially given the specialist expertise of the CAT. But where the Commission follows an unfair procedure the judicial review court will be alert to remedy that.[89]

THE REGULATION OF FINANCIAL SERVICES[90]

Financial services is an area where regulation is clearly needed. The Financial Services and Markets Act 2000[91] brought together the many bodies[92] that previously regulated various forms of financial services. It established a Financial Services Authority which had power to regulate banks, building societies, insurance companies, friendly societies, Lloyd's, investment and pensions advisers, stockbrokers, fund managers and derivative traders.

But the financial and banking crises of 2008 and later revealed the weaknesses of this single regulator with so many diverse responsibilities that it failed to anticipate many difficulties. It was 'the watchdog that didn't bark';[93] its 'light touch' regulation was a failure. The Financial Services Act 2012, consequently, established in its place the Financial Conduct Authority (FCA) as the formal successor of the FSA[94] and also established the Prudential Regulation Authority (PRA).[95]

The FCA has a 'strategic objective' which is 'ensuring that the relevant markets [primarily the financial markets and regulated markets for financial services] function well'.[96] In discharging its general functions the FCA is bound 'so far as is reasonably possible, [to] act

---

[87] Act of 2002, s. 120(6).

[88] See [2001] *JR* 84 (Robertson) (no successful judicial reviews prior to 2001). The intensity of the judicial scrutiny whether of OFT decisions or Competition Commission decisions depends upon the 'statutory context' (*Office of Fair Trading* v. *IBA Health* [2004] EWCA Civ 142, (para. 100 (Carnwath LJ)). Where the question is one of policy review will be less intense than when it simply raises a question of fact (*Unichem Ltd* v. *Fair Trading Office* [2005] CAT 8). For further discussion, see [2006] *JR* 160 (Kennelly).

[89] *Interbrew* v. *Competition Commission and Department of Trade and Industry* [2001] EWHC Admin 367; [2001] UKCLR 954 (failure by Commission to consult over alternative remedy (divestment of Whitbread); decision to ask Director-General of Fair Trading to negotiate undertakings that Interbrew divest itself of Bass quashed). Discussed [2002] *JR* 88 (Robertson). The two cases mentioned in the preceding note are examples of successful challenges.

[90] See Ferran and Goodhart (eds.), *Regulating Financial Services and Markets in the 21st Century* (Oxford: Hart Publishing, 2001) and [2003] *PL* 63 (J. M. Black). See also Hopper, 'Financial Services Regulation and Judicial Review in Black, Muchlinski and Walker (eds.), *Commercial Regulation and Judicial Review* (1998), 63–95.

[91] The Act is very complex and no more than a sketch of its provisions may be given here. For discussion of judicial review and the 2000 Act see [2001] *JR* 255 (A. Henderson).

[92] These include the Self-Regulating Organisations (SROs) (such as the Personal Investment Authority (PIA), the Investment Management Regulatory Organisation (IMRO) and the Securities and Futures Authority (SFA)), the Supervision and Surveillance Branch of the Bank of England, the Building Societies Commission, the Insurance Directorate of the Treasury and the Friendly Societies Commission. The Authority takes the place of the former Securities and Investments Board.

[93] *The Observer*, 24 March 2013.

[94] Although it was commonly said that the FSA was abolished, the Act of 2000, s. 1A(1) as amended by the 2012 Act, s. 6 provides the FSA 'is renamed as the FCA'.

[95] Originally established as a wholly owned subsidiary of the Bank of England, its existence now rests on the Act of 2000, s. 2A as amended by the Act of 2012, s. 6(1).

[96] Act of 2000, s. 1B(2) as amended by the 2012 Act, s. 6; see also s. 1F.

in a way which (a) is compatible with its strategic objective, and (b) advances one or more of its operational objectives', viz., the consumer protection objective, the integrity objective and the competition objective.[97] The FCA's general functions are the making of rules under the Act, preparing and issuing codes under the Act, the giving of general guidance under the Act (considered as a whole), and 'determining the general policy and principles by reference to which it performs particular functions under this Act'.[98] More particularly as the FCA itself says it has 'rule-making, investigative and enforcement powers that [are used] to protect and regulate the financial services industry'. The FCA grants permission to individuals or firms to carry out regulated activities.[99] The Governing Body of the FCA consists mostly of persons appointed by the Treasury (including a chair and chief executive) and the Deputy Governor of the Bank of England for prudential regulation.[100]

The PRA is described by the Bank of England[101] as 'responsible for the prudential regulation and supervision of banks, building societies, credit unions, insurers and major investment firms'. It has 'two statutory objectives[:] to promote the safety and soundness of these firms and, specifically for insurers, to contribute to the securing of an appropriate degree of protection for policyholders... the PRA makes forward-looking judgements on the risks posed by firms to its statutory objectives. Those institutions and issues which pose the greatest risk to the stability of the financial system is the focus of its work.' The PRA too has powers to grant permission to carry out regulated activities.[102] Its Governing Body has a similar structure to that of the FCA save that the Governor of the Bank of England and the Deputy Governor for prudential regulation are chair and chief executive of the PRA respectively.[103]

These new bodies with their objectives, functions and powers spelt out in detail in law mean that financial regulation is more complicated—and the complexities have been barely hinted at in the account here. The extent of the FSA's failures during the financial crisis and after required that the public interest demanded the far-reaching changes outlined in this chapter.

THE REGULATION OF PUBLIC UTILITIES[104]

Notwithstanding significant increases in competition, the denationalised public utilities remain monopoly or near monopoly providers of important services.[105] Some mechanism is necessary in order to prevent them exploiting their position to the detriment of the public. Regulation here also has an important social dimension, in ensuring that the service in question is available to all, is not arbitrarily denied or restricted, and is not overpriced.[106]

[97] Act of 2000, s. 1B as amended by the 2012 Act, s. 6
[98] Act of 2000, s. 1B(6) as amended by the Act of 2012, s. 6.
[99] See the Act of 2000, s. 55N as amended by the Act of 2012, s. 11.
[100] Two members are jointly appointed with the Secretary of State (for Business, Innovation and Skills). See the Act of 2000, Sched. 1ZA (inserted by Act of 2012, s. 2A) for the detail.
[101] At <http://www.bankofengland.co.uk/pra/Pages/default.aspx>. The objectives and functions of the PRA are set out in the Act of 2000, s. 2E–I as amended by the Act of 2012, s. 6(1).
[102] See the Act of 2000, s. 55N as amended by the Act of 2012, s. 11.
[103] See the Act of 2000, Sched. 1ZB (inserted by Act of 2012, s. 2A) for the detail.
[104] See Cosmo Graham, *Regulating Public Utilities: A Constitutional Approach* (Oxford: Hart Publishing, 2000) and Walden and Angel (eds.), *Telecommunications Law and Regulation*, 2nd edn (2005).
[105] See generally, 'The Juridification of Regulatory Relations in the UK Utilities Sectors' in Black, Muchlinski and Walker (eds.) (as above), 16.
[106] The Utilities Act 2000, for instance, imposes specific obligations upon the Secretary of State and OFGEM to 'have regard to the interests of the disabled, pensioners and the poor' (s. 9, s. 13).

The regulation of utilities has principally[107] taken the form of a regulator—either a Director-General or a Regulatory Authority—appointed by the Secretary of State, who wields important powers in the interests of consumers, and whose duty it is to promote efficiency and economy and to promote competition.[108]

Under the statutory scheme each supplier must hold a licence from the Secretary of State or the regulator (most frequently the regulator) which is subject to conditions. The regulator can enforce conditions by making orders, either provisional or final, which have no criminal sanction but allow the consumer to recover the loss resulting from a violation. The regulator can refer a practice to the Competition Commission; and if the Commission reports on it adversely the regulator may prohibit or regulate it by varying the conditions of the supplier's licence. The threat of a reference to the Commission is a powerful lever in the regulators' hands. In imposing sanctions the regulator must take account of any representations by the supplier. He may also generally set the price of the service in question. The similarity in these formal arrangements for the regulation of the several public utilities should not conceal the important functional differences between them and the different challenges that they face. Thus the regulation of telecommunications takes place in circumstances of growing competition while there is little possibility of competition in the water industry. Effective competition has been introduced into the supply of gas and electricity.[109]

The regulation of the railways does not follow this pattern, reflecting the fact that British Rail was divided into many different parts before sale to the private sector. The track and other infrastructure (including signalling) is owned by a not for profit company, Network Rail.[110] The Strategic Rail Authority[111] has broad strategic purposes to promote and develop the use of the railway network and to contribute to an integrated system of transport; and to this end, subject to 'directions and guidance' from the Secretary of State,[112] develops strategies to further these purposes.[113] The SRA has a range of functions. Most prominently, it grants franchises to operate trains on the track to private rail companies. The SRA determines the Passenger Service Requirement (PSR), i.e. the standard of service required to be provided on any particular route, and is also responsible for the distribution of public subsidy to the rail companies. The tender process whereby the franchises (and the subsidy that comes with them) are allocated is largely secret.[114] The

---

[107] Other forms of regulatory bodies are the Civil Aviation Authority (Civil Aviation Act 1982), and OFCOM (constituted by the Office of Communications Act 2000 (above, p. 121). For the Press Complaints Commission and the Advertising Standards Authority see below, pp. 544 and 545. The British Airports Authority, now a commercial company, is regulated by the Civil Aviation Authority in conjunction with the Competition Commission under the Airports Act 1986.

[108] Telecommunications Act 1984, s. 1 (Director-General of Telecommunications); Utilities Act 2000, s. 1 (establishing OFGEM); Water Industry Act 1991, s. 1 (Director-General of Water Services).

[109] The Utilities Act 2000, Part II sets the objectives for OFGEM which include promoting competition.

[110] The track and other assets were transferred to Railtrack, whose shares were owned by the Secretary of State, by orders made under the Railways Act 1993, ss. 84, 85. The shares were thereafter sold to the public. After Railtrack went into administration, it was taken over by Network Rail, a company limited by guarantee.

[111] Established by the Transport Act 2000, s. 202. The SRA takes the place of the Director of Rail Franchising (established by the Railways Act 1993, s. 1) and assumes the residual functions of the British Railways Board which is abolished. See s. 215 of the 2000 Act.

[112] Act of 2000, s. 206(3). The courts insisted that the SRA's predecessor comply with such instructions in R v. Director of Passenger Rail Franchising ex p Save Our Railways [1996] CLC 596 (instruction that PSR be based on that provided by BR justified quashing of PSR that fell below that standard).

[113] Act of 2000, s. 206(1).

[114] Harlow and Rawlings, Law and Administration, 2nd edn (1997), 286–7.

SRA also funds rail consultative committees,[115] and may provide grants in support of railway services.[116] As a last resort it may provide rail services itself.[117]

A franchised rail company, however, requires a licence[118] from the Office of Rail Regulation[119] (ORR)—which has many other functions: the promotion of the use of railways, as well as efficiency, economy and competition[120]—and will need to pay an access charge to Network Rail. The Office of Rail Regulation ensures that the track is accessible to those operators needing access;[121] it enforces the conditions in the licences and may make orders to that effect.[122] The Secretary of State has powers to modify the conditions of licences to prevent the development of monopolies.[123] Rail operators are responsible for safety and undergo a validation process by making a safety case to Network Rail which itself is subject to the safety requirements of the Health and Safety Executive.[124] The Secretary of State, the SRA and ORR must take safety (including the advice of the HSE) into account in exercising their functions.[125]

The powers of the utility regulators have been strengthened by the Competition and Service (Utilities) Act 1992, which empowers them to set standards of performance by regulations, with enforcement by the same system as for breaches of conditions in licences. They are empowered also to determine disputes over charges made to customers under regulations made by the Secretary of State, and for their determinations must give reasons. The Act requires each supplier to establish a complaints procedure.

REGULATION AND JUDICIAL REVIEW

The new emphasis on regulation illustrates the changing style of governmental organisation. In the most obvious case of the privatisation of previously nationalised industries the effect has been to shift power from the hands of a minister, accountable to Parliament, into the hands of an independent regulator.[126] Although the regulator is generally appointed by, and may be dismissed by, the relevant minister, accountability to Parliament for the regulation of the activity in question has generally been confined to appearances before Select Committees.[127] That there are important issues of public policy has already been pointed out and the primary concern here must be with the impact of regulatory regimes in administrative law. Judicial review cannot be considered a suitable substitute for Parliamentary accountability and debate on that issue will doubtless continue.[128]

---

[115] Act of 1993, ss. 2 and 3 and Sched. 2 and 3 as amended by the Act of 2000, s. 229 and Sched. 23.

[116] Act of 2000, s. 211. [117] Act of 2000, s. 213. [118] Act of 1993, s. 8.

[119] Act of 1993, s. 1(1)(a) as amended by Sched. 2 to the Railways and Transport Safety Act 2003. The latter Act transferred the functions of the Rail Regulator to the newly created Office of Rail Regulation (ss. 15 and 16). [120] Act of 1993, s. 4, as amended.

[121] Act of 1993, ss. 17, 18, as amended. ORR may require owners of railway facilities to grant access on terms determined by it. See Winsor v. Bloom [2002] 1 WLR 3002 (CA).

[122] Act of 1993, ss. 54, 57, as amended.

[123] Act of 1993, ss. 13, 14, 15. This will typically follow a reference to the Competition Commission by ORR. [124] Health and Safety Executive, Ensuring Safety on Britain's Railways (1993), paras. 5–6.

[125] Act of 1993, s. 4(3) (Secretary of State and Regulator); Act of 2000, s. 207(3) (SRA).

[126] Sometimes, however, a minister may give directions to a regulator. See Fair Trading Act 1973, s. 12 (general directions in regard to priorities); Railways Act 1993, s. 5 (instructions and guidance).

[127] See Prosser, Law and the Regulators, 295 making proposals to improve accountability. And see the House of Lords Constitution Select Committee Report, The Regulatory State: Ensuring its Accountability (May 2004, HL 68) with proposals for improving accountability.

[128] [1990] PL 329 (J. F. Garner); [1991] PL 15 (C. Graham); [2013] JR 116 (C. Knight).

The drastic powers of the regulators to investigate, to make rules, to impute fault and to impose penalties involve a mixture of legislative, administrative and judicial functions and pose obvious problems of administrative justice. As we have seen, a person aggrieved by the actions of a regulator sometimes has a right of appeal to a tribunal and thereafter to a court. On other occasions that person will have little choice but to seek judicial review of the regulator's decision. There is no difficulty over the principle that such decisions are subject to judicial review.[129] Applications for judicial review have been brought against many regulators including the Monopolies and Mergers Commission, the Office of Fair Trading, the Director-Generals of Water, Electricity, Telecommunications, many financial services regulators, the Takeover Panel, the Stock Exchange, the Bank of England, the Independent Television Commission and the Director of Passenger Rail Franchising.[130] It is thus clear that regulators have no immunity from the rule of law. But the success rate of their antagonists has generally been low. One case of success was where a director general's refusal to modify a power generating licence in a complex situation was quashed by the Court of Appeal on grounds of irrationality and unfairness.[131] Another was where the Director-General of Water Services was required by the court to use enforcement powers in the interests of consumers.[132] A third was where one of the railway regulators exceeded his powers in specifying minimum service levels.[133] A fourth was where the National Lottery Commission allowed one bidder for the licence to run the national lottery to improve its bid, but not the other.[134]

But the Court of Appeal has held that in reviewing a regulatory body the courts should allow a margin of appreciation and intervene only in the case of a manifest breach of principle.[135] It has been recognised that 'the [judicial review] courts [can] play a role in overseeing the decision-making process [of regulators] from the perspective of rationality and legality, and ensuring that decisions are made which are not simply pandering to special interests at the expense of wider public policy goals'.[136] It may be expected, however, that the courts will recognise the expertise of the regulators and be cautious before quashing their decisions,[137] and that they will view sympathetically the dilemmas

[129] See below, p. 539. Cf. Hopper (as above) 72–3, pointing to the difficulties in regard to judicial review of bodies that owe their jurisdiction to contract. See, for instance, *R* v. *Insurance Ombudsman Bureau ex p Aegon Life*, The Times, 7 January 1994. Many of the difficulties over the review of self-regulatory organisations such as IMRO (as above) have been resolved by the Financial Services and Markets Act 2000. In appropriate circumstances private law actions may be brought against regulators: [1995] *PL* 539 (A. McHarg) and see below, p. 660 (breach of statutory duty and misfeasance).

[130] See Black, Muchlinski and Walker (eds.) (as above), 4 (Black, Muchlinski). It has been suggested that sometimes this is 'vanity' judicial review, i.e. it is sought simply as a way of publicising the applicant's case ((1996) *Nottingham LJ* 86 (Marsden)).

[131] *R* v. *Director General of Electricity Supply ex p Scottish Power* (CA., 3 February 1997) for which see [1997] *PL* 400 (C. Scott), discussing regulatory licensing and judicial review.

[132] *R* v. *Director General of Water Services ex p Oldham MBC* (1998) 31 HLR 224 (prepayment system evading statutory safeguards against disconnection).   [133] *ex p Save Our Railways* (as above).

[134] *R* v. *National Lottery Commission ex p Camelot Group plc* [2001] EMLR 3.

[135] *R* v. *Radio Authority ex p Bull* [1997] EMLR 201. And see *Wildman* v. *Ofcom* [2005] EWHC 1573 holding that the regulator has 'a wide measure of discretion and width of decision' (para. 67) and recognising the expertise of the regulator (para. 14). See to like effect *R (Nicholds)* v. *Security Industry Authority* [2006] EWHC 1792 (para. 64) and *R (Centro)* v. *Secretary of State for Transport* [2007] EWHC 2729 ('judicial deference…in the context of the review of the decisions of economic regulators' (para. 32)), *R (London and Continental Stations and Property Ltd)* v. *The Rail Regulator* [2003] EWHC 2607 followed. Also *R (Welsh Water)* v. *Water Services Regulation Authority* [2009] EWHC 3493.

[136] Black and Muchlinski (as above), 14.

[137] There has been some criticism of the courts for misunderstanding the system that is being reviewed (Black and Muchlinski (as above), 16).

faced by regulators such as the FCA and PRA who may destroy a viable business if they intervene too soon but may hasten disaster if they delay.[138] Challenges based upon the irrationality of regulators' decisions have generally failed.[139] And the courts have not allowed challenges based upon the Human Rights Act 1998 to undermine the autonomy of regulators.[140]

But there is a case, in appropriate contexts (e.g. where there is no appeal tribunal or similar remedy), for a more intense form of judicial review.[141] It may avoid 'regulatory capture' (where the regulator comes to act in the interests of the regulated) and secures 'meaningful curial oversight' needed to protect market relations and freedoms. Ultimately, it is argued, that the courts should intervene where a decision is disproportionate rather than irrational to secure fairness and proper respect for the rights of the parties.

Although the usual grounds of judicial review apply in this area, one issue is distinct: as observed above, regulators in performing their tasks will often interpret rules which they have made themselves. This has led to suggestions that the courts should only intervene where the interpretation of the rule by the regulator is irrational.[142] The courts, however, have dealt with such rules as if there was a single correct answer to every question of interpretation and from which the regulator could not lawfully deviate.[143] After all, even if the regulator had the power to make a rule in the terms desired, those affected are surely entitled to the application of the rule as it stands. If the regulator's interpretation were only reviewable on the ground of irrationality, the temptation to interpret the rule in the way that the regulator favours rather than in the actual sense of the words would be irresistible. The regulator is invested with legislative power[144] and his rules should be interpreted accordingly.

---

[138] For judicial comments on this dilemma see below, p. 651. The Barlow Clowes affair (above, p. 79) was a classic example. Particular caution may be anticipated over coercive remedies that may make a bad situation worse. See *Wildman*, para. 14 and the discussion below at p. 540.

[139] *R (London and Continental Stations and Property Ltd)* v. *The Rail Regulator* [2003] EWHC 2607 (Rail Regulator's scheme for calculating compensation to rail service operators for disruption held reasonable and not a breach of HRA 1998, 1st Sched. Pt II, Art. 1); *R (Hunt)* v. *Independent Television Commission* [2003] EWCA Civ 81 (decision that television company had not breached the code of practice by failing to broadcast freelance journalist findings on controversial issue held rational). See also *R (B and ors)* v. *Worcestershire County Council* [2009] EWHC 2915. But requirement of regulator to comply with the principle of proportionality recognised by Moses LJ in *British Telecommunications plc* v. *Director General of Telecommunications* (4 August 2000) (European law context); confirmed *R (British Telecom)* v. *Secretary of State for Business, Innovation and Skills* [2011] EWHC 1021, paras. 206–18 (but wide margin of appreciation appropriate in the circumstances) and *R (Mabanaft)* v. *Secretary of State for Energy and Climate Change* [2009] EWCA Civ 224. Similarly, *R (Sinclair Collis Ltd)* v. *Secretary of State for Health* [2011] EWCA Civ 437.

[140] See *R (London and Continental Stations and Property Ltd)* v. *The Rail Regulator* (above) and *Bertrand Fleurose* v. *The Securities & Futures Authority Ltd* [2001] EWCA Civ 2015 (claim by city trader that enforcement action taken against him by the Securities and Futures Authority was in breach of European Convention (allegedly vague charges and absence of equality of arms) rejected by the Court of Appeal. Applicability of Art. 6(1) accepted but not Art. 6(2)).

[141] See, J. Arancibia, *Judicial Review of Commercial Regulation* (2011) from which the quotations in next sentence come. See also the discussion of the review jurisdiction of the CAT, above, p. 119, and the cases there referred to.

[142] Black, Muchlinski and Walker (eds.) (as above), 156 (Black). See also the discussion of the use of 'evaluative words' in statutes (below, p. 214) and *R (Norwich and Peterborough Building Society)* v. *Financial Ombudsman Service Ltd* [2002] EWHC 2379 there discussed.

[143] Black (as above), 138–42 but pointing out that the courts have adopted purposive approaches in such interpretation (relying primarily on *R* v. *Investor Compensation Scheme ex p Weyell* [1994] QB 749 and *R* v. *Investor Compensation Scheme ex p Bowden* [1995] 3 All ER 605 (HL)).   [144] See below, p. 539.

PART III

EUROPEAN INFLUENCES

6

INCORPORATION OF EUROPEAN LAW

INTRODUCTION

The framework of indigenous institutions—Parliament, the executive and the courts—is no longer adequate to contain British constitutional and administrative law. Large and important areas of European law have been incorporated, and effect must be given to the legislation and judicial decisions of international bodies, which may take precedence not only over the common law but also in some cases over Acts of Parliament. Some of their profound effects have already been noted in the context of sovereignty. The European institutions are:

(a) the European Convention on Human Rights and Fundamental Freedoms (ECHR), incorporated by the Human Rights Act 1998, and

(b) the European Union (formerly the European Economic Community), incorporated by the European Communities Act 1972.

These European institutions are in the form of treaties. By virtue of the Acts of Parliament which incorporate them they have become part of the British constitution, but Parliament has no power to amend them, nor do they themselves contain provisions for amendment. Amendment can be effected only by agreement of the Member States, as by the Protocols added to the Convention on Human Rights and the treaties of Maastricht, Amsterdam and Nice in the case of the European Union. The Lisbon Treaty of 2007 (which entered into force in 2009) makes many amendments to the treaties just mentioned as explained herein.

EUROPEAN HUMAN RIGHTS

The European Convention for the Protection of Human Rights and Fundamental Freedoms was adopted by a group of Western European nations in and after 1950.[1] Today it is subscribed to by the forty-seven member states of the Council of Europe with its reach extending far beyond Western Europe. Its purpose was to provide safeguards against the dictatorial and totalitarian forms of government which had led to the Second World War. It took effect as a treaty ('the Treaty of Rome') under the aegis of the Council of Europe, ratified first by Britain and then by other countries.[2] Britain contributed largely

---

[1] The Convention (Cmd 8969) was signed in Rome in 1950 and the First Protocol in Paris in 1952. References to the Convention follow the revised numbering according to the Eleventh Protocol.

[2] For a fascinating account of the background see [1984] *PL* 86 (Lord Lester).

to its drafting, as may be inferred from many of its provisions. It contained a catalogue of human rights and provisions for a Commission and a Court in Strasbourg to ensure their observation. It imposed obligations on the participating governments to secure that their citizens should enjoy the convention rights with effective remedies in the courts of their own countries.[3] It created a new fundamental law based on rights, in contrast to traditional British law based on liberty, which allowed any action not specifically made illegal. In the first instance complaints of breaches could be brought before the Court only by governments against other governments, and then only if endorsed by the Commission. In 1966, however, Britain accepted both the compulsory jurisdiction of the Strasbourg Court and also the right of individual petition[4] (both optional clauses of the Convention), so that a British citizen could take a complaint against his government to Strasbourg, provided that he had first exhausted domestic remedies and was himself a 'victim' of the injustice.[5] The Commission, if it found the complaint admissible, would itself bring the case before the Court, but it became the practice to allow the complainant to be represented also. In 1998 the Commission stage was eliminated and the former part-time Commission and Court were replaced by a single full-time court which sits in several Chambers of seven judges and sometimes in the Grand Chamber of seventeen.[6] Unlike most European courts, it allows dissenting judgments and makes its decisions by majority. There is one judge for each state, nominated by the state and elected by the Parliamentary Assembly.

The Court adopts a 'living instrument' approach to interpretation under which the meaning of the Convention is not constant but is changed by the Court in response to changing circumstances.[7] Pursuant to this approach the 'Court has read into the Convention, rights that are not explicitly mentioned in the text, such as the right of access to Court.[8] [Moreover] the Court has recognised not only rights the drafters could not have intended to protect, such as the right to vote in EU elections,[9] but also rights that they had intended *not* to protect, such the right not to join a trade union.'[10] While some of these extensions of rights might be widely welcomed the legitimacy of this approach has been questioned. Lord Sumption has remarked extra-judicially that 'the effect of this kind of judicial lawmaking...is to take many contentious issues which would previously have been regarded as questions for political debate, administrative discretion or social convention and transform them into questions of law to be resolved by an international judicial tribunal'.[11]

All complaints of violations are made against the country concerned, as for breach of the duty to secure convention rights to its citizens, whether the offending act is that of

[3] Arts. 1, 13.

[4] For the background see [1998] *PL* 237 (Lord Lester). The right of individual petition is now secured by Art. 34.

[5] Arts. 35, 34 respectively. The latter excludes representative claims by trade unions, amenity societies etc., as noted below.

[6] Eleventh Protocol. For details see [1999] *PL* 219 (A. Mowbray). The *Hood* and *Cable* cases (below) were heard by the Grand Chamber.

[7] First articulated in *Tyrer* v. *UK*, A–26, (1978) 2 EHRR 1 and see *Marckx* v. *Belgium* (1979) 2 EHRR 330. For discussion see Letsas, 'The ECHR as a Living Instrument: Its Meaning and its Legitimacy' available at <http://papers.ssrn.com/sol3/papers.cfm?abstract_id=2021836>.

[8] *Golder* v. *UK*, A–18, (1975) 1 EHRR 524.   [9] *Matthews* v. *UK* (1999) 28 EHRR 361.

[10] *Young, James and Webster* v. *UK* (1982) 4 EHRR 38. Letsas, as above, 12.

[11] 'The Limits of Law', p. 8, being the 27th Sultan Azlan Shah Lecture available at <http://www.supreme-court.gov.uk/docs/speech-131120.pdf>.

a government agency or of a private individual.[12] All domestic remedies must first have been exhausted.[13] If a complaint is found admissible the Court will, before proceeding further, attempt to secure a friendly settlement between the parties, often unsuccessfully. If it finds a violation, it will if necessary 'afford just satisfaction to the injured party',[14] usually in the form of money damages and costs, which the Member State has then to pay.

Unlike most of the other participating countries, Britain did not incorporate the Convention into domestic law.[15] Consequently it could not be enforced in British courts, but only by long and costly proceedings in Strasbourg.[16] The judgments of the Strasbourg Court had no legal effect in Britain and the Convention had no more than the force of a treaty. When decisions were given against Britain the government would pay any money award and would take steps to amend the offending law or practice, but British violations, of which there were many,[17] were exposed to international notoriety. Britain had acceded to the Convention on the assumption that British law would satisfy its obligations, but this proved to be far from the case, even the procedure of habeas corpus being found defective.[18] This unsatisfactory state of affairs was constantly criticised, but was defended by previous governments who feared that the judges would become politicised and would acquire too much power. Ultimately all such objections were overcome by the strength and the logic of the demand for incorporation, which was effected by the Human Rights Act 1998, following the White Paper, *Rights Brought Home*.[19]

For a long time before the Act the Convention was habitually invoked in argument in attempts to clothe it with some legal force. These attempts met with some success in cases where the law was uncertain or ambiguous, and the judges, sensing the need for incorporation, became progressively more favourable, aided by a presumption that Parliament would not intend to legislate contrary to treaty obligations,[20] and by recourse to the doctrine of legitimate expectation.[21] In extra-judicial writings eminent judges suggested that the common law itself should adopt fundamental rights on the same lines as the Convention. But Lord Irvine opposed these ambitious theories, accusing them of 'judicial supremacism' prompted by 'extra-judicial romanticism'.[22] Reform by legislation, he said, was the correct constitutional course, and that has now been taken in the Human Rights Act 1998.

The catalogue of the relevant human rights, as set out in the Convention, will be found in Appendix 2 herein. They are reproduced verbatim in the 1st schedule to the Act, with the exception of Articles 1 and 13 which the Act itself effectuates. Article 1 obliges each

---

[12] See e.g. *A* v. *UK* (1999) 27 EHRR 611 (excessive beating of boy by stepfather; stepfather prosecuted but acquitted; court awarded £10,000 against UK for violation of Art. 3).   [13] Art. 35.

[14] Art. 41.

[15] But did so for many British Commonwealth countries by incorporating its primary provisions in their independence constitutions under which appeals came to the Privy Council. See e.g. *Guerra* v. *Baptiste* [1996] AC 397.   [16] The White Paper (Cm. 3782) mentions 5 years and £30,000 as typical.

[17] By 2002 British violations were more numerous than those of any country except Italy.

[18] See below, p. 505.

[19] Cm. 3782 (1997). The sustained and effective advocacy of Lord Lester of Herne Hill gave impetus to the movement for incorporation.

[20] See below, p. 335 for examples. See generally Lester and Pannick (eds.), *Human Rights Law and Practice*, 2nd edn (2004); Janis, Kay and Bradley, *European Human Rights Law*, 2nd edn (2000); Jacobs and White, *The European Convention on Human Rights*, 3rd edn (2002); Harris, O'Boyle and Warbrick, *Law of the European Convention on Human Rights*; Grosz, Beatson and Duffy, *Human Rights: The 1998 Act and the European Convention*; Lord Cooke in [1999] EHRLR 243.   [21] See below, p. 318.

[22] See [1996] *PL* at 77, where Lord Irvine comments on writings of Lord Woolf MR, Laws J and Lord Cooke of Thorndon; and ibid. at 634.

Member State to secure these rights to everyone within its jurisdiction. Article 13 requires effective domestic remedies.

Most of the rights have qualifications attached to them, the only exceptions being the prohibition of torture and inhuman or degrading treatment or punishment (Article 3), the prohibition of slavery or servitude (Article 4), the prohibition of retrospective criminal liability (Article 7) and the right to marry according to national laws (Article 12). The right to life (Article 2) has to be qualified so as to allow capital punishment and the prohibition of forced labour (Article 4) has to allow for military service and other obligations. The right to personal liberty and security (Article 5), which includes the right to challenge the lawfulness of detention, has numerous exceptions for lawful restraints. The right to a fair and public trial in both civil and criminal matters (Article 6), together with a list of consequential rights, allows for the exclusion of the press and the public on justifiable grounds. Articles 8 to 11 form a group, since they have one special qualification. They provide respectively for respect for private and family life, for freedom of thought, conscience and religion, for freedom of expression and for freedom of assembly and association. The special qualification which is common to all four of them is that any legal restriction upon them may only be such as is 'necessary in a democratic society' for the protection of public order, health or morals or for the protection of the rights of others (ignoring a few differences of wording). Nothing, perhaps, in the Convention better illustrates the new world of interpretation that will confront the judiciary under these clauses. How are they to establish objective standards of democratic necessity? Britain has often been condemned in Strasbourg for laws which failed to pass this test, as in the *Thalidomide*[23] and *Spycatcher*[24] cases (both decisions of the House of Lords). More recently, there was another example, when the Court in Strasbourg held that the statutory limit of £5 on publications in favour of a particular candidate in the period just before an election was disproportionate and so unnecessary in a democratic society.[25] In addition there is the right of property in the First Protocol, which is qualified so as to allow compulsory purchase 'in the public interest'.[26] This protocol provides also for the right to education and the right to free elections. The Sixth Protocol provides for the abolition of the death penalty except in time of war.[27] The Convention has no provision against unreasonable searches and seizures, except through the right of privacy under Article 8, and nothing about the rights of employees, except for the right to join, or not to join, trade unions under Article 11 (freedom of association). It does contain a full anti-discrimination clause (Article 14), but that applies only to the rights specifically protected by the Convention.

Britain has at various times been found by the Strasbourg Court to be in breach of nearly all of the Convention rights. Even the right to life in Article 2 was held violated by the shooting of IRA terrorists by the SAS in Gibraltar in 1988, though only by the votes of ten judges against nine.[28] The right to life, which by Article 2 'shall be protected by law', has been extended by the Strasbourg Court to require a Member State to protect witnesses in legal proceedings or inquiries whose lives might be in danger and to require an effective official investigation where a person has been killed by the use of force—and both

---

[23] *Sunday Times* v. *UK*, A–30, (1979) 2 EHRR 245 (articles intended to help claims by parents of deformed babies prohibited by injunction. Held (by 11 votes to 9) to violate Art. 10, there being no 'pressing social need').

[24] *Observer and Guardian* v. *UK*, A–216, (1991) 14 EHRR 153 (injunction against book revealing official espionage operations but published in the USA held (unanimously) to violate Art. 10; £100,000 costs awarded).   [25] *Bowman* v. *UK* (1998) 26 EHRR 1.

[26] See Appendix 2.   [27] Incorporated in the Human Rights Act 1998, 1st Sched., Pt III.

[28] *McCann* v. *UK*, A–324, (1995) 21 EHRR 97.

requirements have been violated by British decisions, though corrected on appeal.[29] The UK was held liable in respect of inhuman and degrading treatment in the neglect of child welfare by local authorities.[30] Many violations have been found in Acts of Parliament, for example in the legislation on court martial procedures,[31] on trade union closed shops,[32] on homosexual acts in private,[33] on the use of evidence obtained by compulsion,[34] and, as already mentioned, electoral expenses. The Court makes much use of the doctrine of proportionality in condemning restrictions or penalties which are unduly severe. On the other hand it may allow a 'margin of appreciation' to a defendant government, recognising that the national authorities may be the best judges of what measures are suitable or necessary in the circumstances of their own countries, for example as to whether there is a 'public emergency' or a need for 'the protection of morals' and whether the measures are 'strictly required'.[35] But this indulgence is an uncertain quantity. It was not allowed, for example, in the Gibraltar case, despite the deep division among the judges, nor where juvenile murderers were tried in an ordinary court,[36] yet it was allowed in resisting complaints of inadequate compensation on the nationalisation of a shipbuilding company[37] and in the expropriation of certain landlords 'in the public interest'.[38] Nor was it allowed where members of the armed forces were discharged under a policy prohibiting homosexuality, despite the fact that national defence policy might best be left to the national government.[39] The doctrines of proportionality and margin of appreciation are closely connected and often invoked in the same judgment. Prisoners have been a successful class of litigants, for example where the Parole Board's procedures and the scope of judicial review were both found inadequate.[40] Complaints made good against the British government range in importance from the shooting of Irish terrorists to the birching of a schoolboy under the order of a juvenile court.[41] More examples will be found later in this chapter where government liability is illustrated.[42]

All such proceedings arise under the government's primary duties, 'to secure to every-one within their jurisdiction the rights and freedoms defined' etc. (Article 1), and to provide 'an effective remedy before a national authority' (Article 13). Where the domestic remedy is inadequate 'The Court shall if necessary award just satisfaction to the injured party.'[43] It is a firm rule that domestic remedies must first be exhausted[44] and that will now include remedies under the Human Rights Act 1998. There is a time limit

---

[29] *R (A) v. Lord Saville of Newdigate* [2002] 1 WLR 1249 (protection of witnesses at the tribunal of inquiry into deaths in Northern Ireland on 'bloody Sunday' in 1972) and holding the (statutory) tribunal to be a 'public authority'; *R (Amin) v. Home Secretary* [2003] 3 WLR 1169 (murder of prisoner—duty of investigation not satisfied where next of kin unable to participate to safeguard their legitimate interests). But the Art. 2 duty does not extend to the government taking reasonable steps to satisfy itself as to the legality of the invasion of another country (*R (Gentle) v. The Prime Minister* [2008] UKHL 20).

[30] *Z v. UK* (2002) 34 EHRR 97 (damages awarded).

[31] *Findlay v. UK* (1997) 24 EHRR 221. See similarly *Coyne v. UK*, The Times, 24 October 1997; *Hood v. UK* (2000) 29 EHRR 365; and *Cable v. UK* (2000) 30 EHRR 1032. The law was changed by the Armed Forces Act 1996.   [32] *Young, James and Webster v. UK*, A–44, (1982) 4 EHRR 38.

[33] *Dudgeon v. UK*, A–45, (1981) 4 EHRR 149.   [34] *Saunders v. UK* (1997) 23 EHRR 313.

[35] See *Handyside v. UK*, A–24, (1976) 1 EHRR 737.

[36] *T and V v. UK* (2000) 30 EHRR 121 (discretion in enforcing law against obscene publications). See also *Rees v. UK* (1987) 9 EHRR 56.   [37] *Lithgow v. UK*, A–102, (1986) 8 EHRR 429.

[38] *James v. UK*, A–98, (1986) 8 EHRR 123 (unsuccessful complaint by the Duke of Westminster's trustees against the expropriating provisions of the Leasehold Reform Act 1967).

[39] *Smith and Grady v. UK* (1999) 29 EHRR 493.

[40] *Weeks v. UK*, A–114, (1987) 10 EHRR 293; *Thynne, Wilson and Gunnell v. UK*, A–190, (1990) 13 EHRR 666.

[41] *Tyrer v. UK*, A–26, (1978) 2 EHRR 1.   [42] Below, p. 635.

[43] Art. 41. As to this see below, p. 635.   [44] Art. 35.

of six months from the final domestic decision.[45] It is always possible that a litigant may claim that a British judgment does not fulfil his human rights and then take his case to the Strasbourg Court, which will necessarily remain as the ultimate tribunal. This has happened many times.

THE HUMAN RIGHTS ACT 1998

The general structure of the Act

The Act of 1998[46] came fully into force on 2 October 2000.[47] For the sake of clarity the following account of it describes its main features. The numerous subsequent judicial decisions that have added flesh to the bones of the Act have raised a range of important questions which are discussed separately elsewhere. First the general structure of the Act.

The central provision of the Act is in section 6:

6(1) It is unlawful for a public authority to act in a way which is incompatible with a Convention right.

The Convention rights are set out in a schedule which quotes the articles of the Convention verbatim and with the same numbering, including the First and Sixth Protocols but omitting Articles 1 and 13. The contents of the schedule are reproduced in Appendix 2, together with the two omitted articles. The scheduled articles 'are to have effect for the purposes of this Act'.

'Public authority' is not defined with any precision. It 'includes (a) a court or tribunal, and (b) any person certain of whose functions are functions of a public nature', but in relation to a particular act a person is not a public authority by virtue only of (b) 'if the nature of the Act is private'.[48] A 'public authority', accordingly, is defined by the nature of its functions and not by the possession of any particular authority or power. Furthermore, it comes within the definition only in respect of its public, as opposed to its private, functions. Two examples were given by the Lord Chancellor in Parliament: doctors with both National Health Service patients and private patients would be public authorities in respect of the former but not of the latter; and Railtrack would have public functions in relation to railway safety but private functions as a property developer.[49] As explained

---

[45] Art. 35.

[46] See especially (in abundant literature) Clayton and Tomlinson, *The Law of Human Rights* (with annual supplements); Lester and Pannick, *Human Rights Law and Practice*, 2nd edn (2004); Grosz, Beatson and Duffy, *Human Rights: The 1998 Act and The European Convention*; [1999] *CLJ* 509 (I. Leigh and L. Lustgarten); [1999] *PL* 221 (Lord Irvine), 254 (Sir John Laws); [2003] *PL* 308 (Lord Irvine); Fenwick, Phillipson and Masterman, *Judicial Reasoning under the UK Human Rights Act* (2007). See also Gearty, *Principles of Human Rights Adjudication* (2004).

[47] The 1998 Act is not retrospective, so no rights arise under the Act prior to it coming into force (in October 2000). Violations of rights prior to the 1998 Act coming into force, of course, continue to be able to be vindicated by petition to Strasbourg. See *Re McKerr* [2004] UKHL 12 resolving conflicting decisions of other courts (paras. 25–6). *McKerr* concerned the failure properly to investigate the fatal shooting of a civilian by the Royal Ulster Constabulary in breach of Art. 2 (so held by the ECtHR (*McKerr* v. *UK* (2002) 34 EHRR 20) but no remedy under the 1998 Act was available. There is limited retrospective effect provided for in s. 22(4) when a public authority (for instance, a prosecuting authority) brings proceedings. See *R* v. *Lambert* [2001] 3 WLR 206. [48] s. 6(3), (5).

[49] 583 HL Deb. 811 (24 November 1997). But in *Cameron* v. *Network Rail Infrastructure Ltd* [2006] EWHC 1133 it was said that 'running a railway is not intrinsically an activity of government' (para. 29). But by this stage Railtrack had lost its safety functions so the point no longer arises (see above, p. 122).

later the question whether the Act applies where a private body performs a function for a public body has proved controversial.[50]

The definition of 'public authority' was deliberately left vague in order that the courts might make it correspond with the Strasbourg jurisprudence as to bodies which are 'sufficiently public to engage the responsibility of the state'.[51] It is thought that it will cover the BBC, privatised utilities and the Jockey Club, in view of their public functions, so that it may not exactly match the 'public element' which governs the scope of judicial review.[52] The elastic definition and the dichotomy of functions which it demands plainly represent a fertile source of difficulty.[53] These difficulties are further discussed elsewhere.[54]

Courts and tribunals are required by the Act to take account of decisions and opinions of the European Court of Human Rights (sometimes known colloquially as the 'Strasbourg Court' to avoid confusion with the Court of Justice of the European Union[55]) and of the Commission and the Committee of Ministers.[56] In proceedings against public authorities the Court may 'grant such relief or remedy, or make such order, within its powers as it considers just and appropriate'.[57] But it may do so only in favour of a 'victim', since the Convention itself contains this restriction on standing, so that, in contrast to British law, representative bodies such as trade unions and amenity societies cannot sue on behalf of their members.[58] Corporate bodies may themselves have human rights.[59] A 'victim' includes a person at risk of a violation of their Convention rights.[60]

There is a time limit of one year, in the absence of any stricter period, but this may be extended if that is held to be equitable.[61] Relief against judicial acts may be sought only by way of appeal or judicial review, unless rules prescribe otherwise; but it may include damages, which are to be awarded against the Crown, the appropriate minister being made a party.[62] The provisions as to remedies and time limits relate only to proceedings against public authorities; but the requirement to follow the jurisprudence of the Strasbourg Court is not so confined, and that may suffice to supply remedies in proceedings between private parties since the Strasbourg Court commonly awards damages and costs.

---

[50] Below, p. 146.

[51] See the Home Secretary's explanation in (1998) 314 HC Deb. 406, 432 (17 June 1998) and other ministerial statements quoted in Lester and Pannick, *Human Rights Law and Practice*, 30.

[52] See below, p. 532.

[53] Compare the definition in the Public Authorities Protection Act 1893.   [54] Below, p. 146.

[55] Above, p. 160.   [56] s. 2.

[57] s. 8. This is substituted for Art. 13 of the Convention, omitted by the Act as already noted.

[58] s. 7, following Art. 34 of the Convention. See [2000] *CLJ* 133 (J. Miles). See also *Re Medicaments and Related Classes of Goods (No 4)* [2002] 1 WLR 269 (trade association not 'victim').

[59] *County Properties Ltd* v. *Scottish Ministers*, 2000 SLT 965, *The Children's Rights Alliance for England* v. *Secretary of State for Justice* [2012] EWHC 8 (registered charity not 'a victim') and *Northern Ireland Commissioner for Children and Young People, Re Application for Judicial Review* [2007] NIQB 115 (Children's Commissioner established by statutory order not 'a victim'). Note that the Equality Act 2006, s. 30(3)(a) provides that Commission for Equality and Human Rights may institute proceedings for breach of Convention rights and 'need not be a victim or potential victim of the unlawful act'. A non-departmental statutory corporation asserted Art. 1 Protocol 1 rights without comment in *Olympic Delivery Authority* v. *Persons Unknown* [2012] EWHC 1012. But note criticism in Alexander Williams 'The Scope of Section 6 HRA Revisited' at <http://ukconstitutionallaw.org/2013/10/28/alexander-williams-the-scope-of-section-6-hra-revisited/>.

[60] *R (Countryside Alliance)* v. *A-G* [2006] EWCA Civ 817, para. 65 applying *Marckx* v. *Belgium* (1979) 2 EHRR 330. Cf. *Re Judicial Review* [2011] NIQB 5 (a child challenging the introduction of tasers to Northern Ireland not a 'victim').   [61] s. 7(5).

[62] s. 9.

Reconciling the protection of human rights with the supremacy of Parliament

Human rights under the Convention may conflict with Acts of Parliament, as already mentioned, and have done so frequently. The Act addresses this problem with a remarkable amalgam of judicial, legislative and administrative procedures, designed to respect the sovereignty of Parliament while at the same time protecting human rights. In the first place, the court must strive to avoid conflict by benevolent construction. But if that proves impossible, the court may make a 'declaration of incompatibility', whereupon it is for the government and Parliament to take 'remedial action' if they think fit. This is a very different policy from that of the European Communities Act 1972, which incorporated the law of the European Union by providing simply that it should prevail with paramount effect, overriding the sovereignty of Parliament whenever necessary.[63]

The rule of construction is that legislation, both primary and subordinate, and whenever enacted, must be 'read and given effect in a way which is compatible with the Convention rights' 'so far as it is possible to do so'.[64] In other words, instead of seeking the true intention of Parliament at the time of the enactment, the court must adopt the interpretation which is the more favourable to a Convention right. The model for this provision was the New Zealand Bill of Rights Act 1990,[65] though the wording is marginally different. It has been said on high authority that the British formula is slightly stronger.[66]

If no such solution is possible, the court may make a 'declaration of incompatibility'.[67] The declaration must be made at High Court level or above; it does not affect the validity, continuing operation or enforcement of the offending legislation; it is not binding on the parties; and before it is made the Crown must be notified, whereupon a minister or his nominee may be joined as a party.[68] The procedure applies to primary legislation[69] and also to secondary (i.e. delegated) legislation where primary legislation prevents removal of the incompatibility.[70]

Where a declaration of incompatibility is made, and no appeal is pending, or where an incompatibility is revealed by a later decision of the Strasbourg Court, the appropriate minister must consider whether there are 'compelling reasons' for amending the conflicting legislation. If so, he 'may by order make such amendments to the legislation as he considers necessary to remove the incompatibility'.[71] This is a 'remedial order', which must first be laid in draft before Parliament for sixty days with an explanatory statement and approved by resolution of each House. The order may be retrospective to an earlier date, may delegate functions, may amend or repeal any primary or subordinate legislation, but it may not impose criminal guilt retrospectively. The minister may omit to seek Parliamentary resolutions if reasons of urgency make that necessary, but the order must

---

[63] See below, p. 158.

[64] s. 3. See the wide-ranging discussion by Lord Irvine LC, [1999] EHRLR 350. See also [2000] PL 77 (F. Bennion).

[65] s. 6, providing: 'Wherever an enactment can be given a meaning that is consistent with the rights and freedoms contained in this Bill of Rights, that meaning shall be preferred to any other meaning.'

[66] See 583 HL Deb. 1272 (3 November 1997) (Lord Cooke of Thorndon), repeated in R v. Director of Public Prosecutions ex p Kebilene [1999] 3 WLR 972 ('a rather more powerful message') and in [1999] EHRLR 243.

[67] s. 4.

[68] s. 5. Notice should be given as soon as the question of incompatibility is raised: Gunn v. Newman, 2001 SLT 776.

[69] Defined in s. 21(1) and including inter alia prerogative (i.e. non-statutory) Orders in Council.

[70] s. 4.   [71] s. 10.

be laid before Parliament later and will cease to have effect if not approved by resolution of each House.[72]

Constitutional objections to the declaration of incompatibility and remedial orders

This novel procedure was approved by authoritative speakers in the Parliamentary debates as an ingenious method of reconciling fundamental rights with Parliamentary sovereignty. It also allayed fears about giving too much power to the judiciary, and judicial reluctance to sit in judgment on the validity of primary legislation. But these comforts can be obtained only by the sacrifice of constitutional principle. When the minister decides whether or not to make a remedial order, and if so whether it shall be retrospective, he is in effect deciding which party is to win the case: shall it be he whose human rights have been violated, or shall it be he who is in the right under the existing law? The minister's dilemma is likely to be invidious, particularly since the government will often be a party, there may be much money at stake and Parliamentary resolutions may be opposed. But the most serious objection is constitutional. How can it accord with the rule of law to allow the rights of litigants to be determined by executive and legislative discretion? The European Convention itself provides, as does the Act, that 'in the determination of his civil rights and obligations or of any criminal charge against him, everyone is entitled to a fair and public hearing within a reasonable time by an independent and impartial tribunal established by law'.[73] Political decisions by ministers are the reverse of the judicial process required by this fundamental right.[74] Perhaps the only way out of this dilemma, will be for the government to compensate the party damnified either by the remedial order or by a failure to make it, in order to prevent that party from winning an award against it in Strasbourg. But there is still the ironical prospect that the 1998 Act itself may be held to violate the Convention by requiring individual rights to be determined by non-judicial bodies. The ultimate conclusion may be that fundamental rights and Parliamentary sovereignty are, in fact, irreconcilable.

Subordinate legislation

Where subordinate legislation cannot be brought into line with Convention rights without amending primary legislation, it falls under the provisions about declarations of incompatibility discussed above. In other cases of incompatibility the court will have to declare the offending regulations invalid, or disapply them, since under section 6 of the Act it cannot lawfully decide otherwise. The minister who made the regulations will normally have power to amend and so rectify them. He may likewise rectify regulations shown to be incompatible by a later decision of the Strasbourg Court.[75]

Other features of the Act

A minister in charge of a Bill in either House of Parliament is required by the Act to make a written statement, to be published as he thinks best, before Second Reading, saying

---

[72] s. 10 and 2nd Sched.

[73] Art. 6. For this see below, p. 374 (natural justice). For the right to a judicial determination see *Golder* v. *UK*, A–18, (1975) 1 EHRR 524.

[74] But that litigants' rights were intended to be determined in this way is corroborated by the Lord Chancellor in the debates on the Bill: 853 HL Deb. 1108 (27 November 1997). See Grosz, Beatson and Duffy, *Human Rights*, 149, 150.   [75] s. 10.

either that in his view the Bill is compatible with Convention rights or else that, though he cannot make such a statement, the government wishes to proceed with the Bill.[76]

The Convention allows Member States to limit their commitments by derogations and reservations for special reasons. The United Kingdom made a derogation for anti-terrorism laws in Northern Ireland, permitting extended periods of detention without charge, and also a reservation under the First Protocol limiting the right of parental choice in education to what is compatible with efficiency and economy. The texts are scheduled to the Act, which empowers the Secretary of State to amend the schedule as may be required and provides, among other things, for the periodic review of reservations.[77] A further derogation was made in 2001 providing for detention of suspected international terrorists.[78]

The Secretary of State may by order amend the Act so as to accord with any protocol to the Convention.[79]

There are detailed provisions for allowing judges of the Court of Appeal and the High Court and Circuit judges, and their equivalents in Scotland and Northern Ireland, to be appointed to the European Court of Human Rights at Strasbourg, retaining their offices but not their domestic duties.[80] At the time of enactment proposals for a standing commission on human rights were rejected by the government as premature. But in 2006 the Equalities and Human Rights Commission was established[81] with a general duty to encourage the respect for and protection of individual human rights including many other worthy goals (for instance, respect for 'dignity and worth' of individuals).[82]

Parts of the 1998 Act, including the provision for compatibility statements by ministers in charge of Bills, were brought into force in 1999. The principal provisions, however, came into force on 2 October 2000.

Freedom of expression, thought and religion

When the Bill was before Parliament there was anxiety about the possible inhibiting effect of the right of privacy (Article 8) on the right to freedom of expression (Article 10). The right of privacy is strong in Strasbourg but weak in Britain, and it was feared by the media that incorporation of the Convention might mean 'an end to investigative journalism'.[83] Two amendments were made in order to allay these fears.[84] First, where the grant of relief might affect the right to freedom of expression, the court must have particular regard to the importance of that right; and in the case of what is claimed to be journalistic, literary or artistic material, the court must consider how far the material may be publicly available or its publication may be in the public interest, together with any relevant privacy code. Secondly, if the respondent is neither present nor represented, no relief is to be granted unless the court is satisfied that the applicant has taken all practicable steps to notify the respondent or that there are compelling reasons why he cannot do so; and there is to be no restraint on publication before trial unless the court is satisfied that the applicant is

---

[76] s. 19. Parliament has established a Joint Committee on Human Rights, which considers matters relating to human rights in the United Kingdom (but not individual cases). Scrutiny of remedial orders (below, p. 152) is within its remit. For discussion see [2002] PL 323 (D. Feldman).

[77] ss. 14–17 and 3rd Sched.

[78] Derogation Order made on 11 November 2001 (SI 2001 No. 1644), discussed in *A* v. *Home Secretary* [2003] 2 WLR 564. See also Anti-terrorism, Crime and Security Act 2001, s. 30.   [79] s. 1(4).

[80] s. 18 and 4th Sched. Bratza J was appointed as the British judge in 1998.

[81] Equality Act 2006, s. 1.   [82] s. 3.

[83] See 583 HL Deb. 773 (24 November 1997) (Lord Wakeham). See also [1998] PL 254 at 262 (Sir John Laws).   [84] s. 12.

likely to establish his case. The object of this provision is to prevent 'midnight injunctions' being granted *ex parte* to stifle publication of news, except where a strong case can be shown.

This provision shows, incidentally, that the government expected the Act to have 'horizontal effect', as discussed later, since newspapers are not public authorities.

The anxieties of religious bodies led to a further amendment requiring the court to have particular regard to the importance of the right to freedom of thought, conscience and religion where the court's determination might affect the exercise of that right by a religious organisation.[85] The purport of this amendment is far from clear.

THE HUMAN RIGHTS ACT 1998 IN OPERATION

The impact on administrative law

No measure of law reform has had such wide and profound effects on administrative law as has the HRA.[86] Section 6, by providing that it is unlawful for public authorities to act incompatibly with Convention rights, sets new perimeters to the powers of public authorities. A public authority acts beyond its powers if it breaches a Convention right and the task of the judicial review court is simply to keep the authority within its powers.[87] But this means that in principle any breach of Convention rights can be raised in a challenge to a public authority's decision. It would be quite impossible in this book to give an adequate account of every human rights point that might be raised in litigation with a public authority. There are specialist texts (about human rights rather than administrative law) to which reference may be made.[88] But an account must be given in this book of those rights (e.g. procedural rights) of particular importance to administrative law and to those that engage the exercise of discretion. The most prominent of these is the doctrine of proportionality, but an account will also be given of the prohibition against discrimination.

The Article most frequently invoked has perhaps been Article 6, giving the right to the determination of civil rights and criminal liabilities by a fair and public hearing within a reasonable time by an independent and impartial tribunal. Although the Article's demands often mirror those of the common law, its uncompromising terms have encouraged the courts to enforce it in many cases where the more tolerant common law would have allowed exceptions or qualifications. The whole of this subject, both in its domestic and its European aspects, belongs to a later part of this book and need not be investigated here. Likewise the right to liberty and security is discussed later in the context of habeas corpus.

The doctrine of proportionality is becoming ever more prominent, extending the scope of judicial review in human rights cases and perhaps indirectly in the common law also. Very frequently a restriction of a Convention right is alleged and the question becomes whether that may be justified by showing a pressing social need proportionate to the restriction. As will be seen a 'structured proportionality test' has emerged and discussions and debates about the test are endless.[89] What is emerging here is a culture of rights

---

[85] s. 13, discussed but not clarified in *R (Williamson)* v. *Secretary of State for Education and Employment* [2003] 3 WLR 482.

[86] See the assessment by Lord Irvine in [2003] *PL* 308; [2003] *JR* 221 (T. de la Mare and D. Pievsky); and [2002] EHRLR 175 (R. Clayton).

[87] For a persuasive account of the constitutional law of the Act and how it is reconciled with orthodox approaches to judicial review, see Elliott, 'Fundamental Rights as Interpretative Constructs' in Forsyth (ed.) *Judicial Review and the Constitution* (2000) at 269.   [88] Above, p. 131, n. 20 and p. 134, n. 46.

[89] See below, pp. 150 and 306.

in which the crucial question will be whether a restriction of a right is justified.[90] The effect of this reorientation on administrative law is enormous as will be seen throughout this book.

In this flood of enthusiasm for rights based judicial review some sense of perspective should be retained. There are many areas of the law in which human rights issues play only a small or peripheral part.[91] Moreover, even in the most prominent human rights cases, classical administrative law questions will often arise and may be determinative of the outcome.[92] The procedural law that makes the application for judicial review possible remains in place and is the necessary undercarriage for every human rights challenge. Classical administrative law may be transformed by the 1998 Act, it has not been abolished.[93]

The status of decisions of the Human Rights Court

Section 2(1) of the 1998 Act provides that 'a court or tribunal determining a question which has arisen in connection with a Convention right must take into account any…judgment, decision, declaration or advisory opinion of the European Court of Human Rights[94]…whenever made or given, so far as, in the opinion of the court or tribunal, it is relevant to the proceedings'.[95] While such case law is not 'strictly binding' the courts are bound, so Lord Bingham has said, 'in the absence of some special circumstances [to] follow any clear and constant jurisprudence of the Strasbourg court'.[96]

Later in the same speech Lord Bingham used words that have become canonical to describe the duty to ensure uniform interpretation of the Convention: 'It is of course open to member states to provide for rights more generous than those guaranteed by the Convention, but such provision should not be the product of interpretation of the Convention by national courts, since the meaning of the Convention should be uniform throughout the states party to it. The duty of national courts is to keep pace with the Strasbourg jurisprudence as it evolves over time: no more, but certainly no less.'[97]

[90] For a stimulating discussion see Poole, 'Between the Devil and the Deep Blue Sea: Administrative Law in an Age of Rights', *LSE Law, Society and Economy Working Papers 9/2008* available at <http://www.lse.ac.uk/collections/law/wps/>.

[91] For instance, in the judicial review of regulators and commercial judicial review. But also Art. 6(1) is not applicable to many parts of the administrative machine (below, p. 240) and in these areas procedural justice does not depend upon the Convention.

[92] See, for instance, the points of classical administrative law raised (in addition to the human rights points) in the 'control order' cases in the House of Lords. Above, p. 67 and Forsyth, (2008) 67 *CLJ* 1.

[93] There have been several scholarly opinions expressed to the effect that English administrative law is being reformed or reinvented and in the future judicial review will be rights based, by which is understood that the crucial questions will in all cases be whether a right (either from the ECHR or the common law) has been infringed and whether that infringement is justified. See 'The Reformation of English Administrative Law' (2009) 68 *CLJ* 142 (Poole) and 'Reinventing Administrative Law' (Taggart) in Bamforth and Leyland (eds.), *Public Law in a Multi-Layered Constitution* (Hart 2003), ch. 12, 331–4. But as is plain at many points throughout this book, while the impact of the 1998 Act is profound and transformative classical administrative law remains a vital part of our subject. For a critical discussion see 'The Reformation of English Administrative Law? "Rights", Rhetoric and Reality' [2013] *CLJ* 369–413 (Jason) (drawing attention to the conceptual weakness of these views and their vagueness).

[94] Account must also be taken of other less important materials such as decisions and opinions of the Commission (Act of 1998, s. 2(1)(b), (c) and (d)).

[95] See the thoughtful account by Masterman in Fenwick, Phillipson and Masterman (eds.), *Judicial Reasoning under the UK Human Rights Act* (2007), 97.

[96] *R (Ullah)* v. *Special Adjudicator* [2004] UKHL 26, [2004] 2 AC 323, para. 20 (Lord Bingham) following *R (Alconbury Developments Ltd)* v. *Secretary of State for the Environment, Transport and the Regions* [2001] UKHL 23, [2003] 2 AC 295, para. 26.

[97] Ibid. *Ullah* has since being followed many times with this dictum being cited with approval. *Black* v. *Wilkinson* [2013] EWCA Civ 820, para. 28; *Smith* v. *The Ministry of Defence* [2013] UKSC 41, para. 43; *R*

This approach is consistent with the purpose of the 1998 Act as being simply to secure for the individual the benefit of protection of their rights in the domestic courts rather than requiring them to petition Strasbourg. But the following of the 'clear and constant jurisprudence' is not without its critics.[98] As Laws LJ has remarked 'the English court is not a Strasbourg surrogate... [O]ur duty is to develop by the common law's incremental method, a coherent and principled domestic law of human rights... [T]reating the ECHR text as a template for our own law runs the risk of an over-rigid approach'.[99] The same judge has called for the principle just described to 'be revisited' so that 'a municipal jurisprudence' of human rights might develop as part of domestic law.[100] Other judges have spoken of applying the 'principles' gleaned from the Strasbourg decisions rather than treating them as precedents to be followed.[101] And Lord Hope has said that the 'Strasbourg jurisprudence is not to be treated as a straightjacket from which there is no escape.'[102] Lord Steyn has drawn a distinction between the content of the right defined by an article of the Convention and the question of objective justification for restrictions of it. A uniform interpretation had to be adopted to determine the content of the right while the distinctive cultural traditions of the UK would bear on the latter question and influence the conclusion whether the restriction was justified or not.[103]

But notwithstanding these weighty views the House of Lords and the Supreme Court have several times followed Lord Bingham's approach.[104] Whatever its defects it has the advantage, where there is clear Strasbourg jurisprudence, of bringing clarity in an area where this is much needed. Moreover, Convention jurisprudence has even been relied upon to guide the interpretation of the 1998 Act itself since it ensures coherence between an individual's rights in domestic law and before the Strasbourg Court.[105] But some flexibility remains. The local court, and the Supreme Court in particular, 'is not bound to

---

(The Children's Rights Alliance for England) v. *The Secretary of State for Justice* [2013] EWCA Civ 34, para. 49 (but note postscript paras. 62–4). *Ambrose* v. *Harris, Procurator Fiscal, Oban* (Scotland) [2011] UKSC 43, paras. 17, 18, 19, 86. And see *R (Chester)* v. *Secretary of State for Justice* [2013] UKSC 63 where the Supreme Court applied *Hirst* v. *UK (No 2)* (2005) 42 EHRR 41 (holding that the blanket disenfranchisement of prisoners in the UK was a breach of Art. 3 of Protocol No. 1 (the duty to hold free and fair elections)). And see *Home Secretary* v. *AF* [2009] UKHL 28 (discussed, 434-5).

[98] See Masterman, above.

[99] *R (ProLife Alliance)* v. *BBC* [2002] EWCA Civ 297, [2002] 3 WLR 1080, paras. 33–4.

[100] *The Children's Rights Alliance* (above), para. 64. And see also Laws LJ's Third Hamlyn Lecture, 'The Common law and Europe', paras. 34–8 available at <http://www.judiciary.gov.uk/Resources/JCO/Documents/Speeches/laws-lj-speech-hamlyn-lecture-2013.pdf>.

[101] For instance, Lord Sutherland in *Clancy* v. *Caird*, 2000 SLT 546, para. 3.

[102] *Re P* [2008] UKHL 38, para. 50.

[103] *R (S)* v. *Chief Constable of South Yorkshire Police* [2004] UKHL 39, [2004] 1 WLR 2196, at para. 27. Lord Steyn used Art. 8 as an example. But his is but a concrete example of a more general difficulty. The 'margin of appreciation' accorded to national states by Strasbourg 'is not concerned with the separation of powers within the Member State. When it says that a question is within the margin of appreciation of a Member State, it is not saying that the decision must be made by the legislature, the executive or the judiciary. That is a matter for the Member State' (Lord Hoffmann in *Re. P*, above, para. 32) and something that is not uniform across the Member States. See below, p. 308 for discussion of the 'margin of discretion' which takes the place of the 'margin of appreciation' at the domestic level.

[104] For instance, *Huang* v. *Home Secretary* [2007] UKHL 11, [2007] 2 WLR 58; *R (Animal Defenders International)* v. *Secretary of State for Culture, Media and Sport* [2008] UKHL 15, paras. 37 (Lord Bingham) and 53 (Baroness Hale). But contrast Lord Scott at paras. 44–5. And see the more recent cases cited earlier, n 97 for the application of the *Ullah* principle in the Supreme Court.

[105] See, for instance, *R (Al-Skeini)* v. *Defence Secretary* [2007] UKHL 26, [2007] 3 WLR 33 (HL) and *R (Quark Fishing Ltd)* v. *Secretary of State for Foreign and Commonwealth Affairs* [2005] UKHL 57, [2006] 1 AC 529 (extraterritorial effect of the 1998 Act (Lord Bingham dissenting in *Quark*)) and *YL* v. *Birmingham City Council* [2007] UKHL 27, [2007] 3 WLR 112 (meaning of 'public function' in s. 6(1)(b)).

follow every decision of the European court... [as this] would destroy the ability of the court to engage in the constructive dialogue with the European court which is of value to the development of Convention law'.[106] There are prominent examples of the 'clear and consistent' jurisprudence not being followed[107] but, even where flaws are identified in the Strasbourg jurisprudence, the general pattern is to follow it.[108]

Notwithstanding the clarity of the formal law requiring the clear and consistent jurisprudence to be followed, tensions remain. Lord Judge, the retired Lord Chief Justice, has called in a lecture for the 1998 Act to be amended to make it clear that 'the obligation to take account of the decisions of the Strasbourg Court did not mean that our Supreme Court was required to follow or apply those decisions'.[109]

Where there is a conflict between a binding decision of the Supreme Court and a decision of the Strasbourg Court the local court should follow the decision of the Supreme Court.[110]

Compatibility by construction—the art of the 'possible'

Not surprisingly, judges have found difficulty in determining how much liberty they may take under section 3 of the Act in interpreting Acts of Parliament as compatible with Convention rights 'so far as it is possible to do so'.[111] A Supreme Court decision now makes clear[112] that 'the special interpretative duty imposed by section 3 arises only where the legislation, if read and given effect according to ordinary principles, would result in a breach of the Convention rights'.[113] Only if the intent of Parliament, as expressed in legislation, 'gives rise to an incompatibility' is section 3 engaged and the court can 'give effect to legislation in a manner other than the one which Parliament had intended'.[114] Thus

---

[106] *Manchester City Council* v. *Pinnock* [2010] UKSC 45, para. 48 (Lord Neuberger).

[107] The most prominent example in which Strasbourg jurisprudence was taken into account but not followed is *R (Horncastle and ors)* [2009] UKSC 14. The ECtHR case not followed was *Al-Khawaja and Tahery* v. *UK* (2009) 49 EHRR 1. Lord Phillips said that there will 'be rare occasions where this court has concerns as to whether a decision of the Strasbourg Court sufficiently appreciates or accommodates particular aspects of our domestic process. In such circumstances it is open to this court to decline to follow the Strasbourg decision, giving reasons for adopting this course' (para. 8). Consequently the admission of hearsay under the Criminal Justice Act 2003, s. 116 was held not a breach of Art. 6 notwithstanding *Al-Khawaja* to the contrary.

[108] Lord Sumption in *Chester*, above, p. 141, at para. 138 said: 'A wider and perhaps more realistic assessment of the margin of appreciation [by the Strasbourg court in *Hirst*] would have avoided the current controversy. But it would be neither wise nor legally defensible for an English court to say that article 3 of the First Protocol has a meaning different from that which represents the settled view of the principal court charged with its interpretation, and different from that which will consequently apply in every other state party to the Convention.'

[109] 'Constitutional Change: Unfinished Business' given at UCL on the 4 December 2013, para. 46. Lecture available at <http://www.ucl.ac.uk/constitution-unit/constitution-unit-news/constitution-unit/research/judicial-independence/lordjudgelecture041213/>. And see the views of Laws LJ detailed earlier.

[110] *Price* v. *Leeds City Council* [2005] EWCA Civ 289, [2005] 1 WLR 1825, para. 30, to hold otherwise would be to 'subvert the principle of legal certainty' (Lord Phillips). Cf. *D* v. *East Berkshire NHS Trust* [2003] EWCA Civ 1151, [2004] QB 558 (change of circumstances justified departure from HL decision).

[111] See [2003] *PL* 236 (G. Marshall), 319 (Lord Irvine of Lairg). For contrasting views see (2002) 61 *CLJ* 53 (A. Young) and (2002) 118 *LQR* 248 (C. Gearty). See also (2004) 24 *OJLS* 259 (Kavanagh); *Judicial Reasoning under the UK Human Rights Act* (2007, eds. Fenwick, Phillipson and Masterman), 114ff (Kavanagh); and [2004] *PL* 274 (Nicol).   [112] *ANS and anor* v. *ML* [2012] UKSC 30.

[113] Lord Reed, para. 15, relying on *R (Hurst)* v. *London Northern District Coroner* [2007] UKHL 13. Later the judge says that prior to turning to s. 3 the 'court will also apply the presumption, which long antedates the Human Rights Act, that legislation is not intended to place the United Kingdom in breach of its international obligations. Those international obligations include those arising under the Convention' (para. 16).

[114] Para. 15.

it was held that the ordinary meaning of section 31(3)(d) of the Adoption and Children (Scotland) Act 2007 (which permitted, in certain circumstances, the adoption of a child without the parents' consent) was compatible with Article 8; there was no need to have regard to section 3 of the 1998 Act. This approach of turning to section 3 only when the ordinary meaning of the legislation is incompatible is unexceptional constitutionally but none the less salutary. It ensures that lawyers do not mistakenly 'reach for section 3 of the Human Rights Act whenever they hear the words "compatibility with the Convention rights"'.[115] Section 3, in other words, is not a general invitation to rewrite legislation whose compatibility is doubtful.

We may now turn to the application of section 3 itself. In the leading case[116] the House of Lords applied section 3 and held that for the purposes of succession to a statutory tenancy under the Rent Act 1977 the words 'as his or her wife or husband' included a homosexual partner.[117] But the significance of the case lies in what their Lordships said about the approach to the section 3(1) obligation once the section was engaged.

Lord Nicholls, speaking for the majority, said the court had power to 'modify the meaning, and hence the effect, of primary and secondary legislation'. This might require the addition or the subtraction of words from the text[118] although the courts' practice seems to be simply to indicate that the legislation is to be read in a particular way rather than to specify actual textual amendments.

But there must be a limit to what the court can do. Section 3(1) authorises the interpretation not the rewriting of the legislation and the court must not stray from its adjudicative function. Lord Nicholls said:[119]

Parliament, however, cannot have intended that in the discharge of this extended interpretative function the courts should adopt a meaning inconsistent with a fundamental feature of legislation. That would be to cross the constitutional boundary section 3 seeks to demarcate and preserve. Parliament has retained the right to enact legislation in terms which are not Convention-compliant. The meaning imported by application of section 3 must be compatible with the underlying thrust of the legislation being construed. Words implied must... 'go with the grain of the legislation'.

---

[115] Para. 15.

[116] *Ghaidan* v. *Godin-Mendoza* [2004] UKHL 30, [2004] 3 WLR 113 distinguished in *R (Wilkinson)* v. *Inland Revenue* [2005] UKHL 30, para. 18, where the question was whether 'widow' included 'widower' for the purpose of bereavement allowances.

[117] The court concluded that the less favourable treatment of homosexual partners was not justified and so a breach of Arts. 8 and 14. Unless the legislation could be interpreted as compatible under s. 3(1), a declaration of incompatibility would have to be made.

[118] In an important dictum Lord Rogers said this: 'the key to what it is possible for the courts to imply into legislation without crossing the border from interpretation to amendment does not lie in the number of words that have to be read in. The key lies in a careful consideration of the essential principles and scope of the legislation being interpreted. If the insertion of one word contradicts those principles or goes beyond the scope of the legislation, it amounts to impermissible amendment. On the other hand, if the implication of a dozen words leaves the essential principles and scope of the legislation intact but allows it to be read in a way which is compatible with Convention rights, the implication is a legitimate exercise of the powers conferred by section 3(1). Of course, the greater the extent of the proposed implication, the greater the need to make sure that the court is not going beyond the scheme of the legislation and embarking upon amendment' (para. 122).

[119] Paras. 32–3 and note Lord Roger's views expressed in the preceding note. Lord Millett (dissenting) said the court 'can read in and read down; it can supply missing words, so long as they are consistent with the fundamental features of the legislative scheme; it can do considerable violence to the language and stretch it almost (but not quite) to breaking point.... But it is not entitled to give it an impossible one.'

Identifying the limits on section 3(1) thus requires the court to determine the 'fundamental features' of the legislation. When securing compatibility runs up against one of those fundamental features the court's interpretative task ends. It must recognise that it cannot remedy the incompatibility. All it can do is, if appropriate, make a declaration of incompatibility. But the process is an uncertain one as shown by this leading case itself where there was dissent in the House of Lords, although the approaches of Lord Nicholls (for the majority) and Lord Millett (dissenting) to the question were similar.[120] Clearly the language of the statute itself and the policy and purpose underlying it will be important elements in determining the 'fundamental features'. The House of Lords has stressed in another case that section 3(1) did not require the interpreter 'to give the language of [the applicable] statutes acontextual meanings'.[121]

Even though the court may add or subtract words, it seems clear that a specific prohibition or requirement in the statute that is not compatible with the Convention does mark a limit to the court's power. As Lord Rogers said: 'If a provision requires the public authority to take a particular step which is, of its very nature, incompatible with Convention rights, then no process of interpretation can remove the obligation or change the nature of the step that has to be taken... [section 3(1)] does not allow the courts to change the substance of a provision completely, to change a provision where Parliament says that x is to happen into one saying that x is not to happen.'[122] In the end the identification of the 'fundamental features' of the legislation is a matter for judgment. But as the dicta cited here show, the House of Lords is sensitive to the constitutional proprieties and these dicta evince the judiciary's fidelity at a profound level to the existing constitutional order in which even fundamental human rights are subject to the will of Parliament.

Section 3(1) has been relied upon in many cases to secure compatibility with the Convention but they mostly fall outside administrative law.[123] They provide useful

---

[120] Lord Steyn indeed declined to 'formulate precise rules' about the proper limits for the use of s. 3(1) but stressed that the making of a declaration of incompatibility under s. 4 should be a remedy of last resort (para. 50).

[121] *Wilkinson*, above, para. 17 (Lord Hoffmann). Of course, there was 'a strong presumption...that Parliament did not intend a statute to mean something which would be incompatible with [Convention] rights.... But, with the addition of the Convention as background, the question is still one of *interpretation*, i.e. the ascertainment of what...Parliament would reasonably be understood to have meant by using the actual language of the statute (ibid.).

[122] Paras. 109–10. But note the more restrictive approach of Lord Millett in para. 75. Applying Lord Roger's approach the Employment Appeal Tribunal (*Janah* v. *Libya* [2013] UKEAT 0020_13_0410) has found that words could not be added to the State Immunity Act 1978 to secure compliance with Art. 6. The case concerned the claims of domestic staff against their otherwise immune sovereign employers. Langstaff J said that to read the desired words into the statute would 'affect the overall balance struck by the legislature whilst lacking its panoramic vision across the whole of the landscape.... Where Parliament has set out a clear list of those in respect of whom a plea of immunity will fail, and those in respect of whom it will succeed, it would in my view cross the critical line between interpretation and legislation to alter the list by removing one category from the "yes" camp, so as to place it in the "no" camp' (paras. 40–1).

[123] In *R* v. *A (No 2)* [2001] 2 WLR 1546 the House of Lords had to consider the Act which protected women complaining of rape from cross-examination about their previous sexual history, and which might have infringed a defendant's right to a fair trial under Art. 6 by excluding relevant evidence. The House of Lords held that the right to a fair trial was absolute and that relevant evidence should be excluded only where the court was satisfied that the trial would not be unfair. But this bold interpretation was the subject of conflicting views. Lord Steyn held that the protective Act should be read as subject to an implied provision that the right to a fair trial should not be infringed. Lord Hope however held that this course would amount to legislation rather than interpretation, since it contradicted the entire structure of the protective Act. (See similarly *R (Hammond)* v. *Secretary of State for the Home Department* [2005] UKHL 69, [2006] 1 AC 603). *Re S (minors)* [2002] 2 WLR 720 concerned children committed to the care of local authorities. The Court of Appeal had, in the guise of interpretation, imposed a new system of judicial supervision not sanctioned by

guidance as to what may be possible interpretations of statute under this remarkable rule of construction.[124] But a recent case in the House of Lords provided an example in an administrative law context. This case concerned fairness in the making of 'control orders'.[125] The legislation ordained the adoption of a 'special advocate' procedure that did not require full disclosure of the Home Secretary's case to the controlled person, potentially in breach of Article 6(1) requiring a fair hearing. Baroness Hale held in reliance upon section 3(1) that the legislation should be read and given effect 'except where to do so would be incompatible with the right of the controlled person to a fair trial'.[126] Presumably the justification for this reasoning was that the imposition of a procedure in breach of Article 6(1) was not a 'fundamental feature' of the relevant legislation, the Prevention of Terrorism Act 2005.

What is 'possible' under section 3(1) is not defined solely by the 'fundamental features' of the legislation. Even if not precluded by the 'fundamental features' from adopting a particular course, a court may conclude that securing compatibility in the circumstances may inevitably raise practical issues best determined by Parliament. Indeed, wrestling with difficult practical issues may well indicate that the court has slipped from interpretation into legislation.[127]

The last resort: declarations of incompatibility and remedial orders

As Lord Irvine has said, this special technique of interpretation just described 'enables the courts to iron out incompatibilities throughout the statute book',[128] thus avoiding the formalities of declarations of incompatibility except as a last resort. Thus the number of declarations of incompatibility made since the 1998 Act came into force is relatively few in number.[129]

There have been some twenty-eight declarations of incompatibility made (as at April 2013). The most spectacular example thus far was the case in which the House of Lords held that section 23 of the Anti-terrorism, Crime and Security Act 2001 was incompatible with Articles 5 (liberty) and 14 (non-discrimination) of the Convention. Section 23 provided for the indefinite detention without trial of foreign nationals of whom the Home Secretary reasonably believed their presence in the United Kingdom was a threat to national security or whom he reasonably suspected were terrorists, but who could not be deported because of fears for their safety or other considerations.[130] Since it was plain that the threat to the United Kingdom came in part from British citizens the court held that section 23 did not rationally address the threat posed and was not strictly required by

---

Parliament and inconsistent with the policy of the Children Act 1989. This was held to pass 'well beyond the boundary of interpretation', though the House of Lords, while overruling the supervisory scheme, in fact found no incompatibility with Convention rights. *Bellinger* v. *Bellinger*, below, concerned the validity of the marriage of a transsexual. The House of Lords held that s. 3(1) could not be relied upon to secure compatibility. Section 11(c) of the Matrimonial Causes Act 1973 'provides that a marriage is void unless the parties are "respectively male and female"' (para. 1) but it could not be read as including male transsexuals within 'female'. Lord Nicholls and Lord Hope made it clear that the question raised practical issues (e.g. identifying the point at which sex changed) that had to be left to Parliament.

[124] Although unique the s. 3(1) obligation has some similarities with the approach to the interpretation of legislation to secure compatibility with EU law. See below, p. 167.

[125] Control orders are described above, p. 67. The case is *Home Secretary* v. *MB* [2007] UKHL 46, [2007] 3 WLR 681.

[126] Para. 72.　　[127] *Bellinger*, as above.　　[128] [2003] *PL* 308 at 319.

[129] A relatively up-to-date list of declarations of incompatibility will be found at <http://www.lse.ac.uk/humanRights/articlesAndTranscripts/2013/incompatibilityHRA.pdf>.

[130] Act of 2001, s. 23(1) read with s. 21 and the Immigration Act 1971, Sched. 3, para. 2(2).

the exigencies of the situation.[131] It discriminated unjustifiably on the ground of nationality and immigration status. The declaration of incompatibility followed. No remedial order was made but the government's and Parliament's response was the enactment of the Prevention of Terrorism Act 2005, which established the 'control order' regime, discussed elsewhere,[132] to which these suspects (as well as British citizens of like mind) might be subject.

Remedial Orders have thus far been very few in number. The first amended the mental health legislation so as to relieve the patient of the burden of proof.[133] The second amended Naval Courts-Martial procedures to secure fairness in those proceedings.[134] The third amended the Marriage Act 1949 to allow marriage between an individual and the former spouse of their parent or child.[135] Although there are some examples of human rights breaches that remain unremedied several years after the declaration of incompatibility,[136] the paucity of remedial orders simply reflects rather the fact that the government has generally chosen to remedy defects by way of primary legislation either in a Bill introduced for that purpose or by way of an amendment to another Bill. In some cases the defect has been remedied by legislation before the declaration of incompatibility was made. For the reasons given earlier it is preferable that primary legislation rather than the administrative remedial order should be used to remedy human rights failings identified in a declaration of incompatibility.[137]

The functional reach of the HRA: the meaning of 'public authority'

As explained ealier, the 1998 Act does not define clearly the public authorities which are to act compatibly with Convention rights although section 6(3)(b) does include within 'public authority' 'any person certain of whose functions are functions of a public nature'.[138] This lack of clarity has generated much litigation, particularly where a private body performs a service on behalf of a public body.[139] In the leading case the House of Lords was sharply divided.[140]

---

[131] i.e. the court applied the test of proportionality, discussed elsewhere, p. 150 and p. 306.

[132] Above, p. 67.   [133] Mental Health Act 1983 (Remedial) Order SI 2001 No. 3712.

[134] Naval Discipline Act 1957 (Remedial) Order SI 2004 No. 66.

[135] The Marriage Act 1949 (Remedial) Order 2007 No. 438 made following a decision of the Human Rights Court, B and L v. UK (App. No. 36536/02), to the effect that such restrictions breached Art. 12.

[136] For instance, Westminster City Council v. Morris [2005] EWCA Civ 1184, [2006] 1 WLR 505 in which a declaration was made to the effect that the Housing Act, s. 185(4) was incompatible with Art. 14. The subsection provided that a child subject to immigration control should be disregarded in assessing the parent's priority need for accommodation.   [137] Above, p. 137.

[138] Note also Act of 1998, s. 6(5): 'In relation to a particular act, a person is not a public authority by virtue only of subsection (3)(b) if the nature of the act is private'.

[139] Two contrasting decisions of the Court of Appeal are: Poplar Housing Association Ltd v. Donoghue [2001] 3 WLR 183 (housing association (set up by local authority) was a 'registered social landlord' but in law was a private body, nonetheless held a public authority under s. 6 of the HRA and so obliged to respect private and family life (Art. 8) of tenants) and R (Heather) v. Leonard Cheshire Foundation [2002] 2 All ER 936 (independent foundation running care home was discharging the statutory obligations of the local authority, but it remained a private body and not within s. 6). (See [2002] 118 LQR 551 (P. P. Craig)). Parochial Church Council of Aston Cantlow v. Wallbank [2003] UKHL 37 [2004] 1 AC 546, was the only decision of the House of Lords prior to YL. The majority held that a Parochial Church Council, when suing a landowner for money due from him for the repair of the chancel of the parish church, was taking action of a private nature within s. 6(5). The minority stressed 'the strong public flavour of the duty of the PCC to act for its parishioners and the public generally'. See [2004] PL 329 (Oliver); [2004] PL 643 (Sunkin).

[140] YL v. Birmingham City Council [2007] UKHL 27, [2007] 3 WLR 112. Discussed (2007) 66 CLJ 485 (Elliott) and 559 (Palmer). See also [2007] PL 630 (Landau).

That case concerned an elderly woman (YL), suffering from Alzheimer's disease, who lived in a care home run by Southern Cross Health Care, a private company. The relationship between the management of the home and YL's husband and daughter broke down and the result was that Southern Cross wanted to serve a notice to quit on YL. Most of the fees due to Southern Cross in respect of YL's care and accommodation were paid by the local authority (the Birmingham City Council),[141] pursuant to its duty under the National Assistance Act 1948, section 21(1) 'to make arrangements for providing resident accommodation for persons…who by reason of age, illness, disability or any other circumstance are in need of care and attention which is not otherwise available to them'. The 'arrangement' that the council had made to fulfil its duty under section 21(1) was to contract with Southern Cross;[142] but it was Southern Cross who actually provided the care and accommodation to YL. The claimant[143] sought a declaration that Southern Cross was exercising a public function within section 6(3)(b) and requiring her to quit would breach several of her Convention rights.

The majority view was that the provision of such care and accommodation, as opposed to arranging that such care and accommodation was provided by another, was not a public function and so fell outside the subsection. Lord Mance (with whom Lords Scott and Neuberger agreed) approved, as a general approach to the interpretation of section 6, an inquiry into whether the body 'carries out a function of government which would engage the responsibility of the United Kingdom before the Strasbourg organs'.[144] In restricting the reach of section 6(3)(b) the majority was much influenced by considerations that went much wider than the status of care homes. Lord Scott pointed out that Southern Cross 'is neither a charity nor a philanthropist…. It receives no public funding,[145] enjoys no special statutory powers and is at liberty to accept or reject residents as it chooses…It is operating in a commercial market…'[146] Many others who contracted to perform services for the government would also find themselves being treated as public authorities if a wider interpretation were adopted. This would extend not only to other commercial contractors but in certain circumstances to foster parents and private landlords.

The minority (Baroness Hale and Lord Bingham) took the view that while 'there cannot be a single litmus test of what is a function of a public nature, the underlying rationale must be that it is a task for which the public, in the shape of the state, have assumed responsibility, at public expense if need be, and in the public interest.'[147] And as Lord Bingham remarked it was 'hardly a matter of debate' that such a 'social welfare responsibility' had long been accepted by the British state.[148]

It can hardly be denied that the meaning of 'public authority' either in the form of a 'core' authority (section 6(1)) or a 'hybrid' authority (section 6(3)(b)) is vague and unsatisfactory. The determination of the precise reach of the protection afforded by the Human Rights Act will long be a matter of dispute.

The outcome in the YL case proved so controversial[149] that the decision has been overruled by legislation. The Health and Social Care Act 2008 provides in section 145(1) that

---

[141] A top-up fee was paid by YL's relatives.

[142] Such was specifically authorised by the Act of 1948, s. 26.

[143] By her litigation friend and Official Solicitor.

[144] These words come from Lord Rodger in the *Aston Cantlow* case, para. 160, cited with approval by Lord Mance at para. 87.

[145] The fees which it was paid by the council under contract were, of course, public funds but the council did not subsidise the home.   [146] Para. 26.

[147] Para. 65.   [148] Para. 15.

[149] Note particularly the several reports of The Joint Committee on Human Rights being critical of restrictive approaches to the meaning of public authority (2003–4, HL Paper 39/HC 382); (2006–7, HL Paper

'A person who provides accommodation, together with nursing or personal care, in a care home for an individual under arrangements made with [that person by an authority] under the relevant statutory provisions is to be taken for the purposes of subsection (3) (b) of section 6 of the Human Rights Act 1998 ... to be exercising a function of a public nature in doing so.'

This measure is limited to the provision of care, thus the more restrictive approach of the majority will apply to the interpretation of section 6(3)(b) in other areas.[150]

The major difficulty with the more restrictive approach is that it renders it possible, when a public authority contracts with a private party for the performance of one of its functions (typically in the form of a service to an individual), that that individual cannot assert his or her human rights against the party who actually provides the service. Contracting out the service has reduced the protection available to an individual who may be, as was YL, vulnerable.[151] As Lord Woolf said in an earlier case, in this situation 'effective protection of convention rights is lost as a result of the local authorities delegating their responsibilities.'[152]

On the other hand, it should not be supposed that YL's rights were left wholly unprotected. Apart from the criminal law, the civil law and the care home regulatory regime that would protect her in their several ways, Southern Cross had expressly undertaken to observe the Convention rights of residents in its agreement with the council and that same obligation was incorporated into its contract with YL. As Lord Scott remarked: 'Any breach by Southern Cross of YL's Convention rights would give YL a cause of action for breach of contract under ordinary domestic law.'[153]

The degree of protection and the determination of the appropriate measure of protection, in any particular case, is thus both subtle and complicated. The words of the 1998 Act provide little guidance. Although the restrictive approach of the majority in YL and its link to the 'the scope of state responsibility in Strasbourg'[154] provides some help, uncertainty abounds and litigation will doubtless continue.

The approach in later cases has been to apply a test based on an earlier House of Lords decision.[155] There it was said by Lord Nicholls that the factors to be taken into account in deciding whether a particular matter fell within section 6(3)(b) include 'the extent to which in carrying out the relevant function the body is publicly funded, or is exercising statutory powers, or is taking the place of central government or local authorities, or is providing a public service'.[156]

77/HC 410); 8th Report (2007–8 HL Paper 46/HC 303) favouring a general amendment to the 1998 Act rather than the narrow provision adopted (para. 1.6). A Private Member's Bill containing such a general amendment failed.

[150] It may be noted that the s. 145(1) extends only to cases where the local authority makes the arrangement pursuant to its statutory duties. It does not apply to a wholly private arrangement between the individual and the care home. Thus Southern Cross would thus bear Convention obligations in respect of some of its clients and not in respect to others. But it may be noted that the Public Sector Equality Duty (below, p. 325) applies to a 'person who is not a public authority but who exercises public functions' (Equality Act 2010, s. 149(2)).   [151] See the discussion on contracting out and judicial review, above pp. 38–9.

[152] The *Heather* case, above, at 946.   [153] Para. 32.   [154] Lord Mance, para. 87.

[155] The *Aston Cantlow* case, discussed above, p. 146.

[156] Para. 12. But note that in YL Lord Bingham remarked that none of the factors 'is likely to be determinative on its own and the weight of different factors will vary from case to case' (para. 5). Such an approach is not conducive to certainty.

Applying this test the Court of Appeal[157] has held that a registered social landlord was within section 6(3)(b). There was 'substantial public subsidy' of capital sums,[158] and the landlord had a statutory duty to cooperate with the local authority and worked in 'close harmony' with it. Moreover, the 'provision of subsidised housing, as opposed to the provision of housing itself' was a 'governmental function' and its provision a 'public service'. Furthermore, the landlord's charitable objectives placed it 'outside the traditional area of private commercial activity'. All these factors cumulatively brought the landlord within section 6(3)(b).

It remains to remark that it is surprising that in all these decisions nothing has been said about the possibility of the 1998 Act being fully applicable between private parties, i.e. that it operates horizontally.[159] This is discussed separately later.

Clarity has been gained in one area. It has sometimes been said that 'the tests for a functional public authority within the meaning of section 6(3)(b) and for amenability to judicial review are, for practical purposes the same'.[160] But several of the speeches in YL hold that these two processes are distinctly different.[161] There can be no easy read over from the law governing susceptibility to judicial review when a private party performs a public function.[162]

The territorial reach of the HRA and the Convention

Article 1 of the Convention provides that 'the High Contracting Parties shall secure to everyone within their jurisdiction the rights and freedoms defined' in the Convention. The Strasbourg jurisprudence holds that Article 1 applies primarily only in the territory of a state party,[163] but that if that state exercises such effective control over another territory as to enable it to provide the 'full package of [Convention] rights and freedoms' an obligation to secure those rights would arise.[164] In 2007 the House of Lords held that the UK's occupation of parts of Iraq 'fell far short of such control'.[165] But the Strasbourg Court disagreed.[166] It has held that the 'United Kingdom (together with the United States) assumed in Iraq the exercise of some of the public powers normally to be exercised by a sovereign government' and, in particular, 'assumed authority and responsibility for the maintenance of security in South East Iraq. In these exceptional circumstances, the Court considers that the United Kingdom, through its soldiers engaged in security operations in Basrah during the period in question, exercised authority and control over

---

[157] R (Weaver) v. London & Quadrant Housing Trust [2009] EWCA Civ 587 confirming the decision of the Divisional Court: [2008] EWHC 1377. The quotations in this paragraph come from paras. 68–72 (Elias LJ's judgment).   [158] Not the payment of sums for services rendered as in YL.

[159] Below, p. 152.

[160] R (Beer (t/a Hammer Trout Farm)) v. Hampshire Farmers' Markets Ltd [2004] 1 WLR 233 (refusal of licence quashed), para. 14 (Dyson LJ, but the matter was not disputed before him). And see R v. Servite Houses ex p Goldsmith [2001] LGR 55.

[161] Para. 12, 'it will not ordinarily matter whether the body in question is amendable to judicial review' (Lord Bingham); Cf. Lord Mance, paras. 100–1.

[162] Above, p. 539. And see Bevan & Clarke LLP v. Neath Port Talbot County Borough Council [2012] EWHC 236, para. 47: 'It is clear that, because the purpose of attaching liability under section 6 of the 1998 Act is different to the purpose of subjecting a body to public law principles, "it cannot be assumed that because a body is subject to one set of rules it will therefore automatically be subject to the other": Elias LJ in Weaver's case at [37]' (para. 47 per Beatson J). Cf. R (McIntyre) v. Gentoo Group Ltd [2010] EWHC 5 (Admin) at para. 21.

[163] See Bankovic v. Belgium (2001) 11 BHRC 435, para. 61. The Convention reflects an 'essentially territorial notion of jurisdiction, other bases of jurisdiction being exceptional and requiring special justification'.

[164] Words from the head note of Al-Skeini in the House of Lords, below.

[165] R (Al-Skeini) v. Defence Secretary [2007] UKHL 26, [2007] 3 WLR 33 (HL).

[166] Al-Skeini and ors v. UK, 55721/07 [2011] ECtHR 1093, para. 47.

individuals killed in the course of such security operations, so as to establish a jurisdictional link between the deceased and the United Kingdom for the purposes of Article 1 of the Convention.' Consistent with this analysis the Supreme Court has unanimously[167] held[168] that British soldiers, killed by improvised explosive devices[169] while on patrol in occupied Iraq, were within the jurisdiction of the United Kingdom. But it was made plain that this did not engage an obligation to provide the full package of Convention rights. In a significant development the Court held that Convention rights may be 'divided and tailored' to suit the circumstances in which extraterritorial jurisdiction is recognised.[170]

Where an Iraqi civilian died while in British custody on a British military base, the domestic courts had already held that the Convention was engaged.[171]

Since Guantanamo Bay lies outside the jurisdiction of the UK, detainees there have failed to compel the Secretary of State for Foreign Affairs to make diplomatic representations to the United States authorities to secure their release both where the detainee was a British citizen[172] and where the detainee was a resident.[173] But other issues including the justiciability of decisions relating to foreign affairs arise in these cases.

Assessing whether the limitation of a right is justified: the doctrine of proportionality

Articles 8 (private and family life), 9 (freedom of conscience), 10 (freedom of expression) and 11 (freedom of assembly and association) allow for restrictions on these human rights for particular purposes such as national security, national economic policy, crime prevention, public health or morals and the protection of the rights and freedoms of others. Article 10 extends also to the protection of information received in confidence and for maintaining the impartiality of the judiciary.

The leading example on Article 10 is the *Sunday Times* case, where the European Court by a narrow majority found violation in an injunction, granted against the newspaper by the House of Lords to prohibit (as contempt of court) discussion of cases already pending after the thalidomide disaster, holding that 'necessary' indicated a 'pressing social need' and that interference with freedom of expression must be 'proportionate to the legitimate aim pursued' and supported by 'relevant and sufficient reasons'.[174] In the words of Lord Clyde,[175] later endorsed by Lord Steyn, the court must ask itself

---

[167] In an earlier decision (*R (Smith)* v. *Secretary of State for Defence and anor* [2010] UKSC 29) decided before the judgment of the Strasbourg Court in *Al-Skeini*, the Supreme Court was divided on this issue but none the less found that a British soldier (who died of heat exhaustion in Iraq) was not within the jurisdiction of the UK.

[168] *Smith and ors* v. *The Ministry of Defence* [2013] UKSC 41.

[169] To which danger they were vulnerable because of the vehicle in which they were travelling ('Snatch Land Rovers').

[170] See paras. 48–9 departing from *Bankovic* v. *Belgium*, above, which proposed that there should be no such principle.

[171] Another clear case where the Act applies extraterritorially is to British Embassies and Consulates abroad (*R (B)* v. *Secretary of State for the Foreign and Commonwealth Office* [2004] EWCA Civ 1344 (British Consulate in Melbourne dealing with Hazara refugees from Afghanistan)). Another exception applies to vessels and aeroplanes registered in the United Kingdom. See also *R* v. *Secretary of State for Foreign and Commonwealth Affairs ex p Quark Fishing Ltd* [2005] UKHL 57: 1998 Act did not apply to dependent territories (unless specifically extended (Art. 56)).

[172] *R (Abbasi)* v. *Secretary of State for Foreign and Commonwealth Affairs* [2002] EWCA Civ 1598.

[173] *R (Al Rawi)* v. *Secretary of State for Foreign and Commonwealth Affairs* [2006] EWCA Civ 1279, [2007] 2 WLR 1219 (not racial discrimination to distinguish between citizens and residents).

[174] *Sunday Times* v. *UK* (1979) 2 EHRR 245.

[175] *de Freitas* v. *Permanent Secretary of Ministry of Agriculture, Fisheries, Lands and Housing* [1999] 1 AC 69, endorsed by Lord Steyn in *R (Daly)* v. *Home Secretary* [2001] 2 WLR 1622.

whether (i) the legislative objective is sufficiently important to justify limiting a fundamental right; (ii) the measures designed to meet the legislative objective are rationally connected to it; and (iii) the means used to impair the right or freedom are no more than is necessary to accomplish the objective.

Striking the balance between the protection of a fundamental right and the 'pressing social need' that may justify a restriction of that right is one of the most important judicial tasks under the HRA. The application of the structured proportionality test is dealt with in detail elsewhere.[176]

Conflicting human rights

A similar task is the balancing exercise required in the reconciliation of conflicts between different fundamental rights. Intrinsically this is no different from cases where an article allows for exceptions and the question is whether the exception outweighs the rule, for example where the right to a public hearing under Article 6 is negatived by the interest of morals, public order etc., as there provided. But balancing becomes particularly difficult where the main thrust of different articles is in opposite directions. An obvious case is where the right of respect for private and family life under Article 8 is invaded by the exercise of freedom of expression under Article 10. How far should freedom of the press, for example, be restrained for the sake of personal privacy? In striking the balance between Article 8 and Article 10 the courts are creating a right to privacy at common law. At first the courts favoured freedom of expression. Thus a professional footballer failed when he sought to restrain a newspaper from publishing details of his extra-marital affairs. The Court of Appeal held the public had a legitimate interest in being told about a public figure.[177] But the balance has perhaps shifted the other way. Thus a breach of a 'supermodel's' Article 8 rights was found by the House of Lords when a newspaper published photographs of her leaving a clinic where she was being treated for drug addiction.[178] These questions do not engage any aspect of governmental power and are not part of administrative law.

Prohibition of discrimination

Article 14 provides that the Convention rights 'shall be secured without discrimination on any ground such as sex, race, colour, language, religion, political or other opinion, national or social origin, association with a national minority, property, birth or other status.'[179] This creates a powerful basis for challenging a decision of a public authority where it is shown that there was in fact discrimination in securing a Convention right. Indeed Article 14 goes further to cover rights extended by the national legal system but 'within the ambit' of one of the articles of the Convention. Thus while the Convention does not require a scheme for the early release of prisoners lawfully sentenced to a determinate term, if such a scheme is established, it falls 'within the ambit' of Article 5 and must not be discriminatory.[180]

---

[176] Below, p. 306.

[177] A v. B plc [2002] 3 WLR 542. Lord Woolf proposed guidelines that favoured press freedom. Similarly, Re S (a Child) [2003] 3 WLR 1425 where a mother was on trial for murdering her son. The identity of the surviving son not protected. Lord Phillips MR held that the son's Art. 8 rights 'came no way towards outweighing the freedom of expression urged by the press' (no account taken of the 1998 Act, s. 12).

[178] Campbell v. MGN Ltd [2004] UKHL 22, [2004]2 AC 457 (HL).

[179] These words 'other status' are imprecise but do not cover 'differential treatment on any ground whatever' (Clift, below, para. 25 (Lord Bingham)). Thus differentiating between a long-term prisoner sentenced to a determinate term and a prisoner sentenced to a life sentence was not a breach of Art. 14. But discriminating in regard to determination of release date between foreign prisoners (i.e. 'liable to removal' from the UK on completion of sentence) and local prisoners not objectively justified (declaration of incompatibility made).

[180] R (Clift) v. Home Secretary [2006] UKHL 54, [2007] 1 AC 484, para. 18.

A distinction is drawn though between discrimination which offends the respect due for the individual (such as discrimination on grounds of sex or race) and discrimination on other grounds. The former are subjected to severe scrutiny[181] but the latter may be justified by showing rational (or utilitarian) grounds for the discrimination.[182] Thus it was found rationally justifiable to discriminate between residents and non-residents in the level of state pension benefit and a breach of Article 14 was not found.[183] The way these distinctions are drawn is somewhat inchoate: Lord Hoffman remarking in the leading case that whether 'cases are sufficiently [alike to justify a finding of discrimination] is partly a matter of values and partly a question of rationality.' But their Lordships expressed doubt about the somewhat mechanical approach of earlier cases in approaching this issue through a series of questions.[184] Given the value laden nature of these distinctions the outcome of such challenges are difficult to predict; at least the series of questions lends structure and form to the process and will tend to enhance certainty. It may be noted that, notwithstanding the principle of 'strict scrutiny' objective justification for discrimination on ground of gender may in particular circumstances be found.[185]

Remedies and liability

The provisions of the HRA about remedies and liability are explained later in Chapter 20.

Private litigation and 'horizontal effect'

Although, as already pointed out, the HRA provides specific remedies only against public authorities, there is the overriding provision of section 6 that it is unlawful for a public authority to act in a way which is incompatible with a Convention right. Courts or tribunals are specifically included in the definition of public authorities (section 6(2)(a)), so that a court faced with a Convention issue would have to decide it compatibly, whatever the legal proceedings in which the issue arose. The Convention rights would then permeate the whole legal system, in private as much as in public law.[186]

Curiously horizontality is seldom discussed and never relied upon in public law litigation, but is often taken for granted in private litigation with the judges, where necessary, stretching a common law cause of action to uphold Convention rights.[187]

---

[181] 'Article 14 expresses the Enlightenment value that every human being is entitled to equal respect and to be treated as an end and not a means. Characteristics such as race, caste, noble birth, membership of a political party and (here a change in values since the Enlightenment) gender, are seldom, if ever, acceptable grounds for differences in treatment' (Lord Hoffmann, para. 24 in *Carson*, as below).

[182] *R (Carson)* v. *Work and Pensions Secretary* [2005] UKHL 37, [2005] 2 WLR 1369, para. 16 (Lord Hoffmann). The Grand Chamber of the Strasbourg Court has upheld the findings of the domestic courts: *Carson and ors* v. *UK*, 42184/05 [2010] ECtHR 338.   [183] *Carson*, ibid.

[184] See *Wandsworth London Borough Council* v. *Michalak* [2002] EWCA Civ 271, [2003] 1 WLR 617, para. 20, Brooke LJ. If any one of the questions answered no the claim failed. The questions were: (i) Do the facts fall within the ambit of one or more of the substantive Convention provisions? (ii) If so, was there different treatment as respects that right between the complainant on the one hand and other persons put forward for comparison on the other? (iii) Were the chosen comparators in an analogous situation to the complainant's situation? (iv) If so, did the difference in treatment have an objective and reasonable justification?

[185] *Hooper* v. *Secretary of State for Works and Pensions* [2005] UKHL 29 (widowers seeking widows pension benefits); *R (Wilkinson)* v. *Inland Revenue* [2005] UKHL 30 (widowers seeking widows tax allowances).

[186] There is a large literature on this subject. See (2000) 116 *LQR* 217 (Wade); (2000) 11 *LQR* 48 (Buxton); (1999) 62 *MLR* 824 (Phillipson); [1998] *PL* 423 (Hunt).

[187] 'The time has come to recognise that the values enshrined in articles 8 and 10 are now part of the cause of action for breach of confidence': *Campbell* v. *MGN Ltd* [2004] UKHL 22, [2004], 2 AC 457 (HL), para. 17 (Lord Nicholls, dissenting but not on this point). But see the caution expressed in *Douglas* v. *Hello Ltd*, below,

The benefits of the HRA and of Convention rights have been accorded to private parties in actions between landlord and tenant and private complaints against newspapers. Where there was a dispute about succession to a statutory tenancy and, as already noted, the House of Lords allowed a homosexual partner to claim as a 'spouse'; this interpretation under HRA, section 3 had to be adopted, so as to give effect to the partner's Convention rights, since the court was a public authority which must act compatibly with Convention rights even in proceedings between private parties.[188] There have been strong pointers in the same direction in various proceedings against newspapers, which are not public authorities, but where Convention rights have been assumed to be applicable.[189] It was in order to protect newspapers that the government added section 12 to the HRA, as already explained, but that provision would be futile unless newspapers were entitled to claim Convention rights by horizontal application of the Act. In the pawnbroking case already mentioned, where a declaration of incompatibility was refused by the House of Lords, no mention was made of the fact that the case was basically about the rights of private parties.[190]

When injunctions were granted against newspapers in order to protect the future anonymity of two child murderers, the court's duty to enforce their Convention rights was clearly stated by the High Court in a 'horizontal' situation. But it was held also that the court should apply the Convention principles to 'existing causes of action' only and 'cannot hear free-standing applications based directly on the articles of the Convention'.[191]

The protection of human rights in the future

The general verdict of the legal profession on the 1998 Act would probably be that it has been a force for good, revealing many corners of the law where justice and fairness has been found wanting but which, through the Act, have been able to be remedied. But this is not a universal opinion and the Act is often criticised, sometimes unjustly, in the popular press and by politicians.[192] The Act and the Convention do not enjoy a place of pride and respect in the popular mind comparable to that held by the Constitution in the United States. The Strasbourg Court has sometimes found the UK law wanting on a matter on which Parliament is reluctant to change the law to secure compliance.[193] On other occasions it has held that the UK cannot deport individuals whom the government considers

---

para. 50 ('courts not prepared to go so far' as full horizontality) and Baroness Hale in *Campbell* (courts cannot create new cause of action to secure horizontality).

[188] *Ghaidan* v. *Godin-Mendoza* (as above).

[189] See *Douglas* v. *Hello Ltd* [2001] 2 WLR 992; (2003) *CLJ* 443 (Morgan); *Loutchansky* v. *Times Newspapers Ltd* [2002] 2 WLR 640.   [190] *Wilson* v. *Secretary of State for Trade and Industry* [2003] 3 WLR 568.

[191] *Venables* v. *News Group Newspapers Ltd* [2001] Fam 430, paras. 27, 111 (Butler-Sloss P).

[192] In its generally positive *Review of the Implementation of the Human Rights Act* (2006) (available at <http://webarchive.nationalarchives.gov.uk/+/http:/www.dca.gov.uk/peoples-rights/human-rights/pdf/full_review.pdf>) the government recognised that the Act has been 'widely misunderstood by the public' and that 'damaging myths about human rights...have taken root in the popular imagination'. For thoughtful criticism of the Act see [2004] *PL* 829 (Ewing).

[193] Most prominently on the question of the blanket disenfranchisement of prisoners in UK law. See *Hirst* v. *UK (No 2)* (2005) 42 EHRR 41 (Representation of the People Act 1983, s. 3(1) disenfranchising prisoners held a breach of Art. 3 of the First Protocol of the Convention) and *Smith* v. *Scott* [2007] Scot CS CSIH 9 (declaration of incompatibility made). The government's response has been a Draft Voting Eligibility (Prisoners) Bill (available at <http://www.justice.gov.uk/downloads/legislation/bills-acts/voting-eligibility-prisoners/voting-eligibility-prisoners-command-paper.pdf>) which offers Parliament various options (including no change).

to be threats to national security.[194] The domestic courts are also sometimes considered by ministers to be over-protective of certain rights (particularly Article 8). This fuels popular dissatisfaction with the 1998 Act and the European Convention. Public lectures by eminent judges also reveal dissatisfaction with current arrangements, especially over the status of decisions of the Strasbourg Court. Lord Hoffman, for instance, has argued that 'human rights are universal in abstraction but national in application' and this causes him to doubt the legitimacy of an international court acting as mediator 'between the high generalities of the constitutional text and the messy detail of their application to concrete problems'. He gives several examples where the Human Rights Court has accorded too narrow a margin of appreciation to the UK's solution to a difficult problem and instead tried to teach its 'grandmothers [i.e. the House of Lords] to suck eggs'.[195]

All this means that there is significant support for plans to change the current arrangements. After the 2010 General Election the Coalition Government established a Commission on a Bill of Rights which was to consider 'the creation of a UK Bill of Rights that incorporates and builds on all our obligations under the European Convention on Human Rights'.[196] But the Commission's eventual report revealed complex divisions amongst the members. The report thus served neither to crystallise opinion in favour of or against reform nor to make a cogent case for any particular reform. It has been aptly said if reform is ever undertaken the report is unlikely 'to warrant [more than] a footnote'.[197]

What happens in the future will depend upon the tides of politics impossible to predict. But four general comments may be made.

First, human rights adjudication in the UK is primarily concerned with striking a balance between conflicting rights (should a tabloid newspaper's right to 'freedom of expression' under Article 10 outweigh a celebrity's right to 'respect for his private and family life' under Article 8) or pronouncing upon whether the limitation of a particular right—say 'freedom of expression'—is justified as being 'necessary in a democratic society in the interests of national security, public safety or the economic well-being of the country, for the prevention of disorder or crime, for the protection of health or morals, or for the protection of the rights and freedoms of others'.[198] This is a world where balances have to be struck and judgments made. There are no clear measures or easy answers. And self-evidently many such questions are matters upon which reasonable men and women may take different views.

When dealing with such questions the issue is not whether the decision-maker reached the right answer or not—there is no right answer to these questions—but whether the decision-maker had legitimate authority to make that decision. It is not clear that judges are better placed—especially when acute issues of social and political policy are involved—to make such judgments than elected decision-makers or officials accountable to elected representatives. Indeed, Lord Sumption has argued that legislative decisions about rights are to be preferred over judicial ones because 'rights can never be wholly unqualified. Their existence and extent must be constrained to a greater or lesser or lesser

---

[194] The most prominent case is that of *Othman (Abu Qatada) v. UK*, 8139/09 [2012] ECtHR 56 (deportation of suspected terrorist to Jordan found in the circumstances to be a breach of Art. 6 of the Convention). For a summing up of the whole saga see the last case in the UK courts: *Othman (aka Abu Qatada) v. Home Secretary* [2013] EWCA Civ 277. He was eventually deported after the UK and Jordan ratified a treaty that precluded the use of evidence obtained by torture in his trial.

[195] <http://www.judiciary.gov.uk/Resources/JCO/Documents/Speeches/Hoffmann_2009_JSB_Annual_Lecture_Universality_of_Human_Rights.pdf>.

[196] Terms of reference available at <http://www.justice.gov.uk/about/cbr>.

[197] Elliott, 'Damp Squibs in the Long Grass' available at <http://papers.ssrn.com/sol3/papers.cfm?abstract_id=2221888>.

[198] This is discussed in detail above, p. 306 (proportionality).

extent by the rights of others, as well as by some legitimate collective interests. In deciding where the balance lies between individual rights and collective interests, the relevant considerations will often be far wider than anything that a court can comprehend simply on the basis of argument between the parties before it.'[199] This is the case for considerable deference to be shown by the judges—whether of the local courts or the Strasbourg Court—to the considered decisions of the elected authorities.

Secondly, Parliament remains supreme and retains the power and legitimacy to legislate in the field of human rights. Indeed Parliament regularly legislates to strike balances between competing social, moral and political goals (as in the Equality Act 2010). All this is uncontroversial and unexceptional. It is (or should be) equally uncontroversial that Parliament could legislate to change the balance struck between Article 10 and Article 8 or to provide that particular limitations on particular rights are justified or not justified.[200] There may be pragmatic or prudential reasons why Parliament should not do this in general or in particular cases but that it has the authority to do so is not in doubt. Of course, individuals dissatisfied with the protection of their rights by the domestic courts could still petition Strasbourg. In many cases, no doubt, the domestic legislation would be found by the Strasbourg Court to be within the margin of appreciation. But some individuals would doubtless succeed at Strasbourg.

Thirdly, when an individual has succeeded before Strasbourg Article 46(1) of the Convention under which the 'High Contracting Parties undertake to abide by the decision of the Court in any case to which they are parties' applies. The UK has bound itself as a matter of international law to 'abide by' relevant decisions of the Strasbourg Court. This means that the UK (or any other Member State) dissatisfied by a decision of the Court has few remedies. Lord Neuberger explained the position when he said: 'It is true that membership of the Convention imposes obligations on the state to ensure that judgments of the Strasbourg Court are implemented, but those obligations are in international law, not domestic law. And, ultimately, the implementation of a Strasbourg [Court judgment] ... is a matter for Parliament. If it chose not to implement a Strasbourg judgment, it might place the United Kingdom in breach of its treaty obligations, but as a matter of domestic law there would be nothing objectionable in such a course. It would be a political decision, with which the courts could not interfere.'[201]

Ultimately then if there were an irreconcilable clash between domestic law and the UK's treaty obligations a political decision would have to be taken. That decision, if it were not to accept the decision of the Court, would entail either explicit disobedience to the relevant international law or withdrawal from the Convention (and probably the Council of Europe). Both of these options are unpalatable. Explicit disobedience by the government to a legal obligation under international law is offensive to the rule of law; and there would be far-reaching international political repercussions if the UK were to withdraw from the Convention. Choosing between these unpalatable options will be very difficult, but explicit disobedience to the law is contrary to the values and ethos of our subject.

Finally, if reform comes, it will be well to maintain a sense of perspective. Even if the 1998 Act were to be wholly repealed (as is sometimes promised by politicians) that would not be the end of human rights protection in the UK. The values common to the common

[199] 'The Limits of Law' being the 27th Sultan Azlan Shah Lecture, available at <http://www.supreme-court.gov.uk/news/speeches.html>.

[200] Clear legislation would, of course, be followed by the domestic courts (it might have to be particularly clear to prevail over s. 3(1)).

[201] Lord Neuberger, 'Who Are the Masters Now?', Second Lord Alexander of Weedon Lecture, 6 April 2011, at para. 56.

law and the Convention are fundamental and permeate English law; they would not vanish overnight with the repeal of the Act.[202] The common law protected liberty in these islands, and elsewhere, for many centuries without the assistance of the 1998 Act or the Convention.

Moreover, it is wrong to suppose the current arrangements for the protection of rights are incapable of improvement, so that any change would necessarily be retrograde. As we have noted, the 1998 Act is not accepted with enthusiasm by all sections of the public. Lord Sumption touches a crucial point when he says that rights 'are claims against the claimant's own community. In a democracy, they depend for their legitimacy on a measure of recognition by that community. To be effective, they require a large measure of public acceptance through an active civil society. This is something which no purely judicial decision-making process can deliver.'[203] Reform that led to greater public acceptance of the system of protection of fundamental rights would be undeniably beneficial.

THE EUROPEAN UNION

The European Economic Community (EEC) came into being under the Treaty of Rome (now much amended and renamed the Treaty on the Functioning of the European Union (TFEU)), signed by six countries in 1957. In addition there were the European Coal and Steel Community (ECSC) and the European Atomic Energy Community (Euratom), founded in 1951 and 1957 respectively. In 1965 the Merger Treaty amalgamated the institutions of the three communities, so that they shared a single constitutional structure consisting of a Council, a Commission, an Assembly (now Parliament) and a Court of Justice, though in law they remained distinct. France, West Germany, Italy and the Benelux countries were the founder members; Britain, Ireland and Denmark acceded in 1973, Greece in 1981, Spain and Portugal in 1986, Austria, Finland and Sweden in 1995. Ten further countries acceded in 2004 (Cyprus, Czech Republic, Estonia, Hungary, Latvia, Lithuania, Malta, Poland, Slovakia and Slovenia), two more (Bulgaria and Romania) in 2007 and another (Croatia) in 2013.[204]

The objectives of the EU are now set out at length in Article 3 of the TEU (previously the Maastricht Treaty) taking the place of Arts. 2 and 3 of the Treaty of Rome. Apart from worthy general purposes such as the promotion of 'peace, [EU] values and the well-being of its peoples' there are many specific matters mentioned such as the creation of 'an area of freedom, security and justice without internal frontiers, in which the free movement of persons is ensured'; the establishment of 'an internal market' in the interests of 'the sustainable development of Europe based on balanced economic growth and price stability'; 'social exclusion and discrimination' shall be combatted and 'social justice and protection, equality between women and men, solidarity between generations and protection of

---

[202] See Lord Reed, *The Common Law and the ECHR* and Justice Heydon, *Are Bills of Rights Necessary in Common Law Systems?* And see *Osborn v. The Parole Board* [2013] UKSC 61, paras. 55–7 (Lord Reed). See Appendix 3.

[203] 'The Limits of Law', being the 27th Sultan Azlan Shah Lecture, available at <http://www.supremecourt.gov.uk/news/speeches.html>.

[204] There is a very large literature on the law of the EU. Valuable works are Hartley, *Foundations of European Community Law*; Wyatt and Dashwood, *European Community Law*; Craig and De Burca, *EU Law*; Schwarze, *European Administrative Law*; and Nehl, *Principles of Administrative Procedure in EC Law*. See also [2004] *PL* 146 (Schwarze), Anthony, *UK Public Law and European Law: The Dynamics of Legal Integration* (2002) and Craig and De Burca, *The Evolution of EU Law* (2011). For the Lisbon Treaty and its effects see Biondi, Eeckhout and Ripley (eds.), *EU Law after Lisbon* (2012) and Craig, *The Lisbon Treaty: Law, Politics and Treaty Reform* (2010).

the rights of the child' advanced. The article provides for many other things including the establishment of 'an economic and monetary union whose currency is the euro'. Included too is 'eradication of poverty and the protection of human rights'. This latter is particularly important in the light of the European Charter of Fundamental Human Rights as explained later.[205]

The original treaties were modified in 1986 by the Single European Act (SEA) a treaty which extended the powers of the EEC in the economic and environmental fields, including also health and consumer protection among other things. Obstacles to the free movement of goods, capital, services and persons were to be removed before 1993. The SEA also augmented the powers of the European Parliament, as the Assembly then became.

In 1992 the Treaty on European Union (TEU) was signed at Maastricht after much controversy. This treaty was of great political and constitutional importance. It had many and diverse objects, ranging from political affairs on the widest plane to technical schemes such as that for a common European currency. It pointed clearly in the direction of turning the original economic community into a federal union, fulfilling ambitions cherished in some Member States. The three communities remained distinct, but collectively they were christened the European Union (EU). At the same time the EEC became the European Community (EC), recognising that its activities travelled far beyond its original economic objectives. Within the EU, also, there were to be policies of intergovernmental cooperation on two fronts, 'common foreign and security policy' and 'cooperation in the fields of justice and home affairs'. These were two of the three 'pillars' of the European Union. The third pillar was the Community pillar, where policy was predominately formed by the Community institutions rather than through intergovernmental cooperation. The Lisbon Treaty merged the three 'pillars' of the Union into a single legal entity securing a substantial simplification of the law.[206]

Every citizen of a Member State is to be a citizen of the Union, though without much evident legal effect.[207] There is also the 'social chapter', dealing primarily with workers' rights, from which Britain secured the right to opt out, though it later acceded.

The Treaty of Amsterdam, signed in 1997, made numerous amendments of detail, including stronger provisions about discrimination and employment and simplifying the procedures of decision-making. It reorganised and consolidated the EC Treaty and the EU Treaty, with their numerous amendments, by renumbering their articles.[208] It incorporated, *inter alia*, provisions for police and judicial cooperation. Many functions previously part of the justice and home affairs 'pillar' were transferred to the Community pillar.

The Treaty of Nice, signed in 2001, made changes in the composition of the Commission, in the system of voting in the Council, and various institutional reforms including amended rules for the Court of Justice.

The far-reaching changes (designed to enhance the workings of the EU but also to clothe the EU with many of the trappings of statehood) proposed in the Treaty establishing a Constitution for Europe of 2004 (TCE) came to naught when that treaty was rejected in referenda in France and the Netherlands. The successor to the TCE, covering

---

[205] Below, p. 172.

[206] Art. 1 TEU.

[207] But note the 'Citizenship Directive' Regulation 2004/58/EC. Moreover, Art. 11 TEU and Regulation 211/2011 provide a citizens' initiative procedure; if 1 million citizens sign a petition the Commission must consider the matter.

[208] For the text as consolidated and renumbered, see *Blackstone's EC Legislation*, 14th edn, 1.

much the same ground, was the Treaty of Lisbon of 2007.[209] After considerable controversy over ratification in several Member States (and two referenda in Ireland, the second of which approved the Treaty), the Treaty came into force on 1 December 2009. The major changes made by this Treaty included the power to accede to the European Convention on Human Rights (ECHR) and the provision of full legal force to the EU Charter of Fundamental Rights.[210] In addition there was an enhanced role for the European Parliament as explained later[211] and the adoption of qualified majority voting as the default method of decision-making for the Council of Ministers.[212] There are many other changes made and two more may be mentioned: first, the creation of the High Representative for Foreign Affairs and Security Policy and an External Action Service; and, secondly, the adoption of the 'ordinary legislative procedure' under which according to Article 294 TFEU (as explained later) the Council must obtain Parliament's consent under the 'co-decision' procedure for any legislative act. This has significantly increased the power of the Parliament.

THE EUROPEAN COMMUNITIES ACT 1972

This short statute incorporates the law of the EU into British law in the most thoroughgoing manner. It provides that all rights, powers, liabilities, obligations and restrictions deriving from the treaties which 'in accordance with the Treaties are without further enactment to be given legal effect' shall be 'recognised and available in law and enforced, allowed and followed accordingly', and that this includes 'any enactment passed or to be passed'—the words which, as noted already, have prevailed over the principle of Parliamentary sovereignty.[213] Power is given to provide, either by Order in Council or by regulation, for implementing Community law wherever necessary. This power extends to anything that could be effected by Act of Parliament, but it does not authorise taxation, retrospective operation or serious new criminal offences.[214] In legal proceedings any question concerning Community law is to be determined according to the decisions of the European Court of Justice. There are some detailed provisions about customs duties, agricultural policy and other matters, but the basic rules for the wholesale incorporation of Community law are short, comprehensive and (as explained earlier[215]) revolutionary. The Act is supplemented by the European Communities (Amendment) Act 1993, the European Union (Finance) Act 1995, the European Communities (Amendment) Act 2002 and the European Communities (Amendment) Act 2008 (giving effect to the Lisbon Treaty). Mention may also be made here of the European Union Act 2011 which precludes the ratification of any replacement or amendment of TEU or TFEU unless, amongst other things,[216] it has been approved by Act of Parliament and by a majority of those voting in a nationwide referendum.

---

[209] The Report of the House of Lords Select Committee on the European Union ('The Treaty of Lisbon: an impact assessment' HL Paper 62, 2007–08, 13 March 2008) contains much useful information. Available at <http://www.publications.parliament.uk/pa/ld200708/ldselect/ldeucom/62/62.pdf>.

[210] Art. 6 TEU.   [211] Below, p. 161. Art. 294 TFEU (default 'ordinary legislative procedure').

[212] Below, p. 161 (cf. Art. 16(3) TEU).   [213] See s. 2(4) and above, p. 21.

[214] s. 2 and 2nd Sched.   [215] Ibid.

[216] The structure and complexities of the 2011 Act and the attendant formalities are formidable. A statement must be laid before the House (ss. 2(1)(a) and 5). The change must also fall within s. 4 (matters which 'attract…a referendum). This includes the extension of the objectives of the EU, conferring on the EU of a new exclusive competence and the extension of an exclusive competence of the EU.

CONSTITUTION OF THE EU

The principal decision-making bodies of the EU are the Council, the Commission, the European Parliament and the Court of Justice of the EU (CJEU). In addition there are the European Council, the Court of Auditors and the European Central Bank, none of which formed part of the original EEC constitution.[217] These bodies are based in Brussels, except for the Court of Justice which sits in Luxembourg and the Central Bank which sits in Frankfurt. The Parliament sits in Strasbourg and Brussels.

1. *The Council*, properly called the Council of Ministers, consists of a minister from each Member State who must be authorised to commit his government. The ministers will vary with the subject matter, e.g. finance ministers will come for financial business and transport ministers for transport. The presidency of the Council is held by the Member States in turn for six months at a time. Since ministers come only for meetings, continuity is provided by a Committee of Permanent Representatives (COREPER) which manages the procedures and prepares the agenda for the Council. These permanent representatives are the Member States' ambassadors to the EU or else their deputies.[218] Under Article 16(8) TEU the Council now legislates in public, an important step towards proper standards of transparency. The procedure for voting in the Council is described later.

2. *The Commission* is the powerful executive body at the heart of the EU machine. Each Member State may nominate at least one and not more than two commissioners who serve for five years and are renewable.[219] A point of prime importance is that they must be independent of their home governments, and indeed generally. Article 17(3) TEU states 'In carrying out its responsibilities, the Commission shall be completely independent.' Their appointment is now subject to approval by the Parliament. Each commissioner will normally be in charge of one or more portfolios. The portfolios are allotted by the President of the Commission (proposed by the Council[220] and approved by the Parliament), who is in a position of great power, having charge of the general policy and conduct of the Commission. The Commission meets as a body to take decisions, which is done by simple majority vote. There is a large staff of permanent officials organised in departments under director-generals. This is the 'Brussels bureaucracy' which, in contrast to the Council, contains no elective or democratic element and so creates the 'democratic deficit' which raises questions about the EU's political legitimacy.[221] The supervision of the exercise of powers delegated by the Council to the Commissioner is carried out by committees of Member State representatives. This is known as 'comitology' and, to the extent that it excludes supervision by the Parliament, contributes to the democratic deficit.[222]

3. *The European Parliament* was established in 1967, replacing the Assembly originally set up by the Treaty of Rome. It now has some 766 members (MEPs) who since 1979

---

[217] These institutions are now set out in Art. 13 TEU.

[218] Art. 240 TFEU.

[219] Due the growing number of Member States this approach is no longer practical. Article 16(5) TEU provides for a reduction to two-thirds of the number of Member States; membership will be rotated on an equal basis between Member States. These changes will take effect in late 2014.

[220] On a qualified majority vote basis (Art. 17(7) TEU).

[221] But note that Art. 17(8) TEU now provides that the 'The Commission, as a body, shall be responsible to the European Parliament'.

[222] See 'The 2006 Reform of Comitology' (Christiansen and Vaccari) (available at <http://www.eipa.nl/cms/repository/eipascope/Scop06_3_2.pdf>) for comment and description. And see Kaeding and Hardacre, 'The European Parliament and the Future of Comitology after Lisbon' (2013) 19 *ELJ* 382 (new 'delegated acts' regime under Art. 290 TFEU, which empowers the Commission to amend a legislative act by means of a non-legislative act, discussed).

have been directly elected, each Member State having a proportionate number. Under the Treaty of Nice the Parliament is to draw up proposals for election by direct universal suffrage. The MEPs sit in multinational party groupings, thus tending towards a European party system which is a primary need for evolving a genuine parliamentary constitution. The treaties have successively conferred more powers and influence on the Parliament, particularly in budgetary matters.

4. *The European Court of Justice*[223] is, from a lawyer's standpoint, the most impressive of all the EU's institutions. It has vigorously extended its jurisdiction, sometimes beyond the terms of the treaties,[224] and, although in some cases it can enforce its judgments only through national courts, it has established the effective supremacy of EU law throughout the Member States. It has become perhaps the most powerful court in the world, despite the fact that it has jurisdiction only within the boundaries of the treaties. There are now twenty-eight judges, appointed by common accord of the Member States,[225] one judge coming normally from each. In addition there are nine advocates-general one of whom, following the French system, sits with the court (except at first instance) and, after the argument, gives a written opinion advising the court how to decide. Judges are appointed for six years and are renewable. They themselves elect their President for a renewable term of three years. The court may sit in several divisions. There is also a court of first instance (now renamed the General Court),[226] established by the Single European Act, with limited jurisdiction and subject to appeal to the Court of Justice, which lightens the court's constantly increasing caseload. A feature of the court's procedure is that one of the judges (the 'juge-rapporteur') prepares a written summary of the facts and the parties' arguments before the oral hearing, which by British standards is very short. Another contrast with Britain is that dissenting opinions are not given.

The Court's jurisdiction extends, among other things, to enforcing Union law against defaulting Member States, to reviewing the acts and omissions of the various EU bodies and awarding compensation for abuse of power, and to determining by 'preliminary rulings' issues of EU law referred to it by the courts of the Member States. This last is the busiest department of its jurisdiction.

5. *The Ombudsman* is appointed by the Parliament and is removable by the Court of Justice at the Parliament's request.[227] He must be completely independent and may have no other occupation. He may receive complaints from any citizen or resident of the EU about instances of maladministration in the activities of Community institutions or bodies other than the Court of Justice. Complaints may be made to him either direct or through MEPs, and he may act on his own initiative, except where legal proceedings have been taken. Adverse findings are referred to the institution concerned which must reply within three months. The Ombudsman then makes a report to Parliament, but what is to happen thereafter is not explained.

6. *The European Council*, to be distinguished from the Council of Ministers described above, is a political body consisting of the heads of governments of the Member States accompanied by their foreign ministers. It was constituted informally in 1974 and since 1986 is formally established under the Single European Act in order to 'provide the Union with the necessary impetus for its development' and to 'define the general political

---

[223] The abbreviation 'CJEU' refers to the ECJ, the General Court and a number of specialist courts (Art. 19(1) TEU).   [224] See (1996) 112 *LQR* 95 (T. C. Hartley).

[225] Member States consult an independent panel which issues opinions on the suitability of candidates: Arts. 253 and 255 TFEU.

[226] Art. 19(1) TEU. The General Court's jurisdiction is set out in Art. 256 TFEU.

[227] Art. 195 (ex 138E); now Art. 228 TFEU.

directions and priorities'. It has no legal powers, but will concern itself with matters which demand discussion at the highest possible level such as economic policy and proposals for monetary union. It aims to integrate the policies of the Member States and to provide initiatives which the Commission can translate into effective measures. Following the Lisbon Treaty Article 13 TEU establishes the European Council as an EU institution, subject to the supervision of the CJEU. Furthermore the European Council now comprises in addition its own President—another creation of the Lisbon Treaty and who must 'drive forward' the work of the European Council[228]—the President of the Commission and the High Representative of the Union for Foreign Affairs.[229]

LEGISLATIVE POWERS AND PROCEDURES

Following the Lisbon Treaty the most widespread legislative procedure under the Treaties is that is that of the 'ordinary legislative procedure' as set out in Article 294 TFEU.[230] First the Commission submits a proposal to the Council and the Parliament; the Parliament then adopts a position on the proposal and communicates that position to the Council; if the Council agrees with the Parliament's position, the measure is adopted.

But if the Council disagrees, it communicates its reasons to the Parliament and the Parliament either (i) accepts the Council's position, (ii) rejects the Council's position outright (at which point the measure falls) or (iii) proposes amendments for consideration by the Council.

The Council must consider any amendments within three months. If it accepts the amendments, the measure is adopted; but if after three months, the Council does not accept the Parliament's proposed changes, a conciliation committee is convened. The Council may only reach an agreement at this stage by way of qualified majority vote. The Parliament must operate by way of absolute majority vote. The Commission is obliged to take steps to reconcile the institutions' positions.

Finally there is a 'special legislative procedure' in which 'a regulation, directive or Decision' is adopted by the 'European Parliament with the participation of the Council, or by the latter with the participation of the European Parliament'.[231] This is restricted to the admission of new Member States and association agreements with other states and a few special matters such as elections to the Parliament[232] and freedom of movement within the EU.[233]

Voting in the Council, according to the treaty provision in question, is either by simple majority or by qualified majority or by unanimity. The default method is unanimity.[234] As from 1 November 2014 the old provisions in regard to qualified majority voting will no

---

[228] Art. 15(6) TEU. The President is elected by a qualified majority of the European Council for a term of two and a half years (Art. 15(5) TEU).   [229] Art. 15(2) TEU.

[230] There is now (following the Lisbon Treaty) a Protocol on the Application of the Principles of Subsidiarity and Proportionality. It is made pursuant to Art. 3b of the TEU and is available at <http://eur-lex.europa.eu/en/treaties/dat/12007L/htm/C2007306EN.01015001.htm>. The Protocol is complex and provides in outline that the Commission must 'consult widely' before proposing a legislative act (Art. 2); draft texts must be sent to national parliaments accompanied by a detailed statement of compliance with the principles of subsidiarity and proportionality (Arts. 4 and 5); any national parliament may issue a 'reasoned opinion' why it disagrees with the Commission's assessment of subsidiarity and proportionality (Art. 6); if a threshold level of objections is received the Parliament and Commission must review the proposed legislation (Art. 7).   [231] Art. 289(2) TFEU.

[232] Art. 223(1) TFEU.   [233] Art. 21(3) TFEU.

[234] Art. 293(1) TFEU. At the conciliation stage the Council operates according to a qualified majority vote.

longer apply.[235] Under the new provisions a qualified majority is defined as at least 55 per cent of the members of the Council, comprising at least fifteen of them and representing Member States comprising at least 65 per cent of the population of the Union. A blocking minority must include at least four Council members, failing which the qualified majority shall be deemed attained.[236] In special circumstances, for instance, if the Council acts other than on the proposal of the Commission, or if certain members of the Council do not under the Treaties participate in the voting, different rules apply.[237]

Three forms of legally binding legislation are prescribed by the Treaty of Rome:[238]

(a) A *regulation* shall have general application. It shall be binding in its entirety and directly applicable in all Member States.

(b) A *directive* shall be binding, as to the result to be achieved, upon each Member State to which it is addressed, but shall leave to the national authorities the choice of form and methods.

(c) A *decision* shall be binding in its entirety upon those to whom it is addressed.

There may also be recommendations and opinions, but these have no binding force. The merit of the directive was that it allowed for the principle of subsidiarity. Its weak point was that it depended for its efficacy on action by the Member States. Their persistent defaults led to the doctrine of direct effect of directives, discussed later.

SUPREMACY OF EU LAW

The Treaty of Rome imposed a duty on Member States to 'ensure fulfilment of the Community's tasks',[239] but did not specify how this was to be achieved. Perhaps the most striking achievement of the Court of Justice is its doctrine of supremacy, under which national courts must accept that Community law prevails over all domestic legislation and rules of law of whatever kind. Its effect is therefore automatic, and not dependent upon the cumbersome procedures provided in the Treaty for infringements to be prosecuted before the Court of Justice by the Commission or by Member States.

The principle was laid down by the Court in two celebrated cases. In *Costa* the Court said:[240]

In contrast with ordinary international treaties, the Treaty has created its own legal system which, on entry into force of the Treaty, became an integral part of the legal systems of the Member States and which their courts are bound to apply.

And in *Simmenthal* the Court said:[241]

Every national court must, in a case within its jurisdiction, apply Community law in its entirety and protect rights which the latter confers on individuals, and must accordingly set aside any provisions of national law which may conflict with it, whether prior or subsequent to the Community rule.

---

[235] See the 10th edition of this book at p. 166.   [236] Art. 16(4) TEU.

[237] Art. 289(2) and (3) TFEU.

[238] Art. 249 (ex 189) now Art. 288 TFEU.

[239] Art. 10 (ex 5). Article 4 TEU now provides that Member States 'shall take any appropriate measure, general or particular, to ensure fulfilment of the obligations arising out of the Treaties or resulting from the acts of the institutions of the Union'.   [240] *Costa* v. *ENEL*, Case 6/64, [1964] CMLR 425.

[241] *Amministrazione delle Finanze dello Stato* v. *Simmenthal SpA* (*No 2*), Case 106/77, [1978] 3 CMLR 263.

In Britain these rulings came to the test in the *Factortame* cases,[242] where Spanish ship-owners complained that their fleets were excluded from British waters by the requirements of the Merchant Shipping Act 1988 as to the nationality of owners and crews, and that these requirements violated the Community laws on freedom of establishment and discrimination—as, in the end, it was held that they did. In the first case the High Court held, more presciently than the House of Lords, that while a preliminary ruling was sought from the Court of Justice the Act of 1988 must be 'disapplied' (an unprecedented term in British law) and an interim injunction granted against enforcement of the Act, so as to protect the ship-owners from heavy losses in laying up their ships in the meantime. The House of Lords reversed that decision, holding that they had no power to disapply an Act of the sovereign Parliament in an uncertain situation and that, in any case, there was no power in British law to grant an interim injunction against an officer of the Crown (this was wrong, though believed by the judges at the time);[243] but they referred the question of interim protection to the Court of Justice. That court ruled, predictably, that interim protection was just as necessary in Community law as in any other system and that any conflicting rule of national law or sovereignty must be set aside by the national court or tribunal.[244] In the second *Factortame* case, accordingly, the House of Lords accepted these corrections and was obliged to take the revolutionary step of granting an injunction to forbid a minister from obeying an Act of Parliament.[245] There could be no better illustration of the profound effects which the supremacy of Community law can have not only on the domestic law but also on the constitutions of the Member States.

If the incompatibility is clear, the national court may disapply the domestic law without reference to the Court of Justice. This was done by the House of Lords in the *Equal Opportunities* case,[246] where the time thresholds applied to part-time workers under the Employment Protection (Consolidation) Act 1978 as to protection against unfair dismissal and entitlement to redundancy payments were held to conflict both with the Treaty of Rome and with a directive of the EU Council on grounds of sex discrimination. Part-time workers were predominantly women, and it was held that the evidence produced by the government failed to show objective justification for excluding them. Declarations were granted accordingly on judicial review at the instance of the Equal Opportunities Commission.

In cases of this kind the Court of Justice is not content that the offending provisions of national law should be left as they stand and merely treated as dead wood. Community

---

[242] *R* v. *Secretary of State for Transport ex p Factortame Ltd* [1990] 2 AC 85; (*No 2*) [1991] 1 AC 603; (*No 3*) [1992] QB 680; (*No 4*) [1996] QB 404; (*No 5*) [1999] 3 WLR 1062 (HL).

[243] See below, p. 703.

[244] For an example, see *Winner Wetten GmbH* v. *Burgermeisterin der Stadt Bergheim*, Case C-409/06, [2011] CMLR 21, paras. 53–7.   [245] As explained above, p. 21.

[246] *R* v. *Secretary of State for Employment ex p Equal Opportunities Commission* [1995] 1 AC 1. For repercussions in the tribunal system see [1996] *PL* 579 (D. Nicol). When the 2 years' employment qualification was similarly challenged the European Court held that it was for the national court to decide whether there was statistical evidence, objective justification and a legitimate aim of social policy: *R* v. *Secretary of State for Employment ex p Seymour-Smith* [1999] 3 WLR 460 (ECJ). The Court of Appeal had held in the negative ([1997] 1 WLR 473) but the House of Lords allowed the Secretary of State's appeal, [2000] 1 All ER 857. Acts were disapplied in *Bossa* v. *Nordstress Ltd* [1998] ICR 694 and in *Perceval-Price* v. *Department of Economic Development* [2000] IRLR 380. Regulations were disapplied in *Fleming (t/a Bodycraft)* v. *HM Revenue and Customs* [2008] UKHL 2 (no provision for transitional arrangements as required by EU law). And see *Autologic Holdings plc* v. *Commissioners of Inland Revenue* [2005] UKHL 54, [2006] 1 AC 118.

law requires that they should be amended or repealed so that they may not mislead.[247] This is part of the doctrine of legal certainty.

The authority of the Court of Justice is confined to that conferred by the Treaties and it has no inherent jurisdiction. Its doctrines do not automatically apply in British courts unless some specific Community rule is in issue. Thus when the Commission banned the export of British beef and the British government's compensation scheme favoured producers with slaughtering facilities at the expense of those without them, the latter were not entitled to complain under the Community law about discrimination since that law did not derive from a Treaty provision but from 'the common law of the Community' as developed by the Court itself.[248] But when the rates of insurance premium tax, imposed by Act of Parliament, discriminated against travel agencies and in favour of independent insurance companies, and the government could show no objective justification, this was held to be illegal (overriding the Act) as 'state aid' distorting competition and so violating a specific treaty provision.[249]

The success of the Court of Justice in imposing the supremacy of EU law may be contrasted with the lack of success in this respect of the European Communities Act 1972. That Act provided in very general terms for Community law to be 'enforced, allowed and followed' in British courts and 'any enactment passed or to be passed' was expressly made subject to that sweeping provision. Yet the appellate courts, as the first *Factortame* case shows, felt unable to give full scope to these directions, or to the decisions of the Court of Justice which had already established the principle of supremacy. It was only when that Court gave its rulings in the later *Factortame* litigation that the 'new legal order' was fully accepted and disentangled from the restraints and technicalities of domestic law.

ENFORCEMENT THROUGH NATIONAL COURTS

The Court of Justice has no powers of enforcement. It has to rely upon the courts of the Member States and on their duty to fulfil their treaty obligations. Infringements of EU law by a Member State may be brought before the Court by another Member State (Article 227; now Article 259 TFEU) or by the Commission (Article 226; now Article 258 TFEU) and there have been many such proceedings. The commonest procedure, however, is for some national court or tribunal to seek a 'preliminary ruling' from the Court on some question of EC law which has arisen in proceedings before it.[250] Though called 'preliminary', the Court's ruling is normally definitive. The case then returns to the national court which must give effect to the ruling, using its own remedies but disregarding any restrictions of national law which are inconsistent with the ruling. This procedure may be used in ordinary litigation between private parties or in judicial review. A ruling may be sought by any court or tribunal, and must be sought if there is no further judicial recourse possible, as in a decision of the House of Lords.

It is not lawful for a Member State, believing that another Member State is in breach of EU law, to attempt to enforce it by unilateral action. Consequently the British government,

---

[247] See *Commission v. France*, Case 167/73, [1974] CMLR 216. But domestic court not required to reopen a previous judicial decision based on EU law-incompatible domestic legislation: *R v. Budimir (Nikolas)* [2010] EWCA Civ 1486.

[248] *R v. Ministry of Agriculture Fisheries and Food ex p First City Trading* [1997] 1 CMLR 250.

[249] *R v. Commissioners of Customs and Excise ex p Lunn Poly Ltd* [1999] 1 CMLR 1357.

[250] Art. 234 (ex 177); now Art. 267 TFEU. This may be either a matter of the interpretation of the treaty, the validity of acts of the institutions of the Community or the Central Bank, or the interpretation of the statute of a body established by the Council.

supposing that live animals for slaughter were maltreated in Spain, had no right to ban such exports and were held liable to compensate the exporters.[251]

THE DIRECT EFFECT OF EC LAW

The enforcement of EC law through the doctrine of direct effect is the lynch-pin of the Union's legal system, giving it much of the efficiency of a unified jurisdiction as opposed to a collection of international treaties enforceable only by diplomacy. Rights and duties are conferred not only upon states but upon their nationals. In the landmark case of *Van Gend en Loos* the Court of Justice stated the principle:[252]

> The Community constitutes a new legal order of international law for the benefit of which the states have limited their sovereign rights, albeit within limited fields, and the subjects of which comprise not only the Member States but also their nationals. Independently of the legislation of Member States Community law not only imposes obligations on individuals but is also intended to confer on them rights which become part of their legal heritage.

Article 12 of the original treaty, which prohibited new customs duties on imports or exports between Member States, therefore enabled a German firm to reclaim in the Dutch courts customs duty wrongfully imposed by the Dutch government.[253] Since the terms of the treaty were clear and unconditional they were 'ideally adapted to produce direct effects in the legal relationship between Member States and their subjects'. But would this be equally true between those subjects themselves? The Court of Justice answered positively in the *Defrenne* case, where an air hostess successfully sued an independent Belgian airline for violating the principle of equal pay for equal work.[254] The treaty provision was both mandatory and absolute, and also capable of conferring rights on individuals, and so directly applicable in the Belgian court. Even where a provision is capable of elaboration by national legislation, it may, it was held, nevertheless have direct effect in the absence of action by the Member State.

Since the treaty provides that a regulation 'shall be binding in its entirety and directly applicable', EU regulations come naturally within the doctrine of direct effect. They are thus automatically incorporated into domestic law without further ado, and they frequently confer rights on individuals. But a treaty provision or regulation can be given direct effect only if it is clear and unconditional and not dependent upon further action by the Member State.[255]

The difficult problem came with directives, where the Court of Justice had to find ways round a categorical provision of the Treaty of Rome which did not work satisfactorily. It is clear from the Treaty that directives were intended to take effect only indirectly, since they are 'binding as to the result to be achieved', but 'shall leave to the national authorities the choice of form and methods'. This clause put too much faith in the national authorities, which often failed to give effect to directives, and caused the Court of Justice to look

---

[251] See *R* v. *Ministry of Agriculture, Fisheries and Food ex p Hedley Lomas (Ireland) Ltd* [1997] QB 139 (ECJ).

[252] *Van Gend en Loos* v. *Nederlandse Administratie der Belastingen*, Case 26/62, [1963] CMLR 105, [1963] ECR I.					[253] *Van Gend en Loos* (ibid.).

[254] *Defrenne* v. *Sabena* [1976] ECR 455. A later example is *Angonese* v. *Cassa di Risparmio di Bolzano SpA*, Case C-281/98, [2000] ECR I-4139.

[255] *Comitato di Coordinamento per la Difesa della Cava* v. *Regione Lombardia*, Case C-236/92, [1994] ECR I-483.

for ways of circumventing it. In 1974 a measure of direct effect was devised in the *Van Duyn*[256] case, where a Dutch citizen had been refused entry to Britain since she intended to work with the Church of Scientology, an organisation at that time disapproved of by the British government. The treaty provision for freedom of movement allowed exceptions justified by public policy, but a directive restricted them to matters of 'personal conduct'—and no personal misconduct was alleged. The directive had not been incorporated in the British regulations, but the Court of Justice held that it 'would be incompatible with the binding effect attributed to a directive' by the treaty to exclude the possibility that it could be invoked by those concerned and that 'the useful effect of such an act would be weakened if individuals were prevented from relying on it before their national courts'. There was also the argument that a state which had failed to implement a directive ought not to be able to benefit by its own default. As against the terms of the treaty these were not convincing reasons, but the corner had been turned and new horizons opened. Their potentiality was shown by the *Marshall* case,[257] in which the Court of Justice upheld the complaint of a woman employed by a health authority who was compulsorily retired under the age limit of 60 for women, whereas the age limit for men was 65. The British sex discrimination legislation allowed differential retiring ages, but the corresponding directive did not. The directive was held to prevail by direct effect, enabling the woman to sue the health authority in a British court.

A limit, however, was found in the rule that a directive was 'binding upon each Member State to which it is addressed'. It was held that directives could have direct effect only against the state and not against private parties. This is the principle of 'vertical but not horizontal effect'. A broad concept of 'the state' was however adopted, so that it extended to a privatised gas company,[258] a privatised water authority[259] and a voluntary grant-aided school.[260] The test was satisfied if the body provided a public service under state legislation and under some degree of state control and had special powers.[261] It did not cover the (then) publicly owned Rolls-Royce company, since it did not provide a public service.[262] And it does not cover the Motor Insurers' Bureau.[263] Drawing a line round 'the state' in this way produces obvious anomalies, for example as between employees of government agencies and employees of private companies. Nevertheless the Court of Justice decided that it could not do further violence to the treaty, otherwise regulations and directives would be indistinguishable.[264]

---

[256] *Van Duyn* v. *Home Office*, Case 41/74, [1975] Ch 358, [1975] 1 CMLR 1. Judicial review is a satisfactory remedy for Community nationals refused entry to Britain on grounds of public policy: *R* v. *Home Secretary ex p Shingara*, Case C-65/95, [1997] ECR I-3341.

[257] *Marshall* v. *Southampton and South-West Hampshire Health Authority*, Case 152/84, [1986] QB 401, [1986] 1 CMLR 688; and see *Gibson* v. *East Riding of Yorkshire Council* [1999] ICR 662 (working time directive held directly effective so that swimming instructor could claim pay for leave before Britain had implemented the directive).

[258] *Foster* v. *British Gas*, Case 188/89, [1991] 2 AC 306, [1990] 2 CMLR 833.

[259] *Griffin* v. *South-West Water Services Ltd* [1995] IRLR 15.

[260] *National Union of Teachers* v. *Governing Body of St Mary's Church School* [1997] IRLR 242.

[261] A chief constable is included despite his constitutional independence: *Johnston* v. *Chief Constable of the Royal Ulster Constabulary* [1987] QB 129 (ECJ).

[262] *Doughty* v. *Rolls-Royce plc* [1992] IRLR 126.

[263] *Byrne* v. *Motor Insurers' Bureau* [2008] EWCA Civ 574, paras. 48–63. MIB (a private company which compensates victims of uninsured and untraced drivers; every vehicle insurer being required by law to be a member and pay a levy to the MIB) not an emanation of the State because (a) it did not have special powers and (b) it was not controlled by the State.

[264] See *Faccini Dori* v. *Recreb Srl* [1994] ECR I-3325 where the ECJ refused to give effect to a consumer protection directive, unimplemented by Italy, against a private trader, but held that it was for the national

Eventually a way forward was discovered in a doctrine of indirect effect. In the German case of *von Colson*,[265] also a discrimination case, the Court of Justice held that, since a directive was 'binding, as to the result to be achieved' on the Member State, it bound all the authorities of that state including the courts, which therefore had a duty to give effect to it. They must then interpret national law accordingly, and if it conflicts with Community law the 'interpretation' must be that national law is to be set aside. In the German case the plaintiff, an employee of a private company, was accordingly able to recover full compensation for discrimination, despite the fact that German law allowed much less. In this way the Court of Justice, by treating the national court as a state authority, has contrived to achieve generalised direct effect and to rewrite part of the Treaty of Rome. (There is an interesting parallel here with the Human Rights Act 1998, which is noted elsewhere.)[266] The new doctrine was corroborated in the Spanish *Marleasing* case,[267] where one private corporation was suing another to nullify its establishment in Spain as being designed for fraudulent purposes. Spanish law allowed this ground of objection, but the Council directive on the right of establishment for companies did not. The Court of Justice held that the Spanish court must 'interpret' the Spanish law in accordance with the directive and disallow any objection not contained in it. Moreover, the Court of Justice has somewhat relaxed its doctrine, holding that the national court need only interpret the national law 'so far as possible' in conformity with the directive; but that if that is not possible it need not decide *contra legem* by disregarding national law; otherwise it would be giving horizontal effect to directives. This dilemma is unresolved.[268]

How far British courts will feel able to accept this style of 'interpretation' remains to be seen. Before the *Marleasing* decision the House of Lords had already modified a regulation protecting the rights of employees of transferred undertakings so as to make it agree with a directive.[269] But the House had also declined to modify an Act of Parliament, once again in a sex discrimination case, in favour of a woman compulsorily retired at 60 by a private employer contrary to the equal treatment directive of the EU Council, since the directive had no horizontal effect.[270] Lord Templeman said that 'it would be most unfair to the respondent to distort the construction of the 1975 Sex Discrimination Act in order to accommodate the 1976 Equal Treatment Directive' and that 'the respondent could not reasonably be expected to reduce to precision the opaque language which constitutes both the strength and the difficulty of some Community legislation'. The question is whether the Court of Justice, having now broken through all restraints, will consolidate its position in future cases or whether national courts will refuse to accept the horizontal as well as the vertical operation of directives as overriding all forms of domestic law.[271]

---

court to award reparation under national law. Cf. *Werner Mangold* v. *Rüdiger Helm*, Case C-144/04, [2005] ECR I-9981, for criticism see (2007) 9 *CYELS* 81 (Dashwood).

[265] *von Colson* v. *Land Nordrhein-Westfalen*, Case 14/83, [1984] ECR 1891, [1986] 2 CMLR 430.

[266] Above, p. 145.

[267] *Marleasing* v. *La Commercial International de Alimentation*, Case 106/89, [1990] ECR I-4135, [1992] 1 CMLR 688. But see *Kolpinghuis Nijmegen BV* [1987] ECR 3969.

[268] For a recent discussion see *Dominguez* v. *Centre Informatique du Centre Ouest Atlantique*, Case C-282/10, [2012] 2 CMLR 14, para. 25.

[269] *Litster* v. *Forth Dry Dock and Engineering Co* [1990] 1 AC 546, [1989] 2 CMLR 194.

[270] *Duke* v. *GEC Reliance* [1988] AC 618, [1988] 1 CMLR 719. Cf. *Marshall* v. *Southampton Health Authority* (above).

[271] Although the rule against horizontal effect still prevails: see e.g. *El Corte Ingles* v. *Christina Blazquez Rivero*, Case 192/94, [1990] ECR I-1281. For some recent decisions on this issue see *Floe Telecom Ltd* v. *Office of Communications* [2009] EWCA Civ 47, paras. 86–7; and *Assange* v. *Sweden* [2012] UKSC 22, [2012] 2 AC 471, para. 174.

The rigidity of the EU constitution, in which any amendment needs the consent of all Member States, must be taken as the excuse of the Court of Justice for its manipulation of the treaties. Indeed, the Court of Justice has now gone further and developed the direct applicability of 'general principles' of EU Law (primarily non-discrimination). Although asserting that directives do not have direct effect the ECJ has held 'that the need to give full effectiveness to the general principle of non-discrimination on the grounds of age meant that any conflicting national legislation out to be disapplied'.[272]

UNIMPLEMENTED DIRECTIVES: COMPENSATION AND REMEDIES

The Court of Justice has another string to its bow in dealing with Member States which fail to implement directives. This is that individuals who suffer by the default may be able to sue the defaulting state for compensation. There is then no disregard of the TFEU and no difficulty in the reasoning. It is simply an application of the principle that where there is a wrong, there is a remedy.

This solution was found in the Italian *Francovich* case,[273] where Italy had failed to implement a directive requiring Member States to provide legal security for the rights of employees, in particular to unpaid wages, in case of the insolvency of their employer. A number of the former employees of two Italian concerns which went bankrupt were owed large sums for past wages but could not recover them in the absence of the legislation required by the directive. The directive itself was not sufficiently precise to be directly effective, but it was 'inherent in the system of the Treaty' and necessary for 'the full effectiveness of Community rules' that individuals should be able to obtain redress for infringements for which the state was responsible. Three conditions, however, had to be fulfilled. First, 'the result prescribed by the directive should entail the grant of rights to individuals'. Secondly, those rights should be identifiable in the directive. Thirdly, there must be 'a causal link between the breach of the state's obligation and the loss and damage suffered by the injured parties'. The result may then be that the Member State 'manifestly and gravely disregards the limits on its discretion'.[274]

As regards compensation, the Court of Justice held that it was for the defaulting state to make reparation under its own substantive and procedural law, but its rules 'must not be less favourable than those relating to similar domestic claims and must not be so framed as to make it virtually impossible or excessively difficult to obtain reparation'.

The *Francovich* principle will not only be a spur to Member States tempted to procrastinate over directives. It is also to be regarded as one branch of a general doctrine of state liability for breaches of EU law. This doctrine is explained later as a head of government liability.[275]

---

[272] *Kucukdeveci* v. *Swedex GmbH*, Case C-555/07, [2010] 2 CMLR 33, paras. 53–6. The words cited come from Albors-Llorens [2010] *CLJ* 458 at 457. This principle was first applied in *Mangold* v. *Helm* [2006] 1 CMLR 43. See Papadopoulos, 'Criticising the Horizontal Direct Effect of the EU General Principle of Equality' (2011) 4 EHRLR 437.

[273] *Francovich* v. *Italy*, Cases 6 and 9/90, [1993] 2 CMLR 66. See similarly *R* v. *Secretary of State for Social Security ex p Sutton* [1997] ECR I-2163 (ECJ).

[274] *Dillenkofer* v. *Germany* [1996] 3 CMLR 469, elaborating the *Francovich* tests; *R* v. *HM Treasury ex p British Telecom plc* [1996] 2 CMLR 217. This is discussed further below, p. 663.   [275] Below, p. 635.

JUDICIAL REVIEW OF COMMUNITY ACTION

The actions (and inactions) of the authorities of the EU are subject to judicial review by the Court of Justice. The Treaty of Rome, as amended at Maastricht, provides that:

The Court of Justice shall review the legality of acts adopted jointly by the European Parliament and the Council, of the Commission and of the European Central Bank, other than recommendations and opinions, and of acts of the European Parliament intended to produce legal effects vis-à-vis third parties. It shall for this purpose have jurisdiction in actions brought by a Member State, the Council or the Commission on grounds of lack of competence, infringement of an essential procedural requirement, infringement of this Treaty or of any rule of law relating to its application, or misuse of powers.[276]

Secondly the amended treaty now provides that:

Any natural or legal person may, under the conditions laid down in the first and second paragraphs,[277] institute proceedings against an act addressed to that person or which is of direct and individual concern to them, and against a regulatory act which is of direct concern to them and does not entail implementing measures.[278]

The treaty then prescribes a time limit of two months from the publication or notification of the decision or, in their absence, of its discovery by the plaintiff. There is no provision for extension of this short period,[279] but it may be evaded if proceedings are started in the national court and a reference to the ECJ can be obtained.[280] In contrast to Britain, acts and measures are reviewable only if they have legal effect.[281]

The four specified grounds of review (lack of competence etc.) are modelled upon the four traditional *ouvertures* for the *recours pour excès de pouvoir* in French administrative law, which cover the whole field of judicial review much as in Britain. But the rules for standing are interpreted strictly[282] and give much less scope for individual complainants than do the corresponding British rules, which are now relaxed almost to vanishing point.[283] A distinction is made between open and closed categories of persons affected, so that regulations affecting a whole industry cannot be challenged by individual firms, but may be challengeable if the only firms affected are a small and identifiable class. But this did not avail Italian companies disputing a Council regulation restricting the subsidy of Williams pears who claimed that the regulation affected them particularly.[284] Nor does

---

[276] Art. 230 (ex 173); now Art. 263(1) and (2) TFEU (slight differences of wording).

[277] Viz. the conditions described in the preceding paragraph.

[278] Art. 263(4) TFEU. The reference to challenges to regulatory acts suggests a more liberal standard. Regulatory acts are interpreted as 'all acts of general application apart from legislative acts' (*Rutgers Germany GmbH* v. *ECHA*, Case T-96/10, [2013] 3 CMLR 3, para. 57; *Inuit Tapiriit Kanatami* v. *European Parliament*, Case T-18/10, [2012] All ER (EC) 183, paras. 42–5. Note also the more liberal rules under the Aarhus Convention (below, p. 597).

[279] Except for the extensions on account of distance (10 days for Britain) and for unforeseeable circumstances and force majeure allowed by the Court's statute.

[280] See M. J. Beloff in Forsyth and Hare (eds.), *The Golden Metwand*, 289.

[281] *IBM* v. *Commission*, Case 60/81, [1981] 3 CMLR 635. Contrast below, p. 538.

[282] *Plaumann & Co* v. *Commission* [1964] CMLR 29. See e.g. *Government of Gibraltar* v. *Council* [1993] ECR I-4009 (narrow interpretation of 'direct and individual concern'). Similarly held by the ECJ in *Commission* v. *Jégo-Quéré*, Case C-263/02 P, [2004] ECR I-3425 (individual could not seek annulment of a general regulation that does not 'distinguish him individually'). [283] See below, p. 585.

[284] *Calpac* v. *Commission*, Cases 789 and 790/79, [1981] CMLR 26. Contrast *Gestevision Telecino SA* v. *Commission* [1998] All ER (EC) 918 (standing allowed to commercial competitor).

the Court admit representative actions, e.g. by trade unions on behalf of their members or by conservation groups.[285] The jurisprudence of the Court of Justice has been erratic in this difficult area, but will perhaps become more liberal when fears of 'opening the floodgates' recede and the court appreciates that strict rules of standing, just as formerly in Britain, may allow the authorities or individuals to act unlawfully and escape challenge.[286] A movement in this direction is shown by the decision of the Court of Justice, on a preliminary ruling issued to the English Court of Appeal, that a commercial competitor could sue for a breach of Community quality standard regulations committed by another firm importing seedless grapes. The Court stressed the necessity for 'full effectiveness' of Community law without mentioning its conflicting decisions.[287] Furthermore, since Member States, the Council and the Commission always have standing before the Court, individuals and firms may be able to induce them to bring proceedings on their behalf. There is also provision for regulations of the Council and the Commission to be challenged indirectly in other proceedings, as in the British doctrine of collateral pleas, but this applies only to regulations.[288]

Among the grounds of review, which basically reflect the principle of ultra vires, it is notable that 'an essential procedural requirement' is held to include the duty to give a fair hearing to a party adversely affected,[289] and also that 'infringement of the Treaty' includes failure to give reasons for regulations, directives and decisions of the Council and the Commission, which are expressly required.[290]

Where an unlawful act is annulled, it is treated as voidable rather than void. That is to say, it may have legal effect in transactions prior to the judgment. This again contrasts with British law,[291] and may allow rights to be affected by unlawful acts, as may also happen when the very short two-month period of limitation expires. Under the treaty, however, the Court of Justice has discretion to 'state which of the effects of the regulation which it has declared void shall be considered as definitive'.[292] Although nominally confined to regulations, this power has been applied to directives also, particularly where they are kept alive until valid directives replace them.[293] As a general rule the Court will allow the benefit of the annulment only to parties who have begun proceedings before the date of the judgment.[294] Others will have to accept the 'void' act as valid.

Where an act is flagrantly and obviously illegal it is treated as 'non-existent' (as in French administrative law) and so void from the beginning and technically not even reviewable.[295]

A national court has no jurisdiction to review the validity of acts of the EU authorities, but must always seek a ruling from the Court of Justice.[296]

---

[285] *Stichting Greenpeace Council* v. *Commission* [1998] All ER (EC) 620 (standing denied for challenging subsidy for power stations in Canary Islands).   [286] See below, p. 585.

[287] *Muñoz y Cla SA* v. *Frumar Ltd* [2003] 3 WLR 58. In *Union de Pequnos Agricultores* v. *Council* [2002] ECR I-6677 the ECJ adhered to its strict doctrine.

[288] Art. 241 (ex 184); now Art. 277 TFEU.

[289] *Transocean Marine Paint* v. *Commission*, Case 17/74, [1974] ECR 1063, [1974] CMLR 459.

[290] Art. 253 (ex 190); now Art. 296 TFEU.   [291] See below, p. 297.

[292] Art. 231 (ex 174); now Art. 264 TFEU.

[293] See *European Parliament* v. *Council*, Case 295/90, [1992] 3 CMLR 281.

[294] See *Defrenne* v. *Sabena*, Case 43/75, [1976] 2 CMLR 98; *Barber* v. *Guardian Royal Exchange Assurance Group*, Case 262/88, [1990] 2 CMLR 513, balancing the principles of legality and legal certainty; *Commission* v. *AssiDomän Kraft Products AB*, Case 310/97, [1999] All ER (EC) 737.

[295] See *BASF* v. *Commission* [1992] ECR II-315, [1992] 4 CMLR 357.

[296] *Foto-Frost* v. *Hauptzollamt Lübeck-Ost*, Case 314/85, [1988] 3 CMLR 57; *Woodspring DC* v. *Bakers of Nailsea Ltd*, Case C-27/95, [1997] 2 CMLR 266 (ECJ). In *R* v. *Secretary of State for Health ex p Imperial*

LIABILITY OF COMMUNITY AUTHORITIES

The Treaty provides for liability of the Community in tort:[297]

> In the case of non-contractual liability, the Community shall, in accordance with the general principles common to the laws of the Member States, make good any damage caused by its institutions or by its servants in the performance of their duties.

There are no restrictions as to standing and the time limit is five years. But the complainant must show 'a sufficiently serious breach of a superior rule of law for the protection of the individual' and that the EU authority has 'manifestly and gravely disregarded the limits on the exercise of its powers'.[298] 'A superior rule of law' appears to mean any rule of EU law. The mere illegality of an act by itself is not enough, but fault is not essential. Here there may be some conflict with British law, as is explained later.[299] In a series of decisions the Court of Justice has relaxed the strict conditions which it had at first imposed, such as that a reviewable act must first be annulled, so that there is now a wide-ranging remedy against abuse of the drastic powers of the EU authorities.[300]

An example is the second *Mulder* case,[301] in which a dairy farmer had discontinued production for five years under regulations made by the Council and had, as was held in the first case, a legitimate expectation that he would be allowed to resume production in later years. But he was refused licences on the ground that under the regulations they could be allotted only on the basis of the previous year's production, despite the fact that in the previous year he had produced nothing. In awarding damages the Court of Justice held that by failing to take account of the position of farmers in this situation 'the Community legislature manifestly and gravely disregarded the limits of its discretionary power, thereby committing a sufficiently serious breach of a superior rule of law'. Here the 'superior rule of law' was the principle of the protection of legitimate expectations. This may be compared with British cases where regulations have been invalidated for unreasonableness.[302]

EFFECT ON ADMINISTRATIVE LAW

The 'incoming tide' of community law, of which Lord Denning MR spoke thirty-five years ago,[303] has been gaining in strength and volume ever since, and has brought about profound changes both in the constitutional law and the administrative law of Britain. Wide new areas of governmental liability have been opened up and new rights against public authorities have been created, often in favour of private persons and concerns. The enforcement of freedom of establishment and of non-discrimination, to take only two examples, has benefited many plaintiffs, and other EU benefits have similarly added important dimensions to administrative law. An understanding of the source and operation of these new rules, as sketched briefly in the preceding pages, is now indispensable. Examples of their effects in administrative law will be found later in this book, for example in the areas of nullity[304] and breach of duty.[305] An inroad has been made in the doctrine of Parliamentary sovereignty, on which both constitutional and administrative law are founded.[306]

Tobacco Ltd [2002] QB 161, the Court of Appeal questioned the validity of a directive but refused interim relief, Laws LJ (dissenting) holding that the directive was plainly unlawful.

[297] Art. 288 (ex 215); now Art. 340 TFEU. See Wakefield, 'Retrench and Reform: The Action for Damages' (2009) 28 *YEL* 39.   [298] *HNL* v. *Council and Commission* [1978] ECR 1209, [1978] 3 CMLR 566.

[299] Below, p. 663.   [300] See e.g. *Funoc* v. *Commission* [1990] ECR 1-3669.

[301] *Mulder* v. *Council and Commission* [1992] ECR I-3061.   [302] Below, p. 743.

[303] *Bulmer Ltd* v. *Bollinger SA* [1974] Ch 401 at 418.   [304] Below, p. 250.

[305] Below, p. 662.   [306] Above, p. 19.

It is certain, also, that there will be increasing integration and convergence between the two legal systems, with EU law becoming more and more preponderant. Concepts such as proportionality, legitimate expectation and vertical and horizontal effect will infiltrate further into British law, and public authorities will have to be constantly more circumspect in keeping track of their EU obligations. Lawyers will be obliged to 'think European' on an ever-increasing scale.

THE CHARTER OF FUNDAMENTAL RIGHTS OF THE EUROPEAN UNION

The protection of fundamental rights forms 'an integral part of the general principles of law whose observance the [CJEU] ensures.... Respect for human rights is therefore a condition of the lawfulness of Community acts.'[307] Thus the CJEU had the power, even without the Charter, to annul regulations that breach fundamental rights.[308]

The EU Charter on Fundamental Rights gives expression to that 'general principle' of protection and lends form and structure to the process.[309] The Charter was first solemnly proclaimed and the fundamental rights specified were recognised by the Parliament, the Council and the Commission in December 2000 but the legal status of the Charter was unclear. Article 6(1) TEU, as amended by the Lisbon Treaty, now provides that the Charter 'shall have the same legal value as the Treaties [TEU and TFEU]'.

The Charter has been used by the CJEU to strike down legislative acts of the Union.[310] Such use of the Charter seems unexceptional and clearly within the scope of the Charter as set out in Article 51.[311] That article seems to make it clear that, since the Charter is addressed to 'Member States only when implementing Union law', it is inapplicable in cases where Union law does not fall to be applied. Moreover, since the Charter 'does not establish any new power or task for the Community or the Union' the extension of fundamental rights protection into fresh areas is not to be anticipated.

Even so, the United Kingdom and Poland were concerned by the application of the Charter and negotiated a 'Protocol [to the Lisbon Treaty] on the application of the Charter

---

[307] *Kahdi*, below, para. 4.

[308] For a very clear example see *Kadi* v. *Council of the European Union*, Case C-402/05P, [2009] 1 AC 1225 (Grand Chamber annulled a Council Regulation (No. 881/2002 of 27 May 2002) which, in implementing a Security Council Resolution, included the claimant on list of terror suspects subject to an asset freeze but with no right to hearing on decision to list or judicial review afterwards; this violated claimant's 'fundamental rights'). Discussed (2012) 23 *EJIL* 1015–24 (Kokott and Sobotta).

[309] The text will be found at <http://www.europarl.europa.eu/charter/pdf/text_en.pdf>. The chapter headings are: Chapter I (Dignity), Chapter II (Freedoms), Chapter III (Equality), Chapter IV (Solidarity), Chapter V (Citizens' Rights) and Chapter VI (Justice). The rights contained in the Charter must be interpreted to ensure compliance with the ECHR (Art. 51(3)). The EU is not at the time of writing a party to the ECHR but Art. 6(2) TEU provides that the 'Union shall accede' and Protocol No. 14 to the ECHR paves the way for accession (see Art. 17).

[310] For instance, *Association Belge des Consommateurs Test-Achats* v. *Council*, Case C-236/09, [2012] 1 WLR 1933 (Directive provision which empowered Member States to exempt insurance companies from the EU law prohibition on sex discrimination was ruled unlawful because it was incompatible with the Charter prohibition on discrimination).

[311] Art. 51 provides: 'The provisions of this Charter are addressed to the institutions and bodies of the Union with due regard for the principle of subsidiarity and to the Member States only when they are implementing Union law.... 2. This Charter does not establish any new power or task for the Community or the Union, or modify powers and tasks defined by the Treaties.'

of Fundamental Rights of the European Union to Poland and to the United Kingdom'.[312] Article 1 of the Protocol provides that: 'The Charter does not extend the ability of the Court of Justice of the European Union, or any court or tribunal of Poland or of the United Kingdom, to find that the laws, regulations or administrative provisions, practices or action of Poland or of the United Kingdom are inconsistent with the fundamental rights, freedoms and principles that it reaffirms.'

It seems that this article has very little legal effect.[313] It does no more than clarify the existing limitations on the scope of the Charter (as set out in Article 51)[314] but since these were not obviously in need of clarification, the article adds little. It is certainly not and never was an 'opt-out' exempting the UK and Poland from the application of the Charter. But this is not a universal view.[315]

---

[312] The Protocol has the same legal force as a treaty (Art. 51 TEU).

[313] For discussion see Barnard, 'The 'Opt-Out' for the UK and Poland from the Charter of Fundamental Rights: Triumph of Rhetoric over Reality?' in Griller and Ziller (eds.), *The Lisbon Treaty: EU Constitutionalism without a Constitutional Treaty* (Springer, 2008). And Gardner, 'Who's Right about the EU Charter of Fundamental Rights?', available at <http://www.headoflegal.com/>. But in one respect the Protocol is effective: Art. 1(2) provides 'for the avoidance of doubt, nothing in Title IV of the Charter creates justiciable rights applicable to Poland or the United Kingdom except in so far as Poland or the United Kingdom has provided for such rights in its national law'. Title IV deals with employment rights, collective bargaining etc. and Art. 1(2) precludes reliance on the Charter in such matters save to the extent that such rights are already provided for in the relevant national law.

[314] See, for instance, *NS* v. *Home Secretary* [2011] EUECJ C-411/10, [2013] QB 102 where Advocate-General Trstenjak considered that the Protocol 'merely reaffirms the normative content of Article 51 of the Charter of Fundamental Rights, which seeks to prevent...an extension of EU powers or of the field of application of EU law' (para. 169). The Grand Chamber adopted the Advocate General's reasoning (paras. 116–22); also the Home Secretary conceded the ordinary applicability of the Charter in the Court of Appeal (see [2010] EWCA Civ 990, [7]–[8]).

[315] In *R (AB)* v. *Home Secretary* [2013] EWHC 3453 Mostyn J doubted the logic of *NS* and stated the constitutional significance of the ECJ's judgment in NS '[could] hardly be overstated' because '[n]otwithstanding the endeavours of our political representatives at Lisbon [in negotiating the Protocol] it would seem that the...Charter of Rights is now part of our domestic law' (para. 14). Moreover, the Charter would continue to provide enforceable rights in the UK even if the HRA 1998 were repealed (paras. 14–15).

PART IV

POWERS AND JURISDICTION

7

LEGAL NATURE OF POWERS

SOURCES OF POWER

STATUTORY POWERS AND DUTIES

Public administration is carried out to a large extent under statutory powers, conferred upon public authorities by innumerable Acts of Parliament. Statutory duties, imposed similarly, also play their part, but it is a minor one in comparison with powers. This is because duties are obligatory and allow no element of discretion, which raises the most numerous and most characteristic problems of administrative law.

When the question arises whether a public authority is acting lawfully or unlawfully, the nature and extent of its power or duty has to be found in most cases by seeking the intention of Parliament as expressed or implied in the relevant Act. The principles of administrative law are generalised rules of statutory interpretation. Thus the dominating source of power is Parliament, but there are certain other sources which do not have a statutory basis. These are the royal prerogative; corporate and contractual powers; and non-legal and abnormal powers.

ACTS REASONABLY INCIDENTAL

A statutory power will be construed as impliedly authorising everything which can fairly be regarded as incidental or consequential to the power itself; and this doctrine is not applied narrowly.[1] For example, a local authority may do its own printing and bookbinding even though it is not specifically empowered to do so.[2] Buses may be run a short distance beyond the end of the authorised route if there is no other practicable way of turning them round.[3] Housing authorities may charge differential rents according to their tenants' means,[4] may subsidise their tenants,[5] and may insure their effects.[6] A Board charged

---

[1] A-G v. *Great Eastern Railway* (1880) 5 App Cas 473; A-G v. *Smethwick Cpn* [1932] 1 Ch 563. Contrast the more restrictive approach taken in *Ward* v. *Metropolitan Police Commissioner* [2005] UKHL 32, [2005] 2 WLR 1114. 'It is not sufficient that such a power be sensible or desirable. The implication has to be necessary in order to make the statutory power effective to achieve its purpose' (Baroness Hale, para. 24). Thus a magistrate in issuing a warrant to remove a person to a place of safety under the Mental Health Act 1983, s. 135(1) had no power to specify the individuals who should accompany the constable in executing the warrant. Cf. Lord Rodger in paras. 5, 7 adopting the broader view. And in *R (New London College Ltd)* v. *Home Secretary* [2013] UKSC 51 it was held 'the statutory power of the Secretary of State to administer the system of immigration control [under the Immigration Act 1971] must necessarily extend to a range of ancillary and incidental administrative powers not expressly spelt out in the Act, including the vetting of sponsors', viz colleges licensed to sponsor students under Tier 4 of the current points-based system of immigration (Lord Sumption, para. 28; Lord Carnwath, para. 37). See above, p. 61 for the points-based system.

[2] A-G v. *Smethwick Cpn* (above).　　[3] A-G v. *Leeds Cpn* [1929] 2 Ch 291.

[4] *Smith* v. *Cardiff Cpn (No 2)* [1955] Ch 159.

[5] *Evans* v. *Collins* [1965] 1 QB 580; and see *Luby* v. *Newcastle-under-Lyme Cpn* [1965] 1 QB 214.

[6] A-G v. *Crayford Urban District Council* [1962] Ch 575.

with the organisation of the totalisator may make contracts with firms for the collection of off-the-course bets, but may not subsidise one of the firms.[7] The Home Secretary may make charges to prisoners for privileges allowed to them.[8] Statutory powers therefore have considerable latitude, and by reasonable construction the courts can soften the rigour of the ultra vires principle. Although this book contains so many instances of that principle being infringed, it must be remembered that the courts intervene only where the thing done goes beyond what can fairly be treated as incidental or consequential.[9]

Local authorities enjoy a wide 'incidental' power under the Local Government Act 1972: they may do anything 'which is calculated to facilitate, or is conducive or incidental to, the discharge of any of their functions'.[10] The Parole Board has statutory power to do such things 'as are incidental to or conducive to the discharge of... its functions';[11] and thus it has power to institute a special advocate procedure to enable evidence that could not be disclosed to a prisoner to be challenged.[12]

EUROPEAN UNION LAW

Membership of the European Union requires, as already emphasised, that EU law be given overriding legal force.[13] Accordingly it is provided by the European Communities Act 1972 that Community law shall prevail over United Kingdom law, including Acts of Parliament both past and future, in any case of conflict. The Act empowers the Crown (by Order in Council) and any designated minister or department (by regulations) to make any alterations in United Kingdom law that are needed for the purpose of implementing Community obligations or exercising Community rights, or matters related thereto, subject only to a short list of exceptions concerning taxation, retrospective legislation, delegated legislation and limits on criminal fines and imprisonment.[14] In general, therefore, the whole operation of subordinating domestic law to Community law, and of taking advantage of Community rights, can be carried out by ministerial order, and a great many such orders have been made for the purpose of giving effect to Community regulations and directives and to judgments of the European Court in Luxembourg.[15] In the *Factortame* case,[16] where parts of the Merchant Shipping Act 1988 proved to be contrary to Community law, the Act was amended by Order in Council after the European Court had pronounced.[17]

Here therefore is an important source of administrative power. Strictly speaking, it is merely domestic statutory power, since it all flows from the Act of 1972. But that Act opened the door to an external and autonomous system of law beyond the control of Parliament, so that in reality Community law has acquired its own independent force. Regulations and directives issuing from the Council and the Commission in Brussels may have direct effect and so confer rights and duties upon individuals which they can

---

[7] *A-G* v. *Racecourse Betting Control Board* [1935] Ch 34.

[8] *Becker* v. *Home Office* [1932] 2 QB 407.

[9] See *Ski Enterprises* v. *Tongariro National Park Board* [1964] NZLR 884 (exclusive concessions for long terms beyond powers of Board); *Felixstowe Dock & Rly Co* v. *British Transport Docks Board* [1976] 2 Ll R 656 (Board empowered to make agreements incidental to promotion of Bills in Parliament).

[10] s. 111. For the limits of this power see *Crédit Suisse* v. *Allerdale BC* [1997] QB 306 and *R* v. *Richmond LBC ex p McCarthy and Stone* [1992] 2 AC 48 (charging for advice on planning applications not within the section).   [11] Criminal Justice Act 1991, s. 32(7) and Sched. 5, para. 1(2)(b).

[12] *R (Roberts)* v. *Parole Board* [2005] UKHL 45, [2005] 3 WLR 152 discussed, with the special advocate procedure, below at p. 433   [13] Above, p. 21.

[14] s. 2(2) and 2nd Sched.   [15] An example is the Package Travel Regulations 1992 (SI 1992 No. 3288).

[16] For which see above, p. 21.   [17] SI 1989 No. 2006.

enforce in the courts of this country. In particular, the doctrine of direct effect gives the citizen important rights to claim compensation or damages from the government. This is explained in the chapter on government liability.[18]

THE ROYAL PREROGATIVE

In earlier times the Crown[19] wielded extensive powers over its subjects under the royal prerogative, which was part of the common law. In the seventeenth century the Crown had power to imprison people[20] and to impose taxation[21] in its own discretion. But in the course of constitutional history the Crown's oppressive powers have been stripped away, and for administrative purposes the prerogative is now a much-attenuated remnant. Numerous statutes have expressly restricted it, and even where statute merely overlaps it the doctrine is that the prerogative goes into abeyance.[22] It is, in any case, defined by law, that is to say by judicial decisions.[23] Prerogative powers may also, it seems, be atrophied by mere disuse. Although the Crown has been deprived of its former powers of invading the rights and liberties of subjects, there are still a few prerogative powers which can have unwelcome legal effects on individuals. By declaring war the Crown can prevent trade with the enemy and can intern enemy aliens—though in wartime these matters are normally covered by legislation.[24] The Crown has special powers in foreign affairs, e.g. under the doctrine of act of state, which is discussed later.[25] But there is no prerogative power to enforce treaties.[26] The prerogative, in fact, has ceased to be a significant source of administrative power as against the citizen. It still comprises power to take action to preserve the peace,[27] to grant legal favours such as pardons, corporate personality or peerage, and it comprises many constitutional powers, such as the power to summon and dissolve Parliament and to assent to bills.

'Prerogative' power is, properly speaking, legal power which appertains to the Crown but not to its subjects.[28] Blackstone explained the correct use of the term:[29]

> It signifies, in its etymology (from prae and rogo) something that is required or demanded before, or in preference to, all others. And hence it follows, that it must be in it's nature singular and eccentrical; that it can only be applied to those rights and capacities which the king enjoys alone, in contradistinction to others, and not to those which he enjoys in common with any of his subjects; for if once any one prerogative of the crown could be held in common with the subject, it would cease to be prerogative any longer.

---

[18]   Below, p. 662.

[19]   Meaning the Monarch acting in a public or constitutional capacity and not merely as a private individual: see below, p. 689.   [20]   *Darnel's Case* (1627) 3 St Tr 1.

[21]   *Bate's Case* (1606) 2 St Tr 371.

[22]   *A-G v. De Keyser's Royal Hotel* [1920] AC 508; *R v. Home Secretary ex p Northumbria Police Authority* (below). For the development of this rule see P. Craig in Forsyth and Hare (eds.), *The Golden Metwand*, 65.

[23]   *Case of Proclamations* (1611) 12 Co Rep 74; *A-G v. De Keyser's Royal Hotel* (above); *Burmah Oil Co v. Lord Advocate* [1965] AC 75. See [1973] *CLJ* 287 (B. S. Markesinis).

[24]   Much wider powers than those of the prerogative are in fact conferred, as by the Civil Contingencies Act 2004.   [25]   Below, p. 708.

[26]   *Walker v. Baird* [1892] AC 491; below, p. 708.

[27]   *R v. Home Secretary ex p Northumbria Police Authority* [1989] QB 26 (special riot equipment issued to police against wishes of police authority).

[28]   The analysis in the following paragraph was approved in *R v. Secretary of State for Health ex p C* [2000] 1 FLR 627 (Hale LJ) (non-statutory power to maintain index of sex offenders found (but the authority had to act fairly and reasonably)) and was followed in *Shrewsbury and Atcham Borough Council v. Secretary of State for Communities & Local Government* [2008] EWCA Civ 148.   [29]   Bl. Comm. 1, 239.

Although the courts may use the term 'prerogative' in this sense, they have adopted the habit of describing as 'prerogative' every power of the Crown which is not statutory,[30] without distinguishing between powers which are unique to the Crown, such as the power of pardon, from powers which the Crown shares equally with its subjects because of its legal personality,[31] such as the power to make contracts,[32] employ servants and convey land.

Thus the Court of Appeal described the original non-statutory criminal injuries compensation scheme for compensating victims of violent crime out of funds voted by Parliament as established 'under the prerogative'.[33] But anyone may set up a trust or other organisation to distribute money, and for the government to do so involves no unique 'prerogative' power.[34] Similarly the House of Lords has held that the Crown's powers of control over the civil service are part of the royal prerogative,[35] although in their essence they are merely the powers which any employer has over his employees. A true prerogative power, such as the power to declare war or to create a peer, involves something which no subject may do. Similarly the issue or denial of passports is sometimes said to be a prerogative power, but more probably it is merely an administrative practice involving no legal power at all.[36] The Crown's power to make international treaties is also often called a prerogative power.[37]

Questionable attribution of powers to the royal prerogative does not, however, put them beyond the reach of judicial review, as is explained later.[38]

COMMON LAW POWERS OF THE CROWN

As adumbrated, the Crown as a corporation sole[39] has all the powers of a natural person and may enter into contracts and own and convey land and do all the many other things its subjects may do (as just explained, these are sometimes inaccurately called 'prerogative powers'). These are considerable powers in many circumstances and they are generally exercised by ministers on behalf of the Crown.[40] Ministers are, of course, responsible to

---

[30] This loose usage may derive from Dicey, *The Law of the Constitution*, 10th edn, 425: see Wade, *Constitutional Fundamentals*, revised edn, 61.

[31] In law the Crown has two personalities, as a natural person and as a corporation sole: see below, p. 689. For its powers as a natural person see Hogg, *Liability of the Crown*, 2nd edn, 163.

[32] See *A-G of Quebec v. Labrecque* [1980] 2 SCR 1057 at 1082 (Crown, 'in addition to the prerogative', has general capacity to contract under ordinary law).

[33] *R v. Criminal Injuries Compensation Board ex p Lain* [1967] 2 QB 864 at 881, 883. The scheme is now statutory under the Criminal Injuries Compensation Act 1995.

[34] As observed by Lloyd LJ in *R v. Panel on Takeovers and Mergers ex p Datafin plc* [1987] QB, 815 at 848; he added: 'strictly the term "prerogative" should be confined to those powers which are unique to the Crown'.

[35] *Council of Civil Service Unions v. Minister for the Civil Service* [1985] AC 374. For these powers see below, p. 288. For a reservation made by Lord Diplock, see Appendix 1.   [36] See below, p. 289.

[37] As in *Laker Airways Ltd v. Dept of Trade* [1977] QB 643.

[38] Below, p. 481.   [39] See below, p. 689.

[40] This is in accordance with the 'Ram Doctrine' being based on a memorandum dated 2 November 1945 written by Sir Granville Ram, the then First Parliamentary Counsel. The memorandum was only published in 2003 (Lords Hansard, 22 January 2003 (Baroness Scotland)) when it caused a stir ((2003) *PL* 415 (Lester and Weait); (2005) 25 *OJLS* 97 (Cohn)) although it seems to contain no novel principle. The memorandum itself, although much criticised, does not and cannot change the law; it does not grant powers to ministers that they would not otherwise enjoy. See also Harris: 'The "Third Source" of Authority for Government Action Revisited' [2007] 126 *LQR* 225. The Localism Act 2011, s. 1 vests in local authorities the 'power to do anything that individuals generally may do'; it would be surprising if local government had this power but central government lacked it.

Parliament for their exercise and that exercise is subject, when appropriate, to judicial review. Moreover, elementarily, such common law powers cannot be exercised inconsistently with a statute.[41] Equally elementarily, the exercise of these powers is 'circumscribed by public law'.[42] Some consider that it is 'illegitimate' for any exercise of power by ministers not to rest on parliamentary authority,[43] but the common law powers of the Crown have existed for centuries and have been upheld several times in recent years.[44]

CORPORATE POWERS

One lingering effect of the royal prerogative, at least in theory, is on the powers of corporations. The Crown has the prerogative power of incorporation and can thus incorporate bodies by royal charter, for example boroughs, universities and colleges, professional societies, and the British Broadcasting Corporation.[45] But the great majority of corporations, including most trading companies, and many governmental corporations such as county councils, are incorporated by statute. This leads to a difference in the scope of their powers. A corporation incorporated by royal charter 'stands on a different footing from a statutory corporation; the difference being that the latter species of corporation can only do such acts as are authorised directly or indirectly by the statute creating it; whereas the former can, speaking generally, do anything that an ordinary individual can do'.[46]

In other words, the law allows the Crown to create only corporations with complete legal personality and with full power to hold property, make contracts, and so forth. Such corporations may be empowered by their charters to make byelaws, enforceable by fines, provided

[41] *R (Hooper)* v. *Work and Pensions Secretary* [2005] UKHL 29, [2005] 1 WLR 1681 (It would be 'an obvious abuse of power' for the Secretary of State to make extra-statutory payments to widowers (to secure compliance with the Human Rights Convention) when Parliament had clearly expressed its will to favour widows (para. 123 (Lord Brown)).

[42] Attorney-General (Rt Hon. Dominic Grieve QC MP) in evidence to the Constitution Committee (HL). See Thirteenth Report: The Pre-emption of Parliament (24 April 2013), para. 62.

[43] Lester and Weait, at 420. It has long been clear (since well before the publication of Sir Granville Ram's memorandum), that the Crown's (and ministers' powers) did not derive exclusively from Parliament. The crucial point is not their source but that there should be proper accountability including to the law by way of judicial review for their use. Critical evidence was given to the Constitution Committee about the memorandum but the Committee recommended no change in the law (only greater clarity in referring to the common law powers of the Crown) (Recommendations 80–3).

[44] See *ex p C*, above, and *Shrewsbury and Atcham Borough Council* (Secretary of State had power to prepare for local government restructuring, prior to the enactment of the necessary legislation). See also *Hooper*, above, para. 47 (no concluded view expressed but 'good deal of force' in corporation sole analysis (Lord Hoffmann)). But the Court of Appeal in *Shrewsbury and Atcham* was bound to follow *ex p C* and Carnwath LJ expressed some doubt over the constitutional propriety of common law powers of the Crown (paras. 48 and 49). Lord Sumption (speaking for the majority) has said *obiter* in the Supreme Court in *R (New London College Ltd)* v. *Home Secretary* [2013] UKSC 51 that it 'has long been recognised that the Crown possesses some general administrative powers to carry on the ordinary business of government which are not exercises of the royal prerogative and do not require statutory authority... The extent of these powers and their exact juridical basis are controversial... the Court of Appeal [in the cases mentioned earlier in this note] held that the basis of the power was the Crown's status as a common law corporation sole, with all the capacities and powers of a natural person subject only to such particular limitations as were imposed by law... it is open to question whether the analogy with a natural person is really apt in the case of public or governmental action, as opposed to purely managerial acts of a kind that any natural person could do, such as making contracts, acquiring or disposing of property, hiring and firing staff and the like' (para. 28).

[45] The Crown could also make an individual office-holder and his successors a corporation sole. One of the few examples is the Master of Pembroke College, Oxford: Halsbury's *Laws of England*, 4th edn, vol. ix, para. 1233. [46] *A-G* v. *Leeds Cpn* [1929] 2 Ch 291.

that they are reasonable.[47] There are remedies against violation of the charter: it is liable to be revoked in *scire facias* proceedings,[48] members of the corporation can apply for an injunction,[49] and so can the Attorney-General.[50] But the terms of the charter are regarded as a kind of bargain between the corporation and the Crown,[51] and unauthorised transactions are not void as against the rest of the world.[52]

A statutory corporation is entirely different. Its objects and powers are solely those which Parliament has laid down expressly or impliedly in the constituent Act;[53] beyond these it is legally incapable of doing anything, so that any act which is ultra vires is wholly void in law. If therefore it borrows money unlawfully it is not contractually liable to repay because it cannot contract such a debt.[54] If it covenants that it will not exercise a power of compulsory purchase, the covenant is entirely void.[55]

Most governmental corporations are statutory, for example incorporated government departments, county councils, district councils and parish councils. Formerly there were boroughs created by royal charter.[56] But this distinction is now of historical interest only as regards local authorities, all of which became statutory in 1974.[57]

Since a statutory authority's powers are confined by the terms of the statute, any wider powers which a private owner could exercise are not available to them. A dock company in which the docks are vested, accordingly, cannot prevent people from using the docks by relying on an owner's power to exclude whom he wills, if its statutory powers provide only for it to regulate the use of the docks by all comers.[58] A county council may not impose a ban on deer-hunting over its land, relying merely on its powers of ownership and disregarding statutory conditions requiring it to act for the benefit, improvement or development of its area.[59] A public authority's statutory powers must, moreover, be exercised reasonably and in accordance with natural justice, so that it cannot act arbitrarily, for example by denying the use of a football ground in a way that might be lawful for a private landlord or by discriminating unfairly in business transactions. These restraints are explained in later chapters.[60]

There may be traps for innocent parties who contract with local authorities whose undertakings later turn out to be ultra vires and void and therefore unenforceable. This also is explained later.[61]

---

[47] See the *Ipswich Tailors' Case* (1614) 11 Co Rep 53; *Slattery* v. *Naylor* (1888) 13 App Cas 446 at 452. Subject to a few exceptions based on ancient custom or prescription, such byelaws could not bind non-members of the corporation unless empowered by statute: Halsbury's *Laws of England*, 4th edn, ix. 756.

[48] Halsbury (as above), paras. 1332, 1396. An affected person may sue with the Attorney-General's fiat.

[49] *Jenkin* v. *Pharmaceutical Society* [1921] 1 Ch 392.

[50] Either on his own motion or on behalf of an affected person: Halsbury (as above), para. 1342.

[51] *Baroness Wenlock* v. *River Dee Co* (1885) 36 Ch D 674 at 685 n. (Bowen LJ).

[52] *A-G* v. *Leicester Cpn* [1943] Ch 86; *Hazell* v. *Hammersmith and Fulham LBC* [1992] 2 AC 1.

[53] See e.g. *Re Westminster City Council* [1986] AC 668 (unlawful payments by Greater London Council).

[54] *Baroness Wenlock* v. *River Dee Co* (1885) 10 App Cas 354; *Hazell* v. *Hammersmith and Fulham LBC*, above; *Crédit Suisse* v. *Allerdale BC* [1997] QB 306.

[55] *Triggs* v. *Staines UDC* [1969] 1 Ch 10; below, p. 278.

[56] *A-G* v. *Leicester Cpn* [1943] Ch 86. See Hart, *Local Government and Administration*, 9th edn, 309.

[57] See above, p. 91. Where charters were granted under earlier Acts the authority was statutory: *Hazell* v. *Hammersmith and Fulham LBC*, above.

[58] *London Association of Shipowners* v. *London & India Docks Joint Committee* [1892] 3 Ch 242; *British Trawlers Federation Ltd* v. *L & NE Rly Co* [1933] 2 KB 14.

[59] *R* v. *Somerset CC ex p Fewings* [1995] 1 WLR 1037.

[60] See below, p. 355.   [61] Below, p. 676.

CONTRACTUAL POWERS

Public authorities, like other people, frequently acquire powers by contract, for example where a local authority lets houses on lease and under the terms of the lease has power to evict the tenant or to increase the rent. Frequently the contractual power will derive from a statutory power such as, taking the same example, the local authority's power to manage its housing estates, and then the rules of administrative law will apply.[62] Where a public body's contracts are made merely in the exercise of commercial liberty, they generally fall outside administrative law since the ordinary law of contract provides adequate machinery for their enforcement and control. They are not within the scope of the remedies discussed in this book or subject to the system of judicial review. Something will, however, be said later about the use of contracts in the mechanism of government.[63]

NON-LEGAL AND ABNORMAL POWERS

In defiance of strict legal logic the remedies of judicial review have been extended to the control of various bodies which have no legal powers at all but have powerful positions in practice. Examples are the Criminal Injuries Compensation Board as at first created (it is now statutory),[64] the Civil Service Appeal Board and the Stock Exchange Panel on Take-overs and Mergers. The cases of these and other such bodies need to be explained later in the context of the limits of judicial review.[65] None of them were created or given powers by Parliament, so in theory none of them could do any legal act with which administrative law should be concerned. But the courts now treat them as de facto public authorities and hold that their actions are subject to judicial review and to legal remedies, thus recognising 'the realities of executive power'. Here therefore we encounter legally controllable power which has itself no legal basis. New vistas of judicial review have been opened and their boundaries are far from easy to define.

There may even be cases where the principles of judicial review will be applied so as to restrict the powers of a private landowner without any element of contract, for example so as to prevent him from arbitrarily ejecting a race-goer from a racecourse.[66] But such cases, if they exist, lie outside the field of administrative law.

EXPRESS REQUIREMENTS AND CONDITIONS

MANDATORY OR DIRECTORY CONDITIONS

Acts of Parliament conferring power on public authorities very commonly impose conditions about procedure, for example by requiring that a notice shall be served, or that leave to do a certain thing be obtained from another body, or that action shall be taken within a specified time or that the decision shall state reasons. If the authority fails to observe such a condition, is its action ultra vires? Not every defect or omission entails the consequence of invalidity but some do. To decide whether invalidity follows or not requires a 'careful examination of the relevant legislation, to ascertain the purpose of [the] statutory provisions'.[67] If the conclusion is reached that on a true construction non-observance of

---

[62] See *Jones* v. *Swansea City Council* [1990] 1 WLR 54 (reversed on other grounds [1990] 1 WLR 1453).

[63] Below, p. 674.   [64] See below, p. 539.   [65] Below, p. 538.

[66] See *Forbes* v. *New South Wales Trotting Club* (1979) 25 ALR 1 (below, p. 377).

[67] *Director of Public Prosecutions of the Virgin Islands* v. *Penn* [2008] UKPC 29 (Lord Mance, para. 18). This seems the same as the test proposed in *Project Blue Sky Inc*, below. This approach, or something very like

the condition is fatal to the validity of the action, that condition is said to be 'mandatory'. But if the conclusion is reached that non-observance does not lead to invalidity, the condition is said to be 'merely directory'.[68] It should be made crystal clear that there is no suggestion here that affixing the label 'mandatory' or 'directory' to a condition enables the judge to determine the validity of an act mechanically without having regard to the relevant statute. These words are simply convenient shorthand to be used once the court has reached its conclusion regarding the consequences of a breach of the condition.[69]

Sometimes the legislation makes it plain what the effect of non-observance is to be. But more often it does not, and then the court must determine the true import of the legislation. Here the court takes account of, among other things, the inconvenience of holding the condition ineffective against the inconvenience of insisting upon it rigidly.[70] It is a question of construction, to be settled by looking at the whole scheme and purpose of the Act and by weighing the importance of the condition, the prejudice to private rights, and the claims of the public interest.[71] The construction of the Act should not be affected by the facts of the particular case, but those facts may induce the court to withhold a discretionary remedy.[72] The court must look for the statutory intention and seek to do what was just in all the circumstances.[73] In any case, judges faced with these questions of construction may regard categories such as mandatory and directory as presenting, in the well-known words of Lord Hailsham, 'not so much a stark choice of alternatives but a spectrum of possibilities in which one compartment or description fades gradually into another'.[74] But Lord Hailsham's suggestion that these compartments are not logically distinct, and that the choice between them is at the discretion of the court, is open to criticism as explained elsewhere.[75]

---

it, is adopted in several leading decisions: for instance, *R* v. *Soneji* [2005] UKHL 49, para. 23 (Lord Steyn after a extensive comparative analysis said: 'the emphasis ought to be on the consequences of non-compliance, and . . . the question whether Parliament can fairly be taken to have intended total invalidity'). But note the scepticism of Toulson LJ (as he then was) in *TTM* v. *London Borough of Hackney* [2011] EWCA Civ 4 (reference to the imputed intention of the legislature may be 'valuable insofar as it concentrates the mind of the court on the purpose of the particular statutory provision in the wider statutory scheme, although beyond that it can be an oratorical device for clothing the judge's view of the seriousness of the non-compliance on the particular facts with the mantle of the hypothetical view of the legislature' (para. 94).

[68] Sedley LJ described the distinction as 'opaque' (*Sumukan Ltd* v. *Commonwealth Secretariat* [2007] EWCA Civ 1148, para. 42). But properly understood it simply expresses in a convenient way the conclusion reached whether the defect in the procedure leads to invalidity or not. The terminology is not (if it ever was) a way in which the validity or invalidity of an act may be decided upon without recourse to the relevant statute. As the High Court of Australia has said (in *Project Blue Sky Inc* v. *ABA* [1998] HCA 28; (1998) 194 *CLR* 355 at para. 93) 'The classification is the end of the inquiry, not the beginning' (Brennan CJ).

[69] Several leading decisions reject the distinction in terms. For instance, in *R* v. *Soneji*, above, Lord Steyn said that the words had 'outlived their usefulness' (para. 23). But these cases reject the *a priori* affixing of the label, not the *a posteriori* expression of a conclusion. As Lord Roger said in *R* v. *Clarke* [2008] UKHL 8, 'The true significance of the decision in *Soneji* lies . . . in the approval of the view that any classification into mandatory or directory is the end of the relevant inquiry, not the beginning, and that the better test is to ask "whether it was a purpose of the legislation that an act done in breach of the provision should be invalid": *Project Blue Sky Inc* v. *Australian Broadcasting Authority* (1998) 194 CLR 355, 390)' (para. 93).

[70] *R* v. *Rochester (Mayor)* (1857) 7 E & B 910.

[71] *Howard* v. *Bodington* (1877) 2 PD 203; *Coney* v. *Choyce* [1975] 1 WLR 422; *R* v. *Home Secretary ex p Jeyeanthan* (below, p. 188), where Lord Woolf MR expounds the rules. The Secretary of State had applied for leave to appeal in two asylum cases by letter instead of on the prescribed form and omitted the prescribed declaration of truth. Held: the applications were valid.   [72] *Coney* v. *Choyce* (above).

[73] See *ex p Jeyeanthan* (below, p. 185).

[74] *London & Clydeside Estates Ltd* v. *Aberdeen DC* [1980] 1 WLR 226.

[75] Below, p. 251. Note that Lord Woolf (dissenting) in *Seal* v. *Chief Constable of South Wales Police* [2007] UKHL 31, [2007] 1 WLR 1910 supported the 'inherently discretionary' approach of Lord Hailsham (paras. 32–3).

The courts also sometimes vary their terminology, as by contrasting 'imperative' with 'mandatory' (meaning mandatory and directory respectively).[76] In one case the Court of Appeal held that a planning authority could validly give a decision without stating reasons as required by the Act, but called the condition mandatory in the sense that the duty to state reasons could be enforced by mandamus.[77]

It is possible for whole areas of statutory law to be treated as merely directory. This has been held in respect of certain provisions of the Prison Act 1952 and the whole of the prison rules[78] made under it, so that a prisoner not treated in accordance with the Act or the rules has no legal remedy on that account.[79] Yet the same rules have been treated as enforceable in determining a prisoner's right to correspond with his solicitor and to make an application to the court[80] and to receive prompt notice of a disciplinary charge.[81]

Drawing the distinction is often difficult. The same condition may be both mandatory and directory: mandatory as to substantial compliance, but directory as to precise compliance. Where, for example, a local authority was empowered to assess coast protection charges on landowners within six months but did so after twenty-three months, the delay was so excessive that there was total non-compliance with the condition, and the assessments were void; but had the excess been a few days only, they would probably have been valid.[82]

The court may readily find reasons for overlooking irregularities which are trivial or unimportant or merely technical, or which lead to no unjust or unintended consequences.[83] But the court will not overlook non-compliance with a requirement that went to jurisdiction.[84]

PROCEDURAL AND FORMAL REQUIREMENTS

Procedural safeguards, which are so often imposed for the benefit of persons affected by the exercise of administrative powers, are normally regarded as mandatory, so that

---

[76] As in *Howard* v. *Bodington* (above). See also below, p. 188.

[77] *Brayhead (Ascot) Ltd* v. *Berks. CC* [1964] 2 QB 303.   [78] SI 1964 No. 388 as amended.

[79] *Becker* v. *Home Office* [1972] 2 QB 407; *R* v. *Hull Prison Visitors ex p St Germain* [1979] QB 425; *Williams* v. *Home Office (No 2)* [1981] 1 All ER 1211; *R* v. *Parkhurst Prison Deputy Governor ex p Hague* [1992] 1 AC 58. For an exception see *R* v. *Home Secretary ex p Herbage (No 2)* [1987] QB 1077 (below, p. 472).

[80] *Raymond* v. *Honey* [1983] 1 AC 1. See also *Guilfoyle* v. *Home Office* [1981] QB 309 (rules strictly construed by Court of Appeal in rejecting right to correspond with solicitor concerning petition to European Commission of Human Rights).

[81] *R* v. *Board of Visitors of Dartmoor Prison ex p Smith* [1987] QB 106. But see above, p. 57. See also *R* v. *Home Secretary ex p Anderson* [1984] QB 778 (prison rule restricting access to legal advisers held ultra vires).

[82] *Cullimore* v. *Lyme Regis Cpn* [1962] 1 QB 718. Compare *James* v. *Minister of Housing and Local Government* [1968] AC 409.

[83] e.g. *Re Bowman* [1932] 2 KB 621; *R* v. *Dacorum Gaming Licensing Committee* [1971] 3 All ER 666; *Sheffield City Council* v. *Graingers Wines Ltd* [1977] 1 WLR 1119; *R* v. *Home Secretary ex p Jeyeanthan* [2000] 1 WLR 354. See, for further instance, *R (Garland)* v. *Secretary of State for Justice* [2011] EWCA Civ 1335 (non-compliance with prison rule that required disciplinary charge to be laid 'as soon as possible and, save in exceptional circumstances, within 48 hours of the discovery of the offence' did not lead to dismissal of the charge. Hughes LJ said: 'Parliament did not intend that any non-compliance with this rule, however minimal and however devoid of prejudicial effect, should render invalid everything which follows' (para. 25)).

[84] *Rydvist* v. *Secretary of State for Work and Pensions* [2002] 1 WLR 3343 (CA) restricting *ex p Jeyeanthan* (above) to procedural requirements capable of being waived. For waiver see below, p. 201. See also *Ahmed* v. *Kennedy* [2003] 2 All ER 440 (CA) (election petition under the Representation of the People Act 1983 held a nullity: a rule said that the prescribed time periods 'shall not be enlarged' and the notice in question was late and did not contain the required information).

it is fatal to disregard them. Where there is a statutory duty to consult persons affected, this must genuinely be done,[85] and reasonable opportunity for comment must be given.[86] Where a proposal or scheme is required to be published it must be accurately described[87] and anyone entitled to object must be allowed adequate time. Four days' notice of a local authority's scheme for setting up comprehensive schools was held wholly unreasonable and inadequate, so that the scheme was void.[88] An identical scheme had previously been held void and prohibited by injunction, because public notice of it had not been given as required by the Education Act 1944.[89] The object of requiring notice was to give an opportunity for objections to be made to the minister before he decided whether to confirm the scheme. But this procedure was required only where the scheme involved setting up new schools or ceasing to maintain old ones. The local authority had wrongly supposed that they were not ceasing to maintain their former schools. It was held to be clearly implicit in the design of the Act that the minister could not approve the scheme until the statutory procedure had been observed, and it was said:[90]

> it is imperative that the procedure laid down in the relevant statutes should be properly observed. The provisions of the statutes in this respect are supposed to provide safeguards for Her Majesty's subjects. Public Bodies and Ministers must be compelled to observe the law; and it is essential that bureaucracy should be kept in its place.

The same case contains a contrasting example of directory requirements. Objections had been duly invited in respect of other schools covered by the scheme, but the Act also required that their specifications should be approved by the minister. The local authority was proceeding with its scheme without submitting specifications for approval, but it was held that the court would not intervene, in the absence of objection by the minister, even though the local authority was 'flying in the face of the intention which Parliament manifested'.[91]

Contrasting examples also appeared in another comprehensive school case, where the regulations requiring public notice of the scheme were held to be mandatory as regards substantial compliance, but merely regulatory as to some minor details.[92] Substantial compliance also sufficed where a local authority, in arranging for the adoption of a child, failed to notify the mother in writing but in fact made the position clear to her.[93] In a planning case the requirement that a notice of appeal against an enforcement notice should state the grounds of appeal was held to be merely directory, but the time limit for appeal was held to be mandatory.[94] The requirement that a planning application involving a departure from the development plan should be advertised as such has been held to

---

[85] *Grunwick Processing Laboratories Ltd* v. *ACAS* [1978] AC 277; *Agricultural etc. Training Board* v. *Aylesbury Mushrooms Ltd* [1972] 1 WLR 190 (below, p. 755); *R* v. *Camden LBC ex p Cran* [1995] RTR 346. And see *Sumukan Ltd* v. *Commonwealth Secretariat* [2007] EWCA Civ 1148, para. 49.

[86] *Re Union of Benefices of Whippingham and East Cowes, St James'* [1954] AC 245; *Port Louis Cpn* v. *A-G of Mauritius* [1965] AC 1111; and see below, pp. 746 and 755 (delegated legislation).

[87] *Wilson* v. *Secretary of State for the Environment* [1973] 1 WLR 1083 (notice describing land wrongly). See also *Legg* v. *Inner London Education Authority* [1972] 1 WLR 1245; *Coney* v. *Choyce* (above).

[88] *Lee* v. *Dept of Education and Science* (1967) 66 LGR 211. See similarly *R* v. *Brent LBC ex p Gunning* (1985) 84 LGR 168.   [89] *Bradbury* v. *Enfield LBC* [1967] 1 WLR 1311.

[90] Ibid. at 1325 (Danckwerts LJ).   [91] *Bradbury* (above) at 1335 (Diplock LJ).

[92] *Coney* v. *Choyce* [1975] 1 WLR 422. Contrast *Mukta Ben* v. *Suva City Council* [1980] 1 WLR 767 (non-publication of notice of compulsory purchase order not fatal: directory only). See also *R* v. *Immigration Appeal Tribunal ex p Jayeanthan* [1999] 3 All ER 231 (irregularity cured by tribunal).

[93] *Re T* [1986] Fam 160.   [94] *Howard* v. *Secretary of State for the Environment* [1975] QB 235.

be merely directory;[95] but the omission from a planning authority's statutory advertisement of details about the lodging of objections resulted in the invalidity of a planning permission.[96] And the House of Lords has held that a duty to consult was in the particular circumstances not 'a condition precedent' (i.e. was 'merely directory'). The circumstances were whether 'a control order' should be made against a certain individual.[97] The Home Secretary was under a statutory duty to consult with the relevant Chief Officer of Police about whether on the evidence available there is a realistic prospect of prosecuting a particular individual for a terrorism offence.[98] But the failure to consult or to consult properly did not lead to the invalidity of the 'control order'.[99]

In notices affecting private rights, particularly where the effect is penal, scrupulous observance of statutory conditions is normally required. A demand for industrial training levy[100] and a certificate of 'alternative development'[101] have both been held void for failure to indicate, as required by statute, that there was a right of appeal. An enforcement notice is void if it fails to state, as it should, the time allowed for compliance.[102] A demand for a payment is void if it is signed by the borough treasurer instead of by the town clerk.[103] Where an Act requires consent in writing from the local authority for carrying on an 'offensive trade', the requirement of writing is mandatory.[104]

Requirements which are less substantial, and more like matters of mere formality, may fall on either side of the line. Some of the cases concern delegated legislation, and are discussed elsewhere.[105] The omission from a clearance order of a note giving directions for the filling up of the form of order was held to be immaterial.[106] The provision of the Rent Act 1965 that a rent officer should consider 'the rent specified in the application' was held to contain a mandatory condition, so that an application which did not specify the desired rent was a nullity and the defect could not be waived.[107] The court distinguished an earlier case in which the application to a rent tribunal had failed to give the name of the landlord as required by regulations made under the relevant Act. The regulations were held to be merely directory in this respect, since the Act itself contained no such requirement.[108] But many cases show that even where the requirement is in the Act itself, it is possible for it to be held directory only.[109] 'No universal rule can be laid down for the construction of statutes, as to whether mandatory enactments shall be considered directory only or obligatory, with an implied nullification for disobedience.'[110]

---

[95] *R v. St Edmundsbury BC ex p Investors in Industry Commercial Properties Ltd* [1985] 1 WLR 1168; and see *Co-operative Retail Services Ltd v. Taff-Ely BC* (1979) 39 P & CR 223.

[96] *R v. Lambeth LBC ex p Sharp* (1984) 50 P & CR 284.

[97] These orders made under the Prevention of Terrorism Act 2005 are discussed above, p. 66.

[98] Act of 2005, s. 8(2).

[99] *Secretary of State for the Home Department v. E* [2007] UKHL 47, [2007] WLR 720 (HL).

[100] *Agricultural etc. Industry Training Board v. Kent* [1970] 2 QB 19. See similarly *Rayner v. Stepney Corporation* [1911] 2 Ch 312 (closing order void).

[101] *London & Clydeside Estates Ltd v. Aberdeen DC* [1980] 1 WLR 182.

[102] *Burges v. Jarvis* [1952] 2 QB 41.

[103] *Graddage v. Haringey London Borough Council* [1975] 1 WLR 241.

[104] *Epping Forest DC v. Essex Rendering Ltd* [1983] 1 WLR 158 (HL).   [105] Below, p. 755.

[106] *Re Bowman* [1932] 2 KB 621.   [107] *Chapman v. Earl* [1968] 1 WLR 1315.

[108] *Jackson (Francis) Developments Ltd v. Hall* [1951] 2 KB 488; and see *R v. Lincolnshire Appeal Tribunal ex p Stubbins* [1917] 1 KB 1; *R v. Devon and Cornwall Rent Tribunal ex p West* (1974) 29 P & CR 316.

[109] e.g. *Margate Pier Co v. Hannam* (1819) 3 B & Ald 266; *Caldow v. Pixell* (above); *Montreal Street Railway Co v. Normandin* (above).

[110] *Liverpool Borough Bank v. Turner* (1861) 2 De GF & J 507 (Lord Campbell).

A requirement of the prison rules that a charge against a prisoner should be laid 'as soon as possible' was held by the Court of Appeal to be mandatory, thus invalidating a charge laid in May for an offence committed in February.[111]

The possibility that a public authority may have power to waive an otherwise mandatory procedural requirement is mentioned later.[112]

TIME LIMITS

It has often been held that an act may be validly done after the expiry of a statutory time limit. Thus a rating list was upheld even though made and transmitted after the required dates.[113] A local planning authority, which is required by regulations to give notice of its decision within two months, was held able to give a valid decision after three months.[114] An earlier case[115] holding that a delay of over two years would invalidate the decision has been disapproved, but it is not entirely clear that so long a delay may not still be fatal.[116] Even where the time limit is designed as a safeguard of individual freedom the court may, by weighing the public interest against that of the individual, hold that the time limit is directory only, as did a divided Court of Appeal in the case of the ten-day period of notice required for applying for a disqualification notice against a company director.[117]

Time limits may be held to be mandatory where the rights of other persons depend on them or they are of special importance. In an oft-cited case a bishop received a complaint against a clergyman but failed to send a copy of it to the clergyman within the statutory twenty-one days. All subsequent proceedings in the case were void.[118] So was a planning appeal lodged out of time, as mentioned above.[119] So was a scheme of charges for coast protection works which was made long after the appointed time.[120] So was an election petition which was presented after the prescribed time had expired.[121] But time limits governing electoral procedure may sometimes be exceeded with impunity, as where a list of voters was revised after the time appointed by the Act.[122] In New Zealand the court understandably refused to invalidate a general election, even though the Governor-General's warrant was issued unduly late.[123] These are cases where public policy clearly requires some latitude.

FAILURE TO STATE REASONS

The great majority of statutory tribunals are required by the Tribunals and Inquiries Act 1992 to give reasons for their decisions on request. The qualified duty imposed by the Act is often supplemented by an unqualified duty imposed by procedural regulations. The Act

---

[111] *R v. Board of Visitors of Dartmoor Prison ex p Smith* [1987] QB 106.   [112] Below, p. 198.

[113] *R v. Ingall* (1876) 2 QBD 199.

[114] *James v. Minister of Housing and Local Government* [1966] 1 WLR 135, approved on this point [1967] 1 WLR 171 (HL); and see *Chelmsford Rural District Council v. Powell* [1963] 1 WLR 123 (additional ground of appeal allowed out of time); *R v. Inspector of Taxes ex p Clarke* [1971] 2 QB 640.

[115] *Edwick v. Sunbury-on-Thames UDC* [1962] 1 QB 229.

[116] See [1966] 1 WLR at 142 (Lord Denning MR).

[117] *Secretary of State for Trade and Industry v. Langridge* [1991] Ch 402 (9-day notice upheld). And see *R (Garland) v. Secretary of State for Justice* [2011] EWCA Civ 1335, discussed above.

[118] *Howard v. Bodington* (1877) 2 PD 203.

[119] *Howard v. Secretary of State for the Environment* (above, p. 186).

[120] *Cullimore v. Lyme Regis Corporation* [1962] 1 QB 718.

[121] *Devan Nair v. Yong Kuan Teik* [1967] 2 AC 31 and *Ahmed v. Kennedy* [2003] 2 All ER 440 (CA).

[122] *R v. Rochester (Mayor)* (1857) 7 E & B 910.   [123] *Simpson v. A-G* [1955] NZLR 271.

likewise applies to decisions of ministers taken after public inquiries. And other statutes and regulations sometimes impose a like duty. This duty may be broken either because no reasons are given or because the reasons given are inadequate. The general nature of this duty is discussed elsewhere.[124] Here we are concerned with whether the duty to give reasons is mandatory or directory in the particular circumstances.

In the case already mentioned the Court of Appeal held that a condition attached to a grant of planning permission was not invalidated by the planning authority's omission to state reasons in writing as required by the General Development Order.[125] This decision seems reasonable in the circumstances. Planning authorities impose common-form conditions in many cases, and it would be a serious inconvenience to invalidate any condition for which separate reasons were not given. On the other hand, where it is a case of failure to explain the authority's main decision, the court will intervene not merely if no reasons were given but also if they are unsatisfactory. In one such case, where the reasons given by an agricultural arbitrator did not explain what breaches of covenant had been committed by the tenant, this was held to be error on the face of the award and it was set aside.[126] And in a planning case, where the minister's decision on an appeal was accompanied by obscure and unsatisfactory reasons, the decision was quashed for non-compliance with the procedural rules which govern these appeals and require decisions to be reasoned.[127]

Later decisions have clearly held that a statutory duty to give reasons is normally mandatory, so that in default of adequate reasons the decision is a nullity and will be quashed. Decisions of immigration appeal tribunals,[128] employment tribunals[129] and mental health review tribunals[130] have been invalidated accordingly. So have the decisions of ministers taken after statutory inquiries.[131] The whole tenor of the case law is that the duty to give satisfactory reasons is a duty of decisive importance which cannot lawfully be disregarded.

LEAVE OF ANOTHER BODY REQUIRED

The House of Lords was divided on the question whether the requirement that the leave of the High Court should be obtained before a person held under the Mental Health Act 1983 could sue in respect of their detention, was mandatory or directory.[132] The majority held that proceedings brought without the leave of the High Court were a nullity (i.e. the requirement of leave was mandatory).[133] 'Parliament intended' said Lord Brown 'to

---

[124] Below, p. 783.

[125] *Brayhead (Ascot) Ltd* v. *Berks CC* [1964] 2 QB 303. Though misleadingly described as mandatory, the requirement was in effect held to be directory. See likewise *R* v. *Liverpool Cpn ex p Liverpool Taxi Fleet Operators' Association* [1975] 1 WLR 701, where however it is suggested that the court might intervene if the irregularity caused 'significant injury'. In *Greene* v. *Home Secretary* [1942] AC 284 failure to state reasons correctly did not invalidate a detention order.

[126] *Re Poyser and Mills' Arbitration* [1964] 2 QB 247; below, p. 783.

[127] *Givaudan & Co Ltd* v. *Minister of Housing and Local Government* [1967] 1 WLR 250.

[128] *R* v. *Immigration Appeal Tribunal ex p Khan (Mahmud)* [1983] QB 790.

[129] *Norton Tool Co Ltd* v. *Tewson* [1973] 1 WLR 45; *Alexander Machinery (Dudley) Ltd* v. *Crabtree* [1974] ICR 120; *Guest* v. *Alpine Soft Drinks Ltd* [1982] ICR 110; and other cases cited below, p. 784.

[130] *R* v. *Mental Health Review Tribunal ex p Clatworthy* [1985] 3 All ER 699; *R* v. *Mental Health Review Tribunal ex p Pickering* [1986] 1 All ER 99.

[131] Below, p. 803.

[132] *Seal* v. *Chief Constable of South Wales Police*, above. Section 139(2) of the 1983 Act sets out this requirement. The claimant had instituted proceedings without obtaining leave but could not recommence proceedings as the limitation period had passed.

[133] The majority (Lords Brown, Bingham and Carswell) followed *R* v. *Bracknell JJ ex p Griffiths* [1976] AC 314 where criminal proceedings brought without leave were held to be a nullity.

make leave a precondition of any effective proceedings' in order to protect the prospective defendant. 'The very inflexibility of the provision was an integral part of the protection it afforded.'[134]

PROVISIONS AS TO IRREGULARITY

Statutes occasionally make specific provision for the effect of non-observance of their requirements. Thus the Licensing Act 1964, after setting out a list of disqualifying circumstances for justices sitting to grant liquor licences, provides: 'No objection shall be allowed to any justices' licence on the ground that it was granted by justices not qualified to grant it.'[135] The Agriculture Act 1947, after prescribing the mode of appointment of members of agricultural land tribunals, provides that the tribunal's acts shall be valid notwithstanding that it is afterwards discovered that there was a defect in the appointment of a member.[136] The latter provision has been successfully invoked where an appointment appeared to be defective.[137] Procedural regulations sometimes contain similar clauses to the effect that failure to comply with them shall not invalidate the proceedings.[138] It is open to doubt whether such clauses would protect serious procedural errors, and it is unlikely that they would validate any procedure which violated the principles of natural justice.[139]

Irregularities may also be cured under statutory powers of modification. Clearance orders under the Housing Acts, for example, may be confirmed by the minister with or without modification, and he has power to modify an invalid order so as to make it a valid one. Thus where the local authority's order provided that the land acquired might be disposed of in ways not permitted by the Act, the minister modified the order so as to confine the future use of the land to rehousing and thus saved it from invalidity.[140] Similarly an order has been validated by extending an excessively short time limit.[141] Under the Town and Country Planning Act 1990[142] the Secretary of State may correct an error in an enforcement notice in deciding an appeal against it, if satisfied that there will not be injustice.

The common form of enactment which allows the validity of housing, planning and other orders to be challenged only within six weeks gives the court power to quash the order if it is not within the powers of the Act or if failure to comply with requirements of the Act has caused the interests of the applicant to be substantially prejudiced. This formula is discussed in a later chapter, where it is suggested that its two limbs ('not within the powers' and 'failure to comply with requirements') should be interpreted as distinguishing between mandatory and directory conditions.[143]

---

[134] The minority consisted of Lord Woolf and Baroness Hale. For Lord Woolf's discretionary approach, see above and p. 251. Baroness Hale reached a different conclusion on the question of construction of s. 139(2).

[135] s. 193(8). For the restrictive interpretation given to this section see below, p. 397.

[136] Sched.   [137] *Woollett* v. *Minister of Agriculture and Fisheries* [1955] 1 QB 103.

[138] e.g. Plant Variety Rights Tribunal Rules 1965 (SI 1965 No. 1623), r. 21.

[139] See below, p. 373.   [140] *R* v. *Minister of Health ex p Yaffé* [1931] AC 494.

[141] *Re Bowman* [1932] 2 KB 621.

[142] s. 176(2). See *Miller-Mead* v. *Minister of Housing and Local Government* [1963] 2 QB 196.

[143] Below, p. 625.

CONCLUSIVENESS, MISTAKE AND FRAUD

REVOCABLE AND IRREVOCABLE ACTION

It may be necessary to determine whether there is power to revoke or modify the decisions or orders of an administrative authority or tribunal.[144] The question here is whether the authority itself has power to do this. This is different from the question whether some other authority has power to do so, which may be affected by a statutory provision that the decision 'shall be final', as explained elsewhere.[145]

In the interpretation of statutory powers and duties there is a rule that, unless the contrary intention appears, 'the power may be exercised and the duty shall be performed from time to time as occasion requires'.[146] But this gives a highly misleading view of the law where the power is a power to decide questions affecting legal rights. In those cases the courts are strongly inclined to hold that the decision, once validly made, is an irrevocable legal act and cannot be recalled or revised. The same arguments which require finality for the decisions of courts of law apply to the decisions of statutory tribunals, ministers and other authorities.

For this purpose a distinction has to be drawn between powers of a continuing character and powers which, once exercised, are finally expended so far as concerns the particular case. An authority which has a duty to maintain highways or a power to take land by compulsory purchase may clearly act 'from time to time as occasion requires'. But if in a particular case it has to determine the amount of compensation or to fix the pension of an employee, there are equally clear reasons for imposing finality. Citizens whose legal rights are determined administratively are entitled to know where they stand.

There is a third class of cases where there is power to decide questions affecting private rights but where there is also an inherent power to vary an order[147] or power to entertain fresh proceedings and make a different decision. Decisions on licensing applications and other decisions of policy will usually fall into this class, since policy is essentially variable. Thus, decisions on planning applications may be varied at any time if a fresh application is submitted.

There are also cases where a power of review by the body making the decision is expressly given by statute. The social security authorities, for example, have extensive powers to review their decisions on grounds of fresh evidence, change of circumstances, or mere mistakes. Powers of much the same kind have been conferred on employment tribunals. But if it proposes to vary its decision under such a power the tribunal should first hear any party prejudiced.[148] Even where such powers are not expressly conferred,[149] it seems that statutory tribunals have power to correct slips[150] and to set aside decisions

---

[144] On this subject see [1982] *PL* 613 (M. Akehurst).   [145] Below, p. 609.

[146] Interpretation Act 1978, s. 12.

[147] As in *Re Wilson* [1985] AC 750 (justices' order as to payment of fines; Interpretation Act 1978 invoked); *R* v. *Hillingdon LBC ex p London Regional Transport*, The Times, 20 January 1999 (bus-shelter consent revocable).   [148] *Times Newspapers Ltd* v. *Fitt* [1981] ICR 637.

[149] For the position of tribunals, including the statutory power of internal review under the Tribunals, Courts and Enforcement Act 2007, see below, p. 783.

[150] *Akewushola* v. *Secretary of State for the Home Department* [2000] 1 WLR 2295, where Sedley LJ said: 'the maximum power [of a tribunal] must be to correct accidental errors which do not substantively affect the rights of the parties or the decision arrived at' (at p. 2301A).

obtained by fraud[151] or based upon 'a fundamental mistake of fact'.[152] There has been little discussion of the source of these powers; presumably they are implied from the tribunal's statute.[153]

In the absence of such special circumstances the tribunal's decision is irrevocable as soon as it has been communicated to the parties, even though orally[154] and even though the reasons for it remain to be given later.[155]

A mistake may lead to action being taken upon a wholly wrong basis so that some different action needs to be substituted. This happened where a local education authority agreed to pay the cost of school transport for a girl, supposing that she lived more than three miles from the school and that they therefore had a statutory duty to pay. When it was found that the distance was less than three miles, so that they had a power to pay but no duty, they refused to do so. The Court of Appeal rejected the plea that the original decision was irrevocable, since it was not taken in the exercise of any power to determine a question of legal right and could not affect the duty to exercise discretion when the true facts appeared.[156]

CASES OF IRREVOCABILITY

The following cases illustrate situations in which the court will hold administrative decisions to be irrevocable. A local authority, proposing to make up a street and apportion the expense among the frontagers, gave notice that it would follow one of the two alternative statutory procedures. It was held unable to revoke this decision when it later wished to follow the other procedure.[157] Although the court said that the authority's notice would estop it, the true ground of decision was probably that the election, once formally made, was a legal act which there was no power to undo. That was certainly the operative ground where the Westminster Council was held unable to vary an excessive award of compensation to a redundant employee.[158] Similarly where the War Damage Commission had written to the owner of damaged property saying that it had been classified as 'not total loss', so that the statutory compensation would be on a 'cost of works' basis, the Commission were held unable to alter the classification to 'total loss', which they later decided was right.[159] These might be represented as cases of estoppel, but in truth they depend on the

---

[151] Implied in *Fajemisin*, below, para. 37.

[152] *Fajemisin* v. *The General Dental Council* [2013] EWHC 3501 paras. 37–8 (Keith J) in reliance upon *Porteous* v. *West Dorset District Council* [2004] EWCA Civ 244 (local authority had power to retake decision where a fundamental error of fact found); similarly *Crawley Borough Council* v. *B* [2000] EWCA Civ 50, disapproving of *R* v. *Southwark LBC ex p Dagou* (1995) 28 HLR 72 to the opposite effect). But contrast *R (B)* v. *The Nursing and Midwifery Council* [2012] EWHC 1264 per Lang J (para. 35) see above, p. 784.

[153] The High Court has an exceptional power to reopen proceedings it has already determined where it was shown there would otherwise be 'significant injustice' and there was no other remedy (such as an appeal): *Taylor* v. *Lawrence* [2002] EWCA Civ 90, and CPR 40.12, [2003] QB 528, paras. 54–5.

[154] *Lamont* v. *Fry's Metals Ltd* [1985] ICR 566.

[155] *Jowett* v. *Bradford (Earl)* [1977] ICR 342; *R* v. *Cripps ex p Muldoon* [1984] QB 686; *R* v. *Oxford Regional Mental Health Review Tribunal ex p Home Secretary* [1988] AC 120. Contrast *Hanks* v. *Ace High Products* [1978] ICR 1155; *R* v. *Greater Manchester Valuation Panel ex p Shell Chemicals Ltd* [1982] QB 255.

[156] *Rootkin* v. *Kent CC* [1981] 1 WLR 1186.

[157] *Gould* v. *Bacup Local Board* (1881) 50 LJMC 44.

[158] *Livingstone* v. *Westminster Cpn* [1904] 2 KB 109. And see *Battelley* v. *Finsbury Borough Council* (1958) 56 LGR 165 (no power to revoke engagement of employee). Scots examples are *Campbell* v. *Glasgow Police Cmrs.* (1895) 22 R 621; *Blackley* v. *Ayr CC*, 1934 SLT 398.

[159] *Re 56 Denton Road, Twickenham* [1953] Ch 51. See similarly *Akewushola* v. *Home Secretary* [2000] 1 WLR 2295; *Aparau* v. *Iceland Foods plc* [2000] 1 All ER 228 (CA); *Employment and Immigration Commission* v. *Macdonald Tobacco Inc* (1981) 121 DLR (3d) 546.

principle that a statutory power to decide is often a power to decide once and once only. In the case last mentioned Vaisey J accepted the principle in these words:[160]

> where Parliament confers on a body such as the War Damage Commission the duty of deciding or determining any question, the deciding or determining of which affects the rights of the subject, such decision or determination made and communicated in terms which are not expressly preliminary or provisional is final and conclusive, and cannot, in the absence of express statutory power or the consent of the person or persons affected, be altered or withdrawn by that body.

The suggestion that a conclusive decision can be altered with the consent of the person affected needs qualification, since consent by itself cannot confer power which does not exist.[161] If a public authority makes a grant or gives a licence, it will not normally be able to revoke or alter its decision. But if it refuses a grant or a licence, it may be able to allow a renewed application, not because its first decision was not conclusive, but because it has a continuing power, and perhaps duty, to allow applications at any time.[162]

In the War Damage Commission case it was held that the Commission's decision was nonetheless binding because it was conveyed by an informal letter.[163] Where formalities are not prescribed by the Act in such a way as to make them mandatory, there is no reason why informal notification of the decision should not be fully conclusive.

Similarly where an immigration officer gives an immigrant leave to enter and remain in the country, this is conclusive of his right to do so even if the immigration officer acts under a mistake.[164] It is otherwise, of course, if he has no legal authority to grant leave in the circumstances,[165] or if he grants it because of misrepresentation by the immigrant, as explained below.

FRAUD AND MISREPRESENTATION

An order or determination will not be conclusive if it has been obtained by fraud or misrepresentation. Denning LJ once said:[166]

> No judgment of a court, no order of a Minister, can be allowed to stand if it has been obtained by fraud. Fraud unravels everything.

In administrative law, which was not the context of this statement, there is only scanty material to illustrate it, although in principle it ought to be correct. The only field in which there are examples is immigration law, where it is held that leave to enter given by an immigration officer is vitiated if it has been obtained by any kind of fraud, deception or misrepresentation on the part of the immigrant.[167]

A decision of an inferior tribunal obtained by fraud, for example by perjured evidence, may be quashed by the High Court on certiorari.[168]

---

[160] At 56.   [161] Below, p. 198.

[162] See *R v. Hertfordshire CC ex p Cheung*, The Times, 4 April 1986 (student grants, previously refused, allowed after *R v. Barnet LBC ex p Shah* [1982] 2 AC 309 showed that refusals were wrong in law).

[163] As also in *A-G v. Hughes* (1889) 81 LT 679; *Robertson v. Minister of Pensions* [1949] 1 KB 227.

[164] *R v. Home Secretary ex p Ram* [1979] 1 WLR 148.

[165] *R v. Home Secretary ex p Choudhary* [1978] 1 WLR 1177.

[166] *Lazarus Estates Ltd v. Beasley* [1956] 1 QB 702 and 712. Cf. *R v. Wolverhampton Crown Court ex p Crofts* [1983] 1 WLR 204.

[167] *R v. Home Secretary ex p Hussain* [1978] 1 WLR 700; *Same ex p Choudhary* (above); *Same ex p Zamir* [1980] AC 930.

[168] *R v. Gillyard* (1848) 12 QB 527; *R v. Fulham (etc.) Rent Tribunal ex p Gormly* [1951] 2 All ER 1030.

As explained later[169] misrepresentation by a public authority will seldom bring into play the doctrine of estoppel. But such misrepresentation may amount to an abuse of power which the court will control.[170] It may also be a tort for which the court will award damages.[171]

POWER OR DUTY—WORDS PERMISSIVE OR OBLIGATORY

WHEN 'MAY' MEANS 'MUST'

The hallmark of discretionary power is permissive language using words such as 'may' or 'it shall be lawful', as opposed to obligatory language such as 'shall'. But this simple distinction is not always a sure guide, for there have been many decisions in which permissive language has been construed as obligatory. This is not so much because one form of words is interpreted to mean its opposite, as because the power conferred is, in the circumstances prescribed by the Act, coupled with a duty to exercise it in a proper case. Cotton LJ once said:[172]

> I think that great misconception is caused by saying that in some cases 'may' means 'must'. It never can mean 'must', so long as the English language retains its meaning; but it gives a power, and then it may be a question in what cases, where a Judge has a power given him by the word 'may', it becomes his duty to exercise it.

This view of the matter was adopted in a case where the Act provided that the county court 'may' make an order for possession in proceedings by a landlord against a tenant: it was held that, on proof of the relevant facts, the court was bound to make the order.[173] There have been many similar decisions concerning the powers of courts of law, since they have a general duty to enforce legal rights.[174] Public authorities have a duty, likewise, to exercise their powers as the public interest requires.[175]

The application of this doctrine to action of an administrative character is shown by two contrasting decisions of the House of Lords. In *Julius* v. *Lord Bishop of Oxford*[176] the statute said that 'it shall be lawful' for a bishop to issue a commission of inquiry in case of alleged misconduct by a clergyman, either on the application of a complainant or of his own motion; and the question was whether, complaint having been made by a parishioner, the bishop was entitled to refuse to act. The House of Lords held that the permissive wording gave the bishop discretion, and that he had no mandatory duty except, perhaps, to hear and consider the application—as he had done. For it was evident from the form and policy of the Act that the power was given to the bishop in order that he might exercise his judgment and disallow applications which were unsubstantial or unmeritorious.

---

[169] Below, p. 196.   [170] Below, p. 318.

[171] As in *Bennett (Potatoes) Ltd* v. *Secretary of State for Scotland*, 1986 SLT 665 (government inspector without reasonable basis falsely certified potatoes as pest-free: damages awarded for fraudulent misrepresentation though without intent to deceive).

[172] *Re Baker* (1890) 44 Ch D 262 at 270, following *Julius* v. *Lord Bishop of Oxford* (below).

[173] *Sheffield Cpn* v. *Luxford* [1929] 2 KB 180.

[174] See cases catalogued under 'May' in Stroud's *Judicial Dictionary*. Examples are *Shelley* v. *London County Council* [1949] AC 56; *Peterborough Corporation* v. *Holdich* [1956] 1 QB 124; *Re Shuter* [1960] 1 QB 124.   [175] *R* v. *Tithe Commissioners* (1849) 14 QB 459 at 474.

[176] (1880) LR 5 App Cas 214, reviewing cases going back to *Blackwell's Case* (1683) 1 Vern 152, in which permissive words were held mandatory. See also *Lawrence Building Co* v. *Lanarkshire CC*, 1977 SLT 110.

Otherwise clergymen might be harried with innumerable vexatious inquiries. In the contrasting case, *Padfield* v. *Minister of Agriculture, Fisheries and Food*,[177] the question was also whether action need be taken on a complaint. The Agricultural Marketing Act 1958 provided for the reference of certain complaints to a committee of investigation 'if the Minister in any case so directs'. The minister refused to act on a complaint by a group of milk producers against the Milk Marketing Board. But his reasons were held to be inconsistent with the policy of the Act, which was that relevant and substantial complaints should go to the committee in the absence of good reasons to the contrary. The permissive words gave the minister discretion, but he was not entitled to use his discretion in such a way as to thwart the policy of the Act. Primarily, therefore, this is a leading example of the abuse of discretion, and it is in that context that it is considered later.[178]

STATUTORY CONSTRUCTION

Whether a power, expressed in merely permissive language, is accompanied by a duty to exercise it in certain circumstances requires consideration of the whole statutory context in which the power is given. A power to levy rates, for example, is often given in the form that the local authority 'may' levy them for particular purposes or in particular cases, yet the court will readily conclude that where the prescribed conditions exist, there is a duty to impose the rate.[179] Where a licensing authority 'may' grant a licence to an applicant with certain qualifications, the policy of the Act may be that licences are not to be withheld from qualified applicants unless there is some valid objection. Thus where the Home Secretary was given power to license cabs on such conditions as he might by order prescribe, the Court of Appeal doubted whether he was intended to have absolute discretion to put many thousands of cab-drivers out of business even where they fulfilled the conditions.[180] So likewise, where the Act says that a licence 'may be issued' and 'may be revoked' without saying in what circumstances, there may be a duty to issue it and a duty not to revoke it except for a good legal reason: an arbitrary revocation of a television licence by the Home Secretary was accordingly declared unlawful by the Court of Appeal.[181]

Where the Home Secretary 'may by regulations provide' as to immigration appeal procedures, he is held to have a duty to make the regulations, as Parliament must have so intended.[182]

Where a local authority 'may grant permission' for land to be used as a caravan site, this must in some circumstances mean 'shall grant permission', where the context so implies.[183] And where a regulatory power is given for the purpose of policing the fulfilment of prescribed conditions, it is natural to infer a mandatory duty in other cases.[184]

---

[177] [1968] AC 997. See similarly *Car Owners' Mutual Insurance Co Ltd* v. *Treasurer of the Commonwealth of Australia* [1970] AC 527, where the Privy Council held that the Treasurer was obliged to certify that the company had satisfied the requirements for recovery of its deposited funds, despite the statutory condition 'if the Treasurer so certifies'.   [178] Below, p. 297.

[179] *R* v. *Barlow* (1693) 2 Salk 609; *R* v. *Barclay* (1882) 8 QBD 486.

[180] *R* v. *Metropolitan Police Commissioner ex p Holloway* [1911] 2 KB 1131. See also *R* v. *Tynemouth Rural District Council* [1896] 2 QB 451 (building plans disapproved for improper reasons: approval ordered). Contrast *Patmor Ltd* v. *City of Edinburgh District Licensing Board*, 1987 SLT 492.

[181] *Congreve* v. *Home Office* [1976] QB 629; for this case see below, p. 301.

[182] *Singh* v. *Home Secretary* [1992] 1 WLR 1052 (HL).

[183] *Hartnell* v. *Minister of Housing and Local Government* [1965] AC 1134 at 1158 (Lord Reid). See similarly *A-G* v. *Antigua Times Ltd* [1976] AC 16.

[184] As in *R* v. *Newcastle on Tyne Corporation ex p Veitch* (1889) 60 LT 963 (no discretion to withhold approval of plans conforming to building byelaws).

These exercises in statutory interpretation are only another facet of the principle that discretion must be exercised on proper legal grounds and in accord with the policy of the Act.[185] In this way the court may counteract the tendency of legislation to enlarge executive discretion by loosely using the language of power instead of that of duty, in the manner to which government draftsmen are addicted.

The interpretation of permissive language as mandatory in certain circumstances may be assisted by qualifying words in the context, such as 'unless sufficient cause is shown to the contrary'[186] or 'if satisfied that there is proper ground for doing so'.[187] It may also be assisted by the hardship that might otherwise be caused by indefinite delay and uncertainty. It was for this reason that a public authority's power to proceed with a compulsory purchase of land, once the compulsory purchase order was authorised, could be enforced as a duty by the person from whom the land was to be taken, and who might otherwise have been left with unmarketable land on his hands for an indefinite period.[188]

ESTOPPEL

ESTOPPEL AND PUBLIC AUTHORITIES

The basic principle of estoppel is that a person who by some statement or representation of fact causes another to act to his detriment[189] in reliance on the truth of it is not allowed to deny it later, even though it is wrong. Justice here prevails over truth. Estoppel is often described as a rule of evidence, but more correctly it is a principle of law.[190] As a principle of common law it applies only to representations about past or present facts. But there is also an equitable principle of 'promissory estoppel' which can apply to public authorities.[191] In a class by itself is estoppel by judgment, res judicata, which is treated separately.[192] This last is also known as issue estoppel, since it is a rule against the relitigation of the same issue between the same parties.

Legal rules about estoppel and waiver sometimes seem to be applicable to public authorities in the same way that they apply to persons. A city corporation may be estopped from denying that payments made to it in satisfaction of a liability for rates are 'rates actually levied',[193] and a county council may, by giving an employee a certain status for superannuation, estop itself from denying that status later.[194] Similarly a public

---

[185] Below, p. 332. For the *Tower Hamlets ex p Chetnik Developments* case see below, p. 678.

[186] As in *Re Shuter* [1960] 1 QB 142.

[187] As in *Annison v. District Auditor for St Pancras* [1962] 1 QB 489 at 497.

[188] *Birch v. St Marylebone Vestry* (1869) 20 LT 697.

[189] *Norfolk CC v. Secretary of State for the Environment* [1973] 1 WLR 1400 (planning authority erroneously informed applicant that planning permission had been granted; error corrected before applicant had relied to his detriment, so authority not estopped from denying planning permission).

[190] *Canada & Dominion Sugar Co Ltd v. Canadian National (West Indies) Steamships Ltd* [1947] AC 46 at 56.

[191] *Robertson v. Minister of Pensions* [1949] 1 KB 227 (but see below, p. 282); *Roberts & Co Ltd v. Leicestershire CC* [1961] Ch 555 (council estopped from denying terms of contract); the *Crabb* and *Salvation Army* cases (below). When affecting land, as in those cases, it may be called 'proprietary estoppel'.

[192] Below, p. 201.

[193] *North Western Gas Board v. Manchester Corporation* [1964] 1 WLR 64. Cf. *Gould v. Bacup Local Board* (1881) 50 LJMC 44 (election to follow one of the alternative statutory procedures held binding); *Roberts & Co Ltd v. Leicestershire CC* [1961] Ch 555 (council estopped from denying terms of contract).

[194] *Algar v. Middlesex County Council* [1945] 2 All ER 243. But cases of this kind may be better explained by the rule that such determinations are inherently irrevocable: see above, p. 191.

authority which lets land on lease is bound by the usual rule that acceptance of rent with knowledge of a breach of covenant by the tenant amounts to waiver of the lessor's right of forfeiture for the breach.[195] A local authority which agrees that a landowner may have access to a road from a particular plot may not, after the owner has fenced the plot and agreed to sell it, revoke the permission given.[196] If they negotiate the purchase of land for road widening and encourage the owner to incur expenditure on an alternative site, they may not then discontinue the purchase.[197] As several of these cases show, the principle of estoppel applies equally to the Crown.[198]

But, just as with contracts, the ordinary rules must give way where their application becomes incompatible with the free and proper exercise of an authority's powers or the due performance of its duties in the public interest. Where the normal principles of justice are forced to give way, hard cases naturally result. It is possible for a citizen to be seriously misled by a public authority in a manner which ought, under the normal rules, to give rise to an estoppel which would compel the authority to stand by its representations; but nevertheless there may be no legal remedy. These cases, where the rules of public and private law are irreconcilable, will be found in a later section on discretionary power.[199] Some of them concern the Crown.

ESTOPPEL AND ULTRA VIRES

In public law the most obvious limitation on the doctrine of estoppel is that it cannot be invoked so as to give an authority powers which it does not in law possess. In other words, no estoppel can legitimate action which is ultra vires. Thus where an electricity authority, by misreading a meter, undercharged its customer for two years, it was held that the accounts it delivered did not estop it from demanding payment in full,[200] for the authority had a statutory duty to collect the full amount, and had no power to release the customer, expressly or otherwise. Nor could a parish council, which had no power to undertake to allow a neighbouring district to make use of its sewers, be estopped by its long acquiescence from terminating such an arrangement.[201] Where a minister took possession of land under statutory powers of occupation which did not extend to the grant of leases, he was not estopped from denying that he had granted a lease, even though he had expressly purported to 'let' the land to a 'tenant'.[202] The result was the same where the supposed landlord was a local authority which had failed to obtain the requisite consent from the minister, so that the lease was void. Accordingly the local authority was at liberty to deny the validity of their own 'lease', contrary to the rules which govern private lettings.[203] No arrangement between the parties could prevent either of them from asserting the fact that the lease was ultra vires and void. Nor can any kind of estoppel give a tribunal wider jurisdiction than it possesses.[204]

---

[195] Davenport v. R (1887) 3 App Cas 115; R v. Paulson [1921] 1 AC 271. See also Plimmer v. Wellington Cpn (1884) 9 App Cas 699; Orient Steam Navigation Co v. The Crown (1925) 21 Ll. LR 301 (below, p. 701); Canadian Pacific Railway Co v. R [1931] AC 414.   [196] Crabb v. Arun DC [1976] Ch 179.

[197] Salvation Army Trustee Co v. West Yorkshire CC (1980) 41 P & CR 179, explained in A-G of Hong Kong v. Humphreys Estate (Queen's Gardens) Ltd [1987] AC 114.   [198] See n. 196.

[199] Below, p. 281.

[200] Maritime Electric Company v. General Dairies Ltd [1937] AC 610. See likewise R v. Blenkinsop [1892] 1 QB 43 (rate demand too low: no estoppel); Norfolk CC v. Secretary of State for the Environment (above).

[201] Islington Vestry v. Hornsey Urban Council [1900] 1 Ch 695.

[202] Minister of Agriculture and Fisheries v. Matthews [1950] 1 KB 148, citing an unreported decision of the Court of Appeal; R v. Rushbrooke [1958] NZLR 877.

[203] Rhyl UDC v. Rhyl Amusements Ltd [1959] 1 WLR 465.

[204] Secretary of State for Employment v. Globe Elastic Thread Co Ltd [1980] AC 506.

Similarly the principle of estoppel cannot prevent a change of government policy. A government department which encourages an airline to invest in aircraft on the understanding that its licence will be continued is not estopped, if there is a change of government and a reversal of policy, from withdrawing the licence.[205] Many people may be victims of political vicissitudes, and 'estoppel cannot be allowed to hinder the formation of government policy'.

Estoppels have, however, been allowed to operate against public authorities in minor matters of formality, where no question of ultra vires arises. In one case Lord Denning MR said:[206]

> Now I know that a public authority cannot be estopped from doing its public duty, but I do think it can be estopped from relying on technicalities.

He then held that the court could ignore the fact that the proper statutory application had not been made before a planning authority's determination, since the authority itself had led the landowner to suppose that it was not required; and the authority was therefore estopped from taking the objection. The same doctrine was applied in a case where a mother was out of time in lodging a statutory notice of objection to a local authority's order assuming parental rights over her child; the authority was estopped from insisting on the time limit because its officers had misled the mother into supposing that a previous notice of objection was still effective.[207] Where a public authority abuses its powers, a strong *obiter dictum* in the House of Lords holds that it may be estopped.[208]

Estoppel will need further discussion in the context of misleading official advice, where its place is being taken by the doctrine of legitimate expectations.[209]

WAIVER AND CONSENT

PRIMARY RULES

Waiver and consent are in their effects closely akin to estoppel, and not always clearly distinguishable from it. But no rigid distinction need be made, since for present purposes the law is similar.[210] The primary rule is that no waiver of rights and no consent or private bargain can give a public authority more power than it legitimately possesses. Once again, the principle of ultra vires must prevail when it comes into conflict with the ordinary rules of law.[211] A contrasting rule is that a public authority which has made some order or regulation is not normally at liberty to waive the observance of it by exercising a dispensing power. The principle here is that law which exists for the general public benefit

---

[205] *Laker Airways Ltd* v. *Department of Trade* [1977] QB 643. The quotation is from Lawton LJ.

[206] *Wells* v. *Minister of Housing and Local Government* [1967] 1 WLR 1000 at 1007, approved in *Western Fish Products Ltd* v. *Penwith DC* (1978) 38 P & CR 7 (see below, p. 283). *Wells* v. *Minister of Housing and Local Government* was, however, distinguished (but not overruled) in *R (Reprotech (Pebsham) Ltd)* v. *East Sussex County Council* [2003] 1 WLR 348 (HL) discussed in full below, p. 283.

[207] *Re L (AC) (an infant)* [1971] 3 All ER 743; *R* v. *Immigration Appeal Tribunal ex p Patel* [1988] AC 910, where a plea of estoppel was accepted, was plainly a case of abuse of power (below, p. 319).

[208] *R (Anufrijeva)* v. *Home Secretary* [2003] UKHL 36, [2003] 3 WLR 252, para. 35 (Lord Steyn).

[209] Below, p. 319.

[210] But note the distinction drawn in *R (Hill)* v. *Institute of Chartered Accountants In England and Wales* [2013] EWCA Civ 555, a natural justice case discussed more fully above p. 223, between a particular procedure which is not a breach of natural justice because all parties have consented in advance and a breach of natural justice which is waived.

[211] Previous two sentences approved in *Cropp* v. *A Judicial Committee* [2008] NZSC 46.

may not be waived with the same freedom as the rights of a private person. In other cases, where neither of these rules is infringed, waiver and consent may operate in a normal way so as to modify rights and duties.

In one case a tenant had applied to a rent tribunal and obtained an order substantially reducing his rent, but later discovered that the house had been let at a date which put it outside the tribunal's jurisdiction. He then applied to the county court, which in that case would have had jurisdiction. The High Court granted mandamus to compel the county court to decide the case, despite the fact that both parties had previously acquiesced in the rent tribunal's order.[212] The issue was one of jurisdictional fact and the court before which it was raised was obliged to determine it. For the same reasons an agreement with the landlord that the tenancy is furnished, when in fact it is not, cannot estop the tenant from later claiming an unfurnished tenancy.[213] In a planning case concerning a caravan site, the Court of Appeal held that the site-owner could apply for a declaration that the planning authority's enforcement notice was bad in law, even though he had pleaded guilty to contravention of the notice in previous criminal proceedings.[214] If the notice was in reality bad, no previous acquiescence could preclude him from contesting it. Exactly the same point determined an earlier enforcement notice case in which the landowners on whom the notice had been served applied for planning permission on the footing that the notice was valid. They were held entitled, nevertheless, to dispute its validity subsequently.[215] The House of Lords confirmed this principle in a case where a party had acquiesced in proceedings before the Lands Tribunal which were later held to be outside that tribunal's jurisdiction. Lord Reid said: 'in my judgment, it is a fundamental principle that no consent can confer on a court or tribunal with limited statutory jurisdiction any power to act beyond that jurisdiction, or can estop the consenting party from subsequently maintaining that such court or tribunal has acted without jurisdiction.'[216]

It follows that resort to a statutory remedy cannot be a waiver of the right to seek judicial review later.[217]

PROCEDURE AND JURISDICTION

The primary rule is subject to various qualifications. One of these concerns conditions which are merely procedural, but which may nevertheless be mandatory and so affect jurisdiction. Thus where a county court, which for this purpose is analogous to a statutory tribunal, could entertain proceedings against persons residing outside its area only on condition that leave was obtained, it was held that such a person who appeared on the first day as defendant without raising objection could not challenge the court's jurisdiction on a later day.[218] Although the court held that the question 'would come under the head of procedure rather than under the head of jurisdiction', the condition was probably jurisdictional. In an earlier case[219] of a similar kind Erle J had said: 'But jurisdiction is

---

[212] *R* v. *Judge Pugh ex p Graham* [1951] 2 KB 623. See similarly *Farquharson* v. *Morgan* [1894] 1 QB 552; *Wilkinson* v. *Barking Corporation* [1948] 1 KB 721.

[213] *Welch* v. *Nagy* [1950] 1 KB 455; likewise *Chapman* v. *Earl* [1968] 1 WLR 1315 (invalid application by tenant to rent officer: landlord's participation in proceedings not waiver).

[214] *Munnich* v. *Godstone Rural District Council* [1966] 1 WLR 427.

[215] *Swallow & Pearson* v. *Middlesex County Council* [1953] 1 WLR 422.

[216] *Essex Incorporated Congregational Church Union* v. *Essex County Council* [1963] AC 808. See also *London Cpn* v. *Cox* (1867) LR 2 HL 239 at 283; *Bradford City MC* v. *Secretary of State for the Environment* (1986) 53 P & CR 55.   [217] See below, p. 601.

[218] *Moore* v. *Gamgee* (1890) 25 QBD 244.   [219] *Jones* v. *James* (1850) 19 LJQB 257.

sometimes contingent; in such a case, if the defendant does not, by objecting at the proper time, exercise his right of destroying the jurisdiction, he cannot do so afterwards.' This probably reveals the correct principle, that there are some conditions which are jurisdictional only if pleaded at the right time. This conforms, in particular, to the decisions on the rules of natural justice. If a person disqualified by interest or bias takes part in an adjudication, that goes to jurisdiction and renders the decision void. But if the party affected knows the facts and raises no objection at the outset, he is taken to have waived it and cannot raise it later. As explained elsewhere,[220] there is nothing illogical in this. The correct rule, it must be assumed, is that jurisdiction is lost if the objection is raised at the proper time, but not otherwise. Erle J's remark explains why it is fallacious to suppose that a condition cannot be jurisdictional merely because it can be waived. In the House of Lords, in the case already cited, Lord Hodson said: 'Had the question been procedural only no difficulty would have arisen, for the parties had consented to the course taken before the Lands Tribunal.'[221] But he then held that the statutory condition was absolute so that the parties had no power to confer jurisdiction where none existed.

NON-JURISDICTIONAL WAIVER

Where problems of jurisdiction do not arise, a person entitled to the benefit of some statutory rule or condition may be able to waive the benefit of it. Thus one party to an action in the county court may waive the statutory time limit on his opponent's right of appeal.[222] But this doctrine does not apply to planning permission, which under the planning legislation enures for the benefit of the land and its successive owners, so that termination of the permitted operations by one owner does not amount to waiver or abandonment of the permission.[223]

PERSONAL BENEFIT AND PUBLIC POLICY

It may be difficult to decide whether a statutory condition exists solely for a person's benefit so that he may waive it on the principle *quilibet potest renuntiare juri pro se introducto*. It may, on the contrary, embody some public policy which an individual has no power to modify. On this latter ground the Court of Appeal of New Zealand held that the Commissioner of Inland Revenue had no power to waive the thirty-day time limit on appeals from the Taxation Board of Review to the High Court, even though he was willing to do so in a case where the taxpayer's solicitor had been ill.[224] As Turner J put it, 'the due and impartial administration of a revenue statute' is 'a matter in which every citizen has an interest'. In this decision a sound principle may have been carried too far, since it must surely be even more in the public interest that accidents should not prevent tax liability from being correctly adjudicated. In contrast, the Court of Appeal in England in two controversial decisions has shown itself favourable to the contention that a planning authority may waive the prescribed formalities for applications in planning matters.[225]

---

[220] Below, p. 398.
[221] *Essex Incorporated Congregational Church Union v. Essex County Council* [1963] AC 808 at 828. See likewise *Thomas v. University of Bradford (No 2)* [1992] 1 All ER 964 (waiver of irregular procedure by acquiescence).   [222] *Park Gate Iron Co Ltd v. Coates* (1870) LR 5 CP 634.
[223] *Pioneer Aggregates (UK) Ltd v. Secretary of State for the Environment* [1985] AC 132.
[224] *Reckitt & Colman (New Zealand) Ltd v. Taxation Board of Review* [1966] NZLR 1032, following earlier New Zealand and Canadian cases.
[225] *Wells v. Minister of Housing and Local Government* [1967] 1 WLR 1000; *Lever Finance Ltd v. Westminster LBC* [1971] 1 QB 222. But both these cases were distinguished (but not overruled) in *R (Reprotech (Pebsham) Ltd) v. East Sussex CC* [2003] 1 WLR 348 (HL) discussed in full below, p. 283.

But these decisions were strongly motivated by the court's desire to contrive some binding legal basis for the informal advice often given to enquirers by planning authorities and their officers; but to this, as will be shown, there are serious legal objections.[226] The dissenting view of Russell LJ that a planning authority, as 'the guardian of the planning system', is 'not a free agent to waive statutory requirements', and that the law should not be made to conform to 'a thoroughly bad administrative practice',[227] is correct in principle.[228]

NO POWER TO DISPENSE

Where something more than mere procedure or formality is in question, a public authority cannot exercise a dispensing power by waiving compliance with the law. For this would amount to an unauthorised power of legislation. There is therefore no power for a local authority to waive compliance with its binding byelaws;[229] nor is any such power possessed by the minister with whose consent the byelaws are made.[230] Still less is there any power to grant dispensations from the ordinary law, e.g. as to obstruction of the highway.[231]

RES JUDICATA

PRINCIPLES AND DISTINCTIONS

One special variety of estoppel is res judicata. This results from the rule which prevents the parties to a judicial determination from litigating the same question over again, even though the determination is demonstrably wrong. Except in proceedings by way of appeal, the parties bound by the judgment are estopped from questioning it. As between one another, they may neither pursue the same cause of action again, nor may they again litigate any issue which was an essential element in the decision. These two aspects are sometimes distinguished as 'cause of action estoppel' and 'issue estoppel'. It is the latter which presents most difficulty, since an issue 'directly upon the point' has to be distinguished from one which 'came collaterally in question' or was 'incidentally cognisable'.[232] In any case, 'there must be a lis or issue and there must be a decision'.[233]

Like other forms of estoppel already discussed, res judicata plays a restricted role in administrative law, since it must yield to two fundamental principles of public law: that jurisdiction cannot be exceeded; and that statutory powers and duties cannot be fettered.[234] Within those limits, however, it can extend to a wide variety of statutory tribunals and authorities which have power to give binding decisions, such as employment tribunals[235] and commons commissioners.[236] It can extend likewise to the decisions of

---

[226] Below, p. 340.   [227] In the *Wells* case (above) at 1015.

[228] And in the ascendency following the *Reprotech* case (above), discussed below at p. 283.

[229] *Yabbicom v. King* [1899] 1 QB 444; *Bean (William) & Sons v. Flaxton Rural District Council* [1929] 1 KB 450; below, p. 737.   [230] *Bean (William) & Sons v. Flaxton Rural District Council* (above).

[231] *Redbridge LBC v. Jacques* [1970] 1 WLR 1604; *Cambridgeshire CC v. Rust* [1972] 2 QB 426.

[232] These phrases were used in *The Duchess of Kingston's Case* (1776) 20 St Tr 355, 538 n., in which the rules were laid down. See Spencer Bower and Turner, *Res Judicata*.

[233] *Vernon v. Inland Revenue Commissioners* [1956] 1 WLR 1169 at 1178, holding that the Attorney-General was not estopped from disputing the purposes of a charity by having been party to an order of the court which did not put that question in issue.   [234] Below, p. 295.

[235] *McLoughlin v. Gordons (Stockport) Ltd* [1978] ICR 561; *Munir v. Jang Publications Ltd* [1989] ICR 1; *O'Laoire v. Jackel International Ltd (No 2)* [1991] ICR 718.

[236] *Crown Estate Commissioners v. Dorset CC* [1990] Ch 297.

inspectors in planning appeals, so as to prevent an inspector from ruling that houses were used as hostels when another inspector three years earlier had ruled that they were used as hotels and no change of use had occurred meanwhile.[237]

Res judicata is sometimes confused with the principle of finality of statutory decisions and acts, and thus with the general theory of judicial control. If a public authority has statutory power to determine some question, for example the compensation payable to an employee for loss of office,[238] its decision once made is normally final and irrevocable. This is not because the authority and the employee are estopped from disputing it, but because, as explained elsewhere,[239] the authority has power to decide only once and thereafter is without jurisdiction in the case. Conversely, where a statutory authority determines some matter within its jurisdiction, its determination is binding not because of any estoppel but because it is a valid exercise of statutory power. The numerous cases which hold that a decision within jurisdiction is unchallengeable[240] have therefore no necessary connection with res judicata. Res judicata does nothing to make the initial decision binding: it is only because the decision is for some other reason binding that it may operate as res judicata in later proceedings raising the same issue between the same parties.

How easily these questions may appear to overlap may be seen in a case where a school-teacher, who had enlisted for war service, claimed additional pay from the local authority which had undertaken to make up his service pay to the level of his teacher's pay. The dispute was referred to the National Arbitration Tribunal, which ruled against him, and he then brought proceedings in the High Court. The questions were whether there was a 'trade dispute' within the Tribunal's statutory jurisdiction, and whether it had jurisdiction over private (as opposed to national) service agreements. These being answered in the affirmative, the Tribunal's award was held conclusive[241]—from which it followed, the judge said, that it was res judicata.[242] But in fact the case seems to belong to the common class where a specific matter is allotted by statute to a specific tribunal so that the tribunal's award, within its jurisdiction, is conclusive.[243] Where the question in issue is one of jurisdiction, no estoppel can prevent the court from determining it.[244] Once it is determined in favour of the tribunal, no estoppel is needed to bind the parties conclusively. If in the case of the teacher there had been an 'issue estoppel'—if, for example, the tribunal had determined that he belonged to a particular category, and he disputed this in later proceedings against the local authority—a true res judicata might have been pleaded. So where an industrial tribunal found that an employee had been fairly dismissed, he was not allowed to litigate substantially the same issue in a High Court action for breach of contract.[245]

ADMINISTRATIVE CASES

Res judicata in an administrative context is illustrated by a decision of the House of Lords about the making up of Sludge Lane, Wakefield. Adjoining landowners disputed their

---

[237] *Thrasyvoulou* v. *Secretary of State for the Environment* [1990] 2 AC 273. See similarly *Hammond* v. *Secretary of State for the Environment* (1997) 74 P & CR 134. But a certificate of appropriate alternative development creates no estoppel by res judicata or otherwise: *Porter* v. *Secretary of State for Transport* [1996] 3 All ER 693.   [238] As in *Livingstone* v. *Westminster Corporation* [1904] 2 KB 109.

[239] Above, p. 191.   [240] See above, p. 27.

[241] *Re Birkenhead Cpn* [1952] Ch 359.   [242] Ibid. at 379.

[243] e.g. *IRC* v. *Pearlberg* [1953] 1 WLR 331; *Healey* v. *Minister of Health* [1955] 1 QB 221; *R* v. *Paddington etc. Rent Tribunal ex p Perry* [1956] 1 QB 229; *Davies* v. *Price* [1958] 1 WLR 434.

[244] See above, p. 197.   [245] *Green* v. *Hampshire CC* [1979] ICR 861.

liability to contribute to the costs incurred by the Corporation on the ground that Sludge Lane was a public rather than a private road, and so chargeable to the ratepayers generally rather than to the frontagers. A local Act empowered two justices to determine the objection, and they determined it in favour of the frontagers. Three years later the Corporation undertook further works and again attempted to charge the frontagers, who were mostly the same persons as before. The justices refused to reconsider the matter, holding it to be res judicata; and after being reversed in the King's Bench Division and upheld in the Court of Appeal, their decision was upheld in the House of Lords.[246] The House of Lords was prepared to treat the original decision as a judgment in rem,[247] binding on everyone. Lord Davey said that, alternatively, it would bind all who were given notice and an opportunity to object. Such an estoppel would, on ordinary principles, bind their successors in title also.[248]

The House of Lords distinguished *R* v. *Hutchings*,[249] a superficially similar case where the justices had held that the disputed road was a public highway and had dismissed the local board's application for the enforcement of its levy on the frontager. Five years later the same board made another levy on the same frontager which a magistrate upheld. The Court of Appeal held that this was correct and that there was no res judicata. The reason was that the Public Health Act 1875, unlike the local Act in Wakefield, gave the justices no power to determine finally whether the street was public or private. Their only power was to decide whether the levy was properly assessed or not. If its validity was disputed on the ground that it was ultra vires, the magistrate had indeed to determine that issue before proceeding further; but it was only a matter 'incidentally cognisable'. It was thus a point of 'jurisdictional fact' upon which jurisdiction depended, and upon which no estoppel could operate so as to make a wrong decision unchallengeable.[250] It illustrates the 'constitutional principle that a tribunal of limited jurisdiction cannot be permitted conclusively to determine the limits of its own jurisdiction'.[251]

The reasoning of the last-mentioned case has played an important part in a series of later decisions about assessments for rates and taxes. In these it has been repeatedly held that matters decided for the purposes of one year's assessment or of one rating list do not amount to res judicata for the purposes of later assessments or lists. A medical society successfully established before the Lands Tribunal in 1951 that it was entitled to exemption from rates under the Scientific Societies Act 1843. In 1956 a new valuation list had to be made and the valuation officer again attempted to assess the society, and on his appeal to the Lands Tribunal the society pleaded res judicata. Although it was admitted that there had been no relevant change of circumstances, the House of Lords disallowed this plea and ruled that the question must again be decided on its merits.[252] It was held that decisions relating to a different list were irrelevant, since the local valuation court had jurisdiction to determine cases for the purpose of one list only at any one time. The same point has been settled, after some difference of opinion, in a line of income tax cases. Thus where a trust in Ceylon had been held to be a charity, and so exempt from income tax, by the statutory board of review, this was held to be conclusive only in the relevant

[246] *Wakefield Cpn* v. *Cooke* [1904] AC 31. See similarly *Armstrong* v. *Whitfield* (1973) 71 LGR 282 (determination as to public right of way conclusive in later proceedings).

[247] For this see also *A-G* v. *Honeywill* (1972) 71 LGR 81; *Armstrong* v. *Whitfield* (above); *Emms* v. *R* [1979] 2 SCR 1148 (judgment invalidating regulation held binding upon all affected by it).

[248] See Halsbury's *Laws of England*, 4th edn, xvi. 1041.   [249] (1881) 6 QBD 300.

[250] For this see below, p. 209.

[251] *Crown Estate Commissioners* v. *Dorset CC* [1990] Ch 297 at 312 (Millett J), so explaining *R* v. *Hutchings*.

[252] *Society of Medical Officers of Health* v. *Hope* [1960] AC 551.

year of assessment, and to be open to challenge by the Commissioner of Income Tax in any subsequent year.[253] The Privy Council emphasised that the important consideration was the limited nature of the question that was within the tribunal's jurisdiction: each year's assessment was a different operation and there was no 'eadem quaestio' of the kind required for res judicata.

THE SEARCH FOR A PRINCIPLE

The above-mentioned decisions on rates and taxes have carried the doctrine of R v. Hutchings,[254] which they profess to follow, far beyond its apparent boundaries. That case merely illustrates the familiar principle that where jurisdictional questions are raised before a tribunal of limited jurisdiction, the tribunal must necessarily determine them for its own purposes but its determination may always be reviewed in the High Court.[255] It follows that the tribunal's determination cannot be conclusive, whether as res judicata or otherwise. But it is plain that the question whether a taxpayer or ratepayer is entitled to exemption, if raised before a revenue tribunal, is not 'collateral' or 'jurisdictional' in any such sense: it falls squarely within the range of questions which it is the tribunal's business to decide conclusively. The tax and rate cases observe no such distinction, and it is generally accepted that they are anomalous.[256] It should likewise be admitted that no help is to be derived from trying to distinguish judicial from administrative functions[257] (that favourite fallacy):[258] all that res judicata requires is some power to adjudicate. Nor does there appear to be merit in the argument that there is no lis because the taxing or rating officer is a neutral party rather than an opponent.[259] Law based on such sophistries must lack a firm foundation.

Yet a firm foundation exists, and can be traced through a series of judicial opinions. The principle is simply that an assessing officer has a statutory public duty to make a correct assessment on the taxpayer or ratepayer on each occasion, and that no estoppel can avail to prevent him doing so. Just as an electricity company cannot be estopped from charging the full price of electricity, if it has a statutory duty,[260] so an assessing officer 'cannot be estopped from carrying out his duties under the statute'.[261] A county court, similarly, must determine a statutory standard rent on the correct facts, and no estoppel or res judicata from earlier proceedings can discharge the court from this duty.[262] This doctrine fits easily into the framework of public law. It carries altogether more conviction than the formalistic distinctions discussed above, which fail to take account of the special character of public power and duty. Its force is all the more obvious if it is remembered

---

[253] Caffoor v. Commissioner of Income Tax [1961] AC 584, following Broken Hill Proprietary Company Ltd v. Broken Hill Municipal Council [1926] AC 94 and Inland Revenue Commissioners v. Sneath [1932] 2 KB 362; not following Hoystead v. Commissioner of Taxation [1926] AC 155.   [254] Above.

[255] Below, p. 210.

[256] Caffoor (as above) at 599; Crown Estate Commissioners v. Dorset CC [1990] Ch 297 at 311.

[257] Caffoor (as above); and see [1965] PL 237 at 241 (G. Ganz).   [258] See below, p. 416.

[259] The House of Lords lent countenance to this in Society of Medical Officers of Health v. Hope [1960] AC 551. Cf. Inland Revenue Commissioners v. Sneath [1932] 2 KB 362.

[260] See Maritime Electric Company v. General Dairies Ltd [1937] AC 610; above, p. 197.

[261] Society of Medical Officers of Health v. Hope [1960] AC 551 at 568 (Lord Keith), citing the Maritime Electric Company case (above) and the opinion of Lord Parker of Waddington in Inland Revenue Commissioners v. Brooke [1915] AC 478 at 491. See also Bradshaw v. McMullan [1920] 2 IR (HL) 412 at 425; Inland Revenue Commissioners v. Sneath [1932] 2 KB 362 at 382 (Lord Hanworth MR). For a similar principle of public policy in matrimonial law see Hudson v. Hudson [1948] P 292.

[262] Griffiths v. Davies [1943] KB 618; R v. Pugh [1951] 2 KB 623; above, p. 198.

that res judicata, like other forms of estoppel, is essentially a rule requiring a party to accept some determination of fact or law which is wrong.[263] For if the determination is right, no substantive question arises. There are self-evident objections to requiring public authorities to act on wrong assumptions. Public powers and duties, as has been seen elsewhere,[264] cannot be fettered in such ways. There is no inconsistency in giving conclusive force to a tax tribunal's decision on an assessment for the year in question, since that is given the force of law by statute, not by mere estoppel.

The same principle ought to apply in all situations where powers have to be exercised in the public interest. Suppose that certain disciplinary charges are made against a school-teacher whose removal can be required by the education authority only on educational grounds, that no educational grounds are shown before the authority's disciplinary committee, and that the complaint is dismissed. What is the position if it is later discovered that there were in fact good educational grounds on which the teacher ought to have been removed? The answer should be that the education authority always has the power to require removal when such grounds in fact exist; that this is a power which it must exercise in the public interest; that its powers cannot be fettered by any estoppel, by res judicata or otherwise; and that it is therefore free to act on the fresh evidence. The additional dimension of the public interest is what makes the difference.

Where, on the other hand, an immigrant's right to an entry certificate was established in his favour by an adjudicator, but the Home Office later discovered evidence suggesting that he might be an illegal entrant, the court refused to admit that evidence in later proceedings and held that the adjudicator's decision came very close to rendering the immigrant's status res judicata.[265] Thus they treated his status as a matter more of private right than of public interest. The doctrine of res judicata is not entirely rigid and exceptions are sometimes made when the court is unwilling to compel a party to remain bound by a wrong decision.[266]

JURISDICTIONAL AND OTHER LIMITS

No question of res judicata can derogate from the rules that a determination which is ultra vires may always be challenged in the High Court and that no tribunal can give itself jurisdiction which it does not possess. There can therefore be no such thing as jurisdiction by estoppel. But since so many kinds of error, including now mere error of law,[267] are held to go to jurisdiction, the scope of res judicata in administrative law will be restricted unless the courts decide not to press the jurisdictional logic to the limit.

A large class of administrative cases must also be ruled out because they involve public policy. In licensing cases of all kinds it is usually inherent in the system of control that applications may be made at any time and may be renewed. Thus planning permission may be sought repeatedly over many years and each application must be considered on its merits.[268] As will be seen, the discretionary power of a public authority cannot normally be fettered, even by its own decisions.[269] Res judicata rests on the theory of an unchanging

---

[263] This was the reason for the old saying 'estoppels are odious': e.g. *Baxendale* v. *Bennett* (1878) 3 QBD 525 at 529. An instance is *Priestman* v. *Thomas* (1884) LR 9 PD 210, where the estoppel obliged the parties to accept a forged will.   [264] Above, p. 196.

[265] *R* v. *Home Secretary ex p Momin Ali* [1984] 1 WLR 663, no doubt assisted by the fact that the fresh evidence was weak.   [266] See *Arnold* v. *National Westminster Bank plc* [1991] 2 AC 93.

[267] See below, p. 219.   [268] As in *Westminster Bank Ltd* v. *Beverley BC* [1971] AC 551.

[269] Below, p. 271.

law, whereas policy must be free to change at any moment, as the public interest may require.

PREROGATIVE REMEDIES

It is probable that the doctrine of res judicata is inherently inapplicable to proceedings for habeas corpus,[270] certiorari and the other prerogative remedies. Formerly there were grounds for holding that the court's rulings in such cases were not technically judgments capable of producing res judicata.[271] A more persuasive reason is that in these procedures the court 'is not finally determining the validity of the tribunal's order as between the parties themselves' but 'is merely deciding whether there has been a plain excess of jurisdiction or not'.[272] They are a special class of remedies designed to maintain due order in the legal system, nominally at the suit of the Crown,[273] and they may well fall outside the ambit of the ordinary doctrine of res judicata. But the court may refuse to entertain questions which were or could have been litigated in earlier proceedings, when this would be an abuse of legal process;[274] and in the case of habeas corpus there is a statutory bar against repeated applications made on the same grounds.[275]

This reasoning was approved by a Divisional Court and by the Court of Appeal in a case where a London borough, after securing the quashing of the Secretary of State's order to reduce their rate support grant, failed in a further claim that their success in the first proceedings precluded the Secretary of State from later making a similar reduction order. Both courts were of the opinion that the doctrine of issue estoppel was not to be relied upon in proceedings for judicial review.[276]

Another consideration is that the requirement of identity of parties will seldom be satisfied where prerogative remedies are employed. In a wartime case a detainee obtained release on habeas corpus on grounds which the House of Lords in another case held to be insufficient. In an action against the Home Secretary for false imprisonment he claimed that the illegality of his detention was res judicata. The judge held that this plea failed, 'if only because the parties are different'.[277]

---

[270] *Re Hastings (No 2)* [1959] 1 QB 358 at 371; *R v. Pentonville Prison Governor ex p Tarling* [1979] 1 WLR 1417 at 1422.   [271] See Lord Goddard CJ, 'A Note on Habeas Corpus' (1949) 65 *LQR* 30 at 35.
[272] *R v. Fulham etc. Rent Tribunal ex p Zerek* [1951] 2 KB 1 (Devlin J).   [273] See below, p. 500.
[274] See the *Tarling* case (above) and the *Momin Ali* case (below).   [275] Below, p. 503.
[276] *R v. Secretary of State for the Environment ex p Hackney LBC* [1983] 1 WLR 524, [1984] 1 WLR 592, approving the last 10 lines of the preceding paragraph, and confirmed in *R v. Home Secretary ex p Momin Ali* [1984] 1 WLR 663.
[277] *Budd v. Anderson* [1943] KB 642. The report does not say who were the parties to the habeas corpus proceedings. Cf. *R v. Brixton Prison Governor ex p Savarkar* [1910] 2 KB 1056 (different issue).

8

JURISDICTION OVER FACT AND LAW

ERROR OUTSIDE JURISDICTION

OBJECTIVE BOUNDARIES OF SUBJECTIVE POWERS

Wide discretionary powers are very commonly conferred upon ministers and other public bodies, and the courts' powers of review over the exercise of discretion is explained in later chapters. Here we investigate the objective boundaries of these powers and the way in which the courts police them.[1] All discretionary powers have objective limits of some kind, but the problem lies in identifying them. It is easy, for instance, to see that the question whether an alien ought to be deported is for decision by the Home Secretary but that the question whether a person is really an alien must be determined by the court.[2] Other cases, unfortunately, are often less clear.

The same distinction is sometimes expressed in terms of the liberty to err. It is inherent in all discretionary power that it includes the power to decide freely, whether rightly or wrongly, without liability to correction, within the area of discretion allowed by the law. The principle was clearly expressed long ago by Holt CJ,[3] who spoke of

> this diversity, (viz.) that if the commissioners had intermeddled with a thing which was not within their jurisdiction, then all is coram non judice,[4] and that may be given in evidence upon this action; but 'tis otherwise if they are only mistaken in their judgment in a matter within their conusance, for that is not inquirable, otherwise than upon an appeal.

Until fairly recently[5] this liberty to make mistakes within jurisdiction extended to significant mistakes both of law and of fact. The extent to which both these classes of error have been brought within the scope of judicial review will explained below.[6] But it remains true that in all administrative cases there is an area of discretion, its size depending upon the context, within which the administrator has a free hand.[7] When the Home Secretary has complied with all legal requirements for deporting an alien, it remains for him to decide whether to deport or not. As to this the law cannot control him, however mistaken his decision may be thought to be.[8] Parliament has entrusted the exercise of that discretion to the Home Secretary and the courts cannot intervene. But if he orders the deportation of a person who is not an alien, he acts beyond his powers and the courts will stay his hand.

---

[1] We are not here concerned with appeals, which are always statutory.

[2] As explained in *R* v. *Home Secretary ex p Khawaja* [1984] AC 74 in terms of the power to deport an illegal entrant (below, p. 211).

[3] *Fuller* v. *Fotch* (1695) Carthew 346.   [4] i.e. null and void.

[5] The watershed was the *Anisminic* case (below).   [6] See below, p. 230 for the detail.

[7] See e.g. *Anisminic Ltd* v. *Foreign Compensation Commission* [1969] 2 AC 147 at 207 (Lord Wilberforce).

[8] See e.g. *R* v. *Home Secretary ex p Cheblak* [1991] 1 WLR 890.

The principle of objectivity authorises the courts to define that area of freedom. It is only one of the many weapons in their armoury, but it is of primary importance. Without it they would be powerless to prevent serious usurpations. A public authority might then, by making some mistake as to the extent of its powers, do something which the statute never intended to permit. The object of the courts is to prevent this at all costs by standing guard over the frontiers of free discretion. In other words, the minister or other body must not be allowed to be the judge of the extent of his own powers.

In this area 'jurisdiction' is a hard-worked word. Commonly it is used in its broadest sense, meaning simply 'power'. In some contexts it will bear the narrower sense of 'power to decide' or 'power to determine', but there will be no technical difference. In fact, the principle here at work is basically that of ultra vires, which is synonymous with 'outside jurisdiction' or 'in excess of power'.[9]

JURISDICTIONAL AND NON-JURISDICTIONAL FACT

Certain mistakes of fact can carry an administrative authority or tribunal outside its jurisdiction.[10] A rent tribunal, for example, may have power to reduce the rent of a dwelling-house. If it mistakenly finds that the property is a dwelling-house when in fact it is let for business purposes,[11] and then purports to reduce the rent, its order will be ultra vires and void. For its jurisdiction depends upon facts which must exist objectively before the tribunal has power to act. As to these 'jurisdictional facts' the tribunal's decision cannot be conclusive, for otherwise it could by its own error give itself powers which were never conferred upon it by Parliament. The fact that the tribunal's order appears good on its face can avail nothing. It will be quashed on certiorari if the applicant can show that the true facts do not justify it. For this purpose, accordingly, any available evidence may be put before the court.[12]

Although 'jurisdictional fact' and its synonym 'precedent fact' are part of the currency of administrative law,[13] English judges have in the past also spoken of 'collateral questions'. A classic statement comes from a case of 1853[14] in which Coleridge J said:

---

[9] See above, p. 29. An exception to this principle is the doctrine of error of law on the face of the record, explained elsewhere, p. 224.

[10] The earliest recognisable case appears to be *Terry v. Huntington* (1668) Hardr 480 (successful action against commissioners of excise for levying duty on 'low wines' when they had powers only as to 'strong wines'). Hale CB called this 'a stinted, limited jurisdiction' and said: 'though the information before them supposes the matter to be within their power and jurisdiction; yet the party is not thereby concluded, but that he may aver the contrary.' See likewise *Fuller v. Fotch* (1695) Carth 346. In (1929) 45 *LQR* 479 (D. M. Gordon) *St. John's Case* (1601) 5 Co Rep 61b is cited as an early example of collateral fact, but the report is inadequate for this purpose; so is the report of the same case as *Gardener's Case* (1600) Cro Eliz 821: see Rubinstein, *Jurisdiction and Illegality*, 62, 212. On the subject generally see [1984] *OJLS* 22 (J. Beatson); (1987) 103 *LQR* 66 (G. L. Peiris).   [11] As in *R v. Hackney etc Rent Tribunal ex p Keats* [1951] 2 KB 15.

[12] See below, p. 217. Formerly the order had to show jurisdiction.

[13] Probably the first appearance of 'jurisdictional fact' in an English law report was in *Anisminic Ltd v. Foreign Compensation Commission* [1969] 2 AC 147 at 208, 242 (Lord Wilberforce and Browne JJ). See also *R v. Home Secretary ex p Khawaja* [1984] AC 74 where Lord Fraser and Lord Wilberforce use 'precedent fact' also.

[14] *Bunbury v. Fuller* (1853) 9 Ex 111 (assistant tithe commissioner's jurisdiction dependent on fact that land was not previously discharged from tithe; this fact held collateral). Contrast *Tithe Redemption Commission v. Wynne* [1943] KB 756, where the Tithe Act 1936 gave the Commission conclusive jurisdiction over a similar question.

> Now it is a general rule, that no Court of limited jurisdiction can give itself jurisdiction by a wrong decision on a point collateral to the merits of the case upon which the limit to its jurisdiction depends... [Thus the question] whether some collateral matter be or be not within the limits... must always be open to inquiry in the superior Court.

This is merely to say that it is always for the court to enforce the statutory conditions limiting the extent of a power, i.e. to enforce the principle of ultra vires.

Under the classical doctrine many facts would not be jurisdictional, since they would have no bearing on the limits of the power. A rent tribunal's findings as to the state of repair of the property, the terms of the tenancy, and the defaults of landlord or tenant would probably not affect its jurisdiction in any way and would therefore be immune from jurisdictional challenge.[15]

The distinction which has to be made in these cases is that between the primary or central question which the tribunal has power to decide conclusively itself, and other questions which circumscribe the scope of that power. This is what is meant by the contrast made in the above quotation between 'the merits of the case' and a point which is 'collateral', and by the contrasts made by Lord Goddard CJ, as quoted below,[16] between 'the main question which the tribunal have to decide' and other questions on which 'the existence of jurisdiction depends'. In the above examples the central question for the rent tribunal's decision is whether the rent ought to be reduced. No court of law can review their decision on this question if it is validly made within their jurisdiction. The collateral questions, such as whether the letting is furnished or unfurnished, or whether it is for residential or business purposes, or whether a premium has been paid, are questions which determine whether a situation has arisen in which the tribunal may proceed to exercise its primary power. These are therefore questions which a court of law may review in order to keep the tribunal within its proper sphere. Difficult as this distinction may be to apply in some cases, it is clear in principle and fundamental in importance.

JURISDICTIONAL AND NON-JURISIDCTIONAL QUESTIONS OF LAW

In the past a similar distinction was drawn between jurisdictional and non-jurisdictional questions of law. For example, a rent tribunal had power to reduce a rent where it appeared that a premium had been paid; but where the payment had in fact been made in respect of work done by the landlord and not in respect of the grant of the lease, it was not in law a premium. By treating it as such the tribunal made a mistake of law and acted in excess of its powers, and its order was quashed.[17]

Now, however, the courts have taken a new position, holding that every error of law by a tribunal must necessarily be jurisdictional. This is a deduction from the decision of the House of Lords in the *Anisminic* case, which stretched the concept of jurisdictional error of law to such a point that the possibility of non-jurisdictional error was eliminated. This conclusion, which has important repercussions in several areas, must be explained later.[18] For present purposes it means that any error of law made by a tribunal or administrative decision-maker, if material to its decision, may render the decision ultra vires.

---

[15] Thus in *Terry* v. *Huntington* (above) Hale CB said: 'But if they should commit a mistake in a thing that were within their power, that would not be examinable here.' [16] Below, p. 210.

[17] *R* v. *Fulham etc Rent Tribunal ex p Philippe* [1950] 2 All ER 211. Another example is *R* v. *Tottenham District Rent Tribunal ex p Fryer Ltd* [1971] 2 QB 681 (question whether reference to tribunal validly withdrawn). [18] Below, p. 219.

The distinction between errors which do and do not affect jurisdiction would then apply only to errors of fact—if, indeed, the courts do not jettison that concept also.[19]

THE POWER AND DUTY TO DETERMINE
JURISDICTIONAL QUESTIONS

Where a jurisdictional question is disputed before a tribunal, the tribunal must necessarily decide it.[20] If it refuses to do so, it is wrongfully declining jurisdiction and the court will order it to act properly.[21] Otherwise the tribunal or other authority 'would be able to wield an absolutely despotic power, which the legislature never intended that it should exercise'.[22] It follows that the question is within the tribunal's own jurisdiction, but with this difference, that the tribunal's decision about it cannot be conclusive. This also was explained in the classic case:[23]

> Suppose a judge with jurisdiction limited to a particular hundred, and the matter is brought before him as having arisen within it, but the party charged contends that it arose in another hundred, this is clearly a collateral matter independent of the merits; on its being presented, the judge must not immediately forbear to proceed, but must inquire into its truth or falsehood, and for the time decide it, and either proceed or not with the principal subject-matter according as he finds on that point; but this decision must be open to question, and if he has improperly either forborne or proceeded on the main matter in consequence of an error, on this the Court of Queen's Bench will issue its mandamus or prohibition to correct his mistake.[24]

Similarly Lord Goddard CJ explained that[25]

> if a certain state of facts has to exist before an inferior tribunal have jurisdiction, they can inquire into the facts in order to decide whether or not they have jurisdiction, but cannot give themselves jurisdiction by a wrong decision upon them; and this court may, by means of proceedings for certiorari, inquire into the correctness of the decision. The decision as to these facts is regarded as collateral because, though the existence of jurisdiction depends on it, it is not the main question which the tribunal have to decide.

---

[19] This is an uncertain question discussed below, p. 230.

[20] Unless, perhaps, trial by a court is more suitable: see the *Zerek* case (below) at 13 (Devlin J); or unless statute provides otherwise: *R v. Kensington Rent Officer ex p Noel* [1978] QB 1. For a statutory tribunal's jurisdiction to question the validity of regulations see *Chief Adjudication Officer v. Foster* [1993] AC 754, noted below, p. 235.

[21] *R v. Marsham* [1892] 1 QB 371; *R v. Pugh (Judge) ex p Graham* [1951] 2 KB 623; *R v. Camden LB Rent Officer ex p Ebiri* [1981] 1 WLR 881.

[22] *R v. Marsham* (above) at 379.

[23] *Bunbury v. Fuller* (1853) 9 Ex 111 (above). See also *R v. Special Commissioners of Income Tax* (1888) 21 QBD 313 at 319, quoted below, p. 212.

[24] On territorial error see *Vevers v. Mains* (1888) 4 TLR 724; contrast *Re Smith* (1858) 3 H & N 227 and see (1929) 45 *LQR* at p. 486, (1966) 82 *LQR* at p. 518 (D. M. Gordon).

[25] *R v. Fulham etc Rent Tribunal ex p Zerek* [1951] 2 KB 1 at 6 (Devlin J at 10 is equally clear). See similarly *R v. Lincolnshire Justices ex p Brett* [1926] 2 KB 192 at 202; *R v. Pugh (Judge) ex p Graham* [1951] 2 KB 623; *Re Purkiss' Application* [1962] 1 WLR 902 at 914 (Diplock LJ); *Anisminic Ltd v. Foreign Compensation Commission* [1969] 2 AC 147 at 174 (Lord Reid); *R v. Croydon etc Rent Tribunal ex p Ryzewska* [1977] QB 876; *R v. Camden LBC Rent Officer ex p Ebiri* [1981] 1 WLR 881; *R (Ullah) v. Home Secretary* [2003] EWCA Civ 1366, para. 28; *R (YZ and ors) v. Home Secretary* [2011] EWHC 205, para. 92 (Beatson J).

A collateral question is thus to be contrasted with 'the main question', or 'the actual matter committed to its decision',[26] upon which the tribunal's own decision is conclusive.

This doctrine applies just as much to ordinary administrative action as it does to the decisions of courts and tribunals. One instance was where a local authority had power to take land compulsorily for housing provided that it was not 'part of any park, garden or pleasure ground'.[27] An order made by the authority and confirmed by the minister was quashed on the ground that the land was in fact parkland. This on its face was a simple case of ultra vires. But the minister contended that it was for the acquiring authority and himself to determine the facts, and that their findings of fact were conclusive. The Court of Appeal rejected this argument, holding that the fact in question was collateral and applying the classic rule that collateral facts must be determinable ultimately by the court. Luxmoore LJ said:

> In such a case it seems almost self-evident that the court which has to consider whether there is jurisdiction to make or confirm the order must be entitled to review the vital findings on which the existence of the jurisdiction relied upon depends.

It is obvious that, if this were not so, the statutory exemption in favour of parkland would, legally speaking, be illusory.

The Home Secretary's statutory power to deport aliens is similarly limited by the word 'alien'. Whether a person is, in fact or in law, an alien or a British subject is a question which the court must determine in the case of dispute.[28] Alien nationality is the preliminary or collateral condition on which the Home Secretary's power depends. If he could determine this himself conclusively, a British subject mistakenly taken for an alien would have no legal protection, and plainly this would be intolerable. The Home Secretary's power to deport an 'illegal entrant' is limited in the same way, so that it is for the court to decide objectively on the evidence whether a person has or has not entered the country illegally.[29] If the court fails to stand guard over facts and requirements expressed objectively in the Act, it surrenders the rule of law to the rule of executive discretion. It is essential, therefore, that 'where the exercise of executive power depends upon the precedent establishment of an objective fact, the courts will decide whether the requirement has been satisfied'.[30]

---

[26] *R* v. *Lincolnshire Justices* (above) at 202 (Atkin LJ).

[27] *White and Collins* v. *Minister of Health* [1939] 2 KB 838. Another such case is *R* v. *Bradford* [1908] 1 KB 365 (power to license surveyor of highways to excavate from enclosed lands 'not being a...park'. Held: land was a park, so licence was quashed). See the statement of principle by Channell J at 372. See similarly *R* v. *Armagh JJ* [1924] 2 IR 55; *Re Newhill Compulsory Purchase Order* [1938] 2 All ER 163; *R* v. *Blakely ex p Association of Architects of Australia* (1950) 82 CLR 54; *State* v. *Durcan* [1964] IR 279.

[28] *R* v. *Home Secretary ex p Duke of Chateau Thierry* [1917] 1 KB 922 at 930; *Eshugbayi Eleko* v. *Officer Administering Government of Nigeria* [1931] AC 662 at 670; *R* v. *Home Secretary ex p Budd* [1942] 2 KB 14 at 22. In *Khawaja's* case (below) Lord Wilberforce said: 'The best known example of this is *Eshugbayi Eleko* v. *Government of Nigeria* [1931] AC 662, where the discretionary power was exercisable only if the person affected was a native chief, so that whether he was such a chief or not was what is sometimes called a jurisdictional or collateral fact.'

[29] For an example where the House of Lords erred on this fundamental issue, see *R* v. *Home Secretary ex p Zamir* [1980] AC 930, corrected in *R* v. *Home Secretary ex p Khawaja* [1984] AC 74 (below, p. 368); and see *R* v. *Secretary of State for the Environment ex p Tower Hamlets LBC* [1993] QB 632 (council must determine whether homeless person is illegal entrant; Secretary of State's claim to exclusive jurisdiction rejected).

[30] *Khawaja's* case (above) at 110 (Lord Scarman). In *R* v. *Hillingdon LBC ex p Puhlhofer* [1986] AC 484 the House of Lords treated 'accommodation' under the Housing (Homeless Persons Act) 1977 subjectively, but the report fails to make it clear that this was in accordance with the Act, which gives discretion to the housing authority 'if they are satisfied'.

There are many other examples.[31] Any ultra vires case can raise questions of jurisdictional fact if the public authority claims power to decide any question which defines the scope and limits of its power. Where a minister must have 'reasonable cause to believe' something, he may claim that it is for him to decide the question of reasonableness, whereas it is a jurisdictional matter to be decided by the court.[32] It must be remembered that the courts often show themselves unwilling to resign their control of such questions merely because the power is conferred in subjective terms such as 'if the minister is satisfied'. In the rent tribunal case already cited the words were 'where it appears to the tribunal that a premium has been paid', but the court quashed the tribunal's order nevertheless when it was shown that the payment made was not in law a premium, so that the tribunal had misdirected itself in law.[33] Decisions of this kind have become more frequent as the developing law of judicial review has brought discretionary powers under stricter control, as will appear when subjective language is more fully discussed later.[34]

DIFFICULT BORDERLINE CASES

As a general rule, limiting conditions stated in objective terms will be treated as jurisdictional, so that the court will consider any admissible evidence of their non-fulfilment.[35] In the majority of cases these 'limiting conditions' are easy to identify. But there are borderline cases where the question may, on a true view, be part of the matter which the administrative authority is empowered to decide conclusively, so that it is squarely within its jurisdiction. One such was where a taxpayer was entitled to a repayment if 'within or at the end of the year' he could show to the assessing commissioners that he had overpaid. The claims were made two years and more after the relevant year, but passed by the assessing commissioners. The Special Commissioners then refused to pay, holding that the assessing commissioners had no power to accept the claims in the circumstances. But Lord Esher MR held that it was for the assessing commissioners to determine conclusively whether the conditions of claim were satisfied, and that the Special Commissioners were therefore obliged to make the repayment.[36] He distinguished in abstract terms the two situations which the legislature might create:[37]

[31] Numerous examples of questions held to be collateral or not are collected in (1929) 45 *LQR* at pp. 479–82 and in (1960) 1 UBCLR 185 (D. M. Gordon). Examples are *R* v. *Secretary of State for the Environment ex p Davies* (1990) 61 P & CR 487 (CA) ('person having an interest in the land to which an enforcement notice relates'); *State of Queensland* v. *Wyvill* (1989) 90 ALR 611 (whether deceased person 'aboriginal'). But see *Barber* v. *Thames Television plc* [1991] ICR 253 (jurisdictional point first raised on appeal: court refused, in discretion, to consider it). The question whether an asylum-seeker had previously sought asylum in another EU state (so justifying the early return of the asylum-seeker to that state (above, p. 62)) was held not to be a jurisdictional fact in *R (YZ)* v. *Home Secretary* [2011] EWHC 205, para. 109.

[32] See the *Liversidge* and *Rossminster* cases, below, p. 368. *Liversidge* was the most notorious of the lapses from objectivity.

[33] *R* v. *Fulham etc Rent Tribunal ex p Philippe* [1950] 2 All ER 211; above, pp. 213–14. See also *Relton & Sons (Contracts) Ltd* v. *Whitstable Urban District Council* (1967) 201 EG 955 ('where it appears to the appropriate authority that an existing highway should be converted into a new street': no power to decide conclusively that highway was not already a new street, since this was a 'fundamental matter').

[34] Below, p. 357.

[35] The cases usually refer to affidavit evidence since prerogative remedies are in question: e.g. *R* v. *Bolton* (1841) 1 QB 66; *Re Baker* (1857) 2 H & N 219; *R* v. *Bradley* (1894) 70 LT 379; *R* v. *Radcliffe (Judge) ex p Oxfordshire County Council* [1915] 3 KB 418; *R* v. *Board of Control ex p Rutty* [1956] 2 QB 109; *R* v. *Northumberland Compensation Appeal Tribunal ex p Shaw* [1952] 1 KB 338 at 352, 353.

[36] *R* v. *Special Commissioners of Income Tax* (1888) 21 QBD 313. Lindley LJ was doubtful on this question.

[37] Ibid. at 319. This passage was approved by the House of Lords in *Anisminic Ltd* v. *Foreign Compensation Commission* [1969] 2 AC 147.

It may in effect say that, if a certain state of facts exists and is shown to such tribunal or body before it proceeds to do certain things, it shall have jurisdiction to do such things, but not otherwise. There it is not for them conclusively to decide whether that state of facts exists, and, if they exercise the jurisdiction without its existence, what they do may be questioned, and it will be held that they have acted without jurisdiction. But there is another state of things which may exist. The legislature may intrust the tribunal or body with a jurisdiction, which includes the jurisdiction to determine whether the preliminary state of facts exists as well as the jurisdiction, on finding that it does exist, to proceed further or do something more.

A case which naturally falls into the latter category is where a magistrate has jurisdiction to convict on certain facts being proved before him. This is the explanation of the famous 'bum-boat case',[38] in which the magistrates had power to order the forfeiture of any boat suspected of carrying stolen cargo. They were sued in trespass by the owner of a boat so condemned, who wished to show that his vessel was too large to be a boat within the meaning of the Act. The court refused to hear this evidence, holding that the question was within the jurisdiction of the magistrates and that their order, being good on its face, was therefore conclusive. Whether the boat was within the Act was no more jurisdictional than any other ingredient in the situation which the magistrates had to adjudge. In other words, it was within the central area of their jurisdiction and not in any way collateral.

ADMINISTRATIVE CASES

In administrative cases the prescribed statutory ingredients will more readily be found to be collateral. This is probably because, in contrast to the judicial cases just discussed, the central question committed to the administrative authority will commonly be whether to exercise some discretionary power, and the prescribed statutory ingredients will more naturally be regarded as preliminary or collateral conditions. For example, where licensing justices are empowered to grant extensions of hours on 'special occasions', the court will review the question whether there really was a special occasion within the meaning of the Act, which it treats as a jurisdictional condition.[39] As usual with administrative powers, the court is determined to enforce their legal limits and to prevent their abuse. But however strict the court may be, there will always be a residuum of jurisdiction within which the power of determination is conclusive. In a frequently cited case, which may be thought to go too far, justices made an order for the removal of a pauper, who had been in prison for smuggling, from a house belonging to the parish. It was contended that the occupant was not a pauper and that the decision was wrong on the evidence. The court refused to investigate the evidence, holding that the whole matter was within the jurisdiction of the justices and distinguishing cases where their jurisdiction depended upon some objective fact.[40] The statute was not even recited, and no collateral or jurisdictional question was raised—even though it would seem that there might have been room for such

[38] *Brittain v. Kinnaird* (1819) 1 Br & B 432. See likewise *Cave v. Mountain* (1840) 1 M & G 257; *Allen v. Sharp* (1848) 2 Ex 352; *R v. Dayman* (1857) 7 E & B 672 ('new street'); *Ex p. Vaughan* (1866) LR 2 QB 114; *R v. Bradley* (1894) 70 LT 379 (justices empowered to determine conclusively what is 'highway').

[39] *R v. Sussex JJ* [1933] 2 KB 707 (period of summer time: 'clearly . . . excess of jurisdiction'); *R v. Metropolitan Police Commissioner ex p Ruxton* [1972] 1 WLR 232. Similarly as to 'special reasons': *R v. Liverpool Cpn ex p Liverpool Taxi Fleet Operators' Association* [1975] 1 WLR 701: and as to 'special circumstances': *R v. Home Secretary ex p Mehta* [1975] 1 WLR 1087.

[40] *R v. Bolton* (1841) 1 QB 66 (Lord Denman CJ). See similarly *ex p Vaughan* (1866) LR 2 QB 114. Cf. *Allen v. Sharp* (1848) 2 Ex 352; *R v. Young* (1883) 52 LJMC 55.

questions. The case is one of the long series which fall into the second category distinguished by Lord Esher MR and which establish that where the whole matter is considered to be within the jurisdiction of the adjudicating body, its order cannot be quashed by the court merely on the ground that it is mistaken.[41] This elementary rule was often stated in the form that where the subject matter was within the jurisdiction, an order valid on its face was conclusive.[42]

In practice the decisions allow some latitude, providing examples of questions which might have been considered to be collateral being held to be conclusively determinable by an administrative authority.[43] The determining factor is the express or implied intention of Parliament or as it was put in one case 'whether something is in truth a precedent fact...has to depend on the terms of the empowering provision'.[44] Where the Price Commission had to calculate the net profits of a business 'in accordance with generally accepted accounting principles' the Court of Appeal declined to review the Commission's findings of fact as to what these principles were and as to what items were consequently allowable, holding that the legislation clearly implied that these were matters for the Commission and not for the courts; for the statutory scheme of price control required expert, quick and final decisions.[45] But the same court granted a declaration that a method of calculating depreciation, though used only by few companies, would qualify, as a matter of law, as falling within 'generally accepted accounting principles'.[46] These decisions are difficult to reconcile and they illustrate the difficulty that arises in such cases.

EVALUATIVE WORDS

Difficult questions also arise when apparently collateral questions are defined in the statute in a way that leaves the evaluation of the question to the decision-maker, i.e. the jurisdictional condition is so imprecise that there is a range of reasonable interpretations of the condition. In the leading case the Monopolies and Mergers Commission accepted a reference from the minister to investigate local bus services in South Yorkshire on the basis that the statutory and apparently collateral requirement that the relevant area

---

[41] The case is put into correct perspective, and contrasted with cases where jurisdiction is in issue, by Lord Denman CJ himself in *R* v. *Justices of Buckinghamshire* (1843) 3 QB 800; by all the judges in *Ex. p. Vaughan* (1866) LR 2 QB 114; by Sir J. Colville in *Colonial Bank of Australasia* v. *Willan* (1874) LR 5 PC 417 at 443; by Gibson J in *R* v. *Mahony* [1910] 2 IR 695 at 739; by Lord Sumner in *R* v. *Nat Bell Liquors Ltd* [1922] 2 AC 128 at 154; and by Browne J in *Anisminic Ltd* v. *Foreign Compensation Commission* [1969] 2 AC 147 at 242. None of these decisions conflicts in any way with the principle of *Bunbury* v. *Fuller*, above, p. 213. This is explained particularly clearly in *Colonial Bank of Australasia* v. *Willan* (above).

[42] As in *Brittain* v. *Kinnaird* (above); *R* v. *Bolton* (above); *Colonial Bank of Australasia* v. *Willan* (above).

[43] Examples are *R* v. *Dayman; ex p Vaughan*; and *R* v. *Bradley*, cited above. But *Liversidge* v. *Anderson* [1942] AC 206 and *R* v. *Home Secretary ex p Zamir* [1980] AC 930 might be added. For these cases see below, p. 364. Other examples are *R* v. *South Hams DC ex p Gibb* [1995] QB 158 at 170 (whether applicants 'gipsies'); *R* v. *Radio Authority ex p Bull* [1996] QB 169 (whether organisation's objects 'mainly of a political nature'); *R* v. *Home Secretary ex p Onibiyo* [1996] QB 768 at 785 (whether fresh 'claim for asylum').

[44] *R (Lim)* v. *Home Secretary* [2007] EWCA Civ 773, para. 18 (Sedley LJ). 'Breach of condition' of leave to enter the United Kingdom not a 'precedent fact', i.e. is not jurisdictional.

[45] *General Electric Co Ltd* v. *Price Commission* [1975] ICR 1.

[46] *Associated Portland Cement Manufacturers Ltd* v. *Price Commission* [1975] ICR 27, decided within a month of the previous case but not referring to it. In principle the decisions appear contradictory, since in the second the Commission should have been able to find as a fact that generally accepted accounting principles did not admit the method in question. But this does not seem to have been pleaded.

comprised 'a substantial part of the United Kingdom' was fulfilled.[47] On a challenge to the commission's jurisdiction to undertake the investigation the House of Lords held that the 'clear cut approach [as described in the preceding pages] cannot be applied to every case, for the criterion so established may itself be so imprecise that different decision-makers, each acting rationally, might reach differing conclusions when applying it to the facts of a given case. In such a case the court is entitled to substitute its own opinion for that of the person to whom the decision has been entrusted only if the decision is so aberrant that it cannot be classed as rational... [There] is no ground for interference by the court [in this case], since the conclusion at which the commission arrived was well within the permissible field of judgment.'[48] Similarly, another case concerned the limited application of the Freedom of Information Act 2000 to the BBC. The Act did not apply to information held by the BBC for the 'purposes...of journalism, art or literature'.[49] On a challenge to the Information Commissioner's decision to decline to hear a complaint against the BBC, the court held that 'to seek judicially to define [the phrase] as a matter of interpretation [is] both an impossible and a futile exercise.' The decision of the Commissioner was rational and was upheld.

In these cases although the condition appears to be collateral or jurisdictional in truth it is not. Parliament by using the imprecise words ('substantial part', 'purposes of journalism') has entrusted the evaluation of the question to the decision-maker who will be upheld provided he acts fairly and rationally.[50]

Another example of this principle concerns the word 'child', defined as 'a person under the age of eighteen'[51] and used in many sections of the Children Act 1989. To the question whether a person is a child, said Baroness Hale in the Supreme Court, there 'is a right or a wrong answer. It may be difficult to determine what that answer is. The decision-makers may have to do their best on the basis of less than perfect or conclusive evidence.... That does not prevent them from being questions for the courts rather than for other kinds of decision makers.'[52] On the other hand, the question whether a particular 'child' is a 'child in need' for the purpose of engaging the local authority's duty under s. 20(1) of the 1989 Act to provide accommodation for such children, was different. It 'requires a number of different value judgments... it is entirely reasonable to assume that Parliament intended such evaluative questions to be determined by the public authority, subject to the control of the courts on the ordinary principles of judicial review. Within the limits of fair process and "Wednesbury reasonableness" there are no clear cut right or wrong answers.'[53]

As was spelt out in Baroness Hale's judgment, whether a particular question is jurisdictional (and must be got right) is a question of Parliament's intent. Thus where the statutory context is different, the outcome, even where the same words are used, may be different. Thus the Home Secretary, who detained an asylum seeker[54] in the reasonable but mistaken belief that an asylum-seeker was over 18 (and so not 'a child'), was found

---

[47] R v. Monopolies and Mergers Commission ex p South Yorkshire Transport Ltd [1993] 1 WLR 23 (HL). The statute was the Fair Trading Act 1973, s. 64(3). Another good example is Moyna v. Secretary of State for Work and Pensions [2003] UKHL 44, [2003] 1 WLR 1929.

[48] Lord Mustill following Edwards v. Bairstow [1956] AC 14 discussed further below, p. 787.

[49] BBC v. Sugar [2007] EWHC 905. The cited words come from the Act of 2000, s. 7 read with Sched. 1. See now Sugar v. British Broadcasting Corporation and anor [2012] UKSC 4, para. 80 (South Yorkshire approved).

[50] But much depends on context. Thus it was held in R (Norwich and Peterborough Building Society) v. Financial Ombudsman Service Ltd [2002] EWHC 2379 that the Banking Code although to be interpreted purposively 'has [but] one meaning' (para. 71). Even so, the Ombudsman was to be 'afforded considerable leeway in the application of the Code to the circumstances which he finds' (para. 71; emphasis added).

[51] 1989 Act, s. 105.   [52] R (A) v. London Borough of Croydon [2009] UKSC 8, para. 27.

[53] Para. 26.   [54] In terms of the Immigration Act 1971, Sched. 2, para. 16.

not to be in breach of her duty under s. 55 of the Borders, Citizenship and Immigration Act 2009 to ensure that her functions were 'discharged having regard to the need to safeguard and promote the welfare of children who are in the United Kingdom'.[55]

But, as this example shows, determining whether the condition set by the statutory words is fulfilled is 'hard edged' and has to be got right for the decision-maker to stay within his jurisdiction (the 'correctness standard') or whether the condition is not in fact jurisdictional but is entrusted to the decision-maker (and the courts apply a 'rationality standard'), is often difficult. Judges facing such difficult questions are sometimes tempted to manipulate the distinction between law (which is always jurisdictional) and fact (which may be non-jurisdictional and so need only comply with the 'rationality standard') as the following section demonstrates.

THE MALLEABLE BOUNDARY BETWEEN LAW AND FACT

Much of the discussion in this chapter proceeds on the basis that the distinction between a question of law and a question of fact is self-evident. But this is not so; the boundary is often elusive. This is discussed in detail elsewhere (in the context of appeals being permitted on 'a point of law' but not on a question of fact).[56] For the present a leading Supreme Court decision needs to be noted.[57] The case concerned a tragic incident in which the driver of a lorry on a busy road swerved in an unsuccessful attempt to avoid an intending suicide who had jumped into his path. The lorry hit another vehicle causing very serious injury to its driver, Gareth Jones. Mr Jones applied to the Criminal Injuries Compensation Authority (CICA) for compensation. But compensation was only available if the injury was 'directly attributable to…a crime of violence'. The CICA declined to make an award, finding that Mr Jones was not the victim of 'a crime of violence'. The First-tier Tribunal agreed. It was not satisfied that the intending suicide had the necessary intent to be guilty of an offence under s. 20 (malicious wounding) of the Offences Against the Person Act 1861. The Court of Appeal disagreed and it was that decision that came on appeal to the Supreme Court. Lord Hope, for the majority, was clear: a s. 20 offence was 'a crime of violence'. 'The words of the statute', he said, 'admit of only one answer. They speak for themselves….The crime that section 20 defines will always amount to a crime of violence for the purposes of the scheme for compensation for criminal injury.'[58] But whether what the intending suicide had done amounted to a s. 20 offence was a question of fact. The Supreme Court declined to interfere (as the Court of Appeal had done) with the First-tier Tribunal's finding of fact. This conclusion is in itself unexceptional.

But what is noteworthy is how malleable the Supreme Court considered the distinction between law and fact to be. Lord Hope in the lead judgment said:

> it is primarily for the tribunals, not the appellate courts, to develop a consistent approach to these issues [of law and fact], bearing in mind that they are peculiarly well fitted to determine them. A pragmatic approach should be taken to the dividing line between law and fact, so that the expertise of tribunals at the first tier and that of the Upper Tribunal can be used to best effect. An appeal court should not venture too readily into this area by classifying issues as issues of law which are really best left for determination by the specialist appellate tribunals.[59]

---

[55] *R (AA)* v. *Home Secretary* [2013] UKSC 49.   [56] Below p. 789.
[57] *Jones* v. *First Tier Tribunal and anor* [2013] UKSC 19.   [58] Paras. 17–18.
[59] Para. 16. See also Lord Carnwath, paras. 41 and 47. See also Lord Hoffman in *Serco Ltd* v. *Lawson* [2006] UKHL 3, para. 34 recognising 'policy' and 'expediency' playing a part in determining the distinction between law and fact.

Two comments may be ventured. First, the pragmatic approach to the distinction is difficult to reconcile with the general thrust of the law of jurisdiction: to place objective limits on powers. Secondly, much of the discussion in this case takes for granted that while questions of law have to be got right, questions of fact (at least non-jurisdictional questions of fact) are for the primary decision-maker. This sits uneasily with the growing acceptance in other cases of error of material fact as a ground of judicial review. And to consideration of that question we now turn.

DISPUTED QUESTIONS OF FACT

Although the contrast between questions which do and do not go to jurisdiction was in principle clear-cut, it was softened by the court's unwillingness to enter upon disputed questions of fact in proceedings for judicial review.[60] Evidence of facts is normally given on affidavit; and although the rules of court made provision for cross-examination, interrogatories and discovery of documents, and for the trial of issues of fact,[61] the court did not often order them.[62] The judicial review procedure is thus not well adapted for trying disputed facts. If the inferior tribunal had itself tried them, 'the court will not interfere except upon very strong grounds'.[63] There had to be 'a clear excess of jurisdiction' without the trial of disputed facts de novo.[64] Questions of law and questions of fact were therefore to be distinguished, as was explained by Devlin J:[65]

> Where the question of jurisdiction turns solely on a disputed point of law, it is obviously convenient that the court should determine it then and there. But where the dispute turns on a question of fact, about which there is a conflict of evidence, the court will generally decline to interfere.

But a system of judicial review which cannot cope with crucial questions of fact (as jurisdictional facts necessarily are) is seriously defective. One purpose of the procedural reforms made in 1977, and described later,[66] was to remove this defect by providing for cross-examination etc., so that disputed facts could be tried. The correct rule, it is submitted, is that stated by Lord Diplock, that cross-examination should now be allowed whenever the justice of the case so requires, and on the same basis as in ordinary proceedings.[67]

THE 'ORIGINAL JURISDICTION' FALLACY

Many judges have made a contrast between jurisdictional questions determinable at the outset and mere error made within jurisdiction during the course of the inquiry. Thus Lord Sumner said of a magistrate:[68]

> if his jurisdiction to entertain the charge is not open to impeachment, his subsequent error, however grave, is a wrong exercise of a jurisdiction which he has, and not a usurpation of jurisdiction which he has not.

---

[60] For the procedure see below, p. 556.   [61] Ibid.

[62] A rare instance in R v. Stokesley, Yorkshire, Justices ex p Bartram [1956] 1 WLR 254.

[63] Elston v. Rose (1868) LR 4 QB 4 at 7.

[64] R v. Fulham etc Rent Tribunal ex p Zerek [1951] 2 KB 1 at 11, reviewing the authorities. See also Colonial Bank of Australasia v. Willan (1874) LR 5 PC 417 at 442 ('a manifest defect of jurisdiction').

[65] In the Zerek case (above). See likewise Elston v. Rose (above).   [66] Below, p. 549.

[67] O'Reilly v. Mackman [1983] 2 AC 237 at 282; below, p. 569.

[68] R v. Nat Bell Liquors Ltd [1922] 2 AC 128 at 151.

And Lord Reid also once said:[69]

> If a magistrate or any other tribunal has jurisdiction to enter on the inquiry and to decide
> a particular issue, and there is no irregularity in the procedure, he does not destroy his
> jurisdiction by reaching a wrong decision. If he has jurisdiction to go right he has jurisdic-
> tion to go wrong. Neither an error in fact nor an error in law will destroy his jurisdiction.

In their own time and context,[70] and in relation to errors of fact and law, these statements
were unexceptionable. But it does not follow that no sort of error made in the course of the
proceedings can affect jurisdiction. Some question may arise which the tribunal is incompetent to determine;[71] or some point may be decided in bad faith or in breach of natural
justice or on irrelevant grounds or unreasonably, all of which faults go to jurisdiction and
render the proceedings a nullity.[72]

Lord Reid guarded himself with this necessary qualification in a later case,[73] pointing
out that 'the word "jurisdiction" has been used in a very wide sense' and would be better
confined to 'the narrow and original sense of the tribunal being entitled to enter on the
inquiry in question'. In fact 'jurisdiction' has traditionally borne the wide sense, synonymous with 'power'; for plainly a tribunal must not only have jurisdiction at the outset but
must retain it unimpaired until it has discharged its task. Lord Pearce explained this with
impeccable logic in the same case, in words already quoted, pointing out that if a tribunal
in the course of its inquiry addressed itself to the wrong question or violated the rules of
natural justice, it thereby stepped outside its jurisdiction.[74] If the tribunal's determination
is in the end a nullity, it must at some point have exceeded its powers. In the same case
Diplock LJ said:[75]

> 'Jurisdiction' is an expression which is used in a variety of senses and takes its colour from
> its context.

But any attempt to confine 'jurisdiction' to one sort of power rather than another is certain to produce confusion.

THE ESSENTIAL LEGAL POLICY

The distinction between jurisdictional (or collateral) and other questions, emphasised
so strongly in the foregoing discussion, is the lynch-pin of the fundamental policy of the

---

[69] *R v. Governor of Brixton Prison ex p Armah* [1968] AC 192 at 234. Contrast Lord Upjohn's remarks
at 257. See also Lord Devlin's opinion in *Essex Incorporated Congregational Church Union* v. *Essex County
Council* [1963] AC 808, cited above, p. 200.

[70] And under the law as it stood before the *Anisminic* case (below).

[71] See *Colonial Bank of Australasia* v. *Willan* (1874) LR 5 PC 417 at 444: 'There is a third class of cases, in
which the Judge of the inferior court, having legitimately commenced the inquiry, is met by some fact which,
if established, would oust his jurisdiction and place the subject-matter of the inquiry beyond it.' Examples
are then given of question of title to land arising before a tribunal incompetent to try them.

[72] This comment was endorsed by Lord Mustill in *Neill* v. *North Antrim Magistrates' Court* [1992] 1 WLR
1220 (HL).

[73] *Anisminic Ltd* v. *Foreign Compensation Commission* [1969] 2 AC 147 at 171. Lord Reid also said: 'I
understand that some confusion has been caused by my having said ... that if a tribunal has jurisdiction to go
right it has jurisdiction to go wrong.' But more probably confusion would be caused by 'Neither an error in
fact nor an error in law will destroy his jurisdiction', a statement inconsistent with Lord Reid's own decision
in the *Anisminic* case, unless limited to its proper context.

[74] Ibid. at 195, quoted above, p. 32. Lord Wilberforce at 210 was equally impeccable.

[75] In the *Anisminic* case in the Court of Appeal [1968] 2 QB 862 at 889.

law, that no inferior tribunal or authority can conclusively determine the limits of its own jurisdiction.[76] If it could so determine them, it would be uncontrollable and the system of jurisdictions would become incoherent. It is essentially the task of the superior courts to keep all governmental bodies within the bounds of their true powers. Their reasons for clinging so faithfully to their principles have never been given better expression from the bench than in a judgment of Farwell LJ:[77]

> No tribunal of inferior jurisdiction can by its own decision finally decide on the question of the existence or extent of such jurisdiction: such question is always subject to review by the High Court, which does not permit the inferior tribunal either to usurp a jurisdiction which it does not possess...or to refuse to exercise a jurisdiction which it has...Subjection in this respect to the High Court is a necessary and inseparable incident to all tribunals of limited jurisdiction; for it is a contradiction in terms to create a tribunal with limited jurisdiction and unlimited power to determine such limit at its own will and pleasure—such a tribunal would be autocratic, not limited—and it is immaterial whether the decision of the inferior tribunal on the question of the existence or non-existence of its own jurisdiction is founded on law or fact.

If administrative tribunals and authorities could trespass uncontrollably outside their proper fields, there would no longer be order in the legal system. Order can be preserved only if jurisdictional demarcation disputes can always be carried to the regular courts of law, and so brought within a unified hierarchy of authority.

ALL ERROR OF LAW NOW REVIEWABLE

The *Anisminic* case[78] became the leading example of jurisdictional error by a tribunal in the course of its proceedings. It is also an extreme case of an error of law, which might have been considered an error within jurisdiction, being held to be jurisdictional. The Foreign Compensation Commission had rejected a claim for compensation for a property already sold to a foreign buyer on the erroneous ground that the statutory Order in Council required that the successor in title should have been of British nationality at a certain date. The majority of the House of Lords held that this error destroyed the Commission's jurisdiction and rendered their decision a nullity, since on a true view of the law they had no jurisdiction to take the successor in title's nationality into account. By asking themselves the wrong question, and by imposing a requirement which they had no authority to impose, they had overstepped their powers.

But it was soon seen that the concept of jurisdictional error had been stretched to breaking-point. For it requires only a simple verbal manipulation to represent any error of law as the result of the tribunal asking itself a wrong question or imposing some wrong

[76] For this reason it is necessary to reject the so-called 'pure theory of jurisdiction' advocated with great ability and learning by D. M. Gordon QC in articles ranging from (1931) 47 *LQR* 386, 557 to (1966) 82 *LQR* 515, but never adopted or even discussed by an English court. This theory would allow tribunals to determine all relevant questions of fact and law conclusively. For details and criticism see the 7th edn of this book, p. 300.

[77] *R* v. *Shoreditch Assessment Committee ex p Morgan* [1910] 2 KB 859 at 880; approved in *Anisminic Ltd v. Foreign Compensation Commission* [1969] 2 AC 147 at 197, 209 and 233 by Lords Pearce and Wilberforce and by Browne J, who cited it with reference to (1966) 82 *LQR* 226 (Wade). It has often been cited since. It was applied to the Crown Court in *R* v. *Manchester Crown Court ex p Director of Public Prosecutions* [1993] 1 WLR 693.

[78] Above. The case is discussed in (1969) 85 *LQR* 198 (Wade); [1970] *PL* 358 (B. C. Gould); (1971) 34 *MLR* 1 (D. M. Gordon).

requirement. By such logic any and every error of law could be shown to involve excess of jurisdiction. Thus the House of Lords, while purporting to uphold the distinction between errors of law which went to jurisdiction and errors of law which did not, in fact undermined it. A tribunal had now, in effect, no power to decide any question of law incorrectly: any error of law would render its decision liable to be quashed as ultra vires.[79]

This radical conclusion was first drawn by Lord Diplock in a published lecture, saying that the *Anisminic* case 'renders obsolete the technical distinction between errors of law which go to "jurisdiction" and errors of law which do not'.[80] Then it was adopted by Lord Denning MR (supported by Eveleigh LJ but opposed by Geoffrey Lane LJ) in the *Pearlman* case, holding that the decision of a county court could be quashed for error of law, the normal right of appeal having been cut off by statute.[81] Observing that the House of Lords had reduced the former distinction to a mere matter of words, Lord Denning said:

> I would suggest that this distinction should now be discarded.... The way to get things right is to hold thus: no court or tribunal has any jurisdiction to make an error of law on which the decision of the case depends. If it makes such an error, it goes outside its jurisdiction and certiorari will lie to correct it.

Geoffrey Lane LJ, dissenting, pointed out that (as is undoubtedly true) the House of Lords in the *Anisminic* case intended to maintain the established distinction between error of law within jurisdiction and error of law outside jurisdiction;[82] and he held that the county court's error was within jurisdiction, and not therefore subject to judicial review. His opinion was followed, in preference to that of Lord Denning, by the Privy Council in a case from Malaysia, in which they reached the same conclusion as regards the error (if any) in an award of an industrial court.[83] The High Court of Australia has followed the Privy Council.[84]

But Lord Denning's opinion was upheld in two important speeches by Lord Diplock in the House of Lords. The first of these (*Racal*)[85] was concerned with a decision of a High Court judge which statute had made unappealable. A decision of the High Court is not

---

[79] For discussion see (1984) 4 *OJLS* 22 (J. Beatson); I. Hare in Forsyth and Hare (eds.), *The Golden Metwand*, 113.

[80] [1974] *CLJ* 233 at 243 (the de Smith memorial lecture). For a similar comment see (1969) 85 *LQR* at 211.

[81] *Pearlman* v. *Harrow School Governors* [1979] QB 56 (the county court had determined that the installation of central heating was not a 'structural alteration or addition' by a tenant). Lord Denning repeated his proposition, aligning it with Lord Diplock's in the *Racal* case (below), in *R* v. *Chief Immigration Officer, Gatwick Airport ex p Kharrazi* [1980] 1 WLR 1396. See also *Watt* v. *Lord Advocate*, 1979 SLT 137. For an interesting discussion of *Pearlman* see (2011) 74 *MLR* 694–9 (Daly).

[82] Lord Wilberforce had called it 'a crucial distinction which the court has to make': [1969] 2 AC at 210.

[83] *South East Asia Fire Bricks Sdn Bhd* v. *Non-Metallic Mineral Products Manufacturing Employees Union* [1981] AC 363, decided 10 days before the House of Lords gave judgment in the *Racal* case, below.

[84] *Houssein* v. *Under Secretary, Department of Industrial Relations* (1982) 38 ALR 577; *Hockey* v. *Yelland* (1984) 56 ALR 215. See also *Glenvill Homes Pty Ltd* v. *Builders Licensing Board* [1981] 2 NSWLR 608; *New Zealand Engineering etc Union* v. *Court of Arbitration* [1976] 2 NZLR 283; *Eastern (Auckland) Rugby Football Club Inc* v. *Licensing Control Commission* [1979] 1 NZLR 367, where Speight J follows Geoffrey Lane LJ's dissent as preferable 'for conservatively-minded people'.

[85] *Re Racal Communications Ltd*, reported as *Re a Company* [1981] AC 374 (challenge to order of High Court judge authorising compulsory inspection of company's books). Lord Keith concurred with Lord Diplock in general terms. Lord Edmund-Davies supported the Privy Council (in which he had sat) and Geoffrey Lane LJ, and therefore disagreed with Lord Diplock as to the effect of *Anisminic*. Lords Salmon and Scarman merely held (with respect, correctly) that *Anisminic* had nothing to do with the case. *Anisminic* was concerned with judicial review of an inferior tribunal. *Racal* was concerned with appeal from a High Court judge.

subject to judicial review,[86] so the case did not raise any question of error by an inferior tribunal. But Lord Diplock, taking the opportunity to corroborate the view expressed in his lecture, said:

The break-through made by *Anisminic* was that, as respects administrative tribunals and authorities, the old distinction between errors of law that went to jurisdiction and errors of law that did not, was for practical purposes abolished. Any error of law that could be shown to have been made by them in the course of reaching their decision on matters of fact or of administrative policy would result in their having asked themselves the wrong question with the result that the decision they reached would be a nullity.

In the second case (*O'Reilly*),[87] in which prisoners complained of breaches of natural justice in the award of punishments by prison visitors, Lord Diplock said that the decision in *Anisminic*

has liberated English public law from the fetters that the courts had theretofore imposed upon themselves so far as determinations of inferior courts and statutory tribunals were concerned, by drawing esoteric distinctions between errors of law committed by such tribunals that went to their jurisdiction, and errors of law committed by them within their jurisdiction. The breakthrough that the *Anisminic* case made was the recognition by the majority of this House that if a tribunal whose jurisdiction was limited by statute or subordinate legislation mistook the law applicable to the facts as it had found them, it must have asked itself the wrong question, i.e., one into which it was not empowered to inquire and so had no jurisdiction to determine. Its purported 'determination', not being 'a determination' within the meaning of the empowering legislation, was accordingly a nullity.

In 1992 and again in 1998 the House of Lords confirmed these categorical pronouncements. Although both were made in cases where no question of error of law arose, it is clear now that they made an important extension of judicial review in English law. It is clear also that the change was made, once again, by stretching the doctrine of ultra vires. In the case of 1992, Lord Browne-Wilkinson said in the leading speech:[88]

Thenceforward it was to be taken that Parliament had only conferred the decision-making power on the basis that it was to be exercised on the correct legal basis: a misdirection in law in making the decision therefore rendered the decision ultra vires.

And in broader terms he said:

The fundamental principle is that the courts will intervene to ensure that the powers of public decision-making bodies are exercised lawfully.

In the case of 1998[89] Lord Irvine LC said in the leading speech that *Anisminic*

made obsolete the historic distinction between error of law on the face of the record and other errors of law. It did so by extending the doctrine of ultra vires, so that any misdirection in law would render the decision ultra vires and a nullity.

---

[86] The High Court as a court of unlimited jurisdiction cannot act beyond its powers, i.e. act ultra vires and so cannot be subject to judicial review. See in addition to *Racal*, R *(AM (Cameroon)) v. Asylum and Immigration Tribunal* [2008] EWCA Civ 100, para. 11.

[87] *O'Reilly* v. *Mackman* [1983] 2 AC 237 at 278 (below, p. 569).

[88] R v. *Hull University Visitor ex p Page* [1993] AC 682.

[89] *Boddington* v. *British Transport Police* [1999] 2 AC 143 at 154.

Lord Diplock himself had similarly said that unless the decision-maker understood the law correctly and gave effect to it, the court would review for illegality.[90] In the result, the judges have taken a further step in making the courts the conclusive arbiters on all questions of law. Lord Dyson in the Supreme Court has confirmed the approach of the House of Lords remarking that the 'importance of *Anisminic* is that it established that there was a single category of errors of law, all of which rendered a decision *ultra vires*'.[91]

In Australia and Canada the law has moved in the same direction, assisted by legislation,[92] although the High Court of Australia rejects Lord Diplock's reasoning as a matter of common law.[93]

The Supreme Court, though, has spoken (in the *Cart* case) with less clarity.[94] While considering the question whether the Upper Tribunal was subject to judicial review—a claimant had been refused permission by the Upper Tribunal to appeal to it from a decision of the First-tier Tribunal and sought judicial review of that refusal—the court rejected in terms any return to the pre-*Anisminic* law which, it said, would 'lead us back to the distinction between jurisdictional and other errors which was effectively abandoned [in that case]'.[95] There was in the relevant legislation 'no clear and explicit recognition that the Upper Tribunal is to be permitted to make mistakes of law. Certain decisions are unappealable [such as the decision to refuse permission to appeal] and for the most part there are obvious practical reasons why this should be so. But this does not mean that the tribunal must always be permitted to make errors of law when making [such unappealable decisions].'[96]

While this makes plain that all errors of law by the Upper Tribunal are jurisdictional, the Supreme Court also made it clear that the Tribunal would only rarely be subject to judicial review. This was, it seems, because in most cases the right of appeal to the Court of Appeal from the decisions of the Upper Tribunal 'on a point of law'[97] provided an adequate alternative remedy justifying the refusal of permission to apply for judicial review.[98] But this reasoning is not spelt out. Instead the court restricts the availability of judicial review on pragmatic but not principled grounds. The court makes a profoundly pragmatic case that permission to apply for judicial review of the Upper Tribunal should only be granted when the stringent 'second tier appeal criteria'[99] were met.

The Supreme Court thus, while establishing in principle the general availability of judicial review of the Upper Tribunal, has carved away so much of that principle that only rarely will judicial review lie against decisions of the Upper Tribunal. The impact of this decision on administrative law in general is difficult to assess. It may be limited to the Upper Tribunal and so have little general impact;[100] or it may portend the abandonment of jurisdiction as the organising principle of administrative law and its replacement by

---

[90] *Council of Civil Service Unions* v. *Minister for the Civil Service* [1985] AC 374 at 410 (see Appendix 1). See likewise *R* v. *Governors of the Bishop Challoner Roman Catholic Comprehensive Girls' School ex p Choudhury* [1992] 2 AC 182.   [91] *Lumba and Mighty* v. *Home Secretary* [2011] UKSC 12, para. 66.

[92] e.g. Canada (Federal Court Act 1970, s. 28); Australia (Administrative Decisions (Judicial Review) Act 1977, s. 5). These Acts empower the court to quash for error of law generally.

[93] *Public Service Association of South Australia* v. *Federal Clerks' Union* (1991) 102 ALR 161.

[94] *Cart* v. *The Upper Tribunal* [2011] UKSC 28.   [95] Para. 39.   [96] Para. 40.

[97] Act of 2007, s. 13.   [98] As explained below, pp. 600–3.

[99] This test was whether judicial review 'would raise an important point of principle or practice; or...there is some other compelling reason for the Court of Appeal to hear it'. See *PR (Sri Lanka)* v. *Home Secretary* [2011] EWCA Civ 988 on the application of the test ('compelling' meant legally compelling not emotionally or politically compelling).

[100] Although a cottage industry of '*Cart* judicial reviews' with their own civil procedure rule has developed to challenge the refusal by the Upper Tribunal of permission to appeal (below, p. 772).

the court allowing judicial review on a discretionary basis when it is 'rational and proportionate'[101] to do so (which would be a revolutionary change). Its greatest impact may well be on the extent to which courts are subject to judicial review as discussed below.

AN EXCEPTION—COURTS OF LAW

In the longer of the quotations (from *O'Reilly*) from Lord Diplock's speeches above it will be seen that he bracketed together 'inferior courts and statutory tribunals' as liberated by *Anisminic* from the old jurisdictional test for reviewable error of law. But in his earlier speech (in *Racal*) he had said that in the case of courts, such as the county court, there should be no presumption that Parliament had not given them jurisdiction to decide points of law conclusively:[102] it was a matter of construction, and where the Act provided that the court's decision should be final, or final and conclusive, the 'subtle distinctions formerly drawn' might still operate, so that some errors of law might be ultra vires and reviewable but others not—though the reviewing court should be tolerant and not astute to intervene.[103] But when the question arose in the case of a coroner's inquest, which is held to be a court,[104] a divisional court followed Lord Diplock's later opinion and decided that any mistake of law would destroy jurisdiction.[105]

In its 1992 decision[106] the House of Lords has adopted Lord Diplock's earlier view, so that inferior courts must be distinguished from tribunals and other administrative authorities.

These weighty decisions suggest that an error of law by an inferior court, therefore, may still give rise to an argument whether it is jurisdictional or not, and in the latter case it may be immune from judicial review. There are several cases where, there being no appeal from the court's decision, the availability of judicial review for 'a pre-*Anisminic* error of law' has been recognised.[107] And several cases (not always in the context of courts) have referred to the distinction between 'constitutive jurisdiction' (meaning 'entitlement to enter on the inquiry') and 'adjudicative jurisdiction' (meaning 'entitlement to make a valid decision')[108] with the implication that a lack of 'adjudicative jurisdiction' was not a ground of judicial review.

But the Supreme Court in *Cart*, as we have seen, rejected all such distinctions in the case of the Upper Tribunal, by statute a 'superior court of record'.[109] This suggests that all courts—except presumably the High Court as a court of unlimited jurisdiction—stray outside their jurisdiction when they make errors of law and are, in principle, subject to judicial review, save that the Supreme Court will determine, as it did in *Cart*, the actual extent of judicial review allowed.

---

[101] Para. 57.

[102] In *Bulk Gas Users Group* v. *A-G* [1983] NZLR 129 Cooke J suggests that the rival *Pearlman/Racal* and *South East Asia Fire Bricks* propositions can thus be reconciled by regarding the tribunal in the latter case as akin to a court.   [103] In the *Racal* case, above, at 386.

[104] *R* v. *Surrey Coroner ex p Campbell* [1982] QB 661.

[105] *R* v. *Greater Manchester Coroner ex p Tal* [1985] QB 67, where the application failed since no mistake was shown.

[106] *R* v. *Hull University Visitor ex p Page*, above; see also *R* v. *Visitors to the Inns of Court ex p Calder* [1994] QB 1.   [107] Discussed above, p. 219.

[108] *Carter* v. *Ahsan* [2005] ICR 1817, Sedley LJ (dissenting). The body concerned was an Employment Tribunal. Note particularly the discussion by Beatson LJ in *R (Hill)* v. *Institute of Chartered Accountants In England and Wales* [2013] EWCA Civ 555, para. 50. The body concerned was a disciplinary committee.

[109] The Supreme Court did not refer to *Racal* or the other decisions recognising that courts might have power to err as to law within their jurisdiction.

One potential situation will reveal how conceptually threadbare is the approach of the Supreme Court in *Cart*. Suppose that the decision of a tribunal (perhaps that X repay a certain sum) is marred by an error of law. There is no possibility (as *Cart* teaches) of the error being non-jurisdictional, so the decision is void. Judicial review may be precluded either by an alternative remedy (rights of appeal) or non-compliance with the second-tier appeals criteria. But when X is sued for payment he will be able to raise the invalidity of the decision collaterally as of right; and the house of cards will come tumbling down. This, presumably, was the kind of possibility Lord Diplock had in mind in the weighty decisions mentioned above where he contemplated that courts might sometimes make non-jurisdictional errors of law.

ERROR ON THE FACE OF THE RECORD

ERROR WITHIN JURISDICTION

In administrative law, both ancient and modern, an important role has been played by the doctrine that the Court of Queen's Bench could quash any decision of an inferior court or tribunal which displayed error of law upon its face. This ancient head of judicial review has now been made redundant by the wide interpretation of the *Anisminic* case by the House of Lords, under which error of law has become a species of ultra vires, as explained in the preceding section. But until the law was so extended, error on the face was a useful weapon for attacking decisions which, though within jurisdiction, were vitiated by self-evident error. Although the doctrine can now be consigned to the limbo of history, it ought not to pass altogether into oblivion, since until the *Anisminic* era arrived it was an important head of judicial review. But there is no longer a need for the detailed account given in earlier editions of this book.

When in the seventeenth century certiorari was first used to control statutory powers, its primary object was to call up the record of the proceedings into the Court of King's Bench; and if the record displayed error, the decision was quashed. But if the applicant wanted to go outside the record, and bring other evidence to show some abuse of the power, the court would quash only where an excess of jurisdiction could be shown.[110] If the record itself showed an excess of jurisdiction, the court could as well quash for that as for any other defect. If the record did not show it, additional evidence had to be given, and in proceedings for certiorari that had to be done by affidavit. Hence came the rule that affidavits were admitted only to show want of jurisdiction.[111] But that rule emerged only gradually in the eighteenth century.[112] Although it provided the opening through which the wide ultra vires doctrine made its way into the law, this was a development which came later than the jurisdiction to review the record for error of any description, a jurisdiction firmly established in the time of Lord Holt CJ, about the year 1700. Review of the record was therefore the original system of judicial control adopted when the Court of King's Bench took over the work of supervising inferior tribunals and administrative

---

[110] Parts of this passage were adopted by Lawton LJ in *R v. West Sussex Quarter Sessions ex p Johnson Trust Ltd* [1974] 1 QB 24 at 40.

[111] *R v. Bolton* (1841) 1 QB 66; *R v. Nat Bell Liquors Ltd* [1922] 2 AC 128 at 155–6, 160; *R v. Northumberland Compensation Appeal Tribunal ex p Shaw* [1951] 1 KB 711 at 719.

[112] Rubinstein, *Jurisdiction and Illegality*, 70. At p. 69 it is said that *R v. Oulton Inhabitants* (1735) Cas t Hard 169 shows that affidavits were still then refused; but the case does not seem to concern jurisdictional error.

bodies, such as Justices of the Peace and Commissioners of Sewers, after the Star Chamber and the conciliar courts had been abolished.[113]

DECLINE OF NON-JURISDICTIONAL REVIEW

The development of this early system was blighted by parliamentary interference, prompted by judicial pedantry. Review of the record became excessively formal, and many orders were quashed on what one judge described as 'lamentable and disgraceful technicalities'.[114] Parliament remedied this abuse in two different ways: first by inserting 'no-certiorari clauses' in many statutes from the seventeenth century onwards;[115] and secondly by enacting in the nineteenth century that criminal convictions need be supported only by a very short record, omitting the charge and the evidence and the reasoning which were required to be set out previously.[116] No-certiorari clauses simply forbade the court to grant this remedy in many particular cases. The short form of conviction, on the other hand (to quote a celebrated judgment of Lord Sumner)[117]

> did not stint the jurisdiction of the Queen's Bench, or alter the actual law of certiorari. What it did was to disarm its exercise. The effect was not to make that which had been error, error no longer, but to remove nearly all opportunity for its detection. The face of the record 'spoke' no longer: it was the inscrutable face of a sphinx.

The combined effect of these measures was to divert the energies of the courts away from control of the record and towards the development of the ultra vires doctrine. Furthermore, the courts circumvented the no-certiorari clauses by holding that they were intended only to prevent quashing for errors on the formal record within jurisdiction, and not to protect excesses of jurisdiction at all—a doctrine which still plays an important part today.[118] It was for these reasons that the courts were led to concentrate on jurisdictional control, which had a firm constitutional basis,[119] rather than on review of the record, which was often merely formalistic.

THE DOCTRINE REVIVED

The result of this process of evolution was that the power of review for mere error on the face of the record was almost wholly forgotten after 1848 until it was dramatically revived in the *Northumberland* case in 1950.[120] That case[121] turned upon the amount of compensation payable to the clerk to a hospital board in Northumberland who had lost his post in 1949 after the National Health Service was introduced. The Compensation Appeal

---

[113] Holdsworth, *History of English Law*, vi. 56, 112, 263; x. 155. The Court of Session has deplored the lack of any corresponding jurisdiction in Scotland: *Watt* v. *Lord Advocate*, 1979 SLT 137.

[114] *R* v. *Ruyton (Inhabitants)* (1861) 1 B & S 534 at 545.

[115] For these see below, p. 610. Another remedy was to empower the court to correct defects in the record that were not material, as was done by the Quarter Sessions Act 1849 (12 & 13 Vict. c. 45), s. 7.

[116] Summary Jurisdiction Act 1848. The Summary Jurisdiction Act 1857 provided for an appeal by case stated on a point of law; this rendered certiorari unnecessary in many cases (see s. 10).

[117] *R* v. *Nat Bell Liquors Ltd* [1922] 2 AC 128 at 159. See also the account given by Cave J in *R* v. *Bradley* (1894) 70 LT 379.   [118] See below, p. 610.

[119] Above, p. 29.

[120] The Court of Appeal denied its existence in *Racecourse Betting Control Board* v. *Secretary for Air* [1944] Ch 114. The Canadian courts did not fall into this error: *R* v. *Logan ex p McAllister* [1974] 4 DLR 676; *John East Ironworks* v. *Labour Relations Board of Saskatchewan* [1949] 3 DLR 51.

[121] *R* v. *Northumberland Compensation Appeal Tribunal ex p Shaw* [1952] 1 KB 338. See Sawer (1956) *U of WALR* 24; Abel (1963) 15 *U Tor LJ* 102.

Tribunal, misconstruing the regulations, failed to allow him his full period of service, and stated their reasons in their decision. Dismissing the appeal the tribunal stated that there had been these two periods of service, but that in their judgment it was only the second period which should count. The order therefore contained a manifest error of law, and on this ground it was quashed in one of Lord Denning's most celebrated judgments.

This was a timely decision, since there was general dissatisfaction with the numerous tribunals set up under the welfare state which often had to interpret very difficult legislation[122] and from which Parliament had provided few rights of appeal. The reform of the tribunal system is a separate story, related later.[123] The importance of the *Northumberland* decision was that it appeased, at least partially, the public demand for better justice in the welfare state. It also marked the beginning of a new era of judicial review in which the courts became conscious of their powers.

In exercising their control the courts adopted a tolerant standard, recognising that the intention of Parliament was that the new tribunal system should be as free as possible from technical and legalistic disputes. Even where some error of law was shown, the court might decline to intervene.

Specialised tribunals could thus rely upon being leniently judged. But at the same time the *Northumberland* case opened the door to a mass of litigation in which the content of 'the record' was amplified and explained. It came to include not only the formal pleadings and the adjudication but all documentary evidence and any papers referred to in the primary documents.[124] Even spoken words might be part of 'the record' where mistakes were made in oral judgments and statements of reasons.[125]

Judicial review by certiorari had always extended to 'speaking orders', i.e. decisions which contained a statement of reasons, and it was naturally in the reasons that error was most likely to be found. But when this species of review was revived in 1951, and was much in demand, it was often frustrated by the failure of a tribunal to state its reasons, there being usually no obligation to do so. This obstacle was removed in large part by the Tribunals and Inquiries Act 1958 which, as explained elsewhere,[126] introduced a legal right to reasoned decisions from tribunals and inquiries, so that speaking orders could be obtained on demand. It also provided expressly that reasons given under the Act should be treated as incorporated in the record. This made it clear that Parliament accepted the reassertion of the High Court's powers.

REVIEW OF THE RECORD IN WIDER CONTEXT

In the light of later events, the rediscovery of the power of review for error on the face of the record can be seen as the first stage of the movement towards bringing all decisions on questions of law back within the superintendence of the ordinary courts. In the social legislation of the late 1940s statutory tribunals were given an excessive degree of independence, and the lack of rights of appeal was strongly felt.[127] Eventually the Tribunals and Inquiries Act 1958 gave many new rights of appeal on questions of law,[128] thus reducing the need for applications to quash by certiorari. The Act also safeguarded the remedy by certiorari, which was the only remedy for this form of error, against earlier Acts which

---

[122] Sometimes almost too difficult for the House of Lords: see *R v. National Insurance Commissioner ex p Hudson* [1972] AC 944.   [123] See p. 921 of the 9th edn of this book.

[124] *R v. Medical Appeal Tribunal ex p Gilmore* [1957] 1 QB 574.

[125] *R v. Chertsey Justices ex p Franks* [1961] 2 QB 152.   [126] See below, p. 764.

[127] See e.g. *R v. Northumberland Compensation Appeal Tribunal ex p Shaw* [1952] 1 KB 338 at 346 (Singleton LJ): *R v. Medical Appeal Tribunal ex p Gilmore* [1957] 1 QB 574 at 587 (Romer LJ).

[128] Below, p. 764.

had taken it away.[129] This machinery enabled virtually any error of law to be dragged forth into the light for judicial inspection and correction; and the notion that statutory tribunals could be final arbiters on matters of law fell far back from the high-water mark which it had previously attained.

It remained only for the House of Lords, by establishing that all error of law, regardless of the record, was excess of jurisdiction, to widen the powers of the courts still further and to bring to an end, as already explained, the period in which review for error on the face had played such a useful role.

FINDINGS, EVIDENCE AND JURISDICTION

NON-JURISDICTIONAL FACT

It is now necessary to return to questions of fact, in so far as they fall outside the doctrine of jurisdictional fact, already explained. Relatively few findings of fact are jurisdictional, and the question now is how far the large residuum of findings by tribunals and other authorities is subject to judicial review. It must be remembered that the courts have a long-standing dislike of investigating questions of fact in judicial review proceedings,[130] even though the facilities for doing so have been improved.[131]

THE 'NO EVIDENCE' RULE

Findings of fact are traditionally the domain where a deciding authority or tribunal is master in its own house. Provided only that it stays within its jurisdiction, its findings are in general exempt from review by the courts, which will in any case respect the decision of the body that saw and heard the witnesses or took evidence directly. Just as the courts look jealously on decisions by other bodies on matters of law, so they look indulgently on their decisions on matters of fact.

But the limit of this indulgence is reached where findings are based on no satisfactory evidence. It is one thing to weigh conflicting evidence which might justify a conclusion either way, or to evaluate evidence wrongly.[132] It is another thing altogether to make insupportable findings. This is an abuse of power and may cause grave injustice. At this point, therefore, the court is disposed to intervene.

'No evidence' does not mean only a total dearth of evidence. It extends to any case where the evidence, taken as a whole, is not reasonably capable of supporting the finding;[133] or where, in other words, no tribunal could reasonably reach that conclusion on that evidence.[134] This 'no evidence' principle clearly has something in common with the principle that perverse or unreasonable action is unauthorised and ultra vires.[135] It also has some affinity with the substantial evidence rule of American law, which requires that findings be supported by substantial evidence on the record as a whole.[136]

---

[129] Below, p. 617.   [130] See above, p. 217.   [131] See below, p. 556.

[132] *R* v. *Criminal Injuries Compensation Board*, 1997 SLT 291.

[133] *Allinson* v. *General Medical Council* [1894] 1 QB 750 at 760, 763; *Lee* v. *Showmen's Guild of Great Britain* [1952] 2 QB 329 at 345.

[134] *R* v. *Roberts* [1908] 1 KB 407 at 423.   [135] Below, p. 302.

[136] Administrative Procedure Act (USA, 1946), s. 10(e); *Universal Camera Corporation* v. *National Labor Relations Board* 340 US 474 (1951); Schwartz and Wade, *Legal Control of Government*, 228. American administrative procedure facilitates this control by providing a full record of evidence. For the position in Canada see (1972) 37 *Sask LR* 48 (D. W. Elliott).

THE BASIS OF REVIEW

It was held at one time that there could not be a 'no evidence' rule because it could not be forced into the mould of ultra vires. The locus classicus is the celebrated opinion given by Lord Sumner in a Privy Council case from Canada, where a firm had been convicted before a magistrate for selling liquor contrary to the local Liquor Act. The only evidence of the fact of sale was that of an *agent provocateur* of the police. Could the inferior court's decision be quashed as ultra vires (as opposed to being challenged on appeal) because they had no proper evidence before them? In rejecting the contention that 'want of evidence on which to convict is the same as want of jurisdiction to take evidence at all', Lord Sumner said:[137]

> This, clearly, is erroneous. A justice who convicts without evidence is doing something which he ought not to do, but he is doing it as a judge, and if his jurisdiction to entertain the charge is not open to impeachment, his subsequent error, however grave, is a wrong exercise of a jurisdiction which he has, and not a usurpation of a jurisdiction which he has not.... To say that there is no jurisdiction to convict without evidence is the same thing as saying that there is jurisdiction if the decision is right, and none if it is wrong.

The principle was the same for administrative authorities and tribunals and was often stated by Lord Goddard CJ, both in approving a favourite quotation[138] about error within jurisdiction and also when he said:[139]

> If it is acting within its jurisdiction, it is now settled law that absence of evidence does not affect the jurisdiction of the tribunal to try the case, nor does a misdirection by the tribunal to itself in considering the evidence nor what might be held on appeal to be a wrong decision in point of law.

To these authorities can be added statements by Lord Reid and Lord Diplock that lack of evidence raises no question of jurisdiction.[140] And there is no dearth of similar judicial rulings.[141]

But a contrary current of opinion has been gathering force for many years. Lord Atkinson said in 1914 that 'an order made without any evidence to support it is in truth, in my view, made without jurisdiction'.[142] A 'no evidence' doctrine has become established in habeas corpus cases, where in principle the court should intervene on grounds of jurisdiction only.[143] Sometimes judges generalise as if that doctrine was of universal application.[144] Or they may hold that decisions unsupported by evidence are capricious or unreasonable,[145] or given

---

[137] *R v. Nat Bell Liquors Ltd* [1922] AC 128 at 151, described by Lord Denning MR as the darkest moment of the 'black-out of any development of administrative law': *O'Reilly v. Mackman* [1983] 2 AC 237 at 253.

[138] From Halsbury's *Laws of England*, 3rd edn, xi. 62.   [139] *R v. Ludlow* [1947] KB 634.

[140] *R v. Governor of Brixton Prison ex p Armah* [1968] AC 192 at 234; *R v. Governor of Pentonville Prison ex p Sotiriadis* [1975] AC 1 at 30.

[141] A notable instance is *R v. Mahony* [1910] 2 IR 695, where the older law is very fully discussed by Gibson J.

[142] *Folkestone Cpn v. Brockman* [1914] AC 338 at 367.   [143] For these see below, p. 506.

[144] As in *R v. Board of Control ex p Rutty* [1956] 2 QB 109 at 124; *R v. Birmingham Compensation Appeal Tribunal* [1952] 2 All ER 100 (error of statutory interpretation represented as 'no evidence'); *Ashbridge Investments Ltd v. Minister of Housing and Local Government* [1965] 1 WLR 1320 at 1327–8 (representing the case of *White and Collins v. Minister of Health*, discussed above, p. 255, as one of 'no evidence', whereas it was expressly decided on the ground of excess of jurisdiction); *R v. Governor of Brixton Prison ex p Armah* [1968] AC 192 at 257 (wide statement by Lord Upjohn); *R v. Governor of Brixton Prison ex p Ahsan* [1969] 2 QB 222.

[145] As suggested in *Osgood v. Nelson* (1872) LR 5 HL 636 and as held in *R v. A-G ex p Imperial Chemical Industries plc* (1986) 60 TC 1. See also *Minister of National Revenue v. Wrights' Canadian Ropes Ltd* [1947] AC 109; *Argosy Co Ltd v. IRC* [1971] 1 WLR 514.

upon wrong legal grounds,[146] and so ultra vires for other reasons. The House of Lords has held that an immigration officer, who has power to refuse leave to enter the country if satisfied of certain facts, is on 'normal principles' not at liberty to refuse it if there is no evidence to support his decision.[147] The House has similarly quashed a local authority's determination that an immigrant from Bangladesh was 'intentionally homeless' when there was no evidence that the home which he was supposed to have left was ever available to him.[148] The Court of Appeal has quashed a decision of the Secretary of State for Transport when his decision letter stated that he was not satisfied on a number of matters without showing any basis of evidence for his conclusions.[149] In none of these cases was the legal basis of a 'no evidence' rule discussed: it was simply assumed to exist. In one of them Lord Denning MR put 'no evidence' at the head of a list of vitiating errors, saying:[150]

> the court can interfere with the Minister's decision if he has acted on no evidence; or if he has come to a decision to which on the evidence he could not reasonably come; or if he has given a wrong interpretation to the words of the statute; or if he has taken into consideration matters which he ought not to have taken into account, or vice versa; or has otherwise gone wrong in law. It is identical with the position when the court has power to interfere with the decision of a lower tribunal which has erred in point of law.

This was followed by the first clear case in which a minister's order was quashed for 'no evidence'.[151]

Furthermore, the proposition scorned by Lord Sumner ('there is jurisdiction if the decision is right and none if it is wrong') is precisely what the House of Lords has adopted in the case of error of law.[152] If this is combined with the familiar rule that to find facts on no evidence is to err in law, a rule constantly applied in appeals, a simple basis for a no evidence rule emerges. The House of Lords has given it strong corroboration in quashing a decision of magistrates who committed a defendant for trial without any admissible evidence.[153] Although this decision was in a judicial rather than administrative context, the speech of Lord Cooke draws upon administrative law where the logic is identical.

The principles of natural justice may also be invoked, according to a series of opinions of Lord Diplock. In the first of these he indicated that the principles of natural justice require that a tribunal's decisions be based on some evidence of probative value.[154] Speaking in two cases for the Privy Council he held that a minister dealing with an application for registration of citizenship must act on 'evidential material of probative value' if his decision is to be valid,[155] and that the same rule applied, as a matter of natural justice, to a judge acting as a statutory royal commissioner.[156]

---

[146] Examples are *R* v. *Flintshire CC Licensing Committee* [1957] 1 QB 350; *R* v. *Australian Stevedoring Industry Board ex p Melbourne Stevedoring Co* (1953) 88 CLR 100 at 119–20; *Gavaghan* v. *Secretary of State for the Environment* (1989) 60 P & CR 515 (unsupported finding 'not within the powers of this Act').

[147] *R* v. *Home Secretary ex p Zamir* [1980] AC 930.

[148] *R* v. *Hillingdon LBC ex p Islam* [1983] 1 AC 688.

[149] *R* v. *Secretary of State for Transport ex p Cumbria CC* [1983] RTR 129; see similarly *R* v. *Secretary of State for the Environment ex p Knowsley BC*, The Times, 28 May 1991.

[150] *Ashbridge Investments Ltd* v. *Minister of Housing and Local Government* [1965] 1 WLR 1320 at 1326.

[151] *Coleen Properties Ltd* v. *Minister of Housing and Local Government* [1971] 1 WLR 433 (no evidence that purchase of adjacent land for clearance area was reasonably necessary).   [152] Above, p. 219.

[153] *R* v. *Bedwellty JJ ex p Williams* [1997] AC 225, relying on the *Anisminic* and *Page* cases (above, p. 266) as invalidating the committal for error of law.

[154] *R* v. *Deputy Industrial Injuries Commissioner ex p Moore* [1965] 1 QB 456. See also *Burwoods (Caterers) Ltd* v. *SS for Environment* [1972] Est. Gaz. Dig. 1007.

[155] *A-G* v. *Ryan* [1980] AC 718. See also *Ong Ah Chuan* v. *Public Prosecutor* [1981] AC 648 at 671.

[156] *Mahon* v. *Air New Zealand Ltd* [1984] AC 808, where this was a principal ground of decision.

THE 'NO EVIDENCE' RULE NOW ESTABLISHED

Despite lack of any decision reviewing the old authorities against a 'no evidence' rule, it seems clear that this ground of judicial review is now firmly established. There have been so many sporadic references to it on this assumption, and it conforms so well to other developments in administrative law, that the older authorities to the contrary, impressive though they are, must now be consigned to the scrapheap of history. 'No evidence' thus takes its place as yet a further branch of the principle of ultra vires.

The time is ripe for this development as part of the judicial policy of preventing abuse of discretionary power. To find facts without evidence is itself an abuse of power and a source of injustice, and it ought to be within the scope of judicial review. This is recognised in other jurisdictions where the grounds of review have been codified by statute. In Australia the Administrative Decisions (Judicial Review) Act 1977 expressly authorises review on the ground that there was 'no evidence or other material' to justify the decision where some particular matter has to be established,[157] and a somewhat analogous provision has been enacted in Canada.[158]

ERROR OF MATERIAL FACT

Mere factual mistake has become a ground of judicial review, described as 'misunderstanding or ignorance of an established and relevant fact',[159] or acting 'upon an incorrect basis of fact'.[160] In a case where the Secretary of State had power to give directions if he was satisfied that the local education authority were acting unreasonably, Lord Wilberforce, in explaining that such powers were to some extent subject to judicial review, said:[161]

> If a judgment requires, before it can be made, the existence of some facts, then, although the evaluation of those facts is for the Secretary of State alone, the court must inquire whether those facts exist, and have been taken into account, whether the judgment has been upon a proper self-direction as to those facts, whether the judgment has not been made upon other facts which ought not to have been taken into account. If those requirements are not met, then the exercise of judgment, however bona fide it may be, becomes capable of challenge.

Lord Wilberforce approved a remark by Lord Denning MR in another case that the court could intervene if a minister 'plainly misdirects himself in fact or in law'.[162] Effect was given to these ideas when the court quashed a Secretary of State's decision owing to a mistake of fact in his inspector's report which said that a site had never been proposed as green belt when in fact it had been;[163] and when the Court of Appeal held that it could

---

[157] ss. 5, 6. See similarly the Administrative Justice Act 1980 of Barbados, s. 4.

[158] Federal Court Act 1971, s. 28(1). See also Law Reform Commission of Canada, Report No. 14 (1980), recommendation 4.3.

[159] *Secretary of State for Education and Science* v. *Tameside MBC* [1977] AC 1014 at 1030 (Scarman LJ, giving examples). See [1990] *PL* 507 (T. H. Jones), [2004] *JR* 36 (D. Blundell) and [2004] *JR* 184 (Grekos). See also Forsyth and Dring, 'The Final Frontier: The Emergence of Material Error of Fact as a Ground of Judicial Review' in Forsyth, Elliott, Jhaveri, Ramsden and Scully-Hill (eds.), *Effective Judicial Review: A Cornerstone of Good Governance* (2010) at 245.

[160] The *Tameside* case (above) at 1047 (Lord Wilberforce). See similarly *Laker Airways Ltd* v. *Department of Trade* [1977] QB 643 at 706 (Lord Denning MR).   [161] The *Tameside* case (above) at 1047.

[162] *Secretary of State for Employment* v. *ASLEF (No 2)* is seen here in italics whereas appears as roman in pdf, pls ensure[1972] 2 QB 455 at 493, repeated in *Smith* v. *Inner London Education Authority* [1978] 1 All ER 411.

[163] *Hollis* v. *Secretary of State for the Environment* (1982) 47 P & CR 351. See similarly *Simpex (GE) Ltd* v. *Secretary of State for the Environment* (1988) 57 P & CR 306, holding that a decision based on error of fact

quash a local authority's decision which was 'flawed by an error of fact' as to the content of a judgment of the House of Lords.[164] Similarly in New Zealand it was held that a minister's decision was invalid for failure to take into account the true facts, a medical referee having misled him by an inadequate report.[165]

This ground of review has long been familiar in French law,[166] it is accepted by the European Court of Human Rights[167] and it has been adopted in both New Zealand[168] and South Africa.[169]

It is no less needed in this country, since decisions based upon wrong facts are a cause of injustice which the courts should be able to remedy.[170] If a 'wrong factual basis' doctrine should become established, it would be a new branch of the ultra vires doctrine, analogous to finding facts based upon no evidence or acting upon a misapprehension of law.[171] Quoting this passage, the House of Lords has accepted the doctrine but has not as yet applied it.[172] It was emphatically restated, though again not applied, by Lord Slynn in the *Alconbury* case,[173] and has been fully accepted, with both judicial and academic support, by the Court of Appeal.[174] It now seems clear that it has arrived, and that it should consign much of the old law about jurisdictional fact etc., to well-deserved oblivion.

was ultra vires; R v. *Legal Aid Committee No 10 (East Midlands) ex p McKenna* [1990] COD 358. But for a restrictive interpretation of Lord Wilberforce's words see R v. *London Residuary Body ex p Inner London Education Authority,* The Times, 24 July 1987.

[164] R v. *Hertfordshire CC ex p Cheung,* The Times, 4 April 1986 and Lexis (refusal to reconsider students' grant applications quashed). See similarly R v. *Home Secretary ex p Awuku,* The Times, 3 October 1987 (immigration officer's decision quashed for 'material errors of fact' and breach of natural justice); R v. *Parliamentary Commissioner for Administration ex p Balchin* [1997] COD 146. Contrast *Shetland Line (1984) Ltd* v. *Secretary of State for Scotland,* 1996 SLT 653 (error subsequently discovered: relief refused).

[165] *Daganayasi* v. *Minister of Immigration* [1980] 2 NZLR 130 (Cooke J, Richardson J preferring to express no opinion).

[166] CE 20 Jan. 1922, *Trépont,* established 'fait matériellement inexact' as a ground of review.

[167] *Vogt* v. *Germany* A-323 (1996) 21 EHRR 205, requiring 'an acceptable assessment of the relevant facts'.

[168] *New Zealand Fisheries Association Inc* v. *Minister of Agriculture and Fisheries* [1988] 1 NZLR 544 (Cooke P) and *S & D* v. *M and Board of Trustees of Auckland Grammar School* (unreported, 11 June 1998) (Smellie J). In Australia the Administrative Decisions (Judicial Review) Act 1977 provided in s. 5(3)(b) for judicial review where 'the person who made the decision based the decision on the existence of a particular fact, and that fact did not exist'. But this has been interpreted as being little wider than the 'no evidence' rule: *Bond* v. *Australian Broadcasting Tribunal* (1990) 170 CLR 321 at 358.

[169] *Pepkor Retirement Fund* v. *Financial Services Board* 2003 (6) SA 38 (Supreme Court of Appeal), para. 58. And see Hoexter, *Administrative Law* (2007) at 313.

[170] For instance, in *Henry* v. *Parole Board* [2011] EWHC 2081. The Parole Board in deciding not to transfer a prisoner to open conditions thought that he had been convicted of a particularly serious charge (of rape) whereas he had been acquitted of that charge (although convicted of others). Decision not to transfer quashed. [171] See above, p. 229.

[172] R v. *Criminal Injuries Compensation Board ex p A* [1999] 2 AC 330, preferring to decide the case on grounds of natural justice.

[173] *R (Alconbury Development Ltd)* v. *Secretary of State for the Environment, Transport and the Regions* [2003] 2 AC 295, para. 53.

[174] *E* v. *Home Secretary* [2004] EWCA Civ 49 (2 February) (Phillips MR, Mantell and Carnwath LJJ). But the Court of Appeal was not referred to *Adan* v. *Newham LBC* [2001] EWCA Civ 1916, [2002] 1 WLR 2120 (CA) where the jurisdiction had been doubted (Brooke LJ and Steel J; Hale LJ willing to extend *ex p A*). For further authority supporting material error of fact as ground of review, see R *(Marsh)* v. *Lincoln District Magistrates' Court* [2003] EWHC 956 (Admin). *E* has since been followed in R *(Iran)* v. *Home Secretary* [2005] EWCA Civ 982 and *MT (Algeria)* v. *Home Secretary* [2007] EWCA Civ 808. The Competition Appeal Tribunal has held it has jurisdiction 'in a supervisory rather than appellate capacity, to determine whether the [Office of Fair Trading]'s conclusions are adequately supported by evidence, that the facts have been properly found, that all material factual considerations have been taken into account, and that material facts have not been omitted' (*Unichem Ltd* v. *Fair Trading Office* [2005] CAT 8, para. 174). This was said not to contradict *E* (ibid.). For the position in EU law see *Commission* v. *Tetra Laval* (Case C-12/03) [2005] ECR

The Court of Appeal laid down the new position in this dictum:[175]

the time has now come to accept that a mistake of fact giving rise to unfairness is a separate head of challenge in an appeal on a point of law, at least in those statutory contexts where the parties share an interest in co-operating to achieve the correct result.…
Without seeking to lay down a precise code, the ordinary requirements for a finding of
unfairness are… [f]irst, there must have been a mistake as to an existing fact, including a
mistake as to the availability of evidence on a particular matter. Secondly, the fact or evidence must have been 'established', in the sense that it was uncontentious and objectively
verifiable. Thirdly, the appellant (or his advisers) must not have been responsible for the
mistake. Fourthly, the mistake must have played a material (not necessarily decisive) part
in the Tribunal's reasoning.

It has also become clear that the principle is not restricted to asylum or human rights
cases but applies relatively generally.[176] The requirement that the error of fact should have
been 'uncontentious' may prove problematical.[177] It cannot be right that a respondent can
prevent a challenge on this ground by contending against the weight of the evidence that
there was no error. Flexibility will be required in admitting evidence to show the error.[178]

WRONGFUL REJECTION OF EVIDENCE

It was an established rule that if a tribunal wrongly refused to receive evidence on the
ground that it was irrelevant or inadmissible, this error did not go to jurisdiction.[179] But
there was jurisdictional error if the reason for rejecting the evidence was a mistaken belief
by the tribunal that it had no business to investigate the question at all. This was the case
where a magistrate refused to hear evidence, in defence to a charge of failing to pay the
apportioned cost of paving a street, to the effect that the apportionment by the board of
works included improper items.[180] He was thus improperly refusing to allow jurisdictional facts to be disputed. Going somewhat further, the court quashed the refusal of
an inspector, conducting an inquiry into a compulsory purchase order, to hear relevant

I-1113 (courts to establish whether the evidence 'is capable of substantiating the conclusions drawn from it'
(para. 39)). And see the cases in the following note.

[175] *E* v. *Home Secretary*, para. 66 (Carnwath LJ). Discussed [2004] *PL* 788 (Craig) and [2007] *PL* 793
(Williams) and Forsyth and Dring, above. *E* has been followed in *Connolly and ors* v. *Secretary of State for
Communities and Local Government* [2009] EWCA Civ 1059 (planning inspector in error as to planning
history of site; decision quashed); *London Borough of Richmond Upon Thames* v. *Kubicek* [2012] EWHC
3292, paras. 20–2; *Henry* v. *Parole Board* [2011] EWHC 2081, paras. 37–41 (judicial review succeeded on the
basis of error of fact); *R (Pharmacy Care Plus Ltd)* v. *Family Health Services Appeals Unit* [2013] EWHC 824
(judicial review succeeded on the basis of error of fact); and *Macarthur* v. *Secretary of State for Communities
and Local Government* [2013] EWHC 3 (mistake of fact not established). See Appendix 3.

[176] *R (Assura Pharmacy Ltd)* v. *National Health Services Litigation Authority* [2008] EWHC 289 (Admin)
(principle applied to decision to admit pharmacy to the NHS Pharmacy List, but challenge failed since
error in part the responsibility of applicant). See *Pharmacy Care Plus*, above (challenge succeeded). And see
Kubicek, above, para. 26 (principle applies to housing, planning control and asylum).

[177] See *MT (Algeria)*, para. 69. And see *Kubicek*, above (alleged error of fact (whether certain phone calls
made) contentious; applicant failed to provide evidence of contested point; appeal based on alleged error
dismissed).

[178] See *E* at paras. 68–92 for a full discussion (principle of *Ladd* v. *Marshall* [1954] 1 WLR 1489 applicable
but may be departed from exceptionally where justice so requires).

[179] Subject to the new rule for error of law (above, p. 219) and to the possibility that self-misdirection as
to law may be equivalent to declining jurisdiction: *R* v. *Wells Street Magistrate ex p Westminster CC* [1986]
1 WLR 1046.   [180] *R* v. *Marsham* [1892] 1 QB 371.

evidence relating to the owner's conduct as landlord;[181] the court emphasised that the inspector's error was fundamental to the conduct and utility of the inquiry as distinct from a mere error of judgment. In Ontario a labour board's order was quashed where it had refused to receive evidence about resignations from a trade union where the question was whether a majority of employees were members in good standing.[182] In such cases the tribunal can be ordered to determine the question properly.[183]

Whether this 'rather nice'[184] distinction still survives must be doubtful, in the light of the new doctrine that all error of law is ultra vires.[185] It seems most probable that wrongful rejection of evidence, and also wrongful admission of evidence, will be subject to judicial review under the new doctrine.

DISCOVERY OF FRESH EVIDENCE

Where some tribunal or authority has power to decide questions of fact, and no power to reopen its own decisions,[186] its decision cannot be reviewed by the High Court merely on the ground that fresh evidence, which might alter the decision, has since been discovered. This is because the decision is within jurisdiction and there is no basis on which the court can intervene. The remedy of certiorari will therefore not lie in such a case.[187] But, for the same reason, there is an important exception: if the fresh evidence relates to a fact which goes to jurisdiction, so that it may be possible to show subsequently that the decision was without jurisdiction and void, this evidence may be used in later proceedings to invalidate the decision, as explained in the context of res judicata.[188]

Where it is later discovered that an order was outside jurisdiction, the court has inherent power to quash consequential orders made on the footing that the original order was valid, even though the later orders, taken by themselves, were within jurisdiction.[189]

SUMMARY OF RULES

JURISDICTION OVER FACT AND LAW: SUMMARY

At the end of a chapter which is top-heavy with obsolescent material it may be useful to summarise the position as shortly as possible. The overall picture is of an expanding system struggling to free itself from the trammels of classical doctrines laid down in the past. It is not safe to say that the classical doctrines are wholly obsolete and that the broad and simple principles of review, which clearly now commend themselves to the judiciary, will entirely supplant them. A summary can therefore only state the long-established rules

---

[181] R v. Secretary of State for the Environment ex p Kensington and Chelsea RBC, The Times, 30 January 1987.   [182] Toronto Newspaper Guild v. Globe Printing Co [1953] 3 DLR 561.

[183] As in R v. Marsham (above) (mandamus).

[184] R v. Marsham (above) at 378 (Lord Esher MR).   [185] Above, p. 219.

[186] See above, p. 191.

[187] R v. West Sussex Quarter Sessions ex p Johnson Trust Ltd [1974] QB 24 (Lord Denning MR dissenting); and see R v. Home Secretary ex p Momin Ali [1984] 1 WLR 663; Shetland Line (1984) Ltd v. Secretary of State for Scotland, 1996 SLT 653.

[188] See above, p. 206, and R v. Pugh (Judge) [1951] 2 KB 623; R v. Secretary of State for the Environment ex p Powis [1981] 1 WLR 584. Fraud or perjury by a party may also be proved by fresh evidence; ibid.

[189] R v. Middleton, Bromley and Bexley Justices ex p Collins [1970] 1 QB 216 (pleas of guilty on mistaken assumption that earlier conviction was valid; later conviction quashed).

together with the simpler and broader rules which have now superseded them, much for the benefit of the law. Together they are as follows:

Errors of fact
Old rule: The court would quash only if the erroneous fact was jurisdictional.[190]
New rule: The court will quash if an erroneous and decisive fact was

(a) jurisdictional;

(b) found on the basis of no evidence;[191] or

(c) wrong, misunderstood or ignored.[192]

Errors of law
Old rule: The court would quash only if the error was

(a) jurisdictional;[193] or

(b) on the face of the record.[194]

New rule: The court will quash for any decisive error, because all errors of law are now jurisdictional.[195]

---

[190] Above, p. 208. [191] Above, p. 230. [192] Above, p. 230.
[193] Above, p. 209. [194] Above, p. 224. [195] Above, p. 219.

9

PROBLEMS OF INVALIDITY

COLLATERAL PROCEEDINGS

COLLATERAL CHALLENGES ALLOWED

The validity of the act or order may be challenged directly, as in proceedings for certiorari to quash it or for a declaration that it is unlawful. But it may also be challenged collaterally, as for example by way of defence to a criminal charge, or by way of defence to a demand for some payment.[1]

As a general rule, the court will allow the issue of invalidity to be raised in any proceedings where it is relevant. Where some act or order is invalid or void, that should be able to be raised in any proceedings which depend on the validity of that act. An illustration is the House of Lords' decision in the case, mentioned later, where a man prosecuted for carnal knowledge of a detained mental defective was able to plead that the detention order under which the defective was held had not been validly made: the detention order was therefore a nullity and an essential element of the offence was lacking.[2] Many comparable examples are to be found throughout the field of judicial review. A firm may resist a demand for purchase tax by showing that the assessment is made under an invalid regulation,[3] and a ratepayer may similarly resist a rate demand.[4] A local authority's tenant, sued for increased rent, may contend in his defence that the increase was ultra vires and void.[5] Gipsies occupying a local authority's land may resist proceedings for their ejection on the ground that the decision to eject them was unreasonable.[6] The validity of regulations about social security benefit may be disputed before a social security commissioner[7] and the validity of regulations about the registration of land charges may be disputed in proceedings for the recovery of compensation.[8] A local authority may even

---

[1] On collateral challenge see Rubinstein, *Jurisdiction and Illegality*, ch. 3. For a wide-ranging discussion extending to human rights and EU law see [1992] *CLJ* 308 (C. Emery). There is some difficulty over terminology, since the House of Lords has held (in the *Wandsworth* case (below)) that an issue is not truly collateral if it is the central issue which has to be decided. But, as the examples in this section illustrate, it is not the central character of the issue which matters (for any decisive issue is necessarily central) but the nature of the proceedings in which the issue is raised. In the following discussion 'collateral' will be used in its customary sense, as applying to challenges made in proceedings which are not themselves designed to impeach the validity of some administrative act or order.

[2] *Director of Public Prosecutions* v. *Head* [1959] AC 83; cf. *Dillon* v. *R* [1982] AC 484.

[3] *Commissioners of Customs & Excise* v. *Cure and Deeley Ltd* [1962] 1 QB 340. See likewise *R* v. *Commissioners of Customs and Excise ex p Hedges and Butler Ltd* [1986] 1 All ER 164.

[4] *Daymond* v. *Plymouth City Council* [1976] AC 609.

[5] *Wandsworth LBC* v. *Winder* [1985] AC 461, where the House of Lords rejected an argument based on *O'Reilly* v. *Mackman* [1983] 2 AC 237 as to which see below, p. 569, and see similarly *R* v. *Jenner* [1983] 1 WLR 873; *Pawlowski* v. *Dunnington* (1999) 11 Admin LR 565.

[6] *West Glamorgan CC* v. *Rafferty* [1987] 1 WLR 457. Contrast *Waverley BC* v. *Hilden* [1981] 1 WLR 246.

[7] *Chief Adjudication Officer* v. *Foster* [1993] AC 754.

[8] *Ministry of Housing and Local Government* v. *Sharp* [1970] 2 QB 223; below, p. 648.

plead the invalidity of its own repairs notices in resisting tenants' applications for grants to meet the cost of compliance.[9] The invalidity of a local planning authority's breach of condition notice served out of time may be pleaded in defence to a criminal charge of disobedience to it,[10] and so may the invalidity of a byelaw, in whatever court the plea is made.[11] An appeal against convictions for bribery before a statutory tribunal may succeed on the ground that the members of the tribunal were invalidly appointed, so that the tribunal was without jurisdiction.[12] In particular, any questions affecting the jurisdiction of a tribunal can normally be raised in collateral proceedings, for the reasons already explained.[13] The writ of habeas corpus allows a prisoner to raise all questions capable of affecting the validity of his detention, and in most of its applications can be considered a means of collateral attack.[14] A utilities regulator, subject to a ministerial direction purporting to restrict its powers, could issue a determination notice in apparent breach of the direction and await developments.[15]

Two modern decisions of the House of Lords have emphatically reaffirmed the principle, laying stress on the citizen's right, under the rule of law, to defend himself in all respects as a matter of right and not (as in judicial review) as a matter of discretion. In the first case a landowner prosecuted for failure to comply with an enforcement notice served by the local planning authority pleaded that the notice was invalid because it was motivated by bad faith and immaterial considerations. It was held that magistrates' courts were by long usage entitled to allow collateral pleas in criminal cases, so that the validity of any relevant act or order could be challenged before them. In this case, however, there was found to be a contrary intention in the legislation, so that it belongs to the group of exceptional cases discussed later.[16] In the second case, where the defendant was fined for smoking in a railway carriage contrary to railway byelaws, and pleaded that the byelaws were excessively applied, the House of Lords categorically upheld his right to make that plea, though in fact they dismissed it on its merits.[17] Their reasoning, furthermore, applies as much to civil as to criminal cases.[18] They overruled an earlier decision, criticised in a previous edition of this book, which had distinguished between substantive and procedural invalidity and had held that the latter could not be pleaded in defence to a criminal charge but could be challenged only by way of judicial review.[19] In this leading case there are many important observations on the rule of law, ultra vires, 'void or voidable', and the consequences of illegal acts and orders, which are noted elsewhere.[20]

---

[9] R v. Lambeth BC ex p Clayhope Properties Ltd [1988] QB 563.

[10] Dilieto v. Ealing LBC [1998] 3 WLR 1403. As to enforcement notices see R v. Wicks [1998] AC 92, discussed below.

[11] Boddington v. British Transport Police [1999] 2 AC 143, discussed below; R v. Reading Crown Court ex p Hutchinson [1988] QB 384; Staden v. Tarjanyi (1980) 78 LGR 614; Director of Public Prosecutions v. Hutchinson (below).

[12] Bribery Commissioner v. Ranasinghe [1965] AC 172; compare Ranaweera v. Ramachandran [1970] AC 962 (Lord Diplock, dissenting). But no mention was made of the doctrine of officers and judges de facto: see below, p. 238.   [13] Above, p. 210.

[14] As in R v. Board of Control ex p Rutty [1956] 2 QB 109; R v. Brixton Prison Governor ex p Ahsan [1969] 2 QB 22. For these cases see below, p. 503. Rubinstein, Jurisdiction and Illegality, 107.

[15] Mossell (Jamaica) Ltd (t/a Digicel) v. Office of Utilities Regulations and ors (Jamaica) [2010] UKPC 1. In fact the direction was found to be ultra vires and the determination notice lawful in a judicial review initiated by a company in the relevant market.   [16] R v. Wicks [1998] AC 92.

[17] Boddington v. British Transport Police [1999] 2 AC 143. The defence was that power to 'regulate' smoking did not extend to banning it entirely (see below, p. 369). The case is discussed in [1998] PL 364 (Forsyth).

[18] Lord Irvine LC argues (at 159) from the civil case of Wandsworth LBC v. Winder (above) to criminal cases which are a fortiori, as also does Lord Steyn (at 172).

[19] Bugg v. Director of Public Prosecutions [1993] QB 473.   [20] See below, p. 247.

This doctrine cannot be carried to the point of dispensing altogether with some legal requirement such as a licence. If the licensing authority refuses a licence invalidly, for example unreasonably or in breach of natural justice, this cannot be pleaded in defence to a charge of acting without a licence.[21] The application for the licence will remain undetermined and there will be a duty to determine it validly. But no collateral plea can supply a licence which does not exist.

Conversely, but less reasonably, a person may be convicted for selling liquor where his licence is void because of some legal defect.[22] The correct attitude would probably be to treat the defective licence, at least if regular on its face, as a licence de facto, on the same principle as with officers de facto, mentioned later. In some situations the courts have sensibly adopted this type of solution, refraining from pushing the doctrine of nullity to extremes. A case in point is that of officers executing warrants and other orders, who are in general protected if there is no evident invalidity on the face of the warrant or order.[23]

A comparable distinction was made where actions for damages were brought against magistrates and judges of inferior courts on account of orders made by them outside their jurisdiction.[24] If the order was bad on its face the court would treat it as invalid. But if the jurisdictional defect was not visible on the face, the court would require the order first to be quashed in separate proceedings before the action for damages could be entertained.[25] Collateral attack was thus allowed in the first case but not in the second.

COLLATERAL CHALLENGES NOT ALLOWED

There are a number of situations in which the court will not permit an order to be challenged in collateral proceedings. The most obvious is where such proceedings are expressly excluded by statute.[26] Other cases flow partly from the familiar distinctions based on jurisdiction, but partly also they are exceptions to the general rule stated above, made for reasons of convenience.

In some cases it is held that a specific statutory remedy, such as a right of appeal, is the only remedy available. No challenge to the validity of the order can therefore be made in any proceedings other than those prescribed. This class of cases is discussed in connection with remedies.[27] The House of Lords has supplied a strong example in holding that defences based upon bad faith and immaterial considerations cannot be pleaded in a prosecution for disobedience to a local planning authority's enforcement notice requiring the demolition of part of a building.[28] The legislation had its own system for appeals

---

[21] *Quietlynn Ltd* v. *Plymouth CC* [1988] 1 QB 114, which involved such a situation (operation of sex shops without licence), was however decided on contrary intention in the statute, which made a formal decision conclusive: see *R* v. *Wicks* (above) at 117 and *Boddington* v. *British Transport Police* (above) at 160. In fact no invalidity was found.

[22] *R* v. *Downes* (1790) 3 TR 560 (licence granted in private instead of public session); *Pearson* v. *Broadbent* (1870) 36 JP 485 (licence granted under repealed section of Act). See Rubinstein (as above), 43.

[23] *Shergold* v. *Holloway* (1735) 2 Str 1002; *Andrews* v. *Marris* (1841) 1 QB 3; *Demer* v. *Cook* (1903) 88 LT 629. See also Constables Protection Act 1751; *Horsfield* v. *Brown* [1932] 1 KB 355; *Sirros* v. *Moore* [1975] QB 118; *Maharaj* v. *A-G of Trinidad and Tobago (No 2)* [1979] AC 385 at 397.

[24] For their liability see below, p. 670.

[25] *O'Connor* v. *Isaacs* [1956] 2 QB 288 at 304 and cases there cited by Diplock J.

[26] As in *Manchester City Council* v. *Cochrane* [1999] 1 WLR 809.   [27] Below, p. 619.

[28] *R* v. *Wicks* [1998] AC 92, discussed in Forsyth and Hare (eds.), *The Golden Metwand*, 148 (Forsyth). The decision was distinguished in *Dilieto* v. *Ealing LBC* (above, p. 236) on the ground that there was no comparable system of appeals and the issue was one of law only. For another example see *Vestry of St James and St John, Clerkenwell* v. *Feary* (1890) 24 QBD 703.

against enforcement notices and it had progressively restricted the issues which a defendant was permitted to raise otherwise than on appeal. This regime, designed to make enforcement notices speedily and conclusively effective, would be disrupted if collateral pleas were allowed. Another example concerned an anti-social behaviour order (ASBO)[29] where the court held that the validity of the ASBO could not be raised collaterally before the court trying a breach of the order.[30] There was, however, 'a full opportunity' to appeal to the Crown Court.[31]

There may also be cases where, although there is no special statutory remedy, it would be contrary to the scheme of the Act to allow the validity of an order to be disputed collaterally in enforcement proceedings. Such a case was where the mother of a child with scarlet fever refused to obey a magistrate's order for the removal of the child to hospital: when prosecuted for obstructing execution of the order the mother was not allowed to contest its validity, since the intention of the Act was that there should be summary powers for dealing urgently with infectious diseases, without the usual right to notice and hearing; the removal order was therefore to be obeyed, whether right or wrong.[32] The court indicated, however, that its validity might have been challenged directly by certiorari or habeas corpus after the removal.

The findings of criminal convictions may not be attacked collaterally in civil proceedings or before disciplinary tribunals unless fresh evidence of sufficient weight has come to light since the conviction.[33]

The sparseness of these examples, contrasted with the abundance of successful collateral pleas, illustrates the operation of the rule of law in a highly technical area. As Lord Irvine LC has said in exactly this context:[34]

> it is well recognised to be important for the maintenance of the rule of law and the preservation of liberty that individuals affected by legal measures promulgated by executive public bodies should have a fair opportunity to challenge these measures and to vindicate their rights in court proceedings. There is a strong presumption that Parliament will not legislate to prevent individuals from doing so.

OFFICERS AND JUDGES DE FACTO

In one class of cases there is a long-standing doctrine that collateral challenge is not to be allowed: where there is some unknown flaw in the appointment or authority of some officer or judge. The acts of the officer or judge may be held to be valid in law even though

---

[29] ASBOs are made under the Crime and Disorder Act 1998, s. 1 by courts (usually magistrates' courts) on the application of the local authority or chief constable against persons who have caused 'harassment, alarm or distress' to others. It is an offence to breach the terms of an ASBO (s. 1(10)).

[30] *Crown Prosecution Service* v. *T* [2006] EWHC 728 (Admin), [2007], 1 WLR 209 distinguishing *R (W)* v. *Director of Public Prosecutions* [2005] EWHC 1333 (Admin) (challenge possible if order 'plainly invalid' but fear of 'the danger of opening floodgates', para. 12 (Brooke LJ)).

[31] Richards LJ, para. 27 referring to the 1998 Act, s. 4. It may be doubted whether the court would go so far as to convict and imprison a person for breach of a plainly invalid ASBO. In *T* itself the court declined to quash the order of the District Judge upholding the collateral challenge (para. 48).

[32] *R* v. *Davey* [1899] 2 QB 301. Compare *Children's Aid Society of Metropolitan Toronto* v. *Lyttle* (1973) 34 DLR (3d) 127 (collateral challenge to wardship order by way of adoption proceedings not allowed). For discussion in Australian context see [1998] *Public Law Review* 237 (Aronson).

[33] *Hunter* v. *Chief Constable of the West Midlands Police* [1982] AC 529; *Smith* v. *Linskill* [1996] 1 WLR 763; *Re a solicitor*, The Times, 18 March 1996.

[34] *Boddington* v. *British Transport Police* [1999] 2 AC 143 at 161. See also at 173 (Lord Steyn).

his own appointment is invalid and in truth he has no legal power at all.[35] The logic of annulling all his acts has to yield to the desirability of upholding them where he has acted in the office under a general supposition of his competence to do so.[36] In such a case he is called an officer or judge de facto, as opposed to an officer or judge de jure. The doctrine is firmly based in the public policy of protecting the public's confidence in the administration of justice.[37] It is a well-established exception to the ultra vires rule.

The House of Lords applied this principle to an administrative authority so as to uphold a rate levied by a vestry although a number of the vestrymen had not been duly elected. Lord Truro LC described them as vestrymen de facto and said:[38]

> You will at once see to what it would lead if the validity of their acts, when in office, depended upon the propriety of their election. It might tend, if doubts were cast upon them, to consequences of the most destructive kind. It would create uncertainty with respect to the obedience to public officers, and it might lead also to persons, instead of resorting to ordinary legal remedies to set right anything done by the officers, taking the law into their own hands.

In another administrative case the court upheld a distress levied by a collector of land tax who did not have the residential qualification required for his appointment.[39] The same doctrine has been applied to invalidly appointed judges and magistrates: a distress warrant was held valid although granted by a magistrate who had not taken the necessary oath;[40] and when the appointment of a judge of the Supreme Court of New Zealand was found to be void,[41] that did not avail a prisoner whom he had sentenced at the time when he was supposed to be a judge.[42] Similarly, in the days when judges' appointments were automatically determined by the demise of the Crown, their judgments and acts remained valid until news of the monarch's death in fact arrived.[43] And the decision of the Visitors' Panel (hearing an appeal against the decision of Bar Standards Board Disciplinary Tribunal) was upheld when two 'members' of the panel had not been properly nominated.[44]

The decisions indicate that the doctrine will apply only where the office-holder has 'colourable authority' or some colour of title to the appointment. Where the registrar of the Bedford Level company employed a deputy to register land titles within the Level, it was held that registrations effected by the deputy after the death of the registrar was known were invalid: the deputy's authority expired on the death of his principal, and once the

---

[35] For discussion see Rubinstein, *Jurisdiction and Illegality*, 205; Owen Dixon (later Sir O. Dixon CJ), *Res Judicatae* (Melbourne, 1938), i. 285; (1955) 71 *LQR* 100 at 106 (R. B. Cooke); [1978] *PL* 42 (P. Mirfield). There are many American decisions, notably *State* v. *Carroll* (1871) 38 Conn 449, 9 Am 409, where early authorities are reviewed. For an example from Roman law see [1967] *Irish Jurist* 269 (A. M. Honoré), citing a case where a slave was elected praetor.

[36] See *Fawdry & C.* v. *Murfitt (Lord Chancellor intervening)* [2002] 3 WLR 1354 (CA) approving the previous two sentences (at 1361; Hale LJ). This passage was similarly relied upon in *Baldock* v. *Webster* [2004] EWCA Civ 1869, [2006] QB. 315 (para. 10, Laws LJ) and *Russell* v. *Bar Standards Board* (Visitors to the Inns of Court, available at <https://www.barstandardsboard.org.uk/media/1460272/ca_russelll_judgment_12_july_2012.pdf>, para. 38 (Sir Rabinder Singh).

[37] See *Baldock* v. *Webster*, above, and *Fawdry*, above.

[38] *Scadding.* v. *Lorant* (1851) 3 HLC 418 at 447.

[39] *Waterloo Bridge Co* v. *Cull* (1859) 1 E & E 245.

[40] *Margate Pier Co* v. *Hannam* (1819) 3 B & Ald 266.

[41] See *Buckley* v. *Edwards* [1892] AC 387 (appointment invalid since no salary appropriated).

[42] *Re Aldridge* (1893) 15 NZLR 361. This case contains a learned review of the law, except that it makes no mention of *Scadding* v. *Lorant* (above). [43] *Crew* v. *Vernon* (1627) Cro Car 97.

[44] *R (Argles)* v. *Visitors to the Inns of Court* [2008] EWHC 2068.

death was generally known the deputy could not be taken to have any colour of authority to act. Lord Ellenborough CJ said:[45]

> An officer de facto is one who has the reputation of being the officer he assumes to be, and yet is not a good officer in point of law.

So a divorce granted in 1970 by a Rhodesian judge, appointed under the unconstitutional Rhodesian regime established in 1965, was held to be invalid in England, since it was notorious in both countries that the Rhodesian regime had been declared unlawful by Act of Parliament and Order in Council;[46] accordingly the judge had no colour of title to his office in the eyes of English law. The basis of the de facto principle is that the public must be able to rely on the acts of judges and officers so long as there is no reason to suppose that they are not validly appointed. In another case a circuit judge sat in the Queen's Bench Division of the High Court in the wrongful belief that in the particular circumstances he was authorised.[47] His decision was upheld under the de facto doctrine. But the Court of Appeal made it clear the doctrine did not apply to an usurper, i.e. 'someone who knows, even if the world knows not, that he is not qualified to hold the office he is exercising.'[48] The decision of a recorder who knew he was not authorised to sit in the High Court but who thought he was sitting in the County Court was upheld under the doctrine.[49]

The de facto doctrine has a long history and has been applied to a wide variety of officers. It was even said to have applied to the monarchy, so that it might validate acts done in the names of kings whose title to the throne was considered illegitimate and who were kings 'in fact and not in law'.[50] At the other end of the scale the doctrine was invoked from an early date to uphold copyhold titles enrolled by stewards of manors who were not properly appointed.[51] Offices were long considered to be a form of property,[52] and wrongful possession of an office may be compared with wrongful possession of land: just as a wrongful occupier of land may validly exercise an owner's powers (to convey, sue for

---

[45] R v. *Bedford Level Corporation* (1805) 56 East 356 at 368.

[46] *Adams* v. *Adams* [1971] P. 188. For criticism see Lord Denning MR (dissenting) in *Re James* [1977] Ch 41 at 65. The law was changed by SI 1972 No. 1718. See also *Balmain Association Inc* v. *Planning Administrator* (1991) 25 NSWLR 615.

[47] *Coppard* v. *Customs and Excise Commissioners* [2003] 2 WLR 1618 (CA). See also the scholarly treatment of the de facto doctrine in the similar case of *Fawdry & Co* v. *Murfitt (Lord Chancellor intervening)* [2002] 3 WLR 1354 (CA) where, in the event, the judge was held authorised.

[48] Sedley LJ (*Coppard*, para. 17). With usurpers excluded, the court held that the operation of the doctrine did not breach the requirement of Art. 6(1) of the European Convention that 'civil rights and obligations' should be determined by a tribunal 'established by law', i.e. the office as well as the acts of the officer were upheld by the doctrine. Article 6(1) is discussed in general at p. 377. But doubts were expressed by the judge over Art. 47 of the European Union Charter of Fundamental Rights which requires that the tribunal must be 'previously established'; the learned judge thought that these words might exclude the doctrine (para. 38). However, the Court of Appeal has since held in *R (Leathley)* v. *Visitors to the Inns of Court and anor* [2013] EWHC 3097 that the addition of the adverb 'previously' ' does not add to the meaning of "established by law", it merely emphasises the need to prevent *ex post facto* ratification by the Executive of decisions made by those without legal authority' (para. 51; Moses LJ).   [49] *Baldock* v. *Webster*, above.

[50] These words ('en fait et nient en droit') are from the Act of 1461 (1 Edw. IV, c. 1) which on the accession of Edward IV removed doubts as to the judgments given in the reigns of Henry IV, Henry V and Henry VI, then considered usurpers. This Act was said to be declaratory of the common law: see *Re Aldridge* (above) at 369; but this was doubted in *Adams* v. *Adams* (above) at 213. See [1967] *CLJ* 214 (A. M. Honoré); [1972B] *CLJ* at 150 (D. E. C. Yale).

[51] See *Knowles* v. *Luce* (1580) Moore (KB) 109 at 112; *Parker* v. *Kett* (1701) 1 Ld Raym 658.

[52] See (1945) 61 *LQR* 240 at 249 (D. W. Logan).

trespass etc.) against all but the true owner, merely on the strength of the fact of posses-sion,[53] so the wrongful occupier of an office may validly exercise its powers as against members of the public merely on the strength of his authority de facto. Both titles to land and unlawful administrative acts are subject to a similar principle of relativity.[54] In many legal situations it is a mistake to suppose that the consequences of invalidity should be worked out with rigid logic and without regard to facts. The de facto doctrine has even been applied to invalidly enacted legislation.[55] But it did not apply to deficiencies in the appointment of an arbitration tribunal which was governed by contract. The 'common law could [not] make good a want of power' in these circumstances.[56] But the doctrine has been held applicable to Disciplinary Tribunals appointed by the Council of the Inns of Court; although not courts of law they form 'part of the system of public administra-tion of justice'.[57]

In a number of reported cases the possibility of authority de facto does not seem to have been argued, for example where the Privy Council set aside penalties for bribery imposed by the Bribery Commission in Ceylon because the commissioners had not been appointed by the proper body,[58] and where the High Court declared a trial void because the deputy recorder was a solicitor and not a barrister as required by statute.[59]

PARTIAL INVALIDITY

SEVERANCE OF GOOD FROM BAD

An administrative act may be partially good and partially bad. It often happens that a tribunal or authority makes a proper order but adds some direction or condition which is beyond its powers. If the bad can be cleanly severed from the good, the court will quash the bad part only and leave the good standing. One example was where a licensing author-ity allowed an applicant's appeal but wrongly ordered him to pay costs, which it had no power to do; the court quashed only the order as to costs.[60] Another was where a disci-plinary board validly acquitted a public servant on some charges but invalidly convicted him on others.[61] Another was where the Home Secretary's 'tariff policy' for fixing the minimum term of imprisonment for life sentence prisoners contained an unlawful power

---

[53] Megarry and Wade, *Real Property*, 6th edn, 87. The analogy was observed by Manwood CB in *Knowles v. Luce* (above) and *Leak v. Hall* (1597) Cro Eliz 533 (customs officer de facto), and by Sir Owen Dixon in *Res Judicatae* (1938) at 288.   [54] See below, p. 249; as to title to land, Megarry and Wade (as above).

[55] *Manitoba Language Rights Case* [1985] 1 SCR 721, upholding temporarily (until proper re-enactment) nearly a century of legislation not duly enacted in both English and French and citing similar solutions in other countries. See [1989] *PL* at 37 (S. Sedley).

[56] *Sumukan Ltd v. Commonwealth Secretariat* [2007] EWCA Civ 1148, para.52 (Sedley LJ).

[57] *Russell v. Bar Standards Board*, above, para. 45; *Sumukan Ltd*, which appeared to limit the principle to courts or otherwise part of 'the system of public justice', distinguished (*Russell*, para. 48). *Argle*, above, paras. 33–4 followed. To like effect is *R (Leathley) v. Visitors to the Inns of Court and anor* [2013] EWHC 3097, paras. 42–3 (Moses LJ). As the cases cited earlier show the doctrine has been applied to administrative decision-makers such as tax collectors and vestrymen in addition to judges and tribunal members.

[58] *Bribery Commissioner v. Ranasinghe* [1965] AC 172; above, p. 236.

[59] *R v. Cronin* (1940) 27 Cr App R 179. But here there may have been no 'colourable authority'. Contrast *Re James* [1977] Ch 41 at 66; *Campbell v. Wallsend Engineering Co* [1978] ICR 1015 and *Fawdry & Co v. Murfitt* (*Cronin* of 'doubtful authority', para. 57 (Ward LJ)). *Cronin* also doubted in *Director of Public Prosecutions of the Virgin Islands v. Penn (British Virgin Islands)* [2008] UKPC 29, paras. 22–3.

[60] *R v. Bournemouth Licensing Justices ex p Maggs* [1963] 1 WLR 320.

[61] *Bowman v. Stace and State Services Commission* [1972] NZLR 78.

to increase the term.[62] The same principle applies to orders of courts of law, as where an unauthorised order for disqualification or forfeiture is added to a valid conviction.[63] It also seems possible that a single order may be good against some persons and bad against others. In one case, where a training board was under a mandatory duty to consult certain trade organisations and trade unions, the order was held to be good as against those that had been consulted and bad against those that had not been.[64] In this case the remedy was necessarily a declaratory judgment. In another case a Mental Health Review Tribunal ordered the absolute discharge of a patient who had previously been conditionally discharged. When that absolute discharge turned out to be unlawful, the court quashed only the absolute quality of the order, allowing the patient to remain at liberty subject to conditions.[65]

Where an order is not divisible into component parts but is a single whole the court may decline to sever the bad from the good, as it did where the Secretary of State for Transport miscalculated the sum which he ordered the Greater London Council to pay to London Regional Transport and unlawfully overcharged them by some £10m.[66] But there is no 'blue pencil rule' requiring the bad part of the order to be identifiable in the order itself. Thus a local authority's order which appropriated land for planning purposes, but which included a small plot which was outside its powers, was held to be severable and valid as regards the remainder, even though it treated all the land as a single area.[67]

These cases depend not upon rigid rules but upon whether the court finds it possible cleanly to sever the bad from the good.

It may be no easier to draw the line where the authority is empowered to demand information and demands more than is permitted. In the well-known case of *Dyson* v. *Attorney-General*,[68] where the Act required the taxpayer to make a return under penalty, it was held that the tax commissioners' demand was wholly invalid where they included an unauthorised question in the form of return which they required. This was because the penalties of the Act applied to a return which was one and indivisible and which could not be split into good and bad parts.[69] But where the power is to demand such information as is thought necessary or as may be required for some purpose, a demand which is partly within the power and partly in excess of it may be severed, so that it is valid to the extent that it falls within the Act and no further.[70] The mere inclusion of an unauthorised item will not therefore exonerate the recipient. But 'it may well be that if the excess is so entwined with the valid as to be separable from it only with difficulty, then the whole of the requirement will be bad: the subject ought not to be required to perform delicate feats of surgery upon what is in substance a single requirement.'[71]

The court may be particularly disinclined to perform feats of surgery where an invalid condition is one of the terms on which a discretionary power is exercised. If an invalid condition is attached to a licence or to planning permission, the permission without the condition may be such as the licensing authority would not have been willing to grant on

---

[62] *R* v. *Home Secretary ex p Pierson* [1998] AC 539 at 592 (Lord Steyn).

[63] e.g. *R* v. *Llandrindod Wells Justices ex p Gibson* [1968] 1 WLR 598.

[64] *Agricultural, Horticultural and Forestry Industry Training Board* v. *Aylesbury Mushrooms Ltd* [1972] 1 WLR 190. On this and other such cases see below, p. 747.

[65] *R (Home Secretary)* v. *Mental Health Review Tribunal* [2005] EWCA Civ 1616.

[66] *R* v. *Secretary of State for Transport ex p Greater London Council* [1986] QB 556, containing an extensive review of authorities by McNeill J, who quashed the whole order.

[67] *Thames Water Authority* v. *Elmbridge BC* [1983] QB 570.   [68] [1912] 1 Ch 158; below, p. 484.

[69] See Farwell LJ at p. 171.

[70] *Potato Marketing Board* v. *Merricks* [1958] 2 QB 316; *Royal Bank of Canada* v. *IRC* [1972] Ch 665.

[71] Megarry J in the *Royal Bank of Canada* case, above.

grounds of public interest. The right course for the court is then to quash the whole permission, so that a fresh application may be made. An example is where a local authority, in
granting a licence for open-air rock concerts, attached an invalid condition requiring the
promoter to reimburse the cost of policing them. Since the court regarded the condition
as an essential part of the permission, it quashed the whole licence.[72] The House of Lords
approved this practice in a later case in which they held, though by a narrow majority, that
they could not sever a planning condition requiring that the permission should lapse after
three years unless in the meantime detailed plans were approved by the planning authority.[73] Lord Morris then said:[74]

> There might be cases where permission is granted and where some conditions, perhaps
> unimportant or perhaps incidental, are merely superimposed. In such cases if the con-
> ditions are held to be void the permission might be held to endure, just as a tree might
> survive with one or two of its branches pruned or lopped off. It will be otherwise if some
> condition is seen to be a part, so to speak, of the structure of the permission so that if the
> condition is hewn away the permission falls away with it.

Planning conditions do not all necessarily fall into the latter class. Conditions improperly
restricting the 'existing use rights' of owners have been treated as severable;[75] so have conditions which imposed rent control and other excessive restrictions on a caravan site;[76] so
has a condition requiring a developer to provide small shops in addition to a supermarket;[77] and so has a condition requiring any dispute about the observance of conditions to
be referred to a consultant for conclusive determination.[78] A compulsory purchase order
was severed where it wrongly included property which was in good condition and which
was not reasonably necessary for the development of the adjacent clearance area.[79]

Statutory rules and regulations may be partially invalid and raise the same problems as
those considered in this section. That subject is discussed later,[80] but both sections should
be read together.

STANDARD AND BURDEN OF PROOF

THE STANDARD OF PROOF

Nearly all the cases which concern administrative law are civil, as opposed to criminal,
proceedings. The standard of proof of facts, accordingly, is the civil standard, based on the
balance of probabilities, as contrasted with the criminal standard which requires proof

---

[72] *R* v. *North Hertfordshire DC ex p Cobbold* [1985] 3 All ER 486; see likewise *R* v. *Inner London Crown
Court ex p Sitki*, The Times, 26 October 1993. See similarly, *Hall & Co Ltd* v. *Shoreham-by-Sea UDC* [1964] 1
WLR 240 (below, p. 347); *R* v. *Hillingdon LBC ex p Royco Homes Ltd* [1974] QB 720 (below, p. 345).

[73] *Kingsway Investments (Kent) Ltd* v. *Kent CC* [1971] AC 72 (the condition was in fact held valid). See
similarly *Newbury District Council* v. *Secretary of State for the Environment* [1981] AC 578.

[74] Ibid. at 102.

[75] *Hartnell* v. *Minister of Housing and Local Government* [1965] AC 1134 (severability assumed without
discussion); *Allnat London Properties Ltd* v. *Middlesex CC* (1964) 62 LGR 304.

[76] *Mixnam's Properties Ltd* v. *Chertsey UDC* [1965] AC 735 (below, p. 345). Here also severability was
assumed without discussion.

[77] *R* v. *St Edmundsbury BC ex p Investors in Industry Commercial Properties Ltd* [1985] 1 WLR 1168.

[78] *Turner* v. *Allison* [1971] NZLR 833.

[79] *Coleen Properties Ltd* v. *Minister of Housing and Local Government* [1971] 1 WLR 433.

[80] Below, p. 748.

beyond reasonable doubt. Even where, as sometimes in disciplinary proceedings, the language of the Act or regulations has a criminal flavour, speaking of 'offences', 'charges' and 'punishments', the standard of proof remains the civil standard.[81]

But the civil standard is flexible, so that the degree of probability required is proportionate to the nature and gravity of the issue. Where personal liberty is at stake, for example, the court will require a high degree of probability before it will be satisfied as to the facts justifying detention;[82] and the requirement will not be much lower in matters affecting livelihood and professional reputation, or where there is a charge of fraud or moral turpitude.[83] Lord Scarman has indeed said that the choice between the two standards is largely a matter of words, asking how, if a court has to be satisfied of some crucial fact, it can entertain a reasonable doubt.[84]

Disciplinary offences in prisons are evidently treated as criminal, so that the criminal standard applies.[85]

THE BURDEN OF PROOF

Where the validity of an administrative act or order is attacked, the incidence of the burden of proof may vary with the circumstances. The burden of proof naturally lies in the first instance upon the plaintiff or complainant. Whether he can transfer it to the defendant public authority depends upon the nature of the act.

If the act is one which in the absence of statutory power would be a trespass or other wrongful injury, the plaintiff has only to prove the facts which would constitute the wrong and the burden of proof then passes to the public authority, which has to show justification. Thus a government official seizing a man's goods bears the onus of proof that he had power to do so.[86] A highway authority which removes a supposed obstruction can be put to proof of its power, and if it cannot show this it will be liable in damages for trespass.[87] A local authority empowered to eject a tenant for housing purposes must give some evidence that it is acting for those purposes.[88] An immigrant detained on the ground that he landed unlawfully within the previous twenty-four hours is entitled to release by habeas corpus if there is no proof either way of the time at which he landed.[89] Lord Atkin once said:[90]

> In accordance with British jurisprudence no member of the executive can interfere with the liberty or property of a British subject except on the condition that he can support the legality of his action before a court of justice. And it is the tradition of British justice that judges should not shrink from deciding such issues in the face of the executive.

[81] R v. Hampshire CC ex p Ellerton [1985] 1 WLR 749 (disciplinary proceedings against fire officer).

[82] R v. Home Secretary ex p Khawaja [1984] AC 74; and see Eshugbayi Eleko v. Government of Nigeria [1931] AC 662.

[83] Bhandari v. Advocates Committee [1956] 1 WLR 1442; R v. Milk Marketing Board ex p Austin, The Times, 21 March 1983; and see R v. South Glamorgan Health Authority ex p Phillips, The Times, 21 November 1986 (tribunal's rules specified criminal standard).   [84] [1984] AC at 112, 113.

[85] R v. Home Secretary ex p Tarrant [1985] QB 251 at 285.

[86] R v. Inland Revenue Cmrs ex p Rossminster Ltd [1980] AC 952 at 1011. Likewise with compulsory purchase: Prest v. Secretary of State for Wales (1983) 81 LGR 193.

[87] Murray v. Epsom Local Board [1897] 1 Ch 35 at 40.

[88] St Pancras Borough Council v. Frey [1963] 2 QB 586; Harpin v. St Albans Cpn (1969) 67 LGR 479. For doubt on these decisions see Bristol District Council v. Clark [1975] 1 WLR 1443 at 1448 (CA).

[89] R v. Governor of Brixton Prison ex p Ahsan [1969] 2 QB 222.

[90] Eshugbayi Eleko v. Government of Nigeria [1931] AC 662 at 670. See to the same effect R v. Home Secretary ex p Khawaja [1984] AC 74 (below, p. 368).

This was in a case where a Nigerian chief had been deported to another area but the power to do so depended on a number of conditions. The Privy Council held that it was for the executive to show that these conditions existed and they remitted the case to the court in Nigeria.

Where, on the other hand, the administrative act is some decision or order which in itself inflicts no legal wrong, the complainant's task will be to raise a prima facie case of irregularity, and the burden of proof lies upon him. This is equally so where there is an invasion of his liberty or property but he alleges not that the statutory conditions are not satisfied but that there is some ulterior defect, for example bad faith.[91] It has often been laid down that the onus of proof rests upon the party alleging invalidity.[92] In other words, there is a presumption that the decision or order is properly and validly made, a presumption sometimes expressed in the maxim *omnia praesumuntur rite esse acta*.[93]

The House of Lords has more recently approved an earlier version of this rule:[94]

> In the absence of any proof to the contrary, credit ought to be given to public officers, who have acted prima facie within the limits of their authority, for having done so with honesty and discretion.

Judges have likewise spoken of 'the clearly established presumption that statutory duties are duly and properly performed'.[95] An administrative authority cannot therefore be put to proof of the facts or conditions on which the validity of its order must depend, unless the party attacking it can produce evidence which will shift the burden of proof off his own shoulders. How much evidence is required for this purpose will always depend upon the nature of the case. If an order has an apparent fault on its face, the burden is easily transferred. But if the grounds of attack are bad faith or unreasonableness,[96] the plaintiff's task is heavier. So it is also where the authority must be satisfied of something or form some opinion.[97] If no evidence to the contrary is offered, it will be presumed in favour of the authority that it was duly satisfied or of opinion accordingly.[98] Likewise where tax commissioners were empowered to require 'such particulars as they think necessary', but gave no supporting evidence beyond affirming that they did so think, their order was upheld in the absence of positive evidence from the taxpayer that their wide powers had been in any way abused.[99]

A situation in which the presumption of regularity does not apply is where the jurisdiction of an inferior tribunal is challenged in collateral proceedings.[100] This rule, however,

---

[91] *Greene* v. *Home Secretary* [1942] AC 284 as explained in *Ahsan's* case, above.

[92] *Minister of National Revenue* v. *Wright's Canadian Ropes Ltd* [1947] AC 109 at 122; *Associated Provincial Picture Houses Ltd* v. *Wednesbury Cpn* [1948] 1 KB 223 at 228; *Fawcett Properties Ltd* v. *Buckingham County Council* [1959] Ch 543 at 575, affirmed [1961] AC 636.

[93] *Point of Ayr Collieries Ltd* v. *Lloyd-George* [1943] 2 All ER 546.

[94] *Earl of Derby* v. *Bury Improvement Commissioners* (1869) LR 4 Exch 222, approved in *R* v. *Inland Revenue Commissioners ex p TC Coombs & Co* [1991] 2 AC 283.

[95] *Wilover Nominees Ltd* v. *Inland Revenue Commissioners* [1973] 1 WLR 1393 at 1399 (Goulding J), affirmed [1974] 1 WLR 1342.

[96] See *Potato Marketing Board* v. *Merricks* [1958] 2 QB 316 at 331; *Cannock Chase DC* v. *Kelly* [1978] 1 WLR 1 (no obligation on council to justify reasonableness of eviction of tenant).

[97] See the *Point of Ayr Collieries* case, above.

[98] *Stoke-on-Trent City Council* v. *B & Q (Retail) Ltd* [1984] Ch 1, affirmed [1984] AC 754.

[99] *Wilover Nominees Ltd* v. *Inland Revenue Commissioners* [1974] 1 WLR 1342; *R* v. *Inland Revenue Commissioners ex p TC Coombs & Co* (above).

[100] There seems even to have been a presumption of irregularity, in that the order was presumed void unless it showed jurisdiction upon its face: *Taylor* v. *Clemson* (1842) 2 QB 978 at 1031.

is concerned not so much with the initial burden of proof as with the matters that may be put in issue. Willes J expressed it as follows:[101]

> Another distinction is, that whereas the judgment of a superior Court unreversed is conclusive as to all relevant matters thereby decided, the judgment of an inferior Court, involving a question of jurisdiction, is not final.

PERSONAL LIBERTY

In cases of habeas corpus there is a principle which 'is one of the pillars of liberty'

> that in English law every imprisonment is prima facie unlawful and that it is for a person directing imprisonment to justify his act.[102]

Accordingly the detaining authority must be able to give positive evidence that it has fulfilled every legal condition expressly required by statute, even in the absence of contrary evidence from the prisoner. This was held in a case where clandestine immigrants had been arrested but where there was power to detain them only if they had landed within the previous twenty-four hours. The immigrants failed to show that they had landed before that time and the authorities failed to show that they had landed within it. In this situation it was held that they must be released.[103] Accordingly it is not enough for the custodian to make a return which is valid on its face, unless there is no challenge to the conditions which must be satisfied.[104] If there is such a challenge, the custodian must accept the burden of proof of their existence. This rule is indeed an example of the principle stated at the outset, since unjustified detention is trespass to the person. It is particularly important that the principle should be preserved where personal liberty is at stake. It has been corroborated in a decision of the House of Lords which, though not primarily concerned with habeas corpus, explains the burden of proof which lies upon those who have power to detain and remove immigrants, and for this purpose equates habeas corpus with the other remedies of judicial review.[105]

In the past, unfortunately, the protection of liberty has been weakened by judges who have held that a return from the custodian which is valid on its face puts the burden of disproving it upon the prisoner.[106] For the return is merely a statement of the facts which are alleged to justify the detention, and does not in itself provide any evidence of their existence. Administrative detention is a different matter from detention by order of a court of competent jurisdiction, where the return is conclusive.[107] To throw the burden of proof

---

[101] *City of London v. Cox* (1866) LR 2 HL 230 at 262.

[102] *Liversidge v. Anderson* [1942] AC 206 at 245 (Lord Atkin), confirmed in the *Khawaja* case (below) at 110 (Lord Scarman). And see *R v. Home Secretary ex p Ram* [1979] 1 WLR 148.

[103] *Ahsan's* case (above). See also *R v. Home Secretary ex p Badaike*, The Times, 3 May 1977 (habeas corpus granted).   [104] See Lord Parker CJ in *Ahsan's* case (above) at 231.

[105] *R v. Home Secretary ex p Khawaja* [1984] AC 74, especially at 105 (Lord Wilberforce) and 110 (Lord Scarman). Lord Scarman's later statement that a prisoner carries the initial burden of proof is difficult to understand, since the fact of imprisonment makes a prima facie case, as Lord Scarman acknowledges.

[106] *R v. Home Secretary ex p Greene* [1942] 1 KB 87 at 116; *Greene v. Home Secretary* [1942] AC 284 at 295; *R v. Risley Remand Centre Governor ex p Hassan* [1976] 1 WLR 971 (rejecting *Ahsan's* case, above, p. 294, on an unjustifiable distinction between British subjects and aliens and adopting the opinion of the dissenting judge). In *R v. Home Secretary ex p Zamir* [1980] 3 WLR at 253 Lord Wilberforce is reported as saying that it was for the detainee to show that his detention was unlawful; but in [1980] AC at 947 these words are omitted. See also Sharpe, *Habeas Corpus*, 2nd edn, 85.

[107] See *Liversidge v. Anderson* [1942] AC 206 at 245 (Lord Atkin); *Greene v. Home Secretary* (above) at 294 (Lord Maugham, erroneously extending the rule to administrative detention also).

onto administrative prisoners contradicts the principle stated by Lord Atkin[108] and puts the individual in danger of being detained upon allegations which he may have no means of disproving. It was in order to require proper proof of the facts stated in returns by gaolers that the Habeas Corpus Act 1816 empowered the court 'to examine into the truth of the facts set forth in such return' in non-criminal cases.[109] But this protection becomes nugatory if the initial burden of proof is put upon the prisoner. Despite the obvious confusion between allegation and evidence, judges have too readily committed themselves to this dangerous proposition, instead of requiring the custodian to produce at least enough evidence of legality to call for rebuttal. The burden should revert to the prisoner only where his case is based on an allegation of bad faith or breach of natural justice or some such vitiating element, in accordance with the normal rules.[110] If, on the other hand, an allegation of fraud is made, the burden of proof is of course upon the party making it.[111]

INVALIDITY AND VOIDNESS

ALL INVALID ADMINISTRATIVE ACTS ARE VOID IN LAW

An act or order which is ultra vires is a nullity, utterly without existence or effect in law.[112] That is the meaning of 'void', the term most commonly used. In several decisions the House of Lords has made it clear that 'there are no degrees of nullity' and that errors such as bad faith, wrong grounds, and breach of natural justice all necessarily involve excess of jurisdiction and therefore nullity.[113] This was merely to restate what has always been a fundamental rule. Lord Diplock made it clear that 'void' is the correct term in any such context, saying:[114]

> It would, however, be inconsistent with the doctrine of ultra vires as it has been developed in English law as a means of controlling abuse of power by the executive arm of government if the judgment of a court in proceedings properly constituted that a statutory instrument was ultra vires were to have any less consequence in law than to render the instrument incapable of ever having had any legal effect.

---

[108] Quoted above, p. 247. In *Liversidge* v. *Anderson* (above) at 247 Lord Atkin said: 'A minister given only a limited authority cannot make for himself a valid return by merely saying "I acted as though I had authority". His ipse dixit avails nothing.'   [109] See the *Khawaja* case (above) at 110 (Lord Scarman).
[110] As in *R* v. *Brixton Prison Governor ex p Soblen* [1963] 2 QB 243 at 281 (deportation order alleged to be a sham).   [111] *R* v. *Home Secretary ex p Momin Ali* [1984] 1 WLR 663.
[112] For discussion of this group of problems see M. Taggart in Taggart (ed.), *Judicial Review of Administrative Action in the 1980s*, 70, preferring a 'relative theory of invalidity' to the principle of legal relativity mentioned below; and Forsyth in Forsyth and Hare (eds.), *The Golden Metwand*, 141 (describing the theory of the second actor discussed below, p. 251).
[113] *Anisminic Ltd* v. *Foreign Compensation Commission* [1969] 2 AC 147 at 170 (Lord Reid). See likewise *Ridge* v. *Baldwin* [1964] AC 40 at 80; *Crédit Suisse* v. *Allerdale BC* [1997] QB 306. Cf. Lord Bingham in *R (Anufrijeva)* v. *Home Secretary* [2003] UKHL 36 (breach of public law duty did 'not necessarily nullify or invalidate [the] decision' (para. 15)). Cf. also *Charles Terence Estates Limited* v. *Cornwall Council* [2012] EWCA Civ 1439; here a local council sought to rely on the invalidity of certain leases (void, it was said, because of the council's own breach of its 'fiduciary duty' (below, p. 340)) to avoid the payment of rent. Kay LJ said: 'breach of duty, fiduciary or otherwise, may be a defence depending on the circumstances' (para. 37, adopting the language and approach of Hobhouse LJ in *Crédit Suisse* v. *Allerdale BC* (above)). See also Etherton LJ's judgment (esp paras. 49–50) envisaging that an act may be ultra vires for the purposes of public law but not private law. Presumably the public law duty in these cases was directory not mandatory (see above, p. 183).   [114] In the *Hoffmann-La Roche* case (as below) at 365.

Quoting this passage with approval, Lord Irvine LC has said that when an act or regulation has been pronounced by the court to be unlawful, it 'is then recognised as having had no legal effect at all'.[115] This consequence flows from the ultra vires principle or 'equally acceptably' from the rule of law. The voidness of invalid acts also flows from the classic approach to ouster clauses and the necessity of collateral challenge to the rule of law as explained elsewhere.[116] But, as will be seen, an absolute approach to invalidity, although principled and resting upon high authority, poses conundrums that need to be understood in order to be resolved.

VOID ACTS (WHETHER THE DEFECT IS LATENT OR PATENT) MAY APPEAR VALID UNTIL SET ASIDE BY A COURT

The first of these is that an invalid act may not appear to be invalid; and persons will act on the assumption that it is valid. In a well-known passage Lord Radcliffe said:[117]

> An order, even if not made in good faith, is still an act capable of legal consequences. It bears no brand of invalidity upon its forehead. Unless the necessary proceedings are taken at law to establish the cause of invalidity and to get it quashed or otherwise upset, it will remain as effective for its ostensible purpose as the most impeccable of orders.

This is a description of an act that is voidable (i.e. valid until set aside by the court). And in many cases such an act can only be effectively resisted in law by obtaining the decision of the court. The necessity of recourse to the court has been pointed out repeatedly in the House of Lords and Privy Council, without distinction between patent and latent defects.[118] To the same effect is this statement by Lord Irvine LC:[119]

> No distinction is to be drawn between a patent (or substantive) error of law or a latent (or procedural) error of law. An ultra vires act or subordinate legislation is unlawful simpliciter and, if the presumption in favour of its legality is overcome by a litigant before a court of competent jurisdiction, is of no legal effect whatsoever.

Lord Diplock had added that there might be no one entitled to sue, for example if a statutory time limit had expired. In that case the order would have to stand. Cooke J expressed the same idea in a New Zealand case:[120] 'Except perhaps in comparatively rare cases of flagrant invalidity, the decision in question is recognised as operative unless set aside.'

Yet even in the case of flagrant invalidity it remains necessary for the court to pronounce. It cannot be right to say, as Lord Denning MR once did of a defective rating list, that 'there is no need for an order to quash it. It is automatically null and void without

---

[115] *Boddington* v. *British Transport Police* [1999] 2 AC 143 at 158. Confirmed in *McLaughlin* v. *Governor of the Cayman Islands* [2007] UKPC 50 (Lord Bingham) (dismissal of public servant in breach of natural justice void; thus public servant entitled to arrears of salary not damages).

[116] Below, p. 612 (ouster clauses) and above, p. 235 (collateral challenge).

[117] *Smith* v. *East Elloe Rural District Council* [1956] AC 736 at 769.

[118] As by Lord Morris in *Ridge* v. *Baldwin* [1964] AC 40 at 125; by the Privy Council (Lord Wilberforce) in *Calvin* v. *Carr* [1980] AC 574 at 589–90; by Lord Hailsham LC in *London & Clydeside Estates Ltd* v. *Aberdeen DC* [1980] 1 WLR 182 at 189. Lord Morris's remarks were misunderstood by the Privy Council in *Durayappah* v. *Fernando* [1967] 2 AC 337.

[119] *Boddington* v. *British Transport Police* [1999] 2 AC 143 at 158, rejecting the distinction made in *Bugg* v. *Director of Public Prosecutions* [1993] QB 473.

[120] *AJ Burr Ltd* v. *Blenheim Borough* [1980] 2 NZLR 1 at 4.

more ado'. The only difference is, as Lord Irvine LC has pointed out,[121] that the citizen may feel sure enough of his ground to take no action and rely on the invalidity if he should be sued or prosecuted. But that is his decision, and he must accept the risk of uncertainty. Only the court's judgment can eliminate that risk. The availability of collateral challenge at least ensures that the citizen cannot be coerced on the basis of an illegality.

Thus here we see the conundrum that theoretically void administrative acts are functionally voidable.

THE PRESUMPTION OF VALIDITY AND RETROSPECTIVITY

The House of Lords held in 1975 that there is a presumption of validity in favour of a disputed order until set aside by the court. And this is so even where temporary obedience to the disputed order would cause irreparable loss to a party.[122] But their Lordships have since been held that this presumption was 'an evidential matter at the interlocutory stage' and involved no 'sweeping proposition that subordinate legislation must be treated for all purposes as valid until set aside'.[123] 'There is no *rule* that lends validity to invalid acts'.[124] The presumption of validity, therefore, is temporary and procedural only; it does not determine the validity in law of the disputed act.

Moreover, since a void administrative act is, and always has been, non-existent in law, a finding that an act is void will generally be retrospective. The House of Lords so held in the case of a prisoner whose release date had been wrongly calculated so that she remained in prison fifty-nine days longer than she should have.[125] The prison governor had calculated the date in reliance upon the law as it was then laid down. But the Court of Appeal later changed the mode of calculation. The governor could not rely upon either a presumption of validity or the non-retrospectively of the finding that the detention was unlawful. The prisoner recovered damages for wrongful imprisonment from the prison governor. This may seem unfair to the governor who had acted in good faith and reasonably throughout. But that is because the tort of wrongful imprisonment is a tort of strict liability, not because the finding of voidness was retrospective.

THE COURT MAY REFUSE THE REMEDY REQUIRED
TO SHOW VOIDNESS

The second conundrum is that the act may be clearly void but the court may be unwilling (and in some cases not empowered) to grant the necessary legal remedies. The invalid act, being beyond legal challenge, becomes effectively valid. The court may hold that the act or order is invalid, but may refuse relief to the applicant because of his lack of standing,[126] because he does not deserve a discretionary remedy,[127] because he has waived his

[121] [1999] 2 AC at 158. See likewise *London & Clydeside Estates Ltd* v. *Aberdeen* DC (as above) at 189 (Lord Hailsham LC).

[122] *Hoffmann-La Roche & Co* v. *Secretary of State for Trade and Industry* [1975] AC 295. The logic is criticised by Lord Wilberforce in his dissenting speech. The European Court has decided similarly: *Granaria BV* v. *Hoofdproduktschap voor Akkerbouwprodukten* (case 101/78) [1979] 3 CMLR 124.

[123] *R* v. *Wicks* [1998] AC 92 at 116 (Lord Hoffmann).

[124] *Boddington* v. *British Transport Police* [1999] 2 AC 143 at 174 (Lord Steyn).

[125] *R* v. *Governor of Brockhill Prison ex p Evans* [2000] UKHL 48; [2001] 2 AC 19. To similar effect see *Kleinwort Benson Ltd* v. *Lincoln City Council* [1999] AC 153 (but two judges dissented). *Percy* v. *Hall* [1997] QB 924 (constables could make lawful arrests in reliance upon invalid byelaws (not known to be invalid)) was not overruled. [126] As in *Gregory* v. *Camden LBC* [1966] 1 WLR 899.

[127] As in *Lovelock* v. *Minister of Transport* (1980) 40 P & CR 336 (remedy sought too late).

rights,[128] or for some other legal reason. In any such case the 'void' order remains effective and, must be accepted as if it was valid. It seems also that an order may be void for one purpose and valid for another;[129] and that it may be void against one person but valid against another.[130] A common case where an order, however void, becomes valid for practical purposes is where a statutory time limit expires after which its validity cannot be questioned.[131] The statute does not say that the void order shall be valid; but by cutting off legal remedies it produces that result.[132]

Similarly with remedies withheld in discretion: the court may hold that an attack on the validity of some act or order succeeds, but that no remedy should be granted.[133] The court then says, in effect, that the act is void but must be accepted as valid. An example was where in making social security regulations the Secretary of State neglected his mandatory duty to consult organisations concerned: the court granted a declaration to this effect, but declined in its discretion to quash the regulations.[134] The net result of this contradictory course was that the regulations stood, and were in effect valid.

Another example was the case[135] where the court found that the Secretary of State in making the regulations that permitted universities to charge undergraduates substantially enhanced tuition fees had focused insufficiently upon his public-sector equality duties, i.e. duties to have 'due regard' to various important matters, for instance the promotion of 'equality of opportunity and good relations' between different groups of people.[136] But there had been 'very substantial compliance' with the duties and there would be disruption of the plans of many (including those of the claimant students) if the regulations were ineffective; quashing the regulations would not be 'proportionate'.[137] Thus the regulations, found to be legally flawed, were in effect valid.

Remedial discretion will be discussed later[138] but a Supreme Court decision[139] that heralds a new approach to the question should be noted here. The case concerned whether the Supreme Court, having found that certain Orders in Council (which 'froze' the assets of specified individuals suspected of involvement in terrorism) were 'null and void', could suspend the operation of the remedies quashing the Orders. Lord Phillips said that because the Orders were void, 'the court's order, whenever it is made, will not alter the

---

[128] As to waiver see above, p. 198, and below, p. 398.

[129] Approved in R v. Wicks [1998] AC 92 at 109 (Lord Nicholls). Thus it may be valid for the purpose of being appealed against but not otherwise, as explained in Calvin v. Carr [1980] AC 574 at 590 and Crédit Suisse v. Allerdale BC (above).

[130] As in Agricultural etc Training Board v. Aylesbury Mushrooms Ltd [1972] 1 WLR 190 (industrial training order valid against organisations duly consulted but void against those not consulted) approved in the Crédit Suisse case (as above).

[131] As in Smith v. East Elloe RDC [1956] AC 736; R v. Secretary of State for the Environment ex p Ostler (as below).

[132] See O'Reilly v. Mackman [1983] 2 AC 237 at 283F (Lord Diplock); the Crédit Suisse case, above, at 355 (Hobhouse LJ). See also R v. Secretary of State for the Environment ex p Ostler [1977] QB 122 and similar cases cited below, p. 623 (challenge barred by statutory time limit).

[133] This passage was approved by Glidewell LJ in R v. Governors of Small Heath School ex p Birmingham CC (1989) 2 Admin LR 154.

[134] R v. Secretary of State for Social Services ex p Association of Metropolitan Authorities [1986] 1 WLR 1.

[135] R (Hurley and Moore) v. Secretary of State for Business Innovation & Skills [2012] EWHC 201, discussed in more detail in'The Rock and the Sand', (2013) 18 JR 360(Forsyth).

[136] See below, p. 325, for discussion of the Public Sector Equality Duty. The quoted words are from the Equality Act 2010, s. 149. The legislation in force at the time of this case was the equivalent provisions of the Sex Discrimination Act 1975, the Race Relations Act 1976, and the Disability Discrimination Act 1995.

[137] Para. 99 (Elias LJ).   [138] Below, p. 597.

[139] HM Treasury v. Ahmed and ors (No 2) [2010] UKSC 5.

position in law. It will declare what that position is.'[140] He concluded that the 'court should not lend itself to a procedure that is designed to obfuscate the effect of its judgment'.[141] But on every occasion on which a decision is found to be unlawful and void, and a declaration of that voidness or the quashing of the decision is refused, the effect of the original judgment is obfuscated (when it is not gainsaid). Thus this decision promises a distinct narrowing of the scope of remedial discretion.

NULLITY AND RELATIVITY

The truth is that the court will invalidate an order only if the right remedy is sought by the right person in the right proceedings and circumstances. The order may be 'a nullity' and 'void' but these terms have no absolute sense: their meaning is relative, depending upon the court's willingness to grant relief in any particular situation. If this principle of legal relativity is borne in mind, the law can be made to operate justly and reasonably in most cases through the exercise of remedial discretion.[142] This does not mean, as Lord Hailsham LC suggested in an oft-quoted judgment, that categories of analysis (such as nullity, void, voidable, mandatory, directory) should be regarded not as logically distinct but as 'a spectrum of possibilities in which one compartment or description fades gradually into another', and where the choice is to be made at the court's discretion.[143] The fact that it is often difficult to choose between categories does not mean that they do not exist and are not to be sharply distinguished. That is a familiar problem throughout the law. The problems of nullity are soluble by the formulation of principles and by their logical application, not by abandoning the field to free discretion.

THE THEORY OF THE SECOND ACTOR

An important step in developing a principled and practical approach to these conundrums has been the development of the theory of the second actor.[144] This theory, which has attracted significant judicial support,[145] seeks to explain how an unlawful and void

---

[140] Paras. 4–5.   [141] Para. 8.

[142] The previous three sentences approved in *R (New London College Ltd)* v. *Home Secretary* [2013] UKSC 51, para. 45 (Lord Carnwath) and in *White and anor* v. *South Derbyshire District Council* [2012] EWHC 3495, para. 31 (Singh J).

[143] *London & Clydeside* case (as below) at 189. See the contrasting views of this controversial statement in Forsyth and Hare (eds.), *The Golden Metwand* at 145 (Forsyth) and 219 (Lord Cooke). Lord Irvine LC has explained how the statement must be given a restricted meaning, excluding judicial discretion: *Boddington* v. *British Transport Police* [1999] 2 AC 143 at 158. Lord Woolf's most recent support for the 'inherently discretionary' approach of Lord Hailsham will be found in *Seal* v. *Chief Constable of South Wales Police* [2007] UKHL 31, [2007] 1 WLR 1910 at paras. 32–3 (dissenting). Support for Lord Hailsham's approach may also be found in *TTM* v. *London Borough of Hackney and ors* [2011] EWCA Civ 4, para. 88 (Toulson LJ) and *R* v. *Soneji* [2005] UKHL 49, para. 23 (Lord Steyn).

[144] First put forward in Forsyth and Hare (eds.), *The Golden Metwand*, 141 (Forsyth).

[145] The theory has been approved in terms in the House of Lords (*Boddington* at 172 (Lord Steyn)) and the Court of Appeal (*ID and ors* v. *The Home Office* [2005] EWCA Civ 38, para. 81 (Brooke LJ) and the Administrative Court (*AAM (A Child)* v. *Secretary of State for the Home Department* [2012] EWHC 2567, paras. 105–10 (parties agreed that theory applicable); *AAM* overruled in part but 'second actor' not disapproved in *R (AA)* v. *Home Secretary* [2013] UKSC 49). It has also been adopted in several Commonwealth jurisdictions see *Oudekraal* v. *City of Cape Town* 2004 (6) SA 232 (South African Supreme Court of Appeal (Howie P and Nugent JA)) and *Sam Weng Yee and anor* v. *Pan Wai Mei and anor* (Civil Appeal No. C 02/116/2005 (Malaysian Court of Appeal) unreported, judgment of Gopal Sri Ram JCA). See also *A-G.'s Reference No 2 of 2001* [2003] UKHL 68 (para. 123, Lord Hobhouse) and *R* v. *Central London County Court ex p Ax London* [1999] 3 WLR 1 (theory not adopted in terms but result consistent with it). The theory is adopted

administrative act may none the less have legal effect. It is built on the perception that while unlawful administrative acts (the first acts) do not exist in law, they clearly exist in fact. Those unaware of their invalidity (the second actors) may take decisions and act on the assumption that these (first) acts are valid. When this happens the crucial question is whether these latter, or second acts, are valid.

The theory of the second actor holds that the validity of these second acts does not depend upon any presumption of validity or judicial exercise of a discretion to refuse a remedy to an applicant in particular proceedings. It depends upon the legal powers of the second actor. Did that second actor have power to act even though the first act was invalid? Thus in the case discussed above of the man prosecuted for carnal knowledge of a detained mental defective,[146] the decision of the House of Lords meant that the court before which he was charged (the second actor) lacked the power to convict unless the detention order (the first act) was valid. On the other hand, in the case of the landowner prosecuted for failure to comply with an enforcement notice served by the local planning authority,[147] the House of Lords held that notwithstanding the alleged invalidity of the first act (the enforcement notice) the magistrates' court (the second actor) had power to convict.

The strength of the theory is that it shows that a void act is not 'incapable of ever having had any legal effect'. This resolves at a theoretical level many of the difficulties identified in this chapter. Note, however, that the theory provides no immediate guidance as to how the powers of the second actor are to be determined when not expressly laid down in statute.[148] But some principles are beginning to emerge. One such is the way in which the existence of a separate avenue of appeal against the first act will show that the relevant legislation gives the second actor the power to act notwithstanding the invalidity of the first act.[149] Another is the 'value of certainty in a modern bureaucratic state, a value which the legislature should be taken to have had in mind as a desirable objective when it enacts enabling legislation'.[150] This too would tend to enhance the powers of the second actor. Another principle is that the powers of the second actor should be interpreted in a way that is consistent with human rights.[151] This would sometimes enhance the powers of the second actor and would sometimes restrict them depending upon the circumstances.

It must be stressed that these principles assist in the interpretation of the legislation governing the powers of the second actor. The theory does not posit the exercise of discretion by the judge on pragmatic grounds in determining the validity of the second act. It posits an interpretive approach to the determination of the second actor's powers. Thus it

in all but name in *R v. Consolidated Maybrun Mines Ltd* [1998] 1 SCR 706 (Supreme Court of Canada), para. 52. The Supreme Court of Appeal has returned to the theory in *Seale v. Van Rooyen NO* 2008(4) SA 43 (SCA) holding correctly that if 'the first act is set aside, a second act that depends for its validity on the first act must be invalid as the legal foundation for its performance was non-existent' (para. 13). But the decision does not recognise the converse: that if the second act does not depend upon the validity of the first act, setting the first act aside has no effect on the validity of the second act.

[146] Above, p. 235.   [147] Above, p. 237.

[148] The validity of second acts is expressly addressed by statute more frequently than is sometimes realised. See, for instance, Criminal Justice Act 2003, s. 156(6) 'No custodial sentence [the second act]...is invalidated by the failure of the court to obtain and consider a pre-sentence report [the first act] [as required by s. 156(3)]'. See also the Marriage Act 1949, s. 48(2).

[149] Above, p. 237.   [150] *Oudekraal*, para. 37.

[151] This flows readily from the Human Rights Act 1998, s. 3(1) (above, p. 142). Discussed further in 2006 *Acta Juridica* 209 at 221 (Forsyth).

offers not only a conceptual resolution of many of the conundrums in this area but also a practical guide to the resolution of these thorny problems.[152]

The theory has often been referred to and argued over in the courts but often not applied as it should be. Sometimes it is raised in cases in which it is not relevant. For instance, the theory was argued in a case of a man (M) admitted to and detained in a mental hospital under the Mental Health Act 1983, section 3 against the wishes of his nearest relative (which was required in the circumstances).[153] Section 6(3) of the 1983 Act protected hospitals who acted on an application 'which appears to be duly made and to be founded on the necessary medical recommendations'. While this rendered lawful the acts of the hospital it did not render lawful the act of the approved mental health professional (AMHP) (for whom the local authority was responsible) who actually made the application (in the belief that the relative did consent). To suppose (as counsel did) that the lawfulness of the first act (the making of the application) could be determined by the lawfulness of the second act (detention in the hospital) is an attempt to apply the theory back to front. The court was thus right to say that there 'is no issue as to the lawfulness of the conduct of the "second actor" (the hospital trust) in admitting and detaining M. But it does not follow that this either cured the unlawfulness of the AMHP's conduct or meant that M's detention was not a direct consequence of that unlawfulness'.[154]

Another case came tantalisingly close to a second-actor analysis but in the end did not adopt it in terms. This was the case concerning the summary dismissal by a local council of S, its Director of Children's Services (DCS).[155] This followed a scandal in which an ill-treated baby, whose plight was known to the council, had, nonetheless, been killed by its mother and others. The Secretary of State (following an inquiry by Ofsted) made a direction requiring the council to appoint a certain other person to be DCS but without according procedural justice to S. The courts afterwards determined that the direction was unlawful but the council, knowing the lawfulness of the direction was contested, had earlier relied upon it summarily to dismiss S. The Court of Appeal was divided on the validity of the dismissal. Kay LJ (dissenting on this point) thought that there was an 'ill-defined [area]...in which the act of a public authority which is done in good faith on the reasonably assumed legal validity of the act of another public authority, is not ipso facto vitiated by a later finding that the earlier act of the other public authority was unlawful'.[156] Thus the judge recognised that there might be occasions on which the second actor (the local council) could act validly in dismissing an employee notwithstanding the invalidity of the first act (the Secretary of State's direction). But he did not say how that 'ill-defined [area]' was to be identified nor did he attempt an analysis of the powers of the second actor (the local council).

The other judges (Neuberger MR and Burnton LJ) held that the dismissal was null and void, in the main on the ground that the council knew that the validity of the direction was challenged. The council should have stayed the dismissal (there was no urgency) while the lawfulness of the direction was tested by judicial review. The council was doubtless imprudent to press ahead with the dismissal in reliance upon the contested direction. But surely the majority would not change their view if it were not known at the time that the direction would be challenged? S was either in post or not as a matter of law not discretion.

---

[152] This is perceptively noted and discussed by Mark Elliott in *Beatson, Matthews and Elliott's Administrative Law: Text and Materials*, 4th edn (2011), ch. 3.3.4.

[153] *TTM* v. *London Borough of Hackney and ors* [2011] EWCA Civ 4.

[154] Para. 58 (Toulson LJ) also confirming the relevance of the theory to *Ax London* (above).

[155] *R (Shoesmith)* v. *OFSTED and ors* [2011] EWCA Civ 642.   [156] Para. 119.

A second-actor analysis would have asked whether the council had power to dismiss if the direction was invalid. Kay LJ hints at such an analysis when he suggests that acts 'done in good faith on the reasonably assumed legal validity of the act of another public authority'[157] might be upheld. The other judges are robust in their view that the voidness of the direction implied the voidness of the dismissal. But they give no coherent account of the juristic basis of this conclusion.

Given that it was accepted that the DCS was an office holder and protected in that office by the rules of natural justice,[158] a second-actor theorist might conclude that the council lacked power to dismiss a DCS following a direction, if the direction did not comply with the rules of natural justice.

EFFECT ON THIRD PARTIES

If an act or order is held to be ultra vires and void it is natural to assume that, being a nullity, it is to be treated as non-existent by all who would otherwise be concerned. But the judgment of a court binds only the parties to it, so that here also there are problems of relativity. Once again Lord Diplock has supplied the answer:[159]

> Although such a decision is directly binding only as between the parties to the proceedings in which it was made, the application of the doctrine of precedent has the consequence of enabling the benefit of it to accrue to all other persons whose legal rights have been interfered with in reliance on the law which the statutory instrument purported to declare.

In effect, therefore, the court's judgment of nullity operates *erga omnes*, i.e. for and against everyone concerned.

VOID OR VOIDABLE IN THE PAST

The question whether unlawful administrative acts were void or merely voidable became a source of confusion in the period when landmark decisions were revitalising administrative law. Historically there was a sound basis for this distinction. But it is now obsolete, the House of Lords having written its obituary notice decisively. An abbreviated account will now suffice.

'Void or voidable' was a distinction which could formerly be applied without difficulty to the basic distinction between action which was ultra vires and action which was liable to be quashed for error of law on the face of the record. That distinction no longer survives since the House of Lords declared all error of law to be ultra vires.[160] But formerly an order vitiated merely by error of law on its face was intra vires and within jurisdiction, but liable to be quashed because of the exceptional powers of control which the courts established three centuries ago.[161] Such an order was voidable, being intra vires and valid and effective, unless and until the court quashed it.

Lord Irvine LC has since explained how the *Anisminic* case and its sequels, 'by extending the doctrine of ultra vires' so as to embrace any error of law and render the decision a nullity, 'made obsolete the historic distinction between errors of law on the face of the

---

[157] No reference is made to *Oudekraal*, above, on the value of certainty but there are some similarities.
[158] See the discussion at p. 251.
[159] *Hoffmann-La Roche & Co* v. *Secretary of State for Trade and Industry* [1975] AC 295 at 365.
[160] Above, p. 270.   [161] Above, p. 275.

record and other errors of law...Thus, today, the old distinction between void and void-able acts on which Lord Denning relied...no longer applies.'[162]

Before the law was clearly settled in the above sense confusion had been caused by judi-cial suggestions that even ultra vires action might be merely voidable.[163] This paradoxical opinion was first advanced by the dissenting judges in *Ridge v. Baldwin*[164] and some time after that case Lord Denning MR expressed opinions to the effect that irregular admin-istrative acts might be voidable only. But in the end he retracted them. In a case where a court registrar's flawed order was set aside Lord Denning said that 'on being set aside, it is shown to have been a nullity from the beginning and void', and that he would adopt the meanings of 'void' and 'voidable' given in this book.[165]

THE SUPERIOR COURTS

The order of a superior court, such as the High Court, must always be obeyed, no mat-ter what flaws it may be thought to contain. Thus a party who disobeys a High Court injunction is punishable for contempt of court even though it was granted in proceedings deemed to have been irrevocably abandoned owing to the expiry of a time limit.[166] As Lord Diplock explained:

> The contrasting legal concepts of voidness and voidability form part of the English law of contract. They are inapplicable to orders made by a court of unlimited jurisdiction in the course of contentious litigation. Such an order is either irregular or regular. If it is irregular it can be set aside by the court that made it upon application to that court; if it is regular it can only be set aside by an appellate court upon appeal if there is one to which an appeal lies.

Lord Diplock also said that where there was a defect such as breach of the rules of natural justice a party might have the order set aside *ex debito justitiae* (meaning as of right) with-out recourse to the rules about irregularity which give the judge discretion.

An example of a superior court's order being held to be void was where the Court of Appeal allowed an appeal in a case where appeal was expressly prohibited by statute and on further appeal its decision was held by the House of Lords to be without jurisdiction and 'a nullity'.[167] But the 'nullity' of the Court of Appeal's decision was not necessary for the appeal to the House of Lords to succeed and its use in this context may mislead. In any event, the decision had to enjoy sufficient existence to allow it to be appealed and the order of the Court of Appeal must always be obeyed, whatever its legal defects, unless and until it is set aside on appeal. The decision of a court of unlimited jurisdiction cannot be a nullity (although it can be wrong and liable to be set aside). A mirror image of this error is

---

[162] *Boddington v. British Transport Police* (as above) at 154.

[163] The high-water mark of this heresy was perhaps *Durayappah v. Fernando* [1967] 2 AC 337. For discus-sion see (1967) 83 *LQR* 499, (1968) 84 *LQR* 95 (Wade); 31 *MLR* 2 at 138 (M. B. Akehurst); [1981] *CLP* 43 (D. Oliver); Taggart (ed.), *Judicial Review of Administrative Action in the 1980s*, 70.

[164] [1964] AC 40, discussed below, p. 415.

[165] *Firman v. Ellis* [1978] QB 886, generously confirmed in *The Discipline of Law*, 77 ('I confess that at one time I used to say that such a decision was not void but only voidable. But I have seen the error of my ways'). See also *The Discipline of Law*, 108. In *Lovelock v. Minister of Transport* (1980) 40 PLCR 336 Lord Denning said 'I have got tired of all the discussion about "void" and "voidable". It seems to me to be a matter of words—of semantics—and that is all.'

[166] *Isaacs v. Robertson* [1985] AC 97 at 103. See similarly *M v. Home Office* [1994] 1 AC 377, below, p. 704 (disobedience by minister).

[167] *Re Racal Communications Ltd*, reported as *Re a Company* [1981] AC 374; above, p. 220.

to suppose that the decision of an inferior court (of limited jurisdiction) that has exceeded its jurisdiction is voidable not void. The extent to which an invalid order may have effect is determined by an application of the second actor theory.[168] The decision of the Divisional Court[169] holding that the order (an Anti-Social Behaviour Order) made by an inferior court, even if invalid, must be obeyed may be justified, if at all, on the basis of that theory.

A court made by statute 'a superior court of record' is not thereby rendered immune from judicial review; it does not enjoy the unlimited jurisdiction of the High Court and can act beyond its powers. Thus bodies such as the Upper Tribunal,[170] the Special Immigration Appeals Tribunal[171] and the Employment Appeal Tribunal,[172] each established by statute as a 'a superior court of record', may be subject to judicial review in appropriate circumstances.[173] The case in which the Supreme Court made this clear[174] illustrates the vigour with which the courts, in the interests of the rule of law, resist the ouster of judicial review.

---

[168] Above, p. 000.

[169] *Crown Prosecution Service* v. *T* [2006] EWHC 728 (Admin), para. 31 (Richards LJ). It may be that this principle is limited to orders that are good on their face (para. 32). Also, it may be that even courts of limited jurisdiction have unlimited jurisdiction to make particular orders (e.g. injunctions).

[170] Tribunals, Courts and Enforcement Act 2007, s. 3(5).

[171] Special Immigration Appeals Commission Act 1997, s. 1(3). See *G* v. *Home Secretary* [2004] EWCA Civ 265, para. 20 (Suggestion that SIAC although a superior court, subject to judicial review).

[172] Employment Tribunals Act 1996, s. 20(3).

[173] See above, p. 222, for discussion of those circumstances.

[174] *Cart* v. *The Upper Tribunal* [2011] UKSC 28, [2012] 1 AC 663 discussed above, p. 222.

PART V

DISCRETIONARY POWER

10

RETENTION OF DISCRETION

DISCRETIONARY POWER

In this and the next following chapter the rules which govern discretionary power must be examined in detail. All legal power, as opposed to duty, is inevitably discretionary to a greater or lesser extent, but now the emphasis falls upon the nature of discretion itself and the standards upon which the courts insist in order that it may be exercised in a proper and lawful way in accordance with the presumed intentions of the legislature that conferred it. First, in this chapter, come the rules which ensure that discretionary power should be wielded only by those to whom it is given and that they should retain it unhampered by improper constraints or restrictions. Next, in Chapter 11, comes the sovereign principle that powers must be exercised reasonably and in good faith and on proper grounds—in other words, that they must not be abused. This is one of the twin pillars that uphold the structure of administrative law. The other is natural justice, the subject of Part VI. The law can thus control, to a limited but important extent, both the substance of discretionary decisions and the procedure under which they are made.

DELEGATION

INALIENABLE DISCRETIONARY POWER

An element which is essential to the lawful exercise of power is that it should be exercised by the authority upon whom it is conferred, and by no one else. The principle is strictly applied, even where it causes administrative inconvenience, except in cases where it may reasonably be inferred that the power was intended to be delegable. Normally the courts are rigorous in requiring the power to be exercised by the precise person or body stated in the statute, and in condemning as ultra vires action taken by agents, sub-committees or delegates, however expressly authorised by the authority endowed with the power.

One aspect of this principle is the rule that the participation of non-members in the deliberations or decisions of a collective body may invalidate its acts. The decision of a disciplinary committee, for example, is likely to be invalid if any non-member of the committee has taken part in its proceedings.[1] It is not clear that the mere presence of a non-member will be fatal,[2] although in one case Lord Wright MR said:

---

[1] *Lane v. Norman* (1891) 66 LT 83; *Leary* v. *National Union of Vehicle Builders* [1971] Ch 34; *Ward* v. *Bradford Corporation* (1971) 70 LGR 27. But see *Wislang* v. *Medical Practitioners Disciplinary Committee* [1974] 1 NZLR 29.　　　　　　　　　　　　　　　　　　[2] See *Leary* (above) at 53.

It would be most improper on general principles of law that extraneous persons, who may or may not have independent interests of their own, should be present at the formulation of that judicial decision.[3]

A recognised exception is the right of magistrates to have the assistance of their clerk on questions of law.[4]

The maxim *delegatus non potest delegare* is sometimes invoked as if it embodied some general principle that made it legally impossible for statutory authority to be delegated. In reality there is no such principle; the maxim plays no real part in the decision of cases, though it is sometimes used as a convenient label. In the case of statutory powers the important question is whether, on a true construction of the Act, it is intended that a power conferred upon A may be exercised on A's authority by B. The maxim merely indicates that this is not normally allowable.[5] For this purpose no distinction need be drawn between delegation and agency. Whichever term is employed, the question of the true intent of the Act remains. It is true that the court will more readily approve the employment of another person to act as a mere agent than the wholesale delegation of the power itself. But this is due not to any technical difference between agency and delegation but to the different degrees of devolution which either term can cover. The vital question in most cases is whether the statutory discretion remains in the hands of the proper authority, or whether some other person purports to exercise it. Thus where the Act said that an inspector of nuisances 'may procure any sample' of goods for analysis, it was held that the inspector might validly send his assistant to buy a sample of coffee.[6] This might be described as mere agency as opposed to delegation. But that would obscure the true ground, which was that the inspector had in no way authorised his assistant to exercise the discretion legally reposed in himself. For similar reasons there can be no objection to the Commission for Racial Equality using its officers to collect information in its investigations.[7] Another example, which must be close to the boundary, is where a 'selection panel' makes a recommendation of a single candidate for appointment to the appointing body. Since the appointing body could reject the recommendation, unlawful delegation to the selection panel was not found.[8]

EXAMPLES OF DELEGATION

The following are characteristic cases where action was held ultra vires because the effective decision was taken by a person or body to whom the power did not properly belong.

(a) Under wartime legislation local committees were empowered to direct farmers to grow specified crops on specified fields. A committee decided to order eight acres of sugar beet to be grown by a farmer, but left it to their executive officer to decide on which field it should be grown. The farmer, prosecuted for disobedience, successfully pleaded that the direction was void, since the executive officer had no power to decide as to the field.[9] The right procedure would have been for the

---

[3] *Middlesex County Valuation Committee* v. *West Middlesex Assessment Area Committee* [1937] Ch 361.

[4] See *Ward's* case (above) at 33.

[5] For discussion see *Re S. (a barrister)* [1970] 1 QB 160; (1943) 21 *Can BR* 257 (J. Willis); (1972) 2 *Auck ULJ* 85 (P. H. Thorp).   [6] *Horder* v. *Scott* (1880) 5 QBD 552.

[7] *R* v. *Commission for Racial Equality ex p Cottrell & Rothon* [1980] 1 WLR 1580.

[8] *R (Reckless)* v. *Kent Police Authority* [2010] EWCA Civ 1277, para. 32 (Carnwath LJ). Rimmer LJ dissenting. Not even the names of the other candidates on the shortlist were revealed to the appointing body.

[9] *Allingham* v. *Minister of Agriculture and Fisheries* [1948] 1 All ER 780.

committee to have obtained the officer's recommendation and to have decided the whole matter itself.

(b) Registered dock workers were suspended from their employment after a strike. The power to suspend dockers under the statutory dock labour scheme was vested in the local Dock Labour Board. The suspensions were made by the port manager, to whom the Board had purported to delegate its disciplinary powers. The dockers obtained declarations that their suspension was invalid since the Board had no power to delegate its functions and should have made the decision itself.[10]

(c) A local board had power to give permission for the laying of drains. They empowered their surveyor to approve straightforward applications, merely reporting the number of such cases to the Board. It was held that the Board itself must decide each application, and that delegation to the surveyor was unlawful.[11] The result was the same where a local education committee left it to its chairman to fix the date of closure of a school[12] and where the Monopolies Commission allowed its chairman to decide that a company's takeover proposal had been abandoned.[13]

(d) A local authority, having a statutory duty to provide housing for homeless persons, set up a company which purchased houses, financed by a loan from a bank which the council guaranteed. This was held to be impermissible delegation since it transferred the council's functions to the company, over which the council had only limited control.[14]

(e) A chief constable was entitled to delegate to the assistant chief constable his power to extend a police probationer's probation period, but not, it seems, his power to dismiss a probationer.[15]

(f) A local authority's independent appeals panel (which hears appeals by pupils excluded from school) had no power to delegate to the authority's committee services department vital decisions concerning the fairness of appeals before it.[16]

From these typical cases it might be supposed that the question was primarily one of form. Convenience and necessity often demand that a public authority should work through committees, executive officers and other such agencies.[17] The law makes little difficulty over this provided that the subordinate agencies merely recommend, leaving the legal act of decision to the body specifically empowered.[18] It seems that in many such situations the real discretion is being exercised by the body or person that recommends. But the valid

---

[10] *Barnard* v. *National Dock Labour Board* [1953] 2 QB 18. Similarly see *Vine* v. *National Dock Labour Board* [1957] AC 488 (unauthorised delegation to disciplinary committee) and *Young* v. *Fife Regional Council*, 1986 SLT 331 (committee wrongly delegated to sub-committee).

[11] *High* v. *Billings* (1903) 89 LT 550. Similarly *Vic Restaurant Inc* v. *City of Montreal* (1958) DLR (2d) 81 (licensing power delegated to police); *City Cabs (Edinburgh) Ltd* v. *Edinburgh DC*, 1988 SLT 184 (officials acted instead of council).

[12] *R* v. *Secretary of State for Education and Science ex p Birmingham CC* (1984) 83 LGR 79 (Secretary of State's approval quashed).

[13] *R* v. *Monopolies and Mergers Commission ex p Argyll Group plc* [1986] 1 WLR 763 (Secretary of State's consent not quashed: see below, p. 599).   [14] *Crédit Suisse* v. *Waltham Forest LBC* [1997] QB 362.

[15] *R* v. *Chief Constable of Greater Manchester Police*, The Times, 13 July 1999. See also *Rooney* v. *Chief Constable, Strathclyde Police*, 1997 SLT 1261 (chief constable empowered by circular to delegate power to accept resignations, despite statutory regulation to the contrary).

[16] *R (S and anor)* v. *Independent Appeal Panel of Birmingham City Council* [2006] EWHC 2369 (Admin). The decision in question was that not to consolidate several appeals arising out of the same incident.

[17] See below, p. 264.

[18] *Hall* v. *Manchester Cpn* (1915) 79 JP 385 (HL); distinguished in *Cohen* v. *West Ham Cpn* [1933] Ch 814.

exercise of a discretion always requires a genuine application of the mind and a conscious choice by the correct authority.

Thus a public body which blindly rubber-stamps its officers' recommendations will be acting unlawfully, as already seen in the case of the local board which had power to approve drains but allowed its surveyor to approve straightforward applications, merely reporting the numbers of such cases to the board.[19] Similarly a labour relations board, which had power to determine whether a trade union was supported by a majority of employees, could not validly commission one of its officers to determine this question and then merely adopt his decision.[20] In both these cases the decision would have been valid had it been taken on a report and recommendation from the officer which the board genuinely considered before determining the question itself. The same distinction was applied in Ceylon to a board which had power to appoint trustees of a mosque. They consulted a Member of Parliament who supplied a list of names including his own, all of whom the board appointed. It was held that the board had merely adopted a ready-made decision by an outsider and that such appointments were void.[21] There can be no legal objection to a public body obtaining advice and consulting suitable persons, but it is vital that it should genuinely keep the decision in its own hands.

VESTING DISCRETION (OR THE POWER OF VETO) IN ANOTHER AS A FORM OF DELEGATION

Sometimes the judicial aversion to delegation is carried to lengths which make administration difficult, a tendency which is particularly marked in the Canadian cases. In one of these the Governor in Council was empowered to make regulations for the control of immigration with reference to specified criteria such as the immigrant's unsuitability. The court condemned a regulation which denied admission to persons who were unsuitable in the opinion of a special inquiry officer[22]—though it is hard to see how the criterion could have been applied without some such delegation. A clearer case was where an immigration adjudicator, hearing an appeal, found facts which gave a discretion to the Secretary of State but wrongly exercised that discretion himself.[23] But the House of Lords upheld notices issued by a rating authority's subordinate officer where the Act said: 'Where the rating authority are of opinion', and the only opinion formed was that of the subordinate.[24] It was said that the Act plainly contemplated rate-collection by subordinates and this construction was assisted by the very wide powers conferred upon local authorities.[25]

Another legal pitfall is the requirement of some extraneous person's consent, which may be held to put the decision effectively into that person's hands. A county council erred in this respect when it licensed a cinema on condition that no film should be shown which had not been certified by the British Board of Film Censors, an unofficial body established by the film industry.[26] The council were empowered to impose such conditions as they might determine, but this condition was held unreasonable and ultra vires as 'putting the matter into the hands of a third person or body not possessed of statutory or

---

[19] *High* v. *Billings* (1903) 89 LT 550.
[20] *Labour Relations Board of Saskatoon* v. *Spears* [1948] 1 DLR 340.
[21] *Cader* v. *Commissioners for Mosques* (1963) 66 NLR 16.
[22] *A-G of Canada* v. *Brent* [1956] SCR 318.
[23] *R* v. *Home Secretary ex p Malik*, The Times, 18 November 1981.
[24] *Provident Mutual Life Assurance Association* v. *Derby CC* [1981] 1 WLR 173 (Lord Bridge dissenting).
[25] See below, p. 264.   [26] *Ellis* v. *Dubowski* [1921] 3 KB 621.

constitutional authority'. But this case was only just on the wrong side of the line. A similar condition imposed by another council survived challenge since it contained the words 'without the consent of the council' and so preserved the council's own power to decide in the last resort.[27] Thus the court was able to validate an eminently reasonable administrative policy. Similarly in New Zealand, where the Governor-General had power to make regulations for the control of civil aviation, the court upheld a regulation prohibiting the towing of aircraft except with the permission of the Director of Civil Aviation.[28] If the courts make it impossible for conditions of this kind to be imposed, good administration may be hampered for doctrinaire reasons.[29] It is obvious that some dispensing or licensing power will often need to be given to subordinate officials, and that general powers of regulation should be construed so as to permit this in suitable cases.

AGENCY, ADMINISTRATION AND RATIFICATION

Delegation should be distinguished from agency. Although there are plainly similarities between the two concepts, the differences should be noted. An unauthorised act of an agent may generally be ratified by the principal but the unauthorised act of the delegate, in the absence of statutory authority, cannot be ratified by the delegator. Thus the Court of Appeal summarily dismissed the National Dock Labour Board's claim to have ratified the suspension of dock workers who had been invalidly suspended by the port manager, since this was a serious disciplinary action which only the Board itself was competent to take.[30] It dismissed no less firmly a minister's claim to have ratified the irregular requisitioning of a house by a local authority under powers validly delegated by the minister.[31] On the other hand, public authorities are generally allowed to ratify the acts of their agents retrospectively, both under the ordinary rules of agency and under liberal interpretation of statutes.[32] Occasionally the court may even invoke the rules of agency to justify a questionable delegation.[33] Normally a stricter rule prevails, so that where the Act allows proceedings to be instituted by an officer authorised by resolution, a later resolution cannot validly ratify action already taken.[34] It must be emphasised that all these cases turn on the implications of various statutory provisions: there is no rigid rule.

Another difference between agency and delegation is that in appointing an agent a principal does not divest himself of his powers in the same matter, but whether the public authority that delegates its powers retains the power to act concurrently with its delegate is a matter of controversy discussed later.

[27] *Mills* v. *London County Council* [1925] 1 KB 213. See *R* v. *Greater London Council ex p Blackburn* [1976] 1 WLR 550.

[28] *Hookings* v. *Director of Civil Aviation* [1957] NZLR 929, reviewing earlier cases. See likewise *R* v. *Newbury DC ex p Chieveley Parish Council* (1998) 10 Admin LR 676 (planning officer authorised to decide 'subject to there being no objection' from highway authority: valid).

[29] An extreme case is *Re Davies & Village of Forest Hills* (1964) 47 DLR (2d) 392.

[30] *Barnard* v. *National Dock Labour Board* [1953] 2 QB 18. See similarly *Vine* v. *National Dock Labour Board* [1957] AC 488. In both cases the judicial or quasi-judicial nature of the function was emphasised.

[31] *Blackpool Cpn* v. *Locker* [1948] 1 KB 349. See similarly *A-G ex rel Co-operative Retail Services Ltd* v. *Taff-Ely BC* (1979) 39 P & CR 233, affirmed (1981) 42 P & CR 1.

[32] As in *Warwick RDC* v. *Miller-Mead* [1962] Ch 441 (council empowered to sue for nuisance resolved to sue 3 days after writ issued by their solicitors: held valid).

[33] *R* v. *Chapman ex p Arlidge* [1918] 2 QB 298. In *Firth* v. *Staines* [1897] 2 QB 70, there relied upon, the Act expressly authorised subsequent approval.

[34] *Bowyer Philpott & Payne Ltd* v. *Mather* [1919] 1 KB 419 (legal proceedings).

A public authority is naturally at liberty to employ agents in the execution of its powers, as for example by employing solicitors in litigation, surveyors in land transactions, and contractors in road-building. The essential thing is that it should take its decisions of policy itself, and observe any statutory requirements scrupulously.[35] But in general the court is likely to be more strict where the issue is one of substance as opposed to formality.

In one doubtful decision it was held in effect that delegation of its powers by a local planning authority was justified by a general practice, though the practice had no legal basis.[36] In another case Denning LJ said: 'While an administrative function can often be delegated, a judicial function rarely can be. No judicial tribunal can delegate its functions unless it is enabled to do so expressly or by necessary implication'.[37] The decisions in fact show that the courts do not normally allow the delegation even of administrative functions if they involve the exercise of discretion. There is no general principle that administrative functions are delegable. The principle is rather that, where any sort of decision has to be made, it must be made by the authority designated by Parliament and by no one else. On this ground the Director of Public Prosecutions acted unlawfully in delegating legal work to non-legal staff.[38]

Occasionally the court will allow some degree of delegation on the ground that the matter is merely administrative,[39] particularly in the case of a body which has to make investigations, such as the Race Relations Board.[40] It is doubtless correct that the general objections to delegation apply with special force to judicial functions, particularly if they affect personal liberty or are disciplinary.[41] The extent to which the courts will allow the delegation of fair hearings required by the principles of natural justice is explained elsewhere.[42]

STATUTORY POWER TO DELEGATE

Since in practice government demands a great deal of delegation, this has to be authorised by statute, either expressly or impliedly. The whole of the committee system, as operated by local authorities, is dependent upon the powers of delegation conferred by statute, currently by the Local Government Act 1972 (as several times amended). This empowers local authorities, including local planning authorities, to arrange for the discharge of any of their functions by committees, sub-committees or officers of the authority or by any other local authority, or by acting jointly with other local authorities through joint committees etc.[43] Certain functions are excepted, notably the levying of rates and the

---

[35] Thus local authorities taking legal proceedings through their officers must expressly authorise them under the Local Government Act 1972, s. 223; a mere resolution to take proceedings is inadequate: *Bob Keats Ltd* v. *Farrant* [1951] 1 All ER 899. Cf. *Becker* v. *Crosby Cpn* [1952] 2 All ER 1350 (notice to quit signed by wrong officer).

[36] *Lever Finance Ltd* v. *Westminster London Borough Council* [1971] 1 QB 222, now distinguished in *R (Reprotech (Pebsham) Ltd)* v. *East Sussex County Council* [2003] 1 WLR 348 (HL), discussed below, p. 283.

[37] *Barnard* v. *National Dock Labour Board* (above) at 40.

[38] *R* v. *Director of Public Prosecutions ex p Association of First Division Civil Servants* (1988) 138 NLJ Rep. 158.

[39] e.g. *Bridge* v. *R* [1953] 1 DLR 305; *Hookings* v. *Director of Civil Aviation* [1957] NZLR 929. See also the *Provident Mutual Life Assurance* case (above, p. 262).

[40] *R* v. *Race Relations Board ex p Selvarajan* [1957] 1 WLR 1686.

[41] See *R* v. *Chiswick Police Station Superintendent ex p Sacksteder* [1918] 1 KB 578 at 591; *General Medical Council* v. *UK Dental Board* (below).   [42] Below, p. 448.

[43] ss. 101, 102. The Local Government Act 1933, s. 85, gave power to 'delegate' functions to committees, but not to sub-committees. The Act of 1972 avoids using that word. But note *R (Reckless)* v. *Kent Police Authority* [2010] EWCA Civ 1277 distinguishing between a police authority which could delegate under

borrowing of money.[44] Statutory powers of delegation are necessarily very numerous. Ministers' wide powers to provide by Order that certain of their functions should be exercised by another person (typically a commercial company) as part of the contracting out of their functions may also be specifically noted.[45]

Powers to delegate will be construed in the same way as other powers, and will not therefore extend to sub-delegation in the absence of some express or implied provision to that effect. The delegate must also keep within the bounds of the power actually delegated, which may be narrower than that possessed by the delegating authority; it will be no defence that that authority could, had it wished, have delegated wider power.[46]

A statutory power to delegate functions, even if expressed in wide general terms, will not necessarily extend to everything. In the case of judicial and disciplinary functions the court may be disposed to construe general powers of delegation restrictively.[47]

A statutory power to delegate will normally include a power to revoke the delegation when desired.[48] While the delegation subsists it may be arguable whether the delegating authority is denuded of its power or is able to exercise it concurrently with the delegate. This question arose where under statutory authority the executive committee of a county council delegated to a sub-committee its powers to make regulations for the control of rabies; but before the sub-committee had done anything the executive committee, without revoking the delegation, itself issued regulations for the muzzling of dogs. These regulations were upheld, but on inconsistent grounds, one judge holding that the executive committee had resumed its powers and the other that it had never parted with them, and that 'the word "delegate" means little more than an agent'.[49] In a later case the latter view prevailed, on the ground that 'one cannot divest oneself of one's statutory duties'.[50] But the contrary was held by the Court of Appeal where a minister had formally delegated to local authorities his power to requisition houses. By doing this he had for the time being divested himself of his powers, so that an invalid requisition by the local authority could not be cured by their acting in his name; and the court rejected the contention that delegation was a form of agency.[51] The Employment Appeal Tribunal has followed this latter decision holding that 'delegation does imply denudation' so that the Minister for the Civil Service who had delegated his power to determine pay and conditions of civil servants to individual departments lacked the power to act concurrently.[52] The Local Government

---

s. 101 (s. 101 being extended to police authorities by s. 107(3)) and 'the existing members of the police authority' who had power to appoint independent members under reg. 9 of the Police Authority Regulations 2008/630 but no power to delegate (para. 22). Note also the 1972 Act, ss. 101(1)(1A)–(1B) which precludes a local authority from delegating a function to another local authority where that function is the responsibility of that authority's executive. See above, p. 94 for 'executive arrangements'.

[44] s. 101(6).

[45] Under the Deregulation and Contracting Out Act 1994 (discussed above, p. 40), s. 69. The power is subject to certain limitations (no delegation of judicial or legislative functions, or powers of search or seizure or restrictions on personal liberty (s. 71)). See below, p. 675 on 'contracting out'.

[46] *Cook* v. *Ward* (1877) 2 CPD 255; *Blackpool Cpn* v. *Locker* [1948] 1 KB 349.

[47] *General Medical Council* v. *UK Dental Board* [1936] Ch 41.

[48] But not retrospectively: *Battelley* v. *Finsbury Borough Council* (1958) 56 LGR 165 (council unable to repudiate appointment of employee made by committee under delegated power). For revocability see above, p. 191, and *Manton* v. *Brighton Cpn* [1951] 2 KB 393.

[49] *Huth* v. *Clark* (1890) 25 QBD 391 (Lord Coleridge CJ and Wills J).

[50] *Manton* v. *Brighton Cpn* (above). See similarly *Gordon, Dadds & Co* v. *Morris* [1945] 2 All ER 618.

[51] *Blackpool Cpn* v. *Locker* [1948] 1 KB 349.

[52] *Department for Environment, Food and Rural Affairs* v. *Robertson and ors* [2003] UKEAT 0273_03_1012 (Burton J). But the decision is strongly criticised [2005] *JR* 84 (Bailey). The Court of Appeal upheld the decision of the EAT ([2005] EWCA Civ 138) but found it unnecessary to express a view on this point (para. 41, Mummery LJ).

Act 1972 expressly preserves the powers of a local authority concurrently with those delegated to its committees etc.[53]

GOVERNMENT DEPARTMENTS

Departments of the central government have the benefit of a special rule ('the *Carltona* principle') whereby officials may act in their ministers' names without any formal delegation of authority. When powers are conferred upon ministers who have charge of large departments, it is obvious that they will often not be exercised by the minister in person. Parliament is well aware of this, and ministerial powers are therefore taken to be exercisable by officials of the minister's department acting in his name in the customary way.[54] In the leading case the owner of a factory challenged a wartime requisitioning order made on behalf of the Commissioners of Works (as the ministry was then called). The Commissioners had power to requisition land 'if it appears to that authority to be necessary or expedient to do so'. But they themselves never met or transacted business as a body: their powers were exercised entirely by their officials. The requisitioning order was signed by an assistant secretary, who was solely in charge of the case, and it was never considered by any of the Commissioners. The Court of Appeal held that this procedure was open to no legal objection.[55] Lord Greene MR said:[56]

> It cannot be supposed that this regulation meant that, in each case, the minister in person should direct his mind to the matter. The duties imposed upon ministers and the powers given to ministers are normally exercised under the authority of the ministers by responsible officials of the department. Public business could not be carried on if that were not the case. Constitutionally, the decision of such an official is, of course, the decision of the minister. The minister is responsible. It is he who must answer before Parliament for anything that his officials have done under his authority.

Consequently many ministerial powers are exercised by officials who recite 'I am directed by the Minister', 'the Minister is of the opinion', and so forth, when in reality they are acting on their own initiative. If the proper official is acting in his capacity as such, his assumption of ministerial authority is lawful.[57] This doctrine is assumed to extend equally to legislative powers, since it is common practice for officials to issue statutory regulations under powers vested in their ministers.[58]

Strictly speaking, there is no delegation in these cases. Delegation requires a distinct act by which the power is conferred upon some person not previously competent to exercise it. But the authority of officials to act in their ministers' names derives from a general rule of law and not from any particular act of delegation.[59] Legally and constitutionally

---

[53] s. 101(4).

[54] The doctrine is, it seems, 'a common law constitutional power' per Lord Donaldson in the Court of Appeal in *R* v. *Secretary of State for Home Affairs ex p Oladehinde* [1991] 1 AC 254 at 282. As such the principle applied equally to prerogative powers (ibid.).

[55] *Carltona Ltd* v. *Commissioners of Works* [1943] 2 All ER 560. See similarly *Point of Ayr Collieries Ltd* v. *Lloyd-George* [1943] 2 All ER 546; *Re Golden Chemical Products Ltd* [1976] Ch 300.

[56] In the *Carltona* case at 563.

[57] See also *Lewisham BC* v. *Roberts* [1949] 2 KB 608; *Woollett* v. *Minister of Agriculture and Fisheries* [1955] 1 QB 103; *R* v. *Skinner* [1968] 2 QB 700. For the position when the official is not authorised see below, p. 282.

[58] This is the practice, for certain classes of orders, in the Department of the Environment, the Department of Trade, and the Ministry of Agriculture, Fisheries and Food.

[59] *Lewisham BC* v. *Roberts* (above); *R* v. *Skinner* (above).

the act of the official is the act of the minister, without any need for specific authorisation in advance or ratification afterwards.[60] Even where there are express statutory powers of delegation they are not in fact employed as between the minister and his own officials.[61] Such legal formalities would be out of place within the walls of a government department, as is recognised by Parliament's practice of conferring powers upon ministers in their own names. The case is of course different where the official is to be empowered to act in his own name rather than the minister's. Thus the power for inspectors to decide certain kinds of planning appeals must be delegated by the minister by statutory instrument, as required by the Act.[62]

The limits of this doctrine must be noticed. It applies in principle only to the departments of the central government, and not therefore to local government authorities and other statutory bodies,[63] as is plain from the examples already given.[64] It does not, it seems, apply to the police.[65] Even within the central government the powers conferred upon a specified minister could not be exercised in his name by another minister or the latter's officials,[66] until delegation to 'any other servant of the Crown' was authorised by statute in 1992.[67] There may be cases where the power is of such a special kind that the minister must exercise it personally and not through officials.[68] A wartime detention order has been assumed to be one such matter;[69] an order for the deportation of an alien was held to be another in 1918.[70] But in 1990, without reference to the case of 1918, the House of Lords held that the power to make decisions to deport aliens could be exercised on the authority of the Home Secretary by immigration officers, who were Home Office civil servants and not holders of statutory offices.[71] This decision must throw doubt on the indication in an

---

[60] See *R v. Home Secretary ex p Oladehinde* [1991] 1 AC 254 at 284 'The civil servant acts not as the delegate, but as the *alter ego*, of the Secretary of State' (Sir John Donaldson). Cf. Freedland [1996] *PL* 16 at 22 deprecating the *alter ego* fiction and preferring a rule of construction that a power granted to a minister is granted to his department.

[61] See *Carltona Ltd v. Commissioners of Works* (above); *Lewisham BC v. Roberts* (above).

[62] Town and Country Planning Act 1990, 6th Sched.

[63] And this was so held in *R (S and anor) v. Independent Appeal Panel of Birmingham City Council* [2006] EWHC 2369 (Admin) (para. 49, Beatson J relying on the account in this book). But no mention was made of the *Birmingham Justices* case discussed below.   [64] Above, p. 260.

[65] *Nelms v. Roe* [1970] 1 WLR 4. Here it was held that while police officers who normally handled traffic cases had implied delegated authority to sign notices (requiring the identification of drivers) on behalf of a chief constable (who was invested with the statutory power to require identification), but that the police cannot claim the benefit of the *Carltona* doctrine. But this was disapproved in *R (Chief Constable of the West Midlands Police) v. Birmingham Justices* [2002] EWHC 1087 (Admin), as discussed below, p. 268.

[66] But powers conferred upon 'the Secretary of State' are exercisable by any Secretary of State: above, p. 36. And see the discussion of the *Staff Side* case, above, p. 271.

[67] Civil Service (Management Functions) Act 1992. See *Jackson Stansfield & Sons v. Butterworth* [1948] 2 All ER 558, a case which revealed much legal and administrative confusion. Clearer guidance is given by *Lavender & Sons Ltd v. Minister of Housing and Local Government* [1970] 1 WLR 1231, holding that one minister may not share his powers with another: see below, p. 269.

[68] But the *Carltona* principle (or any other principle) does not allow the ignorance of a minister (who makes an order not knowing a crucial fact) to be remedied by the knowledge of his civil servants who advised him without passing on the crucial fact: *R (National Association of Health Stores) v. Department of Health* [2005] EWCA Civ 154: 'It would be an embarrassment both for government and for the courts if we were to hold that a minister or a civil servant could lawfully take a decision on a matter he or she knew nothing about because one or more officials in the department knew all about it' (Sedley LJ at para. 26).

[69] *Liversidge v. Anderson* [1942] AC 206 (see Lord Maugham at 224). But see *Re Golden Chemical Products Ltd* [1976] Ch 300 at 310 (personal exercise of discretion by responsible minister not a 'legal necessity' but in some cases 'a political necessity' (Brightman J)).

[70] *R v. Chiswick Police Station Superintendent ex p Sacksteder* [1918] 1 KB 578 at 585, 591.

[71] *R v. Home Secretary ex p Oladehinde* [1991] 1 AC 254. See also *R v. Home Secretary ex p Doody* [1994] 1 AC 531 (fixing of prisoner's 'tariff period' for parole may be delegated to junior minister).

earlier case that a departmental official could not be authorised to make an order for the return of a fugitive offender.[72]

THE EXTENSION OF THE *CARLTONA* PRINCIPLE BEYOND CENTRAL GOVERNMENT? THE EMERGENCE OF A DOCTRINE OF IMPLIED INEVITABLE POWER TO DELEGATE

Recent decisions, however, lay the foundations for an extension of the *Carltona* principle beyond the powers of central government. In principle there should be no such extension. Local authorities (or other autonomous office holders like chief constables), unlike Ministers, are not accountable to Parliament for all done in their name, so the foundation for the *Carltona* principle is absent. Nonetheless, Sedley LJ held, in a case about whether a chief constable's power to apply to court for an ASBO might be exercised by a subordinate, that there was a distinction to be drawn between 'those offices which are the apex of an organisation itself composed of office-holders or otherwise hierarchically structured, and those offices designated by Parliament because of the personal qualifications of the individual holder'.[73] In the former case the subordinate officers could act on behalf of their superior to whom Parliament had granted the power and who would take legal responsibility for its exercise. In the latter only the officer actually empowered could act. On this approach legal responsibility, not accountability to Parliament, determines the reach of the *Carltona* principle; and it thus extends beyond central government.[74]

This extension of *Carltona* is driven by the need to ensure that administrative efficiency is not undermined by the inability of the chief constable to delegate appropriate powers. This need, however, is better met by the development of a doctrine of implied delegation as was done in a leading decision of the Divisional Court.[75] The case concerned whether the Metropolitan Police Commissioner could delegate his power to set conditions on demonstrations in the vicinity of Parliament.[76] In the absence of express statutory authorisation the Commissioner delegated this power to a Superintendent. Lord Phillips CJ said:

> Where a statutory power is conferred on an officer who is himself the creature of statute, whether that officer has the power to delegate must depend upon the interpretation of the relevant statute or statutes. Where the responsibilities of the office created by statute are such that delegation is inevitable, there will be an implied power to delegate. In such circumstances there will be a presumption, where additional statutory powers and duties are conferred, that there is a power to delegate unless the statute conferring them, expressly or by implication, provides to the contrary.[77]

Applying this doctrine of 'inevitable delegation' the court concluded: 'When the practicalities are considered it is plain that Parliament cannot have intended that the

---

[72] See *R v. Brixton Prison Governor ex p Enahoro* [1963] 2 QB 455 (point assumed but not decided). See also *Minister for Aboriginal Affairs v. Peko-Wallsend Ltd* (1986) 60 ALJR 560.

[73] Sedley LJ in *R (Chief Constable of West Midlands Police) v. Birmingham Justices* (above).

[74] Thus in the *Birmingham Justices*'s case it was held that the Chief Constable's power to make application for an anti-social behaviour order under the Crime and Disorder Act 1998 could be exercised by his subordinate officers.

[75] *Director of Public Prosecutions v. Haw* [2007] EWHC 1931. The provision involved was the Serious Organised Crime and Police Act 2005, s. 134.

[76] Knowing breach of a condition was an offence (s. 134(7)).   [77] Para. 33.

Commissioner should determine the conditions himself';[78] thus the power to set the conditions could be delegated.

Although Lord Phillips said that this approach was 'in practice, indistinguishable from one in which the *Carltona* principle applies'[79] the conceptual differences are obvious from this discussion. Indeed, adoption of a doctrine of 'inevitable delegation' raises no difficulties of principle and is preferable to the awkward extension of *Carltona*. Of course, the courts must be vigilant to ensure that the inevitability of delegation does not slip into the convenience of delegation. Thus a chief constable's power to dismiss a constable must be exercised by the chief constable.[80]

The application of the *Carltona* principle to executive agencies has been persuasively criticised on the ground that ministerial responsibility for such agencies is too weak to justify its application.[81] Administrative convenience should not justify a substitution of legal responsibility for accountability to Parliament.

SURRENDER, ABDICATION, DICTATION

POWER IN THE WRONG HANDS

Closely akin to delegation, and scarcely distinguishable from it in some cases, is any arrangement by which a power conferred upon one authority is in substance exercised by another. The proper authority may share its power with someone else, or may allow someone else to dictate to it by declining to act without their consent or by submitting to their wishes or instructions. The effect then is that the discretion conferred by Parliament is exercised, at least in part, by the wrong authority, and the resulting decision is ultra vires and void. So strict are the courts in applying this principle that they condemn some administrative arrangements which must seem quite natural and proper to those who make them. In this class might be included the case of the cinema licensing authority which, by requiring films to be approved by the British Board of Film Censors, was held to have surrendered its power of control[82] and also the case of the Police Complaints Board, which acted as if it were bound by a decision of the Director of Public Prosecutions when only required to 'have regard' to it.[83] This doctrine has even been applied to voting by local councillors.[84]

Ministers and their departments have several times fallen foul of the same rule, no doubt equally to their surprise. The Minister of Housing and Local Government made it a rule to refuse planning permission for gravel-working on top-class agricultural land whenever the application was opposed by the Minister of Agriculture. The court held that this was to put the decisive power into the hands of the wrong minister and that a decision so taken must be quashed.[85] A decision of the Home Secretary that a prisoner should serve

---

[78] Para. 36.   [79] Para. 33.

[80] *Austin* v. *Chief Constable of Surrey Police* [2010] EWHC 266. And see see *R* v. *Chief Constable of Greater Manchester Police ex p. Lainton* [2000] ICR 1324, para. 28.

[81] Freedland [1996] *PL* 19 at 25–30. But see *R* v. *Secretary of State for Social Security ex p. Sherwin* (1996) 32 BMLR 1 where the *Carltona* principle was applied to a decision of an official in the Benefits Agency not to pay a certain premium. Kennedy LJ said: 'the creation of the Benefits Agency has had no effect whatsoever on the operation of the *Carltona* principle'.   [82] *Ellis* v. *Dubowski*, above, p. 262.

[83] *R* v. *Police Complaints Board ex p Madden* [1983] 1 WLR 447.

[84] *R* v. *Waltham Forest LBC ex p Baxter* [1988] QB 419 (CA), upholding votes based on party policy.

[85] *Lavender & Sons Ltd* v. *Minister of Housing and Local Government* [1970] 1 WLR 1231. For an example of an official abdicating his discretion to a minister see *Simms Motor Units Ltd* v. *Minister of Housing and Local Government* [1946] 2 All ER 201.

a term of at least twenty years was quashed because he acted 'as a rubber stamp' on the advice of the judge or of the parole board without making his own decision.[86]

Clear-cut cases of unlawful dictation have occurred in other jurisdictions where ministers have attempted to interfere for political reasons. In one, the Premier of Quebec gave instructions for the cancellation of a liquor licence where the licensee was supporting an unpopular section of the community;[87] in another, an Indian minister was alleged to have procured the taking-over by the state of businesses belonging to his political opponents.[88] If the minister's intervention is in fact the effective cause, and if the power to act belongs to a body which ought to act independently, the action taken is invalid on the ground of external dictation as well as on the obvious grounds of bad faith or abuse of power.[89]

PERMISSIBLE GUIDANCE AND THE OBJECTIVE ASSESSMENTS OF OTHERS

Clearly these rules ought not to be carried to the length of preventing one government department from consulting another, or of preventing government agencies from acting in accordance with government policy. There must always be a difference between seeking advice and then genuinely exercising one's own discretion, on the one hand, and, on the other hand, acting obediently or automatically under someone else's advice or directions. A licensing authority, for instance, may quite properly take account of government policy in its decisions, provided that it genuinely decides each case itself. A borderline case divided opinions in the High Court of Australia where the majority held that the Director-General of Civil Aviation might refuse import licences for aircraft following the government's policy of not allowing new operators to enter the interstate air freight business.[90]

Similarly, the Audit Commission did not abdicate its discretionary powers when, in assessing the performance of local authorities across the range of their functions, it accepted the rating accorded to councils by the Commission for Social Care Inspection (CSCI) in respect of their social services performance. The process by which the councils were rated by the CSCI was objective. The audit commission had simply 'adopted as its own a series of weightings, produced by the CSCI, which result in a star rating [for the council] in an entirely predictable way.... It is not delegating its decision in any individual case to the CSCI, since the CSCI does not make any such individual decision once it has arrived at the "scores".'[91]

A similar point arises when a decision-maker is obliged in making their decision to have 'due regard' to a relevant consideration (for instance, gender equality) under the Equality Act 2010.[92] These duties are non-delegable and continuing[93] but that does not mean that a third party cannot fulfil the 'due regard' duty provided the 'public authority

---

[86] R v. Home Secretary ex p Walsh [1992] COD 240.

[87] Roncarelli v. Duplessis (1959) 16 DLR (2d) 689 (licensee repeatedly provided bail for Jehovah's Witnesses).   [88] Rowjee v. Andhra Pradesh, AIR 1964 SC 962.

[89] See below, p. 295.   [90] R v. Anderson ex p Ipec-Air Pty Ltd (1965) 113 CLR 177.

[91] Audit Commission for England and Wales v. Ealing London Borough Council [2005] EWCA Civ 556 (para. 27, Keene LJ giving the judgment of the court). The Commission had adopted a rule, not challenged in these proceedings, of penalising sharply a council that was rated poorly by the CSCI. For discussion see [2005] JR 216 (Braier).

[92] These Public Sector Equality Duties ('PSED') are discussed more fully below, p. 325.

[93] R (Brown) v. Secretary of State for Work and Pensions [2008] EWHC 3158 (Aitken LJ), paras. 94–5.

maintains a proper supervision over the third party to ensure it carries out its "due regard" duty'.[94] Moreover, the non-delegable nature of the duties does not prevent the operation of the *Carltona* principle.[95]

Thus in a doubtful case[96] the Secretary of State for Work and Pensions was obliged in carrying out his functions to have 'due regard' to the need 'to promote equality of opportunity between men and women' in determining how police pensions were adjusted for inflation.[97] In fact the equality assessment was carried out by the Treasury and not specifically drawn to the minister's attention when he made the disputed orders. Elias LJ, upholding the orders, said:

> a Minister may rely on workings and a review of effects carried out within his department to satisfy the 'due regard' requirement... without having personally to read an impact assessment, so long as the task has been assigned to officials at an appropriate level of seniority or expertise. Equally... the 'due regard' duty can be discharged by a Minister if he can be satisfied that the relevant equality assessment has been carried out by another government department as well or better placed than his own to undertake the task, particularly where that other department has policy responsibility in relation to the effects under review.[98]

But a later case[99] was more cautious. The case concerned the Secretary of State's decision to reduce the amount of unspent capital grants (for child care and related purposes) from the current year that could be carried forward into the next year. The decision was challenged in part on the ground of non-compliance with the equality duties. Mitting J said that the

> Secretary of State [could] have relied on consideration given by officials to the equality duties who then reported to him in a briefing note that, having given that proper consideration, they were satisfied that the duty to eliminate unlawful discrimination or promote equality of opportunity had been fulfilled... the Secretary of State could... within his own department delegate the task of discharging some of his functions to officials. What is prohibited... is the delegation of that responsibility to outsiders, whether they be another department of state or public authority or private concern.[100]

The court did not accept that 'due regard' had been given to the duty to eliminate unlawful discrimination or promote equality of opportunity.

OVER-RIGID POLICIES

POLICY AND PRECEDENT

An authority can fail to give its mind to a case, and thus fail to exercise its discretion lawfully, by blindly following a policy laid down in advance.[101] It is a fundamental rule for the

[94] Para. 94.   [95] The *Essex County Council* case, below, para. 42.
[96] *R (Staff Side of the Police Negotiating Board)* v. *Secretary of State for Work and Pensions* [2011] EWHC 3175.
[97] The relevant statutory provision at the time was the Sex Discrimination Act 1975, s. 76A.
[98] Para. 89.
[99] *R (Essex County Council)* v. *Secretary of State for Education* [2012] EWHC 1460. The *Staff Side* case was not referred to.
[100] Para. 42. The assessment had not been carried out by another department in this case, so the remark is *obiter*.
[101] For discussion, see (1972) 18 *McGill LJ* 310 (H. L. Molot); [1976] *PL* 332 (D. J. Galligan); [2002] *PL* 111 (C. Hilson); [2009] *JR* 73 (C. J. S. Knight). Note particularly the discussion, paras. 18–23, of formally flexible but substantively rigid policies (and their converse, the formally rigid but substantively flexible policy).

exercise of discretionary power that discretion must be brought to bear on every case: each one must be considered on its own merits and decided as the public interest requires at the time. The Greater London Council was criticised for disregard of this principle when it proceeded to make a large subsidy to the London bus and underground services as a matter of course because the ruling party had promised to do so in their election campaign.[102] They regarded themselves as irrevocably committed in advance, whereas their duty was to use their discretion. Nor may a local authority lawfully refuse all applications for housing for children of families considered to be 'intentionally homeless',[103] since the power to provide housing implies a duty to consider the different circumstances of each child.[104] Nor, for the same reason, may they automatically proceed to recondition sub-standard houses as soon as the owner has failed to comply with an improvement notice.[105] Nor may they refuse to repay rates overpaid if their policy is based upon advice which interprets their statutory discretionary power too narrowly.[106] Where the Secretary of State's policy was to disallow all merely local objections to the allocation of land for gipsies, the court held it unlawful for undue rigidity.[107] The Court of Appeal has held that a local council's resolution might be quashed if councillors voted for it in obedience to the orders of their political party, but not if they conscientiously decided to prefer the party's policy to their own opinions.[108] Another example was where the Home Office took a decision to delay consideration of older asylum applications in order that they might meet the targets set for consideration of the more recent applications. The Court of Appeal considered this a textbook example of unlawful fettering; the decision-makers were prevented by the policy from considering individual cases on their merits.[109]

In enforcing this rule the courts are underlining the difference between judicial and administrative processes. The legal rights of litigants are decided according to legal rules and precedents so that like cases are treated alike. But if an administrative authority acts in this way its decision is ultra vires and void. It is not allowed to 'pursue consistency at the expense of the merits of individual cases'.[110] This doctrine is applied even to statutory tribunals, despite their resemblance to courts of law.[111] But it does not apply to prerogative powers.[112]

---

[102] *Bromley LBC* v. *Greater London Council* [1983] 1 AC 768 (Lords Diplock and Brandon).

[103] See above, p. 57.

[104] *A-G ex rel Tilley* v. *Wandsworth LBC* [1981] 1 WLR 854 (declaration that resolution was unlawful); cf. *R* v. *Accrington Youth Court ex p Flood* (1997) 10 Admin LR 17 (over-rigid policy of sending young offenders to remand centres); *R* v. *North West Lancashire Health Authority ex p A* [2000] 1 WLR 977 (over-rigid policy of refusing medical treatment for transsexuals).   [105] *Elliott* v. *Brighton BC* (1980) 79 LGR 506.

[106] *R* v. *Rochdale MBC ex p Cromer Ring Mill Ltd* [1982] 3 All ER 761. See also the *Tower Hamlets ex p Chetnik Developments* case, below, p. 678.

[107] *R* v. *Secretary of State for the Environment ex p Hatton BC* (1983) 82 LGR 662; and see *R* v. *Home Secretary ex p Bennett*, The Times, 18 August 1986 (Home Office circular set unduly rigid criteria for approval of police rent allowance applications).

[108] *R* v. *Waltham Forest LBC ex p Baxter* [1988] QB 419 (no unlawful fettering of discretion found).

[109] *Home Secretary* v. *R (S)* [2007] EWCA Civ 546 (Carnwath LJ, para. 50).

[110] *Merchandise Transport Ltd* v. *British Transport Commission* [1962] 2 QB 173 at 193. But where the tribunal has adopted a policy it will often be under a duty to apply it consistently. It cannot arbitrarily decide not to follow the policy. See the discussion, above, p. 318. This point is particularly important in the context of legitimate expectations, above, p. 456.

[111] See *R* v. *Greater Birmingham Appeal Tribunal ex p Simper* [1974] QB 543 (tribunal applied rule of thumb instead of exercising discretion: decision quashed); *R* v. *Criminal Injuries Compensation Board ex p RJC*, The Times, 21 January 1978 (discretion fettered by policy statement).

[112] *R (Elias)* v. *Secretary of State for Defence* [2006] EWCA Civ 1293. The official wielding a prerogative power then may lay down a rule (not a policy) that admits of no exception and thus leaves no scope for the argument that exceptional circumstances justify a departure from the rule. The making of the rule will of

Just how far they may enforce a fixed policy is often a difficult question for authorities granting licences or permits. A clear instance was where an applicant for permission to sell pamphlets in public parks for the benefit of the blind was told that the Council had decided to grant no such permits, and could make no exception even in the most deserving case. The court regarded that 'not as the adoption of a policy in the exercise of a discretion but as a refusal to exercise any discretion',[113] and granted mandamus to compel the Council to consider the application.[114] It did not follow that they must give permission, or that they might not follow a policy: their duty was merely to exercise their discretion in each case, and not to shut the door indiscriminately either on all applicants or on applicants who did not conform to some particular requirement.

Consequently a local education authority may follow its own rules in allotting pupils to schools, provided that its motives are not unreasonable, capricious or irrelevant, and provided that it is ready to consider exceptional cases.[115] Where it is at liberty to make a choice between conflicting policies, it may decide to make no exceptions, as where it adopts a policy of making all schools in its area into comprehensive schools and abolishing all grammar schools.[116] But even then it is in a stronger position if it has listened fairly to the objections of parents and others concerned. Similarly, a decision-maker may depart from his usual policy provided he acts fairly and rationally and gives those adversely affected an opportunity to make representations why the usual policy should be followed.[117]

LICENSING AUTHORITIES

The rule has often been canvassed in liquor licensing cases where the licensing justices have adopted some restrictive policy, for example for reducing the number of licences in their area.[118] If the justices refuse renewal of a licence under some new policy without considering the application on its merits, their decision will be quashed.[119] But there can be no objection to a declared policy provided that the application is properly heard and considered in each case. Thus where the justices announced publicly that they would renew restricted licences only subject to the same restrictions, save in very exceptional cases, and subsequently decided a case saying: 'The bench carefully considered the application but is not prepared to alter the policy', the court upheld its decision.[120] The court is careful not to inhibit public authorities from laying down policies, since consistent

course, if justiciable (see above, p. 443) be subject to judicial review. The argument that it is irrational not to allow for exceptional circumstances may sometimes succeed. For discussion see Knight, as above, para. 8.

[113] Quoted from Bankes LJ in *R v. Port of London Authority ex p Kynoch Ltd* [1919] 1 KB 176 at 185.

[114] *R v. London County Council ex p Corrie* [1918] 1 KB 68. Cf. *Sagnata Investments Ltd v. Norwich Cpn* [1971] 1 QB 614 (rigid policy against amusement arcades: no exercise of discretion. This was decided on appeal, not on judicial review). For a case of statutory permission to adopt a rigid policy of refusal see *R v. Herrod ex p Leeds City District Council* [1976] QB 540.

[115] *Cumings v. Birkenhead Cpn* [1972] Ch 12, where Lord Denning MR expounds the rules as to policy.

[116] *Smith v. Inner London Education Authority* [1978] 1 All ER 411.

[117] *R (Mullen) v. Home Secretary* [2004] UKHL 18, [2004] 2 WLR 1140 (Home Secretary, after allowing opportunity for representations, departed from announced policy in regard to ex gratia payments to the victims of 'miscarriages of justice' (applicant was guilty of the crime for which he was convicted but appeal succeeded since his presence in UK for trial secured by executive misconduct): departure upheld).

[118] *Boyle v. Wilson* [1907] AC 45.

[119] *R v. Windsor Licensing Justices ex p Hodes* [1983] 1 WLR 685.

[120] *R v. Torquay Licensing Justices ex p Brockman* [1951] 2 KB 784, distinguishing *R v. Walsall Justices* (1854) 18 JP 757 (refusal to hear any application for new licences) and following *R v. Holborn Licensing Justices* (1926) 42 TLR 778 (fixed policy but case duly considered).

administrative policies are not only permissible but highly desirable. And it is no less desirable that policies should be made public, so that applicants may know what to expect. But the policies must naturally be based on proper and relevant grounds. The justices erred, therefore, in refusing an occasional licence under a policy of never allowing more than two such licences a year to any one applicant.[121] Even though they considered the case and were prepared to make exceptions, they acted on a policy different from that which the Act imposed upon them, which was public convenience. Similarly where the justices had refused a licence to sell liquor to one theatre, and for the sake of consistency felt obliged to refuse one to another theatre which had enjoyed it for fifty years previously, the decision was set aside since the statutory purpose was 'for ensuring order and decency' and the justices' motive was primarily to enforce consistency.[122] These decisions are merely examples of the abuse of discretionary power, discussed elsewhere.[123] None of them is in any way hostile to the adoption of a policy as such.

Bankes LJ stated the basic distinction in a frequently cited judgment. He contrasted two classes of cases: 'cases where a tribunal in the honest exercise of its discretion has adopted a policy, and, without refusing to hear an applicant, intimates to him what its policy is, and that after hearing him it will in accordance with its policy decide against him, unless there is something exceptional in his case'; and 'cases where a tribunal has passed a rule, or come to a determination, not to hear any application of a particular character by whomsoever made'.[124] Accordingly the Port of London Authority, which was empowered to grant or withhold permission for the construction of docks, was allowed to enforce its policy of refusing permission, after due consideration, in cases where the new dock would come into competition with its own docks.

MINISTERS AND NATIONAL POLICY

Ministerial policies are subject to the same principles as the policies of other authorities. Accordingly it was unobjectionable for the Minister of Housing and Local Government, in deciding planning appeals, to follow a policy of discouraging development likely to interfere with the Jodrell Bank radio telescope provided that he judged each individual case fairly.[125] The Home Secretary was likewise entitled to pursue a policy of discrimination against foreign students of 'scientology' by refusing to renew their residence permits, subject to the same qualification;[126] and he might change his policy so as to refuse release on licence ('parole') to certain classes of prisoners in all but the most exceptional cases, so long as each case was examined individually.[127] The Home Secretary fettered his powers unduly when he announced a policy of considering the release of life sentence prisoners on certain grounds only, but he remedied the fault by a later announcement that he would take account of exceptional circumstances.[128] He committed the same fault when he fixed a rigid tariff-period of fifteen years for the minimum term of imprisonment of two boy

---

[121] R v. Rotherham Licensing Justices ex p Chapman (1939) 55 TLR 718 (explained in the Torquay case, above). See also Perilly v. Tower Hamlets London Borough Council [1973] QB 9 (mistaken rule of 'first come first served').   [122] R v. Flintshire CC Licensing Committee ex p Barrett [1957] 1 QB 350.

[123] See particularly R v. Birmingham Licensing Planning Committee ex p Kennedy [1972] 2 QB 140 (unlawful requirement that licences be purchased), below, p. 338.

[124] R v. Port of London Authority ex p Kynoch Ltd [1919] 1 KB 176 at 182.

[125] Stringer v. Ministry of Housing and Local Government [1970] 1 WLR 1281.

[126] Schmidt v. Home Secretary [1969] 2 Ch 149.

[127] Re Findlay [1985] AC 318. Opinions in the Divisional Court and the Court of Appeal were divided.

[128] R v. Home Secretary ex p Hindley [2000] 2 WLR 730.

murderers instead of fixing a term which would be provisional and always reviewable.[129] The law was earlier reviewed by the House of Lords in another case where the Board of Trade had made it a rule to refuse all applications for investment grants for items costing less than £25.[130] The claimants had invested over £4m. in oxygen cylinders, but since each cylinder cost only about £20 the Board refused a grant, after giving full consideration to the case. The Act said merely that the Board 'may make' a grant. The House of Lords upheld the Board's action. Lord Reid said: 'if the Minister thinks that policy or good administration requires the operation of some limiting rule, I find nothing to stop him'. He added the familiar proviso: 'provided that the authority is always willing to listen to anyone with something new to say—of course I do not mean to say that there need be an oral hearing'. But he sounded a caveat against taking Bankes LJ's formula literally in every case; and Lord Dilhorne carried this further, saying: 'it seems somewhat pointless and a waste of time that the Board should have to consider applications which are bound as a result of its policy decision to fail'. There may thus be room for some relaxation of the requirement of consideration of every application on its merits, at any rate in cases involving a national policy where applications are multitudinous. And there is no real difference in this context between a 'policy' and a 'rule'.

In a strongly contrasting case a minister resolved to turn a deaf ear to all pleas for a change of policy and his decision was quashed.[131] He had consulted local authorities generally before obtaining statutory power to reduce the central government's rate support grant to those whose expenditure was in his view excessive. After the Act was passed he refused to receive further representations and decided on reductions in the case of several authorities. He was held to have fettered his discretion unlawfully by settling and announcing his policy before he obtained his powers and then refusing to consider any appeals for exceptions. He had disregarded his duty 'to listen to any objector who shows that he may have something new to say'. He had also disregarded the principles of natural justice.[132]

Sometimes a minister will have power to make regulations covering the same ground as some policy which he has adopted, and it may then be argued that he should enforce his policy openly by making regulations, which may be subject to Parliamentary scrutiny, rather than covertly by exercising discretion in each case. This argument was rejected by the Court of Session in a case where the Secretary of State had refused to approve the appointment of a chief constable on the ground that he came from within the local force.[133] The Secretary of State had both a discretionary power to withhold consent and also power to prescribe the qualifications of chief constables by regulation, but he had made no regulation embodying his policy for rejecting internal appointments. There might perhaps be cases where a regulation-making power could be held to exclude administrative discretion; but where both powers are conferred by the same statute it is reasonable to allow

---

[129] *R v. Home Secretary ex p Venables* [1998] AC 407. Compare *R v. Accrington Youth Court ex p Flood* (1997) 10 Admin LR 17 (rigid policy of sending female young offenders to remand centres instead of to young offender institutions held unlawful).

[130] *British Oxygen Co Ltd v. Board of Trade* [1971] AC 610; cf. *Kilmarnock Magistrates v. Secretary of State for Scotland* (below).

[131] *R v. Secretary of State for the Environment ex p Brent LBC* [1982] QB 593 (Divisional Court).

[132] See below, p. 463.

[133] *Kilmarnock Magistrates v. Secretary of State for Scotland* 1961 SC 350 (Secretary of State's decision upheld). This question has been much litigated in the United States: see Schwartz and Wade, *Legal Control of Government*, 93.

the minister to choose between them; and it is, indeed, his duty to decide every case as he believes the public interest requires at the time.

In another case an authority had statutory power to set the criteria it would use in deciding whether to issue a licence to an individual that permitted employment as a door supervisor ('bouncer').[134] This was a rule-making power and the setting of a rigid rule excluding all convicted of serious criminal offences from consideration was upheld.[135]

INDISCRIMINATE ACTION

It undoubtedly remains true that the court will not accept the indiscriminate use of a power where cases ought to be considered on their own merits. If a local authority has power to refer furnished lettings to a rent tribunal, in order to obtain adjudication of the rent, it may not adopt a rule of referring all tenancies in any block of flats where two or more reductions of rent have previously been ordered, whether or not the tenants have complained.[136] For it is inherent in the power to refer that there should be some reasonable and specified ground for doing so in each particular case. If the authority has power to require owners of unfit houses to repair them, or else to repair them itself at the owner's expense, it may not give standing orders that the latter course shall always be taken without regard to individual circumstances.[137] There can be no substitute for the genuine exercise of discretion on every occasion.

CONTEXT, RIGIDITY AND THE HUMAN RIGHTS ACT

We have already seen that the context in which a policy is applied may affect its rigidity. Where, for instance, the applications are numerous and very similar the policy may almost harden into a rule.[138] On the other hand, where the applications are few in number and the circumstances are very different, greater flexibility will be required. Where the fundamental rights of individuals are involved, the Human Rights Act 1998 may now require a greater degree of flexibility. The decision not to follow the policy will need to be properly made; and in doing this the decision-maker will need to show, as explained elsewhere,[139] that any interference with human rights was proportionate to legitimate aims justifying their restriction.

This was exemplified in a case about the prison service's policy of separating imprisoned mothers from their babies at the age of 18 months.[140] In a narrow range of exceptional circumstances—primarily where the mother would shortly be released—the policy would not be applied. But, because of the human rights context,[141] the Court of Appeal held that the policy should be more flexibly applied. In each case the interference in the child's family life would have to be justified and shown to be proportionate to the legitimate aims of the policy.

---

[134] *Nicholds v. Security Industry Authority* [2006] EWHC 1792, [2007] 1 WLR 2067. The statute was the Private Security Industry Act 2001, s. 7. [135] Paras. 53–4.

[136] *R v. Paddington and St Marylebone Rent Tribunal ex p Bell London & Provincial Properties Ltd* [1941] 1 KB 666 (below, p. 336). Cf. *Wood v. Widnes Cpn* [1898] 1 QB 463 (over-rigid policy of requiring installation of water-closets). [137] *Elliott v. Brighton BC* (1980) 79 LGR 506.

[138] See above, p. 275 (*British Oxygen* case). [139] Below, p. 305.

[140] *R (P and Q) v. Home Secretary* [2001] 1 WLR 2002 (CA). See further below, p. 312.

[141] Art. 8—right to respect for family life—was the right involved.

THE INTERPRETATION OF POLICY

The meaning of a policy may play a vital role in determining whether a policy applies to a particular case and whether, if so, it has been followed or not followed. But interpretation of policy is a vexed issue with conflicting judicial decisions varying with context. On the one hand it is said that if a minister in applying the policy adopts a reasonable meaning of it the judicial review court will not interfere.[142] On the other hand, the test of the 'reasonable and literate man's understanding' of the policy has been applied.[143] The Court of Appeal has now held in the leading case that the true test is the latter one.[144] Applying that test the court rejected the minister's contention that a policy of making ex gratia payments to persons wrongly convicted or charged as a result of serious default on the part of a member of a police force, or of some other public authority, only applied to persons wrongly facing a charge before the domestic courts. Whatever the minister thought, the reasonable man could consider a person wrongly facing extradition proceedings within the policy.

RESTRICTION BY CONTRACT OR GRANT

CONTRACTUAL FETTERS ON DISCRETION

Just as public authorities must have policies, so they must make contracts. Like policies, contracts may be inconsistent with the authorities' proper exercise of their powers. But, unlike policies, contracts are legally binding commitments, and therefore they present more difficult problems. The general principle is the same: an authority may not by contract fetter itself so as to disable itself from exercising its discretion as required by law. Its paramount duty is to preserve its own freedom to decide in every case as the public interest requires at the time.[145] But at the same time its powers may include the making of binding contracts, and it may be most important that it should make them. Since most contracts fetter freedom of action in some way, there may be difficult questions of degree in determining how far the authority may legally commit itself for the future.[146]

Two leading decisions of the House of Lords may be contrasted. In the *Ayr Harbour* case the harbour trustees had been incorporated by a local Act of Parliament with power to acquire compulsorily certain specified land for the purpose of carrying out certain specified works. On the acquisition of one part of the land they wished to give an undertaking to the former owner that he should have unobstructed access from his adjoining land to the harbour, thus reducing the compensation payable for injurious affection of that land. The House of Lords held that any such undertaking would be incompetent.[147] The trustees had specific statutory power to build etc., on the land in question, and they could not strip themselves of this power by making a bargain. Lord Blackburn emphasised that the powers were entrusted to them by the legislature for the public good, and

---

[142] See the discussion in *Raissi* (below), paras. 107–27, especially regarding *In re McFarland* [2004] 1 WLR 1289.

[143] *R v. Criminal Injuries Compensation Board ex p Webb* [1987] QB 74 at 78 (Lawton LJ) applied in *R (Daghir) v. SSHD* [2004] EWHC 243 (Admin).

[144] *R (Raissi) v. Home Secretary* [2008] EWCA Civ 72, [2008] 2 All ER 1023.

[145] See *Denman Ltd v. Westminster Cpn* [1906] 1 Ch 464 at 476.

[146] See [1971] *PL* 288 (P. Rogerson).

[147] *Ayr Harbour Trustees v. Oswald* (1883) 8 App Cas 623.

that a contract purporting to bind them and their successors not to exercise the powers was therefore void.

In the *Birkdale Electricity* case the House of Lords refused to apply this doctrine to an agreement by a statutory electricity company not to raise its charges above those of the adjoining electricity authority, the Corporation of Southport.[148] The company had statutory power to charge what it wished, subject to certain limits, and it was contended that any contract which fettered its exercise of this power could not be binding. But the House of Lords refused to accept an argument which would invalidate many ordinary trading contracts made by statutory authorities in the due management of their businesses. The *Ayr Harbour* case was distinguished as one where the trustees 'renounced a part of their statutory birthright' by offering 'to sterilize part of their acquisition, so far as the statutory purpose of their undertaking was concerned'.[149] In other words, there was a clear incompatibility between their specific statutory purposes and the contract which they wished to make. The electricity company, on the other hand, should have commercial liberty as part of its statutory birthright of selling electricity, and that liberty should include power to make binding contracts. It would be absurd if the existence of statutory powers invalidated 'mere contracts restricting the undertakers' future freedom of action in respect of the business management of their undertaking'.[150]

COMPATIBILITY OF POWERS

The important question is whether there is incompatibility between the purposes of the statutory powers and the purposes for which the contract is made. In cases where there is no commercial element the court is normally ready to condemn any restriction on a public authority's freedom to act in the public interest. Thus a planning authority cannot bind itself by contract either to grant[151] or to refuse[152] planning permission in the future. In one case a local authority designated a sports ground as a proposed public open space, but made a formal agreement with the owner that this designation should cease to operate if the authority had not purchased the land by a certain time, that it would not purchase the land either voluntarily or compulsorily during a certain period, and that it would not make any claim for betterment. All these undertakings were void as clearly incompatible with the authority's duty to preserve its powers intact.[153] On the other hand it has been held to be compatible with the powers of a city council to give a public assurance that it would not increase the number of licensed taxicabs until a local Act of Parliament had been obtained.[154] This was not, apparently, a contractually binding undertaking,[155] but

---

[148] *Birkdale District Electric Supply Company* v. *Southport Cpn* [1926] AC 355, criticising *York Cpn* v. *Henry Leetham & Sons Ltd* [1924] 1 Ch 557 (contract assuring fixed river tolls for 20 years held inconsistent with power to increase tolls as required). [149] *Birkdale* (as above) at 371–2 (Lord Sumner).

[150] As above, at 372.

[151] *Ransom & Luck Ltd* v. *Surbiton BC* [1949] Ch 180 (contract not to revoke permission). But see *Windsor and Maidenhead RBC* v. *Brandrose Investments Ltd* [1983] 1 WLR 509 (relief refused in discretion).

[152] *Stringer* v. *Minister of Housing and Local Government* [1970] 1 WLR 1281 (formal agreement with Manchester University to discourage development in the area of the Jodrell Bank radio telescope).

[153] *Triggs* v. *Staines Urban District Council* [1969] 1 Ch 10.

[154] *R* v. *Liverpool Corporation ex p Liverpool Taxi Fleet Operators' Association* [1972] 2 QB 299. For its 'acting fairly' context see below, p. 465.

[155] Lord Denning MR said: 'So long as the performance of the undertaking is compatible with their public duty, they must honour it.' He also said that 'it certainly was binding unless overridden by some imperative public interest'. No such obligation was mentioned by the other members of the court, but unilateral undertakings have since been held binding in other cases: see below, p. 318.

it influenced the Court of Appeal to hold that the council failed to act fairly and could not lawfully proceed without hearing those affected and paying due regard to its own assurance.

It follows a fortiori that a contract can contain no implied term which conflicts with the freedom to exercise a governmental power. This consideration determined a case where the London Corporation had contracted with a firm of barge-owners for the removal by water of large quantities of refuse, on terms fixed in 1936 which later proved unprofitable to the firm. The Corporation was also the port health authority and responsible for making byelaws. During the period of the contract they made new byelaws imposing more stringent requirements on barges, which would have added to the firm's losses. The firm claimed that the contract for refuse-collecting necessarily implied an undertaking by the Corporation to refrain from altering its byelaws to the firm's disadvantage, and that for breach of this undertaking they were entitled to rescind. The Court of Appeal held that there could be no question of implying a term which, even if express, could not be legally binding, since the Corporation could not contract out of its statutory duties as port health authority.[156] There would seem to be no objection to a term, express or implied, under which the Corporation would undertake, if it should change the byelaws, to compensate the contractor. This is the result achieved in French law by the doctrine of *fait du prince*, under which a government contractor can claim an equitable adjustment if the government, by use of its paramount powers, upsets the calculations on which the contract was made.[157]

The principles which forbid the fettering of public authorities' powers by contract apply equally to covenants and grants in property transactions. If the Crown grants a lease, this cannot prevent the Crown from requisitioning the property under wartime statutory powers.[158] In this case the Crown cannot be said to have 'evicted' the tenant, and thus released him from liability for the rent, since the taking of the premises by requisition was a lawful act. Nor can the usual implied covenant for quiet enjoyment include any implication that the power of requisition will not be exercised, since clearly that power must in the public interest be paramount.[159] Similarly if the government acquires land for national defence, they have overriding power to use the land as an airfield even though it is subject to a restrictive covenant limiting its use to agriculture[160]—and it can make no difference whether the covenant was made by the government itself or by some predecessor in title. A clear case, depending only on the relevant statute and raising no point of doctrine, was that in which a council agreed with its tenants not to vary their tenancies without the consent of a majority of the tenants' representatives. But the council had statutory powers to vary leases without the consent of the tenants. The council's contractual undertaking could not prevent the exercise of these statutory powers.[161]

---

[156] *Cory (William) & Son Ltd* v. *London Corporation* [1951] 2 KB 476. It was conceded that the new byelaws would frustrate the contract, but the firm was claiming immediate rescission as for breach.

[157] See Mitchell, *The Contracts of Public Authorities*, 193. For criticism see P. Rogerson, [1971] *PL* at p. 300, suggesting that an automatic right to compensation unduly favours those who contract with public authorities as compared with other contractors who may suffer equal loss from acts of government. In principle all contractors should cover themselves against this risk, but there are special reasons for implying an indemnity when it is within the power of one contracting party to alter the situation to the disadvantage of the other.   [158] *Commissioners of Crown Lands* v. *Page* [1960] 2 QB 274 (CA).

[159] There is no implied term that the powers shall be exercisable; no covenant can prevent them from being exercisable.

[160] *Marten* v. *Flight Refuelling Ltd* [1962] Ch 115 (covenant by predecessor in title).

[161] *R (Kilby)* v. *Basildon District Council* [2007] EWCA Civ 479.

VALID COMMITMENTS

It would be quite wrong to conclude that a public authority can 'escape from any contract which it finds disadvantageous by saying that it never promised to act otherwise
than for the public good'.[162] There will often be situations where a public authority must
be at liberty to bind itself for the very purpose of exercising its powers effectively. The
Bournemouth Corporation, on acquiring land for a public park, entered into a restrictive covenant with the vendor that the land should be used as a pleasure ground free
from building or erections. The Corporation wished to erect public lavatories, having
specific statutory power to do so in any public park. The Court of Appeal held that they
were bound by their covenant, and refused to accept that there was any analogy with the
Ayr case.[163] The land had been acquired for an express purpose and there was nothing
contrary to that purpose in the observance of the covenant. Similarly a local authority,
on acquiring land for allotments, could validly covenant that it would be used only for
that purpose.[164] If it were otherwise, local authorities would often find it very difficult
to acquire land by agreement. This is another case where the 'statutory birthright' must
include power to make binding promises. And, of course, such a power may be conferred
by statute.[165]

The truth is that multi-purpose authorities, such as local councils, are equipped with a
great many different powers for different purposes, and that some of these may necessarily be inconsistent with others. It cannot be right to restrict the exercise of power which
the authority wishes to use in some particular situation, because some other power, which
the authority does not then wish to use, would then become unusable. A local authority
which has power to maintain public parks may thus quite properly dedicate a park to
public use, even though this makes it impossible in the future for it to exercise its general
powers of letting the land in question.[166]

The Court of Appeal has indicated that in the case of overlapping and conflicting powers the first thing to ascertain is the object for which the land is held. All other powers are
subordinate to the main power to carry out the statutory object and can be used only to
the extent that their exercise is compatible with that object.[167] This principle was applied,
though without being cited, in a case where the Wolverhampton Corporation had granted
to a company the right to use the municipal airport for ninety-nine years. After thirty-five
years the Corporation decided to discontinue the airport and use the land as a housing
estate. But the Vice-Chancellor held that it had no right to do so in breach of its commitment to the company, which had been validly made.[168] He said:

> Obviously, where a power is exercised in such a manner as to create a right extending over
> a term of years, the existence of that right pro tanto excludes the exercise of other statutory
> powers in respect of the same subject matter, but there is no authority and I can see no
> principle upon which that sort of exercise could be held to be invalid as a fetter upon the
> future exercise of powers.

---

[162] *Commissioners of Crown Lands* v. *Page* (above) at 293 (Devlin LJ).

[163] *Stourcliffe Estates Co Ltd* v. *Bournemouth Cpn* [1910] 2 Ch 12. See similarly *R* v. *Hammersmith and
Fulham LBC ex p Beddowes* [1987] QB 1050.

[164] *Leicester (Earl)* v. *Wells-next-the-Sea Urban District Council* [1973] Ch 110.

[165] *Windsor BC* v. *Brandcote Investments Ltd* [1981] 1 WLR 1083 (statutory agreement with planning
authority).   [166] *Blake* v. *Hendon Cpn* [1962] 1 QB 283.

[167] *Blake* v. *Hendon Cpn* (above) at 301–2, following *British Transport Commission* v. *Westmorland
County Council* (below).   [168] *Dowty Boulton Paul Ltd* v. *Wolverhampton Cpn* [1971] 1 WLR 204.

In this case as in many others the court was pressed with the *Ayr* case. But it is quite evident that the doctrine of that case will not be extended to the point where it can be invoked by a public authority as a pretext for escaping from obligations which it has deliberately and properly contracted.

NON-CONTRACTUAL CASES

It has several times been held that a non-contractual undertaking may bind a public body. One case was where a taxicab licensing authority gave a public undertaking not to increase the number of licences for a certain time. Although this was a mere statement of future policy, which in general cannot be restricted by agreement, it was said that the undertaking 'certainly was binding unless overridden by some imperative public interest'.[169] That such an undertaking could create a legal obligation was a novel proposition. But it has since fallen into place as part of the doctrine that breach of an undertaking may lead to inconsistent and unfair action amounting either to an abuse of power[170] or else to a breach of the principles of natural justice.[171]

ESTOPPEL—MISLEADING ADVICE

ESTOPPEL AND DISCRETION

The doctrine of estoppel must be prevented not only from enlarging the powers of public authorities illegitimately, as already explained:[172] it must also be prevented from cramping the proper exercise of their discretion. The principle here is the same as in the case of contracts, already discussed, and it is equally capable of causing hardship.[173] The leading cases concern misleading official rulings.

The employees of public authorities may often be asked to advise or rule upon some question which only their employing authority can decide. Expense may reasonably be incurred in reliance on the advice given, but if it turns out to be wrong there is usually no legal remedy. The authority's freedom to decide as it thinks the public interest requires must on no account be compromised, hard though the result may be. A notable illustration was a case where a company had bought land for use as a builder's yard, on the understanding that it had an existing use right for that purpose, so that no planning permission would be required.[174] In order to make sure of this before committing themselves to the purchase, the company consulted the borough surveyor, an employee of the planning authority, who confirmed that the right existed and that no planning permission was necessary. But this advice was wrong, and eventually the planning authority served an enforcement notice to stop the company from using the land as a builder's yard. It was held, though reluctantly, that this notice was enforceable, and that no advice or assurance from the borough engineer could hamper the planning authority's free and unhindered

---

[169] *R* v. *Liverpool Cpn ex p Liverpool Taxi Fleet Operators' Association* [1972] 2 QB 299 (Lord Denning MR).   [170] See below, p. 318.

[171] See below, p. 417.

[172] Above, p. 196. For discussion see [2003] *JR* 71 (M. C. Elliott); [1981] *CLP* 1 (A. W. Bradley); (1977) 93 *LQR* 398 (P. P. Craig); [1972] *PL* 43 (M. A. Fazal); [1965] *PL* 237 (G. Ganz); (1953) 53 *Col LR* 374 (F. C. Newman).   [173] See the *Laker Airways* case, above, p. 200.

[174] *Southend-on-Sea Corporation* v. *Hodgson (Wickford) Ltd* [1962] 1 QB 416. See also *Brooks and Burton Ltd* v. *Secretary of State for the Environment* (1977) 75 LGR 285, reversed on other grounds, [1977] 1 WLR 1294, but approved on this point in *Western Fish Products Ltd* v. *Penwith DC* [1981] 2 All ER 204.

discretion, which they had a duty to exercise in the public interest. In the same way a local education authority's decision to pay the school transport costs of a pupil could not estop them from revoking it when it was found to have been taken under a mistake as to the facts.[175]

In endeavouring to protect the citizen against such hardships the courts have strained the law and given doubtful decisions. An irregular departmental decision was held binding on the Crown in a case where an army officer claimed a disablement pension on account of war injury. The War Office wrote to him that 'Your disability has been accepted as attributable to military service.' But for this injury the responsible department was the Ministry of Pensions, which the War Office had not consulted. The Ministry later decided that the disability was not attributable and the pension appeal tribunal upheld that decision.

In reliance on the War Office letter the claimant had refrained from getting a medical opinion and assembling other evidence which might have strengthened his case against the Ministry. On appeal to the court, Denning J reversed the decisions of the Ministry and the tribunal, holding that the Crown was bound by the War Office letter.[176] He invoked two doctrines of his own creation: that assurances intended to be acted upon and in fact acted upon were binding; and that where a government department wrongfully assumes authority to perform some legal act, the citizen is entitled to assume that it has the authority. He also dismissed the contentions that estoppels do not bind the Crown ('that doctrine has long been exploded') and that the Crown cannot fetter its future executive action.[177]

The proposition about wrongfully assumed authority was emphatically repudiated by the House of Lords in a later case in which Denning LJ had again put it forward. The question was whether ship repairs, which could be lawfully executed only under written licence, could in effect be validly authorised merely by oral permission from the licensing officer. Could the licensee rely on the licensing officer's purported authority to grant an oral licence? The House of Lords answered this firmly in the negative.[178] Although this was a somewhat stronger case, in that there would otherwise have been a violation of an express statutory prohibition, it would seem necessary to reject the whole notion of estoppel of a public authority by wrongful assumption of statutory authority.[179] For it clearly conflicts with the basic rule that no estoppel can give the authority power which it does not possess. Just as there was no power to license ship repairs orally, so there was no power for the War Office to award pensions which in law were available only from the Ministry of Pensions.

Nevertheless the Court of Appeal has held in a questionable decision a local planning authority bound by wrong statements made by its own officers, in apparent defiance of the rules against both delegation and estoppel. After planning permission had duly been given for the building of a group of houses in London, the builder submitted a revised plan and asked for approval of the variations. The planning officer had lost the file with the original plan and, thinking that the variations were not material, told the builder that no further permission would be needed. In fact the variations brought the new houses much closer to existing houses, and when one of them was already nearly finished the

---

[175] *Rootkin* v. *Kent CC* [1981] 1 WLR 1186.

[176] *Robertson* v. *Minister of Pensions* [1949] 1 KB 227. See also *Re L (AC) (an infant)* [1971] 3 All ER 743.

[177] See below, p. 710.

[178] *Howell* v. *Falmouth Boat Construction Co Ltd* [1951] AC 837. See also *A-G for Ceylon* v. *AD Silva* [1953] AC 461, quoted below, p. 284.

[179] In this context estoppel has a wider sense than estoppel by representations of fact, and includes representations of law. For ostensible agency in contract see below, p. 822.

planning authority refused permission and threatened enforcement. The Court of Appeal granted a declaration that there was already a valid planning permission for the house on the altered site.[180] But in fact the planning officer had no power to grant planning permission at all, and the planning authority itself had not done so in respect of the new site. Lord Denning MR held that the practice of allowing the planning officer to rule that variations were not material gave him 'ostensible authority', since the planning authority might have delegated its powers to him and the builder was entitled to assume that the necessary resolution had been passed.[181] He also stated that a public authority may be bound by representations made by their officer within this ostensible authority if some other person acts on them.[182] These two propositions were virtually the same as those that had been rejected by the House of Lords in the ship-licensing case,[183] but this was not cited.

The unfortunate features of the Court of Appeal's decision were first that it sacrificed the interests of the neighbouring house-owners, who were forced to accept houses over-looking them much more closely than the planning authority would have permitted. Secondly, it sacrificed the public interest, since the court deprived the responsible public authority of the powers of control which the Act assigned to them and to them only. Later Courts of Appeal, being unable to overrule this questionable decision, distinguished it significantly.[184] Although not technically overruled, it has now been strongly criticised by the House of Lords. Its influence must be considered at an end.

The other exception is where the authority waives a procedural requirement relating to some application made to it, whereupon it may be estopped from relying on the lack of formality.[185] As already explained,[186] this is an established exception in cases where it does not hamper the authority in the discharge of its statutory functions.

On the most recent occasion on which the House of Lords has considered the issue it recognised the strength of the criticisms set out in this chapter of the role of estoppel in public law.[187] Their Lordships concluded that 'it is unhelpful to introduce private law concepts of estoppel into planning law' and 'public law has already absorbed whatever is useful from the moral values which underlie the private law concept of estoppel and

---

[180] *Lever Finance Ltd* v. *Westminster London Borough Council* [1971] 1 QB 222 (judgments not reserved) and now distinguished in *R (Reprotech (Pebsham) Ltd)* v. *East Sussex County Council* [2003] 1 WLR 348 (HL), discussed below, p. 283. Sachs LJ held that on the facts the planning authority had delegated its power to the planning officer under Town and Country Planning Act 1968, s. 64; statutory formalities had not been observed, but perhaps they could have been treated as merely directory.

[181] The Town and Country Planning Act 1968, s. 64, was already in force. It was on this ground that the *Southend* case (above, p. 281) was distinguished.

[182] This must mean 'acts on them to his detriment': *Norfolk County Council* v. *Secretary of State for the Environment* [1973] 1 WLR 1400, where Lord Widgery CJ accepted Lord Denning's proposition with this addition. For this case see above, p. 196. See also *Rootkin* v. *Kent CC* [1981] 1 WLR 1186; *A-G* v. *Taff-Ely BC* [1981] 42 P & CR 1.   [183] *Howell* v. *Falmouth Boat Construction Co Ltd* (above).

[184] See *Western Fish Products Ltd* v. *Penwith DC* (1978) 38 P & CR 7, [1981] 2 All ER 204 (unanimous Court of Appeal held that the 'ostensible authority' principle laid down by Lord Denning required that there were special circumstances to justify the applicant in thinking that the officer had authority; the only other context in which estoppel might operate was where a procedural requirement was waived).

[185] The court cites *Wells* v. *Minister of Housing and Local Government* [1967] 1 WLR 1000, where the waiver was by the authority itself, now distinguished in *R (Reprotech (Pebsham) Ltd)* v. *East Sussex County Council* [2003] 1 WLR 348 (HL), discussed below. It seems that officers of the authority may also raise estoppels of this kind: *Re L (AC) (an infant)* [1971] 3 All ER 743 (above, p. 198).   [186] Above, p. 199.

[187] *R (Reprotech (Pebsham) Ltd)* v. *East Sussex County Council* [2003] 1 WLR 348 (HL) (applicant sought unsuccessfully to rely upon planning officer's apparent statement that planning permission was not required for change of use). See [2003] *JR* 71 (M. C. Elliott), [2003] *CLJ* 3 (S. Atrill).

the time has come for it to stand on its own two feet'. As the court foresaw, if estoppel ceased to operate here,[188] the innocent representee would yet be able to rely upon a substantive legitimate expectation.[189] And there are several cases which have relied upon legitimate expectation when earlier they might have rested upon estoppel.[190] Although there is significant overlap between the two doctrines,[191] the substantive protection of legitimate expectations envisages an express judicial weighing of the conflicting interests. So, in principle, the individual interest in upholding the representation might outweigh the public interest in maintaining the planning system on which the public is entitled to rely. But in most cases, since the public interest will generally prove more weighty, there will be little difference.[192]

THE SOLUTION: COMPENSATION

The dilemma which misleading rulings can create is certainly painful. But it does not follow that the right solution is to disregard the public interest, together with the interest of those whom the law is intended to protect. If the force of law is given to a ruling from an official merely because it is wrong, the official who has no legal power is in effect substituted for the proper authority, which is forced to accept what it considers a bad decision.[193] To legitimate ultra vires acts in this way cannot be a sound policy, being a negation of the fundamental canons of administrative law. As the Privy Council said in an analogous case of a Crown officer who made an unauthorised contract:[194]

> It may be said that it causes hardship to a purchaser...if the burden of ascertaining whether or not the Principal Collector has authority to enter into the sale is placed upon him. This undoubtedly is true. But...to hold otherwise would be to hold that public officers had dispensing powers because they then could by unauthorised acts nullify or extend the provisions of the Ordinance. Of the two evils this would be the greater one.

Nor should it make any difference that the decision forced upon the public authority is one which would have been within its powers, as opposed to one which would have been outside them. For decisions which are against the public interest, in the view of the proper authority, are scarcely less objectionable if intra vires than if ultra vires.

The only acceptable solution, therefore, is to enforce the law but to compensate the person who suffered the loss by acting on a ruling from the ostensibly proper official. If the ruling leads to the erection of a house without planning permission, and the planning authority thinks it wrong to give permission, the house should be demolished and the builder should be compensated, in the same way as when a valid planning permission is revoked and compensation is paid for abortive expenditure.

---

[188] Their Lordships in fact distinguished rather than overruled *Lever Finance Ltd* v. *Westminster (City) LBC* [1971] 1 QB 222 and *Wells* v. *Minister of Housing and Local Government* [1967] 1 WLR 732.

[189] See below, p. 318.

[190] See, for instance, *R* v. *Leicester City Council ex p Powergen UK Ltd* [2000] JPL 629.

[191] And both wrestle with the difficulty of a representation made by an ostensibly authorised officer: *South Buckinghamshire DC* v. *Flanagan* [2002] 1 WLR 2601 and *R (Bloggs 61)* v. *Home Secretary* [2003] 1 WLR 2724 (representation by police did not bind prison service).   [192] See Elliott, above, 77–80.

[193] In *Wells* v. *Minister of Housing and Local Government* (above) Russell LJ, dissenting, attributed that policy to the natural indignation that the practice should operate as a trap for the unwary, adding that 'the question is, I think one of law not to be decided by a thoroughly bad administrative practice'.

[194] *A-G for Ceylon* v. *AD Silva* [1953] AC 461 at 480.

The Parliamentary Commissioner for Administration has given a lead in the right direction by obtaining compensation in a number of such cases, for example for an importer who had to pay purchase tax on a car imported on the faith of a prior official assurance that it would be duty-free.[195] The giving of wrong rulings by officials is maladministration and this is the correct basis for redress. French law has found no difficulty in reaching this solution[196] and English law should equally well be able to reach it. It is on all accounts better than manipulating the law so as to uphold acts which are ultra vires or contrary to the public interest, in an attempt to make two wrongs into a right. It is true that many people have to rely on legal or other advice which may prove to be wrong, but there is a special claim to redress where loss is caused by a wrong ruling from a governmental authority on whose guidance the citizen is entitled to rely.

In a growing number of cases a solution has been found in the tort of negligent misstatement, as developed by the courts.[197] Although negligence is not always easy to prove, it is sometimes self-evident in cases of wrong official rulings. A local authority has been held liable for the failure by one of its clerks to search the local register of land charges with due care, thus causing pecuniary loss.[198] A government department has been held liable similarly for negligently advising an exporter that he would be insured against loss when in fact he would not.[199] And other examples are accumulating. Wrong advice or assurances given by officials of planning authorities might make them liable similarly, so as to compensate the misguided developer and avoid the legitimation of wrongful assumption of authority. This head of liability is further discussed below in the wider context of negligent government acts and decisions.[200]

Compensation as a solution has been criticised on the ground that it is a wasteful use of scarce resources.[201] However, the same reproach could be levelled at every use of public funds to remedy maladministration or to pay damages for torts committed by public officials. Justice for the innocent representee has its price.

Misleading official advice may, in addition, be a contributory factor to action by a public authority which is so unfair and inconsistent that it amounts to an abuse of power.[202] Where local authorities wrongly advised students that they were ineligible for grants, thus deterring them from making their applications in time, and then refused grants on the ground that the applications were late, the refusals were quashed as unfair and irrational and an abuse of discretion[203]—a form of maladministration amply illustrated in the following chapter.

---

[195] See above, p. 68.

[196] The Conseil d'État treats misleading official advice as *faute de service*: see CE 10 July 1964, *Duffaut*, Rec. 399; CE 17 Dec. 1965, *Jaquet*, Rec. 699. In both cases planning authorities misled purchasers of land by informing them that there were no restrictions on building, whereas the lands were reserved for an airfield and a university respectively; and when permission to build was later refused, the purchasers recovered compensation from the state. See similarly CE 20 Jan. 1988, *Aubin*, noted in [1988] *PL* 469 (misinformation about unemployment benefit).

[197] *Hedley Byrne & Co Ltd* v. *Heller & Partners Ltd* [1964] AC 465 is the root case.

[198] *Ministry of Housing and Local Government* v. *Sharp* [1970] 2 QB 223.

[199] *Culford Metal Industries Ltd* v. *Export Credits Guarantee Department*, The Times, 25 March 1981.

[200] Below, p. 648.

[201] (1977) 93 *LQR* 398 (P. P. Craig), proposing instead a search by the judge for the balance of public and individual interest; and where the individual interest is more weighty to protect it.

[202] See below, p. 318.

[203] *R* v. *West Glamorgan CC ex p Gheissary*, The Times, 18 December 1985.

11

ABUSE OF DISCRETION

DISCRETION LIMITED BY LAW

It used to be thought to be classical constitutional doctrine that wide discretionary power was incompatible with the rule of law.[1] But this dogma cannot be taken seriously today, and indeed it never contained much truth. What the rule of law demands is not that wide discretionary power should be eliminated, but that the law should control its exercise. Modern government demands discretionary powers which are as wide as they are numerous. Parliamentary draftsmen strive to find new forms of words which will make discretion even wider, and Parliament all too readily enacts them. It is the attitude of the courts by finding limits to such seemingly unbounded powers which is perhaps the most revealing feature of a system of administrative law.[2]

The first requirement is the recognition that all power has legal limits. The next requirement, no less vital, is that the courts should draw those limits in a way which strikes the most suitable balance between executive efficiency and legal protection of the citizen. Parliament constantly confers upon public authorities powers which on their face might seem absolute and arbitrary. But arbitrary power and unfettered discretion are what the courts refuse to countenance. They have woven a network of restrictive principles which require statutory powers to be exercised reasonably and in good faith, for proper purposes only, and in accordance with the spirit as well as the letter of the empowering Act. They have also, as explained in a later chapter, imposed stringent procedural requirements.[3] Here we are concerned with the substance of administrative discretion.

Discretion is an element in all power, as opposed to duty, so that 'abuse of discretion' could be made to include most of administrative law. But it is more convenient to confine this rubric to a central group of rules which are difficult to separate from one another, leaving aside what can readily be classified under other headings. This has the advantage of emphasising the policy of the courts in the area where they have to come closest to sitting in judgment on the merits, as such, of governmental acts and decisions. It is an area where wide choices are open to them. If they choose to shelter behind literal interpretation, and take the words of each Act at face value, they could absolve themselves from many difficult problems. By insisting, as they do, that the implications of an enactment are as significant as its express provisions, and that powers given for public purposes are as it were held upon trust, they embroil themselves with the policy, motives and merits of

---

[1] Dicey, *Law of the Constitution*, 9th edn, 202.

[2] For discussion see Galligan, *Discretionary Power*. For the corresponding law in France see [1986] *PL* 99 (J. Bell); [1987] *PL* 287 (R. Errera). For the USA see Schwartz, *Administrative Law*, 3rd edn, 654; (1986) 54 *Geo Wash L Rev* 469 (C. H. Koch); Schwartz and Wade, *Legal Control of Government*, 260, 262; Davis, *Discretionary Justice*, discusses problems of discretionary power in the United States but says little about the role of the courts. See also Davis, *Discretionary Justice in Europe and America*. For criticism see [1984] *PL* 570 (R. Baldwin and K. Hawkins). [3] Below, p. 373.

administrative action. At the same time they must confine themselves to applying recognisable principles of law, since at all costs they must not expose themselves to the charge of usurping executive power.

Having pushed their doctrines to remarkable lengths in some cases, the courts have staked their claim to a kind of constitutional restraining power. While their paramount duty is loyal obedience to Parliament, it is for them to say what Parliament really means. Parliament—or, more realistically, the government which controls Parliament—is impatient of any restraint, and constantly confers what appear to be unfettered powers, or attempts to take away judicial remedies. The courts, as constantly, react by devising some means of preserving the legal principles of control. In so doing they preserve the rule of law, of which Parliament often appears surprisingly heedless. If legislation were more restrained, the courts would not be called upon to perform such striking feats of interpretation. They are a kind of legal antidote to the unqualified sovereignty of Parliament, redressing the balance of forces in the constitution.

THE JUSTIFICATION FOR REVIEW ON SUBSTANTIVE GROUNDS

In requiring statutory powers to be exercised reasonably, in good faith, and on correct grounds, the courts are still working within the bounds of the familiar principle of ultra vires. The analysis involves no difficulty or mystique. Offending acts are condemned simply for the reason that they are unauthorised. The court assumes that Parliament cannot have intended to authorise unreasonable action, which is therefore ultra vires and void.[4] This is the express basis of the reasoning in many of the cases cited below.[5] Two particularly well-known statements may be instanced. One is from Lord Russell of Killowen CJ, who said that if a local authority's byelaws were manifestly unjust or oppressive

> the Court might well say, 'Parliament never intended to give authority to make such rules; they are unreasonable and ultra vires.'[6]

The other is from Lord Greene MR, who in a judgment discussed later said that where an act was challenged as being unreasonable, the court's only task was

> to see whether the local authority have contravened the law by acting in excess of the powers which Parliament has confided in them.[7]

It is, indeed, self-evident that the decisions rest on this elementary principle, since if the action in question is found to be intra vires the court has no power to interfere. The same result is attained in some cases by saying that, where a decision is bad for unreasonableness, the authority has failed to exercise its discretion at all.[8]

---

[4] Above, p. 27.

[5] e.g. *Short* v. *Poole Corporation* [1926] Ch 66; *Hall & Co Ltd* v. *Shoreham-by-Sea Urban District Council* [1964] 1 WLR 240; *Mixnam's Properties Ltd* v. *Chertsey Urban District Council* [1965] AC 735 at 753 (Lord Radcliffe); *Hartnell* v. *Minister of Housing and Local Government* [1965] AC 1134 at 1173 (Lord Wilberforce); *Roncarelli* v. *Duplessis* (1959) 16 DLR (2d) 689, quoted below, p. 300.

[6] *Kruse* v. *Johnson* [1898] 2 QB 91 at 100.

[7] *Associated Provincial Picture Houses Ltd* v. *Wednesbury Cpn* [1948] 1 KB 223 at 234.

[8] e.g. in *R* v. *St Pancras Vestry* (1890) 24 QBD 371 at 375; *R* v. *Board of Education* [1910] 2 KB 165 at 175; *Williams* v. *Giddy* [1911] AC 381 at 386; *R* v. *Port of London Authority ex p Kynoch* [1919] 1 KB 176 at 183. In licensing cases this analysis may be due to the preference for mandamus as a remedy, based on the mistaken idea that certiorari will not lie: see below, p. 517.

A necessary corollary is that, as usual throughout administrative law, we are concerned with acts of legal power, i.e. acts which, if valid, themselves produce legal consequences. Courts of law have nothing directly to do with mere decisions of policy, such as decisions by the government that Britain shall join the European Communities (even though a treaty is concluded)[9] or that grammar schools shall be replaced by comprehensive schools.[10] Such decisions have no legal impact until statutory powers are conferred or invoked. But as soon as Parliament confers some legal power it becomes the business of the courts to see that the power is not exceeded or abused; and statements of policy relating to the use of such legal powers are within the scope of judicial review.[11]

This logic, fundamental though it should be, is not invariably respected.[12] A number of non-statutory bodies, such as the Criminal Injuries Compensation Authority (in its original form)[13] and the Panel on Takeovers and Mergers (an agency of the London Stock Exchange) have been brought within the scope of judicial review on the same general basis as if they were statutory. These decisions, discussed later,[14] were prompted by the courts' determination to act 'in defence of the citizenry'[15] against abuse of power by important bodies of a governmental or quasi-governmental nature, or by bodies wielding monopolistic power over some profession or activity, and not to let them escape merely because of their non-statutory character.[16] Bold judicial forays have opened up an important new field for administrative law.

THE ROYAL PREROGATIVE

The prerogative powers of the Crown[17] have traditionally been said to confer discretion which no court can question;[18] and there was long a dearth of authority to the contrary. But it may be that this was because the decided cases involved discretions which are, as has been laid down in the House of Lords, inherently unsuitable for judicial review, 'such as those relating to the making of treaties, the defence of the realm, the prerogative of mercy, the grant of honours, the dissolution of Parliament and the appointment of ministers as well as others'.[19] But at the same time the House of Lords held that the court could review a minister's action (forbidding trade union membership by certain civil servants) under authority delegated to him by prerogative Order in Council, so that the principles of natural justice would apply. Administrative action was held to be reviewable in proceedings against the responsible minister without distinction as to the origin of the power, whether statute or common law.[20] In later cases it was held that the dismissal of a civil servant

---

[9] *Blackburn* v. *A-G* [1971] 1 WLR 1037.

[10] *Secretary of State for Education and Science* v. *Tameside Metropolitan Borough Council* [1977] AC 1014; below, p. 360.   [11] See below, p. 321.

[12] Note also the anomaly as to 'decisions', below, p. 517.

[13] It is now a statutory commission under the Criminal Injuries Compensation Act 1995.

[14] Below, p. 538.

[15] Sir John Donaldson MR in *R* v. *Panel on Takeovers and Mergers ex p Datafin plc* [1987] QB 815 at 839.

[16] See (1996) 55 *CLJ* 122 (Forsyth) at 23–5 for discussion of how the common law power to regulate monopolies may justify judicial review in these circumstances.   [17] See above, p. 179.

[18] Bl. Comm. 250, 252.

[19] *Council of Civil Service Unions* v. *Minister for the Civil Service* [1985] AC 374 at 418 (Lord Roskill). For this case see below, p. 474. Despite its title it was an application for judicial review.

[20] So confirming a remark of Lord Devlin in *Chandler* v. *Director of Public Prosecutions* [1964] AC 763 at 809–10. Note the similar attitude of the Court of Appeal in *R* v. *Panel on Takeovers and Mergers ex p Datafin plc* (as above). See also [1973] *CLJ* 287 at 293 (B. S. Markesinis).

involved 'a sufficient public law element' to be subject to judicial review,[21] and that an unfair compensation award by the civil service appeal board should be quashed.[22] Thus today the royal prerogative does not per se confer unreviewable discretion, but that many of the powers contained in it will be of a kind with which the courts will not concern themselves. At one time it was thought that the actions of ministers, authorised by delegation of prerogative power, were reviewable but the actions of the Crown itself (such as the making of an Order in Council) remained unreviewable.[23] But in the *Chagos Islanders* case[24] the Court of Appeal held that 'an Order in Council [made under the prerogative] is an act of the executive and as such is amenable to any appropriate form of judicial review'.[25] Since the monarch always acts on the advice of ministers it is plain that an Order in Council, although in form the act of the sovereign, is in substance an act of the minister who advises Her Majesty; and it is artificial to place it beyond judicial review.[26]

The wide definition of prerogative has been criticised earlier[27] and it continues to pose difficulties in determining the reach of judicial review. The making of treaties, for example, has no effect on the law of this country,[28] so that there is no exercise of power which can concern the courts. It might be called prerogative without power, while the employment of civil servants might be called power without prerogative. A case where there may be neither prerogative nor power is the grant and refusal of passports, which has been claimed to be wholly within the prerogative and discretion of the Crown.[29] A passport is merely an administrative device, the grant or cancellation of which probably involves no direct legal consequences,[30] since there appears to be no justification for supposing that, in law as opposed to administrative practice, a citizen's right to leave or enter the country is dependent upon the possession of a passport.[31] The arbitrary power claimed by the Crown has now been made subject to judicial review along with various other non-legal powers discussed later.[32]

At least it is now judicially recognised that prerogative power is as capable of abuse as is any other power, and that the law can sometimes find means of controlling it. The prerogative has many times been restricted both by judicial decision and by statute.[33] It is

---

[21] *R* v. *Civil Service Appeal Board ex p Bruce* [1989] 2 All ER 907 (relief refused since applicant was taking proceedings in an industrial tribunal). A naval officer's disqualification for promotion was held potentially reviewable in *Bradley* v. *A-G* [1986] 1 NZLR 176.

[22] *R* v. *Civil Service Appeal Board ex p Cunningham* [1991] 4 All ER 310.

[23] Lord Fraser makes this distinction in the *Council of Civil Service Unions* case (as above).

[24] Discussed fully at p. 746.

[25] *R (Bancoult)* v. *Secretary of State for Foreign and Commonwealth* Affairs [2007] EWCA Civ 498, para. 35 (Sedley LJ) and see para.111 (Sir Anthony Clarke MR) 'the principle stated by Lord Scarman [in the CGHQ case]...applies to all exercises of the royal prerogative, including all Orders in Council'. This was confirmed in the same case in the House of Lords ([2008] UKHL 61; paras. 35, 71, 105), although the appeal was upheld on other grounds.

[26] The appropriate remedy would be a declaration against the responsible minister. See above, p. 484.

[27] Above, p. 180. See (1992) 108 *LQR* 626 (B. V. Harris).

[28] *The Parlement Belge* (1879) 4 PD 129; *Walker* v. *Baird* [1892] AC 491; *Blackburn* v. *A-G* [1971] 1 WLR 1037. But it is often called 'prerogative', as in the *Laker Airways* case, below.

[29] See 209 HL Deb. col. 860 (16 June 1958); 764 HC Deb. cols. 1041 et seq. (14 May 1969). The government has refused to agree to a statutory right as advocated in *Going Abroad* (a JUSTICE booklet): 416 HL Deb. col. 558 (22 Jan. 1981).

[30] Under the Immigration Act 1971, 2nd Sched., para. 4(2)(a) an immigration officer may now require production of either a passport or some other document satisfactorily establishing identity and nationality.

[31] See Bl. Comm. (14th edn), i. 265; Halsbury (4th edn), viii. 636; revised edn, Wade, *Constitutional Fundamentals*, 62. For the more favourable law in France see [1986] *PL* 637, [1987] *PL* 464 (R. Errera).

[32] *R* v. *Secretary of State for Foreign and Commonwealth Affairs ex p Everett* [1989] QB 811 (refusal of passport held reviewable but relief refused). See below, p. 538.

[33] As in *Entick* v. *Carrington* (1765) 19 St Tr 1030; *A-G* v. *De Keyser's Royal Hotel* [1920] AC 508; *Burmah Oil Co* v. *Lord Advocate* [1965] AC 75.

for the court to determine the legal limits of the prerogative, and they may include the same requirement of reasonable and proper exercise as applies to statutory powers—though with this difference, that it cannot be based upon the presumed intention of Parliament. In one unusual case, where a Parliamentary basis could be found because action taken by a minister under a treaty was held to be impliedly prohibited by a statute,[34] Lord Denning MR discussed the nature of the prerogative and said:[35]

> Seeing that the prerogative is a discretionary power to be exercised for the public good, it follows that its exercise can be examined by the courts just as any other discretionary power which is vested in the executive.

In today's atmosphere it seems clear that the court would entertain a complaint that, for example, a royal pardon had been obtained by fraud or granted by mistake or for improper reasons.[36] The High Court has gone so far as to review a decision of the Home Secretary not to recommend a posthumous free pardon for a youth hanged for murder forty years previously, on the ground that he considered only an unconditional pardon and failed to take account of other possibilities.[37] Although the court made no order or declaration and merely invited the Home Secretary to look at the matter again, it clearly took a long step towards judicial review of the prerogative of mercy.

A further question is whether the law should concern itself with the Crown's exercise of the ordinary powers and liberties which all persons possess, as in the making of contracts and the conveyance of land. It has hitherto been assumed that in this area the Crown has the same free discretion as has any other person. But where such powers are exercised for governmental purposes it is arguable that the courts should be prepared to intervene, as a matter of public ethics, as a safeguard against abuse. They do not allow local authorities to act arbitrarily or vindictively in evicting tenants, letting sports grounds or placing advertisements, for example.[38] Those are technically statutory powers (since all local authorities are statutory),[39] but they correspond to ordinary powers and liberties.[40] If, as the House of Lords holds, the source of power is irrelevant,[41] it would not seem impossible for judicial review to be extended to this 'third source' of public power[42] which is neither statutory nor prerogative but is a remnant from the days of personal government. But 'the grotesquely undemocratic idea that public authorities have a private capacity is deeply embedded in our legal culture',[43] and such judicial authority as there is is not encouraging.[44]

---

[34] *Laker Airways Ltd* v. *Department of Trade* [1977] QB 643; below, p. 333.

[35] Lord Denning claimed support from Blackstone but did not mention that he insists that the prerogative, within its limits, is uncontrollable by the courts.

[36] According to *Hanratty* v. *Butler*, The Times, 12 May 1971, the discretion is absolute. See likewise *de Freitas* v. *Benny* [1976] AC 239; *Reckley* v. *Minister of Public Safety and Immigration (No 2)* [1966] AC 527 (PC). For criticism see [1996] *PL* 557 (D. Pannick). In 1948, when after the vote in the House of Commons the death penalty for murder was suspended administratively by granting commutation, Lord Goddard CJ suggested that this was contrary to the prohibition of the suspending power in the Bill of Rights 1688: 156 HL Deb. 117 (2 June 1948); compare *Professional Promotions and Services Ltd* v. *A-G* [1990] 1 NZLR 501 (minister's policy on radio licensing violated Bill of Rights 1688).

[37] *R* v. *Home Secretary ex p Bentley* [1994] QB 349. The Home Secretary later procured a qualified pardon.

[38] See below, pp. 295–7.   [39] *Jones* v. *Swansea CC* [1990] 1 WLR 54 at 70, 85.

[40] Note also the use of contracts to enforce policies (below, p. 674).   [41] Below, p. 539.

[42] See B. V. Harris, *The 'Third Source' of Government Action*, (1992) 108 *LQR* 626; (1990) 106 *LQR* 277 (S. Arrowsmith); (1992) 15 NZLR 117 (D. L. Mathieson), discussing comments of Thomas J in *King and New Zealand Medical Association* v. *Clark* (unreported). See also the discussion above, p. 180.

[43] (1993) 13 *Legal Studies* at 189 (J. Alder).

[44] See *R* v. *The Lord Chancellor ex p Hibbit and Saunders* [1993] COD 326 (below, p. 574); the *Hang Wah Chong* case, below, p. 339.

INTENTIONS IMPUTED TO PARLIAMENT

For more than three centuries it has been accepted that discretionary power conferred upon public authorities is not absolute, even within its apparent boundaries, but is subject to general legal limitations. These limitations are expressed in a variety of different ways, as by saying that discretion must be exercised reasonably and in good faith, that relevant considerations only must be taken into account, that there must be no malversation of any kind, or that the decision must not be arbitrary or capricious. They can all be comprised by saying that discretion must be exercised in the manner intended by the empowering Act. As Griffiths LJ has said:[45]

> Now it goes without saying that Parliament can never be taken to have intended to give any statutory body a power to act in bad faith or a power to abuse its powers. When the court says it will intervene if the particular body acted in bad faith it is but another way of saying that the power was not being exercised within the scope of the statutory authority given by Parliament. Of course it is often a difficult matter to determine the precise extent of the power given by the statute particularly where it is a discretionary power and it is with this consideration that the courts have been much occupied in the many decisions that have developed our administrative law since the last war.

In attempting to discover the intention to be imputed to Parliament, the court must some-times pick its way between conflicting presumptions. On the one hand, where Parliament confers power upon some minister or other authority to be used in discretion, it is obvi-ous that the discretion ought to be that of the designated authority and not that of the court. Whether the discretion is exercised prudently or imprudently, the authority's word is to be law and the remedy is to be political only. On the other hand, Parliament cannot be supposed to have intended that the power should be open to serious abuse. It must have assumed that the designated authority would act properly and responsibly, with a view to doing what was best in the public interest and most consistent with the policy of the stat-ute. It is from this presumption that the courts take their warrant to impose legal bounds on even the most extensive discretion. The apparent contradiction of the propositions between which the courts have to steer is well brought out in two contrasting statements by Lord Halsbury. In one case he said:[46]

> Where the legislature has confided the power to a particular body, with a discretion how it is to be used, it is beyond the power of any court to contest that discretion.

But in an earlier case he had already made the necessary qualification:[47]

> 'discretion' means when it is said that something is to be done within the discretion of the authorities that that something is to be done according to the rules of reason and justice, not according to private opinion: *Rooke's Case*; according to law and not humour. It is to be, not arbitrary, vague, and fanciful, but legal and regular. And it must be exercised within the limit, to which an honest man competent to the discharge of his office ought to confine himself.

This passage describes the administrative discretion of justices of the peace in deciding applications for liquor licences. The middle sentence is borrowed from Lord Mansfield,

---

[45]   *R* v. *Commission for Racial Equality ex p Hillingdon LBC* [1982] QB 276.
[46]   *Westminster Cpn* v. *London & North Western Railway Co* [1905] AC 426.
[47]   *Sharp* v. *Wakefield* [1891] AC 173.

who used the same words in describing the discretion of a court of law in allowing bail
to prisoners.[48]

CONFUSING TERMINOLOGY

The legal principles developed to impose the rule of law on the substance of administrative discretion often overlap with each other and they are by their nature difficult to define
precisely. One result of this is that the terminology used by the courts is often confusing
and it may also be used inconsistently. It will be well to set out plainly the various uses of
the terminology and the way that it will be used as far as possible in this book.

A court will often say that a discretionary power has to be exercised reasonably; and
by this it intends to refer compendiously to all the ways in which that power might be
abused.[49] This wide-ranging use of the concept of reasonableness is better captured by a
phrase often used in the ancient cases. There it is held that the decision-maker is bound
to decide according to 'the rule of reason and law'.[50] The rule of reason, as we shall call
the principle, contains within it the several ways in which power might be abused. These
include, in the first place, the rule that the decision-maker should take into account all
relevant considerations and exclude from consideration all irrelevant considerations. It
includes, in the second place, the rule that the power should be exercised for a proper and
not an improper purpose. Subtle questions about the reach and scope of these rules arises
and these are discussed elsewhere.[51] But, in the third place, the rule of reason includes
the rule that a power may be abused when it is exercised to do something 'so absurd that
no sensible person could ever dream that it lay within the powers of the authority'[52] or in
its alternative formulation it led to an outcome 'so outrageous in its defiance of logic or
accepted moral standards that no sensible person who had applied his mind to the question to be decided could have arrived at it'. This third way of abusing a discretionary power
is frequently called *Wednesbury* unreasonableness from the case of that name where the
principle was first articulated in this form. But in the canonical dictum from that case set
out at length elsewhere[53] the judge plainly referred to all the ways in which a discretionary
power could be abused and stressed that 'all these things run into one another'. After all a
decision-maker who acts for an improper purpose (for instance, when he acts out of spite)
will generally make a decision that no sensible person would think lawful. Thus the whole
rule of reason can be referred to as *Wednesbury* unreasonableness; and high authority
supports this usage.[54] Clearly confusion is both possible and common. In addition Lord
Diplock has used the term irrationality as a substitute for '*Wednesbury* unreasonableness' and this formulation has proved influential and is also commonly used.[55] Care and
sensitivity to context is needed to avoid being confused by this terminology. As far as
possible when this book refers to *Wednesbury* unreasonableness it will mean the principle
that the outcome of the decision-making process is so outrageous that the decision must
be unlawful. And when it refers to the rule of reason, or simply reasonableness, it refers
compendiously to all the ways in which a discretionary power may be abused.

Into this melange of different forms of unreasonableness comes the concept of proportionality. As explained elsewhere it applies when human rights are engaged to ensure that

---

[48] *R* v. *Wilkes* (1770) 4 Burr 2527 at 2539.   [49] See the authorities cited below, p. 294.
[50] This phrase comes from *Rooke's Case*, discussed below, p. 293.   [51] Below, p. 323.
[52] Lord Greene in the *Wednesbury* case, below, p. 303.   [53] Set out on p. 303.
[54] Below, p. 294.   [55] Below, p. 295.

any limitation on a human right is proportionate to the social and political considera-tions that justify that limitation.[56] There is much overlap between the rule of reason and a decision flawed for disproportionality.[57] Naturally a disproportionate infringement of a right will often also be contrary to the rule of reason. The co-existence of the principle of proportionality with *Wednesbury* unreasonableness needs to be considered.[58] These and other subtleties are explored in their place.

THE RULE OF REASON

EARLY DECISIONS

The characteristically legal conception of discretion is firmly established and dates at least from the sixteenth century. *Rooke's Case*,[59] referred to by Lord Halsbury, contains a well-known statement made in 1598 which has lost nothing of its accuracy in over 400 years. The Commissioners of Sewers had levied charges for repairing a river bank, but they had thrown the whole charge on one adjacent owner instead of apportioning it among all the owners benefited. In law they had power to levy charges in their discretion. But this charge was disallowed as inequitable and the report proceeds, in Coke's words:

> and notwithstanding the words of the commission give authority to the commissioners to do according to their discretions, yet their proceedings ought to be limited and bound with the rule of reason and law. For discretion is a science or understanding to discern between falsity and truth, between wrong and right, between shadows and substance, between equity and colourable glosses and pretences, and not to do according to their wills and private affections; for as one saith, *talis discretio discretionem confundit*.

In a very similar case of 1609 the same doctrine is repeated;[60] and it recurs elsewhere in Coke's works.[61] In 1647 it is laid down that

> wheresoever a commissioner or other person hath power given to do a thing at his discre-tion, it is to be understood of sound discretion, and according to law, and that this court hath power to redress things otherwise done by them.[62]

An eighteenth-century illustration is the case of the paving commissioners for Wapping, who had power to make alterations in streets 'in such a manner as the commissioners shall think fit'. In order to give a regular incline to a certain street they raised part of it by six feet, thus obstructing the plaintiff's doors and windows. The court held that 'the commissioners had grossly exceeded their powers, which must have a reasonable con-struction. Their discretion is not arbitrary, but must be limited by reason and law.'[63] These words clearly echo the decisions of the previous century.

---

[56] Below, p. 305.

[57] In *Bank Mellat* v. *Her Majesty's Treasury (No 2)* [2013] UKSC 39, Lord Sumption spoke of the 'inevitabl[e] overlap' between the 'requirements of rationality and proportionality' (para. 20). And see *MIAC* v. *Li*, below, p. 316.   [58] Below, p. 316.

[59] (1598) 5 Co Rep 99b.   [60] *Keighley's Case* (1609) 10 Co Rep 139a.

[61] See also Co. Litt. 227b: 'for as by the authority of Littleton, *discretio est discernere per legem, quid sit justum*, that is to discern by the right line of law, and not by the crooked cord of private opinion, which the vulgar call discretion.' See also *Hetley* v. *Boyer* (1614) Cro Jac 336 (Coke CJ). Cf. 4 Co Inst 41.

[62] *Estwick* v. *City of London* (1647) Style 42. See, similarly, *R* v. *Commissioners of Fens* (1666) 2 Keb 43.

[63] *Leader* v. *Moxon* (1773) 2 W Bl 924 (successful action for damages).

SOME LATER AUTHORITIES

That the general principle remains unchanged is shown by an abundance of later statements of high authority, such as Lord Halsbury's already cited. In a case about a local authority's power to erect public conveniences Lord Macnaghten said:

> It is well settled that a public body invested with statutory powers such as those conferred upon the corporation must take care not to exceed or abuse its powers. It must keep within the limits of the authority committed to it. It must act in good faith. And it must act reasonably. The last proposition is involved in the second, if not in the first.[64]

An extensive repertory of similar statements is to be found in the speeches of the Law Lords in *Roberts* v. *Hopwood*, a celebrated case still capable of touching a political nerve. The district auditor had disallowed as 'contrary to law' the over-generous wages paid by the Borough Council of Poplar to their employees under an Act empowering them to pay such wages as they 'may think fit'. What limit should the law set to this apparently unbounded discretion? In upholding the auditor the House of Lords decided unanimously that the Council were not at liberty to pay more than what was reasonable in the light of rates of wages generally.[65] Lord Sumner said that the words 'as they think fit' contained a necessary implication both of honesty and of reasonableness, and that the admitted implication as to bad faith was wide enough to include both.[66]

Lord Wrenbury, dealing with the argument that that Act did not say 'such reasonable wages' or 'as they reasonably think fit', said that to his mind there was no difference in the meaning, whether those words were in or out.[67] He laid down the law as follows:

> A person in whom is vested a discretion must exercise his discretion upon reasonable grounds. A discretion does not empower a man to do what he likes merely because he is minded to do so—he must in the exercise of his discretion do not what he likes but what he ought. In other words, he must, by the use of his reason, ascertain and follow the course which reason directs. He must act reasonably.[68]

VITALITY OF THE PRINCIPLE

The principle of reasonableness has become one of the most active and conspicuous among the doctrines which have vitalised administrative law in the latter half of the twentieth century. Although the principle itself is ancient, the cases in which it was invoked were few and far between until in 1968 the *Padfield* case[69] opened a new era. Today, on the other hand, it appears in reported cases almost every week, and in a substantial number of them it is invoked successfully. Its contribution to administrative law on the substantive side is equal to that of the principles of natural justice on the procedural side.

This doctrine is now so often in the mouths of judges and counsel that it has acquired a nickname, taken from a case decided twenty years before *Padfield*, the *Wednesbury* case.[70] The reports now are freely sprinkled with expressions like 'the *Wednesbury* principle', '*Wednesbury* unreasonableness', or 'on *Wednesbury* grounds'. As Lord Scarman explained:[71]

---

[64] *Westminster Corporation* v. *L & NW Railway* [1905] AC 426 at 430.
[65] *Roberts* v. *Hopwood* [1925] AC 578; below, p. 340.   [66] Ibid. at 604.   [67] Ibid. at 613.
[68] Ibid. at 613.   [69] Below, p. 297.   [70] Below, p. 303.
[71] *R* v. *Secretary of State for the Environment ex p Nottinghamshire CC* [1986] AC 240 at 249.

'*Wednesbury* principles' is a convenient legal 'shorthand' used by lawyers to refer to the classical review by Lord Greene MR in the *Wednesbury* case of the circumstances in which the courts will intervene to quash as being illegal the exercise of administrative discretion.

One of the grounds of review, he added, is 'unreasonableness in the *Wednesbury* sense'. In the same case Lord Bridge referred to the exercise of power 'unreasonably in what, in current legal jargon, is called the "*Wednesbury*" sense'. '*Wednesbury*' is now a common and convenient label indicating the special standard of unreasonableness which has become the criterion for judicial review of administrative discretion. It is explained in that context later, where the key passage from the judgment of Lord Greene MR is set out in full.[72]

In an important ex cathedra statement of the grounds for judicial review Lord Diplock preferred the term 'irrationality', explaining it as 'what can by now be succinctly referred to as *Wednesbury* unreasonableness'.[73] But it is questionable whether 'irrationality' is a better word.[74] Virtually all administrative decisions are rational in the sense that they are made for intelligible reasons, but the question then is whether they measure up to the legal standard of reasonableness. 'Irrational' most naturally means 'devoid of reasons' whereas 'unreasonable' means 'devoid of satisfactory reasons'.[75]

The expression 'arbitrary and capricious' is sometimes used as a synonym for 'unreasonable';[76] and in one case this has been transmuted into 'frivolous or vexatious' and 'capricious and vexatious'.[77] But the meaning of all such expressions is necessarily the same, since the true question must always be whether the statutory power has been abused.

NO UNFETTERED DISCRETION IN PUBLIC LAW

The common theme of all the authorities so far mentioned is that the notion of absolute or unfettered discretion is rejected. Statutory power conferred for public purposes is conferred as it were upon trust, not absolutely—that is to say, it can validly be used only in the right and proper way which Parliament when conferring it is presumed to have intended. Although the Crown's lawyers have argued in numerous cases that unrestricted permissive language confers unfettered discretion, the truth is that, in a system based on the rule of law, unfettered governmental discretion is a contradiction in terms.[78] The real question is whether the discretion is wide or narrow, and where the legal line is to be drawn. For this purpose everything depends upon the true intent and meaning of the empowering Act.

---

[72] Below, pp. 302–3. Among much literature see [1987] *PL* 368 (J. Jowell and A. Lester); [1996] *PL* 59 (Lord Irvine of Lairg); Supperstone and Goudie, *Judicial Review*, 2nd edn, ch. 6 (P. Walker); Sir John Laws in Forsyth and Hare (eds.), *The Golden Metwand*, 185, exploring constitutional and ethical connotations.

[73] *Council of Civil Service Unions* v. *Minister for the Civil Service* [1985] AC 374 at 410. See Appendix 1 for context.

[74] For Lord Donaldson MR's dislike of it see *R* v. *Devon CC ex p G* [1989] AC 573 at 577 ('it is widely misunderstood by politicians, both local and national, and even more by their constituents, as casting doubt on the mental capacity of the decision-maker'); and see the criticism by Carnwath LJ in [1996] *PL* 244 at 253.

[75] e.g. in the *Nottinghamshire* case, above, and in *R* v. *Home Secretary ex p Brind* [1991] 1 AC 696. And see *Minister for Immigration and Citizenship* v. *Li* [2013] HCA 18, (2013) 87 ALJR 618 at para. 30 (recognising distinction between rational and reasonable).

[76] e.g. in *Weinberger* v. *Inglis* [1919] AC 606; *Roncarelli* v. *Duplessis* (above).

[77] *R* v. *Barnet and Camden Rent Tribunal ex p Frey Investments Ltd* [1972] 2 QB 342.

[78] A particularly clear decision to this effect is that of Sachs J in *Commissioners of Customs and Excise* v. *Cure and Deeley Ltd* [1962] 1 QB 340, especially at 366–7.

The powers of public authorities are therefore essentially different from those of private persons. A man making his will may, subject to any rights of his dependants, dispose of his property just as he may wish.[79] He may act out of malice or a spirit of revenge, but in law this does not affect his exercise of his power. In the same way a private person has an absolute power to allow whom he likes to use his land, to release a debtor, or, where the law permits, to evict a tenant, regardless of his motives.[80] This is unfettered discretion. But a public authority may do none of these things unless it acts reasonably and in good faith and upon lawful and relevant grounds of public interest. So a city council acted unlawfully when it refused unreasonably to let a local rugby football club use the city's sports ground,[81] though a private owner could of course have refused with impunity. Nor may a local authority arbitrarily release debtors,[82] and if it evicts tenants, even though in accordance with a contract, it must act reasonably and 'within the limits of fair dealing'.[83] The whole conception of unfettered discretion is inappropriate to a public authority, which possesses powers solely in order that it may use them for the public good.

There is nothing paradoxical in the imposition of such legal limits. It would indeed be paradoxical if they were not imposed. Nor is it a special restriction which fetters only local authorities: it applies no less to ministers of the Crown.[84] Nor is it confined to the sphere of administration: it operates wherever discretion is given for some public purpose, for example where a judge has a discretion to order jury trial.[85] It is only where powers are given for the personal benefit of the person empowered that the discretion is absolute. Plainly this can have no application in public law.

For the same reasons there should in principle be no such thing as unreviewable administrative discretion, which should be just as much a contradiction in terms as unfettered discretion. The question which has to be asked is what is the scope of judicial review, and in a few special cases the scope for the review of discretionary decisions may be minimal.[86] It remains axiomatic that all discretion is capable of abuse, and that legal limits to every power are to be found somewhere.[87]

Before analysing this principle, which has many facets, it will be well to look now at a group of classic decisions which will show its general character, and which come from the period when the courts were breaking through the earlier boundaries and vigorously

---

[79] See *Re Brocklehurst* [1978] Ch 14.

[80] As in *Chapman* v. *Honig* [1963] 2 QB 502 (tenant gave evidence against landlord, who then evicted him. Lord Denning MR dissented).

[81] *Wheeler* v. *Leicester City Council* [1985] AC 1054, explained below, p. 337.

[82] *A-G* v. *Tynemouth Union* [1930] 1 Ch 616.

[83] *Bristol District Council* v. *Clark* [1975] 1 WLR 1443; *Cannock Chase DC* v. *Kelly* [1978] 1 WLR 1, holding that a local authority is under a stricter obligation than a private landlord but need not explain its reasons: *Sevenoaks DC* v. *Emmett* (1979) 39 P & CR 404 (from which the quotation comes). See also *West Glamorgan CC* v. *Rafferty* [1987] 1 WLR 457 (unlawful eviction of gipsies).

[84] e.g. *Commissioners of Customs and Excise* v. *Cure and Deeley Ltd* [1962] 1 QB 340; *Padfield* v. *Minister of Agriculture, Fisheries and Food* (below); *Congreve* v. *Home Office*, below, p. 301; and see the *Tameside* case, below, p. 360.

[85] *Ward* v. *James* [1966] 1 QB 273. For rejection of 'absolute discretion' see at 292 (Lord Denning MR). Similar law governs the discretionary powers of professional bodies and trustees: see e.g. *R* v. *Askew* (1768) 4 Burr 2186 at 2189 (admission to College of Physicians); *Re Baden's Deed Trusts* [1971] AC 424 at 456.

[86] As in the case of some prerogative powers (above, p. 290).

[87] Most of the above section, as it stood in the 6th edition, was approved by the House of Lords in *R* v. *Tower Hamlets LBC ex p Chetnik Developments Ltd* [1988] AC 858 at 872. The relevant passage has since been many times approved. See *Porter* v. *Magill* [2002] 2 AC 357, para. 19 (Lord Bingham) and *R (Attfield)* v. *London Borough of Barnet* [2013] EWHC 2089, para. 39 (Lang J).

extending judicial review. These examples concern ministerial approval, the powers of the police and the revocation of licences. They are all illustrations of the rebellion by the judges against the idea of unfettered discretion.

JUDICIAL REJECTION OF UNFETTERED DISCRETION: DISCRETION MUST BE 'USED TO PROMOTE THE POLICY AND OBJECTS OF THE ACT'

In two strong and almost simultaneous decisions of 1968 the House of Lords and the Court of Appeal boldly applied the law as so often laid down. In one, the House of Lords asserted legal control over the allegedly absolute discretion of the Minister of Agriculture and held that he had acted unlawfully. In the other, related in the next section, the Court of Appeal decided that they had power to condemn discriminatory action by the police in enforcing the criminal law, a species of discretion which is particularly difficult to challenge.

In *Padfield* v. *Minister of Agriculture, Fisheries and Food*[88] the House of Lords had to consider a dispute under the milk marketing scheme established under the Agricultural Marketing Act 1958. The Act provided for a committee of investigation which was to consider and report on certain kinds of complaint 'if the Minister in any case so directs'. The milk producers of the region close to London complained that the differential element in the price fixed for their milk by the Milk Marketing Board was too low, since it ought to reflect the increased cost of transport from other regions but had not been revised since the Second World War. But since that region was in a minority on the Board, and any increase would be at the expense of the other regions, the Board could not be persuaded to act. The minister had power, if the committee of investigation so recommended, to make an order overriding the Board. But he refused to direct the committee to act, saying that since the producers were represented on the board they should be content with 'the normal democratic machinery' of the marketing scheme. His officials also added, incautiously, that if the committee made a favourable report the minister might be expected to take action on it. The whole object of the minister's overriding power, however, was that he might correct the 'normal democratic machinery' where necessary; and the suggestion that he might be embarrassed by a favourable report was, as Lord Reid said, 'plainly a bad reason'. It was held that where there was a relevant and substantial complaint the minister had a duty as well as a power and that he could not use his discretion to frustrate the policy of the Act. Otherwise he would be rendering nugatory a safeguard provided by the Act and depriving the producers of a remedy which Parliament intended them to have. Mandamus was therefore granted to compel the minister to act as the law required.

Lord Reid expressly rejected 'the unreasonable proposition that it must be all or nothing—either no discretion at all or an unfettered discretion'. He said:

> Parliament must have conferred the discretion with the intention that it should be used to promote the policy and objects of the Act; the policy and objects of the Act must be determined by construing the Act as a whole and construction is always a matter of law for the court. In a matter of this kind it is not possible to draw a hard and fast line, but if the Minister, by reason of his having misconstrued the Act or for any other reason, so uses his discretion as to thwart or run counter to the policy and objects of the Act, then

---

[88] [1968] AC 997.

our law would be very defective if persons aggrieved were not entitled to the protection of the court.

Lord Upjohn said that the minister's stated reasons showed a complete misapprehension of his duties, and were all bad in law. The scarcely veiled allusion to fear of parliamentary trouble was, in particular, a political reason which was quite extraneous and inadmissible. One of the fundamental matters confounding the minister's attitude was his claim to 'unfettered' discretion:

> First, the adjective nowhere appears in section 19 and is an unauthorised gloss by the Minister. Secondly, even if the section did contain that adjective I doubt if it would make any difference in law to his powers, save to emphasise what he has already, namely that acting lawfully he has a power of decision which cannot be controlled by the courts; it is unfettered. But the use of that adjective, even in an Act of Parliament, can do nothing to unfetter the control which the judiciary have over the executive, namely that in exercising their powers the latter must act lawfully and that is a matter to be determined by looking at the Act and its scope and object in conferring a discretion upon the Minister rather than by the use of adjectives.

Having thus decisively rejected the notion of unfettered discretion, at the initial stage, the House of Lords went on to indicate that the minister might in the end decline to implement the committee's report, and that the assessment of the balance of public interest would be for him alone. Lord Reid said:

> He may disagree with the view of the committee as to public interest, and, if he thinks that there are other public interests which outweigh the public interest that justice should be done to the complainers, he would be not only entitled but bound to refuse to take action. Whether he takes action or not, he may be criticised and held accountable to Parliament but the court cannot interfere.

In the end, perhaps predictably, the committee reported in favour of the complainants, but the minister refused to take action. No doubt even his ultimate discretion could be abused unlawfully if he could be shown to have acted on inadmissible grounds, e.g. from personal spite. But the distinction drawn by the House of Lords well shows how a statute which confers a variety of discretionary powers may confer wider or narrower discretion according to the context and the general scheme of the Act. Translated into terms of the traditional rule that powers must be exercised reasonably, this means that the standard of reasonableness varies with the situation. The pitfalls which must always be avoided are those of literal verbal interpretation and of rigid standards.

The importance of the House of Lords' decision was underlined by Lord Denning MR:[89]

> The discretion of a statutory body is never unfettered. It is a discretion which is to be exercised according to law. That means at least this: the statutory body must be guided by relevant considerations and not by irrelevant. If its decision is influenced by extraneous considerations which it ought not to have taken into account, then the decision cannot stand. No matter that the statutory body may have acted in good faith; nevertheless the decision will be set aside. That is established by *Padfield* v. *Minister of Agriculture, Fisheries and Food* which is a landmark in modern administrative law.

---

[89] *Breen* v. *Amalgamated Engineering Union* [1971] 2 QB 175 at 190; see similarly *Secretary of State for Employment* v. *ASLEF (No 2)* [1972] 2 QB 455 at 493; *Secretary of State for Education and Science* v. *Tameside Metropolitan Borough Council* [1977] AC 1014.

Another potentially significant aspect of the case was that the House of Lords refused to accept that the court's control could be evaded by omitting to specify the grounds of decision.[90]

Two particularly striking examples of a minister's discretionary power being fettered by the policy of an Act of Parliament are the *Laker Airways* case and the *Criminal Injuries Compensation Board* case. These are explained later.[91]

The Privy Council has held that the discretion of the Malaysian head of state to revoke a proclamation of emergency is not entirely unfettered, and that failure to revoke it after he no longer considers it to be necessary would be an abuse of his discretion.[92]

Two recent cases need to be mentioned here because they propound the heresy that section 25 of the Burial Act 1857 contains an 'unfettered discretion'. That section provides that 'it shall not be lawful to remove any body, or the remains of any body, which may have been interred in any place of burial, without licence under the hand of one of Her Majesty's Principal Secretaries of State'. Lord Neuberger MR has remarked of this section that it 'confers an unfettered discretion' and 'in the absence of special circumstances, it is inappropriate for the court to treat a statutorily conferred discretion with no express limitations or fetters as being somehow implicitly limited or fettered'.[93] Yet as we have seen it is commonplace for the judges to impose limits on apparently unqualified discretions derived from 'the policy and objects of the Act'. And in both the recent cases mentioned the judges, in fact, recognised that such limitations might be imposed and required that the discretion of the Secretary of State, although wide, be exercised in accordance with the rule of reason.[94] Thus the incautious use of the word 'unfettered' to describe a broad statutory discretion does not adumbrate the rejection of the foundational principle of administrative law just described.

NO UNFETTERED DISCRETION IN PUBLIC LAW: DISCRETIONARY POLICE POWERS

The discretion possessed by the police in enforcing the criminal law was considered by the Court of Appeal in a case in which the applicant complained, merely as a citizen, that the police had adopted a policy of not prosecuting London gaming clubs for illegal forms of gaming.[95] The Commissioner's confidential instructions, when revealed to the court, substantially bore out the complaint, being based on the uncertainty of the law and the expense and manpower required to keep the clubs under observation. But while the case was pending the law was clarified, fresh instructions were issued, and the Commissioner undertook to withdraw the former instructions. The court therefore found no occasion to intervene. But they made it clear that the Commissioner was not an entirely free agent as his counsel contended. He had a legal duty to the public to enforce the law and the

---

[90] See below, p. 333.   [91] p. 333.

[92] *Teh Cheng Poh* v. *Public Prosecutor, Malaysia* [1980] AC 458, holding that the duty would be enforceable by mandamus to the responsible ministers.

[93] *R (Rudewicz)* v. *Secretary of State for Justice* [2012] EWCA Civ 499, [2013] QB 410 at para. 30. The other case is *R (The Plantagenet Alliance Ltd)* v. *Secretary of State for Justice* [2013] EWHC B13 (Haddon-Cave J).

[94] An 'obligation to act rationally' and 'in accordance with the general law' (*Rudewicz*, para. 30). Requirement 'to act rationally and in accordance with the general law' and a 'duty to consult' (*Plantagenet Alliance*, para. 21). These limitations can only be implied from the Act, since otherwise, if Parliament intended an unfettered discretion, these limitations would challenge Parliament's will. See above, p. 31. See now Appendix 3.

[95] *R* v. *Metropolitan Police Commissioner ex p Blackburn* [1968] 2 QB 118. See also *Adams* v. *Metropolitan Police Cmr* [1980] RTR 289.

court could intervene by mandamus if, for example, he made it a rule not to prosecute housebreakers. On the other hand the court would not question his discretion when reasonably exercised, e.g. in not prosecuting offenders who for some special reason were not blameworthy in the way contemplated by the Act creating the offence. The court criticised the police policy of suspending observation of gaming clubs, as being clearly contrary to Parliament's intentions; and had it not been changed, they would have been disposed to intervene. But the police have a wide discretion in their operational decisions and their choice of methods, for instance if they call off the pursuit of robbers in a disturbed area because of concern for the safety of their officers,[96] or if their resources of manpower and finance are inadequate for providing continuous protection to exporters of live animals from attacks and obstruction by mobs of protesters.[97]

In 1972 the same public-spirited citizen brought similar proceedings, asking the court to order the police to take more effective action to enforce the law against the publication and sale of pornography. The Metropolitan Police were given instructions not to institute prosecutions or apply for destruction orders without the approval of the Director of Public Prosecutions; and it was shown that much pornographic literature was flagrantly offered for sale without interference by the police. The Court of Appeal found that the efforts of the police had been largely ineffective, but that the real cause of the trouble was the feebleness of the Obscene Publications Act 1959. Accordingly it could not be said that the police were failing in their duty, and an order of mandamus was refused.[98] It was again made clear that if the police were carrying out their duty to enforce the law, the court would not interfere with their discretion; but that the court would do so in the extreme case where it was shown that they were neglecting their duty. And the applicant was commended for having performed a public service by his proceedings.

NO UNFETTERED DISCRETION IN PUBLIC LAW: ABUSE OF LICENSING POWERS

The law was admirably stated by a Canadian judge in a celebrated case where a liquor licence had been unlawfully cancelled for extraneous political reasons, purportedly under an Act which said that the liquor commission 'may cancel any permit at its discretion'. Rand J. said:[99]

In public regulation of this sort there is no such thing as absolute and untrammelled 'discretion', that is that action can be taken on any ground or for any reason that can be suggested to the mind of the administrator; no legislative Act can, without express language, be taken to contemplate an unlimited arbitrary power, exercisable for any purpose, however capricious or irrelevant, regardless of the nature or purpose of the statute. Fraud and corruption in the Commission may not be mentioned in such statutes but they are always implied as exceptions. 'Discretion' necessarily implies good faith in discharging public duty; there is always a perspective within which a statute is intended to operate; and any

---

[96] R v. Oxford ex p Levey, The Times, 1 November 1986; (1987) 151 LG Rev 371.

[97] R v. Chief Constable of Sussex ex p International Trader's Ferry Ltd [1999] 2 AC 418. For this case see below, p. 331.

[98] R v. Metropolitan Police Commissioner ex p Blackburn (No 3) [1973] 1 QB 241. The applicant made another attempt in 1980 but with no better success: The Times, 7 March 1980 (reporting that the applicant referred to Lord Denning MR as 'the greatest living Englishman' and received the retort 'tell that to the House of Lords').

[99] Roncarelli v. Duplessis (1959) 16 DLR (2d) 689 at 705. The other quotations below are from the same judgment.

clear departure from its lines or objects is just as objectionable as fraud or corruption. Could an applicant be refused a permit because he had been born in another Province or because of the colour of his hair? The ordinary language of the Legislature cannot be so distorted.

In this case a restaurant proprietor's liquor licence had been cancelled by the Quebec Liquor Commission at the instigation of the Prime Minister of Quebec, for the reason that the proprietor habitually stood bail for members of the sect of Jehovah's Witnesses, who were a nuisance to the police. The Supreme Court of Canada awarded damages against the Prime Minister and stigmatised the cancellation as

> a gross abuse of legal power expressly intended to punish him for an act wholly irrelevant to the statute, a punishment which inflicted on him, as it was intended to do, the destruction of his economic life as a restaurant keeper within the Province.

And in addition it was said:

> To deny or revoke a permit because a citizen exercises an unchallengeable right totally irrelevant to the sale of liquor in a restaurant is equally beyond the scope of the discretion conferred.

As well as affording an outstandingly clear example of the abuse of executive power, this case illustrates the personal liability of ministers[100] and the possibility of a remedy in damages for maladministration.[101]

In a comparable English case the revocation of television licences by the Home Office was condemned by the Court of Appeal.[102] The Home Secretary had a statutory power to revoke or vary any licence under the Wireless Telegraphy Act 1949, and he elected to use this power to cancel the licences of persons who took them out during the currency of their previous licences in order to avoid a sharp increase in the licence fee. The increase took effect on a fixed date and it was in no way unlawful for a licence-holder to obtain a new licence before that date at the lower fee. The Home Office had no power to prevent this, but they tried to enforce a policy of exacting the higher fee by resorting to their power to revoke licences. This was held to be a clear abuse of the power and also an illegal attempt to levy money for the use of the Crown contrary to the Bill of Rights 1688. Lord Denning MR said:

> But when the licensee has done nothing wrong at all, I do not think the Minister can lawfully revoke the licence, at any rate, not without offering him his money back, and not even then except for good cause. If he should revoke it without giving reasons, or for no good reason, the courts can set aside his revocation and restore the licence. It would be a misuse of the power conferred on him by Parliament: and these courts have the authority—and, I would add, the duty—to correct a misuse of power by a minister of his department, no matter how much he may resent it or warn us of the consequences if we do.

In effect, the Home Office had tried to use their licensing powers to obtain taxing powers which had not been conferred on them. Their handling of the affair was also strongly criticised by the Parliamentary Commissioner for Administration.[103]

---

[100] Below, p. 693.   [101] Below, p. 664.
[102] *Congreve v. Home Office* [1976] QB 629. See (1976) 92 *LQR* 331. The Home Office had issued many thousands of demands and had to undertake a big operation to repay money unlawfully received.
[103] HC 680 (1974–5).

Other examples of the legal limits to the discretion of licensing authorities are given later.[104]

THE STANDARD OF REASONABLENESS

The doctrine that powers must be exercised reasonably has to be reconciled with the no less important doctrine that the court must not usurp the discretion of the public authority which Parliament appointed to take the decision. Within the bounds of legal reasonableness is the area in which the deciding authority has genuinely free discretion. If it passes those bounds, it acts ultra vires. The court must therefore resist the temptation to draw the bounds too tightly, merely according to its own opinion. When a Divisional Court yielded to that temptation by invalidating a Secretary of State's decision to postpone publication of a report by company inspectors, the House of Lords held that the judgments 'illustrate the danger of judges wrongly though unconsciously substituting their own views for the views of the decision-maker who alone is charged and authorised by Parliament to exercise a discretion'.[105] The court must strive to apply an objective standard which leaves to the deciding authority the full range of choices which the legislature is presumed to have intended.[106] Decisions which are extravagant or capricious cannot be legitimate. But if the decision is within the confines of reasonableness, it is no part of the court's function to look further into its merits. 'With the question whether a particular policy is wise or foolish the court is not concerned; it can only interfere if to pursue it is beyond the powers of the authority.'[107] As Lord Hailsham LC has said, two reasonable persons can perfectly reasonably come to opposite conclusions on the same set of facts without forfeiting their title to be regarded as reasonable.[108]

WEDNESBURY UNREASONABLENESS: AN INTRODUCTION

The rule of reason is not therefore the standard of 'the man on the Clapham omnibus'.[109] It is the standard indicated by a true construction of the Act which distinguishes between what the statutory authority may or may not be authorised to do. It distinguishes between proper use and improper abuse of power. It is often expressed by saying that the decision is unlawful if it is one to which no reasonable authority could have come. This is the essence of what is most commonly called '*Wednesbury* unreasonableness', after the now famous case in which Lord Greene MR expounded it as follows:[110]

> It is true that discretion must be exercised reasonably. Now what does that mean? Lawyers familiar with the phraseology used in relation to exercise of statutory discretions often use the word 'unreasonable' in a rather comprehensive sense. It has frequently been used and is frequently used as a general description of the things that must not be done. For instance, a person entrusted with a discretion must, so to speak, direct himself properly in law. He must call his own attention to the matters which he is bound to consider. He

---

[104] Below, p. 342.

[105] *R* v. *Secretary of State for Trade and Industry ex p Lonrho plc* [1989] 1 WLR 525 (Lord Keith).

[106] This passage in its former version was approved by the Court of Appeal in *R* v. *Boundary Commission ex p Foot* [1983] QB 600 (unsuccessful challenge to Commission's decisions fixing boundaries of parliamentary constituencies).   [107] *Short* v. *Poole Cpn* [1926] Ch 66 and 91 (Warrington LJ).

[108] *Re W (an infant)* [1971] AC 682 at 700.   [109] [1933] 1 KB 205 at 224.

[110] *Associated Provincial Picture Houses Ltd* v. *Wednesbury Corporation* [1948] 1 KB 223 at 229, for which see below, p. 344.

must exclude from his consideration matters which are irrelevant to what he has to consider. If he does not obey those rules, he may truly be said, and often is said, to be acting 'unreasonably'. Similarly, there may be something so absurd that no sensible person could ever dream that it lay within the powers of the authority. Warrington LJ in *Short* v. *Poole Corporation*[111] gave the example of the red-haired teacher, dismissed because she had red hair. This is unreasonable in one sense. In another it is taking into consideration extraneous matters. It is so unreasonable that it might almost be described as being done in bad faith; and, in fact, all these things run into one another.

This has become the most frequently cited passage (though most commonly cited only by its nickname) in administrative law. It explains how 'unreasonableness', in its classic rule of reason formulation, covers a multitude of sins. These various errors commonly result from paying too much attention to the mere words of the Act and too little to its general scheme and purpose, and from the fallacy that unrestricted language naturally confers unfettered discretion.

The rule of reason has thus become a generalised rubric covering not only sheer absurdity or caprice, but merging into illegitimate motives and purposes, a wide category of errors commonly described as 'irrelevant considerations', and mistakes and misunderstandings which can be classed as self-misdirection,[112] or addressing oneself to the wrong question.[113] But the language used in the cases shows that, while the abuse of discretion has this variety of differing legal facets, in practice the courts often treat them as distinct. When several of them will fit the case, the court is often inclined to invoke them all. The one principle that unites them is that powers must be confined within the true scope and policy of the Act.

WEDNESBURY: THE CHARACTERISTIC USUAGE

Although the canonical dictum, just cited, stresses that 'all these things run into one another' it is commonplace to single out the final way of acting unreasonably. Thus decisions 'so absurd that no sensible person could ever dream that it lay within the powers of the authority' (Lord Greene MR); or 'so wrong that no reasonable person could sensibly take that view' (Lord Denning MR);[114] or 'so outrageous in its defiance of logic or of accepted moral standards that no sensible person who had applied his mind to the question to be decided could have arrived at it' (Lord Diplock)[115] are often singled out. Such extreme situations are often characterised as *Wednesbury* unreasonable or irrational; this is, in the modern cases, the most characteristic use of the phrase.[116]

---

[111] [1926] Ch 66.

[112] An example of self-misdirection was where the minister was given misleading advice, misunderstood his default powers, and gave invalid directions to a local health authority: *Lambeth LBC* v. *Secretary of State for Social Services* (1980) 79 LGR 61. The mistake was rectified by National Health Service (Invalid Direction) Act 1980.

[113] Examples are *Niarchos* v. *Secretary of State for the Environment* (1977) 76 LGR 480; *Anisminic Ltd* v. *Foreign Compensation Commission* [1969] 2 AC 147 (above, p. 219).

[114] In the *Tameside* case [1977] AC at 1026.

[115] In *Council of Civil Service Unions* v. *Minister for the Civil Service* [1985] AC at 410. For context see Appendix 1.

[116] For a useful account, including suggestions how the test might be clarified: identifying indicia of unreasonableness (illogicality; disproportionality; inconsistency with statute; differrential treatment; unexplained change of policy) see Paul Daly, '*Wednesbury's* Reason and Structure' 2011 *PL* 238.

It might seem from such language that the deliberate decisions of ministers and other responsible public authorities could almost never be found wanting. But, as may be seen in the following pages, there are abundant instances of legally unreasonable decisions and actions at all levels. This is not because ministers and public authorities take leave of their senses,[117] but because the courts in deciding cases tend to lower the threshold of unreasonableness to fit their more exacting ideas of administrative good behaviour.[118]

There is ample room, within the legal boundaries, for radical differences of opinion in which neither side is unreasonable. A number of statements to this effect were made in the Court of Appeal and the House of Lords in the case of the Tameside schools, discussed later.[119] Lord Denning MR pointed out the error of confusing differences of opinion, however strong, with unreasonableness on the part of one side or the other. One party may call the other 'quite unreasonable' when he is well within the legal limits of reasonableness. This was the distinction which the Secretary of State failed to make, as the House of Lords emphatically confirmed. Lord Diplock said:[120]

> The very concept of administrative discretion involves a right to choose between more than one possible course of action upon which there is room for reasonable people to hold differing opinions as to which is to be preferred.

In the same vein Lord Hailsham LC has said that 'not every reasonable exercise of judgment is right, and not every mistaken exercise of judgment is unreasonable'.[121]

Reasonableness does not require reasons to be stated. The only significance of withholding reasons is that if the facts point overwhelmingly to one conclusion, the decision-maker cannot complain if he is held to have had no rational reason for deciding differently,[122] and that in the absence of reasons he is in danger of being held to have acted arbitrarily.[123]

WEDNESBURY NOT 'MONOLITHIC'

Before we turn to consideration of the doctrine of proportionality it needs to be spelt out here that the *Wednesbury* standard is not 'monolithic';[124] it varies according to context. Where the right to life is engaged the House of Lords held in 1987 that 'the basis of the decision must surely call for the most anxious scrutiny'.[125] The effect of this 'anxious scrutiny' is that the human rights context is important in judging whether the decision-maker has exceeded the range of options open to him. The canonical dictum holds that the 'more substantial the interference with human rights, the more the court will require by way of

---

[117] Lord Scarman used this phrase in *R* v. *Secretary of State for the Environment ex p Nottinghamshire CC* [1986] AC 240 at 247.

[118] See the discussion by Lord Lowry, approving the treatment in this book, in *R* v. *Home Secretary ex p Brind* [1991] 1 AC 696 at 765. Cf. [1987] *PL* 368 at 372 (J. Jowell and A. Lester).   [119] Below, p. 360.

[120] [1977] AC at 1064.   [121] *Re W (an infant)* [1971] AC 682 at 700.

[122] *R* v. *Secretary of State for Trade and Industry ex p Lonrho plc* [1989] 1 WLR 525 at 539 (Lord Keith).

[123] See the *Padfield* case, below, p. 297.

[124] Sir John Laws in his important discussion on *Wednesbury* (in Forsyth and Hare (eds.), *The Golden Metwand*, 185) first used this word in this context. Lord Carnwath's ALBA lecture 'From Judicial Outrage to Sliding Scales—Where Next for *Wednesbury*' (12 November 2013) (available at <http://www.supreme-court.gov.uk/docs/speech-131112-lord-carnwath.pdf>) deserves to be noted here. Lord Carnwath advocates a 'pragmatic approach' in which the judge asks whether something has gone wrong that requires the intervention of the court; if the answer appears to be yes then the judge 'looks for a legal hook to hang [judicial intervention] on. And if there is none suitable, [the judge] may need to adapt one' (at 18–19). If correct as a model of the judicial process this pragmatism renders doctrinal analysis otiose.

[125] *R* v. *Secretary of State for the Home Department ex p Bugdaycay* [1987] 1 AC 514, 531 (Lord Bridge).

justification before it is satisfied that the decision is reasonable'.[126] This flexibility in the standard, well established in the law before the enactment of the Human Rights Act 1998, secured a significant measure of protection of fundamental rights at common law.[127] In addition it began the process whereby in fundamental rights cases the focus falls upon whether any infringement of the right is justified. This 'culture of justification' is a prominent facet of the modern law.[128]

This easing of the rigours of *Wednesbury* unreasonableness in the human rights context is matched by a tensing of the rigours where a broad issue of public finance or economic policy is involved, particularly an issue that has been approved by Parliament. In the leading decision[129] Lord Scarman said that he could not accept that 'it is constitutionally appropriate, save in very exceptional circumstances, for the courts to intervene on the ground of "unreasonableness" to quash guidance framed by the Secretary of State and by necessary implication approved by the House of Commons... Such an examination would be justified only if a prima facie case were to be shown for holding that the Secretary of State had acted in bad faith, or for an improper motive, or that the consequences of his guidance were so absurd that he must have taken leave of his senses.'

THE PRINCIPLE OF PROPORTIONALITY

In the law of a number of European countries—the doctrine is Prussian in origin—there is a 'principle of proportionality'[130] which ordains that administrative measures must not be more drastic than is necessary for attaining the desired result.[131] Most significantly, the doctrine is applied by the European Court of Human Rights in Strasbourg (although the word does not appear in the European Convention), and so is taken into account in Britain under the Human Rights Act 1998.[132] The introduction of proportionality into consideration of whether limitations on fundamental rights are justified is one of the most prominent and most far-reaching consequences of the Human Rights Act 1998. The

---

[126] Put forward by David Pannick QC and adopted by Lord Bingham MR in *R v. Ministry of Defence ex p Smith* [1996] QB 517 at 554.   [127] *R v. Home Secretary ex p Brind* [1991] 1 AC 696 at 748.

[128] Below, pp. 139–40. For instance, *R v. Lord Saville of Newdigate ex p A* [1999] 4 All ER 860 (order of statutory tribunal of inquiry denying anonymity to soldier witnesses who fired shots in 'Bloody Sunday' riots of 1972 quashed because identification would endanger their lives).And see *R v. Home Secretary ex p Leech (No 2)* [1994] QB 198 (Home Secretary's wide powers of administration over prisons do not empower prison governors to obstruct prisoners' correspondence with their legal advisers or their access to the courts of law).

[129] *R v. Secretary of State for the Environment ex p Nottinghamshire CC* [1986] AC 240, approved in *R v. Secretary of State for the Environment ex p Hammersmith and Fulham LBC* [1991] 1 AC 521.

[130] There is a voluminous literature on this topic. See (2001) 60 *CLJ* 301 (Elliott); [2002] *PL* 265 (Leigh); (2001) 117 *LQR* 589 (Craig); [2003] *PL* 592 (Jowell); [2004] *PL* 33 (Clayton); [2006] *CLJ* 174 (Rivers); [2007] *JR* 31 (Hickman); Hunt in Bamforth and Leyland (eds.), *Public Law in a Multi-Layered Constitution* (2003) at 350 and particularly Elliott, 'Proportionality and Deference: The Importance of a Structured Approach' in Forsyth, Elliott, Jhaveri, Ramsden and Scully-Hill (eds.), *Effective Judicial Review: A Cornerstone of Good Governance* (2010), 246ff.; Hickman, 'The Substance and Structure of Proportionality' [2008] *PL* 694; J. Rivers, 'Proportionality and Variable Intensity Review' (2006) 65 *CLJ* 174; Gordon, 'Two Dogmas of Proportionality' [2011] *JR* 182; Aharon Barak, *Proportionality: Constitutional Rights and their Limitations* (2012); Arden LJ, 'Proportionality: The Way Ahead?' (2011), available at <http://www.judiciary.gov.uk/Resources/JCO/Documents/Speeches/lj-arden-speech-ukael-proportionality-12112012.pdf>; and Timothy Endicott, 'Proportionality and Incommensurability', available at <http://papers.ssrn.com/sol3/papers.cfm?abstract_id=2086622>.

[131] Schwarze, *European Administrative Law*, 680; (1992) 12 *OJLS* 237 (S. Boyron); P. Walker in Supperstone and Goudie (eds.), *Judicial Review*, 3nd edn, 6.41 (a comprehensive discussion).   [132] s. 2(1).

doctrine has also been adopted by the European Court of Justice in Luxembourg[133] and so it has infiltrated British law by this route, since British law must conform to European Union law.

THE TEST OF PROPORTIONALITY

While the principle of proportionality is easy to state at the abstract level (an administrative measure must not be more drastic than necessary) or to sum up in a phrase (not taking a sledgehammer to crack a nut), applying the principle in concrete situations is less straightforward. But a 'structured proportionality' test has emerged from several decisions[134] for use when assessing whether a decision limiting a right protected under the Human Rights Act 1998 should be upheld or not.

It is typically[135] deployed in determining whether a limitation on the rights protected by Articles 8–11 is justified. Each of these articles has two paragraphs and the second expressly recognises that the right protected in the first may be limited. Thus Article 10(2) provides that the freedom of expression protected in Article 10(1) 'may be subject to such formalities, conditions, restrictions or penalties as are prescribed by law and are necessary in a democratic society, in the interests of national security, territorial integrity or public safety, for the prevention of disorder or crime, for the protection of health or morals, for the protection of the reputation or rights of others, for preventing the disclosure of information received in confidence, or for maintaining the authority and impartiality of the judiciary'. A prohibition on making false reports of fire in a crowded theatre will be readily justified in order to protect public safety. But a restriction on the discussion in

---

[133] See e.g. *R* v. *Intervention Board for Agricultural Produce ex p ED & F Man (Sugar) Ltd* [1986] 2 All ER 115 (excessively severe forfeiture).

[134] The formulation of the test set out below is based upon the advice of the Privy Council in *De Freitas* v. *Permanent Secretary of Ministry of Agriculture, Fisheries, Lands and Housing* [1999] 1 AC 69 at 80 which was adopted by the House of Lords in *R (Daly)* v. *Home Secretary* [2001] UKHL 26, [2001] 2 AC 532, para. 27 (Lord Steyn) and in many other cases. The fourth element in the test set out below is not adopted in these cases but follows from *Huang* v. *Home Secretary* [2007] UKHL 11, [2007] 2 AC 167, para. 19 (adopting the approach of *R* v. *Oakes* [1986] 1 SCR 103) and *R (Razgar)* v. *Home Secretary* [2004] UKHL 27, [2004] 2 AC 368, paras. 17 and 20.

[135] The test of proportionality is less structured in other areas. In EU law, for instance, the orthodox approach is first a test of suitability (is the measure reasonably likely to achieve its objectives) and then a test of necessity (weighing the adverse consequences against the importance of the objectives of the measure) (see Tridimas, *The General Principles of EU Law* (1999) at 91). It should also not be supposed that proportionality is irrelevant to the unqualified articles of the Convention (that lack a limitations clause). In addition the EU test is also less intensive. See *R (Telefonica O2 Europe plc)* v. *Secretary of State for Business, Enterprise and Regulatory Reform* [2007] EWHC 3018, following *Jippes and ors* (Case C-189/01) [2001] ECR I-5689. So if the rule-maker enjoys a wide discretion, the measure adopted must be 'manifestly inappropriate' in terms of the public aim being pursued before intervention is justified (*Spain* v. *Council* (Case C-310/04) [2006] ECR I-7285, para. 99). This was a 'formidable hurdle' for the challenger to surmount (*Telefonica*, para. 17). Similarly, *R (Sinclair Collis Ltd)* v. *Secretary of State for Health* [2011] EWCA Civ 437 (total ban on sale of tobacco in vending machines alleged to be disproportionate); Arden LJ concluded in the circumstances (Neuberger MR concurring; Laws LJ dissenting): 'the test of "least intrusive means" either does not apply or applies with [a] lower level of intensity' (para. 85(d)); regulations upheld. But in *Bank Mellat* it was argued (but rejected in the Court of Appeal ([2011] EWCA Civ 1)) that there was a significant difference between Luxembourg law and domestic law in that the former did not include the element that the means used to impair the right was no more than is necessary to accomplish the objective. Kay LJ was 'not persuaded that the domestic and European tests are significantly different' (para. 21). In the Supreme Court ([2013] UKSC 39) the view of Kay LJ was approved (para. 20 (Lord Sumption) and para. 78 (Lord Reed (dissenting)). Where rights (whether under EU law (see above, p. 172) or the ECHR) are engaged, there may not be much difference. But where, say, the determination of policy is in issue Luxembourg may be less intrusive.

the press of controversial litigation may sometimes be able to be justified as necessary in the interests of national security (protection of the identity and methods of the intelligence services) or to maintain the impartiality of the judiciary (ensuring that a jury is not improperly influenced).[136] At other times such restrictions will not be able to be justified. The pressing social need that supposedly justifies the restriction may be found wanting. It is here that proportionality comes into its own in determining whether the restriction is justified or not. See Appendix 3.

Under the 'structured test' there are four questions which the decision-maker must address. The questions are cumulative in that every one must be satisfactorily answered if the decision is to survive scrutiny. The questions are:

1. Whether the legislative objective is sufficiently important to justify limiting a fundamental right.

2. Whether the measures designed to meet the legislative objective are rationally connected to it.

3. Whether the means used to impair the right or freedom are no more than is necessary to accomplish the objective. (This is the 'necessity question'.)

4. Whether a fair balance has been struck between the rights of the individual and the interests of the community which is inherent in the whole of the Convention. (This is sometimes called 'narrow proportionality'.)

Applying the test is plainly not a mechanical task since each element requires the making of a judgment by the primary decision-maker. But the decision-maker (or the judicial review court when his decision is challenged) cannot avoid these difficult substantive judgments by taking refuge in procedure. The relevant articles of the Convention, Lord Hoffmann has said, are 'concerned with substance, not procedure. [The Convention] confers no right to have a decision [made] in a particular way. What matters is the result'.[137] This shows the extent to which the principle of proportionality departs from classical judicial review where the emphasis falls upon process rather than outcome.

The difficulties of making these judgments are somewhat ameliorated by Lord Bingham's description of the principle. He said:[138] '[I]t is clear that the court's approach to an issue of proportionality under the Convention must go beyond that traditionally adopted to judicial review in a domestic setting.... There is no shift to a merits review, but the intensity of review is greater than was previously appropriate, and greater even than the heightened scrutiny test... The domestic court must now make a value judgment, an evaluation, by reference to the circumstances prevailing at the relevant time'.

But were it possible to calibrate with sufficient precision the extent to which a right was impaired, it would be clear that there would be only one impairment that was 'no more than is necessary to accomplish the objective'. And if only one outcome passes the test of proportionality,[139] there is only one right answer and the test is, in effect, a determination

---

[136] See *Sunday Times* v. *UK* (1979) 2 EHRR 245 discussed above, p. 132.

[137] *R (SB)* v. *Denbigh High School* [2006] UKHL 15, [2006] 2 WLR 719. See also Lord Bingham approving the analysis of Davies in ((2005) 1:3 *European Constitutional Law Review* 511). *Denbigh* was followed in *Belfast City Council* v. *Miss Behavin' Ltd (Northern Ireland)* [2007] UKHL 19, [2007] 1 WLR 1420 (licensing of sex shops). But note particulary Mead, 'Outcomes Aren't All: Defending Process-based Review of Public Authority Decisions under the Human Rights Act' [2012] *PL* 61, 84 ('outcomes are all' reinforces judicial pre-eminence as guardian rather than arbiters of human rights).

[138] *Denbigh High School* (above), para. 30.

[139] Those outcomes that intrude on the right less would obviously not accomplish the objective and so are unacceptable outcomes.

of the merits.[140] That is obviously an unacceptable conclusion; and when the point has been raised the courts have not applied the test literally. In the *Bank Mellat* case, for instance, the 'necessity question' was interpreted as requiring only 'whether a less intrusive measure could have been used without unacceptably compromising the achievement of the objective'[141] rather than no 'more than is necessary to accomplish the objective'.

The rigour of the logic of the test is further ameliorated by the fact that the test of necessity is sensitive to context. So in the context of Protocol 1, Article 1 (where the balance has to be struck between different groups of private interests) it is sufficient that a fair balance is struck between those interests; and the balance struck need not be the least intrusive outcome.[142] In the adoption of a context-sensitive or relative approach to necessity we may note a proper reluctance for the test of proportionality to destroy the distinction between merits and review. This is further illustrated by the development of the concept of deference.

DEFERENCE

It is widely recognised that the primary decision-maker enjoys 'a discretionary area of judgment', i.e. an area into which the court in applying the test of proportionality will not intrude.[143] This is sometimes referred to as according a 'margin of appreciation' to the national authority[144] or a 'margin of discretion'.[145] The word commonly used to describe this (although it is itself controversial)[146] is, however, 'deference';[147] the court is said to show deference to the primary decision-maker. But howsoever it may be phrased, this discretionary area marks the extent to which the decision-maker may exercise an autonomous judgment, i.e. the extent to which the test of proportionality is not a merits review.

---

[140] Blackman J put the point well in *Illinois Election Board* v. *Socialist Worker Party* (1979) 440 US 173, 188–9 when he said: 'a judge would be unimaginative indeed if he could not come up with something a little less "drastic" or a little less "restrictive" in almost any situation and thereby enable himself to strike legislation down'.

[141] Para. 20 (Lord Sumption) and para. 74 (Lord Reed (dissenting)). In the Court of Appeal Kay LJ used a test of whether 'a less intrusive measure' would significantly compromise a 'legitimate aim' (para. 30).

[142] See *R (Clays Lane Housing Co-Operative Ltd)* v. *Housing Corporation* [2004] EWCA Civ 1658, [2005] 1 WLR 2229 (statutory regulator choosing between two social landlords). Kay LJ held that the appropriate test of proportionality under Art. 1 of the First Protocol requires 'a balancing exercise and a decision which is justified on the basis of a compelling case in the public interest and as being reasonably necessary but not obligatorily the least intrusive of Convention rights' (paras. 25 and 22 (necessity varies with context). *Samaroo* v. *Home Secretary* [2001] EWCA Civ 1139 which appeared to favour the least intrusive approach was restricted to its context (Art. 8 rights of family of drugs dealer facing deportation)). See also *Lough* v. *First Secretary of State* [2004] EWCA Civ 905.

[143] The phrase derives from Lester and Pannick, *Human Rights Law and Practice* (1999), para. 3.21 and was approved by Lord Hope in *R* v. *DPP ex p Kebilene* [2000] 2 AC 326 at 381.

[144] This is the phrase used in Strasbourg. It is inappropriate to use in a domestic rather than an international context.

[145] Used by Laws LJ in *R (ProLife Alliance)* v. *BBC* [2002] EWCA Civ 297, para. 33.

[146] See Lord Hoffmann in *R (ProLife Alliance)* v. *BBC* [2003] UKHL 23, paras. 75, 76 deprecating the 'servility' attached to the word deference.

[147] There is again a voluminous literature on this topic. See, in particular, 'Deference: A Tangled Story' [2005] *PL* 346 (Lord Steyn); [2003] *PL* 592 (Jowell); and see (2006) 65 *CLJ* 671 (Allan) (criticism of the concept as either 'empty' or 'pernicious'). See also the sources given above, pp. 140 (Poole) and 305. The nature of deference and the justifications have been the subject of continuing scholarly debate. See further, Allan, 'Judicial Deference and Judicial Review: Legal Doctrine and Legal Theory' (2011) *LQR* 96; Kavanagh, 'Defending Deference in Public Law and Constitutional Theory' (2010) *LQR* 222; and Young, 'In Defence of Due Deferencee (2009) 72 *MLR* 554.

Views differ on the breadth of deference and the justifications for it. On one hand, decisions taken by an elected decision-maker or a decision-maker accountable to elected representatives are said to be entitled to deference on the ground of democratic principle. And the principle is graduated, with greater deference being accorded to an Act of Parliament and less to a decision of the executive.[148] Lord Phillips MR has also remarked that a decision of the Home Secretary refusing leave for a controversial speaker to enter the UK in respect of which he was 'democratically accountable' was entitled to 'a wide margin of discretion'.[149] Others hold that the reason for deference (without any connotation of servility) is one of institutional competence. Where the matter raised is one that the courts are institutionally incompetent to decide, i.e. it concerns the allocation of scarce resources or competing individual needs which the public authority is in a better position to assess than the court, then judicial intervention is inappropriate.[150] Clearly there is considerable overlap between the approach of democratic principle and that of institutional competence since, on the whole, Parliament will allocate powers to institutionally competent decision-makers with the allocation of resources being accorded to democratically accountable decision-makers and the determination of rights to judicial decision-makers. So the debate may not be of great moment, although those who insist upon institutional competence as the only justification doubtless consider this justifies only a narrow doctrine of deference.

Elliott[151] has argued persuasively that the different justifications for deference apply to different questions in the structured test. The third question (the necessity question), for instance, is a question of fact and practicality. A measure of expertise, which the court will generally lack, will be required to assess whether a particular measure is no more intrusive than necessary and yet will achieve the objective. In these circumstances, it is appropriate to defer to the expertise of the official taking the decision. Thus in assessing whether it was necessary to make a 'control order' in a particular case, and whether the particular restrictions placed upon the suspect's rights were necessary to protect the public from the risk of terrorist attack, deference was shown to the assessment of the Home Secretary 'because she is better able than the court to decide what measures are necessary to protect the public from the activities of someone suspected of terrorism'.[152]

On the other hand, in assessing the fourth question (narrow proportionality (to use Elliott's phrase)) the court is not assessing a factual or practical question but is making a value judgment as to where the balance lies between individual rights and the interests of the community. There is often no right answer to such questions and the issue is one of the legitimacy of the decision-maker to make that judgment. Where the democratic process has led the legislator to adopt a particular compromise between the contending interests, that compromise deserves to be respected and deference shown to it.[153]

---

[148] See Laws LJ (dissenting) *International Transport Roth GmbH* v. *Secretary of State for the Home Department* [2002] EWCA Civ 158.

[149] *R (Farrakhan)* v. *Home Secretary* [2002] EWCA Civ 606, para. 74. But the decision was also based on institutional competence (para. 73).

[150] This approach is said to rest on a change in the conception of democracy now applicable following the enactment of the Human Rights Act 1998. Under the new conception fundamental rights trump 'even the overwhelming popular will' ([2003] *PL* 592 at 597 (Jowell)). But the public 'have not spoken yet' on this curbing of their will.   [151] Elliott (2008), as above.

[152] *Home Secretary* v. *AP* [2008] EWHC 2001, para. 66 (Keith J).

[153] e.g. *Kay* v. *London Borough of Lambeth* [2006] UKHL 10, [2006] 2 AC 465 (striking the balance between Art. 8 rights of occupiers of property and the rights of the owners to possession: 'Courts should proceed on the assumption that domestic law strikes a fair balance and is compatible with article 8' (para. 37, Lord Bingham)). See *Manchester City Council* v. *Pinnock* [2010] UKSC 45, [2011] 2 AC 104 (proportionality to be considered when possession sought even of 'demoted (insecure) tenancy') and *London Borough of*

Similarly, where that value judgment is made with due care by a democratically account-able decision-maker the court should not substitute its value judgement for that of the decision-maker. A court 'must not allow itself to become an umpire of a social and eco-nomic controversy that has been settled by due political process'.[154]

Elliott's subtle distinctions just described are valuable but the fact remains that the test of proportionality is complicated and the outcome of its application unpredictable.[155]

CONTINUING DIFFICULTIES WITH PROPORTIONALITY

As pointed out in an earlier chapter[156] human rights adjudication in the UK is primar-ily concerned with striking a balance between conflicting rights or pronouncing upon whether the limitation of a particular right is justified as being 'necessary in a democratic society in the interests of national security, public safety or the economic well-being of the country, for the prevention of disorder or crime, for the protection of health or morals, or for the protection of the rights and freedoms of others'.[157]

The structured test of proportionality, just described, has been developed by the judici-ary as the tool needed to carry out these difficult tasks. There is no doubt that the concept is of great assistance to the judge having to decide these thorny questions and that it lends legitimacy to the judicial process. Using it is a great deal more satisfactory than having the judge decide the issue on his or her assessment of the merits. The concept is now ingrained in the law and may even emerge as a common law principle with a role to play in funda-mental rights cases in the event that the 1998 Act is repealed.

Even so, the law in this area is hardly satisfactory. Two difficulties may, however, be noted. In the first place, the concept leaves the law very uncertain. A four-stage test with each stage requiring a separate judgment would generate uncertainty even if it were not the case that each of those judgments was itself difficult to make and unpredictable. Moreover, the further uncertainty of the degree of deference has to be considered. As it is, the unpredictabilities are cumulative. Only very bold counsel can confidently proffer an opinion, in any particular case, whether the test of proportionality is passed or not. Such uncertainty is not in the broader public interest but there is no easy remedy for it.

In the second place the 'necessity question' is often particularly difficult and unpredict-able since it involves the weighing of apples against pears. This point is best explained by a consideration of the leading case of *Quila* in the Supreme Court.[158] This case concerned a change made to the Immigration Rules 1994[159] that put the age at which a person might be

---

Hounslow v. *Powell* [2011] UKSC 8 (similarly for other insecure tenancies). Similarly in *R (Animal Defenders International)* v. *Secretary of State for Culture, Media and Sport* [2008] UKHL 15, [2008] 2 WLR 781. The limitations on political advertising in s. 321(2) of the Communications Act 2003 were found to be 'neces-sary' (and so no breach of Art. 10 found) on account of the 'great weight' given to the approach adopted by Parliament (para. 33, Lord Bingham). Also, in extradition cases interference with Art. 8 rights would have 'to be extremely serious if the public interest [in extradition] is to be outweighed': *Norris* v. *Government of the United States of America* [2010] UKSC 9, para. 55 and *HH* v. *Deputy Prosecutor of the Italian Republic, Genoa* [2012] UKSC 25 (but one litigant did succeed in resisting extradition; sufficiently severe interference with Art. 8 rights).

[154] *R (Cordant Group plc)* v. *Secretary of State for Business, Innovation and Skills* [2010] EWHC 3442, para. 23 (Kenneth Parker J).

[155] And Elliott's distinctions are not as stark as they have been represented here. For instance, there is an element of legitimacy-based deference even when addressing the necessity question. See the discussion of *Clays Lane Housing Co-Operative Ltd*, above.   [156] Above, p. 154.

[157] For a recent example see *Re W (Children)* [2010] UKSC 12 (Arts. 6 and 8 balanced).

[158] *R (Quila)* v. *Home Secretary* [2011] UKSC 45.   [159] Immigration Rules 1994, r. 277.

granted entry clearance as a spouse or civil partner of a UK settled person up from eighteen to twenty-one years of age. The purpose of this change was to deter forced marriage.[160] The Home Secretary, in making the change to the rule, judged that the increase in age before an application could be made would assist in combating forced marriage. This was because the apparent motive for a significant number of forced marriages was to assist in claims for UK residency or citizenship. By insisting that the spouse or intended spouse was three years older before an application for entry clearance could be made, the rule insured that the pressure to marry on that person while young was eased. Only when they were more mature and more able resist pressure could the application for entry clearance be made.

On the other hand, there were many 'other persons'—far more than the putative forced marriage cases—who were acting in complete good faith and wished to apply to have their spouse or intended spouse join them in the UK. They too fell foul of rule 277 and (unless an exceptional discretion was exercised in their favour) were forced to delay their marriage, or at least to live apart for three years, or live outside the United Kingdom for that period. The Supreme Court concluded—and this is not controversial—that denying the 'other persons' the opportunity to make an application for entry clearance until they were twenty-one was an interference with the respect for their family life required by Article 8(1). So the question to be decided was whether that interference was justified under Article 8(2); or whether it was a disproportionate interference.

The majority of the Supreme Court declined to accord 'a very substantial area of discretionary judgement' to the House Secretary since changes to the immigration rules did not have the 'imprimatur of democratic approval'[161] and went on to conclude that the Home Secretary's evidence that changing the rule would deter forced marriages was 'not robust'.[162] Moreover, there were very much larger numbers of 'bona fide other persons' who would be forced into exile or apart by rule 277 than the number of forced marriages it would deter. Thus rule 277 'is a sledge-hammer but [the Home Secretary] has not attempted to identify the size of the nut. At all events she fails to establish that the interference with the rights of the respondents under article 8 is justified.'[163] It is plain that the majority is more influenced by the injustice to the innocent 'other persons' actually before the court (who in fact had mostly been given exceptional leave to enter by the time the case reached the courts) than by the more uncertain injustice that was or may have been avoided by deterring forced marriages.

Lord Brown, however, dissented sharply. He said:

> The extent to which the rule will help combat forced marriage and the countervailing extent to which it will disrupt the lives of innocent couples adversely affected by it is largely a matter of judgment. Unless demonstrably wrong, this judgment should be rather for government than for the courts. Still more obviously, the comparison between the enormity of suffering within forced marriages on the one hand and the disruption to

---

[160] Lord Wilson, para. 9 explains the position: 'A forced marriage is a marriage into which one party enters not only without her or his free and full consent but also as a result of force including coercion by threats or by other psychological means: section 63A(4) and (6) of the Family Law Act 1996 [as amended]…. The forcing of a person into marriage is a gross and abhorrent violation of her or his rights under, for example, article 16(2) of the Universal Declaration of Human Rights 1948, article 23(3) of the International Covenant on Civil and Political Rights 1966 and article 12 of the ECHR.'

[161] Lord Wilson, at para. 46. See above p. 61 on the status of the immigration rules.

[162] It was of course up to the Home Secretary to justify the infringement of Art. 8(2) and it is clear that little hard evidence was available about forced marriages. This may justify the majority's conclusion. But decisions of this kind have to be made under conditions of imperfect knowledge.

[163] Lord Wilson, at para. 58.

innocent couples within the 18–21 age group whose desire to live together in this country is temporarily thwarted by the rule change, is essentially one for elected politicians, not for judges.

It appears at first sight that the majority and the minority simply take different views over the degree of deference to accord to the Home Secretary's decision to change the rule—and that is just a reflection of the unpredictability of the whole process. But Lord Brown points to a more subtle difference. He says:

> Lady Hale suggests[164]...that: 'The right to marry is just as important as the right not to marry.' But she cannot possibly mean by this that the postponement by up to three years of a couple's wish to live together as man and wife in this country involves just as great a violation of human rights as a forced marriage. What value, then, is to be attached to preventing a single forced marriage? What cost should each disappointed couple be regarded as paying? Really these questions are questions of policy and should be for government rather than us.[165]

Lord Brown thus makes clear here that in balancing the Article 8 infringements suffered by the 'other persons' against the infringements (of Articles 8 and 12 and in some cases Articles 3 and 5) suffered by the victims of forced marriage one is weighing different things against each other. How is one to balance the suffering of the eighteen-year-old forced by threats into an unwanted relationship with the inconvenience of a couple unable to live where they wish to live for three years? These infringements are incommensurable. Striking that balance—particularly when it comprises judgments about whether the rule change is likely to deter forced marriage—is not an obvious judicial task. There is no calculus to mete the depths of human suffering and no scale fine enough nicely to weigh one human rights infringement against another. Judicial decisions presuppose a precision that is foreign to the imperfect muddle that is inevitable in these circumstances.[166] This is not to say that judicial decisions never involve incommensurables[167] but decisions such as these are political and should be taken by politicians. In other words, the case for deference is strong. And at least these difficulties show that proportionality is not the panacea for all the ills of judicial review.

MERITS REVIEW INEVITABLE IN SOME CASES?

The interaction of many such factors is illustrated by a case which investigated the policy of the prison service in separating babies from mothers serving prison sentences at the age of 18 months.[168] Two prisoners challenged this policy under Article 8 of the Convention, in one case successfully and the other not. The Court of Appeal made an elaborate review of numerous relevant considerations such as prison policy and discipline, the welfare of

---

[164] Para. 66.   [165] Lord Brown, at para. 91.

[166] The deterrent effect of the rule change depended upon future human behaviour (which could not be known in advance). See Lord Bingham in *A and ors* v. *Home Secretary* [2004] UKHL 56 (*Belmarsh Prison* case), para. 29; '[the decision is] a pre-eminently political judgment. It involved making a factual prediction of what various people around the world might or might not do, and when (if at all) they might do it, and what the consequences might be if they did.'

[167] See Endicott, above, p. 1 who argues that 'the judicial resolution of disputes over incommensurabilities is not in itself a departure from the rule of law; the rule of law demands a system in which judges reconcile incommensurable interests'; but recognising this it follows that proportionality 'does not bring objectivity or transparency to human rights adjudication' (p. 19). See too the author's analysis of *Quila*.

[168] *R (P and Q)* v. *Home Secretary* [2001] 1 WLR 2002.

the child, the merits of alternative arrangements, the deference due to the prison service as the expert body charged with a sensitive public function and the need to make exceptions in occasional special cases. The court's conclusion, 'following the new *Daly* approach',[169] was that the correct balance, as demanded by proportionality, had not been struck in one of the cases, which was remitted for reconsideration by the prison service, but that it would not intervene in the other. It is difficult not to regard these decisions as clear examples of merits review.

Merits review becomes inevitable if the court should hold that the balance tips so heavily one way that only one decision is possible. There is then no room for a discretionary area of judgment and the court must simply substitute it own opinion. The Court of Appeal explained this clearly in the case of a Nigerian woman who had lived for ten years in this country as an illegal immigrant and had raised a family, but whom, with her children, the Home Secretary decided to deport.[170] The balance had then to be struck between the right to respect for family life (Article 8) and the need, repeatedly recognised at Strasbourg, for effect immigration control. Allowing the mother's appeal, the court held 'there really is only room for one view as to how the balance between these competing interests should be stuck', although the Immigration Appeal Tribunal had held the contrary view.

In another case the Legal Services Commission sought to withdraw funding from a litigant who had succeeded in the lower courts but was now facing an appeal to the Supreme Court; having found that the LSC's decision was 'so unreasonable as to be unlawful'[171] the Supreme Court said that the litigant was 'entitled to an immediate declaration in these proceedings that the only reasonable decision open to the Legal Services Commission is to continue to provide him with public funding for this appeal'.[172]

EXAMPLES OF DEFERENCE

A principle of deference to administrative experience and expertise, which received passing mention in the last-cited case, has become prominent in recent decisions, thus tempering, as already indicated, the stricter criteria of judicial review. It is especially prominent in cases involving foreign affairs, immigration, deportation and prison administration. In substance it adds little to the law which allows a greater or smaller margin of discretion to the executive in such matters, but the term 'deference' has become a symbol for it as a counterweight to the increasingly strict doctrines of judicial review. While the court must decide whether the decision-maker has struck the balance fairly, it must allow the decision-maker 'a discretionary area of judgement'.[173] As Lord Hoffmann said of the limitations on appeals in deportation cases, they arise from the need, in matters of judgment and evaluation of evidence, to show proper deference to the primary decision-maker. This was said in a case where a Pakistani national had been admitted to work as a minister of religion.[174] Finding that he had associations with an Islamic terrorist organisation, the Home Secretary made a deportation order against him on the grounds that his deportation would be 'conducive to the public good in the interests of public security'. His appeal to the Special Immigration Appeals Commission was upheld but an appeal by the Home Secretary succeeded in the Court of Appeal and the House of Lords. Lord Slynn stressed

---

[169] [2001] 1 WLR at 2022.   [170] *Edore* v. *Home Secretary* [2003] 1 WLR 2979.
[171] *JFS* case, below, at para. 22. The LSC was willing to continue to fund if a PCO was obtained (below, p. 563).   [172] *R (E)* v. *Governing Body of JFS* [2009] UKSC 1, para. 23.
[173] See the *Ponting* case (below), para. 70.   [174] *Home Secretary* v. *Rehman* [2001] 3 WLR 877.

the duty of the Commission to give due weight to the assessment and conclusions of the Secretary of State, who 'is undoubtedly in the best position to judge what national security requires even if his decision is open to review'. He must have material on which 'proportionately and reasonably' he can assess the threat to national security.

In a comparable case the Home Secretary refused admission to an American citizen who was the leader of a group known as 'the Nation of Islam' and who wished to meet and address his followers in Britain, who had caused some public disorder.[175] His violent anti-Semitic speeches were considered by the Home Secretary, in a personal decision, to indicate that his presence would pose a significant threat to community relations and would not be conducive to the public good. His appeal, based on Article 10 of the Convention, succeeded in the High Court but failed in the Court of Appeal (the court assuming, though not deciding, that the Convention could benefit someone who was neither a national of, nor present in, the country). It was held that the Home Secretary must be allowed a particularly wide margin of discretion: first, because it was an immigration case, in an area where the Strasbourg jurisprudence is particularly favourable, and was based on a concern for public order; second, because it was the Home Secretary's own personal and informed decision; third, because 'the Secretary of State is far better placed to reach an informed decision . . . than is the court'; and fourthly, because 'the Secretary of State is democratically accountable for this decision, there being no appeal on the "public good" ground. The legislative scheme required the court "to confer a wide margin of discretion on the minister".' The Home Secretary's decision was legitimate, within the limits of Article 10 and was not disproportionate. He had to evaluate the risk of disorder in the light of the political situation in the Middle East and other information available to him but not to the court.

Deference to the prison service and to the police was shown by the Court of Appeal when a prisoner, asserting his 'right to life' under the Convention, was removed from a 'protected witness unit' in which he had been held after assisting the police in discovering drug-smuggling by fellow criminals. It was held that the police and the prison service were generally better placed than the court to assess the risk to the claimant's life and that the court would not in such a case substitute its own opinion for theirs, though in fact the court agreed with it.[176] The Court of Appeal later discussed the principles of review and the 'level of deference' in dismissing a prisoner's complaints against the conditions imposed on his use of a computer, and Arden LJ said: 'it is not for the courts to define how the time of prisoners should be spent or the priorities for the allocation of prison resources'.[177]

These cases illustrate the proposition stated earlier by Sir Thomas Bingham MR in a case where homosexuals had been discharged from the navy under the policy of the Ministry of Defence banning such people from the armed forces:

> Where decisions of a policy-laden, esoteric or security-based nature are in issue even greater caution than normal must be shown in applying the test, but the test itself is sufficiently flexible to cover all situations . . . While the court must properly defer to the expertise of responsible decision-makers, it must not shrink from its fundamental duty to 'do right to all manner of people'.

---

[175] R (Farrakhan) v. Home Secretary [2002] 3 WLR 481.
[176] R (Bloggs 61) v. Home Secretary [2003] 3 WLR 2724.
[177] R (Ponting) v. Governor of HMP Whitemoor [2002] EWCA Civ 224, para. 114.

Showing deference accordingly, the Court of Appeal upheld the Ministry's policy.[178] But the ECtHR rejected it, holding that the intrusion into the claimants' private lives violated Article 8 and could not be justified as 'necessary in a democratic society'.[179]

PROPORTIONALITY AND *WEDNESBURY* UNREASONABLENESS

It is clear that the principles of reasonableness and proportionality cover a great deal of common ground. In the case, for example, where the revocation of a market trader's licence was quashed as being an unreasonably severe penalty for a small offence, the decision could have been based on disproportionality as easily as on unreasonableness.[180] As Lord Hoffmann has said, it is not possible to see daylight between them.[181] They will often be assimilated by the 'margin of appreciation' allowed by European law, which gives latitude for administrative decisions by national authorities in a manner similar to the British doctrine.

Nevertheless a clear difference has emerged and has been corroborated by the House of Lords in a 1991 case that is still the leading case on the status of proportionality in common law.[182] Proportionality, it is held, requires the court to judge whether the action taken was really needed as well as whether it was within the range of courses of action that could reasonably be followed. Proportionality is therefore a more exacting test in some situations and is to be rejected as requiring the court to substitute its own judgment for that of the proper authority. The House has thus closed the door to proportionality in domestic law for the time being. In the case in question the Home Secretary had issued directives to the BBC and the IBA prohibiting the broadcasting of speech by representatives of proscribed terrorist organisations and the applicants, who were journalists involved in broadcasting, unsuccessfully challenged the legality of the directives primarily on the ground of conflict with the European Convention on Human Rights, but also as disproportionate in a sense going beyond the established doctrine of unreasonableness.

In a later case the House of Lords was called upon to apply both the rival doctrines in their respective contexts. Shipments of livestock to Europe were violently obstructed at the port by protesting animal rights groups, and required so much police protection that the police could not adequately cover the rest of their area. When the chief constable, accordingly, reduced police cover at the port to two days a week, traders who were unable to make shipments sought judicial review of his decision, alleging both that it was unreasonable and also that it was disproportionate for enforcing the EU Treaty which prohibits quantitative restrictions on exports and measures having equivalent effect, subject to an exception for (*inter alia*) public policy.[183] The challenge failed on both counts, the former

---

[178] *R* v. *Ministry of Defence ex p Smith* [1996] QB 517 at 556.

[179] *Smith and Grady* v. *UK* (1999) 29 EHRR 493.

[180] *R* v. *Barnsley MBC ex p Hook* [1976] 1 WLR 1052; and see *R* v. *Brent LBC ex p Assegai*, The Independent, 12 June 1987 (citizen banned from access to local authority premises: penalty 'wholly out of proportion' to offence) (1987) 151 *LG Rev* 891; *R* v. *Secretary of State for Health ex p Eastside Cheese Co* [1998] TLR 748 (minister's use of 'draconian power' to prohibit trading in cheese (without compensation) disproportionate when local authority's lesser power (with compensation) would suffice); *Dad* v. *General Dental Council* [2000] 1 WLR 1538 (PC) (suspension of dentist unduly severe). Contrast *R* v. *Secretary of State for Health ex p Eastside Cheese Co* [1999] COD 321, [1999] 3 CMLR 123 (ban on suspected cheese upheld).

[181] In a lecture quoted in *R* v. *Chief Constable of Sussex ex p International Trader's Ferry Ltd* [1998] QB 477 at 495 (Kennedy LJ). For this lecture, an illuminating discussion of the two tests, see (1997) 32 *Ir Jur* 49 (the quotation is at p. 58). [182] *R* v. *Home Secretary ex p Brind* [1991] 1 AC 696.

[183] Arts. 29, 30 (ex 34, 36).

under the domestic *Wednesbury* principle and the latter under the public policy exception in the EU Treaty since the police action was proportionate to the problems to be faced, was suitable and necessary, and well within the margin of appreciation.[184] Of the two tests Lord Slynn said that the difference between them was in practice much less than is sometimes suggested, and that whichever test was adopted, the result was in this case the same.[185]

THE SURVIVAL OF *WEDNESBURY*

Lord Slynn said in the *Alconbury* case, with reference to proportionality: 'Trying to keep the *Wednesbury* principle and proportionality in separate compartments seems to me to be unnecessary and confusing.'[186] And in the *Daly* case Lord Cooke said: 'I think that the day will come when it will be more widely recognised that *Associated Provincial Picture Houses Ltd* v. *Wednesbury Corpn* was an unfortunately retrogressive decision in English administrative law, in so far as it suggested that there are degrees of unreasonableness and that only a very extreme degree can bring an administrative decision within the legitimate scope of judicial invalidation.'[187] Although quoting and sympathising with these weighty opinions, and acknowledging that 'the *Wednesbury* test is moving closer to proportionality', the Court of Appeal has held that 'it is not for this court to perform the burial rites'.[188]

Notwithstanding the apparent persuasiveness of these views the *coup de grâce* has not fallen on *Wednesbury* unreasonableness and now seems unlikely to do.[189] The assimilation of the two doctrines has not been rejected in terms but where a matter falls outside the ambit of the 1998 Act, the *Wednesbury* doctrine, without any reference to proportionality, is regularly relied upon by the courts. Reports of its imminent demise are thus exaggerated. One example is the first instance case about entry clearance to settle in the United Kingdom of veterans previously members of the Brigade of Gurkhas. Entrance clearance for those discharged before 1997 was subject to a policy that was found to be incoherent and irrational in its context; and consequently unlawful.[190] The case was not within the 1998 Act (no breach of Article 14 found) and proportionality was not mentioned. More weightily, the House of Lords, in a case involving a challenge to the lawfulness of a local authority's housing allocation scheme, having found the scheme not in breach of the relevant statutes went on to say that the 'court is in no position to re-write the whole policy and to weigh the claims of the multitude who are not before the court against the claims

---

[184]   *R* v. *Chief Constable of Sussex ex p International Trader's Ferry Ltd* [1999] 2 AC 418.

[185]   Ibid. at 439.

[186]   *R (Alconbury Developments Ltd)* v. *Secretary of State for the Environment, Transport and the Regions* [2001] 2 WLR 1389 at 1406.   [187]   *R (Daly)* v. *Home Secretary* [2001] 2 AC 532 at 548.

[188]   *R (Association of British Civilian Internees: Far East Region)* v. *Secretary of State for Defence* [2003] QB 1397, where the court reviewed and upheld a non-statutory scheme for ex gratia payments of compensation, rejecting claims based on abuse of power and legitimate expectation.

[189]   But this may be different in Australia where the concepts may be assimilated. See *Minister for Immigration and Citizenship* v. *Li* [2013] HCA 18, (2013) 87 ALJR 618 (High Court of Australia) where French CJ said 'a disproportionate exercise of an administrative discretion, taking a sledgehammer to crack a nut, may be characterised as irrational and also as unreasonable simply on the basis that it exceeds what, on any view, is necessary for the purpose it serves' (para. 30). But this was said in the context where there was no Bill of Rights. See also A Wooder, 'An Argument for the Introduction of Proportionality as the General Ground Of Substantive Review' (dissertation, 2013) for a subtle argument that proportionality should supplant *Wednesbury*.   [190]   *R (Limbu)* v. *Home Secretary* [2008] EWHC 2261.

of the few who are'.[191] Thus 'once a housing allocation scheme complies with the [statutory] requirements...the courts should be very slow to interfere on the ground of alleged irrationality'.[192] Proportionality was not mentioned in any of the speeches in the House of Lords; the analysis is classic *Wednesbury*. These examples could be multiplied.[193]

The reasons for the survival of *Wednesbury* are not hard to find. The structured test of proportionality is clearly designed to determine whether a particular limitation of a protected right is justified or not. It is thought apt for the task of weighting rights against rights, or rights against discrete questions of public interest. Since the rights are specifically protected in law the more intense scrutiny that follows from the application of the proportionality test is required.[194] But where protected rights are not engaged, the contending policy considerations that underlie the substance of the decision are much more diffuse, or 'polycentric';[195] the court lacks the expertise and legitimacy to assess them. And the appropriate standard of substantive review is that of the more deferential *Wednesbury*. Thus, in the housing allocation scheme case, there was a strong demand for housing, far in excess of the supply. No one had a legal right to a tenancy and prospective tenants had needs of different intensity. Whatever allocation scheme might be adopted there would be unhappy prospective tenants. While the courts might usefully scrutinise the scheme for perversity, improper purposes and irrelevant considerations there is not much else they might constructively do. Certainly they cannot conjure extra housing out of more intense scrutiny: allocation of scarce resources must be a matter for the elected public authority, not the courts.

But if there are functional reasons for the survival of *Wednesbury* there are conceptual reasons too. *Wednesbury* and proportionality have different starting points and different structures.[196] With proportionality the impugned decision is prima facie an infringement of a protected right and so prima facie beyond power. Thus the infringement needs to be justified and the public authority responsible for the infringement must provide a justification. But with *Wednesbury* the decision impugned is apparently within the power of the decision-maker and it is for the claimant to show that the decision is perverse.[197] These two different tests, in other words, serve different purposes and are not easily merged.

These conceptual differences between the two concepts point to issues of legitimacy. *Wednesbury* is consistent with the doctrine of the separation of powers but proportionality is not. And a change of such a radical nature surely requires some statutory warrant.[198] The survival of *Wednesbury* has been the subject of a lively debate in the learned journals; the tide of that debate has turned. After all, there is no necessary overlap in every case

---

[191] R *(Ahmad)* v. *London Borough of Newham* [2009] UKHL 14, para. 15 (Lady Hale) rejecting the finding in R *(A)* v. *Lambeth London Borough Council* [2002] EWCA Civ 1084; an allocation policy was irrational if it did not contain 'a mechanism for identifying those with the greatest need and ensuring that so far as possible...they are given priority' (para. 18).   [192] Para. 55 (Lord Neuberger).

[193] For instance, R *(E)* v. *Governing Body of JFS* [2009] UKSC 1 (decision of the Legal Services Commission to refuse funding found in the circumstances to be *Wednesbury* unreasonable; proportionality not mentioned). See Appendix 3 for more recent cases.

[194] As Lady Hale remarked in *Ahmad* the position 'would be different...if the most deserving households had a right to be housed, but that is not the law'.

[195] From Lon Fuller, 'The Forms and Limits of Adjudication' (1978) 92 *Harvard Law Review* 353. See the discussion in Goodwin [2012] *PL* 445 at 452 and see R *(British Telecommunications plc)* v. *The Secretary of State for Business, Innovation and Skills* [2011] EWHC 1021 at para. 213: 'it is hard enough for the legislature...to weigh all the possible implications of a range of policy choices that are theoretically open, but is well nigh impossible for a judge'.   [196] Goodwin, above, 446–51.

[197] This point was first put to me by Professor David Feldman in discussion but it overlaps with Goodwin's account, ibid.   [198] See Goodwin, ibid., 450 and Sales, (2013) 129 *LQR* 223.

between rationality and proportionality. A decision may be irrational but not disproportionate and vice versa.

The tussle between *Wednesbury* and proportionality is not an idle or unimportant
question of formal law. At its heart is the question of the intensity of judicial scrutiny of
administrative decisions.

THE RULE OF REASON: PARTICULAR CATEGORIES

INCONSISTENCY AND UNFAIRNESS

Inconsistency of policy may amount to an abuse of discretion, particularly when undertakings or statements of intent are disregarded unfairly[199] or contrary to the citizen's
legitimate expectation.[200] The Privy Council, in holding that the Government of Hong
Kong must honour its published undertaking to treat each deportation case on its merits,
has applied 'the principle that a public authority is bound by its undertakings as to the
procedure it will follow, provided they do not conflict with its duty'.[201] The Supreme Court
in a case about the Home Secretary's policy to review the detention of foreign nationals
awaiting deportation held that 'it was unlawful for [the Home Secretary] to depart from
his published policy unless there were good reasons for doing so'.[202] Thus the failure to
carry out the reviews in accordance with the policy rendered the detention unlawful.
And in an earlier case the Supreme Court[203] held that the 'principle that policy must be
consistently applied is not in doubt' and, hence, it was unlawful for the Home Secretary
to operate an unpublished policy (not to release on bail) inconsistent with his published
policy (to release on bail).

These decisions of the Supreme Court establish no new principle. The Court of Appeal
had earlier made strong comments when quashing the refusal of the Home Office to
allow a Pakistani, settled in England, to bring in his young nephew with a view to his
adoption, since the Home Office had issued a circular specifying the conditions which
need to be satisfied but had, by 'grossly unfair administration', refused admission on an
altogether different ground.[204] In the same way the Court of Appeal held that a public
authority has a duty to act with fairness and consistency in its dealings with the public, and that if it makes inconsistent decisions unfairly or unjustly it misuses its powers.
Consequently the Price Commission was declared unable to issue a new ruling contradicting its previous statement that tax payments were a permissible item of costs for the

---

[199] *R* v. *Inland Revenue Commissioners ex p Preston* [1985] AC 835 (complaint not made good).

[200] See the *Hong Kong* and *Ruddock* cases, below.

[201] *A-G of Hong Kong* v. *Ng Yuen Shiu* [1983] 2 AC 629, approving *R* v. *Liverpool Cpn ex p Liverpool Taxi
Fleet Operators' Association* [1972] 2 QB 299. For these and other 'legitimate expectation' cases see below,
p. 450.

[202] *R (Kambadzi)* v. *Home Secretary* [2011] UKSC 23, previously known as *SK (Zimbabwe)* v. *Secretary of
State for the Home Department*, para. 39 (Lord Hope) (see also, paras. 36 and 69).

[203] *Lumba* v. *Secretary of State for the Home Department* [2011] UKSC 12, para. 26 (Lord Dyson).

[204] *R* v. *Home Secretary ex p Asif Mahmood Khan* [1984] 1 WLR 1337 (Parker LJ). The Home Secretary
'in effect made his own rules, and stated those matters which he regarded as relevant and would consider
in reaching his decision' and 'misdirected himself according to his own criteria and acted unreasonably'
(Dunn LJ).

purpose of calculating increases of price by television programme contractors.[205] The principle that the inconsistent application of policy amounts to abuse of discretion also justifies the decision of the Court of Appeal in the following case.[206] The Home Office had refused an Iraqi Kurd's application for asylum on the ground that he might safely relocate to the Kurdish Autonomous Zone. In so deciding the Home Office's policy of not relying on internal relocation in such cases was inadvertently overlooked.[207] This was found to be 'conspicuous unfairness amounting to an abuse of power' and the challenge succeeded.[208] Concern has been expressed that this formulation tempts the courts into remedying maladministration (overlooking the applicable policy)—which is a matter for the Ombudsman, rather than illegality.[209] But the principle that policy must be consistently applied is not in doubt.

These are revealing decisions. They show that the courts expect government departments to honour their statements of policy[210] or intention, and that there is a clear link between unreasonableness and unfairness. Lord Scarman made an emphatic statement that unfairness in the purported exercise of power can amount to an abuse or excess of power.[211] Fairness is a powerful ally for the litigant and the unexpressed basis of many rules. Although Lord Browne-Wilkinson has said that there is as yet no general principle allowing the quashing of administrative decisions on the simple ground that they are unfair,[212] Lord Steyn in the same case said that the rule of law enforces minimum standards of fairness, both substantive and procedural.[213] The standard may indeed be higher than a minimum.[214] It may be predicted that fairness will in time become the touchstone of reasonableness, and that it will prevail over older rules about estoppel and misleading advice, and about the non-fettering of discretion which have been criticised in an earlier chapter for operating unfairly.[215]

Although there are now decisions of high authority to show that voluntary statements of policy may sometimes be treated almost as binding restrictions in law,[216] it is obvious, on the other hand, that public authorities must be at liberty to change their policies

---

[205] *HTV Ltd* v. *Price Commission* [1976] ICR 170, cited with approval in the *Preston* case (above). Compare *Thames Valley Electric Power Board* v. *NZFP Pulp & Paper Ltd* [1994] 2 NZLR 641 but contrast *R* v. *Inland Revenue Commissioners ex p Matrix-Securities Ltd* [1994] 1 WLR 334 (HL) (tax clearance validly withdrawn).

[206] *R (Rashid)* v. *Home Secretary* [2005] EWCA Civ 744. Discussed [2005] *JR* 281 (Elliott). But the judgments also rely on the applicant's supposed legitimate expectation that the policy would be applied even though the applicant was completely unaware of the policy at the time. As explained elsewhere, the doctrine of legitimate expectation (above, p. 283) protects the trust placed in the promises of officials, so is inapplicable where the individual being unaware of the promises has reposed no trust in the promise. But note the caution in applying this principle in *ZK* v. *Home Secretary* [2007] EWCA Civ 615.

[207] Adopted because the Kurdish authorities did not allow such relocation because of lack of resources.

[208] *Rashid*, para. 54 (Dyson LJ) and see also para. 34 (Pill LJ). A declaration that the claimant was entitled to indefinite leave to remain was made.

[209] *Home Secretary* v. *R (S)* [2007] EWCA Civ 546 (Carnwath LJ, especially para. 41) (delay of four and a half years not abuse of power).

[210] These words and the general account of this topic at this point have been approved twice by the Supreme Court: *Lumba*, para. 26; *Kambadzi*, para. 36.

[211] In the *Preston* case, above, at 872. In *Woods* v. *Secretary of State for Scotland*, 1991 SLT 197 the court rejected the official argument that to discontinue an unfair practice is unfair to others treated unfairly in the past. [212] *R* v. *Home Secretary ex p Pierson* [1998] AC 539 at 575.

[213] Ibid. at 591. New Zealand decisions favour this doctrine: *Northern Roller Milling Co Ltd* v. *Commerce Commission* [1994] 2 NZLR 747.

[214] In the *Unilever* case (above) Simon Brown LJ said that public authorities 'are required to act in a high-principled way, on occasions being subject to a stricter duty of fairness than would apply as between private citizens'. [215] Above, p. 281.

[216] See especially *ex p Pierson* (above); *R* v. *Home Secretary ex p Urmaza* [1996] COD 479.

as the public interest may require from time to time. So where the retirement age for certain civil servants was reduced to 60, their expectation of a longer working life did not avail them.[217] As Lord Diplock said, 'the liberty to make such changes is something that is inherent in our constitutional form of government'. Similarly where the Home Secretary, by a change of prison policy, deferred the date at which certain classes of serious offenders would be considered for release on parole, prisoners disappointed by this change had no legal remedy;[218] and the same was true when the qualifying period for applying for home leave was increased from one-third to a half of the prisoner's sentence.[219] Where a prisoner had given evidence against co-accused and was told by the police that he could be held in a 'protected witness' unit for his own safety, his claim for such protection failed.[220] In these cases the only legitimate expectation was that cases 'will be examined individually in the light of whatever policy the Secretary of State sees fit to adopt'.[221]

In the nursing home case, which is an outstanding example of a substantive right created by legitimate expectation, the Court of Appeal, in a full analysis, put great emphasis on unfairness as a form of abuse of power, treating an unjustified breach of an undertaking by a public authority as equivalent to a breach of contract for substantive as well as for procedural purposes.[222] Only an 'overriding public interest' will outweigh the obligation of a promise, particularly where it is made to an individual or a small group. The law thus accords with the free standing principle of substantive legitimate expectation as established[223] in EU law. Being firmly rooted in European law it is likely to play a progressively more important part in English law, and all the more so because it is so closely allied to fairness. It is illustrated again later in the context of natural justice.[224] It was in that context that the new doctrine first arose, but since it is impossible to separate 'procedural' from 'substantive' cases entirely, the texts on both heads of expectation should be read together.[225]

As the discussion here illustrates, the doctrine of legitimate expectations plays a prominent part in determining whether there has been an abuse of discretion in failing to fulfil a promise made to an individual. But the doctrine of legitimate expectations developed first as an aspect of the law of procedural fairness, not abuse of discretion. Moreover, most legitimate expectations are protected only by an enhancement of procedural, not substantive, protection. Thus the full discussion of legitimate expectations is found elsewhere in this book.[226]

---

[217] *Hughes* v. *Department of Health and Social Security* [1985] AC 776. Compare *R* v. *Criminal Injuries Compensation Board ex p P* [1995] 1 WLR 845 (change of policy favourable to claimants but only as from a fixed date: refusal of earlier claims upheld).   [218] *Re Findlay* [1985] AC 318.

[219] *R* v. *Home Secretary ex p Hargreaves* [1997] 1 WLR 906. The Court of Appeal's rejection of any doctrine of substantive legitimate expectation in this case is eclipsed by their contrary decision in *ex p Coughlan*, above, in which it was distinguished but in effect abandoned.

[220] *R (Bloggs 61)* v. *Home Secretary* [2003] 1 WLR 2724. This was, in any case, a matter for the prison service, not the police. See [2003] *JR* 215 (Iyengar).

[221] *Re Findlay* (above) at 338 (Lord Scarman). See similarly *R* v. *Ministry of Defence ex p Walker* [2000] 1 WLR 806 (HL).   [222] For its procedural origin see below, p. 450.

[223] For EU law see [1996] *CLJ* 289 at 304 (P. P. Craig) and [1987] *PL* at 380 (Forsyth), discussing *Mulder* v. *Minister van Landbauw en Visserij* [1988] ECR 2321 (successful challenge by milk-producer to regulation imposing condition impossible for him to satisfy).   [224] Below, p. 450.

[225] See the discussion at p. 450.   [226] Below, p. 450.

MINISTERIAL POLICY

Ministers' decisions on important matters of policy are not on that account sacrosanct against the unreasonableness doctrine, though the court must take special care, for constitutional reasons, not to pass judgment on action which is essentially political.[227] Examples of justifiable intervention are the *Padfield* and *Congreve* cases already discussed and the *Tameside* case discussed later. Further examples will be found in the context of delegated legislation, since the courts have several times held ministerial regulations to be void for unreasonableness.[228]

A three-judge divisional court provided another striking instance in granting declaratory relief to prisoners serving life sentences whose prospects of release on licence ('parole') were sharply reduced after a change of policy by the Home Secretary.[229] The new policy had first been challenged by other prisoners on the ground that the Parole Board had not been consulted and that the Home Secretary had fettered his discretion, but the House of Lords upheld it.[230] The Home Secretary then decided to make a practice of waiting for three or four years before asking the judge who had passed a life sentence for his opinion on the term of imprisonment which the convict ought to serve. This delay was held to be an unfair restriction on the implementation of the parole policy which in some cases would extend the term of imprisonment unjustly, contrary to what the judge would have advised if consulted at the time of conviction. It was held that a minister could not lawfully maintain a policy when the application of it was, in part at least, shown to give rise to injustice; and that the policy of delayed reference to the judge was unreasonable in the *Wednesbury* sense. The decision is all the more notable in that the unreasonable action was not itself the exercise of a statutory power, as it was in the cases mentioned above, but was merely preparatory to the exercise of the statutory function of referring cases to the Parole Board. The real misdeed, therefore, was the failure to consider whether to take the latter step at the proper time.

A sharply divided House of Lords invalidated the policy of the Home Secretary for setting the 'tariff period' for a prisoner serving a mandatory life sentence.[231] Although none of the various reasons given by the majority judges was expressly based on unreasonableness, they are all related to the abuse of power and the case shows how far the court will now penetrate into the merits of executive policy. The tariff period for the prisoner, i.e. the minimum period considered by the Home Secretary to be necessary for purposes of punishment ('retribution and deterrence') before his possible release could be considered by the Parole Board, had been fixed at twenty years under the policy which the Home Secretary had himself devised for the exercise of his statutory power, in terms unlimited, for the release of life prisoners. 'The concept of a tariff period is not a statutory one. It is a

---

[227] See *R v. Secretary of State for the Environment ex p Nottinghamshire CC* [1986] AC 240 (unsuccessful complaint of unreasonably low 'expenditure target' set by Secretary of State); *R v. Secretary of State for the Environment ex p Hammersmith and Fulham LBC* [1991] 1 AC 521 (unsuccessful challenge to Secretary of State's 'charge-capping' of local authorities); *R v. Home Secretary ex p Brind* [1991] 1 AC 696 (unsuccessful challenge to directive forbidding BBC to broadcast matter from proscribed terrorist organisation); *R v. Secretary of State for Transport ex p Richmond-upon-Thames LBC* [1996] 1 WLR 1460 (unsuccessful challenge to policy for control of airport noise at night).   [228] Below, p. 743.

[229] *R v. Home Secretary ex p Handscomb* (1987) 86 Cr App R 59, partially disapproved on other grounds in *R v. Home Secretary ex p Doody* [1994] 1 AC 531. See also *R v. Home Secretary ex p Walsh* [1992] COD 240 (decision that prisoner should serve 20 years quashed for self-misdirection and unfairness in not disclosing his 'tariff period').   [230] *Re Findlay* [1985] AC 318.

[231] *R v. Home Secretary ex p Pierson* [1998] AC 539. The tariff period was treated as increased because the Home Secretary had withdrawn some of his reasons for setting it at twenty years. See also *R v. Home Secretary ex p Norney* [1995] 7 Admin LR 861 (prolongation of tariff period unreasonable but relief refused).

self-inflicted burden imposed by the Home Secretary on himself by adopting a policy for the exercise of the statutory discretion'.[232] In this case the increased twenty-year tariff was unlawful because the Home Secretary had misconstrued his own policy statement and so erred in law (Lord Goff); and because the Home Secretary, who in fixing terms of imprisonment should act like a judge, had no power to increase a tariff once fixed and communicated to the prisoner (Lord Steyn and Lord Hope). This last reason was strongly contested by the dissenting judges (Lord Browne-Wilkinson and Lord Lloyd) who pointed out that Parliament had given wide discretion to the Home Secretary precisely so that he should exercise it as a minister, responsible to Parliament, rather than as a judge; and as to his misconstruction of his policy statement Lord Browne-Wilkinson said:[233]

> But in my judgment it is not right to adopt such a technical approach to statements made by a minister in Parliament relating to policy matters. If judicial review of executive action is to preserve its legitimacy and utility, it is essential that statements of administrative policy should not be construed as if settled by parliamentary counsel but should be given effect to for what they are, viz. administrative announcements setting out in laymen's language and in broad terms the policies which are to be followed.

The decision of the majority, however, shows how strictly ministers may be held to their statements of policy, rigorously interpreted, and how the rule of law may be invoked to counter anything savouring of retrospective punishment. Tariff-fixing decisions of the Home Secretary have been successfully challenged in a number of other cases for reasons which belong elsewhere in this book.[234]

The present tariff system, however, is due for early abolition, since the European Court of Human Rights has held that the length of a prisoner's detention must be determined by the judiciary and not by the executive.[235] Radical legislation will therefore be necessary.

The policy of banning homosexuals from the armed forces, on which a strong attack was mounted on grounds of unreasonableness and breach of fundamental rights, was upheld in 1995 by the Court of Appeal[236] (though later condemned by the European Court of Human Rights).[237] Sir Thomas Bingham MR said:

> The greater the policy content of the decision, and the more remote the subject matter of the decision from ordinary judicial experience, the more hesitant the court must necessarily be in holding a decision to be irrational. That is good law, and like most good law, common sense. Where decisions of a policy-laden, esoteric or security-based nature are in issue even greater caution than normal must be shown in applying the test, but the test itself is sufficiently flexible to cover all situations.

These are apt words to indicate the limits of the *Wednesbury* test and to prevent undue judicial intervention in major areas of policy.

[232] Ibid. at 571 (Lord Browne-Wilkinson). For the history of this regime and its successive modifications see the *Pierson* case (above). The Home Secretary is not obliged to accept a recommendation from the Parole Board that a prisoner be released on licence: *R v. Home Secretary ex p Stafford* [1999] 2 AC 38. See also *R v. Home Secretary ex p Hindley* [1999] 2 WLR 1253 (tariff of 'whole life' upheld). See above, p. 59 for discussion of changes since these cases.   [233] Ibid. at 327.

[234] See above, p. 269, and below, p. 504.

[235] *T and V* v. *UK* (2000) 30 EHRR 121 (breach of Art. 6 of the Convention).

[236] *R v. Ministry of Defence ex p Smith* [1996] QB 517, affirming a notable judgment of Simon Brown LJ. The House of Lords refused leave to appeal.

[237] *Smith and Grady* v. *UK* (2000) 29 EHRR 493, holding that the *Wednesbury* test set too high a threshold and excluded the considerations of pressing social need and proportionality.

PARLIAMENTARY APPROVAL

Many ministerial orders and regulations are required to be approved by Parliament either positively by resolution or negatively by the expiry of a time limit.[238] This approval ought not, in constitutional principle, to affect the rules of judicial review, since that can be done only by Act of Parliament.[239] 'Parliamentary supremacy over the judiciary is only exercisable by statute.'[240] But where orders and regulations are required to be approved by one or both Houses of Parliament, judicial sensitivity has set an especially high threshold of unreasonableness, crossed only when the minister's order is 'so absurd that he must have taken leave of his senses'.[241] Challenges attempting to satisfy this test in cases with high political content, involving severe central government action against local authorities, have predictably been dismissed by the House of Lords,[242] as also by the Court of Session in Scotland.[243] These were cases where the minister imposed restrictions on local rates, charges or expenditure where he disapproved of the local authority's policy, or where local government boundaries were to be altered. In such situations the minister's order 'is not open to challenge on the grounds of irrationality short of the extremes of bad faith, improper motive or manifest absurdity'.[244] It was in this context that Lord Scarman said: 'Judicial review is a great weapon in the hands of the judges, but the judges must observe the constitutional limits set by our parliamentary system upon their exercise of this beneficent power'.[245]

It is only the criterion of reasonableness that is restricted by this doctrine, and then only in special situations dominated by questions of political judgement. The normal rule is that parliamentary approval does not affect the operation of judicial review, whether for unreasonableness or otherwise. For this the decisions on delegated legislation, which is frequently approved by Parliament, afford ample illustration.[246]

RELEVANT AND IRRELEVANT CONSIDERATIONS

There are many cases in which a public authority has been held to have acted from improper motives or upon irrelevant considerations, or to have failed to take account of relevant considerations, so that its action is ultra vires and void. It is impossible to separate these cleanly from other cases of unreasonableness and abuse of power, since the court may use a variety of interchangeable explanations, as was pointed out by Lord Greene.[247] Regarded collectively, these cases show the great importance of strictly correct motives and purposes. They show also how fallacious it is to suppose that powers conferred in unrestricted language confer unrestricted power.

Lord Esher MR stated the 'irrelevant considerations' doctrine in a case where a vestry had mistakenly fixed the pension of a retiring officer on the erroneous assumption that they had no discretion as to the amount:[248]

---

[238] See below, p. 754.   [239] Above, p. 19.

[240] *M* v. *Home Office* [1994] 1 AC 377 at 395 (Lord Templeman); and see *R* v. *Criminal Injuries Compensation Board ex p P* [1995] 1 WLR 845 at 861 (Evans LJ).

[241] See the *Nottinghamshire* case (above) at 347 (Lord Scarman).

[242] In the *Nottinghamshire* and *Hammersmith* cases, above. Both cases involved positive resolutions of the House of Commons.

[243] In *City of Edinburgh DC* v. *Secretary of State for Scotland*, 1985 SLT 551; *East Kilbride DC* v. *Secretary of State for Scotland*, 1995 SLT 1238.

[244] See the *Hammersmith* case (above) at 597 (Lord Bridge).

[245] In the *Nottinghamshire* case (above) at 250.   [246] Below, p. 737.

[247] Below, p. 365. See [1976] *CLJ* 272 (G. D. S. Taylor).

[248] *R* v. *St Pancras Vestry* (1890) 24 QBD 371 at 375.

But they must fairly consider the application and not take into account any reason for their decision which is not a legal one. If people who have to exercise a public duty by exercising their discretion take into account matters which the courts consider not to be proper for the exercise of their discretion, then in the eye of the law they have not exercised their discretion.

The doctrine applies equally to failure to take account of some consideration which is necessarily relevant, such as the respective costs of rival proposals[249] or the availability of more suitable land.[250] Cooke J explained in a New Zealand case that 'the more general and the more obviously important the consideration, the readier the court must be to hold that Parliament must have meant it to be taken into account'.[251]

Under many statutes the discretion conferred is extensive, and it is no concern of the court to restrict it artificially by limiting the considerations that are relevant. A minister may be entitled to take account of every factor that may affect the public interest,[252] but it does not follow that he is obliged to do so. In another New Zealand case Cooke J pointed out 'the difference between obligatory considerations (i.e. those which the Act expressly or impliedly requires the Minister to take into account) and permissible considerations (i.e. those which can properly be taken into account but do not have to be)'.[253] A decision to take into account (or not to take into account) a permissible consideration will only be able to be challenged on *Wednesbury* grounds.[254] Where there is overlap between different areas of policy, for example housing and planning, the court may decline to make a rigid dichotomy between them so as to confine a housing authority to 'housing' considerations only.[255] The court will intervene in two situations. The first is where the authority has acted on grounds which the statute never intended to allow, for example where fees charged for street traders' licences were based upon what the market would bear rather than administration costs.[256] The second is where the authority has failed to take proper account of something that the statute expressly or impliedly required it to consider,[257] even though it may not have been known at the time.[258] But under this second

---

[249] *Eckersley* v. *Secretary of State for the Environment* [1977] JPL 580; *Prest* v. *Secretary of State for Wales* (1982) 81 LGR 193; *R* v. *Brent LBC ex p Gunning* (1985) 84 LGR 168.

[250] *Brown* v. *Secretary of State for the Environment* (1978) 40 P & CR 285 (provision of land for gipsies). See also *City Cabs (Edinburgh) Ltd* v. *Edinburgh DC*, 1988 SLT 184.

[251] *CREEDNZ* v. *Governor-General* [1981] 1 NZLR 172, applied in *R* v. *Hillingdon Health Authority ex p Goodwin* [1984] ICR 800 (decision to close hospital quashed for failure to take account of doctors' interests) and many other cases.

[252] See e.g. *Rother Valley Railway Co Ltd* v. *Ministry of Transport* [1971] 1 Ch 515.

[253] *Ashby* v. *Minister of Immigration* [1981] 1 NZLR 222 at 224 (admission of South African rugby football team unsuccessfully challenged). See also *CREEDNZ*: 'It is not enough [for invalidity] that a consideration is one that may properly be taken into account, nor even that it is one which many people, including the court itself, would have taken into account if they had to make the decision' but there were 'matters so obviously material to a decision' that they have to be considered even if the statute were silent. This formulation was approved in *Re Findlay* [1985] AC 318 at 333–4 (Lord Scarman).

[254] *R* v. *Secretary of State for Transport ex p Richmond upon Thames LBC (No 1)* [1993] EWHC Admin 1 (Laws J) and confirmed in *R (Hurst)* v. *Commissioner of Police of the Metropolis* [2007] UKHL 13, para. 57 (Lord Brown (for the majority)) (cf. Lord Mance, para. 79 (dissenting)). Unincorporated international obligation (Art. 2 of the European Convention prior to the coming into force of the Human Rights Act 1998) not 'so obviously material' that it had to be taken into account by coroner in deciding whether to resume an inquest in terms of s. 16 of the Coroners Act 1988. See similarly (supporting the general approach) *London Borough of Newham* v. *Khatun and ors* [2004] EWCA Civ 55, para. 35 (Laws LJ).

[255] *Hanks* v. *Minister of Housing and Local Government* [1963] 1 QB 999; see below, p. 325, for this and contrasting cases.   [256] *R* v. *Manchester City Council ex p King* [1991] COD 422.

[257] *CREEDNZ* v. *Governor-General* (above); and see *Ashby* v. *Minister of Immigration* (above).

[258] *R* v. *Immigration Appeal Tribunal ex p Hassanin* [1987] 1 WLR 1448 (cases remitted to appeal tribunals to consider all the relevant circumstances).

head the implied requirement may be wide. In deciding whether to deport an immigrant the Secretary of State 'is bound to take account of all relevant considerations', so that an adjudicator misdirects himself in law if he refuses to take account of the immigrant's special value to his own community.[259] A threat by that community to instigate a strike, on the other hand, would be improper and therefore irrelevant.[260]

Where discretion is conferred upon a minister of the Crown the range of legitimate considerations is likely to be wider than it would be in the case of a judge, who can consider legal relevance only.[261] The decision-maker must take the obligatory relevant considerations into account and if he fails to do so the judicial review court will set him right. But the weight to be attached to any consideration is a matter for the decision-maker.[262] The court will only intervene 'if manifestly excessive or manifestly inadequate weight is given to a relevant consideration'.[263]

THE PUBLIC SECTOR EQUALITY DUTY

The Equality Act 2010, section 149[264]—replacing, consolidating and extending earlier legislation—imposes upon public authorities[265] and others who exercise public functions[266] a duty to have 'due regard to the need to (a) eliminate discrimination, harassment, victimisation and any other conduct that is prohibited by or under this Act; (b) advance equality of opportunity between persons who share a relevant protected characteristic and persons who do not share it; [and] (c) foster good relations between persons who share a relevant protected characteristic and persons who do not share it'.[267] The relevant protected characteristics are defined elsewhere as: 'age; disability; gender reassignment; pregnancy and maternity; race; religion or belief; sex; [and] sexual orientation'.[268]

The breadth of this duty has opened a fresh field of decision-making to judicial review and there have been many challenges based on the alleged absence of 'due regard'. The boldest being perhaps the challenge to the 2010 austerity budget on the ground that it failed to have 'due regard' to equality of opportunity between men and women.[269]

---

[259] R v. Immigration Appeal Tribunal ex p Bakhtaur Singh [1986] 1 WLR 910 (Lord Bridge). See also R v. Immigration Appeal Tribunal ex p Bastiampillai [1983] 2 All ER 844 (failure to take account of immigrant's circumstances); R v. Immigration Appeal Tribunal ex p Kumar [1987] 1 FLR 444 (disregard of husband's proved devotion in alleged marriage of convenience); R v. Home Secretary ex p Bugdaycay [1987] AC 514 (failure to consider danger to asylum-seeker).   [260] Bakhtaur Singh's case (above).

[261] Re Findlay [1985] AC 318 at 333.

[262] Girling v. Secretary of State for the Home Department [2006] EWCA Civ 1779, paras. 27–8 (Sir Anthony Clarke MR) relying upon Tesco Stores Ltd v. Secretary of State for the Environment [1995] 1 WLR 759 at 780 F–G and 784 B–C (no distinction between 'little weight' and 'no weight' given to a particular consideration). To like effect see R (Mavalon Care Ltd) v. Pembrokeshire County Council [2011] EWHC 3371, para. 40 (Beatson J): '[the] judicial review court is not concerned with the weight to be attributed to various factors and will be circumspect in engaging with the conclusions of the primary decision-maker, particularly in relation to complex economic and technical questions'. See also R (British Telecommunications plc and ors) v. Secretary of State for Business, Innovation and Skills [2011] EWHC 1021, paras. 213–14 (Parker J).

[263] R (Mabanaft Ltd) v. Secretary of State for Trade and Industry [2008] EWHC 1052 (Admin), para. 74; appeal dismissed ([2009] EWCA Civ 224).

[264] See [2013] PL 325 (T. Hickman) and Clements, 'The Public Sector Equality Duty' (at <http://www.11kbw.com>) for detailed discussion.   [265] As listed in Sched. 19 of the Act.

[266] s. 149(2).

[267] This is the duty as set out in s. 149(1). Further, more complex, duties are set out in s. 149(3)–(6).

[268] s. 149(7).

[269] R (Fawcett Society) v. Chancellor of the Exchequer [2010] EWHC 3522 (permission refused).

This statutory duty is best conceptualised as the imposition upon the decision-maker of a mandatory relevant consideration,[270] that of having due regard to the need to achieve the worthy goal specified. In a leading case[271] Laws LJ has said 'the duty of due regard is not a duty to achieve a particular result. The courts will not administer section 149 so as in effect to steer the outcome which ought in any particular case to be arrived at. The evaluation of the impact on equality considerations of a particular decision clearly remains the responsibility of the primary decision-maker.' Later he stressed that 'the discipline of the PSED lies in the required quality, not the outcome, of the decision-making process'.[272]

And in another case,[273] Elias LJ described the duty in these words:

> The concept of 'due regard' requires the court to ensure that there has been a proper and con-
> scientious focus on the statutory criteria, but if that is done, the court cannot interfere with
> the decision simply because it would have given greater weight to the equality implications of
> the decision than did the decision maker. In short, the decision maker must be clear precisely
> what the equality implications are when he puts them in the balance, and he must recognise
> the desirability of achieving them, but ultimately it is for him to decide what weight they
> should be given in the light of all relevant factors.

This very proper judicial eschewal of the merits of the decision does not mean that compliance with the duty is straightforward. Laws LJ has held that 'consideration of equality in general is insufficient to amount to "due regard" to the relevant statutory needs. The duty involves analysis of the relevant material with the specific statutory considerations in mind.'[274] It is plain that the PSED sets an important standard for public decision-making. Where the protected characteristics specified in section 149 of the 2010 Act are potentially affected by a forthcoming public measure, the decision-maker is obliged to conduct a rigorous examination of the measure's effects, including due enquiry where that is necessary.

Plainly having 'due regard' is not a 'tick box' exercise. Dyson LJ (as he then was) said in an oft-cited passage that the PSED

> is not a duty to achieve a result, [e.g.] to eliminate unlawful racial discrimination... [or the
> other goals]. It is a duty to *have due regard to the need* to achieve these goals. The distinction
> is vital.... What is *due* regard?...it is the regard that is appropriate in all the circumstances.
> These include on the one hand the importance of the areas of life of the members of the dis-
> advantaged...group that are affected by the inequality of opportunity and the extent of the
> inequality; and on the other hand, such countervailing factors as are relevant to the function
> which the decision-maker is performing.[275]

Thus while it is plain that the decision-maker need not achieve a particular result and that the weight to be attached to the various factors is a matter for him, it is equally plain that the decision-maker faces an onerous and time-consuming task; complying with the duty is an integral part of the decision-making process.[276]

---

[270] See *R (Lunt)* v. *Liverpool City Council* [2009] EWHC 2356, para. 43; *E* v. *The Governing Body of JFS* [2008] EWHC 1535, para. 206.

[271] *R (MA and ors)* v. *Secretary of State for Work and Pensions* [2013] EWHC 2213, para. 72.

[272] Para. 74.

[273] *R (Hurley and Moore)* v. *Secretary of State for Business Innovation & Skills* [2012] EWHC 201, para. 78. To like effect see *Brown* v. *Secretary of State for Work and Pensions* [2008] EWHC Admin 3158, para. 82 (Aitkens LJ) and *R (Baker)* v. *Secretary of State for Communities & Local Government* [2008] EWCA Civ 141, para. 34 (Dyson LJ).

[274] *R (MA)* v. *Secretary of State for Work and Pensions and ors* [2013] EWHC 2213, para. 72.

[275] *Baker*, above, para. 31.

[276] *Secretary of State for Defence* v. *Elias* [2006] EWCA Civ 1293, para. 133 (Mummery LJ) and para. 274 (Arden LJ). See now Appendix 3.

EXAMPLES OF THE DOCTRINE OF RELEVANT CONSIDERATIONS

A clear case of abuse of power prompted by an irrelevant consideration was where some local authorities refused to provide certain newspapers in their public libraries. Their reason for the ban was that they were politically hostile to the newspapers' proprietors, who had dismissed many of their workers when they went on strike. The ulterior political object of the local authorities was irrelevant to their statutory duty to provide 'a comprehensive and efficient library service'.[277] Another example was where the Secretary of State had power to prescribe 'the appropriate contribution' of local authorities to a fund for financing further education, and prescribed a formula based on the rateable resources of each area, so that the richer local authorities were made to subsidise the poorer. It was held that relative resources were an irrelevant consideration, since a local authority's rate fund should be used for the benefit of its own area and there was nothing in the empowering Act to justify the redistribution of resources.[278] Where the Home Secretary refused to release a discretionary life prisoner, despite repeated recommendations from the Parole Board, his decision was quashed because it should have been based solely on future danger to the public, but was influenced by the irrelevant consideration that the prisoner had attempted to escape.[279]

A group of cases concerns the dismissal of schoolteachers. Where education authorities had power to require the dismissal of teachers 'on educational grounds' they acted ultra vires in requiring dismissals in order to save expenditure[280] or because a teacher took an afternoon off in poignant circumstances.[281] But where they had an unrestricted power of dismissal themselves, they were held entitled to dismiss teachers who were married women on the grounds that housewives were less satisfactory and were less in need of employment than single women.[282] These grounds were not alien or irrelevant to the statutory purpose of maintaining efficient schools. But the dismissal of teachers was ultra vires where the sole ground for it was that the teachers refused to collect money for pupils' meals: for the Education Act 1944 expressly provided that the minister could not impose this requirement, and it was not therefore a relevant and valid ground of dismissal.[283]

Incessant litigation over planning and compulsory purchase, illustrated more fully later,[284] has produced a meticulous style of review[285] in which the doctrine of relevant and irrelevant considerations is frequently employed. One case carried it to a new point in quashing a decision of the Secretary of State for paying too much regard to a relevant consideration and so misdirecting himself.[286] His error was to regard a long-expired planning permission as a 'vitally material consideration' requiring the granting of a new permission, when in fact that consideration was relevant but not dominant; and so he came to a

---

[277] R v. Ealing LBC ex p Times Newspapers Ltd (1986) 85 LGR 316.

[278] R v. Secretary of State for Education and Science ex p Inner London Education Authority [1985] 84 LGR 454.

[279] R v. Home Secretary ex p Benson, The Times, 21 November 1988. Contrast R v. Home Secretary ex p Stafford [1999] 2 AC 38.

[280] Hanson v. Radcliffe Urban Council [1922] 2 Ch 490; Sadler v. Sheffield Cpn [1924] 1 Ch 483; R v. Liverpool CC ex p Ferguson [1985] IRLR 501.   [281] Martin v. Eccles Cpn [1919] 1 Ch 387.

[282] Short v. Poole Cpn [1926] Ch 66. Cf. Price v. Rhondda Urban Council [1923] 2 Ch 372.

[283] Price v. Sunderland Cpn [1956] 1 WLR 1253.   [284] Below, p. 344.

[285] Summarised in Seddon Properties Ltd v. Secretary of State for the Environment (1978) 42 P & CR 26.

[286] South Oxfordshire DC v. Secretary of State for the Environment [1981] 1 WLR 1092. Cf. Westminster Renslade Ltd v. Secretary of State for the Environment (1983) 48 P & CR 255; Surrey Heath BC v. Secretary of State for the Environment (1986) 85 LGR 767.

perverse decision. With somewhat similar reasoning the Court of Appeal quashed a compulsory purchase order because the Secretary of State failed to take account of an offer by the landowner which would have made an alternative site less rather than more expensive.[287] It is in decisions such as these that the courts may be said to employ something like the American doctrine of 'hard look review'.[288] But the House of Lords has softened the rigour of this policy by holding that ministerial decision letters may be construed with 'a measure of benevolence'.[289]

Another way of expressing the irrelevant considerations doctrine is to say that a wrong test has been applied. In refusing an application for political asylum on the ground that he was not persuaded that the applicant would be singled out for persecution in his own country, the Home Secretary failed to apply the right test, which was whether the applicant had a well-founded fear of being persecuted for the reasons specified in the international convention on the status of refugees.[290] In the same category, perhaps, was the Home Secretary's 'unreasonable and perverse' decision to refuse concessionary television licences to residents in old people's homes, which the court quashed because he imposed a requirement which was irrelevant to the statutory qualifications.[291]

Nevertheless the House of Lords has held that the Home Secretary, in determining periods of imprisonment under his 'tariff' policy for life prisoners, is in a position analogous to that of a judge passing sentence, and may not therefore take account of public petitions or public opinion or campaigns organised by newspapers.[292] In the case of two boy murderers, for whom he had fixed a tariff of fifteen years, he was held to have misdirected himself in taking account of public demands for a whole-life tariff, and his decision was quashed. This was a majority decision and it was opposed by Lord Lloyd, who rejected the judicial analogy and accepted the relevance of public opinion—as seems natural when the discretion is given by Parliament to a politician rather than to a judge.[293]

QUALIFICATIONS AND EXTENSIONS

There are some situations in which the presence of irrelevant motives will not necessarily be fatal. The most obvious are where they do not in fact affect the action taken or where they operate in the complainant's favour,[294] or where they are merely redundant. Thus where the Broadcasting Complaints Commission declined to entertain a complaint by a party leader that his party was given too little broadcasting time, giving a number of

---

[287] Prest v. Secretary of State for Wales (1982) 81 LGR 193.

[288] The hard look doctrine was originally one of judicial restraint, restricting review of decisions of policy provided that the *agency* had taken a hard look at the whole matter, and decided rationally: *Greater Boston Television Corp.* v. *FCC*, 444 F 2d 841 (1970). But the same title has been given to an intensive technique of review where the *court* investigates relevance of motives, adequacy of evidence and preparatory studies, and other such factors, as in *Sierra Club* v. *Costle*, 657 F 2d 298 (1981) and *Motor Vehicle Manufacturers Association* v. *State Farm Mutual Automobile Insurance Co*, 463 US 29 (1983). In the latter case the Supreme Court set aside the revocation of a government order about car seatbelts for failure to consider the available options and lack of rational connection between the facts and the decision.

[289] Save Britain's Heritage v. No 1 Poultry Ltd [1991] 1 WLR 153 at 165 (HL).

[290] R v. Home Secretary ex p R, The Times, 8 June 1987 (Home Secretary's decision quashed). See similarly R v. Home Secretary ex p Bugdaycay, above, p. 325.

[291] R v. Home Secretary ex p Kirklees BC, The Times, 24 January 1987 (unjustified requirement of exclusive services of housing steward).

[292] R v. Home Secretary ex p Venables [1998] AC 407; and see R v. Home Secretary ex p Furber [1998] 1 All ER 23.

[293] See similarly Lord Lloyd's dissenting speech in R v. Home Secretary ex p Pierson [1998] AC 539, noted above, p. 322.   [294] Hanks v. MHLG (above) at 1020.

good reasons but including the irrelevant reason that the task would be burdensome, their decision was within their lawful discretion.[295] Irrelevant considerations may also be innocuous if the action taken is reasonable in itself. In fixing the level of pay of its employees, which is required by the court to be reasonable, a local authority may act on entirely wrong grounds and yet its payments, if not in themselves excessive, are not unlawful. Of this situation Lord Sumner said:[296]

> If, having examined the expenditure and found clear proof of bad faith, which admittedly would open the account, the auditor found that the councillors' evil minds had missed their mark, and the expenditure itself was right, then the expenditure would not be 'contrary to law' and could not be disallowed.

This therefore appears to be a case where objective and not subjective considerations may prevail. The reasoning was invoked in a later case to justify the payment of children's allowances by way of additional salary.[297]

Objective considerations prevailed also in the Pergau Dam case, where the British government's proposal to grant overseas aid of nearly £70m. for the building of a dam in Malaysia was held to be unlawful as an abuse of power.[298] Under the relevant Act there was power to grant aid 'for the purpose of promoting the development or maintaining the economy' of another country, and it was held that political and economic considerations might legitimately be taken into account. But since on the evidence the whole project was uneconomic, it was held also that it could not have either of the necessary purposes, and on this strict construction it was invalidated.

RELEVANCE OF RESOURCES

A lack of resources, usually financial, often constrains public authorities in deciding how to exercise their duties and powers. As a general rule, impoverishment may not be treated as a relevant reason for failing to perform a statutory duty expressed in objective terms which allow no discretion. The House of Lords made this very clear in a case where the statutory duty of a local authority was to arrange for 'suitable full-time or part-time education', defined as 'efficient education' suitable to the pupil's age, ability, aptitude and any special educational needs.[299] When a cut in government funding compelled the local authority to economise they reduced the home tuition for a handicapped girl from five to three hours a week. It was clear from the Act that the standard of suitability was to be determined purely by educational considerations, so that shortage of funds was irrelevant

---

[295] R v. *Broadcasting Complaints Commission ex p Owen* [1985] QB 1153. See also R v. *Secretary of State for Social Services ex p Wellcome Foundation Ltd* [1987] 1 WLR 1166.

[296] *Roberts* v. *Hopwood* [1925] AC 578 at 604; below, p. 340. Confirmed in R (*Mavalon Care Ltd*) v. *Pembrokeshire County Council* [2011] EWHC 3371, para. 48 (Beatson J).

[297] *Re Walker's Decision* [1944] KB 644; below, p. 342.

[298] R v. *Secretary of State for Foreign and Commonwealth Affairs ex p World Development Movement Ltd* [1995] 1 WLR 386.

[299] R v. *East Sussex County Court ex p Tandy* [1998] AC 714; and see R v. *Sefton MBC ex p Help the Aged* [1997] 4 All ER 532; R v. *Birmingham City Council ex p Mohammed* [1998] 3 All ER 788; B v. *Harrow LBC* [2000] 1 WLR 223 (HC). See also R (*Forest Care Home Ltd*) v. *The Welsh Ministers and anor* [2010] EWHC 3514, para. 46(2) (once an authority has set threshold of need (and an individual crosses that threshold) lack of resources is no excuse; the authority is under a specific duty to an individual, not a target duty). See also R (*T*) v. *Legal Aid Agency* [2013] EWHC 960 following R (*H*) v. *Ashworth Hospital Authority* [2002] EWCA Civ 923 (lack of resources (to give reasons) no justification for inadequate reasons).

and a matter for Parliament only. Otherwise the court would have 'to downgrade a statutory duty to a discretionary power'.

In a contrasting decision, however, a divided House of Lords accepted under-funding as relevant even in the case of a duty.[300] The Act provided that where a local authority was satisfied that it was 'necessary, in order to meet the needs' of a poor person for (*inter alia*) home help, television or recreational facilities, games, outings, facilities for holidays, or meals, 'it shall be the duty' of the authority to make arrangements for them in accordance with the Act. When the local authority, because of lack of funds, withdrew a disabled person's laundry and cleaning services, its action was upheld on the grounds that, since the Act provided no criterion for 'necessary' and 'needs', and the extensive list of welfare benefits showed that those words bore flexible and relative meanings, it was legitimate to take account of resources in determining what was to be treated as necessary or as a need. The logic of this decision is difficult in view of the objective language of the Act; and the dissentient Lords, agreeing with the Court of Appeal, may be thought to have the better of the argument, desirable though it may be to release local authorities from such painful dilemmas. In a later case the Court of Appeal held that in assessing 'necessity' the local authority may consider whether the 'needs', in this case of disabled children, might be met in some way other than the provision of resources by the council, for instance, through the support of their relatives. Thus the council could insist on the children's parents revealing their means.[301]

The decision of the House of Lords is still controversial; the last word has not been heard on this issue. There is much to be said for the view (of Baroness Hale) that:[302] 'There is a clear distinction between need and what is done to meet it. We all need to eat and drink. Resources do not come into it. But there are various ways of meeting that need and it is perfectly sensible to choose the most efficient and economical way of meeting it. Our nutritional needs can met by simple, wholesome food, rather than by giving us the expensive foods that we prefer.' Thus resources are irrelevant to the question of need but may be to the means adopted to meet that need.

Painful dilemmas can equally well arise where an authority has a discretionary power as opposed to a duty, and has to decide how to apportion limited funds in its budget. A local health authority had to decide whether to provide an 11-year-old girl, suffering from acute leukaemia, with very expensive medical treatment which was experimental and had a low chance of success. Concluding that the treatment was not in the girl's best interests, the authority declined to provide it, taking account of its limited resources. The Court of Appeal upheld that decision and Sir Thomas Bingham MR said:[303]

> Difficult and agonising judgments have to be made as to how a limited budget is best allocated to the maximum advantage of the maximum number of patients...it would be totally unrealistic to require the authority to come to the court with its accounts and seek to demonstrate that if this treatment were provided for B. there would be a patient C. who would have to go without treatment.

[300] *R v. Gloucestershire CC ex p Barry* [1997] AC 584. Contrast *R v. Gloucestershire CC ex p Mahfood* (1995) 8 Admin LR 180.

[301] *R (Spink)* v. *London Borough of Wandsworth* [2005] EWCA Civ 302, paras. 44–6 (Lord Phillips MR).

[302] *R (McDonald)* v. *Royal Borough of Kensington and Chelsea* [2011] UKSC 33, para. 41. A 7-member Supreme Court was assembled to hear *R (KM)* v. *Cambridgeshire County Council* [2012] UKSC 23 in order to consider whether *ex p Barry* was rightly decided. But in the event the relevance of resources did not arise.

[303] *R* v. *Cambridge Health Authority ex p B* [1995] 1 WLR 898.

In these discretionary situations it is more likely to be unlawful to disregard financial considerations than to take account of them.

The police, likewise, must be allowed a wide margin of discretion in deciding how best to deploy their limited resources of manpower and finance. Where the loading of live animals for export was obstructed at the port by crowds of animal rights activists, necessitating a level of police protection which interfered with the efficient policing of the rest of the county, the chief constable felt compelled by lack of resources to reduce protection from five days a week to two, and to forbid shipments on other days in order to prevent breaches of the peace. The House of Lords upheld these decisions, despite the shippers' complaints of 'a surrender to mob rule' and the failure of the chief constable to seek a special grant (unlikely to be given).[304] Lord Slynn approved the comment that 'there may well be important and sound reasons for a chief constable's decision not to commit all his force's resources to, nor to exercise his full legal powers in, a given dispute or demonstration'.[305] The police had given due weight to all the relevant considerations, and the court should ask no more. This balancing exercise was what was lacking in a contrasting case where local airport and harbour authorities had banned altogether the shipment of live animals because of disruptive protests. A Divisional Court quashed the bans as being a surrender to the dictates of unlawful pressure groups.[306] The authorities had failed to give any thought to 'the awesome implications for the rule of law of doing what they propose', there was no issue of lack of resources, and no complaint of inaction by the police.

A FLEXIBLE PRINCIPLE

The principle of relevance has a part to play in judicial as well as in administrative decisions. In the time before the enactment of the Human Rights Act 1998, when the European Convention on Human Rights and Fundamental Freedoms had the status of a treaty only and not the force of law, the court would take account of it as a relevant consideration in cases where the law was ambiguous or uncertain. But fundamental rights deserve a special title, which will be found later.

'Irrelevant considerations' as a technique of judicial review provides the court with a weapon of great range and flexibility, which may often approximate to reviewing a decision merely on its merits, undermining the supposedly strict *Wednesbury* principle. Its potentiality is obvious, and equally obvious is the difficulty of reducing it to precise rules. Along with other varieties of unreasonableness it embraces a large area of the ultra vires rule and the decisions are numerous. Many of the best examples can be grouped according to their subject matter under the titles which follow. But these categories must not be regarded as rigid. The courts have many strings to their bow and many of their arguments are interchangeable.[307]

---

[304] R v. *Chief Constable of Sussex ex p International Trader's Ferry Ltd*, above, p. 315. The House also rejected the contention that the police action violated EU law as being measures equivalent to quantitative restrictions on exports, contrary to Art. 34 (now 29) of the EU Treaty. It was held justified by the exception for acts of public policy in Art. 36 (now 30).

[305] (1997) 60 *MLR* 394 at 409 (C. Barnard and I. Hare).

[306] R v. *Coventry City Council ex p Phoenix Aviation* [1995] 3 All ER 37 (the quotation is from Simon Brown LJ). See also *KA Feakins Ltd* v. *Dover Harbour Board* (1998) 10 Admin LR 665 (similar facts, action for breach of statutory duty failed). See discussion of the *Corner House* case at pp. 533 and 563.

[307] See e.g. *Wheeler* v. *Leicester City Council* [1985] AC 1054, where arguments based on unfairness, unreasonableness and abuse of power are intermingled. See also [1987] *PL* 368 (J. Jowell and A. Lester) for various facets of the *Wednesbury* doctrine.

CATEGORIES OF UNREASONABLENESS

OPPOSITION TO THE POLICY OF PARLIAMENT

From time to time public authorities have set their faces against the policy of an Act, and either declined to implement it or else attempted to frustrate it. Needless to say, this is an unlawful motive. In a case under the old poor law, where justices of the peace had discretion to enforce parochial contributions if they 'shall think fit', the justices refused to make an order against one parish because they thought it unfair that, having no paupers, it should be made to contribute, and the justices' order was condemned as arbitrary and illegal.[308] An analogous modern case arose from a London borough council's hostility to the policy of the Rent Act 1957. Certain classes of houses, formerly under requisition, remained in the occupation of tenants whose rents could not be increased 'except so far as the local authority may from time to time determine'; and the local authority had to compensate the owners by paying them the difference between the rent so determined and the rent which would otherwise be payable. The object of the Rent Act 1957 was to allow rents to rise to more realistic levels. Therefore the compensation payable to the owners would be greatly increased unless the local authority approved higher rents for the tenants. The St Pancras borough council refused to do this, being opposed to higher rents generally and wishing to 'protect the tenants from the Rent Act'. Lord Parker CJ held that this policy rendered the council's decision 'purely arbitrary' and disregarded the council's duty to their ratepayers, on whom the cost of the compensation would fall.[309] Their legal duty therefore was to review the rents, taking account of the relevant consideration that rents had been allowed to rise. The district auditor had accordingly been right in disallowing the additional compensation which the council had unlawfully paid. In later proceedings it was held that the councillors responsible had acted honestly but unreasonably, and ought not to be relieved from the auditor's surcharges.[310]

A simple and blatant device aimed at nullifying the effect of an Act of Parliament was where a housing authority, determined not to make a general increase of rents as required by the Act, charged the whole of the required increase onto a single vacant house, putting up its weekly rent from £7 to £18,000. The court had no difficulty in holding this an unlawful abuse.[311]

The *Padfield* case,[312] already discussed, shows the 'statutory policy' doctrine as applied to a minister of the Crown. The House of Lords held that in refusing to refer the milk producers' complaint to the statutory committee the minister had acted so as to frustrate the policy of the Act, despite the fact that its words were merely permissive; and that the political and other reasons given were irrelevant and indicative of unlawful motives. It is particularly important to notice how closely the House of Lords scrutinised the minister's reasons, as governing the validity of the action. One of the reasons given in a departmental letter was that the minister would have to consider whether, if he allowed the producers' complaint to be referred to the statutory committee and they upheld it, he would be expected to give effect to the committee's recommendations. Lord Upjohn said:

> This fear of parliamentary trouble (for, in my opinion, this must be the scarcely veiled meaning of this letter) if an inquiry were ordered and its possible results is alone sufficient

---

[308] *R* v. *Boteler* (1864) 4 B & S 959.   [309] *Taylor* v. *Munrow* [1960] 1 WLR 151.

[310] *Annison* v. *District Auditor for St Pancras* [1962] 1 QB 489.

[311] *Backhouse* v. *Lambeth London Borough Council*, The Times, 14 October 1972.

[312] *Padfield* v. *Minister of Agriculture, Fisheries and Food* [1968] AC 997; above, p. 297.

to vitiate the Minister's decision which, as I have stated earlier, can never validly turn on purely political considerations; he must be prepared to face the music in Parliament.

There could scarcely be a better example of the principle that statutory powers, however permissive, must be used with scrupulous attention to their true purposes and for reasons which are relevant and proper.

The House of Lords also rejected the Crown's argument that the minister need have given no reasons and that therefore such reasons as he volunteered to give could not be criticised. Going still further, the House declared that if in such a case he refused to give any reasons, the court might have to assume that he had no good reasons and was acting arbitrarily.[313] In other words, the minister may not be able to disarm the court by taking refuge in silence. In this way the court would have power to impose, in effect, an obligation to give reasons for discretionary decisions. But the law has not yet reached that point, as explained in a later chapter.[314] Despite the general obligation to act reasonably, a local authority need not give reasons for evicting a tenant,[315] nor need a minister do so for making orders and giving directions for the protection of trading interests.[316]

A determined ministerial attempt to frustrate the policy of an Act was condemned by the Court of Appeal in the *Laker Airways* case.[317] The company had been granted a licence for a low-cost transatlantic air service by the Civil Aviation Authority, one of whose statutory duties was to secure that at least one independent British airline had opportunities to compete with British Airways. In 1975 the government announced a policy of preventing competition and the Secretary of State issued 'guidance' to the CAA, in terms approved by both Houses of Parliament, requiring them to revoke the company's licence. Under the Civil Aviation Act 1971 the Secretary of State had power to give the CAA guidance in the performance of their functions and the CAA had to obey. But the guidance given in this case clearly conflicted with their functions since one of them was to give opportunities to independent airlines. The guidance was therefore ultra vires and invalid.[318] The Secretary of State had also announced that he would withdraw the company's designation as an approved airline under the agreement with the United States, so that it would not obtain landing rights in America. This step was likewise declared to be unlawful. For its object, again, was to frustrate the express provision of the Act about allowing competition and to render licences properly granted by the CAA worthless. The Act, it was held, by necessary implication prohibited the Crown from pursuing this unlawful object, even though the Crown was acting, as it claimed, under the royal prerogative in the sphere of foreign affairs. Lord Denning MR held further that the Crown was abusing the prerogative, as explained earlier.[319] The use of the doctrine of implied prohibition to restrain action which would normally be beyond the court's control is a particularly striking feature of this decision.

---

[313] [1968] AC at 1032, 1053, 1061. See similarly *Secretary of State for Employment* v. *ASLEF (No 2)* [1972] 2 QB 455 at 493 (Lord Denning MR) and *Minister of National Revenue* v. *Wright's Canadian Ropes Ltd* [1947] AC 109 at 123 (below, p. 361); and compare *Fiordland Venison Ltd* v. *Minister of Agriculture* [1978] 2 NZLR 341 (minister's reasons inferred from evidence and held improper; applicant held entitled to licence in the absence of good reasons for refusing it).   [314] Below, p. 440.

[315] *Cannock Chase DC* v. *Kelly* [1978] 1 WLR 1.

[316] *British Airways Board* v. *Laker Airways Ltd* [1985] AC 58.

[317] *Laker Airways Ltd* v. *Department of Trade* [1977] QB 643.

[318] For another mistake by a Secretary of State as to his powers of giving directions see *R* v. *Secretary of State for Social Services ex p Lewisham etc LBC*, The Times, 26 February 1980 (default powers misunderstood).

[319] See above, p. 290.

Failure to take account of the policy of Parliament caused the quashing of a local council's refusal to refund rates overpaid. The council had discretionary power under the Act to make repayments, but had refused to exercise it for various bad reasons, without regard to the Act's policy that injustice should be remedied.[320] And there have been other comparable decisions.[321]

In the most controversial of all these cases there was a radical cleavage of judicial opinion about the proper relationship between the courts and Parliament. The criminal injuries compensation scheme, operated administratively on a non-statutory basis and making payments from funds voted by Parliament, was to be made statutory by the Criminal Justice Act 1988, but its provisions were to come into force 'on such day as the Secretary of State may by order made by statutory instrument appoint'. Before making any such order the Secretary of State (the Home Secretary) decided to abandon the scheme provided for in the Act and to substitute a different scheme (the 'tariff scheme') with a scale of fixed payments and less generous compensation. The new scheme was to be put into force without legislation, in the same manner as the old scheme; and there would be no commencement order under the Act of 1988, which would be repealed *pro tanto* when convenient. There could hardly be a plainer case of administrative frustration of Parliamentary intention. But the question was, ought the court to intervene, or was it a matter for Parliament only? At the instance of the Fire Brigades Union and others the House of Lords by a bare majority, upholding a majority of the Court of Appeal, held that the Home Secretary had a duty to keep the activation of the statutory scheme under continuous consideration, that the introduction of an inconsistent scheme was unlawful frustration of the provision made by Parliament, that the matter was justiciable by judicial review, and that declaratory relief should be given to the firemen's union.[322] Lords Browne-Wilkinson and Nicholls, in the majority, held that the Secretary of State was attempting to pre-empt Parliament's decision whether to preserve the statutory scheme, and that by introducing the tariff scheme he debarred himself from exercising his power to make a commencement order for the purpose that Parliament intended; and that this was an abuse of power and unlawful. Lord Lloyd, assenting, held that the Home Secretary's power was to give effect to, rather than frustrate, the legislative policy enshrined in the Act and allowed him 'to say when, but not whether' that policy should be fulfilled. Lord Keith, in the minority, held that the decision was 'of a political and administrative character quite unsuitable to be the subject of review by a court of law', which 'would be a most improper intrusion into a field which lies peculiarly within the province of Parliament' and a 'usurpation of the function of Parliament'; and Lord Mustill agreed in substance, though less vehemently, with Lord Keith.[323]

Important constitutional issues underlie the conflicting opinions in this case. The Home Secretary was proceeding, realistically, on the footing that 'the intention of Parliament' was in fact the intention of the executive government, which could obtain from Parliament any authority or dispensation that it wanted at any time. The minority judges considered that the courts should not intrude into this relationship. But a great

---

[320] R v. *Tower Hamlets LBC ex p Chetnik Developments Ltd* [1988] AC 858, for which see below, p. 678.

[321] See R v. *Burnham Primary and Secondary Committee ex p Professional Association of Teachers*, The Times, 30 March 1985 (exclusion of teachers' association frustrated policy of Act); R v. *Haberdashers' Aske's Hatcham School Governors ex p Brunyate and Hunt* [1989] 1 WLR 542 (HL) (policy of Education Acts thwarted).

[322] R v. *Home Secretary ex p Fire Brigades Union* [1995] 2 AC 513. After this decision the government's preferred scheme was made statutory by the Criminal Injuries Compensation Act 1995.

[323] Compare the dissent of Neill LJ in R v. *Criminal Injuries Compensation Board ex p P* [1995] 1 WLR 845.

deal of administrative action has a political character, and may affect proceedings in Parliament, for example when orders are approved by resolutions of both Houses and yet may be quashed.[324] To invalidate administrative action which conflicts with statute is essentially the task of the judiciary. As Lord Lloyd said, quoting this book, 'ministerial responsibility is no substitute for judicial review'.

INFRINGEMENT OF FUNDAMENTAL RIGHTS

Two classes of fundamental rights, closely similar and sometimes identical, have to be distinguished. The first class are rights regarded as of special importance by the common law, such as the right of access to the courts.[325] The second class are the rights protected by the European Convention on Human Rights and Fundamental Freedoms, now incorporated into the law by the Human Rights Act 1998. The common law rights affect the operation of the principle of reasonableness since they can be infringed only for especially compelling reasons. Rights under the European Convention, on the other hand, are now statutory rights by virtue of the Act of 1998, with their own independent force. But before the Act those Convention rights would sometimes be taken into account by the courts on the assumption that Parliament would not intend to infringe Convention obligations[326] and this indirect effect may still be important in cases falling outside the Act.

Basic rights such as the right to life, freedom of the person, freedom of speech and the right of access to the courts are protected in the common law by judicial review of special stringency. This may be seen from an important statement by Lord Bridge:[327]

> But I do not accept that this conclusion [the inapplicability of the Convention] means that the courts are powerless to prevent the exercise by the executive of administrative discretions, even when conferred, as in the instant case, in terms which are on their face unlimited, in a way which infringes fundamental human rights... But again, this surely does not mean that in deciding whether the Secretary of State, in the exercise of his discretion, could reasonably impose the restriction he has imposed on the broadcasting organisations, we are not perfectly entitled to start from the premise that any restriction of the right to freedom of expression requires to be justified and that nothing less than an important competing public interest will be sufficient to justify it. The primary judgment as to whether the particular competing public interest justifies the particular restriction imposed falls to be made by the Secretary of State to whom Parliament has entrusted the discretion. But we are entitled to exercise a secondary judgment by asking whether

---

[324] See the *Laker Airways* case, above, p. 333.

[325] For this 'vital constitutional right' see *R v. Lord Chancellor ex p Witham* [1998] QB 575; below, p. 740. The right of access to the court is the duty of the state 'not to place obstacles in the way of access to justice' (per Laws LJ, *R (The Children's Rights Alliance for England) v. The Secretary of State for Justice* [2013] EWCA Civ 34, para. 38). Thus it did not extend to informing prospective claimants of unlawful restraints to which they had been subject in order that they might have access to justice.

[326] *ex p Brind* (below) at 721; *Rantzen v. Mirror Group Newspapers Ltd* [1994] QB 670 at 691.

[327] *R v. Home Secretary ex p Brind* [1991] 1 AC 696 at 748. See also *R v. Home Secretary ex p Bugdaycay* [1987] AC 514 at 531. The resulting state of the law is summarised by Neill LJ in *R v. Secretary of State for the Environment ex p National and Local Government Officers Association* (1992) 5 Admin LR 785 at 798. See also the discussion by Sir John Laws in Forsyth and Hare (eds.), *The Golden Metwand*, 185. And note the influential 'accurate distillation' of the principles laid down in *ex p Bugdacay* and *ex p Brind* put forward by David Pannick QC and adopted by Lord Bingham MR in *R v. Ministry of Defence ex p Smith* [1996] QB 517 at 554. The distillation notes that the human rights context is important in judging whether the decision-maker has exceeded the range of options open to him. The 'more substantial the interference with human rights, the more the court will require by way of justification before it is satisfied that the decision is reasonable'.

a reasonable Secretary of State, on the material before him could reasonably make that primary judgment.

Fundamental rights, accordingly, will be guarded by the law with especial care. This guardianship, according to Lord Bridge, is exercised through the principle of reasonableness; and in the same vein the Court of Appeal has held that the threshold of unreasonableness is lowered and the standard of review becomes more stringent when the right to life is in question.[328] Wide general powers must make way for fundamental rights, for example where it is held that the Home Secretary's wide powers of administration over prisons do not empower prison governors to obstruct prisoners' correspondence with their legal advisers or their access to the courts of law[329] or their interviews with journalists for the purpose of challenging the justice of their convictions,[330] since it is part of their right of access to justice that they should have access to investigative journalism, by which miscarriages of justice have often been exposed. In the latter context Lord Steyn identified 'a fundamental or basic right' bringing into play 'a presumption of general application operating as a constitutional principle'.[331] And Lord Hoffmann said:[332]

> Fundamental rights cannot be overridden by general or ambiguous words. This is because there is too great a risk that the full implications of their unqualified meaning may have passed unnoticed in the democratic process...In this way the courts of the United Kingdom, though acknowledging the sovereignty of Parliament, apply principles of constitutionality little different from those which exist in countries where the power of the legislature is expressly limited by a constitutional document.

The House of Lords is evidently laying the foundations of a more deep-seated doctrine than that of reasonableness,[333] giving effect in the common law to a culture of human rights independent of the Act of 1998.

The statutory rights secured by the Human Rights Act 1998 have already been generally explained.[334] But there may be cases not covered by the Act, for example where the complainant is not a 'victim' within the Act or the Convention but nevertheless has a 'sufficient interest' to seek judicial review.[335] In such cases the court is likely to fall back upon its practice developed before the Act, whereby it would have regard to the Convention principles in cases where the common law was uncertain or a statute was obscure or ambiguous or merely general in its terms.[336]

In a leading example the Court of Appeal, faced with conflicting precedents, held that the right of free expression secured by the Convention entailed that a local authority could not sue for libel when vehemently criticised for bad government—although the House of Lords affirmed the decision on the common law alone, without needing to invoke

---

[328] R v. *Lord Saville of Newdigate ex p A* [1999] 4 All ER 860 (order of statutory tribunal of inquiry denying anonymity to soldier witnesses who fired shots in 'Bloody Sunday' riots of 1972 quashed because identification would endanger their lives).

[329] R v. *Home Secretary ex p Leech (No 2)* [1994] QB 198; *Raymond* v. *Honey* [1983] 1 AC 1.

[330] R v. *Home Secretary ex p Simms* [1999] 3 WLR 328. The House of Lords held that the right was restricted to that purpose only, invalidating (*pro tanto*) a Home Office policy that journalists must undertake not to use the information professionally.   [331] Ibid. at 390.

[332] Ibid. at 341.

[333] Lord Hobhouse however spoke in terms of reasonableness.   [334] Above, p. 129.

[335] See above, p. 135. See Appendix 3.

[336] For full discussion and survey of the pre-Act position see Murray Hunt, *Using Human Rights Law in English Courts*.

the Convention.[337] In a case already cited in the context of proportionality the Home Secretary had issued directives forbidding the BBC and the IBA from broadcasting words spoken by members of organisations proscribed under emergency legislation in Northern Ireland. These directives were challenged by journalists as violating the Convention right of free speech (as well as being disproportionate) but the House of Lords upheld them, finding that the law was clear and that there was no room for the Convention.[338] Room was found for it, however, by the Court of Appeal while the Human Rights Bill was still before Parliament, when the Convention right of privacy was construed as if it were already part of English law, though without affecting the result.[339] But the House of Lords later gave a check to these tendencies, holding that the Act had shown a clear statutory intent to postpone the coming into operation of its central provisions.[340]

PENALISING THE INNOCENT

One element in the abuse of power condemned by the Court of Appeal in the television licences case, already encountered, was the penalising of licence-holders for doing something quite lawful, namely taking out new licences at any time they might wish.[341] The House of Lords emphasised the same point in a later case where a city council had refused, contrary to its previous practice, to allow a local rugby football club to use the city's sports ground because three of its members had played in South Africa.[342] The House held that it was unreasonable thus to punish the club for not conforming to the council's political attitudes, and Lord Templeman said:

A private individual or a private organisation cannot be obliged to display zeal in the pursuit of an object sought by a public authority and cannot be obliged to publish views dictated by a public authority.... The council could not properly seek to use its statutory powers of management or any other statutory powers for the purposes of punishing the club when the club had done no wrong.

The council's decision was therefore quashed, with provision for declaratory or injunctive relief if necessary, thus in effect compelling the council to allow the club to use its sports ground. In a similar case a London borough adopted a policy of boycotting the products of an oil company because it did business in South Africa, and since this was not an unlawful activity the council's resolution was quashed and its enforcement restrained by injunction.[343] The same occurred when, for purely vindictive reasons, a council withdrew all advertising from a newspaper with which it was in dispute.[344] A council's ban on political parties taking part in a community festival was likewise unlawful.[345]

---

[337] *Derbyshire CC v. Times Newspapers Ltd* [1993] AC 534.

[338] *ex p Brind* (above).

[339] *R v. Home Secretary ex p Hargreaves* [1997] 1 WLR 906; *R v. Chief Constable of the North Wales Police ex p AB* [1999] QB 396.

[340] See also *R v. Director of Public Prosecutions ex p Kebilene* [1999] 3 WLR 972 (HL), where the House reversed an imaginative decision of a Divisional Court based on an alleged violation of the presumption of innocence protected by Art. 6 of the Convention. For this case see below, p. 533.

[341] Above, p. 296. See likewise *Roncarelli v. Duplessis*, above, p. 295.

[342] *Wheeler v. Leicester City Council* [1985] AC 1054.

[343] *R v. Lewisham LBC ex p Shell UK Ltd* [1988] 1 All ER 938.

[344] *R v. Derbyshire CC ex p Times Supplements Ltd* (1990) 3 Admin LR 241.

[345] *R v. Barnet LBC ex p Johnstone* (1989) 88 LGR 73.

FINANCIAL MOTIVES

A laudable desire to save public money has led many authorities into the error of using their powers for financial profit when that is not a legitimate purpose. This misdeed may be illustrated by the case of the planning condition which wrongfully required the applicant to provide a strip of roadway at his own expense.[346] Similarly a local authority was not entitled, as a condition of approving building plans, to stipulate that the applicant should provide and pay for sewers outside his own property: this, said Lord Russell CJ, was 'utterly unreasonable'.[347] An education authority which has power to require the dismissal of teachers on 'educational grounds' may not do so merely to save money.[348] Nor may a local authority for reasons of economy restrict the time to be spent on each case by guardians ad litem.[349]

The city of Sydney exceeded its powers of acquiring land for 'carrying out improvements in or remodelling any portion of the city' when it made a compulsory purchase order for land merely in order to obtain the rise in value which the extension of a street would bring about, without any intention of improving or remodelling.[350] In another Australian case a statutory committee was given wide wartime powers to ensure adequate supplies of vegetable seeds, and was also empowered to trade in seeds. It was held that orders prohibiting merchants from dealing in certain seeds would be ultra vires if made primarily for the purpose of improving the profitability of the committee's trading operations rather than for ensuring supplies.[351]

Two liquor licensing cases firmly underline the same point. In one, the licensing justices required the applicant to pay £1,000, which they intended to use to reduce the rates or for some other public purpose. The court had no difficulty in holding that the justices had taken illegitimate factors into account in a wholly unjustifiable way.[352] In the other case an elaborate system had been set up by the statutory licensing planning committee in Birmingham to deal with the licences relating to the many public houses destroyed in the Second World War. With Home Office approval and for some twenty years they had refused to approve applications unless the applicant purchased outstanding licences sufficient to cover his estimated sales. The main object of the policy was to relieve the city of the cost of compensating the holders of the outstanding licences. At the current market price of these licences the proprietors of a large new hotel would have had to pay over £14,000. At their instance the Court of Appeal condemned the whole system as unreasonable.[353] Lord Denning MR said:

> I think it is unreasonable for a licensing planning committee to tell an applicant: 'We know that your hotel is needed in Birmingham and that it is well placed to have an on-licence,

---

[346] Hall & Co Ltd v. Shoreham-by-Sea Urban District Council [1964] 1 WLR 240; below, p. 344.

[347] R v. Tynemouth District Council [1896] 2 QB 219.

[348] Sadler v. Sheffield Cpn [1924] 1 Ch 483; above, p. 327.

[349] R v. Cornwall CC ex p Cornwall Guardians Ad Litem Panel [1992] 1 WLR 427.

[350] Sydney Municipal Council v. Campbell [1925] AC 338. Compare Denman & Co Ltd v. Westminster Cpn [1906] 1 Ch 464 at 476.

[351] Yates (Arthur) & Co Pty Ltd v. Vegetable Seeds Committee (1945) 72 CLR 37. Cf. Bailey v. Conole (1931) 34 WALR 18 (regulations prescribing bus routes invalid since object was to protect state-owned trains from competition).

[352] R v. Bowman [1898] 1 QB 663. See similarly R v. Sheffield Justices ex p Rawson (1927) 44 TLR 43 (offer to pay £1,250 to compensation fund). Cf. Marshall Shipping Co v. R (1925) 41 TLR 285; R v. LCC [1931] 2 KB 215 at 232. Contrast Becker v. Home Office [1972] 2 QB 407 (above, p. 185).

[353] R v. Birmingham Licensing Planning Committee ex p Kennedy [1972] 2 QB 140.

but we will not allow you to have a licence unless you buy out the brewers.' They are taking into account a payment to the brewers which is a thing they ought not to take into account.

The condition was therefore 'bad because it is unreasonable'.

In this class also is to be included the television licence case, already recounted, in which the Court of Appeal held that the Home Secretary could not lawfully exercise his power to revoke a licence for the purpose of compelling the licensee to pay an additional fee which had not been authorised by Parliament.[354] The revocation was invalid not only on general grounds of unreasonableness but also because it was an attempt to levy money for the use of the Crown without the authority of Parliament, contrary to the Bill of Rights 1688.

The Crown is not subject to this branch of the doctrine of unreasonableness when using its ordinary powers as an owner of land. Accordingly there can be no objection to the demand by an official in Hong Kong, acting as land agent for the Crown, for the payment of a high premium as the price of waiving restrictions in a lease of Crown land.[355]

INDISCRIMINATE ACTION

The indiscriminate or excessive use of power is illustrated by the case of a London borough council which made it a rule to refer to the rent tribunal all the tenancies in any block of flats where two or more reductions of rent had been awarded.[356] Although the Act contained no express restriction on the council's power to refer tenancies, it was held that it was an abuse to make a single block reference of over three hundred tenancies without any consideration of the individual cases and without any specific complaint against the landlord. The disputed reference in fact contained so many inaccuracies that it was not a genuine exercise of the power, and furthermore the council had taken account of the irrelevant consideration that the flats were allegedly below the highest building standards. This decision was distinguished in a later case where another London council had considered each case with care in a reference of twenty-two tenancies, and where the only complaint was that most of the tenants themselves did not wish the reference to be made.[357] The council here was plainly acting responsibly and intra vires, within the bounds of its discretion. But the Court of Appeal went out of their way to say that the doctrine of relevant and irrelevant considerations ought not to apply at all to a decision which does not itself infringe rights and merely causes something to be investigated. This novel proposition was probably not intended to make a breach in the long-settled rules of judicial review, since the court appears to have assumed that the 'relevant considerations' doctrine was violated whenever anything which might be thought relevant was not considered or any sort of mistake was made. In reality that doctrine applies only where the relevant considerations neglected or the irrelevant considerations adopted are so serious as to put the decision outside the powers of the statute.[358] The problem disappears if it is understood that the 'relevant considerations' doctrine is necessarily a species of the genus 'ultra vires', and cannot be used to impugn a proper and reasonable decision.

---

[354] *Congreve v. Home Office* [1976] QB 629; above, p. 301.

[355] *Hang Wah Chong Investment Co Ltd v. A-G of Hong Kong* [1981] 1 WLR 1141.

[356] *R v. Paddington etc Rent Tribunal ex p Bell London and Provincial Properties Ltd* [1949] 1 KB 666. Compare *R v. British Coal Corporation ex p Vardy* [1993] ICR 720 (pit closures unreasonable for lack of independent scrutiny).

[357] *R v. Barnet etc Rent Tribunal ex p Frey Investments Ltd* [1972] 2 QB 342.

[358] See *R v. St Pancras Vestry* (1890) 24 QBD 371.

MISPLACED PHILANTHROPY

Statutory authorities have sometimes made use of their wide general powers in order to confer social or economic benefits on particular sections of the community. In several such cases they have gone beyond the true limits of their powers. The policy of the courts is in general hostile to the use of public funds, such as rates, for new social experiments. Local authorities are subject to a fiduciary duty to use their revenues with due restraint.

A classic case in this group is *Roberts v. Hopwood*.[359] A minimum weekly wage of £4 for men and women equally was established in 1920 by the Poplar Borough Council, representing themselves as 'model socialist employers'. This in itself was very substantially above the previous rates, and soon became relatively higher still due to a sharp fall in the cost of living and in wages. But the council insisted on continuing the £4 rate, maintaining that this was within their power to pay their servants 'such salaries and wages as (they) may think fit'. In due course the district auditor disallowed the wage payments, in so far as they exceeded current market rates, as being 'contrary to law', and surcharged the councillors personally. A long struggle over the surcharges began, in the course of which the auditor's ruling was unanimously upheld by the House of Lords, and an order of the Minister of Health, purporting to free the councillors from liability, was held invalid by the High Court. Ultimately, when the surcharges had accumulated far beyond the councillors' personal means, they were remitted by Act of Parliament.[360]

The basis of the decision of the House of Lords, as already noted, was that the wages paid were excessive and unreasonable in such a degree that they were beyond the council's powers. The council's philanthropic purposes were not in law relevant considerations: their duty was not to give their ratepayers' money away in what were in substance gifts, but to take due account of the relevant factor of current market rates. They had misled themselves by 'eccentric principles of socialistic philanthropy'.[361]

Despite remarks such as the last, and despite criticisms from literal-minded people, there is no doubt that this decision was fully in accord with the settled policy of limiting discretionary powers. It was followed where councillors of another London borough were surcharged for failing to increase rents in an attempt to resist the policy of the Rent Act 1957, as already explained.[362] It was also accepted by the Court of Appeal as supporting their decision in the *Birmingham* case, discussed later. It had also been foreshadowed earlier when Farwell LJ had said:[363]

> The auditor does not claim…to exercise any control over questions of policy; but he does claim the right to check and challenge all items of administration. It is not easy to draw the line between policy and administration, or to give a definition except by way of example, but in my opinion the establishment of a works committee would be a question of policy into which the auditor could not go, but the payment of abnormally high wages to the workmen employed by such committee would be a matter of administration.

[359] [1925] AC 578. Contrast *Pickwell* v. *Camden LBC* [1983] QB 962 (payment of wages above national level; auditor's challenge failed).

[360] Audit (Local Authorities) Act 1927, s. 2(6). For a good account of the whole contest and its political background, including the imprisonment of thirty councillors for failing to levy rates, see [1962] PL 52 (B. Keith-Lucas); N. Branson, *Poplarism*. See above, p. 97 for the current system of audit.

[361] *Roberts* v. *Hopwood* (above) at 594 (Lord Atkinson).

[362] *Taylor* v. *Munrow* [1960] 1 WLR 151; above, p. 332.

[363] *R* v. *Roberts* [1908] 1 KB 407 at 435 (unsuccessful appeal by the same auditor who played a leading part in *Roberts* v. *Hopwood*).

Another restrictive decision comes from the general strike of 1926. After the strike, when the poor law guardians had been empowered to give relief to miners' families by way of loan, the Tynemouth guardians resolved to cancel the outstanding debts.[364] This was held to be ultra vires since the guardians, unlike a private creditor, had no power to remit debts,[365] and because, in any case, it was unreasonable to do so where there was no evidence of inability to repay. The idea that runs through these cases is that public money must be administered with responsibility and without extravagance. This appears to mean that it is not available for charity.

The generosity of local authorities, in particular, is restrained by the doctrine that they owe a fiduciary duty to their ratepayers analogous to that of trustees. This means that, in deciding upon their expenditure, they must hold a balance fairly between the recipients of the benefit and the ratepayers who have to bear the cost. The courts have given two notable illustrations of this doctrine. In the first, the Court of Appeal invalidated the Birmingham City Council's concession to old-age pensioners, by which if resident in the city they could travel free of charge on the corporation's buses and trams.[366] These services were operated under Acts of Parliament which empowered the corporation to impose 'such fares and charges as they may think fit'. They were already run at a loss, and the additional cost of the concession was some £90,000 a year. At the instance of a ratepayer the court granted a declaration that the concession was illegal. The corporation's fiduciary duty to its ratepayers meant that it was not free to saddle them with the cost of subsidising one particular class of the community. Philanthropy was no part of the management of a transport undertaking which the corporation ought to operate 'substantially on business lines'. This would not necessarily exclude free or cheap travel for children, which might well be commercially justifiable. But it did exclude concessions made merely 'on benevolent or philanthropic grounds'. Ultimately, however, local authorities were given power to allow free travel to certain specified classes of the community by the Travel Concessions Act 1964.[367]

The second illustration was the invalidation by the House of Lords of the supplementary rate levied by the Greater London Council for the purpose of financing a 25 per cent cut in the London bus and underground fares.[368] This cut was made in fulfilment of electoral promises. But it had to be paid for by all the ratepayers of Greater London, for whom it was exceptionally expensive since it involved a loss of government grant which approximately doubled the rate. In deciding to fulfil its election promises without regard to the exceptional burden thrown upon the ratepayers the GLC was held to have neglected its fiduciary duty to hold the balance fairly, as well as to have failed in its statutory duties. It had power to subsidise the transport services, but it also had a duty to encourage their economic operation rather than to drive them into loss deliberately, leaving the ratepayers to foot the bill.

A paternal concern for human welfare motivated a caravan site licensing authority's requirements that there should be rent control, security of tenure, and no restrictions on the tenants' liberty to shop where they wanted or to form tenants' associations. It will later be seen how the House of Lords invalidated these conditions as being unreasonably remote from the purposes of the Act controlling the use of land for caravan sites.[369]

---

[364] A-G v. Tynemouth Union [1930] 1 Ch 616, also following Roberts v. Hopwood.
[365] See above, p. 295.   [366] Prescott v. Birmingham Cpn [1955] Ch 210.
[367] Concessions already in operation had been legitimated by the Public Service Vehicles (Travel Concessions) Act 1955.   [368] Bromley LBC v. Greater London Council [1983] 1 AC 768.
[369] Mixnam's Properties Ltd v. Chertsey Urban District Council [1965] AC 735; below, p. 341.

PERMISSIBLE PHILANTHROPY

One form of social assistance which the law has allowed is the charging of differential rents to tenants of local authorities.[370] This is held to be reasonably incidental to their managerial powers over their houses. They may therefore adjust rents according to the means of individual tenants, either by granting rebates or by adding surcharges to a low basic rent. This is clearly philanthropy, but it is philanthropy authorised by Parliament. For the underlying policy of the housing legislation, which empowers the authorities to make 'such reasonable charges...as they may determine', is to provide houses for those who cannot afford economic rents, but not to subsidise those who can afford them.[371] This policy was prayed in aid by one tenant of a council house who challenged the legality of a uniform increase of rents on the ground that the council was *not* operating a differential scheme, and did not consider the means of each of its tenants. The court had no difficulty in upholding the council.[372] Here is one field where a wide range of differing social policies is within the bounds of the discretion conferred, and where the court will not (as elsewhere it may)[373] seize upon the word 'reasonable' as importing a rigid legal standard.

Children's allowances have also been held to be a legitimate element in wages paid by local authorities.[374] Following the lead of *Roberts* v. *Hopwood*, the district auditor for Birmingham disallowed the payments and surcharged the councillors, holding that the size of an employee's family was an irrelevant consideration in determining his salary. But the Court of Appeal quashed these orders, on the ground that children's allowances were a recognised benefit which many employers had reasonably paid, and which therefore were within the council's powers. The strength of the council's case was that, instead of increasing all salaries to the pre-war level in terms of real values, they were increasing them selectively in order to benefit the class which suffered most. Since all the salaries were therefore within the range of what the council might reasonably pay, the allowances for children were intra vires. In *Roberts* v. *Hopwood* Lord Sumner had said that even where the motive was improper the expenditure would be lawful if there was no excess over what was reasonable.[375] Here therefore the council's discretion was wide enough to allow some scope for philanthropy.

IMPROPER LICENSING DECISIONS

Miscellaneous licensing powers are very numerous, and are often conferred in widely permissive terms. The courts are vigilant to restrict the discretion of licensing authorities to the true purposes of the empowering Act, and to disallow arbitrary or oppressive refusals or revocations or improper conditions. In licensing there is naturally wide scope for the question of relevant and irrelevant considerations. A century ago, for example, a local authority might not withhold approval of building plans on the ground that the building was unsuitable for the neighbourhood.[376] Today this has become a highly relevant consideration for the refusal of planning permission, although in both cases alike the Acts merely give power to grant or withhold consent.

---

[370] *Leeds Cpn* v. *Jenkinson* [1935] 1 KB 168; *Smith* v. *Cardiff Cpn (No 2)* [1955] Ch 159; *Summerfield* v. *Hampstead Borough Council* [1957] 1 WLR 167.　　　[371] See *Smith* v. *Cardiff Cpn* (above) at 170.
[372] *Luby* v. *Newcastle-under-Lyme Cpn* [1964] 2 QB 64.　　　[373] See below, p. 365.
[374] *Re Walker's Decision* [1944] KB 644.　　　[375] [1925] AC 578 at 604, quoted above, p. 329.
[376] *R* v. *Newcastle on Tyne Cpn ex p Veitch* (1889) 60 LT 963. Cf. *Marshall* v. *Blackpool Cpn* [1935] AC 16 (power to approve plans for access across footpaths to street does not empower refusal of approval of proper plans because access might impede traffic; Act not intended to restrict owner's right of access); *Davies* v. *Bromley Cpn* [1908] 1 KB 170 (plans allegedly rejected out of spite).

Among the many examples of the abuse of licensing powers pride of place is claimed by the three cases, one Canadian and two English, in which ministers have attempted to procure the cancellation of licences for improper reasons. These have already been related.[377] The Court of Appeal quashed the revocation of a market trader's licence on the ground that to deprive him of his livelihood was an excessive penalty in relation to his offence, which was aggravated by abusive language.[378] The similarity with the principle of proportionality in European law has already been noticed.[379]

In the long history of liquor licensing the courts have quashed many decisions of licensing justices and examples have already been given.[380] It has been held irrelevant for the justices, when considering whether the applicant is a fit and proper person, to take account of the way he proposed to do business, the terms agreed between him and the brewery company, and the price of the beer to be supplied.[381] In considering an application for enlarging licensed premises it is an irrelevant ground of refusal that the licensee will obtain a valuable addition to his trade without paying the levy for monopoly value;[382] but this factor is relevant on an application for transfer of the licence to superior premises, since it is then reasonable to insist on a new application.[383] To require the surrender of some other licence as a condition of the grant of a licence is illegitimate.[384] And so is to require a payment.[385] Licensing justices must also pursue a consistent policy and may not refuse renewal of a licence unless their new policy is justified by a genuine change of circumstances.[386] Where a refreshment licence was refused to a theatre which had enjoyed it for over fifty years, on the ground that it should be treated equally with a new theatre where an application had been refused, and because there were other facilities nearby, the licensing committee were held to have given too little weight to the fifty years' enjoyment and too much to rigid consistency.[387] In this case the court was virtually acting as a court of appeal and reversing a decision with which it disagreed. It could not be said that the committee had failed to take into account the rival considerations, each of which was relevant: they had assessed them carefully, but the court assessed them otherwise. Nor could it be said that the decision was so unreasonable as to be beyond the committee's powers.

In other cases the courts have allowed a considerable freedom of discretion to licensing justices, when satisfied that they were acting bona fide for the true purposes of the Licensing Acts.[388] But they abuse their discretion if they require a licensee to enter into a binding undertaking restricting his licence in a case where they are not themselves empowered to impose conditions.[389]

Complication has been caused by the introduction of licensing planning committees from whom a certificate of non-objection must be obtained before application for a justices' liquor licence may be made. The committees have to consider an area as a whole, with reference to the number, nature and distribution of licensed premises and the

---

[377] Above, p. 300.   [378] R v. Barnsley MBC ex p Hook [1976] 1 WLR 1052.
[379] Above, p. 305.   [380] Above, p. 337.   [381] R v. Hyde Justices [1912] 1 KB 645.
[382] R v. Wandsworth Licensing Justices ex p Whitbread & Co Ltd [1921] 3 KB 487 (this levy represents the difference in value between licensed and unlicensed premises and is payable to the exchequer).
[383] R v. Southampton County Confirming Committee ex p Slade [1929] 1 KB 645 (not citing the Wandsworth case, above).   [384] R v. Wandsworth Licensing Justices (above).
[385] See above, p. 337.
[386] R v. Windsor Licensing Justices ex p Hodes [1983] 1 WLR 685.
[387] R v. Flintshire County Licensing Committee ex p Barrett [1957] 1 QB 350.
[388] e.g. Sharp v. Wakefield [1891] AC 173; Leeds Corporation v. Ryder [1907] AC 420.
[389] R v. Edmonton Licensing Justices ex p Baker [1983] 1 WLR 1000.

accommodation and facilities provided in them.[390] It has been held that they may not legitimately insist on a bingo club requiring membership for twenty-four rather than forty-eight hours before supplying liquor,[391] nor may they object to mobile trolley bars being used in cinemas,[392] since these are matters of detail for the licensing justices and irrelevant for the committee's purposes.

Cinema licensing is a field where the courts are reluctant to interfere, since the disputed questions are usually well within the range of the local authority's discretion. Conditions barring children, even when accompanied by adults, from cinemas on Sundays[393] or barring Sunday opening altogether,[394] have been upheld as not unreasonable. The general principles stated by Lord Greene MR in the leading case have already been quoted.[395] He criticised an earlier decision in which the court had disallowed conditions restricting children from attending cinemas after certain hours, and had held that concern for the health and welfare of children generally was not a relevant factor.[396] The 'irrelevant considerations' argument was also rejected in an earlier wartime case where a licence was refused because the cinema company was controlled by enemy aliens.[397] But the Court of Appeal upheld a complaint that the Greater London Council was using an unduly permissive test of obscenity and licensing indecent films, thereby misusing their licensing power.[398]

A good example of irrelevant grounds was where the commissioner of police refused cab licences to all proprietors whose vehicles were on hire-purchase.[399] Another was where a river authority refused to renew a salmon fishery licence because it was in dispute with the owner.[400] In New Zealand the court has condemned a refusal of foreign investment facilities when the motives of the authorities were outside the purposes of the Act.[401]

The planning cases discussed next might also be considered to illustrate illegitimate licensing decisions.

UNREASONABLE PLANNING DECISIONS

The importance of the statutory background and context is well illustrated by a group of planning cases. A local planning authority may grant permission 'subject to such conditions as they think fit',[402] and the court is disposed to construe such conditions benevolently.[403] But it has been repeatedly held that such conditions are invalid unless they 'fairly and reasonably relate to the permitted development'.[404] Many planning conditions have

---

[390] Licensing Act 1964, s. 119, replacing earlier Acts.

[391] *Fletcher* v. *London (Metropolis) Licensing Planning Committee* [1976] AC 150.

[392] *R* v. *London (Metropolis) Licensing Planning Committee ex p Maynard*, The Times, 11 May 1976.

[393] *Harman* v. *Butt* [1944] KB 491; *Associated Provincial Picture Houses Ltd* v. *Wednesbury Cpn* [1948] 1 KB 223.   [394] *London County Council* v. *Bermondsey Bioscope Ltd* [1911] 1 KB 445.

[395] Above, p. 302.   [396] *Theatre de Luxe (Halifax) Ltd* v. *Gledhill* [1915] 2 KB 49.

[397] *R* v. *London County Council ex p London & Provincial Electric Theatres Ltd* [1915] 1 KB 446.

[398] *R* v. *Greater London Council ex p Blackburn* [1976] 1 WLR 550.

[399] *R* v. *Metropolitan Police Commissioner ex p Randall* (1911) 27 TLR 505; cf. *R* v. *Brighton Cpn ex p Thomas Tilling Ltd* (1916) 85 LJKB 1552.

[400] *R* v. *National Rivers Authority ex p Haughey* (1996) 8 Admin LR 567.

[401] *Rowling* v. *Takaro Properties Ltd* [1975] 2 NZLR 62 (doubted by the Privy Council in the sequel case: [1988] AC 473 at 510).

[402] Town and Country Planning Act 1990, s. 70(1) (repeating earlier Acts).

[403] *Fawcett Properties Ltd* v. *Buckingham County Council* [1961] AC 636 at 679; *Hall & Co Ltd* v. *Shoreham-by-Sea Urban District Council* [1964] 1 WLR 240. A condition is not invalid because it depends on events beyond the applicant's control: *Grampian Regional Council* v. *Aberdeen DC* (1983) 47 P & CR 633 (House of Lords upheld condition requiring that a public road should first be closed).

[404] *Pyx Granite Co Ltd* v. *Ministry of Housing and Local Government* [1958] 1 QB 544 at 572 (Lord Denning), affirmed [1960] AC 260.

been condemned by the application of this test. The House of Lords similarly invalidated conditions imposed by a caravan site licensing authority, although it had power to grant licences 'subject to such conditions as the authority may think it necessary or desirable to impose'.[405] Among numerous conditions were: that site rents should be agreed with the authority, that there should be security of tenure comparable to that in rent-controlled houses, that no premium should be charged for a site, and that there should be no restrictions on commercial or political activity. These conditions, designed to benefit the tenants personally rather than to control the use made of the land, were held to be 'a gratuitous interference with the rights of the occupier' and 'wholly unnecessary for the good governance of the site', and therefore ultra vires. Lord Upjohn, who used these words, stressed the principle that conditions such as these must be reasonable.

Planning conditions are likewise unreasonable if, instead of relating to the permitted development, they attempt to restrict the owner's existing use rights in his land; for it is the policy of the legislation to preserve these rights and to give compensation for restriction of them. The House of Lords therefore held a planning condition to be ultra vires and void because it allowed only six caravans to be stationed on the site:[406] for although there had been only six previously, the existing use right included the right to increase the number up to the point where there would be a material change of use. But the principle of this case is confined, it seems, to situations where the owner is given nothing in exchange. If he is given permission for some new development over and above his existing use rights, there may be valid conditions restricting his existing use rights on other land or requiring him to remove buildings on other land. So where British Railways were given permission to rebuild a station subject to a condition that part of the land should always be used as a car park, this condition was valid although it restricted existing use rights in the land in question.[407] A condition requiring the removal of buildings, however, is likely to be void if attached to a permission for their use in some particular way.

Planning conditions sometimes require new buildings to be used for particular purposes.[408] A condition restricting the occupants of new cottages to persons employed in agriculture or forestry was upheld by the House of Lords as being within the policy of the Act.[409] But a Divisional Court held it unreasonable and ultra vires to require a builder to let his houses to persons on the local authority's housing waiting list, for then he was being asked to undertake part of their own duties as housing authority.[410]

A striking example of an invalid planning condition was one which required the landowners to construct a strip of roadway along their entire frontage and to give public right

[405] *Mixnam's Properties Ltd* v. *Chertsey Urban District Council* [1965] AC 735. Compare *A-G's Reference (No 2 of 1988)* [1990] 1 QB 77 (excessively wide anti-nuisance condition in waste disposal licence).

[406] *Hartnell* v. *Minister of Housing and Local Government* [1965] AC 1134, holding the minister's confirming order to be 'unreasonable and ultra vires' (Lord Wilberforce at 1173). See similarly *Allnat London Properties Ltd* v. *Middlesex County Council* [1964] 62 LGR 304 (factory site wrongly restricted); *British Airports Authority* v. *Secretary of State for Scotland*, 1979 SLT 197 (unreasonable restrictions on flying).

[407] *Kingston-upon-Thames Royal London Borough Council* v. *Secretary of State for the Environment* [1973] 1 WLR 1549. See also the *British Airports Authority* case, above.

[408] *Newbury District Council* v. *Secretary of State for the Environment* [1981] AC 578 (condition requiring removal of warehouses after ten years void).

[409] *Fawcett Properties Ltd* v. *Buckingham County Council* [1961] AC 636.

[410] *R* v. *Hillingdon London Borough Council ex p Royco Homes Ltd* [1974] QB 720. See similarly *Lowe (David) & Sons Ltd* v. *Musselburgh Cpn*, 1974 SLT 5; *Westminster Renslade Ltd* v. *Secretary of State for the Environment* (1983) 48 P & CR 255.

of passage over it.[411] The Court of Appeal invalidated this as an attempt to secure a widening of the adjacent road at the landowners' expense, so as to avoid using the powers of the Highways Act 1959 (now 1980), which would require compensation to be paid. The object, i.e. to widen the road, was held to be perfectly reasonable in itself, but the conditions which attempted to put the expense onto the landowner by the use of planning powers were 'so unreasonable that they must be held to be ultra vires'.[412] This decision has several times been approved,[413] though it must not be taken to establish a principle that, where there are two alternative procedures, the more expensive one must be followed.[414] It shows that on the question of reasonableness it is not enough to consider merely the context and purposes of the statute conferring the disputed power: there may be other statutes such as the Highways Act which lay down procedures or confer rights for specific purposes which merely general powers ought not to be capable of overriding, on the principle *generalia specialibus non derogant*. Interaction with other statutes thus imposes still further limits on the indefinite discretionary powers with which statutes are so freely strewn.

The Court may quash the Secretary of State's decision of a planning appeal if it is one which on the evidence he could not reasonably make, as where he refused permission for the continuance of office use in a residential area, when the only reasonable conclusion was that conversion of the premises for residential use was unjustifiably expensive.[415] Where his decision to reopen a planning inquiry can only be described as perverse, that will be quashed likewise.[416] So will be his order for stopping up a road if he fails to take account of the financial loss so inflicted on a restaurant.[417] A local planning authority's decision may be quashed as an abuse of power if it conceals relevant facts or documents.[418]

A way of escape from the strictness of judicial control in this area has been found by many local planning authorities in the device of planning agreements, which they have statutory power to make. An applicant for planning permission will often be willing to agree to give the local authority some benefit, such as land for street widening or office accommodation, if given to understand that he is unlikely to obtain permission otherwise. The legality of this evasive practice has however been questioned.[419]

OVERLAPPING POWERS AND COMPENSATION

Another feature of planning law is that the very wide powers of planning authorities may overlap more specific powers, and that the choice of power may affect the right to compensation. This problem arose where a borough council, as planning authority, persistently

---

[411] *Hall & Co Ltd v. Shoreham-by-Sea Urban District Council* [1964] 1 WLR 240. See similarly *Medina BC v. Proberun Ltd* (1990) 61 P & CR 77 (condition required provision of access on land outside developer's control: held abuse of power and unlawful).

[412] Ibid. at 251 (Willmer LJ). See similarly *Bradford Metropolitan Council v. Secretary of State for the Environment* (1986) 53 P & CR 55 (Secretary of State rightly disallowed condition requiring road-widening as manifestly unreasonable).

[413] By Lord Wilberforce in *Hartnell's* case (above), where similar reasoning was used; by Lord Widgery CJ in the *Hillingdon* case (above); and see *Hoveringham Gravels Ltd v. Secretary of State for the Environment* [1975] 1 QB 754 (Orr LJ).   [414] See below, p. 347 (overlapping powers).

[415] *Niarchos v. Secretary of State for the Environment* (1977) 76 LGR 480; and see *Forkhurst v. Secretary of State for the Environment* (1982) 46 P & CR 89 (inspector's decision quashed as unreasonable); *R v. Secretary of State for the Environment ex p Fielder Estates (Canvey) Ltd* (1989) 57 P & CR 424 (order for new inquiry without consulting parties quashed as irrational).

[416] *Niarchos (London) Ltd v. Secretary of State for the Environment* (1980) 79 LGR 264.

[417] *Vasiliou v. Secretary of State for Transport* [1991] 2 All ER 77.

[418] *R v. Welwyn Hatfield DC ex p Slough Estates plc* [1991] COD 510.   [419] See below, p. 674.

refused planning permission for building alongside a road, because, in its capacity of highway authority, it had nebulous plans for widening the road in the future. Meanwhile the land suffered prolonged 'planning blight'. As highway authority the council had power to prescribe an improvement line under the Highways Act 1959 (now 1980). But the council did not invoke that power, since the Highways Act required compensation to be paid for the blight inflicted, and the Ministry of Transport's policy was to refuse grants towards such compensation since the same result could be attained free of charge by the use of planning powers. Was it lawful for the council to use its general planning powers, which taken by themselves were sufficient, when Parliament had provided a different procedure for this specific purpose and had given a right to compensation? The House of Lords[420] found the solution in a provision that planning powers may be freely exercised despite any other legislation regulating development which was in force before the original planning Act of 1947,[421] which they interpreted so as to include provisions repealing and re-enacting such legislation (as did the Highways Act 1959 as regards improvement lines). But they also gave clear indications that there was no legal objection to the use of planning powers in preference to more specific powers requiring compensation.[422] In a later case Lord Denning MR said, perhaps too broadly, that the House of Lords had held that where there were two such alternative courses of action, a public authority might adopt the one which did not give rise to compensation.[423]

A local planning authority was similarly held to be entitled to grant permission for residential development in an industrial area, with the probability that existing industrial use would become impossible because of the nuisance to future residents, when it had the bona fide intention of making the area residential and at the same time was glad to save the compensation which it would have had to pay if it had made discontinuance orders against the industries.[424] Provided that the planning authority genuinely decided according to their judgment of the public interest, it was immaterial that a substantial part of their motivation was to avoid payment of compensation. The more economical course was justified, also, where the leader of the council sought judicial review of the council's own decision in a planning case, as being vitiated by bias, so saving the making of a revocation order and payment of compensation.[425]

It must be remembered that the planning legislation of 1947 introduced a new philosophy of uncompensated control, so that it may be logical to make this prevail over earlier legislation which paid more respect to rights of property.[426] This reasoning may not necessarily conflict with that adopted by the Court of Appeal in the *Shoreham* case.[427] The basis of the latter may be that a condition requiring a developer to present the public with a free roadway is something quite extraneous to the permitted development and also an unjustifiable demand that he should give up his existing rights of ownership.[428]

---

[420] *Westminster Bank Ltd* v. *Beverley Borough Council* [1971] AC 508, upholding the refusal of planning permission by the local authority and the minister.

[421] Town and Country Planning Act 1962, s. 220, now replaced by s. 335 of the Act of 1990. This provision was not cited in the courts below, nor in *Hall & Co's* case (above).

[422] See especially at 530 (Lord Reid). Similar is *Portion 675 Zandfontein City Council* v. *Sandton City Council* 1995 (4) SA 826.

[423] *Hoveringham Gravels Ltd* v. *Secretary of State for the Environment* [1975] QB 754 at 763. Orr and Scarman LJJ confined their remarks to the planning legislation.

[424] *R* v. *Exeter City Council ex p J. L. Thomas & Co Ltd* [1991] 1 QB 471.

[425] *R* v. *Bassetlaw DC ex p Oxby* [1998] PLCR 283.

[426] See the *Westminster Bank* case (above) at 529, 535.

[427] *Hall & Co Ltd* v. *Shoreham-by-Sea Urban District Council* (above).

[428] This distinction is taken by Orr LJ in the *Hoveringham Gravels* case (above) at 765.

COMPULSORY PURCHASE OF LAND

Wrong or irrelevant purposes have often vitiated compulsory purchase orders or schemes depending upon them, as has already been shown in other contexts.[429] In several cases the illegal element was some bargain with the owner or a third party for putting the land to some use outside the powers of the Act[430] or some plan for disposing of it when the Act required it to be redeveloped.[431] The motives behind a compulsory purchase order made by the Central Land Board were canvassed in a case where, although the House of Lords ultimately upheld the order, a forceful dissenting judgment made out a strong case against it.[432] Under the law then in force persons granted planning permission had to pay a 'development charge', representing the value of the permission, so that development rights were in effect expropriated. Compulsory purchase for public purposes was accordingly effected at 'existing use value' and it was intended that land should change hands at this value. In fact it did not, since the Act did not impose price control, and demand drove up prices. The Central Land Board, empowered to acquire land compulsorily for permitted development, made an order for the acquisition of land which the intending developer was unable to obtain except at a high price. It was suspected that the Board's object was to make an example and to use its powers *in terrorem* for a purpose not authorised by the Act, i.e. to enforce price control.[433] Denning LJ held this to be a usurpation of the legislative powers of Parliament, having a purpose for which Parliament had deliberately refrained from legislating. He said:[434]

> But there is a principle at stake which is far more important than the stopping of one particular piece of profiteering. The principle is that the legislative power in this country resides in Parliament and not in the government departments. [Powers] must not be used for an ulterior object which is not authorised by law, however desirable that object may seem to them to be in the public interest.

But the House of Lords held that the powers conferred were wide enough to cover the Board's objectives.

In another compulsory purchase case the court declined to make a sharp distinction between 'housing' and 'planning' considerations, holding that a housing authority might legitimately take account of factors which were also relevant for the planning authority.[435] In these fields it is obvious that many relevant factors will overlap. On the other hand, a local authority may not use its housing powers merely for the purpose of obtaining a highway;[436] and a caravan site licensing authority, which is concerned with the use of the particular site, cannot lawfully take account of 'pure planning' considerations, such as that the site is in the green belt.[437] There are however numerous aspects such as amenity, transport, schools and shopping facilities which are relevant both to planning and to site licensing, so that here again there is a wide area of common ground.[438] But it was unlawful for the planning authority in exercising compulsory purchase powers to consider an

---

[429] Above, p. 338.
[430] *Denman & Co Ltd* v. *Westminster Cpn* [1906] 1 Ch 464; *London & Westcliff Properties Ltd* v. *Minister of Housing and Local Government* [1961] 1 WLR 519.
[431] *R* v. *Minister of Health ex p Davis* [1929] 1 KB 619.
[432] *Fitzwilliam (Earl)'s Wentworth Estates Co* v. *Minister of Town and Country Planning* [1952] AC 362.
[433] [1951] 2 KB 284 at 300.   [434] [1951] 2 KB at 311.
[435] *Hanks* v. *Minister of Housing and Local Government* [1963] 1 QB 999.
[436] *Meravale Builders Ltd* v. *Secretary of State for the Environment* (1978) 77 LGR 365.
[437] *Esdell Caravan Parks Ltd* v. *Hemel Hempstead Rural District Council* [1966] 1 QB 895 (CA).
[438] Same case at 925 (Lord Denning MR).

'off site' benefit—an undertaking by a developer to develop another unprofitable site—as decisive.[439]

A compulsory purchase order, when confirmed by the minister, authorises the purchase for the particular purpose then specified. If later the purpose changes, the authority no longer holds good. Where, accordingly, a local authority obtained an order for the purpose of road widening and building a market hall, they were unable to enforce it for other purposes after abandoning their earlier plans.[440] But a mere change of circumstances rendering the attainment of the objective more remote will not necessarily have this effect.[441]

Powers of compulsory purchase, like other powers, must be exercised reasonably, and all the more so because they expropriate an owner against his will. An order may be quashed as unreasonable if the authority making it already possesses, or can acquire by agreement, other land which is equally suitable for its purposes.[442]

The acquiring authority is usually empowered to take as much land as it judges to be necessary for the statutory purpose. But where it takes more than could reasonably be considered necessary, it acts ultra vires. It cannot therefore take the whole of the site where it requires no more than a few feet for street widening.[443] The Court of Appeal quashed a compulsory purchase order made ostensibly for a sea-wall but including a large piece of land said to be required for coast protection purposes but in fact intended for a paved access way which was to be a sort of promenade and was not in fact needed for coast protection at all.[444]

TAX CONCESSIONS

Judges have often criticised the practice of the Commissioners of Inland Revenue in making extra-statutory concessions to taxpayers, thereby discriminating between them in their free discretion but without any legal basis.[445] Some of these concessions are made regularly according to published rules;[446] for example, money paid to coalminers in lieu of their entitlement of free coal is, by concession, not assessed to tax. One concession, strongly criticised in the House of Lords, was made under a statute which had been held to make each of a number of joint beneficiaries under a family settlement severally liable for the whole of the tax on the whole income of the fund. Instead of taking steps to amend the law, the tax authorities tempered its application by concession, assessing each taxpayer with his own proportion only. Lord Wilberforce stigmatised this state of affairs

---

[439] *R (Sainsbury's Supermarkets Ltd)* v. *Wolverhampton City Council* [2010] UKSC 20 (rivals wished to develop the same site; authority made CPO to facilitate one rival because of promise to develop another site the authority wished to see developed).

[440] *Grice* v. *Dudley Cpn* [1958] Ch 329 (declarations that notice to treat and compulsory purchase order were no longer effective).

[441] *Simpsons Motor Sales Ltd* v. *Hendon Cpn* [1964] AC 1088 (Lord Evershed at 1126–7 curiously refers to the court's jurisdiction as if it were a branch of equity in the technical sense).

[442] *Brown* v. *Secretary of State for the Environment* (1978) 40 P & CR 285; *Prest* v. *Secretary of State for Wales* (1982) 81 LGR 193.

[443] *Gard* v. *Commissioners of Sewers of City of London* (1885) 28 Ch D 486; *Denman & Co Ltd* v. *Westminster Cpn* [1906] 1 Ch 464; *Bartrum* v. *Manurewa Borough* [1962] NZLR 21 (acquisition for benefit of neighbouring owner rather than for public benefit).

[444] *Webb* v. *Minister of Housing and Local Government* [1965] 1 WLR 755.

[445] See the opinions of Lord Wilberforce, Lord Edmund-Davies and Walton J in the *Vestey* case (below).

[446] HM Revenue & Customs publish a booklet on them with annual supplements. But they are not legally enforceable: *R* v. *HM Inspector of Taxes, Hull ex p Brumfield* [1989] STC 151. See also *R* v. *Customs & Excise Commissioners ex p Cook* [1970] 1 WLR 450; below, p. 530.

as arbitrary, unjust and unconstitutional; for, as Walton J had said at first instance, 'one should be taxed by law, and not be untaxed by concession'. Since the House of Lords held that the oppressive interpretation of the taxing Act was wrong, it was unnecessary to decide whether taxation by administrative discretion was unlawful.[447] But Lord Wilberforce said that unless it was expressly authorised by Act of Parliament 'the courts, acting on constitutional principles, not only should not but cannot validate it'.

In another case, however, the House upheld concessions by which workers in the printing industry were exonerated from liability for arrears of tax on casual earnings, which had been evaded on a large scale for some years. The tax authorities made a concession to the workers under which the arrears would be discharged if proper tax returns were made for the future. Despite evidence that the concession might have been motivated by fear of a printers' strike, it was held to have been made under an arrangement which was within the managerial powers and discretion of the authorities.[448] At the same time it was said that improper concessions might be the subject of intervention by the court. That indeed occurred in a later case where the tax authorities accepted a valuation 'which no reasonable authority properly directing itself could reach', so that it was declared unlawful by the Court of Appeal.[449]

Ultimately the wheel turned full circle when the Court of Appeal, so far from criticising an extra-legal tax concession, enforced it. For more than twenty years the Inland Revenue had accepted late applications by a large company, whose affairs were exceptionally complicated, for allowances for losses which by statute had to be claimed within two years. In 1992 the Revenue suddenly refused a claim for £17m. made late in the customary manner, and insisted on the two-year time limit. This abrupt change of policy was held to be so unfair and unreasonable as to be an abuse of power—although no legal power was involved.[450] The case is a remarkable example of legitimate expectation enforced for the sake of fairness, as discussed earlier in this chapter,[451] and in defiance of an Act of Parliament.

Selective prosecution of tax offenders by the Inland Revenue has passed the test of reasonableness.[452]

UNREASONABLE REGULATIONS

The principle of reasonableness applies just as much to the making of rules and regulations as it does to other administrative action. This is explained in the chapter on delegated legislation, where some striking examples will be found.

MISCELLANEOUS CASES: ALIENS, PRISONERS, UNDUE DELAY

No list of categories will cover all cases, since the possibilities of abuse are infinite.

The courts are always disposed to intervene where the action is arbitrary or oppressive. If the Commission for Racial Equality uses its drastic powers to make a roving

---

[447] *Vestey* v. *Inland Revenue Commissioners* [1980] AC 1148.

[448] *R* v. *Inland Revenue Commissioners ex p National Federation of Self-Employed and Small Businesses Ltd* [1982] AC 617. See also *R* v. *Inspector of Taxes, Reading ex p Fulford-Dobson* [1987] QB 978.

[449] *R* v. *A-G ex p Imperial Chemical Industries plc* (1986) 60 TC 1 (under-valuation of ethane gas).

[450] *R* v. *Inland Revenue Commissioners ex p Unilever* [1996] STC 681. See [1997] *PL* 375 (Forsyth).

[451] Above, p. 318.   [452] *R* v. *Commissioners of Inland Revenue ex p Mead* [1993] 1 All ER 772.

investigation without having reasonable grounds for suspecting racial discrimination, its proceedings may be condemned as unreasonable and vexatious.[453] If an investors' compensation scheme rules out claims on behalf of deceased investors, that rule must be quashed as absurd.[454]

The Home Secretary's formidable discretionary powers in respect of prison administration and immigration, deportation and extradition, are, as already illustrated from leading cases,[455] subject to strict judicial review. Where there had been a delay of ten years in an extradition case, and other circumstances making an extradition order unjust and oppressive, the court quashed it as one which no reasonable minister could make.[456] Where a convicted murderer, released on licence subject to good behaviour, was returned to prison with a postponed release date on account of minor offences the Home Secretary's decision was quashed as perverse and unreasonable.[457] His decisions refusing claims to asylum have been quashed for inadequate reasoning,[458] and for self-misdirection.[459]

The Lord Chancellor's selection of a judge to conduct a particular trial is reviewable for unreasonableness, but the only challenge so far reported has failed.[460]

Where a health authority was opposed to the policy of a ministerial circular about provision of drugs and refused to implement it, the court ordered it to change its policy.[461] This should perhaps be classed as a case of perversity.

A clear instance of 'collateral purpose' was where a chief constable had retired on pension because of infirmity and lived abroad to avoid his creditors. The police authority called him up for medical examination, and when he did not attend, cancelled his pension. It was proved that their object was not to obtain medical information but to bring him within reach of his creditors and he was granted mandamus to restore his pension.[462] An alien may challenge the legality of his deportation on the ground that its real purpose is to comply with a request from his country of origin, so that it is extradition in disguise.[463]

Delay in performing a legal duty may also amount to an abuse which the law will remedy. Where a British 'patrial' was entitled by statute to enter the country 'without let or hindrance', but the Home Office refused her the necessary certificate of patriality except by an administrative procedure which would have made her wait for over a year,[464] the Court of Appeal held that the certificate could not be arbitrarily refused or delayed and ordered its issue, citing Magna Carta 1215: 'to no one will we delay right or justice'.[465] Where police officers were not given the formal notice of complaints made against them for over two years, this excessive delay invalidated the disciplinary proceedings.[466] Where the Advisory, Conciliation and Arbitration Service deferred proceeding with inquiries

---

[453] *R* v. *Commission for Racial Equality ex p Hillingdon LBC* [1982] QB 276.

[454] *R* v. *Investor Compensation Scheme Ltd ex p Bowden* [1993] COD 278.

[455] See above, pp. 318, 321. [456] *R* v. *Home Secretary ex p Sinclair* [1992] Imm AR 293.

[457] *R* v. *Home Secretary ex p Cox* (1993) 5 Admin LR 17.

[458] *R* v. *Home Secretary ex p Chahal* [1992] COD 214.

[459] *R* v. *Home Secretary ex p P* [1992] COD 295.

[460] *R* v. *Lord Chancellor ex p Maxwell* [1997] 1 WLR 104.

[461] *R* v. *North Derbyshire Health Authority ex p Fisher*, (1998) 10 Admin LR 27.

[462] *R* v. *Leigh (Lord)* [1897] 1 QB 132. Similarly a local authority may not use its power to acquire land, even by agreement, where its real object is to remove gipsies from it: *Costello* v. *Dacorum DC* (1980) 79 LGR 133.

[463] *R* v. *Brixton Prison Governor ex p Soblen* [1963] 2 QB 243 at 302. For this case see below, p. 353.

[464] *R* v. *Home Secretary ex p Phansopkar* [1976] QB 606. See also *R* v. *Durham Prison Governor ex p Hardial Singh* [1984] 1 WLR 704 (delay in effecting deportation). [465] Magna Carta 1215, c. 29.

[466] *R* v. *Merseyside Chief Constable ex p Calveley* [1986] QB 424.

into a recognition issue at the instance of a trade union, the House of Lords held that excessive deferment, amounting to abdication of the Service's functions, would be unlawful; but the majority also held that the deferment was not excessive in the circumstances.[467] Likewise the House has held that delay by the tax authorities may, if unfair, amount to abuse of power; but again the complaint failed on the facts.[468]

It may be possible for total inactivity to amount to abuse of discretion. The Privy Council has suggested that this would be the case if the Malaysian head of state failed to revoke a proclamation of emergency once he no longer considered it necessary for its proper purpose.[469] That is another way of saying that in those circumstances he would become subject to a legal duty to proclaim the end of the emergency.

MIXED MOTIVES

DUALITY OF PURPOSE

Sometimes an act may serve two or more purposes, some authorised and some not, and it may be a question whether the public authority may kill two birds with one stone. The general rule is that its action will be lawful provided that the permitted purpose is the true and dominant purpose behind the act, even though some secondary or incidental advantage may be gained for some purpose which is outside the authority's powers. There is a clear distinction between this situation and its opposite, where the permitted purpose is a mere pretext and a dominant purpose is ultra vires.[470]

A leading example is the decision of the House of Lords upholding the legality of the subway crossing the foot of Whitehall in London.[471] The Westminster Corporation had no power to construct subways, but they had power to construct public conveniences. They located the conveniences under the street with access from both sides, so that a subway naturally resulted. The House of Lords had no doubt that the 'primary object of the council was the construction of the conveniences with the requisite and proper means of approach thereto and exit therefrom'.[472] Accordingly 'that the public may use it for a purpose beyond what the statute contemplated is nothing to the purpose'.[473] Distinguishing the opposite situation, Lord Halsbury said:

> I quite agree that if the power to make one kind of building was fraudulently used for the purpose of making another kind of building, the power given by the Legislature for one purpose could not be used for another.

And Lord Macnaghten said:

> In order to make out a case of bad faith it must be shown that the corporation constructed this subway as a means of crossing the street under colour and pretence of providing public conveniences which were not really wanted at that particular place.

---

[467] *Engineers' and Managers' Association* v. *ACAS* [1980] 1 WLR 302.

[468] *R* v. *Inland Revenue Cmrs ex p Preston* [1985] AC 835.

[469] *Teh Cheng Poh* v. *Public Prosecutor, Malaysia* [1980] AC 458 (suggesting that mandamus might lie against members of the cabinet on whose advice he would act).

[470] This paragraph was approved by the House of Lords in *R* v. *Southwark Crown Court ex p Bowles* [1998] UKHL 16, [1998] 2 WLR 715 (Lord Hutton) (production of documents order made under Criminal Justice Act 1998, s. 93H quashed; not clear that predominant purpose of order was to facilitate the confiscation of criminal proceeds (the express purpose of s. 93H) rather than the investigation of crime (the subsidiary purpose).   [471] *Westminster Cpn* v. *London and North Western Railway* [1905] AC 426.

[472] Ibid. at 433 (Lord Macnaghten).   [473] Ibid. at 428 (Lord Halsbury).

The Court of Appeal closely followed these statements in upholding the power of a city corporation to make and improve a roadway even though their immediate motive was to attract speed trials of motor cars.[474] The speed trials indeed provided the occasion for the work being done at the particular time; but that was no reason why the corporation could not use its road-making powers for an improvement which was shown to be genuine and desirable in its own right, and which could not be said to be a merely pretended purpose for the sake of a different and unlawful objective. By contrast, the Inner London Education Authority acted unlawfully in launching an expensive publicity campaign in protest against cuts in its expenditure imposed by the government. The ILEA had power to publish information on local government affairs, but 'a, if not the, major purpose' of their campaign was to persuade the public that they were being hardly treated, and this purpose was unauthorised.[475]

The same distinction was made by the Court of Appeal where an order for the deportation of an alien to the United States was challenged on the ground that the Home Secretary was in fact motivated by a request from the United States for the surrender of the alien. Since the offence with which the alien was charged was not a legal ground of extradition, it was argued that the Home Secretary's real object was unlawful extradition, and that the deportation order was a mere disguise. Lord Denning MR said that everything depended upon the purpose with which the act was done:[476]

> If, therefore, the purpose of the Home Secretary in this case was to surrender the applicant as a fugitive criminal to the United States of America because they had asked for him, then it would be unlawful. But if the Home Secretary's purpose was to deport him to his own country because the Home Secretary considered his presence here to be not conducive to the public good, then the Home Secretary's action is lawful. It is open to these courts to inquire whether the purpose of the Home Secretary was a lawful or an unlawful purpose. Was there a misuse of the power or not? The courts can always go behind the face of the deportation order in order to see whether the powers entrusted by Parliament have been exercised lawfully or no.

On the facts the court found that there was every reason to suppose that the Home Secretary was acting from proper 'deportation' motives. His power to deport, and his power to prescribe the country of destination, was in no way diminished by the fact that he was at the same time assisting the United States government, and might indeed be glad to do so.

OVERLAPPING MOTIVES

Cases where the dominant motive is improper are, of course, cases of ultra vires, and a number of them have been cited in the context of wrong purposes and irrelevant considerations. Examples are the case of the caravan site licensing authority which wrongly attempted to act as a planning authority in order to protect the green belt,[477] and the case

---

[474] R v. Brighton Cpn ex p Shoosmith (1907) 96 LT 762.

[475] R v. Inner London Education Authority ex p Westminster CC [1986] 1 WLR 28. See similarly R v. Greater London Council ex p Westminster CC, The Times, 27 December 1984; R v. Lewisham LBC ex p Shell UK Ltd [1988] 1 All ER 938.

[476] R v. Brixton Prison Governor ex p Soblen [1963] 2 QB 302; and see R v. Bow Street Magistrates ex p Mackeson (1981) 75 Crim App R 24, where the court quashed charges on account of 'disguised extradition' by way of deportation from Zimbabwe.

[477] Esdell Caravan Parks Ltd v. Hemel Hempstead Rural District Council [1966] 1 QB 895; above, p. 348.

of the town council which compulsorily acquired land ostensibly for coast protection but in reality for public amenity.[478] Similarly the High Court of Australia invalidated a local authority's scheme for the resumption (acquisition) of land for road improvement, since a substantial part of the land was to be sold off and not therefore acquired for 'the improvement and embellishment of the area'.[479] The High Court said:[480]

> But the evidence establishes that one purpose at least of the Council in attempting to acquire the land now required to construct the new road is to appropriate the betterments arising from its construction. In *Municipal Council of Sydney* v. *Campbell*[481] this was the sole purpose. But in our opinion it is still an abuse of the Council's powers if such a purpose is a substantial purpose in the sense that no attempt would have been made to resume this land if it had not been desired to reduce the cost of the new road by the profit arising from its re-sale.

Where schoolteachers can be dismissed only on 'educational grounds' it has been said that this means educational grounds only, so that if the grounds are both educational and non-educational, the power is not well exercised.[482] But if in fact there were sufficient educational grounds, and these supplied the true motive, it seems unlikely that additional non-educational grounds would vitiate the dismissal.

An alternative criterion may be found by invoking the doctrine of irrelevant considerations. If the decision has been materially influenced by an unauthorised purpose, it can be said that an irrelevant consideration has been taken into account, so that the decision cannot stand.[483]

GOOD FAITH

BAD FAITH NOT DISHONESTY

The judgments discussed in the last few pages are freely embellished with references to good and bad faith. These add very little to the true sense, and are hardly ever used to mean more than that some action is found to have a lawful or unlawful purpose. It is extremely rare for public authorities to be found guilty of intentional dishonesty: normally they are found to have erred, if at all, by ignorance or misunderstanding. Yet the courts constantly accuse them of bad faith merely because they have acted unreasonably or on improper grounds. Again and again it is laid down that powers must be exercised reasonably and in good faith. But in this context 'in good faith' means merely 'for legitimate reasons'. Contrary to the natural sense of the words, they impute no moral obliquity.

Lord Sumner said in *Roberts* v. *Hopwood*,[484] dealing with the power of a local board to pay 'such wages as they think fit':

---

[478] *Webb* v. *Minister of Housing and Local Government* [1965] 1 WLR 755; above, p. 349.

[479] *Thompson* v. *Randwick Cpn* (1950) 81 CLR 87; cf. *Hanks* v. *Minister of Housing and Local Government* [1963] 1 QB 999.   [480] Ibid. at 106.

[481] [1925] AC 338; above, p. 338.

[482] *Sadler* v. *Sheffield Cpn* [1924] 1 Ch 483 at 504. For other such cases see above, p. 327.

[483] *Hanks* v. *Minister of Housing and Local Government* (above); *R* v. *Inner London Education Authority ex p Westminster CC* (above); and see *R* v. *Home Secretary ex p Yiadom* [1998] INLR 489 (relevant reasons not vitiated by one irrelevant reason).

[484] [1925] AC 578 at 603.

Firstly, the final words of the section are not absolute, but are subject to an implied quali-fication of good faith—'as the board may bona fide think fit.'...Bona fide here cannot simply mean that they are not making a profit out of their office or acting in it from private spite, nor is bona fide a short way of saying that the council has acted within the ambit of its powers and therefore not contrary to law. It must mean that they are giving their minds to the comprehension and their wills to the discharge of their duty towards the public, whose money and local business they administer.

Still more pithily, Vaughan Williams LJ had said in an earlier case:[485]

You are acting mala fide if you are seeking to acquire land for a purpose not authorised by the Act.

And Lord Greene MR, in the passage already quoted, treated bad faith as interchangeable with unreasonableness and extraneous considerations.[486] Bad faith therefore scarcely has an independent existence as a distinct ground of invalidity. Any attempt to discuss it as such would merely lead back over the ground already surveyed. But a few examples will illustrate it in its customary conjunction with unreasonableness and improper purposes.

If a local authority were to use its power to erect urinals in order to place one 'in front of any gentleman's house', then 'it would be impossible to hold that to be a bona fide exercise of the powers given by the statute'.[487] If they wish to acquire land, their powers are 'to be used bona fide for the statutory purpose and for none other'.[488] If they refer numerous cases en masse to a rent tribunal without proper consideration, this is not 'a valid and bona fide exercise of the powers'.[489] If a liquor licence is cancelled for political reasons, the minister who brought this about is guilty of 'a departure from good faith'.[490] Such instances could be multiplied indefinitely. Cases of misfeasance in public office, where the misfeasor knows that he is acting outside his powers, could be added to the collection.

MOTIVES AND MALICE, ABUSE OF PROCESS

The courts no less frequently use the words 'good faith' in their ordinary sense, imply-ing personal honesty and good intentions. In the licensing cases where the authorities wrongly demanded a money payment or the buying-in of suspended licences, the court in each case emphasised that the unlawful conditions were imposed in perfectly good faith, i.e. in what was genuinely thought to be in the public interest.[491] The same words were freely used in both senses in a decision condemning a district council's compul-sory purchase order for land allegedly required for coast protection: at first instance the order was held to be 'an abuse of power and a flagrant invasion of private rights which the council has tried to cover up by means which do them no credit'.[492] But the Court of Appeal decided that it was not necessary to go so far as to hold the council 'guilty of bad

---

[485] *Westminster Cpn* v. *London and North Western Railway Co* [1904] 1 Ch 759 at 767, followed in *Webb* v. *Minister of Housing and Local Government* [1965] 1 WLR 755 at 784.   [486] Above, p. 303.

[487] *Biddulph* v. *Vestry of St George, Hanover Square* (1863) 33 LJ Ch 411.

[488] *Denman* v. *Westminster Cpn* [1906] 1 Ch 464 at 476; above, p. 348.

[489] *R* v. *Paddington etc Rent Tribunal ex p Bell London & Provincial Properties Ltd* [1949] 1 KB 666; above, p. 339.   [490] *Roncarelli* v. *Duplessis* (1959) 6 DLR (2d) 689 at 707; above, p. 300.

[491] *R* v. *Bowman* [1898] 1 QB 663 at 667; *R* v. *Birmingham Licensing Planning Committee ex p Kennedy* [1972] 2 QB 140 at 147.

[492] *Webb* v. *Minister of Housing and Local Government* [1964] 1 WLR 1295 at 1305.

faith'.[493] Elsewhere in this case 'mala fide' was used merely to mean 'for an unauthorised purpose'.[494] Such opprobrious terms would be more suitably restricted to the rare cases of actual dishonesty, as Megaw LJ has advocated:[495]

> I would stress—for it seems to me that an unfortunate tendency has developed of loose-ness of language in this respect—that bad faith, or, as it is sometimes put, 'lack of good faith', means dishonesty: not necessarily for a financial motive, but still dishonesty. It always involves a grave charge. It must not be treated as a synonym for an honest, though mistaken, taking into consideration of a factor which is in law irrelevant.

It is a pity that this good advice is not more generally accepted. The various categories of ultra vires can more fittingly be described by words which do not impute dishonesty.

Where actions for damages are brought, bad faith may be described as malice, as is shown by the cases of misfeasance in public office.[496] An unsuccessful plaintiff alleged that a borough corporation had rejected his building plans out of malice, because he had previously been in litigation with them.[497] The cancellation of a liquor licence on political grounds, mentioned above, was held to be malicious and therefore actionable under the law of Quebec.[498] Rand J said:

> What could be more malicious than to punish this licensee for having done what he had an absolute right to do in a matter utterly irrelevant to the Alcoholic Liquor Act?

Allegations of fraud played a leading part in a decision of the House of Lords about a compulsory purchase order.[499] The question at issue was whether judicial remedies were wholly barred by statute,[500] but the House assumed that the effect of fraud (which was not in fact proved)[501] would normally be to vitiate any act or order. It was said that fraud or corruption were covered by the phrase mala fides, but that 'its effects have happily remained in the region of hypothetical cases'.[502] In a different context Denning LJ has said:[503]

> No judgment of a court, no order of a Minister, can be allowed to stand if it has been obtained by fraud. Fraud unravels everything.

But in administrative law there is a dearth of material to illustrate this statement.

Where a prisoner wanted in England was unlawfully returned by the South African police and extradition procedures were ignored the House of Lords stayed the prosecution on grounds of abuse of process and violation of the rule of law.[504]

It is clear that the court cannot question the validity of an Act of Parliament on the ground that it was obtained by misrepresentation or fraud.[505]

---

[493] [1965] 1 WLR 755 at 777.   [494] Ibid. at 784.

[495] *Cannock Chase DC* v. *Kelly* [1978] 1 WLR 1. See the Court of Appeal's similar protest against this 'debasement of the currency of language' in *Western Fish Products Ltd* v. *Penwith DC* (1978) 38 P & CR 7 at 22, [1981] 2 All ER 204 at 215.   [496] See below, p. 664.

[497] *Davis* v. *Bromley Cpn* [1908] 1 KB 170.   [498] *Roncarelli* v. *Duplessis*, above, p. 300.

[499] *Smith* v. *East Elloe Rural District Council* [1956] AC 736.   [500] For this see below, p. 619.

[501] *Smith* v. *Pywell*, The Times, 29 April 1959.   [502] [1956] AC at p. 770 (Lord Somervell).

[503] *Lazarus Estates Ltd* v. *Beasley* [1956] 1 QB 702 at 712.

[504] *R* v. *Horseferry Road Magistrates' Court ex p Bennett* [1994] 1 AC 42.

[505] *Pickin* v. *British Railways Board* [1974] AC 765.

SUBJECTIVE LANGUAGE

A FAVOURITE DEVICE

Words such as 'if the minister is satisfied that...' or 'if it appears to the board that...' are a very common feature of statutory powers. They have an important bearing on jurisdictional questions.[506] Their evident intention is to make the minister or the board the sole judge of the existence of the conditions which make the power exercisable. They indicate that instead of judging objectively whether the conditions in fact exist, the court is merely to judge subjectively whether the requisite state of mind exists in the minister or the board. But courts have an ingrained repugnance to legislative devices for making public authorities judges of the extent of their own powers, or for exempting them from judicial control.[507] Although a number of decisions have given to such expressions a very nearly literal meaning, a number of others have developed lines of attack which have been able to penetrate behind the ostensible 'satisfaction' or 'appearance' and deal with the realities.

There is a subjective element in all discretion, and expressions such as 'if the minister is satisfied' differ only in degree from a power to act 'as he thinks fit'. The limits of that type of power have already been explained: the minister must act reasonably and in good faith, and upon proper grounds. In principle the same limits should operate however subjective the language, in order that the courts may always afford protection against an abuse of power such as the Act cannot have been supposed to authorise. But in some of the situations where such words are employed it is plain not only from the language but also from the context that the discretion granted is exceptionally wide. The most obvious example is powers to do whatever is 'necessary or expedient' in time of war or emergency.

POWERS TO DO WHAT IS 'NECESSARY OR EXPEDIENT'

The Emergency Powers (Defence) Act 1939 empowered His Majesty by Order in Council to make such defence regulations 'as appear to him to be necessary or expedient for securing the public safety... and for maintaining supplies and services essential to the life of the community'. Plainly the courts were not to sit in judgment on the question of necessity or expediency or on the government's motives.[508] But if it could have been shown that a defence regulation was made for some quite extraneous purpose, for example to punish a political party which was no threat to public safety, the court in principle should have been able to intervene. Such challenges as were made fell far short of this improbable example and consequently failed. But in one case under the corresponding Canadian legislation the Privy Council held that the court could intervene in a hypothetical case of bad faith or of unauthorised purposes.[509] Lord Radcliffe said:[510]

> Parliament has chosen to say explicitly that [the Governor] shall do whatever things he may deem necessary or advisable. That does not allow him to do whatever he may feel

---

[506] See above, p. 207.   [507] See below, p. 218.

[508] *R v. Comptroller-General of Patents ex p Bayer Products Ltd* [1941] 2 KB 306; *Progressive Supply Co v. Dalton* [1943] Ch 54; *Point of Ayr Collieries Ltd v. Lloyd-George* [1943] 2 All ER 547; *Carltona Ltd v. Commissioners of Works* [1943] 2 All ER 560; *Demetriades v. Glasgow Cpn* [1951] 1 All ER 457; *Hackett v. Lander* [1917] NZLR 947. See the discussion of emergency powers by Turner J in *Reade v. Smith* [1959] NZLR 996 at 1000. And see discussion below, p. 749, n. 230.

[509] *A-G for Canada v. Hallett & Carey Ltd* [1952] AC 427 at 444. See similarly *Lipton Ltd v. Ford* [1917] 2 KB 647.   [510] Ibid. at 450.

inclined, for what he does must be capable of being related to one of the prescribed purposes, and the court is entitled to read the Act in this way.

The Privy Council applied this test in judging the validity of emergency regulations made
in Cyprus for imposing collective fines on communities which harboured terrorists,
finding that the regulations were clearly related to the prescribed purposes of securing
public safety and public order for which the Governor might make 'such Regulations as
appear to him to be necessary or expedient'.[511] The regulations themselves required the
Commissioner to 'satisfy himself' as to certain facts. The argument that his own declaration was conclusive was rejected, since it was open to a party to show that there was no
ground on which he could be satisfied. But in fact it was held that he had ample grounds.

The United Nations Act 1946 empowers His Majesty by Order in Council to make provision 'as appears to Him necessary or expedient' to give effect to any relevant resolution
of the Security Council of the United Nations. A series of Security Council resolutions
required member states to freeze the assets of those involved in international terrorism;
the Security Council maintained a list of such persons but those listed were not informed
why they were included nor afforded any right to challenge their listing in court. The UK
gave effect to these resolutions by two Orders in Council one of which went further than
the Security Council required in that it empowered the Treasury to freeze the assets of
those reasonably suspected by the Treasury of facilitating terrorism. Clearly the effect of
these Orders was gravely to infringe the rights of those affected both to their property and
access to the courts; was that justified by the UK's obligation to give effect to the Security
Council resolutions?

Since the test of reasonable suspicion went beyond what the Security Council required,
it lay outwith the powers granted in the 1946 Act.[512] Freezing the assets of those listed
was, on the other hand, required by a Security Council resolution, but there was no means
whereby those listed could challenge before an independent and impartial judge the
decision to list them as terrorists, with the consequence that their assets were frozen.[513]
The relevant provisions of the Order had the effect of depriving those listed access to an
effective remedy and infringing their right to property. Lord Roger said that 'by enacting
the general words of section 1(1) of the 1946 Act, Parliament could not have intended to
authorise the making of [an Order] which so gravely and directly affected the legal right
of individuals to use their property and which did so in a way which deprived them of any
real possibility of challenging their listing in the courts'.[514]

Given the context—international terrorism and fidelity to international obligations—
in which this case arose this was a bold decision;[515] but it was a principled one with the
reasons given for the quashing of the relevant parts of the Orders being compelling.
Moreover, as is plain from the judgments this was not 'judicial interference with the will
of Parliament. On the contrary [the case] upholds the supremacy of Parliament in deciding whether or not measures should be imposed that affect the fundamental rights of
those in this country.'[516]

---

[511] *Ross-Clunis* v. *Papadopoullos* [1958] 1 WLR 546.

[512] *Ahmed* v. *HM Treasury* [2010] UKSC 2, para 61. Relying here on the principle in *R* v. *Secretary of State
for the Home Department ex p Pierson* [1998] AC 539 and *R* v. *Secretary of State for the Home Department
ex p Simms* [2000] 2 AC 115 that fundamental rights cannot be overridden by general or ambiguous words.
Above, p. 336.   [513] Para. 81.

[514] Para. 185

[515] Lord Brown dissented; he considered that the UK had no alternative but to uphold its obligations
under the UN Charter (para. 204).   [516] Para. 157.

THE LITERAL APPROACH

In ordinary legislation the requirement that the authority shall be 'satisfied' as to certain things is one of the commonest devices for conferring wide discretion. There have been times when the courts have taken it at face value and held that the authority has merely to declare itself to be satisfied in order to be free of all legal control. But this was when judicial control was at an exceptionally low ebb, so that the decisions of that time—as in the case of so many other fundamental rules—cannot be treated as sound.[517] Both before and since the courts have, more characteristically, refused to allow themselves to be disarmed, and for various reasons have held that the requisite 'satisfaction' cannot exist.

Of the less characteristic cases the leading example is the Court of Appeal's decision about the restoration of war damage at Plymouth.[518] The minister had made an order for the compulsory purchase of a badly damaged area of the city under an Act which empowered him to do so 'where the Minister... is satisfied that it is requisite, for the purpose of dealing satisfactorily with extensive war damage, in the area of the local planning authority, that a part or parts of their area... should be laid out afresh and redeveloped as a whole'. Owners objected that what was in fact proposed was merely restoration and repair, not redesign and redevelopment, and that 'the minister can only be "satisfied" if at the time of the order he has before him evidence sufficient in law to entitle him to be so "satisfied" '. This, said the court, 'imports an objective test into a matter to which such a test is entirely inappropriate'.[519] The tenor of the cases of this period was that attempts to dispute the minister's right to be 'satisfied' must be rejected.[520]

THE OBJECTIVE APPROACH

But many decisions reject the literal approach, and show that the court, more characteristically, is not content to relinquish control. An ordinance in Singapore provided machinery for the demolition of houses without compensation 'whenever it appears to the Board that... a dwelling place... is in such a condition as to be unfit for human habitation'. By using an English housing standard which was not a standard of unfitness for habitation the board were held by the Privy Council to have applied a wrong and inadmissible test and to have acted beyond their powers.[521] Where a minister had power to confirm a compulsory purchase notice 'if he is satisfied that the conditions specified' in the Act are fulfilled, the court quashed his confirmation order because his stated grounds were that the land was substantially diminished in value, whereas the Act required him to be satisfied that the land was incapable of reasonably beneficial use.[522] A compulsory purchase

---

[517] See above, p. 11.

[518] *Robinson* v. *Minister of Town and Country Planning* [1947] KB 702. For similarly worded powers see *Franklin* v. *Minister of Town and Country Planning* [1948] AC 87; *Re Trunk Roads Act 1936* [1939] 2 KB 515.

[519] Ibid. at 714.

[520] e.g. *R* v. *Ludlow ex p Barnsley Cpn* [1947] KB 634; *Re Beck and Pollitzer's Application* [1948] 2 KB 339; *Land Realisation Co Ltd* v. *Postmaster-General* [1950] Ch 435.

[521] *Estate and Trust Agencies (1927) Ltd* v. *Singapore Improvement Trust* [1937] AC 898 (prohibition granted).

[522] *R* v. *Minister of Housing and Local Government ex p Chichester Rural District Council* [1960] 1 WLR 587. See similarly *Metropolitan Life Insurance Co* v. *International Union of Operating Engineers Local 796* (1970) 11 DLR (3d) 336 ('If the Board is satisfied' as to membership of trade union: wrong test of membership and wrong question determined); *R* v. *Australian Stevedoring Industry Board* (1953) 88 CLR 100 ('Where the Board is satisfied' that a port employer is unfit to be registered: no basis for such finding and determination vitiated by irrelevant motive).

order which could be made 'where it appears to the authority' that compulsory powers were necessary was quashed by the Court of Appeal where it was shown that it did not so appear.[523] The Privy Council similarly set aside a minister's order under an Act which empowered him to take over the management of schools in Ceylon 'where the minister is satisfied' that a school 'is being administered in contravention of any of the provisions of this Act'.[524] The minister had based his order on a past default which had been made good, whereas the Act required him to be satisfied that there was maladministration existing at the time of the order. 'There was therefore no ground on which the minister could be "satisfied" at the time of making the Order' and 'he failed to consider the right question.'

An impressive instance of subjective language being swept aside on grounds of unreasonableness was the case where purchase tax regulations were condemned by the High Court.[525] Regulations could be made by the Commissioners of Customs and Excise 'for any matter for which provision appears to them to be necessary' for the administration of the tax. The offending regulation provided that in default of a proper return they might themselves determine the tax due, and that the taxpayer should have only seven days to dispute it. This was held invalid as wholly unreasonable and wholly unprotected by the subjective words. Language of this kind is merely one of many devices for disarming the courts. It was described in this case as a 'drafting mechanism' employed for the exclusion of the jurisdiction of the court on the footing that 'modern drafting technique is to use words which do not exclude jurisdiction in terms but positively repose arbitrary power in a named authority'.[526] The hardening judicial attitude to this device may be compared with the attitude to clauses which oust the jurisdiction of the courts directly, which has changed similarly during the same period of time.[527]

Yet another pointer in the same direction was the statement by Lord Denning MR in a Housing Act case where there was power to modify a clearance order 'if the Minister is of opinion' that any land should not have been included. The minister's order was upheld, but Lord Denning said that the court could quash it if the minister had acted on no evidence or unreasonably or had gone wrong in law.[528] Similarly where the Act said 'Where it appears to the Secretary of State...that there are reasons for doubting' whether workers wished to take part in a strike, the Court of Appeal held that those words did not put his decision beyond scrutiny by the court and that it would be invalid in law if it were not one which he could reasonably reach on the facts before him—as was not, however, established in the case itself.[529] There is an obvious affinity between this class of decisions and those which have introduced the 'no evidence' principle discussed in Chapter 8.

THE *TAMESIDE* CASE

The tendency just described was powerfully reinforced by the House of Lords, unanimously upholding a unanimous Court of Appeal, in the case of the Tameside schools.[530] After a local election the new council proceeded to reverse their predecessors' scheme, already in an advanced stage of execution, for introducing comprehensive schools. The

---

[523] *Webb* v. *Minister of Housing and Local Government* [1965] 1 WLR 755.

[524] *Maradana Mosque Trustees* v. *Mahmud* [1967] 1 AC 13.

[525] *Commissioners of Customs and Excise* v. *Cure & Deeley Ltd* [1962] 1 QB 340; below, p. 744.

[526] Ibid. at 364 (Sachs J).   [527] Below, p. 611.

[528] *Ashbridge Investments Ltd* v. *Minister of Housing and Local Government* [1965] 1 WLR 1320 at 1326, quoted above, p. 229.   [529] *Secretary of State for Employment* v. *ASLEF (No 2)* [1972] 2 QB 455.

[530] *Secretary of State for Education and Science* v. *Tameside Metropolitan Borough Council* [1977] AC 1014.

Secretary of State, who favoured comprehensive schools, issued a statutory direction to the new council to carry out the original scheme. The Act empowered him to issue directions if he was 'satisfied...that any local authority...have acted or are proposing to act unreasonably' in their statutory functions.[531] When the new council resisted he applied for an order of mandamus to force them to comply. This was refused by the Court of Appeal and the House of Lords on the ground that he must have misdirected himself in law and misunderstood the meaning of 'unreasonable' in the Act. It was not enough that he should personally disagree with the council's policy, or even that he should genuinely think that it was unreasonable. There had to be evidence that the council was acting in a way in which no reasonable council would act.[532] Since the real issue was a disagreement over policy, and the administrative difficulties were shown to be easily soluble, the Secretary of State was not legally entitled to be satisfied as the Act required, and his directions were invalid. Lord Wilberforce said:[533]

> The section is framed in a 'subjective' form—if the Secretary of State 'is satisfied'. This form of section is quite well known, and at first sight might seem to exclude judicial review. Sections in this form may, no doubt, exclude judicial review on what is or has become a matter of pure judgment. But I do not think that they go further than that. If a judgment requires, before it can be made, the existence of some facts, then, although the evaluation of those facts is for the Secretary of State alone, the court must inquire whether those facts exist, and have been taken into account, whether the judgment has been made upon a proper self-direction as to those facts, whether the judgment has not been made upon other facts which ought not to have been taken into account.

Little authority was cited for this objective approach, but the House adopted it unanimously. The Privy Council has since held that an emergency power of detention exercisable 'if the Governor is satisfied' as to acts prejudicial to public safety etc., requires that the Governor should be able to show reasonable grounds, though here there was a helpful constitutional context.[534]

It does not follow that words such as 'if the minister is satisfied' are now of little significance. For it may be material whether the question for the minister is 'a matter of pure judgment', as Lord Wilberforce put it, or a matter which can be established objectively by accepted legal standards, as can unreasonableness. Lord Denning MR expressed the same thought in the Court of Appeal:[535]

> Much depends on the matter about which the Secretary of State has to be satisfied. If he is to be satisfied on a matter of opinion, that is one thing. But if he has to be satisfied that someone has been guilty of some discreditable or unworthy or unreasonable conduct, that is another.

The minister may therefore be a free agent to the extent that, in the words of Lord Greene MR, 'no objective test is possible'.[536] And even where it is a question of discreditable or unreasonable conduct the court may hold that the facts supporting the exercise of discretion are not open to review because of the nature of the legislation. The Department of Trade may investigate a company's affairs 'if it appears' to them that there are

---

[531] Education Act 1944, s. 68. The Education Act 1976, passed after the *Tameside* case, gave wider compulsory powers to the Secretary of State.   [532] See above, p. 303.
[533] *Tameside* (above) at 1047.   [534] *A-G of St Christopher* v. *Reynolds* [1980] AC 637.
[535] [1977] AC at 1025.
[536] *Robinson* v. *Minister of Town and Country Planning* [1947] KB 702 at 713. See also *Thornloe & Clarkson Ltd* v. *Board of Trade* [1950] 2 All ER 245; *Adegbenro* v. *Akintola* [1963] AC 614.

circumstances suggesting malpractice, but the department will not be put to proof of these circumstances, since summary powers are a quid pro quo for the legal privileges which limited companies enjoy.[537]

Nevertheless the *Tameside* case is undoubtedly a landmark, manifesting the same judicial resistance to statutes which attempt to confer arbitrary power as appears in the *Anisminic* case[538] and elsewhere.

OTHER EXAMPLES

In two immigration cases where the law gave a right of entry to a Commonwealth citizen 'who satisfies an immigration officer' that he has means of support or comes for a course of study, the court treated these questions as purely objective: it quashed or upheld the immigration officer's ruling according to its own view of the law and the facts,[539] at the same time stating that it was not a court of appeal, but had to see that the Act had been administered fairly and properly construed.[540] Similarly a local authority could not lawfully be 'satisfied' that a homeless person was not 'vulnerable' when they misconstrued the latter word as requiring some substantial disability.[541]

In a case where the minister had to be satisfied by medical certificates that a person was a defective, Lord Denning said that 'satisfied' meant 'reasonably satisfied', and that if no reasonable person would have been satisfied, the minister's order would be liable to be quashed.[542] This in fact was done where a minister had power to dispense with a public inquiry into a road scheme if he was satisfied that it was unnecessary. It was held that a reasonable minister could not have been so satisfied since there were numerous objections and strongly conflicting interests.[543] These were not the first cases in which the duty to act reasonably was brought to bear upon subjective discretionary power: the same qualification had been suggested in a Housing Act case a quarter of a century earlier.[544]

The court is always likely to disregard subjective language if there is any indication that the action taken is outside the scope of the statute. Thus a council's highway order was quashed on the ground that the highway was already partly a street, although they were empowered to make the order 'where it appears to the appropriate authority that an existing highway should be converted into a new street'.[545] Where a new street already existed they were without power, and the wide subjective language could not give them final authority over 'fundamental matters such as this'. Nor will such language afford protection where the excess of power is founded on a mistake of law. A rent tribunal's rent-fixing order was accordingly quashed in so far as it was based on a premium not in fact paid by the tenant.[546] There was power to reduce the rent 'where... it appears to the tribunal that... a premium has been paid', but the payment had been made in consideration of work done by the landlord and was therefore not in law a premium, i.e. a payment

---

[537] *Norwest Holst Ltd* v. *Secretary of State for Trade* [1978] Ch 201.   [538] Below, p. 613.

[539] *R* v. *Chief Immigration Officer Lympne Airport ex p Amrik Singh* [1969] 1 QB 333 (quashed); *R* v. *Immigration Appeals Adjudicator ex p Khan* [1972] 1 WLR 1058 (upheld). See similarly *R* v. *Diggines ex p Rahmani* [1986] AC 475 (quashed).   [540] *Amrik Singh's* case (above) at 342.

[541] *R* v. *Waveney DC ex p Bowers* [1983] QB 238; and see *Kelly* v. *Monklands DC*, 1986 SLT 169.

[542] *Director of Public Prosecutions* v. *Head* [1959] AC 83 at 110; cf. *Reade* v. *Smith* [1959] NZLR 996, below.

[543] *R* v. *Secretary of State for the Environment ex p Binney*, The Times, 8 October 1983.

[544] *Re Bowman* [1932] 2 KB 621 at 634 (hypothetical case where no material, information or representation before local authority to justify clearance order).

[545] *Relton & Sons (Contracts) Ltd* v. *Whitstable UDC* (1967) 201 EG 955.

[546] *R* v. *Fulham etc Rent Tribunal ex p Philippe* [1950] 2 All ER 211.

in consideration of the grant of a lease. No court confronted with so patent an error is likely to allow it to stand.

Where the matter to be decided is a wholly objective matter and involves no question of 'pure judgment', then the words 'if the Secretary of State is satisfied' may be given no value at all. There is simply an investigation into whether the objective condition set in the legislation is established. Thus in a case where the Home Secretary could not deprive a naturalised British citizen of his citizenship 'if he is satisfied that the order would make a person stateless',[547] the Supreme Court held [548] 'the inquiry is a straightforward exercise both for the Secretary of State and on appeal: it is whether the person holds another nationality at the date of the order'.[549] The 'word "satisfied"...adds nothing to' the argument.[550]

TAX CASES

Tax authorities are commonly invested with very wide powers, freely embellished with subjective language. Sometimes, moreover, they assume them without statutory authority, as in the case of extra-statutory concessions, already discussed.[551] Their powers of search and seizure may also be very extensive.[552] Here may be mentioned some of their more ordinary powers, as where they are empowered to call for 'such particulars as they think necessary' for specified purposes. In principle these powers are subject to the control of the court in case they may be exercised unreasonably or oppressively,[553] but in their nature they are so wide that attempts to challenge them will often fail.

Taxing Acts sometimes give the revenue authorities arbitrary powers of assessment, and the courts naturally strive to impose some control upon these. A striking example was the case where purchase tax regulations were held invalid because they allowed the taxpayer no adequate opportunity to dispute the assessment, as explained above.[554] In some cases it has been held that, however subjectively the power is worded, the authorities must at least act on evidence which could reasonably justify their assessment. A Canadian minister was empowered to disallow for tax purposes 'any expense which he in his discretion may determine to be in excess of what is reasonable or normal'. On appeal the Privy Council held that the Act made the minister 'the sole judge of the fact of reasonableness or normalcy [sic]' and that the court was not at liberty to substitute their opinion for his.[555] But they went on to refer to the familiar rule of judicial review requiring reasonableness. Although the case was in fact an appeal, the Privy Council applied the 'review' standard of reasonableness, and they set aside the minister's ruling because no evidence was produced which would reasonably justify it. They said:

> The court is, in their Lordships' opinion, always entitled to examine the facts which are shown by evidence to have been before the Minister when he made his determination. If those facts are in the opinion of the court insufficient in law to support it, the determination cannot stand. In such a case the determination can only have been an arbitrary one.

This case is a remarkable contrast to *Liversidge* v. *Anderson*, discussed later.[556]

---

[547] British Nationality Act 1981, s. 40(4). The power to deprive the citizen of citizenship in certain circumstances is found in s. 40(2) and (3).   [548] *Home Secretary* v. *Al-Jedda* [2013] UKSC 62.
[549] Para. 32.   [550] Para. 31.   [551] Above, p. 349.
[552] See the *Rossminster* case, below, p. 367.
[553] *Royal Bank of Canada* v. *Inland Revenue Commissioners* [1972] Ch 665; *Clinch* v. *Inland Revenue Commissioners* [1974] QB 76; *Wilover Nominees Ltd* v. *Inland Revenue Commissioners* [1974] 1 WLR 1342.
[554] *Customs & Excise Commissioners* v. *Cure & Deeley Ltd* [1962] 1 QB 340 (above, p. 360).
[555] *Minister of National Revenue* v. *Wrights' Canadian Ropes Ltd* [1947] AC 109.
[556] Below p. 366.

Another Privy Council case from Guyana, also on appeal, concerned a tax assessment which could be made only 'where...the Commissioner is of opinion that the person is liable to pay tax'. It was held that on the facts he could have formed no reasonable opinion to this effect, and the assessment was annulled.[557]

THE CROWN

Certain Australian decisions have suggested an exception in favour of the Crown's representatives, i.e. the Governor-General and State Governors.[558] According to this, subjective language of the 'if satisfied' or 'if of opinion' type would render the Crown representative's action immune from judicial review on the basis of bad faith, irrelevant considerations, misconception of the meaning of the matters to be considered, or 'some other miscarriage'. No such exception is recognised by the Privy Council, as has already been seen;[559] nor is it recognised in New Zealand. In the leading New Zealand case the Supreme Court condemned a regulation made by the Governor-General which author-ised the compulsory transfer of pupils between schools and which was held to be in conflict with the principle of parental choice on which the Act was founded.[560] The Act empowered regulations which 'in the opinion of the Governor-General' were required 'for any purpose which he thinks necessary in order to secure the due administration of this Act'. The Court held that it could always inquire whether the Governor-General could reasonably have formed the necessary opinion, and whether he had acted on an untenable view of a question of law.

The suggested exception seems to be contrary to principle and unlikely to be followed. In a later decision the High Court of Australia has decided that the powers of the Crown's representatives are reviewable on normal principles.[561] The distinction which needs to be made has nothing to do with the empowered authority's position in the administrative hierarchy: it should be based on the nature of the matters on which it must satisfy itself. In time of war or grave emergency these are likely to be so wide and difficult of proof that it can hardly be supposed that the court will be in a position to question them.[562] In other contexts the principles of judicial review should have their normal operation. As Turner J said in the New Zealand case:[563]

> Cases dealing with war regulations promulgated in time of great national danger must, in my opinion, be carefully examined before being used too hastily as a touchstone for the validity of regulations made under more normal conditions.

No case could better illustrate this truth than the decision of the House of Lords in *Liversidge* v. *Anderson*,[564] discussed later.

---

[557] *Argosy Co Ltd* v. *Inland Revenue Commissioners* [1971] 1 WLR 514.

[558] See *Australian Communist Party* v. *The Commonwealth* (1951) 83 CLR 1 at 179–80 (Dixon J); *R* v. *Martin* (1967) 67 SR (NSW) 404.

[559] *A-G for Canada* v. *Hallett & Carey Ltd* [1952] AC 427 at 444; above, p. 357.

[560] *Reade* v. *Smith* [1959] NZLR 996.

[561] *R* v. *Toohey ex p Northern Lands Council* (1982) 151 CLR 170; *FAI Insurances Ltd* v. *Winneke* (1982) 41 ALR 1; *Minister for Arts* v. *Peko-Wallsend* (1987) 75 ALR 218.

[562] See *Re Chemicals Regulations* [1943] 1 DLR 248.

[563] *Reade* v. *Smith* (above) at 1000.   [564] [1942] AC 206; below, p. 366.

FORMALITIES

It does not appear that it is essential to recite the minister's satisfaction or opinion, as the case may be, in the text of the order, since the court is sometimes prepared to assume it or to accept a subsequent statement.[565] In former times a full recital was required, in accordance with the old rule, now obsolete, that the order of an inferior tribunal or authority must show on its face the facts necessary to give it jurisdiction.[566] Good practice of course requires that the proper recital should be made. The House of Lords confirmed this where a judge granted warrants of search and seizure to tax officials under an Act authorising him to grant them 'if...satisfied' that there was reasonable ground for suspicion. The warrants did not recite that he was so satisfied, but it was held that this recital, though desirable, was not essential to their validity.[567]

STATUTORY REASONABLENESS

OBJECTIVE CONDITIONS

A condition requiring some degree of reasonableness will often be prescribed by statute. If the language is objective, the authority will have to be prepared to show that the condition is fulfilled in a way which satisfies the court. If a sound building may be included in a clearance area if that is 'reasonably necessary', a minister's decision to include it will be quashed if there is no evidence of any necessity.[568] If a licensing authority has power to revoke a trader's licence if it has 'reasonable cause to believe' that the licensee has committed malpractices, the authority must show causes which the court judges to be reasonable.[569] This is simply the ordinary doctrine that empowers the court to judge whether statutory conditions are satisfied. The case is of course different if the power is worded subjectively, as where a legal aid committee may refuse aid 'if it appears unreasonable' to grant it in any case.[570] Such a subjective formula may restrict the court's control—though, as has been seen, it may be rash to count on the court accepting it at face value.[571]

In the ordinary case where the court is the judge, the standard will be the familiar legal standard of the reasonable man. But it by no means follows, because the standard of reasonableness is objective, that it is also rigid. There may be a broad band of different decisions or policies all of which fall within the range of reasonableness, and two opposite policies may be equally reasonable. Under the Housing Act 1985 housing authorities 'may make such reasonable charges for the tenancy or occupation of the houses as they may determine',[572] but this leaves them at liberty either to fix their rents at flat rates which make no allowance for the tenant's personal circumstances[573] or, alternatively, to impose a scheme of differential rents which subsidises the poorer tenants at the expense of the

---

[565] R v. *Comptroller-General of Patents ex p Bayer Products Ltd* [1941] 2 KB 306 at 314 (but the sense is doubtful); *Land Realisation Co Ltd* v. *Postmaster-General* [1950] Ch 435; *Thornloe & Clarkson Ltd* v. *Board of Trade* [1950] 2 All ER 245; *Union Motors Ltd* v. *Motor Spirits Licensing Authority* [1964] NZLR 146. See also *Liversidge* v. *Anderson* (below) at 224. Contrast R v. *Martin* (above).

[566] Rubinstein, *Jurisdiction and Illegality*, 170, citing R v. *Whittles* (1849) 13 QB 248.

[567] R v. *Inland Revenue Commissioners ex p Rossminster Ltd* [1980] AC 952 (Lord Salmon dissenting). No decisions on this point were mentioned in the speeches.

[568] *Coleen Properties Ltd* v. *Minister of Housing and Local Government* [1971] 1 WLR 443.

[569] *Nakkuda Ali* v. *Jayaratne* [1951] AC 66.

[570] R v. *Legal Aid Committee No 1 (London) Legal Aid Area ex p Rondel* [1967] 2 QB 482.

[571] Above, p. 359.   [572] s. 24.   [573] *Luby* v. *Newcastle-under-Lyme Cpn* [1964] 2 QB 64.

ratepayers.[574] In the same way the authority may fix rents at overall rates which take no account of the differing costs of construction of different houses.[575] Of none of these different courses could it be said that it was 'manifestly unjust' or 'could find no justification in the minds of reasonable men' within the *Wednesbury* test previously explained.[576] The housing authority was 'applying what is, in effect, a social policy upon which reasonable men may hold different views'.[577] The degree of objectivity in the test of reasonableness can therefore vary widely with the statutory context and purpose.

'REASONABLE CAUSE TO BELIEVE'

Objectivity may be reduced to vanishing point if the circumstances are strong enough—or, at least, this happened in *Liversidge* v. *Anderson*, a case of emergency powers in wartime. The Defence (General) Regulations 1939 provided: 'If the Secretary of State has reasonable cause to believe any person to be of hostile origin or associations... he may make an order against that person directing that he be detained'. By all accepted canons of interpretation this language required the Secretary of State to show cause which the court would adjudge to be reasonable.[578] If the Secretary of State had been intended to be the sole judge of the grounds of detention, the Regulation should have used a subjective formula such as 'the Secretary of State, if satisfied...' And indeed those very words had been used in the original form of the Regulation,[579] which had been criticised in Parliament and amended into the objective form. Nevertheless, when a detainee challenged the Secretary of State's grounds, all the courts held that in the circumstances of the war there could be no judicial review of the reasonableness of the Secretary of State's grounds of belief.[580]

Viscount Maugham said that despite the prima facie meaning of the vital words, they might have a different and subjective meaning where the thing to be believed was essentially something within the knowledge of the Secretary of State and a matter for his exclusive discretion. This proposition was vehemently denied by Lord Atkin in his lone dissenting speech,[581] in which he contended that 'the words have only one meaning' and 'have never been used in the sense now imputed to them'. He protested against 'a strained construction put on words with the effect of giving an uncontrolled power of imprisonment to the minister', and denied that the words 'if a man has' could ever mean 'if a man thinks he has'. His caustic remarks about judges, who 'show themselves more executive minded than the executive', arguments which 'might have been addressed acceptably to the Court of King's Bench in the time of Charles I' and Humpty Dumpty's use of a word to mean 'just what I choose it to mean' gave rise to some unusual public controversy.[582] Legal opinion was for the most part on Lord Atkin's side on the question of construction.[583] When a similar form of words came before the Privy Council in a post-war case,

---

[574] *Smith* v. *Cardiff Cpn (No 2)* [1955] Ch 159.

[575] *Summerfield* v. *Hampstead Borough Council* [1957] 1 WLR 167.

[576] See *Luby* (as above) at 71.

[577] *Luby* (as above) at 72. An obvious case of illegal abuse was *Backhouse* v. *Lambeth Borough Council*, above, p. 332.   [578] Above, p. 207.

[579] SR & O 1939 No. 978. See *Liversidge* v. *Anderson* [1942] AC 206 at 237.

[580] *Liversidge* v. *Anderson* [1942] AC 206 (action for false imprisonment); and see *Greene* v. *Home Secretary* [1942] AC 284 (habeas corpus).

[581] Another lone dissent was that of Stable J in *R* v. *Home Secretary ex p Budd* [1941] 2 All ER 749, affirmed [1942] 1 All ER 373.

[582] For an account of this and for the case generally see (1970) 86 *LQR* 33, (1971) 87 *LQR* 161 (R. F. V. Heuston) and A. W. B Simpson, *In the Highest Degree Odious: Detention without Trial in Wartime Britain* (1992).   [583] Professor Heuston's articles (above) give a good survey.

where the statute gave power to cancel a textile dealer's licence 'where the Controller has reasonable grounds to believe that any dealer is unfit to be allowed to continue as a dealer', the Judicial Committee held that the 'reasonable grounds' formula bore its usual objective sense, so that the Controller was required to show that his grounds were reasonable in the eyes of the court.[584] Lord Radcliffe said that it would be a very unfortunate thing if the *Liversidge* case were regarded as laying down any general rule. He added that the formula must be intended to limit an otherwise arbitrary power, but that if it was to be conclusively interpreted by the man who wielded the power, the value of the intended restraint was in effect nothing.

In 1963 Lord Reid referred dismissively to 'the very peculiar decision of this House in *Liversidge* v. *Anderson*'[585] and by then it was already clear that the decision was regarded as an aberration. It remained for Lord Diplock to say in 1979:[586]

> For my part I think the time has come to acknowledge openly that the majority of this House in *Liversidge* v. *Anderson* were expediently and, at that time, perhaps, excusably wrong and the dissenting speech of Lord Atkin was right.

And Lord Scarman said in the same case that the ghost of that decision need no longer haunt the law.

It will not always be the case, however, that the governmental authority can at once be put to proof of the reasonableness of its grounds. For if criminal proceedings are in prospect, the information will be protected by 'public interest immunity'[587] until the proceedings are concluded or a reasonable time has elapsed without proceedings being brought. This was the position, as the House of Lords held, where officers of the Inland Revenue had carried out an elaborate and drastic raid on the homes and offices of two tax consultants and had seized large quantities of papers. They had obtained search warrants authorising them to seize and remove anything which they had reasonable cause to believe might be required for the purposes of legal proceedings for tax offences involving fraud. Since many of the papers had been seized and removed without scrutiny, the Court of Appeal held that the tax officers could not have had reasonable cause to believe that they might be required. But the House of Lords held that this was not proved and that the issue could be litigated only after criminal proceedings were either concluded or abandoned.[588]

STATUTORY UNREASONABLENESS

As well as prescribing conditions in terms of reasonableness, statutes may prescribe them in terms of unreasonableness. The objective legal standard of reasonableness, as already explained, is then again the criterion, though in the negative sense. In the Tameside comprehensive school case,[589] where the Secretary of State was required to be satisfied that the local authority had acted unreasonably, the House of Lords disallowed his intervention because he had evidently misdirected himself as to the meaning of 'unreasonably': the evidence showed that the local authority's plan to restore grammar schools, though it raised difficulties, was not so impracticable that no reasonable authority could have adopted it.

---

[584] *Nakkuda Ali* v. *Jayaratne* [1951] AC 66, followed in *Registrar of Restrictive Trading Agreements* v. *WH Smith & Son Ltd* [1969] 1 WLR 1460.   [585] *Ridge* v. *Baldwin* [1964] AC 40 at 73.

[586] In the *Rossminster* case (below) at 1011.   [587] Explained below, p. 715.

[588] *R* v. *Inland Revenue Commissioners ex p Rossminster Ltd* [1980] AC 952.

[589] Above, p. 360.

OBJECTIVITY FORSAKEN AND RESTORED

Scarcely had the House of Lords completed the obsequies of *Liversidge* v. *Anderson* when they held in an immigration case that objective words might be interpreted subjectively so as to give a minister an area of discretionary power. This serious lapse and its prompt correction[590] deserve to be put alongside *Liversidge* v. *Anderson* as another example of the House of Lords forsaking the principle of objectivity and later eating its words.

Under the Immigration Act 1971 an immigration officer may detain an 'illegal entrant' who may then be removed from the country by the Home Secretary. An 'illegal entrant' is defined in the Act as a person entering or seeking to enter unlawfully.[591] The question whether his entry was or was not unlawful ought therefore to be decided upon the objective facts. But the House of Lords held that 'the whole scheme of the Act' indicated the contrary, and that the court could intervene only if the Home Secretary was acting on no evidence or in a way in which no reasonable person could do.[592] It was said that, although there were no words such as 'in the opinion of the Secretary of State', such a formula was not necessary; and that the nature and process of the powers conferred upon immigration officers was incompatible with any requirement for the establishment of precedent objective facts which the court could verify. In less than three years, fortunately, the House reversed itself in a closely similar case, holding that 'illegal entrant' was a precedent or jurisdictional fact to be determined on all the evidence by the court, and that on the facts the Home Secretary had failed to show that one of the appellant immigrants was an illegal entrant.[593] The House restored the principle that the court must be the final judge of objectively stated facts. Why it was ever denied is even harder to understand than in *Liversidge* v. *Anderson*, since there was no situation of emergency. The explanation may be that the rapid expansion of judicial review had led judges to suppose that its rules for the review of discretionary decisions were the only operative restraints on the executive,[594] forgetting the independent and more fundamental principle of objectivity.[595]

AMBIGUOUS LANGUAGE: 'REQUIRED', 'REGULATE'

Many words take their colour from their context, and this may make the difference between objective and subjective construction. One such word is 'required'. If a public authority is empowered to take land 'required' for certain purposes, does it have to show to the court that there is a real need or is it the sole judge of the need itself? Can 'required' mean merely 'desired'? The decisions show that there is no rigid rule, even on similar words in similar Acts. Thus in one case where the question was whether a local authority was obliged to dispose of land as 'not required' for a sewage works, the judge held on the evidence that the land was likely to be required in the future and so should be retained.[596]

---

[590] *R* v. *Home Secretary ex p Zamir* [1980] AC 930. Corrected in *R* v. *Home Secretary ex p Khawaja* [1984] AC 74.

[591] For the precise meaning see *R* v. *Naillie* [1993] AC 674; *R* v. *Secretary of State for the Environment ex p Tower Hamlets LBC* [1993] QB 632.

[592] *R* v. *Home Secretary ex p Zamir* [1980] AC 930. The only reasoned speech was that of Lord Wilberforce. The House approved *R* v. *Home Secretary ex p Hussain* [1978] 1 WLR 700. See similarly *R* v. *Home Secretary ex p Choudhary* [1978] 1 WLR 1177, but contrast the cases cited above, p. 361.

[593] *R* v. *Home Secretary ex p Khawaja* [1984] AC 74 (above, p. 244). See also *R* v. *Home Secretary ex p Bugdaycay* [1987] AC 514.

[594] This seems probable from some unsound statements made in the lower courts and reviewed in the speech of Lord Wilberforce in *Khawaja*.   [595] For which see above, p. 207.

[596] *A-G* v. *Teddington Urban District Council* [1898] 1 Ch 66. And see *Stocker* v. *Minister of Health* [1938] 1 KB 655 at 663.

Clearly he regarded the words as objective. And 'requisite' has been interpreted similarly.[597] But in another case it was held that it was solely for the local authority to decide whether land was 'not required' for its original purpose, so that it could be appropriated to other purposes.[598] The Court of Appeal, though not without some reluctance,[599] has declared itself in favour of the latter interpretation.[600] Russell LJ construed 'not required' as meaning 'not needed in the public interest of the locality', and said that 'the local authority is better qualified than the court to judge, assuming it to be acting bona fide and not upon a view that no reasonable local authority could possibly take'.

But just as this permissive interpretation is subject to the usual requirements of good faith and reasonableness, so it must also be subject to the rule about illegitimate purposes.[601] The Court of Appeal accordingly condemned a compulsory purchase order made by a district council for land 'required by them' for coast protection work when it appeared that a substantial part of the land was to be used for purposes of public amenity and was not needed for coast protection.[602] At first instance the order was quashed on the ground of bad faith, but on appeal the council was absolved from that charge. 'Required' was held to mean 'properly required' for the correct purpose, and since in fact the land was required for a different purpose, the order could not stand. The difference between this and the cases mentioned in the preceding paragraph is clear. The former cases are concerned only with whether land is or is not needed for an admittedly valid purpose. In this last case there is the additional feature of an illegitimate purpose, outside the powers of the Act in question. The case then becomes one of ultra vires which no court is likely to condone.

Another ambiguous word, common in administrative law, is 'regulate'. It has several times been decided that a power to regulate does not extend to a power to prohibit, the assumption being that a power to regulate implies the continued existence of what is to be regulated.[603] But the contrary has also been held where the context was suitable,[604] as it was when the House of Lords held that the Railways Board were entitled to impose a general ban on smoking in trains under their power to regulate 'the use and working of, and travel on, their railways'.[605] Power to prohibit, furthermore, may include power to regulate, as by making some activity subject to the grant of permission.[606]

---

[597] *R v. Secretary of State for the Environment ex p Powis* [1981] 1 WLR 584.

[598] *A-G v. Manchester Cpn* [1931] 1 Ch 254.

[599] *Per* Buckley and Lawton LJJ. The *Webb* case (below) was not cited.

[600] *Dowty Boulton Paul Ltd v. Wolverhampton Cpn (No 2)* [1976] Ch 13.   [601] Above, p. 300.

[602] *Webb v. Minister of Housing and Local Government* [1965] 1 WLR 755.

[603] *Toronto Cpn v. Virgo* [1896] AC 88; *Birmingham and Midland Omnibus Co v. Worcestershire CC* [1967] 1 WLR 409; *Tarr v. Tarr* [1973] AC 254.

[604] *R v. British Airports Authority ex p Wheatley* (1983) 81 LGR 794 (control of taxicabs at airport).

[605] *Boddington v. British Railways Board* [1999] 2 AC 143.

[606] *Foley v. Padley* (1984) 54 ALR 609.

PART VI

NATURAL JUSTICE

12

NATURAL JUSTICE AND LEGAL JUSTICE

PROCEDURAL JUSTICE

Just as the courts can control the substance of what public authorities do by means of the rules relating to reasonableness, improper purposes, and so forth, so through the principles of natural justice they can control the procedure by which they do it. In so doing they have imposed a particular procedural technique on government departments and statutory authorities generally. The courts have, in effect, devised a code of fair administrative procedure based on doctrines which are an essential part of any system of administrative justice.

Procedure is not a matter of secondary importance. As governmental powers continually grow more drastic, it is only by procedural fairness that they are rendered tolerable. A judge of the United States Supreme Court has said: 'Procedural fairness and regularity are of the indispensable essence of liberty. Severe substantive laws can be endured if they are fairly and impartially applied'.[1] One of his colleagues said: 'The history of liberty has largely been the history of the observance of procedural safeguards.'[2] The work of British judges in devising procedural safeguards is the theme of this Part of the book, as also of the following Part on remedies. But Article 6(1) of the European Convention on Human Rights (ECHR),[3] which has legal effect under the Human Rights Act 1998, now supplements the common law of procedural justice in many administrative cases and plays an important role.[4] However, the judges have developed, and continue to develop, techniques that ensure that the Convention is flexibly applied in a way that is sensitive to the administrative context.[5]

Lawyers are a procedurally minded race, and it is natural that administrators should be tempted to regard procedural restrictions, invented by lawyers, as an obstacle to efficiency. It is true that the rules of natural justice restrict the freedom of administrative action and that their observance costs a certain amount of time and money. But time and money are likely to be well spent if they reduce friction in the machinery of government; and it is because they are essentially rules for upholding fairness and so reducing grievances that the rules of natural justice can be said to promote efficiency rather than impede it. Provided that the courts do not let them run riot, and keep them in touch with the standards which good administration demands in any case, they should be regarded

---

[1] *Shaughnessy* v. *United States*, 345 US 206 (1953) (Jackson J).

[2] *McNabb* v. *United States*, 318 US 332 (1943) (Frankfurter J).

[3] When applicable, this article provides for 'a fair and public hearing…by an independent and impartial tribunal established by law'. The full text is given in Appendix 2.

[4] See below, p. 377. Article 6 also applies to 'the determination…of any criminal charge'.

[5] Discussed in detail, ibid.

as a protection not only to citizens but also to officials. Moreover, a decision which is made without bias, and with proper consideration of the views of those affected by it, will not only be more acceptable; it will also be of better quality. Justice and efficiency go hand in hand, so long at least as the law does not impose excessive refinements.[6]

Judgments of the highest courts confirm that the rules of natural justice are not imposed simply to ensure better decisions but also because, as Lord Reed has said, 'justice is intuitively understood to require a procedure which pays due respect to persons whose rights are significantly affected'.[7] Those affected by the decision should be respected 'as beings capable of explaining themselves'.[8]

ADMINISTRATIVE JUSTICE AND NATURAL JUSTICE

In its broadest sense natural justice may mean simply 'the natural sense of what is right and wrong'[9] and even in its technical sense it is now often equated with 'fairness'.[10]

But in administrative law natural justice is a well-defined concept which comprises two fundamental rules of fair procedure: that a man may not be a judge in his own cause; and that a man's defence must always be fairly heard.[11] In courts of law and in statutory tribunals it can be taken for granted that these rules must be observed. But so universal are they, so 'natural', that they are not confined to judicial power. They apply equally to administrative power, and sometimes also to powers created by contract. Natural justice is one of the most active departments of administrative law.

There are both broad and narrow aspects to consider. The narrow aspect is that the rules of natural justice are merely a branch of the principle of ultra vires. Violation of natural justice is then to be classified as one of the varieties of wrong procedure, or abuse of power, which transgress the implied conditions which Parliament is presumed to have intended. Just as a power to act 'as he thinks fit' does not allow a public authority to act unreasonably or in bad faith, so it does not allow disregard of the elementary doctrines of fair procedure. As Lord Selborne once said:[12]

> There would be no decision within the meaning of the statute if there were anything of that sort done contrary to the essence of justice.

---

[6] See Galligan, *Due Process and Fair Procedures: A Study of Administrative Procedures* (1996) distinguishing between instrumental (efficient application of rules) and non-instrumental (treating the person affected with respect and dignity) justifications for procedural justice. This distinction is discussed further in Elliott, *Beatson, Matthews and Elliott's Administrative Law Text and Materials*, 4th edn (2011), 342–6 and (1998)18 *OJLS* 497 (Allan).

[7] *Osborn* v. *The Parole Board* [2013] UKSC 61, paras. 67–72. The purpose of natural justice is also discussed by Lord Phillips in *Home Secretary* v. *AF and anor* [2009] UKHL 28, paras. 60–3, rejecting a distinction between 'a fair procedure [non-instrumental] and a procedure that produces a fair result [instrumental]'. Lord Hoffman in the same case recognised the importance of non-instrumental justifications but also recognised that they were not absolute (para. 72). See further below, pp. 436 (oral hearings) and 424 (hearing would make no difference).

[8] Waldron, 'How Law Protects Dignity' [2012] *CLJ* 200 at 210 (cited with approval by Lord Reed at para. 68).   [9] *Voinet* v. *Barrett* (1885) 55 LJQB 39 at 41 (Lord Esher MR).

[10] Below, p. 417.

[11] See Marshall, *Natural Justice*; Jackson, *Natural Justice* (2nd edn); Flick, *Natural Justice* (2nd edn). The two rules do not seem to have been bracketed together before the decision of the House of Lords in *Spackman* v. *Plumstead District Board of Works* (below).

[12] *Spackman* v. *Plumstead District Board of Works* (1885) 10 App Cas 229 at 240.

Quoting these words, the Privy Council has said that 'it has long been settled law' that a decision which offends against the principles of natural justice is outside the jurisdiction of the decision-making authority.[13] Likewise Lord Russell has said:[14]

it is to be implied, unless the contrary appears, that Parliament does not authorise by the Act the exercise of powers in breach of the principles of natural justice, and that Parliament does by the Act require, in the particular procedures, compliance with those principles.

Thus violation of natural justice makes the decision void, as in any other case of ultra vires. This effect is discussed more fully later.[15] For the moment it is enough to note that the rules of natural justice thus operate as implied mandatory requirements, non-observance of which invalidates the exercise of the power.

In its wider aspect the subject contains the very kernel of the problem of administrative justice: how far ought both judicial and administrative power to rest on common principles? How far is it right for the courts of law to try to impart their own standards of justice to the administration? When special powers to take action or to decide disputes are vested in administrative bodies with the very object of avoiding the forms of legal process, is there yet a residuum of legal procedure which ought never to be shaken off? The judges have long been conscious of this problem, and it has prompted them to some of their more notable achievements. Rules of common law, which became in effect presumptions to be used in the interpretation of statutes, developed and refined the rules of natural justice over a period of centuries. Since the decisions to which the rules apply are very various, they have to be flexibly applied and their precise content depends on the circumstances. But their general applicability to governmental action is today beyond doubt.

POST-WAR VICISSITUDES

After the Second World War natural justice suffered a setback, and the whole subject threatened to become unsettled, in a manner which is all too characteristic of case law. This was closely connected with a parallel confusion over the remedy of certiorari.

A turning-point came in 1963 with the decision of the House of Lords in *Ridge* v. *Baldwin*.[16] This marked an important change of judicial policy, indicating that natural justice was restored to favour and would be applied on a wide basis. A spate of litigation followed in its wake, and many new questions were elucidated. The process is likely to continue, as the courts build up their code of administrative procedure and explore the implications of what they call 'fair play in action'.[17] The citizen's right to have his case properly heard, before he suffers in some way under the official rod, can cover a whole series of procedural steps, from the initial objection to the final decision.

The litigation since 1963 has helped to make public authorities aware of the law's requirements, thereby improving administrative standards. In the courts the rules have been clarified and their enforcement has become more consistent. The legal conception of procedural justice, has now a secure bridgehead in the territory of administration. Judges are no longer deterred by the disparaging remarks of some of their predecessors,

[13] *A-G* v. *Ryan* [1980] AC 718. Even the order of a superior court may be set aside for violation of natural justice: *Isaacs* v. *Robertson* [1985] AC 97, for which see above, p. 255.

[14] *Fairmount Investments Ltd* v. *Secretary of State for the Environment* [1976] 1 WLR 1255 at 1263. And see *Ridge* v. *Baldwin* [1964] AC 40 at 80 ('a decision given without regard to the principles of natural justice is void' (Lord Reid)).　　　　　　　　　　　　　　　　　　　　　　　[15] Below, pp. 403, 419.

[16] [1964] AC 40.　　　[17] See below, p. 417.

such as 'the expression [natural justice] is sadly lacking in precision'[18] and 'that the judiciary should presume to impose its own methods on administrative or executive officers is a usurpation'.[19] Such comments are out of line with the current of authority which has flowed for several hundred years. In *Ridge* v. *Baldwin* Lord Reid made an apt reply:[20]

> In modern times opinions have sometimes been expressed to the effect that natural justice is so vague as to be practically meaningless. But I would regard these as tainted by the perennial fallacy that because something cannot be cut and dried or nicely weighed or measured therefore it does not exist. The idea of negligence is equally insusceptible of exact definition...and natural justice as it has been interpreted in the courts is much more definite than that.

NATURAL JUSTICE IN THE COMMON LAW

The rules requiring impartial adjudicators and fair hearings can be traced back to medieval precedents, and, indeed, they were not unknown in the ancient world. In their medieval guise they were regarded as part of the immutable order of things, so that in theory even the power of the legislature could not alter them. This theory lingered into the seventeenth and faintly even into the eighteenth century. It reached its high-water mark in *Dr Bonham's* case (1610), where Chief Justice Coke went so far as to say that the court could declare an Act of Parliament void if it made a man judge in his own cause, or was otherwise 'against common right and reason'.[21] This was one of his grounds for disallowing the claim of the College of Physicians to fine and imprison Dr Bonham, a doctor of physics of Cambridge University, for practising in the City of London without the licence of the College of Physicians. The statute under which the College acted provided that fines should go half to the king and half to the College, so that the College had a financial interest in its own judgment and was judge in its own cause.

No modern judge could repeat this exploit, for to hold an Act of Parliament void is to blaspheme against the doctrine of parliamentary sovereignty.[22] As we shall see, there are plenty of cases under modern statutes where authorities are in a sense (sometimes even a financial sense) judges in their own affairs. Coke's opinion was by no means clear law even in his own time although it was approved by at least one contemporary Chief Justice.[23] Natural justice, natural law, the law of God and 'common right and reason' were all aspects of the old concept of fundamental and unalterable law. They no longer

---

[18] *R* v. *Local Government Board ex p Arlidge* [1914] 1 KB 160 at 199 (Hamilton LJ). And see *Maclean* v. *Workers' Union* [1929] 1 Ch 602 at 604 (Maugham J).

[19] *Local Government Board* v. *Arlidge* [1915] AC 120 at 138 (Lord Shaw), followed by derogatory comments on natural justice.   [20] [1964] AC 40 at 64.

[21] 8 Co Rep 113b at 118a. It has been suggested (by Moses J) that 'the right of review of a determination of statutory entitlement...carries with it a right to independent and impartial review' (*R (Bewry)* v. *Norwich City Council* [2001] EWHC Admin 657, para. 29. Insofar as this judgment supposes a common law right to an independent and impartial decision-maker removable only by primary legislation, it may be doubted: *McLellan* v. *Bracknell Forest Borough Council and anor* [2001] EWCA Civ 1510, para. 75.

[22] See the discussion of sovereignty, above, p. 19.

[23] Hobart CJ in *Day* v. *Savadge* (1614) Hobart 85, who said 'even an Act of Parliament made against natural equity, as to make a man judge in his own case, is void in itself, for *jura naturae sunt immutabilia* and they are *leges legum*'. And see *City of London* v. *Wood* [1701] 12 Mod 669 (Holt CJ approving Coke's opinion).

represent any kind of limit to the power of statute.[24] Natural justice has had to look for a new foothold, and has found it as a mode not of destroying enacted law but of fulfilling it. Its basis now is in the rules of interpretation. The courts presume that Parliament, when it grants powers, intends them to be exercised in a right and proper way. 'Where wide powers of decision-making are conferred by statute', Lord Browne-Wilkinson has observed, 'it is presumed that Parliament implicitly requires the decision to be made in accordance with the rules of natural justice'.[25] Since Parliament seldom makes provision to the contrary, this allows considerable scope for the courts to devise a set of canons of fair administrative procedure, suitable to the needs of the time and the context in which the issue arises.

The courts also apply similar doctrines in the private sphere, in the interpretation of contracts. Members of trade unions or clubs, for example, cannot normally be expelled without being given a hearing, for their contracts of membership are held to include a duty to act fairly: by accepting them as members and receiving their subscriptions the trade union or club impliedly undertakes to treat them fairly and in accordance with the rules.[26]

The courts are not always willing to be confined by rigid categories, and in some cases they have held that there is a duty of procedural fairness even where there is neither statute nor contract upon which to base it. The Court of Appeal has held that the Panel on Take-overs and Mergers, part of the Stock Exchange's system of self-regulation which has no statutory or contractual basis, is subject to judicial review, and must observe the principles of natural justice, because it operates in the public sphere and exercises immense power de facto.[27] This and other such cases are discussed later.[28] The High Court of Australia has held that the owner of a racecourse who admits the public has a 'moral duty' not to eject any individual arbitrarily and without hearing him fairly, and that if he does so his act is 'ultra vires and void'.[29] The courts have in the past asserted common law powers to impose standards of fairness upon some kinds of monopolies; and these decisions are perhaps to be seen as analogous to those powers.[30]

THE EUROPEAN CONVENTION AND NATURAL JUSTICE IN ADMINISTRATIVE PROCEEDINGS

The European Convention does not refer specifically to administrative proceedings. Article 6(1),[31] however, provides for 'a fair and public hearing within a reasonable time by an independent and impartial tribunal established by law'. But it only applies to the 'determination' of an individual's 'civil rights and obligations or of any criminal charge

[24] In 1871 Willes J described the above-quoted remark of Hobart CJ as 'a warning rather than an authority to be followed': *Lee v. Bude & Torrington Junction Rly* (1871) LR 6 CP 576 at 582. But see the discussion above, p. 238.

[25] *R v. Home Secretary ex p Pierson* [1998] AC 539 at 550. See also Lord Steyn at 505 and Lord Mustill in *R v. Home Secretary ex p Doody* [1994] AC 531 at 560 (Parliament presumed to intend power to be exercised in a manner that is fair in all the circumstances).   [26] See below, p. 407.

[27] *R v. Panel on Takeovers and Mergers ex p Datafin plc* [1987] QB 815 (not a natural justice case).

[28] See below, p. 532.

[29] *Forbes v. New South Wales Trotting Club* (1979) 25 ALR 1. Contrast *Heatley v. Tasmanian Racing and Gaming Commission* (1977) 14 ALR 519 at 538, holding that an owner's rights of property may be exercised without regard to natural justice.   [30] See below, p. 545.

[31] For the full text, see Appendix 2. For discussion see [2003] *PL* 753 (P. P. Craig); [2005] *JR* (P. Sales QC); [2006] *JR* 57 (M. Westgate); [2006] *JR* 78 (J. Cooper).

against him' and the jurisprudence of the Court of Human Rights shows that there is no 'determination' of an individual's 'civil rights and obligations'[32]—which was originally intended to mean broadly *private law* rights[33]—in many administrative proceedings. Moreover, disciplinary proceedings where the liberty of the accused is not at risk do not involve a 'criminal charge'.[34] But if they deprive the accused of the liberty to practise a profession they do determine his rights and Article 6(1) is applicable.[35] A fixed penalty

[32] The Court, in accordance with its usual approach, gives both 'civil rights and obligations' and 'criminal charge' 'an autonomous Convention meaning' independent of the national legal system involved. It has been held by the Court that Art. 6(1) 'does not in itself guarantee any particular content for rights and obligations' (*James* v. *UK* (1986) 8 EHRR 81, para. 81). The suggestion in *Osman* v. *UK* (2000) 29 EHRR 245, [1999] 1 FLR 193 (wide immunity accorded to police for negligence in investigation and suppression of crime, held a breach of Art. 6(1)) that there is a substantive facet to Art. 6(1) has not since found favour: *Barrett* v. *Enfield LBC* [1999] 3 WLR 79 at 85 (Lord Browne-Wilkinson) and *DP and JC* v. *UK* (2003) 36 EHRR 14 (Art. 6(1) only applicable to disputes over rights arguably 'recognised under domestic law' (para. 123)). This was confirmed in *Mathews* v. *Ministry of Defence* [2003] UKHL 4, [2003] 1 AC 1163, so a substantive bar to a serviceman recovering damages from the MOD, in the particular circumstances, did not engage Art. 6(1). The article only protected the right of access to the courts where the right in question was at least arguably recognised in domestic law and the restriction on access was procedural. *R (Kekoe)* v. *Secretary of State for Work and Pensions* [2005] UKHL 48, [2005] 3 WLR 252(HL) (parent caring for child had no right to recover or enforce a claim for maintenance against absent parent; Art. 6(1) not engaged). And see *Crosbie* v. *Secretary of State for Defence* [2011] EWHC 879 (army chaplain had no right to extension of commission; Art. 6(1) not engaged).

[33] *Lecompte, Van Leuven and De Meyere* v. *Belgium* (1981) 4 EHRR 533 (and many other decisions). The Court and Commission have not defined with clarity the boundary between public and private law but have proceeded inductively on a case by case basis. See Harris, O'Boyle and Warbrick, *Law of the European Convention on Human Rights*, 2nd edn (2005), for discussion. See the discussion in *Runa Begum* v. *Tower Hamlets LBC* [2003] 2 AC 430 (HL), especially paras. 30–44 (Lord Hoffmann) and paras. 84–94 (Lord Millett) noting 'the unsettled state of the jurisprudence of the Strasbourg court'.

[34] Thus a disciplinary matter affecting liberty may concern a 'criminal charge' even though it is considered administrative in the relevant legal system: *Engel* v. *Netherlands*, A 22 (1976); *X* v. *UK* (military discipline) and *Campbell and Fell* v. *UK*, A 80 (1984) (prison discipline). It was confirmed in *Ezeh and Connors* v. *UK* (2004) 39 EHRR 1 that a prison disciplinary offence that led to the imposition of 'additional days' of imprisonment amounted to a 'criminal charge', and engaged the full protection of Art. 6 (including right to representation (Art. 6(3)(b)). But Art. 6 is not engaged in this way with 'lifers' (on whom additional days cannot be imposed) (*Tangney* v. *Governor of HMP Elmley and Home Secretary* [2005] EWCA Civ 1009)). A recall to prison of a prisoner released on licence is also not criminal (*R (Smith and West)* v. *Parole Board* [2005] UKHL 1, [2005] 1 WLR 350, para. 40). Tax penalties are 'criminal' (*Bendenoun* v. *France* A 284 (1994); cf. *Schouten and Meldrum* v. *Netherlands* A304 (1994)). Article 6(1) is applicable to road traffic offences even where the national law does not consider them criminal: *Ozturk* v. *FRG*, A 73 (1984).

[35] *Le Compte, Van Leuven and de Meyere* v. *Belgium* (1982) 4 EHRR 1, and *Mattu* v. *The University Hospitals of Coventry and Warwickshire NHS Trust* [2012] EWCA Civ 641. 'The right to carry on one's profession is undoubtedly a civil right' (para. 50, *obiter*). But Art. 6(1) does not apply to disciplinary proceedings which may end an individual's employment but leave him or her still able to practise their profession by finding employment elsewhere. Thus, in *Mattu*, Art. 6(1) found not applicable to proceedings to dismiss a medical practitioner from his employment by a health authority. But does apply to proceedings before the GMC which determine whether the practitioner can continue to practise. And see, to like effect, *R (G)* v. *X School* [2011] UKSC 30 (Art. 6(1) not applicable unless proceedings directly decisive of civil rights; thus not applicable to disciplinary proceedings by employer (X School) (dismissal for gross misconduct (inappropriate relationship with pupil)); but Art. 6(1) applicable to proceedings before the Independent Safeguarding Authority (which determined whether G could work with children at all) and to which the school was bound to report the dismissal. In *X School* the Supreme Court approved and applied the test laid down by Laws LJ in the Court of Appeal ([2010] EWCA Civ 1) but reached a different conclusion and allowed the appeal. Laws LJ said: 'where an individual is subject to two or more sets of proceedings...and a "civil right [or] obligation" enjoyed or owed by him will be determined in one of them, he may (not

scheme to penalise carriers who bring clandestine entrants into the UK has been held to be criminal, since the objective of the scheme was to deter dishonesty and carelessness.[36]

Thus Article 6(1) does not impose a general duty upon administrative bodies to provide a fair and impartial hearing to those affected by their decisions. The circumstances of each case must be investigated to see whether Article 6(1) is engaged. The various matters to which Article 6(1) has been held by the Court or the Commission to be applicable (or inapplicable) are sketched later.

But the domestic courts have established two general restrictions on the scope of Article 6(1). First of all, the suggestion 'that the effect of the Human Rights Act 1998 (giving a domestic civil remedy for violations of Convention rights)[37] was to convert all claims of infringement of Convention rights into civil rights within the meaning of Article 6' is not well founded. The reach of Article 6(1) was determined by the 'nature of the proceedings and not the articles of the Convention which are alleged to be violated'.[38] Thus Article 6(1) was not applicable to a decision to segregate a prisoner even though his Article 8 rights were (arguably) engaged by the segregation.[39]

Secondly, the Supreme Court has held that decisions 'that cases where the award of services or benefits in kind is not an individual right of which the applicant can consider himself the holder, but is dependent upon a series of evaluative judgments by the provider as to whether the statutory criteria are satisfied and how the need for it ought to be met, do not engage article 6(1)'.[40] Thus the duties of local authorities to house homeless persons (under Part VII of the Housing Act 1996) do not engage Article 6(1). One result of this is that many, but not all welfare schemes will fall outside the scope of Article 6(1).[41] Many regulatory schemes will also involve such evaluative judgments and so are excluded from the protection of Article 6(1). There is significant sensitivity to the possibility that extending too broad a reach to Article 6(1) will lead to the judicialisation of administrative decision-making.[42]

The following matters have all been held not to engage Article 6(1) on the ground that there is no determination of the applicant's civil rights and obligations: immigration

---

necessarily will) by force of Article 6 enjoy appropriate procedural rights in relation to any of the others if the outcome of that other will have a substantial influence or effect on the determination of the civil right or obligations' (para. 37).

[36] *International Transport Roth GmbH* v. *Home Secretary* [2002] 3 WLR 344 (CA) (per Simon Brown LJ and Jonathan Parker LJ; contra Laws LJ). Once recognised as criminal the further protections (including the presumption of innocence) contained in Art. 6(2) and (3) are engaged.

[37] See above, p. 129, and below, p. 635.

[38] *R (King and ors)* v. *Secretary of State for Justice* [2012] EWCA Civ 376, para. 56 (Kay LJ).

[39] There was no common law right to associate that was determined by the decision to segregate.

[40] *Tomlinson and ors* v. *Birmingham City Council* [2010] UKSC 8 (this case appears in some reports as *Ali* v. *Birmingham City Council*), para. 49 Lord Hope. Cf. Lord Collins preferring the lack of precision of the statutory duty (para. 58); there was no right to any particular accommodation.

[41] *R (A)* v. *London Borough of Croydon* [2009] UKSC 8.

[42] These domestic decisions on the reach of Art. 6(1) seem consistent with the decision of the ECtHR in *Crompton* v. *UK* (2010) 50 EHRR 36. 'Whereas in *Bryan*, the issues to be determined required a measure of professional knowledge or experience and the exercise of administrative discretion pursuant to wider policy aims, in *Tsfayo* the Housing Benefits Review Board ('HBRB') was deciding a simple question of fact, namely whether there was 'good cause' for the applicant's delay in making a housing benefit claim...No specialist expertise was required to determine this issue. Nor could the factual findings in *Tsfayo* be said to be merely incidental to the reaching of broader judgments of policy or expediency which it was for the democratically accountable authority to take' (para. 73).

and deportation,[43] entitlement to tax benefits,[44] the payment of discretionary grants,[45] public employment (but subject to growing exceptions),[46] the procedures adopted by official investigations (such as a DTI inquiry),[47] the revocation of a licence by the Parole Board,[48] disciplinary proceedings in employment (even if the employer is a public authority)[49] and freezing orders made under statute to deny access to funds to persons suspected of terrorism.[50] This is not a complete list.[51]

On the other hand, there are cases where administrative proceedings are considered to be 'decisive' of civil rights even where that is not their purpose. For instance, where a contract for the sale of land was conditional upon the grant of permission by an administrative tribunal to use the land for non-agricultural purposes, Article 6(1) was held to apply to the proceedings of that tribunal.[52] For similar reasons Article 6(1) generally applies to matters directly regulating property rights and commercial activity through the grant of licences (or similar devices).[53] Claims for welfare benefits must be considered with particular care. Where the law defines the right with precision (e.g. the payment to the claimant of a particular sum) Article 6(1) will be engaged; but where an evaluative judgment has to

---

[43] *X, Y, Z, V and W* v. *UK* (App. No. 3325/67) (1967) 10 YB 528; *Uppal and Singh* v. *UK* (App. No. 8244/78) (1979) 17 D & R 149 (entry); *Agee* v. *UK* (App. No. 7729/76) (1976) 7 DR 164 (deportation); *Maaouia* v *France*(App. No. 39652/98) [2000] ECtHR 455 (confirming *Agee* but pointing out that deportees are protected by Protocol 7, Art. 1).

[44] *Huber* v. *Austria* (App. No. 8903/80) (1981) 21 D & R 246; *Ferrazini* v. *Italy* (App. No. 44759/98) [2001] STC 1314. But proceedings for the recovery of overpaid tax are within Art. 6(1): *National and Provincial Building Society* v. *UK* (1997) 25 EHRR 127 (including judicial review of regulations designed to prevent such recovery).

[45] *X* v. *Sweden* (App. No. 6776/74) (1976) 2 D & R 123 and *B* v. *Netherlands* (App. No. 11098/84) (1985) 43 D & R 198 (criminal injuries compensation). Cf. *Rolf Gustafson* v. *Sweden* (1997) 25 EHRR 623.

[46] *X* v. *UK* (App. No. 8496/79) (1981) 21 D & R 168; *Maillard* v. *France* (1999) 27 EHRR 232. But the 'public employment' exception is weakening. In *Pellegrin* v. *France*, 28541/95, [1999] ECtHR 140 (8 December 1999) the Human Rights Court held that civil servants who did not wield a portion of the State's sovereign power fell within Art. 6(1). Civil servants who did wield such powers (such as the armed forces and the police) owed a special bond of trust and loyalty to the State and this justified their exclusion from the protection of Art. 6(1). A further step was taken in *Vilho Eskelinen and ors* v. *Finland*, 63235/00, [2007] ECtHR 314 where the court held that for a civil servant to be outside Art. 6(1) 'national law must have expressly excluded access to a court' for that category of staff and 'the exclusion must be justified on objective grounds in the State's interest'. In *Crosbie* v. *Secretary of State for Defence* [2011] EWHC 879 an army chaplain's exclusion from Art. 6(1) was held 'objectively justified' (para. 114).

[47] *Fayed* v. *UK*, A 294, (1994) 18 EHRR 393 (investigation did not determine rights).

[48] *R (Smith)* v. *Parole Board (No 2)* [2003] EWCA Civ 1269, [2004] 1 WLR 421.

[49] *R (G)* v. *X School* [2011] UKSC 30; *Mattu* v. *The University Hospitals of Coventry and Warwickshire NHS Trust* [2012] EWCA Civ 641.

[50] *Secretary of State for the Foreign Office & Commonwealth Affairs* v. *Maftah and anor* [2011] EWCA Civ 350, paras. 24–6 (while the freezing order had an impact on civil rights, it did not determine them as required by Art. 6(1)).

[51] See the full accounts in [1984] PL 89 (Boyle); (1998) 1 European Public Law 347 (Bradley); Harris, O'Boyle and Warbrick, *Law of the European Convention on Human Rights*, 2nd edn (2009), 170; Janis, Kay and Bradley, *European Human Rights Law: Text and Materials*, 3rd edn (Oxford, 2008), 787ff. and Grosz, Beatson and Duffy, *Human Rights: The 1998 Act and the European Convention* (2000), 227–9. Cooper (above) lists the matters within and without Art. 6(1).

[52] *Ringeisen* v. *Austria*, A 13, (1971) 1 EHRR 455. The administrative decision must be directly decisive; a remote connection is insufficient: *Lecompte, Van Leuven and De Meyere* case (above). Planning appeals do engage Art. 6(1) since they affect the value (and enjoyment) of land (*Ortenburg* v. *Austria* (1995) 19 EHRR 524 (appeal against grant of planning permission)).

[53] *Hakansson and Sturesson* v. *Sweden*, A 171 (1990); *Bentham* v. *Netherlands* (1986) 8 EHRR 1: *Tre Traktorer Aktiebolag* v. *Sweden* (1989) 13 EHRR 309. And *Sporrong and Lonnroth* v. *Sweden* (App. Nos. 7151/75; 7152/75) [1982] ECtHR 5 (expropriation proceedings).

be made (is this accommodation suitable?) the claim will fall outside the article.[54] The fair administration of justice, as protected by Article 6(1), is considered of such importance that the Court has said that it is not to be restrictively interpreted.[55]

Article 6(1) is thus potentially relevant in many cases and a close analysis of the relevant domestic law in the light of the decisions of the Court will often be required. Where Article 6(1) is engaged domestic courts and tribunals will take into account the authoritative interpretations laid down by the Court.[56] There have been influential warnings against 'undermining the imperative of legal certainty by excessive debates over how many angels can dance on the head of the Article 6 pin'.[57] But some uncertainty is inherent in the extension of Article 6(1) to administrative proceedings. The court may decline to enter into consideration of whether Article 6(1) is applicable if it considers that it would not 'afford any greater protection' than the 'common law duty of procedural fairness'.[58]

THE CURATIVE EFFECT OF ACCESS TO A COURT OF 'FULL JURISDICTION'

Even where Article 6(1) does apply, the European Court has not insisted that the public authority or other primary decision-maker should comply with every aspect of it. This is fortunate since many administrative decision-makers do not comply with the essentially judicial standards of impartiality and independence required by Article 6(1). What the Court does insist upon is that the applicant aggrieved by the decision of the primary decision-maker should be able to bring the dispute before a court of 'full jurisdiction'. If this is possible, the procedure as a whole is compliant and the defect at first instance is cured. Thus the crisp question often arises whether the application for judicial review (or other judicial remedy) is sufficient to remedy any falling short of the standards of Article 6(1) by the original decision-maker.[59] The principle that access to the judicial review court may cure a defect, provided that the procedure as a whole complies with Article 6(1), is well recognised.[60]

The House of Lords has stressed that the curative principle is to be flexibly applied in a way that is sensitive to the context in which it arises. 'Full jurisdiction' Lord Hoffmann has

---

[54] *Feldbrugge* v. *Netherlands* (1986) 8 EHRR 425 (sickness benefit claim associated with private contract of employment and contributory) made plain that Art. 6(1) was applicable to claims for benefits analogous to insurance claims. *Salesi* v. *Italy* (1993) 26 EHRR 1122 (claim for wholly state-funded non-contributory disability pension) upheld the applicability of the article, even where there was no private law analogy, to individual, economic claims to rights flowing from specific statutory rules. See to like effect *Mennitto* v. *Italy* (2000) 34 EHRR 1122. But as adumbrated the domestic courts now hold that Art. 6(1) is not engaged where 'evaluative judgments' have to be made, e.g. whether certain accommodation was suitable: *Tomlinson*, para. 49. This new approach departs from that assumed (but not decided) in *Runa Begum*, viz. that Art. 6(1) was applicable even to welfare schemes that granted benefits in kind. The relationship between the reach of Art. 6(1) and the 'curative principle' is discussed below, p. 382.
[55] *Delcourt* v. *Belgium* (1973) 1 EHRR 355.   [56] Human Rights Act 1998, s. 2(1).
[57] *R (Beeson's Personal Representatives)* v. *Secretary of State for Health* [2002] EWCA 1812, para. 15 (Laws LJ).   [58] *Smith and West*, above, para. 44 (Lord Bingham).
[59] See [2003] *JR* 90 (R. Clayton and V. Sachdeva). Similar issues may arise in considering whether a right of appeal to a court of law from a tribunal decision suffices for compliance with Art. 6(1). See below, p. 381.
[60] *Bryan* v. *UK* (1995) 21 EHRR 342 and *Alconbury Developments* below.

said means 'full jurisdiction to deal with the case as the nature of the decision requires'.[61] Moreover, Lord Bingham has pointed to the relationship between the reach of the Article 6(1) and the intensity of the judicial scrutiny required to cure non-compliance at first instance: 'the narrower the interpretation given to "civil rights", the greater the need to insist upon review by a judicial tribunal exercising full powers. Conversely, the more elastic the interpretation given to "civil rights", the more flexible must be the approach to the requirement of independent and impartial review if the emasculation (by over judicialisation) of administrative welfare schemes is to be avoided.'[62] Thus the more administrative and less judicial the decision-making process set up by Parliament may be the less intensive will be the judicial scrutiny of the decision to secure compliance. The fact that 'the legality of virtually all government decisions' may be subjected to judicial scrutiny allows English law to 'view with equanimity the extension of the scope of Article 6'. This allows the courts to have proper regard 'to democratic accountability, efficient administration and the sovereignty of Parliament' in setting the measure of procedural justice in any particular case.[63]

Lord Hoffmann's equanimity in this regard should not develop into complacency. The Human Rights Court has clearly signalled that there are limits to the operation of the curative principle. Where judicial review cannot adequately set right what has gone wrong at first instance, the principle will not operate and reforms to administrative procedures will be required to comply with Article 6(1).[64] Similarly, the consequences of the initial decision may be so profound that non-compliance with Article 6(1) cannot be cured.[65] And in another case[66] Laws LJ has suggested that the 'curative' principle is applicable only when there is an administrative or executive decision which is subject to judicial review; it has no application when the second procedure does not control or correct errors of the initial process.

As foreshadowed above, however, the common law imposes a far-reaching and sophisticated duty of procedural fairness upon those who decide administrative matters.

---

[61] *R (Alconbury Developments Ltd)* v. *Secretary of State for the Environment* [2001] UKHL 23, [2001] 2 WLR 1389, para. 87 approved by Lord Bingham in *Runa Begum* (as above), para. 5.

[62] *Runa Begum* (as above), para. 5. And in *R (Wright)* v. *Secretary of State for Health* [2009] UKHL 3, para. 23 Baroness Hale said: 'What amounts to "full jurisdiction" varies according to the nature of the decision being made. It does not always require access to a court or tribunal even for the determination of disputed issues of fact. Much depends upon the subject matter of the decision and the quality of the initial decision-making process. If there is a "classic exercise of administrative discretion", even though determinative of civil rights and obligations, and there are a number of safeguards to ensure that the procedure is in fact both fair and impartial, then judicial review may be adequate to supply the necessary access to a court, even if there is no jurisdiction to examine the factual merits of the case.'

[63] The quotations come from Lord Hoffmann's speech in *Runa Begum* (para. 35).

[64] These limitations are discussed at p. 392. See *Kingsley* v. *UK* 35605/97 [2000] ECtHR 528 (non-compliance with Art. 6(1) where judicial review unable to order decision retaken by impartial and independent body) and *Tsfayo* v. *UK* (App. No. 60860/00) [2006] ECtHR 981 (judicial review court unable to correct finding of fact by non-complying first instance body) and (2007) 66 *CLJ* 487 (Forsyth).

[65] As in *Wright*, above 382, where a declaration was made that the Care Standards Act 2000, s. 82(4)(b) was incompatible with Art. 6(1). The section provided for the provisional inclusion (without a hearing) of a care worker on a list of persons unsuitable to work with vulnerable adults, where the care worker has been dismissed by their employer on the ground of misconduct that put a vulnerable adult at risk. Such listing prevents the care worker from working in that field. Although there was a review procedure and a right of appeal to the Care Standards Tribunal, non-compliance at first instance could not be cured.

[66] *R (G)* v. *X School* [2010] EWCA Civ 1, paras. 42–3; but the suggestion was left open in the Supreme Court [2011] UKSC 30, para. 84 (Lord Dyson). The case is discussed further at p. 378.

Although there are bound to be some difficult cases,[67] the incorporation of the Convention should not entail many fundamental changes of practice, and those that it will require should be beneficial. None the less, the uncertainty in Convention law discussed in this chapter ensures that, even if the decision is eventually reached that either Article 6(1) is inapplicable or that there has been compliance with it, there is ample scope for administrative action to be challenged on the ground of non-compliance.

---

[67] Primarily over the requirement of a determination 'by an independent and impartial tribunal'.

13

THE RULE AGAINST BIAS

JUDICIAL AND ADMINISTRATIVE IMPARTIALITY

'NO MAN A JUDGE IN HIS OWN CAUSE'

Nemo judex in re sua.[1] A judge is disqualified from determining any case in which he may be, or may fairly be suspected to be, biased.[2] The classic example of an offence against this rule in the regular courts of law is that of Lord Chancellor Cottenham in 1852, who in a Chancery suit had affirmed a number of decrees made by the Vice-Chancellor in favour of a canal company in which Lord Cottenham was a shareholder to the extent of several thousand pounds. Lord Cottenham's decrees were set aside by the House of Lords on account of his pecuniary interest;[3] but the House then itself dealt with the appeal on its merits, and affirmed the decrees of the Vice-Chancellor.[4] It was not shown that Lord Cottenham's decision was in any way affected by his interests as a shareholder; in fact it was clearly not affected at all, for Lord Campbell said:[5]

> No one can suppose that Lord Cottenham could be, in the remotest degree, influenced by the interest that he had in this concern; but, my Lords, it is of the last importance that the maxim, that no man is to be a judge in his own cause, should be held sacred. And that is not to be confined to a cause in which he is a party, but applies to a cause in which he has an interest...And it will have a most salutary influence on [inferior] tribunals when it is known that this high Court of last resort, in a case in which the Lord Chancellor of England had an interest, considered that his decree was on that account a decree not according to law, and was set aside. This will be a lesson to all inferior tribunals to take care not only that in their decrees they are not influenced by their personal interest, but to avoid the appearance of labouring under such an influence.

A modern case, where the offending interest was of a non-pecuniary kind, has become equally well known, since it is the source of the quotation, overworked but nonetheless true, that 'justice should not only be done, but should manifestly and undoubtedly be seen to be done'.[6] A solicitor was acting for a client who was suing a motorist for damage

---

[1] See generally [2000] *PL* 45 (D. G. T. Williams) and 'The Modern Approach to Bias' (James Maurici), available at <http://www.adminlaw.org.uk/docs/James%20Maurici%20-%20July%202007.doc>.

[2] The suggestion by Coke CJ in *Egerton v. Lord Derby* (1613) 12 Co Rep 114 (and elsewhere) that this rule would prevail over an Act of Parliament has not been followed: *Parish of Great Charte v. Parish of Kennington* (1742) 2 Str. 1173. See also [1974] *CLJ* 80 (D. E. C. Yale).

[3] *Dimes v. Grand Junction Canal* (1852) 3 HLC 759. Non-pecuniary interest is sufficient where the judge is one of the parties. See *R v. Bow Street Magistrate ex p Pinochet Ugarte (No 2)* [2000] 1 AC 119 (HL), discussed below, p. 385, for a modern example.   [4] See 3 HLC 794.

[5] 3 HLC at 793.

[6] *ex p McCarthy*, below at 259. To like effect see Atkin LJ in *Shrager v. Basil Dighton Ltd* [1924] 1 KB 274 at 284. Lord Bingham MR's remark that: '[This] famous aphorism...is no longer, it seems, good law': (*R v. Inner West London Coroner ex p Dallaglio* [1994] 4 All ER 139 at 162) is mistaken. See the discussion below, p. 394.

caused in a road accident. The solicitor was also acting clerk to the justices before whom the same motorist was convicted of dangerous driving and he retired with them when they were considering their decision. The fact that the clerk's firm was acting against the interests of the convicted motorist in other proceedings was held to invalidate the conviction, even though it was proved that the justices had not in fact consulted the clerk and that he had scrupulously refrained from saying anything prejudicial.[7]

AUTOMATIC DISQUALIFICATION IN CERTAIN CASES

The case concerning Lord Chancellor Cottenham, just described, is an example of the rule that a direct pecuniary interest disqualifies the decision-maker. It became the rule that any direct pecuniary interest, however small, was a disqualification,[8] and this rule was applied rigorously.[9] Indeed, in a prominent modern case, the House of Lords has affirmed that the principle of automatic disqualification in fact extends beyond pecuniary and proprietary interests.[10] It applies equally where the judge is himself a party or has a relevant interest in the subject matter of the litigation, even if he has no financial interest in its outcome. The case concerned an appeal before the House of Lords in which the Crown Prosecution Service sought to overturn the quashing by the Divisional Court of extradition warrants made against a former head of state. Amnesty International (AI) was given leave to intervene in the proceedings before the House of Lords. Unknown to the representatives of the former head of state at the time, one of the law lords was in fact an (unpaid) director and chairperson of Amnesty International Charity Limited (AICL), a company under the control of Amnesty International which was formed to carry out the charitable parts of Amnesty International's activities. The law lord, who did not disclose his links with AI, had no financial interest in the outcome and was not a party to the proceedings, but the 'substance of the matter is that AI...and AICL are all various parts of an entity or movement working in different fields towards the same goals'.[11] This was enough automatically to disqualify the law lord; and the matter was reheard before a differently constituted Appeal Committee. The circumstances of this case were most unusual; it is difficult to see what other non-pecuniary interests will suffice other than the obvious one where the judge is a party.[12]

The automatic disqualification rule has been subject to telling criticism.[13] If the circumstances are such that there is no reasonable apprehension of bias (perhaps because

---

[7] R v. Sussex Justices ex p McCarthy [1924] 1 KB 256.

[8] R v. Rand (1866) LR 1 QB 230; R v. Meyer (1875) 1 QBD 173; R v. Farrant (1887) 20 QBD 58; R v. Barnsley Licensing Justices ex p Barnsley and District Licensed Victuallers' Association [1960] 2 QB 167.

[9] See e.g. R v. Cambridge Recorder (1857) 8 E & B 637. In R v. Farrant (above) it was held that a magistrate who made a bet on the result of the case would be disqualified for pecuniary interest. But this rule was rejected by the High Court of Australia in Ebner v. Official Trustee (2000) 205 CLR 337 (action by Official Trustee to set aside transfer of property to bankrupt's spouse; the judge was beneficiary of trust which owned shares in creditor bank that would benefit if transfer set aside: held no rule of automatic disqualification and no reasonable apprehension of bias).

[10] R v. Bow Street Magistrate ex p Pinochet Ugarte (No 2), above.

[11] Ibid. at 135 (Lord Browne-Wilkinson).

[12] The automatic disqualification rule was held inapplicable in Meerabux v. A-G of Belize [2005] UKPC 12, [2005] 2 WLR 1307 (PC) (complaint made to Governor General by Bar Association alleging misbehaviour by judge; constitutional Advisory Council convened to consider complaint, chaired by another judge who was (as required by law) a member of Bar Association); no 'personal or pecuniary' interest found, no automatic disqualification.

[13] See, particularly, [2000] PL 456 (Olowofoyeku) (automatic disqualification no better than reasonable apprehension of bias at protecting the integrity of the administration of justice; and the consequences of the rule 'draconian' (at 475)).

the financial interest involved is trivial) justice may be better served by upholding rather than quashing the impugned decision. There have been influential suggestions in the courts that the automatic disqualification rule might be assimilated into the test of apprehension of bias;[14] only if such an apprehension existed would the automatic disqualification rule apply. But for the moment the automatic disqualification rule remains the law. As we shall see the modern test of apprehension, that of the 'fair-minded and well-informed observer' (shortly to be described) is itself criticised for uncertainty. At least the automatic disqualification rule is relatively certain.

A HISTORY OF THE TEST OF BIAS: 'REAL LIKELIHOOD', 'REAL DANGER', 'REASONABLE SUSPICION' AND 'REAL POSSIBILITY' AND 'THE FAIR-MINDED AND WELL-INFORMED OBSERVER'

In cases where there is no automatic disqualification it then has to be determined whether the judge's or decision-maker's interest in the matter is sufficient to justify disqualification. What is the test of apparent bias? This question has a tangled history although the modern test, set out later, is now relatively clear. Much confusion has been caused in the past by the concurrent use of differently formulated tests for disqualifying bias. In the past many judges have laid down and applied a 'real likelihood' formula, holding that the test for disqualification is whether the facts, as assessed by the court, give rise to a real likelihood of bias;[15] and this test has naturally been emphasised in cases where the allegation of bias was far-fetched.[16] Other judges have employed a 'reasonable suspicion' test, emphasising that justice must be seen to be done, and that no person should adjudicate in any way if it might reasonably be thought that he ought not to act because of some personal interest.[17]

In 1954 a Divisional Court, after reviewing authorities, decided firmly in favour of real likelihood.[18] But in 1968 the Court of Appeal decided equally firmly in favour of reasonable suspicion,[19] although Lord Denning MR interwove this with the other test. This decision reasserted 'justice must be seen to be done' as the operative principle. But 'it left a legacy of some confusion'[20] in 'a somewhat confusing welter of authority'.[21] In 1993 the House of Lords affirmed the 'real likelihood' test in a criminal case,[22] though preferring

---

[14] *R (Kaur) v. Institute of Legal Executives Appeal Tribunal* [2011] EWCA Civ 1168, [2012] 1 All ER 1435. Automatic disqualification and apparent bias could be brought together into 'a single over-arching requirement: that judges should not sit or should face recusal or disqualification where there is a real possibility on the objective appearances of things, assessed by the fair-minded and informed observer... that the tribunal could be biased' (para. 45, Rix LJ). And see *Meerabux*, above, para. 23 (Lord Hope) (no need for automatic disqualification if modern test for apprehension of bias available).

[15] *R v. Rand* (1866) LR 1 QB 230; *R v. Sunderland Justices* (1901) 2 KB 357; *Frome United Breweries Co v. Bath Justices* [1926] AC 586; *R v. Camborne Justices ex p Pearce* [1955] 1 QB 41; *Healey v. Rauhina* [1958] NZLR 945; *Hannam v. Bradford Corporation* [1970] 1 WLR 937.

[16] See *R v. Camborne Justices*, above.

[17] The numerous decisions include *R v. Gaisford* [1892] 1 QB 381; *R v. Sussex Justices ex p McCarthy* [1924] 1 KB 256; *Cooper v. Wilson* [1937] 2 KB 309 at 324, 344; *Metropolitan Properties Co (FGC) Ltd v. Lannon* [1969] 1 QB 577.

[18] *R v. Camborne Justices ex p Pearce*, above. See similarly *R v. Nailsworth Licensing Justices ex p Bird* [1953] 1 WLR 1046.   [19] *Metropolitan Properties Co (FGC) Ltd v. Lannon* [1969] 1 QB 577.

[20] *R v. Gough* (below) (Lord Goff).

[21] *Hannam. v. Bradford Cpn* [1970] 1 WLR 937 (Widgery LJ).

[22] *R v. Gough* [1993] AC 646 (juror recognised accused's brother as her next-door neighbour, but not until after the verdict: held, no real danger of bias). But where a juror knew vital witnesses and did not reveal

to state it in terms of 'real danger',[23] so as to emphasise that 'the court is thinking in terms of possibility rather than probability of bias'. In a significant passage Lord Goff added: 'I think it unnecessary, in formulating the appropriate test, to require that the court should look at the matter through the eyes of a reasonable man, because the court in cases such as these personifies the reasonable man; and in any event the court has first to ascertain the relevant circumstances from the available evidence, knowledge of which would not necessarily be available to an observer in court at the relevant time.'

This change of perspective—from the point of view of the reasonable observer to that of the court in possession of all the relevant evidence—led the Court of Appeal to conclude in one case[24] that 'by the time the legal challenge comes to be resolved, the court is no longer concerned strictly with the appearance of bias but rather with establishing that there was actual although unconscious bias'.[25] '[If] despite the appearance of bias', Lord Bingham MR said, 'the court is able to examine all the relevant material and satisfy itself that there was no danger of the alleged bias having in fact caused injustice, the impugned decision will be allowed to stand'.[26]

The change in perspective may be illustrated by a case in which a lay member of the Restrictive Practices Court applied for employment with a consultancy firm, not recalling that a director of that firm was a principal expert witness in a case before the court.[27] By the time set for hearing it was clear that there was no suitable employment for the lay member with that firm and that a full explanation including an undertaking not to seek employment with that firm in the future, had been given to the parties. While a judge who accepted the lay member's explanation might conclude there was 'no real danger' of bias, the fair-minded observer, the Court of Appeal decided, might have concluded that the lay member's favourable estimation of the firm that led to the application for employment 'indicated a partiality to them which could not be undone' by the explanation.

THE MODERN TEST

Since the jurisprudence of the European Convention on Human Rights insists that the appearance of bias, even if there is no actual bias, is sufficient to taint a decision as a breach of Article 6(1)[28] the 'real danger' test, interpreted as in the first-mentioned case, introduced a discrepancy between the Convention and the common law in ensuring impartial decision-making. In addition it disregarded the hallowed principle that justice must be seen to be done. The House of Lords, in recognition of this discrepancy, has now made 'a modest adjustment'—in truth a substantial adjustment—to the real danger test and

---

this to the court, a real danger was found: *R* v. *K*, The Times, 14 April 1995. See also *R* v. *Wilson and Strason* (1996) 8 Admin LR 1.

[23] But the real danger test did not find favour in some commonwealth jurisdictions: *Moch* v. *Ned Travel (Pty) Ltd* 1996 (3) SA1 (AD); *Webb* v. *R* (1994) 181 CLR 41; *Doherty* v. *McGlennan*, 1997 SLT 444. In *Roylance* v. *The General Medical Council (No 2)* [2000] 1 AC 311, the Privy Council did not find it necessary to choose between the different tests.

[24] *R* v. *Inner West London Coroner ex p Dallaglio* [1994] 4 All ER 139. For criticism see [1996] *JR* 102 (Rayment).

[25] Simon Brown LJ at 152. And if the decision-maker is shown not to know about the disqualifying interest no question of unconscious bias can arise: *Locabail (UK) Ltd* v. *Bayfield Properties Ltd* (above) para. 18 and *Auckland Casino Ltd* v. *Casino Control Authority* [1995] 1 NZLR 142 at 148.

[26] *Ex p Dallaglio*. This is the context in which Lord Bingham MR remarked that Lord Hewart's famous dictum was not good law.

[27] *Re Medicaments and Related Classes of Goods (No 2)* [2001] 1 WLR 700 (CA) (judgment of Lord Phillips MR proposing the 'modest adjustment' discussed below, p. 387).   [28] See below, p. 391.

ensured consistency between the Convention and the common law.[29] The case concerned
a leading counsel, a Recorder, who had been appointed by the Lord Chancellor to serve as
a part-time judge in the Employment Appeal Tribunal. He was briefed to appear before
an EAT which included lay members who had previously sat with him in his role as judge.
The test of bias laid down was 'whether the fair-minded and informed observer, having
considered the facts, would conclude that there was a real possibility that the tribunal was
biased'.[30] Applying this test the House of Lords concluded that it was reasonably possible
that that observer might consider that the recorder's submissions would carry particular
weight, perhaps subconsciously, with the lay members with whom he had sat in the past.[31]

This change in the test—and the shift in perspective—was firmly based in the necessity
of ensuring public confidence in the administration of justice.[32] The House of Lords made
clear though that the 'fair-minded and well-informed observer' would adopt a 'balanced
approach'[33] and was 'neither complacent nor unduly sensitive or suspicious'.[34] Although
aware of legal traditions that might enhance impartiality, he or she might be critical of
them.[35] The fair-minder observer is not an insider.

THE APPLICATION OF THE 'THE FAIR-MINDED AND WELL-INFORMED OBSERVER' TEST

Although the 'fair-minded and well-informed observer' test is now very well established
in formal law, its application has proved problematical. The test is, of course, not 'hard
edged' so a measure of uncertainty in its application is inevitable. But the difficulties with
the test are deeper than uncertainty in its application.

The classic statements of the test make it clear that the 'fair-minded and well-informed
observer' may 'be assumed to have access to all the facts that are capable of being known
by members of the public generally, bearing in mind that it is the appearance that these
facts give rise to that matters, not what is in the mind of the particular judge or tribunal
member who is under scrutiny'. But when in possession of all those facts, it is noteworthy
how seldom the 'fair-minded and well-informed observer' apprehends a possibility of bias.

Lord Rogers in a scintillating lecture[36] has expressed some scepticism about the
'fair-minded and well-informed observer'. He said:

> the whole point of inventing this fictional character is that he or she does not share the
> viewpoint of a judge. Yet, in the end, it is a judge or judges who decide what the observer

---

[29] *Lawal* v. *Northern Spirit Ltd* [2003] UKHL 35 following a dictum in *Porter* v. *Magill* [2001] UKHL 67,
[2002] 2 WLR 37 (HL) (discussed (2002) 61 *CLJ* Re 249 (R. Williams); (2002) 118 *LQR* 364 (J. Rowbottom)).
The 'modest adjustment' was first proposed in *Medicaments and Related Classes of Goods (No 2)* [2001] 1
WLR 700 (CA) (discussed above, p. 387). And see *Nwabueze* v. *General Medical Council* [2000] 1 WLR 1760
(PC).

[30] The cited words come from Lord Phillips's judgment in *Re Medicaments and Related Classes of Goods
(No 2)* (para. 85) adopted by Lord Hope in *Porter* v. *Magill* (para. 103) and Lord Bingham in *Lawal* (para. 14).
The test is discussed in [2005] *JR* 78 (Hanif).

[31] That this was a reasonable apprehension in such circumstances was shown by the specific rules that
precluded part-time judges in Employment Tribunals from appearing before ETs containing lay members
with whom they had previously sat.

[32] The Strasbourg jurisprudence (as well as the traditional common law) stressed this. See, for instance,
Belilos v. *Switzerland* (1988) 10 EHRR 466, para. 67, and below, p. 391.   [33] Ibid.

[34] Lord Bingham in *Lawal* (ibid.) adopting a phrase of Kirby J in *Johnson* v. *Johnson* (2000) 200 CLR 488
(para. 53).   [35] Ibid.

[36] *Bias and Conflicts of Interests–Challenges for Today's Decision-Makers* being the 24th Sultan Azlan
Shah Law Lecture.

would think about any given situation. Moreover, the well-informed observer is supposed to know quite a lot about judges—about their training, about their professional experience, about their social interaction with other members of the legal profession, about the judicial oath and its significance for them etc. Endowing the well-informed observer with these pieces of knowledge is designed to ensure that any supposed appearance of bias is assessed on the basis of a proper appreciation of how judges and tribunals actually operate. The risk is that, if this process is taken too far, . . . the judge will be holding up a mirror to himself. To put the matter another way, the same process will tend to distance the notional observer from the ordinary man in the street who does not know these things. And yet the whole point of the exercise is to ensure that judges do not sit if to do so would risk bringing the legal system into disrepute with ordinary members of the public.

And there have indeed been cases in which it may well be thought that the judge held up a mirror to himself. In one case, for instance, a judge was held not disqualified in a case where one party's solicitors were already acting for that judge in relation to his will. The judge, in fact, met with the solicitors to execute a codicil to his will on the day of closing speeches and the day before he gave judgment.[37] The 'legal traditions and culture of this jurisdiction' (said Lord Woolf) would be known to the fair-minded observer who would consequently not suspect bias.

As we have seen the whole shift of perspective to the 'fair-minded and well-informed observer' was designed to secure public confidence in the administration of justice.[38] But, with due respect to Lord Woolf, the public whose confidence is to be secured is not as well informed about the applicable 'legal traditions and culture' as an experienced judge. And if that confidence is to be built, the fair-minded observer should not be imbued with all the knowledge of an experienced judge. Although this case purports to apply the 'fair-minded and well-informed observer' test, in fact it represents a shift of perspective back to whether the judge perceives a real danger of bias.

In a leading case a difference of view on this issue became apparent in the Privy Council.[39] The case concerned a financial and political dispute following a general election in Belize that led to a change of government. A payment of $10 million had been made to the Belize Bank by Venezuela and the dispute centred on whether these moneys should have been transferred to the Central Bank of Belize or whether the payment could be retained in settlement of a debt owed to the Belize Bank by the government of Belize. In the event, the Central Bank, in the exercise of statutory powers, issued a directive requiring the Belize Bank to credit the Central Bank's account with the $10 million forthwith. Such a directive was subject to appeal to an Appeal Board and that Board consisted of three members: the Chief Justice (or his nominee) and two persons with relevant knowledge appointed by the Finance Minister (provided that they were not serving members of the Central Bank or of any other bank or financial institution). At least two members, one of whom was required to be the Chief Justice (or his nominee) had to support any decision of the Board for it to be valid.

---

[37] *Taylor* v. *Lawrence* [2002] EWCA Civ 90, [2003] QB 528 (no 'significant injustice' justifying reopening of appeal).

[38] Confidence in the administration of justice by the unsuccessful litigant in the case just discussed has certainly not been secured. Several complaints against the judge involved have been made (but not upheld); and correspondence over the matter continues.

[39] *Belize Bank Ltd* v. *A-G (Belize)* [2011] UKPC 36.

The incoming Prime Minister who was also Minister of Finance had expressed himself robustly on the dispute, clearly favouring one side of the dispute; he was also the person who had to appoint two members of the Board. On the nomination of a senior civil servant two appropriately experienced persons were appointed; but would the 'fair-minded and well-informed observer' apprehend the real possibility of bias?

The majority of the Privy Council found that the 'fair-minded and well-informed observer' would not apprehend the real possibility of bias. But it is noteworthy that they were influenced by the nature of the jurisdiction in which the question arose. Lord Dyson for the majority, in finding that the fair-minded observer would not apprehend bias said: 'the Board should recognise that the judges of Belize are better equipped than we are to assess how the fair-minded and informed Belizean would view matters, also bearing in mind that Belize is a small country with a small pool of persons who would be likely to satisfy the statutory criteria for appointment as lay members of the Appeal Board'.[40] On the other hand, Lord Brown asked 'in the light of the appointment procedure adopted…[h]ow could it not strike such an observer that [the senior civil servant] may well have chosen these two Board members, and [the Prime Minister] so speedily have accepted his choice, because each felt confident that these two would instinctively be more sympathetic, ie predisposed, to the Central Bank's and government's cause than [Belize Bank]?'[41]

Viewed purely through the prism of the 'fair-minded and well-informed observer' test Lord Brown may be thought to be right. But in small jurisdictions qualified persons may be few in number and likely to be known to the parties; this may make the 'fair-minded and well-informed observer' test impractical. The doctrine of necessity, it may be thought, is where such considerations of size should play their role rather than in the distortion of the test.

FANCIFUL ALLEGATIONS OF BIAS

While the test of bias is unsatisfactory in application, clarity may be sought in the actual decisions. It may be noted that, generally, a challenge based on a personal interest or connection between the judge and the parties or witnesses is more likely to succeed than one based upon membership of particular organisations or institutes that may be thought to have an interest in the dispute.

A line must be drawn between genuine and fanciful cases. A justice of the peace is not disqualified, merely because he subscribes to a society for preventing cruelty to animals, from hearing a prosecution instituted by the society.[42] Where a county council had prosecuted a trader under the Food and Drugs Act, it was held no objection that the justices' clerk was a member of the council, upon proof that he was not a member of the council's Health Committee, which had in fact directed the prosecution.[43] The Court of Appeal, in this case, protested against the tendency to impeach judicial decisions 'upon the flimsiest pretexts of bias', and against 'the erroneous impression that it is more important that justice should appear to be done than that it should in fact be done'. Similarly, a deputy High Court judge was not disqualified because the solicitors' firm of which he was a partner

---

[40] Para. 75.   [41] Para. 112.

[42] R v. Deal Justices (1881) 45 LT 439. Cf. R v. Burton ex p Young [1897] 2 QB 468 and contrast R v. Huggins [1895] 1 QB 563.

[43] R v. Camborne Justices ex p Pearce [1955] 1 QB 41. Cf. R v. Minister of Agriculture and Fisheries ex p Graham [1955] 2 QB 140.

was, without his knowledge, involved in related litigation.[44] And a judge who was the director of a property company, which was the landlord of one of the parties, was not disqualified.[45] The judge did not know of this link but even if he had known there could in the circumstances 'not be a real danger of bias. The interest was so minimal, that no reasonable and fair-minded person sitting in court would have considered there was a real as opposed to a fanciful danger of a fair trial not being possible.'[46] On the other hand, where the judge had expressed himself vigorously but properly in law journal articles on the legal issues that subsequently arose before him he had crossed 'the ill defined line' and the Court of Appeal concluded that there was a real danger that 'a lay observer with knowledge of the facts' would not have excluded the possibility of unconscious bias.[47] Judicial criticism of the law must in the future be expressed in measured and restrained language.

MATTERS WHICH WILL NOT FOUND AN OBJECTION ON THE GROUND OF BIAS

In a leading case the Court of Appeal, speaking with the special authority of the Lord Chief Justice, the Master of the Rolls and the Vice-Chancellor together, laid down that, while everything will depend upon the facts and the nature of the issue to be decided, objections could not be based on religion, ethnic or national origin, gender, age, class, means or sexual orientation of the judge. Nor, ordinarily, would the judge's educational, social, employment or service background, nor his political associations, professional associations (e.g. membership of an Inn of Court), membership of social, sporting or charitable bodies (including Masonic associations), prior judicial decisions or views expressed in textbooks, lectures or articles, nor the fact that he had in the past received instructions from a party (or the parties' legal representatives) be relevant. But a history of personal friendship or animosity between the judge and a member of the public associated with the case (e.g. as party or witness)[48] may disqualify the judge.[49]

BIAS AND ARTICLE 6(1)

When Article 6(1) of the European Convention on Human Rights applies[50] it entitles those affected to the determination of their 'civil rights and obligations' or of any 'criminal charge' against them 'by an independent and impartial tribunal established

---

[44] *Locabail (UK) Ltd* v. *Bayfield Properties Ltd* [2000] 2 WLR 870 (CA).

[45] *R* v. *Bristol Betting and Gaming Licensing Committee ex p O'Callaghan* (heard with the *Locabail* case). See similarly *R* v. *Mulvihill* [1990] 1 WLR 438 (bank robber's appeal on the ground that judge held shares in the bank robbed failed since no one could reasonably suspect unfairness). [46] Ibid. at 906.

[47] *Timmins* v. *Gormely* (heard with the *Locabail* case). The phrase 'ill defined line' comes from *Vakauta* v. *Kelly* (1989) 167 CLR 568 at 571. Similarly, a senior Scottish judge who had published a newspaper article which painted a vivid but negative picture of the Convention's impact on the law, created a 'legitimate apprehension' in defendants that he would not act impartially in the protection of their Convention rights, and his decision was set aside (*Hoekstra* v. *Lord Advocate* [2001] 1 AC 216 (PC)).

[48] Thus a judge who had known a witness for thirty years was disqualified (*AWG Group Ltd* v. *Morrison* [2006] EWCA Civ 6, [2006]1 WLR 1163(CA) (recusal 'not a discretionary case management decision' in which inconvenience might outweigh the breach of impartiality).

[49] *Locabail (UK) Ltd* v. *Bayfield Properties Ltd* above. The principles laid down in this case are formally limited to judicial decision-makers (para. 3). The line was clearly crossed in *Howell* v. *Millais* [2007] EWCA Civ. 720 (judge refused to recuse himself).

[50] See above, p. 377 for an account of when it applies. Most of the bias cases concern criminal trials (which fall directly within Art. 6(1)) thus the Convention is frequently referred to in that area.

by law'. As explained above,[51] many administrative proceedings will be found to determine 'civil rights and obligations' and so the protection of the common law will be
overlaid with that of the Convention. In the Human Rights Court's jurisprudence,
the concept of impartiality is tested both subjectively—was there in fact bias?[52]—and
objectively—were there guarantees in place to exclude any legitimate doubt as to the
impartiality of the tribunal?[53] There is a clear relationship between the objective test
of bias and the home-grown principle that justice must be seen to be done. Indeed,
the importance of the appearance of impartiality has often been stressed by the court
which has stated that what 'is at stake is the confidence which the courts in a democratic society must inspire in the public and, above all, as far as criminal proceedings
are concerned, in the accused'.[54] The common law and the European Convention both
view impartiality as fundamental characteristics of fair procedure and in principle
there should be little conflict between them. And, the House of Lords has made 'a
modest adjustment' to the common law to ensure that there is congruence between the
two systems of protection.[55]

In one important respect, however, the Convention appears in conflict with the common law on bias. Many administrative decision-makers—for instance, ministers, civil
servants and local government employees—do not have the judicial independence or
impartiality required for compliance with Article 6(1). They lack security of tenure, they
are often open to influences from their employer and, as administrative decision-makers,
will often be influenced by policy in a way that is inappropriate for judicial officials.
Compliance with Convention standards of independence and impartiality appears to
require far-reaching and inconvenient reforms in administrative decision-making.

As explained earlier,[56] however, the European Court has not insisted that administrative decision-makers should comply with every aspect of Article 6(1). Non-compliance
can be cured by access to a court of 'full jurisdiction'. This has provided the means, particularly in regard to independence and impartiality, whereby the application of Article
6(1) is reconciled, without grave disruption, to existing administrative practice and law.
The European Court of Human Rights has signalled that where the procedure overall
remains unfair, there will be no curative effect.[57] This will be of particular significance in
cases of necessity.[58] Further difficult questions arise over the limits of this principle, for
instance, where the court to which there is access is one of 'full jurisdiction' etc. For the
detail reference should be made to the earlier discussion.

English law has not come up to Convention standards of impartiality and independence in other cases, but this has generally been because statutory provisions have been
found wanting.[59] In Scotland it has been held that temporary Sheriffs, appointed with no

---

[51]   Above, p. 377.   [52]   This is, of course, only established very rarely.
[53]   *Piersack* v. *Belgium*, A 53 (1982) 5 EHRR 169 and *Hauschildt* v. *Denmark*, A 154 (1989) 12 EHRR 266.
[54]   *Fey* v. *Austria*, A 255-A (1993) para. 30.   [55]   Above p. 387.   [56]   Above, p. 381.
[57]   See *Kingsley* v. *UK* (App. No. 35605/97), The Times, 9 January 2001, discussed below, p. 397.
[58]   Below, p. 395.
[59]   Courts martial procedure, for instance, until reform by the Armed Forces Act 1996 placed the decision to prosecute as well as the appointment of the court and the prosecuting and defending officers in
the hands of the convening officer who could vary the verdict. See *Findlay* v. *UK* (1997) 24 EHRR 221.
The reformed procedure is generally compliant: *Morris* v. *UK* (2002) 34 EHRR 1253 (procedure generally
compliant but considering that junior officers on court compromised independence); *R* v. *Spear* [2002] 3
WLR 437 (HL) (trial of civil offence by courts martial not in itself incompatible; upholding presence of
junior officers (ECtHR not fully informed)). Naval courts-martial were reformed by Remedial Order. See
above, p. 146.

security of tenure and subject to annual renewal by the Lord Advocate,[60] were not 'independent' as required by Article 6(1).[61]

ADMINISTRATIVE DECISIONS

Most decided cases on bias concern decisions of courts of law. The question now is how far the same rules can be applied to administrative decisions.

It was natural for the rule against bias to be applied generally to the functions of justices of the peace, whether judicial or administrative, and in this way the rule was readily adapted to administrative action. Thus in the eighteenth and nineteenth centuries, during the time when local government was mostly in the hands of the justices, many of their decisions were invalidated for bias in such matters as highway administration, poor law administration and liquor licensing. In 1705 the Court of Queen's Bench quashed a highway order because of the participation of a justice who was also the surveyor of the highway whose conduct was in question, and Holt CJ treated the case as analogous to one before a court of law.[62] Many similar decisions followed.[63] Twentieth-century judges have generally enforced the rule against bias in administrative proceedings no less strictly than their predecessors,[64] as exemplified by the following cases.

The mere presence of a non-member while a tribunal is deliberating is enough to invalidate the proceedings. Thus the proceedings of a Watch Committee, hearing an appeal by a police sergeant against his dismissal by his chief constable, were fatally flawed by the presence of the chief constable, whose mind was made up and who was in effect the respondent, during the committee's deliberations.[65] For similar reasons the court quashed the decision of a disciplinary committee which had consulted privately with the chief fire officer who had reported a fireman for indiscipline.[66] But the tribunal's clerk may sometimes attend.[67]

---

[60] In accordance with the Sheriff Courts (Scotland) Act 1971, s. 11.

[61] *Starrs* v. *Procurator Fiscal Linlithgow*, The Times, 17 November 1999. And *Singh* v. *Home Secretary*, The Times, 21 January 2004 (part-time immigration adjudicator not independent).

[62] *Foxham Tithing Case* (1705) 2 Salk 607.

[63] e.g. *Great Charte* v. *Kennington* (1730) 2 Str 1173; *R* v. *Cheltenham Commissioners* (1841) 1 QB 467; and the curious case of *R* v. *Great Yarmouth Justices ex p Palmer* (1882) 8 QBD 525.

[64] The proposition that different rules governed administrative proceedings to those that governed judicial proceedings was crisply rejected in *R* v. *Secretary of State for the Environment ex p Kirkstall Valley Campaign Ltd* [1996] 3 All ER 304 at 325 (Sedley J). Cf. *Eves* v. *Hambros Bank (Jersey) Ltd* [1996] 1 WLR 251 (Jurat, who had been director of bank, entitled to sit as judge in proceedings, to which defaulting mortgagor not party, confirming bank's tenancy over mortgaged property).

[65] *Cooper* v. *Wilson* [1937] 2 KB 309 (but in fact it was held that the sergeant had succeeded in resigning before his dismissal). Contrast *Kilduff* v. *Wilson* [1939] 1 All ER 429. And see *R* v. *Hendon Rural District Council ex p Chorley* [1933] 2 KB 696 establishing the same point in a planning context. Cf. *Samuel Smith Old Brewery (Tadcaster)* v. *City of Edinburgh Council*, 2001 SLJ 977 (convenor of development control committee declared interest and vacated chair, but remained present in place allocated to non-member councillors: decision upheld).   [66] *R* v. *Leicestershire Fire Authority ex p Thompson* (1978) 77 LGR 373.

[67] *Barrs* v. *British Wool Marketing Board*, 1957 SLT 153 and *McDonnell, Petitioner*, 1987 SLT 486 (allowing attendance) but contrast *ex p McCarthy* (above) and *R* v. *Birmingham Magistrates' Court ex p Ahmed* [1994] COD 461 (disallowing attendance in a judicial context). A justices' clerk may question a fine defaulter about his means but must do so impartially: *R* v. *Corby JJ ex p Mort*, The Times, 13 March 1998.

PREDETERMINATION, PREVIOUS INVOLVEMENT, POLICY AND THE APPEARANCE OF BIAS

The appearance of bias and predetermination are distinct concepts. Predetermination consists in 'the surrender by a decision-making body of its judgment',[68] for instance, by failing to apply his mind properly to the task at hand or by adopting an over-rigid policy. The decision is unlawful but not because it may appear biased (although in many cases it will). On the other hand, a decision-maker may apply his mind properly to the matter for decision and make a decision that is exemplary save that, because of some prior involvement or connection with the matter, the fair-minded observer would apprehend bias. The decision is once more unlawful but for a completely different reason. Only in rare cases will the distinction between these two concepts be significant.

The difference between predetermination and the appearance of bias has not always been appreciated. In one case the Court of Appeal considered the position wherein a protestor against opencast mining spoke briefly with the chairman of the Planning Decision Committee who told her he was 'going to go with the Inspector's Report'(which favoured the conditional grant of permission).[69] The court correctly treated this as if it were a case of 'possible predetermination' but it sought to apply the test of the fair-minded observer apprehending bias.[70] It found that the fair-minded observer would not apprehend bias and the decision was upheld. And in a later case in the Court of Appeal it was conceded that there were no 'closed minds', but the case proceeded to consider whether the fair-minded observer might nonetheless perceive a real possibility of predetermination.[71]

The significance of the conceptual distinction between predetermination and the apprehension of bias lies in the fact that administrative decision-makers, unlike judicial decision-makers, will often, quite rightly, be influenced, formally or informally, in their decision by policy considerations. They will naturally approach their task with a legitimate predisposition to decide in accordance with their previously articulated views or policies.[72] The fair-minded observer knows this, appreciates that there is no question of personal interest, and does not apprehend bias where there is simply a predisposition to decide one way rather than the other in accordance with previous policies. But where the question is whether the decision-maker has closed his mind and slipped from predisposition to predetermination it seems unnecessarily complicated to involve the fair-minded observer.

How the rule against bias applies in the context of policy-based administrative decisions (such as the decision of a planning authority) has long been a vexed issue. At times it has been suggested that less onerous rules in regard to bias apply to administrative decisions than apply to judicial decisions. But it is now clear that in accordance with general principle the same approach to bias should be adopted to both administrative and judicial decisions.[73] The distinction between predetermination and predisposition set out here, it is submitted, satisfactorily shows how the rule against bias applies in the context of policy-based administrative decisions.

---

[68] *Per* Sedley J in the *Kirkstall Valley* case at 317 (above).

[69] *National Assembly for Wales v. Condron* [2006] EWCA Civ. 1573 (Richards LJ).

[70] The judge relied upon *Georgiou v. Enfield LBC* [2004] EWHC 779 at para. 31. He considered that *Porter v. Magill* [2001] UKHL 67, [2002] 2 WLR 37 (HL) had collapsed the *Kirkstall Valley* approach to predetermination.

[71] *R (Lewis) v. Persimmon Homes Teesside Ltd* [2008] EWCA Civ. 746 adopting the *Georgiou*, above, approach.   [72] See further the discussion below, p. 402.

[73] *R v. Secretary of State for the Environment ex p Kirkstall Valley Campaign Ltd* [1996] 3 All ER 304 at 325 (Sedley J). Cf. *R v. Hereford and Worcester CC ex p Wellington Parish Council*, 94 LGR 159 (Harrison J).

In many of the contexts in which this question arises the decision-maker will be an elected councillor and a member of a political party. The courts have consistently declined to intervene where an administrative decision is influenced by the party political views of the elected decision-maker.[74] An influential case concerned the proposed construction of a rugby 'school of excellence' on land owned by the local council.[75] The council commenced negotiations for the disposal of the land to the rugby union and developers and granted planning permission for the development. Before terms could be agreed for the sale local elections were held in which the proposed development was an issue. A party opposed to the development came to power and passed a resolution not to sell the land in question to the developers. This latter decision was challenged by the developers on the ground that it was predetermined. The judge was pressed to apply the fair-minded observer test to this question but expressed his doubts.[76] Consistent with the analysis of predetermination above he held that in the absence of 'positive evidence' of a closed mind 'prior observations' favouring a particular decision would not suffice to justify quashing that decision.[77] In any event section 25(2) of the Localism Act 2011 now provides that a local authority decision-maker 'is not to be taken to have had, or to have appeared to have had, a closed mind when making the decision just because (a) the decision-maker had previously done anything that directly or indirectly indicated what view the decision-maker took, or would or might take, in relation to a matter, and (b) the matter was relevant to the decision'.[78]

These decisions also invite the comment that some of them might have been based more suitably on the rule of necessity, shortly to be explained.[79] When Parliament has empowered the same body both to undertake development and to grant planning permission, that body must perform both these functions as best it can despite the inevitable conflict between its roles as developer and as planner. This is the problem of indivisible authority discussed later. But this does not mean that the test of bias cannot apply to an administrative decision where it affects only particular members of a deciding body, who can be disqualified without making that body incompetent to act.

Where there is no dispute of fact, the procedure whereby a planning authority may grant planning permission in respect of land which it owns, has been held compliant with Article 6(1).[80]

INDIVISIBLE AUTHORITIES: CASES OF NECESSITY

In most of the cases so far mentioned the disqualified adjudicator could be dispensed with or replaced by someone to whom the objection did not apply. But there are many cases

---

[74] R v. Waltham Forest LBC ex p Baxter [1988] 1 QB 419; R v. Amber Valley District Council ex p Jackson [1984] 3 All ER 501 (Woolf J) confirmed in R (Lewis) v. Redcar and Cleveland Borough Council [2008] EWCA Civ 746, paras. 69–70 and R (Berky) v. Newport City Council [2012] EWCA Civ 378, para. 28.

[75] R (Island Farm Development Ltd) v. Bridgend County Borough Council [2006] EWHC 2189 (Admin); and see also Bovis Homes Ltd v. New Forest plc [2002] EWHC 483 (Admin) at paras. 111–13 (appearance of bias by one councillor sufficient (para. 103) but doubted in Berky, para. 30).

[76] Collins J, para. 30 distinguishing Porter v. Magill on the ground that it concerned a quasi-judicial decision. See also R (Loudon) v. Bury School Organisation Committee [2002] EWHC 2749 (Admin).

[77] And see the discussion in the Persimmon Homes case, above, para. 61.

[78] This provision is applicable when an 'allegation of bias or predetermination, or otherwise' calls the validity of a decision into question (s. 25(1)). Parliament has thus not committed itself on the conceptual distinction between the rule against bias and predetermination. [79] Below.

[80] R (Kathro) v. Rhondda Cynon Taff CBC [2001] EWHC 527 (Admin), [2002] Env LR 15.

where no substitution is possible, since no one else is empowered to act. Natural justice then has to give way to necessity;[81] for otherwise there is no means of deciding and the machinery of justice or administration will break down.[82] The Article 6(1) requirement of an independent and impartial decision-maker is, as the Human Rights Court has made clear,[83] more absolute and less mindful of administrative convenience. Compliance with the Convention standard will thus sometimes pose difficulties.

These will be discussed later, but first an account of the common law necessity principle is required. Necessity made an appearance in *Dimes* v. *Grand Junction Canal*, already recounted.[84] Before the appeal could proceed from the Vice-Chancellor to the House of Lords, the Lord Chancellor had to sign an order for enrolment. But it was held that his shareholding in the company, which disqualified him from hearing the appeal, did not affect the enrolment, since no one but he had power to effect it. 'For this is a case of necessity, and where that occurs the objection of interest cannot prevail.'[85] Comparable situations have occurred in modern cases. For instance, the government of Saskatchewan called upon the court to determine whether the salaries of judges were liable to income tax; and the Privy Council confirmed that the court was right to decide it, as a matter of necessity.[86]

In administrative cases the same exigency may easily arise. Where statute empowers a particular minister[87] or official to act, he will usually be the one and only person who can do so. There is then no way of escaping the responsibility, even if he is personally interested. Transfer of responsibility is, indeed, a recognised type of ultra vires.[88] In one case it was unsuccessfully argued that the only minister competent to confirm a compulsory purchase order for land for an airport had disqualified himself by showing bias and that the local authority could only apply for a local Act of Parliament.[89] The court will naturally not allow statutory machinery to be frustrated in this way. It is generally supposed, likewise, that a minister must act as best he can even in a case where he, for instance, himself owns property which will be benefited if he approves a development plan. Such cases of private and personal interest are conspicuous by their absence in the law reports. But there have been cases involving public funds. The Local Government Superannuation Act 1937 gave employees of local authorities statutory rights to pensions under certain conditions, but provided that any question concerning these rights should be decided first by the local authority, and then in case of dispute by the minister, whose decision on questions of fact was to be final. The Court of Appeal held that there was no escape from these clear provisions although they were trenchantly criticised by Scott LJ.[90]

Nevertheless no change was made when the next Local Government Superannuation Act was enacted in 1953.[91] There could hardly be a better example to show how remote from the modern world are the ideas expressed in Dr Bonham's case.[92]

---

[81] See [1982] *PL* 628 (R. R. S. Tracey).

[82] In *Great Charte* v. *Kennington* (1730) 2 Str 1173 it was said that where there were no justices who were not ratepayers 'it might be allowed to prevent a failure of justice'.

[83] *Kingsley* v. *UK* (2002) 35 EHRR 177, discussed below.   [84] Above, p. 384.

[85] (1852) 3 HLC at 787 citing authority as early as 1430.

[86] *The Judges* v. *A-G for Saskatchewan* (1937) 53 TLR 464 (the Saskatchewan court's decision was adverse to the judges).

[87] But if he is 'the Secretary of State', another Secretary of State can act in his stead: above, p. 36; *London and Clydeside Estates Ltd* v. *Secretary of State for Scotland*, 1987 SLT 459 at 463.

[88] See above, p. 260.

[89] *Re Manchester (Ringway Airport) Compulsory Purchase Order* (1935) 153 LT 219 (no bias was found).

[90] *Wilkinson* v. *Barking Cpn* [1948] 1 KB 721.

[91] See s. 21. Under the Superannuation Act 1972, s. 11, a question of law can be referred to the High Court.

[92] Above, p. 376.

Similarly in a New Zealand case the Privy Council held that a marketing board could not be prevented from making a zoning order allotting the milk produced by a certain district to a certain dairy company, even though the board had given the company a large loan and therefore had a pecuniary interest in its prosperity.[93] Both the power to make zoning orders and the power to make loans to dairy companies were expressly conferred by statute on the board and on no one else, so that 'although the board may find itself placed in an unenviable position', it was bound to exercise both powers if the statutory scheme was to be workable. The same doctrine should, perhaps, have been invoked in English cases where local authorities had to exercise different functions one of which could prejudice the other.[94]

Doubt has been cast on these principles by a case decided in the European Court of Human Rights.[95] What had happened was that the chairwoman of the Gaming Board had in a speech indicated that she and the Board did not regard the applicant as a fit and proper person to have conduct of a casino. The Gaming Board thereafter unsurprisingly found that the applicant was not a fit and proper person to hold a gaming licence. The Court of Appeal concluded that there was no real danger of bias and dismissed the application for judicial review. But the court also said that even if there was such a danger only the Gaming Board could make the decision and so the rule against bias gave way to necessity. Before the ECtHR the applicant complained that the proceedings before the Gaming Board were unfair and that the review by the High Court could not adequately remedy the matter because of the restricted nature of judicial review. The ECtHR held that because there was no remedy for the lack of the necessary impartiality before the English courts, English law was in breach of Article 6. Had the English courts been able to quash the decision and remit it for decision to a different tribunal or had they been able to make the fresh decision themselves, the procedure would have been compliant.

As this case shows, where Article 6(1) is applicable, little reliance can be placed upon necessity in the future. This has the potential to cause administrative difficulty although generally the only remedy available will often be to seek a declaration of incompatibility.[96]

STATUTORY DISPENSATION

So strictly did the courts apply the rule against bias that Parliament attempted to mitigate it by granting exemption in particular cases. Difficulty arose especially in the case of justices of the peace, who often had other public functions which might disqualify them from adjudicating. An Act of 1742 allowed them to make orders in poor law cases despite the fact that they were themselves among the ratepayers who would benefit.[97] But the courts put a narrow interpretation upon all such provisions, holding that any departure from the universally acknowledged principle of natural justice required clear words of enactment.[98] Rules which exempt from disqualification licensing committee members

---

[93] *Jeffs* v. *New Zealand Dairy Production and Marketing Board* [1967] 1 AC 551. See likewise *NZI Financial Cpn Ltd* v. *New Zealand Kiwifruit Authority* [1986] 1 NZLR 159 (statutory membership of export licensing authority); *Laws* v. *Australian Broadcasting Tribunal* (1990) 93 ALR 435 (tribunal must perform statutory function even if biased).   [94] See above, p. 395.

[95] *Kingsley* v. *UK* (2002) 35 EHRR 177. See [2002] *PL* 407 (I. Leigh).   [96] See above, p. 145.

[97] Justices Jurisdiction Act 1742.

[98] *Mersey Docks Trustees* v. *Gibbs* (1866) LR 1 HL 93 at 110; *Frome United Breweries Co Ltd* v. *Bath Justices* [1926] AC 586.

from hearing appeals when they were involved in earlier applications were found to create a danger that the decision of the licensing committee (the first instance decision-maker) would be unconsciously favoured on appeal and so these rules were not in compliance with Article 6(1).[99]

Parliament may also adopt the somewhat contradictory policy of forbidding a person to act in cases where he has some disqualifying interest but of validating his action if he should do so. Thus the Local Government Act 1972 makes it a criminal offence for a member of a local authority to take part in or vote on any contract or other matter in which he has a pecuniary interest;[100] but the Act provides in general terms that the acts of anyone elected to office and acting in that office shall be valid and effectual notwithstanding disqualification.[101]

WAIVER OF OBJECTION

The right to object to a disqualified adjudicator may be waived, and this may be so even where the disqualification is statutory.[102] But it has to be clear that the person alleged to have waived his right to object to an adjudicator 'has acted freely and in full knowledge of the facts'.[103] And if counsel has advised the applicant inadequately as to his right to object to an adjudicator, he will not be taken to have waived his right to object.[104]

The court normally insists that the objection shall be taken as soon as the party prejudiced knows the facts which entitle him to object. If, after he or his advisers know of the disqualification, they let the proceedings continue without protest, they are held to have waived their objection and the determination cannot be challenged.[105] In the past this rule has been strictly applied, so much so that the practice was to refuse certiorari to quash the decision unless it was specifically shown in the affidavits that the applicant had no knowledge of the disqualifying facts at the time of the proceedings.[106] But in one case, where the litigant had appeared in person before the justices, certiorari was granted even though he knew the facts at the trial, since he did not know that he was entitled to raise his objection then, and there can be no waiver of rights of which the person entitled is unaware.[107]

[99] R (Chief Constable of Lancashire) v. Crown Court at Preston [2001] EWHC 928 (Admin), [2002] 1 WLR 1332.   [100] s. 94. The Secretary of State has a dispensing power: s. 97.

[101] s. 82.

[102] Wakefield Local Board of Health v. West Riding and Grimsby Rly Co (1865) 1 QB 84.

[103] R v. Bow Street Magistrate ex p Pinochet (No 2) [2000] 1 AC 119 at 137 (per Lord Browne-Wilkinson).

[104] Smith v. Kvaerner Cementation Foundations Ltd [2006] EWCA Civ. 242 (counsel, in good faith, had conveyed a 'vigorous recommendation of the qualities of his head of chambers' (the disqualified adjudicator) which made it difficult for the applicant to object). See also Jones v. DAS Legal Expenses Insurance Co [2003] EWCA Civ. 1071 for detailed guidance on judicial conduct when issue arises.

[105] R v. Byles ex p Hollidge (1912) 77 JP 40; R v. Nailsworth Licensing Justices ex p Bird [1953] 1 WLR 1046; Thomas v. University of Bradford (No 2) [1992] 1 All ER 964 (waiver of correct procedure); R v. Lilydale Magistrates Court ex p Ciccone [1973] VR 122; and see R v. Antrim Justices [1895] 2 IR 603; Tolputt (H) & Co Ltd v. Mole [1911] 1 KB 836; Corrigan v. Irish Land Commission [1977] IR 317; Locabail (UK) Ltd v. Bayfield Properties Ltd [2000] 2 WLR 870 ('It is not open to [the litigant] to wait and see how her claims…turned out before pursuing her complaint of bias…[She] wanted to have the best of both worlds. The law will not allow her to do so' (Lord Woolf MR, Lord Bingham LCJ and Scott V-C)).

[106] R v. Williams ex p Phillips [1914] 1 KB 608; R v. Kent Justices (1880) 44 JP 298.

[107] R v. Essex Justices ex p Perkins [1927] 2 KB 475.

CAUSES OF PREJUDICE

Thorny questions often arise when a judge is required to adjudicate on a matter on which he has expressed a view in another capacity. In the leading case, a judge, who had previously been a minister of the Crown, was precluded from hearing an appeal in which the legal effect of section 21 of the Crown Proceedings Act 1947[108] was a central issue, since he had, as a minister, expressed a clear and considered view in Parliament on that very matter. Lord Bingham said: 'The fair-minded and informed observer, having considered the facts, would conclude that there was a real possibility that Lord Hardie [the judge], sitting judicially, would subconsciously strive to avoid reaching a conclusion which would undermine the very clear assurances he had given to Parliament.'[109]

INTERMINGLING OF FUNCTIONS

A common problem is where an adjudicator has already been concerned with the case in some other capacity. This is particularly prone to arise in the case of magistrates, who may also be members of local authorities or of other administrative bodies. Difficult questions of degree frequently arise, since the court must try to avoid impeding the work of citizens who give their services in more than one capacity, while at the same time the principle of fair and unbiased decisions must at all costs be upheld.

One class is where the adjudicator has supported the application, complaint or prosecution which comes to be adjudicated.[110] A justice who has proposed a prosecution,[111] or has voted for it,[112] as a member of a local authority is naturally disqualified; but he may act, it seems, if he was merely present at a meeting which resolved to institute proceedings, provided that he took no active part,[113] despite the fact that he may well have been influenced by things said at the meeting. In some situations mere membership, without

---

[108] See below, pp. 704, 705, n. 124.

[109] *Davidson* v. *Scottish Ministers* [2004] UKHL 34, para. 17 (criticised [2005] *PL* 225 (Blom-Cooper)). The European Court has found violations of Art. 6 of the Human Rights Convention in similar circumstances: *Procola* v. *Luxembourg* (1995) 22 EHRR 193 (members of Conseil d'État had in their advisory capacity scrutinised a regulation and then, in their judicial capacity, adjudicated on it) and *McGonnell* v. *UK* (2000) 30 EHRR 289 (planning permission refused as being contrary to development plan; judge (the Bailiff of Jersey) presiding at the challenge to the refusal had previously presided, as Deputy Bailiff, over the States of Deliberation (a non-judicial body) that adopted the plan). But where the prior involvement was merely formal (and not 'structural') it will be upheld: *Pabla Ky* v. *Finland* (App. No. 47221/99) [2004] ECtHR 279 (specialist judge also member of legislature but no prior involvement in matter before court). Similarly, *Panton and Panton* v. *The Minister of Finance and the Attorney General* [2001] UKPC 33 (judge had previously, as Attorney-General, formally certified statute's constitutionality before royal Assent; not precluded from hearing challenge to that statute's validity). But in *R* v. *Home Secretary ex p Al-Hasan* [2005] UKHL 13, [2005] 1 WLR 688 (HL) a deputy prison governor was precluded from adjudicating in disciplinary proceedings on whether an order (to submit to a 'squat search') was lawful because he was present when the governor confirmed the order.

[110] *R* v. *Sunderland Justices* [1901] 2 KB 357 (councillors supporting road-widening scheme sat as justices and granted liquor licence for premises involved in the scheme); *R* v. *Caernarvon Licensing Justices* [1948] WN 505. Contrast *R* v. *Nailsworth Licensing Justices ex p Bird* [1953] 1 WLR 1046. See also *R* v. *Ely Justices ex p Burgess* [1992] COD 21 (justices travelled in car with prosecutor: conviction quashed).

[111] *R* v. *Gaisford* [1892] 1 QB 381. See similarly *Re French and Law Society of Upper Canada (No 2)* (1973) 41 DLR (3d) 23.

[112] *R* v. *Milledge* (1879) 4 QBD 332; *R* v. *Lee ex p Shaw* (1882) 9 QBD 394; *R* v. *Henley* [1892] 1 QB 504 (justice present: resolution unanimous).

[113] *R* v. *Pwllheli Justices ex p Soane* [1948] 2 All ER 815, distinguishing *R* v. *Henley*, above. But in these cases there were statutory provisions.

participation, may invalidate the adjudication. Thus where a local education authority had to decide whether to prohibit the dismissal of a schoolteacher whom the governors of the school had resolved to dismiss, the Court of Appeal found objectionable bias because three members of the local authority's sub-committee, which resolved not to prohibit the dismissal, were governors; yet those members had not attended the governors' meeting which resolved upon the dismissal.[114] It was observed that members of a body such as a board of governors might be thought to have a built-in tendency to support their colleagues, and ought not therefore to sit in judgment on their decisions.[115] In a contrasting case, where a student at a teacher training college was expelled for having a man living with her in her room, the Court of Appeal upheld the expulsion even though it was effected by the board of governors who had taken it upon themselves to refer the case to the disciplinary committee which recommended expulsion.[116]

Mere membership of a prosecuting body, however, raises questions of degree, and there may be a situation where a member who was inactive in the matter is not disqualified.[117] Thus a solicitor may sit as a magistrate on a prosecution brought by the Council of the Law Society,[118] and a member of a society for preventing cruelty to animals may adjudicate on a prosecution brought by the society;[119] and, a fortiori, past membership is unobjectionable.[120] A judge may refuse a paper application for permission to appeal, yet sit on that appeal when heard.[121] And a consultant may sit on a mental health review tribunal where he is employed by the NHS Trust responsible for the patient before the tribunal.[122]

Where functions are delegated or entrusted to committees or sub-committees, an overlap of membership may be objectionable on grounds of bias. This was plainly so where the London County Council used a committee for hearing applications for music and dancing licences and three members of the committee not only sat as members of the Council (though taking no part) when considering the committee's adverse recommendation, but also instructed lawyers to oppose the application before the Council.[123] The House of Lords followed this decision in a similar situation where justices referred a licence application to the compensation authority and instructed a lawyer to oppose it before that authority; three of the same justices not only sat but also voted as members of the compensation authority, and the decision of the authority was accordingly set aside.[124] But it was not irregular for invigilators to sit on the examinations board that decided whether a candidate had made improper use of notes.[125]

A particularly clear case of irregularity is where a person sits with an appellate body to hear an appeal against a decision of his own,[126] as did the chief constable in the Liverpool

---

[114] *Hannam v. Bradford Cpn* [1970] 1 WLR 937.   [115] Ibid. at 946 (Widgery LJ).

[116] *Ward v. Bradford Cpn* (1971) 70 LGR 27, not citing *Hannam v. Bradford Cpn*, above. Compare *Haddow v. Inner London Education Authority* [1979] ICR 202.

[117] As in *R v. Camborne Justices ex p Pearce* [1955] 1 QB 41; above, p. 386.

[118] *R v. Burton ex p Young* [1897] 2 QB 468. And see *Leeson v. General Medical Council* (1889) 43 Ch D 336; *Re S. (a barrister)* [1981] QB 683.   [119] *R v. Deal Justices* (1881) 45 LT 439.

[120] *Allinson v. General Medical Council* [1894] 1 QB 750.

[121] *Senguptor v. Holmes* [2002] EWCA Civ. 1104, The Times, 19 August, 2002 (CA) (application for permission renewed orally before two different judges, and granted).

[122] *R (PD) v. West Midlands and North West MHRT* [2003] EWHC 2469.

[123] *R v. London County Council ex p Akkersdyk* [1892] 1 QB 190.

[124] *Frome United Breweries Co Ltd v. Bath Justices* [1926] AC 586.

[125] *R v. Manchester Metropolitan University ex p Nolan* [1994] ELR 380.

[126] Judges may however do this and often did so in earlier times: see *Hamlet v. General Municipal Boilermakers and Allied Trades Union* [1987] 1 WLR 449; *R v. Lovegrove* [1951] 1 All ER 804.

police case mentioned earlier.[127] Many rating cases have revealed other objectionable intermixtures of functions, for example where an employee of a town council, who took the minutes of its rating committee, acted also as a clerk to the assessment committee.[128]

It has been held that the fact that a magistrate has been subpoenaed as a witness is no ground for prohibiting him from sitting at the hearing of the same case.[129]

OTHER CAUSES OF PREJUDICE

Objectionable bias may be found in a wide variety of situations and relationships. Any indication that an adjudicator has prejudged the case, or any indication that he might do so, will normally disqualify him—as it did where a magistrate prepared a statement of the sentence halfway through the trial.[130] A judge who in the absence of a prosecutor, took over the prosecution was also at fault[131] as was the magistrate who read a newspaper (law report) during the defendant's evidence.[132] Another case was where certain justices were directors and shareholders of a hotel which applied for a liquor licence; they sat with the licensing justices, who granted a licence, but before doing so they resigned their director-ships and sold their shares. Even though they then had no pecuniary interest, their object from the start was to procure the grant of a licence, which was therefore quashed.[133] In another case a justice who joined in refusing a licence, and who belonged to a strict tem-perance sect, stated afterwards that he would have been a traitor to his position if he had voted in favour; and since this clearly indicated bias from the outset, the order of refusal was bad.[134] But a licensing justice is not disqualified by the mere fact that he is a teetotal-ler.[135] Nor, provided that a fair trial is given, does it matter that a justice showed from the bench that he held strong views on some relevant matter,[136] or that a member of a com-mittee responsible for licensing sex shops had previously published his opinion that none should be allowed.[137] As was said in one licensing case, 'preconceived opinions—though it is unfortunate that a judge should have any—do not constitute such a bias, nor even the expression of such opinions, for it does not follow that the evidence will be disregarded'.[138]

Among other obvious cases of prejudice are personal friendship or hostility[139] and family or commercial relationship.[140] A justice was disqualified where he was a friend of

[127] *Cooper* v. *Wilson* [1937] 2 KB 309; above, p. 393. See similarly *Taylor* v. *National Union of Seamen* [1967] 1 WLR 532 (trade union official who had dismissed plaintiff presided at appeal and presented case against him); *R* v. *Barnsley Metropolitan Borough Council ex p Hook* [1976] 1 WLR 1052 (revocation of mar-ket trader's licence: prosecuting officer sat with appeal committee).

[128] *R* v. *Salford Assessment Committee ex p Ogden* [1937] 2 KB 1.

[129] *R* v. *Farrant* (1887) 20 QBD 58.   [130] *R* v. *Romsey Justices ex p Gale* [1992] COD 323.

[131] *R* v. *Wood Green Crown Court ex p Taylor*, The Times, 25 May 1995.

[132] *R* v. *Marylebone Magistrates Court ex p Joseph*, The Times, 7 May 1993.

[133] *R* v. *Hain* (1896) 12 TLR 323. See similarly *Meadowvale Stud Farm Ltd* v. *Stratford CC* [1979] 1 NZLR 342 (shareholders sat on county council).

[134] *R* v. *Halifax Justices ex p Robinson* (1912) 76 JP 233; cf. *Goodall* v. *Bilsland* (1909) SC 1152. In *M'Geehen* v. *Knox* (1913) SC 688 the facts were nearly as strong, yet the order stood.

[135] *R* v. *Nailsworth Licensing Justices ex p Bird* [1953] 1 WLR 1046.

[136] *ex p Wilder* (1902) 66 JP 761 (justice showed prejudice against motor cars). Cf. the *Hoekstra* case, above p. 391.   [137] *R* v. *Reading BC ex p Quietlynn Ltd* (1986) 85 LGR 387.

[138] *R* v. *London County Council, re Empire Theatre* (1894) 71 LT 638. See *Whitford Residents Association* v. *Manukau City Cpn* [1974] 2 NZLR 340; *R* v. *Commonwealth Conciliation and Arbitration Commission ex p Angliss Group* (1969) 122 CLR 546.

[139] As in *R* v. *Handley* (1921) 61 DLR 656; cf. *White* v. *Kuzych* [1951] AC 585. The statement to the contrary in *Maclean* v. *Workers' Union* [1929] Ch 602 goes too far.

[140] See *R* v. *Rand* (1866) LR 1 QB 230 at 232–3.

the mother of one of the parties and that party had let it be known that the justice would be on her side;[141] but the court distinguished this sharply from cases of mere acquaintance or business contact. Bias was found where a member of an industrial tribunal was the mother-in-law of a professor who had sat on the internal appeal committee of a college which dismissed allegations of sex discrimination and unfair dismissal.[142] But a former professional adviser would normally be allowed to adjudicate in the case of a client,[143] and a builder is not disqualified from sitting on a planning committee merely because the applicant is a commercial rival.[144] A non-voting chairman of a university disciplinary committee who knew sensitive information about the student concerned was not disqualified.[145]

There can normally be no objection to a member of a tribunal sitting in an application by a party who has previously appeared before him on another application.[146]

DEPARTMENTAL OR ADMINISTRATIVE BIAS

It is self-evident that ministerial or departmental policy cannot be regarded as disqualifying bias. One of the commonest administrative mechanisms is to give a minister power to make or confirm an order after hearing objections to it. The procedure for the hearing of objections is subject to the rules of natural justice in so far as they require a fair hearing and fair procedure generally. But the minister's decision cannot be impugned on the ground that he has advocated the scheme or that he is known to support it as a matter of policy. The whole object of putting the power into his hands is that he may exercise it according to government policy. Otherwise the situation might resemble the pathetic picture painted by the Committee on Ministers' Powers in their report of 1932,[147] where they suggested that a minister might be put in a dilemma where his impartiality would be in inverse ratio to his efficiency:

> An easy-going and cynical Minister, rather bored with his office and sceptical of the value of his Department, would find it far easier to apply a judicial mind to purely judicial problems connected with the Department's administration than a Minister whose head and heart were in his work... Parliament should be chary of imposing on Ministers the ungrateful task of giving judicial decisions in matters in which their very zeal for the public service can scarcely fail to bias them unconsciously.

Attempts to represent government policy as objectionable on grounds of natural justice are usually complaints of predetermination, alleging that the effective decision was taken in advance, thus rendering the hearing futile and the result a foregone conclusion. In the case already mentioned, where the minister had confirmed a compulsory purchase order for the acquisition of land for an airport, it was contended that the minister was disqualified because the Air Council, of which the minister was a member, had expressed a provisional view in favour of the scheme before objections were invited; but this was held to be

---

[141] *Cottle* v. *Cottle* [1939] 2 All ER 535.

[142] *University College of Swansea* v. *Cornelius* [1988] ICR 735.

[143] *Re Polites ex p The Hoyts Cpn Pty Ltd* (1991) 100 ALR 634.

[144] *R* v. *Holderness BC ex p James Roberts Developments Ltd* (1992) 5 Admin LR 470.

[145] *R* v. *Board of Governors of Sheffield Hallam University ex p Rowlett* [1994] COD 470. But the application was allowed on other grounds.

[146] *R* v. *Oxford Regional Mental Health Review Tribunal ex p Mackman*, The Times, 2 June 1986. Contrast *R* v. *Downham Market Magistrates Court ex p Nudd*, The Times, 14 April 1988.

[147] Cmd 4060 (1932), 78.

perfectly proper and not prejudicial.[148] Where, before a planning application was due to come before a local authority, the members of a political party controlling the authority agreed to support the application, their political predisposition did not disqualify them, since it was 'almost inevitable, now that party politics play so large a part in local government, that the majority group on a council would decide on the party line'.[149] The key to all these decisions is the fact that if Parliament gives the deciding power to a political body, no one can complain that it acts politically. The principles of natural justice still apply, but they must be adapted to the circumstances.[150]

A dramatic contest over a prior political commitment concerned the order for the new town at Stevenage.[151] Here the issue was whether the minister had truly complied with the statutory requirement that after the objections had been heard at an inquiry 'the minister shall consider the report' of the inspector.

The Minister of Town and Country Planning had determined that Stevenage should be the first of the new towns under the New Towns Act 1946. Strong objections were made and were fully heard by a ministry inspector at a public inquiry. The minister confirmed the designation order. But before considering the report he had addressed a public meeting in Stevenage where he met heckling and jeering and is reported to have said 'it is no good your jeering, it is going to be done'. The objectors argued that the minister had declared in advance that his mind was made up and that he would not consider the report impartially. But the House of Lords, reversing both courts below, held that the minister need only follow the statutory procedure and had no judicial or quasi-judicial duty. This might at the time have unsettled the 'basic English' of administrative law. But as the judges grew more sensitive to natural justice it soon became clear that its principles applied to the procedural part of such statutory procedures even though the final decision was one of policy, so that the minister had a quasi-judicial duty of the kind explained earlier.

EFFECTS OF PREJUDICE

VOID OR VOIDABLE?

In the case of Lord Cottenham's judgment, cited at the outset of this discussion,[152] the judges advised the House of Lords that the disqualifying interest made the judgment not void but voidable.[153] This has sometimes been repeated as if it were true of administrative cases involving bias, thus producing the concept of a voidable administrative act, already criticised. But Lord Cottenham's case had nothing to do with administrative powers. His judgment was given in the Court of Chancery, one of the superior courts of law, and it would naturally be valid unless and until reversed on appeal. It could therefore correctly be described as voidable as opposed to being void from the beginning.

---

[148] *Re Manchester (Ringway Airport) Compulsory Purchase Order* (1935) 153 LT 219; above, p. 396.

[149] *R v. Amber Valley DC ex p Jackson* [1985] 1 WLR 298 (Woolf J). And see *Turner v. Allison* [1971] NZLR 833. See also *Old St Boniface Residents' Association v. City of Winnipeg* (1990) 75 DLR (4th) 385. Contrast *Anderton v. Auckland CC* [1978] 1 NZLR 657.   [150] See *R v. Amber Valley DC* (above).

[151] *Franklin v. Minister of Town and Country Planning* [1948] AC 87, discussed in '"Quasi-judicial" and its Background' (1949) 10 *CLJ* 216 (Wade).   [152] Above, p. 384.

[153] *Dimes v. Grand Junction Canal* (1852) 3 HLC 759 at 785. Parke B added a dictum about decisions of magistrates, but the authorities he cited did not support him: see (1968) 84 *LQR* at p. 108.

But where an administrative act or decision is subject to judicial review, as opposed to appeal, the court can intervene on one ground only: ultra vires.[154] The court necessarily intervenes on the basis that the vitiated act is ultra vires, i.e. wholly unauthorised by law and thus void. There is no valid analogy with an appeal from a court of law. Judgments dealing with administrative decisions therefore proceed on the footing that the presence of bias means that the tribunal is improperly constituted, so that it has no power to determine the case; and accordingly its decision must be void and a nullity.[155] Thus the reviewing court's jurisdiction fits correctly into the framework of the ultra vires principle, whereas the notion of a voidable decision does not. A long line of judges of high authority have agreed with Lord Esher's observation that the participation of a disqualified person 'certainly rendered the decision wholly void'.[156]

This analysis is corroborated by the nature of the remedies which the courts have granted. In a police discipline case, already mentioned, the Court of Appeal granted a declaration that the officer's dismissal was a nullity.[157] But a declaratory judgment is a useless remedy where the decision is merely voidable: merely to declare that a decision is voidable achieves nothing. But if it is void and a nullity, a declaration as to this is effective. Second, the court will quash for bias even where there is a statutory 'no certiorari' clause;[158] but such a clause can be ignored only where the decision is ultra vires and void.[159]

The logic of the situation is in no way weakened by the fact that the right to object on the ground of bias can be waived in the manner already mentioned.[160] This has sometimes been supposed to show that bias must render the decision voidable only.[161] But this follows only if 'void' is given the absolute meaning criticised earlier and not the relative meaning which it ought to bear. Waiver is only one of many factors which may induce the court to refuse relief:[162] it may do so in its discretion for many reasons, however void the decision in question, and then the decision must be accepted as valid. Channell J once observed that the right to object on the ground of bias could be lost by waiver 'no matter whether the proceedings...are void or voidable'.[163] That question is merely irrelevant. Furthermore, there is no reason why the rule of law which says that a biased decision is void should not itself contain the qualification that it operates only if the right to object is not waived.[164]

---

[154] Formerly there was the ground of error on the face of the record: above, p. 224. See also the general discussion: above, p. 27.

[155] For fuller discussion see (1968) 84 *LQR* at p. 101. For other aspects of 'void or voidable' see above, p. 247.

[156] *Allinson* v. *General Medical Council* [1894] 1 QB 750. In agreement are *R* v. *Cheltenham Commissioners* (1841) 1 QB 467 (decision 'invalid' despite no certiorari clause, therefore ultra vires); *R* v. *Nat Bell Liquors Ltd* [1922] 2 AC 128 at 160 ('without jurisdiction'); *Cooper* v. *Wilson* [1937] 2 KB 309 at 344 ('a nullity'); *R* v. *Paddington etc Rent Tribunal ex p Kendal Hotels Ltd* [1947] 1 All ER 148; *R* v. *Paddington etc Rent Tribunal ex p Perry* [1956] 1 QB 229 at 237 ('no jurisdiction'); and see *Anisminic Ltd* v. *Foreign Compensation Commission* [1969] 2 AC 147 at 171.   [157] *Cooper* v. *Wilson* [1937] 2 KB 309; above, p. 393.

[158] *R* v. *Cheltenham Commissioners* (1841) 1 QB 467; *R* v. *Hertfordshire Justices* (1845) 6 QB 753.

[159] See below, p. 610.   [160] Above, p. 398.

[161] See Rubinstein, *Jurisdiction and Illegality*, 221; (1926) 42 *LQR* 523 (D. M. Gordon).

[162] As explained above, p. 251. See (1968) 84 *LQR* at 109 (Wade).

[163] *R* v. *Williams ex p Phillips* [1914] 1 KB 608.   [164] See above, p. 198 (waiver and jurisdiction).

14

THE RIGHT TO A FAIR HEARING

AUDI ALTERAM PARTEM

'HEAR THE OTHER SIDE'

It is fundamental to fair procedure that both sides should be heard: *audi alteram partem*, 'hear the other side'. This is the more far-reaching of the principles of natural justice, since it can embrace almost every question of fair procedure, or due process, and its implications can be worked out in great detail. It is also broad enough to include the rule against bias, since a fair hearing must be an unbiased hearing; but in deference to the traditional dichotomy, that rule has already been treated separately.

The right to a fair hearing has been used by the courts as a base on which to build a kind of code of fair administrative procedure, comparable to 'due process of law' under the Constitution of the United States

The courts took their stand several centuries ago on the broad principle that bodies entrusted with legal power could not validly exercise it without first hearing the person who was going to suffer. This principle was applied very widely to administrative as well as to judicial acts, and to the acts of individual ministers and officials as well as to the acts of collective bodies such as justices and committees. Even where an order or determination is unchallengeable as regards its substance, the court can at least control the preliminary procedure so as to require fair consideration of both sides of the case. Thus the law makes its contribution to good administration.

Since the courts have been enforcing this rule for centuries, and since it is self-evidently desirable,[1] it might be thought that no trained professional, whether judge or administrator, would be likely to overlook it. But the stream of cases that come before British and Commonwealth courts shows that overlooking it is one of the most common legal errors to which human nature is prone. When a Lord Chief Justice,[2] an Archbishop of Canterbury[3] and a three-judge Court of Appeal[4] have strayed from the path of rectitude,

---

[1] But see the discussion above, p. 373 on the justifications for procedural fairness.

[2] *Abraham* v. *Jutsun* [1963] 1 WLR 658 (Divisional Court ordered solicitor to pay costs without hearing him in his defence; order set aside by Court of Appeal as made per incuriam). Sir William Scott, the future Lord Stowell, excommunicated an ecclesiastical offender without a hearing and was liable in damages: *Beaurain* v. *Scott* (1813) 3 Camp 388.

[3] *R* v. *Archbishop of Canterbury* (1859) 1 E & E 545 (Archbishop dismissed curate's appeal on consideration of his written petition of appeal only: mandamus granted).

[4] *B* v. *W* [1979] 1 WLR 1041 (court acted on document not disclosed to appellant). In *Hadmor Productions Ltd* v. *Hamilton* [1983] 1 AC 191 Lord Diplock accused Lord Denning MR of violating natural justice by relying upon a speech in a debate in the House of Lords without first informing counsel. But in *Mahon* v. *Air New Zealand* [1984] AC 808 at 838 he spoke tolerantly of such judicial lapses.

it is not surprising that it is one of the more frequent mistakes of ordinary mortals. The courts themselves must take some of the blame, for they have wavered in their decisions, particularly in the period of about fifteen years which preceded *Ridge* v. *Baldwin*.

AN ANCIENT RULE OF WIDE APPLICATION

According to one picturesque judicial dictum, the first hearing in human history was given in the Garden of Eden:[5]

> I remember to have heard it observed by a very learned man upon such an occasion, that even God himself did not pass sentence upon Adam, before he was called upon to make his defence. 'Adam, says God, where art thou? Hast thou not eaten of the tree, whereof I commanded thee that thou shouldst not eat?' And the same question was put to Eve also.

This was in *Dr. Bentley*'s case, in which the University of Cambridge had deprived that recalcitrant scholar of his degrees on account of his misconduct in insulting the Vice-Chancellor's court; but he was reinstated on a mandamus from the Court of the King's Bench, on the ground that deprivation was unjustifiable and that, in any case, he should have received notice so that he could make his defence, as required by 'the laws of God and man'. This is a nice example of the old conception of natural justice as divine and eternal law.[6]

A century previously the same doctrine had made an appearance in an equally notorious case of contumacy, where a freeman of the borough of Plymouth had threatened and scandalised the mayor and was disfranchised. It was similarly held that the penalty was unjustified, in the absence of any special power of disfranchisement; and that even if there had been such a power, the removal would be void because it was not shown that a hearing had first been given.[7] In this case also the remedy was a mandamus for restoration. Coke's report quotes from Seneca:[8]

> quicunque aliquid statuerit parte inaudita altera, aequum licet statuerit, haud aequus fuerit.

This contains the same message as does the law about bias, that where natural justice is violated it is no justification that the decision was in fact correct.[9]

The early decisions mainly concerned restoration to offices.[10] In the first half of the nineteenth century natural justice began to affect ecclesiastical affairs. In one case a bishop had appointed a curate, at the vicar's expense, to perform the duties of the vicar whom the bishop considered to be negligent. The bishop did not call on the vicar to make

---

[5] *R* v. *University of Cambridge* (1723) 1 Str 557 (Fortescue J).   [6] See above, p. 376.

[7] *Bagg's Case* (1615) 11 Co Rep 93b. The most celebrated of his misdeeds was that he 'turning the hinder part of his body in an inhuman and uncivil manner towards the aforesaid Thomas Fowens, scoffingly, contemptuously, and uncivilly, with a loud voice, said to the aforesaid Thomas Fowens, these words following, that is to say, "Come and kiss".'

[8] *Medea* 199–200, cited also in *Boswell's Case* (1606) 6 Co Rep 48b at 52a; *R* v. *University of Cambridge* (1723) 1 Str 557 at 561; *R* v. *Archbishop of Canterbury* (1859) 1 E & E 545; Bl. Comm. ix. 283.

[9] Seneca's sentiment is exactly reproduced in *Earl* v. *Slater & Wheeler (Airlyne) Ltd* [1973] 1 WLR 51 (dismissal without hearing held intrinsically unfair, even though fully justified).

[10] Examples are *Protector* v. *Colchester* (1655) Style 452; *Campion's Case* (1658) 2 Sid 97.

any defence; and for this reason the court held the whole process to be void.[11] The exercise of a drastic power required that the vicar should be given the opportunity to answer the charges made against him. Bayley B said:

> When the bishop proceeds on his own knowledge I am of the opinion also that it cannot possibly, and within the meaning of this Act, appear to the satisfaction of the bishop, and of his knowledge, unless he gives the party an opportunity of being heard, in answer to that which the bishop states on his own knowledge to be the foundation on which he proceeds.

It was already clear from decisions of this kind that the courts would apply the principle of natural justice to cases of an administrative character. They did so no less vigorously when the modern statutory authorities, equipped with new powers of many kinds, began to proliferate as the nineteenth century progressed. The same principle was extended beyond the sphere of administrative law, to such bodies as societies and clubs. It was held to be an implied term of each member's contract of membership that he could not be expelled without a fair hearing.[12] In a case where a member of a mutual insurance society was purportedly expelled for suspicious conduct, but without a hearing, it was held that the expulsion was absolutely void, so that he was still a member in law; and it was said:[13]

> This rule is not confined to the conduct of strictly legal tribunals, but is applicable to every tribunal or body of persons invested with authority to adjudicate upon matters involving civil consequences to individuals.

Subsequently this doctrine found a fruitful field of application in protecting members and officers of trade unions from unfair expulsion or other penalties.[14] Here likewise the basis for natural justice was an implied term in the contract of membership. Denning LJ said of trade union committees:[15]

> These bodies, however, which exercise a monopoly in an important sphere of human activity, with the power of depriving a man of his livelihood, must act in accordance with the elementary rules of justice. They must not condemn a man without giving him an opportunity to be heard in his own defence: and any agreement or practice to the contrary would be invalid.

That the last ten words represent the law has since been decided definitely.[16]

How far the same rules apply in university disciplinary proceedings is discussed below.[17]

---

[11] *Capel* v. *Child* (1832) 2 C & J 558. See also *Bonaker* v. *Evans* (1850) 16 QB 162; *R* v. *North ex p Oakey* [1927] 1 KB 491.

[12] *Dawkins* v. *Antrobus* (1881) 17 Ch D 615; *Fisher* v. *Keane* (1878) 11 Ch D 853. Cf. *Wright* v. *Jockey Club*, The Times, 16 June 1995 (no liability for loss caused by unfair hearing).

[13] *Wood* v. *Woad* (1874) LR 9 Ex 190 (Kelly CB). And see *Byrne* v. *Kinematograph Renters Society Ltd* [1958] 1 WLR 762.

[14] As e.g. in *Burn* v. *National Amalgamated Labourers' Union* [1920] 2 Ch 364; *Lee* v. *Showmen's Guild* [1952] QB 329; *Lawlor* v. *Union of Post Office Workers* [1965] Ch 712; *Leary* v. *National Union of Vehicle Builders* [1971] Ch 34; *Edwards* v. *SOGAT* [1971] Ch 354; *Breen* v. *Amalgamated Engineering Union* [1971] 2 QB 175; *Stevenson* v. *United Road Transport Union* [1976] 3 All ER 29.

[15] *Abbott* v. *Sullivan* [1952] 1 KB 189 at 198.

[16] *Edwards* v. *SOGAT* (above); *Enderby Town Football Club* v. *Football Association* [1971] Ch 591 at 606.

[17] Below, p. 469.

THE RIGHT TO A FAIR HEARING AND ARTICLE 6(1) OF THE HUMAN RIGHTS CONVENTION

The enactment of the Human Rights Act 1998 and the incorporation of the European Convention on Human Rights and Fundamental Freedoms brought a new dimension to this subject. As explained earlier,[18] the most germane article of the Convention, Article 6(1), applies to many but not all administrative proceedings. It only applies to administrative proceedings that determine the 'civil rights and obligations' of individuals. When it does apply it requires that there should be 'a fair and public hearing within a reasonable time'.[19] There clearly will be occasions on which the application of Article 6(1) will impose obligations upon decision-makers that go beyond those imposed by the common law. Thus unreasonable delay will amount to a breach of Article 6(1) even though, in the absence of prejudice, it is not a breach of the common law.[20] Furthermore, while the common law does not as yet impose a general duty to give reasons for a decision,[21] where Article 6(1) applies, the decision-maker must give a reasoned judgment so as to enable the individual affected to decide whether to appeal.[22] The requirements of a 'public hearing' and the public pronouncement of judgment[23] may also impose fresh obligations upon some administrative decision-makers.[24] It has already been noted that not all administrative decision-makers will satisfy the test of 'independence and impartiality' required by Article 6(1).[25]

However, the vigour of the wide-ranging and sophisticated common law requirement of a fair hearing, shortly to be further described, should not be underestimated. Its protection of procedural due process will extend further into the administrative machine and will generally be as, or more, extensive than that afforded by Article 6(1). Although there will be occasions on which reliance will properly be placed upon Article 6(1) and the relevant decisions of the European Court, the common law will continue to dominate in this area.

ADMINISTRATIVE CASES

A CLASSIC EXAMPLE

The numerous new administrative authorities, both local and central, which came into being in the nineteenth and twentieth centuries opened up a large new territory for the principles of natural justice. The character of the authority was not what mattered: what mattered was the character of the power exercised. If the exercise of that adversely affected legal rights or interests, it must be exercised fairly.

One case of 1863 is especially noteworthy, both because it stated the law in short judgments of great clarity, and also because it has played an important part in the revival in the

---

[18] Above, p. 377.   [19] See Appendix 2 for the text of Art. 6(1).
[20] *Procurator Fiscal* v. *Watson and Burrows* [2002] UKPC D1, [2004] 1 AC 379, para. 85 (Lord Hope) and *Porter* v. *Magill* [2001] UKHL 67, [2002] 2 AC 357 (same principles apply to civil and criminal proceedings) discussed Lambert and Strugo [2005] JR 253. See Appendix 3.   [21] See below, p. 440.
[22] *Hadjianastassiou* v. *Greece* (1992) 16 EHRR 219 (in the context of a criminal case); *Garcia Ruiz* v. *Spain* (1999) 31 EHRR 589 and *Ruiz Jorija* v. *Spain* (1994) 19 EHRR 553. And see *English* v. *Reimbold and Strick* [2002] 1 WLR 2409 (CA), paras. 8–14 (judicial not administrative decision).
[23] A previously unmentioned requirement of Art. 6(1).   [24] These will be noted as they arise.
[25] See above, pp. 377 and 392.

1960s of the right to be heard: *Cooper v. Wandsworth Board of Works*.[26] Under an Act of 1855 it was provided that no one might put up a building in London without giving seven days' notice to the local board of works; and that if any one did so, the board might have the building demolished. A builder nevertheless began to erect a house in Wandsworth without having given due notice and when his building had reached the second storey the board of works sent men late in the evening who demolished it. The board did exactly what the Act said they might do in exactly the circumstances in which the Act said they might do it. And their action was, of course, purely administrative. Nevertheless, the builder brought a successful action for damages for the injury to his building, merely on the ground that the board had no power to act without first asking him what he had to say for himself. Erle CJ said:

> I think the board ought to have given notice to the plaintiff and to have allowed him to be heard. The default in sending notice to the board of the intention to build, is a default which may be explained. There may be a great many excuses for the apparent default. The party may have intended to conform to the law. He may have actually conformed...though by accident his notice may have miscarried...I cannot conceive any harm that could happen to the district board from hearing the party before they subjected him to a loss so serious as the demolition of his house; but I can conceive a great many advantages which might arise in the way of public order, in the way of doing substantial justice, and in the way of fulfilling the purposes of the statute, by the restriction which we put upon them, that they should hear the party before they inflict upon him such a heavy loss.

Two of the other judgments in this case are important. Willes J said:

> I am of the same opinion. I apprehend that a tribunal which is by law invested with power to affect the property of one of Her Majesty's subjects, is bound to give such subject an opportunity of being heard before it proceeds: and that the rule is of universal application, and founded on the plainest principles of justice. Now, is the board in the present case such a tribunal? I apprehend it clearly is.

And Byles J also said:

> It seems to me that the board are wrong whether they acted judicially or ministerially. I conceive they acted judicially, because they had to determine the offence, and they had to apportion the punishment as well as the remedy. That being so, a long course of decisions beginning with *Dr. Bentley's* case, and ending with some very recent cases, establish that, although there are no positive words in a statute, requiring that the party shall be heard, yet the justice of the common law will supply the omission of the legislature.

These last two quotations bring out clearly two especially important aspects: the universality of the principle, which make it applicable to almost the whole range of administrative powers; and the presumption that it will always apply, however silent about it the statute may be.

How wide its application was to be is illustrated by many later decisions. Whether the case concerned the cancellation of a Crown lease in Queensland,[27] the condemnation of a house in Manchester as unfit for human habitation,[28] the compulsory transfer of

---

[26] (1863) 14 CB (NS) 180; approved in *Ridge v. Baldwin* [1964] AC 40; *Durayappah v. Fernando* [1967] 2 AC 337; *Wiseman v. Borneman* [1971] AC 297.

[27] *Smith v. R* (1878) 3 App Cas 614 (power to cancel in case of non-residence or abandonment: held, 'a judicial function').   [28] *Hall v. Manchester Cpn* (1915) 84 LJ Ch 732.

indentured labour in Trinidad,[29] or the refusal of a pension to a Canadian police officer obliged to resign,[30] the court uniformly insisted that the power could be validly exercised only after a fair hearing of the party adversely affected.

'JUDICIAL' AND 'QUASI-JUDICIAL' ACTS

The above quotations show very clearly how the courts justified their interventions. They held that every judicial act is subject to the procedure required by natural justice; and they then denominated the great majority of administrative acts as 'judicial' for this purpose. Instead of saying, as was in fact the truth, that natural justice must be observed in both judicial and administrative acts, the courts stretched the meaning of 'judicial' in an unnatural way. Another graphic example is a statement by Willis J in a case which in essentials was the same as *Cooper* v. *Wandsworth Board of Works*:

> In condemning a man to have his house pulled down, a judicial act is as much implied as in fining him £5; and as the local board is the only tribunal that can make such an order its act must be a judicial act, and the party to be affected should have a notice given him…in the present case there is nothing in the Act of Parliament to limit the natural inference as to the nature of the act.[31]

Every administrative act was thus treated as 'judicial' if it adversely affected any person's rights or entailed a penalty.[32] Exactly the same abuse of language was adopted in requiring a 'duty to act judicially' as a condition of the availability of the remedies of certiorari and prohibition; and to this an unprofitable discussion must be devoted elsewhere.[33] When in time the courts came to forget the paradoxical sense which they had invented for 'judicial', they found themselves in difficulty. If every power affecting some person's rights is called 'judicial', there is virtually no meaning left for 'administrative'.

The term 'quasi-judicial' accordingly came into vogue, as an epithet for powers which, though administrative, were required to be exercised as if they were judicial, i.e. in accordance with natural justice.[34] This at least was less of a misnomer than 'judicial', and made it easier for the courts to continue the work of developing their system of fair administrative procedure. 'Quasi-judicial' was the subject of a classic discussion and definition by the Committee on Ministers' Powers,[35] who emphasised that a judicial decision consists of finding facts and applying law whereas a quasi-judicial decision consists of finding facts and applying administrative policy. The latter term was much used in the housing cases, related below.

---

[29] *De Verteuil* v. *Knaggs* [1918] AC 557.

[30] *Lapointe* v. *L'Association de Bienfaisance et de Retraite de la Police de Montreal* [1906] AC 535.

[31] *Hopkins* v. *Smethwick Local Board of Health* (1890) 24 QBD 713. See similarly *Masters* v. *Pontypool Local Government Board* (1878) 9 Ch D 677. One of the many examples is *R* v. *London County Council ex p Commercial Gas Company* (1895) 11 TLR 337 (report of gas examiner held 'a judicial proceeding' and quashed for failure to grant hearing).

[32] See the discussion in *Barnard* v. *National Dock Labour Board* [1953] 2 QB 18 and *Vine* v. *National Dock Labour Board* [1957] AC 488, where the removal of a dock worker from the register was held to be a judicial act, though described also as quasi-judicial.   [33] Below, p. 513.

[34] An early example of its use is in *Mersey Docks Trustees* v. *Gibbs* (1866) LR 1 HL 93 at 110.

[35] Cmd 4060 (1932), 73. See above, p. 32.

LORD LOREBURN'S EPITOME

Of all the classical expositions of the general principle, the most frequently quoted has been from a speech of Lord Loreburn in the House of Lords in 1911. The House had to decide whether the Board of Education had properly determined a dispute between a body of school managers and the local education authority of Swansea, which had refused to pay teachers in church schools the same wage as teachers in the authority's own schools. The House of Lords upheld the quashing of the Board's decision; for the Board had not dealt with the question which arose under the Act, which was whether they could legitimately discriminate between the two classes of schools.[36] But the Lord Chancellor, Lord Loreburn, spoke about the Board's duties in general terms:

> Comparatively recent statutes have extended, if they have not originated, the practice of imposing upon departments or officers of State the duty of deciding or determining questions of various kinds. In the present instance, as in many others, what comes for determination is a matter to be settled by discretion, involving no law. It will, I suppose, usually be of an administrative kind; but sometimes it will involve matter of law as well as matter of fact, or even depend upon matter of law alone. In such cases the Board of Education will have to ascertain the law and also to ascertain the facts. I need not add that in doing either they must act in good faith and listen fairly to both sides, for that is a duty lying upon every one who decides anything. But I do not think they are bound to treat such a question as though it were a trial. They have no power to administer an oath, and need not examine witnesses. They can obtain information in any way they think best, always giving a fair opportunity to those who are parties in the controversy for correcting or contradicting anything prejudicial to their view.

Although the case itself involved no breach of natural justice, Lord Loreburn's epitome of the general principle was so apt that it has been quoted with approval again and again.[37] Experience has shown that there are remarkably few true exceptions to this 'duty lying upon every one who decides anything', at any rate anything which may adversely affect legal rights or liberties. At the same time the passage acknowledges, though not with complete accuracy,[38] the practical limitations which the administrative character of a power may impose.

STATUTORY HEARINGS

STATUTORY INQUIRIES AND HEARINGS:
THE *ARLIDGE* CASE

A characteristic technique adopted as a way of resolving disputes about the exercise of statutory powers is that of the public inquiry (coupled with a public hearing) before an inspector who conducts the inquiry and then lays a report before the relevant minister (or other authority) for decision. Clearly such procedures engage the rules of natural justice

---

[36] *Board of Education* v. *Rice* [1911] AC 179.

[37] The central part is also reproduced almost verbatim by Lord Denning MR in *Re Pergamon Press* [1971] Ch 388 at 399–400.

[38] In *General Medical Council* v. *Spackman* [1943] AC 627 at 638 Lord Atkin pointed out that the Evidence Act 1851 gave power to administer oaths, and that witnesses tendered ought to be examined in many cases. On these questions see below, pp. 437, 777 and 811.

both in regard to the conduct of the hearing before the inspector and then in regard to the actual decision by the minister or other relevant authority.

Local Government Board v. *Arlidge*,[39] a 1914 decision of the House of Lords exemplifies the issues that arise. A public inquiry had been held on an appeal to the Local Government Board by the owner of a house against which the Hampstead Borough Council had made a closing order on the ground that it was unfit for human habitation. The owner complained to the court that the Board had dismissed his appeal without a fair hearing because he was not allowed to appear before the officer of the Board who made the decision or to see the report of the inspector who held the inquiry. The argument that prevailed in the House of Lords was that by entrusting the power to a government department, Parliament must have intended that the department should act in its normal manner, and should therefore be able to take its decision without making public its papers and without having to conduct itself like a court of law.

In thus attempting to reconcile the procedure of a government department with the legal standard of a fair hearing the House of Lords stressed the limits that must be set to the judicialisation of administrative procedure. But in setting their faces against the disclosure of the inspector's report they missed an important opportunity. The decision will be based on the report but the appellant can hardly make meaningful representations to the decision-maker without having seen the report. It took over forty years for this mistake to be corrected, when it finally came to be understood that the supposed analogy between the report and any other departmental papers was misconceived. But even now the law formally stands where the House of Lords left it in the *Arlidge* case,[40] and the necessary reforms have been made administratively, following the report of the Franks Committee of 1957, as explained elsewhere.[41] The *Arlidge* case was therefore a turning-point, in which the law failed to keep abreast of the standard of fairness required.

THE *ERRINGTON* CASE AND THE *LIS* PROBLEM

A line of other housing cases dealt with the same dilemma, and particularly with the question how far a government department could retain its normal administrative freedom while at the same time performing its quasi-judicial function of deciding a contested issue. For example, the ministry responsible for housing would frequently be in close touch with the local authority promoting a housing scheme: administratively regarded, the central and local authorities ought to work in collaboration; but legally regarded, the ministry which was given the task of deciding disputes between local authorities and objectors to their schemes, ought to hold the scales evenly between the local authority and the objectors, and not favour one party at the expense of the other. The solution devised by the courts was that the minister's freedom is unfettered up to the point where the scheme is published and objection is lodged. From that point onwards there is an issue, a *lis*, between the local authority and the objectors, and the minister is no longer free to deal with one party without due consideration of the other.[42]

---

[39] [1915] AC 120.

[40] See *Denby (William) & Sons Ltd* v. *Minister of Health* [1936] 1 KB 337; *Steele* v. *Minister of Housing and Local Government* (1956) 6 P & CR 386.   [41] Below, p. 764.

[42] See particularly *Marriott* v. *Minister of Health* (1935) 52 TLR 63; *Fredman* v. *Minister of Health* (1935) 154 LT 240; *Denby (William) & Sons Ltd* v. *Minister of Health* [1936] 1 KB 337; *Errington* v. *Minister of Health* (below); *Steele's* case, above.

The leading case is the Court of Appeal's decision on the Jarrow clearance order, *Errington* v. *Minister of Health*.[43] A public inquiry had been held but after receiving the report the ministry made efforts to persuade the Jarrow Corporation to accept a less expensive scheme. The Corporation resisted and asked the minister to receive a deputation. The minister replied that in view of his quasi-judicial function he did not think he ought to receive a deputation representing one side only. But it was arranged that an official of the ministry and also the inspector who had held the inquiry should visit Jarrow and confer with the local authority on the site. After this meeting the Corporation submitted further evidence and argument to the ministry. In the end the minister confirmed the order. But the objectors impugned it, and with success, on the ground that these dealings between the Corporation and the ministry after the public inquiry had been closed were a breach of natural justice. For at that stage issue had been joined, and evidence had been heard, yet the ministry were giving a further hearing to one party behind the back of the other.

In accordance with the doctrine of the *lis*, complainants uniformly failed where they took exception only to events which had happened before their objections were lodged and the *lis* arose. The court refused to set aside orders on the ground that the ministry advised the local authority before they published their proposals,[44] or because the ministry encouraged them to suppose that their order would be likely to be confirmed.[45] Nor did natural justice require that the minister should disclose documents or advice available in his department before issue was joined, and on which his decision was based.[46] But the court uniformly insisted on the observance of fair procedure once the quasi-judicial stage was reached.[47]

Although by inventing the principle of the *lis* the courts contrived to infuse a measure of natural justice into the statutory procedure at the point where it was most needed, the mixture of administrative and judicial responsibilities made it difficult for the ministry to fulfil their functions. As soon as an objection was lodged, they must either give up their normal dealings with the local authority, or else they must allow the objectors to intrude into the daily work of the department. What made the position seem artificial was the idea that the local authority was a party to the dispute, and that the minister was an independent judge. In fact, the two authorities were working—or should have been working—hand in glove, one at the local and one at the national level. Both were wielding administrative power, and there was no real difference in the nature of their activities.[48] If the scheme had been promoted by a local office of the ministry, instead of by the local corporation, any amount of subsequent consultation might have taken place and have been passed over as ordinary departmental work. The notion of the *lis*, therefore, was not the true key to the problem. Ultimately the key was found in the distinction between evidence

---

[43] [1935] 1 KB 249. For later decisions to the same effect see below, p. 429. Contrast *Horn* v. *Minister of Health* [1937] 1 KB 164 and *Re Manchester (Ringway Airport) Compulsory Purchase Order* (1935) 153 LT 219, where no prejudicial communication was shown between the ministry and a party to the dispute.

[44] *Frost* v. *Minister of Health* [1935] 1 KB 286.   [45] *Offer* v. *Minister of Health* [1935] 1 KB 249.

[46] *Miller* v. *Minister of Health* [1946] KB 626; *Price* v. *Minister of Health* [1947] 1 All ER 47; *Summers* v. *Minister of Health* [1947] 1 All ER 184; *B Johnson & Co (Builders) Ltd* v. *Minister of Health* [1947] 2 All ER 395.

[47] See *Stafford* v. *Minister of Health* [1946] KB 621; *R* v. *Housing Appeal Tribunal* [1920] 3 KB 334 (tribunal empowered to dispense with hearing; local authority's statement not disclosed to appellant: decision quashed); *R* v. *Secretary of State for Wales ex p Green* (1969) 67 LGR 560 (objector led to suppose that inquiry would be held, so made summary objections only; minister's order quashed).

[48] This comment was approved by Lloyd LJ in *R* v. *Secretary of State for the Environment ex p Southwark LBC* (1987) 54 P & CR 226.

of a general character, used by the minister to guide him on policy,[49] and evidence of the facts of the local situation investigated at the inquiry. But this more sophisticated solution was not reached in litigation over natural justice.[50] It was reached by reforms of administrative procedure made after the report of the Franks Committee on Tribunals and Inquiries (1957), and belongs to a later chapter.[51]

THE RETREAT FROM NATURAL JUSTICE

THE BREAK WITH TRADITION

In the Stevenage case[52] the House of Lords had held that the deciding minister's function was 'purely administrative' and in no way judicial or quasi-judicial. Yet, as amply illustrated earlier,[53] it was essentially to administrative acts that the epithets 'judicial' and 'quasi-judicial' had been applied, in order to impose the legal standard of fair procedure on judicial and administrative conduct alike. Forgetting this tradition, and following the backward lead of the House of Lords, the courts began to hold that natural justice had no application to ordinary administrative action unless it could also be categorised as 'judicial' or 'quasi-judicial'.

The first clear denial of the role of natural justice occurred in a case from Ceylon in which the Privy Council held that a textile trader could be deprived of his trading licence without any kind of hearing.[54] The charge against him was that his firm had falsified paying-in slips when banking coupons under the scheme of control. The Controller in fact arranged an inquiry at which the trader and his witnesses were heard. The Supreme Court of Ceylon, following familiar English authorities, held that the circumstances demanded a fair hearing, but that it had in fact been given. The Privy Council agreed that a fair hearing had been given—but, going out of their way to raise the question, they held that it had never been necessary.

The judgment, delivered by Lord Radcliffe, stated that there was no ground for holding that the Controller was acting judicially or quasi-judicially; that he was not determining a question but withdrawing a privilege; and that nothing in the regulations or in the conditions of his jurisdiction suggested that he need proceed by analogy to judicial rules.[55] It said that the power 'stands by itself on the bare words of the regulation'. It assumed that there was nothing to consider beyond the bare words, and that the right to a hearing could be determined as if the question had never before arisen in an English court.

Not long afterwards the Queen's Bench Division held that a London taxi-driver's licence could be revoked without a hearing by the Metropolitan Police Commissioner.[56] Here again, the licensing authority did not in fact act without granting a hearing: the driver was

---

[49] See *Kent CC* v. *Secretary of State for the Environment* (1976) 33 P & CR 70 (minister free to consult another minister about policy).

[50] But see *Darlassis* v. *Minister of Education* (1954) 52 LGR 304, discussed below, p. 809, where remarks favour the more sophisticated solution.   [51] See below, p. 807.

[52] *Franklin* v. *Minister of Town and Country Planning* [1948] AC 87 discussed earlier, p. 403.

[53] Above, p. 410.

[54] *Nakkuda Ali* v. *Jayaratne* [1951] AC 66, criticised in (1951) 67 *LQR* 103 (Wade). As to wartime decisions, see *Ridge* v. *Baldwin* [1964] AC 40 at 73 (Lord Reid).

[55] In *David* v. *Abdul Cader* [1963] 1 WLR 834 at 839 Lord Radcliffe expressed a view more sympathetic to judicial control of licensing functions.

[56] *R* v. *Metropolitan Police Commissioner ex p Parker* [1953] 1 WLR 1150. Contrast *R* v. *City of Melbourne ex p Whyte* [1949] VLR 257 (cancellation of taxi-driver's licence requires observance of natural justice).

allowed to appear before the licensing committee, but the committee would not allow him to call a witness to controvert the evidence of the police. He complained that the hearing given to him had not been full and fair. Lord Goddard CJ said that the Commissioner could summarily withdraw a licence without any sort of hearing or inquiry.

These two notorious decisions threatened to undo all the good work of earlier judges. They exposed English law to the reproach that, though a man must be heard before being expelled from his trade union or his club, he need not be heard before being deprived of his livelihood by a licensing authority.

THE RIGHT TO BE HEARD REINSTATED

RIDGE V. BALDWIN

The tide turned once again in 1963,[57] when the House of Lords went back to the classic authorities in *Ridge* v. *Baldwin*,[58] a case which is an important landmark.

The chief constable of Brighton had been tried and acquitted on a criminal charge of conspiracy to obstruct the course of justice. Two other police officers were convicted, and the judge twice commented adversely from the bench on the chief constable's leadership of the force. Thereupon the Brighton Watch Committee, without giving any notice or offering any hearing to the chief constable, unanimously dismissed him from office. His solicitor then applied for a hearing and was allowed to appear before a later meeting. The Committee confirmed their previous decision, but by a vote of nine against three. The chief constable exercised his right of appeal to the Home Secretary, but his appeal was dismissed. Finally he turned to the courts of law, claiming a declaration that his dismissal was void since he had been given no notice of any charge against him and no opportunity of making his defence. This was refused by the High Court and by a unanimous Court of Appeal. But it was awarded by the House of Lords by a majority of four to one.

The initial dismissal was not only a breach of the principles of natural justice: it was contrary to the express provisions of the statutory regulations governing police discipline, which in cases of misconduct required notice of the charge and an opportunity for self-defence.

A police authority was, as the law then stood, empowered to dismiss any constable 'whom they think negligent in the discharge of his duty, or otherwise unfit for the same'.[59] Therefore in the authority's eyes the constable must be convicted of negligence or unfitness before they have power to deprive him of his office. This makes the case considerably stronger than many of the older natural justice cases, and it is certain that the judges who decided those cases would have held that no holder of a public office could be removed from it without notice of the charge and a fair hearing. For how could the committee convict for negligence or unfitness without hearing the defence? It was on this simple and general ground that the majority upheld the chief constable's rights. Lord Morris said:[60]

---

[57] Favourable signs had appeared shortly beforehand: *Ceylon University* v. *Fernando* [1960] 1 WLR 223; *Kanda* v. *Government of Malaya* [1962] AC 322; *Hoggard* v. *Worsborough Urban District Council* [1962] 2 QB 93.

[58] [1964] AC 40. Academic comment on this beneficial decision was surprisingly unfavourable: (1964) 80 *LQR* 105 (A. L. Goodhart); [1964] *CLJ* 83 (A. W. Bradley). But Lord Reid, in a press interview given on his retirement after 26 years in the House of Lords, singled it out as the decision which he remembered with greatest satisfaction: The Times, 14 January 1975. It will surely now be accepted as worthy of that high honour.   [59] Municipal Corporations Act 1882, s. 191.

[60] [1964] AC at 114.

My Lords, here is something which is basic to our system: the importance of upholding it far transcends the significance of any particular case.

The hearing given to the chief constable's solicitor was held to be irrelevant, since even then no notice of any specific charge was given, and natural justice was again violated.

THE 'JUDICIAL' FALLACY REPUDIATED

The leading speech of Lord Reid in *Ridge* v. *Baldwin* is of the greatest significance because of its extensive review of the authorities, which inevitably exposed the fallacies into which the decisions of the 1950s had lapsed. He attacked the problem at its root by demonstrating how the term 'judicial' had been misinterpreted as requiring some superadded characteristic over and above the characteristic that the power affected some person's rights. The mere fact that the power affects rights or interests is what makes it 'judicial', and so subject to the procedures required by natural justice.[61] In other words, a power which affects rights must be exercised 'judicially', i.e. fairly, and the fact that the power is administrative does not make it any the less 'judicial' for this purpose. Lord Hodson put this point very clearly:[62]

> the answer in a given case is not provided by the statement that the giver of the decision is acting in an executive or administrative capacity as if that were the antithesis of a judicial capacity. The cases seem to me to show that persons acting in a capacity which is not on the face of it judicial but rather executive or administrative have been held by the courts to be subject to the principles of natural justice.

Thus at last was verbal confusion cleared away and thus the House of Lords restored the classic doctrine of *Cooper* v. *Wandsworth Board of Works*, aptly celebrating the centenary of that case, and approving in particular the statements that the right to a hearing was 'of universal application' and that 'the justice of the common law will supply the omission of the legislature'.[63]

Lord Reid emphasised the universality of the right to a fair hearing: whether the cases concerned property or tenure of an office or membership of an institution, they were all governed by one principle. He also said:[64]

> We do not have a developed system of administrative law—perhaps because until fairly recently we did not need it...But I see nothing in that to justify our thinking that our old methods are any less applicable today than ever they were to the older types of case. And if there are any dicta in modern authorities which point in that direction then, in my judgment, they should not be followed.

This led to the conclusion that *Nakkuda Ali* v. *Jayaratne*, holding that a licensing authority did not need to act judicially in cancelling a licence, was based on 'a serious misapprehension of the older authorities and therefore cannot be regarded as authoritative'. In a later case Lord Denning MR pithily summed up the situation:[65]

---

[61] See likewise *A-G* v. *Ryan* [1980] AC 718. This point is of great importance also for determining the scope of certiorari as a remedy: see below, p. 516.   [62] [1964] AC 130.

[63] Above, p. 409. For further approval of *Cooper* v. *Wandsworth Board of Works* see *Wiseman* v. *Borneman* [1971] AC 297.   [64] [1964] AC at 72.

[65] *R* v. *Gaming Board for Great Britain ex p Benaim and Khaida* [1970] 2 QB 417 at 430. See also *Pagliara* v. *A-G* [1974] 1 NZLR 86; *Heatley* v. *Tasmanian Racing and Gaming Commission* (1977) 14 ALR 519 (statutory ban placed on race-goer from entering public racecourse: fair hearing required).

At one time it was said that the principles (sc. of natural justice) only apply to judicial proceedings and not to administrative proceedings. That heresy was scotched in *Ridge* v. *Baldwin*.

At another time it was said that the principles do not apply to the grant or revocation of licences. That too is wrong. *R* v. *Metropolitan Police Commissioner ex p Parker* and *Nakkuda Ali* v. *Jayaratne* are no longer authority for any such proposition.

Even more concisely, the Privy Council said:[66]

the Minister was a person having legal authority to determine a question affecting the rights of individuals. This being so it is a necessary implication that he is required to observe the principles of natural justice when exercising that authority; and if he fails to do so, his purported decision is a nullity.

And Lord Diplock said in the House of Lords that the right of a man to be given 'a fair opportunity of hearing what is alleged against him and of presenting his own case is so fundamental to any civilised legal system that it is to be presumed that Parliament intended that a failure to observe it should render null and void any decision reached in breach of this requirement'.[67]

'ACTING FAIRLY'

Although *Ridge* v. *Baldwin* sorted out the confusion caused by the artificial use of the word 'judicial' to describe functions which were in reality administrative, it did not eliminate this misnomer from the law. A means of doing so, however, appeared in a later line of cases which laid down that powers of a purely administrative character must be exercised 'fairly', meaning in accordance with natural justice—'which after all is only fair play in action'.[68] 'Natural justice is but fairness writ large and judicially'.[69] By this simple verbal shortcut the misuse of the term 'judicial' can be avoided altogether. At last we reach the result directly instead of by a devious path: administrative powers which affect rights must be exercised in accordance with natural justice.[70] As Lord Diplock put it:[71]

Where an Act of Parliament confers upon an administrative body functions which involve its making decisions which affect to their detriment the rights of other persons or curtail their liberty to do as they please, there is a presumption that Parliament intended that the administrative body should act fairly towards those persons who will be affected by their decisions.

This development dates from a case of 1966 where an immigration officer at London Airport had refused to admit a boy from Pakistan on the ground that he appeared to be well over the age of 16, under which age he would have been allowed to enter with his father. Lord Parker CJ held that even if an immigration officer is not acting in a judicial or quasi-judicial capacity, he must nevertheless act fairly.[72] He added that he realised

---

[66] *A-G* v. *Ryan* [1980] AC 718 (opinion delivered by Lord Diplock, holding that a minister in the Bahamas had failed to give a fair hearing to an applicant for registration as a citizen).

[67] *O'Reilly* v. *Mackman* [1983] 2 AC 237 at 276.

[68] A much-quoted remark of Harman LJ in *Ridge* v. *Baldwin* [1963] 1 QB 539 at 578.

[69] Lord Morris in *Furnell* v. *Whangarei High Schools Board* [1973] AC 660 at 679.

[70] On this development see (1975) 25 *U Tor LJ* 280 (D. J. Mullan); (1978) 28 *U Tor LJ* 215 (M. Loughlin); (1979) 96 *SAfLJ* 607 (L. G. Baxter).

[71] *R* v. *Commission for Racial Equality ex p Hillingdon LBC* [1982] AC 779.

[72] *Re HK (an infant)* [1967] 2 QB 617. See similarly *R* v. *Birmingham City Justice ex p Chris Foreign Foods (Wholesalers) Ltd* [1970] 1 WLR 1428.

that he was overstepping the line which earlier cases had drawn, according significance to whether there was or was not a duty to act judicially or quasi-judicially. Salmon LJ likewise held that the immigration officer, acting in an administrative capacity, must act 'fairly in accordance with the ordinary principles of natural justice', although he thought that he had a quasi-judicial capacity since he had statutory power to 'make a decision affecting basic rights of others'. The court did not, however, intervene, since it found on the facts that the officer had acted fairly.

Although this decision was plainly founded on a misapprehension as to the state of the law,[73] it supplied such a simple and attractive basis for natural justice that it was followed with alacrity, and it was not long before its principle was adopted by the Court of Appeal.[74] Speaking of inspectors appointed by the Board of Trade to make a report on the affairs of a company, which might have grave consequences, Lord Denning MR said:[75]

> Seeing that their work and their report may lead to such consequences, I am clearly of the opinion that the inspectors must act fairly. This is a duty which rests on them, as on many other bodies, even though they are not judicial or quasi-judicial, but only administrative.

As this and other opinions show, the courts still find difficulty in ridding themselves of the idea that if the function is administrative it is therefore not quasi-judicial. They still shrink from reverting to the traditional doctrine, that an administrative power which may gravely affect a person's position must be exercised judicially, despite 'Lord Reid's momentous speech in *Ridge* v. *Baldwin*, since which emphasis upon the distinction between judicial and non-judicial decisions is no longer good law'.[76] The fallacy that 'quasi-judicial' and 'administrative' mean two basically different things appears to be almost ineradicable.

Notwithstanding the clear statements in the original decision that 'acting fairly' was required by the rules of natural justice, judges unable to accept the logic of *Ridge* v. *Baldwin* have attempted to differentiate them, suggesting that natural justice applies only to judicial or quasi-judicial functions and 'acting fairly' to administrative or executive functions—thus compounding the old fallacy with a new one.[77] But it is now clearly settled, as is indeed self-evident, that there is no difference between natural justice and 'acting fairly', but that they are alternative names for a single but flexible doctrine whose content may vary according to the nature of the power and the circumstances of the case.[78] In the words of Lord Denning MR, 'the rules of natural justice—or of fairness—are not cut and dried. They vary infinitely'.[79] Attempts to represent natural justice and 'acting fairly'

---

[73] *Ridge* v. *Baldwin* was not cited and *Nakkuda Ali* v. *Jayaratne* was discussed and distinguished as if it were still good law. Judgment was not reserved.

[74] *R* v. *Gaming Board for Great Britain ex p Benaim and Khaida* [1970] 2 QB 417 at 430: *Re Pergamon Press* [1971] Ch 388 at 399. See also *R* v. *Kent Police Authority ex p Godden* [1971] 2 QB 662; *R* v. *Liverpool Corporation ex p Liverpool Taxi Fleet Operators' Association* [1972] 2 QB 299; *Maxwell* v. *Department of Trade and Industry* [1974] QB 523; *R* v. *Race Relations Board ex p Selvarajan* [1975] 1 WLR 1686; *Fraser* v. *Mudge* [1975] 1 WLR 1132.   [75] *Re Pergamon Press* (above).

[76] Stephen J in *Salemi* v. *Minister for Immigration (No 2)* (1977) 14 ALR 1 at 30.

[77] As in *Pearlberg* v. *Varty* [1972] 1 WLR 534 at 547; *Bates* v. *Lord Hailsham* [1972] 1 WLR 1373, mostly corrected in *McInnes* v. *Onslow-Fane* [1978] 1 WLR 1520 at 1530. By exploiting this supposed distinction the Supreme Court of Canada, having precluded itself from applying 'natural justice' to administrative action, accepted the duty to 'act fairly': *Re Nicholson and Haldimand-Norfolk Police Commissioners* (1979) 88 DLR (3d) 671. See also *Flexman* v. *Franklin CC* [1979] 2 NZLR 690.

[78] e.g. *Re Pergamon Press Ltd* [1971] Ch 388 at 399; *R* v. *Home Secretary ex p Hosenball* [1977] 1 WLR 766 at 784; *O'Reilly* v. *Mackman* [1983] 2 AC 237 at 275 (Lord Diplock); *Lloyd* v. *McMahon* [1987] AC 625 at 702 (Lord Bridge); *Salemi* v. *Minister for Immigration (No 2)* (1977) 14 ALR 1.

[79] *R* v. *Home Secretary ex p Santillo* [1981] QB 778.

as two different things are a sure sign of failure to understand that *administrative* powers are subject to the principles of natural justice as explained throughout this chapter. Lord Scarman neatly combined both points in observing that the courts have extended 'the requirement of natural justice, namely the duty to act fairly, so that it is required of a purely administrative act'.[80]

'Acting fairly' is a phrase of such wide implications that it may ultimately extend beyond the sphere of procedure. It was suggested in one case that it included a duty of acting with substantial fairness and consistency.[81] But when Lord Denning MR said much the same thing (that not only must there be a fair hearing but 'the decision itself must be fair and reasonable') the House of Lords repudiated his opinion.[82] On the other hand, fairness may not necessarily comprise the whole domain of natural justice. Inspectors investigating the affairs of companies, who are subject to the duty to act fairly, are not required to be free from bias.[83] Yet the same phrase has been used to describe a duty to act honestly and without bias or caprice but without any need to disclose the charge or give a hearing.[84] Judges seem to be using it in a variety of different situations, so that it has no precise meaning except when used as a synonym for natural justice.

VOID OR VOIDABLE

Ridge v. *Baldwin* brought with it a rash of conflicting opinions about whether failure to give a fair hearing rendered the dismissal of the chief constable void or voidable.[85] In the long history of the cases on natural justice as applied to administrative action this question had never before been agitated, for the simple reason that the logic of the situation excluded it. It had always previously been held that a breach of the rules of natural justice resulted in the determination being null and void, in the same way as any other act which was ultra vires. For the duty to act fairly, just like the duty to act reasonably,[86] was enforced as an implied statutory requirement, so that failure to observe it meant that the administrative act or decision was outside the statutory power, unjustified by law, and therefore ultra vires and void. This assumption was so well understood that it was rarely spelled out in judgments.[87] As explained already,[88] there was no other basis on which the courts could intervene. The majority of the House of Lords in *Ridge* v. *Baldwin* decided entirely consistently with this hypothesis, holding expressly that the chief constable's dismissal was void. Lord Reid said:[89]

> Then there was considerable argument whether in the result the watch committee's decision was void or merely voidable. Time and time again in the cases I have cited it has been

---

[80] *Council of Civil Service Unions* v. *Minister for the Civil Service* [1985] AC 374 at 407.

[81] *HTV Ltd* v. *Price Commission* [1976] ICR 170 at 189 (Scarman LJ); above, p. 318.

[82] *Chief Constable of North Wales Police* v. *Evans* [1982] 1 WLR 1155, perhaps giving Lord Denning's words a wider meaning than he intended. In *Daganayasi* v. *Minister of Immigration* [1980] 2 NZLR 130 Cooke J said that 'fairness need not be treated as confined to procedural matters'. See also above, p. 335 as to unfairness amounting to abuse of power.

[83] *R* v. *Secretary of State for Trade ex p Perestrello* [1981] QB 19.

[84] *McInnes* v. *Onslow-Fane* [1978] 1 WLR 1520.

[85] For discussion see (1967) 83 *LQR* 499, (1968) 84 *LQR* 95 (Wade); (1968) 31 *MLR* 2, 138 (M. B. Akehurst).

[86] See above, p. 287.

[87] It was spelled out with perfect clarity in *Anisminic Ltd* v. *Foreign Compensation Commission* [1968] 2 QB at 890 (Diplock LJ), [1969] 2 AC at 171 (Lord Reid), 195 (Lord Pearce) and 207 (Lord Wilberforce). Yet another proof is that failure to give a fair hearing renders the decision 'not within the powers of this Act' for the purposes of statutory remedies: below, p. 625. See also the quotations above, p. 374.

[88] Above, p. 28.   [89] [1964] AC at 80.

stated that a decision given without regard to the principles of natural justice is void and that was expressly decided in *Wood* v. *Woad*.[90] I see no reason to doubt these authorities. The body with the power to decide cannot lawfully proceed to make a decision until it has afforded to the person affected a proper opportunity to state his case.

Lord Morris and Lord Hodson likewise held that the decision of the watch committee was void, and could be called voidable only in the sense that unless and until the chief constable contested it, it may appear valid and would be treated as valid.[91]

But the dissentient judges who would have held that the chief constable had no right to a fair hearing were of opinion that the watch committee's decision was not void but voidable. As expounded by Lord Evershed in the House of Lords, the motive was a desire to enlarge judicial discretion.[92] This policy is open to the objection that it would introduce dangerous uncertainty—one might say, palm-tree injustice. Natural justice has for centuries been enforced as a matter of law and not of discretion.[93] An end was put to such arguments when the House of Lords later reaffirmed that an order made contrary to natural justice was outside jurisdiction and void.[94]

FAIR HEARINGS—GENERAL ASPECTS

SCOPE AND LIMITS OF THE PRINCIPLE

Ridge v. *Baldwin* reinstated the right to a fair hearing as 'a rule of universal application' in the case of administrative acts or decisions affecting rights; and, in Lord Loreburn's oft-repeated words, the duty to afford it is 'a duty lying upon every one who decides anything'.[95] The decision gave the impetus to a surge of litigation over natural justice, in which the courts have been able to consider many of its facets and to build up something like a canon of fair administrative procedure. For the most part the numerous decisions have served only to show the correctness of the above-quoted words, sweeping though they are. Natural justice has achieved something like the status of a fundamental right.[96]

For example, the courts have repudiated earlier suggestions that the principles of natural justice do not apply to disciplinary bodies: 'they must act fairly just the same as anyone else; and are just as subject to control by the courts'.[97] Disadvantaged groups such as prisoners,[98] immigrants[99] and gipsies[100] have succeeded in invalidating decisions made against them when they have not been treated fairly. At the other end of the spectrum of power, public authorities themselves are now given the benefit of natural justice, as illustrated at the end of this section. Basically the principle is confined by no frontiers.

---

[90]   (1874) LR 9 Ex 190.   [91]   Above, p. 247.

[92]   [1964] AC at 91. But *Osgood* v. *Nelson*, from which support is claimed, does not in fact support this proposition: see (1968) 84 *LQR* at 112.

[93]   For a case following the dissident judges see *Durayappah* v. *Fernando* [1967] 2 AC 337.

[94]   *Anisminic Ltd* v. *Foreign Compensation Commission* [1969] 2 AC 147; and see *A-G* v. *Ryan* [1980] AC 143.   [95]   Above, p. 411.

[96]   In *Fraser* v. *State Services Commission* [1984] 1 NZLR 116 at 121. Cooke J said *obiter*, in the context of natural justice, that 'it is arguable that some common law rights may go so deep that even Parliament cannot be accepted by the courts to have destroyed them'.

[97]   *Buckoke* v. *Greater London Council* [1971] Ch 655 (Lord Denning MR).

[98]   See below, p. 471.   [99]   See above, p. 362.

[100]   *R* v. *Brent LBC ex p MacDonagh*, 22 March 1999 (gipsies entitled to hearing after assurance from local authority).

On the other hand it must be a flexible principle. The judges, anxious as always to preserve some freedom of manœuvre, emphasise that 'it is not possible to lay down rigid rules as to when the principles of natural justice are to apply: nor as to their scope and extent. Everything depends on the subject-matter'.[101] Their application, resting as it does upon statutory implication, must always be in conformity with the scheme of the Act and with the subject matter of the case. 'In the application of the concept of fair play there must be real flexibility'.[102] There must also have been some real prejudice to the complainant: there is no such thing as a merely technical infringement of natural justice.[103]

Sometimes urgent action may have to be taken on grounds of public health or safety, for example to seize and destroy bad meat exposed for sale[104] or to order the removal to hospital of a person with an infectious disease.[105] In such cases the normal presumption that a hearing must be given is rebutted by the circumstances of the case.[106] So it was when the Secretary of State for Transport provisionally suspended the permit of a Romanian airline because its pilots had failed the British civil aviation examinations,[107] and where a local authority prohibited the sale of allegedly dangerous toys as 'an emergency holding operation'.[108] The presumption is rebutted also, for obvious reasons, where the police have to act with urgency, e.g. in making arrests.[109]

Even in cases not involving urgency it may be equally clear that no hearing is required. A decision to prosecute or bring legal proceedings,[110] or to carry out a search,[111] damaging though it may be to the accused, does not entitle him to be consulted or shown the evidence in advance. The same applies to a decision by the Department of Trade to appoint inspectors to investigate suspicious circumstances in the affairs of a company: it may injure the company's reputation, but that risk has to be accepted as the price of the legal privileges enjoyed by companies; and in many cases prior warning would frustrate the objects of the legislation.[112] Nor need a minister offer a hearing to a local authority before calling in their local plan for his approval or consult them about objections to it received by him.[113] In resolving to adopt a slum-clearance scheme a local authority need not first give a hearing to an objecting landowner, since under the statutory procedure this resolution is the initial step and the Act provides amply for the hearing of objections at a statutory inquiry.[114] Sometimes a right of appeal may imply that no earlier hearing is necessary.[115] And it is always possible for hearings to be excluded by the scheme of the legislation.[116] But where the grant of a fair hearing is consistent with the exercise of the legal power, the law leans strongly in its favour. Judges of the highest authority have approved

[101] R v. Gaming Board for Great Britain ex p Benaim and Khaida [1970] 2 QB 417 at 439 (Lord Denning MR). For cases of national security see below, p. 473. But see now Appendix 3.

[102] Re Pergamon Press Ltd [1971] Ch 388 at 403 (Sachs LJ).

[103] George v. Secretary of State for the Environment (1979) 77 LGR 689.

[104] White v. Redfern (1879) 5 QBD 15.   [105] R v. Davey [1899] 2 QB 301.

[106] But 'urgency' did not justify the denial of procedural justice in R (Shoesmith) v. OFSTED and ors [2011] EWCA Civ 642, para. 60. Discussed above, p. 253.

[107] R v. Secretary of State for Transport ex p Pegasus Holdings (London) Ltd [1988] 1 WLR 990.

[108] R v. Birmingham City Council ex p Ferrero Ltd [1991] 3 Admin LR 613, discussed below, p. 603.

[109] Grech v. Minister of Immigration (1991) 105 ALR 107.

[110] Wiseman v. Borneman [1971] AC 297 at 308 (Lord Reid); Nicol v. A-G of Victoria [1982] VR 353.

[111] R v. Leicester Crown Court ex p Director of Public Prosecutions [1987] 1 WLR 1371.

[112] Norwest Holst Ltd v. Secretary of State for Trade [1978] Ch 201. But as to the conduct of the investigation see below, p. 822.

[113] R v. Secretary of State for the Environment ex p Southwark LBC (1987) 54 P & CR 226 (plan rejected by minister).   [114] Fredman v. Minister of Health (1935) 154 LT 240.

[115] Below, p. 446.

[116] As in Commissioner of Business Franchises v. Borenstein [1984] VR 375; Building Construction Federation v. Minister for Industrial Relations [1985] 1 NSWLR 197.

the epigram of Byles J, that 'the justice of the common law will supply the omission of the legislature'.[117] Nor is this presumption to be excluded merely for the sake of administrative convenience: 'convenience and justice are often not on speaking terms'.[118]

THE PRESERVATION OF FLEXIBILITY

In order to preserve flexibility the courts frequently quote general statements such as the following:[119]

> The requirements of natural justice must depend on the circumstances of the case, the nature of the inquiry, the rules under which the tribunal is acting, the subject-matter to be dealt with, and so forth.

To the same effect is a passage, much cited, in a speech of Lord Bridge in the House of Lords:[120]

> My Lords, the so-called rules of natural justice are not engraved on tablets of stone. To use the phrase which better expresses the underlying concept, what the requirements of fairness demand when any body, domestic, administrative or judicial, has to make a decision which will affect the rights of individuals depends on the character of the decision-making body, the kind of decision it has to make and the statutory or other framework in which it operates. In particular, it is well-established that when a statute has conferred on any body the power to make decisions affecting individuals, the courts will not only require the procedure prescribed by the statute to be followed, but will readily imply so much and no more to be introduced by way of additional procedural safeguards as will ensure the attainment of fairness.

But the flexibility of natural justice does not imply a variable standard of procedural justice. As Sedley J has observed:

> The well attested flexibility of natural justice does not mean that the court applies differential standards at will, but that the application of the principles (which, subject to known exceptions, are constant) is necessarily as various as the situations in which they are invoked.[121]

In other words the courts apply the same principles in many different situations. Ample illustration will be found in the remainder of this chapter.

The principle is in no way limited to particular categories of cases such as interference with property, dismissal from office, and charges of personal misconduct. It applies equally to the allocation of compensation for a 'well maintained' house as between landlord and tenant,[122] to the banning of one member of the public from local authority premises which are open to others,[123] to the removal of a name from a list of approved

---

[117] Above, p. 409; approved in *Ridge* v. *Baldwin* [1964] AC 40; *Durayappah* v. *Fernando* [1967] 2 AC 337, *Wiseman* v. *Borneman* [1971] AC 297. But 'it is not to be used to frustrate the intention of the legislature': *Norwest Holst Ltd* v. *Secretary of State for Trade* (above) (Ormrod LJ).

[118] *General Medical Council* v. *Spackman* [1943] AC 627 at 638 (Lord Atkin). See *R* v. *Hull Prison Visitors ex p St Germain (No 2)* [1979] 1 WLR 1401.

[119] *Russell* v. *Duke of Norfolk* [1949] 1 All ER 109 at 118 (Tucker LJ).

[120] *Lloyd* v. *McMahon* [1987] AC 625 at 702. And to similar effect see *R (West)* v. *Parole Board* [2005] UKHL 1, [2005]1 WLR 350 (para. 27 (Lord Bingham)).

[121] *R* v. *Home Secretary ex p Moon* (1996) 8 Admin LR 477 at 480.

[122] *Hoggard* v. *Worsborough Urban District Council* [1962] 2 QB 93.

[123] *R* v. *Brent LBC ex p Assegai*, The Times, 18 June 1987.

foster-parents,[124] or of approved contractors,[125] and to the right to be heard at a coroner's inquest.[126] The scope of the principle is at least as wide as it was under the old authorities cited earlier in this chapter. If anything, it is now wider, partly owing to the general administrative duty to act fairly which has now been repeatedly recognised. It is just as applicable in favour of public authorities as against them, as a series of decisions now shows. Thus a municipal council in Ceylon dissolved by the minister under his default powers was entitled to a fair hearing before the minister could legally make the order.[127] A local authority's rate support grant, as mentioned above, could not lawfully be reduced without giving the authority a fair hearing. A ministerial order requiring the Greater London Council to make the maximum payment to London Regional Transport was quashed for the same reason.[128] And where a mental health review tribunal discharged a patient without notifying the Secretary of State, so that he had no opportunity to be heard, the tribunal's order was set aside in 'a classic case of a failure of natural justice'.[129]

SUPPLEMENTATION OF STATUTORY PROCEDURES

Many cases cited in this chapter illustrate the way in which the principles of natural justice are used to supplement procedures which themselves provide for a hearing or inquiry, with or without detailed regulation of the procedure. As Lord Reid said:[130]

> For a long time the courts have, without objection from Parliament, supplemented procedure laid down in legislation where they have found that to be necessary for this purpose. But before this unusual kind of power is exercised it must be clear that the statutory procedure is insufficient to achieve justice and that to require additional steps would not frustrate the apparent purpose of the legislation.

Or, in the words of Lord Bridge:

> In particular, it is well-established that when a statute has conferred on any body the power to make decisions affecting individuals, the courts will not only require the procedure prescribed by the statute to be followed, but will readily imply so much and no more to be introduced by way of additional procedural safeguards as will ensure the attainment of fairness.[131]

Citing these words Lord Sumption has said:[132]

---

[124] R v. Wandsworth LBC ex p P. [1988] 87 LGR 370. Similarly, R v. Secretary of State for Health ex p C [2000] FLR 627 (fairness required in maintenance of non-statutory child care index of persons unsuitable to work with children).   [125] R v. Enfield LBC ex p TF Unwin (Roydon) Ltd (1989) 1 Admin LR 51.

[126] Annetts v. McCann (1990) 97 ALR 177.

[127] Durayappah v. Fernando (above). See likewise R v. Secretary of State for the Environment ex p Norwich City Council [1982] QB 808; Balmain Association Inc v. Planning Administrator (1991) 25 NSWLR 615.

[128] R v. Secretary of State for Transport ex p Greater London Council [1986] QB 556.

[129] R v. Oxford Regional Mental Health Review Tribunal ex p Home Secretary [1986] 1 WLR 1180, affirmed [1988] AC 120.

[130] Wiseman v. Borneman [1971] AC 297 at 308. See also R v. Hull Prison Visitors ex p St Germain [1979] 1 WLR 1401 at 1408; R v. Home Secretary ex p Abdi [1996] 1 WLR 298 at 313 (HL).

[131] Lloyd v. McMahon [1987] AC 625 at 702. Several of the judgments emphasise this point.

[132] Bank Mellat v. HM Treasury [2013] UKSC 39, para. 35. The fact that the Orders in this case were laid before Parliament made no difference: 'it is not possible to say that procedural fairness is sufficiently guaranteed by Parliamentary scrutiny' (para. 47). But note the dissenting judges. Lord Hope said: 'the evident intention of Parliament that the Treasury should have power to make orders of the kind contemplated...without prior consultation' (para. 153).

The duty of fairness governing the exercise of a statutory power is a limitation on the discretion of the decision-maker which is implied into the statute. But the fact that the statute makes some provision for the procedure to be followed before or after the exercise of a statutory power does not of itself impliedly exclude either the duty of fairness in general or the duty of prior consultation in particular, where they would otherwise arise. As Byles J observed in *Cooper v Board of Works for the Wandsworth District* (1863) 14 CB(NS) 190, 194, 'the justice of the common law will supply the omission of the legislature.'

No statutory procedure is likely to cover every possibility of unfairness. Gaps may therefore be filled by resorting to 'the justice of the common law'. Thus objectors at public inquiries must be given a fair opportunity to meet adverse evidence, even though the statutory provisions do not cover the case expressly,[133] inquiries must not be unfairly renewed;[134] adjournments must be granted where fairness so demands;[135] and rival applications must be treated fairly.[136] And issues that 'the public law principle of fairness' requires to be taken separately, must be heard and decided separately.[137]

WHERE A FAIR HEARING 'WOULD MAKE NO DIFFERENCE'

Procedural objections are often raised by unmeritorious parties with weak cases. Judges may then be tempted to refuse relief on the ground that a fair hearing could have made no difference to the result. But in principle it is vital that the procedure and the merits should be kept strictly apart, since otherwise the merits may be prejudged unfairly. Lord Wright once said:[138] 'If the principles of natural justice are violated in respect of any decision it is, indeed, immaterial whether the same decision would have been arrived at in the absence of the departure from the essential principles of justice. The decision must be declared to be no decision.' On another occasion, Sedley LJ said that even judges found it 'seductively easy to conclude that there can be no answer to a case of which you have only heard one side'.[139]

The dangers were vividly expressed by Megarry J, criticising the contention that 'the result is obvious from the start':[140]

---

[133] *Errington v. Minister of Health* [1935] 1 KB 249 and other cases cited below, p. 428. And see *Steele v. Minister of Housing and Local Government* (1956) 6 P & CR 386 (inspector and minister must act judicially in accordance with natural justice).

[134] *R v. Secretary of State for the Environment ex p Fielder Estates (Canvey) Ltd* (1989) 57 P & CR 424.

[135] *Majorpier Ltd v. Secretary of State for the Environment* (1989) 59 P & CR 453.

[136] *Lakin Ltd v. Secretary of State for Scotland*, 1988 SLT 780.

[137] *Raji v. General Medical Council* [2003] UKPC 24, [2003] 1 WLR 1052 (PC), para. 16 (Professional Conduct Committee of the GMC not free to decide whether to restore practitioner to register at the same time as it decided whether he could make further applications for restoration).

[138] *General Medical Council v. Spackman* [1943] AC 627 at 644; and see *Annamunthodo v. Oilfields Workers' Trade Union* [1961] AC 945 at 956 (Lord Denning).

[139] *Secretary of State for the Home Department v. AF and ors* [2008] EWCA Civ 1148, para. 113.

[140] *John v. Rees* [1970] Ch 345 at 402. Approved in *R (Amin) v. Home Secretary* [2003] UKHL 51, [2003] 3 WLR 1169 (HL), para. 52 (Lord Steyn). See similarly many other cases including *ex p Fanneran* (below) at 359 (Rougier J), *R (Shoesmith) v. OFSTED and ors* [2011] EWCA Civ 642, para. 74 (Kay LJ); *ML (Nigeria) v. Home Secretary* [2013] EWCA Civ 844, para. 10 (Moses LJ); and *Ibrahim v. London Borough of Wandsworth* [2013] EWCA Civ 20, para. 19 (Sedley LJ). Given all this weighty authority it ought to be noted that Lord Phillips in *Home Secretary v. AF and anor* [2009] UKHL 28, para. 62 was not 'convinced' by this principle where the decision-maker has but 'a low threshold to cross' before making an adverse finding; cogent evidence, even if not disclosed to the individual concerned, would take the decision-maker over that threshold. *AF (No 3)* is discussed more fully below, p. 435.

As everybody who has anything to do with the law well knows, the path of the law is strewn with examples of open and shut cases which, somehow, were not; of unanswerable charges which, in the event, were completely answered; of inexplicable conduct which was fully explained; of fixed and unalterable determinations that, by discussion, suffered a change.

The last few words are especially apt for administrative decisions. They were adopted in a later case where the court quashed a Secretary of State's order reducing a local authority's rate support grant for failure to grant them a hearing at the proper time.[141] Even though it was 'certainly probable' that the decision would have been the same, since all the arguments had been fully rehearsed at an earlier stage, the court declined to hold that a hearing would have been a useless formality. In another case it has been held that it is a breach of natural justice for a magistrates' court to order the destruction of a dog under the Dangerous Dogs Act 1991 without hearing the owner, even where the court has no discretion but to order the destruction, since the procedure was fundamentally faulty. The argument that it would not have made any difference 'is to be treated with great caution. Down that slippery slope lies the way to dictatorship'.[142] In the leading case Bingham LJ gave six reasons why such a holding should be a very rare event, although the court then proceeded so to hold in validating the dismissal of a probationer police constable for obesity, a physical fact which could not be gainsaid, even though an adverse report about him was not disclosed.[143] And in a difficult case where the police did not disclose adverse reports on ex-prisoners before informing their neighbours that they were convicted paedophiles, the Court of Appeal held that although the reports, or at least their gist, should have been disclosed, the omission was immaterial since disclosure would have made no difference.[144]

This question profoundly affected the course of *Ridge v. Baldwin*. The argument favoured by the lower courts, and in Lord Evershed's dissenting speech, was that natural justice need not be enforced in the absence of a miscarriage of justice or some probable effect on the result.[145] The House of Lords rejected this reasoning decisively, but nevertheless it has made a reappearance in several later cases. In one, a university student had been rusticated without a hearing and in breach of natural justice, but the courts refused him relief on the ground that his offence was of the kind that merited a severe penalty and the penalty inflicted on him was perfectly proper.[146] In another case, where a schoolteacher's dismissal was annulled by the House of Lords because he had not been fairly heard, it was said that a man had no right to be admitted to state his own case unless he could show that he had a case of substance to make, since the 'court does not act in vain'; and that it need not be determined whether a hearing was required where it 'could only be a useless formality' because there was nothing that the person affected could say against the

---

[141] *R v. Secretary of State for the Environment ex p Brent LBC* [1982] QB 593, followed in *Simpex (GE) Holdings Ltd v. Secretary of State for the Environment* (1988) 57 P & CR 306 at 324. Contrast *R v. Secretary of State for the Environment ex p Hammersmith and Fulham LBC* [1991] 1 AC 521.

[142] *R v. Ealing Magistrates' Court ex p Fanneran* [1996] 8 Admin LR 351 at 356 (Staughton LJ).

[143] *R v. Chief Constable of Thames Valley Police ex p Cotton* [1990] IRLR 64 (medical report had advised that constable's weight made him unfit for full duty). Bingham LJ quotes his 6 points in [1991] *PL* at 72.

[144] *R v. Chief Constable of North Wales Police ex p AB* [1998] 3 WLR 57.

[145] See [1963] 1 QB at 556 (contention that no hearing was required since police officer had convicted himself out of his own mouth). See also *Byrne v. Kinematograph Renters Society Ltd* [1958] 1 WLR 762. For criticism see above, p. 420; [1975] *PL* 27 (D. H. Clark).

[146] *Glynn v. Keele University* [1971] 1 WLR 487; see below, p. 427.

action taken.[147] Much the same was said by the Court of Appeal where car-hire drivers were banned from London Airport because of repeated and persistent offences against the regulations.[148] There may be cases where it is merely futile to grant relief, as where food hawkers were refused street trading consent without being allowed to see objections which had been lodged but which, as was found when the judge inspected them, could not have affected the decision.[149]

Judges are naturally inclined to use their discretion when a plea of breach of natural justice is used as the last refuge of a claimant with a bad case. But that should not be allowed to weaken the basic principle that fair procedure comes first, and that it is only after hearing both sides that the merits can be properly considered. A distinction might perhaps be made according to the nature of the decision. In the case of a tribunal which must decide according to law, it may be justifiable to disregard a breach of natural justice where the demerits of the claim are such that it would in any case be hopeless. But in the case of a discretionary administrative decision, such as the dismissal of a teacher or the expulsion of a student, hearing his case will often soften the heart of the authority and alter their decision, even though it is clear from the outset that punitive action would be justified.[150] This is the essence of good and considerate administration, and the law should take care to preserve it.

RELIEF REFUSED IN DISCRETION

Closely akin to the subject of the foregoing paragraphs, and overlapping it in some cases, is the question of the court's discretion. The remedies most used in natural justice cases—the quashing order, the prohibiting order, the mandatory order, the injunction and the declaration—are discretionary, so that the court has power to withhold them if it thinks fit; and from time to time the court will do so for some special reason, even though there has been a clear violation of natural justice.[151]

The House of Lords exercised discretion in an unusual way in the case of a police probationer who had been unjustly required to resign. Since he was the holder of an office, and since he was held entitled to treat himself as unlawfully dismissed, he should have been granted mandamus so as to reinstate him. The House of Lords shrank from this because 'in practice it might border on usurpation of the powers of the chief constable', and they declared the probationer entitled only to the remedies of unlawful dismissal.[152] In other words, the House were not willing to protect this particular office specifically in

---

[147] *Malloch v. Aberdeen Cpn* [1971] 1 WLR 1578 at 1595 (Lord Wilberforce), 1600 (Lord Simon), criticised by D. H. Clark (as above). For this case see below, p. 465. See also *Wislang v. Medical Practitioners Disciplinary Committee* [1973] 1 NZLR 29 (fact that defence was likely to be unsuccessful taken into account in refusing relief in discretion); *Stininato v. Auckland Boxing Association* [1978] 1 NZLR 1 (relief refused to boxer denied licence because of complaints).

[148] *Cinnamond v. British Airports Authority* [1980] 1 WLR 582 (Shaw and Brandon LJJ).

[149] *R v. Bristol City Council ex p Pearce* (1984) 83 LGR 711.

[150] For an example see Wade, *Towards Administrative Justice*, 10. In *Ridge v. Baldwin* the hearing later given to the chief constable's solicitor induced 3 members of the watch committee to change their minds: [1964] AC 40 at 47; and see at 68 (Lord Reid).

[151] For a general statement see *Hoffmann–La Roche v. Secretary of State for Trade and Industry* [1975] AC 295 at 320 (Lord Denning MR). For discretionary remedies generally see below, p. 596.

[152] *Chief Constable of the North Wales Police v. Evans* [1982] 1 WLR 1155 (Lord Brightman). Lord Bridge was in favour of granting mandamus. Contrary to its title and the report (at 1157), this was an application for judicial review. For further discussion see (1983) 99 *LQR* 171, (1985) 101 *LQR* 154 (Wade).

the circumstances of the case,[153] feeling perhaps that the chief constable's hand ought not to be forced.

Discretion has been exercised in several cases where fair hearings have not been given to university students in disciplinary proceedings. One is in the case of the rusticated student mentioned above, in which an injunction was refused.[154] In another, students who had been required to withdraw for failure in examinations ought to have been given a hearing, but they delayed for seven months before taking legal action and the court declined to grant prerogative remedies to 'those who sleep upon their rights'.[155] Academic discipline is discussed further below.[156]

Where it is by the applicant's own default, or by that of his advisers, that his case cannot be heard, the courts have sometimes been willing to exercise discretion in his favour. But the House of Lords reversed such a decision in a deportation case where the applicant missed the hearing of his appeal because his solicitor wrote to him at the wrong address,[157] and this decision appears to mark the end of these indulgences.

Judicial discretion in withholding remedies is very carefully exercised and is a good deal less dangerous than some other arguments which have been used as excuses for condoning breaches of natural justice. Nevertheless it needs to be exercised with constant regard to the dangers mentioned in the preceding section.[158]

WHO IS ENTITLED TO SUE?

It seems plain that denial of a fair hearing is a wrong which is personal to the party aggrieved. If he himself waives the objection and does not complain, it is not the business of other people to do so, for as against them there is nothing wrong with the decision.[159] In the Ceylon case already mentioned, accordingly, the proper person to challenge the minister's action was the municipal council itself, which had not been lawfully dissolved.[160] Since in fact the proceedings were brought by the mayor personally, he failed as not being the proper plaintiff. The Privy Council held that this was because the minister's order was merely voidable, as already explained. The true reason, it is submitted, is to be found by asking what is the condition to be read into the statute. That condition need not be that any order made without giving a hearing is void: it should rather be that such an order is void unless accepted by the person concerned. The same point could be expressed in terms of locus standi, but more probably it is inherent in the principle of natural justice itself.

Similarly if in *Ridge* v. *Baldwin* the chief constable had not contested his dismissal, a third party could not have contested some order made by his successor on the ground that the former chief constable's dismissal was void, so that he was still in office.[161] It would be absurd to imply into any statute a condition capable of producing that effect.

---

[153] For specific protection of offices see below, p. 490.   [154] *Glynn* v. *Keele University* (above).

[155] *R* v. *Aston University Senate ex p Roffey* [1969] 2 QB 538. The application for prerogative remedies was probably misconceived: see (1974) 90 *LQR* 157 (Wade).   [156] Below, p. 469.

[157] *R* v. *Home Secretary ex p Al-Mehdawi* [1990] 1 AC 876. Contrast *R* v. *Diggines ex p Rahmani* [1985] QB 1109 (affirmed on other grounds [1986] AC 475); *R* v. *Immigration Appeal Tribunal ex p Enwia* [1984] 1 WLR 117 at 130.   [158] Remedial discretion is discussed fully at p. 596.

[159] *Hoffman–La Roche & Co* v. *Secretary of State for Trade and Industry* [1975] AC 295 at 320 (Lord Denning MR); *Credit Suisse* v. *Allerdale BC* [1997] QB 306 at 356 (Hobhouse LJ); *R* v. *Home Secretary ex p Jeyeanthan* [2000] 1 WLR 354 at 365.

[160] *Durayappah* v. *Fernando* [1967] 2 AC 337; above, p. 420.

[161] As pointed out in *Durayappah* v. *Fernando*, above, at 353, saying that it was 'a matter of ordinary common sense'. It might also have been affected by the doctrine of officers de facto: see above, p. 238.

Consequently there is no contradiction in saying that a breach of natural justice can be waived but that if it is not waived the act is void.[162]

It does not follow that no third party can ever complain of a breach of natural justice, though this may be true as regards denial of a fair hearing. If a biased licensing authority grants an application, this is a wrong done not to the applicant but to other interested parties and to the public interest generally. In that case the court may suitably grant a remedy, as happened in one such case.[163]

Where the Secretary of State calls in a local plan for decision by himself instead of by the local planning authority, that authority has no right to be heard since it is not sufficiently affected.[164] Nor, probably, has a shareholder in a company the listing of whose shares is cancelled by the stock exchange, when the company itself does not complain.[165]

Sometimes third parties may be seriously affected and then they may be entitled to claim fair treatment. In one case an insurance company was prohibited by LAUTRO from accepting further business from a particular agent. Under LAUTRO's rules only the company was entitled to appeal, and the company did not do so. The agent himself was given no opportunity of resisting the prohibition, which seriously damaged his business. The Court of Appeal held that LAUTRO had a duty to act fairly towards the agent as well as towards the company, and that where for the protection of the public the prohibition had to be issued urgently, the agent should have the right to apply for its rescission and also a right of appeal. But the agent's complaint was that he was not consulted before the notice of prohibition was served, and in this he failed, since LAUTRO was in the dilemma that so often besets regulatory authorities and was justified in acting with urgency.[166]

THE RIGHT TO KNOW THE OPPOSING CASE

A proper hearing must always include a 'fair opportunity to those who are parties in the controversy for correcting or contradicting anything prejudicial to their view'.[167] Lord Denning has added:

> If the right to be heard is to be a real right which is worth anything, it must carry with it a right in the accused man to know the case which is made against him. He must know what evidence has been given and what statements have been made affecting him: and then he must be given a fair opportunity to correct or contradict them.[168]

Accordingly where a chief constable required a police probationer to resign on account of allegations about his private life which he was given no fair opportunity to rebut the House of Lords granted him the remedies of unlawful dismissal.[169] The Court of Appeal

---

[162] See above, p. 419, and (1968) 84 *LQR* at 109 (Wade).

[163] R v. *Hendon Rural District Council ex p Chorley* [1933] 2 KB 696.

[164] R v. *Secretary of State for the Environment ex p Southwark LBC* (1987) 54 P & CR 226.

[165] R v. *International Stock Exchange of the United Kingdom and the Republic of Ireland Ltd ex p Else (1982) Ltd* [1993] QB 534 (dealing with both domestic and EC law).

[166] R v. *Life Assurance Unit Trust Regulatory Organisation Ltd ex p Ross* [1993] QB 17, not applying to the dictum of Lord Diplock in *Cheall* v. *APEX* [1983] 2 AC 190, where the case was much weaker. See also R v. *LAUTRO Ltd ex p Tee* (1994) 8 Admin LR 289.

[167] Above, p. 411. See below, p. 434, for discussion of whether this common law principle is less extensive than the disclosure required under Art. 6(1).

[168] *Kanda* v. *Government of Malaya* [1962] AC 322. See similarly *A-G* v. *Ryan* [1980] AC 718 (application for citizenship refused without disclosing grounds).

[169] *Chief Constable of the North Wales Police* v. *Evans* [1982] 1 WLR 1155; see similarly R v. *Home Secretary ex p Benwell* [1985] QB 554; R v. *Chief Constable of Thames Valley Police ex p Stevenson*, The Times, 22 April 1987; R v. *Chief Constable of Avon & Somerset ex p Clarke*, The Independent, 27 November 1986.

likewise quashed the refusal of renewal of a taxi-driver's licence because an adverse medical report was not disclosed to him;[170] and the High Court quashed the entry on a child abuse register of the name of a suspect who was not told about the accusation.[171] Where a police officer was dismissed in Malaya, after a hearing before an adjudicating officer, the Privy Council declared the dismissal void because the adjudicating officer was in possession of a report of a board of inquiry which made charges of misconduct but which was not available to the police officer.[172] A similar case in England led to the quashing by certiorari of a decision of an Industrial Injuries Commissioner.[173] After hearing the case the Commissioner obtained, as he was empowered to do, a report from an independent medical expert; but the parties were not notified and were therefore unable to comment on the report. The Commissioner had, in effect, taken further evidence, unknown to the parties, between the hearing and the decision.[174] The same principle applies where a party is allowed to know only part of the real charge against him, as where a minister made it clear in a later speech that he had acted partly on grounds which he had not notified to the person against whom he made his order.[175] Another case in the same class is where a tribunal decides a case on some point which has not been argued before it, without giving the party an opportunity to comment on it.[176] Another is where a rent tribunal, having inspected the property before the hearing, fails to inform the landlord of unfavourable conclusions formed at the inspection.[177] Another is where a tribunal follows some previous decision of its own without disclosing it.[178] And where the Home Secretary is considering whether to refer a prisoner's case to the Court of Appeal on the ground that there may have been a miscarriage of justice, the prisoner is 'in the vast majority of cases' entitled to the expert witnesses' reports prepared on his case.[179] A fair procedure must be followed when exercising the prerogative of mercy. Thus the Governor-General of Jamaica who chaired the committee, the Jamaican Privy Council, which decided[180] whether to reprieve a convicted murderer sentenced to death, had to ensure that notice of

---

[170] R v. Assistant Metropolitan Police Commissioner ex p Howell [1986] RTR 52. See likewise R v. Secretary of State for Health ex p Gandhi [1991] 1 WLR 1053 (failure to disclose papers needed by doctor appealing against non-appointment).

[171] R v. Norfolk CC Social Services Department ex p M. [1989] QB 619. Contrast R v. Harrow LBC ex p D. [1990] Fam. 133 (written submissions allowed: procedure held fair).

[172] Kanda v. Government of Malaya (above); similarly Shareef v. Commissioner for Registration of Indian and Pakistani Residents [1966] AC 47. The same principle has been applied to the ejection of a housing authority's tenant: Re Webb and Ontario Housing Cpn (1978) 93 DLR (3d) 187; and to the discharge of a soldier from the army: State (Gleeson) v. Minister for Defence [1976] IR 280; and to the non-reappointment of magistrates: Macrae v. A-G for New South Wales (1987) 9 NSWLR 268.

[173] R v. Deputy Industrial Injuries Commissioner ex p Jones [1962] 2 QB 677.

[174] See similarly Taylor v. National Union of Seamen [1967] 1 WLR 532 (evidence heard in accused party's absence); Kane v. University of British Columbia (1980) 110 DLR (3d) 311.

[175] Maradana Mosque Trustees v. Mahmud [1967] 1 AC 13. See also R v. Home Secretary ex p Awuku, The Times, 3 October 1987 (Home Secretary's decision quashed since based on facts which immigrant was given no opportunity to explain); R v. Bedfordshire CC ex p C (1986) 85 LGR 218 (council's refusal to return child to father quashed since based on mother's allegations not put to him).

[176] R v. Industrial Injuries Commissioner ex p Howarth (1968) 4 KIR 621; Sabey (H) & Co v. Secretary of State for the Environment [1978] 1 All ER 586 (public inquiry); TLG Building Materials v. Secretary of State for the Environment (1980) 41 P & CR 243 (public inquiry).

[177] R v. Paddington etc Rent Tribunal ex p Bell London Properties Ltd [1949] 1 KB 666.

[178] R v. Criminal Injuries Compensation Board ex p Ince [1973] 1 WLR 1334 at 1345.

[179] R v. Home Secretary ex p Hickey (1995) 7 Admin LR 549.

[180] Governor General is bound to act on the Jamaican Privy Council's advice: Constitution of Jamaica 1962, s. 90(2).

the date of the crucial meeting and all the documents before the committee were available to the condemned man.[181]

A group of cases concerning statutory public inquiries also falls into this class. As already explained, natural justice does not require a minister to disclose all the information about a proposed housing scheme which his department collected before any objection to the scheme was lodged.[182] Nor need he necessarily disclose other schemes in his department which might possibly affect the scheme in question.[183] But after objection is lodged he must not receive evidence from one party without disclosing it to the others, as is shown by the case of the Jarrow clearance order.[184] The inspector who holds the inquiry must also take care to disclose all the material facts to all concerned. Compulsory purchase orders have been quashed where the inspector during his site inspection asked the residents about their wishes and failed to inform the objectors of the answers, even though it was not clear that the answers had prejudiced the objectors' case;[185] and where the inspector based his recommendations upon what he had himself seen on his site inspection, without disclosing to the objectors that this raised questions quite different from those ventilated at the inquiry.[186] In such cases the inspector ought to give the parties a fair opportunity to comment on the new evidence.[187] Likewise the minister, when considering the inspector's report, ought not to take account of new factual evidence relating to the particular case without giving the parties an opportunity to comment on it.[188] But for this situation there are usually statutory rules, explained elsewhere.[189]

Disclosure of the charge or of the opposing case must be made in reasonable time to allow the person affected to prepare his defence or his comments.[190] He must have fair notice of any accusation against him, and this is commonly included in the right to a fair hearing by calling it the right 'to notice and hearing'. At an inquiry, for example, any person who might be affected by adverse findings should be given fair warning so that he can defend himself against them at the hearing.[191] But notice may not be indispensable as to matters where no fact is in dispute and there is no prejudice to the party charged.[192]

As several of the above-mentioned cases show, natural justice often requires the disclosure of reports and evidence in the possession of the deciding authority. A licensing

---

[181] *Lewis* v. *A-G of Jamaica* [2001] AC 50 (PC); *de Freitas* v. *Benny* [1976] AC 239 (PC); *Reckley* v. *Minister of Public Safety (No 2)* [1996] AC 527 not followed.   [182] Above, p. 412.

[183] *Rea* v. *Minister of Transport* (1982) 48 P & CR 239 (claim that motorway schemes were interdependent: disclosure not required).

[184] *Errington* v. *Minister of Health* [1935] 1 KB 249, discussed above, p. 413, and citing other cases. See also *Lake District Special Planning Board* v. *Secretary of State for the Environment* (1975) 236 EG 417; *Reading BC* v. *Secretary of State for the Environment* (1985) 52 P & CR 385, where a planning authority was given the benefit of this rule; *British Muslims' Association* v. *Secretary of State for the Environment* (1987) 57 P & CR 205 (inspector spoke with council officers: decision quashed).

[185] *Hibernian Property Co Ltd* v. *Secretary of State for the Environment* (1973) 27 P & CR 197.

[186] *Fairmount Investments Ltd* v. *Secretary of State for the Environment* [1976] 1 WLR 1255 (inspector noticed signs of unsafe foundations).

[187] Compare *Second City (South West) Ltd* v. *Secretary of State for the Environment* (1990) 60 P & CR 498 (failure to disclose change of policy). As to site inspections see *Winchester City Council* v. *Secretary of State for the Environment* (1978) 36 P & CR 455.

[188] *Geraghty* v. *Minister for Local Government* [1976] IR 153. Compare *R* v. *Secretary of State for Education and Science ex p Islam* (1992) 5 Admin LR 177 (refusal of grant-aided status for school quashed for non-disclosure of changed circumstances).

[189] Below, p. 807. See also *Pfizer Co Ltd* v. *Deputy Minister of National Revenue* (1975) 68 DLR (3d) 9.

[190] *R* v. *Thames Magistrates' Court ex p Polemis* [1974] 1 WLR 1371; *Brentnall* v. *Free Presbyterian Church of Scotland*, 1986 SLT 471.   [191] *Mahon* v. *Air New Zealand Ltd* [1984] AC 808.

[192] See *Davis* v. *Carew-Pole* [1956] 1 WLR 833.

authority must disclose any objections lodged with it so that the applicant may reply to them.[193] A prisoner whose release on parole is revoked is entitled to be notified of adverse facts to be put before the parole board.[194] Where a police officer was compulsorily retired after being examined by a medical officer chosen by the police authority, the Court of Appeal held that natural justice had been violated because the police officer's own doctor had not been allowed to see the report of an inquiry and a medical report made to the police authority, though it was also held that these need not necessarily be disclosed to the police officer himself.[195] A tribunal must disclose reports and evidence bearing upon the case before it, although it may use its own knowledge and experience as to general questions.[196] The decision of an assessment committee was therefore quashed when it failed to disclose a report by an expert valuer which made it fix a rating assessment at a figure higher than that contended for by the rating authority; and the majority of the Court of Appeal held that it made no difference whether the report was obtained before or after the assessment was objected to or whether the report was of a general or specific character.[197] In New Zealand the decision of a town planning committee was held to be void because at the hearing given to the parties the committee failed to disclose a long report from its planning officer about the case;[198] and the dismissal of a civil servant was invalid because an adverse report about him was not disclosed.[199] In Australia the court has rejected the plea that the undisclosed material was not considered or would have made no difference.[200]

LIMITS TO THE RIGHT TO SEE ADVERSE EVIDENCE

In some administrative situations there are limits to the broad principles stated above. The court must always consider the statutory framework within which natural justice is to operate, and a limit may sometimes necessarily be implied. What is essential is substantial fairness to the person adversely affected. But this may sometimes be adequately achieved by telling him the substance of the case he has to meet, without disclosing the precise evidence or the sources of information. The extent of the disclosure required by natural justice may have to be weighed against the prejudice to the scheme of the Act which disclosure may involve.[201] In a leading case the Court of Appeal applied these considerations to the procedure of the Gaming Board in granting certificates of consent to persons wishing to operate gaming clubs.[202] It was the Board's duty to investigate the

---

[193] R v. *Huntingdon DC ex p Cowan* [1984] 1 WLR 501 (objections to entertainments licence not disclosed: refusal quashed).

[194] R v. *Home Secretary ex p Georghiades* (1992) 5 Admin LR 457. For other cases concerning prisoners see below, p. 471.

[195] R v. *Kent Police Authority ex p Godden* [1971] 2 QB 662. See likewise R v. *London County Council ex p Commercial Gas Co* (1895) 11 TLR 337 (reports of gas testing must be disclosed).

[196] R v. *National Insurance Commissioner ex p Viscusi* [1974] 1 WLR 646; *Freeland* v. *Glasgow Licensing Board*, 1980 SLT 101; and see below, p. 777.

[197] R v. *Westminster Assessment Committee ex p Grosvenor House (Park Lane) Ltd* [1941] 1 KB 53. Scott LJ considered that a report obtained before the objection was lodged was part of the committee's expert knowledge and need not be disclosed.　　　　　[198] *Denton* v. *Auckland City* [1969] NZLR 256.

[199] *Fraser* v. *State Services Commission* [1984] 1 NZLR 116.

[200] *Minister for Immigration* v. *Taveli* (1990) 94 ALR 177.

[201] But the statutory exclusion of the duty to give reasons does not limit the duty to disclose the adverse case (*ex p Fayed*, below, p. 442).

[202] R v. *Gaming Board for Great Britain ex p Benaim and Khaida* [1970] 2 QB 417. Cf. *Ainsworth* v. *Criminal Justice Commission* (1991) 106 ALR 11.

credentials of applicants and to obtain information from the police and other confidential sources. Such sources, it was held, need not be divulged if there were objections properly based on the public interest. The Board must, however, give the applicant an indication of the objections raised against him so that he can answer them, as fairness requires. The same doctrine was applied to the preparation of a report by inspectors appointed by the Board of Trade to investigate the affairs of a company: their duty to act fairly did not require them to disclose the names of witnesses or the transcripts of their evidence, or to show to a director any adverse passages in their proposed report in draft.[203] But, without quoting chapter and verse, they must give him a fair opportunity to contradict what is said against him, as by giving him an outline of the charge; and if their information is so confidential that they cannot reveal it even in general terms, they should not use it.[204] Similarly, the Home Secretary in considering an application for naturalisation in which all the statutory requirements, save good character, were not in dispute, was obliged to identify the matters causing him difficulty and to provide an opportunity for the applicants to make representations about those matters.[205]

In the first two cases mentioned above, the authorities were held to have acted properly, since they had given fair hearings on the substance of the charges. But in the last case the minister had not disclosed even the gist of matters causing difficulty and his decision was quashed. Similarly an immigration officer, who gave a suspected illegal immigrant a full opportunity to understand and contradict the case against him but who did not reveal reports which he had obtained when making inquiries was held to have acted fairly.[206] Lord Denning MR said that 'the rules of natural justice must not be stretched too far'. But he made it clear that the duty to act fairly applied in the same way to the investigations of the Race Relations Board (now the Commission for Racial Equality) and its committees.[207] This duty likewise obliges the Monopolies and Mergers Commission, in examining a proposed company takeover, to ensure that the parties understand the issues and arguments which will be decisive, but they need not necessarily disclose to one party every piece of evidence submitted by the other, provided always that there is no manifest unfairness.[208] A professional body in considering whether to approve an applicant as suitable for appointment to a senior post, was not obliged to disclose confidential reports containing consultants' opinions on the applicant's suitability.[209]

---

[203] Re Pergamon Press Ltd [1971] Ch 388; and see Maxwell v. Department of Trade and Industry [1974] QB 523 (no duty to disclose inspectors' proposed conclusions); Campbell v. Mason Committee [1990] 2 NZLR 577. See also Ceylon University v. Fernando [1960] 1 WLR 223 (student suspended for cheating in examination not offered opportunity to confront accuser, but adequately informed of case to be met: student's suspension upheld); O'Rourke v. Miller (1985) 58 ALR 269.

[204] Cf. Canterbury Building Society v. Baker (1979) 2 NSWLR 265. As to cases involving national security see below, p. 473.

[205] R v. Home Secretary ex p Fayed [1997] 1 All ER 228 (CA). See also R v. Home Secretary ex p McAvoy [1998] 1 WLR 790 (prisoner whose security status was under review was entitled to gist of reports made to the review body but not to the reports in full. A prisoner was not entitled to detailed information (which was confidential) about the basis on which he was categorised as an exceptional high risk prisoner: R v. Home Secretary ex p Mulkerrins [1998] COD 235.

[206] R v. Home Secretary ex p Mughal [1974] QB 313. And see Lim v. Minister of the Interior, Malaya [1964] 1 WLR 554; Herring v. Templeman [1973] 3 All ER 569.

[207] R v. Race Relations Board ex p Selvarajan [1975] 1 WLR 1686.

[208] R v. Monopolies and Mergers Commission ex p Matthew Brown plc [1987] 1 WLR 1235. Compare Public Disclosure Commission v. Isaacs [1988] 1 WLR 1043 (commission investigating allegations not required to disclose details to complainant).

[209] R v. Joint Higher Committee on Surgical Training ex p Milner (1995) 7 Admin LR 454.

THE 'SPECIAL ADVOCATE'/'CLOSED MATERIAL' PROCEDURE

Administrative decision-makers will often need to act in reliance on confidential or intelligence sources. But the public interest will be harmed if the identities of these sources as well as the detail of the information they provide are revealed to those affected by the decision. This makes securing procedural fairness in such cases very difficult, if not impossible.[210] The limits that the common law allows to be placed on the right to see adverse evidence have just been described.

But a fresh approach to this dilemma is revealed in the special advocate/closed material procedure.[211] This procedure is expressly authorised by statute in several situations touching national security, most prominently when the lawfulness of a 'Terrorism Prevention and Investigation Measures Order' is tested before the relevant court.[212] In essence, instead of disclosing the sensitive material to the person affected, it is disclosed to a special advocate appointed by the Attorney-General or the decision-maker. The special advocate then deals with that material as the occasion demands in a closed session (at which the person affected is not present).

This procedure clearly attempts to secure procedural fairness and is fairer than simply denying the sensitive material altogether to the person affected. But the absence of communication between the special advocate and his client, the person affected, means that the special advocate cannot know what answers the person affected may have to the matters raised in the sensitive material. He will thus be unable to put those answers to the decision-maker. And the person affected will be similarly unable to put his response to the tribunal since he does not know what the sensitive material contains. While the special advocates are conscientious and expert the procedure cannot secure procedural fairness in all cases. It is no surprise that the procedure is much criticised. Lord Bingham has remarked that the specially appointed advocate would inevitably be 'taking blind shots at a hidden target.'[213]

The Supreme Court has held that 'it is not for the courts to extend [this] controversial procedure beyond the boundaries which Parliament has chosen to draw for its use thus far'[214] and thus such procedure can only be introduced by legislation. But the procedure

---

[210] Lord Roger in the *Roberts* case pointed out the acute difficulties (in para. 111). The case concerned concealing from a prisoner, appearing before the Parole Board, the evidence of an informer to the effect that the prisoner was involved in drug dealing and breaches of prison discipline. The Board feared that revealing this evidence to the prisoner would put the informer at risk. Requiring the informer to give evidence at the risk of his life would raise issues under Arts. 2 and 3 of the Human Rights Convention. If the Board closed its eyes to the informer's evidence and decided whether to release the prisoner on licence without regard to it, the Board would be in breach of its duty to protect the public. If the Board used the evidence but did not disclose it to the prisoner, it denied his right to a fair procedure.

[211] The procedure has Canadian origins but was its adoption in the UK was 'encouraged' by the Human Rights Court in *Chahal* v. *UK* (1996) 23 EHRR 413 recognising that there were techniques that might protect sources and still 'accord the individual a substantial measure of procedural justice' (para. 131). Cf. *Al-Nashif* v. *Bulgaria* (2002) 36 EHRR 655, para. 97.

[212] The Terrorism Prevention and Investigation Measures Act 2011, Sched. 4, or the Counter-Terrorism Act 2008, Pt 6. TPIMs take the place of 'control orders' and are discussed elsewhere (above, pp. 72–3). The Employment Tribunals Act 1996, s. 10(6) permits the procedure in employment tribunal proceedings where national security is engaged.

[213] *Roberts*, para. 18. The quoted words come from *Coles* v. *Oldhams Press Ltd* [1936]1 KB 416 at 426 (Lord Hewart CJ).

[214] *Al Rawi and ors* v. *The Security Service and ors* [2011] UKSC 34, [2012] 1 AC 531 (Lord Dyson, para. 47). This case concerned civil claims for damages against the defendants alleging complicity by the defendants in the claimants' mistreatment by foreign powers (including detention at Guantanamo Bay). The defendants as part of their defence wished to place before the court 'security sensitive material'—presumably the evidence

need not be expressly authorised by statute; necessary implication of the power will suffice. Thus the Parole Board has been held to be impliedly authorised to adopt it in deciding whether to release a mandatory life prisoner on licence.[215] And the Supreme Court[216] (which has no express power to hold a closed material procedure) has held that its statutory powers under the Constitutional Reform Act 2005, section 40 (2) and (5) to decide an appeal 'from any order or judgment of the Court of Appeal' and to determine 'any question necessary...for the purposes of doing justice in an appeal' was sufficient to vouchsafe the required power. But the House of Lords and the Supreme Court that decided these cases were sharply divided, reflecting the acute clash of the principles involved. The last word has not been heard on where that balance is to be struck.

DISCLOSING THE 'GIST' AND THE COMPATIBILITY OF THE SPECIAL ADVOCATE PROCEDURE WITH ARTICLE 6(1)

As discussed above the usual right to know the opposing case may be limited where to reveal all would be to compromise confidential sources or harm national security. In these cases natural justice requires that the substance or 'gist' of the case to be answered has to be disclosed. Where a duly authorised closed material procedure is held but the closed hearing deals only with minor or confirmatory matters, the 'gist' is readily revealed and there has been adequate disclosure.

But where the substance of the case is dealt with in the closed session, there clearly has been no disclosure of the 'gist'. In these circumstances the question will often be whether there has been compliance with Article 5(4) (procedural fairness in determination of lawfulness of detention) or Article 6(1) (procedural fairness in the determination of civil rights).

The Human Rights Court in a passage that has become canonical has said:[217]

> the special advocate could perform an important role in counterbalancing the lack of full disclosure and the lack of a full, open, adversarial hearing by testing the evidence and putting arguments on behalf of the detainee during the closed hearings. However, the special advocate could not perform this function in any useful way unless the detainee was provided with sufficient information about the allegations against him to enable him to give effective instructions to the special advocate. While this question must be decided on a case-by-case basis, the Court observes generally that, where the evidence was to a large extent disclosed and the open material played the predominant role in the determination, it could not be said that the applicant was denied an opportunity effectively to

[215] R (Roberts) v. Parole Board [2005] UKHL 45, [2005] 3 WLR 152. Lord Bingham held that 'the ordinary rules of procedural fairness' could not be removed save by 'clear and express' words (para. 30). And Lord Steyn said that 'Parliament does not lightly override fundamental rights' (para. 93). But Lord Woolf for the majority (Lord Brown and Lord Carswell) held that the special advocate procedure was authorised by Criminal Justice Act 1991, Sched. 5, para. 1, granting power to the Parole Board to 'to do such things...as are incidental to or conducive to the discharge' of its functions. It has been recognised in a criminal trial that the special advocate procedure may be necessary in exceptional circumstances 'in the interests of justice' (R v. H [2004] UKHL 3, [2004] 2 WLR 335). The context was the need to hear the defence on a public interest immunity application; no breach of Art. 6(1) was found.

[216] Bank Mellat v. Her Majesty's Treasury [2013] UKSC 38, paras. 38–42.

[217] A v. UK (2009) 49 EHRR 29, para. 220.

challenge the reasonableness of the Secretary of State's belief and suspicions about him. In other cases, even where all or most of the underlying evidence remained undisclosed, if the allegations contained in the open material were sufficiently specific, it should have been possible for the applicant to provide his representatives and the special advocate with information with which to refute them, if such information existed, without his having to know the detail or sources of the evidence which formed the basis of the allegations. An example would be the allegation made against several of the applicants that they had attended a terrorist training camp at a stated location between stated dates; given the precise nature of the allegation, it would have been possible for the applicant to provide the special advocate with exonerating evidence, for example of an alibi or of an alternative explanation for his presence there, sufficient to permit the advocate effectively to challenge the allegation. Where, however, the open material consisted purely of general assertions and [court's] decision to uphold the certification and maintain the detention was based solely or to a decisive degree on closed material, the procedural requirements of article 5(4) would not be satisfied.

Relying on this passage Lord Phillips in the House of Lords held[218] (in a control order case in which the case against AF was to be found only in the closed material) that

the controlee must be given sufficient information about the allegations against him to enable him to give effective instructions in relation to those allegations. Provided that this requirement is satisfied there can be a fair trial notwithstanding that the controlee is not provided with the detail or the sources of the evidence forming the basis of the allegations. Where, however, the open material consists purely of general assertions and the case against the controlee is based solely or to a decisive degree on closed materials the requirements of a fair trial will not be satisfied, however cogent the case based on the closed materials may be.

Thus while it is clear that a closed material procedure is not *ipso facto* a breach of Articles 6(1) or 5(4)[219]—on the contrary, the closed material procedure will play 'an important role in counterbalancing the lack of full disclosure'—there will be cases in which what is disclosed in the open proceedings is too little and too general so that the proceedings as a whole do not comply with the relevant article.

When such cases arise—and they will not be rare[220]—the court will have the choice of making a declaration of incompatibility or reading down the relevant statute to secure compliance with the relevant article. Moreover, cases will be very fact sensitive and uncertainty will abound.

Thus it may be helpful to note the importance of context. Where the right to liberty is at stake or the ill-treatment of detainees is alleged, the courts will be more robust in their insistence on the highest standards of procedural propriety. But where the issues at stake are employment rights (and non-discrimination)[221] or fairness in the exercise of a naturalisation discretion[222] the courts may more readily find the special advocate procedure

---

[218] *Home Secretary* v. *AF and anor* [2009] UKHL 28, para. 59.

[219] *Home Office* v. *Tariq* [2011] UKSC 35. But note that there will also be non-compliance when the closed material procedure is ordered by the minister rather than the court (Lord Mance, para. 11).

[220] Because often the crucial evidence will be derived from intelligence sources and dealt with in the closed hearing.   [221] *Tariq*.

[222] *R (AHK)* v. *Secretary of State for the Home Department (Practice Note)* [2009] EWCA Civ 287. In *Tariq*, at 27, Lord Mance said: 'cases where the state is seeking to impose on the individual actual or virtual imprisonment are in a different category to the present, where an individual is seeking to pursue a civil claim for discrimination against the state which is seeking to defend itself'. The same, it seems, applies to naturalisation cases.

acceptable. Most of the cases have concerned judicial proceedings; non-disclosure on cogent grounds should fare better in administrative proceedings.[223]

But the courts have shown reluctance to approve the application of a procedure as compliant with Convention Rights until the matter has been finally decided.[224] And they have made it clear that the procedure is only to be used as a last resort, after 'strenuous efforts' have been made to secure fairness by other means (e.g. revealing the gist of the adverse evidence to the individual perhaps in a redacted form).[225]

PROCEDURE GENERALLY

A 'hearing' will normally be an oral hearing.[226] In the leading case the House of Lords has held that 'an oral hearing is most obviously necessary to achieve a just decision in a case where facts are at issue... [but] there are other cases where an oral hearing may well contribute to a just decision'.[227] This case concerned the procedures adopted by the Parole Board in deciding whether prisoners who had been released on licence and subsequently recalled to prison, should be re-released. Their Lordships found in the circumstances that an oral hearing had to be held to reflect the interests at stake, both the safety of the public and the liberty of the individual. In a later case,[228] where the issue was whether the Parole Board should hold an oral hearing in deciding whether to release certain prisoners on licence or transfer them to open conditions, the Supreme Court said that an oral hearing should be held in such cases 'whenever fairness to the prisoner requires such a hearing in the light of the facts of the case and the importance of what is at stake'.[229] The Supreme Court added: 'the purpose of holding an oral hearing is not only to assist it in its decision-making, but also to reflect the prisoner's legitimate interest in being able to participate in a decision with important implications for him, where he has something useful to contribute'. Consistent with this clear recognition of the non-instrumental value of an oral hearing,[230] the court added that when in doubt a 'it will be prudent for the [Parole Board] to allow an oral hearing'.

But in many cases it may suffice to give an opportunity to make representations in writing, provided that any adverse material is disclosed and provided, as always, that the demands of fairness are substantially met. In another case the House of Lords dealt with the example of the Liverpool councillors who had failed to make a valid rate and were

---

[223] *Tariq*, para. 27 following *R (AHK) v. Secretary of State for the Home Department (Practice Note)* [2009] EWCA Civ 287.

[224] Compliance with Art. 5(4) (right to liberty) was to be assessed after the completion of the proceedings when regard could be had to evidence of what had occurred (*Roberts*). Compliance with Art. 6(1) also to be assessed after the procedure was complete (*Secretary of State for the Home Department v. MB* [2007] UKHL 46, [2007] WLR 681) (leaving open whether there could be compliance when the decision only justified on the basis of closed material).   [225] *MB*, para. 66 (Baroness Hale).

[226] *R v. Immigration Tribunal ex p Mehmet* [1977] 1 WLR 795 (tribunal's decision and resulting deportation order quashed for failure to afford oral hearing).

[227] *R (West) v. Parole Board* [2005] UKHL 1, [2005] 1 WLR 350, para. 31 (Lord Bingham). This result flowed from the common law duty of procedural fairness not Art. 6(1). Article 5(4), however, does require an oral hearing in such cases: *Hussain v. UK* (1996) 22 EHRR 1. In the *Osborne* case below, the Supreme Court stressed that '[c]ompliance with the common law duty should result in compliance also with the requirements of article 5(4) in relation to procedural fairness' (para. 2 xii).

[228] *Osborn v. The Parole Board* [2013] UKSC 61, para. 2 (Lord Reed).

[229] The court then set out the 'circumstances' that might render an oral hearing necessary. The most significant indicator of the need for an oral hearing is where important facts are in dispute or where 'significant explanation or mitigation is advanced which needs to be heard orally in order fairly to determine its credibility' (para. 2).   [230] Discussed above, p. 374.

surcharged by the district auditor for wilful misconduct. The auditor gave them full particulars of his complaints and offered to consider their representations in writing, which they duly made without asking to be heard orally. The Court of Appeal held that this procedure fell short of fairness, since the charges were serious, they attributed bad faith, and past practice had almost invariably been to give oral hearings in surcharge cases. The House of Lords held the contrary, finding that in dealing with a group of forty-nine councillors acting collectively, none of whom asked to be heard orally, the auditors had adopted a procedure which was both suitable and fair in all the circumstances.[231]

In various situations practicalities may justify dispensing with oral hearings.[232] It has been held that a statutory board, acting in an administrative capacity, may decide for itself whether to deal with applications by oral hearing or merely on written evidence and argument, provided that it does in substance 'hear' them;[233] and that dealing with an appeal on written communications only is not contrary to natural justice.[234] The visitor of a college may similarly deal with an appeal on written submissions only[235] and a student may be rusticated from his college without an oral hearing, if he has been told the nature of the complaints against him and given a fair opportunity to state his case in writing.[236] A licensing authority may give a 'hearing' on paper,[237] provided that the applicant is allowed to reply to any objections known to the authority.[238] An immigrant appealing against a deportation order need not be offered an interview.[239] Some statutory tribunals have power to dispense with oral hearings,[240] but if they do so, they must be careful to give a party a fair opportunity to comment on any adverse statement submitted.[241] Large numbers of planning appeals are disposed of on paper, but in those cases the appellant previously waived his right to a statutory hearing.[242] A number of tribunals may dispense with hearings under their statutory rules in certain circumstances.[243]

Where an oral hearing is given, it has been laid down that a tribunal must (a) consider all relevant evidence which a party wishes to submit; (b) inform every party of all the evidence to be taken into account, whether derived from another party or independently; (c) allow witnesses to be questioned; (d) allow comment on the evidence and argument on the whole case.[244] Failure to allow the last two rights, which include the

---

[231] *Lloyd* v. *McMahon* [1987] AC 625.

[232] See 'The Economics of Procedural Fairness' in *Johns* v. *Release on Licence Board* (1987) 9 NSWLR 103 at 113 (Kirby P), mentioning the need for cost–benefit analysis.

[233] See *R* v. *Local Government Board ex p Arlidge* [1914] 1 KB 160 at 191, approved in *R* v. *Immigration Appeal Tribunal ex p Jones (Ross)* [1988] 1 WLR 477; *R* v. *Amphlett (Judge)* [1915] 2 KB 223 (district wages board); *Jeffs* v. *New Zealand Dairy Board* [1967] 1 AC 551 (dairy zoning order); *R* v. *Harrow LBC ex p D*. [1990] Fam. 133 (child abuse register).

[234] *Stuart* v. *Haughley Parochial Church Council* [1935] Ch 452, affirmed [1936] Ch 32 (lay electoral commission).   [235] *R* v. *Bishop of Ely* (1794) 5 TR 475 at 477 (Buller J).

[236] *Brighton Cpn* v. *Parry* (1972) 70 LGR 576. See also *Ayanlowo* v. *Commissioners of Inland Revenue* [1975] IRLR 253 (dismissal of probationer civil servant: letter sufficient).

[237] *Kavanagh* v. *Chief Constable of Devon and Cornwall* [1974] QB 624. And see *British Oxygen Co Ltd* v. *Board of Trade* [1971] AC 610 at 625 (Lord Reid).

[238] *R* v. *Huntingdon DC ex p Cowan* [1984] 1 WLR 501.

[239] *R* v. *Home Secretary ex p Malhi* [1991] 1 QB 194.   [240] See below, p. 775.

[241] *R* v. *Housing Appeal Tribunal* [1920] 3 KB 334. To like effect see *R* v. *Law Society ex p Ingham Foods Oy Ab* [1997] 2 All ER 666.   [242] See below, p. 814. The procedure is now statutory.

[243] See below, p. 775.

[244] *R* v. *Deputy Industrial Injuries Commissioner ex p Moore* [1965] 1 QB 456 at 490 (Diplock LJ). See also *Asher* v. *Secretary of State for the Environment* [1974] Ch 208 (district auditor); *R* v. *Secretary of State for the Environment ex p Stewart* (1978) 77 LGR 431 (inquiry: evidence wrongly excluded); *R* v. *North Yorkshire FHSA ex p Wilson* [1991] 8 Admin LR 613 (decision-maker not obliged to hear argument on irrelevant consideration).

right of cross-examination,[245] has led to the quashing of punishments awarded by prison visitors (who used to exercise disciplinary powers in prisons) in a series of cases.[246] In one, the visitors refused to allow prisoners to call witnesses because of the administrative inconvenience of bringing them from distant prisons to which they had been dispersed after a riot, and for other inadequate reasons.[247] In another, a prisoner was not allowed to question his own witness or to comment on the evidence.[248] In a third, there was a witness unknown to the prisoner but known to the investigating officer, who failed to inform the visitors.[249] This last case shows that natural justice may be violated by the conduct of those who bring forward the accusation as well as by that of the tribunal—as also does a later case, where a prosecution was instigated by a detective who concealed his own criminal record.[250] But a mistake by the applicant's own advisers, even though it deprives him of the opportunity to be heard in an appeal against deportation, will not entitle him to relief, since he has not been the victim of unfair procedure.[251] Where there is a charge of serious misconduct it is especially important, as the Court of Appeal has emphasised,[252] that procedural fairness should be carefully observed. In various other contexts, however, it is scarcely less important.

Failure to allow cross-examination by an objector at a statutory inquiry has led to the quashing of the Secretary of State's decision,[253] though not where the objections went beyond the proper scope of the inquiry.[254] And the order of a Scottish magistrate who ordered the destruction of a large quantity of cheese on grounds of food safety without allowing cross-examination of the food safety experts was reduced (quashed).[255] On the other hand there are many administrative proceedings in which formal testimony and cross-examination are inappropriate, the inquiry being informal.[256] When offering a hearing after an investigation the Commission for Racial Equality need not produce

[245] For dicta favourable to a right of cross-examination see *Osgood* v. *Nelson* (1872) LR 5 HL 636 at 646; *Marriott* v. *Minister of Health* (1936) 154 LT 47 at 50; *R* v. *Newmarket Assessment Committee ex p Allen Newport Ltd* [1945] 2 All ER 371 at 373.

[246] In the past prison visitors had important disciplinary functions but these were removed as recommended in the Woolf Report, *Prison Disturbances, April 1990*, Cm. 1456 (1991). For the former disciplinary functions of prison visitors see above, p. 58.

[247] *R* v. *Hull Prison Visitors ex p St Germain (No 2)* [1979] 1 WLR 1401, an exemplary judgment of Geoffrey Lane LJ. See likewise *Re Cheeung and Minister of Employment and Immigration* (1981) 122 DLR (3d) 41 (adjudicator refused to allow immigration officer to be called as witness: deportation order set aside).

[248] *R* v. *Gartree Prison Visitors ex p Mealy*, The Times, 14 November 1981.

[249] *R* v. *Blundeston Prison Visitors ex p Fox-Taylor* [1982] 1 All ER 646.

[250] *R* v. *Knightsbridge Crown Court ex p Goonatilleke* [1986] QB 1 (it being a case of one man's word against another's, the conviction was quashed).

[251] *R* v. *Home Secretary ex p Al-Mehdawi* [1990] 1 AC 876 (solicitor sent letters to wrong address). See above, p. 425. But where the default is that of the tribunal the position is different: *Fisher* v. *Hughes* [1998] COD 281 (applicant represented by deaf person, tribunal failed to provide trained interpreter: proceedings unfair).   [252] In the *Hull Prison* case (above).

[253] *Nicholson* v. *Secretary of State for Energy* (1978) 76 LGR 693; and see *Errington* v. *Minister of Health* [1935] 1 KB 249 at 272; *Wednesbury Cpn* v. *Ministry of Housing and Local Government (No 2)* [1966] 2 QB 275 at 302; cf. *National Companies and Securities Commission* v. *News Corporation Ltd* (1984) 52 ALR 417.

[254] *Bushell* v. *Secretary of State for the Environment* [1981] AC 75. For this question see below, p. 804.

[255] *Errington* v. *Wilson*, The Times, 2 June 1995 (Court of Session).

[256] See *Re Pergamon Press Ltd* [1971] Ch 388 at 400; *Herring* v. *Templeman* [1973] 3 All ER 569 (no witnesses allowed); cf. *Ceylon University* v. *Fernando* [1960] 1 WLR 223 at 253 (opportunity to cross-examine not requested); *O'Rourke* v. *Miller* (1984) 58 ALR 269 (police probationer not allowed to cross-examine); *Re Irvine and Restrictive Trade Practices Commission* (1987) 41 DLR (4th) 429 (statutory inquiry, no right to cross-examine).

witnesses for cross-examination.[257] It has been said that even the Crown Court, when acting administratively in a licensing appeal, need not allow cross-examination.[258]

It is clear that the strict legal rules of evidence need not be observed.[259] In an industrial injury case the Commissioner was therefore held entitled to take into account evidence given at a hearing of medical reports made in previous cases, although in a court of law these might have been inadmissible under the rule against hearsay.[260] But this dispensation is subject to the overriding obligation to give a genuinely fair hearing. The admission of hearsay evidence may make it all the more necessary to allow it to be tested by cross-examination, and if that is not practicable the right course in some cases may be to exclude the evidence from consideration.[261] Where hearsay evidence was the sole evidence of many of the serious allegations made, the arguments in favour of cross-examination of that evidence were 'formidable' and had to be allowed to secure fairness.[262]

It has twice been held that natural justice demands that the decision should be based on some evidence of probative value.[263]

The right to representation by a lawyer or other person may prove to be a part of natural justice in suitable cases, but this is not as yet clearly established. It may exist in the case of a formal tribunal[264] or investigation[265] if there is no provision to the contrary,[266] but regulations excluding it have been upheld.[267] In cases concerning non-statutory domestic tribunals the Court of Appeal has favoured the right of legal representation where a serious charge was made,[268] but has held that it may be excluded by an association's rules.[269] It may also be excluded, as both the Court of Appeal and the House of Lords have held, in disciplinary proceedings which demand a rapid hearing and decision, as in the case of offences committed by prisoners,[270] though on some occasions it has been held that principles of fairness must be observed.[271] There is also a right in criminal cases to legal assistance

---

[257] *R v. Commission for Racial Equality ex p Cottrell & Rothon* [1980] 1 WLR 1580.

[258] *Kavanagh v. Chief Constable of Devon and Cornwall* (above).

[259] *Mahon v. Air New Zealand Ltd* [1984] AC 808.

[260] *R v. Deputy Industrial Injuries Commissioner ex p Moore* (above); and see the *Kavanagh* case (above); *Miller (TA) Ltd v. Minister of Housing and Local Government* [1968] 1 WLR 992 (hearsay evidence at statutory inquiry). The Supreme Court of the Irish Republic does not permit the 'laissez-faire attitude' of these decisions: *Kiely v. Minister for Social Welfare* [1977] IR 267.

[261] See the *Hull Prison* case (above) at 1409.

[262] *R (Bonhoeffer) v. General Medical Council* [2011] EWHC 1585, para. 43 (the witness in question feared reprisals if he gave oral evidence).

[263] *R v. Deputy Industrial Injuries Commissioner ex p Moore* (above); *Mahon v. Air New Zealand Ltd* [1984] AC 808. See the discussion of the 'no evidence' rule above, p. 237. But a tribunal may accept statements agreed between the parties without violating natural justice: *R v. Oxford Local Valuation Panel ex p Oxford CC* (1981) 79 LGR 432.

[264] *R v. Assessment Committee, St Mary Abbotts, Kensington* [1891] 1 QB 378.

[265] *R v. Commissioner of Police ex p Edwards* (1977) 32 FLR 183.   [266] See below, p. 782.

[267] *Maynard v. Osmond* [1977] QB 240 (police discipline regulations). The Court of Appeal took account of the fact that there could be legal representation on appeal to the Home Secretary. Contrast *Joplin v. Chief Constable of Vancouver* (1985) 20 DLR (4th) 314 (police regulation excluding right to counsel held ultra vires on grounds of fairness).

[268] *Pett v. Greyhound Racing Association* [1969] 1 QB 125, not followed in *(No 2)* [1970] 1 QB 46 (Lyell J).

[269] *Enderby Town Football Club Ltd v. Football Association Ltd* [1971] Ch 591. See also *London Passenger Transport Board v. Moscrop* [1942] AC 332; *Tait v. Central Radio Taxis (Tollcross) Ltd*, 1987 SLT 506. In *R (G) v. X School* [2011] UKSC 30 arrangements in which an employee (a school teaching assistant) was allowed a trade union representative or work colleague to attend disciplinary hearing but not a solicitor passed without comment, once it was established that Art. 6(1) not applicable (see above, p. 378).

[270] *Fraser v. Mudge* [1975] 1 WLR 1132; *R v. Maze Prison Visitors ex p Hone* [1988] AC 379.

[271] *R v. Home Secretary ex p Tarrant* [1985] QB 251 (visitors held that representation could not be allowed: decisions quashed); *ex p Hone* (above). Contrast *R v. Risley Remand Centre Visitors ex p Draper*, The Times, 24 May 1988 (prisoner pleaded guilty: refusal of representation upheld); *Abbas v. Home Secretary,*

and representation under Article 6(2) of the European Convention on Human Rights.[272] A party conducting his case in person will normally be allowed the assistance of a friend to give advice and take notes.[273]

Arrangements for hearings must be fair and justice may not be sacrificed to speed.[274] Wrongful refusal of an adjournment, when reasonably requested, may amount to refusal of a fair hearing, particularly where the party affected is thereby disabled from appearing at all.[275] The Takeover Panel of the Stock Exchange narrowly escaped from having its investigation of a company invalidated when it refused adjournments in a manner which was 'insensitive and unwise' but which did not in fact cause injustice.[276] Natural justice was violated by the exclusion from a juvenile court of a social worker who might have assisted a boy who was convicted,[277] and by alteration of the time and place of a hearing without notice.[278]

Lord Denning MR has summed up the procedure in the case of an investigating body such as the Commission for Racial Equality which is under a duty to act fairly:[279]

> The investigating body is, however, the master of its own procedure. It need not hold a hearing. It can do everything in writing. It need not allow lawyers. It need not put every detail of the case against a man. Suffice it if the broad grounds are given. It need not name the informants. It can give the substance only. Moreover, it need not do everything itself. It can employ secretaries and assistants to do all the preliminary work and leave much to them. But, in the end, the investigating body itself must come to its own decisions and make its own report.

REASONS FOR DECISIONS

The principles of natural justice do not, as yet, include any general rule that reasons should be given for decisions.[280] Nevertheless there is a strong case to be made for the giving of reasons as an essential element of administrative justice. The need for it has been sharply exposed by the expanding law of judicial review, now that so many decisions are liable to be quashed or appealed against on grounds of improper purpose, irrelevant considerations and errors of law of various kinds. Unless the citizen can discover the reasoning behind the decision, he may be unable to tell whether it is reviewable or not, and so he may be deprived of the protection of the law. A right to reasons is therefore an indispensable

---

1993 SLT 502 (rule against representation of deportees before advisory panel upheld). The disciplinary jurisdiction of the visitors has now been abolished: see above, p. 58.

[272] *Campbell and Fell* v. *UK*, ECtHR (1984) Series A, No. 80 (prisoners' claim succeeded). See the ECtHR judgment discussed in the *Maze Prison* case (above) at 187. And see *P, C & S* v. *UK* (2002) 35 EHRR 31.

[273] *R* v. *Leicester City Justices ex p Barrow* [1991] 2 QB 260, deprecating the term 'McKenzie friend', for which see below, p. 782.

[274] *R* v. *Portsmouth City Council ex p Gregory & Moss* [1991] 2 Admin LR 681.

[275] *Priddle* v. *Fisher & Sons* [1968] 1 WLR 1478; *Re M (an infant)* [1968] 1 WLR 1897; *Rose* v. *Humbles* [1972] 1 WLR 33; *Lucy* v. *Royal Borough of Kensington and Chelsea* [1997] COD 191. Contrast *Ostreicher* v. *Secretary of State for the Environment* [1978] 1 WLR 810 (religious objection to date of inquiry).

[276] *R* v. *Panel on Takeovers and Mergers ex p Guinness plc* [1990] 1 QB 146.

[277] *R* v. *Southwark Juvenile Court ex p J.* [1973] 1 WLR 1300.

[278] *Supermarchés Jean Labrecque Inc* v. *Labour Court* (1987) 43 DLR (4th) 1.

[279] *R* v. *Race Relations Board ex p Selvarajan* [1975] 1 WLR 1686; and see *R* v. *Commission for Racial Equality ex p Cottrell & Rothon* (above); same *ex p Hillingdon LBC* [1982] AC 779.

[280] *R* v. *Home Secretary ex p Doody* [1994] 1 AC 531 at 564E ('the law does not *at present* recognise a general duty to give reasons for administrative decisions' (emphasis added)). No general duty has developed since *ex p Doody*: *R* v. *Minister of Defence ex p Murray* [1998] COD 134.

part of a sound system of judicial review. Natural justice may provide the best rubric for it, since the giving of reasons is required by the ordinary man's sense of justice. It is also a healthy discipline for all who exercise power over others. 'No single factor has inhibited the development of English administrative law as seriously as the absence of any general obligation upon public authorities to give reasons for their decisions.'[281]

The need for this obligation was recognised both by the Committee on Ministers' Powers of 1932[282] and by the Committee on Administrative Tribunals and Enquiries of 1957,[283] and the latter's recommendation was implemented by the Tribunals and Inquiries Act 1958, as explained elsewhere,[284] which required reasons to be given on request by statutory tribunals and by ministers after statutory inquiries. American federal law has a comparable requirement.[285] In Australian federal law the right to reasons has been extended to administrative decisions generally.[286] But the High Court of Australia emphatically reversed an attempt by the New South Wales Court of Appeal to introduce a right to reasons as a general rule of common law.[287] A more enlightened doctrine prevails in the European Union, where the Council and the Commission are required to state the reasons for their regulations, directives and decisions.[288] And as already noted,[289] Article 6(1) of the European Convention on Human Rights, where it applies, requires the giving of reasons.

Notwithstanding that there is no general rule requiring the giving of reasons,[290] it is increasingly clear that there are many circumstances in which an administrative authority which fails to give reasons will be found to have acted unlawfully. The House of Lords has recognised 'a perceptible trend towards an insistence on greater openness... or transparency in the making of administrative decisions'[291] and consequently has held that where, in the context of the case, it is unfair not to give reasons, they must be given.[292]

---

[281] *Administration under Law* (a JUSTICE booklet), 23. For further discussion of the point see [1998] *JR* 158; (1998) 18 *OJLS* 497.   [282] Cmd 4060 (1932), 80, 100.

[283] Cmnd 218 (1957), paras. 98, 351.   [284] Below, p. 764.

[285] Administrative Procedure Act of 1946, s. 8(b).

[286] Administrative Decisions (Judicial Review) Act 1977, s. 13. The Administrative Law Act 1978, s. 8, of Victoria is similar. Both Acts require reasons in writing to be given on request.

[287] *Public Service Board of New South Wales* v. *Osmond* (1986) 60 ALJ 209 (Board dismissed New South Wales civil servant's appeal against non-promotion and refused to state reasons). The case for the right to reasons is strongly argued by Kirby CJ in the court below, [1984] 3 NSWLR 447, and in Taggart (ed.), *Judicial Review of Administrative Action in the 1980s*, where the editor also criticises the High Court's decision. In Canada, on the other hand, a common law duty for administrative decision makers to give reasons is recognised 'in certain circumstances', including where the decision has 'important significance for an individual' or where there is a right of appeal: *Baker* v. *Canada (Minister of Citizenship and Immigration)* [1999] 2 SCR 817.

[288] Treaty of Rome, Art. 190. A regulation is invalid if reasons are not given: *REWE* v. *Hauptzollamt Kiel* [1982] 1 CMLR 449. Other EU provisions may apply where Art. 190 does not. Thus information may only be denied to the public by EU institutions after stating the particular ground (of several listed) on which the denial is founded (Code of Conduct on Access to Information (adopted by Commission Decision 94/90 pursuant to Declaration No. 17 in the Maastricht Treaty 1992)); and those grounds will be narrowly construed (*WWF UK* v. *Commission* Case T-105/95 [1997] ECR II-1).   [289] Above, p. 408.

[290] The suggestion, in *R* v. *Lambeth LBC ex p Walters* (1994) 26 HLR 170, that there was such a duty has been disapproved twice by the Court of Appeal (*R* v. *Kensington and Chelsea Royal LBC ex p Grillo* (1996) 28 HLR 94 and *R* v. *Home Secretary ex p Duggan* [1994] 3 All ER 277). Judges, but not magistrates, are under a general duty to give reasons. *Flannery* v. *Halifax Estate Agencies Ltd* [2000] 1 WLR 377 at 381.

[291] *ex p Doody* (above).

[292] Moreover, the authority seeking not to give reasons must show that that procedure is not unfair: *ex p Doody* at 561A.

There is no closed list of the circumstances in which fairness will require reasons to be given but the more important examples may be given here. First, decisions that appear aberrant without reasons have to be explained, so that it may be judged whether the aberration is real or apparent. Thus an award of abnormally low compensation to an unfairly dismissed prison officer by the Civil Service Appeal Board, which made it a rule not to give reasons, was quashed by the Court of Appeal, holding that natural justice demanded the giving of reasons both in deciding whether dismissal was unfair and in assessing compensation, since other employees were entitled to appeal to industrial tribunals which were obliged by law to give reasons.[293] Similarly, where the decision-maker departs from a previously adopted policy (even if not published) fairness will require that departure to be explained.[294] Thus a health authority's refusal, without giving reasons, to follow the policy of the National Health Service Executive to introduce a new (and expensive drug) was quashed.[295]

Then, second, there are cases in which the interests concerned (for instance, personal liberty) are 'so highly regarded by the law that fairness requires that reasons…be given as of right'.[296] The House of Lords has held that a mandatory life prisoner should be able to make meaningful representations to the Home Secretary on what his 'tariff period'[297] should be, thus where the Home Secretary was minded to depart from the judicial recommendation of 'tariff' he has to disclose his reasons to the prisoner.[298] Similarly, given the benefits attached to citizenship, fairness would require reasons to be given for the denial of an application for naturalisation were it not that statute specifically excluded that duty.[299] And reasons had to be given when certifying that medication should be given to a competent but non-consenting mental patient.[300] Even the DPP may in exceptional circumstances be required to give the reasons why he decided not to prosecute.[301]

And, third, it is always possible that the failure to give reasons for a decision may justify the inference that the decision was not taken for a good reason.[302] But these cases are not

---

[293] R v. Civil Service Appeal Board ex p Cunningham [1991] 4 All ER 310. Cf. Lawrie v. Commission for Local Authority Accounts, 1994 SLT 1185 (no apparent irrationality and Commission an administrative, not a judicial body: no duty to give reasons).   [294] R v. Home Secretary ex p Urmaza [1996] COD 479.

[295] R v. North Derbyshire Health Authority ex p Fisher (1998) 10 Admin LR 27.

[296] R v. Higher Education Funding Council ex p Institute of Dental Surgery [1994] 1 WLR 242 at 263, per Sedley J interpreting ex p Doody.

[297] i.e. that period considered necessary to meet the needs of retribution for the offence and general deterrence.

[298] ex p Doody (above). See also R v. Home Secretary ex p Murphy [1997] COD 478 (mandatory life prisoner entitled to reasons why Parole Board's recommendation that he be transferred to open prison not accepted); R v. Home Secretary ex p Duggan [1994] 3 All ER 277 (mandatory life prisoner entitled to reasons why he continued to be classified as category A (and so not eligible for parole)); R v. Home Secretary ex p Follen [1996] COD 169 (prisoner entitled to reasons why Parole Board's recommendation that he be released on licence not accepted).

[299] R v. Home Secretary ex p Fayed [1997] 1 All ER 228. Under the British Nationality Act 1981, s. 44(2) the Home Secretary 'shall not be required to assign any reasons for the grant or refusal of any application under this Act'.

[300] R (Wooder) v. Feggetter and anor [2002] 3 WLR 591 (CA), paras. 24, 25 (per Brooke LJ) (decision based on the common law, not the Human Rights Act 1998; cf. Sedley LJ, paras. 46, 47 relying on Art. 8 of the European Convention).

[301] R v. DPP ex p Manning [2001] QB 330 (inquest jury verdict of unlawful killing on death in custody: reasons for decision not to prosecute required). Cf. R v. Solicitor-General ex p Taylor [1996] COD 61 (A-G need not give reasons in declining to prosecute in particular cases).

[302] R v. Secretary for Trade and Industry ex p Lonrho plc [1989] 1 WLR 525 at 540 ('if all the other known facts and circumstances appear to point overwhelmingly in favour of a different decision, the decision-maker, who has given no reasons, cannot complain if the court draws the inference that he had no rational reason for his decision' (Lord Keith). And see Padfield v. Minister of Agriculture, Fisheries and Food [1968] AC 997.

concerned with a legal duty to give reasons but with proving that there was some other flaw in the decision-making process.

As explained above, an important consideration underlying the extension of the duty to give reasons, referred to in many cases, is that in the absence of reasons the person affected may be unable to judge whether there has been 'a justiciable flaw in the [decision-making] process';[303] and thus whether an appeal, if available, should be instituted or an application for judicial review made. Since today there are few exercises of governmental power which are not subject to judicial review,[304] it will be rare that a person affected by a decision—for which reasons were not given—will not be able to say that the absence of reasons has denied him effective recourse to judicial review. A general duty to give reasons is latent in this argument; and the courts seem willing to see sufficient weight given to it to enable such a duty to develop.[305] The Court of Appeal has stressed that a judge's reasons should address the issues critical to the decision so that the parties can assess whether to appeal.[306] Application for permission to appeal to the High Court (from an arbitrator's award) or to the Privy Council from the court below may, however, be dismissed without reasons.[307] In these cases there is no further remedy and so reasons could not buttress a further appeal.

The time has now surely come for the court to acknowledge that there is a general rule that reasons should be given for decisions, based on the principle of fairness which permeates administrative law, subject only to specific exceptions to be identified as cases arise. Such a rule should not be unduly onerous, since reasons need never be more elaborate than the nature of the case admits, but the presumption should be in favour of giving reasons, rather than, as at present, in favour of withholding them.

THE ADEQUACY OF REASONS

Given that statute now frequently requires reasons or it is clear that the common law requires reasons, disputes often concern whether the reasons given are adequate. In the leading case the House of Lords has said that

> The reasons for a decision must be intelligible and they must be adequate. They must enable the reader to understand why the matter was decided as it was and what conclusions were reached on the 'principal important controversial issues', disclosing how any issue of law or fact was resolved. Reasons can be briefly stated, the degree of particularity required depending entirely on the nature of the issues falling for decision. The reasoning

---

[303] *ex p Institute of Dental Surgery* at 256 approved in *ex p Matson* at 776 and *ex p Murray* at 136. And in *ex p Doody* (above) Lord Mustill said (at 565) 'To mount an effective attack on the decision...[the person affected] has [in the absence of reasons] virtually no means of ascertaining whether...the decision-making process has gone astray'. See also *R v. Inland Revenue Commissioners ex p Coombe & Co* (1989) 2 Admin LR 1 (order quashed since court cannot perform its review function in absence of reasons).

[304] Below, p. 532.

[305] Significantly, Lord Neill, for long a proponent of a general statutory duty to give reasons, now favours continued judicial development (in 'The Duty to Give Reasons' in Forsyth and Hare (eds.), *The Golden Metwand and the Crooked Cord* (1998), 183).

[306] *English v. Emery Reimbold & Strick Ltd* [2002] 1 WLR 2409 (CA), paras. 18, 19. This conclusion reached notwithstanding an 'unwelcome' 'cottage industry' manufacturing application for permission to appeal on ground of insufficient reasons (para. 2). See also *R v. Lambert* [2002] 1 SCR 869.

[307] *Mousaka Inc v. Golden Seagull Maritime Inc* [2002] 1 WLR 395 (arbitrator's award: provision of reasons in the circumstances 'completely worthless') (approved *North Range Shipping Ltd v. Seatrans Shipping Corp.* [2002] 1 WLR 2397 (CA)); *Webb v. UK* (1997) 24 EHRR CD 73 (Privy Council: held by the Human Rights Commission compliant with Art. 6(1)).

must not give rise to a substantial doubt as to whether the decision-maker erred in law, for example by misunderstanding some relevant policy or some other important matter or by failing to reach a rational decision on relevant grounds. But such adverse inference will not readily be drawn. The reasons need refer only to the main issues in the dispute, not to every material consideration.... Decision letters must be read in a straightforward manner, recognising that they are addressed to parties well aware of the issues involved and the arguments advanced.[308]

The courts often warn themselves against imposing too onerous a duty to give reasons.[309] Thus there are cases in which reasons need not be given even where fairness may appear to require reasons. Reasons do not need to be given for refusals of appointments or promotions or examination failures,[310] or for a reduction of research funds depending upon academic judgment.[311] And there is no general duty on the Professional Conduct Committee of the General Medical Council to give reasons for its findings of fact.[312] Where the case for reasons is strong but there is some countervailing reason to restrict the duty, the tendency is to accept or require only brief reasons. The publication of a short press notice containing 'brief reasons' sufficed when the Secretary of State made a controversial decision following a complex consultation process that would increase the amount of aircraft noise near Heathrow.[313] Where an alderman's election had to be confirmed by the Court of Aldermen, the court had to explain 'in short reasons' its decision not to confirm even if different members of the court had had different reasons for their conclusion.[314] Similarly, where the Millennium Commission rejected an application for funding on the ground that the application 'was less attractive than others', this was sufficient compliance with the duty.[315] Where a challenge to a decision notice made by the Financial Services Authority involved a full rehearing (in which the reasons played little part) the reasons need simply explain why the decision was made and not deal with every submission made by the recipient of the decision notice.[316]

---

[308] *South Bucks District Council* v. *Porter (No 2)* [2004] UKHL 33, [2004] 1 WLR 1953, para. 26 (Lord Brown) relying upon *Re Poyser and Mills' Arbitration* [1964] 2 QB 467, 478 and *Save Britain's Heritage* v. *Number 1 Poultry Ltd* [1991] 1 WLR 153. In a planning context 'substantial prejudice' by the 'person aggrieved' is an additional requirement (r. 19(1) of the Town and Country Planning Appeals (Determination by Inspectors) (Inquiries Procedure) (England) Rules 2000 (SI 2000 No. 1625) read with s. 288(5)(b) of the Town and Country Planning Act 1990).

[309] In *Institute of Dental Surgery* (above) at 257A (approved in *ex p Murray* (above) at 136 and *Asha Foundation*, below, para. 25) the following grounds for denying a duty to give reasons were given: 'it may place an undue burden upon decision-makers; demand an appearance of unanimity when there is diversity; call for articulation of sometimes inexpressible value judgments; and offer an invitation to the captious to comb the reasons for previously unsuspected grounds of challenge' (Sedley J).

[310] See *ex p Cunningham* (above) at 316 (Lord Donaldson MR). But in *Bradley* v. *A-G* [1988] 2 NZLR 454, non-promotion of a naval officer was held to entitle him to a hearing and in *R* v. *University of Cambridge ex p Evans* [1998] ELR 515 Sedley J considered it 'arguable' that non-promotion of a university lecturer required reasons (*sed quaere*). Legitimate expectation may make a difference, as it did in the New Zealand case.

[311] *R* v. *Higher Education Funding Council ex p Institute of Dental Surgery* [1994] 1 WLR 242 but since doubted on this point by Sedley LJ himself (*Wooder*, above, para. 41).

[312] *Gupta* v. *General Medical Council* [2001] UKPC 1, [2002] 1 WLR 1691 (PC) (but a serious flaw in the committee's fact finding may thus go undetected).

[313] *R* v. *Secretary of State for Transport ex p Richmond-upon-Thames LBC (No 4)* [1996] 4 All ER 903.

[314] *R* v. *City of London Corporation ex p Matson* [1997] 1 WLR 765.

[315] *R (Asha Foundation)* v. *The Millennium Commission* [2003] EWCA Civ 88 (an explanation of rejection had been promised).

[316] *R (Willford)* v. *Financial Services Authority* [2013] EWCA Civ 677, paras. 49–52.

Where permission to apply for judicial review is granted, the decision-maker has a duty of candour to the court and must reveal why the challenged decision was made.[317]

Thus the question arises whether a failure to give reasons at or about the time of the disputed decision, may be remedied by reasons given much later in the respondent's affidavit responding to the grant of permission. If the duty to give reasons is an element of natural justice, the failure to give reasons, like any other breach of natural justice, should render the disputed decision void.[318] And a void decision could not be validated by late reasons even if they show that the decision was justified. Consistent with this analysis the Court of Appeal has quashed a decision that an applicant was intentionally homeless notwithstanding that the bad reasons given when the decision was made were supplemented by good reasons given in the respondent's affidavit.[319] 'It is not ordinarily open', the Court of Appeal said in another case,[320] 'to a decision maker, who is required to give reasons, to respond to a challenge by giving different or better reasons.' There is always the danger that the decision-maker in giving supplementary reasons may drift 'perhaps subconsciously, into ex post facto rationalisation' of the decision.[321] Thus decision-makers should not be given 'a second bite at the cherry'. European law requires reasons to be given with the decision.[322]

But the courts are reluctant to quash sound decisions marred only by a technical failure of reasons.[323] The Court of Appeal has said that to quash a judicial decision simply because of a failure to give adequate reasons 'is likely to be a disproportionate and inappropriate response'.[324] Thus where a judge's decision is appealed simply on the ground of inadequate reasons, the judge should have an opportunity to amend his reasons.[325] Similarly, the seeking of an amplification of reasons by the Employment Appeal Tribunal from the

---

[317] R v. Lancashire County Council ex p Huddleston [1986] 2 All ER 941 at 945. Cf Marshall and ors v. Deputy Governor of Bermuda [2010] UKPC 9 ('duty of candour was to provide the court, where necessary, with the material needed to make an informed decision' (para. 32); thus not breached when information sought not necessary for that decision).   [318] See above, p. 419.

[319] R v. Westminster City Council ex p Ermakov [1996] 2 All ER 302, followed in R (Wall) v. Brighton and Hove City Council [2004] EWHC 2582 (reasons could not be reconstructed after the event) and R (Richards) v. Pembrokeshire CC [2004] EWCA Civ 1000. See also, R v. South West Thames Mental Health Review Tribunal ex p Demetri [1997] COD 445, R v. Croydon LBC ex p Graham (1994) 26 HLR 286 and Akel v. Immigration Appeal Tribunal [1996] COD 50; and Nash v. Chelsea College [2001] EWHC 538 (Admin).

[320] R (S) v. Brent LBC [2002] EWCA Civ 693, para. 26 (Schiemann LJ).

[321] Adami v. Ethical Standards Officer [2005] EWCA Civ 1754, para. 24 (Auld LJ). See also Barke v. SEETEC Business Technology Centre Ltd [2005] EWCA Civ 578.

[322] Michel v. European Parliament Case 195/80, [1981] ECR 2861.

[323] Some of the cases are: R v. Northampton County Council ex p W [1998] COD 108 (affidavit 'amply justified…decision'); R v. Home Secretary ex p Jahromi (1996) 8 Admin LR 197 (national security case; affidavit lifted reasons above the 'bare minimum'); and R v. Camden LBC ex p Mohammed (1997) 9 Admin LR 639 ('if the matter was capable of being put right [by late reasons, the court] should allow the process to be completed'). Note also that a powerful Divisional Court (Lord Parker CJ, Cooke J and Bridge J) held in Mountview Court Properties Ltd v. Devlin (1970) 21 P & CR 689, [1970] RVR 451 that failure to comply with a statutory duty to give reasons did not itself amount to an error of law justifying the quashing of the decision (although unsatisfactory reasons might reveal such a flaw). But this decision has since been doubted: R v. Northants CC ex p Marshall [1998] COD 457 (Sedley J) and Crake v. Supplementary Benefits Commission [1982] 1 All ER 498 (Woolf J).

[324] Adami, as above, para. 26. And see Office of Fair Trading v. IBA Health Ltd [2004] EWCA Civ 142, para. 106 'nothing unusual…for the stated reasons to be amplified by evidence before the Court' (Carnwath LJ).

[325] The procedure is explained in English v. Emery Reimbold & Strick Ltd, above, paras. 25 and 26. The trial judge may suo motu amplify his reasons when an application for permission to appeal is made or the appeal court may adjourn to afford him that opportunity when an application is made to it for permission to appeal. See [2007] JR 82 (Olley). See also Aerospace Publishing Ltd v. Thames Water Utilities Ltd [2006] EWCA Civ 717 (principle did not apply where permission to appeal already granted).

Chairman of the Employment Tribunal has been upheld by the Court of Appeal.[326] And in another case the Court of Appeal approved the remission of an inadequately reasoned decision back to the Standards Committee that made it.[327] But the courts have refused to allow the amplification of reasons in other cases.[328]

Where the reasoning of the decision-maker is exemplary but the account given of that reasoning is defective, it is appropriate to allow the error to be set right provided that is done soon after the error is discovered. But this principle must be applied with caution. Amplification of reasons can too easily be transmuted into improvement or replacement of reasons that do not reflect the actual reasoning of the decision-maker.

APPEALS

Natural justice does not require that there should be a right of appeal from any decision.[329] This is an inevitable corollary of the fact that there is no right of appeal against a statutory authority unless statute so provides.[330]

Whether a hearing given on appeal is an acceptable substitute for a hearing not given, or not properly given, before the initial decision is in some cases an arguable question. In principle there ought to be an observance of natural justice equally at both stages; and accordingly natural justice is violated if the true charge is put forward only at the appeal stage.[331] If natural justice is violated at the first stage, the right of appeal is not so much a true right of appeal as a corrected initial hearing: instead of a fair trial followed by appeal, the procedure is reduced to unfair trial followed by fair trial. This was pointed out by Megarry J in a trade union expulsion case, holding that, as a general rule, a failure of natural justice in the trial body cannot be cured by a sufficiency of natural justice in the appellate body.[332] He distinguished a Canadian case in which a law student had been refused leave to take a degree: he had been allowed to submit only a written statement to the faculty council, but on appeal had been given a full oral hearing and represented by counsel in a fully judicial proceeding, and the Supreme Court of Canada held that the appeal cured any earlier defect.[333] In New Zealand, also, it has been held that a fair appeal does not normally redeem a failure of natural justice at first instance, though it may be taken into account in considering the award of discretionary remedies.[334] Nor does a full hearing on appeal justify cancellation of a taxi-driver's licence[335] or dismissal of a school-teacher[336] without an initial hearing.

---

[326] The *Barke* case, as above.   [327] *Adami*, as above.

[328] *VK* v. *Norfolk County Council and the Special Educational Needs and Disability Tribunal* [2004] EWHC 2921. Amplification was considered but not allowed in *Dunster Properties* v. *First Secretary of State* [2006] EWHC 2079.   [329] *Ward* v. *Bradford Cpn* (1971) 70 LGR 27.

[330] See below, p. 771.

[331] *Annamunthodo* v. *Oilfields Workers' Trade Union* [1961] AC 945.

[332] *Leary* v. *National Union of Vehicle Builders* [1971] Ch 34. See also *R* v. *Aston University Senate ex p Roffey* [1969] 2 QB 538; *Glynn* v. *Keele University* [1971] 1 WLR 487; *Re Cardinal and Cornwall Police Commissioners* (1973) 42 DLR (3d) 323; *Fagan* v. *Coursing Association* (1974) 8 SASR 546 at 562; *Hall* v. *New South Wales Trotting Club* [1976] 1 NSWLR 323.

[333] *King* v. *University of Saskatchewan* (1969) 6 DLR (3d) 120. Megarry J in *Leary* (above) would if necessary have declined to follow this decision. See also *Pillai* v. *Singapore City Council* [1968] 1 WLR 1278, where the question was governed by rules of procedure for the dismissal of employees; *Re Clark and Ontario Securities Commission* (1966) 56 DLR (2d) 585; *Twist* v. *Randwick Municipal Council* (1976) 12 ALR 379 at 387; *Re Harelkin and University of Regina* (1979) 96 DLR (3d) 14.

[334] *Reid* v. *Rowley* [1977] 2 NZLR 472; *Wislang* v. *Medical Practitioners Disciplinary Committee* [1974] 1 NZLR 29.   [335] *Moran* v. *A-G* [1976] IR 400.

[336] *Pratt* v. *Wanganui Education Board* [1977] 1 NZLR 476.

According to the Privy Council, however, Megarry J's 'general rule' was too broadly stated, since in some cases members of organisations, whose rights depend upon contract, 'should be taken to have agreed to accept what in the end is a fair decision, notwithstanding some initial defect'. An appeal to the committee of the Australian Jockey Club was held, for this reason, to cure an initial decision of the stewards which failed to observe the principles of natural justice in disqualifying the owner of a horse found to have been raced improperly.[337] But the Privy Council emphasised that their reservations applied to domestic disputes which have to be settled by agreed procedure under contractual rules. Those cases technically fall outside administrative law, since they do not concern governmental action.

Squarely within the field of public law, however, is the case of the Liverpool councillors, in which the House of Lords followed the lead of the Privy Council. The councillors had been surcharged by the district auditor with losses resulting from their failure to make a valid rate. It was held that they had been given a fair hearing, but that, in any case, a defective hearing would have been cured by the full rehearing of their case on their appeal to the High Court.[338] It was stressed that the scope of the statutory appeal was as ample as it could be and more ample than that of judicial review;[339] and a distinction was drawn between full appeals where all the evidence may be examined and limited appeals on questions of law only or where the appellate body does not investigate findings of fact.[340] It is only where the appellate body can enter into the merits and determine the issue itself that the House of Lords' reasoning applies; and in that case it is hard to deny that a fair hearing has been given, even though two fair hearings were legally due. And an appeal may have greater curative effect where the appeal tribunal has original as well as appellate jurisdiction.[341] As already noted[342] access to a court of 'full jurisdiction' may cure non-compliance with Article 6(1) of the Human Rights Convention by the initial decision-maker. And in a later similar case[343] involving councillors surcharged by the district auditor for wilful misconduct, the extensive powers of the High Court on Appeal secured compliance both with Article 6(1) and the common law duty of fairness.

A similar principle—although the appeal body was not a court—was applied in a school discipline case.[344] It was found that while Parliament had intended that pupils were entitled to fairness at each stage of the procedure before exclusion, it had also intended that the appeal to an independent appeal tribunal, rather than judicial review, should be the normal remedy for the aggrieved pupil. This was shown by the IAP's hearing of all the evidence and its extensive powers.[345]

---

[337] *Calvin v. Carr* [1980] AC 574, approving the judgment of Cooke J in *Reid v. Rowley* (above). See also *Murray v. Greyhound Racing Control Board of Queensland* [1979] Qd. R 111. *Calvin v. Carr* was followed in *Modahl v. British Athletic Federation Ltd* [2001] EWCA Civ 1447, [2002] 1 WLR 1192 (CA) ('where an apparently sensible appeal structure has been put in place [by contract] the parties should [be] taken [to] have agreed to accept what is in the end a fair decision' (para. 61, Latham LJ)).

[338] *Lloyd v. McMahon* [1987] AC 625. See similarly *R v. Visitors to the Inns of Court ex p Calder* [1994] QB 1 (Stuart-Smith LJ); *Re Chromex Nickel Mines Ltd* (1970) 16 DLR (3d) 273. Contrast *O'Laughlin v. Halifax Longshoremen's Association* (1972) 28 DLR (3d) 315; *Pollock v. Alberta Union of Provincial Employees* (1978) 90 DLR (3d) 506; *Colpitts v. Australian Telecommunications Commission* (1986) 70 ALR 554.

[339] Ibid. at 709 (Lord Bridge).

[340] Ibid. at 716 (Lord Templeman). Note the reservations of Staughton LJ in *ex p Calder*, above.

[341] As in *Clark v. Young* [1927] NZLR 348; *Twist v. Randwick Municipal Council* (1976) 12 ALR 379; *R v. Marks ex p Australian Building Federation* (1981) 35 ALR 241; *Marine Hull Insurance v. Hereford* (1985) 62 ALR 253; contrast *Courtney v. Peters* (1990) 98 ALR 645.   [342] Above, p. 381.

[343] *Porter v. Magill* [2002] 2 WLR 37 (HL), paras. 92–4 (Lord Hope) (adoption of unlawful housing policy for political reasons led to loss to council of £31 million).

[344] *R (Dr) v. Head Teacher of St George's Catholic School and ors* [2002] EWCA Civ 1822.

[345] Paras. 37, 38.

It is always possible that some statutory scheme may take the further step and imply that an 'appeal' is to be the only opportunity of a hearing. It is surprising that this question has not been settled under the Town and Country Planning Acts. If planning permission is refused by the local planning authority the applicant may appeal to the Secretary of State who must, if requested, hold an inquiry or hearing.[346] But does this absolve the local planning authority from giving a fair hearing before refusing the initial application? In 1952 a judge said that it did,[347] but that was at the time when judicial concern for natural justice was at its lowest ebb. In 1987, by contrast, a judge held that a planning authority was in breach of its duty to act fairly in not giving rival traders an opportunity to oppose a grant of permission for an amusement area and arcade.[348]

The existence of a full right of appeal on the merits may be taken into account in holding that the scheme of the Act does not require a hearing for some preliminary administrative step, as where an inspector of taxes applied for leave to raise assessments outside the usual time on grounds of fraud, wilful default or neglect.[349]

The Court of Appeal on one occasion held that the exercise of a right of administrative appeal (by a police officer to the Home Secretary) deprived the appellant of his right to complain to the court of a denial of natural justice at the initial stage. Here there was clearly a confusion between a right of appeal on the merits of the case and judicial review of the legality of the whole proceedings; and the decision was duly reversed by the House of Lords.[350]

DELEGATED HEARINGS

Does natural justice require that 'the one who decides must hear'?[351] In other words, may the hearing be given by one body, e.g. a committee of the deciding authority, and the decision itself by another?

Where the deciding authority is a minister or central government department, it must be assumed that Parliament intends the department to operate in its usual way, so that the minister's duties may be performed by subordinate officials.[352] In other cases, the courts allow some relaxation of the normal rule which requires statutory powers to be exercised by the precise person or body on whom they are conferred and makes it impossible for them to be legally exercised by others, e.g. sub-committees.[353] The Privy Council has held that a dairy board, in making zoning orders affecting milk producers, may appoint a person or persons to receive evidence and submissions from interested parties; and that if, before deciding to make an order, the board is fully informed of the evidence and submissions, there will be no breach of natural justice.[354] In some circumstances, it was added, an accurate summary of the evidence and submissions might suffice. But since the board had merely acted on the report of a committee of inquiry which held a public hearing

---

[346] Town and Country Planning Act 1990, s. 79(2), replacing earlier Acts.

[347] Parker J *obiter* in *Hanily* v. *Minister of Local Government and Planning* [1952] 2 QB 444 at 452.

[348] *R* v. *Great Yarmouth BC ex p Botton Bros Arcades Ltd* (1987) 56 P & CR 99. See similarly *R* v. *Monmouth DC ex p Jones* (1985) 53 P & CR 108 (planning permission quashed since objector not given opportunity to explain his case).

[349] *Pearlberg* v. *Varty* [1972] 1 WLR 534; and see *Wiseman* v. *Borneman* [1971] AC 297.

[350] *Ridge* v. *Baldwin* [1963] 1 QB 539, reversed [1964] AC 40; and see *Annumunthodo* v. *Oilfields Workers' Trade Union* [1961] AC 945.   [351] For this American proposition see the 9th edn, p. 991.

[352] *Local Government Board* v. *Arlidge* [1915] AC 120; see above, p. 266.   [353] See above, p. 260.

[354] *Jeffs* v. *New Zealand Dairy Production and Marketing Board* [1967] 1 AC 551. Contrast *Re Macquarie University ex p Ong* (1989) 17 NSWLR 113 (committee specifically empowered).

on its own initiative and did not report the evidence to the board, the board's order was quashed.[355] The Court of Appeal decided similarly in a licensing case where a licensing panel failed to report the applicant's submissions or the objections to them to the committee which made the decision,[356] even though delegation of the hearing was authorised by statutory rules.

There is no breach of natural justice if the deciding authority appoints a committee to investigate and report, then discloses the report to the person affected and gives him a fair hearing before itself.[357] There is here no delegation of any of the authority's powers or duties.

HEARING HELD AFTER DECISION

What is an administrative authority to do if it has failed to give a fair hearing, so that its decision is quashed or declared void? It still has the duty to give a proper hearing and decide the case, but it has prejudiced itself by its defective decision, which it may well have defended in legal proceedings. It cannot be fair procedure to take a decision first and hear the evidence afterwards, even though the first decision is legally a nullity. But usually the only possible course is for the same authority to rehear the case.[358] For that authority will be the only authority with statutory power to proceed, and there is therefore 'a case of necessity' of the kind we have already met.[359] In the case of a tribunal with variable membership the court may order the hearing to be held by a differently constituted tribunal.[360]

It was acknowledged in *Ridge* v. *Baldwin* that, if there was no such alternative, the original body would have to reconsider the case as best it could. Lord Reid said:[361]

> if an officer or body realises that it has acted hastily and reconsiders the whole matter afresh, after affording to the person affected a proper opportunity to present his case, then its later decision will be valid.

But in that case the hearing, when given by the watch committee, was defective in that the charges were not fully disclosed, so that the second decision was as void as the first. A Canadian case, arising out of disciplinary proceedings by the Toronto Stock Exchange, affords an example of the second decision being valid, since everything possible was done to hold a full and fair hearing on the second occasion.[362] Likewise the Secretary of State for the Environment, whose decision to reduce a local authority's rate support grant was quashed because he failed to hear their objections at the proper stage, validly came to the same decision as before after hearing the objections correctly.[363]

A different but comparable situation is where the hearing is given after action has been decided upon, but in time to prevent the decision being void. This happened in Trinidad where the Governor had power to transfer the indentures of immigrant workers from one estate to another. The Governor made an order for such a transfer without consulting the

---

[355] The *Jeffs* case (above); and see *Wislang* v. *Medical Practitioners Disciplinary Committee* [1974] 1 NZLR 29 (statutory requirement of 'full report' not satisfied).

[356] *R* v. *Preston BC ex p Quietlynn Ltd* (1984) 83 LGR 308 (refusal of sex shop licence quashed).

[357] *Osgood* v. *Nelson* (1872) LR 5 HL 636.

[358] As in *R* v. *Secretary of State for the Environment ex p Hackney LBC*, below.

[359] Above, p. 395. But the limitations imposed by Art. 6(1) on the operation of the principle of necessity should be noted (see above, p. 396).

[360] As in *Metropolitan Properties (FGC) Ltd* v. *Lannon* [1969] 1 QB 577.   [361] [1964] AC at 79.

[362] *Posluns* v. *Toronto Stock Exchange* (1968) 67 DLR (2d) 165.

[363] *R* v. *Secretary of State for the Environment ex p Hackney LBC* [1984] 1 WLR 592.

estate owner, but as soon as he heard that the owner objected he gave him a fair hearing. He then declined to cancel the order. Since the hearing was given while there was still power to cancel the order, the procedure was held valid.[364] In Canada the cancellation of a vehicle permit was upheld even though the holder was given only the opportunity to persuade the Registrar afterwards that the cancellation should be revoked.[365] Since the initial decision in such cases will almost inevitably have a prejudicial effect, the law ought to be slow to admit such dubious procedure.

LEGITIMATE EXPECTATION

INTRODUCTION

The classic situation in which the principles of natural justice apply is where some legal right, liberty or interest is affected, for instance where a building is demolished or an office-holder is dismissed or a trader's licence is revoked. But good administration demands procedural justice in other situations also. Where some boon or benefit has been promised by an official (or has been regularly granted by the official in similar circumstances), that boon or benefit may be legitimately expected by those who have placed their trust in the promises of the official. It would be unfair to dash those expectations without at least granting the person affected an opportunity to show the official why his discretion should be exercised in a way that fulfils his expectation. Hence there has developed a doctrine of the protection of legitimate expectations[366] primarily in the context of natural justice (although as will be seen below it extends beyond procedure in exceptional cases). The doctrine is a welcome addition to the armoury of the courts in ensuring that discretions are exercised fairly. But as will be seen it has been attended by some conceptual confusion where clarity is required. The phrase 'legitimate expectation' (which is 'much in vogue')[367] must not be allowed to collapse into an inchoate justification for judicial intervention.

THE REASONS FOR THE PROTECTION OF LEGITIMATE EXPECTATIONS

As adumbrated in the previous paragraph the protection of legitimate expectations is often considered to be required by fairness.[368] On the other hand the abuse of power has

---

[364] *De Verteuil* v. *Knaggs* [1918] AC 557. See similarly *Pagliara* v. *A-G* [1974] 1 NZLR 86. Compare *Vestry of St James and St John Clerkenwell* v. *Feary* (1890) 24 QBD 703.

[365] *Registrar of Motor Vehicles* v. *Canadian American Transfer Ltd* (1972) 26 DLR (3d) 112. Contrast *Re McGavin Toastmaster Ltd* (1972) 31 DLR (3d) 370 (Manitoba Human Rights Commission required undertakings from company before hearing it: proceedings set aside as unduly prejudicial).

[366] For discussion, with European comparisons, see (1988) *CLJ* 238 (Forsyth). See also Jowell and Oliver (eds.), *New Directions in Judicial Review*, 37 (P. Elias); (1992) 108 *LQR* 79 (P. P. Craig); and [2011] *JR* 429 (Forsyth). For criticism of the doctrine by the High Court of Australia see *Annetts* v. *McCann* (1991) 97 ALR 177. See particularly, *Actions Against Public Officials* (2009) ch. 2 (R. Moules). See also [2004] *PL* 564 (Sales and Steyn), [2011] *PL* 330 (Reynolds) and (2010) 30 *Legal Studies* 633 (Watson).

[367] *R (EB (Kosovo))* v. *Home Secretary* [2008] UKHL 41, para. 31 (Lord Scott).

[368] See, for instance, *R* v. *Inland Revenue Commissioners ex p MFK Underwriting* [1990] 1 WLR 1545, at 1569H–1570A (Bingham LJ); *CCSU* v. *Minister for the Civil Service* [1985] AC 374 at 415C–G (Lord Roskill).

been considered the 'root concept' justifying the protection of legitimate expectations.[369] Particularly in the European context 'legal certainty', i.e. that 'the individual ought to be able to plan his or her action on the basis [that the expectation will be fulfilled]'[370] is also relied upon. But as Lord Justice Laws has remarked; 'Abuse of power...catches the moral impetus of the rule of law....But it goes no distance to tell you, case by case, what is lawful and what is not.'[371] And similar remarks could be made about the other reasons for protecting of legitimate expectations.

A further and more satisfactory reason for the protection of legitimate expectations lies in the trust that has been reposed by the citizen in what he has been told or led to believe by the official.[372] Good government depends upon trust between the governed and the governor. Unless that trust is sustained and protected officials will not be believed and government becomes a choice between chaos and coercion.[373] The protection of trust as a concept has its origins in German law and it plainly overlaps with the protection of 'legal certainty'.[374] But it has this particular advantage: it is a simple concrete question of fact whether trust has been reposed in an official's promise, so this principle does go 'some distance' to indicate which expectations should be protected and which should not. It captures precisely why legitimate expectations should be protected.

CREATING THE EXPECTATION: SOME EXAMPLES

As Lord Bridge in 1986 set out clearly there are two ways in which legitimate expectations may be created. He said:[375] 'The courts have developed a relatively novel doctrine in public law that a duty of consultation may arise from a legitimate expectation of consultation aroused either by a promise or by an established practice of consultation'.

A case of a 'promise' was where the government of Hong Kong announced that certain illegal immigrants, who were liable to deportation, would be interviewed individually and treated on their merits in each case. The Privy Council quashed a deportation order where the immigrant had only been allowed to answer questions without being able to put his own case, holding that 'when a public authority has promised to follow a

---

[369] The phrase comes from *R v. Secretary of State for Education ex p Begbie* [2000] 1 WLR 1115 (CA), 1129 (Laws LJ). Abuse of power is also much relied upon in *R v. North and East Devon Health Authority ex p Coughlan* [2000] 2 WLR 622.

[370] Craig, (*Administrative Law*. 6th edn, 2012), para. 20-004. But note the criticisms by Reynolds, above p. 450, of legal certainty in this context.

[371] *Abdi v. Secretary of State for the Home Department* [2005] EWCA Civ 1363, para. 67.

[372] See (1988) *CLJ* 238 (Forsyth) first advancing trust as the basis of protection. And see now particularly, 'Legitimate Expectations and the Protection of Trust in Public Officials' [2011] *PL* 330 (Reynolds).

[373] Previous two sentences cited in *Board of Governors of Loreto Grammar School, Re Judicial Review* [2011] NIQB 30, para. 95 (McCloskey J) and approved on appeal; *Re Loreto Grammar School's Application for Judicial Review* [2012] NICA 1, [2013] NI 41, para. 43 (Girvan LJ).

[374] See the discussion in Forsyth (1988), as above, pp. 242ff.

[375] *Re Westminster City Council* [1986] AC 668 at 692. Lord Diplock made a formal statement in the *Council of Civil Service Unions* case (below) at 408, saying that the decision must affect some other person either:(a) by altering rights or obligations of that person which are enforceable by or against him in private law; or (b) by depriving him of some benefit or advantage which either (i) he had in the past been permitted by the decision-maker to enjoy and which he can legitimately expect to be permitted to continue to do until there has been communicated to him some rational grounds for withdrawing it on which he has been given an opportunity to comment; or (ii) he has received assurance from the decision-maker will not be withdrawn without giving him first an opportunity of advancing reasons for contending that it should not be withdrawn.

One case which does not seem to be covered is that of a first-time applicant for a licence (below, p. 463).

certain procedure, it is in the interest of good administration that it should act fairly and should implement its promise, so long as implementation does not interfere with its statutory duty'.[376] Another example was where the Court of Appeal quashed the refusal of the Home Office to admit an immigrant when this was contrary to the legitimate expectation created by one of its published circulars.[377] And where a government department encouraged a company to suppose that it would receive a grant, it could not lawfully refuse the grant without first granting a hearing.[378] In several such cases the expectation is of some actual grant or benefit rather than merely of a hearing, and it is difficult to divide them cleanly from cases of unreasonableness.[379]

A case of 'established practice' was where civil servants employed in secret work in the government communications headquarters were prohibited from belonging to trade unions. Since there was a well-established practice of consultation in such matters, but no consultation had been offered, the House of Lords held that the procedure would have been unfair and unlawful had there not been overriding considerations of national security.[380] For the same reason a local education authority acted unlawfully in proceeding with a school reorganisation without adequately consulting parents, since this was habitually done in such cases under the emphatic advice of the Secretary of State.[381] In 'a classic example of legitimate expectation' the court quashed the government's and British Coal's decision to close a large number of collieries in disregard of the established colliery review procedure and without consulting the miners and trade unions affected. It was held that only a substantially similar review procedure, including some form of independent scrutiny, would satisfy the expectations legitimately held.[382]

WHEN IS AN EXPECTATION LEGITIMATE?

It is not enough that an expectation should exist; it must in addition be legitimate. But how is it to be determined whether a particular expectation is worthy of protection? This is a difficult area since an expectation reasonably entertained by a person may not be found to be legitimate because of some countervailing consideration of policy or law. A crucial requirement is that the assurance must itself be clear, unequivocal and unambiguous.[383] Many claimants fail at this hurdle after close analysis of the assurance. The test is 'how on a fair reading of the promise it would have been reasonably understood by

---

[376] A-G of Hong Kong v. Ng Yuen Shiu [1983] 2 AC 629. Another 'promise' case, in effect one of legitimate expectation, is R v. Liverpool Cpn ex p Liverpool Taxi Fleet Operators' Association [1972] 2 QB 299, for which see above, pp. 336 and 338. See also Cole v. Cunningham (1983) 49 ALR 123.

[377] R v. Home Secretary ex p Asif Mahmood Khan [1984] 1 WLR 1337; above, p. 338.

[378] R v. Secretary of State for Transport ex p Sherriff & Sons Ltd, The Times, 18 December 1986.

[379] See (1992) 108 LQR 79 at 92 (P. P. Craig).

[380] Council of Civil Service Unions v. Minister for the Civil Service [1985] AC 374.

[381] R v. Brent LBC ex p Gunning (1985) 84 LGR 168. See also Walsh v. Secretary of State for Scotland, 1990 SLT 526 (prisoner's legitimate expectation of release frustrated by transfer to Scotland: detention held contrary to natural justice).

[382] R v. British Coal Cpn ex p Vardy [1993] ICR 720. The decision also violated statutory employment law.

[383] ex p MFK Underwriting Agencies Ltd and ex p Matrix-Securities Ltd. Confirmed R (Bancoult) v. Secretary of State for Foreign and Commonwealth Affairs [2008] UKHL 61, para. 60 (Lord Hoffmann). Thus an undertaking to work 'on the feasibility of resettling the Ilois' on the Chagos Islands and to change the law to permit resettlement did not amount to an 'unequivocal assurance' that the Ilois could return; no legitimate expectation found (para. 134 (Lord Carswell)). Cf. Lord Mance (para. 285). For further examples see R (Elayathamby) v. Home Secretary [2011] EWHC 2182 and R (Luton Borough Council & Nottingham City Council and ors) v. Secretary of State for Education [2011] EWHC 217; and R (Royal Brompton and Harefield NHS Foundation Trust) v. Joint Committee of Primary Care Trusts [2012] EWCA Civ 472.

those to whom it was made'.[384] But different judges may take different views of the same assurance, thus leading to uncertainty.[385]

Some points are relatively clear. First of all, for an expectation to be legitimate it must be founded upon a promise or practice by the public authority that is said to be bound to fulfil the expectation. Thus a statement made by a minister cannot found an expectation that an independent officer will act in a particular way.[386] Similarly, an election promise made by a shadow minister did not bind the responsible minister after the change of government.[387] And a prisoner (who had provided the police with information about his drug trafficking associates) was allegedly promised by the police that he would serve his sentence in a 'protected witness unit'. But that unit was part of the prison service and the police had no authority to bind the prison service.[388]

Similar difficulties arise in regard to the question whether a promise made by one minister can bind another minister. The House of Lords was divided in a case about whether the Minister of Health could issue guidance to NHS employers (denying employment to international medical graduates (IMGs) unless there were no suitable resident candidates) which severely restricted the benefits of the Home Secretary's Highly Skilled Migrant Programme (HSMP) to IMGs.[389] Lord Scott held that the continued existence of the HSMP could not fetter the Minister of Health's freedom to issue guidance to the NHS employers as the public interest ordained.[390] But the majority disagreed and Lord Rogers held that both ministers were 'formulating the policies of a single entity, Her Majesty's Government';[391] and that consequently the guidance was unfair as not consistent with the legitimate expectations derived from the Home Secretary's scheme.

Second, clear statutory words, of course, override any expectation howsoever founded.[392] But this is simply a particular example of an ultra vires expectation discussed separately below.

---

[384] R (Association of British Civilian Internees: Far East Region) v. Secretary of State for Defence [2003] EWCA Civ 473, [2003] QB 1397, at para. 56 (Dyson LJ) approved in Paponette, below, para. 30 (Lord Wilson).

[385] See the different views in the House of Lords of the assurance in Bancoult (previous note). And in Paponette and ors v. A-G of Trinidad and Tobago (Trinidad and Tobago) [2010] UKPC 32 the majority of the Privy Council thought that the assurance was sufficiently 'clear, unequivocal and unambiguous' to require the authority to justify its departure from it. But Lord Brown, dissenting, found the assurance 'more…an aspiration than a guarantee' (para. 60). See also R (Davies and anor) v. Revenue and Customs [2011] UKSC 47 for different views in the Supreme Court on whether a Revenue booklet containing statements on when a taxpayer would be 'non-resident' was sufficiently clear. A 'confusing presentation [in the booklet] would be likely to have lacked the clarity required by the doctrine of legitimate expectation' (para. 37). See further Re Loreto Grammar School's Application for Judicial Review [2012] NICA 1, [2013] NI 41 for another example (Court of Appeal and first instance judge taking different views).

[386] R v. DPP ex p Kebilene, above (DC) (statement by minister could not found expectation concerning the future decisions of the Director of Public Prosecutions).

[387] ex p Begbie, above. Moreover, the correction of an error in a letter from the decision-maker is generally not an abuse of power (para. 84). This aspect of ex p Begbie followed in R (Capital Care Services UK Ltd) v. Home Secretary [2012] EWCA Civ 1151 (employment agency licensed as sponsor in error; revocation of licence upheld).

[388] R (Bloggs 61) v. Home Secretary [2003] 1 WLR 2724 (promise not within the police's ostensible authority).

[389] R (BAPIO Action Ltd) v. Home Secretary [2008] UKHL 27, [2008] 2 WLR 1073. See (2008) CLJ 453 (Elliott). [390] Ibid., para. 29.

[391] Ibid., para. 34. It may be recalled that Ministers may generally exercise each others' powers. Above, p. 52. And see also, below, p. 705 (divisibility of the Crown).

[392] R v. DPP ex p Kebilene [1999] 3 WLR 972 (HL) (no legitimate expectation that prosecutorial discretion would be exercised in accordance with the European Convention, since the Human Rights Act 1998, s. 22, clearly postponed the operation of the Convention). See above, p. 134. And see R v. Secretary of State for Education ex p Begbie [2000] 1 WLR 1115 (CA) (to give effect to expectation that the state funding for private

Third, the notification of a relevant change of policy destroys any expectation founded upon the earlier policy.[393] This again is discussed separately below.

Fourth, there is no artificial restriction on the material on which a legitimate expectation rests may be based. Thus a legitimate expectation can be founded upon an unincorporated treaty, but it is seldom that the terms of the treaty will be sufficiently precise or known to the individual concerned.[394]

Fifth, the individual seeking protection of the expectation must themselves deal fairly with the public authority. Thus taxpayers seeking revenue clearance for their proposals must make full disclosure before the Revenue's assurances will be binding.[395]

Sixth, consideration of the expectation may be beyond the jurisdiction of the court. For instance, when it would involve questioning proceedings in Parliament contrary to the law of parliamentary privilege.[396]

THE ULTRA VIRES EXPECTATION

An expectation whose fulfilment requires that a decision-maker should make an unlawful decision, cannot be a legitimate expectation.[397] It is inherent in many of the decisions,[398] and express in several,[399] that the expectation must be within the powers of the

---

schooling of a class of children would continue until the end of their schooling, would fetter the minister's statutory discretion to allow such funding in exceptional cases). And see *R (Bloggs 61)* v. *Home Secretary* [2003] 1 WLR 2724.

[393] *Fisher* v. *Minister of Public Safety (No 2)* [1999] 2 WLR 349 (any expectation that prisoners would not be executed while their petition was being considered by Inter-American Commission on Human Rights dashed by letters to the prisoners' solicitors stating date beyond which the government would not wait for the IACHR's decision) and many other cases. *Fischer* was distinguished in *Lewis* v. *A-G of Jamaica* [2001] 2 AC 50. The latter decision, however, rested on a constitutional right to 'the protection of the law' which was held wide enough to encompass petition to the IACHR. See further p. 461 (change of policy).

[394] Although the dictum from *Teoh*, see below, p. 455, n. 406, founding a legitimate expectation on the terms of a treaty was approved *obiter* in *R* v. *Home Secretary ex p Ahmed* [1999] COD 69 (Lord Woolf MR), the principle has not since been adopted: *R* v. *DPP ex p Kebilene* [1999] 3 WLR 175 (DC) (ratification of the European Convention does not found legitimate expectation that it would be followed): 'It was generally assumed at the time [in 1950] that ratification would have no practical effect on British law or practice, as proved for many years to be the case. It cannot plausibly be said that [this] gives rise to any legitimate expectation today'; and *R* v. *Home Secretary ex p Behluli* [1998] COD 328 (no legitimate expectation that asylum applications would be dealt with in accordance with the Dublin Convention (see above, p. 62); statements relied upon lacked 'the requisite degree of clarity and certainty'). Cf. *R* v. *Uxbridge Magistrates' Court ex p Adimi* [2001] QB 667 (asylum seekers had a legitimate expectation that they would not be prosecuted for using false documents contrary to Art. 31 of the UN Convention Relating to the Status of Refugees, Cmd 9171 (1951)). *Teoh* was also approved, *en passant*, in *Higgs* v. *Minister of National Security* [2000] 2 AC 228 (PC), 241. And note Laws LJ's principled doubts in *European Roma Rights Centre* v. *Immigration Officer At Prague Airport* [2003] EWCA Civ 666, para. 100.

[395] *R* v. *Inland Revenue Commissioners ex p MFK Underwriting Agencies Ltd* [1990] 1 WLR 1545; *same ex p Matrix-Securities Ltd* [1994] 1 WLR 334.

[396] *R (Wheeler)* v. *Office of the Prime Minister* [2008] EWHC 1409, para. 49 (alleged expectation that Referendum Bill would be introduced into Parliament).

[397] See Moules, as above, ch. 2, paras. 1.70–1.87 and (2004) *CLJ* 261 (Elliott). Note that it is not the representation itself which is ultra vires but the conduct promised which is.

[398] See *Bloggs 61*, above and *R* v. *Secretary of State for Education ex p Begbie* [2000] 1 WLR 1115 (CA).

[399] For instance, *Bibi* (Schiemann LJ) and *Al Fayed* v. *Advocate General for Scotland*, 2003 SLT 747 (OH). Similarly, Gibson LJ in *Rowland* v. *The Environment Agency* [2003] EWCA Civ 1885, paras. 67–9 (ultra vires statements led adjacent landowner to believe that certain public water was private). And see *Van Schalkwyk* v. *The Chief Financial Officer*, Case No. 1570/2007, 5 July 2007 (High Court of South Africa) (overpaid civil servants unable to use ultra vires representation to resist claim for repayment).

decision-maker before any question of protection arises. There are good reasons why this should be so: an official cannot be allowed in effect to rewrite Acts of Parliament by making promises of unlawful conduct or adopting an unlawful practice.[400]

But are innocent representees who reasonably placed their trust in ultra vires promises left remediless? The Human Rights Court has held that an ultra vires legitimate expectation—in the context of the lease of real property—was protected as a possession under Article 1 Protocol 1 of the Human Rights Convention; and the victim was entitled to 'just satisfaction', i.e. damages.[401] This result is consistent with the proposal made earlier in this book that innocent representees, even in non-human rights cases, should be compensated.[402] This is not upholding an ultra vires representation but simply recognising that the undoubted fact of the representation may be an element in establishing that the compensation should be paid.[403] The making of an ultra vires representation should also be recognised as maladministration entitling the representeee to petition the Ombudsman.[404]

It has been suggested that as an alternative the judges should weigh 'legal certainty' (the expectation) against 'legality' (the ultra vires doctrine) and give judgment according to where that balance falls.[405] This latter, and bold alternative, need not be adopted in the light of the availability of compensation where justice requires. The protection of the trust placed in an expectation is important; but it is not as important as upholding the rule of law.

KNOWLEDGE

Whether an expectation exists is, self-evidently, a question of fact. If a person did not expect anything, then there is nothing that the doctrine can protect. So a person unaware of an undertaking made by a public authority cannot expect compliance with that undertaking.[406] After all where no trust has been reposed in the promise or undertaking of the official there is no reason why any subsequently discovered expectation should be protected.

But in a leading decision the Court of Appeal (discussed elsewhere)[407] has held that it would be 'grossly unfair if the court's ability to intervene depended at all upon

---

[400] R v. Ministry of Agriculture, Fisheries and Food ex p Hamble (Offshore) Fisheries Ltd [1995] 2 All ER 714, 731.

[401] Stretch v. UK (2004) 38 EHRR 12 (an option to extend lease was beyond the powers of the landlord (a local authority)). And see Pine Valley v. Ireland (1991) 14 EHRR 319 (land purchased in reliance upon planning permission afterwards quashed). See Moules, as above, para. 1.79ff. for a full account of the ECtHR cases.   [402] Above, p. 284. For discussion of 'just satisfaction', see p. 635.

[403] See Moules, para. 1.85 linking this issue to the question of how void acts may sometimes have legal effect (above, p. 269).   [404] Above, p. 68.

[405] This latter alternative, originally put forward by Professor Craig (Administrative Law, 7th edn, 2012, paras. 22-039 et seq.) draws support from the judgment of May LJ in Rowland, paras. 114–120 who recognises that its adoption would amount to legislation. Discussed [2005] PL 729 (Hannett and Busch).

[406] R v. Secretary of State for National Heritage ex p J Paul Getty Trust [1997] Eu LR 407 (statement of which Trust was unaware could not found legitimate expectation) and Chundawara v. Immigration Appeal Tribunal [1988] Imm. AR 161 (unincorporated but ratified treaty of which claimant unaware could not found legitimate expectation). Cf. majority judgment in Minister of Ethnic Affairs v. Teoh (1995) 128 ALR 353 ('It is not necessary that a person seeking to set up such a legitimate expectation should be aware of the Convention [upon which the expectation was founded] or should personally entertain the expectation', at 365; contra however McHugh J at 383). See (1996) 112 LQR 50 (M. Taggart). But note the case of Lam, below.

[407] R (Rashid) v. Home Secretary [2005] EWCA Civ 744. Discussed [2005] JR 281 (Elliott). Discussed above, p. 318.

whether the particular claimant had or had not heard of a policy'.[408] Here the Home Office had refused an Iraqi Kurd's application for asylum on the ground that he might safely relocate to the Kurdish Autonomous Zone. In so deciding the policy of not relying on internal relocation in such cases (of which the Kurd was quite unaware) was inadvertently overlooked.

A decision by an official not to honour an undertaking (or apply a policy) may, even where those affected were unaware of the undertaking (or the policy), be flawed for many reasons. It may, for instance, amount to unfair discrimination where the undertaking has been honoured in many other cases. Or it may be that the decision is flawed through a failure to apply a policy consistently. And this last indeed is the ground on which the case just mentioned should have been decided.

Indeed where there is no knowledge of the policy allegedly disregarded, inconsistency in the application of policy rather than frustration of a legitimate expectation is the appropriate ground of review. This view has been gathering strength. The Supreme Court has said that '[t]he principle that policy must be consistently applied is not in doubt'.[409] Consequently, the Supreme Court found that the Home Secretary had 'unlawfully exercised the statutory power to detain [the appellants] pending deportation because she applied an unpublished policy which was inconsistent with her published policy'.[410]

But to bring such 'no expectation' cases under the rubric 'legitimate expectation' is to deprive that concept of clear meaning. The phrase 'protection of legitimate expectations' is not an imprecise alternative for securing fairness or avoiding abuse of power. Legitimate expectations bear, it is submitted, on the narrow issue of whether trust has been reposed in the official. Thus if no trust has been reposed, the concept has nothing to add to an inquiry into what fairness requires in the circumstances or whether the power concerned has been abused. This heresy first saw the light of day in the High Court of Australia which has effectively abandoned it.[411]

RELIANCE

Although a person who seeks to rely upon an expectation must be aware of it, the better view is that he need not have relied to his detriment upon it for that would be to assimilate

---

[408] Ibid., para. 25. But now see Appendix 3.

[409] Para. 26 (Lord Dyson) and similarly *SK (Zimbabwe)* v. *Secretary of State for the Home Department* [2011] UKSC 23, para. 36 (Lord Hope to similar effect). And see now *Secretary of State for the Home Department* v. *Rahman* [2011] EWCA Civ 814, para. 42 Stanley Burton LJ. See the same judge's view in *Occam's Razor, Administrative Law and Human Rights* available at <http://www.adminlaw.org.uk/library/publications.php>.

[410] Para. 169 per Lord Dyson who makes no mention of legitimate expectations in his judgment. Cf Lord Phillip's dissent which makes extensive mention of legitimate expectations that policy be applied but it is plain, it is submitted, that legitimate expectations add nothing to the analysis.

[411] The High Court of Australia in *Re Minister for Immigration and Multicultural Affairs ex p Lam* (2003) 214 CLR 1 has greatly restricted *Teoh* even if it is formally not yet overruled. Callinan J said: 'if a doctrine of "legitimate expectation" is to remain part of Australian law, it would be better if it were applied only in cases in which there is an actual expectation, or that at the very least a reasonable inference is available that had a party turned his or her mind consciously to the matter in circumstances only in which that person was likely to have done so, he or she would reasonably have believed and expected that certain procedures would be followed' (para. 143). See Appendix 3.

legitimate expectations to estoppel.[412] But a taxpayer, it seems, must rely upon a representation from the Revenue before his expectation will be protected.[413] Reliance, however, provides strong evidence of the existence of the expectation.[414] And an applicant who has relied to his detriment upon a statement by an official will find the courts readier to protect his expectation.

Disclosure and reliance are, however, inappropriate requirements in many cases. While a taxpayer cannot expect the Revenue to be bound by a personal assurance given when the full nature of the taxpayer's scheme has not been disclosed, nothing more than proof that the claimant falls within the terms of the published policy should be required when the legitimate expectation is founded upon the announcement of such a policy. And the only reliance that a prisoner will be able to place in a promise of home leave or consideration for parole will be to use it to kindle hope.

CLASSES OR CATEGORIES OF EXPECTATION

Expectations may broadly be divided into two groups.[415] An expectation may, first of all, be a procedural expectation where a particular procedure not otherwise required has been promised. Thus in the case discussed earlier where the government of Hong Kong announced that certain illegal immigrants would be interviewed before deportation a procedural expectation was established.[416] Second, what is expected may be a particular or favourable decision by the authority. Thus where the Home Secretary had specified the criteria applicable to a decision to allow a child to enter the UK with a view to adoption there was a substantive expectation that those criteria (which were satisfied by the applicant) and not others would be used when the decision was taken.[417]

---

[412] R v. Ministry of Agriculture, Fisheries and Food ex p Hamble Fisheries (Offshore) Ltd [1995] 2 All ER 714 (reliance not required; 'legitimate expectation is [not] another name for estoppel' (Sedley J)); R v. Home Secretary ex p Jaramillo-Silva [1995] 7 Admin LR 445 (CA) ('reliance and detriment as such are not necessarily required in every legitimate expectation case' (Simon Brown LJ)). For criticism see [1998] J R 196 (Bamforth). For the relationship between legitimate expectations and estoppel, see above, p. 283.

[413] R v. Inland Revenue Commissioners ex p Matrix-Securities Ltd [1994] 1 WLR 334 ('advance' clearance undertaking to tax a Docklands property development in a certain way given by revenue but withdrawn before funds invested: no protection of expectation). Confirmed in Oxfam v. Revenue and Customs [2009] EWHC 3078 (Ch). Sales J said that in cases like this one (change of policy after assurance to individual taxpayer) 'the absence of detrimental reliance on the part of the person to whom the assurance is given is fatal to the argument that to modify the assurance would involve an abuse of power' (para. 50 (remark not limited to revenue cases)).

[414] See ex p Begbie, below, where the absence of reliance was said by Gibson LJ to be 'very much the exception, rather than the rule'. And to like effect: R (Bibi) v. Newham LBC [2002] 1 WLR 237 (CA) (reliance not required as matter of law, but reliance was a relevant consideration in deciding whether it was unfair for the authority to resile from their promise).

[415] In R v. Devon County Council ex p Baker (below) at 88 Simon Brown LJ identified 4 categories of legitimate expectation. One category consisted of a legitimate expectation of fairness discussed and rejected above. The other 3 categories are substantive expectations substantively protected (category (1), substantive right), substantive expectations procedurally protected (category (2), interest or benefit that triggers duties of fairness and reasonableness) and procedural expectations procedurally protected (category (3), special procedural entitlement)—discussed now. Category 1 expectations—substantive expectations, substantively protected—are discussed, above, p. 320.   [416] A-G of Hong Kong v. Ng Yeun Shui, above, p. 452.

[417] R v. Home Secretary ex p Asif Mahmood Khan [1984] 1 WLR 1337.

THE PROTECTION OF LEGITIMATE EXPECTATIONS ENHANCES BUT DOES NOT REPLACE THE DUTY TO ACT FAIRLY

Even where no promise of a benefit has been made and there is no established practice of granting that benefit, the person concerned is, elementarily, entitled to be treated fairly.[418] But he is not entitled to rely upon his expectation of a benefit unless it is founded upon some promise or established practice. To do this is to confuse the protection of legitimate expectations with the duty to act fairly. As Simon Brown LJ has said, it is 'superfluous and unhelpful' to contend that a claimant has 'a legitimate expectation that the public body will act fairly towards him'.[419] The doctrine of legitimate expectation thus extends the procedural protection that would otherwise be applicable; it enhances but does not replace the duty to act fairly.

THE PROCEDURAL PROTECTION OF PROCEDURAL EXPECTATIONS

Procedural expectations are protected simply by requiring that the promised procedure be followed. If the decision-maker has promised to follow a particular procedure it will be held to that save in very exceptional circumstances—for instance, where national security justifies a departure from the expected procedure.[420] A leading case may serve as an example. The Secretary of State for Education, after a change of government, decided to cease funding certain school building programmes favoured by his predecessor. This decision was taken without consulting the local (education) authorities who had been fully and continuously engaged with earlier consultations over the programme with the department.

THE PROCEDURAL PROTECTION OF SUBSTANTIVE EXPECTATIONS

Substantive expectations are often protected procedurally, i.e. by extending to the person affected an opportunity to make representations before the expectation is dashed. Thus where recommended applicants for hospital posts were rejected in breach of a long-established practice because they had complained about bad conditions, they were

---

[418] Thus stall-holders in a market are entitled to be consulted before charges are increased: *R v. Birmingham City Council ex p Dredger* [1993] COD 340. But residents in an old people's home to whom no promise of consultation has been made need not be consulted before the local authority closes the home: *ex p Baker* (below).

[419] *R v. Devon County Council ex p Baker* [1995] 1 All ER 73 at 89 adopting the approach of *A-G for New South Wales v. Quin* (1990) 93 ALR 1 at 39. Cf. *R v. Secretary of State for Wales ex p Emery* [1996] 1 All ER 1 (no need for knowledge of practice or promise). Some South African cases hold that, if it is fair and reasonable to expect a hearing, a hearing is legitimately expected: *Minister of Justice, Transkei v. Gemi* 1994 (3) SA 28; cf. *Ngema v. Minister of Justice, Kwazulu* 1992 (4) SA 349. For criticism see Kahn (ed.), *The Quest for Justice: Essays in Honour of M M Corbett* (1995), pp. 204–6 (Forsyth). And see *R v. Home Secretary ex p Hindley* [2000] 2 WLR 730 at 737 (mandatory life prisoner had no expectation that Home Secretary would not impose a 'whole-life' tariff, since she was unaware of the provisional decision to that effect).

[420] As in the *CCSU* case, above, p. 452.

held entitled to a hearing before rejection.[421] The person affected is not entitled to a favourable decision but the trust which he has reposed in the decision-maker's undertaking should be protected.

The requirement of a fair procedure in such circumstances should not surprise. The decision-maker must clearly make a proper decision before dashing the expectation. And, elementarily, that requires procedural fairness. An appropriately tailored requirement of interview, consultation, or notice then follows.

THE FURTHER PROTECTION OF SUBSTANTIVE EXPECTATIONS: THE EXPECTATION AS A MANDATORY RELEVANT CONSIDERATION

The decision-maker deciding to dash a substantive expectation must, again on elementary principles, take into account all relevant considerations. One clear relevant consideration will be the existence of the substantive legitimate expectation.[422] Where a housing authority, supposing wrongly (as the House of Lords later held) that they had a legal duty, promised permanent accommodation to families of refugees it was held that this created legitimate expectations, but that for the court to enforce them would conflict with the authority's allocation policy and that it was for the authority to consider the case on the basis that the expectations were legitimate.[423] The Court of Appeal held that 'the Authority is under a duty to consider the applicants' applications for suitable housing on the basis that they have a legitimate expectation that they will be provided by the Authority with suitable accommodation'.[424] The court did not order the expectation to be fulfilled but it had to be properly taken into account.

THE FURTHER PROTECTION OF SUBSTANTIVE EXPECTATIONS: IRRATIONALITY

By similar reasoning the conclusion may be reached that a decision to dash a substantive expectation may be quashed where it is irrational. Two Court of Appeal decisions may serve as contrasting examples.[425] A change in prisoners' home leave policy meant that certain prisoners' first home leave took place significantly later than they were led to expect when they entered the prison; but the court held that this change was not irrational and their expectations were not protected.[426] But a decision by the Revenue to abandon a twenty-year-old practice of allowing a taxpayer, because of the complexity of its affairs, to make late claims for loss relief was irrational; and the expectation of the practice continuing was protected.[427]

---

[421] *Administrator, Transvaal* v. *Traub* 1989 (4) SA 731. For English authority recognising this category, see *Schmidt* v. *Home Secretary* [1969] 2 Ch 149 (the first legitimate expectation case in English law), *R* v. *Secretary of State for Transport ex p Richmond upon Thames LBC* [1994] 1 WLR 74 at 92G and *ex p Baker* at 88.

[422] See Moules, as above, para. 1.106.

[423] *R (Bibi)* v. *Newham LBC* [2002] 1 WLR 237 (CA). And see *R (ABCIFER)* v. *Secretary of State for Defence* [2003] EWCA Civ 473, [2003] QB 1397, paras. 74–5.   [424] Ibid., para. 62 (Schiemann LJ).

[425] *R* v. *Home Secretary ex p Hargreaves* [1997] 1 WLR 906 and *R* v. *Inland Revenue Commissioners ex p Unilever plc* [1996] STC 681 (decision also based upon fairness). For comment see [1997] *PL* 375 (Forsyth) and (1997) 56 *CLJ* 1 (Bamforth). And see above, p. 318.   [426] *ex p Hargreaves* (above).

[427] *ex p Unilever plc* (above).

THE SUBSTANTIVE PROTECTION OF LEGITIMATE EXPECTATIONS

The courts have gone further still in the protection of substantive expectations. They have required the fulfilment of the expectation unless an overriding public interest ordains otherwise. In the leading case a health authority which, for practical and financial reasons, wished to close a specially built home for very seriously injured long-term patients, in breach of its promise to the residents that it was their 'home for life', was prevented from doing so.[428] The Court of Appeal, in rejecting rationality as the appropriate standard of review, held that it was for the court to judge 'whether there [was] a sufficient overriding interest to justify a departure from what has previously been promised'.[429] This approach is consistent with European law which balances the protection of the general public interest against the individual's legitimate expectation.[430]

Substantive protection clearly involves the court in aspects of the decision-making process (e.g. the allocation of resources) generally considered beyond the bounds of judicial competence and authority. Substantive protection will impinge upon the decision-maker's freedom of action; it will fetter his discretion. An influential dictum holds that, for these reasons, 'the doctrine of [substantive protection of] legitimate expectation[s] should be narrowly construed'.[431] Thus it is clear that only exceptionally will such protection be afforded.[432] Substantive protection will generally require that the promise is made only to a small group (such as the residents of a care home). A general announcement of policy made to a large group (such as prisoners) is unlikely to be protected substantively.[433] Moreover, said the Court of Appeal in the care home case, 'the promise or representation

---

[428] R v. North and East Devon Health Authority ex p Coughlan [2000] 2 WLR 622. For criticism see [2000] JR 27 (Elliott).   [429] Lord Woolf, Sedley and Mummery LJJ concurring.

[430] See Mulder v. Minister of Landbouw and Visserij [1998] ECR 2321 and Mulder v. Council and Commission Cases, C-104/89 and C-37/90 [1992] ECR I-3061 discussed fully (1996) 55 CLJ 289 (Craig). A similar approach was adopted by Sedley J in R v. Ministry of Agriculture, Fisheries and Food ex p Hamble Fisheries (Offshore) Ltd [1995] 2 All ER 714 but this was rejected as a 'heresy' in ex p Hargreaves as explained above, p. 320.

[431] Re Loreto Grammar School's Application for Judicial Review [2012] NICA 1, [2013] NI 41, para. 46 (Girvan LJ).

[432] Apart from Coughlan, successful substantive protection has been very limited. See R v. Department of Education and Employment ex p Begbie [2000] 1 WLR 1115 (no protection); R (Bibi) v. Newham LBC [2001] EWCA Civ 607 (expectation considered mandatory relevant consideration); Henry Boot Homes Ltd v. Bassetlaw District Council [2002] EWCA Civ 983 (no protection: legitimate expectation 'very exceptional' in planning law). R (Bloggs 61) v. Home Secretary [2003] EWCA Civ 686 (no protection); R (Association of British Civilian Internees: Far East Region) v. Secretary of State for Defence [2003] EWCA Civ 473 (no 'clear and unequivocal' undertaking); Rowland v. Environment Agency [2003] EWCA Civ 1885 (no protection)); R (Rashid) v. Home Secretary [2005] EWCA Civ 744 (not true legitimate expectation case (above, p. 318)); R (Abdi and Nadarajah) v. Home Secretary [2005] EWCA Civ 1363 (no protection); R (Bancoult) v. Secretary of State for Foreign and Commonwealth Affairs (No 2) [2007] EWCA Civ 498 (appeal to House of Lords upheld); R (S) v. Home Secretary [2007] EWCA Civ 546 (case not decided on legitimate expectation); R (BAPIO Action Ltd) v. Home Secretary [2007] EWCA Civ 1139 (legitimate expectation upheld in the House of Lords (above, p. 453)); R (Niazi) v. Home Secretary [2008] EWCA Civ 755 (no protection); R (Elayathamby) v. Home Secretary [2011] EWHC 2182 (no protection) and R (Luton Borough Council & Nottingham City Council and ors) v. Secretary of State for Education [2011] EWHC 217 (no substantive protection); R (Godfrey) v. Southwark LBC [2012] EWCA Civ 500 (no protection); Naik v. Secretary of State for the Home Department [2011] EWCA Civ 1546 (no protection); R (W) v. Secretary of State for Education [2011] EWHC 3256 (substantive legitimate expectation (that no further action would be taken) but overriding public interest (child protection) shown).

[433] The size of the group affected also played a role in Ng Siu Tung v. Director of Immigration [2002] 1 HKLRD 561 discussed (2002) 10 Asia Pacific Law Review 29 (Forsyth and Williams).

[would normally have] the character of a contract'.[434] In a later case the Court of Appeal said that the assurance relied upon to found a substantive legitimate expectation had to be 'pressing and focussed' in nature.[435]

However, even after a sufficiently pressing and focused assurance, the public authority may avoid substantive protection if it is able to show an overriding public interest justifying the dashing of the expectation.[436] Lord Justice Laws has emerged as the champion of the view that the substantive legitimate expectation, once established, should be treated as akin to a fundamental right, and so requiring any departure from it to be justified by 'the requirement of proportionality'.[437]

While successful substantial protection is rare, there are some successes to be noted. A pharmacist wishing to retrain as a medical practitioner received an individual, clear and unequivocal assurance from the General Medical Council that a particular course (at an overseas university) would be recognised as a primary medical qualification (PMQ). But the GMC refused to recognise that qualification after the pharmacist had expended large sums and effort on obtaining it. A substantive expectation was found and the GMC compelled to recognise the PMQ.[438] A member of a taxi association received clear and unequivocal assurances directed to the association from the government that if they agreed to a move of a taxi stand the association would be able to manage and control their own affairs there. In fact, the new stand was under the control of a competitor who charged the taxis a fee. No overriding public interest justifying the frustration of the legitimate expectation was found.[439]

CHANGE OF POLICY AND LEGITIMATE EXPECTATIONS

As we have seen (for instance, when the policy on prisoners' home leave was changed) a public authority's change of policy may be challenged as a denial of a substantive legitimate expectation. Generally speaking, though, all that can be legitimately expected is that the policy as it exists at the time will be applied to the case at hand. As the Court

---

[434] *R v. North and East Devon Health Authority ex p Coughlan* [2001] QB 213, para. 59. Indeed, through the prism of private law *Coughlan* is explicable as an example of the Health Authority being held to a bad bargain as it would be held to any unfavourable contract. Seen in this way the case raises no difficulties of principle involving the allocation of resources or intruding into the merits. But now there is a fresh difficulty: where a public authority contracts in a way that fetters its discretion it must show that it has the statutory power to do so or else the contract is ultra vires and void (above, p. 278). There has been little consideration of this in the decided cases. First pointed out by Pascoe (unpublished Part II dissertation, Cambridge, 2011).

[435] *Niazi*, above, para. 41 (Laws LJ).

[436] While 'initial burden lies on an applicant to prove the legitimacy of his expectation' the 'onus shifts to the authority to justify the frustration of the legitimate expectation. It is for the authority to identify any overriding interest on which it relies to justify the frustration of the expectation' (*Paponette*, above, para. 37).

[437] *Niazi*, above, para. 62 (Laws LJ). And see *Abdi v. Secretary of State for the Home Department* [2005] EWCA Civ 1363, paras. 68 and 69. And the test will be 'whether denial of [the] expectation is in the circumstances proportionate to a legitimate aim pursued. Proportionality will be judged, as it generally is to be judged, by the respective force of the competing interests arising in the case' (Laws LJ). For discussion of the doctrine of proportionality in fundamental rights cases, see above, p. 306. For a case in which the test was applied, see *R (X) v. Headteachers and Governors of Y School* [2007] EWHC 298 (school uniform policy precluding wearing the niqab, proportionate in the circumstances).

[438] *R (Patel) v. General Medical Council* [2013] EWCA Civ 327.

[439] *Paponette and ors v. A-G of Trinidad and Tobago* [2010] UKPC 32. But note Lord Brown's dissent and the fact that the decision was also justified as a failure to treat the legitimate expectation as a mandatory relevant consideration.

of Appeal has remarked that the 'doctrine of substantive legitimate expectation plainly cannot apply to every case where a public authority operates a policy over an appreciable period. That would expand the doctrine far beyond its proper limits. The establishment of any policy, new or substitute, by a public body is in principle subject to *Wednesbury* review. But a claim that a substitute policy has been established in breach of a substantive legitimate expectation engages a much more rigorous standard'.[440] Thus the court laid down a specific undertaking given to a particular individual or group of individuals would be required for substantive protection. Where there was no undertaking but the impact of the authority's past conduct on those affected was 'pressing and focused', procedural protection (i.e. consultation and notice) would be required.[441]

FAIR HEARINGS—PARTICULAR SITUATIONS

WIDE DISCRETIONARY POWER

It is of the essence of natural justice that it should be observed generally in the exercise of discretionary power. The mere fact that the discretion conferred is wide is no reason for weakening this principle. Although it has been said that there has in the past been some correlation between wide discretionary power and absence of a duty to observe natural justice,[442] this scarcely seems to be supported except by decisions which are explicable on other grounds. At any rate, now that the frontiers of natural justice have been advanced considerably (and, as a Lord Chancellor has added, rightly),[443] there seems to be no detectable correlation of this character. All discretionary powers have limits of some kind, and whether those limits are widely or narrowly drawn, the discretion ought to be exercised fairly, just as it must also be exercised reasonably.[444]

This is corroborated, in particular, by cases in which the power has been conferred in wide subjective language but the rules of natural justice have been held applicable. One example is the case of the bishop who was empowered to act against a vicar 'when satisfied either of his own knowledge or by affidavit' of the vicar's default.[445] Another is the case of the colonial governor empowered to act 'on sufficient ground shown to his satisfaction'.[446] Even the favourite statutory formulae which represent the ultimate in wide discretion, 'Where the Minister is satisfied'[447] and 'If it appears to the Minister',[448] which purport to make the extent of his powers depend upon his own state of mind, do not exclude the right to a fair hearing. Nor does a local authority's power to divide a payment between landlord and tenant 'in such shares as the authority think equitable in the circumstances'[449]

---

[440] *Niazi*, above, paras. 34–5.

[441] *Niazi*, above, para. 49. Curiously Laws LJ refers to such procedural protection of substantive expectations as a 'secondary case of procedural expectation'.

[442] De Smith, *Judicial Review of Administrative Action*, 4th edn, 186 (but now see 5th edn, 415). One of the few true examples seems to be *Re Barnett* [1967] 2 NSWR 746, but the reasoning invites criticism. Another may be the case of offices held at pleasure: see below, p. 468. Note also the *Essex County Council* case, below, p. 473.   [443] *Pearlberg* v. *Varty* [1972] 1 WLR 534 at 540 (Lord Hailsham LC).

[444] Above, p. 293.

[445] *Capel* v. *Child*, above, pp. 406–7. But contrast *Abergavenny (Marquis)* v. *Bishop of Llandaff* (1888) 20 QBD 460.   [446] *De Verteuil* v. *Knaggs*, above, p. 410.

[447] *Maradana Mosque Trustees* v. *Mahmud* [1967] 1 AC 13.

[448] *Durayappah* v. *Fernando* [1967] 2 AC 337.

[449] *Hoggard* v. *Worsborough Urban District Council* [1962] 2 QB 93. Compare *Re Webb and Ontario Housing Corporation* (1978) 93 DLR (3d) 187 (housing authority required to act fairly in terminating lease)

exclude the right. Nor does the Home Secretary's wide discretion in granting or refusing naturalisation to an alien.[450]

CASES DETERMINED BY POLICY

Closely akin to the question of wide discretionary power is the question of policy. Policy is of course the basis of administrative discretion in a great many cases, but this is no reason why the discretion should not be exercised fairly vis-à-vis any person who will be adversely affected. The decision will require the weighing of any such person's interests against the claims of policy; and this cannot fairly be done without giving that person an opportunity to be heard. The cases of slum-clearance and similar orders, already discussed,[451] are a clear illustration of decisions based upon policy which are nevertheless subject to the principles of natural justice.

The plainest possible case of 'pure policy' occurred where a minister refused to meet a delegation of London borough council representatives protesting against his decision to reduce their rate support grant on account of their excessive spending. His policy had been fully discussed with them and debated in Parliament before the passing of the Act empowering the cuts. But fairness demanded that their objections should be heard at some point between the granting of the power and its exercise, particularly since the borough councils would otherwise have a statutory right to the normal rate support grant. For this failure to observe natural justice, as well as for the unlawful fettering of his discretion, the minister's decision was quashed.[452]

LICENSING AND COMMERCIAL REGULATION

As the preceding section has illustrated, licensing cases often contain a large element of policy, since the licensing authority will commonly be free to grant or withhold licences as it thinks best in the public interest. Very extensive licensing powers are possessed by the central government, local authorities, the police, magistrates, tribunals and other authorities, and in many cases they give what might be called powers of commercial life or death over a person's trade or livelihood.[453] Local authorities license such things as cinemas, nursing homes, road vehicles, animal boarding establishments, knackers' yards, fireworks factories, pawnbrokers and slaughterhouses. Police licensing powers cover, *inter alia*, firearms, pedlars, taxicabs and taxi-drivers. Many of these arrangements might be thought to cry out for administrative rationalisation and procedural regularity, but before *Ridge* v. *Baldwin* only the licensing of public-houses and places of entertainment, which has been in the hands of magistrates since the sixteenth century, had made much contribution to the case law. Although it was firmly established that this form of licensing was a judicial function, and therefore subject to natural justice,[454] this was so far from

---

but contrast *Sevenoaks DC* v. *Emmett* (1979) 78 LGR 346 (council not required to give hearing or reasons when ejecting tenant).

[450] *R* v. *Home Secretary ex p Fayed* [1997] 1 All ER 228.   [451] Above, p. 412.

[452] *R* v. *Secretary of State for the Environment ex p Brent LBC* [1982] QB 593. And see similarly *R* v. *Secretary of State for Transport ex p Greater London Council* [1986] QB 556.

[453] For licensing powers see Street, *Justice in the Welfare State*, 70; Hart, *Local Government*, 9th edn, 756; Glanville Williams (1967) 20 *Current Legal Problems* 81.

[454] *Frome United Breweries Co* v. *Bath Justices* [1926] AC 586 is a leading example. See further below, p. 515.

being recognised as a general principle that the Privy Council was able to hold in 1950 that a trader's licence could be cancelled without fair procedure of any kind.[455]

Ridge v. Baldwin transformed the situation;[456] and in particular the courts have shown a strong disposition to bring licensing functions generally within their doctrine that administrative powers must be exercised fairly. Nor is the duty excluded because the licence is in the form of a contract with a local authority, since all authorities' powers are statutory.[457] Nor is the principle confined to cases of cancellation or suspension on grounds of misconduct, where the claims of natural justice are obviously strongest. It is recognised that licensing is a drastic power, greatly affecting the rights and liberties of citizens, and in particular their livelihoods, and that this alone demands fair administrative procedure. Thus where a street trader, allowed to sell food under an informal arrangement with the local authority, was summarily given notice to quit, the decision was quashed because she had not first been given a hearing, even though she was a mere temporary licensee; and the court stressed the duty of fairness where livelihood is at stake.[458]

It seems, furthermore, that no distinction is drawn in principle between initial applications for the grant of licences and the revocation or non-renewal of licences already granted.[459] Subject to what was said about decisions of policy,[460] a first-time applicant for a licence should normally be allowed to state his case before being refused, and in particular where the refusal is on personal grounds. It was said in a case of 1916:[461]

> Persons who are called upon to exercise the functions of granting licences for carriages and omnibuses are, to a great extent, exercising judicial functions; and though they are not bound by the strict rules of evidence and procedure observed in a court of law, they are bound to act judicially. It is their duty to hear and determine according to law, and they must bring to that task a fair and unbiased mind.

In approving this passage Lord Denning MR said that according to the modern judicial vocabulary such persons act administratively but are required to act fairly.[462]

Where a licence is due for renewal the case is still stronger, and may be reinforced by 'legitimate expectation', as in the case of the taxi-driver mentioned earlier.[463]

---

[455] Above, p. 414.

[456] See Banks v. Transport Regulation Board (Vic) (1968) 119 CLR 222 at 233 (Barwick CJ); Murdoch v. New Zealand Milk Board [1982] 2 NZLR 108; (1967) 2 NZULR 282 (J. A. Farmer). As to taxi-drivers see Moran v. A-G [1976] IR 400 (no hearing: cancellation invalid); R v. Assistant Metropolitan Police Commissioner ex p Howell (below).

[457] Jones v. Swansea CC [1990] 1 WLR 54 70, at 85. In ex p Binks (below) the court preferred to base its decision on the 'public law' character of market licensing. For criticism see (1990) 106 LQR 277 at 281 (S. Arrowsmith).

[458] R v. Wear Valley DC ex p Binks [1985] 2 All ER 699. In R v. Basildon DC ex p Brown (1981) 79 LGR 655, there discussed, a similar licence was validly terminated by 3 months' notice, written representations having first been received. Compare R v. Barnsley MC ex p Hook [1976] 1 WLR 1052, above, p. 401.

[459] In McInnes v. Onslow-Fane [1978] 1 WLR 1520 at 1529 Megarry V-C says that there is a substantial distinction between 'application cases' and 'forfeiture cases' and that this is well recognised in the case of membership of a social club. But that is a case based upon contract (above, p. 407) where a member has the protection of his contract of membership and an applicant has not. It does not follow that any such distinction applies to the exercise of statutory powers. Nor is it correct that in application cases 'in all normal circumstances there are no charges and so no requirement of an opportunity to be heard in answer to the charges'. Applicants are often prejudiced by unfavourable information possessed by the licensing authority, as in the Gaming Board case, below. Cf. A-G v. Ryan [1980] AC 718 (above, p. 417).

[460] Above, p. 463.

[461] R v. Brighton Cpn ex p Thomas Tilling Ltd (1916) 85 LJKB 1552 (Sankey J).

[462] In R v. Liverpool Cpn ex p Liverpool Taxi Fleet Operators' Association [1972] 2 QB 299.

[463] R v. Assistant Metropolitan Police Commissioner ex p Howell [1986] RTR 52. See also R v. Huntingdon DC ex p Cowan (above), and Lord Diplock's statement in Council of Civil Service Unions v. Minister for

On the basis of these authorities the duty to observe natural justice is now extremely wide. But it is probably safe to say that there must be many thousands of adverse licensing decisions annually in which no hearing is in fact given. These will mostly occur at the two extremes of the scale of importance: both in much petty administrative licensing by local authorities and the police; and also in the case of certain wide powers of commercial and industrial regulation under which many decisions are made from day to day and which have no statutory procedural safeguards.

OFFICES AND EMPLOYMENTS

A line has to be drawn between an office which gives its holder a status which the law will protect specifically, on the one hand, and, on the other hand, a mere employment under a contract of service. Offices used in old times to be looked upon as a form of property which could be held and recovered in specie: if the holder was wrongfully removed he could obtain restoration by mandamus; or he might be granted prohibition or an injunction. Nowadays he can also obtain a declaration that his removal was void, and that he is therefore still in office, as was done in *Ridge* v. *Baldwin*, since this remedy likewise operates specifically. In other words, he is removable only by a due and lawful exercise of the power of removal, failing which he remains legally in office. A servant under a mere contract of service enjoys no such protection, according to a long-established rule of law: whatever his contractual rights, he can always be dismissed and his remedy lies in damages for breach of contract.[464] In other words, there is always a power to dismiss him, even though under the contract there is no right to do so. The principle is that one man will not be compelled to employ another against his will. By contrast, the law will give specific protection to a status such as membership or office in a trade union, association or club, even though it is merely contractual; this is a less personal relationship, and an injunction or declaration may be granted so as to preserve the status.[465] A statutory status, such as that of a registered dock worker, will be protected similarly,[466] subject always to the discretion of the court in awarding remedies.[467]

The distinction is of importance for the purposes of the right to be heard. If an office-holder is removed without a hearing in a case where he has a right to one, he can recover his office specifically. But if in a similar situation a mere servant is dismissed, his dismissal remains legally effective and there is no remedy by which he can compel his employer to continue to employ him. The law then holds that the right to a fair hearing has no application in a mere relationship of master and servant. This is not because justice does not so require (for in many cases it does) but because the law will not restore the employment specifically. For this reason the Privy Council refused certiorari to a university lecturer who had been dismissed without a hearing from his post in Ceylon—though the case itself looked more like one of statutory status since the university's power to dismiss was statutory and was restricted (just as in *Ridge* v. *Baldwin*) to cases of incapacity or misconduct.[468] Lord Wilberforce has said that he could not follow this decision and has commented:[469]

---

the *Civil Service* [1985] AC 374 at 408 (see Appendix 1); *Smitty's Industries Ltd* v. *A-G* [1980] 1 NZLR 355; *FAI Insurances Ltd* v. *Winneke* (1982) 41 ALR 1 (legitimate expectation of renewal of approval to provide worker's compensation insurance).

[464] See below, p. 490. [465] See above, p. 407. [466] See below, p. 452.
[467] See the *North Wales Police* case (above), p. 426.
[468] *Vidyodaya University Council* v. *Silva* [1965] 1 WLR 77, following the *Barber* case (below). Contrast *McCarthy* v. *Calgary RC School District* (1979) 101 DLR 48 (school superintendent: office).
[469] *Malloch* v. *Aberdeen Cpn* [1971] 1 WLR 1578 at 1595, at 1596, citing the *Barber*, *Palmer* and *Vidyodaya* cases and *Glynn* v. *Keele University* [1971] 1 WLR 487.

A comparative list of situations in which persons have been held entitled or not entitled to a hearing, or to observation of the rules of natural justice, according to the master and servant test, looks illogical and even bizarre. A specialist surgeon is denied protection which is given to a hospital doctor; a university professor, as a servant, has been denied the right to be heard, a dock labourer and an undergraduate have been granted it; examples can be multiplied.

Although the law makes such a sharp distinction between office and service in theory, in practice it may be difficult to tell which is which. For tax purposes 'office' has long been defined as a 'subsisting, permanent substantive position which has an existence independent of the person who fills it',[470] but for the purposes of natural justice the test may not be the same.[471] Nor need an office necessarily be statutory,[472] although nearly all public offices of importance in administrative law are statutory. A statutory public authority may have many employees who are in law merely its servants, and others of higher grades who are office-holders.[473] A prison officer holding the office of constable, has the rights of an office-holder,[474] but a nursing officer employed by a local health authority is an ordinary employee.[475] In England it has been held that a consultant surgeon employed in the National Health Service by a regional hospital board is a mere contractual servant, despite the 'strong statutory flavour' attaching to the contract.[476] But where, as happened in Scotland, a surgeon similarly employed was denied a hearing before the hospitals board when they decided to reject a report in the surgeon's favour by their appeals committee, it was held that the appeals procedure, as set out in a departmental circular, was 'an inherent condition of his contract of service' and that the breach of natural justice nullified the dismissal.[477] This case therefore departed from the usual rule that a contract of service will not be specifically enforced; and an exception to that rule has been admitted in England in abnormal circumstances.[478] Even a contractual servant may be able to have his dismissal declared void if there are statutory procedural safeguards which have not been observed, so that in effect the power to dismiss is statutory.[479]

---

[470] Approved by the House of Lords in *Edwards* v. *Clinch* [1982] AC 845, holding (by 3:2) that a surveyor engaged from time to time to hold public inquiries was not the holder of an office.

[471] For tax purposes 'office' has to be distinguished from 'profession', whereas for purposes of natural justice it has to be distinguished from 'employment'.

[472] See e.g. *Fisher* v. *Jackson* [1891] 2 Ch 84 (school established under deed of trust: schoolmaster granted injunction against dismissal without hearing); *Stevenson* v. *United Road Transport Union* [1976] 3 All ER 29 (trade union officer: declaration granted).

[473] *Malloch* v. *Aberdeen Cpn* [1971] 1 WLR 1578 at 1582 (Lord Reid). Lord Wilberforce (at 1596) defined 'pure master and servant cases' more narrowly as involving 'no element of public employment or service, no support by statute, nothing in the nature of an office or a status which is capable of protection.' By this criterion all public employees would appear to count as office-holders, but that may not have been intended. See also *Social Club (102) Ltd* v. *Bickerton* [1977] ICR 911: *R* v. *Brent LBC ex p Assegai*, The Times, 18 June 1987 (school governor: protected office; Lord Wilberforce's criterion applied). In Ireland the protection of natural justice has been given to a fireman (*R (Hennessy)* v. *Department of the Environment* [1980] N. Ireland Bulletin No. 6) and an army private (*State (Gleeson)* v. *Minister for Defence* [1976] IR 280).

[474] *R* v. *Home Secretary ex p Benwell* [1985] QB 554.

[475] *R* v. *East Berkshire Health Authority ex p Walsh* [1985] QB 152. For this and the *Benwell* case see below, p. 575.

[476] *Barber* v. *Manchester Regional Hospital Board* [1958] 1 WLR 181 (declaration refused). See similarly *Francis* v. *Kuala Lumpur Councillors* (above). The *Barber* case was doubted in *Irani* v. *Southampton Health Authority* [1985] ICR 590, but in *R* v. *Trent Regional Health Authority ex p Jones*, The Times, 19 June 1986, a consultant surgeon in the national health service was held to be employed under an ordinary contract of service.

[477] *Palmer* v. *Inverness Hospitals Board* 1963 SC 311, cited with apparent approval in *Malloch's* case, below.   [478] See below, p. 490.

[479] *Malloch* v. *Aberdeen Cpn* [1971] 1 WLR 1578 at 1596 (Lord Wilberforce) (schoolteacher).

EXTENDED EMPLOYMENT PROTECTION

Radical changes in the rights of contractual employees were made by the Industrial Relations Act 1971 (replaced first by the Employment Protection (Consolidation) Act 1978, and now by the Employment Rights Act 1996),[480] giving protection against unfair dismissal. This new right is enforceable in employment tribunals, which must have regard to the code of practice, now issued by ACAS, which requires formal procedure and an opportunity for the employee to state his case; and apart from the code, fairness alone will require this in most cases.[481] But the tribunal has no power to restore the employment specifically: it may recommend reinstatement or re-engagement, and if the employer refuses it may award compensation.[482] Where the dismissal was in fact justified, failure to give a fair hearing will involve no loss and therefore no compensation.[483]

The employment protection legislation, it has now been held, 'has substantially changed the position at common law so far as dismissal is concerned', so that 'even the ordinary contract of master and servant now has many of the attributes of an office', and the court can intervene by way of injunction and declaration. An employee of the BBC, whose contract contained elaborate procedural rights of appeal, would by this decision have been protected against dismissal in breach of those rights, had she not elected to avail herself of a different procedure.[484]

A distinction is evidently developing between contracts containing express procedural rights, which the court now seems disposed to protect specifically, and contracts containing no such rights, where the employee has only the statutory protection. There is a clear tendency to extend the ambit of natural justice in the field of employment, as fairness undoubtedly demands. In some sense it may already be said, as in New Zealand, that the requirements of fairness apply to virtually all employment relationships, whether public or private.[485]

SUSPENSION FROM OFFICE

Suspension from office, as opposed to dismissal, may be nearly as serious a matter for the employee, but the courts have wavered between two different views. One is that the employer needs a summary power to suspend without hearing or other formality as a holding operation, pending inquiries into suspicions or allegations.[486] The other is that 'suspension is merely expulsion pro tanto. Each is penal, and each deprives the member concerned of the enjoyment of his rights of membership or office'.[487] Taking the former view in a controversial decision, a majority of the Privy Council held that a schoolteacher in New Zealand need not be given a hearing before being suspended without pay pending

---

[480] Pt X. As to civil servants see above, p. 51.

[481] *Earl v. Slater & Wheeler (Airlyne) Ltd* [1973] 1 WLR 51; and see *Polkey v. Dayton (AE) Services Ltd* [1988] AC 344. [482] s. 106, as continued by the Act of 1974 (above).

[483] See the *Earl* case (above).

[484] *R v. British Broadcasting Cpn ex p Lavelle* [1983] 1 WLR 23 (Woolf J). See likewise *Irani v. Southampton Health Authority* [1985] ICR 590 (injunction granted to protect contractual dismissal procedures).

[485] *Marlborough Harbour Board v. Goulden* [1985] 2 NZLR 378. They apply to the transfer of an officer to other duties if it is made for disciplinary as opposed to administrative reasons: *Poananga v. State Services Commission* [1985] 2 NZLR 385. Contrast *Bullen v. State Services Commission* [1985] 1 NZLR 402.

[486] *Lewis v. Heffer* [1978] 1 WLR 1061 (party officers suspended 'as a matter of good administration'); cf. *R v. Cole* (1979) 27 ACTR 13 (suspension without hearing valid, but not as to withholding of pay).

[487] *John v. Rees* [1970] Ch 345 (Megarry J). See also *R v. Committee of Lloyd's ex p Posgate*, The Times, 12 January 1983.

the determination of a disciplinary charge against him on which he would be fully heard in accordance with statutory regulations.[488] Although it was recognised that suspension without pay might involve hardship and also a temporary slur on the teacher, it was held that he had accepted this possibility in the terms of his employment and that the disciplinary procedure as a whole was fair. It has been said also that a police officer need not be heard before being suspended from duty pending investigation of charges of misconduct.[489]

OFFICES HELD AT PLEASURE

Where the holder of an office is subject to removal 'at pleasure', as opposed to removal 'for cause' such as unfitness or neglect of duty, it has been held that he has no right to be heard before removal.[490] In *Ridge* v. *Baldwin* Lord Reid approved the decision of 1844 on which the rule rests, though admitting that it had been doubted.[491] He stated that since no reasons need be given for the removal, the court could not determine whether it would be fair to hear the officer's case. But this is circular reasoning, and it is unsatisfying on grounds of justice as well as of logic. As already explained, natural justice does not necessarily require the giving of reasons for decisions, but nevertheless it does require fair notice of the case to be met, and this requirement of notice is something quite different from a duty to give reasons for the decision when taken.[492] If the officer is subject to some accusation, justice requires that he should be allowed a fair opportunity to defend himself, whatever the terms of his tenure. To deny it to him is to confuse the substance of the decision, which may be based on any reason at all, with the procedure which ought first to be followed. It is then an example of the fallacy, already mentioned, that the argument for natural justice is weaker where the discretionary power is wide.

It is therefore not surprising that Lord Hatherley LC said that he was not altogether satisfied with the reasoning of the decision of 1844,[493] and that it has been more enthusiastically distinguished than followed.[494] Reviewing the position in 1971, the House of Lords held that a Scottish schoolteacher, who by statute held his appointment 'during the pleasure' of the school board, could not validly be dismissed without a hearing.[495] Lip-service was paid to the decision of 1844, but it was distinguished on the ground that the teacher was entitled by statute to three weeks' notice of the proposal to dismiss him, and that the only possible reason for this was to enable him to prepare his defence, which

---

[488] *Furnell* v. *Whangarei High Schools Board* [1973] AC 660 (Lords Reid and Dilhorne dissenting).

[489] *Norwest Holst Ltd* v. *Secretary of State for Trade* [1978] Ch 201 at 224, repeated in *Cinnamond* v. *British Airports Authority* [1980] 1 WLR 582 at 590 (Lord Denning MR).

[490] *R* v. *Darlington School Governors* (1844) 6 QB 682 (dismissal of schoolmaster by governors of chartered grammar school), following *R* v. *Stratford-on-Avon (Mayor)* (1670) 1 Lev 291. In *Tucker* v. *British Museum Trustees*, The Times, 8 December 1967, the Court of Appeal held that a senior scientific officer of the British Museum had no right to be heard before dismissal, since he held an 'office, employment or service' terminable at the trustees' pleasure; whether he held an office was therefore not decided.

[491] [1964] AC at 66.

[492] See above, pp. 431 and 440 and in particular the *ex p Fayed* case, where the Act expressly ruled out any duty to give reasons but did not affect the requirement of notice.

[493] *Dean* v. *Bennett* (1870) 6 Ch App 489.

[494] See *Willis* v. *Childe* (1851) 13 Beav 117 (schoolmaster removed by grammar school trustees: power to remove on such grounds as they deemed just held not a power to remove at pleasure).

[495] *Malloch* v. *Aberdeen Cpn* [1971] 1 WLR 1578 (dismissal held a nullity). Cf. *Coutts* v. *Commonwealth of Australia* (1985) 59 ALR 699; *Knight* v. *Indian Head School Division (No 19)* [1990] 1 SCR 653. If there is a statutory duty to dismiss, natural justice is excluded: *Scott* v. *Aberdeen Cpn*, 1976 SLT 141.

the board ought accordingly to hear. Lord Reid partly refuted the explanation which he had himself given in *Ridge* v. *Baldwin*, saying that 'it seems to me perfectly sensible for Parliament to say to a public body: you need not give formal reasons but you must hear the man before you dismiss him'.[496]

Why then should this sensible provision not normally be implied, in accordance with the general presumption in favour of a fair hearing? Lord Wilberforce, though uphold-ing the case of 1844 'as a general principle', observed that the very possibility of dismissal without reason given, which might vitally affect a man's career or pension, made it all the more important for him to be able to state his case.[497] In other words, the basis of the 'gen-eral principle' is wrong, at least if justice is the criterion. Lord Wilberforce also said that the rules of natural justice were to be excluded only where there was 'no element of public employment or service, no support by statute, nothing in the nature of an office or a status which is capable of protection'. This formula leaves no room for officers not protected by natural justice, especially when they are public and statutory. It was adopted in the case of a school governor appointed under statute by a local authority, who was held entitled to the opportunity to make representations in writing before being removed from his office.[498] The way now lies open, therefore, for the abandonment of the precedent of 1844, which is clearly out of line with the duty to act fairly as it exists today.

The key to the problem, it is submitted, is to be found not in the terms on which the office is held, but in the specific protection of the office. It is this which distinguishes offices on the one hand from mere contractual employment on the other. In a perfect world even a mere employee would doubtless have a right to be heard before dismissal for misconduct, and to some extent he now has one by statute.[499] But since the law lacks any mechanism for restoring his employment specifically, it cannot supply the remedy which is usually wanted. In the case of offices, membership, status, and so forth it is able to do so; and it would seem right therefore to protect the officer or member against wrongful deprivation of every kind and to accord him the procedural rights without which depriva-tion is not fair and lawful. Whether he is removable for cause or at pleasure should make no difference.

ACADEMIC DISCIPLINE

The right to a fair hearing has been invoked in a number of cases by senior and junior members of universities and colleges, though not as yet with success. The courts have in general held that academic disciplinary proceedings require the observance of the prin-ciples of natural justice,[500] but equally they have refused to apply unduly strict standards, provided that the proceedings are substantially fair. Universities and colleges have in many cases established detailed disciplinary procedures under their own internal rules, often with rights of appeal.

A university lecturer was in one case held by the Privy Council to be a mere contractual employee, so that he could be dismissed without a hearing as explained in the preceding section.[501] This decision has been criticised by high authority[502] and may not now be a safe guide. But it is at least possible that academic staff of some grades may in law be mere

---

[496] Ibid. at p. 1582.   [497] Ibid. at p. 1597.
[498] *R* v. *Brent LBC ex p Assegai*, The Times, 18 June 1987.   [499] Above, p. 467.
[500] For disciplinary cases generally see above, p. 420.
[501] *Vidyodaya University* v. *Silva* [1965] 1 WLR 77; above p. 465.
[502] Lord Wilberforce in *Malloch* v. *Aberdeen Cpn* [1971] 1 WLR 1578 at 1596.

servants. More probably holders of established posts would be regarded as office-holders and so entitled to the benefit of natural justice. Jurisdiction will be in the visitor if the case turns upon internal rules. But if it comes within the statutory law of employment protection, protecting against unfair dismissal, the statutory law is overriding.[503] Elaborate dismissal procedures for universities and colleges have been instituted under the Education Reform Act 1988.[504] To that extent Parliament has transferred the jurisdiction of the visitor to special statutory bodies and tribunals.

Students have the protection of their contracts of membership: it will be implied that in return for their fees they will be treated in accordance with the university or college rules, and natural justice will operate in the same way as with members of a trade union or association,[505] though jurisdiction will in most cases lie with the visitor as explained above. Before being expelled for failure in examinations[506] or for misconduct[507] they are entitled to be treated fairly and given a hearing—though clearly this does not apply to the conduct of examinations themselves.[508] In one case students expelled for failure in examinations succeeded in showing that they had not been treated in accordance with natural justice by the examiners, but this was because the examiners had themselves decided that they be asked to withdraw after taking into account personal factors as well as examination marks; and relief was refused in discretion owing to undue delay in bringing the proceedings.[509] In another case a student who had been fined and rusticated for exhibiting himself nude on the campus was able to show that the Vice-Chancellor had failed to observe the requirements of natural justice since he had given the student no hearing initially but had merely informed him that he could appeal against the penalties.[510] Once again, relief was refused in discretion, since the facts were not contested and the penalties were obviously proper; but this reasoning is dangerous,[511] and the judge himself recognised that such discretion ought to be exercised sparingly.

PRELIMINARY AND ADVISORY ACTS, INVESTIGATIONS AND REPORTS

Natural justice is concerned with the exercise of power, that is to say, with acts or orders which produce legal results and in some way alter someone's legal position to his disadvantage. But preliminary steps, which in themselves may not involve immediate legal consequences, may lead to acts or orders which do so.[512] In this case the protection of fair

---

[503] See *Thomas v. University of Bradford* [1987] AC 795 at 824.

[504] ss. 202–8. For the complicated transitional position see *Pearce v. University of Aston in Birmingham (No 1)* [1991] 2 All ER 461, *(No 2)* ibid. 469.

[505] See *Herring v. Templeman* [1973] 3 All ER 569 at 585. In his Report on the Sit-in at Cambridge University (1973, para. 154) Lord Devlin said that the foundation of the disciplinary power was the contract of matriculation.

[506] *R v. Aston University Senate ex p Roffey* [1969] 2 QB 538 (it was conceded that the university had no visitor: see *Patel v. Bradford University Senate* [1978] 1 WLR 1488 at 1501, [1979] 1 WLR 1066 at 1068); and see *Brighton Cpn v. Parry* (1972) 70 LGR 576 (unsatisfactory work).

[507] *Ceylon University v. Fernando* [1960] 1 WLR 223; *Ward v. Bradford Cpn* (1971) 70 LGR 27.

[508] See *Thorne v. University of London* (above).

[509] *R v. Aston University Senate ex p Roffey* (above).

[510] *Glynn v. Keele University* [1971] 1 WLR 487; and see *R v. Oxford University ex p Bolchover*, The Times, 7 October 1970, quoted in *Glynn's* case.   [511] See above, p. 424.

[512] In *Peko-Wallsend Ltd v. Minister for Arts, Heritage and Environment* (1986) 70 ALR 523 a mining company was held entitled to put its case to the cabinet before they proposed part of a national park for designation under an international convention which under Australian legislation would then empower the government to prohibit the company's operations if it so wished.

procedure may be needed throughout, and the successive steps must be considered not only separately but also as a whole. The question must always be whether, looking at the statutory procedure as a whole, each separate step is fair to persons affected.[513]

The House of Lords considered this question in an income tax case where the tax authorities, before they could take the taxpayer before the tribunal which determines whether the object of some transaction is tax avoidance, were required to show a prima facie case to the tribunal. The tribunal refused to allow the taxpayer to be represented, or to see the evidence submitted to it by the authorities, at that stage. The House of Lords upheld this ruling, since the taxpayer would have full opportunity to state his case to the tribunal in the later proceedings.[514] As Lord Reid said, every public officer who has to decide whether to prosecute ought first to decide whether there is a prima facie case, but no one supposes that he need consult the accused. There was nothing inherently unjust in the procedure, which as a whole was found to be fair in its statutory context. But the House of Lords strongly reaffirmed the general doctrine of the right to a fair hearing, and held that there was nothing about the determination of a prima facie case which automatically excluded it:[515] the procedure must pass the test of fairness at each and every stage.

In general, however, the courts are favourable to the observance of natural justice in the making of preliminary investigations and reports which may lead to serious legal consequences to some person.[516] The Commission for Racial Equality and its committees must act fairly in making their investigations, though considerable latitude is allowed as to its procedure.[517] Inspectors investigating the affairs of a company under statutory powers must give the directors a fair opportunity to meet criticisms, even though the object is merely to make a report.[518] A police officer threatened with compulsory retirement is entitled to have the report of a preliminary inquiry disclosed to his own doctor.[519] A gas company should be given the opportunity to comment on an adverse report by a gas tester which might lead to an order against it by the local authority.[520] These are really instances of the right to know the opposing case.[521] But an academic board considering a student's record and recommending his expulsion was not obliged to give him a hearing since it merely made a recommendation and there was adequate opportunity for his case to be heard by the governing body when considering the recommendations.[522]

PRISONERS' RIGHTS

The benefit of the principles of natural justice was extended to prisoners, as already noted, when they were charged with serious disciplinary offences before boards of prison

---

[513] See (1974) 12 *Osg HLJ* 179 (R. D. Howe).

[514] *Wiseman* v. *Borneman* [1971] AC 297, Lord Wilberforce concurring with hesitation and holding that the tribunal must disclose the official evidence for the taxpayer's use at the hearing, and that the tribunal had a residual duty of fairness in case prejudicial evidence was introduced unfairly. See similarly *Balen* v. *Inland Revenue Cmrs* [1978] 2 All ER 1033; *Moran* v. *Lloyds* [1981] 1 Ll R 423.

[515] Contrast *Parry-Jones* v. *Law Society* [1969] 1 Ch 1.

[516] See *R* v. *Agricultural Dwelling-house Advisory Committee ex p Brough* [1897] 1 EGLR 106.

[517] Above, p. 440.

[518] *Re Pergamon Press Ltd* [1971] Ch 388; above, p. 432; and see *State (McPolin)* v. *Minister for Transport* [1976] IR 93 (preliminary wreck inquiry: shipowner entitled to contest evidence given by crew). Contrast *Guay* v. *Lafleur* (1965) 47 DLR (2d) 226 (taxpayer not entitled to participate in inquiry into his affairs by tax authorities. The decision was later reversed by statute). For this and other Canadian cases see (1974) 12 *Osg HLJ* 179 (R. D. Howe). [519] *R* v. *Kent Police Authority ex p Godden* [1971] 2 QB 662; above, p. 418.

[520] *R* v. *London County Council ex p Commercial Gas Co* (1895) 11 TLR 337.

[521] Above, p. 431. [522] *Herring* v. *Templeman* [1973] 3 All ER 569.

visitors, who for this purpose have now been abolished.[523] In one case the Court of Appeal held that judicial review did not extend to the disciplinary decisions of prison governors in the day-to-day administration of prisons, which at that time might impose penalties including loss of remission of sentence up to twenty-eight days.[524] The case recalled earlier decisions, since shown to be unsound, where the court refused relief against the exercise of disciplinary powers on the ground that it would undermine disciplinary authority.[525] The House of Lords, however, has now held that a prison governor adjudicating in this way 'bears all the classic hallmarks of an authority subject to judicial review', and has overruled the earlier decision.[526] The door has thus been opened for the operation of judicial review generally and for the rules of natural justice in particular. In sufficiently serious cases governors cannot deny prisoners legal representation.[527] The House of Lords has eliminated the supposed exception with a decision firmly based upon broad principle, which should ensure the full measure of procedural justice for prisoners. Non-disciplinary action, such as the transfer of a troublesome prisoner to a segregation unit, is another matter.[528]

Since procedural fairness is a fundamental matter, it may in addition be possible to claim it under another decision of the Court of Appeal which holds that judicial review is not excluded where a prison governor is alleged to be violating rights which are fundamental.[529] One fundamental right is that of access to the courts,[530] but that does not necessarily entitle a prisoner to appear in person or to be conveyed to court free of charge if he has the ability to pay.[531]

EXCEPTIONS

LIMITATIONS AND EXCEPTIONS

Only an arbitrary boundary can be drawn between cases where the right to a fair hearing is excluded by the nature of the subject matter and cases where there is some special exception. It has already been explained how the right may be excluded by the very nature of the power, for instance where urgent action has to be taken to safeguard public health or safety,[532] by the absence of 'legitimate expectation'; by the dubious doctrine that a hearing would make no difference; by the refusal of remedies in discretion; and by the rule that employees can be dismissed at pleasure.[533] On rare occasions also, it may be excluded by express legislation.[534] Here we must consider such residual exceptions as remain.

---

[523] Above, p. 59.

[524] R v. Camphill Prison Deputy Governor ex p King [1985] QB 735 (leave to appeal refused by House of Lords). In R v. Hull Prison Visitors ex p St Germain [1979] QB 425 dicta in the Court of Appeal had been conflicting. The Court of Appeal in Northern Ireland refused to follow the Camphill decision: R v. Maze Prison Governor ex p McKiernan [1985] NILR Bulletin No. 6, p. 6. For the current disciplinary powers of governors see above, p. 59.　　　　[525] Above, p. 418.

[526] Leech v. Parkhurst Prison Deputy Governor [1988] AC 533, a natural justice case.

[527] Ezeh v. UK (2003) 15 BHRC 145 discussed above, p. 58.

[528] Williams v. Home Office (No 2) [1981] 1 All ER 1211 (hearing not required).

[529] R v. Home Secretary ex p Herbage (No 2) [1987] QB 1077 (allegation that conditions of imprisonment were cruel and unusual punishment contrary to Bill of Rights 1688: leave to apply for judicial review granted).　　　　[530] Raymond v. Honey [1983] 1 AC 1.

[531] R v. Home Secretary ex p Wynne [1993] 1 WLR 115 (HL).　　　　[532] Above, p. 420.

[533] Above, pp. 424, 465 and 481 respectively.　　　　[534] See above, p. 145.

In truth the lesson of the host of cases that have been brought before the courts is that exceptions are conspicuous by their absence wherever genuine administrative power has been exercised under statute with any serious effect on a person's property, liberty or livelihood. Where a right to be fairly heard has been denied, it is more probably a case of a bad decision than of a true exception. The rule must come close to deserving the judicial tributes quoted earlier: 'a principle of universal application', 'a duty lying upon everyone who decides anything'.

LEGISLATION

There is no right to be heard before the making of legislation, whether primary or delegated, unless it is provided by statute.[535] Accordingly an association of practising solicitors could not insist on being consulted before the Lord Chancellor made an order abolishing scale fees in conveyancing for solicitors generally—nor did it make any difference that the Act in this case specifically required consultation with the Law Society.[536] The same exception was probably the determining factor in the refusal of a hearing to a local authority which wished to dispute the siting of runways at Stansted Airport, which the government had determined to authorise by a special development order, thus avoiding the procedure of an ordinary application for planning permission.[537] It was held that the power to make such an order was 'a purely administrative or legislative power fully exercisable discretionarily' for which the minister was responsible only to Parliament. Of the three different grounds comprised in these words, the most plausible may be that the power was legislative. But it is not convincing, since a special development order is limited to specified land and is no more general than, say, a slum-clearance scheme. In a case where regulations banned trading in oral snuff generally, but impinged almost exclusively on a single company which had been 'led up the garden path' and denied a fair opportunity to dispute the expert advice given to the government, the court quashed the regulations for unfairness, without mentioning the difficulty that they were legislation.[538] But the Supreme Court has since made clear that where subordinate legislation is 'targeted against "designated persons"' those persons will have a right to be consulted.[539]

NATIONAL SECURITY

The right to a fair hearing may have to yield to overriding considerations of national security. The House of Lords recognised this necessity where civil servants at the government communications headquarters, who had to handle secret information vital to national security, were abruptly put under new conditions of service which prohibited

---

[535] For the practice of consultation see below, p. 755.

[536] *Bates* v. *Lord Hailsham* [1972] 1 WLR 1373; below, p. 746. Similarly, *R (BAPIO Action Ltd)* v. *Home Secretary* [2007] EWCA Civ 1139, para. 47 (Sedley LJ) (point not considered in the House of Lords (above)). Contrast *R* v. *The Lord Chancellor ex p The Law Society* (1994) 6 Admin LR 833 (Law Society had legitimate expectation of consultation on legal aid regulations, but no relief given). No legitimate expectation of consultation found in the *BAPIO* case.

[537] *Essex County Council* v. *Ministry of Housing and Local Government* (1967) 66 LGR 23. Compare *CREEDNZ* v. *Governor-General* [1981] 1 NZLR 172, where it was held that a right to make representations would be inconsistent with the scheme of the legislation.

[538] *R* v. *Secretary of State for Health ex p United States Tobacco International Inc* [1992] 1 QB 353. See also *South African Roads Board* v. *Johannesburg City Council* 1991(4) SA 1.

[539] *Bank Mellat* v. *HM Treasury* [2013] UKSC 39, para. 47 (Lord Sumption) (financial measures targeted against particular banks). This case is discussed above, pp. 308, 423.

membership of national trade unions. Neither they nor their unions were consulted, in disregard of an established practice, and their complaint to the courts would have been upheld on grounds of natural justice, had there not been a threat to national security. The factor which ultimately prevailed was the danger that the process of consultation itself would have precipitated further strikes, walkouts, overtime bans and disruption generally of a kind which had plagued the communications headquarters shortly beforehand and which were a threat to national security. Since national security must be paramount, natural justice must then give way.[540]

The Crown must, however, satisfy the court that national security is at risk. Despite the constantly repeated dictum that 'those who are responsible for the national security must be the sole judges of what the national security requires',[541] the court will insist upon evidence that an issue of national security arises, and only then will it accept the opinion of the Crown that it should prevail over some legal right. There is also the proviso that the opinion of the Crown should not be one which no minister could reasonably have held. 'There is no abdication of the judicial function, but there is a common sense limitation recognised by the judges as to what is justiciable.'[542]

---

[540] *Council of Civil Service Unions v. Minister for the Civil Service* [1985] AC 374 (declaratory relief against minister's instructions refused on application for judicial review).
[541] *The Zamora* [1916] 2 AC 77 at 107 (Lord Parker of Waddington).
[542] [1985] AC at 406 (Lord Scarman). The proviso as to reasonableness is the preceding sentence.

PART VII

REMEDIES AND LIABILITY

15

ORDINARY REMEDIES

RIGHTS AND REMEDIES

Rights depend upon remedies.[1] Legal history is rich in examples of rules of law which have been distilled from the system of remedies, as the remedies have been extended and adapted from one class of case to another. There is no better example than habeas corpus. This remedy, since the sixteenth century the chief cornerstone of personal liberty, grew out of a medieval writ which at first played an inconspicuous part in the law of procedure: it was used to secure the appearance of a party, in particular where he was in detention by some inferior court. It was later invoked to challenge detention by the king and by the Council; and finally it became the standard procedure by which the legality of any imprisonment could be tested. The right to personal freedom was almost a by-product of the procedural rules.

This tendency has both good and bad effects. It is good in that the emphasis falls on the practical methods of enforcing any right. Efficient remedies are of the utmost importance, and the remedies provided by English administrative law are notably efficient. But sometimes the remedy comes to be looked upon as a thing in itself, divorced from the legal policy to which it ought to give expression. In the past this has led to gaps and anomalies, and to a confusion of doctrine to which the courts have sometimes seemed strangely indifferent.

For a long time there were anomalies caused by the fact that the remedies employed in administrative law belong to three different families. There is the family of ordinary private law remedies such as damages, injunction and declaration. Although their origins lie in private law, they played and continue to play a vital role in public law. Then there is a special family of public law remedies, principally certiorari, prohibition and mandamus,[2] collectively known as the prerogative remedies. There is also a third family of statutory remedies for special situations, which may sometimes exclude all other remedies or which may extend the scope of ordinary remedies as does the Human Rights Act 1998.[3]

Prior to the reforms of 1977 damages, injunctions and declarations were sought in an ordinary action, as in private law; but prerogative remedies had to be sought by a procedure of their own, which could not be combined with an ordinary action. It was thus not possible to seek certiorari and a declaratory judgment in the alternative, although this would often be a desirable course. This anomaly, though it gave rise to little difficulty in practice, was an obvious target for law reform; and in 1977 it was removed by the provision of a comprehensive procedure, the 'application for judicial review' (now called the 'claim for judicial review'), under which remedies in both families became interchangeable.[4]

---

[1] On remedies generally (Chs. 15–18) see Lewis, *Judicial Remedies in Public Law*, 4th edn (2008).
[2] Whose names have recently changed as explained below, p. 500.   [3] Below, p. 619.
[4] Below, p. 549.

This reform caused new difficulties and uncertainties but, as explained below, they have been significantly eased recently.[5]

All the remedies mentioned in this and the following chapters are remedies for obtaining judicial review, i.e. for challenging the legality of some public authority's action (or inaction). Appeals (usually to a tribunal), though in some sense a form of remedy, are fundamentally different and are dealt with in Chapter 23.

The present chapter is concerned with the remedies of private law which play a part in public law. First come the remedies related to powers (actions for damages, injunctions, declarations and relator actions). A final section contains such remedies as private law supplies for the enforcement of duties.

ACTIONS FOR DAMAGES

The possibilities of suing governmental authorities, including the Crown, for damages for unjustified tortious injury and for breach of contract are governed by the principles of official and personal liability, explained in Chapters 20 and 21. Damages as a remedy therefore need no more than a bare mention here.

Except in cases of personal injury, e.g. from highway and industrial accidents, actions for damages have in the past played a relatively small role in litigation against administrative authorities. But recently the courts have been called upon to investigate new possibilities of liability, sometimes with positive and sometimes with negative results. It is now clear that what might be called administrative torts are a subject of importance, and often of difficulty, in administrative law. As will be seen in due course, the remedy of damages, which has always been an essential element in the protection of the citizen against public authorities, is gaining greater prominence as a means of ensuring that powers are exercised responsibly, in good faith and with due care.

INJUNCTIONS

GENERAL

The injunction is the standard remedy of private law for forbidding the commission of some unlawful act, e.g. a tort or breach of contract. Its sanction is imprisonment or fine for contempt of court, or attachment of property. Although now statutory,[6] historically it is an equitable remedy, since it derives from the former Court of Chancery, and accordingly it has a discretionary character. In administrative law the most important remedies are discretionary—injunctions, declarations and certiorari, for example. But the discretion must be exercised judicially and according to settled principles. The only marked effect is that there is a tendency for the court to refuse the remedy where the plaintiff has some other equally good remedy, or where he has been guilty of delay or in some other way he has forfeited the court's sympathy. This characteristic of remedies is explained later.[7]

It is also possible for the court to grant a mandatory injunction, i.e. a positive order to do some act rather than a negative order to refrain.[8] Mandatory injunctions play a

---

[5] Below, p. 584.   [6] Senior Courts Act 1981, s. 37.   [7] Below, p. 596.

[8] In R v. Kensington and Chelsea Royal LBC ex p Hammell [1989] QB 518 the court granted an interlocutory mandatory injunction for the housing of a homeless person pending judicial review. A tenant's

restricted part in public law because there is a special procedure for enforcing the performance of a public duty in the prerogative remedy of mandamus, dealt with below. But where a public authority's duty is analogous to a private person's, e.g. in managing a housing estate, a mandatory injunction may be a suitable remedy.[9] There may also be more scope for mandatory injunctions now that there is a dichotomy between public and private law and some duties are assigned to the latter category.[10]

Injunctions are as readily available against ministers, officials and public authorities generally as they are against private persons, and they are quite often granted to prohibit wrongful or unlawful action.[11]

Although primarily a remedy against tort and other actionable wrongs, the injunction is also used as a remedy in public law against unauthorised action by governmental and public bodies, even though the action in question would not be a tort or breach of contract. This appears most clearly in cases where the Attorney-General, as the nominal plaintiff in a relator action, as explained below, obtains an injunction to prohibit either some breach of the criminal law or else some ultra vires act by a public authority, such as illegal local government expenditure. Injunctions are also awarded to private individuals also merely on the ground that a public authority was proposing to act ultra vires.[12]

The courts are not deterred by the fact that an injunction against a public authority is a particularly drastic step, bringing the machinery of government to a halt. They do not lend a ready ear to pleas of administrative inconvenience. 'Even if chaos should result, still the law must be obeyed.'[13] With these defiant words the Court of Appeal granted an interim injunction against a local authority's reorganisation of eight existing schools into new comprehensive schools, already approved by the Secretary of State and on the point of taking effect, since the authority had not followed the statutory procedure which required public notice and opportunity for objection.[14] The court firmly disregarded the plea that it would cause excessive disruption to reverse all these completed plans.

The most drastic of all such interventions was when the House of Lords granted an interim injunction forbidding a minister from obeying an Act of Parliament because the Act was in conflict with European Community law.[15]

The appropriate procedure for obtaining an injunction against a public authority in any 'public law' case is now an application for judicial review. Many claims against public authorities may however fall into the 'private law' category, for example where an injunction is sought against a threatened tort such as a nuisance. The dichotomy is explained in Chapter 18.

EXAMPLES OF INJUNCTIONS

The injunction may be used to prevent the commission or continuance of any tort or breach of contract. Just as damages were awarded for trespass against the Wandsworth board of works when it pulled down a building without giving the owner a hearing, so in

statutory right to buy is enforceable by mandatory injunction: Housing Act 1985, s. 138; *Taylor* v. *Newham LBC* [1993] 1 WLR 444.

[9] *Parker* v. *Camden LBC* [1986] Ch 162, holding also that the court would not usurp the local authority's duty by appointing a receiver and manager.

[10] See *Cocks* v. *Thanet DC* [1983] 2 AC 286, discussed below, p. 572.

[11] But note the discussion below, p. 704 (*M* v. *Home Office*).   [12] Below, p. 479.

[13] Lord Denning MR in the *Bradbury* case (below).

[14] *Bradbury* v. *Enfield London Borough Council* [1967] 1 WLR 1311.

[15] *R* v. *Secretary of State for Transport ex p Factortame Ltd (No 2)* [1991] 1 AC 603; above, p. 162.

a case at Rotherham an injunction was granted to restrain the corporation from carrying out a demolition order without a proper hearing of the owner's appeal for exercise of the statutory power of postponement.[16] The only difference in the latter case was that the owner was able to act before the blow had fallen, and to prevent it from falling. The citizen is in a far stronger position if he can challenge the local authority before it has committed itself to action, and the value in this respect of the remedy by injunction need hardly be stressed.

Cases of nuisance created by public authorities are suitably remedied by injunction, as illustrated in a later chapter.[17] In the Derwent pollution case, there mentioned,[18] it was argued that the corporation, since it was responsible for a vital public service, ought not to be prohibited by injunction from supplying it, but should be liable (if at all) only in damages. If this had been right, then the corporation could in effect have compulsorily expropriated the owners of the fishing rights subject to payment of damages by way of compensation. To say that the sewage-disposal arrangements were an urgent necessity for public health, while the fishing rights were of relatively minor importance, did not alter the case at all: for it still remains true that private rights can be expropriated only by statutory authority, and no such authority was to be found. Accordingly the corporation was ordered to cease from polluting the rivers within a specified time, and they were thus compelled to make new arrangements. Needless to say, a public authority can be relied upon to respect the court's order. But it is not unknown, where an authority has been tardy in its obedience, for the courts to fine or imprison its members or officers for contempt.[19]

Confidential material may be protected by injunction. A public authority which obtains documents or information by compulsory power may use them only for the purposes for which the compulsory power was given, and use for other purposes may be restrained by injunction.[20] Detailed reports made by the Police Complaints Authority to the complainant and the police force in question are confidential and will be protected similarly.[21]

INJUNCTIONS AGAINST THE WORLD

The long-settled rule was that an injunction would be binding only against a specified party to a lawsuit. But a radical change has occurred since the introduction of the Human Rights Act 1998, which imposes on the court the obligation of acting compatibly with the Human Rights Convention and its European jurisprudence. Holding that 'we are entering a new era', the High Court held that it could (as it did) grant injunctions 'against the world' so as to forbid indefinitely the publication by newspapers or others of information disclosing the identity and whereabouts of two child murderers who were to be protected after their release from prison.[22]

---

[16] *Broadbent* v. *Rotherham Cpn* [1917] 2 Ch 31. For the *Wandsworth* case see above, p. 409. See also *Repton School Governors* v. *Repton Urban District Council* [1918] 2 KB 133.　　　　　[17] Below, p. 641.

[18] *Pride of Derby and Derbyshire Angling Association Ltd* v. *British Celanese Ltd* [1953] Ch 149; below, p. 643.　　　　　[19] Below, p. 521.

[20] *Marcel* v. *Metropolitan Police Commissioner* [1992] Ch 225 (subject, however, to rights of third parties).

[21] *Police Complaints Authority* v. *Greater Manchester Police Authority* (1990) 3 Admin. LR 757 (police authority restrained from publishing report in its favour). See also *Dalgleish* v. *Lothian and Borders Police Board*, 1992 SLT 721.

[22] *Venables* v. *News Group Newspapers Ltd* [2001] Fam 430 (Butler-Sloss P).

INTERIM PROTECTION

Where there is imminent danger of irreparable injury and damages would not be an adequate remedy, the court may grant an interim injunction[23] so as to preserve the position of the parties pending trial. The court must assess the strength of the case and the balance of convenience, and its discretion is very wide.[24] In a case in which interim relief was sought even before permission had been granted the court had to weigh the protection of journalistic sources against national security; not unexpectedly national security proved weightier and relief was refused to the claimant.[25]

When an interim injunction is granted before trial, the party protected must normally give an undertaking in damages so that, if he loses at the trial, the party restrained is compensated for any loss suffered meanwhile. Formerly the court would grant an interim injunction to the Crown without any such undertaking, the doctrine being that 'the Crown does not undertake'. But the House of Lords has decided that this indulgence to the Crown is no longer justified, since the plain implication of the Crown Proceedings Act 1947 is that the Crown should so far as possible be treated like other litigants.[26] But in the case of the Crown, and also of other public authorities charged with enforcing the law, the court in its discretion may dispense with the undertaking. Thus a local authority was able to obtain an interim injunction against shops opening unlawfully on Sundays without having to give an undertaking which, if its action proved to be contrary to European Community law, might have imposed heavy liability.[27]

THE CROWN AND ITS SERVANTS

The Crown is immune from ordinary legal process but its servants are not.[28] No injunction can therefore be granted against the Crown itself, but a declaration in lieu of an injunction may be granted under the Crown Proceedings Act 1947 in cases where the Act applies, which are mostly actions in tort and contract and are actions against the Crown itself. After years of doubt it was settled that the Act did not prevent the grant of injunctions against servants of the Crown. But by an illogical distinction under two decisions of the House of Lords, it was held that the Act permits only declarations of a final character (thus ruling out interim relief) in proceedings against the Crown under the Act of 1947, whereas both interim and final injunctions are available against Crown servants in judicial review proceedings, which are governed by the Senior Courts Act 1981. This is a story of controversy and confusion and of the highest constitutional importance. It is best told in the context of the Act of 1947 in the chapter on Crown Proceedings.

---

[23] A *Mareva* injunction (to forbid dealing with assets generally) may be granted to a public authority: *Securities and Investments Board* v. *Pantell SA* [1990] Ch 426.

[24] See *American Cyanamid Co* v. *Ethicon Ltd* [1975] AC 396; *R* v. *Secretary of State for Transport ex p Factortame Ltd (No 2)* [1991] 1 AC 603. And see *National Commercial Bank Jamaica Ltd* v. *Olint Corp Ltd (Jamaica)* [2009] UKPC 16 ('the court should take whichever course seems likely to cause the least irremediable prejudice to one party or the other' (para. 16 (Lord Hoffmann)).

[25] *R (Miranda)* v. *Home Secretary* [2013] EWHC 2609, paras. 27–35 (Beatson LJ and Parker J). Thus the police investigation of the material seized (while the journalist's assistant was transiting through Heathrow) could continue to establish whether there were 'reasonable grounds for suspecting that a person "is or has been concerned in the commission, preparation or instigation of acts of terrorism"' (Terrorism Act 2000, s. 40(1)(b)). But the refusal was for only a short period (8 days) before a full *inter partes* hearing could be held.

[26] *Hoffmann-La Roche & Co* v. *Secretary of State for Trade and Industry* [1975] AC 295. For this case see above, p. 247. For the Act see below, p. 694.

[27] *Kirkless MBC* v. *Wickes Building Supplies Ltd* [1993] AC 227.

[28] *M* v. *Home Office* [1994] AC 377.

INJUNCTIONS FOR ENFORCEMENT OF STATUTES

An important use of the injunction, very different from those already described, is for the purpose of forbidding disobedience to statutes, for example in the case of constantly repeated offences where the statutory penalties are inadequate. Since only the Attorney-General may seek injunctions for this purpose, except where statute has provided otherwise, the practice is explained below, in the section on relator actions.[29]

TENURE OF PUBLIC OFFICE: INJUNCTION IN NATURE OF *QUO WARRANTO*

Since 1938 the injunction has been made available by statute to prohibit the usurpation of a public office, in place of the former proceedings known as *quo warranto*. This was originally a prerogative writ which the Crown could use to inquire into the title to any office or franchise claimed by a subject. It fell out of use in the sixteenth century and was replaced by the information in the nature of *quo warranto*, which in form was a criminal proceeding instituted in the name of the Crown by the Attorney-General or by a private prosecutor.[30] These informations were abolished by the Administration of Justice (Miscellaneous Provisions) Act 1938[31] (now replaced by the Senior Courts Act 1981)[32] which provided that where any person acts in an office to which he is not entitled and an information would previously have lain against him, the High Court may restrain him by injunction and may declare the office to be vacant if need be; and that no such proceedings shall be taken by a person who would not previously have been entitled to apply for an information. Consequently the old law of *quo warranto* is still operative,[33] but the remedy is now by injunction and declaration. The procedure is similar to that for prerogative remedies and must now be by 'application for judicial review'.[34] But there seems to be no record of its having been used.

The remedy as now defined applies to usurpation of 'any substantive office of a public nature and permanent character which is held under the Crown or which has been created by any statutory provision or royal charter'.[35] But it must not be a case of 'merely the function or employment of a deputy or servant held at the will and pleasure of others'.[36] Here once again we meet the difference between office and mere contractual employment.[37] The procedure was typically used to challenge the right to such offices as those of freeman or burgess of a borough, mayor, town councillor, sheriff, justice of the peace, county court judge, chief constable or member of the General Medical Council.[38] But the alleged usurper had to be in possession of the office and to have acted in it.[39]

For challenging the qualifications of a member of a local authority there are special statutory provisions under the Local Government Act 1972.[40] Proceedings may be instituted in the High Court or a magistrates' court, but only by a local government elector for the area concerned, and only within six months of the defendant having acted as a

---

[29] Below, p. 496.   [30] Bl. Comm. iii. 263.   [31] s. 9.   [32] s. 30.

[33] For the leading example, see *R* v. *Speyer, R* v. *Cassel* [1916] 1 KB 595, affirmed [1916] 2 KB 858. For a short history of the procedure, see the judgment of Lord Reading CJ at first instance.

[34] Senior Courts Act 1981, s. 31: see below, p. 550. The pre-1938 practice, as with the prerogative remedies, was to obtain a rule nisi for the information.   [35] Senior Courts Act 1981, s. 30.

[36] *Darley* v. *R* (1846) 12 Cl & F 520 at 541 (Tindal CJ, advising the House of Lords).

[37] See above, p. 490.   [38] Halsbury's *Laws of England*, 4th edn, vol. i, para. 171.

[39] *R* v. *Tidy* [1892] 2 QB 179; Administration of Justice (Miscellaneous Provisions) Act 1938, s. 9(2).

[40] s. 92, replacing s. 84 of the Act of 1933.

member; if the defendant merely claims to be entitled to act, proceedings lie in the High Court only. The various remedies include declarations, injunctions and financial penalties.

DECLARATIONS

DEVELOPMENT OF THIS REMEDY

Declaratory judgments play a large part in private law and are a particularly valuable remedy for settling disputes before they reach the point where a right is infringed.[41] The essence of a declaratory judgment is that it states the rights or legal position of the parties as they stand, without changing them in any way; though it may be supplemented by other remedies in suitable cases. Typical applications are for finding the meaning of some provision in a will, or whether a statute applies to some particular case, or whether a contract has been properly performed. In administrative law there are additional advantages, as in cases where it is difficult to choose the right remedy or where the ordinary remedy is for some reason unsatisfactory.

The common law, with its insistence on compulsory remedies and its horror of maintenance and procedural abuse, long refused to countenance judgments that were merely declaratory; and so did the Court of Chancery. But they were needed inevitably in proceedings against the Crown, since in that case there was no means of enforcement, so that they were in regular use in connection with petitions of right[42] and on the equity side of the Exchequer. Scots law had the action of declarator, which Lord Brougham attempted to import into England with only small success at first. Acts of 1850 and 1852 empowered the Court of Chancery to make declarations of right, but they were construed as narrowly as possible by a still mistrustful judiciary.[43] Even the Judicature Acts 1873–5 did not implant any such power generally in the remodelled judicial system. It arrived finally only with the rules of court of 1883. It must therefore be considered a statutory rather than an equitable remedy. The surprising thing is that this form of relief, indispensable in any modern system of law, should be so recent an invention.

The rules of court of 1883 provided that:

> No action or proceedings shall be open to objection, on the ground that a merely declaratory judgment or order is sought thereby, and the Court may make binding declarations of right whether any consequential relief is or could be claimed, or not.[44]

This is still the rule today,[45] and the courts have grown accustomed to using it very freely. A declaratory judgment by itself merely states some existing legal situation. It requires no one to do anything and to disregard it will not be contempt of court.[46] By enabling a party

---

[41] See generally Woolf and Zamir, *The Declaratory Judgment*, 2nd edn; P. W. Young, *Declaratory Orders* (1975).   [42] For the petition of right, now abolished, see below, p. 691.

[43] Court of Chancery, England, Act 1850; Court of Chancery Procedure Act 1852. Section 50 of the latter Act was in nearly as wide a form as the later rule of court, but it was construed as allowing declaratory relief only where some other equitable relief could have been awarded: see *Dyson* v. *A-G* [1911] 1 KB 410 at 417 and 422.

[44] RSC Ord. 25 r. 5, upheld as intra vires in *Guaranty Trust Co of New York* v. *Hannay & Co* [1915] 2 KB 536.   [45] RSC 1965, Ord. 15 r. 16, now replaced by CPR Sched. 1, 15.16.

[46] *Webster* v. *Southwark LBC* [1983] QB 698, where however the court approved the issue of a writ of sequestration against the property of councillors who in deliberate breach of statutory duty had refused the use of a hall for an election meeting of a National Front candidate. The court's order had been merely declaratory since it was assumed that it would be respected. Otherwise a compulsory order might have been

to discover what his legal position is, it opens the way to the use of other remedies for giving effect to it, if that should be necessary. But it cannot be used to resolve matters which are not justiciable in the courts, such as civil servants' superannuation allowances[47] or claims based upon the European Convention on Human Rights[48] (before it was incorporated) or perhaps (or perhaps not), the proceedings of Royal Commissions.[49] The declaration is a discretionary remedy. This important characteristic probably derives not from the fact that the power to grant it was first conferred on the Court of Chancery, but from the discretionary power conferred by the rule of court. There is thus ample jurisdiction to prevent its abuse; and the court always has inherent powers to refuse relief to speculators and busybodies, those who ask hypothetical questions[50] or those who have no sufficient interest.[51] As was said by Lord Dunedin[52]

> The question must be a real and not a theoretical question; the person raising it must have a real interest to raise it; he must be able to secure a proper contradictor, that is to say, some one presently existing who has a true interest to oppose the declaration sought.

In other words, there must be a genuine legal issue between proper parties.

DECLARATIONS AGAINST PUBLIC AUTHORITIES

In administrative law the great merit of the declaration is that it is an efficient remedy against ultra vires action by governmental authorities of all kinds, including ministers and servants of the Crown, and, in proper cases even, the Crown itself. If the court will declare that some action, either taken or proposed, is unauthorised by law, that concludes the point as between the plaintiff and the authority. If then his property is taken, he has his ordinary legal remedies; if an order is made against him, he can ignore it with impunity; if he has been dismissed from an office, he can insist that he still holds it.[53] All these results flow from the mere fact that the rights of the parties have been declared. This is a particularly suitable way to settle disputes with governmental authorities, since it involves no immediate threat of compulsion, yet is none the less effective.

The landmark in this use of the declaration is the famous case of *Dyson* v. *Attorney-General* (1911–12).[54] It was one of the repercussions of Lloyd George's budget

---

granted. The contumacious conduct of the defendants was a decisive factor. Nevertheless the decision seems questionable.

[47] *Nixon* v. *A-G* [1930] 1 Ch 566. See also *Gouriet* v. *Union of Post Office Workers* [1978] AC 435. But the position may now be different: below, p. 485.

[48] *Malone* v. *Metropolitan Police Commissioner* [1979] Ch 344 (telephone tapping).

[49] In Britain royal commissions have no statutory or other powers. In New Zealand they are statutory and have power to award costs, and so are subject to judicial review: *Mahon* v. *Air New Zealand Ltd* [1984] AC 808; and likewise in Australia: *Ross* v. *Costigan* (1982) 41 ALR 319. See also *Peters* v. *Davison* [1999] 2 NZLR 164 (review for error of law).

[50] As in *Re Barnato* [1949] Ch 258; *Harrison* v. *Croydon London Borough Council* [1968] Ch 479.

[51] See below, p. 585.

[52] *Russian Commercial and Industrial Bank* v. *British Bank for Foreign Trade Ltd* [1921] 2 AC 438 at 448, summarising Scots law applicable in England. See *HM (Iraq) and anor* v. *Secretary of State for the Home Department* [2011] EWCA Civ 1536 (late withdrawal of legal aid meant that certain refugees were unrepresented in their appeal before the Upper Tribunal; there was no contradictor and inadequate steps taken by UT to secure representation; appeal upheld).

[53] As in *Ridge* v. *Baldwin* [1964] AC 40; above, p. 415.

[54] [1911] 1 KB 410, holding that the procedure was admissible: [1912] 1 Ch 158, holding that the demand was ultra vires. For a recent parallel see *R* v. *Customs and Excise Commissioners ex p Hedges and Butler Ltd* [1986] 2 All ER 164 (regulation allowing demand for all records of business held excessive and ultra vires; declaration granted).

proposals for a tax on land values, which the House of Lords rejected in 1909 with results disastrous to themselves. Under the Act as finally passed in 1910 the Commissioners of Inland Revenue were empowered to demand from landowners, under threat of penalty, factual information which could be used in valuing their lands. But the demands sent out (more than eight million) required in addition a statement of the annual value of the land, a demand not authorised by the Act. At the instance of a landowner, who brought proceedings against the Attorney-General, the Court of Appeal granted a declaration that the demands were wholly ineffective in law. By seeking a declaration the owner was able to take the initiative, and the court rejected the Crown's argument that his right course was to take no action and then dispute the demand when he was sued for the penalty. Fletcher Moulton LJ said:[55]

> So far from thinking that this action is open to objection on that score, I think that an action thus framed is the most convenient method of enabling the subject to test the justifiability of proceedings on the part of permanent officials purporting to act under statutory provisions. Such questions are growing more and more important, and I can think of no more suitable or adequate procedure for challenging the legality of such proceedings. It would be intolerable that millions of the public should have to choose between giving information to the Commissioners which they have no right to demand and incurring a severe penalty.

On the other hand, declarations cannot be granted merely because a party prefers to attack rather than defend. If that is his only motive, the court may say to him 'Wait until you are attacked and then raise your defence', and dismiss his action.[56] Nor, if a criminal prosecution has been instituted against him, can he ask for a declaration that he has committed no offence.[57] Everything therefore depends upon the merits of his motives for seeking this remedy. But the *Dyson* case gave a fair wind to the action for a declaration as a defensive weapon against the executive power.[58] As the quotation shows, the court considered that a question as to the legality of administrative action was in itself a good reason for asking for judicial intervention at the earliest possible moment. The decision is all the stronger for the fact that the Inland Revenue were not threatening any tort. They were merely making a demand which they had no power to make, and therefore no power to enforce.

Even where there is no immediate demand or threat, a declaration may be granted to settle some doubtful question of law on which an authoritative ruling is needed. One such case was where a company wished to know whether its quarrying operations required planning permission and obtained an emphatic judgment in their favour from the House of Lords.[59] In two other cases the House granted declarations to settle arguments about the legality of action recommended in circulars issued by government departments, which themselves had no direct legal force. One was where nurses were stated to be allowed to perform certain functions under the Abortion Act 1967.[60] The other was where doctors

---

[55] [1912] 1 Ch at 168.

[56] [1911] 1 KB at 417 (Cozens-Hardy MR). And see *Smeeton* v. *A-G* [1920] 1 Ch 85 at 96–8. This argument was rejected in *Ealing LBC* v. *Race Relations Board* [1972] AC 342, holding that the council need not wait for the board to start proceedings but could seek a declaration that their action was lawful.

[57] *Imperial Tobacco Ltd* v. *A-G* [1981] AC 718. And see *R (Taylor)* v. *Wigan and Leigh Magistrates Court* [2012] EWHC 1127 (advisory declaration sought; application described as 'hopeless').

[58] See the strong remarks of Farwell LJ, [1911] 1 KB at 424.

[59] *Pyx Granite Co Ltd* v. *Ministry of Housing and Local Government* [1960] AC 260, for which see below, p. 606.   [60] *Royal College of Nursing* v. *Department of Health and Social Security* [1981] AC 800.

were said to be entitled to give contraceptive advice to girls aged under 16 in certain circumstances without informing their parents.[61] In both cases the official advice was upheld, as it was also where a local authority sought a declaration that a government circular about the community charge omitted essential details.[62] But a local authority's press release was declared unlawful when it conflicted with statutory provisions for consumer protection.[63] In none of these cases did the court object on the ground that the circulars had no legal force.

Thanks to its flexibility and convenience the declaratory judgment has flourished as a general remedy in administrative law and has been used as a primary technique for extending judicial review. Before the reforms of 1977 this remedy was also preferred because it had important procedural advantages as compared with certiorari, as explained later.[64]

THE CROWN AND ITS SERVANTS

Throughout the case of *Dyson* v. *Attorney-General* the Court of Appeal emphasised that the declaration was granted against the Attorney-General, as representing the Crown. In fact the Act had conferred the power upon the Commissioners of Inland Revenue,[65] not upon the Crown itself, so that the decision conformed to the principle that officers of the Crown are subject to legal remedies whereas the Crown itself is immune.[66] Since statutory executive powers are almost always conferred on ministers in their own names, it is very common for a litigant to seek a declaration against a minister, with or without some other remedy, as a means of challenging some questionable act or order. If there is no obvious minister the Attorney-General may still be sued. Thus where a prince of Hanover wished to establish his claim to British nationality under the somewhat dubious authority of an Act of Queen Anne's reign, he obtained a declaration that he was a British subject by bringing an action against the Attorney-General.[67]

The immunity of the Crown itself is no longer intact, however, since at least some of the powers of the royal prerogative may now be challenged in proceedings for declarations in judicial review.[68] Actions for declarations have been entertained against the responsible minister or agent, as if the power belonged to the minister or agent rather than to the Crown.[69] Civil servants have thus been able to dispute the legality of their restriction or dismissal in proceedings against the minister for the civil service[70] or

---

[61] *Gillick* v. *West Norfolk and Wisbech Area Health Authority* [1986] AC 112. Lord Bridge there says (at 193) that the *Royal College of Nursing* case (above) effected 'a significant extension of the court's power of judicial review'; and the *Gillick* case is so treated by Sir John Donaldson MR in *R* v. *Panel on Takeovers and Mergers ex p Datafin plc* [1987] QB 815. But on this there is no clear majority view in the House of Lords. Nor is it clear why the case was not within the previous rules. For comment see (1986) 102 *LQR* 173 and below, p. 571.

[62] *R* v. *Secretary of State for the Environment ex p Greenwich LBC* [1989] COD 530. See also *R* v. *Deputy Governor, Parkhurst Prison ex p Hague* [1992] 1 AC 58 (prisons department circular declared contrary to prison rules). Contrast *R* v. *Home Secretary ex p Westminster Press Ltd* (1991) 4 Admin. LR 445. See (1992) 109 *LQR* at 462 (B. V. Harris).

[63] *R* v. *Liverpool City Council ex p Baby Products Association* [2000] COD 91 (warning against unsafe baby walkers). Contrast *R* v. *Inland Revenue Commissioners ex p Bishopp* (1999) 11 Admin. LR 575 (no review of pre-transaction rulings). [64] Below, p. 546.

[65] Today such an action would be brought against the Commissioners themselves.

[66] Below, p. 693. [67] *A-G* v. *Prince Ernest Augustus of Hanover* [1957] AC 436.

[68] Above, p. 288.

[69] *Pyx Granite Co Ltd* v. *Ministry of Housing and Local Government* [1960] AC 260 and *Congreve* v. *Home Office* [1976] QB 629 are notable examples.

[70] *Council of Civil Service Unions* v. *Minister for the Civil Service* [1985] AC 374 (prohibition of membership of trade unions).

the civil service appeal board even though their employer was the Crown itself;[71] and where the Crown was visitor to a university, a declaration could be sought against the Lord President of the Council as the relevant Crown agent.[72] In the expanding field of judicial review the declaration has proved to be a useful device for evading the short-comings of traditional remedies such as certiorari and mandamus, which do not lie against the Crown; and since the government will respect the court's decision, it is in practice equally effective.

Crown immunity has also been abolished in wide areas of liability by the Crown Proceedings Act 1947, under which the declaration plays an important part, as explained elsewhere.[73]

OTHER AUTHORITIES

Declarations are freely available against other authorities. A child's guardian may obtain a declaration that a county council is wrongly refusing to accept children in its schools,[74] a police officer may obtain a declaration that he has not been validly dismissed;[75] a dock worker may obtain a declaration that he has been wrongfully removed from the register, thereby preserving his right to employment under the dock labour scheme.[76] In principle, any act of a public authority may be challenged in declaratory proceedings claiming that it is ultra vires and void. Declarations have been granted against unlawful tax demands,[77] street works charges,[78] compulsory purchase orders,[79] conditions imposed on planning permission,[80] enforcement notices,[81] coast protection charges,[82] and threats of trespass under alleged rights of way.[83] The plaintiff must have the necessary standing to sue[84] and the case must not be one where the remedy is expressly or impliedly excluded by statute.[85] But otherwise there is no limit to the variety of ultra vires acts which can be challenged by the use of this flexible remedy. It has been held that the jurisdiction to grant it 'should receive as liberal a construction as possible'.[86] But the relief sought must always relate to 'rights and liabilities that are enforceable in the courts, and not merely moral, social or political rights or liabilities'.[87]

---

[71] R v. Civil Service Appeal Board ex p Bruce [1989] ICR 171 (unsuccessfully in both cases).

[72] R v. Hull University Visitor ex p Page [1993] AC 682. See also R v. Committee of the Lords of the Judicial Committee of the Privy Council ex p Vijayatunga [1990] 2 QB 444, entitled in the Law Reports 'R v. HM The Queen in Council…'.   [73] Below, p. 701.

[74] Gateshead Union Guardians v. Durham CC [1918] 1 Ch 146.

[75] Cooper v. Wilson [1937] 2 KB 309; Ridge v. Baldwin [1964] AC 40.

[76] Vine v. National Dock Labour Board [1957] AC 488.

[77] Bowles v. Bank of England [1913] 1 Ch 57; Dyson v. A-G [1912] 1 Ch 159.

[78] Elsdon v. Hampstead Borough Council [1905] 2 Ch 633.

[79] Grice v. Dudley Cpn [1958] Ch 329.

[80] Hall & Co Ltd v. Shoreham-by-Sea Urban District Council [1964] 1 WLR 240; and see Pyx Granite Co Ltd v. Ministry of Housing and Local Government [1960] AC 260.

[81] Francis v. Yiewsley & West Dayton Urban District Council [1958] 1 QB 478.

[82] Cullimore v. Lyme Regis Cpn [1962] 1 QB 718.   [83] Thornhill v. Weeks [1913] 1 Ch 438.

[84] See below, p. 585.   [85] See below, p. 605.

[86] Guaranty Trust Co of New York v. Hannay & Co [1915] 2 KB 536 at 572 (Bankes LJ).

[87] Malone v. Metropolitan Police Commissioner [1979] Ch 344 at 352 (Megarry V-C).

SPECIAL CASES: ADVISORY DECLARATIONS

Advisory declarations[88] are sought from time to time by parties keen to clarify a legal question not yet the subject of a dispute. There has been a distinct judicial reluctance in the past to give advisory judgments or opinions, particularly on the application of the government.[89]

But today it is clear that the courts do have the jurisdiction to make advisory declarations.[90] They are considered 'valuable tools... [but they] should be sparingly used. Their essential purposes are, first, to reduce the danger of administrative activities being declared illegal retrospectively, and, second, to assist public authorities by giving advice on legal questions which is then binding on all.'[91] There must be 'a serious justiciable issue' against a party with 'a true interest to oppose', or as the House of Lords has put it, 'a proper contradictor'.[92] Declarations that certain conduct is not a crime are only granted in 'truly exceptional cases'.[93]

Further useful applications of the declaration are for the determination of some disputed question of status;[94] for settling whether advice given in government circulars is correct in law;[95] for enabling a public authority to ascertain its own duties or powers;[96] and for the resolution of some dispute between two public authorities.[97] The Law Commission

---

[88]   i.e. a declaration sought prior to a dispute arising to clarify an important legal question. The question must be neither hypothetical (based upon facts that have not occurred and which may never occur) nor academic (having no practical purposes (such as the meaning of a repealed statute)). See Beatson, 'Prematurity and Ripeness for Review' in Forsyth and Hare (eds.), *The Golden Metwand and the Crooked Cord* (1998), 221 at 243ff. and Elvin [2006] *JR* 307.

[89]   The historical reasons for this are canvassed in Zamir and Woolf, *The Declaratory Judgment*, 4th edn (2011), para. 4.044. The reluctance may be gauged by the following words of Lord Diplock: 'the jurisdiction of the court is not to declare the law generally or to give advisory opinions; it is confined to declaring contested legal rights, subsisting or future, of the parties represented in the litigation before it and not those of anyone else' (*Gouriet* v. *Union of Post Office Workers* [1978] AC 435 at 501). And Elias LJ has said that where there is no contradictor the 'court is asked to determine the question of principle divorced from any plausible factual scenario in which the question might arise' (*R (Weaver)* v. *London & Quadrant Housing Trust* [2009] EWCA Civ 587, para. 90).

[90]   See e.g. *R* v. *The Secretary of State for Employment ex p the Equal Opportunities Commission* [1994] 2 WLR 409 (HL) (words 'advisory declarations' not used but a declaration was made where there was no formal decision under challenge). See also *Oxfordshire County Council* v. *Oxford City Council* [2006] UKHL 25, [2006] 2 WLR 1235, paras. 131 (Baroness Hale) and 97 (Lord Scott).

[91]   *R (CND)* v. *The Prime Minister of the UK* [2002] EWHC 2777 (Admin) in para. 46 (Simon Brown LJ). Declaration that UK in breach of UN resolution refused; 'domestic courts are the surety for the lawful exercise of public power only with regard to domestic law; they are not charged with policing United Kingdom's conduct on the international plain' (para. 36 (Simon Brown LJ)). Similarly *R (Al-Haq)* v. *Secretary of State for Foreign & Commonwealth Affairs* [2009] EWHC 1910 (no declaration that UK in the circumstances in breach of customary international law).

[92]   *Re S (hospital patient)* [1996] Fam. 1 citing the House of Lords. Here a friend, opposing a relative, was allowed to seek a declaration as to the right of custody of an incapacitated patient. Declarations about the treatment of incapacitated patients is the most common use of the advisory declaration, e.g. *Airedale NHS Trust* v. *Bland* [1993] AC 789.

[93]   *Imperial Tobacco Limited* v. *A-G* [1981] AC 718 (prosecution pending). And see *R (Rushbridger)* v. *A-G* [2003] UKHL 38, [2004] AC 357 (far-fetched attempt by journalists to obtain a declaration that the Treason Act 1848, s. 3 did not apply to persons like themselves who advocated republicanism without any intent to achieve this unlawfully or by force. There was no prosecution threatened (last prosecution under the 1848 Act was in 1880s); case insufficiently exceptional but it was equally hypothetical). See [2006] *JR* 36 (Robinson).   [94]   *A-G* v. *Prince Ernest Augustus of Hanover* (above).

[95]   As illustrated above, p. 481.   [96]   *Wimbledon & Putney Conservators* v. *Tuely* [1931] Ch 90.

[97]   e.g. *Gateshead Union Guardians* v. *Durham County Council* (above); *Surrey County Council* v. *Ministry of Education* [1953] 1 WLR 516; *R* v. *London Transport Executive ex p Greater London Council* [1983] QB 484 (GLC's policy of subsidising London transport fares declared lawful).

has in fact recommended that the High Court should be expressly empowered to grant advisory declarations.[98]

SPECIAL CASES: INTERIM DECLARATIONS

The courts have several times said that there is 'no such order known to English law as an interim declaration'.[99] The reason for this is that since a declaratory order 'has effect, between the parties to the proceedings in which it was made, as a conclusive definition of their legal rights, it should only be made as a final order. The notion of an interim declaration is…a contradiction in terms'.[100] CPR Part 25.1(1)(b), however, now provides that 'The court may grant…an interim declaration' thus trumping the common law's logic.[101] The principles on which the court may make an interim declaration are somewhat under-developed[102] but it seems the same principles as govern the grant of interim injunctions apply.[103] The advantage of this novel remedy is that while it is not coercive it does address the interim position.[104] Neither does it require the party seeking an interim declaration to give an undertaking in damages.[105] In addition it may be helpful when interim relief is sought pending a reference to the European Court to determine the compatibility of primary legislation with European law.[106] But interim declarations are only sporadically and rarely made.[107]

The interim declaration will prove useful where an interim injunction is excluded by statute[108] and in other circumstances too where early guidance from the courts on the correct course of conduct is required.[109]

OTHER MATTERS

Non-statutory authorities of certain kinds are now subject to judicial review and therefore to declaratory court orders. This development is discussed at the end of the next chapter.

[98] Law Com. No. 226, para. 8.12.

[99] Fox v. Riverside Health Trust (1993) 6 Admin. LR 250. See also R v. Secretary of State for the Environment ex p Royal Society for the Protection of Birds (1995) 7 Admin. LR 434 (HL).

[100] St George's Healthcare NHS Trust v. S [1998] 2 FLR 728 at 755. The phrase 'contradiction in terms' was used in this context by Diplock LJ said in International General Electric v. C&E Commissioners [1962] Ch 784 at 790. Upjohn LJ in the same case 'could not understand how there can be such an animal'.

[101] The introduction of the interim declaration had been recommended by the Law Commission in (Law Com. No. 226, Administrative Law: Judicial Review and Statutory Appeals (1994). Discussed [2001] JR 10 (Solomon).

[102] R v. Independent Television Commission ex p TVDanmark 1 Limited [2000] EWHC 389 (Admin) Mr Beatson QC granted an interim declaration where he found a 'prima facie case' (para. 32) of an error of law by the respondent.

[103] See above, p. 481.

[104] Lord Woolf in Re M [1994] AC 377 (see below, p. 704) 'saw advantages' in interim declarations (which were not then available) as avoiding the difficulty there encountered over issuing interim injunctions against ministers.

[105] Above, p. 481.

[106] See the discussion in Elliott, Beatson, Matthews and Elliott's Administrative Law: Text and Materials, 4th edn (2011), 416–19 discussing R v. Ministry of Agriculture Fisheries and Food ex p Monsanto plc [1998] QB 1161.

[107] Their most common use remains dealing with the treatment of patients with impaired mental capacity: The NHS Trust v. T [2004] EWHC 1279 (Fam).

[108] For instance, under the Crown Proceedings Act 1947, s. 21. See below, p. 703.

[109] Bank of Scotland v. A Ltd [2001] EWCA Civ 52; [2001] 1 WLR 751 (bank seeking guidance when client suspected of money laundering).

A declaration may also be sought against a statutory tribunal so as to challenge the validity of its decision—and, occasionally, to tell it positively what it ought to decide.[110] Although it has been suggested that, where the tribunal has merely to make a determination which it does not itself enforce, the proper defendant is not the tribunal but the person entitled to enforce the decision,[111] declarations have in several cases been granted against tribunals and similar bodies on account of decisions which were ultra vires.[112] There would seem to be no reason why this direct challenge should not be allowed, just as it is where the remedy is certiorari.

OFFICES AND EMPLOYMENTS

As explained earlier, the law will not specifically enforce a contract of service between master and servant: the master always has power to dismiss the servant, even though in breach of contract, and the servant's remedy is to sue for damages.[113] In special circumstances the court may depart from this rule,[114] but normally it is observed uniformly. Accordingly a dismissed employee cannot obtain a declaration that his dismissal was a nullity, for in that case his employment would still continue and the court would be enforcing the contract of employment specifically.[115] This does not mean that a declaration will never be granted to a dismissed employee: he may obtain a declaration that his dismissal was a breach of contract, thus establishing his right to damages.[116] But he cannot claim a declaration that will prolong his employment.

To this rule there now appears to be an exception in respect of dismissal procedures. Where a contract of employment provides rights of appeal or other procedural rights, the court may grant an injunction or declaration to prevent the employee being denied these rights.[117] This specific enforcement is akin to the enforcement of the principles of natural justice in such cases, as already explained.[118]

An office, as opposed to mere employment, may be protected specifically, as has also been seen above; and the same applies to a statutory status, such as that of a registered dock worker.[119] This is why police officers can be removed from their posts only by a valid exercise of the statutory power of dismissal.[120] On the same principle a declaration was granted against the dismissal of a schoolteacher on 'educational grounds' (as the Act

---

[110] As in *Barty-King* v. *Ministry of Defence* [1979] 2 All ER 80.

[111] *Anisminic Ltd* v. *Foreign Compensation Commission* [1968] 2 QB 862 at 911 (Diplock LJ).

[112] *Taylor* v. *National Assistance Board* [1957] P 101 at 111, affirmed [1958] AC 532; *Anisminic Ltd* v. *Foreign Compensation Commission* [1969] 2 AC 147; and see *Lee* v. *Showmen's Guild* [1952] 2 QB 329 at 346; *Barnard* v. *National Dock Labour Board* [1953] 2 QB 18 at 41; *Punton* v. *Ministry of Pensions and National Insurance (No 1)* [1963] 1 WLR 186; *(No 2)* [1964] 1 WLR 226.   [113] Above, p. 465.

[114] As in *Hill* v. *Parsons* [1972] Ch 305, where an injunction to enforce continuing employment was granted on the ground that damages were an inadequate remedy. The plaintiff had been dismissed under a closed shop policy, but might have been protected by the Industrial Relations Act 1971 coming into force within the period of notice to which he was entitled. See also *Taylor* v. *National Union of Seamen* [1976] 1 WLR 532; *Powell* v. *Brent LBC* [1988] ICR 176.

[115] *Barber* v. *Manchester Regional Hospital Board* [1958] 1 WLR 181 (doubted but corroborated as mentioned above, p. 541); *Francis* v. *Kuala Lumpur Councillors* [1962] 1 WLR 1411.

[116] This appears to be the explanation of *McClelland* v. *Northern Ireland General Health Services Board* [1957] 1 WLR 594, though it is only in the dissenting speech of Lord Keith (at 609) that the point appears clearly. The report is inadequate as to the relief sought.

[117] *R* v. *British Broadcasting Corporation ex p Lavelle* [1983] 1 WLR 23; *Irani* v. *Southampton Health Authority* [1985] ICR 590.   [118] Above, p. 539.

[119] *Barnard* v. *National Dock Labour Board* [1953] 2 QB 18; *Vine* v. *National Dock Labour Board* [1957] AC 488.   [120] *Cooper* v. *Wilson* [1937] 2 KB 309; *Ridge* v. *Baldwin* [1964] AC 40.

required) when no such grounds existed,[121] and against the dismissal of schoolteachers who had refused to collect money for pupils' meals, since the Education Act provided (as the court held) that teachers could not be required to act as collectors.[122] A limited statutory power of dismissal is one of the marks of a protected office or status. The ambiguous position of many public employees has been explained in the context of natural justice.[123]

In these employment cases injunctions are commonly sought and granted together with declarations and according to the same rules.[124]

DECLARATION IN RELATION TO PREROGATIVE REMEDIES

Since 1977 the remedies of declaration and injunction have become available interchangeably with the prerogative remedies of certiorari, prohibition and mandamus under the procedure of application for judicial review.[125] The scope of declaration and injunction is therefore now coextensive with that of those remedies as explained below under their respective titles. One example of this extended scope concerns non-statutory functions to which judicial review is now extended, as explained in a later place.[126] But it is no longer allowable to seek declarations against public authorities by the ordinary procedure of private law, as was freely allowed before 1977. They must be sought by the new procedure, which has created serious problems in the past.[127]

It was formerly a defect of the declaratory judgment that it was useless in cases of mere error on the face of the record, where the disputed determination was held to be intra vires but nevertheless liable to be quashed by certiorari.[128] Merely to declare that a determination was intra vires, even though mistaken, effected nothing; whereas certiorari 'quashed' and positively removed the offending determination out of the way. This difficulty was eliminated by the doctrine,[129] that every error of law by a tribunal amounts to excess of jurisdiction which necessarily means that an erroneous determination must be ultra vires, and a declaration to that effect will, as usual, invalidate it.

FITTING THE REMEDY TO THE CASE

In granting declarations, as they do so freely, the courts do not always observe that they may not fit the facts. An example was where a probationer police officer had resigned from the force under an unjustified threat of dismissal. The Court of Appeal granted him a declaration that the chief constable's decision to dismiss him was void, despite the fact that the chief constable's only legal power was to dismiss, which in fact he did not do, and he had no specific power to make a decision.[130] On appeal the House of Lords substituted a different declaration, recognising that the Court of Appeal's order could not effect the probationer's reinstatement, and that an order of mandamus was the only satisfactory remedy.[131] This case

---

[121] *Martin* v. *Eccles Cpn* [1919] 1 Ch 387 (a touching story).

[122] *Price* v. *Sunderland Cpn* [1956] 1 WLR 1253; and see *Smith* v. *Macnally* [1912] 1 Ch 816; *Sadler* v. *Sheffield Cpn* [1924] 1 Ch 483; *Gorse* v. *Durham CC* [1971] 1 WLR 775; *Jones* v. *Lee* [1980] ICR 310.

[123] Above, p. 538.   [124] See cases in n. 120 above.   [125] Below, p. 648.

[126] Below, p. 635.   [127] For which see below, p. 659.

[128] Above, p. 268. The defect was established in *Punton* v. *Ministry of Pensions and National Insurance (No 2)* [1964] 1 WLR 226.   [129] See above, p. 264.

[130] *Chief Constable of North Wales Police* v. *Evans* [1982] 1 WLR 1155 (application for judicial review).

[131] See at 1165 (Lord Bridge) and 1176 (Lord Brightman). But mandamus was not awarded because 'it might border on usurpation of the powers of the chief constable' (at 1176, Lord Brightman). So the proper remedy was withheld in discretion.

may be classed with others, explained below,[132] where there has been a misfit between the remedy and the case because it was supposed that every administrative power was a power of decision.

DISCRETIONARY REMEDY

Finally, and most importantly, the declaration is a discretionary remedy. The court may refuse it if it thinks fit, for example if persons who are directly interested in the proceedings are not joined as parties.[133] But this characteristic is best explained later, since injunction, declaration and the prerogative orders are all discretionary remedies, and the same principles govern them all.[134]

RELATOR ACTIONS

A HYBRID PROCEDURE

A relator action is an action brought by the Attorney-General at the relation (i.e. at the instance) of some other person claiming an injunction or declaration, or both,[135] in order to prevent some breach of the law. By lending his name for this purpose the Attorney-General enabled the injunction and declaration, which were basically remedies for the protection of private rights,[136] to be converted into remedies of public law for the protection of the public interest. They thus acquired a hybrid character even before the reforms of 1977 discussed in Chapter 19.

ATTORNEY-GENERAL'S ROLE

The Attorney-General may if he prefers act independently, ex officio.[137] But in practice he acts at the instance of the relator, whom he requires to instruct solicitor and counsel, who must certify that the statement of claim is proper for the Attorney-General's acceptance and that the relator will be responsible for costs.[138] Once the Attorney-General has accepted, 'he virtually drops out of the proceedings…the actual conduct of the proceedings is entirely in the hands of the relator who is responsible for the costs of the action'.[139] Having conferred the necessary standing on the relator, therefore, the Attorney-General shows no further concern with the public interest, but leaves the case to proceed like private litigation.

It has long been axiomatic that it rests entirely in the discretion of the Attorney-General to decide whether or not he will lend his name.[140] But what rules, if any, the

---

[132] Below, p. 609.   [133] *London Passenger Transport Board* v. *Moscrop* [1942] AC 332.

[134] Below, p. 694.

[135] Most commonly an injunction. An example of declaration is *A-G ex rel Tilley* v. *Wandsworth LBC* [1981] 1 WLR 854.

[136] A plaintiff may sue in his own name where interference with a public right causes him special damage: *Boyce* v. *Paddington Borough Council* [1903] 1 Ch 109.

[137] The reason why this was not in practice done has been said to be that there was no satisfactory system for awarding costs prior to the Administration of Justice (Miscellaneous Provisions) Act 1933, s. 7: *Hoffmann-La Roche* v. *Secretary of State for Trade & Industry* [1975] AC 295 at 363 (Lord Diplock).

[138] *A-G ex rel McWhirter* v. *Independent Broadcasting Authority* [1973] QB 629 at 647 (Lord Denning MR). The relator may be joined as a party in suitable cases.   [139] As preceding note.

[140] *London County Council* v. *A-G* [1902] AC 165 at 169 (Lord Halsbury LC). For a modern example, see *R* v. *Solicitor-General ex p Taylor* [1995] COD 61.

Attorney-General follows for this purpose are not known. There is no published information about his practice,[141] which can only be guessed from the reported cases in which he has consented to act. It seems that he will normally lend his name where the proceedings are against a local authority, and perhaps also where a local authority is the relator. It seems also that he never does so where the proceedings are against a minister or a department of the central government. The relator action is therefore a one-sided as well as an uncertain procedure: it is a weapon in the hands of the central government which is made available on unspecified grounds against local and other subordinate authorities, but not against the central government itself.

A relator action may be brought against a public authority that is acting, or threatening to act, ultra vires; and equally it may be brought against any private individual or body who is committing a public nuisance or otherwise violating public law.[142] The commonest defendants to relator actions are local authorities, particularly where ratepayers challenge the validity of their local authority's expenditure, suing under the Attorney-General's name.

Relator actions fall outside the Crown Proceedings Act 1947, so that their scope and procedure remain unchanged.[143]

LOCAL AUTHORITIES

There is a standardised practice by which a ratepayer may dispute the validity of the local authority's expenditure in a relator action, sometimes called a 'ratepayer's action'. A typical case was where the London County Council, being empowered by statute to purchase and operate tramways, purchased a tramway company and also carried on a bus service which the company had run. The proprietors of a rival bus service, who were also ratepayers, caused the Attorney-General to sue for an injunction against the operation of buses by the Council, which was duly granted.[144] The Attorney-General appears to allow actions against local authorities with a free hand. In one case a local authority, after there had been much fire and flood damage on its housing estates, made a contract with an insurance company for the collective insurance of its tenants' effects. The staff trade union of a rival insurance company, acting apparently merely in their own interests as its employees, were allowed to bring a relator action challenging the legality of the contract— which was in fact held lawful.[145] The Court of Appeal expressed some curiosity as to these proceedings, but held that they could not question the Attorney-General's practice or the relator's standing.

Whether it was necessary for ratepayers to resort to relator actions in such cases became uncertain when in 1954 the Court of Appeal awarded a declaration to a ratepayer suing in his own name.[146] But the Court made no mention of the question of standing, and it has

---

[141] In the *McWhirter* case (above) at 656 Lawton LJ said: 'In the course of this hearing the Attorney-General gave the court information about the attitude which he and his predecessors in modern times have taken towards relator actions.... Much of this information is not available, as far as I know, in any of the practitioners' textbooks.'

[142] But it is not available to a local authority against breach of contract or covenant by the other party, for which the local authority should sue in its own name: *A-G ex rel Scotland* v. *Barratt* (1990) 60 P & CR 475.

[143] See s. 23(3).

[144] *London County Council* v. *A-G* [1902] AC 165. See similarly *A-G* v. *Fulham Cpn* [1921] 1 Ch 440 (expenditure on municipal laundry ultra vires).

[145] *A-G* v. *Crayford Urban District Council* [1962] Ch 575.

[146] *Prescott* v. *Birmingham Cpn* [1955] Ch 210; above, p. 341. *Bradbury* v. *Enfield Borough Council* [1967] 1 WLR 1311 (see above, p. 479) appears to be a comparable case.

since been held that the decision was inadvertent and not, on this question, a precedent to be followed.[147] A ratepayer may be able to proceed unassisted under the procedure of application for judicial review, explained later, provided that he can obtain the leave of the court.[148] But whether this new avenue is open to him has not yet been established.

Local authorities have now been given a special statutory power to take action for the benefit of their areas. Formerly they could not bring proceedings for the general public benefit without the assistance of the Attorney-General, unless their own rights of property were in some way affected.[149] The courts rejected claims by local authorities, suing by themselves, for injunctions against public nuisances,[150] against obstruction of highways,[151] and against the withdrawal of bus services.[152] For such purposes local authorities therefore needed to use relator actions. However, the Local Government Act 1972[153] now provides as follows:

> Where a local authority deem it expedient for the promotion or protection of the interests of the inhabitants of their area, they may prosecute or defend or appear in any legal proceedings and, in the case of civil proceedings, may institute them in their own name.

These words have been held to remove the difficulty, so that a local authority[154] is able to obtain an injunction against unlawful Sunday trading merely in its own name.[155] As a rule, therefore, the Attorney-General's consent will no longer be needed in such cases. Local authorities can also take proceedings against statutory nuisances in their own name under the Public Health Act 1936.[156]

As regards injunctions for enforcing obedience to statute, as explained below,[157] a local authority has been held to have no power to proceed in its own name, even to enforce its own byelaws.[158] But this also may now be permitted by the Act of 1972, assuming that the enforcement of the criminal law by injunction counts as 'civil proceedings'.

WHERE THE ATTORNEY-GENERAL DECLINES TO ACT

It has been laid down by decisions of the House of Lords that if the Attorney-General declines to consent to a relator action, the court cannot question his exercise of his discretion nor can it allow a private person to sue in his own name merely in the capacity of a member of the public. In 1977 the House had occasion to disapprove two dramatic decisions in which the Court of Appeal had attempted to throw open the door to the public-spirited citizen wishing to prevent a breach of the law by a public authority. In the first of these it was held that if the Attorney-General refused leave in a proper case, or his machinery worked too slowly, an offended or injured member of the public could in the

---

[147] *Barrs* v. *Bethell* [1982] Ch 294 (Warner J). And see *Collins* v. *Lower Hutt City Cpn* [1961] NZLR 250; *Cowan* v. *Canadian Broadcasting Cpn* (1966) 56 DLR (2d) 578.   [148] Below, p. 550.

[149] *Thorne Rural District Council* v. *Bunting* [1972] Ch 470.

[150] *Prestatyn Urban District Council* v. *Prestatyn Raceway Ltd* [1970] 1 WLR 33.

[151] *Hampshire County Council* v. *Shonleigh Nominees Ltd* [1970] 1 WLR 865.

[152] *Sinfield* v. *London Transport Executive* [1970] Ch 550.   [153] s. 222.

[154] But not a local development corporation: *London Docklands Development Cpn* v. *Rank Hovis Ltd* (1985) 84 LGR 101.

[155] *Solihull Council* v. *Maxfern Ltd* [1977] 1 WLR 127; *Stoke-on-Trent City Council* v. *B & Q (Retail) Ltd* [1984] AC 754; *Barking and Dagenham LBC* v. *Essexplan Ltd* (1982) 81 LGR 408. See likewise *Burnley BC* v. *England* (1978) 76 LGR 393 (breach of byelaw excluding dogs from parks); *Kent CC* v. *Batchelor (No 2)* [1979] 1 WLR 213 (enforcement of tree preservation orders); *City of London Cpn* v. *Bovis Construction Ltd* [1992] 3 All ER 697 (injunction against noise nuisance while prosecution pending).   [156] s. 100.

[157] Below, p. 496.   [158] *Devonport Cpn* v. *Tozer* [1903] 1 Ch 759.

last resort apply to the court himself. Lord Denning MR said that it was a matter of high constitutional principle that the court should thus assist to stop a government department or public authority transgressing the law. But these remarks were *obiter*, since before final judgment was given the Attorney-General intervened and lent his name to the proceedings. The relator's complaint was that the Independent Broadcasting Authority was about to allow the transmission of an indecent television programme, contrary to its statutory duty to see that programmes did not offend against good taste and decency.[159]

The second case was an attempt by a private citizen to restrain a threatened breach of the criminal law by trade unions, when unions of post office workers were planning to boycott communications with South Africa, despite the fact that improper interference with mail and telegrams is a statutory offence.[160] The Attorney-General declined to proceed, but Lord Denning MR held that an injunction could be granted at the suit of a private plaintiff and the other members of the court were willing to grant declaratory relief. The House of Lords reversed this decision and disapproved the remarks in the earlier case.[161] They held that to act in the public interest was the Attorney-General's exclusive right. His role was substantial and constitutional and he was free to consider the public interest generally and widely. He was therefore free to take account of any circumstances, political or otherwise. His decision was not subject to judicial review.[162]

This decision contained sweeping remarks about the Attorney-General's exclusive right to represent the public interest; and for a time it seemed that the House of Lords had administered a sharp check to the tendency towards liberality in allowing it to be vindicated by private citizens. But later events have shown otherwise. This must be explained in another place[163] as part of the law of standing, which the House of Lords has put upon a new and more generous basis, following procedural reforms in the law of remedies. Their above-mentioned decision, it now appears, ought to be confined to its peculiar subject matter, which is the use of civil proceedings for the purpose of enforcing the criminal law. That is a highly abnormal procedure and there may be good reasons for allowing only the Attorney-General to employ it.

OBSERVATIONS ON THE RELATOR ACTION

The relator action is one of the useful devices, like the prerogative remedies, by which the Crown's procedural privileges have been made available to the ordinary citizen, to the advantage not only of himself but of the public interest. It imposes a measure of control on situations where otherwise any number of members of the public might attempt to bring uncoordinated actions, resulting in general confusion. Basically it is a regulated form of *actio popularis*, available to all and sundry whom the Attorney-General is willing to assist; and his practice appears to be cooperative, save only where the complaint is against the central government or where he is unwilling to act for political reasons.

Nevertheless the situation is far from logical.[164] In effect, the Attorney-General himself determines the plaintiff's standing to sue. But this is a matter which should be determined

---

[159] *A-G ex rel McWhirter* v. *Independent Broadcasting Authority* [1973] QB 629. After viewing the programme the court refused relief. See also *Wilson* v. *Independent Broadcasting Authority* (below), an interesting Scots parallel.   [160] For injunctions in aid of the criminal law see below, p. 496.

[161] *Gouriet* v. *Union of Post Office Workers* [1978] AC 435. For discussion see Edwards, *The Attorney-General, Politics and the Public Interest*, 129 and 140.

[162] See ibid. at 478 (Lord Wilberforce). For a review of authorities see *R* v. *Solicitor-General ex p Taylor* (1995) 8 Admin. LR 206.   [163] Below, p. 584.

[164] See the criticisms of Ormrod LJ in *Gouriet* v. *Union of Post Office Workers* [1977] QB 729 at 776.

by known rules of law, and not by the undisclosed practice of a minister of the Crown. Nor is there any logic in withholding this remedy against the central government, as seems to be the present practice. The use of the relator action has therefore been an impediment to the development of satisfactory rules of law as to the ability of citizens to litigate in the general public interest. There is no such system in Scots law, which allows individuals with very general interests (e.g. as voters or members of political bodies) to sue on their own account in order to prevent breach by a public body of a duty owed by that body to the public.[165]

Now, however, the House of Lords has provided a prospect of a more uniform and liberal system under the new procedure of application for judicial review, whereby the public-spirited citizen may be enabled 'to vindicate the rule of law' in his own name, unimpeded by 'outdated technical rules of locus standi'.[166] This generous judicial policy has much reduced the need for relator actions, which are now scarce items in the law reports.

ENFORCEMENT OF OBEDIENCE TO STATUTE

It remains to mention a very different use of the relator action, where it operates not as a defence against the abuse of authority, but as a weapon in the hands of authority to prevent the deliberate and flagrant disregard of statute. The Attorney-General, acting on the application of a local authority or other relator, may apply for an injunction to prevent contravention of statute, or abuse of statutory rights, by any offending person. Disobedience then becomes contempt of court, punishable by fine and imprisonment in the court's discretion. The typical situation is where there are repeated offences and the statutory penalties are not an adequate deterrent.[167]

In one case the defendant had often broken the provisions of the Town and Country Planning Act by using his land as a site for caravans without permission. He refused to pay fines, and was eventually sentenced to imprisonment for non-payment. But the local planning authority also moved the Attorney-General to apply for an injunction to prohibit illegal use of the land, and the injunction was granted.[168] It was held that there was jurisdiction to grant this additional remedy to prevent violation of the public policy enforced by the Act, and the fact that the Act contained its own provisions for enforcement did not fetter the Attorney-General's discretion, as an administrative matter, to ask for an injunction either as an alternative to or in addition to the statutory penalties.[169]

The Attorney-General, acting for a local authority, was granted an injunction to restrain the use of a hotel without a certificate of fire precautions.[170] The local authority was prosecuting the owner as the Act authorised in a magistrates' court, but was concerned at a serious fire risk during the period before the charge could be heard. Lord Denning MR said:

---

[165] *Wilson v. Independent Broadcasting Authority*, 1979 SLT 279 (interdict granted against IBA to prevent broadcasting of one-sided political programmes). Contrast *Scottish Old People's Welfare Council, Petitioners*, 1987 SLT 179.   [166] See below, p. 589.

[167] See *A-G v. Harris* [1961] 1 QB 74, where a flower-seller with over a hundred convictions for obstruction, punishable only by fine, was restrained by injunction from offending again—and offended again and was committed for contempt of court. For an account of this case see Edwards, *The Law Officers of the Crown*, 290.   [168] *A-G v. Bastow* [1957] 1 QB 514.

[169] See similarly *Runnymede BC v. Ball* [1986] 1 WLR 353.

[170] *A-G v. Chaudry* [1971] 1 WLR 1614. And see *Stafford Borough Council v. Elkenford Ltd* [1977] 1 WLR 324.

Whenever Parliament has enacted a law and given a particular remedy for the breach of it, such remedy being in an inferior court, nevertheless the High Court always has reserve power to enforce the law so enacted by way of an injunction or declaration or other suitable remedy. The High Court has jurisdiction to ensure obedience to the law whenever it is just and convenient to do so.

It is not only in the case of repeated offences that this jurisdiction may be invoked. But mere infringement of the criminal law is not enough: it must be shown that the offender is deliberately and flagrantly flouting it.[171]

Now that local authorities can bring proceedings in their own name they can dispense with the assistance of the Attorney-General, as already explained.[172]

Whether it is right to increase statutory penalties by the use of injunctions is a debatable question. The House of Lords have more than once emphasised that this remedy should be regarded as anomalous and exceptional, since it is not normally for the civil courts to enforce the criminal law, to increase statutory penalties, and to convict (in effect) on a civil standard of proof.[173] As Lord Templeman has said:[174]

> Where Parliament imposes a penalty for an offence, Parliament must consider that the penalty is adequate and Parliament can increase the penalty if it proves to be inadequate. It follows that a local authority should be reluctant to seek and the court should be reluctant to grant an injunction which if disobeyed may involve the infringer in sanctions far more onerous than the penalty imposed for the offence.

The House of Lords have also emphasised that the procedure is one which only the Attorney-General can put into motion (save where statute provides otherwise).

ENFORCEMENT OF DUTIES

PUBLIC DUTIES

As well as illegal action, by excess or abuse of power, there may be illegal inaction, by neglect of duty.[175] Public authorities have a great many legal duties, under which they have an obligation to act, as opposed to their legal powers, which give them discretion whether to act or not. The remedies so far investigated deal with the control of powers. The remedies for the enforcement of duties are necessarily different. The most important of them, mandamus, belongs among the prerogative remedies in the next chapter. The 'ordinary' remedies noted here play only a minor part.

CRIMINAL PROSECUTION

The natural way for a statute to enforce a public duty in the case of a private person is to invoke the criminal law, for example by making it an offence to fail to make an income-tax return. The common law took the same approach to the problem of making public authorities carry out their duties. Wilful neglect of a public duty was held to be an

---

[171] *Stoke-on-Trent City Council* v. *B & Q Ltd* [1984] AC 754. See also *Nottingham City Council* v. *Zain* [2001] EWCA Civ 1248, [2002] 1 WLR 607 (local authority seeking to restrain criminal activities which also constituted a public nuisance).　　　　　　　　　　　　　　　　　　　　[172] Above, p. 493.

[173] *Gouriet* v. *Union of Post Office Workers* [1978] AC 435; *Stoke-on-Trent CC* v. *B & Q Ltd* (above).

[174] In the *Stoke-on-Trent* case (above).　　　　[175] See Harding, *Public Duties and Public Law*.

indictable offence, punishable by fine or imprisonment.[176] It was impossible, of course, to indict the Crown.[177] But the inhabitants of counties, townships and parishes were often indicted for failure to repair highways and bridges. When these duties were transferred to statutory highway authorities, it was possible to indict them also. The legal basis of this procedure was that a public nuisance (a crime) had been perpetrated. But in 1959 it was abolished in favour of statutory proceedings which anyone may institute against the highway authority, with the ultimate sanction that the complainant may carry out the work himself and recover the cost from the defaulting authority.[178]

It was often laid down in the past that disobedience of a statute or neglect of the duties of a public office was a criminal offence unless Parliament had provided some other sanction or remedy.[179] This is illustrated by the decision that an indictment would lie against an overseer of the poor for not receiving a pauper under a justices' order;[180] and by the case of a magistrate who was indicted, but acquitted, for failing to take proper steps to suppress a riot.[181] Where the duty was statutory the offence was sometimes called contempt of statute. Indictment is obviously an unsatisfactory remedy, and has not often been used in recent times.[182] Modern statutes are not to be presumed to create criminal offences unless they do so clearly, and the doctrine of contempt of statute is regarded as obsolete.[183]

PRIVATE LAW REMEDIES

The ordinary remedies of private law are sometimes effective in case of breach of duty by public authorities. Actions for damages play an important part where breach of statutory duty is held to be an actionable wrong, as explained in the chapter on liability of public authorities.[184]

Injunctions are in general not used. To enforce a duty requires a mandatory injunction, which the court will grant only where the duty is owed to the plaintiff personally, i.e. where he has a legal right to protect. Thus the court made a mandatory order against the police for the return of passports and other documents which were being detained unlawfully.[185] Although there is no reason in principle why a mandatory injunction should not be granted against a public authority, the prerogative remedy of mandamus is usually more suitable, particularly since the procedure is quicker and the rules as to standing are less strict. Where the duty is owed to the public generally and not to the plaintiff personally an injunction to enforce performance of a duty will not be granted.[186]

[176] See *R* v. *Hall* [1891] 1 QB 747, reviewing authorities; Holdsworth, *History of English Law*, x. 147.

[177] Nevertheless Dowdell, *A Hundred Years of Quarter Sessions*, 125, records an indictment against the King in 1670 for non-repair of Hampton Bridge; but it was 'not pressed'.

[178] Highways Act 1959, s. 59, replaced by Highways Act 1980, s. 56.

[179] Co. Inst. ii. 163; Bl. Comm. iv. 122 and other authorities cited in *R* v. *Horseferry Road Justices ex p Independent Broadcasting Authority* [1987] QB 54.   [180] *R* v. *Davis* (1754) Sayer 163.

[181] *R* v. *Pinney* (1832) 3 B & Ad 947.

[182] An example is *R* v. *Dytham* [1979] QB 722 (alleged failure by police officer to stop fight).

[183] *R* v. *Horseferry Road Justices* (above) where the court quashed a summons issued against the IBA for breach of statutory duty in respect of a television programme. The Law Commission have recommended the abolition of the doctrine (Law Com. No. 76 (1976), p. 142).   [184] Below, p. 660.

[185] *Ghani* v. *Jones* [1970] 1 QB 693.

[186] *Glossop* v. *Heston and Isleworth Local Board* (1879) 12 Ch D 102; *Bradbury* v. *Enfield London Borough Council* (1967) 1 WLR 1311; *Wood* v. *Ealing London Borough Council* [1967] Ch 364 (see under default powers, below).

In principle, also, there is no reason why the plaintiff should not seek a declaratory judgment, i.e. a declaration, that a public authority has some legal duty towards him personally. This has occasionally been done successfully.[187] But in accordance with the general rule that a declaration can only declare the legal position of the plaintiff, he will have to show that it is to himself particularly that the duty is owed.[188]

GENERAL AND SPECIFIC DUTIES

A *power* enables an authority to do what would otherwise be illegal or ineffective. It is always subject to legal limits, and it is safe to assume that Parliament did not intend it to be exercised beyond those limits. A *duty*, on the other hand, may or may not be legally enforceable.[189] Parliament has become fond of imposing duties of a kind which, since they are of a general and indefinite character, are perhaps to be considered as political duties rather than as legal duties which a court could enforce. Many such duties may be found in statutes concerned with social services and nationalisation. Thus the opening words of the National Health Service Act 1977 are

> It is the Secretary of State's duty to continue the promotion in England and Wales of a comprehensive health service...

The Coal Industry Nationalisation Act 1946 charged the Coal Board with the duties of 'working and getting coal in Great Britain', 'making supplies of coal available', and so on. Current legislation furnishes an abundance of such examples.

Only in the unlikely event of its making total default would any of the above-mentioned authorities be at risk of legal compulsion in respect of its general duties. But as soon as duties become sufficiently specific, the courts do not shrink from enforcing them. This was shown dramatically by the House of Lords and the Court of Appeal when they quashed the supplementary rate levied by the Greater London Council for the purpose of subsidising passenger transport in London.[190] The Council had power to subsidise the London Transport Executive, but they also had a duty to have regard to the Executive's own duties, which required it not to accumulate deficits and to operate with due regard to economy. The Council's general duty was to promote the provision of 'integrated, efficient and economic transport facilities' in London. But in calling upon the Executive to lower its fares, thereby accumulating a large deficit, the Council was in breach of its duty to have regard to the Executive's duties, as well as in breach of its fiduciary duty to its ratepayers.[191] The courts analysed the amalgam of general and specific duties and powers in the Transport (London) Act 1969, concluding that the Executive had a duty to minimise avoidable losses and the council a duty not to prevent them from doing so.

---

[187] As in *Gateshead Union* v. *Durham County Council* [1918] 1 Ch 146.
[188] *Clark* v. *Epsom Rural District Council* [1929] 1 Ch 287.
[189] The Post Office's general duties are expressly made unenforceable: Post Office Act 1969, s. 9(4): above, p. 114.　　　　　　　　　　　　　　　[190] *Bromley LBC* v. *Greater London Council* [1983] 1 AC 768.
[191] For the latter duty see above, p. 340.

16

PREROGATIVE REMEDIES

REMEDIES OF PUBLIC LAW

NATURE OF PREROGATIVE REMEDIES

We enter now the realm of the prerogative remedies, and we meet something like a system of public law. These are remedies which, if not always designed from the first for the control of governmental duties and powers, have long been in use for that purpose especially. Their hallmark is that they are granted at the suit of the Crown, as the title of every case indicates. They are 'prerogative' because they were originally available only to the Crown and not to the subject. By obtaining orders of the court in the form of mandamus, certiorari or prohibition, the Crown could ensure that public authorities carried out their duties, and that inferior tribunals kept within their proper jurisdiction. These were essentially remedies for ensuring efficiency and maintaining order in the hierarchy of courts, commissions and authorities of all kinds.

By the end of the sixteenth century these remedies had become generally available to ordinary litigants (some had done so much earlier), and an applicant could begin proceedings in the Crown's name without seeking any permission or authority.[1] The Crown lent its legal prerogatives to its subjects in order that they might collaborate to ensure good and lawful government. Habeas corpus would test the legality of any prisoner's detention at his own or some friend's instance. Certiorari and prohibition were designed for preventing the usurpation or abuse of power of inferior bodies, judicial and administrative alike. These three remedies played a most important part in the development of administrative law. By a process of evolution characteristic of our legal history, the Crown's prerogative powers have been converted into machinery for the protection of the subject.

Nowadays all these remedies issue from the High Court and they must still be sought by a special form of procedure.[2] They are all discretionary remedies, with the exception of habeas corpus. They are the prerogative orders.[3] The procedural peculiarities of the prerogative remedies were formerly important since they entailed certain disadvantages as compared with the remedies of private law such as declaration and injunction.[4] The procedural reforms introduced by Civil Procedure Rules Part 54[5] changed the names of the specific prerogative orders most used in judicial review. Certiorari becomes a 'quashing

---

[1] For the history of the prerogative remedies see Henderson, *Foundations of English Administrative Law*; de Smith, *Judicial Review of Administrative Action*, 3rd edn, Appendix. This appendix does not appear in the most recent editions of de Smith. But much the same ground is covered in S. A. de Smith, 'The Prerogative Writs' (1951–3) 11 *CLJ* 40. [2] For this see below, p. 546.

[3] Previously they were the prerogative writs. See Administration of Justice (Miscellaneous Provisions) Act 1938, s. 7, replaced by Senior Courts Act 1981, s. 29. Habeas corpus, which was too sacred to be tampered with, remains a writ. [4] Below, p. 546.

[5] Discussed below, p. 550.

order', prohibition a 'prohibiting order' and mandamus becomes a 'mandatory order'.[6] The writ of habeas corpus is untouched.

There were other prerogative writs which could be used at the instance of a subject, such as scire facias for rescinding royal charters and grants, and ne exeat regno for preventing a subject from leaving the realm. The latter writ seems now to be obsolete as a weapon of the Crown, but it is still in use by ordinary litigants as a remedy to prevent a debtor from absconding, if the applicant can show that the debtor's absence from the realm would materially prejudice him.[7] It has been suggested also that the writ might prove useful in public law as a means of preventing an immigrant being deported before his application to the court has been decided.[8] The modern use of the writ is yet another instance of the conversion of the Crown's legal armoury into remedies beneficial to the subject.

The remedies to be discussed first are habeas corpus (together with its human rights counterpart), certiorari (the quashing order) and prohibition (the prohibiting order). These are grouped together since they are all remedies for the control of powers. Mandamus (the mandatory order) then follows, being the primary remedy for enforcing public duties.

HABEAS CORPUS

THE HISTORIC WRIT

The writ of habeas corpus[9] plays a part in administrative law, since some administrative authorities and tribunals have powers of detention. The cases most likely to arise are those where some person is detained as an illegal immigrant or in order that he may be deported, or as being of unsound mind. A writ of habeas corpus challenging the legality of the detention is the traditional means of challenging the validity of the administrative order which caused it. If the court orders the applicant's release, that in effect quashes the order, an additional certiorari for this purpose being unnecessary.[10]

Prized and historic though it is, the remedy of habeas corpus, with its problems and technicalities as described in the following pages, may be destined to give place to the much simpler, more direct and more comprehensive provision for 'the right to liberty and security' conferred by Article 5 of the Human Rights Convention under the Human Rights Act 1998. Although those provisions have nothing to do with any prerogative writ, they are most conveniently explained alongside habeas corpus so that the remedies protecting personal liberty may be seen together. The text of Article 5 is given in Appendix 2 and it will be discussed at the end of this account of the ancient writ.

The procedural deficiencies of the prerogative remedies, to be noticed later, were particularly acute in the case of habeas corpus. No right of appeal used to exist against refusal of the writ in cases of imprisonment where there was a charge of a criminal nature—a grave

---

[6] Reading the decided cases will require, for some time to come, knowledge of both names and it would be anachronistic to use the new names in old contexts. Hence the old names have not been systematically excised from this book. Furthermore, the old names are frequently used in quotations from judgments; it would be inappropriate to 'update' these. Readers will simply have to be familiar with both the old and new names.

[7] Felton v. Callis [1969] 1 QB 200, where Megarry J explains the history and modern application of the writ. In Parsons v. Burk [1971] NZLR 244 the writ was refused to a private litigant who wished to prevent a New Zealand football team from visiting South Africa.

[8] R v. Home Secretary ex p Muboyayi [1992] 1 QB 244 at 258 (Lord Donaldson MR).

[9] See Sharpe, Habeas Corpus, 3rd edn with A. D. R. Zellick (2010) and P. Halliday, Habeas Corpus from England to Empire (2010).   [10] Below, p. 505.

and irrational defect which was not remedied until 1960.[11] Likewise there was no appeal against the issue of the writ, i.e. against the release of the prisoner. Here again the Act of 1960 provided for appeal and empowered the court, in a criminal case, to order the detention of the prisoner meanwhile;[12] but in a civil case the prisoner was to be released at once,[13] and the only use of the appeal was to allow the authorities to test the correctness of the decision.[14] The Act did not alter the old rule against disputing the facts stated in the gaoler's return to the writ,[15] but this was in practice allowed by admitting evidence of the facts before the writ was issued,[16] and in civil cases the rule was expressly abolished by the Habeas Corpus Act 1816.[17]

The famous Habeas Corpus Act 1679, designed to prevent various abuses including prolonged imprisonment on criminal charges without bail, was drawn so specifically in terms of seventeenth-century procedure that some of its safeguards were probably ineffective in modern conditions.[18] But these are matters of little significance in practice. The courts can usually be relied upon to find their way round anachronistic obstacles. The writ may be applied for by any prisoner, or by anyone acting on his behalf, without regard to nationality, since 'every person within the jurisdiction enjoys the equal protection of our laws'.[19] It may be directed against the gaoler, often the appropriate prison governor, or against the authority ordering the detention, e.g. the Home Secretary.[20] The writ will issue not only against the custodian or the authority ordering detention, but also against anyone who has 'the reasonable prospect of being able to exert control over [the detainee's] custody or to secure his production to the court'.[21]

The writ is not discretionary, and it cannot therefore be denied because there may be some alternative remedy.[22] Nor is leave of any kind required before it can be sought: it issues as of right.[23] There is no time limit. The defence will not always be statutory. There

---

[11]   Administration of Justice Act 1960, s. 15, amended by the Access to Justice Act 1999, s. 65.

[12]   ss. 5, 15. In some Commonwealth countries there may still be no appeal, as in the case of the Trinidad rebellion: *A-G of Trinidad and Tobago* v. *Phillip* [1995] 1 AC 396 (PC). Absence of appeal from the grant of the writ at common law or under the prerogative confirmed in *Foxhill Prison Superintendent* v. *Kozeny* [2012] UKPC 10 (PC) (Bahamas).   [13]   s. 15(4).

[14]   See *R* v. *Home Secretary ex p Virk* [1996] COD 134 ('only an academic right...in the realms of cloud cuckoo land', said Popplewell J). The Law Commission has recommended a review of the habeas corpus appeal system: Law Com. No. 226, para. 11.32.

[15]   The theoretical remedy seems to have been an action for a false return: see Wilmot's *Opinion on Habeas Corpus*, Wilm. 77 at 106; the *Rutty* case (below) at 124. For such an action in an analogous case see *Brasyer* v. *Maclean* (1875) LR 6 PC 398; below, p. 766.   [16]   See Sharpe (as above), 66.

[17]   *R* v. *Board of Control ex p Rutty* [1956] 2 QB 109 at 124; *R* v. *Home Secretary ex p Khawaja* [1984] AC 74 at 110, where Lord Scarman quotes the Act. Even before the Act the court would sometimes admit affidavit evidence in the interests of justice: see *Goldswain's* case (1778) 2 W Bl 1207 at 1211. The Act may cut both ways, since the evidence may reveal good grounds for the detention which are not shown in the detention order: *Re Shahid Iqbal* [1979] QB 264, Boreham J forcefully dissenting.

[18]   *R* v. *Campbell* [1959] 1 WLR 646. Section 6 of the Habeas Corpus Act 1679, there discussed, was repealed by the Courts Act 1971, 11th Sched., Pt IV.

[19]   *R* v. *Home Secretary ex p Khawaja* (above) at 112.   [20]   As in cases cited below.

[21]   *Secretary of State for Foreign and Commonwealth Affairs* v. *Rahmatullah* [2012] UKSC 48, para. 45. An individual (R) was detained by UK forces in Iraq and handed over to US forces who removed him to Afghanistan; this was done under a Memorandum of Understanding between the US and UK that such detainees would returned on request; writ issued against Secretary of State; but US asserted detention was lawful and refused to return; held sufficient return to the writ. *Secretary of State for Home Affairs* v. *O'Brien* [1923] 2 KB 361 applied. In effect the UK was required to request the return of the detainee from the US. See Roach, (2013) 82 *Mississippi LJ* 907 at 963.

[22]   *R* v. *Pentonville Prison Governor ex p Azam* [1974] AC 18 at 31 and 41. But see the *Muboyayi* and *Cawley* cases discussed below, p. 503 and the *Hilali* case below, p. 504.

[23]   *R* v. *Home Secretary ex p Khawaja* (above) at 111, confirmed in *Secretary of State for Foreign and Commonwealth Affairs* v. *Rahmatullah* [2012] UKSC 48, para. 41 (Lord Kerr): 'the most important thing

is a 'common law doctrine of necessity' which may justify detention of those who are a danger to themselves or others or incapable of consenting to medical treatment.[24]

It may be noted that the belief, previously held, that an applicant could renew his application for the writ on the same grounds before any number of judges successively has been rejected both by the courts[25] and by Act of Parliament;[26] that the writ will not issue to Northern Ireland[27] or to a colony or foreign dominion overseas where there are courts competent to grant the writ,[28] but may issue to a protectorate;[29] and that the authority detaining the applicant carries the burden of proof of every fact prescribed by statute as a condition of the power of detention.[30]

The procedure is governed by special rules of court,[31] which have not been affected by the rules for 'application for judicial review' introduced for other remedies in 1977. The writ may be applied for *ex parte*, i.e. without notice to the custodian, with the support of an affidavit made by or on behalf of the prisoner; the court will then normally adjourn the case for argument between the parties, with or without requiring the prisoner to be brought before it. The modern practice is not to require the production of the prisoner unless there are special circumstances, but to order his release if the imprisonment is found to be unlawful, whereupon the writ of habeas corpus is issued. The writ may also be issued at an earlier stage if there is a danger that the prisoner may be deported before the court can decide his case.[32] In that case he is not seeking release but is asking for continuance of his detention.

Ordinary cases of ultra vires do not call for detailed discussion. One such case was where a magistrate made an order for the detention of a mental defective, which he had power to do if she was 'found neglected'. Since the evidence showed that she had not been found neglected, within the proper meaning of those words, she was released on habeas corpus.[33] This appears to have been an ordinary case of error as to jurisdictional fact. Where a Nigerian chief was deported to another part of the country and the Crown did not show that the conditions which would have justified the deportation under the local Ordinance were fulfilled, the Privy Council held that habeas corpus would be granted if these were not duly established by the Crown before the Nigerian court, for otherwise the deportation would be ultra vires.[34] Where illegal entrants from Vietnam were imprisoned

---

to be said about habeas corpus…is that entitlement to the issue of the writ comes as a matter of right…if detention cannot be legally justified, entitlement to release cannot be denied by public policy considerations, however important they may appear to be'.

[24] See *R v. Bournewood Community and Mental Health NHS Trust ex p L* [1999] 1 AC 458.

[25] *Re Hastings (No 2)* [1959] 1 QB 358; *Re Hastings (No 3)* [1959] Ch 368; and see *R v. Brixton Prison Governor ex p Osman (No 5)* [1993] COD 219. For the question of res judicata see above, pp. 205–6.

[26] Administration of Justice Act 1960, s. 14(2), banning repeated applications on the same grounds unless supported by fresh evidence (this means evidence which could not reasonably have been put forward previously: *R v. Pentonville Prison Governor ex p Tarling* [1979] 1 WLR 1417).

[27] *Re Keenan* [1972] 1 QB 533. It may issue to the Channel Islands and the Isle of Man: *Ex p. Brown* (1864) 5 B & S 280.   [28] Habeas Corpus Act 1862.

[29] *Ex p. Mwenya* [1960] 1 QB 241 relied upon by the Supreme Court of the United States in *Rasul v. Bush* (2004) 542 US 466 to hold that habeas corpus could issue to Guantanamo Bay which was under the control of the United States even though sovereignty vested in Cuba. See also *Boumediene v. Bush*, 553 US 723 (2008). See also below, p. 709.

[30] *R v. Governor of Brixton Prison ex p Ahsan* [1969] 2 QB 222; see above, p. 246.

[31] RSC Ord. 54, reproduced in CPR 1998, Sched. 1.

[32] See *R v. Home Secretary ex p Muboyayi* [1992] 1 QB 244; [1993] *PL* 24 (M. Shrimpton).

[33] *R v. Board of Control ex p Rutty* [1956] 2 QB 109 (Hilbery and Devlin JJ, Lord Goddard CJ concurring but evidently on grounds of 'no evidence': see below, p. 506).

[34] *Eshugbayi Eleko v. Government of Nigeria* [1931] AC 662.

in Hong Kong under an ordinance authorising their detention 'pending removal' the Privy Council freed them by habeas corpus when it became clear that their removal was impracticable.[35] The celebrated Daisy Hopkins, committed by the Vice-Chancellor of Cambridge to the Spinning-house for her presumption in 'walking with a member of the University', was released on habeas corpus on the ground that this was not an offence known to the law.[36]

Review by means of habeas corpus is naturally available only where the tribunal which has made the order for detention is subject to review by the High Court. Habeas corpus will not therefore be granted on an allegation that an order for committal for contempt of court, made by one of the superior courts, was made on the authority of a judge with a disqualifying interest contrary to the principles of natural justice.[37] A statute[38] that provided that the decision to detain pending extradition should 'be questioned in legal proceedings only by means of an appeal' may exclude habeas corpus. Where there is no right of appeal habeas corpus is not excluded;[39] but where there is a right of appeal the House of Lords has said that the 'remedy of habeas corpus must be taken to have been excluded by the clear and unequivocal' words of the statute.[40]

Where there has been excessive delay in bringing a prisoner up for trial,[41] or in executing an order for his deportation,[42] he can use habeas corpus so as to bring himself before the court and the court will give suitable directions by declaration or otherwise. In the contrary situation, where the deportation may take place before the court has been able to decide his case, he may seek a habeas corpus quia timet, to protect him meanwhile.[43] But habeas corpus will not avail to challenge the conditions of detention, provided that the detention itself is lawful.[44] A prisoner retains all his personal rights and remedies, except in so far as the law deprives him of them.[45] In case of maltreatment he can use ordinary or prerogative remedies, including certiorari and a mandatory order.[46] If he claims the

---

[35] *Tan Te Lam* v. *Superintendent of Tai A Chau Detention Centre* [1997] AC 97. Contrast *R (Khadir)* v. *Home Secretary* [2005] UKHL 39, [2005] 3 WLR 1 distinguishing *Hardial Singh* (below) and *Tan Te Lam*. A failed asylum seeker remained 'liable to detention' 'pending removal' under Sched. 2 of the 1971 Act (discussed above, pp. 72–3) for so long as the Home Secretary was intent upon removal. Persons 'liable to detention' may be granted temporary admission (subject to stringent conditions) instead of being detained. And this was granted to Khadir. His judicial review of Home Secretary's refusal of exceptional leave to remain (which was subject to less stringent conditions) was refused.

[36] *ex p.* *Hopkins* (1891) 61 LJ QB 240, 17 Cox CC 444. See [2000] *PL* 31 (Simon Brown LJ).

[37] *ex p.* *Dimes* (1850) 14 QB 554 (committal for contempt for disobeying an injunction of the Court of Chancery). Compare above, p. 384.					[38] Extradition Act 2003, s. 34.

[39] *Nikonovs* v. *The Governor of HMP Brixton and the Republic of Latvia* [2005] EWHC 2405 (Admin). The 'strongest words' required to remove 'the ancient remedy of habeas corpus' para. 18; Scott Baker LJ).

[40] *Re Hilali* [2008] UKHL 3, para. 21 (Lord Hope) followed in *Ignaoua* v. *The Judicial Authority of the Courts of Milan* [2008] EWHC 2619 (new evidence subsequent to appeal insufficient to overcome s. 34).

[41] *R* v. *Brixton Prison Governor ex p Walsh* [1985] AC 154.

[42] *R* v. *Durham Prison Governor ex p Hardial Singh* [1984] 1 WLR 704. Followed in *Re Mahmod (Wasfi Suleman)* [1995] Imm AR 311 and *R (I)* v. *Home Secretary* [2003] INLR 196 (CA) both deportation cases. See also *R (A)* v. *Home Secretary* [2007] EWCA Civ 804 (reasonableness of period of detention to be judged by the court and a risk of absconding and a refusal to accept voluntary repatriation 'likely . . . to be decisive factors' in determining reasonableness (detention for more than 18 months upheld in the unusual circumstances)). Note, as discussed above, the different rule that applies to those liable to detention pending 'removal' rather than deportation.

[43] *R* v. *Home Secretary ex p Muboyayi* [1992] 1 QB 244, holding also that Immigration Act 1971, Sched. 2, para. 18(4) (detained person to be 'deemed to be in legal custody') does not bar habeas corpus.

[44] *ex p.* *Rogers* (1843) 7 Jur 992; *R* v. *Wandsworth Prison Governor ex p Silverman* (1952) 96 Sol J 853.

[45] *Raymond* v. *Honey* [1983] 1 AC 1 at 10.					[46] As illustrated above, p. 437.

right to be moved to another prison,[47] or to be held under better conditions[48] he can apply for judicial review, but normally the court will not interfere with the management of a prison.[49] Non-observance of the prison rules will not normally entitle him to sue.[50]

While habeas corpus for the most part deserves its high reputation as a bulwark of personal liberty, it has several times been weakened by unfortunate decisions, particularly in wartime and immigration cases.[51] The case law is 'riddled with contradictions'.[52] It has also failed to measure up to the standards of the European Convention on Human Rights, which is likely to provide a better remedy in many cases, as explained below.

HABEAS CORPUS AND JUDICIAL REVIEW

Before it was established that all error of law is ultra vires[53] the House of Lords in the *Armah* case[54] indicated that the scope of review on habeas corpus was as wide as that on certiorari; and that, therefore, it extended to mere error on the face of the record, even though made (as was then supposed) within jurisdiction.[55] Evidently the court no longer confines itself to the grounds of detention stated in the return to the writ, but will examine the validity of preliminary steps, so that any legal flaw in those steps will invalidate the detention.[56]

Accordingly habeas corpus will be granted if it can be shown that the order of detention is ultra vires on any of the normal grounds, such as absence of a necessary condition or a wrong finding of jurisdictional fact; or if the order is vitiated by error of law; or if it is supported by no evidence. There is no logical reason for distinguishing habeas corpus cases from others, since all depend alike on legality. If the grounds of detention are flawed by any of these errors at any stage, the prisoner should be entitled to the writ when his liberty is at stake.[57]

Nevertheless the Court of Appeal has held that 'the evolution of the new and extended system of judicial review' justifies 'confining the ambit of the writ of habeas corpus' to cases where the challenge is to 'a precedent fact'[58] as opposed to 'a prior underlying

---

[47] *R v. Home Secretary ex p McAvoy* [1984] 1 WLR 1408 (application failed); *Thomson, Petitioner,* 1989 SLT 907.　　　　　　　　　　　　　　[48] *R v. Home Secretary ex p Herbage (No 2)* [1987] QB 1077.

[49] *R v. Home Secretary ex p Herbage* [1986] QB 872. A change to stricter confinement, even though unjustified, gives no right to damages for false imprisonment: *R v. Gartree Prison Visitors ex p Sears,* The Times, 20 March 1985.　　　　　　　　　　　　　　[50] See above, p. 57.

[51] See above, p. 368, also [1982] *PL* 89 (C. Newdick).

[52] Law Com. No. 226 (1994), para. 11.2.　　　[53] See above, p. 219.

[54] *R v. Governor of Brixton Prison ex p Armah* [1968] AC 192. In *R v. Home Secretary ex p Khawaja* [1984] AC 74 the House of Lords emphasised the common ground between habeas corpus and judicial review: see at 105 (Lord Wilberforce), 110 (Lord Scarman). This judicial review case contains much about habeas corpus.

[55] See above, p. 224.

[56] At one time the prisoner would have had to obtain a quashing order to quash the detention order at the same time as habeas corpus to secure his release, in order to succeed on this ground. But to insist upon a separate quashing order was pointless formalism, since the habeas corpus brought the whole question of the validity of the detention before the court. It therefore became the practice to receive the depositions of evidence as if there had been a certiorari and to treat them as part of the record, in the same way as used to be done in reviewing magistrates' decisions before 1848. If error of law then appeared, habeas corpus would be granted, thus in effect quashing the detention order. For this see Bacon's Abridgement (1768), iii, 6, cited in *ex p Armah* (above) at 234 and 254. And see *Gibson* v. *Government of the United States of America* [2007] UKPC 52, [2007] 1 WLR 2367 (PC) confirming 'the wide scope of a habeas corpus application in extradition proceedings' (para. 20) (Lord Brown) and approving the account given above of why a quashing order is not required.

[57] This reading of the authorities is supported by the Law Commission in their report *Administrative Law: Judicial Review and Statutory Appeals,* Law Com. No. 226 (1994), para. 11.19. For dissenting comment see [2000] *PL* 31 (Simon Brown LJ).　　　　　　[58] For this (alias jurisdictional fact) see above, p. 207.

administrative decision'; and that in the latter case the challenge can be made only by the procedure of judicial review.[59] The applicant, a rejected asylum-seeker detained pending deportation, wished to argue that the rejection of his claim was unlawful but this, it was held, could be argued only on judicial review since the rejection was 'a prior underlying administrative decision'. The refusal of habeas corpus was evidently correct on the facts,[60] but the court's general proposition conflicts with the decisions of the House of Lords just cited and with the principle that any element of illegality in the detention is a ground for habeas corpus. Otherwise there will be circuity and complexity of proceedings, even though the court will sometimes waive formalities and allow one procedure to be converted into another in the face of the court.[61] Since habeas corpus and judicial review may be sought in the same proceeding[62] the danger of a fatal mistake in choice of remedies can be eliminated by seeking them both. But unless this is done there is a procedural dichotomy similar to that made notorious by *O'Reilly* v. *Mackman*, discussed elsewhere.[63] The Court of Appeal's novel proposition was emphatically criticised by the Law Commission on a number of grounds, including the substitution of discretionary remedies for a remedy as of right, which 'could be seen as eroding ancient and vital constitutional liberties', and the unsuitability of the time limit and leave requirements of judicial review.[64] Yet in a later case, where magistrates had ignored mandatory conditions in issuing warrants of commitment for young offenders, a Divisional Court refused habeas corpus and elected to follow the Court of Appeal, though aware of the adverse authority and criticism.[65] When the new judicial review procedure was introduced in 1977 care was taken to leave habeas corpus wholly intact, and how the new procedure justifies 'confining the ambit' of that classic remedy, or enforcing the use of judicial review, is not apparent.[66] This is the latest unhappy event in a long and unfortunate judicial story.

EVIDENCE AND PROOF

The status of 'no evidence' as a ground of review has already been explained.[67] In habeas corpus cases, however, it was established earlier than elsewhere, indicating that personal liberty is entitled to the benefit of every doubt.[68] The House of Lords granted habeas corpus in the *Armah* case[69] to release a detainee whose return to Ghana had been requested

---

[59] *R* v. *Home Secretary ex p Muboyayi* [1992] QB 244.

[60] The applicant was seeking decision of his asylum application on its merits (as opposed to release), arguing that France was not a 'safe country' to which he could be deported summarily. His remedy should therefore have been a mandatory order on judicial review. [61] As it did in *ex p Muboyayi* (above).

[62] See *R* v. *Home Secretary ex p Harshad Patel* (1994) 7 Admin. LR 56. Both remedies were sought and granted together in *ex p Hopkins* (above). [63] Discussed below, p. 569.

[64] Law Com. No. 226 (1994), Pt XI, paras. 5–20. For further discussion and criticism see [1992] PL 13 (Le Sueur): (1997) 113 LQR 55 (Wade); [2000] PL 31 (Simon Brown LJ).

[65] *R* v. *Oldham JJ. ex p Cawley* [1997] QB 1. Contrast *Re S-C (mental patient)* [1996] QB 599, where the Court of Appeal, though quoting from *Muboyayi* at length, granted habeas corpus on the ground that the detention of the patient was plainly ultra vires, being based on a false application by a social worker. See also *Re Barker*, The Times, 14 October 1998.

[66] In *Re Mulcahy* (1992) 6 Admin. LR 229 Laws J said that 'if all underlying processes could be gone into on habeas corpus the distinction between judicial review and habeas corpus would disappear altogether'. But the distinction between 'as of right' and discretion would remain; and the wide overlap was recognised by the House of Lords in the *Khawaja* case (above). For discretion as a shift from the rock to the sand, see below, p. 596. [67] Above, p. 230.

[68] See Sharpe, *Habeas Corpus*, 2nd edn, 78, 85, and in [1990] CLJ 422.

[69] Above. See also *R* v. *Governor of Brixton Prison ex p Schtraks* [1964] AC 556, recognising the same principle but refusing habeas corpus since the evidence before the magistrate was sufficient and the court would not review his finding on the merits.

by the Ghanaian government under the Fugitive Offenders Act 1881 on charges of corruption and extortion. This the magistrate was empowered to order on the production of evidence raising 'a strong or probable presumption that the fugitive committed the offence'. It was held that the court could investigate 'whether any magistrate, properly applying his mind to the question, could reasonably have come to the conclusion that a strong or probable presumption had been made out'.[70] It was further held that the depositions of evidence did not satisfy this test, and that there was therefore no evidence to support the magistrate's order. Since an order based on no evidence was erroneous in law, and the depositions were part of the record of the magistrate's proceedings, his order could have been quashed on certiorari and habeas corpus was therefore granted.

There have been contrasting views expressed *obiter* whether a court can make a fresh determination of a vital issue of fact (age of the detainee).[71]

'No evidence', being confirmed as error of law, is now a firm ground for both certiorari and habeas corpus alike.[72] But it may well be that where there are other regular procedures for its correction, the court will not allow habeas corpus to be used instead. Otherwise innumerable applications might be made by persons convicted on criminal charges and attempting to use habeas corpus as, in effect, an additional form of appeal.[73]

The law as to the burden of proof is of the greatest importance in habeas corpus cases. Although some of the decisions have created serious problems, the law is now in a more creditable state, thanks to the decision of the House of Lords in the *Khawaja* case.[74] This has been explained already in its general context,[75] dealing with the standard of proof as well as with the burden.

PERSONAL LIBERTY AS A HUMAN RIGHT

A wide-ranging right to liberty and security of the person is conferred by Article 5 of the European Convention on Human Rights, enforced by the Human Rights Act 1998. There is considerable overlap between the rights protected by Article 5 and the writ of habeas corpus. In particular, Article 5(4) provides that anyone 'deprived of his liberty by arrest or detention shall be entitled to take proceedings by which the lawfulness of his detention shall be decided speedily by a court and his release ordered if the detention is not lawful'. A breach of Article 5 is often a ground on which the writ of habeas corpus is sought.

The full text of Article 5 is given elsewhere.[76] In summary it provides that no one may be deprived of his liberty save in the specified cases and in accordance with a procedure prescribed by law. The specified cases include lawful conviction by a competent court; disobedience to a lawful court order or default on legal obligation; arrest for production in court on reasonable suspicion; prevention of infectious diseases, detention of persons of unsound mind, alcoholics, drug addicts or vagrants; illegal immigrants and persons

---

[70] These are the words of Lord Parker CJ in *R v. Governor of Brixton Prison ex p Mourat Mehmet* [1962] 2 QB 1 at 10, approved in the *Armah* case (above) by Lords Reid and Pearce. The Extradition Act 1989 no longer requires a 'strong or probable presumption' but requires evidence which would justify trial in this country.

[71] *R (AA) (Appellant) v. Home Secretary* [2013] UKSC 49, para. 53 (Lord Toulson) and para. 56 (Lord Carnwath).

[72] *R v. Bedwellty JJ. ex p Williams* [1997] AC 225 (see above, p. 232). This was not a habeas corpus case, but Lord Cooke's observations on the habeas corpus cases are important, explaining how Lord Diplock's reservations in *R v. Governor of Pentonville Prison ex p Sotiriadis* [1975] AC 1 at 30 are superseded.

[73] The Court 'cannot grant writs of habeas corpus to persons...who are serving sentences passed by courts of competent jurisdiction': *Re Featherstone* (1953) 37 Cr App R 146 at 147 (Lord Goddard CJ).

[74] *R v. Home Secretary ex p Khawaja* [1984] AC 74.   [75] Above, p. 246.   [76] Appendix 2.

awaiting deportation or extradition. Every person so arrested must be informed promptly and intelligibly of the reasons for his arrest and of any charge against him. Everyone arrested for production in court must be brought promptly before a judge or judicial officer and is entitled to trial within a reasonable time or to release on bail, conditionally or otherwise. As already mentioned, a detained person may take proceedings by which lawfulness of his detention shall be decided speedily by a court and shall be released if detention is unlawful. Everyone arrested or detained in contravention of this Article shall have an enforceable right to compensation.

Among the numerous claimants who have benefited from Article 5 have been particularly mental patients and prisoners. In a case where prisoners were detained pending proceedings for their extradition it was held that the lawfulness of their detention should be determined by the magistrates' court, the Article 5 jurisdiction being additional to the High Court's jurisdiction in habeas corpus; and that since under section 6 of the 1998 Act all courts must decide compatibly with the Convention and since the case would depend upon findings of fact, the magistrates' court was the more suitable forum to determine the question of committal for trial.[77] Questions of adequacy of evidence and fairness, on the other hand, would be best determined by the trial court. It is not clear how Article 5 allows jurisdiction to be divided in this way or why, in accordance with that Article, the magistrates' court should not make the initial determination of all questions governing the lawfulness of the detention.

The express right to compensation contained in Article 5(5) is notable as being the only such right given specifically, the general right to an effective remedy under Article 13 having been omitted by the Human Rights Act 1998, as mentioned earlier.[78] In a group of mental health cases damages (for undue delays) were awarded and the measure of damages was fully discussed.[79]

Undue delay has led to numerous violations of the right to a prompt trial. Where a mental health review tribunal adopted a practice of not listing for hearing detained patients' applications for discharge until eight weeks from the date of application, the Court of Appeal held the practice unlawful under Article 5.[80] So similarly was the practice of the Parole Board in imposing a delay of up to three months in considering a prisoner's application for release on licence after the expiry of his 'tariff period'; and lack of resources was no defence.[81]

Prison disciplinary procedures such as loss of remission for a drug offence[82] and recall to prison by the Parole Board for breach of conditions of release[83] have been held compatible with Article 5. Similarly the procedures to recall to prison from home detention curfew by the Secretary of State are compatible with Article 5.[84]

Two infringements of Article 5 led to declarations of incompatibility. In the first, the Act of Parliament had placed on a mental patient the burden of proof of his right to be discharged, and in due course the Act was amended by remedial order.[85] In the second case a

---

[77] R (Kashamu) v. Brixton Prison Governor [2002] 2 WLR 907 (DC). Judicial review was granted to quash the direct judge's decision that habeas corpus was the only remedy and the case was remitted to him.

[78] Above, p. 131.

[79] R (KB) v. South London Mental Health Review Tribunal [2003] 3 WLR 185. See below, p. 639.

[80] R (C) v. London South and West Region Mental Health Review Tribunal [2002] 1 WLR 176. The remedial order SI 2001 No. 3712 amends Mental Health Act 1983. See above, p. 146.

[81] R (Noorkaiv) v. Home Secretary [2002] 1 WLR 3284; and see R (A) v. Home Secretary [2003] 1 WLR 330.

[82] R (Greenfield) v. Home Secretary [2001] 1 WLR 1731, [2002] 1 WLR 545.

[83] R (Sim) v. Parole Board [2003] 2 WLR 1374; West v. HM Prison Bure [2013] EWCA Civ 604, para. 39.

[84] R (Whiston) v. Secretary of State for Justice [2012] EWCA Civ 1374 (recall not a fresh deprivation of liberty).

[85] R (H) v. London North and East Region Mental Health Review Tribunal [2001] 3 WLR 512.

discretionary life prisoner had been transferred to a mental hospital and he could obtain release only if the Home Secretary referred his case to the Parole Board. This discretionary barrier was held to be incompatible with his positive right to have the lawfulness of his detention decided speedily by a court under Article 5(4). No remedial order has yet been made.[86]

Detention of alien asylum seekers pending decision of their claims, not being unduly prolonged and not disproportionate, was held to be lawful under the provision of Article 5 about immigration.[87] After the terrorist outrages of September 2001 in the United States, and the derogation made by the United Kingdom in consequence, the Court of Appeal held that the Special Immigration Appeals Commission was entitled to conclude that there was an emergency threatening the life of the nation and that the detention of non-nationals whose presence was believed by the Home Secretary to be a risk to national security on objective, justifiable and relevant grounds was not incompatible with Article 5 (or with Articles 3 and 14).[88]

THE QUASHING ORDER (CERTIORARI) AND THE PROHIBITING ORDER (PROHIBITION)

COMMON PRINCIPLES

The quashing order and the prohibiting order are complementary remedies, based upon common principles, so that they can be classed together. A quashing order issues to quash a decision which is ultra vires.[89] A prohibiting order issues to forbid some act or decision which would be ultra vires. The quashing order looks to the past, a prohibiting order to the future. In this way they are respectively comparable to the declaration and injunction in the sphere of private law remedies. Like private law remedies, they may be sought separately or together. Unlike private law remedies, they have never been dependent on the applicant showing a specific personal right. Nominally they are granted to the Crown, and the Crown always has sufficient interest to call upon public bodies to act lawfully.

Quashing and prohibiting orders are discretionary remedies, and must be sought by the procedure of judicial review. Both these features are explained in the following chapters.[90]

THE QUASHING ORDER

The quashing order is used to bring up into the High Court the decision of some inferior tribunal or authority in order that it may be investigated. If the decision does not pass the test, it is quashed—that is to say, it is declared completely invalid, so that no one need respect it.

The underlying policy is that all inferior courts and authorities have only limited jurisdiction or powers and must be kept within their legal bounds. This is the concern of the Crown, for the sake of orderly administration of justice, but it is a private complaint

---

[86] R (D) v. Home Secretary [2003] 1 WLR 1315.
[87] R (Saadi) v. Home Secretary [2002] 1 WLR 356 (CA) affirmed [2002] 1 WLR 3131 (HL).
[88] A v. Home Secretary [2003] 2 WLR 564. For this see above, p. 137.
[89] Or, formerly, vitiated by error on the face of the record.
[90] Below, pp. 549 and 596. See below p. 551 for discussion of the changing nomenclature of these remedies.

which sets the Crown in motion. The Crown is the nominal plaintiff but is expressed to act on behalf of the applicant, so that an application by Smith to quash an order of (for instance) a rent tribunal would be entitled *R (Smith)* v. *The Rent Tribunal*.[91] The court will then decide whether the tribunal's order was within its powers. There are normal rights of appeal both for the applicant and the tribunal.[92]

The form of the old writ was that of a royal demand to be informed (certiorari) of some matter, and in early times it was used for many different purposes.[93] It became a general remedy to bring up for review in the Court of King's Bench any decision or order of an inferior tribunal or administrative body. Its great period of development as a means of controlling administrative authorities and tribunals began in the later half of the seventeenth century, and its wide modern application was promoted particularly by Holt CJ.[94] Something was needed to fill the vacuum left by the Star Chamber, which had exerted a considerable degree of central control over justices of the peace, both in their judicial and their administrative functions, but was abolished in 1640. There was also the problem of controlling special statutory bodies, which had begun to make their appearance. The Court of King's Bench addressed itself to these tasks, and became almost the only coordinating authority until the modern system of local government was devised in the nineteenth century. The most useful instruments which the Court found ready to hand were the prerogative writs. But not unnaturally the control exercised was strictly legal, and no longer political. Certiorari (or quashing order) would issue to call up the records of justices of the peace and commissioners for examination in the King's Bench and for quashing if any legal defect was found. At first there was much quashing for defects of form on the record, i.e. for error on the face. Later, as the doctrine of ultra vires developed, that became the dominant principle of control.

Failure to return the record into the High Court was punishable as contempt; in the seventeenth century commissioners of sewers several times found themselves fined and incarcerated for disobedience.[95]

THE PROHIBITING ORDER

The prohibiting order developed alongside the quashing order as part of the system of control imposed by the Court of King's Bench.[96] It was a similar remedy, but was prospective rather than retrospective. Primarily it lay to prohibit an inferior tribunal from doing something in excess of its jurisdiction. In what might be called the jurisdictional

---

[91] Sometimes this case will be referred to, somewhat laboriously, as *R (on the application of Smith)* v. *The Rent Tribunal*. In the past it would have been entitled *R* v. *The Rent Tribunal ex parte Smith* but now the Latin 'ex parte' must be avoided.

[92] See e.g. *R* v. *Immigration Appeal Tribunal ex p Alexander* [1982] 1 WLR 430.

[93] Originally it issued out of the Chancery or the King's Bench: Holdsworth, *History of English Law*, i. 228, 658.

[94] See the quotation below, p. 514. In *Groenvelt* v. *Burwell* (1700) 1 Ld Raym 454 at 469 Holt CJ said: 'for it is a consequence of all jurisdictions to have their proceedings returned here by certiorari, to be examined here... Where any court is erected by statute a certiorari lies to it; so that if they perform not their duty, the King's Bench will grant a mandamus.'

[95] See *Hetley* v. *Boyer* (1614) Cro Jac 336; *Smith's Case* (1670) 1 Vent 66; Bacon's Abridgement, ii. 542.

[96] Formerly prohibition was commonly awarded on the direct application of the party rather than at the suit of the Crown: *London Corporation* v. *Cox* (1867) LR 2 HL 239 at 279. A modern example is *Turner* v. *Kingsbury Collieries Ltd* [1921] 3 KB 169. The opinion of the judges delivered by Willes J in *London Corporation* v. *Cox* is a classic source of information on prohibition. See also Bl. Comm. iii. 113; Holdsworth, *History of English Law*, i. 228, 656. All the superior courts could grant the writ: Bl. Comm. iii. 112.

warfare of the seventeenth century it was an important weapon of the King's Bench when that court struck down the pretensions of competing jurisdictions such as those of the Court of Admiralty and the ecclesiastical courts. Later, like the quashing order, it developed into part of the regular mechanism of judicial control both of inferior tribunals and of administrative authorities generally. In a much-cited case Atkin LJ said:[97]

> I can see no difference in principle between certiorari and prohibition, except that the latter may be invoked at an earlier stage. If the proceedings establish that the body complained of is exceeding its jurisdiction by entertaining matters which would result in its final decision being subject to being brought up and quashed on certiorari, I think that prohibition will lie to restrain it from so exceeding its jurisdiction.

Typical modern examples are its use to prevent an electricity authority from proceeding with a scheme which was outside its powers;[98] to prevent the execution of a decision vitiated by a breach of the principles of natural justice;[99] to prevent a housing authority from requiring the demolition of a house which was improperly condemned;[100] to prevent a rent tribunal from proceeding with a case outside its jurisdiction;[101] and to prevent a local authority from licensing indecent films.[102] In the last-mentioned case[103] Lord Denning MR said of a prohibiting order:

> It is available to prohibit administrative authorities from exceeding their powers or misusing them. In particular, it can prohibit a licensing authority from making rules or granting licences which permit conduct which is contrary to law.

Although a prohibiting order was originally used to prevent tribunals from meddling with cases over which they had no jurisdiction, it was equally effective, and equally often used, to prohibit the execution of some decision already taken but ultra vires. So long as the tribunal or administrative authority still had some power to exercise as a consequence of the wrongful decision, the exercise of that power could be restrained by a prohibiting order.[104]

Quashing and prohibiting orders frequently go hand in hand, as where a quashing order is sought to quash the decision and a prohibiting order to restrain its execution. But either remedy may be sought by itself. Where only a prohibiting order is applied for to prevent the enforcement of an ultra vires decision, as happened in the last-cited case, the effect is the same as if a quashing order had been granted to quash it; for the court necessarily declares its invalidity before prohibiting its enforcement. A prohibiting order is a remedy strictly concerned with excess of jurisdiction.[105]

The court will not be disposed to issue a prohibiting order if the effect will be to prevent Parliament from considering some proposal or report. If its presentation should be shown to be unlawful, the court will prefer to state the legal position by a declaratory judgment.[106]

---

[97] *R v. Electricity Commissioners ex p London Electricity Joint Committee Co (1920) Ltd* [1924] 1 KB 171 at 206. [98] *R v. Electricity Commissioners* (above).

[99] *R v. North ex p Oakey* [1927] 1 KB 491 (ecclesiastical court: no notice to vicar of order against him); *R v. Liverpool Cpn ex p Taxi Fleet Operators' Association* [1972] 2 QB 299 (licensing authority not to act before giving fair hearing). Similarly a biased adjudicator may be prohibited from acting: *R v. Kent Police Authority ex p Godden* [1971] 2 QB 662.

[100] *Estate and Trust Agencies (1927) Ltd v. Singapore Improvement Trust* [1937] AC 898.

[101] *R v. Tottenham and District Tribunal ex p Northfield (Highgate) Ltd* [1957] 1 QB 103.

[102] *R v. Greater London Council ex p Blackburn* [1976] 1 WLR 550. [103] Ibid. at 559.

[104] See the *Estate and Trust Agencies* case (above).

[105] Rubinstein, *Jurisdiction and Illegality*, 94.

[106] *R v. Boundary Commission for England ex p Foot* [1983] QB 600 (report of Boundary Commission: complaint not upheld).

Occasionally a prohibiting order will lie where a quashing order will not, e.g. to an ecclesiastical court. This is explained below.[107]

Disobedience of a prohibiting order is punishable as contempt of court.[108]

SCOPE OF THESE REMEDIES

Quashing and prohibiting orders are employed primarily for the control of inferior courts, tribunals and administrative authorities. Crown courts,[109] county courts, justices of the peace, coroners and all statutory tribunals[110] are liable to have their decisions quashed or their proceedings prohibited, except where Parliament provides otherwise—and sometimes even when it does.[111] So are all other public authorities, whether their functions are judicial or administrative.[112] Minsters' decisions are frequently quashed by the quashing order.

In earlier times the prohibiting order was often used to restrict the jurisdiction of tribunals existing by virtue of common law, such as the ecclesiastical and admiralty courts. But both quashing and prohibiting orders, in their modern applications for the control of administrative decisions, lie primarily only to statutory authorities. The reason for this is that nearly all public administrative power is statutory. Powers derived from contract are matters of private law and outside the scope of prerogative remedies.[113] In refusing to grant a quashing or prohibiting order against arbitrators appointed privately under a contract of apprenticeship Lord Goddard CJ said:[114]

> But the bodies to which in modern times the remedies of these prerogative writs have been applied have all been statutory bodies on whom Parliament has conferred statutory powers and duties which, when exercised, may lead to the detriment of subjects who may have to submit to their jurisdiction.

But the existence of statutory power is no longer the sole touchstone, since judicial review has been extended to a number of non-statutory bodies.[115] The scope of review covers all varieties of ultra vires and unlawful action, including unreasonableness, breach of natural justice and error of law, as explained in Chapter 18.

Where the bad part of a decision is severable from the good, a quashing order may be granted to quash the bad part only. Severability is discussed elsewhere.[116]

An authority or tribunal whose decision is quashed has failed to dispose of the case and may normally be called upon to begin again and do so properly.[117] It will not suffice merely to ratify the invalid decision.[118]

---

[107] p. 534.   [108] Bl. Comm. iii. 113.

[109] See below, p. 537, for particulars affecting this and other courts.

[110] Including the Patents Appeal Tribunal, though consisting of a High Court judge: *Baldwin & Francis Ltd* v. *Patents Appeal Tribunal* [1959] AC 663; and an election court: *R* v. *Cripps ex p Muldoon* [1984] QB 68, affirmed [1984] QB 686.   [111] As in the *Anisminic* case, below, p. 612.

[112] Including the Commissioners of Inland Revenue: *R* v. *Inland Revenue Commissioners ex p National Federation of Self-Employed and Small Businesses Ltd* [1982] AC 617.   [113] See below, p. 535.

[114] *R* v. *National Joint Council for Dental Technicians ex p Neate* [1953] 1 QB 704 at 707.

[115] See below, p. 533.   [116] Above, p. 241.

[117] An example is *Kingswood DC* v. *Secretary of State for the Environment* (1987) 57 P & CR 153.

[118] *R* v. *Rochester upon Medway City Council ex p Hobday* (1989) 58 P & CR 424.

'JUDICIAL' FUNCTIONS

Originally quashing and prohibiting orders lay to control the functions of inferior courts, i.e. judicial functions. But the notion of what is a 'court' and a 'judicial function' has been greatly stretched, so that these remedies have grown to be comprehensive remedies for the control of all kinds of administrative as well as judicial acts. This is because the judges very naturally saw no reason to abdicate the control which they achieved at the zenith of their power in the eighteenth century. In that age the chief organs of local government were the justices of the peace, who in addition to their regular judicial business had many administrative functions such as the upkeep of roads and bridges, the licensing of ale-houses and the administration of the poor law. These administrative duties were discharged in the most judicial style possible: not only were the justices themselves primarily judicial officers, whose proceedings naturally tended to follow legal patterns—they were almost completely free from central political control.[119] Maitland epitomised the position of 'the amphibious old justice who did administrative work under judicial forms':[120]

> Whatever the justice has had to do has soon become the exercise of a jurisdiction; whether he was refusing a licence or sentencing a thief, this was the exercise of jurisdiction, an application of the law to a particular case. Even if a discretionary power was allowed him, it was none the less to be exercised with a 'judicial discretion'; it was not expected of him that he should have any 'policy'; rather it was expected of him that he should not have any 'policy'.

Local administration thus had a strong judicial tradition. When, in the nineteenth century, most of the administrative functions of the justices were transferred to elected local councils or to new statutory authorities, they carried this tradition with them. Political control was imposed, but a judicial technique was inherited. The courts had fallen into the habit of calling many administrative acts 'judicial', meaning simply that the person wielding the power was required by law to keep within his jurisdiction and to observe the elements of fair procedure, such as the principles of natural justice. For a long time this abuse of language was masked by the mixture of functions which were performed by justices of the peace. When these functions were later sorted out, the label 'judicial' still stuck to administrative acts. Quashing and prohibiting orders were still described as remedies for the control of judicial functions, and for preventing excess of jurisdiction. But 'jurisdiction' had become synonymous with 'power', and in fact quashing and prohibiting orders were used to control all kinds of irregular administrative acts, from those of justices to those of ministers. Their scope expanded automatically with the development of the doctrine of ultra vires.

THE 'ELECTRICITY COMMISSIONERS' FORMULA

Discussion of the scope of the modern law begins with a classic statement made by Atkin LJ in 1923. The case concerned an electricity scheme for the London area, where the Electricity Commissioners had statutory power to make schemes for grouping electricity authorities into districts for the general improvement of the supply. Any scheme was subject to confirmation by the Minister of Transport and to approval by both Houses of

---

[119] Thus when the government were in need of recruits under the Militia Acts during the Seven Years War they had to move the Court of King's Bench for writs of mandamus to the county authorities. This was the height of 'judicial' administration. See Holdsworth, introduction to Dowdell, *A Hundred Years of Quarter Sessions*, ix; *History of English Law*, x. 156.   [120] *Collected Papers*, i. 478.

Parliament; it was also subject to the usual public inquiry procedure in case of objection. There was a difference of opinion between the London County Council, which wanted one district for the whole area, and the electric supply companies, who wanted two districts. The Commissioners attempted to compromise by making a scheme under which there was only one district, but the district authority was to be required to delegate its powers to two committees, so that there would be a division of the kind that the companies wanted. The companies, however, challenged the legality of the scheme, and the Court of Appeal held it ultra vires on the ground that the Act did not permit the Commissioners to set up two authorities in the form of one.[121] A writ of prohibition was granted against the Commissioners at the instance of the companies, who had applied for it only a few days after the public inquiry had opened. It was objected that the function was not judicial but executive; that the application was premature as nothing decisive had yet happened; and that in any case the court should not intervene where the scheme had to be approved by Parliament.[122] All these objections were swept aside, and the court made it plain that any statutory authority acting ultra vires could be called to order by the prerogative writs— by prohibition, to prevent them proceeding further with an unauthorised scheme, and by certiorari, to declare that any decision already taken was ineffective. The judgments explained how this wide power had been exercised for centuries. It had been said in a case of 1700:[123]

> For this court will examine the proceedings of all jurisdictions erected by Act of Parliament. And if they, under pretence of such Act, proceed to incroach jurisdiction to themselves greater than the Act warrants, this Court will send a certiorari to them, to have their proceedings returned here.

This was restated in modern terms by Atkin LJ in the case of 1923 in what has become the definitive statement, approved in many later cases:

> Wherever any body of persons having legal authority to determine questions affecting the rights of subjects, and having the duty to act judicially, act in excess of their legal authority, they are subject to the controlling jurisdiction of the King's Bench Division exercised in these writs.[124]

Canonical though these words are, they require much interpretation. Though they overstate the true position in one respect,[125] in almost every other respect they understate it, the scope of the remedies being in reality substantially wider. For instance, the requirement of 'legal authority' is no longer invariable, since extra-legal bodies are now sometimes subject to the remedies.[126] Nor, for the same reason, are the remedies concerned

---

[121] R v. Electricity Commissioners ex p London Electricity Joint Committee Co (1920) Ltd [1924] 1 KB 171.

[122] See above, pp. 19 and 323.

[123] R v. Glamorganshire Inhabitants (1700) 1 Ld Raym 580. The words are evidently those of Holt CJ. Certiorari was granted to bring up an order of justices for a rate for the repair of Cardiff bridge, despite the objection that 'it was a new jurisdiction erected by a new Act of Parliament, the trust and the execution of which is reposed in the justices, and this Court has nothing to intermeddle with it'.

[124] [1924] 1 KB at 205. Similar language was used by Brett LJ in R v. Local Government Board (1882) 10 QBD 309 at 321; but since the Court of Appeal there declined to decide whether the quashing order would lie to a central government department, they left a large area of doubt.

[125] Read literally they could include bodies having a contractual duty to act judicially (i.e. fairly) such as disciplinary committees of trade unions and clubs. But in their context they are confined to the area of public law. For this see below, p. 525.

[126] See below, p. 538. Nor did this formula cover error of law on the face of the record, which at the time had been forgotten (above, p. 224).

only with the 'rights' of subjects in the sense of legal rights. Nor are they limited to 'subjects', since aliens lawfully within the realm in time of peace have the same civil rights as British citizens.[127] Nor need the power be exercised by a 'body of persons' in the plural: the principle applies equally to an individual minister or official.[128]

ACTING 'JUDICIALLY'

The above quotations of 1700 and 1923, though separated by so long an interval of time, are essentially similar in meaning. But the former speaks of 'jurisdiction', the latter of persons 'having the duty to act judicially'. The former is the more accurate, since 'jurisdiction' can easily include all kinds of administrative power, whereas 'the duty to act judicially' suggests a judicial as opposed to an administrative function.[129] In reality nothing could be plainer than that the acts controlled, both in the cases themselves and in many other cases decided both before and since, were administrative acts.

In the *Electricity* case the Court of Appeal cited a long series of precedents where a quashing order or a prohibiting order, or both, had issued to administrative authorities such as the Board of Education, the Poor Law Commissioners, the Tithe Commissioners, inclosure commissioners, and licensing justices. Plenty of other authorities could be added to this list including ministers of the Crown. The truth was that quashing and prohibiting orders were general remedies for the judicial control of both judicial and administrative decisions, and could be invoked just as freely where a minister made an invalid clearance order[130] or a local authority wrongfully granted a licence[131] or planning permission,[132] as where justices of the peace convicted without jurisdiction. But the courts failed to give candid expression to this truth. At two different times they threw themselves into confusion by forgetting that in this context they had made 'judicial' a synonym for 'administrative', and by drawing the false inference that an act which was administrative could not be judicial in the sense required.

The first occasion was in the late nineteenth century, when it was suddenly held that the decisions of liquor licensing authorities, since they were administrative, were not subject to certiorari.[133] This fallacy was soon corrected,[134] and the House of Lords explained how licensing functions, though administrative in nature, are subject to certiorari.[135] Nevertheless the aberration left a permanent mark, for it led to the use of a mandatory

---

[127] *Johnstone* v. *Pedlar* [1921] 2 AC 262.   [128] See below, p. 515.

[129] An administrative (or quasi-judicial) decision is a decision determined by the policy or expediency of the moment, as opposed to a judicial decision which is determined according to some rule or principle of law: see above, p. 31.

[130] As in *R* v. *Minister of Health ex p Davis* [1929] 1 KB 619 (prohibition); *R* v. *Minister of Health ex p Yaffé* [1930] 2 KB 98 (certiorari), reversed on other grounds [1931] AC 494. Whether certiorari lay to a minister or central government department was left open in *R* v. *Local Government Board* (1882) 10 QBD 309; that it did so lie was accepted without argument in *Board of Education* v. *Rice* [1911] AC 179.

[131] As in *R* v. *London County Council ex p Entertainment Protection Association* [1931] 2 KB 215. See similarly *R* v. *London County Council ex p Commercial Gas Co* (1895) 11 TLR 337 (breach of natural justice: certiorari granted); *R* v. *Greater London Council ex p Blackburn* [1976] 1 WLR 550 (licensing of indecent films: prohibition).

[132] *R* v. *Hendon Rural District Council ex p Chorley* [1933] 2 KB 696 (breach of natural justice); *R* v. *Hillingdon London Borough Council ex p Royco Homes Ltd* [1974] QB 720 (permission vitiated by unreasonable conditions).   [133] *R* v. *Sharman* [1898] 1 QB 578; *R* v. *Bowman* [1898] 1 QB 663.

[134] *R* v. *Woodhouse* [1906] 2 KB 501, reversed on other grounds, *Leeds Cpn* v. *Ryder* [1907] AC 420.

[135] *Frome United Breweries Co* v. *Bath Justices* [1926] AC 586 (Lord Sumner). Counsel contesting this proposition in 1953 was told that he was about 60 years too late: *R* v. *Brighton Borough Justices* [1954] 1 WLR 203.

order as a substitute for the quashing order in liquor licensing cases, which still lingers on illogically.[136]

Confusion again began to reign about 1950 in the erroneous decisions on natural justice discussed in an earlier chapter.[137] By overlooking the fact that these remedies had long been used to control administrative functions, the courts relapsed into a profound muddle. The Court of Appeal went so far as to suggest that the quashing order might not lie in matters determined by policy and expediency.[138] Yet the *Electricity Commissioners* case itself arose out of a question of pure policy and expediency: how best to organise the electricity companies in London. Policy and expediency play a dominant role in licensing functions, but there is abundant authority for the control of licensing authorities by a quashing order.[139]

The law was once again saved from its own backsliding in *Ridge v. Baldwin*,[140] where Lord Reid reinterpreted Atkin LJ's words about 'the duty to act judicially'. This was a case of a breach of natural justice remedied by a declaratory judgment, as has been seen. But Lord Reid perceived the close parallel with cases where quashing and prohibiting orders were applied for. He explained how 'judicial' had been made a stumbling-block in earlier cases which had treated it as a superadded condition.[141] In the correct analysis it was simply a corollary, the automatic consequence of the power 'to determine questions affecting the rights of subjects'. Where there is any such power, there must be the duty to act judicially. In the *Electricity Commissioners* case the Court of Appeal 'inferred the judicial element from the nature of the power'. Atkin LJ might therefore have said

...and *accordingly* having the duty to act judicially...

Lord Reid explained how any other interpretation was impossible to reconcile with a long line of unquestionable authorities, including the *Electricity Commissioners* case itself,[142] and Lord Hodson criticised the fallacy of saying that 'the giver of the decision is acting in an executive or administrative capacity as if that was the antithesis of a judicial capacity'.[143] Thus the law was for the second time brought back onto its course. Quashing and prohibiting orders were once again recognised as general remedies for the control of administrative decisions affecting rights, simply giving effect to the principle that powers of decision must be exercised lawfully.[144]

The quashing order thus performs a function not unlike that of a declaratory judgment: by quashing the court declares that some purported decision or determination is irregular or futile and therefore of no effect in law. The result is to establish that no one need take heed of it. The question at issue has not been lawfully determined, and the responsible authority must start again and determine it properly. The difference from a declaratory judgment is that quashing positively invalidates the offending decision or act, whereas a declaration of invalidity merely leaves it exposed to other remedies if required.

---

[136] *R v. Cotham* [1898] 1 QB 802; see below, p. 527.   [137] Above, p. 414.

[138] *R v. Manchester Legal Aid Committee ex p RA Brand & Co Ltd* [1952] 2 QB 413.

[139] As in the *Woodhouse* and *Frome* cases, above.   [140] [1964] AC 40; above, p. 415.

[141] Notably *R v. Legislative Committee of the Church of England ex p Haynes-Smith* [1928] 1 KB 411 at 415.

[142] [1964] AC at 75.   [143] [1964] AC at 130.

[144] The Privy Council's disparaging reference to Lord Reid's analysis in *Durayappah v. Fernando* [1967] 2 AC 337 at 349 was marred by unfathomable reasoning and factual inaccuracy as noted above. For the correct view see *O'Reilly v. Mackman* [1983] 2 AC 237 at 279 (Lord Diplock).

DECISIONS, DETERMINATIONS AND ACTS

'It cannot be too clearly understood that the remedy by way of certiorari only lies to bring up to this court and quash something which is a determination or a decision'.[145] This was said in a case where the court refused to grant the remedy to quash a mere report, being the report of the visitors of a hospital as to the need for continued detention of a mental defective. The power to order continued detention rested in another body, the board of control, who were required to consider the report of the visitors before deciding. Consequently the visitors had no power to make any decision affecting the rights of anyone: they could merely recommend, and their report was no more than a piece of evidence which the board of control were required to obtain.[146] Had they not obtained it, or had it not been a proper resort as required by the Act, a quashing order would have issued to quash the decision of the board.

A quashing order was similarly refused against justices who had power to license cinemas but who made it their practice to approve or disapprove plans for building cinemas and then to grant or refuse licences accordingly.[147] The object was to save abortive expenditure, but the statute gave no power to approve plans. An applicant aggrieved at the refusal of his plans was therefore unable to have the refusal quashed by a quashing order, nor for the same reason could he enforce consideration of his plans by a mandatory order.

As the law has developed, quashing and prohibiting orders have become general remedies which may be granted in respect of any decisive exercise of discretion by an authority having public functions, whether individual or collective.[148] The matter in question may be an act rather than a legal decision or determination, such as the grant or refusal of a licence,[149] the making of a rating list on wrong principles,[150] the taking over of a school,[151] the dismissal of employees who have statutory protection[152] or the issue of a search warrant.[153] They will lie where there is some preliminary decision, as opposed to a mere recommendation, which is a prescribed step in a statutory process which leads to a decision affecting rights, even though the preliminary decision does not immediately affect rights itself. Where a telegraph operator was entitled to claim compensation for telegraphist's cramp on production of a medical certificate from a medical officer specified in the Act, the refusal of a certificate by a different and unauthorised medical officer was quashed as being 'so much waste paper'.[154] The court thus removed what would otherwise have been a legal obstacle to claiming a certificate from the proper officer. In the same way a quashing order was granted to quash a medical certificate stating that a boy was an imbecile and incapable of benefiting from attendance at school, when one of the signatory doctors had not himself seen the boy and the question was, in any case, for determination by the Board of Education under the Act.[155] Even a report may be quashed if it is substantially

---

[145] R v. St Lawrence's Hospital Statutory Visitors ex p Pritchard [1953] 1 WLR 1158 at 1166 (Parker J). See Appendix 6.

[146] See also R v. Macfarlane (1923) 32 CLR 518 (immigration board's recommendation for deportation not subject to certiorari or prohibition).   [147] R v. Barnstaple Justices ex p Carder [1938] 1 KB 385.

[148] Despite the reference to 'any body of persons' in the classic formula (above, p. 514).

[149] Above, p. 295.

[150] R v. Paddington Valuation Officer ex p Peachey Property Corporation Ltd [1966] 1 QB 380.

[151] Maradana Mosque Trustees v. Mahmud [1967] 1 AC 13.

[152] R v. British Coal Corporation ex p Vardy [1993] ICR 720.

[153] The Court of Appeal quashed search warrants in R v. Inland Revenue Commissioners ex p Rossminster Ltd [1980] AC 952, though the House of Lords held that the warrants were lawful; and see R v. Tillett ex p Newton (1969) 14 FLR 101.   [154] R v. Postmaster-General ex p Carmichael [1928] 1 KB 291.

[155] R v. Boycott ex p Keasley [1939] 2 KB 651. The report confirming the certificate and the letter transmitting it were also quashed as being consequential to the certificate.

a decision rather than a mere recommendation, e.g. where the Act provides that it shall be final.[156] There is no magic in the word 'report'. The question is whether some issue is being determined to some person's prejudice; and the court's ability to intervene has been increased by the new doctrine that decisions which are wholly non-statutory may nevertheless be reviewable wherever there is a 'public element'.[157]

The courts are accustomed to granting the quashing order so freely that they sometimes do so, illogically, where it does not fit the facts and other remedies would be more suitable. In one such case, where a local authority had a statutory duty to provide accommodation for a homeless person, the Court of Appeal quashed their decision to take no action.[158] Yet this 'decision' was not made under any specific power to decide any question. The local authority had merely stated its unwillingness to perform its duty, and the natural remedy was a mandatory order. A quashing order was also granted to quash a 'determination' of the Commission for Racial Equality to hold a formal investigation into alleged discrimination, when in fact there was no distinct power to make such a determination, but a prohibiting order could have been granted to forbid an unauthorised investigation.[159] Cases of this kind are now common. So long as public authorities act in the spirit of the court's order, no problems arise. But it is obvious that to 'quash' a 'decision' that by itself has no legal effect must be an impotent remedy in cases of disobedience unless some further order, such as a mandatory order or an injunction, will be granted if necessary.[160] If confusion and complication are to be avoided, judicial review must be accurately focused upon the actual exercise of power and not upon mere preliminaries. The House of Lords perhaps appreciated this point in refusing to review letters in which a minister refused to accept that legislation about unfair dismissal and redundancy pay was sexually discriminatory or contrary to European Community law.[161] That was a case of prematurity, where the issue was not ripe for review.[162] Other such examples have already been given in the context of natural justice.[163]

The emphasis now given to decisions, whether or not made under a legal power of decision, is greatly extending the scope of the quashing order. It appears to derive from opinions of Lord Diplock. In a case where the Act provided that a tax officer, under a

[156] As in R v. London County Council ex p Commercial Gas Co (1895) 11 TLR 337 (gas tester's report made in breach of natural justice). But a mere statement of opinion, such as that a licence will be necessary, is not reviewable: R v. London Waste Regulation Authority ex p Specialist Waste Management Ltd [1989] COD 288. See also R v. Secretary of State for Employment ex p Equal Opportunities Commission (below).

[157] See below, p. 532. In R v. Ethical Committee of St Mary's Hospital ex p H [1988] 1 FLR 512 it was assumed that judicial review might lie to quash the advice of an informal and non-statutory committee as well as a consultant's decision to refuse fertilisation treatment to a woman; but relief was refused on the merits. In R v. Metropolitan Police Commissioner ex p P (1995) 8 Admin. LR 6 a mere police caution, given contrary to guidelines, was quashed.

[158] R v. Hillingdon LBC ex p Streeting [1980] 1 WLR 1425. For criticism see (1985) 101 LQR 153. In contrast to the American 'certiorarified mandamus' (below, p. 547) this might be called 'mandamusified certiorari'.

[159] R v. Commission for Racial Equality ex p Hillingdon LBC [1982] QB 276. See also the Court of Appeal's order in the North Wales Police case (above, p. 491), which presents the same problem in the context of the declaration.

[160] In Wheeler v. Leicester City Council [1985] AC 1054, where on judicial review the House of Lords upheld the quashing of the council's decision not to allow a club to use their football ground, instead of granting prohibition or an injunction; it was recognised (at 1079) that further relief might be needed.

[161] R v. Secretary of State for Employment ex p Equal Opportunities Commission [1995] 1 AC 1, holding the minister wrong on both issues of substance, however.

[162] See J. Beatson, Prematurity and Ripeness for Review in Forsyth and Hare (eds.), The Golden Metwand, 221.

[163] Above, p. 470. See also R v. Inland Revenue Commissioners ex p Bishopp [1999] COD 354 (informal opinions of IRC not reviewable).

power of entry and search, 'may seize and remove' anything reasonably believed to be required as evidence of tax fraud, Lord Diplock said that the seizure 'involves a decision by the officer as to what documents he may seize', and said that 'Parliament has designated a public officer as decision-maker'.[164] He then discussed the question of 'setting aside his decision', either for error on the face of the record or else as being ultra vires. Yet the Act gave no power to decide anything: it gave power to seize evidence and it was the act of seizure, rather than any decision, which was in dispute. Then in a later case Lord Diplock said: 'The subject matter of every judicial review is a decision made by some person (or body of persons) whom I will call the "decision-maker" or else a refusal by him to make a decision.'[165] Yet many cases of judicial review necessarily turn upon the legality of acts, as opposed to decisions.[166] When an order is quashed, for example, it is the legality of the order itself, and not of the decision to make it, with which the law is concerned. The attempt to extract a 'decision' out of every legal act led the House of Lords into an unsound dichotomy, as explained later.[167]

QUASHING NULLITIES

Over a century ago there was a short-lived fallacy that 'certiorari will not lie to quash nullities'.[168] It seems that the court would sometimes refuse certiorari to quash a patently ineffective act, for example where an inquisition was held by a coroner's clerk instead of by the coroner himself, since new proceedings would have to be taken and the void proceedings could simply be disregarded.[169] Yet the fact remained that the matter was brought before the court and the court held that the act was a nullity. This fallacy died a natural death, since certiorari was constantly in use for quashing acts which were ultra vires and nullities, as is shown by most of the cases cited in the foregoing discussion of this remedy.[170]

But in two modern cases Lord Denning said that in the case of an order which is a nullity there is 'no need for an order to quash it' and that it is 'automatically null and void without more ado'.[171] The difficulties of this proposition have already been pointed out.[172] However null and void a decision may be, there is no means by which its nullity can be established except by asking the court to say so.[173] Lord Denning's successor pointed this out very clearly in the case of the Takeover Panel, quoted below.[174] If for example a licensing authority refuses a licence for wrong reasons or in breach of natural justice, so that its decision is ultra vires and void, nothing will avail the applicant except a judicial decision quashing the refusal and ordering a proper determination.[175] In other situations, such as

---

[164] The *Rossminster* case (above) at 1013.

[165] *Council of Civil Service Unions* v. *Minister for the Civil Service* [1985] AC 374 at 408. See Appendix 1 for the context.

[166] In *West* v. *Secretary of State for Scotland*, 1992 SLT 636 at 650. The Court of Session more accurately speaks of 'acts or decisions' as the subjects of judicial review.

[167] *Cocks* v. *Thanet DC* [1983] 2 AC 286, for which see below, p. 572.

[168] Rubinstein, *Jurisdiction and Illegality*, 83.   [169] *Re Daws* (1838) 8 Ad & E 936.

[170] A good example is *R* v. *Postmaster-General ex p Carmichael* [1928] 1 KB 291; above, p. 517.

[171] *Director of Public Prosecutions* v. *Head* [1959] AC 83 at 111; *R* v. *Paddington Valuation Officer ex p Peachey Property Corporation Ltd* [1966] 1 QB 380 at 402. For comment see (1967) 83 *LQR* at 521.

[172] Above, p. 248.   [173] As to the presumption of validity see above, p. 269.

[174] Below, p. 540.

[175] See especially *London & Clydeside Estates Ltd* v. *Aberdeen DC* [1980] 1 WLR 182 at 189, where Lord Hailsham LC emphasises the need to go to the court except in extreme situations where the position is obvious to all concerned.

that mentioned in the preceding paragraph, it is possible to ignore a void order only if the public authority makes no attempt to enforce it.

THE CROWN

Prerogative remedies do not lie against the Crown, since it is at the suit of the Crown that they are sought. But they lie against ministers and officials and since the practice is to give statutory powers to ministers or other government agencies as such rather than to the Crown, the Crown's immunity is of little consequence.[176] The correct remedy for use against the Crown itself, in the cases where such proceedings are allowed, is an action for a declaratory judgment against the responsible minister.[177] The same is true in matters which may concern Parliament for which a declaratory judgment is more suitable than a prohibiting order.[178]

THE MANDATORY ORDER

NATURE OF THIS REMEDY

The prerogative remedy of a mandatory order has long provided the normal means of enforcing the performance of public duties by public authorities of all kinds.[179] Like the other prerogative remedies, it is normally granted on the application of a private litigant, though it may equally well be used by one public authority against another. The commonest employment of a mandatory order is as a weapon in the hands of the ordinary citizen, when a public authority fails to do its duty by him. The quashing order and a prohibiting order deal with wrongful action, a mandatory order deals with wrongful inaction. The prerogative remedies thus together cover the field of governmental powers and duties.

Mandamus reached the zenith of its utility in the eighteenth century, when as well as protecting the citizen it played a conspicuous part in the machinery of government. It proved to be one of the few effective instruments of public policy in the era between the abolition of the Star Chamber in 1640 and the creation of the modern system of local government in the nineteenth century. During that interregnum the business of administration was mainly in the hands of local magistrates and other authorities who enjoyed an extraordinary measure of independence. A mandamus from the King's Bench was virtually the only effective means of forcing some such body to carry out its duties under common law or Acts of Parliament. We have already seen an example of its use in that heyday of the rule of law.[180]

The essence of a mandatory order is that it is a royal command, issued in the name of the Crown from the Court of King's Bench (now the Queen's Bench Division of the High Court), ordering the performance of a public legal duty. It is a discretionary remedy, and the Court has full discretion to withhold it in unsuitable cases. It has never lost the wide scope which the courts gave it in the eighteenth and early nineteenth centuries, when it was so vital a part of the mechanism of the state. But in the highly organised administrative system of the modern state it has no longer this prominent role to play. Governmental

---

[176] See above, pp. 36–7, and below, p. 689; *M v. Home Office* [1994] AC 377 at 417.
[177] See above, p. 486.   [178] *R v. Boundary Commission for England ex p Foot* [1983] QB 600.
[179] See Harding, *Public Duties and Public Law*, ch. 3.   [180] Above, p. 513, n. 119.

bodies today respond more naturally to the political stimulus, and the ultimate legal sanction has to be invoked only in a handful of stubborn cases.

Disobedience to a mandatory order is a contempt of court, punishable by fine or imprisonment.[181] A mandatory order is therefore very like a mandatory injunction: both are commands from the court that some legal duty be performed. But the two remedies have different spheres. The injunction is an equitable remedy, and it is rare to find mandatory injunctions outside private law. A mandatory order is a common law remedy, based on royal authority, which is used only in public law.

CHANGING SCOPE

Originally the writ of mandamus was merely an administrative order from the sovereign to his subordinates. But from early times it was made generally available through the Court of King's Bench, as was natural when the central government had little administrative machinery of its own. The writ would issue to enforce the terms of royal charters and by the seventeenth century it was in common use to compel the admission or restoration of freemen or burgesses to their offices or rights in borough corporations.[182] Another early use for it was to enforce the rights of members of universities;[183] and Lord Mansfield said that he had seen a report of a mandamus in the time of Edward III commanding the University of Oxford to restore a member who had been banished.[184] Lord Holt and Lord Mansfield favoured the free use of the writ for the enforcement of public duties of all kinds, for instance against inferior tribunals which refused to exercise their jurisdiction or against municipal corporations which did not duly hold elections, meetings, courts and so forth. Lord Mansfield said in sweeping terms:[185]

> It was introduced, to prevent disorder from a failure of justice, and defect of police. Therefore it ought to be used upon all occasions where the law has established no specific remedy, and where in justice and good government there ought to be one.... The value of the matter, or the degree of its importance to the public police, is not scrupulously weighed. If there be a right, and no other specific remedy, this should not be denied. Writs of mandamus have been granted, to admit lecturers, clerks, sextons, and scavengers, &c., to restore an alderman to precedency, an attorney to practice in an inferior court, &c.

This was in a case where a writ issued for the admission of a Presbyterian preacher whose only title was under a trust deed, showing that the duty enforced need be neither statutory nor under royal charter.[186] Furthermore, the duty was public only in the sense that it was a duty to execute a charitable trust. Mandamus used to be employed for enforcing the admission of copyholders in manors, where it was a matter of private duty only.[187]

---

[181] As to officers of the Crown, see *M v. Home Office* [1994] AC 377 (below, p. 689) (contempt of court by minister). As to other authorities, see *R v. Poplar Borough Council ex p London County Council (No 2)* [1922] 1 KB 95, granting a mandamus under which members of the defaulting council were imprisoned. Enforcement against a corporate body is against its members personally as individuals. For the political background, a story of great interest, see [1962] *PL* 52 (B. Keith-Lucas).

[182] The landmark here was *Bagg's Case* (1615) 11 Co Rep 93b, recounted above, p. 406, but there were 15th- and 16th-century precedents: see *Middleton's Case* (1574) 3 Dyer 332b.

[183] As in *R v. St John's College, Cambridge* (1693) 4 Mod 233; *R v. University of Cambridge* (1723) 1 Str 557; *R v. Vice-Chancellor of Cambridge* (1765) 3 Burr 1647; *R v. Chancellor of Cambridge* (1794) 6 TR 89; *Tapping on Mandamus* (1848) 267. But this is subject to the exclusive jurisdiction of any visitor: see below.

[184] *R v. Askew* (1768) 4 Burr 2185 at 2189. Oxford University was ordered by mandamus in 1396 to expel Lollards: *Tapping on Mandamus*, 269.   [185] *R v. Barker* (1762) 3 Burr 1265 at 1267.

[186] It may also show Lord Mansfield's leaning towards incorporating equity into the common law.

[187] See *R v. Powell* (1841) 1 QB 352; *R v. Garland* (1879) LR 5 QB 269.

An example of mandamus enforcing a duty existing at common law is *Dr. Bentley's* case,[188] mentioned elsewhere, where the writ was granted to restore him to his degrees which had been unlawfully taken away by the Vice-Chancellor's court of Cambridge University. Where a university or college has a visitor, mandamus may be granted to require the visitor to act, and to hear the parties fairly,[189] but the court will not otherwise interfere with his exercise of his jurisdiction, provided that he keeps within it.[190] There was much litigation on such questions in the eighteenth century.

Although the older authorities have not been invalidated, mandamus has in practice acquired a more precise scope than that which Lord Mansfield advocated. Modern government is based almost exclusively on statutory powers and duties vested in public bodies, and a mandatory order is the regular method of enforcing the duties. The plethora of ancient and customary jurisdictions no longer exists. The introduction in the nineteenth century of the modern system of local government, and the provision by the state in the twentieth century of social services and benefits which were previously a matter for private charity, have sharpened the distinction between bodies and activities which are governmental and those which are not. As the picture has come into focus, the proper sphere of a mandatory order has become clearer. A mandatory order now belongs essentially to public law. It seems safe to say that it would not be granted today to enforce the duties of trustees, even where these are statutory, since for this there are sufficient remedies in private law. Nor will it be granted to enforce the private rights of shareholders against companies,[191] though courts entertained such cases previously.[192]

Today the majority of applications for a mandatory order are made at the instance of private litigants complaining of some breach of duty by some public authority. But public authorities themselves may still use the remedy, as they did in the past, to enforce duties owed to them by subordinate authorities. When the borough council of Poplar refused to pay their statutory contribution to the London County Council for rates, the county council obtained a mandamus ordering the proper payments to be made;[193] and when they were not made, the county council obtained writs of attachment for the imprisonment of the disobedient councillors.[194] Statutes also may provide for a mandatory order as a remedy for one public authority against another, as observed later in the case of default powers.[195]

Within the field of public law the scope of a mandatory order is still wide and the court may use it freely to prevent breach of duty and injustice:

> Instead of being astute to discover reasons for not applying this great constitutional remedy for error and misgovernment, we think it our duty to be vigilant to apply it in every case to which, by any reasonable construction, it can be made applicable.[196]

For the sake of this principle technical difficulties may be overcome. The court can, for example, order the fulfilment of a duty even though a statutory time limit for its

---

[188] *R v. University of Cambridge* (1723) 1 Str 557; above, p. 406. The University's charters had been confirmed by statute, but the duty to restore was evidently at common law. The court held that it could intervene because the University did not claim to have a visitor.

[189] *R v. Bishop of Lincoln* (1785) 2 TR 338 n.

[190] For university visitors see above, p. 469, below p. 537.

[191] *Davies v. Gas Light and Coke Co* [1909] 1 Ch 708, holding that the proper remedy was injunction.

[192] See *R v. London and St Katherine's Docks Co* (1874) 44 LJQB 4.

[193] *R v. Poplar Borough Council ex p London County Council (No 1)* [1922] KB 72.

[194] *Same (No 2)* [1922] 1 KB 95.   [195] Below, p. 629.

[196] *R v. Hanley Revising Barrister* [1912] 3 KB 518 at 529 (Darling J).

performance has expired;[197] and if the defaulting officer has been replaced by a successor, the latter may be ordered to make good his predecessor's default.[198]

DISCRETIONARY REMEDY

Like quashing and prohibiting orders, a mandatory order is a discretionary remedy.[199] What this means is explained later.[200] It may therefore be refused to an applicant who has been guilty of undue delay, as where nine years were allowed to elapse before claiming a refund of tax.[201] It may also be refused where a public authority has done all that it reasonably can to fulfil its duty,[202] or where the remedy is unnecessary, as where a tribunal undertakes to rehear the case according to law after its decision has been quashed.[203] In the case of the police, to whom a mandatory order may issue if they refuse to perform their duty, the court may prefer to explain their duty to them in general terms and leave them to act on their own responsibility in any particular situation.[204] The court always retains discretion to withhold the remedy where it would not be in the interests of justice to grant it.[205] But where no such question arises the remedy will be granted, and the court may even deny that discretion exists.[206]

MODERN STATUTORY DUTIES

Typical applications of a mandatory order in modern cases are to enforce statutory duties of public authorities to make a rate,[207] to refer a complaint to a statutory committee,[208] to decide a dispute between education authorities on proper grounds,[209] to determine an application for a licence,[210] to reconsider an application for a licence on proper grounds,[211] to appoint an inspector of a company,[212] to adjudicate between landlord and tenant,[213] to approve building plans,[214] to pay college lecturers,[215] to pay a police pension,[216] to improve conditions of imprisonment[217] and to implement an employment scheme.[218] Where the duty is to reach a decision the order will usually be 'to hear and determine according to law', the law being indicated by the court.[219] In other cases the order will be

---

[197] *R v. Farquhar* (1870) LR 9 QB 258; *R v. Hanley Revising Barrister* (above); *R v. Woodbury Licensing Justices* [1960] 1 WLR 461.　　　　　　　　　　　[198] *R v. Hanley Revising Barrister* (above).

[199] *R v. Churchwardens of All Saints, Wigan* (1876) 1 App Cas 611 at 622.　　　[200] Below, p. 596.

[201] *Broughton v. Commissioner of Stamp Duties* [1899] AC 251. An extreme case is *R v. Leeds to Liverpool Canal Co* (1840) 11 A & E 316 (65-year delay fatal).

[202] *R v. Bristol Cpn ex p Hendy* [1974] 1 WLR at 503 (duty to rehouse tenant).

[203] *R v. Northumberland Compensation Appeal Tribunal ex p Shaw* [1952] 1 KB 338 at 357.

[204] *R v. Metropolitan Police Cmr ex p Blackburn* [1968] 2 QB 118; *R v. Devon and Cornwall Chief Constable ex p Central Electricity Generating Board* [1982] QB 458.

[205] As in *R v. Garland* (1879) LR 5 QB 269.　　　[206] *R v. Bishop of Sarum* [1916] 1 KB 466 at 470.

[207] *R v. Poplar Borough Council (No 1)* [1922] 1 KB 72.

[208] *Padfield v. Minister of Agriculture, Fisheries and Food* [1968] AC 997.

[209] *Board of Education v. Rice* [1911] AC 179.

[210] *R v. Tower Hamlets London Borough Council ex p Kayne-Levenson* [1975] QB 431.

[211] *R v. London County Council ex p Corrie* [1918] 1 KB 68; and see the liquor licensing cases cited below, p. 527.　　　　　　　　　　[212] *R v. Board of Trade ex p St. Martin's Preserving Co Ltd* [1965] 1 QB 603.

[213] *R v. Pugh (Judge)* [1951] 2 KB 623 (mandamus to require county court to hear case).

[214] *R v. Tynemouth Rural District Council* [1896] 2 QB 219 (the conditions for approval being satisfied).

[215] *R v. Liverpool City Council ex p Coade*, The Times, 10 October 1986.

[216] *R v. Leigh (Lord)* [1897] 1 QB 132.

[217] *R v. Home Secretary ex p Herbage (No 2)* [1987] QB 1077.

[218] *R v. Liverpool City Council ex p Secretary of State for Employment*, [1989] COD 404.

[219] As in (e.g.) *R v. St Pancras Vestry* (1890) 24 QBD 371.

to act according to law, with or without further details and instructions which the court may add. Occasionally a mandatory order may be sought to enforce a non-statutory duty, such as the duty of the police to prosecute offenders against the law,[220] or the duty of a local authority to produce documents which a councillor reasonably needs for the proper performance of his duties as such.[221]

A statutory duty must be performed without unreasonable delay, and this may be enforced by a mandatory order. A mandatory order was granted on this ground against the Home Secretary when the Home Office insisted that a would-be immigrant who was legally entitled to enter the country 'without let or hindrance' should wait for over a year in the queue of applicants for entry certificates.[222]

Obligatory duties must be distinguished from discretionary powers. With the latter a mandatory order has nothing to do: it will not, for example, issue to compel a minister to promote legislation.[223] Statutory duties are by no means always imposed by mandatory language with words such as 'shall' or 'must'. Sometimes they will be the implied counterparts of rights, as where a person 'may appeal' to a tribunal and the tribunal has a correlative duty to hear and determine the appeal.[224] Sometimes also language which is apparently merely permissive is construed as imposing a duty, as where 'may' is interpreted to mean 'shall'.[225] Even though no compulsory words are used, the scheme of the Act may imply a duty.

Having developed from a piece of purely administrative machinery, a mandatory order was never subject to the misguided notion which at one time afflicted its less fortunate relative the quashing order, that it could apply only to 'judicial' functions. Administrative or ministerial duties of every description could be enforced by a mandatory order. It was, indeed, sometimes said that this remedy did not apply to judicial functions,[226] meaning that where a public authority was given power to determine some matter, a mandatory order would not lie to compel it to reach some particular decision. The law as to this is explained below under 'Duty to exercise jurisdiction'.

The fact that the statutory duty is directory as opposed to mandatory, so that default will not invalidate some other action or decision,[227] is no reason for not enforcing it by a mandatory order.[228]

Considerations of public policy may render a statutory duty unenforceable, for example under the rule that no one may profit from his own crime. A widow convicted of killing her husband cannot therefore claim widow's benefit under the Social Security Act 1975,[229] and a woman who has committed perjury and forgery in the course of marrying a British subject cannot compel the Home Secretary to register her as a British subject also.[230] A mandatory order was also refused in one exceptional case where compliance with a statutory duty might have endangered life.[231]

---

[220] See below, p. 295.
[221] See R v. Barnes Borough Council ex p Conlan [1938] 3 All ER 226 and cases there cited.
[222] R v. Home Secretary ex p Phansopkar [1976] QB 606; above, p. 352.
[223] R v. Secretary of State for Employment ex p Equal Opportunities Commission [1994] 1 AC 1.
[224] See below: 'Duty to exercise jurisdiction'.   [225] For this see above, p. 194.
[226] As in R v. London Justices [1895] 1 QB 214, 616.   [227] For this distinction see above, p. 183.
[228] Brayhead (Ascot) Ltd v. Berkshire County Council [1964] 2 QB 303 at 313–14.
[229] R v. Chief National Insurance Commissioner ex p Connor [1981] QB 758.
[230] R v. Home Secretary ex p Puttick [1981] QB 767.
[231] R v. Registrar-General ex p Smith [1991] 2 QB 393 (copy of birth certificate refused because of danger to applicant's mother, whose name he did not know).

CONTRACTUAL DUTIES DISTINGUISHED

A distinction which needs to be clarified is that between public duties enforceable by a mandatory order, which are usually statutory, and duties arising merely from contract. Contractual duties are enforceable as matters of private law by the ordinary contractual remedies, such as damages, injunction, specific performance and declaration. They are not enforceable by a mandatory order, which in the first place is confined to public duties and secondly is not granted where there are other adequate remedies.[232] This difference is brought out by the relief granted in cases of ultra vires. If for example a minister or a licensing authority acts contrary to the principles of natural justice, quashing and mandatory orders are standard remedies. But if a trade union disciplinary committee acts in the same way, these remedies are inapplicable: the rights of its members depend upon their contract of membership, and are to be protected by declaration and injunction, which accordingly are the remedies employed in such cases.[233]

But occasionally the courts appear to have overlooked the distinction. Lord Campbell CJ once said that 'a legal obligation, which is the proper substratum of a mandamus, can arise only from common law, from statute, or from contract',[234] a loose dictum which need not necessarily mean that Lord Campbell thought that mandamus was a remedy for breach of contract. In a university disciplinary case, already mentioned, the High Court proceeded as if the rights of students to be treated in accordance with natural justice could be enforced by a mandatory order, although the university had no statutory powers and the rights of its student members were evidently contractual.[235] The authority of this case has been shaken as regards the appropriate remedies, which should have been injunction and declaration.[236] It is possible that a mandatory order would lie to enforce rights flowing directly from the charter of a university or college for which there was no other remedy.[237] But rights flowing merely from a contract of membership should not be within the scope of a mandatory order.

DUTY TO EXERCISE JURISDICTION

A court or tribunal has a public duty to hear and decide any case within its jurisdiction which is properly brought before it. A mandatory order is frequently granted to enforce this duty on the part of inferior courts and statutory tribunals, which will be ordered to hear and determine according to law. Thus magistrates, licensing justices, county courts, statutory tribunals, ministers, officials, university visitors[238] and other jurisdictions subject to the High Court can be prevented from refusing jurisdiction wrongfully. A county court judge, who mistakenly declined to hear an action for possession by mortgagees on the ground that the county court had no jurisdiction, was ordered to hear and determine the case on a mandatory order from the Queen's Bench Division.[239] The same occurred where a county court judge refused to investigate the correctness of jurisdictional facts on which the validity of a rent tribunal's decision depended, and which were properly disputed before him,[240] and where a minister declined to decide an appeal about public rights of way.[241] Refusal to receive evidence on some relevant point may also amount to

[232] See below, p. 528.   [233] As in the cases cited below, p. 535.
[234] Ex p. Napier (1852) 18 QB 692 at 695.
[235] R v. Aston University Senate ex p Roffey (1969) 2 QB 538; below, p. 537.
[236] Herring v. Templeman [1973] 3 All ER 569 at 585; below, p. 537.   [237] See above, p. 469.
[238] R v. Dunsheath ex p Meredith [1951] 1 KB 127; R v. Hull University Visitor ex p Page [1993] AC 682.
[239] R v. Briant (Judge) [1957] 2 QB 497.   [240] R v. Pugh (Judge) [1951] 2 KB 623.
[241] R v. Secretary of State for the Environment ex p Burrows [1991] 2 QB 354.

refusal of jurisdiction, so that a mandatory order will go to compel a magistrate to receive it; though this has to be distinguished from a decision by the magistrate, within the scope of his discretion, that the evidence is irrelevant.[242] Refusal to consider a party's case also has to be distinguished from refusal to accept his argument. As Lord Goddard CJ said:[243]

> to allow an order of mandamus to go there must be a refusal to exercise the jurisdiction. The line may be a very fine one between a wrong decision and a declining to exercise jurisdiction; that is to say, between finding that a litigant has not made out a case, and refusing to consider whether there is a case.

If the inferior court or tribunal merely makes a wrong decision within its jurisdiction, as opposed to refusing to exercise it, a mandatory order cannot be employed to make it change its conclusion.[244] This is merely the familiar rule that the court cannot interfere with action which is intra vires.

An instance of a mandatory order to a statutory tribunal was where a housing appeal tribunal dismissed an appeal by a company wishing to build a picture house without giving them a hearing as required by law. This was a breach of an implied statutory duty; the decision was accordingly quashed by a quashing order and a mandatory order issued to require the tribunal to exercise its jurisdiction properly.[245] The same remedies were likewise granted where an immigration tribunal wrongly refused leave to appeal.[246]

The basis of all such cases is that the court or tribunal has a legal duty to hear and determine the case which is correlative to a statutory right of some person to apply or appeal to it. But now that the courts will grant a quashing order to quash decisions of non-statutory bodies, which can have no statutory duties, it seems that they will also grant a mandatory order to require the body to hear and determine—though it may be difficult to add the usual words 'according to law'.[247] Since this anomalous jurisdiction[248] is already established, it is only logical to extend it to a mandatory order, thus completing the system of judicial review.

A mandatory order has also been granted anomalously, as it would appear, to enforce what the court called 'a rule of practice'. Magistrates had refused to authorise legal aid by counsel for a man charged with murder; and though the statute gave them discretion as to the type of aid to be granted, it was held that there was a practice of allowing counsel in trials for murder, and that the practice was obligatory.[249] But perhaps this case ought to be regarded as one of an unreasonable decision, or of a duty implied in the statute, in which case quashing and mandatory orders would be normal remedies.

The position where there is a duty to hear and determine, but discretion as to the correct determination, must be distinguished from that where there is a discretion not to act in the matter at all. The Parliamentary Commissioner for Administration, who 'may investigate' complaints of maladministration, and is expressly given discretion whether to initiate any investigation,[250] cannot therefore be ordered by a mandatory order to entertain a complaint, since this is a matter of discretion and not of duty.[251]

---

[242] R v. Marsham [1892] 1 QB 371 (a mandatory order granted). For this question see above, p. 232.

[243] R v. Goods Vehicles Licensing Authority ex p Barnett Ltd [1949] 2 KB 17 at 22.

[244] R v. London Justices [1895] 1 QB 616 at 637; Smith v. Chorley Rural Council [1897] 1 QB 678; R v. Goods Vehicles Licensing Authority (above). [245] R v. Housing Appeal Tribunal [1920] 3 KB 334.

[246] R v. Immigration Appeal Tribunal ex p Shezada [1975] Imm. AR 26.

[247] A mandatory order was granted in R v. Criminal Injuries Compensation Board ex p Clowes [1977] 1 WLR 1353 (the Board was then non-statutory).

[248] For review of non-statutory bodies see below, p. 538.

[249] R v. Derby Justices ex p Kooner [1971] 1 QB 147.

[250] Parliamentary Commissioner Act 1967, s. 5(1), (5). See above, p. 81.

[251] Re Fletcher [1970] 2 All ER 527. Compare Environmental Defence Society Inc. v. Agricultural Chemicals Board [1973] 2 NZLR 758 (power rather than duty).

THE MANDATORY ORDER AND THE QUASHING ORDER

A mandatory order is often used as an adjunct to a quashing order. If a tribunal or authority acts in a matter where it has no power to act at all, a quashing order will quash the decision and a prohibiting order will prevent further unlawful proceedings. If there is power to act, but the power is abused (as by breach of natural justice or error of law), the quashing order will quash and a mandatory order may issue simultaneously to require a proper rehearing. An example is *Board of Education* v. *Rice*, cited elsewhere:[252] the Board's decision was ultra vires since they had addressed their minds to the wrong question; consequently it was quashed by a quashing order and the Board were commanded by a mandatory order to determine the matter according to law, i.e. within the limits indicated by the House of Lords.

But either remedy may be used by itself. Defective decisions are frequently quashed by a quashing order without any accompanying mandatory order. Once the decision has thus been annulled, the deciding authority will recognise that it must begin again and in practice there will be no need for a mandatory order. If on the other hand a mandatory order is granted without a quashing order, the necessary implication is that the defective decision is a nullity, for it is only on this assumption that the a mandatory order can operate. A simple mandatory order therefore does the work of a quashing order automatically. Normally a mandatory order is not used by itself in this elliptical way. But, by a curious practice, this use of it has become habitual in liquor licensing cases, so that the standard remedy for judicial control of licensing justices' decisions is a mandatory order rather than a quashing order.[253] This is because it was those cases which were first bedevilled by illogical doubts as to whether licensing was a judicial function for the purposes of a quashing order;[254] and though the doubts were long ago swept away, the habit lives on.

In the *Paddington* rating case, where the validity of the whole rating list was attacked (though unsuccessfully), Lord Denning MR suggested that, in order to avoid administrative inconvenience, an invalid rating list might be kept in operation by withholding a quashing order for the time being, and that meanwhile a mandatory order might issue against the rating authority to enforce the preparation of a valid list.[255] But this was on the hypothesis that an invalid list was voidable rather than void, a heresy criticised elsewhere.[256] As Salmon LJ more logically observed, a mandatory order could not be granted if there was a valid valuation list in being; it could be granted only on the footing that a legal list had never been made at all.[257] In an earlier case Lord Denning himself had said:[258]

> The cases on mandamus are clear enough: and if mandamus will go to a tribunal for such
> a cause, then it must follow that certiorari will go also: for when a mandamus is issued to
> the tribunal, it must hear and determine the case afresh, and it cannot well do this if its

---

[252] [1911] AC 179; above, p. 411.

[253] Examples are *R* v. *Weymouth Licensing Justices ex p Sleep* [1942] 1 KB 465; *R* v. *Flintshire County Licensing Committee ex p Barrett* [1957] 1 QB 350 (licence refused on irrelevant grounds); *R* v. *Birmingham Licensing Planning Committee ex p Kennedy* [1972] 2 QB 140 (similar); *Fletcher* v. *London (Metropolis) Licensing Planning Committee* [1976] AC 150 (similar). The first such case was *R* v. *Cotham* [1898] 1 QB 802. In some American States, where the fallacy over judicial functions persists, mandamus has taken the place of certiorari and is known as 'certiorarified mandamus'; see below, pp. 547–8.

[254] See above, p. 515.

[255] *R* v. *Paddington Valuation Officer ex p Peachey Property Co Ltd* [1966] 1 QB 380 at 402; below p. 625.

[256] Above, p. 254.   [257] In the *Paddington* case (above) at 419.

[258] *Baldwin & Francis Ltd* v. *Patents Appeal Tribunal* [1959] AC 663 at 693–4.

previous order is still standing. The previous order must either be quashed on certiorari or ignored: and it is better for it to be quashed.

Although both quashing and mandatory orders are discretionary remedies, the court's discretion must be limited by the basic rules of judicial control. Unless the rating list disputed in the *Paddington* case had been void, the court would have had no power to intervene.

REQUIREMENT OF DEMAND AND REFUSAL

It has been said to be an 'imperative rule' that an applicant for a mandatory order must have first made an express demand to the defaulting authority, calling upon it to perform its duty, and that the authority must have refused.[259] But these formalities are usually fulfilled by the conduct of the parties prior to the application, and refusal to perform the duty is readily implied from conduct.[260] The substantial requirement is that the public authority should have been clearly informed as to what the applicant expected it to do, so that it might decide at its own option whether to act or not.[261]

The court does not insist upon this condition where it is unsuitable. As Channell J said:[262]

> The requirement that before the court will issue a mandamus there must be a demand to perform the act sought to be enforced and a refusal to perform it is a very useful one, but it cannot be applicable to all possible cases. Obviously it cannot apply where a person has by inadvertence omitted to do some act which he was under a duty to do and where the time within which he can do it has passed.

An obvious case where no demand need be made is where a mandatory order is used as a substitute for a quashing order to quash a decision, as explained in the preceding section.

EFFECT OF ALTERNATIVE REMEDIES

A mandatory order is not to be granted where the law provides some other adequate remedy. At one time this rule was very strictly applied, in conformity with the doctrine that a mandatory order was a supplementary remedy, to be invoked where there was no specific remedy for enforcing some right.[263] A mandatory order was thus refused where there was a possibility of obtaining a tax refund by way of petition of right.[264] An extreme instance, criticised later, was where the House of Lords held that ministerial default powers were an adequate remedy for an individual aggrieved by the failure of a local authority to provide sewers as required by law.[265] This view of a mandatory order was expounded by Bowen LJ:[266]

---

[259] *Tapping on Mandamus*, 282.

[260] See *The State (Modern Homes Ltd)* v. *Dublin Corporation* [1953] IR 202.

[261] *R* v. *Brecknock & Abergavenny Canal Co* (1835) 3 Ad & E 217 (mandamus refused on this ground); *R* v. *Commissioners of Public Utilities ex p Halifax Transit Cpn* (1970) 15 DLR (3d) 720.

[262] *R* v. *Hanley Revising Barrister* [1912] 3 KB 518 at 531.

[263] Above, p. 523. See e.g. *R* v. *Gamble* (1839) 11 A & E 69.

[264] *Re Nathan* (1884) 12 QBD 461 (but it was also held that no duty to the applicant existed).

[265] *Pasmore* v. *Oswaldtwistle Urban District Council* [1898] AC 387; below, p. 630.

[266] *Re Nathan* (above) at 478.

A writ of mandamus, as everybody knows, is a high prerogative writ, invented for the purpose of supplying defects of justice. By Magna Charta the Crown is bound neither to deny justice to anybody, nor to delay anybody in obtaining justice. If, therefore, there is no other means of obtaining justice, the writ of mandamus is granted to enable justice to be done. The proceeding, however, by mandamus, is most cumbrous and most expensive; and from time immemorial accordingly the courts have never granted the writ of mandamus where there was another more convenient, or feasible remedy within the reach of the subject.

A mandatory order may therefore be refused where there is an adequate right of appeal. Where the statute provides a right of appeal or other remedy, it may well be held that the statutory remedy is intended to be exclusive, so that a mandatory order is inapplicable.[267] But where licensing justices had rejected an application without giving reasons as the statute required, with the consequence that the applicant could not tell upon what grounds he might appeal, a mandatory order was granted to require the justices to hear and determine according to law.[268] The Court of Appeal has held that ratepayers may challenge the validity of the local authority's rating list as a whole, despite the existence of a right of appeal against any particular assessment.[269] This once again illustrates that the court will not require an applicant to exercise a right of appeal on the merits when his complaint is of lack of jurisdiction or ultra vires.

Today a mandatory order has largely lost the character of a residual remedy. As noted earlier, it has become the regular remedy for enforcing the statutory duties of public authorities, and its procedure is no longer 'cumbrous and expensive'. Accordingly the courts have grown accustomed to awarding it more freely, even where some other remedy exists. Thus the Local Government Board obtained a mandatory order against a local authority which refused to appoint a vaccination officer, even though the Act empowered the board, in case of default, to make the appointment themselves.[270] Similarly the London County Council were granted a mandatory order to compel the Poplar Borough Council to pay a precept for rates, even though the Act provided that they might enforce their claim by levying distress—a wholly inadequate remedy, as the court held.[271]

It is expressly provided that the new remedies introduced by the Crown Proceedings Act 1947 shall not limit the discretion of the court to grant a mandatory order.[272]

STATUTORY PROTECTION

A mandatory order has been given the same protection as the quashing order against statutes passed before 1 August 1958 which purport to exclude the powers of the High Court to question orders or determinations.[273] This provision must be explained later.

---

[267] *R v. City of London Assessment Committee* [1907] 2 KB 764; *R v. Thomas* [1892] 1 QB 426 at 429; *Stepney Borough v. Walker & Sons Ltd* [1934] AC 365.   [268] *R v. Thomas* [1892] 1 QB 426.
[269] *R v. Paddington Valuation Officer ex p Peachey Property Corporation Ltd* [1966] 1 QB 380.
[270] *R v. Leicester Guardians* [1899] 2 QB 632; see below, p. 631.
[271] *R v. Poplar Borough Council ex p London County Council (No 1)* [1922] 1 KB 72.
[272] Crown Proceedings Act 1947, s. 40(5).
[273] Tribunals and Inquiries Act 1992, s. 12, replacing earlier Acts; below, p. 617.

THE CROWN AND ITS SERVANTS

It is inherent in the nature of the prerogative remedies that, since they emanate from the Crown, they cannot lie against the Crown itself.

> That there can be no mandamus to the Sovereign, there can be no doubt, both because there would be an incongruity in the Queen commanding herself to do an act, and also because disobedience to the writ of mandamus is to be enforced by attachment.[274]

This is no impediment in the case of quashing and prohibiting orders, since they lie to control inferior jurisdictions and they apply to all the ministers of the Crown and other public authorities upon whom powers are conferred by Parliament in their own names. But it is serious in the case of a mandatory order, since the Crown itself has public duties. How is their performance to be enforced?

There is a clear distinction as to the duties of Crown servants. Where the Crown servant is merely the instrument selected by the Crown for the discharge of the Crown's duty, any complaint of default must be made against the Crown and not against the servant. No mandatory order can then lie. For example, an army officer disputed the terms of his retiring pay and compensation, which had to be determined under the terms of a royal warrant (a prerogative instrument making regulations as to terms of service in the army), and sought a mandatory order against the Secretary of State for War in order to enforce what he thought were his rights under the royal warrant. In fact the royal warrant imposed no legal obligation on the Crown. But even if it did, the action could not succeed, since the Secretary of State was merely one of the Crown's servants who owed no legal duty as such to any individual affected by the warrant.[275] Similarly no mandatory order will issue to the Treasury to pay monies appropriated by Parliament for a given purpose, since the money is granted to the Crown, and even though it is in the hands of the Treasury, they are merely the instrument of the Crown for handling the money.[276]

On the other hand, where Parliament has imposed a duty on particular persons acting in some particular capacity, a mandatory order will issue notwithstanding that those persons are servants of the Crown and acting on the Crown's behalf. This is because the legal duty is cast upon them personally, and no orders given to them by the Crown will be any defence. If therefore the Act requires 'the Minister' to do something, a mandatory order will lie to compel the minister to act.[277] Similarly a mandatory order was granted against the Special Commissioners of Income Tax, acting as servants of the Crown, commanding them to authorise repayment to a taxpayer where the Act said that 'the ... Commissioners shall issue an order for the repayment, etc.'[278] The Crown Proceedings Act 1947 does nothing to impede this use of a mandatory order as in the past.[279]

Nevertheless it should make no difference in principle whether the duty is cast upon the Crown as such or upon some government department or other agency of the Crown. It is a pity that this untidy situation was left unaltered by the Crown Proceedings Act 1947, which in other respects put the Crown effectively onto the same footing as a private person. Logically the Act ought to have empowered the court to make a declaratory

---

[274] *R* v. *Powell* (1841) 1 QB 352 at 361.   [275] *R* v. *Secretary of State for War* [1891] 2 QB 326.

[276] *R* v. *Lords Commissioners of the Treasury* (1872) LR 7 QB 387.

[277] As in *Padfield* v. *Minister of Agriculture, Fisheries and Food* [1968] AC 997; *R* v. *Home Secretary ex p Phansopkar* [1976] QB 606. In the case of 'the Secretary of State' the mandatory order will evidently issue to the person responsible in practice. For doubts suggested by the *Town Investments* case see above, p. 36.

[278] *R* v. *Special Commissioners of Income Tax* (1888) 21 QBD 313. See similarly *R* v. *Special Commissioners of Income Tax ex p Dr Barnardo's Homes* [1920] 1 KB 26; *R* v. *Commissioners of Customs and Excise ex p Cook* [1970] 1 WLR 450 at 455.   [279] See below, p. 695.

order against the Crown in lieu of a mandatory order. There would seem to be no reason why the court should not itself fill this lacuna by exercising its ordinary jurisdiction to grant declaratory relief. The reason why the question has not arisen is probably that the statutory duties of the Crown, as opposed to those of specific ministers and government departments, are very few. If they were numerous and important, some remedy for their enforcement would be indispensable.

The Privy Council has suggested another solution to this problem of royal immunity, saying that a mandatory order could be awarded against cabinet ministers requiring them to advise the Crown to perform its duty. This was in the context of the proclamation of a security area in Malaysia which the Crown had power to revoke and also, according to the Privy Council, a duty to revoke if its continuance could no longer be considered necessary, i.e. if failure to revoke it would be an abuse of discretion.[280] But the facts of the case provided no occasion for applying this interesting theory.

The Crown or a government department may itself be granted a mandatory order, for example for compelling a local authority to levy a rate to finance a payment due to the Treasury.[281]

PROCEDURE

A mandatory order must be sought by 'application for judicial review' in the same way as quashing and prohibiting orders, as described in the next chapter. Permission to apply for the order must therefore be obtained before the application itself can be heard, and evidence is normally taken by affidavit. Undue delay is a ground for withholding the remedy in discretion, subject to the same qualifications as regards hardship, prejudice to rights, and detriment to good administration as apply in the case of quashing and prohibiting orders.[282] No action may be instituted against anyone in respect of anything done in obedience to a mandatory order.[283] Disobedience to a mandatory order is punishable as a contempt of court, by fine or imprisonment.[284] Without prejudice to its power to punish disobedience as contempt, the court may direct that the default be made good by the party who obtained the mandatory order at the cost of the disobedient party.[285]

---

[280] *Teh Cheng Poh v. Public Prosecutor* [1980] AC 458. The Constitution of Malaysia (Art. 40) requires the Yang di-Pertuan Agong to act in accordance with ministerial advice in most matters.

[281] *R v. Maidenhead Cpn* (1882) 9 QBD 494. 　　[282] See below, p. 558.

[283] Ord. 53 r. 10. No directly analogous provision exists in CPR 54, however.

[284] *R v. Poplar Borough Council ex p London County Council (No 2)* [1922] 1 KB 95; above, p. 521. In the case of a corporation, which cannot be imprisoned, the members responsible should be named in the writs of attachment; but in the *Poplar* case this requirement was held to be waived by members who appeared and persisted in disobedience. 　　[285] Ord. 45 r. 8, applying also to other mandatory orders.

17

BOUNDARIES OF JUDICIAL REVIEW

MARGINAL SITUATIONS

REVIEWABLE FUNCTIONS

Although judges often speak as if judicial review were itself a remedy, it must be remembered that it is merely a procedure for obtaining the remedies specified in the Senior Courts Act 1981, namely the quashing order, the prohibiting order and the mandatory order and (in suitable circumstances) declaration and injunction as described in the preceding two chapters. The scope of judicial review, therefore, is the same as the scope of these remedies. Their boundaries, as set out already, are fairly clear (despite the wide range of declaratory relief), but in the non-statutory area they are uncertain. The leading case is the *Datafin* decision, which excludes cases based on contract (as was already established) and holds that possibly the only other requirement is 'what can be described as a public element, which can take many different forms'.[1] In the absence of any more positive guidance the outer limits of judicial review can only be inferred from the catalogue of the borderline cases.[2]

Faced with such an ill-defined field, it is not surprising that judges have preferred to evade the problem rather than confront it. When the Referendum Party complained that the television authorities (BBC, ITVA and ITC) had allowed it too little broadcasting time before the 1997 general election, the Divisional Court preferred to reject the complaint on its merits.[3] But the Court of Appeal has since treated the BBC as fully reviewable,[4] and it was held that the ITVA and the ITC, being statutory, were clearly reviewable. But the statutory powers and duties are possessed by many bodies, for example commercial companies and trustees, having no public element and quite outside the range of judicial review. Nor will judicial review normally be granted where there is a suitable alternative remedy such as a statutory appeal procedure.[5]

---

[1] See below, p. 539.

[2] On the scope of review see [1987] *PL* 356 (Forsyth); [1992] *PL* 1 (D. Pannick); [1993] *PL* 239 (N. Bamforth). Note particularly (2009) 125 *LQR* 491 (C. Campbell) arguing powerfully that 'a monopoly power test could plausibly be employed by the courts as the *sole* test for determining the availability of judicial review'. The common law's regulation of monopoly power goes a considerable way towards justifying judicial review of non-statutory power (see (1996) *CLJ* 122 (Forsyth) at 124–6) but it does not explain why monopolistic private power is not subject to judicial review (e.g. why there is no judicial review of the decision to close the only supermarket in an isolated town).

[3] *R v. British Broadcasting Corporation ex p Referendum Party* (1997) 9 Admin LR 553. See also *Scottish National Party* v. *Scottish Television plc*, 1998 SLT 1395 (operation under statutory licence may make corporation reviewable).   [4] *R (Prolife Alliance)* v. *BBC* [2002] 3 WLR 1080.

[5] *R (Sivasubramaniam)* v. *Wandsworth County Court* [2003] 1 WLR 475; and see below, p. 601.

Judicial review therefore covers a very wide range of tribunals and public authorities. Its remedies may equally be granted against public corporations where their constitutions and functions are suitable. This was the case with the licensing decisions of the Independent Television Commission[6] and in one case,[7] but not in another,[8] with a decision of British Coal to close collieries. The status of the National Trust (statutory),[9] has been left open, although prima facie it has the public element mentioned below; and so has that of the Press Complaints Commission (non-statutory).[10] The Independent Broadcasting Authority was held to be subject to judicial review in exercising statutory powers but not in exercising its voting powers in the applicant company.[11] Reviewable also was a 'farmers market' set up originally by a local authority under statutory powers but later transferred to a non-profit making company managed by the farmers themselves, though with some local authority assistance. The Court of Appeal held it to be reviewable.[12] But the decisions of a 'pub watch' scheme[13] were not reviewable.[14]

The court has granted review of a decision to prosecute[15] or not to prosecute,[16] or to continue or discontinue a prosecution, but not of a law officer's refusal to cite a newspaper for contempt of court.[17] The House of Lords has however held that decisions about prosecutions are not amenable to judicial review where the complaint could equally well be made in the course of trial, since otherwise trials would be unacceptably delayed by collateral proceedings.[18] Where the accused has been unlawfully repatriated from a foreign country the court may stay the prosecution on the ground of abuse of process.[19] In general 'the courts are very slow to interfere' in decisions to investigate and prosecute crime.[20]

Prisoners may be awarded judicial review and have applied for it successfully against disciplinary decisions of prison visitors (which previously had disciplinary functions in prisons), for example where there has been a failure of natural justice.[21] The House of Lords has now abolished the former exception under which the court would not intervene

---

[6] *R v. Independent Television Commission ex p TSW Ltd* [1996] EMLR 291 (application unsuccessful).

[7] *R v. British Coal Cpn ex p Vardy* [1993] ICR 720. State-owned enterprises in New Zealand may be reviewable: *Mercury Energy Ltd* v. *Electricity Corporation of New Zealand* [1994] 1 WLR 521.

[8] *R v. National Coal Board ex p National Union of Mineworkers* [1986] ICR 791 (commercial decision not reviewable).

[9] *Ex p. Scott* [1998] 1 WLR 226 (claim failed since it should have been brought under Charities Act 1993).

[10] *R v. Press Complaints Commission ex p Stewart-Brady* (1997) 9 Admin LR 274. See *R v. Criminal Cases Review Commission ex p Pearson* [1999] 3 All ER 498 (Commission reviewable).

[11] *R v. Independent Broadcasting Authority ex p Rank Organisation plc*, The Times, 14 March 1986. See similarly as to sale of land: *R v. Bolsover DC ex p Pepper*, The Times, 15 November 2000.

[12] *R (Beer t/a Hammer Trout Farm)* v. *Hampshire Farmers' Markets Ltd* [2004] 1 WLR 233. See above, p. 139.

[13] i.e. a scheme whereby local publicans agree *inter alia* to 'ban' from all local pubs particular individuals alleged to be guilty of misconduct. Such schemes are often supported by the police and local authorities.

[14] *R (Boyle)* v. *Haverhill Pub Watch and ors* [2009] EWHC 2441 and *R (Proud)* v. *Buckingham Pubwatch Scheme and anor* [2008] EWHC 2224 (difficulty in identifying defendant).

[15] *R v. Chief Constable of Kent ex p L* (1991) 93 Cr App R 416; *R v. Croydon Justices ex p Dean* [1993] QB 769 (breach of undertaking not to prosecute: committal quashed); and see *R v. Inland Revenue Commissioners ex p Mead* [1993] 1 All ER 772.

[16] *R v. Director of Public Prosecutions ex p Camelot plc* (refusal to prosecute rival lottery company; the reasoning seems questionable); *R v. DPP ex p Duckenfield* (1999) 11 Admin LR 611. And note *R (Corner House Research)* v. *The Serious Fraud Office* [2008] UKHL 60 (decision of Director of the Serious Fraud Office to halt an investigation into fraud in the award of contracts for the sale of arms challenged but upheld).

[17] *R v. Solicitor-General ex p Taylor* [1996] COD 61.

[18] *R v. DPP ex p Kebilene* [1999] 3 WLR 972. Exception is made for bad faith or exceptional circumstances.

[19] *R v. Horseferry Road Magistrates' Court ex p Bennett* [1994] AC 42 (decided on assumed facts).

[20] *Corner House Research*, para. 31.   [21] See above, p. 471.

against decisions of prison governors in their day-to-day management of prisons.[22] Relief may also be granted where the governor is claimed to have infringed a fundamental right, such as the right not to be subjected to 'cruel and unusual punishment' contrary to the Bill of Rights 1688.[23]

Decisions of the Legal Aid Board are reviewable.[24] So are statutory functions of independent schools.[25] No success has attended attempts to challenge the assignment of particular judges for the trial of particular cases.[26] The decision by a health authority not to consent to pay damages by way of periodical payments is not subject to judicial review.[27] Neither are the non-statutory recommendations sometimes made by Mental Health Review Tribunals.[28]

SPECIAL JURISDICTIONS

Ecclesiastical courts are not subject to review by the quashing order, since ecclesiastical law is a different system from the common law on which the ordinary courts will not sit in judgment.[29] But a prohibiting order will lie, not only to restrain the ecclesiastical court from exceeding its jurisdiction,[30] but also to prevent it from executing decisions marred by error of law, provided that the error is one which the court is competent to correct.[31] Historical reasons lie behind this distinction. It is devoid of logic, since if the court is prepared to assert control by a prohibiting order it might as well do so by a quashing order.

It seems probable that the law used to be similar for other special jurisdictions such as those of visitors of universities, colleges and charities who have jurisdiction to determine internal disputes within those bodies;[32] but visitorial jurisdiction has now been held to be subject to judicial review in the ordinary way,[33] save only in respect of error of fact or law, for which visitors enjoy a supposed ancient immunity.[34] The same immunity is enjoyed by the judges of the High Court when acting as visitors to the Inns of Court, though in other respects they are subject to judicial review.[35]

Where there is a breakdown of law and order and the ordinary courts cannot operate, and martial law is imposed by force of arms, the court cannot interfere with the actions

---

[22]   *Leech* v. *Parkhurst Prison Deputy Governor* [1988] AC 533.

[23]   *R* v. *Home Secretary ex p Herbage (No 2)* [1987] QB 1077 (allegation of cruel conditions of imprisonment: leave to apply for mandatory order granted).

[24]   *R* v. *Legal Aid Board ex p Donn & Co* [1996] 3 All ER 1.

[25]   *R* v. *Cobham Hall School ex p S* [1998] ELR 389.

[26]   *R* v. *Lord Chancellor ex p Maxwell* [1997] COD 22; *R* v. *Lord Chancellor ex p Stockler* [1997] COD 24.

[27]   *R (Hopley)* v. *Liverpool Health Authority* [2002] EWHC 1723.

[28]   *C and anor* v. *Birmingham and Solihull Mental Health NHS Trust and anor* [2013] EWCA Civ 701.

[29]   *R* v. *St Edmundsbury and Ipswich Diocese (Chancellor) ex p White* [1948] 1 KB 195. See also *R* v. *Chancellor of Chichester Consistory Court ex p News Group Newspapers Ltd* [1992] COD 48; *R* v. *Provincial Court of the Church in Wales ex p Williams* [1999] COD 163.

[30]   e.g. *R* v. *North* [1927] 1 KB 491 (prohibiting order to Consistory Court for decision contrary to natural justice).

[31]   Bl. Comm. iii. 112, giving examples; *Veley* v. *Burder* (1841) 12 Ad & E 265, esp. at 311 (prohibiting order to prevent ecclesiastical court enforcing irregular church rate); Rubinstein, *Jurisdiction and Illegality*, 98. See also the *Chichester* case, above.

[32]   Bl. Comm. iii. 112 applies this doctrine to numerous jurisdictions; and see (1970) 86 *LQR* 531 at 544 (J. W. Bridge).

[33]   *Thomas* v. *University of Bradford* [1987] AC 795; *R* v. *Committee of the Lords of the Judicial Committee of the Privy Council ex p Vijayatunga* [1990] 2 QB 444. See above, p. 469.

[34]   *R* v. *Hull University Visitor ex p Page* [1993] AC 682. See below, p. 537.

[35]   *R* v. *Visitors to the Inns of Court ex p Calder* [1994] QB 1.

of the military or with the proceedings of courts-martial set up in such a situation. The ordinary courts-martial regularly established under military law in normal conditions are subject to quashing and prohibiting orders and to judicial review generally.[36]

The High Court is beyond the scope of these remedies, not being subject to judicial review.[37] But a judge of the High Court, when acting as a statutory tribunal, has no such immunity.[38] Bodies—such as the Upper Tribunal, the Special Immigration Appeals Commission and the Courts-Martial Appeal Court—established by statute as 'superior court[s] of record' are not for that reason exempt from judicial review.[39] The Crown Court counts for this purpose as an inferior court, but is by statute exempt from review 'in matters relating to trial on indictment'.[40]

CONTRACTUAL BODIES, DOMESTIC TRIBUNALS, UNIVERSITIES ETC.

Tribunals whose jurisdiction is confined to the internal affairs of some profession or association, and which are commonly called domestic tribunals, have not until recently appeared among the numerous tribunals against which quashing and the prohibiting orders have been granted. Where their powers are statutory, as in the case of the Disciplinary Committee of the General Medical Council[41] and the Disciplinary Committee of the Law Society,[42] there is no apparent difficulty in fitting them into Atkin LJ's formula as bodies having legal authority to determine questions affecting rights.[43] There have been other comparable cases.[44] Even non-statutory bodies have been brought within the scope of judicial review, so that statutory powers are no longer an indispensable requirement for prerogative remedies. These exceptional cases are explained separately below.[45]

Where a disciplinary body has no statutory powers its jurisdiction will normally be based upon contract. Members of trade unions, business associations and social clubs and also students in universities and colleges have, as we have seen, contractual rights based on their contracts of membership, with implied terms which protect them from unfair expulsion.[46] The same applies to religious bodies outside the established

---

[36] *R v. Wormwood Scrubs Prison Governor ex p Boydell* [1948] 2 KB 193 (habeas corpus and quashing order granted). The Courts-Martial Appeal Court is an exception, as noted below.

[37] *Re Racal Communications Ltd* [1981] AC 374.

[38] *R v. Master of the Rolls ex p McKinnell* [1993] 1 WLR 88 (appeal under Solicitors Act 1974).

[39] *Cart v. The Upper Tribunal* [2009] EWHC 3052 (Laws LJ) upheld in the Supreme Court: [2011] UKSC 28. Discussed above, pp. 222–3.

[40] Senior Courts Act 1981, s. 29(3). The purpose is to avoid delay: see the *Kebilene* case (above). The exemption has caused much difficulty: see *Re Smalley* [1985] AC 622; *Re Ashton* [1994] 1 AC 9; and see [1990] *PL* 50 (R. Ward). Contrast *M v. Isleworth Crown Court* [2005] EWHC 363 (bail decision 'at early stage' of proceedings does not relate to trial on indictment, so subject to judicial review), *R (Shergill) v. Harrow Crown Court* [2005] EWHC 648 (bail decision after arraignment but before substantive commencement of trial, subject to judicial review) and *R (TH) v. Wood Green Crown Court* [2006] EWHC 2683, [2007] 1 WLR 1670 (denial of bail to hostile witness during the course of trial, not subject to judicial review (but habeas corpus available)).

[41] Medical Acts, 1956–78.   [42] Solicitors Act 1974, Pt II.

[43] *R v. General Medical Council ex p Gee* [1986] 1 WLR 226 at 237, also [1986] 1 WLR 1247 (CA) and [1987] 1 WLR 564 (HL); *R v. General Medical Council ex p Colman* [1990] 1 All ER 489.

[44] *R v. Committee of Lloyds ex p Posgate*, The Times, 12 January 1983 (cf. the cases discussed below, p. 540); *R v. Pharmaceutical Society of Great Britain ex p Sokoh*, The Times, 4 December 1986; *R v. Code of Practice Committee of the British Pharmaceutical Industry* (1990) 3 Admin LR 697.

[45] Above, p. 538.   [46] Above, pp. 377 and 469.

church.[47] In these cases declaration and injunction are the appropriate remedies. Quashing and prohibiting orders are quite out of place, since the Crown's supervisory powers over public authorities are not concerned with private contracts. A quashing order will therefore not issue where all the rights asserted are contractual.[48] As Lord Parker CJ said:[49]

> Private or domestic tribunals have always been outside the scope of the quashing order since their authority is derived solely from contract, that is, from the agreement of the parties concerned.

On the same principle, contracts of employment are equally beyond the scope of quashing and prohibiting orders. Thus where a university in Ceylon dismissed a lecturer from his post, it was held that his position was merely that of an employee under an ordinary contract of master and servant, and that in such a case a quashing order would not lie.[50] There have been similar rulings on applications made by employees of the Crown Prosecution Service[51] and of a district health authority[52] and of the BBC.[53]

Here again a distinction is to be drawn between a mere contract of employment and tenure of a public office. An office-holder unlawfully dismissed may have his dismissal quashed by a quashing order, so that he remains in office.[54] In the past, nevertheless, public offices were in practice protected by ordinary actions for declaration and injunction.[55]

Universities and colleges may or may not have statutory powers. If they have, the court may treat them as statutory public authorities which are subject to quashing and prohibiting orders as well as to declaration and injunction.[56] But the mere fact that the university is established by statute does not necessarily make its powers statutory: it may engage its employees under ordinary contracts of service.[57] If there is no statutory constitution, but merely incorporation by charter, there is no basis for disciplinary rules other than contract. As Lord Devlin said in a published report about misconduct by students:[58]

---

[47] See R v. Chief Rabbi ex p Wachmann [1992] 1 WLR 1036; R v. Imam of Bury Park Jami Masjid Luton ex p Sulaiman Ali [1994] COD 142; R v. Provincial Court of the Church in Wales ex p Williams [1999] COD 163; above, p. 535.

[48] Law v. National Greyhound Racing Club Ltd [1983] 1 WLR 1302; R v. Corporation of Lloyds ex p Briggs [1993] 1 Lloyd's Rep. 176 (relations between Lloyd's and 'names' held to be contractual only); R v. Panel of the Federation of Communication Services Ltd ex p Kubis (1999) 11 Admin LR 43. See also the Datafin case, below, p. 540.

[49] R v. Criminal Injuries Compensation Board ex p Lain [1967] 2 QB 864 at 882. See similarly Lee v. Showmen's Guild of Great Britain [1952] 2 QB 329 at 346 (Denning LJ).

[50] Vidyodaya University Council v. Silva [1965] 1 WLR 77. See similarly R v. Post Office ex p Byrne [1975] ICR 221.   [51] R v. Crown Prosecution Service ex p Hogg (1994) 6 Admin LR 778.

[52] R v. East Berkshire Health Authority ex p Walsh [1985] QB 152.

[53] R v. British Broadcasting Corporation ex p Lavelle [1983] 1 WLR 23. See below, p. 574.

[54] As in R v. Home Secretary ex p Benwell [1985] QB 554 (prison officer).

[55] As in Cooper v. Wilson [1937] 2 KB 309 and Ridge v. Baldwin [1964] AC 40 (police officers: declarations).

[56] As in the case of city technology colleges, constituted by ministerial order: R v. Governors of Haberdashers' Aske's Hatcham College Trust ex p Tyrell [1995] COD 399 (college's refusal to admit pupil held reviewable but relief refused). The court may have a choice where, as in that case, there are both statutory and contractual functions. See also Naik v. University of Stirling, 1994 SLT 449 (royal grant of powers: judicial review for student competent); King v. University of Saskatchewan (1969) 6 DLR (3d) 120.

[57] As in the Vidyodaya case (above); and see Fekete v. Royal Institution for the Advancement of Learning [1969] BR 1 (Quebec), affirmed (1969) 2 DLR (3d) 129. The Universities of Oxford and Cambridge are ancient universities by prescription but have statutory power to make their own statutes. How they should be classified is uncertain.   [58] Report on the Cambridge Sit-in, 1973, para. 154.

Contract is the foundation of most domestic or internal systems of discipline... The power to discipline should be derived from the acceptance of it by the student in the contract of matriculation.

Non-statutory discipline may therefore be controlled by the ordinary remedies for breach of contract such as injunction, declaration or damages, but not by quashing or prohibiting orders. But it must be remembered that any dispute over the interpretation and administration of the university's internal rules comes within the exclusive jurisdiction of the visitor, if there is one, even where there is a relationship of contract.[59] A visitor is subject to quashing and prohibiting orders if he had no power to adjudicate or if he abused his power or violated the rules of natural justice. But, by a special exception, his decision is not reviewable for mere error of fact or law. If he refuses to act he is compellable by a mandatory order.[60]

The courts will, in any case, be reluctant to enter into 'issues of academic or pastoral judgment which the university was equipped to consider in breadth and in depth but on which any judgment of the courts would be jejune and inappropriate. That undoubtedly included such questions as what mark or class a student ought to be awarded or whether an aegrotat was justified.'[61]

The contractual basis of the rights of students appears to have been overlooked by the High Court in one case, where it was held that the student complainants had not been treated in accordance with natural justice, but that they had delayed too long to be entitled to quashing and mandatory orders.[62] It has since been made clear once again that contractual rights are outside the scope of the quashing order altogether, so that this remedy was not available to a Post Office employee alleging that he was dismissed in breach of his terms of employment.[63] But if the dismissal was in breach of statutory restrictions a quashing order will lie to quash it.[64]

The contrast between contractual and non-contractual situations has been sharpened by the divorce of public and private law, discussed in the following chapter with further examples of employments, offices and other heads of liability.[65] If contract is made into a rigid barrier against judicial review, victims of abuse of power may be left without remedy where they are not themselves parties to a contract under which some public service is administered. 'Government by contract' is now so extensive that the case for controlling it may become irresistible.[66]

---

[59] Above, p. 469.

[60] For all these propositions see *R* v. *Hull University Visitor ex p Page* [1993] AC 682. Judges acting as visitors to the Inns of Court are a tribunal of appeal, not of review, in disciplinary cases but are themselves liable to limited judicial review as stated above, p. 534. See also *R* v. *Council of Legal Education ex p Eddis* (1994) 7 Admin LR 357.

[61] *Clark* v. *University of Lincolnshire and Humberside* [2000] 1 WLR 1988 (Sedley LJ). As to academic judgment see also above, p. 444.

[62] *R* v. *Aston University Senate ex p Roffey* [1969] 2 QB 538, criticised in *Herring* v. *Templeman* [1973] 3 All ER 569 at 585. See also *R* v. *Fernhill Manor School ex p Brown* (1993) 5 Admin LR 159 (expulsion from school: remedy in contract only). Contrast *R* v. *Cobham Hall School ex p S* [1998] ELR 389) (pupil withdrawn by head from government assisted places scheme (which was established by statute); decision subject to review). [63] *R* v. *Post Office ex p Byrne* [1975] ICR 221, repeating the above criticism.

[64] *R* v. *British Coal Corporation ex p Vardy* [1993] ICR 720. [65] Below, p. 574.

[66] See below, p. 674.

REALMS BEYOND THE LAW

NON-STATUTORY ACTION

Judicial review is designed to prevent the excess and abuse of power and the neglect of duty by public authorities. In the past there was a clear test for determining the limits of the court's jurisdiction: 'power' meant legal power conferred by Act of Parliament. Subject to the special rules governing individual remedies, it was only necessary to ascertain that the power was statutory before invoking the aid of the court. Nor was it difficult to distinguish public authorities from other recipients of statutory powers such as commercial companies and trustees. If the power was granted for governmental purposes, its exercise was controllable by the remedies of administrative law. The same could likewise be said of duties. The scope of judicial review was defined by the classic formula of the *Electricity Commissioners* case which, at least after *Ridge* v. *Baldwin*, was well understood.[67]

The law has been driven from these familiar moorings by the impetus of expanding judicial review, which has been extended to two kinds of non-statutory action. One is where bodies which are unquestionably governmental do things for which no statutory power is necessary, such as issuing circulars or other forms of information. Examples have already been given to show how the courts will entertain actions disputing statements of law, and even of policy, in government statements and circulars, although mere statements and circulars in themselves have no legal effect.[68] The other category is where judicial review is extended to bodies which, by the traditional test, would not be subject to judicial review and which, in some cases, fall outside the sphere of government altogether. A variety of commercial, professional, sporting and other activities are regulated by powerful bodies which are devoid of statutory status and may yet have an effective monopoly. In their willingness to 'recognise the realities of executive power'[69] and in their desire to prevent its abuse the courts have undertaken to review the decisions of a number of such bodies, while in other cases they have refused. The limits of this new jurisdiction have been explored in a series of judgments and they are by no means certain. At the present stage they are best discussed case by case, as in the paragraphs below. The first in order of time, and by a long interval, was the case of the Criminal Injuries Compensation Board.

These judicial forays into areas beyond the law have constitutional implications. The rule of law now operates in territory previously supposed to be beyond its reach. Where the court undertakes, as illustrated below, to enforce the self-made rules of a non-statutory (and non-contractual) body, those rules become in effect legislation, though in no way authorised by Parliament.[70] Other novel phenomena are likely to reveal themselves. Although the House of Lords has not expressly approved this novel jurisdiction, it has recognised it indirectly.[71]

For obvious constitutional reasons there can be no judicial review of parliamentary proceedings of any kind.[72]

---

[67] Above, p. 516.   [68] Above, p. 486.

[69] See the *Takeover Panel* case, below. See also D. Oliver in Forsyth (ed.), *Judicial Review and the Constitution*, ch. 14.

[70] A point noted by Popplewell J in the *Pharmaceutical Industry* case (below, p. 542).

[71] In *ex p Walker*, below.

[72] *R v. Parliamentary Commissioner for Standards ex p Al Fayed* [1998] 1 WLR 669 (relief refused). But this does not apply to the Parliamentary Commissioner for Administration: see above, p. 82.

THE CROWN AND THE PUBLIC SERVICE

Powers of the Crown which are treated as within the royal prerogative are now, in appropriate cases, within the scope of judicial review, as already explained.[73] These include decisions of the Civil Service Appeal Board,[74] whose powers derive from prerogative Orders in Council without any statutory basis, though the Board carries the Secretary of State's statutory approval for the purposes of the law of unfair dismissal. The court has declined to extend its control beyond the Appeal Board into day-to-day discipline, so that the removal of an offending civil servant to another department with loss of seniority is not reviewable.[75] But review may be granted where civil service regulations are not observed.[76] The grant or refusal of passports, which remains a non-statutory function, is another example of the extended range of judicial review.[77]

NON-STATUTORY BODIES SET UP BY THE GOVERNMENT

The function of the (former) Criminal Injuries Compensation Board was to adjudicate claims and award compensation to victims of violent crime. It was constituted merely administratively as a non-statutory body, which it remained until reconstituted by Parliament in 1995.[78] There was a published scheme which was debated in Parliament, but not enacted, so that in law the rules of the scheme were mere administrative instructions from the Home Secretary to the Board. Funds for the Board were voted annually by Parliament. The court readily granted quashing orders to quash decisions of the Board which were not in accordance with the informal rules of the scheme or with the principles of reasonableness and fairness.[79] The extension of judicial review did not seem far-reaching when it was made in 1967, since the Board was clearly part of the machinery of government, was under parliamentary and ministerial control, and was analogous with many statutory tribunals. But a breach had been made in the logical boundaries of judicial review and twenty years later the breach was exploited in a way which opened up entirely new vistas.

The Home Office Policy and Advisory Board for Forensic Pathology is a non-statutory body, set up by the Home Office, with responsibility amongst other things for accreditation of forensic pathologists including the maintenance of a register of the same. It has 'a vital role... [underpinning] the proper functioning of the criminal justice system and... [preventing] miscarriages of justice'. It is unsurprisingly subject to judicial review.[80]

---

[73] Above, p. 37.

[74] *R v. Civil Service Appeal Board ex p Bruce* [1989] 2 All ER 907 (claim failed); *R v. Civil Service Appeal Board ex p Cunningham* [1991] 4 All ER 310 (Board's decision quashed); *R v. Civil Service Appeal Board ex p Chance* [1993] COD 116 (Board's decision quashed).

[75] *R v. Lord Chancellor's Department ex p Nangle* [1992] 1 All ER 897. And see *R (Tucker) v. Director General of the National Crime Squad* [2003] ICR 599 (secondment to National Crime Squad not reviewed).

[76] *Jackson v. Secretary of State for Scotland*, 1992 SLT 572 (rule concerning retirement on health grounds disregarded). [77] See above, p. 289.

[78] Criminal Injuries Compensation Act 1995, replacing the Board by a panel of adjudicators. For the failure of the Home Secretary's attempt to introduce another non-statutory scheme see above, p. 334. See also *R v. Ministry of Defence ex p Walker* [2000] 1 WLR 806 (HL) (non-legal compensation scheme for armed forces overseas).

[79] *R v. Criminal Injuries Compensation Board ex p Lain* [1967] 2 QB 864 (claim failed). Examples of successful claims are *R v. Criminal Injuries Compensation Board ex p Schofield* [1971] 1 WLR 926; *ex p Tong* [1976] 1 WLR 1237 (CA); *ex p Clowes* [1977] 1 WLR 1353 (mandatory order also granted); *ex p Cummings* (1992) 4 Admin LR 747 (reasons inadequate). A duty of fairness and reasonableness was to be inferred from the voting of funds by Parliament: *R v. Criminal Injuries Compensation Board ex p P* [1995] 1 WLR 845.

[80] *R (Heath) v. Home Office Policy and Advisory Board for Forensic Pathology* [2005] EWHC 1793.

THE PANEL ON TAKEOVERS AND MERGERS

This unincorporated association in the City of London monitors a code of rules, promulgated by itself, governing company takeovers and mergers. It is 'without visible means of legal support', having neither statutory nor contractual powers.[81] Yet it wields 'immense power de facto', since violations of the code, adjudged by itself, may lead to exclusion from the stock exchange or investigation by the Department of Trade and Industry or other sanctions. The Court of Appeal has held that it must 'recognise the realities of executive power...in defence of the citizenry', and be prepared to grant judicial review of the panel's rulings so as to prevent abuse of 'the enormously wide discretion which it arrogates to itself'.[82] But, except in case of violation of natural justice, declaration will usually be a more suitable remedy than the quashing or mandatory order; and even then, in view of the disruptive effect of legal proceedings on urgent commercial transactions, review may be 'historic rather than contemporaneous', so as to prevent future error and relieve against unjust penalties, but otherwise to let the instant decision stand. This illustrates 'a very special feature of public law decisions, such as those of the panel, namely that however wrong they may be, however lacking in jurisdiction they may be, they subsist and remain fully effective unless and until they are set aside by a court of competent jurisdiction'.[83] It also illustrates the flexible use of discretionary remedies to meet novel legal situations.

Although the function of the takeover panel was, as a matter of law, outside the machinery of government, the court emphasised that, as a matter of fact, the panel performed an important public duty and the Secretary of State deliberately relied upon it 'as the centrepiece of his regulation of that market' in conjunction with the statutory regulation of investment business. Lloyd LJ held this to be 'an implied devolution of power' and held the panel to be established 'under authority of the Government', despite the lack of legal connection. The courts are evidently determined not to allow any powerful quasi-governmental body to opt out of the legal system, even where there may be good reasons for avoiding the law's delays and uncertainties. The court's criteria, furthermore, are extremely wide. 'Possibly the only essential elements are what can be described as a public element, which can take many different forms, and the exclusion from the jurisdiction of bodies whose sole source of power is a consensual submission to its jurisdiction.'[84] This generous formula invites litigants to assert a 'public element' in many situations where otherwise they could find no legal foothold.[85] It is now the source of great uncertainty. It seems that it may be used as a substitute, and a much less precise one, for the classic formula of Atkin LJ, 'any body of persons having legal authority to determine questions affecting the rights of subjects',[86] even in cases which clearly fall within that formula.[87]

---

[81] Now, however, the rules will probably be made statutory by endorsement under the Financial Services and Markets Act 2000, s. 143.

[82] *R v. Panel on Takeovers and Mergers ex p Datafin plc* [1987] QB 815. The application failed on the merits. The quotations are from Sir John Donaldson MR. The decision expressly follows *R v. Criminal Injuries Compensation Board ex p Lain* (above). For comment see (1987) 103 *LQR* 323 (Wade); [1987] *PL* 356 (Forsyth).

[83] The same point is made above, p. 254, on 'void or voidable'.

[84] Sir John Donaldson MR (at 838). In *R v. Spens* [1991] 4 All ER 421 it is said that relations with the Panel are consensual, but this probably means 'voluntary' rather than 'contractual'.

[85] Unsuccessful examples are *R v. Fernhill Manor School ex p Brown* (1992) 5 Admin LR 159 (expulsion of pupil from independent school); *R v. Ethical Committee of St Mary's Hospital ex p H* [1988] 1 FLR 512 (above, p. 518). But a city technology college constituted by statutory order is reviewable: *R v. Governor of Haberdashers' Aske's Hatcham College Trust ex p Tyrell* [1995] COD 399, discussing the *Datafin* and other non-statutory cases.   [86] Above, p. 514.

[87] As for example in *R v. Visitors to Lincoln's Inn ex p Calder* [1994] QB 1, where reviewability is attributed to the 'public element' rather than to the classic formula.

In the cases so far reported the complaints against the Panel were not made good,[88] so that there is as yet no example to show how the court might give effect to its imaginative propositions about adapting remedies to financial transactions. The court evidently contemplated some form of 'prospective overruling' as can be found elsewhere in the law, as is noted later.[89]

'Consensual submission' may not necessarily mean the acceptance of specific contractual obligations, as opposed to voluntary participation or activity.[90] Contractual obligations belong to private law, so that where the only rights asserted are covered by such obligations, judicial review will be refused.[91] For this reason many commercial, social and sporting associations will lie outside the field of public law.

RECOGNISED SELF-REGULATORY ORGANISATIONS

Officially recognised bodies that regulate sectors of financial markets, are in principle amenable to judicial review, even when their powers are not statutory.[92] But a statutory basis is now provided in most cases by the Financial Services and Markets Act 2000 described elsewhere.[93] Decisions of the Stock Exchange are similarly reviewable.[94] But Lloyd's of London is not a self-regulatory body and is not subject to review.[95] The Medical Defence Union which provides discretionary membership benefits, including legal advice and indemnity against claims, to doctors and dentists is not 'so woven into the fabric of public regulation or into a system of government or governmental control as to make it subject to judicial review'.[96]

THE ADVERTISING STANDARDS AUTHORITY

This authority was set up by the advertising industry for voluntary self-regulation, charged with maintaining respectable standards in advertising. Its only sanction is that it can call upon newspapers and other 'media', which have undertaken to cooperate, to refuse advertising from offending firms. Complaints are adjudicated by its council under its published rules, with no right of appeal. It has no legal basis of any kind. Yet when the council upheld a complaint against an advertiser the High Court quashed its decision for violation of natural justice, since they had not themselves seen all the material submitted by the defence.[97] The court found the 'public element' in the fact that the practice of the

---

[88] R v. Panel on Takeovers and Mergers ex p Guinness plc [1990] 1 QB 146 (Panel's refusal to grant adjournments criticised but upheld); R v. Panel on Takeovers and Mergers ex p Al Fayed (1992) 5 Admin LR 337 (refusal to adjourn disciplinary proceedings upheld).

[89] Below, p. 599. See also above, p. 249 (retrospectivity).

[90] In rejecting a claim against the Press Complaints Commission the court left the question of its reviewability open: R v. Press Complaints Commission ex p Stewart-Brady [1997] COD 93.

[91] See above, pp. 513 and 535.

[92] Bank of Scotland v. Investment Management Regulatory Organisation Ltd, 1989 SLT 432; R v. Financial Intermediaries Managers and Brokers Regulatory Association ex p Cochrane [1990] COD 33; R v. Life Assurance Unit Trust Regulatory Organisation Ltd ex p Ross [1993] QB 17.   [93] Above, p. 120.

[94] R v. International Stock Exchange of the United Kingdom and the Republic of Ireland Ltd ex p Else (1982) Ltd [1993] QB 534.

[95] R (West) v. Lloyd's of London [2004] EWCA Civ 506 and R v. Lloyd's of London ex p Briggs [1993] 1 Lloyd's Rep 176.   [96] R (Moreton) v. Medical Defence Union Ltd [2006] EWHC 1948.

[97] R v. Advertising Standards Authority ex p Insurance Service plc (1990) 2 Admin LR 77. See also R v. Advertising Standards Authority ex p Vernons Organisation Ltd [1992] 1 WLR 1289 (order restraining publication of decision pending judicial review refused as inconsistent with freedom of speech); R v. Advertising Standards Authority ex p Direct Line Financial Services Ltd [1997] COD 20 (leave to apply granted).

Director of Fair Trading was to intervene under the statutory regulations about misleading advertisements only if the ASA had failed to deal properly with the complaint. If the
ASA had not existed, said the court, the Director-General would no doubt have acted.
Like the Takeover Panel, the ASA played a part, at one remove, in a system of governmental control.

THE PRESS COMPLAINTS COMMISSION

This commission was established by the newspaper and magazine industry in 1991,
replacing the former Press Council. It is wholly non-statutory. It publishes a code of
practice and adjudicates complaints, frequently for invasion of privacy. Its only sanctions are reprimand and publicity. In a case where the Commission had rejected a complaint of photography of a patient in a hospital without his consent, in apparent breach of
the code, the Court of Appeal held that the Commission need not consider the question
of a breach if they were clearly of the view that no censure was required. Dismissing the
application for leave to apply for judicial review, the court in fact reviewed the decision,
while at the same time holding, paradoxically, that the question of the amenability of
the Commission to judicial review should await a decision after full argument on a more
suitable occasion.[98]

THE BAR COUNCIL

The General Council of the Bar deals with complaints against barristers through its professional conduct committee, which can bring charges before a disciplinary tribunal.
After a quarrel between two Queen's Counsel, one of whom accused the other of mis-
handling money, the committee put forward a charge of breach of proper professional
standards. The complainant, arguing that this was too mild a charge, sought declaratory
relief by judicial review. The High Court upheld the committee's decision on its merits,
without questioning the availability of review.[99] Yet the Bar Council and its committees
have no statutory or other legal power in such a case.

THE PHARMACEUTICAL INDUSTRY

The pharmaceutical industry has a code of practice committee which advises on the commercial products which can be recommended to doctors. It has no statutory status or
powers, but an adverse recommendation will mean that there may be no market for the
product. On an application for judicial review by an aggrieved manufacturer the High
Court held that the committee's decisions were reviewable, though the complaint failed
on its merits.[100] The judge expressed great reluctance to add to the range of cases which
might swamp the courts with what were essentially domestic issues of private law; but he
felt compelled to follow the authorities mentioned above.

---

[98] R v. *Press Complaints Commission ex p Stewart-Brady* (1997) 9 Admin LR 274.
[99] R v. *General Council of the Bar ex p Percival* (1990) 2 Admin LR 711.
[100] R v. *Code of Practice Committee of the British Pharmaceutical Industry ex p Professional Counselling
Aids Ltd* (1990) 3 Admin LR 697.

REGULATION OF SPORT

Sport is regulated on a national basis by a number of powerful bodies such as the Jockey Club, the Football Association, the National Greyhound Racing Club and the British Boxing Board of Control. They have no statutory basis or authority, but in practice they may operate a monopoly so that all participants in the sport must accept their control or else be excluded; and their disciplinary powers may have very serious consequences for trainers, coaches, organisers and so forth. Where membership of such a body is contractual there may be express or implied terms about fair treatment which the member can enforce in private law. But where there is no such membership private law offers no protection against abuse of the controlling body's power, despite occasional indications to the contrary.[101] Here there is a vacuum of justice which the law ought to fill.

The courts, however, have almost uniformly declined to regard bodies controlling sport as coming within public law. In one case, where the disciplinary committee of the Jockey Club had disqualified a steward from acting as chairman of boards of inquiry, the High Court was sympathetic to judicial review but held that it was bound by authority rejecting review of the National Greyhound Racing Club.[102] In a later decision the Court of Appeal refused review of a decision of the disciplinary committee of the Jockey Club disqualifying a racehorse and fining its trainer, when both owner and trainer were in contractual relationship with the Club.[103] The decisive factor was that the powers of the Jockey Club were 'in no sense governmental', but derived from the consent of racehorse owners to be bound by its rules. A complaint of unfair procedure could not therefore be remedied by judicial review, though it might still be remediable by an action for breach of contract. The High Court similarly declined to review a decision of the Football Association to establish a premier league for football, holding that the Association was a domestic body existing in private law only and that it would be a 'quantum leap' to bring it within the law for controlling government organs.[104] But Scots law has made that leap without difficulty[105] and so, it

---

[101] See the decision of Sir Robert Megarry V-C in *McInnes* v. *Onslow-Fane* [1978] 1 WLR 1520, favouring limited review of the (non-statutory) British Boxing Board of Control's decisions on applications for licences. See also *Nagle* v. *Fielden* [1966] 2 QB 633 where the question was whether the Jockey Club's refusal to grant a trainer's licence to a woman might be unlawful as being arbitrary and unreasonable and also contrary to public policy and to 'the right to work'.

[102] *R* v. *Jockey Club ex p Massingberd-Mundy* [1993] 2 All ER 207, following *Law* v. *National Greyhound Racing Club Ltd* [1983] 1 WLR 1302. See the similarly sympathetic but negative decision in *R* v. *Jockey Club ex p RAM Racecourses Ltd* [1993] 2 All ER 207, where the proprietors of a new racecourse were allotted no race meetings and a claim based on legitimate expectation failed. Had the court not been bound by *Law* these decisions might have been different. For discussion see [1989] *PL* 95 (M. J. Beloff).

[103] *R* v. *Disciplinary Committee of the Jockey Club ex p Aga Khan* [1993] 1 WLR 909 followed in *R (Mullins)* v. *The Jockey Club* [2005] EWHC 2197 (criticism of *Aga Kahn* rejected but recognising that the existence of a contract did not in itself exclude judicial review (para. 29)). And judicial review like principles may be applied in contractual litigation over the Jockey Club's disciplinary jurisdiction (*Bradley* v. *Jockey Club* [2005] EWCA Civ 1056).

[104] *R* v. *Football Association Ltd ex p Football League Ltd* [1993] 2 All ER 833.

[105] *St Johnston Football Club Ltd* v. *Scottish Football Association*, 1965 SLT 171 (breach of natural justice, relief granted); and see *West* v. *Secretary of State for Scotland* (below). For discussion of the position in Scotland see [2005] *PL* 681 (Munro). Even sports clubs (rather than national bodies) are subject to judicial review: *Irvine* v. *Royal Burgess Golfing Society of Edinburgh* 2004 SCLR 386 (member suspended for wearing wrong shoes) and *Crocket* v. *Tantallon Golf Club*, 2005 SLT 663 (member who complained repeatedly about others wearing overcoats in the lounge expelled). These are matters more appropriately dealt with as contractual disputes.

seems, has the law in New Zealand[106] and in Canada.[107] And in one English case, where a rugby football disciplinary committee had suspended a player for fighting, the High Court granted an interim injunction to lift the suspension until it could be determined whether the proceedings lacked basic fairness, the judge observing that sport was now big business and that it was naive to pretend that it could be conducted as it was not many years ago.[108] This decision, though out of line with the authorities, is surely likely to outlive them.

THE AWARD OF CONTRACTS

The decision of a public authority to award a contract to one person rather than another is generally seen as a matter of private law and not subject to judicial review.[109] The courts would no more intervene than they would in a private individual's choice of tailor. Thus the decision of a local authority to terminate its contract with the owner of a care home which provided care for dementia patients was not subject to judicial review.[110] Decisions of local authorities in regard to setting the fees paid to care homes have been subject to review but these decisions are 'public functions'.[111]

Although there have been no notable successes in England,[112] judicial review is not entirely excluded where 'there is a public law element in the decision,… [or] the obligation involves suggested breaches of duties or obligations owed as a matter of public law'.[113] An unsuccessful tenderer may have remedies in private law[114] or under the EU public procurement regulations,[115] but will not be able to succeed in an application for judicial review unless he can show some broader breach of public law other than simple

---

[106] *Finnigan* v. *New Zealand Rugby Football Union Inc (No 2)* [1985] 2 NZLR 181 (interim injunction granted against football union's decision to send a team to South Africa; the proceedings were discontinued: *(No 3)* [1985] 2 NZLR 190).

[107] *Re Parks and B.C. School Sports* (1997) 145 DLR (4th) 174.

[108] *Jones* v. *Welsh Football Union*, The Times, 6 March 1997 (Ebsworth J), affirmed by CA, The Times, 6 January 1998. The complaint was that the player had not been allowed to challenge adverse evidence. It is not clear whether it was based on contract, tort or judicial review.

[109] See, for instance, *Mass Energy Ltd* v. *Birmingham City Council* [1994] Env. LR 298 (CA) at 306 (Glidewell LJ) (local authority obliged by statute to contract for construction of incinerator); *R* v. *The Lord Chancellor ex p Hibbit and Saunders* [1993] COD 326 (unfair treatment of firm tendering for court services). Cf. *R (Cookson & Clegg Ltd)* v. *Ministry of Defence* [2005] EWCA Civ 577 (leave to appeal from decision denying permission to apply for judicial review of decision to award contract granted).

[110] *R (Broadway Care Centre Ltd)* v. *Caerphilly CBC* [2012] EWHC 37 (this notwithstanding that Health and Social Care Act 2008 s. 145 (discussed above, p. 147) provided that the provision of such care was a public function); *R (Forest Care Home Ltd)* v. *Pembrokeshire CC* [2010] EWHC 3514 not followed.

[111] *R (Redcar and Cleveland Independent Providers Association and ors)* v. *Redcar and Cleveland Borough Council* [2013] EWHC 4 (setting of fees a 'public function' and no contract with an individual provider involved). *R (Bevan & Clarke LLP)* v. *Neath Port Talbot CBC* [2012] EWHC 236 followed. See also *R (Mavalon Care Ltd)* v. *Pembrokeshire CC* [2011] EWHC 3371.

[112] But see *R(A)* v. *B Council* [2007] EWHC 1529 (judicial review of decision to remove claimant from list of approved transport contractors).

[113] *R (Menai Collect Ltd)* v. *The Department of Constitutional Affairs* [2006] EWHC 724 (Admin), para. 41 (McCombe J) approved in *R (Gamesa Energy UK Ltd)* v. *National Assembly for Wales* [2006] EWHC 2167, para. 61 (Gibbs J). Both these cases concerned alleged unfairness in pre-tender scoring procedure. The Privy Council has also said that intervention may be justified where the decision is tainted by 'fraud, corruption or bad faith': *Mercury Energy Limited* v. *Electricity Corporation of New Zealand* [1994] 1 WLR 521 and *Williams Construction Limited* v. *Blackburn* [1995] 1 WLR 102.

[114] See Scott LJ in the *Mass Energy* case (at 313) considering whether submission of a tender may constitute a contract between the tenderer and the invitor which might found a duty of fairness.

[115] Discussed below, p. 676.

unfairness to himself. Where a contract is inconsistent with the applicable regulations the court may make a declaration to that effect.[116]

MISCELLANEOUS CASES

The British Council when operating a scheme for the accreditation of schools teaching English as a foreign language is not subject to judicial review.[117] Judicial review has predictably been refused against religious authorities.[118]

CONTRASTING POLICIES

In drawing the line as explained above the courts have set limits to the use of judicial review, which is essentially a mechanism for enforcing legality in government, as a means of remedying the shortcomings of private law. In many spheres of life, whether commercial, social, sporting or religious, a great deal of power is exercised in matters which have nothing to do with government, and particularly in the case of monopolies the law should be able to prevent unfairness and abuse.[119] An element of this appeared in the ancient common law rule that tradesmen in 'common callings' such as innkeepers, common carriers and ferrymen might make only reasonable charges and might not discriminate between customers;[120] and the same principle is seen in modern legislation against monopolies, unfair contracts and discrimination. Such a system would lie beyond administrative law, but would draw strength from it. New laws and new remedies would be needed, while judicial review remained confined to the sphere of government and to the upholding of the rule of law.

In Scots law, by contrast, the distinction between public and private law is rejected and the supervisory jurisdiction of the Court of Session is available wherever a decision-making power is conferred on some body, whether by statute or private contract or some other instrument,[121] and that body exceeds or abuses its power or fails in its duty.[122] The court may intervene if any such body violates its own constitution or rules or errs in law or infringes natural justice, even if it is the governing body of a private association. Judicial review may extend to the decisions of religious[123] and sporting[124] bodies if they act irregularly, oppressively or unfairly. Justice can thus be done in cases which lie beyond the reach of the rigid English system with its misguided public and private law dichotomy, and procedural obstacles and dilemmas are avoided.

---

[116] R (The Law Society) v. Legal Services Commission [2007] EWCA Civ 1264, [2008] 2 WLR 803 (Unified Contract (between LSC and firms of solicitors) inconsistent with Public Contract Regulations 2006).

[117] R (Oxford Study Centre Ltd) v. British Council [2001] EWHC 207 (remedy in contract available).

[118] R v. Chief Rabbi ex p Wachmann [1992] 1 WLR 1036; R v. Imam of Bury Park Jami Masjid ex p Sulaiman Ali [1992] COD 132.

[119] See Hoffmann LJ in the Aga Khan case (above) at 932 and the suggestions of Sir Harry Woolf [1986] PL 220 at 224 and Sir Gordon Borrie [1989] PL 552.

[120] See M. Taggart in Joseph (ed.), Essays on the Constitution, 214 (a full survey); [1991] PL 538 (P. Craig); P. Craig, 'Public Law and Control over Private Power' in Taggart (ed.), The Province of Administrative Law, 196; [1997] PL 630 (D. Oliver). And see Colin Campbell, 'Monopoly Power as Public Power for the Purposes of Judicial Review' (2009)125 LQR 491.

[121] Emphasis is put upon the 'tripartite relationship' between the body conferring the jurisdiction, the body exercising it and the citizen affected by it. But this may not be an inflexible requirement: Naik v. University of Stirling, 1994 SLT 449; Jobaen v. University of Stirling, 1995 SLT 120.

[122] West v. Secretary of State for Scotland, 1992 SLT 636, where the law is fully expounded by Lord President Hope. Grounds of review are held to be the same as in England but procedure is different and problem-free: see below, p. 659. See also Boyle v. Castlemilk East Housing Co-operative Ltd, 1998 SLT 56.

[123] As in M'Donald v. Burns, 1940 SLT 325 (sisters expelled from Roman Catholic convent; action held competent). [124] As in St Johnston Football Club Ltd v. Scottish Football Association Ltd (above).

18

PROCEDURE OF JUDICIAL REVIEW

INTRODUCTION

Chapters 15 and 16 described the remedies, some originating in private law and the others in public law, that might be sought by a claimant seeking to challenge the lawfulness of a public authority's decision. Chapter 17 set out the boundaries of such challenges by delimiting the kinds of decisions and the kinds of bodies subject to challenge. The central topic of this chapter is the vehicle used in the modern law to obtain all these remedies, 'the application for judicial review'. But the development of the application is complicated and intertwined with the historical deficiencies and peculiarities of the remedies themselves. Thus the chapter commences with an account of the defects in the prerogative remedies that spurred the creation of the application.

THE DEFECTS OF PREROGATIVE REMEDIES PRIOR TO THE REFORMS OF 1977

PROCEDURAL PECULIARITIES

For a long time the prerogative remedies as a body suffered from hereditary procedural defects. They had escaped the radical reforms of the nineteenth century in which the old forms of action, with their exclusive character and their multifarious peculiarities, were swept away. The prerogative remedies were left on one side, so that they remained as isolated survivors from the old era. They thus retained their own special procedure, which was of a summary and limited character and could not be combined with applications for other remedies.

Such changes as were made did not cure the two major deficiencies. The first of these was the procedural incompatibility which made it impossible to seek a quashing order and a declaration (for example) in one proceeding.[1] The second deficiency was the lack of interlocutory facilities: prerogative remedy procedure made no provision for obtaining disclosure of relevant documents by the other side[2] or for serving interrogatories, which were normal facilities in an ordinary action and were therefore available in ordinary proceedings for injunctions or declarations. These incongruities were unjustifiable survivals, especially when judicial review was developing so rapidly after about 1960.

---

[1] For attempts to mitigate this by allowing amendment of the proceedings see *Metropolitan Properties Ltd* v. *Lannon* [1968] 1 WLR 815, reversed [1969] 1 QB 577; *Chapman* v. *Earl* [1968] 1 WLR 1315.

[2] *Barnard* v. *National Dock Labour Board* [1953] 2 QB 18 at 43 (Denning LJ). In practice there was no disclosure in prerogative order procedure.

OTHER PECULIARITIES

A feature of prerogative remedy procedure which remains unaltered in the modern procedure is that evidence is taken on affidavit, i.e. by sworn statements in writing rather than orally. It is possible, but exceptional, for the court to allow cross-examination on the affidavits.[3] If the case turns upon a conflict of evidence,[4] quashing and prohibiting orders may therefore involve difficulties. It was said of them[5] that they

> afford speedy and effective remedy to a person aggrieved by a clear excess of jurisdiction by an inferior tribunal. But they are not designed to raise issues of fact for the High Court to determine *de novo*...Where the question of jurisdiction turns solely on a disputed point of law, it is obviously convenient that the court should determine it there and then. But where the dispute turns on a question of fact, about which there is a conflict of evidence, the court will generally decline to interfere.

The Crown has a privileged position for obtaining its own prerogative remedies. Where the Attorney-General applies for a quashing order on the Crown's behalf, he does not require permission to apply, and there is no time limit.[6] But the court retains all its normal control over the merits of the case.[7] Likewise the Crown may obtain a prohibiting order in case of an excess of jurisdiction, even though the party affected cannot do so because his conduct has disentitled him to the remedy.[8]

THE QUASHING ORDER (CERTIORARI) VERSUS DECLARATORY JUDGMENT

One result of these procedural handicaps and incompatibilities was that a kind of rivalry developed between certiorari (and prohibition) on the one hand and the declaratory judgment on the other. This is worth brief notice because it formed the background to the subsequent reforms.

The story goes back more than fifty years, to a time when it seemed that certiorari and prohibition might almost be put out of business by the rapidly developing remedy of declaration, aided where necessary by injunction. In legal history a shift of this kind from inferior to superior remedies is a familiar method of progress.

The advantages of the declaration were brought into prominence in 1953 in *Barnard v. National Dock Labour Board*.[9] Dock workers in London had been dismissed for refusing to operate a new system for the unloading of raw sugar, and began actions for declarations that their dismissal was illegal. When they obtained disclosure of documents they found that the vital order had been made not by the local board but by the port manager, who had no power to make it. Thus they won their case. But had they applied

---

[3] When this was allowed for special reasons in *R v. Stokesley, Yorkshire, Justices ex p Bartram* [1956] 1 WLR 254 Lord Goddard CJ said that it was probably 'the first case in recent history', and that no one knew of a precedent. See also *George v. Secretary of State for the Environment* (1979) 77 LGR 689.

[4] As it may well do in a case of jurisdictional fact or breach of natural justice.

[5] *R v. Fulham etc Rent Tribunal ex p Zerek* [1951] 2 KB 1 at 11 (Devlin J). See likewise *R v. Pugh (Judge)* [1951] 2 KB 623; above, p. 217.

[6] *R v. Amendt* [1915] 2 KB 276; *Re Application for Certiorari* [1965] NI 67. It is presumed that the Senior Courts Act 1981 (below, p. 558) does not bind the Crown.   [7] *R v. Amendt* (above).

[8] *Board v. Perkins* (1888) 21 QBD 533 at 535.   [9] [1953] 2 QB 18.

for certiorari they would probably have been unable to discover the irregularity[10] and they would have been out of time, more than six months having expired. The Court of Appeal observed that certiorari was 'hedged round by limitations' and that it was right to grant declarations and injunctions in order to prevent statutory tribunals from disregarding the law.

This policy of encouraging litigants to circumvent the limitations of certiorari was twice approved by the House of Lords in later cases. In one case the question was whether planning permission was needed for quarrying operations in the Malvern Hills, and, if so, whether conditions imposed by the minister were valid.[11] The time limit for certiorari had expired and the quarrying company asked instead for declarations as to its rights. These were granted by the House of Lords, and the minister's argument that the right remedy, if any, was certiorari was rejected on the ground that the two remedies are in no way mutually exclusive.

But then it was found that the declaration had its own deficiencies. It lacked the 'public' character of the prerogative remedies, so that it might be refused to a plaintiff on the ground that he had not the necessary personal standing. It also had the serious (at that time) weakness that it was useless in cases of error on the face of the record. It began to be realised that the prerogative remedies represented the nucleus of a system of public law, operating in the name of the Crown, whose importance might be as great in the future as it had been in the past. Two contrasting statements by Lord Denning will illustrate the swing of opinion. In 1949 he said in a public lecture:[12]

> Just as the pick and shovel is no longer suitable for the winning of coal, so the procedure of mandamus, certiorari and actions on the case are not suitable for the winning of freedom in the new age. They must be replaced by new and up-to-date machinery, by declarations, injunctions and actions for negligence... The courts must do this. Of all the great tasks that lie ahead, this is the greatest.

But in 1959 he said judicially:[13]

> There is nothing more important, to my mind, than that the vast number of tribunals now in being should be subject to the supervision of the Queen's courts. This can only be done if the remedy by certiorari is maintained in the full scope which the great judges of the past gave to it... this historic remedy has still a valuable part to play: or at any rate, it should have, if we wish any longer to ensure that the rights of the people are determined according to law.

The solution, then, was evidently to be found by preserving all the various remedies but making them interchangeable under a unified system of procedure, the 'application for judicial review'.

---

[10] This was true also of *Anisminic Ltd* v. *Foreign Compensation Commission* [1969] 2 AC 147 as related by Lord Diplock in *O'Reilly* v. *Mackman* [1983] 2 AC 237 at 278.

[11] *Pyx Granite Co Ltd* v. *Ministry of Housing and Local Government* [1960] AC 260. See *Vine* v. *National Dock Labour Board* [1957] AC 488 for another example.

[12] *Freedom under the Law*, 126.

[13] *Baldwin & Francis Ltd* v. *Patents Appeal Tribunal* [1959] AC 663 at 697.

THE CREATION OF THE APPLICATION FOR JUDICIAL REVIEW AND SUBSEQUENT DEVELOPMENTS

PROPOSALS AND REFORMS

By about 1970 it had become obvious that the dilemmas and anomalies which disfigured the law of remedies could be eliminated by simple procedural reforms under which the virtues of each separate remedy could be preserved. The pioneering measures were enacted in Ontario in 1971[14] and in New Zealand in 1972.[15] Their central feature was to provide for a single form of application to the court under which the court might award any one or more of the remedies of certiorari, prohibition, mandamus, declaration or injunction. There was supplementary provision for a uniform interlocutory process by which disclosure of documents, interrogatories etc. were available, regardless of the remedies sought.[16]

For England the Law Commission in 1971 tentatively proposed a much more drastic plan.[17] There was to be an 'application for review' which was to be 'an exclusive remedy not only where an administrative act or order is challenged directly, but also where it is challenged collaterally in an action for tort or contract and in other cases which essentially involve the exercise of public powers'. This proposal was criticised[18] for aiming to create a dichotomy between public and private law, despite the fact that in the British system these are closely interlocked.

In 1976, however, the Law Commission put forward a much simpler and less problematical scheme.[19] All proposals for exclusive remedies were dropped—and, it was recommended simply that by an 'application for judicial review', made in accordance with rules of court, an applicant might seek any one or more of the five remedies of mandamus, certiorari, prohibition, declaration or injunction. This and accompanying proposals as to interlocutory procedure and other matters were implemented by the Rule Committee of the Supreme Court. This led to the reform of Order 53 of the Rules of the Supreme Court and the creation of the 'application for judicial review'.[20] Some of the reforms have since been incorporated in the Senior Courts Act 1981. Analogous reforms were made in Scotland in 1985.[21]

The Act of 1981 gave statutory force to a number of the primary provisions, so removing any doubt that they might have been beyond the powers of the Rule Committee. The subsequent replacement of Order 53 by Civil Procedure Rules, Part 54 in 2000 is described below.

---

[14] Judicial Review Procedure Act 1971.   [15] Judicature Amendment Act 1972.

[16] Later legislation in Australia went even further enumerating the grounds of judicial review: the Administrative Decisions (Judicial Review) Act 1977.

[17] Remedies in Administrative Law (published Working Paper No. 40, 1971).

[18] By the senior author in an unpublished memorandum of December 1971, expressing fears which were largely fulfilled by O'Reilly v. Mackman (below).

[19] Report on Remedies in Administrative Law (Law Com. No. 73), 1976, Cmnd 6407.

[20] SI 1977 No. 1955. For a statistical survey and comment on the procedure see (1987) 50 MLR 432 (M. Sunkin).

[21] Act of Sederunt (Rules of Court Amendment No. 2) (Judicial Review) 1985, SI No. 500 (as amended by SI 1990 No. 705), requiring 'application for judicial review' to be used in any application for 'the supervisory jurisdiction of the court', thus establishing an exclusive procedure. See The Laws of Scotland (Stair Memorial Encyclopedia) vol. i, para. 345; [1987] PL 313 (A. W. Bradley). the Encyclopedia contains a valuable account of administrative law in Scotland by Professor Bradley. See also Judicial Review in Scotland (C. M. G. Himsworth) in Supperstone and Goudie (eds.), Judicial Review, 3rd edn, and also above, p. 545.

THE APPLICATION FOR JUDICIAL REVIEW

The basis of the reformed procedure is now laid down in section 31 of the Senior Courts Act 1981 in the two following subsections.

> (1) An application to the High Court for one or more of the following forms of relief, namely—
>
>   (a) a mandatory order, a prohibiting or a quashing order;
>
>   (b) a declaration or injunction under subsection (2); or
>
>   (c) an injunction under section 30 restraining a person not entitled to do so from acting in an office to which that section applies,[22]
>
> shall be made in accordance with rules of court by a procedure to be known as an application for judicial review.
>
> (2) A declaration may be made or an injunction granted under this subsection in any case where an application for judicial review, seeking that relief, has been made and the High Court considers that, having regard to—
>
>   (a) the nature of the matters in respect of which relief may be granted by mandatory, prohibiting or quashing orders;
>
>   (b) the nature of the persons and bodies against whom relief may be granted by such orders; and
>
>   (c) all the circumstances of the case,
>
> it would be just and convenient for the declaration to be made or the injunction to be granted, as the case may be.

The object of the 'having regard' provisions is to confine the new procedure to the sphere of judicial review, i.e. the control of governmental powers and duties. That is the sphere within which the prerogative remedies themselves operate. 'The purpose of section 31 is to regulate procedure in relation to judicial review, not to extend the jurisdiction of the court.'[23] It would be just as unsuitable, for example, to apply for judicial review in seeking an injunction against a tort or breach of contract by a public authority as it would be to seek a prohibiting order for the same purpose.

THE 'CLAIM FOR JUDICIAL REVIEW' AND THE CIVIL PROCEDURE RULES, PART 54

The application for judicial review, just described, with its foundation in section 31 of the Senior Courts Act 1981 supplemented by the provisions of RSC, Order 53 has been further reformed as part of Lord Woolf's far-reaching Civil Justice Reforms.[24] Although Lord Woolf's Report made important recommendations about judicial review,[25] changes

---

[22] For this see above, p. 482.

[23] *Law v. National Greyhound Racing Club Ltd* [1983] 1 WLR 1302 (Lawton LJ); and see *R v. Inland Revenue Commissioners ex p National Federation of Self-Employed and Small Businesses Ltd* [1982] AC 617 at 639 and 648; *R v. British Broadcasting Corporation ex p Lavelle* [1983] 1 WLR 23; *Davy v. Spelthorne BC* [1984] AC 262 at 278.

[24] See Lord Woolf, *Access to Justice: The Final Report to the Lord Chancellor on the Civil Justice System in England and Wales* (1997).   [25] *Access to Justice*, above, ch. 18.

were only made after a further report, the Bowman Report into the Crown Office.[26] These reforms are now implemented through Part 54 of the Civil Procedure Rules which takes the place of RSC Order 53.[27]

The most obvious changes have been in nomenclature, Latin being generally avoided. Certioriari becomes a 'quashing order', prohibition becomes a 'prohibiting order' and mandamus becomes a 'mandatory order'.[28] And the application for judicial review which has to be proceeded by an application for leave has become a 'claim for judicial review'[29] for which 'permission'[30] must be obtained. The Crown Office List has been renamed the 'Administrative Court'.[31] For some considerable time to come lawyers will need to be familiar with both sets of names. Practice will require use of the new names, while reading other than the most recent decided cases and other materials will require knowledge of the earlier names.

While the new procedure under CPR Part 54 is similar in its essential features to the RSC Order 53 procedure, the changes that have been made are significant in several areas.[32] The detailed changes are noted below.[33] Furthermore, claims under Part 54 are subject to the 'overriding objective' of CPR Part 1, viz., 'of enabling the court to deal with cases justly and at proportionate cost'. This, subject to a requirement of practicality, requires that the parties should be on 'an equal footing' and the case is dealt with in ways which are proportionate to the sums involved, the importance and complexity of the cases and the means of the parties.[34]

THE JUDICIAL REVIEW CLAIM FORM

An application for judicial review has to be made on the prescribed form[35] which among many other things requires to be stated the names and addresses of the parties (claimant and defendant) and other interested parties, the decision to be judicially reviewed, the detailed grounds for review and the relief sought. A statement of facts must be made and its truth certified. Relevant documents must be listed and attached. Once complete, the claim form must be filed with the court via the Administrative Court Office.[36]

[26] *Review of the Crown Office List* (LCD, 2000). Bowman was asked to 'put forward costed recommendations for improving the efficiency of the Crown Office List…[that do] not compromise the fairness or probity of proceedings, the quality of decisions, or the independence of the judiciary'.

[27] Pt 54 is subordinate legislation made under the Civil Procedure Act 1997, s. 2 by the Civil Procedure Rules Committee. See SI 2000 No. 2092 (Sched. 1). Pt 54 applies to all applications for judicial review lodged after 2 October 2000.   [28] For these changes see r. 54.1 in particular and Pt 54 in general.

[29] This change of name may be doubted since the Senior Courts Act 1981, s. 31(1) refers to the procedure 'to be known as an application for judicial review'.

[30] This is also open to doubt since the 1981 Act, s. 31(3) refers to the 'leave of the High Court' being required. This change of name provides a rare example of the civil justice reforms substituting a Latin word (permission) for an English one (leave).   [31] *Practice Direction* [2000] 1 WLR 1654.

[32] For comment see [2001] *PL* 4 (Fordham); [2001] *PL* 11 (Sunkin); [2000] 5 *Web JCLI* (Cornford) [2001] *JR* 138 (Smith).   [33] See, in particular, below, pp. 550, 551 and 558.

[34] For the full definition see CPR Pt 1.2 (as amended).

[35] This is now form N461 (Judicial Review Claim form). It is available at <http://www.hmcourts-service. gov.uk/courtfinder/forms/n461_e0407.pdf> (under Order 53 it was Form 86A). Guidance notes on filling in the form will be found at the same place.

[36] See <http://www.hmcourts-service.gov.uk/HMCSCourtFinder/Search.do?court_id=697> for the details of the Office's work. A process of regionalisation of the Administrative Court is under way and 'fully operational offices of the Administrative Court [are established] in Cardiff, Birmingham, Manchester and

PERMISSION/LEAVE TO APPLY

As foreshadowed, a necessary preliminary step[37] in making a claim for judicial review is obtaining the permission of the court. In the past the application for leave was made *ex parte*, i.e. without notice to the defendant and other parties involved. An important change made by CPR 54 is that the claim form must be served on 'the defendant and...unless the court otherwise directs, any person the claimant considers to be an interested party'.[38] The significance of this is that the permission stage is now an inter partes procedure. The defendant has an opportunity in their acknowledgement of service to land a 'knock-out blow' on the application for permission.

Hearing both sides at the permission stage is intended to ensure, in the interests of efficiency, that permission is not granted in inappropriate cases. The test for whether permission should be granted remains whether an arguable case has been shown,[39] although now the court will be aware of the defendant's case. Consideration of the defendant's case—even if only in summary—sometimes leads to the conclusion that the claimant's case is unarguable, thus leading to the denial of permission in cases in which it would otherwise be granted. These changes have been criticised as unlikely to lead to a more efficient procedure and as being unfair to claimants.[40] Although some lawyers find even the most obvious propositions 'arguable', the grant of permission requires 'a realistic prospect of success'.[41]

Permission may also be refused because of delay or the availability of an alternative remedy or because the claim is premature.[42]

That hearing will be 'on paper' with the judge deciding after having read the claim form and the defendant's summary of grounds for contesting the claim. But if permission is refused, the claimant may request reconsideration of the decision at an oral hearing.[43] Should the judge record that 'the application is totally without merit[44]...the claimant may not request that decision to be reconsidered at a hearing'.[45] This recent reform may deny an applicant any right to make oral submissions or to respond to the acknowledgement of service.[46]

Leeds'. Although the bulk of judicial review work originates in London, it is possible to file claim forms regionally, and deal with permission applications and substantive hearings regionally.

[37] The first step is generally writing a 'letter before claim' to the defendant to identify the issues in dispute and avoid litigation. This is not a legal requirement but it is required under the 'Pre-action Protocol' ([2001] *JR* 197) other than in urgent cases. Non-compliance with the protocol will be taken into account in managing the case and determining costs. In *R (S)* v. *Hampshire CC* [2009] EWHC 2537 non-compliance with the protocol was one of the grounds for refusing permission.

[38] CPR 54.7. Service must take place within 7 days of filing of the claim form with the court. Service must be acknowledged within 21 days (CPR 54.8).

[39] See e.g. *R* v. *Income Tax Special Commissioners ex p Stipplechoice* [1985] 2 All ER 465. Bowman favoured a presumption in favour of permission where arguability was shown (ch. 7, paras. 13 and 14) but this was not implemented in terms. For discussion of arguability, see [2007] *JR* 000 (Fordham).

[40] See [2000] *PL* 649–68 (Bridges, Meszaros and Sunkin) and [2001] *PL* 11 (Cornford and Sunkin).

[41] *Sharma* v. *Deputy Director of Public Prosecutions* [2006] UKPC 57 para. 14(4) (Lord Bingham). Speculation is discouraged, so potential arguability will not suffice (ibid.). But there is some flexibility in the test which is sensitive to context.   [42] *Sharma*, ibid. Fordham, above, para. 6.

[43] CPR 54.12(3). The defendant cannot apply to set aside an order granting permission (CPR 54.13).

[44] This finding must be in accordance with CPR 23.12 which requires the court to record the finding in its order and consider whether to make a civil restraint order (preventing the applicant from making further claims or applications without the permission of a named judge).

[45] CPR 54.12(7). This reform is one of the results of the Lord Chancellor's programme to reform judicial review. See 'Reform of Judicial Review: The Government Response', available at <http://consult.justice.gov.uk/digital-communications/judicial-review-reform>.

[46] For discussion see the ALBA Seminar paper 'The Early Stages of Judicial Review: The Changing Landscape' (Buley), at <http://www.adminlaw.org.uk/docs/ALBA%20Seminar%20June%202013%20by%20Buley.pdf>.

The still dissatisfied claimant may apply to the Court of Appeal for permission to appeal against the refusal of permission.[47]

Where after a contested hearing permission is granted on one ground but not on another, the ground on which permission was refused will not generally be able to be raised in the substantive hearing. But if the claimant shows 'substantial justification' this will be allowed.[48]

As explained elsewhere[49] the Upper Tribunal[50] is subject to judicial review when permission has been refused to appeal from a decision of the First-tier Tribunal. Such applications (known as *Cart* judicial reviews) are now governed by CPR 54.7A. The application must be filed 'no later than 16 days after the date on which notice of the Upper Tribunal's decision was sent to the applicant';[51] and permission may only be granted where the claim is 'arguable' and either the 'claim raises an important point of principle or practice; or ... there is some other compelling reason to hear it'.[52] '[E]xtreme consequences for the individual could not, of themselves' amount to 'a compelling reason'.[53] If permission is refused there is no right to an oral hearing.[54]

CRITICISM OF THE REQUIREMENT OF PERMISSION/LEAVE

The requirement of permission, which formerly applied only to the prerogative remedies, has thus been extended to declarations and injunctions when sought for the purpose of judicial review, its justification being that it enables many unmeritorious cases to be disposed of summarily if an arguable case cannot be shown. In principle it seems wrong to impose this special requirement on proceedings against public authorities, who ought not to be treated more favourably than other litigants.[55] It is notably absent from the statutory judicial review procedures which impose six-week time limits,[56]

---

[47] The right of appeal is contained in the Senior Courts Act 1981, s. 18; the procedure to be adopted is in CPR 52. The Court may give permission to appeal or it may give permission to claim judicial review in which case the claim proceeds in the High Court, unless the Court of Appeal orders otherwise (CPR 52.15). Note that the application for permission to appeal 'must be made within 7 days of the decision of the High Court to refuse to give permission to apply for judicial review' (CPR 52.15(2)). The application found by the High Court judge to be 'totally without merit' may still, with permission, be appealed to the Court of Appeal but CPR 52.15(1A)(b) now provides that in such circumstances 'the application [for permission to appeal] will be determined on paper without an oral hearing'. While such an applicant is unable to make oral representations to the Court of Appeal he will, at least, be able on paper to ventilate his criticisms of the acknowledgement of service.

[48] *R (Smith)* v. *Parole Board* [2003] 1 WLR 2548 (CA) (prisoner on licence recalled to prison claimed judicial review for alleged breach of Art. 5 and Art. 6; permission granted at contested hearing to argue Art. 6, subsequently allowed to argue Art. 5 because claims so closely interrelated; no new legal or factual point need to have risen). Cf. *R (Opoku)* v. *Principal of Southwark College* [2003] 1 WLR 234 (new material required). [49] Above, p. 222.

[50] The role and functions of the Upper Tribunal and the First-tier Tribunal are described below, p. 770.

[51] Discretionary relief from this rule available in 'exceptional' circumstances: *R (Kelway)* v. *Upper Tribunal* [2013] EWHC 2575, para. 43.

[52] These criteria are applicable only to the grant of permission: *R (HS)* v. *Upper Tribunal* [2012] EWHC 3126, paras. 32–3.

[53] *JD (Congo)* v. *Home Secretary* [2012] EWCA Civ 327, para. 26; *PR (Sri Lanka)* v. *Home Secretary* [2011] EWCA Civ 988, para. 36. An example of the criteria being satisfied is *A* v. *Home Secretary* [2013] EWHC 1272 (multiple errors by authorities including treating German national as a Ghanian). See also *R (Kuteh)* v. *Upper Tribunal* [2012] EWHC 2196, para. 51. [54] CPR 54.7A (7) and (8).

[55] The leave requirement is defended by Lord Woolf, *Protection of the Public—A New Challenge*, 19 and by The Law Commission, Law Com. No. 226, Pt V, but criticised by the *Justice/All Souls Review*, 153.

[56] Below, p. 619.

and also from corresponding procedures in other jurisdictions.[57] It would be open to grave objection if the applicant did not enjoy the right of appeal against refusal of permission.[58]

The empirical evidence of the actual operation of the permission requirement raises important questions.[59] In a particularly valuable paper Bondy and Sunkin have pointed to a sharp decline in the rate of success in permission applications (from 58 per cent in 1996 to 22 per cent in 2006).[60] The decline commenced before the introduction of the inter partes permission procedure (which may none the less account for some of the decline since its introduction). It may be that other factors (the coming into force of the Human Rights Act 1998, for instance) have led to a growth in applications in which an arguable case was not shown. Earlier empirical evidence shows a high success rate for renewed applications, suggesting a high rate of error at the initial stage, where the judge makes only 'a quick perusal of the material', as Lord Diplock described it.[61] The degree of arguability may vary widely, and new developments in this expanding branch of the law may be rejected at the outset as unarguable.[62] The success rate may be markedly different with different judges. Procedure also is variable, being sometimes oral and sometimes written. It is now generally inter partes. Defects of this kind are perhaps inevitable with such summary and informal procedure. But they may be enough to counterbalance such advantages as the permission stage may have.

THE RESPONSE AND THE DUTY OF CANDOUR

If permission is granted, the respondent and other interested parties have thirty-five days after service of the order giving permission in which to respond.[63] The response will contain the detailed grounds on which the application is resisted as well as the relevant written evidence (usually including affidavits from those involved). In making their response defendants are under a duty of candour 'to lay before the court all the relevant facts and reasoning underlying the decision under challenge'.[64] Good practice suggests that the key documents should be exhibited to the respondent's affidavit.[65] But judgment is called for. It is 'not necessary to flood the court with needless paper'.[66] A failure of candour may lead

---

[57] In Scotland there is no requirement of leave: see [1987] PL at 315 (A. W. Bradley); [1992] PL at 634 (W. J. Wolffe). In Australia, where there is also no requirement of leave, the Administrative Review Council has concluded that the requirement is wrong for 'sound reasons of both principle and pragmatism': Report No. 26, 1986, para. 66. Nor is it to be found in judicial review procedures in New Zealand and Canada.

[58] In the Administration of Justice Bill 1985, clause 43, the government proposed to abolish this right of appeal, but after much protest the clause was dropped.

[59] For detailed evidence and commentary see [1992] PL 102 (A. P. Le Sueur and M. Sunkin); M. Sunkin, L. Bridges and G. Meszaros, *Judicial Review in Perspective*, 2nd edn (1995).

[60] [2008] PL 647 (Bondy and Sunkin) at 656–7. See also Nason, above, para. 3.12.

[61] In *R v. Inland Revenue Commissioners ex p National Federation of Self-employed and Small Businesses Ltd* [1982] AC 617 at 644.

[62] A striking example is *R v. Panel on Takeovers and Mergers ex p Datafin plc* [1987] QB 815. See also the *Stipplechoice* case, above; *R v. Stratford-on-Avon DC ex p Jackson* [1985] 1 WLR 1319.

[63] CPR 54.14. Under RSC Order 53 the time to respond was 56 days.

[64] *Tweed v. Parades Commission for Northern Ireland* [2006] UKHL 53, [2007] 1 AC 650, para. 54 (Lord Brown). And see *R v. Lancashire CC ex p Huddleston* [1986] 2 All ER 941 (CA). Judicial review is a game played 'with all the cards face upwards on the table and the vast majority of cards will start in the authority's hands' (at 946; Parker LJ). There are many cases to like effect. See also the discussion by Sanders 2008, as below. [65] See below, p. 556.

[66] *Tweed*, as above, para. 56 (Lord Brown).

to an order for disclosure,[67] or an adverse inference being drawn, or a costs penalty[68] or, ultimately, punishment for contempt.[69]

Once the responses have been filed and served the application moves, subject to inter-locutory and other applications, toward the substantive hearing with argument and, of course, judgment.

THE CHANGED REMEDIAL LANDSCAPE

All the remedies mentioned are made interchangeable by being made available 'as an alternative or in addition' to any of them.[70] In addition, the court may award damages if they are claimed in the application and if they could have been awarded in an action at the same time.[71] If a claim to prerogative remedies is not opposed a declaration may still be granted to support a 'parasitic' claim for damages.[72] A declaration may also be granted where no prerogative remedy is available, as in a claim that an Act of Parliament conflicts with European Union law.[73] Even where no prerogative remedy is sought, the application is usually entitled in the name of the Queen.[74]

The novel 'substitutionary remedy' is created by CPR 54.19(3) and may be noted here. Where a quashing order has been made the court may 'in so far as any enactment per-mits, substitute its own decision' for that of the quashed decision. Since in most cases the relevant enactments will not so permit, this remedy is of limited scope.[75] For the judicial review court to substitute its decision for that of an administrative body raises difficult issues of principle—at any rate when there is more than one decision that can be lawfully taken.[76] But the power has several times been exercised, perhaps more readily when it is a decision of a judicial body that is being substituted.[77]

---

[67]   As below, p. 537.

[68]   For an example, see *R (Shoesmith)* v. *Ofsted and ors* [2010] EWHC 852 (see Ruling) (indemnity costs awarded against Ofsted for failure of candour.   [69]   See the discussion in Sanders 2008, as below.

[70]   Ord. 53 r. 2. The availability of all the remedies in the alternative is only implicit in CPR Pt 54.

[71]   Senior Courts Act 1981, s. 31(4). See *R* v. *Northavon DC ex p Palmer* [1994] COD 60. See Appendix 2 for the extension of this power to restitution and recovery of a sum due.

[72]   *R* v. *Northavon DC ex p Palmer* (1993) 6 Admin LR 195.

[73]   *R* v. *Secretary of State for Employment ex p Equal Opportunities Commission* [1995] 1 AC 1, not citing Lord Wilberforce's statement to the contrary in *Davy* v. *Spelthorne BC* (above) at 277–8.

[74]   As in *R* v. *London Transport Executive ex p Greater London Council* [1983] QB 484. Contrast *Chief Constable of North Wales* v. *Evans* [1982] 1 WLR 1155; *Council of Civil Service Unions* v. *Minister for the Civil Service* [1985] AC 374 (both cases of judicial review).

[75]   For examples of its exercise see *R (Mowlem plc)* v. *HM Assistant Deputy Coroner for the District of Avon* [2005] EWHC 1359 (substitution of words in coroner's jury's inquisition since the words substituted could not be objected to by the jury as unreflective of their reasonable determination (para. 26)) and *Meir Galandauer* v. *Snaresbrook Crown Court* [2006] EWHC 1633 (order for defence costs quashed on judi-cial review and new order made under CPR 54.19(3)). See for further discussion *R (Wheeler)* v. *Assistant Commissioner House of the Metropolitan Police* [2008] EWHC 439 (disciplinary matter); *R (Bramall)* v. *Law Society* [2005] EWHC 1570; and *R (Haracogkou)* v. *Department for Education and Skills* [2001] EWHC 678. The words cited are from the 2008 amendment to CPR 54.19 which are narrower than those used in the ear-lier version. See also the discussion in 'Procedural Update and Costs, 4–5 Gray's Inn Square, Judicial Review Conference, 2008 (Brown and Loveday).

[76]   See *R (Dhadly)* v. *London Borough of Greenwich* [2001] EWCA Civ 1822, para. 16 (May LJ). Cf. *Mowlem*, as above.

[77]   See above, p. 397 for the possible application of CPR 54.19(3) in cases where a decision is quashed for the appearance of bias.

A similar but narrower power for the court to 'substitute its decision for the decision in question' was created by a 2007 amendment to section 31 of the Senior Courts Act 1981. The decision must have been made by a court or tribunal, it must have been quashed on the ground that there was an error of law and 'without the error, there would have been only one decision which the court or tribunal could have reached'.[78]

PROCEDURAL DETAILS: DISCLOSURE, CROSS-EXAMINATION AND INTERIM RELIEF

Order 53 remedied in part the procedural deficiencies previously associated with the procedure for obtaining the prerogative remedies. In particular, it made uniform inter-locutory facilities—disclosure of documents,[79] interrogatories and cross-examination—available although subject to control of the court.[80]

In practice, however, discovery was ordered only in limited circumstances.[81] The applicant needed to show that discovery was 'necessary…for disposing fairly of the cause',[82] and this he rarely succeeded in doing without access to the documents. This will continue to be the case under the CPR with disclosure of documents—the new name for discovery—only being required when the court so orders.[83] The duty under the general Pre-Action Protocol 'to act reasonably in exchanging information and documents relevant to the claim'[84] as well as the defendant's duty of candour to the court once permission has been granted[85] offsets in part this generally parsimonious approach to disclosure. The duty of candour, for instance, means that it is 'ordinarily good practice' for a public authority to exhibit in its evidence any document 'significant to its decision'.[86]

A new direction was signalled when the House of Lords held that 'a more flexible and less prescriptive principle' was called for in disclosure, especially when the court was called upon to assess whether a restriction on a Convention right satisfied the test of proportionality.[87] Assessing proportionality called for a careful factual assessment raising issues that went beyond the predominantly legal issues raised in a straightforward judicial review challenge (and which justified a restrained approach to disclosure). The court thus instituted a procedure whereby on a disclosure summons, the disclosure would be

---

[78] 1981 Act, s. 31(5A) as added by the Tribunals, Courts and Enforcement Act 2007, s. 141. This innovation is similar to that proposed by the Law Commission in 1996.

[79] Previously discovery of documents.   [80] Order 53 r. 8.

[81] But *Norwich Pharmacal* disclosure against third parties (*Norwich Pharmacal Co* v. *Customs and Excise Commissioners* [1974] AC 133) is in principle available in judicial review when 'necessary in order to dispose fairly of the claim or to save costs' (CPR 31.17(3)(b)): *R (Omar)* v. *Secretary of State for Foreign & Commonwealth Affairs* [2011] EWCA Civ 1587.

[82] Order 24 rr. 8 and 13(1). Thus unless there was a prima facie case for suggesting that the respondent's evidence is incorrect or inadequate disclosure would not be ordered (*Tweed*, as below, para. 29 (Lord Carswell).

[83] CPR 54.16 read with the Judicial Review Practice Direction, para. 2.1, 12 ([2000] *JR* 222, 224). The general provisions governing disclosure are in CPR 31.

[84] Para. 7 (<http://www.justice.gov.uk/courts/procedure-rules/civil/rules/pd_pre-action_conduct>).

[85] See below, p. 552; and see also p. 444. For discussion see [2006] *JR* 194 (Sanders) and 'Candour and Disclosure in Claims for Judicial Review' (Paper given at ALBA conference, 27 July 2008 (Sanders)).

[86] *Tweed*, as below, para. 41 (Lord Bingham). If the duty of candour is complied with the question of ordering disclosure should only arise when the respondent considers a good reason exists (confidentiality or public interest immunity justifies).

[87] Above, p. 306. The cited words come from para. 32 (Lord Carswell) in *Tweed*, as below.

made in the first instance to the judge alone who would consider whether the documents assisted in assessing proportionality (and if they did not, refuse disclosure).[88] If they did assist, the court would address questions of preserving confidentiality (through redaction of the documents) and public interest immunity.[89]

Cross-examination was also only rarely allowed under Order 53. On the whole judicial review is not concerned with factual disputes and is ill suited to resolve such disputes. In the absence of oral testimony courts rely on 'affidavit evidence without the benefit of cross-examination', and generally 'take the facts where they are in issue as they are deposed to' by the public authority.[90] But factual disputes can arise—for instance, over the existence of a jurisdictional fact or the truthfulness of a particular witness—where justice requires that cross-examination be ordered.[91] Especially in the human rights context cross-examination may prove necessary more frequently.[92] When, as is often the case in disputes over the application of the European Convention, 'a hard-edged question [where t]here is no room for legitimate disagreement'[93] arises and which the court has to decide, then cross-examination must be allowed.[94] When cross-examination was ordered then it followed that 'disclosure was needed to enable effective and proper cross-examination to take place'.[95]

CPR 54, apparently through inadvertent error, removes any express power to cross-examine in claims for judicial review.[96] But the Administrative Court has held that, nonetheless, it retains the power to order cross-examination under CPR 32.1 (power to control evidence).[97] As an alternative, Collins J has suggested that where a factual dispute arises the court may consider ordering that the application for judicial review proceeds 'as if a writ action. This will enable full discovery in the normal way and the hearing of witnesses', i.e. cross-examination.[98]

Where a prohibiting or quashing order is sought, the court may direct a stay of the challenged proceedings. It was held accordingly that a stay could be granted to prevent the implementation of decisions of the Secretary of State for the reorganisation of county

---

[88] *Tweed v. Parades Commission for Northern Ireland* [2006] UKHL 53, [2007] 1 AC 650, paras. 32–41 (Lord Carswell), 56–8 (Lord Brown). The case concerned a challenge to a decision of the Parades Commission imposing restrictions on a proposed procession alleged to be disproportionate infringement of the claimant's Arts. 9, 10 and 11 rights.

[89] Ibid.

[90] *R v. Board of Visitors of Hull Prison ex p St Germain* [1979] 1 WLR 1401 at 1411 (Lane LJ) confirmed in *R (Al-Sweady) v. Secretary of State for Defence* [2009] EWHC 2387, para. 17.

[91] See e.g. *R v. Waltham Forest LBC ex p Baxter* [1988] QB 419 and *R v. Derbyshire County Council ex p Times Supplements Ltd* (1991) 3 Admin LR 241 (cross-examination revealed that the councillors 'displayed an unworthy lack of candour').

[92] e.g. *R (Wilkinson) v. Broadmoor Hospital Authority* [2001] EWCA Civ 1545, [2002] 1 WLR 419 (CA) (consideration of whether patient might be treated without consent).

[93] *R v. Monopolies & Mergers Commission ex p South Yorkshire Transport Ltd* [1993] 1 WLR 23 at 32 D–F.

[94] *R (Al-Sweady and ors) v. Secretary of State for Defence* [2009] EWHC 2387, paras. 18–19 (complicated disputes over whether breaches of Arts. 2, 3 and 5 by British troops in occupied Iraq shown).

[95] *Al-Sweady*, para. 22. Note criticism of Secretary of State for failure to disclose; indemnity costs ordered (para. 44). See Appendix 3.

[96] See [2001] JR 138 (M. Smith) for criticism. CPR 8.6(3) permits, even in Pt 8 proceedings (which concerns cases that are 'unlikely to involve a substantial dispute of fact'), directions to witnesses to attend for cross-examination. But CPR 54.16(1) provides that CPR 8.6 does not apply to claims for judicial review.

[97] *R (PG) v. Ealing LBC* [2002] EWHC 250.

[98] *R (Maiden Outdoor Advertising Ltd) v. Lambeth LBC* [2003] EWHC 1224, para. 37. Questions of procedural exclusivity were dismissed in accordance with the flexible approach discussed below.

schools, although in the circumstances the stay was not needed.[99] Where other remedies are sought the court may grant interim relief as in an ordinary action.[100] The court also has power to grant an interim declaration.[101] Where damages are available and are an adequate remedy, an interim injunction will generally be refused. Otherwise the court will consider where the 'balance of convenience' lies and grant or withhold the relief accordingly.

OTHER DETAILS

When quashing with a quashing order the court may remit the case to the tribunal or deciding body with a direction to decide in accordance with the court's findings.[102] This removes the need for a mandatory order in addition.

Whether an unincorporated association may apply for judicial review is uncertain.[103] A positive answer is recommended by the Law Commission.[104]

DELAYED APPLICATIONS/CLAIMS

Good administration requires that important decisions, on which many other decisions and actions will depend, should not be able to be set aside long after the event by a successful application or claim for judicial review.[105] For this reason the question of whether there has been 'undue delay' in the bringing of a claim has long been important in applying for judicial review.[106] The fundamental provisions are sections 31(6) and (7) of the Senior Courts Act 1981 which are in the following terms:

(6) Where the High Court considers that there has been undue delay in making an application for judicial review, the court may refuse to grant—

    (a) leave for the making of the application; or

    (b) any relief sought on the application,

---

[99] *R v. Secretary of State for Education and Science ex p Avon CC* [1991] 1 QB 558 (CA), holding that the power to order a stay of 'proceedings' when permission is granted extended to preventing the implementation of the administrative proceedings or decision under challenge; so that a stay could be used as a form of interim relief against administrative authorities. See also *Ex p. Ewing* [1991] 1 WLR 388; *R v. Home Secretary ex p Muboyayi* [1992] 1 QB 244 at 269; *Scotia Pharmaceuticals International Ltd* v. *Department of Health* [1993] COD 408. But contrast *Minister for Foreign Affairs, Trade and Industry* v. *Vehicles and Supplies Ltd* [1991] 1 WLR 550, where the Privy Council held the corresponding provision in Jamaica to apply to the staying of judicial proceedings only: *Avon* case was not cited. *Avon* was followed in preference to the Privy Council decision in *R (H)* v. *Ashworth Hospital Authority and ors* [2002] EWCA Civ 923 (stay of mental health tribunal decision considered). The law on this point awaits final determination by the Supreme Court, but now that interim relief in the form of injunctions and declarations is available even against ministers (see p. 705), the question is no longer acute. The power to grant a stay in an application for judicial review is now vouchsafed by CPR 54.10(2).

[100] The statutory power is found in the 1981 Act, s. 31(2). And see CPR Pt 24.1 and previously Ord. 53 r. 3(10). Urgent applications (which usually seek interim relief) are made on a special form (N463). For the procedural detail see [2004] *JR* 256 (Markus). See above, p. 705, for discussion of the grant of interim injunctions against ministers of the Crown.   [101] Discussed above, p. 488.

[102] Senior Courts Act 1981, s. 31(5).

[103] See *R v. Darlington BC ex p Association of Darlington Taxi Owners* [1994] COD 424 (refused); *R v. Tower Hamlets LBC ex p Tower Hamlets Combined Traders Association* [1996] COD 248 (allowed); *R v. Traffic Commissioners ex p 'Brake'* [1996] COD 248 (discussed).

[104] Law Com. No. 226, para. 5.38.

[105] For discussion, critique and examples, and for European parallels see Forsyth and Hare (eds.), *The Golden Metwand*, 267 (M. J. Beloff).

[106] For discussion of the law prior to CPR Pt 54, see the 8th edn of this book, pp. 647–9.

if it considers that the granting of the relief sought would be likely to cause substantial hardship to, or substantially prejudice the rights of, any person or would be detrimental to good administration.

(7) Subsection (6) is without prejudice to any enactment or rule of court which has the effect of limiting the time within which an application for judicial review may be made.

These provisions are supplemented by CPR 54.5 which, apart from an important amendment shortly to be described, is in the following terms:[107]

1. The claim form must be filed (a) promptly; and (b) in any event not later than 3 months after the grounds to make the claim first arose.

2. The time limit in this rule may not be extended by agreement between the parties.

3. This rule does not apply when any other enactment specifies a shorter time limit for making the claim for judicial review.

The claim must be made 'promptly' which means that in appropriate cases there may be 'undue delay' even when brought within the three month limit. These cases are, primarily, where a successful claim would cause 'substantial hardship' or 'prejudice the rights' of 'any person' or would be 'detrimental to good administration'.[108] But the House of Lords has said that the possibility of 'undue delay' within the three-month limit may be 'productive of unnecessary uncertainty and practical difficulty'.[109]

Nonetheless when the application is made within three months of the grounds for the application arising[110] as required by CPR 54.5 (1)(b), success in resisting a claim for lack of promptness will be relatively unusual. Generally such examples will concern planning or similar matters where there will be significant prejudice to third parties if permission is granted; much will depend upon the precise facts.[111]

---

[107] The infelicitous drafting that led to similar but conflicting provisions in Order 53 r. 4 and s. 31(6) and (7), described as 'this muddle' and as 'in truth, nonsense' (by Lloyd LJ in *R v. Dairy Quota Tribunal ex p Caswell* [1989] 1 WLR 1089 at 1094), has been in large measure resolved (by interpretation rather than amendment). For discussion see the 8th edn, p. 648 and *The Golden Metwand* (as above), 267, 272 (M. J. Beloff). Thus 'application for judicial review' in s. 31(6) and (7) means 'application for leave' not the substantive application (*R v. Dairy Quota Tribunal ex p Caswell* [1990] 2 AC 738 at 747). Under CPR 54 this will be the filing of the claim form since that is the application for 'permission'. Note the discussion below on the 'good reason' for delay in Order 53 r. 4.

[108] 1981 Act, s. 31(6). See *R (Burkett) v. Hammersmith & Fulham LBC* [2002] 1 WLR 1593 (HL) for discussion and rejection of the proposition that in planning cases the rule of thumb should be that the claim was made within 6 weeks.

[109] *Burkett* (above) (Lord Steyn). Lord Steyn pointed out that in 'truly urgent cases the court would in any event in its ultimate discretion or under section 31(6) of the 1981 Act be able to refuse relief where it is appropriate to do so'. Lord Steyn (para. 53) expressed some doubt whether the requirement of promptness was sufficiently certain to be human rights compliant. But this suggestion has been robustly rejected by the Human Rights Court (*Lam v. UK* (App. No. 41671/98)). See [2005] JR 249 (Taylor). And see *Hardy v. Pembrokeshire County Council* [2006] EWCA Civ 240. And note the position in regard to community law discussed below, p. 560, where the requirement of promptness was found to be insufficiently certain to be compliant with European law.

[110] See also *R (Burkett) v. Hammersmith & Fulham LBC* rejecting the proposition in *R v. Secretary of State for Trade and Industry ex p Greenpeace* [1998] COD 59 that where the impugned action takes place in stages the challenge should be launched against the earlier stage rather than the final and decisive stage (analysis of Forsyth ([1998] JR 8) approved). But this has been distinguished in *R (Nash) v. Capita plc and ors* [2013] EWHC 1067 as applicable only when the earlier stages were 'preliminary, provisional or contingent in the sense discussed in *Burkett*' (para. 49 (Underhill J).

[111] *Finn-Kelcey v. Milton Keynes Council and anor* [2008] EWCA Civ 1067 (application made 4 days from 3-month limit; planning matter (windfarm); permission refused); *R (Macrae) v. Heath* [2012] EWCA Civ 457

A grant of permission precludes the later dismissal of the application on account of undue delay if there is no finding of the specified hardship, prejudice or detriment; and if there is, the court should refuse relief for that reason rather than for delay.[112]

Order 53 rule 4 allowed the three-month limit to be extended where 'good reason' for the extension was shown. CPR 54.5, however, contains no similar provision although it spells out that time may not be extended by agreement between the parties. The court, however, retains power under CPR 3.1(2)(a) to 'extend or shorten the time for compliance with any rule, practice direction or court order (even if an application for extension is made after the time for compliance has expired)'. Thus the absence of a specific power to extend in this context is unlikely to be significant. And the previous cases of 'good reason' will continue to provide guidance. The courts were inclined to be generous in finding 'good reason' for extending the three-month period, thereby tempering the unduly severe time limit.[113] Time taken in applying for legal aid or for ministerial intervention in a planning dispute,[114] or in seeking to exhaust alternative remedies,[115] may justify delay if the applicant cannot fairly be criticised in the circumstances. Even where he can, the court may allow him to proceed with the case if the issues are of general importance and need to be resolved.[116]

One example of detriment to good administration is provided by a decision of the House of Lords, in which relief was refused on a delayed application because it would have required the reopening of dairy produce quotas for several past years with great administrative complications.[117] Another was where a belated challenge to a land reclamation scheme might have caused heavy financial losses.[118]

The ECJ has held[119] that the arrangements described above[120] where the duration of a limitation period 'is placed at the discretion of the competent court, is not predictable in its effects' and fails the test of legal certainty. Thus an applicant raising a community law question within the three-month limit could not be defeated by the requirement of promptness.[121] Where the same application raises both community points and domestic law points it seems that the ordinary rule will apply to the domestic points but a promptness requirement may not be able to be applied to the community law points.[122]

(planning matter; application within 2 days of the limit; permission granted because the authority's failure to provide adequate reasons explained the delay in applying).

[112] R v. Criminal Injuries Compensation Board ex p A [1999] 2 WLR 974 (HL).

[113] See M. J. Beloff (as above) at 276.

[114] R v. Stratford-on-Avon DC ex p Jackson (above), allowing both excuses. Contrast Atherton v. Strathclyde Regional Council, 1995 SLT 557.

[115] R v. Rochdale MBC ex p Cromer Ring Mill Ltd [1982] 3 All ER 761; R v. Home Secretary ex p Ruddock [1987] 1 WLR 1482 (telephone tapping).   [116] See R v. Collins ex p MS [1998] COD 52.

[117] R v. Dairy Produce Quota Tribunal ex p Caswell [1990] 2 AC 738, 749–50 (Lord Goff). See also R (Lichfield Securities Ltd) v. Lichfield District Council [2001] PLCR 519 and R (Gavin) v. Haringey LBC [2003] EWHC 2591 taking different views on whether relief could be refused simply on detriment to good administration being shown (Gavin) or only where hardship or prejudice shown (Lichfield Securities).

[118] R v. Swale BC ex p Royal Society for the Protection of Birds (1990) 2 Admin LR 790. See also R v. Bradford MBC ex p Sikander Ali (1997) 6 Admin LR 589 (possible disruption of school allocation system); R v. Leeds City Council ex p Leeds Industrial Co-operative Society Ltd (1996) 73 P & CR 70.

[119] Uniplex (UK) [2010] EUECJ C-406/08, [2010] 2 CMLR 47, paras. 39–41. [2010] CJQ 297 (Knight).

[120] The Uniplex case concerned the 'promptness' requirement in reg. 47 of the Public Contracts Regulations 2006 (SI 2006/5) which was in identical terms to CPR 54.5.

[121] R (Buglife) v. Medway Council [2011] EWHC 746 (Uniplex 'applied general and core principles of Community Law which are applicable to all directives' (para. 61) and R (U & Partners (East Anglia) Ltd) v. Broad Authority and Environment Agency [2011] EWHC 1824, paras. 37–47.

[122] R (Berky) v. Newport City Council and ors [2012] EWCA Civ 378.

The important amendment referred to above excludes from the rules just described applications for judicial review that relate to decisions made by 'the Secretary of State or local planning authority under the planning acts'.[123] In these cases the 'the claim form must be filed not later than six weeks after the grounds to make the claim first arose'. Also excluded from the usual rule are judicial review challenges to decisions 'governed by the Public Contracts Regulations 2006'. Here the basic rule is that the challenge 'must be started within 30 days beginning with the date when, '[a contractor, a supplier or a services provider] first knew or ought to have known that grounds for starting the proceedings had arisen'.

STANDING

The Senior Courts Act1981, s. 31(3) provides that:

> the court shall not grant leave to make such an application unless it considers that the applicant has a sufficient interest in the matter to which the application relates.

The Law Commission had recommended in 1976 this 'sufficient interest' formula in order to allow further development of the law about standing, which they recognised was changing to meet new situations.[124] The wisdom of this advice was shown by the decision of the House of Lords in the *Inland Revenue Commissioners* case, in which the House made use of the new rule to remodel the law radically. CPR 54, unlike Order 53,[125] contains no provision on standing, relying instead upon development through the common law.[126] That subject must be reserved for later discussion in the context of the whole law about standing.[127]

COSTS AND HELP WITH COSTS

The general rule is that 'the unsuccessful party will be ordered [by the court] to pay the costs of the successful party' although the court has a discretion to make a different order.[128] The costs recovered by a successful party are those not 'unreasonably incurred or...unreasonable in amount'.[129] This general rule serves as a powerful deterrent to discourage claimants from making claims and defendants from defending them, unless a vital interest is at stake. In general an unsuccessful claimant will need to pay only one

---

[123] *R* v. *Newbury DC ex p Chieveley Parish Council* (1998) 10 Admin LR 676.

[124] Cmnd 6407 (1976), para. 48.   [125] Which repeated the statutory formula.

[126] See the discussion in Cornford (above) in section 'Standing and Third Party Intervention', suggesting that this was to avoid a decision to accord standing explicitly on public interest grounds.

[127] Below, p. 584.

[128] CPR 44.3. The statutory power is found in the Senior Courts Act 1981, s. 51(1). In exercising this discretion the court may, apart from any party's success in the proceedings, take into account many factors including the conduct of the parties (prior to and during the proceedings) and any admissible offer of settlement (CPR 44.3(4) and (5)). See generally [2005] *JR* 139 (Leventhal).

[129] CPR 44.4(1). The award may be made on a 'standard' or the more generous 'indemnity' basis. With 'standard' costs the award must be 'proportionate to the matters in issue' and any doubt as to whether costs were reasonable and proportionate being resolved in favour of the paying party. CPR 44.4(2) and (3). Principles governing indemnity costs are discussed [2004] *JR* 202 (Riley) (conduct of parties and failure of the losing party to comply with the pre-action protocol important factors in influencing court's decision to award indemnity costs).

set of defendant's costs.[130] Where the application for judicial review is settled and the claimant secures all the relief he sought he will generally be awarded all his costs.[131] But where the claimant is only partly successful he will be awarded only a proportion of his costs depending upon the court's assessment of the reasonableness of the unsuccessful part of the claim.[132] Where it is not possible in the circumstances to identify a successful party the court may make no order for costs.[133]

More detailed rules apply in regard to costs at the permission stage. The defendant is obliged to file a acknowledgement of service once a claim form has been served on him.[134] Thus if permission is thereafter refused, the defendant can generally recover the costs of preparing and filing that acknowledgement.[135] But the defendant is not obliged to appear at the hearing when, after refusal 'on the papers', the application for permission is renewed orally. Thus if the defendant is represented at that hearing, he can not recover those costs,[136] save in exceptional circumstances.[137] Where permission is granted, then permission costs are costs in the cause.[138]

Sometimes the court may make no order as to costs. The Court of Appeal has said that 'a claim brought partly or wholly in the public interest, albeit unsuccessful, may properly result in a restricted or no order for costs'.[139] And there are other circumstances too where no order as to costs is made. For instance, where a successful defendant had unreasonably rejected a suggestion of mediation from the judge no order was made.[140] And where the decision challenged is that of a court or tribunal, and the court or tribunal is not represented in the judicial review proceedings (although it may place an affidavit or witness statement before the court) costs orders are not made in the absence of misconduct or abuse.[141] But the Court of Appeal has recognised that a successful applicant should 'be fairly compensated out of a source of

---

[130] *Bolton MDC* v. *Secretary of State for the Environment* [1995] 1 WLR 1176 (a second defendant's costs may be awarded if that defendant raises some important issue not raised by the first defendant (whose decision is under challenge); a third defendant's costs will only be awarded very rarely). But as Lord Lloyd remarked (at 1178): 'As in all questions to do with costs, the fundamental rule is that there are no rules.' One set of costs 'to be shared by the [two] interested parties' was ordered in *R (Boyle)* v. *Haverhill Pub Watch and ors* [2009] EWHC 2441, para. 45 (Judge Mackie).

[131] *R (M)* v. *Croydon LBC* [2012] EWCA Civ 59, paras. 60–1 applying the principles set out in *R (Boxall)* v. *Waltham Forest LBC* (2001) 4 CCLR 258. And see *R (Bahta)* v. *Secretary of State for the Home Department* [2011] EWCA Civ 895.

[132] *Croydon LBC*, para. 62.

[133] *Croydon LBC*, para. 63 but some qualification when it was clear which party would have won if the case had gone to trial.   [134] CPR 54.8.

[135] See *R (Leach)* v. *Commissioner for Local Administration* [2001] EWHC 445 (Collins J) (paras. 14–21) and see *Mount Cook Land Ltd* v. *Westminster CC* [2003] EWCA Civ 1346 (Auld LJ) (para. 76).

[136] This is in accord with CPR Pt 54 Practice Direction Judicial Review, para. 8.5 (no obligation to attend permission hearing unless directed by court) and para. 8.6 ('court will not generally make an order for costs against claimant'). Para. 8.6 was applied in *Mount Cook* (para. 72).

[137] A non-exhaustive list of such circumstances was provided in *Mount Cook* (para. 76). These include the hopelessness of the claim (and persistence in the claim after its hopelessness was evident), abuse of process (use of judicial review for collateral ends) and whether the unsuccessful claimant has had, in effect, the advantage of an early substantive hearing of the claim.

[138] Practice Statement (Judicial Review: Costs) [2004] 1 WLR 1760. This may include reasonable preparation costs but it is for the defendant to justify these (*Davey* v. *Aylesbury Vale DC* (below), para. 21; and see para. 32 (Sir Anthony Clarke MR) needless costs at pre-permission stage not to be encouraged). And see *Ewing* v. *Office of the Deputy Prime Minister* [2005] EWCA Civ 1583.

[139] Sedley LJ in *Davey* v. *Aylesbury Vale DC* [2007] EWCA Civ 1166, para. 21.

[140] *Dunnett* v. *Railtrack plc* [2002] EWCA Civ 303. And see *R (Nurse Prescribers Ltd)* v. *Secretary of State for Health* [2004] EWHC 403. Cf. Pre-Action Protocol, para. 3.4 'no party . . . should be forced to mediate'.

[141] *R (Davies No 2)* v. *HM Deputy Coroner for Birmingham* [2004] EWCA Civ 207, [2004] 1 WLR 2739.

public funds and not be put to irrecoverable expense in asserting his rights after a coroner (or other inferior tribunal) has gone wrong in law'.[142] Thus the court indicated that costs might be awarded in such cases even where the judge adopts a neutral stance assisting only on questions of jurisdiction and procedure.[143]

Where the 'issues raised are truly ones of general public importance'[144] the court may make a protective costs order (PCO).[145] This is an order made by the court (at any stage of the proceedings but usually after permission has been granted)[146] to the effect that, irrespective of the outcome of the judicial review, the court will make no order as to costs against the claimant[147] or that any order will not exceed a stated sum.[148] In the past the rule was that the claimant should have no private interest—so the typical applicant for a PCO was a pressure group rather than an individual with a direct interest.[149] This requirement has been significantly diluted and the current approach is to apply the requirement of a direct interest 'flexibility'. By this is meant that private interest should not be a disqualifying factor but its weight and importance in the overall context of the case should be taken into consideration by the judge.[150] Thus if the party seeking the PCO is acting to protect his own interest only the order should be refused, but if his interest is marginal in comparison to the public interest a PCO may receive more favourable consideration. Clearly it remains that case that the public interest must require that the issues raised should be resolved.[151]

---

[142] *Davies (No 2)*, para. 47 (detailed judgment of Brooke LJ) but costs were not in fact awarded. See *R (Touche) v. Inner North London Coroner* [2001] EWCA Civ 383, where costs were awarded against a coroner.

[143] *Davies (No 2)*, para. 47. The court regretted the fact that the government had not acted on the Law Commission's recommendation (Report No. 226 (1994), para. 10.6) that the judicial review court should be able to order costs paid out of central funds in appropriate public interest challenges.

[144] *R v. Lord Chancellor ex p CPAG* [1999] 1 WLR 347 at 358 (Dyson LJ).

[145] These have been much discussed although they are still relatively rare. See [2005] *JR* 206 (Stein and Beagent); [2006] *JR* 171 (Jaffey); [2006] *PL* 429 (Clayton); [2003] *PL* 697 (Chakrabarti and others). See particularly 'Litigating in the Public Interest—Report of the Working Group on Facilitating Public Interest Litigation' (July 2006). The Working Party was set by Liberty and chaired by Kay LJ. The report contains much valuable discussion and thoughtful criticism.

[146] *Corner House Research*, below, para. 78. Application should be made on the face of the claim form supported by full evidence of anticipated costs. But a PCO has been made *ex parte* (with the defendant at liberty to apply for variation): *Campaign against Arms Trade v. BAE Systems* [2007] EWHC 330.

[147] See generally *Corner House Research*, below.

[148] As a 'balancing factor', if a PCO is made, 'the liability of the defendant for the applicant's costs if the defendant loses will…be restricted to a reasonably modest amount' *Corner House Research*, below, para. 76(2).

[149] Several applications have failed where the claimant had a personal interest: *Goodson v. HM Coroner for Bedfordshire and Luton* [2005] EWCA Civ 1172 (claimant the daughter of the deceased); *R (A and ors (disputed children)) v. Home Secretary* [2007] EWHC 2494 (claimant had personal interest even though Home Secretary had conceded liability). But the requirement of personal interest is justifiably criticised (*Wilkinson v. Kitzinger* [2006] EWHC 835 (suggesting requirement should be flexibly applied)). Where the issues do truly engage the public interest and the matter is otherwise apt for a PCO, the personal interest of the claimant should not preclude making an order that would enable the public interest to be served. *Litigating the Public Interest* concluded 'that the lack of a private interest should not be a condition for obtaining a PCO' (para. 83). See also *Weir and ors v. Secretary of State for Transport and anor (No 1)* [2005] EWHC 812 (*Corner House* principles applicable only in public law challenges). For further scepticism, see *Compton*, as below and *R (England) v. Tower Hamlets LBC* [2006] EWCA Civ 1742.

[150] See *Morgan and anor v. Hinton Organics (Wessex) Ltd* [2009] EWCA Civ 107, paras. 88–9 (Laws LJ relying on the criticism in the authorities outlined in the previous note). See also *Buglife*, above, approving *R (Bullmore) v. West Hertfordshire Hospitals NHS Trust* [2007] EWHC 1350.

[151] In addition to the requirements mentioned in the text, the leading case, *R (Corner House Research) v. Secretary of State for Trade and Industry* [2005] EWCA Civ 192 (para. 76) also requires (1) that, having regard to the means of the parties and the likely costs, a PCO would be 'fair and just' and (2) that the claimant will probably discontinue the proceedings and will be acting reasonably in so doing if a PCO is not made. Furthermore, the merits of the application would be enhanced if counsel for the claimant were acting pro bono.

Although a PCO was originally said to be made only 'exceptionally', there is no longer, if there ever was, a separate requirement of 'exceptionality'.[152] PCOs have been made: to enable the legality of the Iraq war to be tested (although in the event the question was held non-justiciable);[153] to enable the legality of the closure of a Minor Injuries Unit at a local hospital to be tested;[154] and to test the legality of a scheme of experiments on animals.[155] An attempt by the Legal Services Commission to specify that the respondent (who was publically funded in the lower courts) would not be funded by the Commission in the Supreme Court unless he obtained a PCO failed.[156]

PCOs ensure that some important challenges made in the public interest are heard. But should not costs be awarded from central funds, as the Law Commission has recommended, to support challenges made in the public interest? Public authorities should expend their limited resources on their core functions, not litigation. It is not clear why public authorities, rather than the taxpayer generally, should underwrite challenges brought in the public interest.

The costs of the claimant and the defendant in a relatively straightforward judicial review may easily amount to several tens of thousands of pounds by the time that judgment is given. Thus many potential claimants can only consider judicial review if financial assistance is available from the Legal Aid Agency (LAA).[157] Under the Legal Aid, Sentencing and Punishment of Offenders Act 2012, the Lord Chancellor 'must secure that legal aid is made available in accordance with' the 2012 Act.[158] To this end he is given power to designate a civil servant as Director of Legal Aid Casework and to give him directions (although not in any individual case).[159] To provide the necessary assistance to the Director the LAA has been established as an executive agency in the Lord Chancellor's Department.

'Civil legal services',[160] the Act of 2012 continues, 'are to be made available to an individual' if they are (a) 'described in Part 1 of Schedule 1' and (b) 'the Director has determined that the individual qualifies for the services in accordance with this Part'.[161] Part 1 of Schedule 1 is very complex with many exclusions qualifying the general principle of availability; it is impossible to summarise the mosaic of entitlements and exceptions

---

[152] See R (Buglife) v. Thurrock Thames Gateway Development Corp [2008] EWCA Civ 1209, para. 18. The exceptionality requirement derives from Corner House, above and Compton, below. It is now clear that there is no separate requirement of exceptionality. But there is a particular reluctance to make PCO in a high costs case where one or both parties are publically funded (Governing Body of JFS, paras. 24–5).

[153] R (CND) v. The Prime Minister [2002] EWHC 2712.

[154] R (Compton) v. Wiltshire Primary Care Trust [2008] EWHC 880 (doubts whether general public interest requirement satisfied). See now the same case on appeal [2008] EWCA Civ 749: the requirements of Corner House (including absence of private interest) not 'to be read as statutory provisions, nor…in an over-restrictive way' (para. 23 (Waller LJ; Buxton LJ dissenting)).

[155] R (British Union for the Abolition of Vivisection) v. Home Secretary [2006] EWHC 250.

[156] R (E) v. Governing Body of JFS and anor [2009] UKSC 1 (decision to withdraw funding found to be unlawful; declaration made that funding continue). And see Weaver v. London Quadrant Housing Trust [2009] EWCA Civ 235.

[157] An executive agency (above, p. 37) established in the Department of Justice that took the place of the Legal Aid Commission which has 'cease[d] to exist' (Legal Aid, Sentencing and Punishment of Offenders Act 2012, s. 38(1)).

[158] s. 1(1). For detail see Ling and Pugh, LAG Legal Aid Handbook 2013/14 (2013).

[159] Act of 2012, s. 4(3) and (4).

[160] A concept broader than representation; it includes advice and assistance with mediation and other forms of dispute resolution (Act of 2012, s. 8).   [161] S. 8.

here. The upshot is that there are many areas in which legal aid for judicial review applications is not available (and for which they were previously available).[162] Those areas excluded of particular significance for judicial review include housing, many welfare issues and most aspects of immigration.[163] On the other hand, even where a matter is not within the scope of Part 1, if the Director has made an 'exceptional case determination', 'civil legal services' will be available.[164] Such a determination is made if failure to provide civil legal services would be a breach of an individual's Convention rights or of an individual's rights under EU law to legal services or representation at an inquest into the death of a member of the individual's family (and the Director has made a 'wider public interest determination').

Of course, it is for the Director to determine that an individual 'qualifies' for the services. Although the Act leaves much to be filled in by regulation, in essence the individual's case must pass 'a merits test' (is the case strong enough; are contested legal proceedings appropriate?) and a 'means test' (covering both income and capital). Only a person of very modest means is likely to satisfy the test.

If funding is not obtained from the LAA, assistance may be available under a conditional fee arrangement or on a pro bono basis.[165]

The Aarhus Convention[166] (which deals with decision-making in environmental matters) and to which both the UK and EU are party, requires that the remedies provided to enforce the rights secured by the Convention shall be, amongst other things, 'not prohibitively expensive'. This principle has been given effect in EU law.[167] As a result a fixed costs regime has been established for Aarhus Convention cases.[168] A party to an Aarhus Convention claim[169] 'may not be ordered to pay costs exceeding the amount prescribed in Practice Direction 45'.[170] The amount currently prescribed where a claimant is ordered to pay costs is '£5,000 where the claimant is claiming only as an individual and not as, or on behalf of, a business or other legal person; [and] in all other cases, £10,000'. And where the defendant is ordered to pay costs, the amount currently prescribed is £35,000.[171] Naturally the unsuccessful claimant will still have his own legal costs to pay but this cap on costs will doubtless spur environmental litigation. The effect of this cap is to shift the burden of much environmental litigation (even when the claimant is unsuccessful) onto the shoulders of the decision-making public authorities. This fixed costs regime takes the place of the nearly automatic PCO regime that had become established previously in Aarhus Convention claims.[172]

---

[162] There is an online tool (at <http://www.gov.uk/legal-aid/eligibility>) to assist in determining eligibility, And see <http://www.gov.uk/check-legal-aid>. [163] See Pt 1.

[164] Act of 2012, s. 10.

[165] See <http://www.barprobono.org.uk>.

[166] Convention On Access To Information, Public Participation In Decision-Making And Access To Justice In Environmental Matters, Agreed at Aarhus, Denmark, on 25 June 1998.

[167] Directive 2003/35/EC of the European Parliament and of the Council of 26 May 2003, Art. 7.

[168] It was preceded by a Ministry of Justice Consultation Paper 'Cost Protection for Litigants in Environmental Judicial Review Claims'.

[169] CPR 45.44 provides a procedure to determine whether a case is an Aarhus Convention claim or not. Respondents will doubtless fight hard to establish that the claim in not an Aarhus Convention claim in order to increase the costs risk on the claimant. [170] CPR 45.43.

[171] Practice Direction 45, para. 5.1.

[172] R (Garner) v. Elmbridge Borough Council and ors [2010] EWCA Civ 1006.

THE APPLICATION FOR JUDICIAL REVIEW IN ACTION

Since its establishment the actual operation of the application for judicial review has been subject to study not from the point of view of doctrinal law but from the point of view of statistical analysis.[173] This has yielded many valuable insights into the application for judicial review. The variation in the rates of success on permission applications has already been noted; regionalisation of the Administrative Court is considered elsewhere.

The growth of the number of applications for judicial review is striking. In 1998 there were about 4,500 applications and by 2012 this had reached 12,400 in that year.[174] This puts great pressure on judicial resources and leads to delays and irritation. But most of the growth in numbers of applications has been in immigration and asylum; indeed, apart from immigration and asylum, the growth in numbers has been modest.[175] In a significant change most immigration and asylum judicial reviews have been transferred, as from 1 November 2013, to the Upper Tribunal.[176] This means that the pressure on the Administrative Court should be significantly eased and tends to undermine the Ministry of Justice's concerns over the growth of applications that has spurred the government's programme for the reform of judicial review.[177]

THE REGIONALISATION OF THE ADMINISTRATIVE COURT

The regionalisation of the Administrative Court in April 2009—the establishment of offices of the Administrative Court in Cardiff, Birmingham, Manchester and Leeds and arranging for applications to be heard in courts in these centres—needs to be noted. This development enhances access to justice for claimants by allowing applications to be heard closer to the claimant's locality.[178] But, on the other hand, it may be thought that regionalisation will lead to more fragmented and less specialist public law litigation. Assessment of these questions is much assisted by valuable empirical studies of the process and effect of regionalisation.[179] While Cardiff is, in terms of the number of applications, the smallest regional centre, there is a constitutional aspect to its work in that the Welsh Ministers can be held to account to the local courts; a separate Welsh Administrative Court may be

---

[173] Some of the literature is: (1987) 50 *MLR* 432 (M. Sunkin); [2000] *PL* 649–68 (Bridges, Meszaros and Sunkin); [2001] *PL* 11 (Cornford and Sunkin); [2008] *PL* 647 (Bondy and Sunkin); and M. Sunkin, L. Bridges and G. Meszaros, *Judicial Review in Perspective*, 2nd edn (1995). But, since literature in this area dates readily, the latest examples should be noted and are relied upon for the statistics in the rest of this section. These are (2013) 76 *MLR* 223–53 (Nason and Sunkin) and 'Regionalisation and Trends in Administrative Court Claims' (2013) (Nason, unpublished). In addition the Lord Chancellor's 'Further Reform' Consultation Paper, below p. 567, contains a useful account of the latest statistics.

[174] 'Further Reform', para. 9.

[175] 'Further Reform', para. 10, recognises that the growth in civil judicial review apart from immigration and asylum has been 'at a much slower rate' and appends a graph showing a growth from 2007 to 2012 from approximately 2,000 to approximately 2,600. But Nason (above, para. 3.5) shows growth from 2007 to 2012 in 'Ordinary' civil judicial review (excluding immigration) from 2,071 to 2,091 (rising to 2,153 in 2013).

[176] Crime and Courts Act 2013, s. 22 amending the Senior Courts Act 1981, s. 31A.

[177] This change may, of course, have resource implications for the tribunal system. The government's intention is to introduce similar reforms to the tribunal system as those introduced into judicial review proper.

[178] This is of particular importance in the case of homelessness judicial reviews which affect only the individual and the relevant local authority.

[179] See 'The Regionalisation of Judicial Review: Constitutional Authority, Access to Justice and Specialisation of Legal Services in Public Law' (2013) 76 *MLR* 223–53 (Nason and Sunkin) and 'Regionalisation and Trends in Administrative Court Claims' (2013) (Nason, unpublished).

emerging.[180] Although there has been modest growth in the number of applications made in the regions—so now 16.6 per cent are heard in the regions—judicial review remains dominated by London with more than 82 per cent of applications (11,998) in 2012–13.[181]

FURTHER REFORMS

Some recent reforms—the shortening of time limits in some cases and the effect of a finding that a particular claim was totally without merit—to judicial review procedure have already been noted. These reforms were the result of a Ministry of Justice programme to reform judicial review based upon concern that there was massively increased use of judicial review leading to a waste of time and money dealing with unmeritorious claims 'brought simply to generate publicity or to delay the implementation of a decision that was properly made'.[182]

Now further reforms are in train. A further consultation paper has been published and it outlines several potentially far-reaching changes to the procedure of judicial review.[183] It contains many proposals, some of which are unformed and imprecise as befits their status as part of a consultation paper. Not all of them can be discussed here.

Some of the proposals are uncontroversial and would be widely welcomed, for instance the creation of a Planning Court in the High Court[184] to hear planning judicial reviews or the extension of the 'leapfrogging' appeals procedure to enable more important cases to reach the Supreme Court earlier. But most of the proposals are likely to be criticised.

Substantive reforms are planned to the law of standing. These proposals are currently inchoate and will require primary legislation to implement. The currently unformed proposal will be considered below when the law of standing is considered.[185]

The next proposed reform to be noted here is that providers of legal services should only be funded by the Legal Aid Agency in respect of work done in preparing the application for permission, if the application for permission is granted.[186] This change will throw the risk of unfunded costs squarely onto the shoulders of the providers and will doubtless act as a powerful deterrent[187] against frivolous litigation; only very strong applications where the provider is confident that permission will be granted will be made. It may be doubted whether it is appropriate that this risk should be borne entirely by the private service provider. (Special arrangements will be made for cases which settle before the permission decision is made.[188]) This proposal has predictably led to concern about access to justice and, should this proposal be implemented in its current form, it may be anticipated that there would be some judicial response—perhaps an easing of the requirement of arguability for permission.[189]

---

[180] For the statistics see Nason, above, para. 3. In 2012–13 there were only 200 applications made in Cardiff (and some of those derived from south-west England). The biggest regional centre is Manchester (with 954); Birmingham (with 764) and Leeds (with 494) follow well behind.

[181] Nason, above, para. 3.

[182] Foreword to the 'Judicial Review: Proposals for Further Reform' Consultation Paper (September 2013) available at <http://www.official-documents.gov.uk/document/cm87/8703/8703.pdf>.

[183] 'Further Reform', above. Any implementation of these proposals will be noted in Appendix 3 where an account of cl. 52 of the Criminal Justice and Courts Bill 2014 will be found.

[184] See below, pp. 770, 595.   [185] See below, p. 584. But see Appendix 3.

[186] Para. 118 n. 119, some costs still recoverable.

[187] The strength of the deterrent is enhanced by the fact that the greater part of the work in preparing an application for judicial review is frequently done in preparing the application for permission.

[188] Para. 124.

[189] See the discussion above, p. 554 (variation in the success rate of permission applications).

The Consultation further recommends that, contrary to the current position where the claimant who loses after an oral permission hearing does not bear the respondent's costs (since the respondent was not obliged to attending the hearing), the unsuccessful claimant in these circumstances should bear the respondent's costs.[190] Once more this would be a powerful deterrent against the pursuit of frivolous litigation.

Further related proposals that are likely to be controversial are the restriction of the availability of Protective Costs Orders where there is a private interest involved, and where there is no private interest a PCO should be denied if the claim is 'political' or 'campaigning'. As an alternative, the power to make PCOs may be removed in non-environmental cases. Another proposal is that interveners should bear their own costs; indeed they might bear the costs of other parties incurred in meeting the intervener's unsuccessful arguments.

It remains to be seen how many of these proposals are implemented and in quite what form. But it is difficult to avoid the impression that notwithstanding the lip service paid in the consultation paper to judicial review as 'a crucial check to ensure lawful public administration'[191] in fact the Ministry of Justice is sceptical of the value of judicial review and suspects abuse too readily. Adverse changes may be made to the application for judicial review but the subjection of the exercise of executive power to the law is ingrained in our subject; it is a task that will not be readily set aside by the courts.

THE DIVORCE OF PUBLIC AND PRIVATE LAW

AN EXCLUSIVE PROCEDURE?

In preparing the ground for the new procedure adopted in 1977 the Law Commission emphasised that they did not intend it to be exclusive. They were clearly of opinion that ordinary actions for a declaration or injunction, as contrasted with applications for prerogative orders, and also public law issues raised collaterally in ordinary actions or criminal proceedings, should remain unaffected.[192] Their object was to remove the procedural disadvantages of the prerogative remedies and to allow declarations and injunctions to be sought along with them, but not to deprive the litigant of the choice of procedures which he had enjoyed previously and which the courts had for several decades encouraged him to exploit to the full.

This policy, however, contained a grave flaw. Before 1977 there was only one procedure by which any one remedy could be sought. After 1977, according to the Law Commission's plan, there would have been two quite different procedures by which declaration and injunction could be sought in the public law field, one under Order 53 and the other by ordinary action. Between these two procedures there were sharp contrasts. The former was subject to obtaining leave of the court and to a very short time limit extendable only at the court's discretion, and its facilities for disputing questions of fact were in practice limited. The latter was free from all these restraints. How then could it make sense to allow a choice of procedures for obtaining the same remedies under which the restrictions of one could simply be evaded by recourse to the other?[193] They could no longer

---

[190] Para. 39.
[191] Foreword. [192] Law Com. No. 73 (as above), para. 34.
[193] e.g. *Heywood* v. *Hull Prison Visitors* [1980] 1 WLR 1386; *Re Tillmire Common, Heslington* [1982] 2 All ER 615 (originating summons seeking declaration as to error of law by commons registration authority disallowed). Contrast *Steeples* v. *Derbyshire CC* [1985] 1 WLR 256 (decided in 1981), the last reported example of the former procedure.

claim, as they had done before the reforms, that it was reasonable to allow the defects of the ancient prerogative remedies to be evaded by the use of ordinary actions. It was now quite a different matter for the courts to allow its evasion at the litigant's option. This was the reasoning which led to the decision of the House of Lords in *O'Reilly* v. *Mackman*, in which the divorce of public and private law was proclaimed in categorical terms. Judicial review by declaration and injunction in an ordinary action, which the courts had encouraged with great success for many years, was suddenly held to be an abuse of the process of the court. Yet in the changed circumstances, and for the reasons just explained, some such result was probably inevitable.[194]

Under the former law the prerogative remedies had, indeed, represented a separate system of public law since they were confined to the sphere of governmental powers and duties. But that system was not exclusive, and much benefit resulted from the availability of declaratory judgments in ordinary actions begun by writ or originating summons, which the courts in their discretion allowed freely. It was the availability of the alternative procedure of private law for public law purposes which made it unnecessary for the sphere of public law to be strictly defined. Now, however, it is ordained that public and private law procedures are mutually exclusive; and since the dividing line between them is impossible to draw with certainty, a great deal of fruitless litigation has resulted. As will be seen below, however, the border between public and private law is beginning to open. And the problem of procedural exclusivity, while still serious, is becoming less intense.

The dichotomy which has been imposed, and which must now be explained, must be accounted a setback for administrative law. It has caused many cases, which on their merits might have succeeded, to fail merely because of choice of the wrong form of action. It is a step back towards the time of the old forms of action which were so deservedly buried in 1852. It has produced uncertainty as to the boundary between public and private law, since these terms have no clear or settled meaning. Procedural law, which caused very little difficulty before 1977, is now full of doubts and pitfalls. Nor are these in any way necessary, as may be seen from a comparison with judicial review legislation and practice in Scotland,[195] Australia, New Zealand and Canada, where procedural obstacles have been avoided. Nor do there appear to be countervailing benefits in the English reforms. As will be seen, the House of Lords has expounded the new law as designed for the protection of public authorities rather than of the citizen. Such are the misfortunes which can flow from the best-intentioned reforms.

O'REILLY V. MACKMAN

The sole issue in this case[196] was whether the court could grant declaratory relief in ordinary actions begun by writ or originating summons at the instance of prisoners disputing the validity of punishments awarded by a board of prison, the then disciplinary authority visitors. The plaintiffs were four inmates of Hull prison, who sued (three by writ and one by originating summons) for declarations that the visitors' awards were void for breach

---

[194] The Law Commission itself says 'perhaps inevitable': Law Com. No. 226 (1994), para. 3.2.

[195] For a full discussion, see *West* v. *Secretary of State for Scotland*, 1992 SLT 636, rejecting the public/private law dichotomy and explaining the simpler procedure of judicial review in Scotland. For this important decision see [1992] *PL* 625 (W. J. Wolffe). See also *Judicial Review in Scotland* (C. M. G. Himsworth) in Supperstone and Goudie (eds.), *Judicial Review*, 2nd edn, 19.14. For the scope of review in Scots law see above, p. 545. For the rules of procedure see SI 1985 No. 500; SI 1990 No. 705.

[196] [1983] 2 AC 237, noted in (1983) 99 *LQR* 166 and discussed in (1985) 101 *LQR* 180. In the Court of Appeal Lord Denning MR decided in the same sense as the House of Lords.

of the prison rules and for violation of natural justice. They chose the ordinary forms of action because they expected substantial disputes on questions of fact and wanted to be sure that they could call oral evidence. As the trial judge said, this was clearly a rational choice.[197] The House of Lords held that in view of the new Order 53 the proceedings should be struck out as an abuse of the process of the court;[198] and that the only available procedure in such a case, since it was a matter of public law, was application for judicial review.

Lord Diplock's speech, in which the whole House concurred summarily, is an outstanding feat of analysis and synthesis, ranging widely over the landmarks of administrative law. Observing that the distinction between private law and public law 'has itself been a latecomer to the English legal system', he attributed its arrival to the expansion of judicial review over the previous thirty years. He took the opportunity to restate his doctrine of jurisdictional error and to broaden Atkin LJ's *Electricity Commissioners* formula[199] by eliminating the 'duty to act judicially' in accordance with Lord Reid's speech in *Ridge v. Baldwin*.[200] He pointed out that *Anisminic* was an action by writ for a declaration where the vital facts had been obtained only upon disclosure of documents, so that a quashing order would have been useless. In the most striking part of the speech he then presented the restrictions of prerogative remedy procedure, both before and after 1977, as designed to protect public authorities against irresponsible and protracted litigation, emphasising the following:

1. the need to obtain leave to apply

2. the need to file affidavits from the outset, so that the case has to be stated on oath and with the utmost good faith, 'an important safeguard against groundless or unmeritorious claims', in contrast with the unsworn pleadings of an ordinary action

3. the court's power on granting leave to impose terms as to costs or security

4. very speedy procedure, 'available in urgent cases within a matter of days rather than months'

5. the time limit, now reduced to three months and extended to all forms of relief.

'The public interest in good administration', Lord Diplock explained, 'requires that public authorities and third parties should not be kept in suspense as to the legal validity of a decision' disputed by a litigant.

Lord Diplock accepted that the disadvantages of the prerogative writ procedure, particularly the absolute bar on disclosure of documents, justified the use of ordinary actions for declarations before 1977, as the House of Lords had allowed in *Ridge v. Baldwin, Anisminic* and other cases, even though the safeguards imposed in the public interest were thereby evaded. But those disadvantages had now all been removed by the new Order 53. Disclosure of documents, interrogatories and cross-examination were now allowable wherever the justice of the case required, though cross-examination would be needed only on rare occasions, since issues of fact would seldom be crucial because of the court's limited function on review.[201] To allow ordinary actions for public law remedies might subject public authorities to lengthy delays which would defeat the policy of the reforms

---

[197] [1983] 2 AC at 249 (Peter Pain J).

[198] They were 'blatant attempts to avoid the protections for the defendants for which Order 53 provides' (at 285).

[199] Above, p. 514.   [200] Above, p. 516.   [201] For criticism, see above, p. 217.

and the interests of good administration. To do so, therefore, was as a general rule contrary to public policy and an abuse of the process of the court. There might be exceptions, such as collateral pleas of public law issues in claims arising under private law (an exception which was to prove important later),[202] or cases where none of the parties objected to ordinary procedure.[203] But the classes of cases where the new procedure was mandatory, and any further exceptions, should be left for future decision on a case-to-case basis.

THE NEED FOR A SINGLE PROCEDURE

It is undoubtedly right that public authorities should not be harassed by vexatious legal procedures and that disputes about their powers and duties should be settled expeditiously. But it is questionable whether the logic of *O'Reilly* v. *Mackman* is as compelling as Lord Diplock maintained. For several decades before 1977 the courts were actively encouraging ordinary actions for declarations in order to evade the handicaps of a quashing order, yet it did not appear that public authorities were lacking any protection which they could properly claim. In the case of baseless actions they could, like other litigants, apply for pleadings to be struck out, and they often did so. Points of law could be tried as preliminary issues, often saving trial of the facts. Public authorities did not appear to feel the need of the procedural privileges on which the House of Lords laid such stress. The Public Authorities Protection Act had been repealed in 1954[204] with general approval. Despite some incongruities, public and private law worked harmoniously together without any need for exclusive forms of action, and the system of remedies efficiently supported the great expansion of administrative law during those years.

The period since *O'Reilly* v. *Mackman*, on the other hand, has one of unprofitable litigation about which of two exclusive procedures a litigant should use. The need for law reform is clearly greater now than it was before 1977. The first necessity is to abandon mutually exclusive procedures and institute a single comprehensive procedure, which ought to be the same for both public and private law. Instead of putting declaration and injunction into the group of the prerogative remedies, as was in effect done in 1977, the prerogative remedies ought to be sought, at least initially, by the same procedure as applies to ordinary remedies.[205] Once the initial step is taken, it can be decided whether the case should be tried by judicial review procedure, which is best suited to the summary disposal of questions of law, or by ordinary procedure, which is best suited to the trial of disputed facts. That decision should be taken by a judicial officer, perhaps a master in suitable cases. Where the validity of a public authority's action (or inaction) was challenged, either party could apply for expedited procedure and evidence by affidavit, and the public authority could apply for dismissal of the claim on the ground of undue delay. In this way claims of whatever kind could be sorted out and directed into the right channels at the interlocutory stage. Cases of judicial review should still have a prerogative-style title with the Queen as the nominal plaintiff, in order to preserve the important public interest

---

[202] See below, p. 576.

[203] An example is *Securities and Investments Board* v. *Financial Intermediaries, Managers and Brokers Regulatory Association Ltd* [1992] Ch 268. But jurisdiction for judicial review cannot be created by agreement: *R* v. *Durham City Justices ex p Robinson*, The Times, 31 January 1992.

[204] See below, p. 622.

[205] See the comments in *New Directions in Judicial Review* 5 at 16 (M. Beloff QC); (1991) 107 *LQR* 298 at 314 (S. Fredman and G. Morris).

element. No case could then be lost by choice of the wrong procedure before its merits ever came before the court.

PROBLEMS OF DICHOTOMY

As soon as *O'Reilly* v. *Mackman* was decided the courts had to undertake surgical operations in order to sever public from private law.[206] Never having had to do this previously, they naturally encountered difficulty.

Their work made a mystifying start in a decision of the House of Lords delivered on the same day as *O'Reilly* v. *Mackman* and coordinated with that case.[207] Proceedings had been started in the county court for a declaration that a district council was in breach of its duty to provide permanent accommodation for the plaintiff under the Housing (Homeless Persons) Act 1977.[208] He found himself taken to the House of Lords on the preliminary issue whether he should have sought judicial review in the High Court. The House of Lords held that there was now 'a dichotomy between a housing authority's public and private law functions': their decision[209] whether they were satisfied that the plaintiff fulfilled the statutory conditions was a matter of public law, but their obligation to provide housing, if so satisfied, was a matter of private law enforceable by ordinary remedies. Since the plaintiff was challenging the decision of the housing authority, he could proceed only by judicial review in the High Court in accordance with *O'Reilly* v. *Mackman*. The difficulty in this case is to understand how a single statutory duty (to provide housing in certain circumstances) can be dichotomised in indefinable terms of functions. The remedy for enforcing the duty should have been a mandatory order (necessarily by judicial review in the High Court) so that it was correct to disallow an ordinary action.[210] But the fallacy of the dichotomy was shown by a later case[211] in which a homeless applicant failed to obtain a mandatory injunction in the county court in exactly the circumstances in which the House of Lords had said that he should succeed, namely where the duty to house the applicant was accepted but he claimed that the house was inadequate. The Court of Appeal held, surely correctly, that the duty and its fulfilment were inseparable elements of the same composite duty, which must be either public or private and could not be both. It remained for the House of Lords to hold, rejecting the reasoning of the original case, that the homeless persons legislation created no private right by way of statutory duty, so that judicial review was the only remedy available.[212]

A similar misunderstanding defeated the owner of a decommissioned fishing vessel who sued for the government grant by ordinary action when his proper remedy (in the absence of private law right) was a mandatory order, available only by judicial review.[213]

---

[206] For criticism, see *Administrative Justice—Some Necessary Reforms* (the JUSTICE/All Souls Report, 6.18 (Sir P. Neill); (1987) 103 *LQR* 34 (J. Beatson); [1985] *CLJ* 415 (Forsyth); (1985) 101 *LQR* 150 (Wade); [1994] *PL* 51 (A. Tanney); [1994] *PL* 69 (S. Fredman and G. Morris). For approval see [1986] *PL* 220 at 232 (Sir Harry Woolf), repeated in his Hamlyn Lectures, *Protection of the Public—A New Challenge*, 27; the Law Commission's report (Law Com. No. 226), discussed below, p. 581.

[207] *Cocks* v. *Thanet DC* [1983] 2 AC 286. See comment in (1983) 99 *LQR* at 169 and [1984] *PL* at 20 (P. Cane).   [208] Now Pt III of the Housing Act 1985.

[209] For such 'decisions' see above, p. 516.

[210] As the House of Lords in effect confirmed in *O'Rourke* v. *Camden LBC* (below), criticising the decision in *Cocks* v. *Thanet DC* (above).

[211] *Mohram Ali* v. *Tower Hamlets LBC* [1993] QB 407; see also *Tower Hamlets LBC* v. *Abdi* (1992) 91 LGR 300; and see *R* v. *Northavon DC ex p Palmer* (1993) 6 Admin LR 195.

[212] *O'Rourke* v. *Camden LBC* [1988] AC 188.

[213] *Cato* v. *Minister of Agriculture, Fisheries and Food* [1989] 3 CMLR 513. See also *R* v. *Kidderminster District Valuer ex p Powell* [1992] COD 54 (district valuer's valuation of police house: judicial review).

Yet when a candidate in a local government election sued to enforce the local authority's statutory duty to provide him with a room for an election meeting, and the local authority claimed that he should have applied for judicial review, it was held to be a matter of private law suitable for an action by writ claiming a declaration and injunction.[214] Such are the results of the attempt to dichotomise the duties of public authorities.

The impossibility of dividing public and private law cleanly is illustrated by another case where the House of Lords gave a variety of different reasons for allowing an action by writ for a declaration to be brought against a government department. The department had issued a circular to local health authorities to the effect that doctors could in some circumstances give contraceptive advice and treatment to girls under 16 without parental consent. Mrs Gillick, a mother of five young girls, sued by writ for a declaration that to act on this advice would infringe her parental rights. Her claim failed on the merits, but the House of Lords approved the procedure used.[215] Of the various reasons given[216] the simplest was that the defendants raised no objection—an exception expressly recognised in *O'Reilly* v. *Mackman*,[217] presumably on the ground that if a public authority chooses to waive its procedural privileges, the logic of that decision no longer applies. Another reason, put forward by Lord Scarman, was that 'the private law content of her claim was so great as to make her case an exception to the general rule'; and, abandoning the mutual exclusivity of *O'Reilly*, he held that she was entitled to proceed either by ordinary action or by judicial review. It might, indeed, be expected that she could bring an ordinary action for a declaration as to her personal legal rights without being caught in the *O'Reilly* entanglement, as had for so long been allowed in classic cases such as *Dyson*[218] and *Pyx Granite*.[219] No mention was made of those authorities in the *Gillick* case and it is not clear how they now stand.[220] But the case did indicate that the House of Lords was avoiding a collision course and was disinclined to press the logic of *O'Reilly* to its limit.

From this point onwards the stream of decisions is best divided into categories as follows.

ACTIONS IN TORT

Claims to remedies in tort are based on the infringement of private law rights and are in principle ineligible for judicial review, even though brought against public authorities. An action for damages for negligence, for example, must be brought against a public authority by the same procedure as against a private defendant. The House of Lords made this clear in a planning case where the plaintiff sued by writ for damages for negligent official

---

[214] *Ettridge* v. *Morrell* (1986) 85 LGR 100.

[215] *Gillick* v. *West Norfolk and Wisbech Area Health Authority* [1986] AC 112. The effective defendant was the Department of Health and Social Security. For comment see (1986) 102 *LQR* 173. On the question whether the scope of judicial review has been extended to include such cases see above, p. 538.

[216] Others were that it was a pre-*O'Reilly* case (Lord Fraser, contra Lord Scarman) and that it was a collateral issue (Lord Scarman).

[217] [1983] 2 AC at 285. This may also explain *R* v. *Doncaster MBC ex p Brain* [1986] 85 LGR 233 (declaration that land was statutory 'open space' granted on judicial review).

[218] *Dyson* v. *A-G* [1911] 1 KB 410 (above, p. 484).

[219] *Pyx Granite Co Ltd* v. *Ministry of Housing and Local Government* [1960] AC 260 (above, p. 485).

[220] Perhaps *Dyson* would now require judicial review since the validity of a departmental demand was challenged but *Pyx Granite* would not since no administrative action was disputed. On the latter point see *O'Reilly* at 281. *Pyx Granite* was quoted with approval by Lord Fraser in *Wandsworth LBC* v. *Winder* [1985] AC 461 at 510. See also *R* v. *Bromley LBC ex p Lambeth LBC*, The Times, 16 June 1984 (declaration that local authorities might lawfully subscribe to association of London authorities granted on judicial review).

advice which had prevented him from appealing in time against an enforcement notice, and also claimed, in the alternative, an injunction against its enforcement and an order to set it aside on the ground that it was invalid. It was held that the first claim could proceed but that the second and third claims must be struck out, since they could be raised only by judicial review.[221] The claim to damages raised no issue of public law since it assumed the validity of the enforcement notices, whereas the other claims impugned it. A litigant ought to be able to pursue alternative claims in one proceeding, but this can be done by seeking judicial review and making an alternative claim to damages as the rules allow.

Despite the House of Lords' ruling, the High Court later dismissed as an abuse of process an action for damages and breach of statutory duty brought against a local authority for alleged failure to make proper provision for a child in their care. Since it was claimed that the degree of negligence was such as to render their conduct ultra vires,[222] this was held to be 'a substantial public law element' which made judicial review the only available procedure, even though public and private law rights were intermingled.[223] Similarly where a landowner disputed the legality of a highway closing order it was held that judicial review was his only remedy and that his action in tort for nuisance must fail.[224] If these decisions are right, litigants are faced with insoluble dilemmas.

EMPLOYMENT AND CONTRACTUAL RELATIONSHIPS

Contractual and commercial obligations are enforceable by ordinary action and not by judicial review.[225] An employee of the BBC failed in her application for a quashing order to quash her dismissal by the Corporation since the ordinary contractual obligations of master and servant had never been within the scope of the prerogative remedies, which had not been extended by Order 53 and the Senior Courts Act 1981.[226] A civil servant also failed in attempting to have a disciplinary penalty quashed, since his proper course was to sue for breach of contract.[227] The Court of Appeal similarly rejected an application for a quashing order to quash the dismissal of a male nurse by a health authority.[228] Lord Donaldson MR said that '[e]mployment by a public authority does not per se inject

---

[221] *Davy* v. *Spelthorne BC* [1984] AC 262. See also *An Bord Bainne Co-operative Ltd* v. *Milk Marketing Board* [1984] 2 CMLR 584 (action for damages and injunction against the Board for price discrimination contrary to EEC law properly brought by ordinary action); *Garden Cottage Foods Ltd* v. *Milk Marketing Board* [1984] AC 130 at 144 (House of Lords ruled similarly); *Bourgoin SA* v. *Ministry of Agriculture, Fisheries and Food* [1986] QB 716 (dicta); *Lonrho plc* v. *Tebbitt* [1992] 4 All ER 161 (action for damages for misuse of minister's power: ordinary action allowed).

[222] For this point see below, p. 650.

[223] *Guevara* v. *Hounslow LBC*, The Times, 17 April 1987. In general wardship proceedings are preferable in the case of children in care: *R* v. *Newham LBC ex p McL* [1988] 1 FLR 416.

[224] *The Great House at Sonning Ltd* v. *Berkshire CC* (1996) 95 LGR 350.

[225] See *R* v. *Lord Chancellor ex p Hibbit and Saunders* [1993] COD 326 (complaint by a firm of shorthand writers that their tender for court services was unfairly rejected held a purely commercial matter and ineligible for judicial review).

[226] *R* v. *British Broadcasting Corporation ex p Lavelle* [1983] 1 WLR 23 (decided before *O'Reilly* v. *Mackman*). Leave to continue as if by writ was granted.

[227] *R* v. *Lord Chancellor's Department ex p Nangle* [1992] 1 All ER 897; alternatively it was held to be a mere matter of internal discipline with no element of public law.

[228] *R* v. *East Berkshire Health Authority ex p Walsh* [1985] QB 152. Leave to continue as if by writ was refused. See similarly *R* v. *Trent Regional Health Authority ex p Jones*, The Times, 19 June 1986 (consultant surgeon: no sufficient 'statutory underpinning'); *Doyle* v. *Northumberland Probation Committee* [1991] 1 WLR 1340 (probation officers' claim for breach of contract: private law). Contrast *R* v. *Salford Health Authority ex p Janaway* [1989] AC 537 (dismissal of secretary by health authority: judicial review).

any element of public law.' It could be different if there were statutory 'underpinning' of the employment such as statutory restrictions on dismissal, which would support a claim of ultra vires, or a statutory duty to incorporate certain conditions in the terms of employment, which could be enforced by a mandatory order. A sufficient 'statutory underpinning' was found immediately afterwards in a case where the Home Secretary's decision to dismiss a prison officer was quashed for violation of natural justice.[229] Unlike the male nurse, he was held not to be under a contract of employment[230] but appointed to an office and subject to a statutory code of discipline which had not been fairly applied. His dismissal was therefore ultra vires, and judicial review was the right way to contest it. But when a deputy police surgeon sought judicial review, complaining similarly that his dismissal was in breach of natural justice, he failed on the ground that he should have proceeded by writ, since his rights were contractual only.[231] So did a probationary prosecutor dismissed by the Crown Prosecution Service, though the court's attitude might have been different if there had been any infringement of the 'constitutional principle' of the prosecutor's independence.[232] Cases of this kind, in which contract, office and regulations are mixed in uncertain quantities, show well the snares that entrapped litigants[233] before the case of a health service doctor, discussed below, heralded a change.[234] Again and again claimants failed, not because their cases were bad, but because they could not tell which procedure to follow. Again and again public authorities pleaded, often with ill-deserved success, that the wrong avenue was chosen.

Private law also regulates associations and bodies whose relations with their members are governed by contract, however powerful their licensing and disciplinary powers may in fact be. Where a greyhound trainer disputed the suspension of his trainer's licence and sued by originating summons for declarations, the national association's objection that he should have proceeded by judicial review was disallowed by the Court of Appeal, which emphasised that the new rules did not extend public law remedies to private law relationships.[235] The same is presumably true in the case of trade unions,[236] and in the case of private, but not state, schools.[237] But where disciplinary powers are statutory, judicial review now seems to be favoured, even in the case of professional associations which, being outside the sphere of government, were formerly outside the scope of the prerogative remedies.[238] It was generally

---

[229] *R* v. *Home Secretary ex p Benwell* [1985] QB 554. See likewise *R* v. *Home Secretary ex p Attard* (1990) 2 Admin LR 641 (prison officer suspended without pay: judicial review granted without dispute).

[230] See above, p. 490.

[231] *R* v. *Derbyshire CC ex p Noble* [1990] ICR 808. An additional reason was that conflicting evidence made judicial review unsuitable—an example of judicial reluctance to implement the reform of 1977 (above, p. 260). There was a lack of statutory underpinning in *R* v. *Leeds City Council ex p Cobleigh* [1997] COD 69 (disposal of land by council: judicial review refused).

[232] *R* v. *Crown Prosecution Service ex p Hogg* (1994) 6 Admin LR 778.

[233] See (1991) 107 *LQR* 298, [1994] *PL* 69 (S. Fredman and G. Morris).

[234] The *Roy* case (below).

[235] *Law* v. *National Greyhound Racing Club Ltd* [1983] 1 WLR 1302.

[236] See *R* v. *Inland Revenue Commissioners ex p National Federation of Self-employed and Small Businesses Ltd* [1982] AC 617 at 639 (Lord Diplock).

[237] *R* v. *Fernhill Manor School ex p Brown* [1992] COD 446.

[238] As in *R* v. *Committee of Lloyd's ex p Posgate*, The Times, 12 January 1983; *R* v. *Pharmaceutical Society of Great Britain ex p Sokoh*, The Times, 4 December 1986; *R* v. *General Medical Council ex p Gee* [1987] 1 WLR 564; *Colman* v. *General Medical Council*, The Times, 14 December 1988 (why the case was so entitled does not appear). See above, p. 535. Perhaps the same may happen with public utilities. In *R* v. *Midlands Electricity Board ex p Busby*, The Times, 28 October 1987, the court entertained an (unsuccessful) application for judicial review against a 'decision' of the Board to require a domestic customer to pay in advance for electricity under his agreement with the Board.

safer to seek judicial review in any case of doubt, since, in case of mistake the application for judicial review could be converted into a private law proceeding as if begun by writ (or 'claim form' in the modern jargon). But if the proceedings began by writ the reverse process was possible only exceptionally.[239]

DEFENSIVE AND COLLATERAL PLEAS

An important question was whether issues of public law might be raised by way of defence, or as collateral issues, in proceedings of any kind. On a rigorous interpretation of *O'Reilly v. Mackman* it was argued that a defendant who wished to attack the validity of some official act or order should do so by separate proceedings for judicial review,[240] and apply for an adjournment of the main proceedings meanwhile. But the House of Lords, once again refraining from the extreme course, held that it would be wrong to deprive a defendant of the opportunity to raise any available defence as a matter of right. The question arose when a tenant of a local authority refused to pay an increase of rent on the ground that the local authority's decision raising the rent from £12.06 to £18.53 was void for unreasonableness. The local authority applied to strike out this defence to its action in the county court for the rent, and for possession, claiming that the issue could be raised only by application for judicial review; and it took the tenant to the House of Lords on this preliminary question alone. The House held that it could not be an abuse of the process of the court to raise the familiar defence of ultra vires, which can normally be pleaded as a collateral issue,[241] when the defendant was not able to select the procedure adopted.[242] 'In any event,' Lord Fraser said, 'the arguments for protecting public authorities against unmeritorious or dilatory challenges to their decisions have to be set against the arguments for preserving the ordinary rights of private citizens to defend themselves against unfounded claims.' A defendant is entitled to make his defence as a matter of right, whereas judicial review proceedings are subject to the discretion of the court.

This principle has since been held by the Court of Appeal to be confined to persons who are 'seeking to raise a true defence'; and it was denied to gipsies resisting a local authority's eviction action because they did not deny that they were trespassers but contended that the local authority was in breach of its statutory duty to provide sites for them and so was acting unreasonably.[243]

This principle has been several times upheld in civil proceedings. In one case a financial adviser, who had given 'unsuitable advice' to an individual, had been directed by the Financial Services Ombudsman to make certain payments to that individual to make

---

[239] See above, p. 558, and below, p. 579 (Lord Woolf's third suggestion).

[240] This was the opinion of Ackner LJ in the *Wandsworth* case (below) and also of the county court judge, who had granted a stay so that judicial review might be sought, but the High Court refused leave. For a similar view see [1986] *PL* at 234 (Woolf LJ). [241] See above, p. 235.

[242] *Wandsworth LBC v. Winder* [1985] AC 461. See *Dwr Cymru Cyfyngedig v. Corus UK Ltd* [2006] EWHC 1183 (the principle of *Winder* applied to a dispute between private parties, where one wished to challenge a public law decision as part of its defence; this point not the subject of appeal ([2007] EWCA Civ 285)). Contrast *Aspin v. Estill* (1987) 60 TC 549, where the Court of Appeal held that the General Commissioners of Income Tax could not consider a plea by a taxpayer that the Inland Revenue had misled him and abused their power. But in *Pawlowski (Collector of Taxes) v. Dunnington* (1999) 11 Admin LR 565, the Court of Appeal allowed a defence of 'no evidence' to be raised against a direction issued by the Inland Revenue, following the *Winder* case. See to like effect *Rhondda Cynon Taff CBC v. Watkins* [2003] 1 WLR 1864.

[243] *Avon CC v. Buscott* [1988] QB 656, approving *Waverley BC v. Hilden* (below). Compare *West Glamorgan CC v. Raffery* [1987] 1 WLR 457, where a gipsy sought judicial review successfully on similar grounds.

good the harm occasioned by following the advice. The adviser was held entitled to raise as a defence to an application for an injunction to enforce the direction the invalidity of the Ombudsman's direction.[244]

The House of Lords' principle also applies where a defence involving a public law challenge is raised against a criminal charge. On a prosecution for violation of a byelaw the Crown Court or a magistrates' court must decide upon the validity of the byelaw if this is raised by way of defence.[245] On the other hand a firm prosecuted for operating a sex shop without a licence cannot escape by pleading that its application for a licence had been wrongfully refused, since this cannot alter the fact of the offence.[246] Nor can gipsies escape conviction for disregarding planning enforcement notices by pleading that the local authority was in breach of its duty to provide sites for them, since that cannot alter the fact that they had no planning permission.[247]

Special consideration needs to be given to the position where a tenant or a licensee of land raises public law or human rights defences when the landowner seeks possession. Collateral challenge has been held by the Court of Appeal to be confined to persons who are 'seeking to raise a true defence'; and it was denied to gipsies resisting a local authority's eviction action. They did not deny that they were trespassers but contended that the local authority was in breach of its statutory duty to provide sites for them and so was acting unreasonably.[248] But the more recent jurisprudence[249] supports allowing the tenant or licensee to challenge on public law grounds the decision to seek possession.[250] In addition the tenant or licensee can raise their dispossession as an infringement of their Article 8 rights (respect for home).[251] These are the two 'gateways' for a challenge recognised by the House of Lords in the leading case. But the challenge based on either gateway must

[244] *Bunney* v. *Burns Anderson plc and Financial Ombudsman Service Ltd* [2007] EWHC 1240 (the 'procedural reasons which led to the formulation of the principle in *O'Reilly* v. *Mackman* have lost much of their force since the introduction of the CPR [and] they never applied to defendants who wished to challenge public law decisions upon which a private cause of action against them was asserted' (para. 47, Lewison J). Followed by the Competition Appeal Tribunal in *Orange Personal Communications Services Ltd* v. *Office of Communications* [2007] CAT 36. Cf. *Financial Services Authority* v. *Matthews* [2004] EWHC 2966 ('Anyone from a legal background would know that the only way of challenging an Award [of the Personal Investment Authority Ombudsman] would be by Judicial Review' (Peter Smith J).

[245] *Boddington* v. *British Railways Board* [1999] 2 AC 143 (discussed above, p. 236). And see *R* v. *Reading Crown Court ex p Hutchinson* [1987] QB 384; *R* v. *Oxford Crown Court ex p Smith* (1989) 2 Admin LR 389 (planning authority's notice).

[246] *Quietlynn Ltd* v. *Plymouth City Council* [1988] QB 114, where the result is correct but the decision that such defences cannot now be raised in criminal proceedings is erroneous: see the *Reading Crown Court* case (above).

[247] *Waverley BC* v. *Hilden* [1989] 1 WLR 246, holding that this plea could be made only by way of judicial review and refusing, on the merits, to grant a stay for that purpose.

[248] *Avon CC* v. *Buscott* [1988] QB 656, approving *Waverley BC* v. *Hilden* (below). Compare *West Glamorgan CC* v. *Raffery* [1987] 1 WLR 457, where a gipsy sought judicial review successfully on similar grounds.

[249] See *Kay* v. *Lambeth LBC* [2006] UKHL 10, [2006] 2 WLR 570. These conjoined cases with complicated facts were decided by a (divided) 7-member appeal committee all of whom gave substantive judgments, making it difficult to understand precisely what was decided. But the Court of Appeal has isolated the issues with clarity in *Doherty* v. *Birmingham CC* [2006] EWCA Civ 1739 (Carnwath LJ giving the judgment of the court). In para. 22 the court helpfully set out what was decided in *Kay* v. *Lambeth LBC*. See now *Doherty* in the House of Lords, below.   [250] Ibid., para. 110 (Lord Hope).

[251] Ibid., para. 110 (Lord Hope). Which is the ground on which the licensee succeeded before the Strasbourg court in *Connors* v. *UK* (2005) 40 EHRR 9 189 (having failed to obtain permission for judicial review).

be 'seriously arguable'.[252] The upshot is that in many situations the 'court is entitled to say that the legislation itself strikes a fair balance between the rights of the individual and the interests of the community, so that there is no room for the court to strike the balance in the individual case.'[253]

The rationale for procedural exclusivity is undermined by the general availability of collateral challenge, because the judicial review 'safeguards' of permission and the short time limits are sidestepped when the invalidity of a decision of a public authority is raised by right as a defence to civil or criminal proceedings. But, as explained elsewhere,[254] the general availability of collateral challenge is a requirement of the rule of law. Fidelity to the rule of law requires that procedural exclusivity give way.

JUDICIAL PROTESTS AND PROPOSALS

In a relatively early case Lord Wilberforce gave an apt warning:[255]

> The expressions 'private law' and 'public law' have recently been imported into the law of England from countries which, unlike our own, have separate systems concerning public law and private law. In this country they must be used with caution, for, typically, English law fastens, not upon principles but upon remedies.... Before the expression 'public law' can be used to deny a subject a right of action in the court of his choice it must be related to a positive prescription of law, by statute or by statutory rules. We have not yet reached the point at which mere characterisation of a claim as a claim in public law is sufficient to exclude it from consideration by the ordinary courts: to permit this would be to create a dual system of law with the rigidity and procedural hardship for plaintiffs which it was the purpose of the recent reforms to remove.

Judicial protests have since become more vehement, mostly in cases where defendants have applied for the striking out of some claim on the ground that it should have been brought by judicial review and the decision on the striking out application is appealed by itself. Pointing to the confusion in the case law, Henry J called it 'a formidable extra hurdle for plaintiffs' and said that the forms of action abolished in 1854 'appeared to be in danger of returning to rule us from their graves'.[256] In a decision where the sole issue was which procedure to use, the House of Lords, reversing the Court of Appeal which had reversed the trial judge, held that ordinary procedure was allowable for disputing the interpretation of a condition in a telecommunications licence.[257] Lord Slynn spoke of the need to avoid 'the over-rigid demarcation between procedures reminiscent of earlier disputes as to the forms of action' and said:

> In the absence of a single procedure allowing all remedies—quashing, injunctive and declaratory relief, damages—some flexibility as to the use of different procedures is

---

[252] Ibid., para. 110 (Lord Hope). The majority view was that a challenge under Art. 8 had to be to the domestic law under which the possession order is made, i.e. a challenge based upon the defendants' individual circumstance was not possible. *Kay* was confirmed by the House of Lords in *Doherty v. Birmingham CC* [2008] UKHL 57, paras. 19, 22 (Lord Hope), para. 61 (Lord Scott) (although recognition that some cases might 'straddle' the gateways).

[253] *Belfast City Council v. Miss Behavin' Ltd* [2007] UKHL 19, para. 36 (Baroness Hale approving *Kay*).

[254] Above, pp. 235 and 236.

[255] *Davy v. Spelthorne BC* [1984] AC 262 at 278.

[256] *Doyle v. Northumbria Probation Committee* [1991] 1 WLR 1340 at 1348.

[257] *Mercury Communications Ltd v. Director General of Telecommunications* [1996] 1 WLR 48.

necessary. It has to be borne in mind that the overriding question is whether the proceedings constitute an abuse of the process of the court.

The procedural dilemma was again the sole issue before the Court of Appeal when the Customs and Excise Commissioners asserted that a claim in restitution for a statutory relief from excise duty could be made only by way of judicial review. Reversing the trial judge, the court held that the claimant could use an ordinary action for restitution.[258] Saville LJ said:

It is now well over 100 years ago that our predecessors made a great attempt to free our legal process from concentrating upon the form rather than the substance, so that the outcome of cases depended not on strict compliance with intricate procedural requirements, but rather on deciding the real dispute over the rights and obligations of the parties . . . This is only the most recent such case, for over the last decade or so there has been a stream of litigation on this subject, much of it proceeding to the House of Lords. The cases raise and depend upon the most sophisticated arguments, such as the distinction and difference between what is described as 'public' as opposed to 'private' law . . . The cost of this litigation, borne privately or through taxation, must be immense, with often the lawyers the only people to gain. Such litigation brings the law and our legal system into disrepute, and to my mind correctly so . . . the courts have to address difficult and complex questions which in my view, under a proper system, it should not be necessary even to ask, let alone answer.

A claim to a statutory benefit was also in issue in the Court of Appeal when a city council resisted a pension fund's claim for housing improvement grants on the ground that it should have been brought by judicial review.[259] This unmeritorious defence prompted Lord Woolf MR, in rejecting it, to suggest guidelines which might help to reduce litigants' dilemmas. He prefaced his suggestions by saying:

This appeal raises yet again issues as to the relationship between public and private law proceedings. It illustrates the fact that, despite the hopes to the contrary, a very substantial volume of the resources of the parties and the courts are still being consumed to little or no purpose over largely tactical issues as to whether the correct procedure had been adopted. . . . I have little doubt that the amount of the costs already incurred far exceeds the sum in issue in the proceedings but the parties and the courts have yet to turn their attention to the merits of the dispute.

Lord Woolf then made three suggestions. First, in case of doubt it is safer to opt for judicial review and so avoid 'arid arguments' as to the right procedure. Second, where application is made to strike out an ordinary action, the court should ask itself whether leave (now permission) to apply for judicial review would have been granted. If so, there should be no objection based on abuse of process. Third, it should be remembered that a case can always be transferred to the Crown Office list (now the Administrative Court) as an alternative to being struck out.[260] If the procedure chosen has no significant disadvantages for the parties, the public or the court, Lord Woolf said, then it should not normally be regarded as constituting an abuse.

---

[258] *British Steel plc* v. *Customs and Excise Commissioners* [1997] 2 All ER 366. See similarly Saville LJ (dissenting) in *The Great House at Sonning* case, above, p. 574.

[259] *Trustees of the Dennis Rye Pension Fund* v. *Sheffield CC* [1998] 1 WLR 840.

[260] But the 3-month time limit may have expired, unless the court is willing to extend it.

SIGNS OF LIBERALITY

Into the welter of procedural pitfalls and conflicting judicial opinions a more favourable wind began to blow. In the case of a prison officer suspended without pay for refusing to work a new shift system, which he claimed was contrary to his conditions of service, the Court of Appeal rejected the Home Office's objection that judicial review should have been sought and held that conditions of service, where it was arguable that they were contractual, were to be treated as matters of private law for which ordinary actions would lie.[261]

Taking a step further in a notable decision, the House of Lords held that private law rights, whether contractual or statutory, were enforceable by ordinary action notwithstanding that they might involve a challenge to a public law act or decision. In this case the remuneration of a doctor in the National Health Service had been reduced by the local committee on the ground of insufficient time devoted to general practice, as required by statutory regulations, and he sued for the amount deducted. The committee pleaded the usual objection and at first instance they succeeded. But on appeal it was held that a claim to pay, even though governed by statutory regulations and by a discretionary decision of the committee, was essentially a matter of private right and enforceable by ordinary action, free from the constraints of judicial review.[262] Lord Lowry said 'if Dr Roy has any kind of private law right, even though not contractual, he can sue for its alleged breach'. He approved a distinction made in the Court of Appeal: if the committee had initially refused to take Dr Roy onto their panel of doctors, he would have had no private right to assert and judicial review would be his only remedy; but when he took employment with the committee, he acquired private rights to pay and conditions of service in accordance with the regulations. Lord Steyn has similarly pointed out that under the House of Lords' decisions the primary focus of the rule of procedural exclusivity is situations in which an individual's sole aim was to challenge a public law act or decision. It does not apply in a civil case when an individual seeks to establish private law rights which cannot be determined without an examination of the validity of a public law decision.[263]

In thus liberating the whole area of private right by exploiting the exception which Lord Diplock himself had suggested,[264] the House of Lords made it clear that it made no difference whether the private right was asserted in attack[265] or in defence.[266]

Although there may still sometimes be difficulty in identifying 'private right', particularly in non-contractual relationships,[267] many litigants will now have been freed from the dangers of what Lord Lowry called 'a procedural minefield'.

Lord Lowry also contrasted the two possible interpretations of *O'Reilly* v. *Mackman*. The 'broad approach' was that proceedings challenging a public law act or decision were

---

[261] *McClaren* v. *Home Office* [1990] ICR 824.

[262] *Roy* v. *Kensington and Chelsea Family Practitioner Committee* [1992] 1 AC 624. For a discerning discussion, see (1993) 13 *Legal Studies* 183 (J. Alder).

[263] *Boddington* v. *British Transport Police* [1999] 2 AC 143; *Pawlowski* v. *Dunnington* (1999) 11 Admin LR 565.   [264] See above, p. 571.

[265] As in *Shears Court (West Mersey) Management Co Ltd* v. *Essex CC* (1986) 85 LGR 479 (landowner may sue in trespass contesting council's determination as to public right of way).

[266] Endorsing an earlier remark of Goff LJ in *Wandsworth LBC* v. *Winder* [1985] AC 461 at 480, criticised by Sir Harry Woolf in [1986] *PL* 220 at 233. See [1992] *CLJ* 308 (C. Emery). Contrast *Tower Hamlets LBC* v. *Abdi* (1992) 9 LGR 300.

[267] e.g. in *R* v. *Home Secretary ex p Benwell* (above), which was not cited in *Roy*.

required to employ judicial review only when private law rights were not at stake. The 'narrow approach', which was that of Lord Diplock in the original decision, was that all such proceedings must be by judicial review, subject only to some exceptions where private law rights were involved. Lord Lowry declared his strong preference for the broad approach, though unfortunately he found it unnecessary to decide categorically. He gave a series of good reasons for a liberal attitude even if the narrow approach should be adopted. The whole tenor of the case is in favour of the broad approach and in favour of relief from Lord Diplock's rigid logic.

The House of Lords corroborated this position in 2000, holding that an individual's claim to statutory compensation (as distinct from a challenge to the legality of the whole compensation scheme) could properly be brought by ordinary action.[268]

THE CIVIL PROCEDURE RULES, CHANGING JUDICIAL ATTITUDES AND THE DECLINE OF PROCEDURAL EXCLUSIVITY?

Lord Diplock's speech in *O'Reilly* v. *Mackman* was a brilliant judicial exploit, but it turned the law in the wrong direction, away from flexibility of procedure and towards a rigidity reminiscent of the bad old days of the forms of action a century and a half ago. The well-intentioned reforms of 1977 became a classic example of the remedy being worse than the disease. Although the House of Lords is now clearly disposed towards relaxation and future decisions are likely to continue the process, the root cause of the dichotomy will be difficult to extirpate judicially, and new legislation is needed.[269]

Lord Woolf's report, published in 1996 was wide-ranging, but here we are concerned primarily with his chapter on the Crown Office List now renamed the Administrative Court.[270] He states that his objective is to secure greater uniformity in cases which 'can at present be bedevilled by disputes as to procedure' which are 'wholly undesirable procedural wrangles'.[271] He recommends that the form of application for judicial review, instead of being a separate claim form, should follow the standard claim form. After various recommendations on procedural details he says:[272]

> The recommendations which I have made are intended to bridge the divide between public and private law claims by bringing the two procedures together. The same statements of case will be used in both, so that there will be no need for a claim in one area to be treated as though it has been begun by another procedure. It is nevertheless important that the safeguards of the three month time limit and of standing, which are necessary in judicial review claims, should not be bypassed, but these can be retained without making it an abuse of process to adopt the wrong procedure.

The report then explains how objections to the use of private law procedure could be referred to the Crown Office for a case management conference without the court having

---

[268] *Steed* v. *Home Secretary* [2000] 1 WLR 1169 (claim for interest on delayed payment of compensation for surrender of handguns; Home Secretary's claim that judicial review was the only permissible procedure dismissed).

[269] Surprisingly the Law Commission reporting in 1994 did not recognise the gravity of the central problem of procedural exclusivity or penetrate to its heart (*Administrative Law: Judicial Review and Statutory Appeals*, Law Com. No. 226, Pt III, para. 3.15).   [270] *Access to Justice*, ch. 18.

[271] Ibid., para. 2.   [272] Ibid., para. 26.

to consider whether the issues are in public or private law, and leaving questions of standing and time limits to the final hearing.

Although many particulars remain to be clarified, Lord Woolf's proposals amount
in substance to a unified procedure of the kind suggested in this book.[273] They were
not implemented in the first instalment of his reforms, introduced in 1999,[274] perhaps
because they conflict so directly with the recommendations of the Law Commission. But
Lord Woolf has said: 'I am reasonably confident that the rejection of proceedings on the
basis of the wrong choice of procedure will soon be a problem of the past.'[275]

The fulfilment of this overdue reform was foreshadowed in a case where a university
student sued the university in contract, alleging wrongful treatment in examinations.[276]
The new Civil Procedure Rules had been introduced but CPR 54 had not yet been made.
The university, which had no visitor, pleaded that she could proceed only by judicial
review, for which she was out of time, under the strict doctrine of O'Reilly v. Mackman. In
rejecting this plea, and so allowing the action to proceed, the Court of Appeal observed that
the ground had shifted considerably since that decision; and that the new Civil Procedure
Rules introduced the principle that the mode of commencement of proceedings should not
matter. The Court of Appeal in effect envisaged that the new Civil Procedure Rules provided
a substitute for the provisions of the then Order 53 that protected public authorities.

The Court of Appeal in this case looked forward to the further reform of the procedure for judicial review along the lines proposed by Lord Woolf. CPR 54, however, when
eventually made did not in terms abandon procedural exclusivity.[277] Claims for judicial
review, indeed, fall within CPR 8 as proceedings 'unlikely to involve a substantial dispute
of fact'. But the protections for public authorities—the requirement of permission and the
short time limits—are retained and prerogative remedies will only be available in a claim
for judicial review brought under CPR 54.2. This leaves the way clear for claimants to seek
advantage through the adoption of one procedure or another and for courts to resist this
by the adoption of procedural exclusivity.

Lord Woolf, however, had reasoned in the case of the university student that it was not
generally necessary to strike out a claim which was more appropriate for judicial review
but which had been brought by ordinary action under Part 7 or 8 of the CPR. The reason
for this was that CPR 24 allowed summary judgment to be given against the claimant
where, for instance, the claimant was seeking to evade the short time limit in CPR 54[278]
or otherwise misusing the ordinary procedure. While this easing of the rigours of procedural exclusivity is welcome, Lord Woolf does not address the converse situation. This
is when a claim that should be brought by ordinary action is brought by way of judicial
review in order to secure a prerogative remedy. This may yet generate fruitless litigation.
Where it is uncertain which procedure to use it may be prudent to bring both.[279]

---

[273] Above, p. 571; similarly in the 8th edn, p. 653.

[274] Under the Civil Procedure Rules 1998. As explained above, p. 550. CPR 54 was not made at this stage.

[275] (1998) 114 LQR 579 at 589.

[276] Clark v. University of Lincolnshire and Humberside [2000] 1 WLR 1988. Cf. [2004] JR 140 (R. Bateson)
arguing that the impact of Clark is restricted to 'wrongly brought' applications for judicial review, to the
exclusion of 'wrongly brought' private claims.

[277] And as we have seen (above, p. 551) there is a separate claim form for judicial review (N461).

[278] Sedley LJ (para. 17) said that 'the unfair exploitation of the longer limitation period for civil suits'
might be addressed by the intervention of the court to deny 'worthwhile relief'.

[279] This is the suggestion of the authors of De Smith's Judicial Review, 6th edn (2007), p. 168. The suggestion is that both proceedings would be consolidated and heard together. For a case where this was an issue
see R (Cookson and Clegg) v. MOD [2005] EWCA Civ 577 (Pt 7 or judicial review).

On the other hand, the rigours of exclusivity have been further abated by the rules which allow, subject to the court's discretion, the transfer of claims both out of Part 54 and into Part 54 if the claim has been commenced in the wrong way.[280] In the changed climate brought about by the more flexible rules of the CPR and the changing judicial attitudes, litigants no longer raise procedural exclusivity points, perceiving rightly that it would not advance their suit.

The CPR did not abolish procedural exclusivity but has provided the route whereby this unwelcome innovation has, in large measure, crept unsung from the scene.[281] But the principle has not been abolished; there remain rare cases in which the form of the procedure adopted is determinative of the outcome of litigation.[282]

[280] e.g. *R* v. *Association of British Travel Agents ex p Sunspell Ltd*, The Independent, 27 November, 2000 (ABTA's contractual relationship with agents precluded judicial review of its decisions; *Clark* relevant only to procedure). CPR 54.20 (out of Pt 54) and CPR 30.5 (into Pt 54). Under RSC Order 53 only transfer out of the application for judicial review expressly provided for and even then it was set about with technicality. See *R* v. *East Berkshire Health Authority ex p Walsh* [1985] QB 152. See Woolf LJ in [1986] *PL* 220 at 232 for discussion of transfer into Order 53. A two-way transfer system such as that which now exists under the CPR was recommended by the Law Commission (Law Com. No. 226, para. 5.38).

[281] In the few recent cases in which procedural exclusivity has been considered it has seldom been determinative of the outcome and the more flexible judicial attitude has been evident. See, for instance, *R (Wilkinson)* v. *Broadmoor Special Hospital* [2001] EWCA Civ 1545 (Brooke LJ (para. 62): 'it cannot and should not matter whether proceedings in respect of forcible treatment of detained patients are brought by way of an ordinary action in tort, an action under section 7(1) of the 1998 Act, or judicial review'). But note *Stancliffe Stone Company Ltd* v. *Peak District National Park Authority* [2004] EWHC 1475 (declaratory relief refused since matter, that could have been brought by judicial review, fell far outside the judicial review time limit).

[282] Thus *North Dorset District Council* v. *Trim* [2010] EWCA Civ 1446 concerned a private law claim seeking a declaration that a breach of condition notice was unlawful (since it was served more than 10 years after the alleged breach). The action was struck out as an abuse of process. Carnwath LJ said: 'the exclusivity principle is in my view directly applicable in the present case. The service of a breach of condition notice is a purely public law act. There is strong public interest in its validity, if in issue, being established promptly, both because of its significance to the planning of the area, and because it turns what was merely unlawful into criminal conduct... It does not come within any other categories identified... as requiring a more flexible approach' (para. 26). *Trim* was followed in *R (Townsend)* v. *Secretary of State for Works and Pensions* [2011] EWHC 3434 and distinguished in *BB and ors* v. *The Home Office* [2011] EWHC 1446. Procedural exclusivity was also determinative in *Jones* v. *Powys Local Health Board* [2008] EWHC 2562 (claim struck out; in substance claim was pure public law: dispute seeking reimbursement of nursing care and accommodation fees); Plender J said that 'the present proceedings by writ rather than by application for judicial review deprives the [health boards] of protection that they would otherwise have enjoyed and is inconsistent with the just conduct of the proceedings' (para. 39). *Sed quaere*. The protection involved here was the permission requirement and the proper approach (following Lord Woolf in *Dennis Rye*, above p. 579) was only to strike out if, had the matter been brought by judicial review, permission would not have been granted. See Appendix 3.

19

RESTRICTION OF REMEDIES

THE OLD LAW OF STANDING

THE PROBLEM OF STANDING

It has always been an important limitation on the availability of remedies that they are awarded only to litigants who have sufficient locus standi, or standing.[1] The law starts from the position that remedies are correlative with rights, and that only those whose own rights are at stake are eligible to be awarded remedies. No one else will have the necessary standing before the court.

In private law that principle can be applied with some strictness. But in public law it is inadequate, for it ignores the dimension of the public interest. Where some particular person is the object of administrative action, that person is naturally entitled to dispute its legality and other persons are not. But public authorities have many powers and duties which affect the public generally rather than particular individuals. If a local authority grants planning permission improperly, or licenses indecent films for exhibition, it does a wrong to the public interest but no wrong to any one in particular. If no one has standing to call it to account, it can disregard the law with impunity—a result which would 'make an ass of the law'.[2] An efficient system of administrative law must find some answer to this problem, otherwise the rule of law breaks down.

Having grown to a considerable extent out of private law, administrative law has traditionally contained a number of restrictive rules about standing. But as governmental powers and duties have increased, and as public interest has gained prominence at the expense of private right, more liberal principles have emerged. The prerogative remedies, in particular, have shown their worth, since they exist for public as well as private purposes and provide the nucleus of a system of public law. The Attorney-General (who always has standing) also can act in the public interest and will sometimes, though not always, do so. The resources of the legal system are adequate to solve the problems, which are basically problems of judicial policy.

---

[1] For this subject see Lewis, *Judicial Remedies in Public Law*, 5th edn (2014), ch. 10; Supperstone and Goudie (eds.), *Judicial Review*, 3rd edn, ch. 15; *Standing in Public Interest Litigation* (1985, Report No. 27, Law Reform Commission, Australia—an extensive study); Eleventh Report (1978), Public and Administrative Law Reform Committee, New Zealand; L. Stein (ed.), *Locus Standi*; S. M. Thio, *Locus Standi and Judicial Review*; J. Vining, *Legal Identity* (discussing United States law); P. Van Dijk, *Judicial Review of Government Action and the Requirement of Interest to Sue* (discussing Anglo-American, European and international law). See (2002) 65 *MLR* 1 (C. Harlow) criticising the expansion of pressure group standing. And see Hare, *The Law of Standing in Public Interest Adjudication*, in M. Andenas and D. Fairgrieve (eds.), *Judicial Review in International Perspective: Liber Amicorum in Honour of Lord Slynn of Hadley*, Vol. II (2000), 301–18.

[2] *Steeples v. Derbyshire CC* [1985] 1 WLR 256 at 296 (Webster J). See also *Minister of Justice v. Borowski* (1982) 130 DLR (3d) 588.

Judges have in the past had an instinctive reluctance to relax the rules about standing. They fear that they may 'open the floodgates' so that the courts will be swamped with litigation. They fear also that cases will not be best argued by parties whose personal rights are not in issue. But recently these instincts have been giving way before the feeling that the law must somehow find a place for the disinterested, or less directly interested, citizen in order to prevent illegalities in government which otherwise no one would be competent to challenge.

THE HISTORY OF THE CURRENT LAW

Formerly there were different rules of standing for different remedies, as might be expected in a system which operates with a mixture of private law and public law remedies. The private law remedies of injunction and declaration were for the most part available only to parties whose own rights were in issue. The prerogative remedies, on the other hand, were nominally sought by the Queen and might be awarded at the instance of anyone whom the court considered to be deserving. The strict rules as to injunction and declaration could sometimes be evaded with the assistance of the Attorney-General sometimes bringing the action at the instance of an individual who lacked standing in a relator action as explained earlier.[3] The generous rules for the prerogative remedies, on the other hand, were tightened in an illogical way by making them stricter for mandamus than for certiorari and prohibition.

The situation was transformed by the introduction in 1977 of the application for judicial review.[4] The remedies in both groups then became available in a single proceeding and it became obvious (as indeed it had been beforehand) that a uniform rule about standing ought to apply to them all. The provision in the rules of court, now embodied in the Senior Courts Act 1981, appeared to leave this question open. But when it came before the House of Lords in the *Inland Revenue Commissioners* case[5] the majority opinion was that a uniform rule had been established. This is the basis of the new law of standing discussed below.[6] Since the *Inland Revenue Commissioners* case there has been little sign that the distinctions between the standing rules for various remedies that previously applied have any effect on the practice of the courts. No detailed account of the historical rules (other than the sketch just given) will be given here; the interested reader is referred to the accounts given in earlier editions of this book.

THE NEW LAW OF STANDING

THE REFORMED PROCEDURE

When the application for judicial review was introduced in 1977 the prerogative remedies, declaration and injunction all became available in a single form of proceeding, in which the first step was to obtain the court's permission to apply. The Senior Courts Act 1981[7] provides that the 'court shall not grant leave[8] to make such an application unless it

---

[3] Above p. 492.   [4] Above, p. 549.

[5] *R v. Inland Revenue Commissioners ex p National Federation of Self-Employed and Small Businesses Ltd* [1982] AC 617, explained below, p. 586.   [6] Below, p. 585.

[7] s. 31(3).

[8] The modern jargon (blessed by CPR 54) uses 'permission' (above, p. 551) but 'leave' is the statutory word.

considers that the applicant has a sufficient interest in the matter to which the application relates'.

Standing for the purposes of this procedure is thus first of all made a 'threshold question', to be determined at the stage of the initial application for leave. At this point the court can reject 'simple cases in which it can be seen at the earliest stage that the person applying for judicial review has no interest at all, or no sufficient interest',[9] and so 'prevent abuse by busybodies, cranks and other mischief-makers'.[10] The Law Commission has recommended a 'two-track system' under which standing would be refused unless the applicant has been or would be adversely affected, or the court considers that it is in the public interest for the application to be made.[11]

By requiring the interest to be 'in the *matter* to which the application relates' the rule suggests also that standing is to be related to the facts of the case rather than (as previously) to the particular remedy sought, so that one uniform test should apply to all the remedies alike. Extra-judicially Lord Denning MR has expressed the view that the rule 'lays down one simple test' and gives standing to 'an ordinary citizen who comes asking that the law should be declared and enforced'.[12] The House of Lords has now indicated that this may indeed be its result.

THE *INLAND REVENUE COMMISSIONERS* CASE

The House of Lords gave a new and liberal but somewhat uncertain character to the law of standing in the *Inland Revenue Commissioners* case.[13] This decision was to some extent a result of the above-mentioned procedural reforms. But in fact the rules gave the House a wide choice of solutions and their decision is an act of judicial policy which is clear in its general thrust if not in all particulars. In general it may be said to crystallise the elements of a generous and public-oriented doctrine of standing which had previously been sporadic and uncoordinated.

Application for judicial review was made by an association of taxpayers who resented the fact that the Inland Revenue had agreed to waive large arrears of income tax due from some 6,000 workers in the newspaper printing industry who for some years had collected pay under false names and defrauded the revenue. The applicants complained that the Inland Revenue had failed in their duty to administer the tax laws fairly as between different classes of taxpayers and that they had been unduly influenced by the fact that the printing workers might cause serious disruption by striking if their cooperation could not be obtained. The remedies sought were a declaration that the Inland Revenue had acted unlawfully and an order of mandamus requiring them to collect the arrears of tax. The Divisional Court granted leave *ex parte* but upon hearing both parties held, as a preliminary matter, that the applicants had not 'sufficient interest'. The Court of Appeal reversed them and the House of Lords reversed the Court of Appeal. The House of Lords' decision may be summarised as follows.

1. It was right to grant leave on the *ex parte* application.[14]

2. It was wrong to treat standing as a preliminary issue for determination independently of the merits of the complaint. 'In other words, the question of sufficient

---

[9] [1982] AC at 630C (Lord Wilberforce). [10] [1982] AC at 653G (Lord Scarman).
[11] Law Com. No. 226 (1994), paras. 5.20, 5.22. [12] *The Discipline of Law*, 133.
[13] *R v. Inland Revenue Cmrs ex p National Federation of Self-Employed and Small Businesses Ltd* [1982] AC 617. For comment see [1981] *PL* 322 (P. Cane).
[14] Decided unanimously. But note that today permission (leave) is not dealt with *ex parte*. Above, p. 552.

interest can not, in such cases, be considered in the abstract, or as an isolated point: it must be taken together with the legal and factual context.'[15] It 'is not simply a point of law to be determined in the abstract or upon assumed facts—but upon the due appraisal of many different factors revealed by the evidence produced by the parties, few if any of which will be able to be wholly isolated from the others'.[16]

3. On the facts (not considered by the lower courts), the applicants had failed to show any breach of duty by the Inland Revenue. Their wide managerial powers allowed them to make 'special arrangements' of the kind in question, despite their legal duty to act fairly as between one taxpayer and another.[17]

4. But if it had been shown that the Inland Revenue had yielded to improper pressure, or had committed a breach of duty of sufficient gravity, the applicants might have succeeded.[18] Such rare cases apart, the assessment of one taxpayer is not the business of another, individual assessments being confidential.[19] Rating assessments are another matter.[20]

5. The law as to standing is now the same for all the remedies available under Order 53.[21] Mandamus is not subject to stricter rules than certiorari.[22] Injunction and declaration are available where certiorari would be available.[23]

The testing of an applicant's standing is thus made a two-stage process.[24] On the application for permission (stage one) the test is designed to turn away hopeless or meddlesome applications only. But when the matter comes to be argued (stage two), the test is whether the applicant can show a strong enough case on the merits, judged in relation to his own concern with it. As Lord Scarman put it:[25] 'The federation, having failed to show any grounds for believing that the revenue has failed to do its statutory duty, have not, in my view, shown an interest sufficient in law to justify any further proceedings by the court on its application.' He added that had reasonable grounds for supposing an abuse been shown, he would have agreed that the federation had shown a sufficient interest to proceed further.

The novel aspect of the second-stage test, as thus formulated, is that it does not appear to be a test of standing but rather a test of the merits of the complaint. The essence of standing, as a distinct concept, is that an applicant with a good case on the merits may have insufficient interest to be allowed to pursue it. The House of Lords' new criterion would seem virtually to abolish the requirement of standing in this sense. However

---

[15] [1982] AC 617 at 630D (Lord Wilberforce). Lords Diplock and Scarman agreed, Lord Fraser disagreed, as also does Scots law: *Scottish Old People's Welfare Council, Petitioners*, 1987 SLT 179, holding that 'the matter of locus standi is logically prior to and conceptually distinct from the merits of the case'; but in fact the court decided the merits first.   [16] Ibid. at 656D (Lord Roskill).

[17] Decided unanimously.   [18] Decided unanimously.

[19] Ibid. at 633C (Lord Wilberforce), 646E (Lord Fraser), 663A (Lord Roskill).

[20] Ibid. at 632H (Lord Wilberforce); 646D (Lord Fraser); *Arsenal Football Club Ltd* v. *Ende* [1979] AC 1, explained below, p. 628.   [21] No change is made by CPR 54 discussed above, p. 554.

[22] Ibid. at 640D (Lord Diplock), 646A (Lord Fraser—probably), 653C (Lord Scarman), 656G (Lord Roskill) and 631A (Lord Wilberforce—against). See also *R* v. *Metropolitan Police Cmr ex p Blackburn*, The Times, 7 March 1980. Cf. *R* v. *Inspectorate of Pollution ex p Greenpeace Ltd (No 2)* [1994] 4 All ER 329 (stricter test for mandamus).

[23] Ibid. at 639D (Lord Diplock), 646A (Lord Fraser—possibly), 648A (Lord Scarman), 656G (Lord Roskill—probably).

[24] See ibid. at 630C (Lord Wilberforce), 642E (Lord Diplock), 645E (Lord Fraser).

[25] Ibid. at 654H; likewise at 644D (Lord Diplock).

remote the applicant's interest, even if he is merely one taxpayer objecting to the assessment of another, he may still succeed if he shows a clear case of default or abuse. The law will now focus upon public policy rather than private interest.[26] Standing is thus today seldom a determining issue in applications for judicial review. If the merits are weak, the application will fail without consideration of standing and if the merits are strong, denial of relief for lack of standing will prove more than judicial flesh and blood can bear.[27]

Another, though minor, curiosity is that the House of Lords repeatedly used the formula of section 31(3) of the Senior Courts Act 1981, viz. 'a sufficient interest in the matter to which the application relates', as the second-stage test whereas section 31(3) makes it the first-stage test. Since they are substantially different tests, the same formula will hardly do for both. This may be another indication that the second-stage test is not in fact based upon a distinct concept of standing. That, again, is tantamount to saying that standing has been abolished as a restrictive principle of public law.

A CITIZEN'S ACTION?

A recurrent theme of the speeches in the *Inland Revenue Commissioners* case is the 'change in legal policy'[28] which has greatly relaxed the rules about standing in recent years. This was put at its highest by Lord Diplock, who related it to 'that progress towards a comprehensive system of administrative law that I regard as having been the greatest achievement of the English courts in my judicial lifetime'.[29] He spoke of 'a virtual abandonment of the former restrictive rules as to the locus standi' of applicants for prerogative orders[30] and he approved the widest implications of the award of a prohibiting order to a citizen seeking to prevent a local authority from licensing indecent films.[31] He also approved the eloquent words of Lord Denning MR in the same case:

I regard it as a matter of high constitutional principle that if there is good ground for supposing that a government department or a public authority is transgressing the law, or is about to transgress it, in a way which offends or injures thousands of Her Majesty's subjects, then any one of those offended or injured can draw it to the attention of the court of law and seek to have the law enforced, and the courts *in their discretion*[32] can grant whatever remedy is appropriate.

Lord Diplock expressed the same point in his own words:[33]

It would, in my view, be a grave lacuna in our system of public law if a pressure group, like the federation, or even a single public-spirited taxpayer, were prevented by outdated technical rules of locus standi from bringing the matter to the attention of the court to vindicate the rule of law and get the unlawful conduct stopped.

Although Lord Diplock's speech was the most far-reaching in its terms, it is fully consistent with the majority view that the real question is whether the applicant can show some substantial default or abuse, and not whether his personal rights or interests are involved.[34]

---

[26] For arguments for and against such an 'open system' see [1990] *PL* 342 (Sir K. Schiemann).
[27] But the choice of remedy may be influenced by considerations of standing.
[28] [1982] AC 617 at 656G (Lord Roskill).   [29] Ibid. at 641C.   [30] Ibid. at 640C.
[31] *R v. Greater London Council ex p Blackburn* [1976] 1 WLR 550; above, p. 515.
[32] Lord Diplock's italics.   [33] [1982] AC 617 at 644E.
[34] Approved in the *World Development Movement* case (below, p. 592) at 395 (Rose LJ), holding that 'standing should not be treated as a preliminary issue, but must be taken in the legal and factual context of the whole case'.

In effect, therefore, a citizen's action, or *actio popularis*, is in principle allowable in suitable cases. Whether the case is suitable will depend upon the whole factual and statutory context, including any implications that can fairly be drawn from the statute as to who are the right persons to apply for remedies.[35] In fact the possibility of a citizen's action has long existed in the case of the prerogative remedies; but now the court may, in its discretion, grant a declaration or an injunction also. Although the House of Lords had laid it down in 1977 that only the Attorney-General could sue on behalf of the public for the purpose of preventing public wrongs, and that declarations could be granted only to litigants whose own legal position was in issue,[36] the House held that these sweeping statements were inapplicable to judicial review of governmental powers, to the prerogative remedies and to declarations and injunctions available in the application for judicial review.[37] Lord Diplock pointed out that neither the Attorney-General's practices, nor the doctrine of ministerial responsibility to Parliament, were adequate to fill the 'grave lacuna' which would exist otherwise.[38]

UNIFORMITY OF RULES OF STANDING UNDER THE SENIOR COURTS ACT 1981 AND THE CPR PART 54

The House of Lords has thus made it clear that the creation of the application for judicial review signalled a rationalising and simplifying of the tangle of different rules, sketched above, which used to complicate the subject of remedies. The changes were, as Lord Roskill said, 'intended to be far-reaching'.[39] He continued:

> They were designed to stop the technical procedural arguments which had too often arisen and thus marred the true administration of justice, whether a particular applicant had pursued his claim for relief correctly, whether he should have sought mandamus rather than certiorari, or certiorari rather than mandamus, whether an injunction or prohibition, or prohibition rather than an injunction, or whether relief by way of declaration should have been sought rather than relief by way of prerogative order. All these and like technical niceties were to be things of the past. All relevant relief could be claimed under the head of 'judicial review', and the form of judicial review sought or granted (if at all) was to be entirely flexible according to the needs of the particular case. The claims for relief could be cumulative or alternative under rule 2 as might be most appropriate.

Not all the law lords were willing to go so far and to hold that the old technical rules could now be forgotten,[40] but in the years since there has been little sign that different rules of standing might be adopted for different remedies. There was a similar difference of opinion as to the discretion which the court may exercise.[41] But the House of Lords is clearly determined to prevent technicalities from impeding judicial review so as to protect illegalities and derelictions committed by public authorities. The law about standing

---

[35] [1982] AC 617 at 646C (Lord Fraser).

[36] *Gouriet v. Union of Post Office Workers* [1978] AC 435; above, p. 495.

[37] [1981] AC 617 at 639A (Lord Diplock), 649F (Lord Scarman), 657H (Lord Roskill). Compare the liberal Scots doctrine in *Wilson v. IBA*, 1979 SLT 279 (above, p. 496). [38] [1982] AC 617 at 644E.

[39] Ibid. at 657E.

[40] See ibid. at 631E (Lord Wilberforce), 646A (Lord Fraser). Lord Diplock (at 640A) and Lord Roskill (at 656E) said that decisions earlier than 1950 were no longer to be relied upon.

[41] Contrast Lord Diplock's 'unfettered discretion' (at 642E) with Lord Fraser's rejection of 'uncontrolled discretion' (at 646A).

has moved forward, and the more progressive interpretations of it are probably the more likely to prove right in the future.[42]

LATER DECISIONS ON STANDING: GENERAL

Since the decision of the House of Lords the law has continued to reflect the liberal character of their ruling and the elasticity of 'sufficient interest' for the purposes of judicial review. The House of Lords' condemnation of the practice of treating standing as a preliminary issue has inclined the courts to decide adversely on the merits of the case, taking standing for granted, where this offers an easier route to the solution. The Court of Appeal dealt in this way with challenges made by the Leader of the Opposition and three local authorities to proposals published by the Boundary Commission for the reorganisation of parliamentary constituencies; the alleged illegalities were clearly not made out, so that there was no need for the court to express any opinion about standing.[43] In none of these cases dealt with below has it been suggested that there is any remaining difference as regards standing between the various remedies available by way of judicial review. The question of standing is held to go to the jurisdiction of the court, so that it is not open to the respondent to waive the objection and thus confer jurisdiction by agreement.[44]

THE 'PUBLIC-SPIRITED TAXPAYER' OR CITIZEN AND THE CITIZEN WITH A 'SINCERE CONCERN FOR CONSTITUTIONAL ISSUES'

Lord Diplock's 'single public-spirited taxpayer' has also received encouragement. In the capacity merely of a taxpayer and elector an individual was able to dispute (though unsuccessfully) the legality of the government's undertaking to pay its contribution of some £121 million to the European Economic Community, claiming that the draft Order in Council laid before Parliament was ultra vires.[45] Quoting the House of Lords' decision, Slade LJ referred to the 'change in legal policy' and to the 'virtual abandonment' of the old restrictive rules. 'If only in his capacity as a taxpayer', he said, the applicant should have standing, and on the serious question raised the right of challenge should not belong to the Attorney-General alone. Another taxpayer, public-spirited no doubt but also self-interested, achieved standing on the same question as in the *Inland Revenue Commissioners* case, namely whether one taxpayer could complain that the Inland Revenue had treated another taxpayer too leniently.[46] The applicant was a chemical company which contended that the Inland Revenue had accepted from competitor companies an unduly low valuation of ethane contrary to the Oil Taxation Act 1975. Although this was 'one of the rare cases' where one taxpayer could complain of the treatment of another, it would seem that such an applicant with a genuine and substantial complaint is likely to be accorded standing. And on this occasion the complaint was upheld.

---

[42] For comments on legal policy, see [1990] *PL* 342 (Sir K. Schiemann). For a detailed study see the Australian Law Reform Commission's Report No. 27 (1985).

[43] *R v. Boundary Commission for England ex p Foot* [1983] QB 600.

[44] *R v. Secretary of State for Social Services ex p Child Poverty Action Group* [1990] 2 QB 540.

[45] *R v. Her Majesty's Treasury ex p Smedley* [1985] QB 657 (Sir John Donaldson MR not deciding positively). Contrast *Wilson v. Grampian Regional Council*, 1993 SLT 588.

[46] *R v. A-G ex p Imperial Chemical Industries plc* (1986) 60 TC 1. In *R v. Camden LBC ex p H* [1996] ELR 360, the victim of a school shooting incident was granted judicial review on the ground that the decision of the governors was faulty and too lenient.

Citizens with a 'sincere concern for constitutional issues' have been able to challenge the lawfulness of the ratification of treaties without their standing being called into question.[47] But their challenges have generally failed for other reasons.

Other individual applicants have had mixed fortunes, but on the whole have fared well. Although the court made no order, a peace 'activist' concerned over whether insurgents captured by British forces were ill treated when transferred to the Afghan authorities secured substantial judicial scrutiny of the MOD's policy and its implementation.[48] A journalist, in the capacity of a public-spirited citizen, has been able to obtain a declaration that it was unlawful for a magistrates' court to conceal the identity of the justices as a matter of policy.[49] The press, 'as guardian and watchdog of the public interest', was entitled to raise this 'matter of national importance'. It is held that every holder of a television licence has an interest in the quality of the programmes, so that a breach by the Independent Broadcasting Authority of its duty to monitor controversial programmes effectively was remedied by a declaration at the instance of a lady offended by the film *Scum*.[50] On the other hand an opponent of cigarette smoking was denied standing to seek to restrain the BBC from broadcasting a snooker championship sponsored by a tobacco company, since he was no more affected than anybody else and so could proceed only with the aid of the Attorney-General.[51] The apparent inconsistency of these decisions may be due to the fact that standing is no longer a matter separate from the merits of the complaint. A public duty may amount to a sufficient interest to confer standing, so that a minister may challenge a local authority's budgetary estimates,[52] and a chief constable's duty to secure the restoration of stolen property can justify his application for an injunction to prevent its dissipation in a third party's hands.[53] In Canada a citizen was allowed to complain that statutory provisions about abortion conflicted with the right to life in the Canadian Bill of Rights;[54] but in New Zealand a doctor was not allowed to challenge a duly certified abortion with which he had no connection.[55]

If a personal right or interest is in issue the case is still stronger. A gipsy living on a caravan site may apply for an order that the Secretary of State should direct the local authority to fulfil its statutory duty to provide an adequate site.[56] No objection was raised to the standing of a mother of five young girls who sued a government department for a declaration that contraceptive advice given to her daughters without her knowledge, as proposed in a departmental circular, would infringe her rights as a parent, even though no such advice had been given and she was in no different position from any similar parent.[57] The holder of a gaming licence who objects to the grant of a licence to another company

---

[47] *R v. Secretary of State for Foreign Affairs ex p Lord Rees Mogg* [1993] EWHC Admin 4, [1994] QB 552. Standing was not even mentioned in the permission hearing in *R (Wheeler) v. Office of the Prime Minister and the Foreign Secretary* [2008] EWHC 936 (Admin) (application for declaration that referendum should be held on the Lisbon Treaty).

[48] *R (Evans) v. Secretary of State for Defence* [2010] EWHC 1445 (standing it seems not raised by MOD).

[49] *R v. Felixstowe Justices ex p Leigh* [1987] QB 582 (mandamus in respect of a particular decision refused since the journalist could show no sufficient interest in the identity of the justices).

[50] *R v. Independent Broadcasting Authority ex p Whitehouse*, The Times, 14 April 1984. In *Ogle v. Strickland* (1987) 71 ALR 41 priests were allowed standing to oppose registration of an allegedly blasphemous film, their vocation giving them a special interest.

[51] *Holmes v. Checkland*, The Times, 15 April 1987.

[52] *R v. London Borough of Haringey ex p Secretary of State for the Environment* [1991] COD 135.

[53] *Chief Constable of Kent v. V* [1983] QB 34.

[54] *Minister of Justice v. Borowski* (1981) 130 DLR (3d) 588.

[55] *Wall v. Livingstone* [1982] 1 NZLR 734.

[56] *R v. Secretary of State for the Environment ex p Ward* [1984] 1 WLR 834.

[57] *Gillick v. West Norfolk and Wisbech Area Health Authority* [1986] AC 112 (the active defendant was the DHSS). Contrast *R (Bulger) v. Home Secretary* [2001] EWHC Admin 119 (father of murdered child lacked

may proceed by judicial review.[58] So may a barrister who complains that a disciplinary decision in a case reported by him was too lenient.[59]

REPRESENTATIVE BODIES

State agencies, amenity societies and other representative bodies have profited from the relaxation of the former restrictions. The Equal Opportunities Commission, in the light of its statutory duty 'to work towards the elimination of discrimination', was able to contend (successfully) that European Union law against sex discrimination was violated by British legislation which excluded part-time workers from compensation for unfair dismissal and from redundancy payments, since many more women than men were in part-time employment.[60] Where a government department had failed to review cases of benefits wrongfully refused, contrary to social security regulations, because the administrative cost far outweighed the amount at stake, standing was accorded to the Child Poverty Action Group, acting in the interests of claimants; but at the same time standing was refused to the Greater London Council who were held not to have a sufficient interest.[61] In the same way the National Union of Mineworkers had standing to represent one of its members, but the Trades Union Congress had not.[62] The Royal College of Nursing was entitled to sue a government department in order to settle a doubtful question as to the legality of nurses performing certain functions in terminating pregnancy.[63] A local action group were able to proceed against a district council in an attempt to force them into action to prevent the demolition of listed buildings.[64] An environmental defence society had standing to challenge the authorisation of a nuclear generator.[65] A similar society with worldwide concerns was allowed to contest (successfully) the government's proposed overseas development grant of £316 million for the construction of the Pergau dam in Malaysia on the ground that, being uneconomic the project was not within statutory authority.[66] In New Zealand an environmental group had standing to oppose the construction of an aluminium smelter by disputing the validity both of the government's order[67] and of the company's planning application,[68] and members of

---

standing to challenge tariff period (see above, p. 59) set for murderer; his standing was limited to the impact of the decision on him personally).

[58] *Patmor Ltd v. City of Edinburgh District Licensing Board*, 1987 SLT 492; contrast *Matchett v. Dunfermline DC*, 1993 SLT 537; and see *R v. Department of Transport ex p Presvac Engineering Ltd* (1992) 4 Admin LR 121 (trade competitor allowed standing).

[59] *R v. General Council of the Bar ex p Percival* [1991] 1 QB 212 (relief refused). But a litigant may not complain that her counsel was insufficiently remunerated: *R v. Legal Aid Board ex p Bateman* [1992] 1 WLR 711.

[60] *R v. Secretary of State for Employment ex p Equal Opportunities Commission* [1995] 1 AC 1, Lord Jauncey dissenting on the question of standing.

[61] *R v. Secretary of State for Social Services ex p Greater London Council*, The Times, 16 August 1984. The standing of the CPAG was accepted by the Court of Appeal in a similar case: *R v. Secretary of State for Social Services ex p Child Poverty Action Group* [1990] 2 QB 540. Contrast *Scottish Old People's Welfare Council, Petitioners*, 1987 SLT 179 (standing refused to welfare organisation disputing legality of circular on social security payment for severe weather).

[62] *R v. Chief Adjudication Officer ex p Bland*, The Times, 6 February 1985.

[63] *Royal College of Nursing v. Department of Health and Social Security* [1981] AC 800.

[64] *R v. Stroud DC ex p Goodenough* (1980) 43 P & CR 59 (no relief granted).

[65] *R v. Inspectorate of Pollution ex p Greenpeace Ltd (No 2)* [1994] 4 All ER 329.

[66] *R v. Secretary of State for Foreign and Commonwealth Affairs ex p World Development Movement Ltd* [1995] 1 WLR 386. See similarly *R v. Secretary of State for the Environment ex p Friends of the Earth Ltd* (1994) 7 Admin LR 26 (claim for proper enforcement of water quality standards: standing allowed).

[67] *Environmental Defence Society Inc v. South Pacific Aluminium Ltd (No 3)* [1981] 1 NZLR 216.

[68] (As above) *(No 4)* [1981] 1 NZLR 530. Contrast *Everyone v. Tasmania* (1983) 49 ALR 381, where the High Court of Australia held that 'mere intellectual or emotional concern' was not enough.

football clubs in New Zealand were allowed standing to challenge the decision of the football union to send a team to South Africa.[69] Australian aborigines were also able to oppose plans for a smelter in Victoria, having a special interest in the land concerned.[70] The Campaign for Nuclear Disarmament even had standing to apply for an advisory declaration as to the legality of the use of armed force against Iraq (although the claim was dismissed primarily as non-justiciable).[71]

In contrast to these decisions the High Court refused standing to a trust company formed for the purpose of preserving the remains of the Rose Theatre in London; which the Secretary of State refused to list as an ancient monument.[72] A series of propositions was laid down by the judge as to standing, but they did not include any allowance for the strength, or rather weakness, of the case, which according to the House of Lords' doctrine should have been the dominant factor. It is significant, also, that the judge first dealt fully with the merits, rejecting the claim, before coming to the question of standing and deciding it restrictively. If, however, the applicants could have shown any possibility that the Secretary of State had acted improperly the decision on standing should have been different, since otherwise no one would have had standing and the law could have been violated with impunity. The case is best regarded as one where an arguable issue was not shown. In a later case no point was taken on the standing of a company formed in order to bring the application for judicial review.[73] Nor, despite conflicting authorities, are unincorporated associations likely to be held disqualified from suing in their own names.[74] But the agent (not the employer) of a group of musicians lacked standing to challenge.[75]

A Palestinian NGO was denied standing (at the permission stage) to challenge the UK's foreign policy in regard to Israel.[76] The NGO had 'no right even arguably' and should not be granted standing.

THE THIRD PARTY OR NEIGHBOUR IN PLANNING MATTERS

The problem of the standing of neighbours and third parties alleging the illegality of a planning permission[77] may now at last be resolved. In one case, where the grant of permission for a 'leisure centre' was held to be vitiated by bias, a neighbour was able to sue both because his land adjoined the proposed development and, apparently, because he

---

[69] Finnigan v. New Zealand Rugby Football Union Inc [1985] 2 NZLR 159.

[70] Onus v. Alcoa of Australia Ltd (1981) 149 CLR 27.

[71] R (Campaign for Nuclear Disarmament) v. Prime Minister [2002] EWHC 2777. See now Appendix 3.

[72] R v. Secretary of State for the Environment ex p Rose Theatre Trust Co [1990] 1 QB 504, not followed in R v. Somerset CC ex p Dixon [1992] COD 323 (for reasons explained by Sedley J at 327 (note)) and in R v. HM Inspectorate of Pollution ex p Greenpeace [1994] 4 All ER 329 (Otton J distinguishing Rose Theatre on ground that the trust was formed to bring the challenge).

[73] R (Legal Remedy UK Ltd) v. Secretary of State for Health [2007] EWHC 1252 (challenge to the fairness of the appointment process of junior doctors; but the company (unlike the Rose Theatre Trust) represented many junior doctors with a personal interest).

[74] See above, p. 592. No standing point was taken when an unincorporated association challenged in R (West End Street Traders Association) v. City of Westminster [2004] EWHC 1167.

[75] R (R70 World Ltd) v. Deputy High Commissioner, Lagos [2006] EWHC 330 (agent of musicians refused visa unable to challenge refusal (musicians themselves would only have been able to challenge by way of appeal)).

[76] R (Al-Haq) v. Secretary of State for Foreign and Commonwealth Affairs [2009] EWHC 1910, para. 48 (Pill LJ; Cranston J concurring). See too R (Hasan) v. Secretary of State for Trade and Industry [2008] EWCA Civ 1312.

[77] Gregory v. Camden London Borough Council [1966] 1 WLR 899; Bray v. Faber [1978] 1 NSWLR 335.

was a ratepayer.[78] A hostile precedent of 1966[79] was obviated by the 'considerable development in the field of administrative law' and the new law of judicial review. In another case, where a number of rival companies had applied for permission to build a supermarket, an unsuccessful applicant challenged the legality of the permission eventually granted without their standing being questioned.[80]

COMMERCIAL COMPETITORS AND ULTERIOR MOTIVES

As this last-mentioned case shows commercial enterprises will often seek to challenge the decisions of public authorities that benefit their rivals, e.g. a challenge to the grant of planning permission that enables a competitor to compete more effectively. The mere fact that the applicant is a commercial rival is not in itself sufficient to establish standing. But a rival does have an interest in seeing that the law is consistently applied. Thus a glass manufacturing firm could challenge the more lenient pollution control regime applied to its competitor.[81] The claimant had 'a proper interest to seek to ensure that [its] few competitors are subject to the same consistency of approach'.[82] But judicial 'dissatisfaction' has been expressed 'at the way the availability of the remedy of judicial review can be exploited—some might say abused—as a commercial weapon by rival potential developers to frustrate and delay their competitors' approved developments, rather than for any demonstrated concern about potential environmental or other planning harm.'[83]

And in another case it was said that 'if a claimant seeks to challenge a decision in which he has no private law interest, it is difficult to conceive of circumstances in which the court will accord him standing, even where there is a public interest in testing the lawfulness of the decision, if the claimant is acting out of ill-will or for some other improper purpose. It is an abuse of process to permit a claimant to bring a claim in such circumstances.'[84] Even so, a farmer, whose land had been used for the incineration of many slaughtered animals during the foot and mouth epidemic, had standing to challenge the Secretary of State's plans for the disposal of the remains, even though it was said the challenge was brought simply to bolster the compensation due to him.[85]

STRICTER EUROPEAN DOCTRINES

The progressive relaxation of the rules about standing is not reflected in the law of the European Union or in the law of European human rights. The European rules have been

---

[78] *Steeples* v. *Derbyshire CC* [1985] 1 WLR 256 (decided in 1981, before the House of Lords' decisions in the *Inland Revenue Commissioners* case and *O'Reilly* v. *Mackman*). See similarly *R* v. *Somerset CC ex p Dixon* (above). [79] The *Gregory* case, above, n. 77.

[80] *R* v. *St Edmundsbury BC ex p Investors in Industry Commercial Properties Ltd* [1985] 1 WLR 1168 (complaint not upheld) and see *R* v. *Ceredigion CC ex p McKeown* [1997] COD 465; *R* v. *St Edmundsbury DC ex p Walton* (1999) 11 Admin LR 648 (planning consent quashed for unlawful delegation). Cf. *Consumers Co-operative Society (Manawatu) Ltd* v. *Palmerston North CC* [1984] 1 NZLR 1 (standing allowed to commercial rival).

[81] *R (Rockware Glass Ltd)* v. *Chester City Council and Quinn Glass Ltd* [2005] EWHC 2250.

[82] Ibid., para. 174 (Judge Gilbert).

[83] *R (The Noble Organisation Ltd)* v. *Thanet District Council* [2005] EWCA Civ 782 (para. 64 (Auld LJ)) (challenge to the grant of planning permission to a commercial rival without an environmental impact assessment as was arguably required; appeal refused on the merits not standing).

[84] *Feakins* (below), para. 23 (Dyson LJ).

[85] *R (Feakins)* v. *Secretary of State for the Environment* [2003] EWCA Civ 1546 (motive of claimant relevant but not, in this case, determining).

briefly explained and illustrated in an earlier chapter.[86] They disallow actions by representative bodies on behalf of their members, so that the numerous English examples of successful claims by trade unions, environmental bodies and amenity societies have no European counterparts. Claims under the European Convention on Human Rights, incorporated in similar words by the Human Rights Act 1998, can be made only by a 'victim' who has himself suffered a wrong.

PROPOSED REFORMS

The Ministry of Justice in its consultation paper 'Judicial Review Proposals for Further Reform'[87] expresses its concern that in the current rules 'too wide an approach is taken to who may bring a claim, allowing judicial reviews to be brought by individuals or groups without a direct and tangible interest in the subject matter to which the claim relates, sometimes for reasons only of publicity or to cause delay'. Thus the government is consulting upon 'whether claimants without a direct or tangible interest ought to be able to bring a judicial review'.

The government is clearly out of sympathy with the policy that has driven the liberalisation of the rules of standing, viz. that the public interest (and the rule of law) is served by allowing persons without a direct interest to test the lawfulness of a contested decision. At any rate the government considers that the executive and the legislature rather than the judiciary should determine where the public interest lies.[88] The heart of the consultation on standing is whether one of the 'existing alternatives' to standing should be adopted for judicial review. These alternatives are: first, the stricter test of standing in EU law;[89] secondly, the 'victim' test used in the European Convention and the Human Rights Act 1998;[90] thirdly, the 'person aggrieved' test used in statutory appeals;[91] and, fourthly, the test for the civil public funding of judicial review claims which is 'the potential to produce a benefit for the individual, a member of the individual's family or the environment'.[92]

Legislation replacing the requirement of 'sufficient interest' with one of the stricter tests just mentioned would reverse the policy of the law of standing since the *Inland Revenue Commissioners* case. In fact, as the consultation paper itself makes clear, there are only a small number of judicial reviews each year where the applicant lacks a direct interest.[93] So the impact on the number of applications for judicial review made each year is likely to be modest. Moreover, should one or other of the stricter tests be imposed, it seems likely that in many cases an individual with a personal interest will be found to make the claim instead of the representative body. And the person or body without a personal interest, who might otherwise be a claimant, will seek to join the proceedings as an intervener.[94] The government has now abandoned its plans to reform the law of standing. See Appendix 3.

---

[86] Above, pp. 174 (EU), 143 (ECHR).   [87] Published September 2013.   [88] Para. 80.

[89] Above, p. 94.   [90] Above, p. 135.   [91] Below, p. 620.   [92] Above, p. 564.

[93] There are around 50 such applications for judicial reviews a year (para. 78). Of these 30% are environmental judicial reviews to which it is accepted the stricter tests will not be able to be applied. The government accepts that EU law and the Aarhus Convention mean that more liberal standing rules will be applied to environmental claims under EU law or the Convention (para. 81).

[94] CPR 54.17 provides that, on application to the court, which must be made promptly, 'any person' may file evidence and make representations to the court. But interveners, even on the winning side, may not get their costs (above, p. 568).

DISCRETION, EXHAUSTION, IMPLIED EXCLUSION

DISCRETION AND ITS CONSEQUENCES

The most active remedies of administrative law—declaration, injunction, the quashing order (certiorari), the prohibiting order (prohibition), the mandatory order (mandamus)—are discretionary and the court may therefore withhold them if it thinks fit. In other words, the court may find some act to be unlawful but may nevertheless decline to intervene.[95] In contrast, habeas corpus may be claimed as of right and so may remedies in tort, contract or restitution.

Such discretionary power may make inroads upon the rule of law, and must therefore be exercised with the greatest care. The following passage from an earlier edition of this book has thrice been approved judicially:[96]

> There are grave objections to giving the courts discretion to decide whether governmental action is lawful or unlawful: the citizen is entitled to resist unlawful action as a matter of right, and to live under the rule of law, not the rule of discretion. 'To remit the maintenance of constitutional right to the region of judicial discretion is to shift the foundations of freedom from rock to sand.'[97] The true scope for discretion is in the law of remedies, where it operates within narrow and recognised limits and is far less objectionable. If the courts were to undermine the principle of ultra vires by making it discretionary, no victim of an excess or abuse of power could be sure that the law would protect him.

Lord Bingham in an influential article has said 'the rights and obligations of citizens should depend on clear rules publicly stated and not on the whims, prejudices or predilections of the individual decision-maker', yet this was not the case when remedies depended upon the exercise of discretion. Consistency with the rule of law meant that 'the [remedial] discretion ... [was] strictly limited and the rules for its exercise clearly understood'.[98]

In any normal case the remedy accompanies the right. But the fact that a person aggrieved is entitled to a quashing order *ex debito justitiae* does not alter the fact that the court has power to exercise its discretion against him, as it may in the case of any discretionary remedy. This means that he may have to submit to some administrative act which is *ex hypothesi* unlawful. For, as has been observed earlier, in many situations, a void act is in effect a valid act if the court will not grant relief against it.[99]

Nevertheless distinctions may have to be drawn according to the nature of the remedy sought, and according to the differences between public and private law remedies. The quashing order and the prohibiting order have as their primary purpose the preservation of order in the legal system by preventing excess and abuse of power, rather than the final determination of private rights.[100] If a quashing order is refused in discretion, the applicant is not prevented from disputing the legality of the administrative decision in other

---

[95] See 'Should Public Law Remedies be Discretionary?' [1991] *PL* 64 (Lord Justice Bingham), discussing examples; Lord Cooke of Thorndon, 'The Discretionary Heart of Administrative Law' in Forsyth and Hare (eds.), *The Golden Metwand*, 203, discussing arbitrariness, discretionary relief and alternative remedies; also, Forsyth, 'The Rock and the Sand: Jurisdiction and Remedial Discretion' [2013] *JR* 360.

[96] 6th edn, 354, quoted in *Bugg* v. *Director of Public Prosecutions* [1993] QB 473 at 499 (Woolf LJ and Pill J), *R* v. *Wicks* [1998] AC 92 at 121 (Lord Hoffmann) and *Boddington* v. *British Transport Police* [1998] UKHL 13, [1999] 2 AC 143 at 176.   [97] *Scott* v. *Scott* [1913] AC 417 at 477 (Lord Shaw).

[98] Bingham at 64 (both quotations).

[99] Above, p. 247. This and the preceding paragraph were approved by the Court of Appeal in *R* v. *Governors of Small Heath School ex p Birmingham CC* (1989) 2 Admin LR 154 at 167.   [100] Above, p. 509.

proceedings, e.g. by suing his tenant for the original rent after a rent tribunal has ordered a reduction and an application for a quashing order has failed.[101] In other words, he cannot be met with a plea of res judicata, and he may always show, if he can, that the tribunal has no jurisdiction.[102] It would be logical to extend the same doctrine to all the remedies now obtainable by judicial review.

There is an inevitable tension between the rule of law and remedial discretion. Where a claimant establishes that an impugned decision is unlawful but is denied the fruits of that victory through the exercise of discretion to deny a remedy, the rule of law is undermined. And there are 'grave objections' to this. At the same time, it is clear as a matter of law[103] that all the relevant remedies are discretionary and that the denial of a remedy sometimes serves the public interest—for instance, by the avoidance of administrative chaos or the harm to innocent third parties that might otherwise result.

But the emergence of the principle that all errors of law are jurisdictional[104] implies certain limits on the operation of remedial discretion. These jurisdictional limits, as will be seen, narrow the scope of remedial discretion considerably. Where an error of law is shown the impugned decision will be legally non-existent and void. When the courts have this in mind they hesitate to breathe life into an illegality by denial even of a declaration that the impugned decision is unlawful. In the leading Supreme Court decision (*Ahmed No 2*)[105] the court had found, for reasons that need not now concern us,[106] that certain Orders in Council that froze the funds of a number of individuals suspected of involvement in terrorism were 'ultra vires and void'.[107] The Treasury asked the Supreme Court not to deny relief but to take the smaller step of suspending the quashing orders and other relief for a period so that Parliament could pass primary legislation to enable similar freezing orders to be lawfully imposed.[108] Lord Phillips speaking for the majority said:

> the court's order, whenever it is made, will not alter the position in law. It will declare what that position is. It is true that it will also quash the [Orders in Council], but these are provisions that are ultra vires and of no effect in law. The object of quashing them is to make it quite plain that this is the case. The effect of suspending the operation of the order of the court would be, or might be, to give the opposite impression. It would suggest that, during the period of suspension of the quashing orders, the provisions to be quashed would remain in force... [the] court should not lend itself to a procedure that is designed to obfuscate the effect of its judgment.[109]

This logic implies a significant narrowing of remedial discretion; once the court finds an error of law is shown, the impugned decision is null and void; to deny that by refusing relief would 'obfuscate' the court's judgment. Consistent with the Supreme Court's approach (but with very different facts) is the case where a constable challenged the order[110] of the Police Appeals Tribunal to limit the 'back pay' to which he was entitled. The Tribunal accepted that the order challenged was void (since the Tribunal had been *functus officio* when

---

[101] See above, p. 198.

[102] For res judicata in relation to prerogative remedies see above, p. 206.

[103] The discretionary nature of the remedies, both prerogative and private, derives primarily from the common law. But remedial discretion has in significant measure the imprimatur of statute. See the Senior Courts Act 1981, s. 31(2) and (6). Note also the Town and Country Planning Act 1990, s. 288(5).

[104] Above, p. 219.   [105] *HM Treasury* v. *Ahmed and ors (No 2)* [2010] UKSC 5.

[106] Above, p. 358.   [107] Paras. 177 and 187.

[108] Such a request was made, and granted, in similar circumstances by the Court of Final Appeal in Hong Kong: *Koo Sze Yiu and anor* v. *Chief Executive of the HKSAR* [2006] HKCFA 74.   [109] Paras. 4–8.

[110] In fact the order challenged was an amending order purporting to amend an earlier order in which the constable had been granted full pay during his period of suspension.

it was made) but 'argued that the court should decline to quash the order as a matter of discre-tion on the ground that to do so would result in injustice'.[111] The court refused to stay its hand remarking that: 'It is a fundamental requirement of the rule of law—viewed as a safeguard against arbitrary power—that decision-makers act within the powers conferred on them by law and do not exceed those powers. That fundamental requirement would be subverted if it were to be accepted as a proper reason for refusing to quash an invalid decision of a tribunal that the invalid decision is one which the court thinks it would have been desirable or just for the tribunal to make had it been within its power to make it.'[112]

On the other hand, there are several decisions since *Ahmed* (including decisions of the Supreme Court)[113] that have continued to exercise remedial discretion freely as if it were unexceptional to breathe life into an invalid act.

The supposition in the past that the rules for the exercise of remedial discretion were stricter in the EU context than in a purely domestic case has been shown to be false;[114] the same rules govern in both circumstances.[115]

EXAMPLES OF REFUSAL OF RELIEF

An applicant may lose his claim to relief because his own conduct has been unmerito-rious[116] or unreasonable.[117] Examples of this have already been given in the context of natural justice.[118] An applicant may also have raised his objection too late.[119] If a party appearing before a tribunal knows that it is improperly constituted because one of the

---

[111] *Baker v. Police Appeals Tribunal* [2013] EWHC 718, para. 1 (Leggatt J). No reference was made to *Ahmed (No 2)*. It is clearly spelt out in this judgment that, since the order was void, even if relief was refused its nullity would be shown in a collateral challenge, for instance if the constable sued for the pay due to him, the invalid order would not avail the police force as a defence to that claim. See the discussion of collateral challenge, at p. 235.   [112] Para. 41.

[113] *R (KM) v. Cambridgeshire County Council* [2012] UKSC 23 (deficit found in decision-maker's reason-ing about extent of support due to severely disabled man but amplification of reasoning in the judicial review made it 'pointless' to quash the decision; see above, p. 445 for curing defects in reasons) and *Walton v. The Scottish Ministers* (below, p. 598). Another prominent case refusing relief although illegality had been deter-mined was *R (Hurley and Moore) v. Secretary of State for Business Innovation & Skills* [2012] EWHC 201.

[114] *Berkeley v. Secretary of State for the Environment and ors* [2000] UKHL 36. Environmental Impact Assessment required by EU law not carried out; planning permission quashed; court refused to exercise discretion ('In the Community context, unless a violation is so negligible as to be truly de minimis and the prescribed procedure has in all essentials been followed, the discretion (if any exists) is narrower [than in domestic law]: [because of]...the obligation of national courts to ensure that Community rights are fully and effectively enforced' (Lord Bingham)).

[115] In *Walton v. The Scottish Ministers* [2012] UKSC 44 Lord Carnwath said: 'Where the court is satisfied that the applicant has been able in practice to enjoy the rights conferred by the European legislation...I see nothing in principle or authority to require the courts to adopt a different approach merely because the pro-cedural requirement arises from a European rather than a domestic source.'

[116] As in *R v. Kensington General Commissioners of Income Tax ex p Polignac* [1917] 1 KB 486 (material facts suppressed in affidavit); *White v. Kuzych* [1951] AC 585 (breach of contract); *Windsor and Maidenhead RBC v. Brandrose Investments Ltd* [1983] 1 WLR 509 (council ought not to have litigated); *R v. Secretary of State for Education and Science ex p Birmingham CC* (1984) 83 LGR 79 (council changed its mind about school closure and pleaded its own procedural error to nullify Secretary of State's confirmation order); *R v. Brent LBC ex p Dorot Properties Ltd* [1990] COD 378 (ratepayer with bad record: order for refund of over-payment refused). Contrast *Taylor v. Newham LBC* [1993] 1 WLR 444 (no discretion to refuse enforcement by injunction of tenant's statutory right to buy).

[117] As in *Ex. p. Fry* [1954] 1 WLR 730; *Fulbrook v. Berkshire Magistrates Courts Committee* (1970) 69 LGR 75.   [118] Above, p. 426.

[119] As in *R v. Stafford Justices ex p Stafford Corporation* [1940] 2 KB 33; *R v. Aston University Senate ex p Roffey* [1969] 2 QB 538; *R v. Herrod ex p Leeds City Council* [1976] QB 540, but see [1978] AC 403; *R v.*

members has an interest in the case, but raises no objection at the time, he may be refused a remedy.[120] He is treated, in effect, as having waived the objection by accepting the tribunal's jurisdiction. It is a general rule that the court will not intervene in favour of an applicant who has allowed a court or authority to proceed to a decision without setting up an objection of which he was aware at the time—'except perhaps upon an irresistible case, and an excuse for the delay, such as disability, malpractice, or matter newly come to the knowledge of the applicant'.[121]

The court may also withhold remedies for objective reasons—a tendency which has come to the fore with the widening ambit of judicial review.[122] The Court of Appeal gave a notable example in a case where a takeover bid had been referred to the Monopolies and Mergers Commission.[123] The chairman of the Commission, being satisfied by assurances from the bidding company, decided that the controversial part of the proposals had been abandoned, and obtained the Secretary of State's consent to discontinuing the reference. But under the statutory procedure it should have been the Commission itself, and not the chairman alone, who decided the question of abandonment. It was therefore a case of ultra vires delegation. But a rival company, also a bidder, was refused certiorari to quash the discontinuance of the reference. The court considered that the Commission would have reached the same conclusion as the chairman and that account should be taken of the demands of good public administration. These were that substance should prevail over form; that there should be speed of decision, especially in the financial field; that the Secretary of State could protect the public interest; that the statutory scheme was not intended to benefit rival companies; and that decisiveness and finality were vital. The result was that the reference stood discontinued, despite the procedural illegality.

Another striking case was where the court declined to quash unlawful regulations. Before making regulations for the housing benefits scheme the Secretary of State had a mandatory duty to consult organisations representing housing authorities, but his consultation with them was so inadequate both as to time and as to substance that he was held to have failed to consult. The court granted a declaration to this effect but refused to quash the regulations by certiorari or to declare them void, since they had already been acted upon by local authorities and had been consolidated into new regulations which had not been challenged. Since the applicants did not object to the substance of the regulations, there was no point in invalidating them. So, unlawful though they were, they took effect.[124] In this and the similar cases cited the decisions amounted to a disguised form of prospective overruling, denying relief to the party but establishing the invalidity for the future.[125]

Another example of effect being given to unlawful regulations—the regulations that permitted a very substantial increase in university fees—was the case in which, although

Secretary of State for the Environment ex p Walters (1998) 30 HLR 328 (also involving defective consultation and third party interests).

[120] R v. Williams ex p Phillips [1914] 1 KB 608; above, p. 398.

[121] London Cpn v. Cox (1867) LR 2 HL 239 at 283; Broad v. Perkins (1888) 21 QBD 533.

[122] See e.g. R v. Brent LBC ex p O'Malley (1997) 10 Admin LR 265 (defective consultation but effect minimal); R v. South Tyneside MBC ex p Cram (1997) 10 Admin LR 477 (disruptive pupil caused threat of teachers' strike—mandamus refused).

[123] R v. Monopolies and Mergers Commission ex p Argyll Group plc [1986] 1 WLR 763.

[124] R v. Secretary of State for Social Services ex p Association of Metropolitan Authorities [1986] 1 WLR 1. See similarly R v. Secretary of State for Social Services ex p Association of Metropolitan Authorities (1993) 5 Admin LR 6; R v. Rochdale MBC ex p Schemet [1993] COD 113; R v. North West Thames Regional Health Authority ex p Daniels [1994] COD 44; R v. Sheffield City Council ex p Hague, The Times, 20 August 1999.

[125] See above, p. 249.

a non-technical breach of the minister's public sector equality duties (PSED)[126] in making the regulations was shown, all relief was refused on the ground that it was 'disproportionate' and inconvenient (in that many people had relied upon the validity of the regulations).[127]

The freedom with which the court can use its discretion to mould its remedies to suit special situations is shown by two decisions already encountered. One was the case where the House of Lords refused mandamus to a police probationer wrongly induced to resign, although he made out a good case for that remedy, in order not to usurp the powers of the chief constable, and instead granted him an unusual form of declaration to the effect that he was entitled to the remedies of unlawful removal from office except for reinstatement.[128] The other was the case of the Takeover Panel, where in fact no relief was granted but the Court of Appeal explained the novel way in which remedies should be employed in future cases, with the emphasis on declaration rather than quashing orders and on 'historic rather than contemporaneous' relief.[129] The same freedom to mould remedies exists in European Union law, where the European Court of Justice may declare non-retroactivity when holding some act or regulation to be void.[130]

The court may also exercise a discretion not to interfere with the internal discipline of forces such as the police and fire brigades.[131] Where time is needed for making arrangements to comply with the court's judgment, a prohibiting order may be withheld in discretion, with liberty to apply for it again later.[132]

EXHAUSTION OF REMEDIES—(A) THE PRINCIPLE

In principle there ought to be no categorical rule requiring the exhaustion of administrative remedies before judicial review can be granted. A vital aspect of the rule of law is that illegal administrative action can be challenged in the court as soon as it is taken or threatened. There should be no need first to pursue any administrative procedure or appeal in order to see whether the action will in the end be taken or not.[133] An administrative appeal on the merits of the case is something quite different from judicial determination of the legality of the whole matter. This is merely to restate the essential difference between review and appeal, which has already been emphasised. The only qualification is that there may occasionally be special reasons which induce the court to withhold discretionary remedies where the more suitable procedure is appeal, for example where an appeal is already in progress,[134] or the object is to raise a test case on a point of law.[135]

In the *Electricity Commissioners* case, accordingly, even though the minister might in the end not have confirmed the scheme, the proceedings were halted by prohibition as

---

[126] Above, p. 325.   [127] *Hurley and Moore*, above, para. 99 (Elias LJ).

[128] *Chief Constable of North Wales Police* v. *Evans* [1982] 1 WLR 1155 (above, p. 425).

[129] *R* v. *Panel on Takeovers and Mergers ex p Datafin plc* [1987] QB 815 (above, p. 540).

[130] See e.g. *Société des Produits de Mais SA* v. *Administration des Douanes et Droits Indirects* [1988] 1 CMLR 459; and above, p. 170.

[131] *Ex p. Fry* (above); *Buckoke* v. *Greater London Council* [1970] 1 WLR 1092.

[132] *R* v. *Greater London Council ex p Blackburn* [1976] 1 WLR 550.

[133] Where there is a right of appeal within a time limit, RSC Ord. 53 r. 3(8) empowered the court to adjourn an application for a quashing order until the appeal is determined or the time limit has expired. There is no express equivalent power in CPR 54.

[134] As in *R* v. *Civil Service Appeal Board ex p Bruce* [1989] 2 All ER 907 (civil servant appealed to industrial tribunal); *Nahar* v. *Strathclyde Regional Council* (above); *R* v. *Commissioner for the Special Purposes of the Income Tax Acts ex p Napier* [1988] 3 All ER 166; *Wardle* v. *A-G* [1987] 1 NZLR 296.

[135] *R* v. *Chief Adjudication Officer ex p Bland*, The Times, 6 February 1985.

soon as it was shown that the scheme would be invalid.[136] Where a police officer, invalidly dismissed by a watch committee, did not exercise his statutory right of appeal to the Home Secretary, this was held no bar to his obtaining a declaration from the court.[137] Similar decisions have many times been given.[138] A redundant vestry clerk was not obliged to pursue his right of appeal to the Treasury before obtaining mandamus to require the local authority to compute his compensation correctly.[139] A vicar did not have to appeal to the Court of the Arches before obtaining prohibition against a Consistory Court which had not given him a hearing.[140] A planning permission vitiated by unreasonable conditions may be quashed at once with a quashing order, even though there is a right of appeal to the Secretary of State and a further appeal to the High Court on a question of law.[141] A doctor contesting the legality of a deduction from his pay by a health service committee need not first follow the prescribed procedure of making representations to the Secretary of State.[142] These decisions confirm what was said in one of the classic cases: 'A party is not concluded by not appealing against a nullity'.[143] If the order is one which the applicant is entitled for any reason to have quashed as a matter of law, it is pointless to require him first to pursue an administrative appeal on the merits.

The same principle applies in habeas corpus cases, so that a detained immigrant need not go through the procedure of immigration appeals before he can apply for his release on the ground that he is detained illegally.[144] Domestic tribunals such as trade union disciplinary committees are also subject to the same rule,[145] even though their jurisdiction is based upon contract and even though the terms of the contract expressly purport to exclude the jurisdiction of the court[146]—for this the court will not allow.

A paradoxical contention, occasionally put forward, is that the exercise of an administrative appeal implies a waiver of judicial remedies. In *Ridge* v. *Baldwin* the Court of Appeal held that since the chief constable had appealed to the Home Secretary unsuccessfully he had thereby waived his right to seek a declaration from the court that his dismissal was legally invalid.[147] The House of Lords reversed this decision, which rests on an obvious confusion between appeal on the merits of the case and judicial review of the legality of the whole proceeding. Since these are quite different things, it would be an illogical trap if they were mutually exclusive. Administrative remedies are highly

---

[136] [1924] 1 KB 171; above, p. 514.   [137] *Cooper* v. *Wilson* [1937] 2 KB 309.

[138] See e.g. *Burder* v. *Veley* (1841) 12 Ad & E 263; *White* v. *Steele* (1862) 12 CBNS 383 at 409; *London Cpn* v. *Cox* (1867) LR 2HL 239 at 278; *R* v. *Comptroller-General of Patents ex p Parke Davis & Co* [1953] 1 All ER 862 at 865 (affirmed on other grounds, [1954] AC 321); *R* v. *Wimbledon Justices ex p Derwent* [1953] 1 All ER 390; *Graddage* v. *Haringey London Borough Council* [1975] 1 WLR 241; *R* v. *Galvin* (1949) 77 CLR 432; *Bell* v. *Ontario Human Rights Commission* (1971) 18 DLR (3d) 1; *Martin* v. *Ryan* [1990] 2 NZLR 209.

[139] *R* v. *Stepney Cpn* [1902] 1 KB 317.

[140] *R* v. *North ex p Oakey* [1927] 1 KB 491, citing earlier cases.

[141] *R* v. *Hillingdon Borough Council ex p Royco Homes Ltd* [1974] 1 QB 720. Compare *Munnich* v. *Godstone Rural District Council* [1966] 1 WLR 427.

[142] *Roy* v. *Kensington and Chelsea and Westminster Family Practitioner Committee* [1992] 1 AC 624.

[143] *Bunbury* v. *Fuller* (1853) 9 Ex 111 at 135.

[144] *R* v. *Governor of Pentonville Prison ex p Azam* [1974] AC 18 at 31, 41.

[145] *Lawlor* v. *Union of Post Office Workers* [1965] Ch 712; *Leigh* v. *National Union of Railwaymen* [1970] Ch 326.

[146] *Leigh* v. *National Union of Railwaymen* (above). Contrast *White* v. *Kuzych* [1951] AC 585, decided when the attitude of the courts was different.

[147] *Ridge* v. *Baldwin* [1963] 1 QB 539, reversed [1964] AC 40. See also *Annamunthodo* v. *Oilfield Workers' Trade Union* [1961] AC 945. For sound statements see *Ackroyd* v. *Whitehouse* [1985] 2 NSWLR 239 at 248 (Kirby P); *Mensah* v. *Home Secretary*, 1992 SLT 177.

desirable and people should be encouraged to use them. But to allow unlawful action to stand, merely because it has been appealed against on its merits, is indefensible.

EXHAUSTION OF REMEDIES—(B) CONFLICTING OPINIONS

In the past three decades the case law has produced a crop of judicial statements which conflict with the principle just explained.[148] It has been said that, where there is some right of appeal, judicial review will not be granted 'save in the most exceptional circumstances'; and that the normal rule is that the applicant 'should first exhaust whatever other rights he has by way of appeal'.[149] A decision of the Court of Appeal goes further and suggests that, in the absence of a point of law, the existence of alternative dispute mechanisms or statutory complaint procedures is sufficient to preclude judicial review.[150] These propositions have been prompted by the rapid growth of applications for judicial review and a judicial desire to limit them. The Law Commission also supports them and favours a general rule requiring the exhaustion of alternative remedies before judicial review is allowed.[151] This is, however, a controversial subject and there is an issue of principle.

In a tax case, where the complainant had failed to show abuse of power by the commissioners, Lord Scarman said that it was 'a proposition of great importance' that 'a remedy by way of judicial review is not to be made available where an alternative remedy exists', and that 'it will only be very rarely that the courts will allow the collateral process of judicial review to be used to attack an appealable decision'.[152] But he at once went on to say that judicial review would be available had the commissioners done something equivalent to an abuse of power. Lord Templeman said that 'judicial review should not be granted where an alternative remedy is available', but almost in the same breath he neatly epitomised the familiar grounds which in such a case would allow review,[153] and he added, significantly, that the case in hand was exceptional in that the appeal procedure could not operate if the conduct of the commissioners was unlawful.[154] In another tax case Sir John Donaldson MR said that 'it is a cardinal principle that, save in the most exceptional circumstances, [the judicial review] jurisdiction will not be exercised where other remedies were available and have not been used'.[155] He repeated these words when in fact granting judicial review to police officers, despite their having lodged appeals to

---

[148] For discussion, mostly antithetical to the views here expressed, see Lewis, *Judicial Remedies in Public Law*, 5th edn, 11–043; [1992] *CLJ* 138 (C. Lewis); J. Beatson in Forsyth and Hare (eds.) *The Golden Metwand*, 230: Lord Cooke of Thorndon, ibid., 203. See also the interesting discussion in [2005] *JR* 350 (Moules) arguing that the principle (not rule) that alternative remedies should be exhausted should be weighed with other principles in deciding whether to grant permission.

[149] *R v. Chief Constable of Merseyside Police ex p Calveley* [1986] QB 424 at 435 (May LJ). In Scotland the rules of court require resort to appeal if available: see *O'Neill v. Scottish Joint Negotiating Committee for Teaching Staff*, 1987 SLT 648.

[150] *R (Cowl) v. Plymouth CC* [2001] EWCA Civ 1935, [2002] 1 WLR 803 (CA) ('heavy obligation not to resort to litigation if at all possible': para. 27) (Lord Woolf). See [2002] *PL* 203 (Le Sueur).

[151] Law Com. No. 226 (1994), paras. 5.33, 5.35, not mentioning any problem of principle.

[152] *R v. Inland Revenue Commissioners ex p Preston* [1985] AC 835 at 852 (allegations of unfairness and abuse of power not upheld). See likewise *R v. Inland Revenue Commissioners ex p Opman International UK* [1986] 1 All ER 328.

[153] 'Where a decision-making authority exceeds its powers, commits an error of law, commits a breach of natural justice, reaches a decision which no reasonable tribunal could have reached, or abuses its powers.'

[154] [1985] AC 835 at 862. For this supposed difficulty see below, p. 600.

[155] *R v. Epping and Harlow General Commissioners ex p Goldstraw* [1983] 3 All ER 257 at 262 (no case for judicial review shown): see similarly *R v. Panel on Takeovers and Mergers ex p Guinness plc* [1990] 1 QB 146 at 177.

the Home Secretary, after they had been unfairly dismissed in a typical natural justice case which had nothing exceptional about it.[156] In a case which was indeed exceptional the Court of Appeal accepted the 'very strong dicta' quoted above and rejected the criticism of them in this book.[157] Those dicta led also to the denial of judicial review of a magistrates' court's conviction of a motorist who had appealed to the Crown Court but had been given an unfair trial. It was held that a fair retrial by that court was the proper remedy despite the citation of about a dozen precedents in favour of judicial review.[158]

Deeper research produced a very different result in another magistrates' court case where an irregular conviction was quashed on judicial review despite the right of appeal to the Crown Court.[159] Numerous authorities going back to 1924 showed that judicial review had constantly been allowed for quashing convictions vitiated by unfairness, bias or procedural irregularity, rights of appeal notwithstanding. Remarks of Lord Caldecote CJ in a case of 1942 make an almost comical contrast with the dicta of Lord Scarman and Lord Donaldson:[160]

> It remains to consider the argument that the remedy of certiorari is not open to the appellant because others were available. It would be ludicrous in such a case as the present for the convicted person to ask for a case to be stated. It would mean asking the court to consider as a question of law whether the justices were right in convicting a man without hearing his evidence. That is so extravagant an argument as not to merit a moment's consideration.

Quoting these remarks, and omitting all mention of the contrary dicta, Lord Bingham CJ said that to refuse judicial review for unfairness or bias 'would be to emasculate the long-established supervisory jurisdiction of this court over magistrates' courts, which has over the years provided an invaluable guarantee of the integrity of proceedings in those courts'. The long line of decisions brings out what the dicta ignore, namely that appeal and review exist for different purposes, the first concerning merits and the second concerning legality,[161] and that review of legality is the primary mechanism for enforcing the rule of law under the inherent jurisdiction of the court. If an applicant can show illegality, it is wrong in principle to require him to exercise a right of appeal. Illegal action should be stopped in its tracks as soon as it is shown.[162]

---

[156] R v. Chief Constable of Merseyside Police ex p Calveley (above) at 433, May and Glidewell LJJ concurring. See similarly R v. Inspector of Taxes ex p Kissane [1986] 2 All ER 37 (allegation of improper decision by tax inspector: judicial review granted despite availability of appeal).

[157] R v. Birmingham City Council ex p Ferrero Ltd [1993] 1 All ER 530. The exceptional factor was danger to children from the sale of certain toys, which required immediate prohibition. 'Common sense dictates that protection of the public must take precedence over fairness to the trader' (Taylor LJ). See also R v. Ministry of Defence Police ex p Sweeney [1998] COD 122. See also R v. Humberside CC ex p Bogdal (1992) 5 Admin LR 405 (need to protect occupants of old people's home); R v. Special Educational Needs Tribunal ex p Fairpo [1996] COD 180; R v. Brighton and Hove BC ex p Nacion (1999) 11 Admin LR 472 (clear statutory intent). Contrast the allowance of judicial review in R v. Devon CC ex p Baker [1995] 1 All ER 73 (point of law); R v. Bristol Magistrates' Court ex p Doles [1994] COD 139 (natural justice); R v. Falmouth and Truro Health Authority ex p South West Water Services Ltd [1999] COD 305 (lack of consultation); R v. Wiltshire CC ex p Lazard Bros Ltd, The Times, 31 December 1997 (plain error of law).

[158] R v. Peterborough Magistrates' Court ex p Dowler [1997] QB 911.

[159] R v. Hereford Magistrates' Court ex p Rowlands [1998] QB 110, rejecting the reasoning of ex p Dowler (above). For comment on these decisions see [1997] PL 589 (Wade).

[160] R v. Wandsworth JJ ex p Read [1942] 1 KB 281.

[161] See Kemper Reinsurance v. Minister of Finance [1998] 3 WLR 630 (PC).

[162] For comment on this see Lord Cooke of Thorndon in The Golden Metwand, 215.

For this purpose there should be no relevant difference between civil and criminal cases. Nor should the much-extended scope of judicial review be allowed to restrict its use as a matter of principle.[163] But it has to be recognised that what ought to be a clear distinction has been blurred by the overlap in the area of error of law, which is now held to be a form of ultra vires, and so a ground for judicial review, but which is particularly suitable for correction on appeal.[164] In addition there may be classes such as planning cases,[165] tax cases,[166] employment cases,[167] and immigration cases[168] for which specialised appeal systems exist, where the court may reasonably hold that appeal is the normal remedy, subject always to the grant of review in case of excess or abuse of power, breach of natural justice, and so forth.[169] What does not seem right is to insist that there is something exceptional about judicial review, that remedies given for different purposes must be exhausted first, and that the choice of remedies depends upon convenience, speed, expertise and other factors which, being imponderable, produce procedural dilemmas and potential traps for litigants. Where appeal lies to a minister, as in many planning cases, that is plainly an unsatisfactory alternative to judicial review in any case turning on questions of law.

In reality the courts are better than their word.[170] When genuine grounds for judicial review are alleged or there is some clear advantage to judicial review, it is the refusal rather than the grant of review which is the exceptional course.[171] A leading Court of Appeal case

---

[163] For a contrary view see J. Beatson in *The Golden Metwand*, 221 and sources there cited.

[164] But see *R v. Peterborough City Council ex p Hanif* [1992] COD 491 (taxi-cab licence: appeal to lay magistrates on point of law unsuitable); *R v. Leeds City Council ex p Mellor* [1993] COD 352 (appeal to Crown Court unsuitable); *R v. Leeds City Council ex p Hendry*, The Times, 20 January 1994 (similar).

[165] *R v. Epping Forest DC ex p Green* [1993] COD 81; *R v. Home Secretary ex p Watts* [1997] COD 152.

[166] See e.g. *R v. Commissioners for the Special Purposes of the Income Tax Acts ex p Napier* [1988] 3 All ER 166; *R v. Poole Justices ex p Benham* (1991) 4 Admin LR 161; *Horley Development Inc v. CIR* [1996] 1 WLR 727; *R v. Commissioners of Customs and Excise ex p Bosworth Beverages Ltd*, The Times, 24 April 2000.

[167] As in *R v. Secretary of State for Employment ex p Equal Opportunities Commission* [1995] 1 AC 1 (review refused to individual applicant, who could appeal, but granted to EOC, which could not).

[168] As in *R v. Home Secretary ex p Swati* [1986] 1 WLR 477; *R v. Home Secretary ex p Capti-Mehmet* [1997] COD 61. Contrast *Choi v. Home Secretary*, 1996 SLT 590 (review allowed). See also *Lim* (below).

[169] As in *Accountant in Bankruptcy v. Allans of Gillock Ltd*, 1991 SLT 765; *Macksville Hospital v. Mayze* (1987) 10 NSWLR 708.

[170] For a case in which the Court of Appeal was not better than their word see *R (Lim) v. Home Secretary* [2007] EWCA Civ 773. Here a removal order was made by an immigration officer against a Malaysian citizen for alleged breach of condition of leave to enter (working for the 'Riverbank' restaurant instead of the 'Lucky Star') (Immigration and Asylum Act 1999, s. 10(1)). There was a right of appeal to the Asylum and Immigration Tribunal but this could not be exercised while the immigrant remained in the UK (i.e. there was only an 'out of country' appeal) (Nationality, Immigration and Asylum Act 2002, s. 92). Nonetheless, the existence of this right of appeal justified the denial of judicial review. *Sivasubramaniam* (below, n. 219) followed and *Khawaja v. Home Secretary* [1984] 1 AC 74 (where an 'out of country' appeal did not preclude judicial review) distinguished. The hardship (losing job, income and home) before 'out of country' appeal could be heard did not render the case exceptional (even though the judge found that the hardship 'seems impossible to justify'!). The first instance decision of Lloyd Jones J ([2006] EWHC 3004 (Admin)) following *Khawaja* and finding exceptional circumstances justifying judicial review is to be preferred.

[171] *R (AM (Cameroon)) v. The Asylum and Immigration Tribunal* [2008] EWCA Civ 100 is a good example of this showing the court's fidelity to fairness prevailing over the pragmatic preference for alternative remedies. The applicant was an asylum seeker who was given a grossly unfair appeal hearing against the Home Secretary's decision to reject his application for asylum (failure to allow important evidence to be given by telephone link, *inter alia*). The appellant applied both for judicial review and to a High Court judge for the review of the tribunal's decision under s. 103A. The permission judge (Beatson J) ordered that an oral permission hearing take place and this should be linked to any application under the statutory procedure. But in fact no linked hearing took place and the High Court judge under the statutory procedure (Bean J), surprisingly, refused to order reconsideration by the AIT. The Court of Appeal rejected the argument that Beatson J should have refused permission because of the alternative remedy and ordered that AM's application for judicial review should be allowed to proceed. Moreover, the decision of Bean J, finding that there

concerned the summary dismissal by an unfair procedure by the relevant local authority of a Director of Children's Services following a scandal that led to the death of a child.[172] The DCS sought judicial review of her dismissal and the Court of Appeal held this was not barred by the fact that she could have brought proceedings in an Employment Tribunal. Kay LJ said that the judge below 'was wrong to defer to the Employment Tribunal proceedings. The alternative remedy was not "equally convenient and effective".'[173] This was because, if judicial review succeeded, the dismissal would be a nullity which would entitle the DCS to her remuneration in the interim not subject to the Employment Tribunal limits on compensation.

Lord Justice Bingham recorded his impression that the exhaustion doctrine 'is more often proclaimed than applied', and he questions whether 'in practice the reality quite matches the rhetoric'. He does not find the arguments for the principle altogether convincing, and he concludes that where unlawful, as opposed to unjustified, treatment is shown, the court should grant relief regardless of alternative remedies.[174]

Notwithstanding the views of Lord Bingham just cited, the judges remain reluctant to allow judicial review where there is an alternative remedy. But the focus has fallen upon whether the alternative remedy is an adequate alternative. Lord Phillips has said in the Supreme Court that the 'power of the High Court to conduct judicial review subsists alongside ... statutory provisions for appeal. It is not, however, the practice of the Court to use this power where a satisfactory alternative remedy has been provided by Parliament. Where this is not the case the power of judicial review is a valuable safeguard of the rule of law.'[175] The claimant who seeks judicial review where there is an alternative faces an uphill struggle. But the jurisdiction of the High Court to grant judicial review, even in the face of an alternative, is not in doubt and an unsatisfactory alternative remedy—or for that matter an 'equally convenient and effective'[176] remedy—may be easier to establish than the 'most exceptional circumstances' some cases require.[177]

DOES A STATUTORY REMEDY EXCLUDE ORDINARY REMEDIES?

Many statutory schemes contain their own system of remedies, e.g. by way of appeal to a tribunal or to a minister. There may then be a choice of alternative remedies either under the Act or according to the ordinary law. On the other hand it may be held that the statutory scheme impliedly excludes the ordinary remedies. If its language is clear enough it may exclude them expressly.[178]

As a general rule, the courts are reluctant to hold that ordinary remedies are impliedly excluded, particularly where the statutory remedy is in the hands of an administrative body. The House of Lords adopted this policy in granting a declaration that certain

---

had been no unfairness in the hearing, did not stand in the way of the judicial review. That decision could be exceptionally set aside by the court which made it in accordance with *Taylor* v. *Lawrence* [2003] QB 528 and *Seray-Wurie* v. *Hackney London Borough Council* [2002] EWCA Civ 909. Thus the court picked a path through this maze of error and technicality to secure fairness for the asylum seeker. Contrast *M and G* [2004] EWCA Civ 1731, and in *Y* [2005] EWHC 2845.

[172] *R (Shoesmith)* v. *OFSTED and ors* [2011] EWCA Civ 642. See above, p. 252 for the other issues in the case.   [173] *R* v. *Essex County Council ex p EB* [1997] ELR 327 at 329, per McCullough J.

[174] In a lecture printed in [1991] *PL* 64 (at 72).

[175] *Cart* v. *The Upper Tribunal* [2011] UKSC 28, para. 71.

[176] *R* v. *Essex County Council ex p EB* [1997] ELR 327 at 329, per McCullough J.

[177] *R (Willford)* v. *Financial Services Authority* [2013] EWCA Civ 677, para. 37.

[178] Below, p. 619.

quarrying operations did not need planning permission, even though the Act provided that application might be made to the local planning authority to determine whether planning permission was required in any case.[179] Here the plaintiff was merely seeking to establish that the planning legislation did not affect his ordinary legal liberties, which the ordinary courts protect. Lord Simonds said:[180]

> It is a principle not by any means to be whittled down that the subject's recourse to Her Majesty's courts for the determination of his rights is not to be excluded except by clear words. That is…a 'fundamental rule' from which I would not for my part sanction any departure. It must be asked, then, what is there in the Act of 1947 which bars such recourse. The answer is that there is nothing except the fact that the Act provides him with another remedy. Is it, then, an alternative or an exclusive remedy? There is nothing in the Act to suggest that, while a new remedy, perhaps cheap and expeditious, is given, the old and, as we like to call it, the inalienable remedy of Her Majesty's subjects to seek redress in her courts is taken away.

There are two differences between this situation and that discussed in the previous section on exhaustion of other remedies. In the first place, the previous section deals with remedies which exist for different purposes, either merits or legality, whereas here the remedies exist for the same purpose. In the second place, the exhaustion of other remedies may not preclude a later application for judicial review, if grounds for it can still be shown and any necessary extension of time obtained.[181] Here, on the other hand, the question is whether the statutory remedy is exclusive.

The court's interpretation may be determined by convenience. Prerogative relief will not be granted to a ratepayer wishing to challenge the correctness of a rating assessment, since the rating legislation provides a detailed procedure for that purpose which impliedly excludes other remedies.[182] But if the validity of the whole rating list is challenged, prerogative relief may be sought, since to challenge every one of the many thousands of assessments would be excessively inconvenient.[183] It is not, however, clear why this distinction should not rest simply on that between legality and correctness, irrespective of convenience, since the ordinary jurisdiction of the High Court to quash illegal acts will not be excluded by the existence of an administrative appeal on the merits, as the decisions in the previous section show.

On the other hand there are situations where the statutory remedy is the only remedy. For example, where a taxing statute gives a right of appeal to the Commissioners of Inland Revenue on a disputed assessment, the court will not grant a declaration that the taxpayer is entitled to certain allowances,[184] or that he is not the owner of the property assessed.[185]

---

[179] *Pyx Granite Estates Ltd* v. *Ministry of Housing and Local Government* [1960] AC 260. See also *Slough Estates* v. *Slough Borough Council* [1968] Ch 299 (appeal to minister and action for declaration pursued concurrently on question whether planning permission effective: conditions as to costs imposed by court); *Ealing LBC* v. *Race Relations Board* [1972] AC 342 (statutory procedure for legal proceedings by the board held no bar to action for declaration against the board).   [180] Ibid. at 286.

[181] *Ridge* v. *Baldwin* [1964] AC 40 was such a case. See above, p. 415.

[182] *Stepney Cpn* v. *John Walker & Sons Ltd* [1934] AC 365. See similarly *British Railways Board* v. *Glasgow Cpn*, 1975 SLT 45. Compare *R (Balbo B&C Auto Transport)* v. *Home Secretary* [2001] 1 WLR 1356 (judicial review refused).

[183] *R* v. *Paddington Valuation Officer ex p Peachey Property Co Ltd* [1966] 1 QB 380 at 399. See also the remarks as to convenience in *R* v. *Hillingdon London Borough Council ex p Royco Homes Ltd* [1974] QB 720 at 728, though that case belongs properly to the previous section: above, p. 601.

[184] *Argosam Finance Co Ltd* v. *Oxby* [1965] Ch 390. Compare *Harrison* v. *Croydon London Borough Council* [1968] Ch 479.

[185] *Re Vandervell* [1971] AC 912. Contrast *Thorne Rural District Council* v. *Bunting* [1972] Ch 470.

Similarly where a river authority is given a statutory right to recover certain expenses in a magistrates' court, it cannot obtain a declaration from the High Court that its claim is good;[186] and where Trinity House were empowered to grant pilotage certificates, with a provision for complaint to the Board of Trade if they failed to do so without reasonable cause, disappointed applicants could not complain to the court.[187] These are cases where the right given by the statute does not exist at common law, and can be enforced only in the way provided by the statute. 'The right and the remedy are given *uno flatu*, and the one cannot be dissociated from the other.'[188] The same logic is applied to the important class of cases where the Act prescribes a procedure for the making and consideration of objections to some proposed order and then provides that a person aggrieved may question its validity, after it has taken effect, within a short period of time but not otherwise.[189] This statutory procedure is exclusive, and rules out any challenge except as expressly permitted by the Act.[190]

A still clearer case is where the power of determination is expressly conferred by the Act on a named authority. The court could not entertain an action for a declaration that a claimant to superannuation benefits under the National Health Service Act 1946 was a 'mental health officer' since the Act and regulations validly made under it provided that 'any question arising under these regulations as to the rights or liabilities of an officer...shall be determined by the Minister'.[191] Strong judicial comments have been made on enactments of this kind where the minister might have an interest in the result;[192] and a narrow construction has sometimes been put upon them in order to preserve the court's control over the limits of any act which is ultra vires.[193] In any case of excess or abuse of power the court may intervene in the usual way.[194] Disciplinary decisions of the Financial Services Authority under the Financial Services and Markets Act 2000, which contains a detailed statutory scheme for challenging actions by the Authority (by way of appeal to the Financial Services and Markets Tribunal and thence to the Court of Appeal on a point of law), are only subject to judicial review 'in the most exceptional circumstances'.[195] Dissatisfied tenderers for government contracts will often be able under EU procurement law to apply to the High Court to set aside an award as well as an injunction and damages.[196] Judicial review of such decisions will then not be available unless the alternative statutory scheme is 'inadequate to assert complaints which the subject legitimately wishes to make'.[197]

---

[186] *Barraclough* v. *Brown* [1897] AC 615. See the *Pyx Granite* case (above) at 286 and 300. See also *Cook* v. *Ipswich Local Board of Health* (1871) LR 6 QB 451; *Wake* v. *Sheffield Corporation* (1883) 12 QBD 142; *Vestry of St James and St John, Clerkenwell* v. *Feary* (1890) 24 QBD 703; *Re Al-Fin Corporation's Patent* [1970] Ch 160; *Wilkes* v. *Gee* [1973] 1 WLR 742.

[187] *Jensen* v. *Trinity House* [1982] 2 Lloyd's R 14. But if the Board of Trade 'should misdirect itself in law or in fact', judicial review could be granted (Lord Denning MR).

[188] *Barraclough* v. *Brown* (above) at 622. See also *Turner* v. *Kingsbury Collieries Ltd* [1921] 3 KB 169.

[189] For this class see below, p. 619.

[190] *R* v. *Cornwall CC ex p Huntington* [1994] 1 All ER 694, rejecting challenges to rights of way modification orders not yet in effect.   [191] *Healey* v. *Minister of Health* [1955] 1 QB 221.

[192] *Wilkinson* v. *Barking Cpn* [1948] 1 KB 721 at 728; above, p. 396.

[193] *Martin* v. *Eccles Cpn* [1919] 1 Ch 387, and cases there cited.

[194] *Healey* v. *Minister of Health* (above) at 227. Ouster clauses in contracts are void as against public policy in so far as they attempt to exclude the courts from deciding questions of law, e.g. where the rules of an association give its council exclusive and final power to interpret its rules: see *Barker* v. *Jones* [1954] 1 WLR 1005; compare *Leigh* v. *National Union of Railwaymen* [1970] Ch 326.

[195] *R (Davies)* v. *Financial Services Authority* [2003] EWCA Civ 1128, [2004] 1 WLR 185 (CA) followed in *R (Willford)* v. *Financial Services Authority* [2013] EWCA Civ 677 (appeal to Upper Tribunal excluded judicial review of decision notice).   [196] Above, p. 676.

[197] *R (Cookson)* v. *MOD* [2005] EWCA Civ 811 (para. 20, Buxton LJ). See [2006] JR 26 (Zar).

Difficult cases may arise out of ministerial 'default powers', i.e. special powers under which ministers may take steps to compel local authorities to carry out their functions properly. Since these are special statutory remedies, they are discussed later. But it may be noted that the existence of the minister's default power is sometimes held to imply the exclusion of other remedies, and that this interpretation is open to criticism.[198]

PROTECTIVE AND PRECLUSIVE (OUSTER) CLAUSES

PRESUMPTION IN FAVOUR OF JUDICIAL REVIEW

Acts of Parliament frequently contain provisions aimed at restricting, and sometimes at eliminating, judicial review, and various forms of these provisions must now be investigated. But first it must be stressed that there is a presumption against any restriction of the supervisory powers of the court. Denning LJ said in one case:[199]

> I find it very well settled that the remedy by certiorari is never to be taken away by any statute except by the most clear and explicit words.

The Court of Appeal has re-emphasised this rule in interpreting the provision of the Mental Health Act 1983 which prohibits the bringing of civil proceedings for anything done without bad faith or negligence in executing the Act. It was held that this language was unsuitable to include judicial review, so that a mental patient could proceed with her application for certiorari and declaration contesting the legality of her admission to hospital.[200] Furthermore, as is mentioned below, restriction of judicial review may violate both human rights and EU law.[201]

But the courts draw a distinction between the ousting of judicial review (which they will in the interests of the rule of law resist, if necessary, by artificial interpretations of statute) and the allocation of the power of review from one judicial body to another (which is found to be constitutionally acceptable). Thus the House of Lords has said that this 'strict approach... [to ouster clauses] is not appropriate if an effective means of challenging the validity of a maintenance assessment is provided elsewhere'.[202] And the Supreme Court has said[203] that section 65 of the Regulation of Investigatory Powers Act 2000 'has not ousted judicial scrutiny of the acts of the intelligence services; it has simply allocated that scrutiny... to the IPT';[204] hence the jurisdiction of the Administrative Court was excluded in the relevant matter.[205]

---

[198] See below, p. 631.   [199] R v. Medical Appeal Tribunal ex p Gilmore [1957] 1 QB 574 at 583.

[200] Ex p. Waldron [1986] QB 824. This accords with the definition of 'civil proceedings' in the Crown Proceedings Act 1947: see above, p. 481. Contrast Hutchins v. Broadcasting Corporation [1981] 2 NZLR 593 (protection against 'civil proceedings' restricts judicial review).   [201] Below, p. 618.

[202] Farley v. Child Support Agency and anor [2006] UKHL 31, para. 18. Thus the Child Support Act 1991, s. 33(4) provided that a magistrates' court asked by the Secretary of State to make a liability order against an absent parent 'shall not question the maintenance assessment under which the payments of child support maintenance fell to be made'. This provision was not interpreted with the 'strictness appropriate to a provision which purports to exclude the jurisdiction of the court' because there were other routes to challenge the Secretary of State's decision (ibid.).

[203] R (A) v. B [2009] UKSC 12, para. 23. See also R (Ignaoua) v. Home Secretary [2013] EWHC 2512 (full discussion; certificate from Home Secretary under powers under the Justice and Security Act 2013 terminating claimant's application for judicial review upheld; claimant could make the same application to SIAC).

[204] Investigatory Powers Tribunal.

[205] Whether an intelligence officer could publish a book about his work in the Security Service; Art. 10 rights asserted.

'FINAL AND CONCLUSIVE' AND SIMILAR CLAUSES

Many statutes provide that some decision shall be final. That provision is a bar to any appeal.[206] But the courts refuse to allow it to hamper the operation of judicial review. As will be seen in this and the following sections, there is a firm judicial policy against allowing the rule of law to be undermined by weakening the powers of the court. Statutory restrictions on judicial remedies are given the narrowest possible construction, sometimes even against the plain meaning of the words.[207] This is a sound policy, since otherwise administrative authorities and tribunals would be given uncontrollable power and could violate the law at will. 'Finality is a good thing but justice is a better.'[208]

If a statute says that the decision or order[209] of some administrative body or tribunal[210] 'shall be final' or 'shall be final and conclusive[211] to all intents and purposes' this is held to mean merely that there is no appeal: judicial review of legality is unimpaired. 'Parliament only gives the impress of finality to the decisions of the tribunal on condition that they are reached in accordance with the law'.[212] This has been the consistent doctrine for three hundred years.[213] It safeguards the whole area of judicial review, including (formerly) error on the face of the record as well as ultra vires. In the leading case the Court of Appeal granted certiorari to quash the decision of a medical appeal tribunal which had, by misconstruction of the complex 'paired organ' regulations, miscalculated the rate of disablement benefit payable to a colliery pick sharpener whose one good eye had been injured.[214] The Act provided that the tribunal's decision 'shall be final', but the court would not allow this to impede its normal powers in respect of error of law.[215]

The normal effect of a finality clause is therefore to prevent any appeal. There is no right of appeal in any case unless it is given by statute.

A provision for finality may be important in other contexts, for example when the question is whether the finding of one tribunal may be reopened before another,[216] or whether an interlocutory order is open to appeal,[217] or whether an action in tort will lie.[218] And when a statute provided that there should be 'no appeal' from the decision of a county court judge to refuse permission to appeal, judicial review of that decision was not precluded.[219]

---

[206] It precludes the Court of Appeal's jurisdiction 'however expressed': Senior Courts Act 1981, s. 18(1)(c).

[207] See (1956) 3 *U of Queensland LJ* 103 (D. C. M. Yardley).

[208] *Ras Behari Lal* v. *King-Emperor* (1933) 60 IA 354 at 361 (Lord Atkin).

[209] As in *Pollway Nominees Ltd* v. *Croydon LBC* [1987] AC 79 (repairs notice under Housing Act 1969 served on wrong party: held a nullity despite provision making it 'final and conclusive').

[210] Inferior courts of law may be protected by a finality clause in respect of error of law: above, p. 223.

[211] The words 'and conclusive' add nothing: *Hockey* v. *Yelland* (below).

[212] *Gilmore* (below) at 585 (Denning LJ).

[213] *R* v. *Smith* (1670) 1 Mod 44; *R* v. *Plowright* (1686) 3 Mod 94. See *R* v. *Nat Bell Liquors Ltd* [1922] 2 AC 128 at 159–60; *Gilmore* (below) at 584.

[214] *R* v. *Medical Appeal Tribunal ex p Gilmore* [1957] 1 QB 574. See also *R* v. *Berkley and Bragge* (1754) 1 Keny 80 at 100; *Tehrani* v. *Rostron* [1972] 1 QB 182; *Hockey* v. *Yelland* (1984) 56 ALR 215.

[215] This was a case of error of law on the face of the record but the same applies with errors that take the decision-maker beyond his powers: *Pyx Granite Co Ltd* v. *Ministry of Housing and Local Government* [1960] AC 261; *Ridge* v. *Baldwin* [1964] AC 40.

[216] As in *R* v. *National Insurance Commissioners ex p Hudson* [1972] AC 944 (decisions of national insurance local tribunals held final as against medical boards and tribunals later assessing disablement. A special House of Lords of 7 was divided by 4 to 3. The majority decision was reversed by the National Insurance Act 1972, s. 5).

[217] *R* v. *Lands Tribunal ex p London Cpn* [1981] 1 WLR 985 (order for disclosure of documents held appealable).   [218] *James* v. *Department of Employment* [1989] QB 1 (action for negligence barred).

[219] *R (Sivasubramaniam)* v. *Wandsworth County Court* [2002] EWCA Civ 1738, [2003] 1 WLR 475 (implied exclusion of judicial review rejected (in reliance on *Gilmore*) (paras. 44–5). But, even so, permission

There are many other varieties of protective or preclusive clauses, for example where it is provided that a person detained for deportation 'shall be deemed to be in legal custody';[220] or that hospital managers may detain a mental patient where the application for admission 'appears to be duly made'; or that the application 'shall be sufficient authority' for the managers.[221] The courts must be careful to confine such provisions strictly to their limited meaning, and the Court of Appeal sharply criticised one interpretation which might have validated an unlawful detention.[222]

The effectiveness of all forms of preclusive clause is now in question under human rights and EU law, as explained later.[223]

A provision that a determination 'shall be conclusive for all purposes' or that a certificate 'shall be conclusive evidence' of something might be expected to be interpreted in the same way as a finality clause, so as not to restrict judicial review. But this is not always the case, as will be seen below in the context of the Tribunals and Inquiries Act 1992.[224]

'NO CERTIORARI' CLAUSES

An even bolder, though equally justifiable, judicial policy was that certiorari would be granted to quash an act or decision which was ultra vires even in the face of a statute saying expressly that no certiorari should issue in such a case. When in the seventeenth century the court began to use certiorari in the modern way, it was excessively prone to quash the decisions of justices for trivial defects of form. Parliament retaliated by providing in many statutes that no certiorari should issue to remove or quash decisions made under the Act. The court said of such a clause:[225]

> The doctrine of defects and variances in the examinations and grounds of removal before the trial of appeals had been mischievous; and the statute in question was a most beneficial alteration of the law, designed to check a practice which had introduced lamentable and disgraceful technicalities.

But, while giving full effect to these clauses for their proper purposes, the court refused to allow them to interfere with the court's control over excess of jurisdiction; for otherwise (once again) subordinate tribunals would have become a law unto themselves. The court limited the clause to excluding the jurisdiction to quash for error of law on the face of the record. In any case of ultra vires, therefore, the court continued to grant certiorari regardless of the 'no certiorari' clause. In an early case the Commissioners of Sewers claimed the benefit of a statute of 1571, providing that they should not be compellable to make any return of their actions, and disobeyed writs of certiorari from the King's Bench; but since they had rated lands outside their jurisdiction, they were fined and imprisoned for contempt, Kelynge CJ saying that the court would take care not to allow uncontrollable

---

will only be granted exceptionally, e.g. jurisdictional error ('in the narrow pre-*Anisminic* sense' (see above, pp. 209–10)) or a denial of a fair hearing (para. 54). See [2005] *JR* 244 (Kellar). See *Gregory* v. *Turner* [2003] EWCA Civ 183 ('fundamental departure from rules of natural justice' required for judicial review) and *Sinclair Gardens Investments (Kensington) Ltd* v. *The Lands Tribunal* [2005] EWCA Civ 1305.

[220] Immigration Act 1971, 2nd Sched., para. 18, wrongly held in *R* v. *Home Secretary ex p Cheblak* [1991] 1 WLR 890 to restrict the right to habeas corpus, but correctly interpreted in *R* v. *Home Secretary ex p Muboyayi* [1992] 1 QB 244.   [221] Mental Health Act 1983, s. 6.

[222] *Re S-C (mental patient)* [1996] QB 599, disapproving *R* v. *Managers of South Western Hospital ex p M* [1993] QB 683.   [223] Below, p. 618.

[224] See below, p. 617, and *Piper* v. *St Marylebone Justices* [1928] 2 KB 221.

[225] *R* v. *Ruyton (inhabitants)* (1861) 1 B & S 534 at 545.

jurisdictions.[226] In 1759 Lord Kenyon CJ disregarded an express no certiorari clause in an Act of 1690 where justices made an order outside their jurisdiction,[227] and a long succession of similar cases followed.[228] Denning LJ said of them:[229]

> In stopping this abuse the statutes proved very beneficial, but the court never allowed those statutes to be used as a cover for wrongdoing by tribunals. If tribunals were to be at liberty to exceed their jurisdiction without any check by the courts, the rule of law would be at an end.

This epitomises the court's determination to preserve regularity in the legal system, and to construe every Act of Parliament as intended to uphold it. 'The consequence of holding otherwise', it was said in one case, 'would be that a Metropolitan magistrate could make any order he pleased without question'.[230]

The only form of error that these clauses would protect, therefore, was mere error within jurisdiction on the face of the record. It was indeed primarily at that branch of judicial control, and the abuse of it, that the clauses were aimed.

'No certiorari' clauses were extremely common until about a century ago.[231] They are of relatively rare occurrence today since Parliament uses other devices, to be explained shortly. But occasional examples are to be found in modern statutes, such as the County Courts Act 1959.[232] By enacting them repeatedly in similar form Parliament made it clear that it was content with the construction put upon them by the courts.

All such clauses enacted before August 1958 are now subject to the provision, explained below, which restores the full powers of the court to grant quashing and mandatory orders.[233]

'AS IF ENACTED' CLAUSES

Another form of protective clause is to the effect that a statutory order shall 'have effect as if enacted in this Act' and that confirmation by the minister shall be 'conclusive evidence that the requirements of this Act have been complied with, and that the order has been duly made and is within the powers of this Act'.[234] Even this formula should not protect a flagrant case of ultra vires,[235] despite a judicial ruling that it makes an order unchallengeable.[236] The House of Lords has held that the 'as if enacted in this Act' formula applies only to orders which themselves conform to the Act, since it is only such orders that the Act

---

[226] *Smith's* case (1670) 1 Vent 66; compare 1 Mod 44; *R v. Plowright* (1686) 3 Mod 94.

[227] *R v. Derbyshire Justices* (1759) 2 Ld Kenyon 299.

[228] e.g. *R v. West Riding of Yorkshire Justices* (1794) 5 TR 629; *R v. Cheltenham Commissioners* (1841) 1 QB 467 (breach of natural justice); *R v. Gillyard* (1848) 12 QB 527; *Colonial Bank of Australasia* v. *Willan* (1874) LR 5 PC 417; *Ex p. Bradlaugh* (1878) 3 QBD 509; *R v. Hurst ex p Smith* [1960] 2 QB 133; compare *R v. Worthington-Evans ex p Madan* [1959] 2 QB 145.

[229] *R v. Medical Appeal Tribunal ex p Gilmore* [1957] 1 QB 574 at 586. See also *R v. Northumberland Compensation Appeal Tribunal ex p Shaw* [1951] 1 KB 711 at 716 (Lord Goddard CJ), affirmed [1952] 1 KB 338.

[230] *Ex p. Bradlaugh* (above). But mere error on the face of the record could not be controlled: *R v. Chantrell* (1875) LR 10 QB 587 (certiorari refused to bring up a case stated).

[231] See under Certiorari in index to Ruffhead's *Statutes at Large*, ix. 232. A typical example is Highway Act 1835, s. 107.   [232] s. 107. On this see *R v. Hurst; R v. Worthington-Evans* (above).

[233] Tribunals and Inquiries Act 1992, s. 12; below, p. 617.

[234] e.g. Smallholdings and Allotments Act 1908, s. 39(3); Housing Act 1925, 3rd Sched., para. (2).

[235] See Report of the Committee on Ministers' Powers, Cmd 4060 (1932), 40.

[236] Certiorari to quash a compulsory purchase order protected by this formula was refused in *Ex p. Ringer* [1909] 73 JP 436; and see *Reddaway* v. *Lancashire County Council* (1925) 41 TLR 422.

contemplates.[237] Thus the court could still control procedural or other legal errors, and the exclusion clause would be virtually meaningless. This type of clause came into use in the nineteenth century. But it is now in disuse, since Parliament has resorted to a different formula which, instead of attempting to give statutory validity to defective acts, protects them by removing judicial remedies. To this we must turn next.

More about 'as if enacted' clauses will be found in the chapter on delegated legislation.[238]

'SHALL NOT BE QUESTIONED' CLAUSES

Modern legislation has adapted itself to the wide variety of remedies available in administrative law, and has evolved a comprehensive provision that the order or determination[239] to be protected 'shall not be questioned in any legal proceedings whatsoever'. Most commonly of all it is framed so as to take effect only after a time limit, before which remedies may be sought. But that type of provision raises different problems and needs separate discussion. Wide enactments designed to oust the jurisdiction of the courts entirely in respect of all remedies have come to be known as 'ouster clauses'. However they are worded, they are interpreted according to the same principle.

The law as now settled by the House of Lords is that these ouster clauses are subject to exactly the same doctrine as the older no certiorari clauses, namely, that they do not prevent the court from intervening in the case of excess of jurisdiction. Violation of the principles of natural justice, for example, amounts to excess of jurisdiction, so that where a minister refused an application for citizenship without giving the applicant a fair hearing the Privy Council invalidated his decision notwithstanding a statute providing that it 'shall not be subject to appeal or review in any court'.[240]

Wide as the doctrine of ultra vires is, the House of Lords made it even wider for the purpose of minimising the effect of ouster clauses. This they did in the leading case of *Anisminic Ltd.* v. *Foreign Compensation Commission*.[241] That case was a high-water mark of judicial review. But for judges in later cases it presented an acute dilemma.

The crucial words were the provision of the Foreign Compensation Act 1950 that a determination of the Commission 'shall not be called in question in any court of law'.[242] Yet a determination of the Commission was questioned for five years before successive courts, and, as a fitting climax, the House of Lords granted a declaration that it was ultra vires and a nullity. The House held:

    (a) (unanimously) that the ouster clause did not protect a determination which was outside jurisdiction; and

---

[237] *Minister of Health* v. *R ex p Yaffé* [1931] AC 494.   [238] Below, p. 751.

[239] Sometimes even anything 'which purports to be' an order to determination: below, p. 616.

[240] *A-G* v. *Ryan* [1980] AC 718. Whether the same reasoning applies to an ouster clause in a Commonwealth country's constitution was left an open question in *Harrikissoon* v. *A-G of Trinidad and Tobago* [1980] AC 265. See also *McDaid* v. *Clydebank DC*, 1984 SLT 162 (planning enforcement notice not served and so a nullity; time for appeal expired: ouster clause held no bar to judicial review); *Renfrew DC* v. *McGourlick*, 1987 SLT 538 (housing order ultra vires; ouster clause no bar).

[241] [1969] 2 AC 147, restoring a notable judgment of Browne J, for which see [1969] 2 AC at 223, [1969] *CLJ* 230. The case is discussed in (1969) 85 *LQR* 198 (Wade). For a Scottish parallel see *Campbell* v. *Brown* (1829) 3 W & S 441 (cited in *West* v. *Secretary of State for Scotland*, 1992 SLT 636) in which the Court of Session asserted its jus supereminens in the face of an express ouster clause. For an American parallel see *Lindahl* v. *Office of Personnel Management*, 105 S Ct 1620 (1985), explained in context with *Anisminic* in 38 *Administrative Law Review* 33 (B. Schwartz).   [242] s. 4(4).

(b) (by a majority)[243] that misconstruction of the Order in Council which the Commission had to apply involved an excess of jurisdiction, since they based their decision 'on a ground which they had no right to take into account',[244] and sought 'to impose another condition, not warranted by the order'.[245]

Question (b) has been considered elsewhere already, in the context of ultra vires action.[246] But it is significant here also, since it shows clearly the great determination of the courts to uphold their long-standing policy of resisting attempts by Parliament to disarm them by enacting provisions which, if interpreted literally, would confer uncontrollable power upon subordinate authorities.

DECISIONS THAT 'MAY BE QUESTIONED IN LEGAL PROCEEDINGS ONLY BY MEANS OF AN APPEAL'

The Extradition Act 2003 provides the decision of the judge in extradition proceedings might 'be questioned in legal proceedings only by means of an appeal'.[247] In the particular circumstances there was no right of appeal; but unsurprisingly the court held that habeas corpus was not precluded.[248] The release of a detainee who had not been brought before the court 'as soon as practicable' as required by the Act[249] was ordered.

ANISMINIC AND AFTER

The Foreign Compensation Commission, which has to adjudicate claims for compensation against funds paid by foreign governments to the British government for the expropriation of British property abroad, had rejected a claim for some £4m. in respect of a manganese mine in the Sinai peninsula after the Suez hostilities of 1956. The reason was that the claimants had sold their undertaking to the United Arab Republic before the date of the treaty of 1959 under which the compensation fund was established, and that they did not therefore comply with a provision of the Order in Council, duly made under the Act, requiring that claimants and their successors in title should be British nationals at that date. But it was held that the Commission were misled by 'unfortunate telescopic drafting',[250] and that the requirement about the nationality of successors in title did not apply where the original owner was the claimant. This meant that the Commission had entered into matters which it had no jurisdiction to consider and had imposed a condition which it had no jurisdiction to impose. Consequently it had exceeded its jurisdiction, and the ouster clause was no impediment to intervention by the court.

Under this decision the only effect of a 'shall not be questioned' clause was to prevent judicial review for such errors as could be said to be within jurisdiction.[251] This was the same doctrine as had for so long been applied to no certiorari clauses, so that the House of Lords' decision on question (a) represented no change of judicial policy. The remarkable

---

[243] Lords Reid, Pearce and Wilberforce, Lords Morris and Pearson dissenting.
[244] [1969] 2 AC at 175 (Lord Reid).   [245] [1969] 2 AC at 214 (Lord Wilberforce).
[246] Above, p. 219.   [247] s. 34.
[248] *Nikonovs* v. *HM Prison Brixton* [2005] EWHC 2405 (Admin) (para. 18) (It 'would in my judgment require the strongest words in a provision such as section 34 to remove the ancient remedy of habeas corpus' (Scott Baker LJ)). Neither was judicial review excluded (para. 15).
[249] s. 4(3) and note s. 4(5) ('If subsection (3) is not complied with…the judge must order his discharge').
[250] [1969] 2 AC at 214 (Lord Wilberforce).
[251] As in *A-G* v. *Car Haulaways (NZ) Ltd* [1974] 2 NZLR 331.

feature of the case was the decision of the majority on question (b), which made a juris-dictional error out of what would more naturally, at that time, have been treated as a mere error of law (misconstruction) within jurisdiction.

The House of Lords had in fact extended their concept of jurisdictional error to such an extreme point that judges were driven to conclude that the basic distinction between jurisdictional and non-jurisdictional error, upon which the *Anisminic* judgment pur-ported to be founded, had been rendered unintelligible. All error of law now appeared to be jurisdictional error, so that the decision of any administrative tribunal or authority could be quashed for such error, regardless of its nature.[252]

According to the logic of the House of Lords, 'shall not be questioned' clauses must now be totally ineffective. Every error of law is jurisdictional; and error of fact, if material, is either jurisdictional or unreviewable anyway.[253] So there is no situation in which these clauses can have any effect. The policy of the courts thus becomes in effect one of diso-bedience to Parliament. Under the basic distinction which formerly obtained, and which the House of Lords supposed that they were upholding in the *Anisminic* case, judges could at least say that they were obeying Parliament in some situations, while resisting ouster clauses in others. But now they seem to have lost sight of the reasons which justified their attitude originally. Ouster clauses are still being enacted,[254] and the conflict with Parliament is as yet unresolved.

WIDER CONSIDERATIONS

The *Anisminic* case and its sequels were the culmination of the judicial insistence, so often emphasised in this work, that administrative agencies and tribunals must at all costs be prevented from being sole judges of the validity of their own acts. If this were allowed, to quote Denning LJ again, 'the rule of law would be at an end'.[255] Lord Wilberforce expressed the same idea in different words:[256]

> What would be the purpose of defining by statute the limit of a tribunal's powers if, by means of a clause inserted in the instrument of definition, those limits could safely be passed?

This is the identical point that was made so clearly by Farwell LJ in the *Shoreditch* case, quoted earlier, when he said that subjection to the jurisdictional control of the High Court was 'a necessary and inseparable incident to all tribunals of limited jurisdiction'.[257] That passage was quoted with approval in the *Anisminic* case as correctly expressing the fun-damental principle which maintains a coherent and orderly legal system.

In order to preserve this vital policy the courts have been forced, in effect, to rebel against Parliament. The object of the ouster clause in question in the *Anisminic* case was to keep the distribution of compensation outside the courts altogether,[258] since proved claims will normally exceed the available compensation and they must all be finally settled before the claimants can be paid their dividend. In the *Pearlman* case the object of the legislation was

---

[252] Above, p. 220.

[253] Above, p. 230.   [254] See below, p. 615.   [255] Above, p. 611.

[256] [1969] 2 AC at 208.

[257] *R* v. *Shoreditch Assessment Committee ex p Morgan* [1910] 2 KB 859 at 880; above, p. 219. This was cited by Browne J (see [1969] 2 AC at 233) with reference to (1966) 82 *LQR* 226 and was approved in the House of Lords by Lords Pearce and Wilberforce in the *Anisminic* case at 197, 209.

[258] Witness the specific exemption of the Commission from s. 11 of the Tribunals and Inquiries Act 1958: below, p. 617.

to make the county court's decision final, so as to save further litigation between landlord and tenant. The intention of Parliament was clear in both cases. In refusing to enforce it the court was applying a presumption which may override even their constitutional obedience, namely that jurisdictional limits must be legally effective. This is tantamount to saying that judicial review is a constitutional fundamental which even the sovereign Parliament cannot abolish and that any attempt to abolish it is an abuse of legislative power.[259] There is no incongruity, therefore, in the extra-judicial suggestions of Lord Woolf MR, that judicial obedience to Parliament should stop short of legislation 'removing or substantially impairing the entire reviewing role of the High Court on judicial review', since 'there are even limits on the supremacy of Parliament which it is the courts' inalienable responsibility to identify and uphold'.[260] But it would be wise for Parliament and the courts not to test these propositions to breaking point,

Parliament is mostly concerned with short-term considerations and is strangely indifferent to the paradox of enacting law and then preventing the courts from enforcing it. The judges, with their eye on the long term and the rule of law, have made it their business to preserve a deeper constitutional logic, based on their repugnance to allowing any subordinate authority to obtain uncontrollable power.[261] Needless to say, they have maintained throughout that they are correctly interpreting Parliament's true intentions. In the *Anisminic* case they did so behind a dense screen of technicalities about jurisdiction and nullity; and Lord Wilberforce bravely said:[262]

> In each task they are carrying out the intention of the legislature, and it would be misdescription to state it in terms of a struggle between the courts and the executive.

That this is fair comment, at least at the most sophisticated level of legal thought, is shown by the fact that the policy of the judges has been wisely tolerated by Parliament. The restricted meaning given to no certiorari clauses was never made the object of a legislative counter-attack. After the *Anisminic* decision the government did indeed propose a more elaborate ouster clause to empower the Foreign Compensation Commission to interpret the Orders in Council for itself and making its interpretations unquestionable. But after criticism both in and out of Parliament[263] this proposal was dropped, and instead provision was made for a right of appeal direct to the Court of Appeal, but no further, on any question as to the jurisdiction of the Commission or the interpretation of the Orders in Council; and all restriction of remedies was removed as regards breaches of natural justice.[264] So far, therefore, from joining issue with the courts over their recalcitrance, Parliament to a large extent restored the judicial remedies which the ouster clause had vainly attempted to take away.

Parliament has not, however, abandoned its attempts to devise a really judge-proof formula.[265] In the Act just discussed it is provided that, apart from the remedies

---

[259] See Wade, *Constitutional Fundamentals*, 66. But see Lord Irvine LC's critical comment in [1999] *EHRLR* 350 at 362, citing *R v. Lord Chancellor ex p Witham* [1998] QB 575 as showing that there must be some formula strong enough to prevail.

[260] See [1995] *PL* 57 at 68 (a published lecture). For criticism of Lord Irvine QC see above, p. 31.

[261] This passage approved in *Oakley v. Animal Ltd* [2005] EWHC 210, para. 84 (Prescott QC sitting as a Deputy High Court judge).   [262] [1969] 2 AC at 208.

[263] 776 HC Deb. col. 568; 299 HL Deb. col. 640; letters in *The Times*, 1 and 4 February 1969.

[264] Foreign Compensation Act 1969, s. 3(2), (10). Since breach of natural justice goes to jurisdiction (above, p. 419), questions of natural justice can apparently be taken either to the Court of Appeal direct or else raised in ordinary proceedings with unrestricted rights of appeal. In view of the specific provision, it might be held that only the latter course was open.

[265] In 2004 there was a determined attempt by the government to find a judge-proof formula that would place the decisions of the Asylum and Immigration Tribunal (see above, p. 63) above the law and to deny asylum seekers and immigrants any significant access to the courts. But although this proposal was passed

specified, 'anything which purports to be a determination' of the Commission shall not be called in question in any court of law.[266] The Interception of Communications Act 1985 tries a slightly different line of attack: 'The decisions of the Tribunal (including any decisions as to their jurisdiction) shall not be subject to appeal or liable to be questioned in any courts'.[267] The latter formula appears also in the Security Service Act 1989,[268] in the Police Act 1997[269]and in the Regulation of Investigatory Powers Act 2000.[270] Nevertheless it is taken for granted in the courts that an ouster clause will not prevent judicial review on jurisdictional grounds.[271] When the Home Secretary's refusal of an application for naturalisation was challenged, he conceded that judicial review was not ousted by the provision in the Act[272] that his decision 'shall not be subject to appeal to, or review in, any court' and the Court of Appeal confirmed the concession, holding also that a provision that he should not be required to give reasons for grant or refusal did not exempt him from observing fair procedure and allowing the applicant to know the substance of the case against him, and being given an opportunity to contest it.[273]

Ouster clauses which take effect only after a period of time, such as six weeks, are a different matter altogether, as explained below.[274]

by the House of Commons the weight of criticism led to it being withdrawn in the House of Lords. The proposal, contained in the Asylum and Immigration (Treatment of Claimants, etc.) Bill 2004, excluded all the 'supervisory' jurisdiction of the High Court and challenges to any 'decision on jurisdiction'. The ouster clause went on to exclude challenges 'to determine whether a purported determination, decision or action of the Tribunal was a nullity' on any ground including 'lack of jurisdiction, irregularity, error of law, breach of natural justice or any other matter'. The only significant ground of challenge not excluded was 'dishonesty, corruption or bias'. The criticism will be found collected in 'The Ouster Debate' in [2004] JR 95ff., but note also the tellingly critical Reports of the Joint Committee on Human Rights on the Bill (HL 35/HC 304, 10 February 2004) and the House of Commons Constitutional Affairs Committee in its Second Report (HC 211-I, 2 March 2004 and the weighty criticism from the Lord Chief Justice, Lord Woolf, giving the Squire Centenary Lecture in Cambridge (see (2004) 63 CLJ 317). The 'forcible' but private representations made by Lord Irvine of Lairg (see the Lord Chancellor's statement in the Lords (Hansard, 15 March 2004, col. 51) also played their part. Access to the courts to force a review of a decision of the AIT remains limited and subject to very short time limits (above, p. 63) but the courts are not wholly excluded and they exhibit ingenuity to ensure fairness in decision-making. See R (AM (Cameroon) v. Asylum and Immigration Tribunal and the Home Secretary [2008] EWCA Civ 100 discussed above, p. 604, n. 171. For as long as Parliament remains supreme the possibility will exist that legislation will be enacted using words clear enough to deny all access to the courts, contrary to the rule of law. But as this incident shows strong forces support the fundamental right of access to the courts and in this case those forces prevailed. For other accounts of this incident see the sources referred to above.   [266] Foreign Compensation Act 1969, s. 3(3), (9).

[267] s. 7(8).

[268] s. 5(4).   [269] s. 91(10). See n. 259, above, for Lord Irvine's comment.

[270] s. 67(8). See A v. B [2008] EWHC 1512 (exclusive jurisdiction of investigatory powers of tribunal rejected).

[271] Similarly in the High Court of Australia: Darling Casino Ltd v. New South Wales Casino Control Authority (1997) 143 ALR 55.

[272] British Nationality Act 1981, s. 44(2). The same clause did not prevent the quashing of a similar refusal flawed by restrictive interpretation of the statutory requirements: R v. Home Secretary ex p Mehta [1992] COD 484.

[273] R v. Home Secretary ex p Fayed [1998] 1 WLR 763 (Home Secretary's decisions quashed 'so that they can be retaken in a manner which is fair').

[274] Below, p. 619.

STATUTORY REFORM

Just as the judges have opposed ouster clauses which attempt to restrict judicial control, so lawyers generally are hostile to them as opening the door to dictatorial power. The Committee on Ministers' Powers recommended in 1932 that they 'should be abandoned in all but the most exceptional cases',[275] and in 1957 the Franks Committee recommended that no statute should contain words purporting to oust the prerogative remedies.[276] The Tribunals and Inquiries Act 1992, replacing the Acts of 1958 and 1971, has done something towards fulfilling the latter recommendation. Section 12 provides that:

> any provision in an Act passed before 1st August 1958 that any order or determination shall not be called into question in any court, or any provision in such an Act which by similar words excludes any of the powers of the High Court, shall not have effect so as to prevent the removal of the proceedings into the High Court by order of certiorari or to prejudice the powers of the High Court to make orders of mandamus.

In the Act of 1958 the Foreign Compensation Commission was specifically excepted;[277] and there is an important exception still in force, for time-limited ouster clauses, as explained in the next section. Further exceptions were any order or determination of a court of law; and discretionary decisions on questions of nationality.[278]

The remedy of a quashing order has therefore been restored, along with the mandatory order, in cases governed by pre-1958 ouster clauses which fall within the section. It seems also that a post-1958 clause which substantially re-enacts a pre-1958 clause will be treated as pre-1958 for this purpose. For the Court of Appeal has held that the provision that any determination of a supplementary benefit appeal tribunal 'shall be conclusive for all purposes' does not exclude review by quashing order, although contained in the Supplementary Benefit Act 1966[279] which replaced the National Assistance Act 1948,[280] and this was held to be due to the above-cited section of the Tribunals and Inquiries Act.[281] Another possibility might be that 'shall be conclusive' clauses are to be construed in the same way as 'final and conclusive' clauses, discussed above. But, without referring to its above-cited decision, the Court of Appeal later held that a pre-1958 provision making a registrar's certificate 'conclusive evidence' of compliance with statutory registration requirements is unaffected by the Tribunals and Inquiries Act.[282] There is thus a conflict of authorities as to what are 'similar words' for the purposes of the Act.

This last decision also holds that a 'conclusive evidence' clause is equally unaffected by the *Anisminic* principle, i.e. that it effectively precludes judicial review.[283] This produces the paradox that the strongest form of ouster clause may fail to protect some ultra vires decision or act whereas the weaker one may succeed in doing so.

---

[275] Cmd 4060 (1932), 65.   [276] Cmnd 218 (1957), para. 117.

[277] s. 11(3), now repealed in view of the Foreign Compensation Act 1969 (above).

[278] For the exceptions see Tribunals and Inquiries Act 1992, s. 12(3).

[279] ss. 18(3), 26(2). This is the same as the Ministry of Social Security Act 1966: see Social Security Act 1973, s. 99(18).   [280] s. 14(4).

[281] *R* v. *Preston Supplementary Benefits Appeal Tribunal ex p Moore* [1975] 1 WLR 624 at 628.

[282] *R* v. *Registrar of Companies ex p Central Bank of India* [1986] QB 1114 at 1182. The *Preston* case was cited in argument but not in the judgments.

[283] See particularly at 1175–6 (Slade LJ), stressing that the *Anisminic* principle rests on a presumption which is rebuttable. The European Court of Justice holds that a clause of this kind is unlawful in a case where, as in sex discrimination cases, European Community law requires an effective judicial remedy: *Johnston* v. *Chief Constable of the Royal Ulster Constabulary* [1987] QB 129 (ECJ).

For no apparent reason the Tribunals and Inquiries Act assumed that quashing and mandatory orders were the only relevant remedies in England, ignoring declaratory judgments and injunctions, though it may now be possible to obtain those remedies under the Senior Courts Act 1981, since that Act has made them interchangeable with quashing and mandatory orders.[284]

PARTIAL OUSTER CLAUSES

Instead of providing that an act or order may not be questioned at all, statute may provide that it shall not be questioned on certain specified grounds. Thus under the Town and Country Planning Act 1990 the validity of an enforcement notice may not be questioned in any proceedings whatsoever, except by way of appeal under the Act on certain grounds, including (for example) that there has been no breach of planning control.[285] Since the statutory appeal procedure is in any case more convenient, and provides for an appeal to the court on a point of law, the court will enforce the statute according to its terms.[286]

Such an enactment is scarcely to be distinguished from a provision that all questions of a certain kind shall be determined in the manner provided by the Act and not otherwise. Such provisions are enforced without judicial resistance,[287] as already noticed,[288] since they do not purport to protect any excess or abuse of power.

OUSTER CLAUSES AND HUMAN RIGHTS

The European Convention on Human Rights, now incorporated as law by the Human Rights Act 1998, provides by Article 6 that everyone is entitled to a fair and public hearing by an independent and impartial tribunal when their civil rights and obligations are determined. Ouster clauses, whether total or partial, may come into conflict with this right to a judicial determination, since they have the effect of cutting off judicial remedies, at least in so far as the courts allow them to operate.

In a case from Northern Ireland, where contractors complained that their tender for work on a power station had been unlawfully rejected because they were Roman Catholics, the Secretary of State had issued a statutory certificate that the rejection was on grounds of national security or public safety. Under the Act this certificate was made 'conclusive evidence' of the purpose stated in it, and the complaint therefore failed in the High Court. But the European Court of Human Rights held that Article 6 was violated, since the right not to suffer religious discrimination and to have it enforced judicially was disproportionately restricted by the *ipse dixit* of the minister.[289] It ought to have been possible to provide a fairer procedure, while yet safeguarding national security.

A legal immunity, on the other hand, may likewise cut off judicial remedies without engaging Article 6. Whether immunity exists is a matter of substantive domestic law and means that there is no civil right to which Article 6 can apply. That is the position with

---

[284] In *Ridge v. Baldwin* [1964] AC 40 at 120–1 Lord Morris expressed the opinion that the Act protected the declaratory judgment in the same way as certiorari. In *O'Reilly v. Mackman* [1983] 2 AC 237 at 278 Lord Diplock said that the Act of 1971 suggested a parliamentary preference for certiorari. There is no such discrimination in Scotland: Act of 1992, s. 12(2).

[285] s. 285, replacing earlier provisions to the same effect.

[286] *Square Meals Frozen Foods Ltd v. Dunstable Corporation* [1974] 1 WLR 59.

[287] e.g. *Healey v. Minister of Health* [1955] 1 QB 221.   [288] Above, p. 607.

[289] *Tinnelly & Sons Ltd v. UK* (1999) 27 EHRR 249. For a parallel in EU law see *Johnston v. Chief Constable of the Royal Irish Constabulary* (above, also below, p. 741).

diplomatic immunity, for example.[290] The same is true where the claim is time-barred under a statute of limitation.[291] Likewise, since there is no duty of care under English law, failure by a local authority to use its powers to protect neglected children falls outside Article 6.[292] The question is whether there is a mere procedural bar to access to the court, as in the Northern Irish case, or a true immunity denying any civil right.

This difficult distinction confronted the House of Lords where a naval mechanic had contracted asbestosis and claimed damages in tort under the Crown Proceedings Act 1947. The Secretary of State issued a certificate under the Act certifying that the illness was attributable to service for pension purposes, which barred any action under the law then in force.[293] The House of Lords held that it was part of the substantive law of remedies against the Crown, under which the Crown had always had immunity at common law and had retained a remnant of that immunity under the certification procedure. The claim therefore failed. The House emphasised that the existence of an immunity, and so the non-existence of a civil right, might always be provided in domestic law. A 'procedural bar', on the other hand, prevented the fair trial of an otherwise existing civil right. The distinction so made, however, may be logically indefinable, and the European Court of Human Rights has confessed that 'it may sometimes be no more than a question of legislative techniques whether the limitation is expressed in terms of the rights or its remedy'.[294] The European Court has also in effect withdrawn its earlier and much criticised decision that the immunity of the police for negligence in investigating crime amounted to a violation of Article 6.[295]

Many ouster and similar clauses of the kind discussed in this chapter may be vulnerable as procedural bars. The Human Rights Act may provide the judges with a powerful tool in their work, well advanced but not yet complete, of demolishing unjustified obstacles to judicial review.

EXCLUSIVE STATUTORY REMEDIES

STATUTORY REVIEW PROVISIONS

A prominent feature of many modern statutes is a provision which allows judicial review to be sought only within a short period of time, usually six weeks, and which thereafter bars it completely. These provisions have become common, particularly in statutes dealing with the compulsory acquisition and control of land. They are therefore of great importance in administrative law. Their primary object is to make it safe for public money to be spent, for example on housing schemes, hospitals or motorways, without the danger that the order acquiring the land might later be invalidated. If the six weeks elapse without legal proceedings being started, the public authority can go ahead with its plans in the knowledge that they cannot be upset subsequently. Where any statutory scheme depends

---

[290] *Fogarty* v. *UK* (2001) 34 EHRR 302.   [291] *Stubbings* v. *UK* (1996) 23 EHRR 213.

[292] *Z* v. *UK* (below).

[293] *Matthews* v. *Ministry of Defence* [2003] 2 WLR 435. (The amending Act of 1947 (below, p. 698) was not in force at the relevant time).

[294] *Fayed* v. *UK* [1994] 18 EHRR 393 at 430. In *Wilson* v. *First County Trust Ltd* (*No 2*) [2003] 3 WLR 568 the House of Lords held that legislation making a pawnbroking agreement unenforceable unless it contained prescribed terms was compatible with Art. 6.

[295] See *Z* v. *UK* (2002) 34 EHRR 97, 138 explaining that in *Osman* v. *UK* (1998) 29 EHRR 245 the court had acted on an erroneous view of English law. For that case see below, p. 655.

upon the authority being able to acquire a secure title to land, a preclusive clause of this kind plays a key role.

But these clauses do not merely cut off remedies after the period of six weeks. They also prescribe how judicial review may be sought within that period, and upon what grounds. Except as provided by the Act itself, the order is not to be questioned in any legal proceedings whatsoever. The whole basis of judicial review is therefore changed. Instead of depending, as it normally does, upon the inherent powers of the court at common law, it depends upon the terms of the Act. These clauses have therefore introduced a form of statutory review which, though in general similar to review at common law, may reveal important differences, according to the interpretation adopted by the courts.

THE STANDARD FORMULA

The first example of this type of review clause was provided by the Housing Act 1930.[296] Later Acts have not altered the formula in any important respect, so that it may be taken as the type. It provides that with respect to clearance orders and compulsory purchase orders made under the Act the following provisions shall have effect:

(3) If any person aggrieved by an order desires to question its validity on the ground that it is not within the powers of this Act or that any requirement of this Act has not been complied with, he may, within six weeks after the publication of the notice of confirmation, make an application for the purpose to the High Court, and where any such application is duly made the court—

   (i)   may by interim order suspend the operation of the order either generally or in so far as it affects any property of the applicant until the final determination of the proceedings; and

   (ii) if satisfied upon the hearing of the application that the order is not within the powers of this Act or that the interests of the applicant have been substantially prejudiced by any requirement of this Act not having been complied with, may quash the order either generally or in so far as it affects any property of the applicant.

(4) Subject to the provisions of the last preceding subsection, an order shall not, either before or after its confirmation, be questioned by prohibition or certiorari or in any legal proceedings whatsoever, and shall become operative on the expiration of six weeks from the date on which notice of its confirmation is published in accordance with the provisions of subsection (2) of this section.

Later versions, such as those in the Acquisition of Land Act 1981[297] (dating from 1946), which governs a great many compulsory purchase orders, and in the denationalising statutes, which govern enforcement orders made by regulatory authorities,[298] omit the reference to prohibition or certiorari and use the generalised form of ouster clause: 'shall not...be questioned in any legal proceedings whatsoever'.[299] The final words include criminal proceedings, thus

---

[296] s. 11.   [297] s. 25.

[298] e.g. Telecommunications Act 1984, s. 18(3); Gas Act 1986, s. 30(3); Electricity Act 1989, s. 27(3); Railways Act 1993, s. 57.

[299] These words do not restrict judicial review of a local authority's resolution to make a compulsory purchase order (*R v. Camden LBC ex p Comyn Ching & Co* (1983) 47 P & CR 417; but contrast *R v. Central Manchester Development Cpn ex p Merlin Great Northern Ltd* [1992] COD 262) or of a minister's decision refusing confirmation (*Islington LBC v. Secretary of State for the Environment* (1980) 43 P & CR 300).

ruling out a collateral plea in defence to a criminal charge.[300] It has been suggested that they do not include appeals to the Secretary of State under the planning legislation,[301] but the contrary seems equally possible.

Similar provisions are found in numerous statutes, primarily but not exclusively[302] in connection with compulsory acquisition and control of the use of land. The Town and Country Planning legislation contains a complex series of sections which apply the usual formula to a wide variety of orders and decisions.[303] It is not applied to the decisions of local planning authorities on applications for planning permission, which may therefore be challenged by ordinary procedures,[304] but it applies to the Secretary of State's decisions on planning appeals and to cases which he calls in for his own initial decision and to a long list of other matters; and there are special provisions restricting challenge to enforcement notices on a number of specified grounds which can be raised only by way of appeal.[305]

In all the clauses now under discussion it is enacted that the court 'may' suspend or quash the offending order. This indicates that the statutory remedy is discretionary,[306] like the other principal remedies of administrative law.[307] But if the statutory conditions are fulfilled the court will normally quash, unless the error is merely technical.[308] There is no provision for declaration or injunction.

If application is made to the High Court within the six weeks, the normal rights of appeal to the higher courts may be exercised without additional restriction as to time.

The statutory formula has generated many problems,[309] of which three in particular stand out:

1. Is judicial review absolutely cut off after six weeks?
2. What is the scope of review if the action is duly brought within the six weeks?
3. What is the meaning of 'any person aggrieved'?

In addition there are a number of other questions of construction, such as the meaning of 'substantially prejudiced'.

EFFECT OF EXPIRY OF THE SIX WEEKS

In cases decided prior to the *Anisminic* case it was held that after the expiry of the period of six weeks judicial review of the validity of the order was absolutely cut off. In *Smith v. East Elloe Rural District Council*,[310] where it was alleged that a local authority had taken land for housing under a compulsory purchase order made wrongfully and in bad faith, the House of Lords refused to allow the action to proceed since it was brought more than six weeks after publication of the notice of confirmation. This was a majority decision,[311]

---

[300] *R* v. *Smith* (1984) 48 P & CR 392.

[301] *Westminster City Council* v. *Secretary of State for the Environment* [1984] JPL 27.

[302] e.g. Medicines Act 1968, s. 107 (licensing system for control of medicines).

[303] Town and Country Planning Act 1990, ss. 284–8, replacing earlier Acts.

[304] As in *R* v. *Hillingdon Borough Council ex p Royco Homes Ltd* [1974] QB 720.   [305] s. 243.

[306] *Errington* v. *Minister of Health* [1935] 1 KB 249 at 279; *Miller* v. *Weymouth Cpn* (1974) 27 P & CR 498; *Kent CC* v. *Secretary of State for the Environment* (1976) 75 LGR 452.   [307] Above, p. 596.

[308] *Peak Park Joint Planning Board* v. *Secretary of State for the Environment* (1980) 39 P & CR 361.

[309] See (1975) 38 *MLR* 274 (J. Alder).

[310] [1956] AC 736. The House allowed an action for a declaration of wrongful action to proceed against the clerk to the council on the footing that the validity of the order was not questioned: for this see below, p. 666.   [311] Lords Reid and Somervell dissented.

but in an earlier case the Court of Appeal had decided similarly where a minister's certificate that requisitioned land should be retained, which the Act required to be treated as a compulsory purchase order, was challenged on the ground that it had been confirmed by an irregularly appointed tribunal.[312] The only exception was a case where an order confirming a coast protection scheme, which was not to be questioned in any proceedings whatsoever after six weeks, was followed by a compulsory purchase order for the land required, and the legal proceedings were started within six weeks of the compulsory purchase order but more than six weeks after the confirmation order.[313] The validity of the compulsory purchase order depended upon the validity of the confirmation order, and for the purpose of challenging the compulsory purchase order, which was quashed, the Court of Appeal allowed proof of the invalidity of the confirmation order, which was vitiated by failure to comply with the requirements of the Act. This is the one example of the court insisting on its powers of review after the expiry of the six weeks, in a case where it felt that an order had been improperly made.

In the cases in which the 'shall not be questioned' provision was applied literally, no reference was made to the long-established policy of preserving judicial review, or to the earlier authorities on 'no certiorari' clauses which the House of Lords reactivated in the *Anisminic* case.[314] Furthermore, the *East Elloe* case was for this reason criticised in the *Anisminic* case, Lord Reid and Lord Pearce saying that they did not regard it as a binding authority, and Lord Wilberforce saying that he could not regard it as a reliable solvent of any similar case.[315] The House of Lords did not suggest that there was any fundamental difference between absolute ouster clauses and ouster clauses which operated only after a prescribed time: if anything they tended to emphasise their similarity.[316] The question therefore is whether an order protected by a time-limited ouster clause can be challenged in proceedings brought after the expiry of the time limit on any of the grounds which would render it ultra vires, such as bad faith, wrong grounds, or violation of natural justice, in accordance with the principle of the *Anisminic* case.

Both reason and authority dictate a negative answer. Public authorities would be in an impossible position if their compulsory purchase, housing, planning and similar orders were exposed to invalidation by the court after they had invested much public money, for example in building on land compulsorily purchased. It is true that the remedy is discretionary,[317] and that the court might therefore confine it to cases where this objection did not apply. But it is now clear that the court will, despite the *Anisminic* dicta, make a distinction between absolute ouster clauses and time-limited ouster clauses. The latter might well be regarded not as ousting the jurisdiction of the court but merely as confining the time within which it can be invoked. In other words, clauses of this type might be regarded as analogous to statutes of limitation, setting limits of time within which action must be brought. There is no judicial criticism of statutes of limitation as 'ousting the jurisdiction of the court', though this is exactly what they do; and the courts formerly made no difficulties about enforcing the Public Authorities Protection Act 1893

---

[312] *Woollett* v. *Minister of Agriculture and Fisheries* [1955] 1 QB 103; and see similarly *Cartwright* v. *Ministry of Housing and Local Government* (1967) 65 LGR 384 (grant of planning permission and compulsory purchase order for ring road).

[313] *Webb* v. *Minister of Housing and Local Government* (1965) 1 WLR 755 (scheme under Coast Protection Act 1949 included land not genuinely 'required' and did not require compulsory purchase).

[314] [1969] 2 AC 147; above, p. 612.

[315] [1969] 2 AC at 171, 200, 210. In the *East Elloe* case no reference was made to the decisions about 'no certiorari' clauses and bad faith such as *R* v. *Gillyard* (1848) 12 QB 527; *Colonial Bank of Australasia* v. *Willan* (1874) LR 5 PC 417.

[316] See [1969] 2 AC at 170 (Lord Reid), 200 (Lord Pearce), 210 (Lord Wilberforce).

[317] See above, p. 621.

(repealed in 1954)[318] which set a time limit of six months, later extended to a year,[319] on actions against public authorities acting in execution or intended execution of any Act of Parliament. On this basis the *East Elloe* and *Anisminic* decisions can be reconciled.

A number of decisions have adopted this solution. In 1972 a Scots court rejected a challenge made more than six weeks after a compulsory purchase order, distinguishing the *Anisminic* case since the statute there made no provision for questioning the order at any stage,[320] and in another such case challenge was held to be barred even where the order had not been served on the owner of the land and an innocent purchaser was deceived.[321] The Court of Appeal has decided similarly in a case where breach of natural justice and bad faith were alleged in the case of compulsory purchase orders for a trunk road scheme, under which much work had already been done but which the complainant had not challenged within the six weeks because he had not known of the supplementary plans which would affect his property.[322] Lord Denning MR mentioned the analogy with a limitation period and pointed also to the public interest in imposing finality where action had already been taken under the disputed orders; and the House of Lords refused leave to appeal. Similar decisions have since multiplied.[323]

The same logic evidently governs cases where the difficulty is not the expiry of a time limit, for example where an order may be challenged only for a prescribed period after it has taken effect. In one such case the court refused an application made before the order had taken effect and rejected arguments about fundamental invalidity based on the *Anisminic* case.[324]

THE TIME LIMIT

The real question, in the case of time-limited ouster clauses, should be whether the time limit is reasonable. In the *East Elloe* case Lord Radcliffe described six weeks as 'pitifully inadequate'.[325] In 1932 the Committee on Ministers' Powers recommended that the period should be at least three months and preferably six months[326] And the Law Commission has suggested but subsequently abandoned a general time limit of one year for actions seeking judicial review of administrative acts.[327] But in their formal report on remedies in 1976 they abandoned this proposal.[328]

---

[318] Law Reform (Limitation of Actions, etc.) Act 1954.

[319] Limitation Act 1939, s. 21.

[320] *Hamilton v. Secretary of State for Scotland*, 1972 SLT 233 (averment of receipt of new evidence after inquiry and failure to consult objectors).

[321] *Martin v. Bearsden and Milngavie DC*, 1987 SLT 300.

[322] *R v. Secretary of State for the Environment ex p Ostler* [1977] QB 122. Lord Denning MR suggested a variety of reasons including one based on void or voidable, which he later recanted: see above, p. 306. Goff LJ found difficulty in the analogy of a limitation period, but in effect adopted it by holding that literal construction was easier where the order was one which needed to be acted upon promptly.

[323] *Jeary v. Chailey Rural District Council* (1973) 26 P & CR 280 (following *East Elloe*, distinguishing *Anisminic*); *Routh v. Reading Corporation* (1971) 217 EG 37 (following *East Elloe*, not mentioning *Anisminic*); *Westminster City Council v. Secretary of State for the Environment* [1984] JPL 27 (following *Ostler*); *R v. Secretary of State for the Environment ex p Kent* (1988) 57 P & CR 431 (following *Ostler*); see also (1975) 38 *MLR* 274 (J. Alder); (1980) 43 *MLR* 173 (N. P. Gravells).

[324] *R v. Cornwall CC ex p Huntington* [1992] 3 All ER 566 (public right of way order).

[325] [1956] AC at 769.   [326] Cmd 4060 (1932), 62.

[327] Law Com. Working Paper No. 40 (1971), para. 123, abandoned in Law Com. No. 73, Cmnd 6407 (1976), para. 7.

[328] Law Com. No. 73, Cmnd 6407 (1976), para. 7. For the proposals generally see above, p. 549.

The time to be allowed ought to be a fair compromise between the expedition needed for proceeding with public works and development of land and the time reasonably required for legal advice and investigation by the citizen whose property is being taken or whose interests are affected. The danger is that Parliament pays little attention to these provisions in Bills and enacts them sometimes too freely at the instance of government departments.

The period of six weeks begins to run from the date on which the decision letter or order was signed and dated, not from the date when it was posted, and there is apparently no obligation as to its notification.[329]

SCOPE OF REVIEW: 'POWERS', 'REQUIREMENTS' AND 'SUBSTANTIAL PREJUDICE'

It is important to ascertain the scope of judicial review provided by the standard time-limited ouster clause where the action is duly brought within the six weeks or other prescribed period. Ordinary review at common law is replaced by a statutory formula specifying two grounds on which the court may quash: (a) that the order is 'not within the powers of this Act'; and (b) 'that any requirement of this Act has not been complied with'. These are evidently intended to be distinct, because for ground (b) there is the additional requirement that 'the interests of the applicant have been substantially prejudiced'. This last requirement does not apply to ground (a).[330]

It has been held that a breach of natural justice, brought about by improper consultation or receipt of evidence after a formal inquiry, renders the order liable to be quashed on both grounds, there being substantial prejudice to the objecting party for the purposes of ground (b).[331] The power to quash on ground (a) follows from the fact that a breach of natural justice is an ultra vires act which makes the decision void and a nullity.[332] The same applies to a decision vitiated by failure to take account of some relevant consideration,[333] or by error of law, since that is now also ultra vires.[334] But where the only objection was that a statutory report was defective in form,[335] or that owing to a slip a minister's confirmation order did not agree with the decision letter stating his reasons for extending the time within which a use of land had to be discontinued,[336] it was held that these flaws were merely non-compliance with the requirements of the respective Acts; and that since

---

[329] *Griffiths* v. *Secretary of State for the Environment* [1983] 2 AC 51.

[330] The contrary was held in *Re Manchester (Ringway Airport) Compulsory Purchase Order* (1935) 153 LT 219, but probably wrongly.

[331] *Errington* v. *Minister of Health* [1935] 1 KB 249 at 268 (Greer LJ: not within powers of Act), 279 (Maugham LJ: non-compliance with requirement and substantial prejudice), 282 (Roche LJ agreeing with Maugham LJ); *Hibernian Property Co Ltd* v. *Secretary of State for the Environment* (1973) 27 P & CR 197 (Browne J: both grounds); *Fairmount Investments Ltd* v. *Secretary of State for the Environment* [1976] 1 WLR 1255 (House of Lords; both grounds). See also *R* v. *Secretary of State for the Environment ex p Ostler* [1977] QB 122; *Lithgow* v. *S of S for Scotland*, 1973 SLT 81.   [332] Above, p. 375.

[333] *Eckersley* v. *Secretary of State for the Environment* (1977) 34 P & CR 124; *North Surrey Water Co* v. *Same* [1976] 34 P & CR 140; *Spackman* v. *Same* [1977] 1 All ER 257.

[334] See above, p. 219; *Peak Park Joint Planning Board* v. *Secretary of State for the Environment* (1979) 39 P & CR 361.

[335] *Gordondale Investments Ltd* v. *Secretary of State for the Environment* (1971) 70 LGR 158.

[336] *Miller* v. *Weymouth Cpn* (1974) 27 P & CR 468. See also *Re Bowman* [1932] 2 KB 621 (minor formal defect in clearance order: no substantial prejudice); *Steele* v. *Minister of Housing and Local Government* (1956) 6 P & CR 386 (clearance order containing redundant statement: no substantial prejudice).

the objectors had not been misled in any way and had suffered no substantial prejudice, the court had no power to quash the orders. These decisions suggest that the court may attempt to differentiate grounds (a) and (b) by a distinction between substantial breaches of the law and minor or procedural irregularities.[337]

Substantial prejudice was found to have been caused where a local authority served an invalid improvement notice in respect of a cottage,[338] and where a minister advertised his intention to take land for road improvements but misdescribed the land so that persons who would have wished to object were not informed of their opportunity to do so.[339] But where notice of a compulsory order was served upon one only of two joint owners, who were husband and wife, and both were in fact fully aware of the order, there was no prejudice at all.[340]

Since judges have commented on the difficulty of distinguishing between ground (a) and ground (b),[341] and have favoured a narrow construction of ground (a) in order to find some meaning for ground (b),[342] it may be suggested that the difficulty would disappear if they were construed with reference to the well-known distinction between statutory requirements which are mandatory and those which are directory. Neglect of a mandatory requirement renders an order ultra vires and void, whereas neglect of a directory requirement has no invalidating effect at all.[343] Neglect of a mandatory requirement therefore makes an order 'not within the powers of this Act', just as much as does bad faith or a breach of natural justice. There is no need to confine such cases to ground (b) merely because they are cases of non-compliance with some requirement. Ground (b) may well be intended for the case of neglect of merely directory requirements. Although such neglect does not affect the validity of the order, and therefore does not fall within ground (a), it would be reasonable to empower the court to quash the order where an irregularity of this class has in fact caused substantial prejudice to the aggrieved person. The scope of judicial review under ground (b) would then go further than at common law, though always subject to proof of substantial prejudice and subject also to the discretion of the court. The forms of words used in the standard clause suggest that precisely this may have been the legislative intention. If that were established, the distinction between grounds (a) and (b) would then be a familiar one, and their combined effect would be eminently reasonable.

SCOPE OF REVIEW: THE *EAST ELLOE* CASE

In the foregoing commentary it is assumed that, as both the words of the Acts and the decisions indicate, 'not within the powers of this Act' means ultra vires for any of the normal reasons, e.g. bad faith or unreasonableness or breach of natural justice. But in the

---

[337] See the *Gordondale* case (above) at 167 (Megaw LJ); *Bugg* v. *Director of Public Prosecutions* [1993] QB 473 (disapproved as noted above, p. 236).

[338] *De Rothschild* v. *Wing Rural District Council* [1967] 1 WLR 740 (in this case the requirement of substantial prejudice was made applicable to invalid improvement notices: Housing Act 1964, s. 27(3)).

[339] *Wilson* v. *Secretary of State for the Environment* [1973] 1 WLR 1083.

[340] *George* v. *Secretary of State for the Environment* (1979) 77 LGR 689.

[341] See the *Gordondale* case (above) at 167 (Megaw LJ); *Miller* (above) at 478 (Kerr J). In *George* v. *Secretary of State for the Environment* (above) Lord Denning MR suggests that, where the defect is a breach of natural justice the two grounds are almost indistinguishable, since an actionable breach of natural justice must involve substantial prejudice.

[342] As in *Hamilton* v. *Secretary of State for Scotland*, 1972 SLT 223 at 240. See also *Hamilton* v. *Roxburgh County Council*, 1971 SLT 2 for another case of narrow construction.

[343] As explained above, p. 183.

East Elloe case a remarkable variety of opinions were expressed on the meaning of these innocent-looking words. It was treated as a case where, as Lord Simonds said, 'plain words must be given their plain meaning'.[344] But there was little agreement about what the plain meaning might be.

Lord Reid was of opinion that the whole area of bad faith and unreasonableness fell outside the statutory clause altogether, and remained an available ground of challenge even after the six weeks;[345] and Lord Somervell held that fraud was not a matter of ultra vires at all, and could be alleged at any time likewise.[346] Lords Simonds, Morton and Radcliffe opposed these views, holding that challenge for fraud, as for any other reason, was barred after the six weeks. But Lord Morton also held that the Act allowed challenge only for violation of express statutory requirements,[347] so that many kinds of unlawful action would not be challengeable even within the six weeks. This extraordinary conclusion would allow uncontrollable abuse of statutory power and cannot conceivably have been intended by Parliament. The case shows what paradoxes can result from using literal verbal interpretation as a substitute for legal principle.

Later decisions have sensibly turned a blind eye to this confusion, though Lord Denning MR[348] expressed his preference for the opinion of Lord Radcliffe,[349] that the words 'not empowered to be granted under this Act' (equivalent to 'not within the powers of this Act') embraced the whole range of the varieties of ultra vires, without any need 'to pick and choose'.

The key to the true interpretation of these statutory clauses must surely be to presume, following Lord Radcliffe and Lord Denning, that Parliament did not intend to authorise any of the abuses normally controlled by the courts of law, but intended only to set a short time limit within which proceedings must be initiated. 'Not within the powers of this Act' is simply a draftsman's translation of 'ultra vires', comprising all its varieties such as bad faith, breach of natural justice, irrelevant considerations, error of law[350] and breach of statutory requirements.[351] The other parts of the clause then fall easily into place if interpreted as suggested above. The draftsman may have been rash to attempt to express the whole subject of judicial review in a statutory formula; but he could scarcely have foreseen the fate that was in store for it.

STANDING: 'ANY PERSON AGGRIEVED'

The statutory remedy may be invoked by 'any person aggrieved'. This is the same phrase as is used at common law to define standing for obtaining quashing and prohibiting orders, and as has been seen it bears a very wide meaning in that context, so that virtually anyone concerned in any way personally falls within it.[352] It has also been used in many statutes, where its meaning ought to be equally wide; for in earlier times the usual phrase was 'any person who feels aggrieved' or 'any person who thinks himself aggrieved', which made

---

[344] *Smith* v. *East Elloe RDC* [1956] AC 736 at 751, for which see above, p. 621.   [345] Ibid. at 763.

[346] Ibid. at 772.   [347] Ibid. at 755.

[348] In *Webb* v. *Minister of Housing and Local Government* [1965] 1 WLR 755 at 770.

[349] [1956] AC at 708.

[350] Above, p. 219. This interpretation was adopted in *Peak Park Planning Board* v. *Secretary of State for the Environment* (1980) 39 P & CR 361.

[351] *Save Britain's Heritage* v. *Number 1 Poultry Ltd* [1991] 1 WLR 153 (HL) (Secretary of State's planning decision challenged for failure to give adequate reasons as required by statutory rules, but no legal error shown).   [352] *R* v. *Thames Magistrates' Court ex p. Greenbaum* (1957) 55 LGR 129.

it clear that the grievance was purely subjective.[353] When this was abbreviated to 'any person aggrieved' the meaning should have remained the same, as indeed is the natural sense of the words,[354] corroborated by at least one statute.[355]

But in some cases the courts interpreted this apparently guileless phrase as expressing a requirement of standing, and treated it as meaning 'any person affected'.[356] In particular, they were reluctant to hold that a public authority was a person aggrieved for the purpose of a statutory right of appeal, so that a local planning authority was not allowed to appeal against the quashing of its own enforcement notice.[357] By glossing the natural meaning of the words the courts introduced so much ambiguity that judges vainly appealed to Parliament to rescue them from their own confusion.[358] Now, however, the Court of Appeal has established that a public authority may be a person aggrieved, and that those words include the losing party in legal proceedings.[359] The question arose on the statutory six-weeks formula of the Town and Country Planning Act 1959 in a case where a landowner had objected to an application for permission to work chalkpits on neighbouring land, alleging that the minister had rejected his inspector's findings on the basis of evidence taken after the inquiry and not disclosed. He brought his action within the six weeks, but it was held that, genuinely aggrieved though he was, he was not a person aggrieved within the meaning of the Act.[360] As a mere neighbour he had no rights under the Act, since the question whether permission should be granted is one between the applicant and the planning authority, and the grant of permission affects no one's legal rights adversely. He could have applied for the quashing of the order only if he had been one of the specified classes of persons having a statutory right to have their representations considered by the minister. Since then, however, statutory rules of procedure for planning inquiries have been made[361] which confer this status on persons allowed to appear at the inquiry at the inspector's discretion. This has made an important difference, and members of a local preservation society, allowed by the inspector to appear at the inquiry, have been held to be persons aggrieved and so entitled to challenge the validity of the order.[362] In any

---

[353] e.g. Highway Act 1835, s. 72 ('if any person shall think himself aggrieved'); Public Health Act 1875, s. 268 ('deems himself aggrieved'); London County Council Act 1947, s. 64 (similar). The National Insurance Act 1911, s. 66(1) referred to 'any person who feels aggrieved'. In the National Insurance Act 1965, s. 65(3) this had become 'any person aggrieved'. The phraseology evolved similarly in rating law: see *Arsenal Football Club Ltd* v. *Ende* [1979] AC 1 at 15. Even the 'feels aggrieved' formula can be restrictively interpreted: see *R* v. *Ipswich Justices ex p Robson* [1971] 2 QB 340.

[354] *R* v. *Surrey Assessment Committee* [1948] 1 All ER 856.

[355] Parliamentary Commissioner Act 1967, s. 12(1), defining 'person aggrieved' as the person 'who claims or is alleged' to have sustained injustice.

[356] See *Ex p. Sidebotham* (1879) 14 Ch D 458 at 465. There are many Australian decisions under the Administrative Decisions (Judicial Review) Act 1977, e.g. *Right to Life Association (NSW)* v. *Secretary, Department of Health* (1995) 128 ALR 238.

[357] *Ealing Cpn* v. *Jones* [1959] 1 QB 384. Contrast *A-G of the Gambia* v. *N'Jie* [1961] AC 617.

[358] In the *Ealing* case (above) and the *Buxton* case (below).

[359] *Cook* v. *Southend BC* [1990] 2 QB 1, overruling *R* v. *London Quarter Sessions ex p Westminster Corporation* [1951] 2 KB 508 and so also *R* v. *Southwark LBC ex p Watts* (1989) 88 LGR 86.

[360] *Buxton* v. *Minister of Housing and Local Government* [1961] 1 QB 278. Compare *Simpson* v. *Edinburgh Cpn*, 1960 SC 313 (neighbour unable to dispute planning permission).

[361] For these rules see below, p. 809.

[362] *Turner* v. *Secretary of State for the Environment* (1973) 28 P & CR 123; and see *Sevenoaks UDC* v. *Twynam* [1928] 2 KB 440 (objector without special personal interest held to be person aggrieved); *Wilson* v. *Secretary of State for the Environment* [1973] 1 WLR 1083 (objectors conceded to be persons aggrieved); *Times Investments Ltd* v. *Secretary of State for the Environment* (1991) 61 P & CR 98 (successor in title); *North East Fife DC* v. *Secretary of State for Scotland*, 1992 SLT 373. If the Act requires the Secretary of State to 'consider all objections' all objectors may be persons aggrieved: *Nicholson* v. *Secretary of State for*

case, since a neighbour is a person aggrieved for the purpose of obtaining a quashing order (when not barred by statute) to quash a planning decision,[363] it is hard to understand why these identical words should be held to debar him from the corresponding remedy under the Act.

The root of the problem is that the common statutory formula contains no other provision about standing, but allows 'any person aggrieved' to apply to the court. Judges have therefore felt that any question of standing must be resolved by interpreting these words restrictively. Since standing depends upon indefinable factors which vary from one case to another, the interpretations have become inconsistent. There has evidently been some confusion of two different questions: whether a person is at liberty to apply to the court; and whether, having done so, he has shown sufficient standing to be entitled to a remedy. There seems to be no reason to hold that, because he passes the first test, he necessarily passes the second. In any case, the statutory formula expressly makes the remedy discretionary, thus giving ample scope for withholding remedies from applicants with inadequate standing. Thus in a planning case it should be possible to hold that a neighbour is a 'person aggrieved', even though he may be denied a remedy because of the implication of the planning legislation that a neighbour has no standing to challenge a grant of planning permission. By disentangling the two questions the court could avoid laying down a restrictive rule.[364]

As already observed in the case of other remedies, the current tendency is to relax requirements as to standing, and this is in accordance with an enlightened system of public law.[365] The House of Lords has given the subject a new and broader basis in the *Inland Revenue Commissioners* case,[366] and the principles of that decision should be applicable also to special statutory remedies. In several cases the courts had already favoured a generous interpretation of 'person aggrieved' and it is now less likely that these words will be made an obstacle to any person who may reasonably consider himself aggrieved. Judicial statements suggest that they are likely to cover any person who has a genuine grievance of whatever kind—and that is tantamount to any person who reasonably wishes to bring proceedings.[367] The House of Lords construed them liberally in a rating case, holding that a ratepayer had standing to object to the under-assessment of another property in the same area, but that the interest of a taxpayer would be too remote.[368]

INTERIM SUSPENSION ORDER

One noteworthy element in the common form of time-limited statutory remedy is that it empowers the court to make an interim order suspending the operation of the order

---

Energy (1978) 76 LGR 693; *Lovelock* v. *Minister of Transport* (1980) 40 P & CR 336. See also *Environmental Defence Society Inc* v. *South Pacific Aluminium Ltd (No 3)* [1981] 1 NZLR 216 and contrast *Burke* v. *Minister of Housing and Local Government* (1957) 8 P & CR 25. A technical change of legal personality may not matter: *R* v. *Hammersmith and Fulham LBC ex p People Before Profit Ltd* (1981) 45 P & CR 364.

[363] *R* v. *Hendon Rural District Council ex p Chorley* [1933] 2 KB 696; *R (Bryson)* v. *Ministry of Development* [1967] NI 180.

[364] Cf. the analogous reasoning in *R* v. *Darlington BC ex p Association of Darlington Taxi Owners* [1994] COD 424.   [365] Above, p. 585.

[366] Above, p. 585.

[367] See the remarks of Lord Denning in *A-G of the Gambia* v. *N'Jie* [1961] AC 617 at 634 and *Maurice* v. *London County Council* [1964] 2 QB 362 at 377 (where the statute said 'who may deem himself aggrieved'). In the latter case the interpretation in the *Buxton* case (above) was disapproved.

[368] *Arsenal Football Club Ltd* v. *Ende* [1979] AC 1. But the law of rating provided a special context.

challenged, pending the result of the proceedings. In principle this should be a useful power which ought to be available as an adjunct to all remedies by which unlawful orders can be set aside. In 1977 provision was made for it in proceedings for judicial review, though subject to some uncertainty.[369] What is needed is a general power to suspend the operation of an administrative order until its validity can be determined, so as to protect persons affected who would otherwise have to obey the order in the meantime, thereby perhaps suffering irreparable loss.[370]

In fact, however, it does not appear that the courts have availed themselves of their suspending power under time-limited statutory remedies. The reason probably is that where the validity of an order is in dispute, a public authority cannot safely proceed to do anything, in case it should turn out that the order was void and its acts were ultra vires, perhaps with consequent liabilities in tort. Interim suspension of disputed orders, therefore, is virtually automatic in many situations, at any rate in cases involving the compulsory taking of land, which form so large a proportion of those covered by time-limited statutory remedies.

DEFAULT POWERS

DEFAULT POWERS: EXCLUSIVE EFFECT

It is common for ministers to be given statutory powers to compel local authorities to fulfil their duties, together with power for the minister to step in and remedy the default himself.[371] Thus the Education Act 1996 provides that if the minister is satisfied that a local authority has failed to discharge any duty under the Act, the minister may by give them such directions as he thinks expedient for performing the duty; and that any such directions may be enforced by mandatory order on the minister's application.[372] Under the Public Health Act 1936 the minister may cause a local inquiry to be held if complaint is made to him, or he is himself of opinion, that a local authority have failed to discharge their functions under the Act; he may then, if satisfied as to the failure, give them directions for making good the default; and if they do not, he may by order transfer any of their functions to a county council or to himself, the expense being charged to the defaulting authority.[373] Similar default powers are conferred by the National Health Service Act 1977.[374] The Town and Country Planning Act 1990 contains more limited powers which the Secretary of State may enforce by mandatory order.[375] The Housing Act 1985 empowers the Secretary of State to act as he may think necessary or expedient for enforcing tenants' 'right to buy' from local authorities, if difficulties are put in their way,[376] and the Local Government Act 1985 contains default powers in case local planning authorities fail in their duty to make unitary development plans.[377]

---

[369] RSC Ord. 53 r. 3(10); above, p. 558.   [370] See above, p. 249.

[371] For a list of default powers to which local authorities are subject see 58 HC Deb. (WA) 249 (11 April 1984); [1984] PL 485.

[372] See s. 497A (2), (3), (4), (4A) and (4B) of the 1996 Act (as amended) for the detail. For a recent example of the exercise of the s. 497A(4B) power see R (Shoesmith) v. OFSTED and ors [2011] EWCA Civ 642.

[373] s. 322. The Public Health Act 1875, s. 299 was the prototype of these powers.   [374] s. 85.

[375] ss. 100, 104.

[376] s. 164. See R v. Secretary of State for the Environment ex p Norwich CC [1982] QB 808.

[377] 1st Sched., para. 13.

Powers of this kind are a standard administrative mechanism for enabling the central government to deal with an inefficient or recalcitrant local authority. The mere fact of their existence puts a powerful lever in the minister's hands. In principle they should be powers of last resort and rarely used. But tensions between central and local government call them into play. Ministers have sometimes been armed with such a complex battery of default powers that they have misunderstood them and acted unlawfully.[378]

One legal effect of these default powers is that the courts are prone to treat them as exclusive remedies, impliedly excluding other remedies for the enforcement of the duty. The principle is the same as that already explained in connection with powers, but in the case of duties the courts seem less disposed to allow ordinary remedies to be used as alternatives. A learned judge once said:

> Where an Act creates an obligation and enforces the performance in a specified manner, we take it to be a general rule that performance cannot be enforced in any other manner.[379]

The House of Lords approved this proposition in a case where the owner of a paper mill was trying to force the local authority to build sewers adequate to the discharge of effluent from his mill.[380] Under the Public Health Act 1875 the local authority had the duty to provide such sewers as might be necessary for effectually draining their district. The Act also provided that if complaint was made to the Local Government Board about failure to provide sewers, the Board after duly inquiring into the case might order performance of the duty within a fixed time, and might enforce their order by mandatory order, or else appoint some person to perform the duty. This scheme of enforcement was held to bar the right of a private person to seek a mandatory order on his own account, since the Act implied that his right course was to complain to the Board. The same principle has several times been applied in proceedings for injunctions[381] or declarations[382] against local education authorities in connection with the provision or administration of schools, the courts holding that their obligations in these matters were remediable only by means of the Secretary of State's default power. That was also the only remedy where a local authority was accused of failing to provide temporary accommodation for persons in urgent need under the National Assistance Act 1948,[383] and, in a similar case, of failing to follow ministerial directions and guidance.[384]

---

[378] As in *Lambeth LBC v. Secretary of State for Social Services* (1980) 79 LGR 61; *R v. Secretary of State for Transport ex p Greater London Council*, The Times, 31 October 1985 (discretionary power mistaken for duty).

[379] *Doe v. Bridges* (1831) 1 B & Ad 847 at 859 (Lord Tenterden CJ). For this rule and its later relaxation see [1998] *PL* 407 at 416 (Sir R. Carnwath).

[380] *Pasmore v. Oswaldtwistle Urban District Council* [1898] AC 387. See also *Clark v. Epsom Rural District Council* [1929] 1 Ch 287 (sewers); *R v. Kensington LBC ex p Birdwood* (1976) 74 LGR 424 (refuse).

[381] *Bradbury v. Enfield London Borough Council* [1967] 1 WLR 1311 (failure to submit plans and obtain approval before establishing new schools); *Wood v. Ealing London Borough Council* [1967] Ch 364 (duty to provide sufficient schools). Contrast *Meade v. Haringey LBC* [1979] 1 WLR 637 (duty to keep schools open enforceable by parents).

[382] *Cumings v. Birkenhead Cpn* [1972] Ch 12 (duty to provide sufficient schools): *Watt v. Kesteven County Council* [1955] 1 QB 408 (duty to have regard to wishes of parents); and see *R v. Northampton CC ex p Gray*, The Times, 10 June 1986 (choice of parent governors).

[383] *Southwark London Borough Council v. Williams* [1971] Ch 734. See similarly *Roberts v. Dorset CC* (1976) 75 LGR 79; *Wyatt v. Hillingdon LBC* (1978) 76 LGR 727.   [384] *Ex p. P* (1999) 31 HLR 154.

DEFAULT POWERS: NON-EXCLUSIVE EFFECT

On the face of it, it is strange that the courts should thus regard default powers as a substitute for ordinary legal remedies. A default power is an administrative device of last resort which is rarely used and which has as its object the internal efficiency of the executive machinery of the state. It is suitable for dealing with a general breakdown of some public service caused by a local authority's default, but it is quite unsuitable as a remedy for defaults in individual cases. As a judge once said, a power of this kind is not really a legal remedy at all, and certainly not an equally convenient and beneficial remedy for an individual so as to exclude the remedy of a mandatory order.[385] Scots law also rejects the English doctrine.[386] A better explanation of the cases mentioned above is probably that the nature of the duty made it unsuitable for enforcement by private action or that, in other words, Parliament did not intend to make it a duty owed to individuals personally. Thus in the case of the sewers Lord Halsbury LC said that

> it would be extremely inconvenient that each suitor in turn should be permitted to apply for a specific remedy against the body charged with the care of the health of the inhabitants of the district in respect of drainage.

In the case under the National Assistance Act Lord Denning MR likewise said:[387]

> It cannot have been intended by Parliament that every person who was in need of temporary accommodation should be able to sue the local authority for it.

It is reasonable to suppose that the general obligations of public authorities in the areas of health, education and welfare are not intended to be enforceable at the suit of individuals. It is unrealistic to suppose that ministerial default powers supply an adequate alternative remedy.

This last point is recognised by the courts in a number of situations. They will not accept default powers as a substitute for ordinary remedies in a case of breach of statutory duty causing personal injury;[388] or where something is done which is positively forbidden by the Act;[389] or where something is done which is ultra vires.[390] In these situations it would plainly be wrong to deprive an injured or affected person of his ordinary legal rights. Furthermore, the duty of a body such as a local education authority may sometimes be owed to an individual and therefore enforceable by him. Parents who are obliged to send their children to school under criminal penalties have a legal right to have them accepted by the local education authority in accordance with their statutory duty. Consequently where an authority refused to accept poor children in its schools without a special payment which it was not entitled to demand, the guardians of the children were

---

[385] *R v. Leicester Guardians* [1899] 2 QB 632 at 639 (Darling J). See also *R v. Inner London Education Authority ex p Ali* (1990) 2 Admin LR 822; *R v. Secretary of State for Education ex p Prior* [1994] COD 197, citing a helpful dictum of Woolf J.

[386] *Docherty (T.) Ltd v. Burgh of Monifieth*, 1971 SLT 13 (local authority ordered to construct sewers); *Walker v. Strathclyde Regional Council (No 1)*, 1986 SLT 523; *Wilson v. Independent Broadcasting Authority*, 1979 SLT 279; *MacKenzie's Trustees v. Highland Regional Council*, 1995 SLT 218.

[387] *Southwark London Borough Council v. Williams* [1971] Ch 734 at 743.

[388] *Ching v. Surrey CC* [1910] 1 KB 736; *Reffell v. Surrey County Council* [1964] 1 WLR 358 (failure to keep school buildings safe; pupil injured).

[389] *Bradbury v. Enfield London Borough Council* [1967] 1 WLR 1311 (ceasing to maintain school without giving opportunity for objection).

[390] *Cumings v. Birkenhead Cpn* [1972] Ch 12 (Lord Denning MR); *Meade v. Haringey LBC* [1979] 1 WLR 637. See also *R v. Secretary of State for the Environment ex p Ward* [1984] 1 WLR 834.

granted a declaration that the children must be accepted.[391] Where an authority closed schools which it had a duty to keep open, it was held by the Court of Appeal that the minister's default power was not exclusive but left open all the established remedies for breach of statutory duty.[392] In a relator action brought on behalf of a member of the public for an injunction against the broadcasting of an indecent television programme, contrary to the statutory duty of the broadcasting authority, the same court rejected the argument that the complainant's only remedy was to apply for a ministerial intervention under the Television Act 1964.[393]

---

[391] *Gateshead Union* v. *Durham County Council* [1918] 1 Ch 146. The court would have granted an injunction also if necessary.   [392] *Meade* v. *Haringey LBC* (above).

[393] *A-G ex rel McWhirter* v. *Independent Broadcasting Authority* [1973] QB 629 at 649 (no breach of duty was found).

20

LIABILITY OF PUBLIC AUTHORITIES

CATEGORIES OF LIABILITY

Any attempt to describe the liability of public authorities to pay monetary damages or compensation runs at once into difficulties of classification.[1] In the first place, there is the problem of the Crown. Crown liability for torts such as trespass and negligence has a very different history from the liability of local authorities and other governmental bodies. But since the Crown Proceedings Act 1947 the Crown has in principle been put on the same footing as public authorities generally. To treat the Crown in an entirely separate compartment would therefore mean segregating materials and illustrations which are best grouped together; but to deal adequately with the Crown in one single discussion would require too many digressions. The course which will be followed here will be to treat matters involving the Crown as part of the general law so far as they rest on the same principles; but the history and peculiarities of Crown proceedings, together with certain connected matters, must be relegated to the next chapter.

Inevitably, also, there will be overlap with the chapter on remedies. The law of liability can never be cleanly detached from the law of remedies, so that reference back may be needed. Liability under European Union law is in a class by itself, and in view of the supremacy of EU law over national law can suitably be treated first.

LIABILITY UNDER EUROPEAN UNION LAW

VARIETIES OF LIABILITY

An important new head of government liability was created when Britain acceded to the European Communities in 1973 under the European Communities Act 1972, as explained earlier.[2] Breach of Community obligations may make the government liable to pay compensation or damages under rules which are in continuous development by the European Court of Justice in Luxembourg.

Community obligations may arise both directly from the EU Treaty and also from regulations, directives and decisions issued by the EU Council and the Commission. Treaty

---

[1] For discussion see Staunton, Skidmore, Harris and Wright, *Statutory Torts* (2003); Fairgrieve, *State Liability in Tort: A Comparative Law Study* (2003); Law Commission's Report (No. 322) 'Administrative Redress: Public Bodies and the Citizen' (available at <http://lawcommission.justice.gov.uk/docs/lc322_Administrative_Redress_Public_Bodies_and_the_Citizen.pdf>); and Price, 'The Influence of Human Rights on State Negligence Liability in England and South Africa' (unpublished PhD thesis, Cambridge 2012).   [2] Above, p. 189.

provisions and regulations may have direct effect and may confer rights enforceable in national courts.[3] Although originally directives were to be implemented by the Member State by methods of its own choice,[4] the European Court has developed the doctrine that a directive, if unconditional and sufficiently precise, may have direct effect, without national legislation, against the government which is failing to implement the directive, including any body which is a government agency according to national law.[5] Thus where an area health authority dismissed a woman employee because she had reached the age of 60, when the corresponding age for men was 65, the European Court, holding that certain provisions of the directive of the EC Council prohibiting sex discrimination in employment were directly effective, decided that the dismissed employee could rely on the directive in a British court or tribunal and so claim both a retiring age of 65, despite British legislation specifically permitting differential retiring ages, and full financial compensation, despite the limit imposed by British law.[6]

Directives which are directly effective are enforceable as such only against national authorities and not against other individuals or bodies, the principle being that the state may not take advantage of its own failure to implement Community law. In a case such as that just related, therefore, a claim against a private employer would have failed. This anomaly of 'vertical but not horizontal effect' can be indirectly remedied in two ways, as has been explained earlier: one is by extending the meaning of national authorities so as to include any body which provides a public service under state authority and enjoys special powers; the other is by treating national courts as national authorities, which may thus be obliged to give effect to directives even against private parties.[7] State liability may also be incurred, as already explained, where the state has failed to translate a directive into national law, as where the Italian government had failed to give effect to a directive requiring state guarantees for wages owed to employees by bankrupt employers and the European Court held that the employees could sue the Italian government in the Italian courts for damages.[8] For this purpose it is immaterial whether or not the directive has direct effect (in the Italian case it did not, since it was held to lack precision). The principle is simply that the state must bear the liability for its failure to embody the directive in national law. Even though governments may not always bear liability for violations of the Treaty or of Community regulations,[9] the generality of the propositions laid down by the Court points distinctly in that direction. These propositions are discussed below in the context of breach of duty, and they conflict with the Court of Appeal's decision that the

[3] EU Treaty, Art. 249 (ex 189); *Van Gend en Loos* case [1963] CMLR 105; *Defrenne* v. *Sabena (No 2)* [1976] CMLR 98. An example concerning regulations is *R* v. *Minister of Agriculture ex p Cox* [1993] 2 CMLR 917.

[4] EU Treaty, Art. 249 (ex 189).

[5] *Van Duyn* v. *Home Office* [1975] Ch 358 (ECJ); the *Marshall* case (below).

[6] *Marshall* v. *Southampton and South West Hampshire Area Health Authority* [1986] QB 401 (ECJ); *(No 2)* [1994] QB 126 (ECJ), [1994] AC 530 (HL).

[7] See above, p. 165, and the decisions there cited. It may be noted that a claimant may succeed in obtaining damages against a Member State when court adjudicating at last instance makes 'a manifest error of Community law' causing damage (Case C-224/01, *Köbler* v. *Republik Österreich* [2003] ECR I-10239). But 'a considered but wrong judgment' on the point (whether to make a reference to the ECJ) 'is not properly described as *ipso facto* a manifest breach of the case law of the Court of Justice' (*Cooper* v. *HM A-G* [2010] EWCA Civ 464, para. 107 (Arden LJ)).

[8] *Francovich* v. *Italian Republic* [1991] ECR I-5357, [1993] 2 CMLR 66 (ECJ) (above, p. 168). See [1993] *CLJ* 272 (R. Cantara). See also *Emmott* v. *Minister for Social Welfare* [1993] ICR 8 (Irish Republic's failure to implement directive: domestic time limit overridden).

[9] Alternative interpretations are discussed in [1993] *PL* 151 at 160 (C. Lewis and S. Moore). For useful discussion of the principles of liability see P. P. Craig in (1997) 113 *LQR* 67 and in Beatson and Tridimas (eds.), *New Directions in European Public Law*, ch. 6.

government is not liable in damages for loss caused by a ministerial order which is invalid because of conflict with the EU Treaty.[10]

Despite the uncertainty which surrounds some important points, it is clear that the decisions of the European Court have opened up a wide new category of government liability. The Court is evidently determined to ensure that the principle of supremacy of European law is reinforced by a stringent system of remedies and that governments which default on their Community obligations shall be responsible for making reparation.

LIABILITY FOR BREACH OF HUMAN RIGHTS

ENFORCEABLE HUMAN RIGHTS

The Human Rights Act 1998 has opened up new vistas of liability for public authorities. In the long period between Britain's acceptance of the right of individual petition in 1966 and the incorporation of 'the Convention rights' into domestic law by the Act of 1998 the Convention had no more than the force of a treaty and could not create domestic legal liability.[11] But the rights secured by it are now clothed with legal force by the Act, already explained generally together with the list of the protected rights.[12] The Act came fully into force on 2 October 2000, although the courts, by intelligent anticipation, had woven parts of it into the doctrines of reasonableness and natural justice before its date of commencement.[13] After that date there began, as had been expected, a copious flow of proceedings against public authorities. Important heads of liability under the Act have been explained elsewhere in this book, both in the general account (Chapter 6) and also in particular contexts such as the right to personal liberty (Chapter 16), the right to a fair and impartial hearing (Chapters 13 and 14) and the right to effective remedies (Chapter 19). Other areas will be illustrated in this present chapter.

The Act makes comprehensive provision for remedies, in particular against public authorities, in the ordinary courts and at the instance of individual claimants, for breaches of Convention rights. The citizen may now make his claim against a public authority in the appropriate court or tribunal, and in any legal proceedings, provided that he satisfies the Convention's requirement of himself being a 'victim' of the alleged breach.[14] He must sue within a year unless the court or tribunal considers it equitable to extend the time.[15] A case against the UK may still be taken to Strasbourg on a complaint that domestic law fails to satisfy the Convention.

REMEDIES—GENERAL

The Act's specific provisions about remedies have their roots in Article 41 of the Convention which provides that the European Court 'shall, if necessary, afford just satisfaction to the injured party'. Since the Act requires domestic courts to 'take into account' the judgments, decisions and opinions of the European Court and of the (former) Commission,[16] domestic courts will normally follow European case law in the absence of good reasons

[10] Below, p. 662.
[11] Where possible statute is interpreted or the common law developed to secure compliance with treaty obligations and international law. Above, p. 131 and Price, above p. 142 n. 7.   [12] Above, p. 129.
[13] See above, p. 335, for an example; and *R (Mahmood)* v. *Home Secretary* [2001] 1 WLR 840 as discussed in *R (Daly)* v. *Home Secretary* [2001] 1 WLR 840 (Lord Steyn).
[14] s. 7(1). For the 'victim' rule see above, p. 596.   [15] s. 7(5).   [16] s. 2(1).

for departing from it.[17] Unfortunately the European Court has not developed clear principles for the award of compensation. The Law Commission attempted to clarify the law and practice on damages in a full discussion published in 1998, but found difficulty in crystallising a mass of case law into positive rules and observed that there would be much scope for judicial discretion.[18]

In the case of any act (or proposed act) of a public authority the court may 'grant such relief or remedy, or make such order, within its powers as it considers just, and appropriate'.[19] Remedies which issue only from the High Court, such as quashing and mandatory orders, will remain so restricted, but otherwise the whole field of remedies is open. A tribunal's power to provide 'an appropriate remedy' may be extended by ministerial order.[20] Damages may be awarded only where, allowing for any other relief, the court holds that this is necessary to afford 'just satisfaction', and account must be taken of the principles applied by the European Court.[21]

All the rulings and practices of the European Court whether before or after the Act, are now relevant material for enforcing it. The Convention provides that if the law of the Member State allows only partial reparation, the Court 'shall, if necessary, afford just satisfaction to the injured party'.[22] The Court habitually awards both damages and costs in a manner comparable with the practice of British courts, and these awards are binding under the Convention.[23] There are therefore many precedents for the claims that can be made under the Act. The Act provides, however, that damages for a judicial act (since courts and tribunals count as public authorities), if done in good faith, may not be awarded except as specifically provided in the case of unlawful detention;[24] nor may a judicial act be challenged otherwise than by way of appeal or judicial review or under ministerial rules (if any).[25]

REMEDIES—INJUNCTIONS AND POSSESSION ORDERS

All remedies under the Act are discretionary. But the court's discretion is not unfettered and Convention principles require that remedies should be just and proportionate both to social needs and to individual circumstances. Thus the House of Lords allowed appeals against injunctive orders obtained by local authorities against gipsies using land for caravan sites in breach of planning control, remitting their cases to the High Court for reconsideration, which would require balancing of the need for planning control in the public interest against any resulting personal hardship and any failure to respect a person's home under Article 8.[26] In contrast, where a tenant's lease was terminated and he held over unlawfully, the House of Lords held by a majority that the premises factually remained his home, but that Article 8 would not help him since it could not defeat a legal owner's right to possession.[27] In this case the House of Lords was sharply divided. And in a later case a still divided House of Lords held that a tenant or licensee can raise as a defence to a possession order a deficiency in the domestic law infringing his Article 8 rights; but he could not raise a defence based on his personal circumstances.[28] These disagreements in the House of Lords turn on whether Article 8 can displace the established law about

---

[17] As explained above, p. 140.   [18] Law Com. No. 266, Cm. 4853.   [19] s. 8(1).
[20] s. 7(11).   [21] s. 8(3), (4).   [22] Art. 41.   [23] Art. 46.
[24] s. 9(3). Any award is to be made against the Crown (s. 9(4)). See above, p. 507 discussing the special provision in Art. 5 for compensation for detention.   [25] s. 9(1).
[26] *South Bucks DC* v. *Porter* [2003] 2 WLR 1547.   [27] *Harrow LBC* v. *Qazi* [2003] 3 WLR 792.
[28] *Kay* v. *Lambeth LBC* [2006] UKHL 10, [2006] 2 WLR 570, para. 110 (Lord Hope). Discussed more fully above, p. 577.

ownership and possession of property, which is itself protected in the First Protocol. The local authorities' claims to possession were subject to judicial review and subject also to the rule against evicting an occupier without a court order;[29] rules which themselves show the law's respect for the occupier's home, and under which, in any case, the court must act compatibly with Convention rights.[30] But to confer new property rights on an unlawful occupier is another matter altogether. As Lord Scott in the first case said, Article 8 was intended to deal with the arbitrary intrusion by state or public authorities into a citizen's home life and not to amend the social housing legislation of a Member State. There is ample scope for that Article to operate within its proper sphere, but the right to remove unlawful occupiers is 'necessary in a democratic society...for the protection of the rights and freedoms of others'.[31]

REMEDIES—DAMAGES

Infringements of human rights under the HRA may be regarded as a new species of tort or else as an additional form of breach of statutory duty or else as *sui generis*.[32] Whatever classification is adopted, the Convention requirement of 'just satisfaction', as well as the special provision for compensation in Article 5, makes it clear that compensation equivalent to money damages may be awarded. But the 1998 Act makes it clear that an award should not be made unless it is 'necessary to afford just satisfaction' and in assessing this account should be taken of other relief and remedies available.[33] As will be seen below, awards of damages in 'just satisfaction' are not common.

Rules and principles for the assessment of damages in the European Court are however conspicuous by their absence. The Law Commission's study, already mentioned, gave many examples from a variety of countries but led to few conclusions. Typical Strasbourg awards were of £12,000 against the UK for delays and maladministration in arranging the adoption of a child;[34] of sums totalling £43,000 against Italy for the arrest and maltreatment of a suspected Mafia member[35] and of £5,000 against France for distress and anxiety caused by delays in proceedings against a hospital.[36]

There are still relatively few reported English decisions on damages since the HRA came into force. But the first case to reach the House of Lords has begun the clarification of the principles applicable.[37] The case concerned a prisoner who challenged the fairness of the disciplinary proceedings that had led to him being awarded twenty-one 'additional days' of imprisonment. By the time the matter reached the House of Lords, the Home Secretary had conceded that the proceedings had been unfair,[38] so it was only necessary

---

[29] Protection from Eviction Act 1977, s. 3.   [30] HRA s. 6(1), (3).   [31] Art. 8(2).

[32] See (2009) 72 *MLR* 750 (Varuhas) for the argument that 'just satisfaction' should be conceptualised as a tort. The question may be important in determining issues such as causation, remoteness and quantum.

[33] Act of 1998, s. 8(3). In *Anufrijeva*, below, Lord Woolf laid down that, in applying for permission, claimants should explain why recourse should not be had to alternative remedies (internal complaints procedures or the Ombudsman) (para. 81). This was done in order to encourage a 'proportionate resolution' to damages claims, laying down further that 'no more than three authorities' should be cited in support of a claim etc. (ibid.).   [34] *H* v. *UK* (1987) 10 EHRR 95.

[35] *Labita* v. *Italy* (1995) 20 EHRR 535.

[36] *H* v. *France* (1989) 12 EHRR 74.

[37] *R (Greenfield)* v. *Home Secretary* [2005] UKHL 14, [2005] 1 WLR 673. See [2006] *JR* 230; [2005] *PL* 429 (Clayton). *Greenfield* followed in *Van Colle* v. *Chief Constable of Hertfordshire Police* [2007] EWCA Civ 325; [2007] 1 WLR 1821.

[38] The proceedings had been conducted by a deputy controller (who was insufficiently independent for a matter involving 'additional days') who had denied legal representation (required in the particular circumstances). See further at p. 59.

for their Lordships to decide on the prisoner's claim for damages for violation of Article 6. Lord Bingham, who gave the only substantive speech, stressed that 'the primary aim' of the Convention was to promote the uniform protection of human rights.[39] Member States are bound to this obligation and thus the expectation is that they will act promptly to prevent a repetition of any violation found by the ECtHR. Consequently, when the court finds that there has been a violation, that finding is often 'in itself, just satisfaction for the violation... [The] focus of the Convention is on the protection of human rights and not the award of compensation.'[40]

Where a procedural right, such as Article 6, has been violated it is generally not clear that the challenged decision would have been different had the right not been violated. Thus, save exceptionally, any damage that flows from an adverse decision is not caused by the violation.[41] Consequently, the House of Lords made appropriate declarations regarding the fairness of the disciplinary proceedings but no damages were awarded. Where awards are made for Article 6 violations (for instance, where there has been exceptional delay and aggravation caused by the violation) they 'have been noteworthy for their modesty'.[42]

Violations of articles other than Article 6 are often treated similarly, with the finding of a violation being considered 'just satisfaction', especially where non-pecuniary damages are sought.[43] But the requirement of causation will be more straightforwardly met by a violation of a substantive human right as opposed to a procedural violation. Nonetheless, awards are still modest.[44]

QUANTUM OF DAMAGES IN HUMAN RIGHTS CASES

Section 8(4) of the 1998 Act provides that in determining the amount of any award of damages the court 'must take into account the principles applied by the European Court of Human Rights in relation to the award of compensation under Article 41 of the Convention'. As Lord Bingham has said, the 1998 Act 'is not a tort statute.... the purpose of incorporating the Convention in domestic law was not to give the victims better remedies at home than they could recover in Strasbourg but to give them the same remedies without the delay and expense of resort to Strasbourg.'[45] Thus an English, or domestic law, scale of damages which will generally be more generous should not be applied.[46] And the English courts in making awards for violations of human rights will have to grapple with the sometimes contradictory Strasbourg cases.

Damages may be claimed for pecuniary loss (such as loss of earnings or profits). But claims can also be made for non-pecuniary loss, for instance, where the defendant has

---

[39] *Greenfield*, para. 7.   [40] Ibid., para. 9.

[41] Causation is an obvious prerequisite for an award of damages. See *Greenfield*, para. 14 and *Kingsley v. UK* (2001) 35 EHRR 177, para. 40.

[42] *Greenfield*, para. 17. To like effect see *Anufrijeva*, para. 75.

[43] For instance, in *TH v. The Crown Court Wood Green* [2006] EWHC 2683, [2007] 1 WLR 1670 where the court said that if it had found a violation of Art. 5, that finding would have been 'just satisfaction' (para. 42).

[44] See *Anufrijeva*, below, para. 75.   [45] *Greenfield*, para. 19.

[46] Ibid., not following suggestions to the contrary in *KB*, below and in *R (Bernard) v. Enfield LBC* [2002] EWHC 2282, [2003] HLR 27 (Council in breach of duty to provide suitably adapted accommodation to severely disabled claimant: full tort damages awarded). Compare (2000) 49 *ICLQ* 517 (Carnwath). Cf. also *Anufrijeva*, para. 74 (ordinary civil law principles not applicable but 'rough guidance' in Judicial Studies Board's guidance and the level of awards made by the Criminal Injuries Compensation Board. Reliance upon these sources may be justified on the basis that s. 8(4) does not preclude such reliance, as long as it does not displace taking into account the principles of the ECtHR.

suffered 'some loss of real opportunities' as a result of the violation. But such awards are rare given the difficulty of establishing the casual connection.[47] Another head of non-pecuniary loss that may be awarded in extreme cases is 'physical or mental suffering', but the court has 'been sparing in making these awards'.[48] In this context it seems improbable that exemplary or aggravated damages will be awarded.

SOME EXAMPLES

The High Court awarded damages in six cases out of a group of eight, where applicants to mental health review tribunals had suffered excessive delays in breach of Article 5(4). The awards ranged from £750 to £4,000; but in the other two cases, following the common Strasbourg practice, it was held that a finding in the claimant's favour was sufficient just satisfaction without damages.[49] Similarly, another group of cases raised questions concerning alleged breaches of Article 8. This resulted in a full opinion on damages under the HRA from a powerful Court of Appeal.[50] Three claims for damages, all based on maladministration and delay, alleged neglect of special needs, impoverishment and failure to allow entry to an accepted refugee's family. None of the claims succeeded, but the Court made an important survey of the subject of damages and of a Member State's obligations under Article 8. Although that article does not provide a right to a home, it may require the provision of welfare support, including housing, in special circumstances; and neglect of this duty may justify damages. The Strasbourg jurisprudence shows, however, that the Court will not regard mere delay as infringing Article 8 unless its consequences are serious; and regard must be had to resources. A case was brought against the police by the parents of a murdered man. He had been murdered shortly before he was due to give evidence for the prosecution at the trial (for theft) of another man who was subsequently convicted of his murder. The failure of the police to protect him was found by the trial judge to be a violation of both Articles 2 and 8 and this was upheld by the Court of Appeal. But the trial judge's award of £50,000 (£15,000 to the deceased's estate and £17,500 to each parent) was reduced on appeal, after taking into account the Strasbourg authorities, to £25,000 (£10,000 to the deceased's estate and £7,500 to each parent).[51]

PROCEDURAL POINT

A claim for damages alone cannot be brought by judicial review proceedings.[52] A claim for damages alleging wrongdoing by a public body under the 1998 Act should be brought in the Administrative Court, but by ordinary claim.[53]

---

[47] *Greenfield*, paras. 12–15.   [48] *Greenfield*, para. 16.

[49] *R (KB) v. South London and South and West Region Mental Health Review Tribunal* [2003] 3 WLR 385.

[50] *Anufrijeva v. Southwark LBC* [2003] EWCA Civ 1406, [2004] QB 1124, [2004] 2 WLR 603, [2004] 1 All ER 833 (CA), Lords Woolf LCJ and Phillips MR both sitting.

[51] *Van Colle v. Chief Constable of Hertfordshire Police* [2007] EWCA Civ 325, [2007]1 WLR 1821. Discussed [2008] *CLJ* 239 (Steele). The finding of liability was overturned in the House of Lords (*Hertfordshire Police v. Van Colle* [2008] UKHL 50) discussed below, p. 654, but no adverse comment was made on the size of these awards.   [52] Above, p. 555.

[53] *Anufrijeva*, above, para. 81 and see *TH v. The Crown Court Wood Green* [2006] EWHC 2683, [2007] 1 WLR 1670.

LIABILITY IN TORT GENERALLY

GENERAL PRINCIPLES

Public authorities,[54] including ministers of the Crown,[55] enjoy no dispensation from the ordinary law of tort and contract, except in so far as statute gives it to them.[56] Unless acting within their powers, they are liable like any other person for trespass, nuisance, negligence and so forth. This is an important aspect of the rule of law.[57] Similarly they are subject to the ordinary law of master and servant, by which the employer is liable for torts committed by the employee in the course of his employment, the employee also being personally liable. Examples are furnished by many classic cases. In *Cooper* v. *Wandsworth Board of Works*[58] the board was held liable in damages in an ordinary action of trespass: as has been seen, it was acting outside its powers because it caused its workmen to demolish a building without first giving the owner a fair hearing; therefore it had no defence to an action for damages for trespass. The famous cases which centred round John Wilkes in the eighteenth century, and which denied the power of ministers to issue general warrants of arrest and search, took the form of actions for damages against the particular servants who did the deeds, who were sued in trespass just as if they were private individuals.[59]

The claimant, if injured by an employee in the course of his employment, may sue the master or the servant or both, since both are liable, but in most cases he will naturally choose to sue the master. He must, however, be able to show some recognised legal wrong. But there are some situations where an officer of central or local government has an independent statutory liability by virtue of his office, because the statute imposes duties upon him as a designated officer rather than on the public authority which appoints him. In that case the employee only will be liable. Thus an action failed against a local authority when their inspector of animals had seized supposedly infected sheep in a market, since the statutory order empowered the inspector but not the local authority to seize infected animals; and it made no difference that the local authority had a statutory duty to appoint the inspector and power to dismiss him.[60] But if the duties of the designated officer are in fact carried out by employees of the local authority, that authority may be liable in the same way as for its other employees. This last proposition was applied by the Court of Appeal where a junior employee of a local authority negligently certified that no local land charges were registered against land which was being sold, so that an incumbrancer lost a charge over the land, although the statutory duty of issuing certificates rested specifically upon the local authority's clerk as registrar.[61] In cases where the designated officer alone is liable, his employer (whether the Crown or a local authority) will normally indemnify him; but this is only a matter of grace.[62]

---

[54] See Street, *Governmental Liability*, ch. 2; Hogg, *Liability of the Crown*, ch. 4; Harlow, *Compensation and Government Torts*; Arrowsmith, *Civil Liability and Public Authorities*; Aronson and Whitmore, *Public Torts and Contracts*; (1980) 98 *LQR* 413 (P. P. Craig). For an acute critique of what is seen as undue indulgence to plaintiffs, see [1989] *PL* 40 (J. A. Weir).   [55] See below, p. 693.

[56] It is also worth noting that 'The breach of a public law right by itself gives rise to no claim for damages. A claim for damages [against a public authority] must be based upon a private law cause of action' (Lord Browne-Wilkinson in *X (minors)*, below, at 165 ([1995] 3 WLR 152).

[57] Previous 3 sentences approved in *ID* v. *The Home Office* [2005] EWCA Civ 38, [2006] 1 WLR 1003, para. 56.   [58] (1863) 14 CB (NS) 180; above, p. 409.

[59] *Entick* v. *Carrington* (1765) 19 St Tr 1030; *Leach* v. *Money* (1765) 19 St Tr 2002; *Wilkes* v. *Wood* (1763) 19 St Tr 1153.   [60] *Stanbury* v. *Exeter Cpn* [1905] 2 KB 838.

[61] *Ministry of Housing and Local Government* v. *Sharp* [1970] 2 QB 223. For this case see below, p. 648. For the liability of the Chief Constable for the torts of the constables in his force, see above, p. 103.

[62] Same case, at 269, 275.

Another rule which emerged in the course of Wilkes's legal adventures was that oppressive or unconstitutional action by servants of the government could justify an award of exemplary or punitive damages, i.e. damages which take into account the outrageous conduct of the defendant and not merely the actual loss to the plaintiff. This is one of the special cases in which exemplary damages are allowed, according to the law as declared by the House of Lords.[63] So the position here is that the law is sterner with the government than with the citizen. Examples in the governmental area are rare, but one occurred when the Court of Appeal upheld an award of exemplary damages to a Sikh woman who had suffered sex and racial discrimination as an applicant for a post at a local authority college.[64] Such aggravated damages will not, however, be awarded in actions for public nuisance or negligence.[65]

The Supreme Court has held[66] (by a majority) in a false imprisonment case[67] that 'vindicatory damages' were not available to mark the importance of the right infringed. Lord Dyson, for the majority, thought that the introduction of such a principle would lead to '[u]ndesirable uncertainty' and saw 'no justification for letting such an unruly horse loose on our law.... [T]he purpose of vindicating a claimant's common law rights is sufficiently met by (i) an award of compensatory damages, including (in the case of strict liability torts) nominal damages where no substantial loss is proved, (ii) where appropriate, a declaration in suitable terms and (iii) again, where appropriate, an award of exemplary damages.'[68] Lady Hale, on the other hand, said that there 'must be some recognition of the gravity of the breach of the fundamental right which resulted in false imprisonment, and account should be taken of the deterrent effect of an award lest there be the possibility of further breaches'.[69]

NUISANCE AND INEVITABLE INJURY

What is duly done under statutory authority is lawful action of which no one is entitled to complain. A public authority will therefore not be liable in tort where the injury is the inevitable consequence of what Parliament has authorised, as is the nuisance caused by the running of trains on a railway authorised to be operated on a particular line,[70] or by the erection of a barrier on a pavement.[71] There is no liability for a nuisance necessarily implied by the empowering Act even if not expressly authorised.[72] Thus the House of

---

[63] *Rookes* v. *Barnard* [1964] AC 1129 at 1226; and see *Ashby* v. *White* (1703) 2 Ld Raym 938 at 956; *Broome* v. *Cassell & Co Ltd* [1972] AC 1027; *A-G of St Christopher* v. *Reynolds* [1980] AC 637; *Kuddus* v. *Chief Constable of Leicestershire Constabulary* [2001] 2 WLR 1789 (misfeasance in public office). For awards of exemplary damages against the police see *George* v. *Commissioner of Metropolitan Police* The Times, 31 March 1984; *Connor* v. *Chief Constable of Cambridgeshire* The Times, 11 April 1984; *Treadaway* v. *Chief Constable of West Midlands* The Times, 25 October 1994. Nationalised industries were not 'governmental' for this purpose: *AB* v. *South West Water Services* (below). [64] *Bradford CMC* v. *Arora* [1991] 2 QB 507.

[65] *AB* v. *South West Water Services Ltd* [1993] QB 507.

[66] *Lumba (WL)* v. *Secretary of State for the Home Department* [2011] UKSC 12; *A-G of Trinidad and Tobago* v. *Ramanoop* [2005] UKPC 15, recognising vindicatory damages only applied to infringements of constitutional rights.

[67] The claimants secured only nominal damages since, if the Home Secretary had not made the error which rendered their detention unlawful, they would have been lawfully detained. Case discussed above, p. 318.

[68] Para. 101. Lords Phillips, Rodger, Walker, Brown, Collins and Kerr, concurring on this point.

[69] Para. 180. Lord Hope and Walker dissenting on this point.

[70] *Hammersmith Rly Co* v. *Brand* (1869) LR 4 HL 171. A claim for statutory compensation was also rejected: see below, p. 684. [71] *Dormer* v. *Newcastle upon Tyne Cpn* [1940] 2 KB 204.

[72] In the nineteenth century a distinction was drawn between a nuisance expressly authorised (such as that consequent upon the construction of a railway track) and that which was not inevitable (such as that

Lords held that, even though the operation of an oil refinery was only authorised by necessary implication, the neighbours who complained of excessive smell, vibration and noise had no remedy in so far as the nuisance was the inevitable result of the authorised operation. Statutory provision is now made for compensation where the value of an interest in land is depreciated through authorised public works.[73]

Rights over property are similarly overridden where a public authority acquires land which is subject to some third party right such as a right of way or a restrictive covenant. No such right can prevent the authority from exercising its statutory powers;[74] and to the extent that the right is expropriated, there is, as mentioned below, a statutory claim to compensation.[75] But the right is not extinguished, and may be enforced in any situation where it does not conflict with action based on statutory authority. For example, the Air Ministry may set up an aerodrome on land compulsorily purchased, even though the land is subject to a covenant that it shall be used only for agriculture; but if the Ministry lets the aerodrome to a company for commercial flying, the company may be restrained by injunction from breaking the covenant.[76]

These are cases where private interests must suffer inevitably. But in many situations there is no such inevitability. If there is a choice of sites or methods, some of which will injure private rights and some of which will not, a public authority may have a duty to choose the latter. In each case the court has to consider whether Parliament presumably intended to permit the infringement. The presumption is that infringement is to be avoided unless reasonably necessary, and the onus of proving necessity is on the public authority.[77] In an early case where paving commissioners were empowered to carry out paving works as they should think fit, damages were awarded against them for raising a street so as to obstruct doors and windows, since they had acted, as Blackstone J said, 'arbitrarily and tyrannically'.[78]

A leading case was decided by the House of Lords under an Act which gave power to build hospitals in London for the benefit of the poor. A hospital was built at Hampstead for smallpox and other contagious diseases, and neighbouring residents obtained an injunction against it on the ground that, sited where it was, it was a nuisance.[79] The District Managers were unable to show that such a hospital in such a place was expressly or impliedly authorised by the Act: the Act gave no compulsory powers, it made no provision for compensation, and the inference was that it was not designed to permit interference with private rights. This principle may also apply even where the Act authorises a specific undertaking on a specific site. The Manchester Corporation was empowered to build and operate an electric power station on certain land outside the city, but this did not prevent a farmer from obtaining an injunction and damages on the ground that the Corporation had not used all reasonable diligence to prevent the creation of a nuisance by sulphurous fumes and contamination of grass.[80] Furthermore, the House of Lords held

---

from the running of trains (since the railway company was at liberty not to operate trains). See *Vaughan v. Taff Vale Rly Co* (1960) 5 H & N 679 and *Jones v. Festiniog Rly Co* (1868) LR 3 QB 733. But as the case now discussed shows, this distinction is no longer drawn.

[73] Below, p. 684.

[74] *Kirby v. Harrogate School Board* [1896] 1 Ch 437; *Re Simeon and Isle of Wight RDC* [1937] Ch 525; *Marten v. Flight Refuelling Ltd* [1962] Ch 115.   [75] Below, p. 682.

[76] *Marten v. Flight Refuelling Ltd* (above).   [77] See *Manchester Cpn v. Farnworth*, below.

[78] *Leader v. Moxton* (1773) 3 Wils KB 461.

[79] *Metropolitan Asylum District v. Hill* (1881) 6 App Cas 193; similarly *Fletcher v. Birkenhead Corporation* [1907] 1 KB 205 (local authority's waterworks pumped out silt from beneath plaintiff's house, causing subsidence); *Tate & Lyle Ltd v. Greater London Council* [1983] 2 AC 509 (power to construct ferry terminal does not justify adoption of a design which diverts silt to plaintiffs' jetty).

[80] *Manchester Cpn v. Farnworth* [1930] AC 171.

that the degree of nuisance which might have to be accepted as inevitable would vary with the state of scientific knowledge from time to time, so that the Corporation would have to keep abreast of the best current practice in this respect in order to discharge the onus lying upon them. Lord Dunedin said:[81]

> When Parliament has authorised a certain thing to be made or done in a certain place, there can be no action for nuisance caused by the making or doing of that thing if the nuisance is the inevitable result of the making or doing so authorised. The onus of proving that the result is inevitable is on those who wish to escape liability for nuisance, but the criterion of inevitability is not what is theoretically possible but what is possible according to the state of scientific knowledge at the time, having also in view a certain common sense appreciation, which cannot be rigidly defined, of practical feasibility in view of situation and of expense.

This 'criterion of inevitability' will depend in each case on the true implications of the empowering statute, and this may pose difficult questions of construction. A contrasting case concerned a river authority which, in dredging a river, deposited the spoil along the banks and thus raised their height. This prevented the river, when in flood, from overflowing into its usual flood channels, and the diversion of flood waters caused the collapse of a bridge belonging to the plaintiff. But the plaintiff failed in an action for nuisance, since it was held that the injury 'was clearly of a kind contemplated by the Act'.[82] The depositing of soil along river banks was a normal accompaniment of dredging, and if any owner of land which would be injured thereby could obtain an injunction, the river authority could in many cases be prevented from exercising its powers.[83] It was said also that there was an important distinction between powers to execute particular works (such as the building of power stations or hospitals) and powers to execute a variety of works of specified descriptions (such as river drainage works); and that the principle of avoiding injury to private rights, except where demonstrably necessary, applied only to the former.[84] But the decisive point was probably that the Land Drainage Act 1930 gave a right to compensation for injury done, with the implication that this was intended to be in substitution for the ordinary remedies of private law.

If a public authority commits an unauthorised nuisance, it is no defence that it is taking the most reasonable action possible in the public interest, or that the injury done is relatively unimportant in relation to the benefit to the public. Thus an injunction was granted at the instance of an angling club whose fishing rights in the river Derwent were injured by pollution from the sewage works of the Derby Corporation.[85] The Corporation had a statutory duty to provide a sewerage system and had originally provided an adequate one. But the growth of the city had overloaded it, and the Corporation had taken to discharging inadequately treated sewage into the river. The Court of Appeal rejected the argument that the Corporation's duty to act in the public interest gave it some sort of immunity from injunctions. The court did, however, suspend the operation of the injunction for sixteen months so as to give the Corporation reasonable time to make better arrangements.

---

[81] Ibid. at p. 183.

[82] *Marriage* v. *East Norfolk Rivers Catchment Board* [1950] 1 KB 284. Cf. *Lagan Navigation Co* v. *Lambeg Bleaching etc Co* [1927] AC 226.

[83] This argument, which recurs through the cases (e.g. in *Allen* v. *Gulf Oil Refining Ltd*, below, n. 425), may be fallacious, since injunction is a discretionary remedy which need not necessarily be granted in an action for damages at common law. See [1982] *CLJ* 87 (S. R. Tromans).

[84] *Marriage* at p. 307 (Jenkins LJ).

[85] *Pride of Derby and Derbyshire Angling Association Ltd* v. *British Celanese Ltd* [1953] Ch 149.

In the *Derby* case the Corporation itself caused the nuisance by discharging the effluent from its own plant. If it had reached the river merely by overflowing from the sewers, without any action on the Corporation's part, the Corporation would have done nothing to incur liability. This situation arose at Ilford through sewage overflowing through a manhole, due to the growth of the population and the overloading of what was previously an adequate sewerage system. A householder whose premises were flooded failed in an action for nuisance, since the Corporation themselves had committed no unlawful act.[86] This has nothing to do with the distinction between misfeasance and nonfeasance, mentioned below.[87] The point is simply that the cause of the injury is not any act of the Corporation but the use of the sewers by other people whom the Corporation has no power to prevent. If the overflow had been caused by a housing estate built by the Corporation, the result might have been different.[88] The Corporation would also have been liable if they had diverted the overflow from one man's land to another's, even though that minimised the injury.[89] For their failure to provide a more adequate sewage system there is only the statutory remedy of complaint to the minister.[90] The Public Health Act 1936 provides for compensation for injury caused by the exercise of powers of this kind;[91] but the exercise of some power must be the cause of the injury.

That Act, like many other Acts, used to contain an express 'nuisance clause' providing that the local authority shall not create a nuisance.[92] Clauses of this kind may be interpreted as excluding strict liability, i.e. liability without fault, under the rule in *Rylands* v. *Fletcher* in case of accidents caused by the escape of noxious things such as sewage or gas,[93] if indeed that rule applies at all to statutory authorities providing public services (see below). A provision that an authority shall not create a nuisance, or shall not be exonerated from liability for nuisance, does not affect its non-liability for nuisances inevitably resulting from the performance of its duties and the exercise of its powers.[94]

A public authority which itself deliberately creates a nuisance cannot escape liability by pleading that it was acting outside its powers.[95] But unauthorised action by its servants or agents, if outside the powers of the authority, might well be outside the scope of their employment. The principle of vicarious liability, explained below with reference to negligence, applies equally to nuisance and other torts.

The grant of planning permission, for example to build a factory, under the Town and Country Planning Acts confers no right to commit nuisances or to infringe private rights.[96] The scheme of the planning legislation is 'to restrict development for the benefit of the public at large and not to confer new rights on any individual members of

---

[86] *Smeaton v. Ilford Cpn* [1954] Ch 450. Confirmed in *Marcic* v. *Thames Water Utilities Ltd* [2003] 3 WLR 1603 (HL), paras. 55–6 (Lord Hoffmann). But see now *Dobson and ors* v. *Thames Water Utilities Ltd (No 2)* [2011] EWHC 3253 where the claimants were in part successful applying the qualification to *Allen* v. *Gulf Oil Refining Ltd* [1981] AC 1001. Discussed below, p. 684.   [87] Below, p. 658.

[88] See the *Smeaton* case at 463.   [89] See ibid. at 465.   [90] See above, p. 629.

[91] s. 278.

[92] s. 31 (now repealed). See *Radstock Co-operative Society Ltd* v. *Norton-Radstock Urban District Council* [1968] Ch 605.

[93] See *Smeaton* v. *Ilford Cpn* (above) and cases there cited. For the rule in *Rylands* v. *Fletcher* see below, p. 659.

[94] See Public Utilities Street Works Act 1950 as applied in *Department of Transport* v. *North West Water Authority* [1984] AC 336.   [95] *Campbell* v. *Paddington Cpn* [1911] 1 KB 869.

[96] *Buxton* v. *Minister of Housing and Local Government* [1961] 1 QB 278 (Salmon J), from which the quotation comes (at 283). See *Wheeler* v. *JJ Saunders Ltd* [1996] Ch 19 (malodorous pig farm not justified by planning permission); *Delyn BC* v. *Solitaire (Liverpool) Ltd* (1995) 93 LGR 614 (planning permission for market does not authorise infringement of council's market rights).

the public, whether they live close to or far from the proposed development'. Planning permission merely removes a statutory impediment, and thus *pro tanto* restores to the successful applicant the liberty to develop his own property, subject to the rights of his neighbours, which he would otherwise enjoy at common law. But there may be some 'interplay between planning permission and the law of nuisance', since planning permission for a major development may lead to a change in the character of a neighbourhood and so alter the standard of amenity by which nuisance must be judged.

This factor was decisive in a case where the local authority had granted planning permission for the operation of a commercial port, which necessarily involved heavy lorry traffic at night and disturbance to neighbours, and later sued on their behalf in nuisance. The claim was held to fail when judged 'by reference to the present character of the neighbourhood pursuant to the planning permission', despite the undoubted disturbance.[97] By observing that Parliament had delegated to the local planning authority the task of balancing the competing interests the judge seemed to imply that the planning permission legitimated the nuisance, but he stressed also the change in the character of the neighbourhood which should probably have been the sole criterion. There is a danger of confusing public policy with private interests in a doctrine which 'would transform a matter of legal right into one of administrative decision making',[98] and 'the court should be slow to acquiesce' in it.[99] It is unlikely that Parliament would have intended to authorise planning authorities to inflict uncompensated injury to the private rights of citizens.

A local authority may be liable in nuisance for failing to remove gipsies from its land[100] or for their depredations on the land of neighbours,[101] and for allowing trees in the highway to cause the subsidence of a neighbouring house.[102]

NEGLIGENCE

NEGLIGENCE AND PUBLIC AUTHORITIES—BASIC PRINCIPLES

The law governing the liability of public authorities for the tort of negligence is confusing unless some basic principles are kept constantly in mind.[103]

In the first place, negligence is a common law cause of action. For a claimant to succeed in such an action against a public authority, he or she will need to establish all the elements of the tort that would have to be established if a private body or person was being sued.[104] The only significant difference is that 'a common law duty of care may arise in the

---

[97] *Gillingham BC* v. *Medway (Chatham) Dock Co Ltd* [1993] QB 343, from which the quotation comes.

[98] Pill LJ in *Hunter* v. *Canary Wharf Ltd* [1987] AC 655 at 668, where the question is discussed in the Court of Appeal, rejecting the relevance of planning permission, but not in the House of Lords.

[99] Peter Gibson LJ in the *Wheeler* case, above. See also *Ports of Auckland Ltd* v. *Auckland City Council* [1999] 1 NZLR 601, not following 'the bungle of the *Gillingham* case'.

[100] *Page Motors Ltd* v. *Epsom BC* (1981) 80 LGR 337.

[101] *Lippiatt* v. *South Gloucestershire Council* [2000] 1 QB 51.

[102] *Russell* v. *Barnet LBC* (1984) 83 LGR 152.

[103] The law has been much clarified by Lord Browne-Wilkinson's luminous speech in *X (minors)* v. *Bedfordshire CC* [1995] 2 AC 633, [1995] 3 WLR 152 (HL) which is discussed more fully below and from which much of what follows is drawn. See Booth and Squires, *The Negligence Liability of Public Authorities* (2006).

[104] These elements being that the claimant should have suffered actionable damage (generally not pure economic loss) as a result of the defendant breaching a duty of care owed to the claimant. Whether there was a duty of care is determined by precedent and, in novel cases, by whether the harm was reasonably foreseeable,

performance of statutory functions',[105] and thus to decide whether such a common law duty arises requires consideration of the statutory context. Most importantly, 'a common law duty of care cannot be imposed on a statutory duty if the observance of such common law duty of care would be inconsistent with, or have a tendency to discourage, the due performance by the local authority of its statutory duties.'[106]

Second, a public authority cannot be held liable for doing what Parliament has authorised. So when a discretionary power is exercised and causes harm the question arises whether that harm was authorised by the statute, or whether it fell outside the scope of the authorisation. In determining this question the carelessness of the authority in exercising its power will come under consideration, for a sufficiently careless exercise will take the authority outside the protection of the statute. On the other hand, where the decision involves a question of policy it will generally fall within the area of authorisation and liability will not be imposed. Deciding these questions raise subtle and difficult issues to be discussed below.[107] Of course, even where the authority is careless and the matter does not fall within the 'policy immunity' the claimant may fail if some other element of the tort of negligence (for instance, proximity) is absent.

Third, the word 'negligence' is often used when the word 'carelessness' is more apt, and this can confuse. To say that a defendant is 'negligent' in its performance of a statutory duty does not mean that, without more, it will be liable for any damage that may be caused. There is no common law duty of care (establishing the tort of negligence) consequent upon simple 'carelessness', but the use of the word 'negligence' in this context can suggest otherwise.[108]

Fourth, the normal principles of vicarious liability generally apply.[109] So public authorities are liable for the torts of their employees committed in the course of their employment in the same way that private employers are.

VICARIOUS LIABILITY OF PUBLIC AUTHORITIES

The liability of statutory bodies for the negligence of their servants and agents, acting within the scope of their employment, was firmly established by the House of Lords in 1866. The plaintiff's ship had been damaged by hitting a mudbank which the harbour board's employees had negligently allowed to block the entrance of one of the docks. It was held that public bodies created by statute must in principle bear the same liabilities for the torts of their servants as were borne by private employers, subject only to any contrary statute.[110] The fact that the public body was acting solely for the public benefit and for no profit was immaterial. Nor was there any room for the defence that employer and employee were all alike holders of public offices with no vicarious liability. This argument

---

whether the relationship between the parties was sufficiently 'proximate' and whether the imposition of a duty of care was in the circumstances 'fair, just and reasonable'. See *Caparo Industries plc* v. *Dickman* [1990] 2 AC 605 (HL) at 617–18 (Lord Bridge). New duties of care in novel situations are developed 'incrementally and by analogy with established categories [of liability]' (*Murphy* v. *Brentwood DC* [1991] 1 AC 398 at 461 (Lord Keith)) rather than by the application of abstract principle.

[105]   *X (minors)*, Lord Browne-Wilkinson at 169H. The mere breach of a statutory duty does not comprise the tort of negligence, although it may amount to the separate tort of breach of statutory duty (discussed below).   [106]   Ibid., Lord Browne-Wilkinson at 173E.

[107]   At p. 651.

[108]   See the detailed discussion by Lord Browne-Wilkinson in *X (minors)* at 166–9.

[109]   But see the discussion below, p. 647 for a qualification to this.

[110]   *Mersey Docks and Harbour Board Trustees* v. *Gibbs* (1866) LR 1 HL 93.

exonerates an intermediate employee in a hierarchy such as the civil service.[111] But it cannot exonerate the true employer. In a later case Lord Blackburn stated:[112]

> It is now thoroughly well established that no action will lie for doing that which the legislature has authorised, if it be done without negligence, although it does occasion damage to anyone; but an action does lie for doing what the legislature has authorised, if it be done negligently.

This was a case where a reservoir company had statutory power to make use of a certain stream but neglected to clean it out, so that their use of it caused flooding and made them liable.

The principle that public authorities are vicariously liable for their employees in the same way as private employers is qualified in one respect. If the authority is not directly liable because the decision in question falls within the 'policy immunity', as explained above, then 'to recognise such a vicarious liability on the part of the authority may so interfere with the performance of [its] duties that it would be wrong to recognise any liability on the part of the authority'.[113] But Lord Slynn has said that it is for the local authority to establish this and 'the circumstances where it could be established would be exceptional'.[114] Even though individual employees will exercise discretion in the implementation of their employer's policy, that discretion is likely to be towards the operational end of the spectrum.

It is open to doubt, however, whether there is vicarious liability for exemplary damages awarded against the tortfeasor.[115]

EXAMPLES OF PUBLIC AUTHORITIES HELD LIABLE FOR THE TORT OF NEGLIGENCE: SOME ILLUSTRATIVE EXAMPLES

There are infinite varieties of actionable negligence, an account of which belongs to the law of tort. But the courts have extended the principle of liability to certain acts of public authorities which are of a peculiarly governmental character.[116]

In 1970 the House of Lords held the Crown (the Home Office) liable for damage done by escaping Borstal boys. These were boys with criminal records who had been taken out on a training exercise in charge of Borstal officers who had instructions to keep them in custody but who neglected to do so; they escaped and damaged a yacht, the owner of which was the successful plaintiff.[117] Despite the novel nature of the claim, and the contention that there was no liability for the acts of persons other than servants or agents, it was held that the custody of these dangerous boys imposed a duty to take reasonable care that they

---

[111] See below, p. 693. [112] *Geddis* v. *Proprietors of Bann Reservoir* (1873) 3 App Cas 430 at 455.

[113] *Phelps*, below, n. 150, at 790 (Lord Slynn). [114] Ibid.

[115] See *Kuddus* v. *CC of Leicestershire* [2001] 2 WLR 1789 (HL) (case of misfeasance not negligence) where the question was left open by Lords Slynn, Mackay and Nicholls, but Lord Scott was firmly opposed, while the principle was generally favoured by Lord Hutton. In *Rowlands* v. *The Chief Constable of Merseyside Police* [2006] EWCA Civ 1773 (para. 47) Moore-Bick LJ said 'that it is desirable as a matter of policy that the courts should be able to make punitive awards against those who are vicariously liable for the conduct of their subordinates'.

[116] See [1973] *PL* 84 (G. Ganz); (1976) 92 *LQR* 213, (1978) 94 *LQR* 428 (P. P. Craig).

[117] *Dorset Yacht Co Ltd* v. *Home Office* [1970] AC 1004 (discussed further below). See similarly *Whannel* v. *Secretary of State for Scotland*, 1989 SLT 907 (attack by Borstal boy on prisoner). On the comparable French law, which now extends to prisoners released on licence, see (1969) 27 *CLJ* 273 (C. J. Hamson) and [1987] *PL* 465.

could not injure the public. This was an application of the doctrine of the law of tort that a duty of care arises from a relationship of proximity where the damage done is the natural and probable result of the breach of duty. In this decision the House of Lords took a noteworthy step towards spreading over the whole community the price that has to be paid for experimental penal policies, rather than requiring it to be borne by the individual victim. In the same way a local authority was held liable for negligent custody of a boy, known to be an incendiary, who escaped and burned down a church.[118] The police may be liable for negligently allowing confidential information to be stolen if this results in injury to another person.[119] On the other hand, a health authority was not liable for the abuse and murder of a child by an outpatient at a hospital maintained by the authority as the damage was insufficiently proximate.[120]

PARTICULAR SITUATIONS: MISLEADING ADVICE

Liability for negligence in administrative office work is illustrated by a planning case in which a government department successfully sued a local authority for damages.[121] A clerk of the local authority had carelessly overlooked a compensation notice entered in the local land charges register, so that it failed to operate against a later purchaser of the land affected; and accordingly, when planning permission was granted and the compensation paid for a previous refusal should have been repayable, the ministry were unable to recover it.

It seems this last case should be considered an example of the tort of negligent misstatement, for which damages are recoverable where the plaintiff justifiably relied upon the misstatement.[122] That tort is now proving important as a head of government liability, particularly in connection with misleading official advice, the problems of which were explained earlier.[123] It has enabled a firm to recover damages from a government department which wrongly advised them that they were covered by export credit insurance against default by a foreign company;[124] and purchasers of land to recover damages from local authorities who overlooked proposals for a subway[125] and for road widening[126] in

---

[118] Writtle (vicar) v. Essex CC (1979) 77 LGR 656.

[119] Swinney v. Chief Constable of Northumbria Police (No 2) (1999) 11 Admin LR 811 (informer's identity shown by papers stolen from locked car but no negligence found).

[120] Palmer v. Tees HA (2000) 2 LGLR 69 (CA).

[121] Ministry of Housing and Local Government v. Sharp [1970] 2 QB 223. But an official whose decisions are subject to appeal owes no duty of care: Jones v. Department of Employment [1989] QB 1 (social security adjudication officer). Statutory defences against personal liability were given by Land Charges Act 1972, s. 10(6) and Local Land Charges Act 1975, s. 10(6).

[122] Recognised by the House of Lords in Hedley Byrne & Co Ltd v. Heller & Partners Ltd [1964] AC 465 and applied by the Court of Appeal in Esso Petroleum Co Ltd v. Mardon [1976] QB 801.

[123] Above, p. 281.

[124] Culford Metal Industries Ltd v. Export Credits Guarantee Dept. The Times, 25 March 1981. Other examples are Windsor Motors Ltd v. District of Powell River (1969) 4 DLR (3d) 155 (municipality liable for negligence of inspector who recommended a car dealer to rent a site on which his business was forbidden by zoning byelaws); Jung v. District of Burnaby (1978) 91 DLR (3d) 592 (negligent misstatement about fire regulations); Christchurch Drainage Board v. Brown The Times, 26 October 1987 (drainage board failed to warn applicant for building permit of flood danger); Meates v. A-G [1983] NZLR 308 (government liable for negligent assurances about future subsidies to industry). A disclaimer of liability may be effective: Hadden v. Glasgow DC, 1986 SLT 557; Vaughan v. Edinburgh DC, 1988 SLT 191.

[125] Coats Patons (Retail) Ltd v. Birmingham Cpn (1971) 69 LGR 356 (disclaimer of liability held ineffective).

[126] Shaddock & Associates Pty Ltd v. Parramatta City Council (1981) 36 ALR 385, where Gibbs CJ and Stephen J held that the duty of care extends to public bodies which make a practice of supplying information. See likewise Bell v. City of Sarnia (1987) 37 DLR (4th) 438.

answering planning enquiries. Claims for loss caused by negligent mortgage valuations have also succeeded,[127] as have claims against district auditors by local authorities.[128] The principle has been extended to planning authorities who negligently grant invalid planning permissions under which the developer later suffers loss,[129] or valid permissions where the right to object is negligently denied to a neighbour.[130] At this point the cases merge with those of negligent discretionary decisions, discussed in the following section. They may be noted also as examples of actionable negligence causing economic loss only, as the House of Lords has recognised in its important decision noted below.[131]

CARELESS INSPECTION AND CONTROLS

There was for a time, following a Court of Appeal decision in 1971 approved by the House of Lords in 1978, an extensive liability on public authorities who carelessly carried out their duties to inspect buildings.[132] The Court held a local council liable in damages for the careless inspection and passing of the defective foundations of a house, at the instance of a later purchaser. The builder sold the house to a purchaser who then sold it to the plaintiff, who found that it subsided badly, and sued the council for the cost of repair and loss of value. After various attempts to limit the wide duties of care so unexpectedly thrust upon local authorities, a special House of seven law lords in 1990 abandoned their former position and overruled their earlier decision as well as several others.[133]

In this case the local council had referred the plans of a house to consulting engineers, who had culpably failed to see their defects.[134] Twelve years later cracks appeared in the walls and foundations and the owner sold the house at a loss. His action to recover the loss from the council was dismissed by the House of Lords. It was held that it was wrong, as a matter of policy, to impose liability for pure economic loss resulting from the negligent passing of the plans. It was not decided, however, whether negligence in administering building regulations or byelaws might entail liability in case of personal injury or impaired health or damage to some different property. The overruling of the earlier House of Lords decision has relieved local authorities of much the greater part of the novel liability created by that decision. It indicates also the House of Lords' preference for developing the categories of negligence 'incrementally by analogy with established categories' rather than by 'massive extension of a prima facie duty of care',[135] and their

---

[127] *Westlake v. Bracknell DC* [1987] 1 EGLR 161; *Harris v. Wyre Forest DC* [1990] 1 AC 831 (disclaimer of liability held ineffective under Unfair Contract Terms Act 1977).

[128] *West Wiltshire DC v. Garland* [1995] Ch 297. There was also liability for breach of statutory duty (below, p. 661).   [129] *Lambert v. West Devon Borough Council* (1997) 96 LGR 45.

[130] *Craig v. East Coast Bays City Council* [1986] 1 NZLR 99 (breach of authority's duty, based on proximity, to notify neighbour whose view was spoiled: damages awarded).

[131] *Murphy v. Brentwood DC*, below.

[132] *Dutton v. Bognor Regis UDC* [1972] 1 QB 373. The House of Lords decided similarly in *Anns v. Merton LBC* [1978] AC 728. *Anns* was followed in Canada (*Kamloops v. Nielsen* [1984] 10 DLR (4th) 641, S Ct) and New Zealand (*Invercargill City Council v. Hamlin* [1996] AC 624). In Australia it was at first rejected (*Sutherland Shire Council v. Heyman* (1985) 60 ALR 1) but the High Court later changed direction (*Bryan v. Maloney* (1995) 69 ALJR 375). In the *Invercargill* case the Privy Council recognised that the common law might vary in different jurisdictions.

[133] *Murphy v. Brentwood DC* [1991] 1 AC 398. For discussion and criticism see [1991] *CLJ* 58 (D. Howarth).

[134] The Court of Appeal held the council responsible for the engineers' negligence [1991] 1 AC at 407, 435) but the House of Lords did not decide that question (see at 472, Lord Keith).

[135] Quotations from Brennan J in the *Sutherland Shire Council* case above.

recognition of the merits of a pragmatic policy in an area where general principles are elusive and indefinable. It does not affect established categories of liability for economic loss, either in ordinary cases of careless damage to property or in special cases such as those of the escaping Borstal boys or cases of negligent misstatement, as discussed above, or other cases where 'a special relationship of proximity' exists, usually involving 'an element of reliance'.[136]

NEGLIGENT DISCRETIONARY DECISIONS: INVALIDITY OF THE DECISION NOT THE TOUCHSTONE OF LIABILITY

In holding the Home Office liable for the negligent custody of Borstal boys, as explained above, the House of Lords related the degree of carelessness to the degree of unreasonableness which will render a discretionary decision ultra vires. Lord Reid put this as follows:[137]

> When Parliament confers a discretion... there may, and almost certainly will, be errors of judgment in exercising such a discretion and Parliament cannot have intended that members of the public should be entitled to sue in respect of such errors. But there must come a stage when the discretion is exercised so carelessly or unreasonably that there has been no real exercise of the discretion which Parliament has conferred. The person exercising the discretion has acted in abuse or excess of his power. Parliament cannot be supposed to have granted immunity to persons who do that. The present case does not raise the issue because no discretion was given to these Borstal officers. They were given orders which they negligently failed to carry out.

The same point was made by Lord Wilberforce when he said that 'in the case of a power, liability cannot exist unless the act complained of lies outside the ambit of the power'.[138] But it is difficult to see how these statements amount to more than the truism that what is done within the limits of statutory authority is not actionable. They do not supply an answer to the difficult question, which is how far into the concentric circles of authority should legal liability penetrate.

They have since been justly criticised by Lord Browne-Wilkinson, saying that it is neither helpful nor necessary to introduce public law concepts as to the validity of a decision into the question of liability at common law for negligence.[139] The real problem is not whether the act of the public authority is valid or invalid, but whether it falls within the scope of the statutory authorisation. And Lord Slynn remarked in another case that the acts of the authority 'may amount to an excess of power, but that is not in my opinion the test to be adopted: the test is whether the conditions [for negligence] have been satisfied'.[140]

---

[136] See *Murphy* v. *Brentwood DC* (above) at 481 (Lord Bridge).

[137] *Dorset Yacht Co*, above, at 1031. See also 1068–9 (Lord Diplock); 1037 (Lord Morris). And see the *Writtle* case, above, p. 648.   [138] *Anns* v. *Merton LBC* [1978] AC 728 at 758.

[139] See the *X (minors)* case, below, p. 651 at 736.

[140] *Barrett*, below, at 572C and see Lord Hutton at 586D–E. See further Price, above, 147–9 calling this the abandonment of the 'public law hurdle'.

NEGLIGENT DISCRETIONARY DECISIONS:
THE POLICY-OPERATIONAL DISTINCTION

A more serviceable criterion may be found in the distinction, also made by Lord Wilberforce,[141] between 'the area of policy or discretion', where there is a choice of courses of action, and 'the operational area' where a chosen course of action is carried out, saying that 'the more "operational" a power or duty may be, the easier it is to superimpose upon it a common law duty of care'.[142] Taking an example from a well-known American case, he pointed to the difference between a decision whether or not to build a lighthouse and a failure, after one had been built, to keep the light in working order.[143] Lord Grieve in the Court of Session said similarly that the duty of care in exercising a statutory power 'does not arise until the discretionary stage of its exercise has ceased and the executive stage has begun'.[144]

The distinction between policy and operations has not always proved straightforward to apply and while not the 'touchstone of liability',[145] it does provide helpful guidance. Lord Browne-Wilkinson in X (minors) expressed the current principle in these words:[146]

> Where Parliament has conferred a statutory discretion on a public authority, it is for that authority, not for the courts, to exercise the discretion: nothing which the authority does within the ambit of the discretion can be actionable at common law. If the decision complained of falls outside the statutory discretion, it *can* (but not necessarily will) give rise to common law liability. However, if the factors relevant to the exercise of the discretion include matters of policy, the court cannot adjudicate on such policy matters and therefore cannot reach the conclusion that the decision was outside the ambit of the statutory discretion. Therefore a common law duty of care in relation to the taking of decisions involving policy matters cannot exist.

This dictum makes clear that policy is vital to the judicial task in considering whether there is a duty of care in the context of a statutory discretion.[147] Where policy plays a significant role in the exercise of the discretion, the matter will be considered within the statutory authorisation. But where policy is absent, i.e. the matter lies towards the operational end of the spectrum, liability may follow if all the other elements of the tort are established.

The sort of decisions that will fall within the policy immunity are ministers' decisions on such matters as the allocation of scarce resources or the distribution of risks. These are altogether unsuitable for actions in negligence.[148] To these may be added the decisions of regulators who must choose between intervention 'with immediate and probably disastrous effect' and non-intervention based on hopes of recovery.[149] As Lord

---

[141] *Anns* v. *Merton LBC* (above), at 754. The distinction was described as 'promising' and 'a guide' in deciding whether the issue is justifiable in *Barrett* v. *Enfield LBC* (below) (Lord Slynn, 567) discussed below, p. 655.

[142] For criticism see [1986] *CLJ* 430 (S. H. Bailey and M. J. Bowman) and the speeches of Lord Hoffmann in *Stovin* v. *Wise* [1996] AC 923 and of Lord Browne-Wilkinson in *X (minors)* v. *Bedfordshire CC* [1995] 2 AC 633.   [143] *Indian Towing Co* v. *US* (1955) 350 US 61.

[144] *Bonthrone* v. *Secretary of State for Scotland* (1981) reported in 1987 SLT 34 (no liability for alleged official negligence in encouraging vaccination of infants without adequate warning of risk).

[145] *Rowling* v. *Takaro Properties Ltd* [1988] AC 473 at 501 (Lord Keith).   [146] At 172–3.

[147] Policy decisions 'involve the weighing of competing public interests' or are otherwise non-justiciable (Lord Slynn in Phelps at 653A–B).   [148] Citing Craig, *Administrative Law*, 1st edn, 534–8.

[149] *Yuen Kun Yeu* v. *A-G of Hong Kong* [1988] AC 175. And see *Davis* v. *Radcliffe* [1990] 1 WLR 821, emphasising the delicacy and difficulty of such decisions, militating against the imposition of a duty of care. See also *Minories Finance Ltd* v. *Young* [1989] 2 All ER 105 (Bank of England not liable for failure to supervise collapsed bank).

Browne-Wilkinson has said 'the courts should proceed with great care before holding liable in negligence those who have been charged by Parliament with the task of protecting society from the wrongdoing of others'.[150]

The court in determining whether there is a common law duty of care in any particular case will, of course, have close regard to the statutory context in which the matter arises. But two points may be noted in this context. The first concerns the relationship between the tort of breach of statutory duty[151] and the common law duty of care in the context of a statutory discretion. The cases establish that where 'no private law claim will lie for breach of statutory duty, a claim in negligence will rarely, if ever, lie where the carelessness relied upon is merely the failure to perform the statutory duty'.[152] Second, the way in which public authority implements its duties in practice may amount to an assumption of responsibility and so assist in the recognition of a common law duty of care.[153] A relationship between claimant and defendant may establish a common law duty of care even where there is no private law breach of statutory duty.

THE LIABILITY, DIRECT AND VICARIOUS, OF LOCAL AUTHORITIES FOR DISCRETIONARY DECISIONS IN THE FIELD OF CHILD WELFARE AND EDUCATION

X (minors) concerned several alleged breaches by local authorities of their duties to children. And to each case the principles just discussed were applied. The lead case concerned allegations that the council had failed to protect certain children against child abuse. Many reports of abuse and neglect of the children were made by the police, the family's GP and the head teacher to the county council, but little was done to protect the children (although eventually they were taken into foster care). The relevant legislation provided that when intervention by the local authority 'was necessary in the interests of the welfare of the child, it shall be the duty of the local authority to receive the child into their care'.[154] Lord Browne-Wilkinson concluded that 'the task of the local authority was...extraordinarily delicate' with conflicting considerations tugging it in different directions. After a full analysis of all the relevant statutes he concluded that a 'common law duty of care would cut across the whole statutory scheme for the protection of children at risk'. The children's action failed. One of the other cases concerned a claim by a child who had suffered from an erroneous decision by a social worker that the child was being abused by her mother's co habitee and so had to be removed from the home. The action based on the council's vicarious liability for the negligence of the social worker also failed. The social worker advised the council, not the claimant, and had assumed no responsibility to her.[155] These two cases, with the council facing action whatever it did, illustrate why a bona fide

---

[150] X (minors) v. Bedfordshire CC [1995] 2 AC 633 at 751, discussing and supporting the Privy Council's decision. See also Harris v. Evans [1998] 1 WLR 1285 (no liability for Health and Safety Executive's notice prohibiting bungee jumping). Cf. Phelps v. Hillingdon LBC [2001] 2 AC 618 (liability in particular circumstances for educational psychologist's failure to diagnose dyslexia), discussed below, p. 661.

[151] Discussed below, p. 660.

[152] Carty v. Croydon LBC [2005] EWCA Civ 19, [2005] 1 WLR 2312, para. 21 (Dyson LJ) following Gorringe v. Calderdale Metropolitan Borough Council [2004] UKHL 15, [2004] 1 WLR 1057 (council's duty to 'promote road safety' (Highways Act 1988, s. 39) did not give claimant private law right of action for breach of statutory duty, and so a duty of care in negligence could not be created by that duty alone; failure to paint 'Slow' on road at dangerous point did not found an action). See particularly Lord Scott, para. 71 and Lord Hoffmann, para. 32. See also (2011) 127 LQR 260 (Nolan).

[153] See Lord Browne-Wilkinson in X (minors) at 170A.　　　　[154] Child Care Act 1980, s. 2(2).

[155] A point on which Lord Nolan dissented.

decision whether to intervene or not to intervene, will rarely found a common law action for negligence.[156]

The final group of cases concerned the local authorities' duties in regard to the education of children with special needs, including dyslexia. The allegations in the several cases were that the councils had failed to diagnose the relevant learning disorder and failed to refer the child to an educational psychologist. As in the child abuse cases, the court found that the aim of the Education Act 1981 (which provided for the education of children with special educational needs) 'was to provide for the benefit of society as a whole an administrative machinery to help one disadvantaged section of society. The statute provides its own detailed machinery for securing that the statutory purpose is performed. If, despite [this] the scheme fails to provide the benefit intended that is a matter... [for the] Ombudsman.' Thus there was no common law duty of care.[157]

If claimants were generally disappointed by the outcome in *X (minors)*, they have enjoyed some success since, as the principles laid down have been applied. In one case a 17-year-old claimant, who had been in local authority care for most of his life, claimed that the council had failed to protect him from physical, emotional, psychiatric and psychological injury in several ways. The House of Lords distinguished between cases (such as *X (minors)*) where the decision was whether to take a child into care and the treatment of a child already in care.[158] In respect of the latter there could be a common law duty of care. The claimant's claim was not struck out.

In another leading case the claimant sought to hold the educational authority vicariously liable for the negligence of an educational psychologist in failing to diagnose her dyslexia (which was subsequently diagnosed privately). The conduct of the psychologist fell towards the operational end of the spectrum and, moreover, the fact that the psychologist owed a duty to the council did not mean that no duty was owed to the child.[159] As adumbrated in *X (minors)* there might be a common law duty in these circumstances. The claimant's claim was not struck out.

NEGLIGENT DISCRETIONARY DECISIONS: FURTHER ILLUSTRATIVE EXAMPLES

Two cases illustrate the policy–operational distinction. A chief constable was held not liable in negligence for not equipping his force with a particular CS gas device which might have avoided damage to the plaintiff's shop (this was a policy decision); but he was liable for failing to have fire-fighting equipment on hand when the use of a more dangerous CS gas device set the shop on fire (this was an operational decision).[160] On a motion to strike out pleadings

---

[156] But as pointed out elsewhere (p. 662) the common law here laid down may be eclipsed by the Human Rights Act 1998; see Price, above, at 161–2 and the statements to that effect in the Court of Appeal *East Berkshire* case, above, para. 85 (Lord Phillips MR).

[157] In one of the education cases there was more success for the claimant. Here the allegation was that the headmaster and teaching advisers (including educational psychologists) had failed properly to advise him. There was no incompatibility between the statutory scheme and such a duty, and so the appeal against a refusal to strike out was dismissed. See *X (minors)* at 196 distinguishing between the educational psychologist in the education cases and doctors and social workers in the child abuse cases.

[158] *Barrett* v. *Enfield LBC* [2001] 2 AC 550 (HL). The bar on a child suing its parents for negligence did not apply to a local authority. [159] *Phelps* v. *Hillingdon LBC* [2001] 2 AC 618.

[160] *Rigby* v. *Chief Constable of Northamptonshire* [1985] 1 WLR 1242 (police siege of gunsmith's shop occupied by violent psychopath). See similarly *Minister for Administering Environmental Planning* v. *San Sebastian Pty Ltd* [1983] 2 NSWLR 268 (no state liability for negligently prepared development plan); *Sasin* v. *Commonwealth of Australia* [1984] 52 ALR 299 (government not liable for approval of design of aircraft

it was held that the government could not be liable for adopting a policy of immunisation against whooping cough, but could be liable for careless or misleading advice about the performance of inoculations.[161] Failure to act on inspectors' reports of an airline's breaches of safety regulations in Canada rendered the government liable for deaths in an air crash, since this was clearly operational negligence.[162]

On the other hand the House of Lords predictably dismissed an action by the mother of a girl murdered by the 'Yorkshire ripper', based on allegations of negligence in the efforts of the police to capture him, since the police owed no duty of care to individual members of the public in such circumstances.[163] It was held also that in the investigation and suppression of crime the police are immune on grounds of public policy from actions for negligence, except where there is a special degree of proximity. Even when the victim of a savage attack had informed the police of the repeated threats of violence made to him by his ex-partner and had provided all his ex-partner's contact details so the police could intervene, he did not recover when the police failed to protect him.[164]

When the Court of Appeal treated this qualified immunity as absolute, and struck out a claim by the victim of a mentally deranged teacher, the European Court of Human Rights

---

seat belt). Contrast *Just* v. *The Queen in right of British Columbia* (1989) 64 DLR (4th) 689 (highway inspection system 'operational': injury caused by rockfall may ground action for damages).

[161] *Department of Health and Social Security* v. *Kinnear*, The Times, 7 July 1984; and see *Ross* v. *Secretary of State for Scotland*, 1990 SLT 13 (policy of vaccination not challengeable).

[162] *Swanson* v. *The Queen in right of Canada* (1991) 80 DLR (4th) 741. And see *Brewer Bros* v. *The Queen in right of Canada* (1991) 80 DLR (4th) 321 (failure to take adequate security from grain elevator company: government liable for financial loss on company's bankruptcy). Contrast *Philcox* v. *Civil Aviation Authority* The Times, 8 June 1995 (claim for negligent inspection of aircraft failed).

[163] *Hill* v. *Chief Constable of West Yorkshire* [1989] AC 53. See also *Elguzouli-Daf* v. *Commissioner of Police of the Metropolis* [1995] QB 335 (Crown Prosecution Service: no duty of care); *Kinsella* v. *Chief Constable of Nottinghamshire* The Times, 24 August 1999 (property damaged during search: immunity upheld). Contrast *Costello* v. *Chief Constable of Northumbria Police* [1999] 1 All ER 550 (immunity negated by assumed responsibility). The police owe no duty of care in disciplinary investigations: *Calveley* v. *Chief Constable of Merseyside* [1989] AC 1228. The public policy that justifies absolute immunity in regard to evidence given by police officers and others in court, does not extend to wrongdoing, such as fabrication of evidence, in the course of investigation: *Darker* v. *Chief Constable of the West Midlands Police* [2001] 1 AC 435 (HL). The House of Lords has held in *Brooks* v. *Commissioner of the Metropolitan Police* [2005] UKHL 24, [2005] 1 WLR 1495, para. 30 (Lord Steyn) that: 'the core principle of *Hill* has remained unchallenged in our domestic jurisprudence and in European jurisprudence for many years. If a case such as the Yorkshire Ripper case...arose for decision today I have no doubt that it would be decided in the same way.' But their Lordships indicated that the breadth of the immunity in *Hill* might be reviewed in later cases. The continuing correctness of *Hill* was again affirmed in the House of Lords in *Smith* v. *Chief Constable of Sussex Police* heard with *Hertfordshire Police* v. *Van Colle* [2008] UKHL 50. The *Hill* immunity was based upon several heads of public policy of which the most important were 'first...that the existence of a duty of care would alter, detrimentally, the manner in which the police performed their duties in as much as they would act defensively out of apprehension of the risk of legal proceedings. [And] second that time and resources would have to be devoted to meeting claims brought against the police which could better be directed to their primary duties' (para. 89 (Lord Phillips)). Lord Bingham, dissenting, while upholding *Hill* held that where 'a member of the public (A) furnishes a police officer (B) with apparently credible evidence that a third party whose identity and whereabouts are known presents a specific and imminent threat to his life or physical safety, B owes A a duty to take reasonable steps to assess such threat and, if appropriate, take reasonable steps to prevent it being executed' (para. 44). *Hill* has not been followed in several other jurisdictions (*Carmichele* v. *Minister of Safety and Security* (2001) 12 BHRC 60 (South Africa) and *Odhavji Estate* v. *Woodhouse and ors* [2003] 3 SCR 263 (Canada); cf. *Sullivan* v. *Moody* [2002] LRC 251 (Australia)). See also *Desmond* v. *Chief Constable* [2011] EWCA Civ 3 (no duty of care owed by CC to individual applying for an enhanced criminal record certificate under the Police Act 1997 (CC fulfilling statutory duty not undertaking something he was not obliged to do)). [164] *Smith*, above.

found, in a decision, which has since been several times disapproved,[165] that the right to a fair trial under Article 6 had been violated, since the victim was denied the opportunity of showing special proximity, which possibly existed.[166] A distinction is now drawn by the Human Rights Court between an immunity from suit which denies the litigant access to the court (and is a breach of Article 6) and a substantive rule of law (such as the rule currently under discussion) which is wholly a matter for domestic law.[167] However, it is still possible that Article 2 (the right to life) is engaged when the police fail in their duty. The European Court has laid down that where the police knew or ought to have known at the time of the existence of a real and immediate risk to the life of an identified individual or individuals from the criminal acts of a third party and that they failed to take measures within the scope of their powers which, judged reasonably, might have been expected to avoid that risk, a breach of Article 2 would be found.[168] No breach of Article 2 was found by the House of Lords in the case of a man who had been murdered shortly before he was due to give evidence for the prosecution at the trial (for theft) of another man who was subsequently convicted of his murder. The threats made were of 'trouble' or 'danger' and in the circumstances it was reasonable for the police not to anticipate 'a real and immediate risk'.[169]

The police may be liable in negligence for the suicide of a prisoner known to be suicidal.[170] No duty of care is owed by a fire brigade in answering a call or in fighting a fire, except in so far as some additional danger is created by the brigade's own negligence. There was no liability, therefore, when the brigade left the scene of several fires without making sure that they were all extinct,[171] but another brigade were liable when they mistakenly ordered the sprinkler system to be turned off and so created a new danger.[172]

Nearer to the 'policy' end of the spectrum there have been attempts to sue regulatory bodies for negligence, but these have mostly been unsuccessful.[173] When depositors who had lost money in a bank failure in the Isle of Man sued the Treasurer and members of the Finance Board for failure to supervise the bank effectively, their claim was struck out by the Privy Council as untenable.[174] The same fate befell depositors with a finance company in Hong Kong, whose claims were based on the failure of the Commissioner of

---

[165] See above, p. 378. In addition to the cases there discussed see *Z* v. *UK* (2002) 34 EHRR 3 (*Osman* to be 'reviewed'), and *D* v. *East Berkshire NHS Trust* [2003] EWCA Civ 1151, [2004] 2 WLR 58 (CA).

[166] *Osman* v. *UK* [1999] 1 FLR 193. The European Court in effect decided what should be the limits of the English law of negligence rather than any issue of procedural rights under ECHR Art. 6. See the criticism of Lord Browne-Wilkinson in *Barrett* v. *Enfield LBC* [2001] 2 AC 550 (HL) and compare the same court's attitude to ouster clauses, above, p. 618 which may be open to similar criticism. See also Lord Hoffmann's criticism in (1999) 62 *MLR* 159; and also (1999) 59 *CLJ* 4 (T. Weir) and *Palmer* v. *Tees Health Authority* (2000) 2 LGLR 69.   [167] *Z* v. *UK*, above.

[168] *Osman*, as above, para. 116. The threshold test of 'a real and immediate risk to life' is a high one and seldom satisfied (*Re Officer L* [2007] UKHL 36, [2007] 1 WLR 2135, para. 20).

[169] *Van Colle*, above. Contrary to suggestions in *R (A)* v. *Lord Saville of Newdigate* [2001] EWCA Civ 2048, [2002] 1 WLR 1249 (at para. 28) the threshold is not lowered because the victim was a witness assisting the prosecution. See *Van Colle*, paras. 34, 70.

[170] *Reeves* v. *Commissioner of Police of the Metropolis* [1999] 3 WLR 363 (HL) (damages reduced because of contributory fault).

[171] *Capital & Counties plc* v. *Hampshire CC* [1997] QB 1004, reporting 4 such cases decided together. The law is similar for coastguards: *OLL Ltd* v. *Secretary of State for Transport* [1997] 3 All ER 897.

[172] Ibid.

[173] The one spectacular success was achieved not through the courts but through the Parliamentary Commissioner: above, p. 79.

[174] *Davis* v. *Radcliffe* [1990] 1 WLR 821, emphasising the delicacy and difficulty of such decisions, militating against the imposition of a duty of care. See also *Minories Finance Ltd* v. *Young* [1989] 2 All ER 105 (Bank of England not liable for failure to supervise collapsed bank).

Deposit-taking Companies to refuse the company registration or to revoke its licence.[175] The Privy Council pointed out the 'very difficult choice' confronting a regulator who must choose between intervention 'with immediate and probably disastrous effect' and non-intervention based on hopes of recovery. As Lord Browne-Wilkinson has said 'the courts should proceed with great care before holding liable in negligence those who have been charged by Parliament with the task of protecting society from the wrongdoing of others'.[176] And Clarke J has said:[177]

the exercise of the powers and duties of a supervisor in this field involves the balancing of many different factors in the interests both of the public generally and of both existing and future depositors. The interests of these and other different groups may conflict so that it makes no real sense to hold that a duty of care or a statutory duty is owed to only one or some of those groups.

In contrast, the Court of Appeal of New Zealand decided that a minister's refusal of consent to a financial transaction rendered him liable in negligence where he plainly should have taken legal advice and by neglecting to do so made an unlawful decision.[178] But the Privy Council reversed them, holding that the minister had not acted negligently in the circumstances, and that, in any case, it was questionable whether liability for negligence ought to be imposed in such cases in addition to the existing liability for acting in bad faith.[179] It is not every careless decision, therefore, which will involve liability, even if damage is caused. A statutory power of decision may include power to decide wrongly and even carelessly. A minister or official making a decision is allowed a margin of error which is not allowed, for example, to the driver of a motor vehicle. The distinction between the 'policy' and 'operational' areas is evident, although the Privy Council were sceptical of its value as a touchstone of liability. They inclined rather to suggest that ministers' decisions on such matters as the allocation of scarce resources or the distribution of risks were altogether unsuitable for actions in negligence.[180]

Although important questions remain to be answered, there is a clear tendency, in England at least, against applying the ordinary law of negligence to discretionary administrative decisions. The decisions of licensing authorities, for example, may be held ultra vires and quashed if proper attention is not given to the case. But there is no indication that actions for damages will lie for any resulting loss, merely because negligence can be shown.[181] The Court of Appeal has held that there is no liability in tort for the negligent handling of a planning application, even though this is plainly in the 'operational' class.[182]

---

[175] *Yuen Kun Yeu* v. *A-G of Hong Kong* [1988] AC 175.

[176] *X (minors)* v. *Bedfordshire CC* [1995] 2 AC 633 at 751, discussing and supporting the Privy Council's decision. See also *Harris* v. *Evans* [1998] 1 WLR 1285 (no liability for Health and Safety Executive's notice prohibiting bungee jumping). Cf. *Phelps* v. *Hillingdon LBC* [2001] 2 AC 618 (liability in particular circumstances for educational psychologist's failure to diagnose dyslexia), discussed below, p. 661.

[177] *Three Rivers DC* v. *Bank of England (No 3)* [1996] 3 All ER 558 at 601. For this case, where the law of misfeasance was invoked, see below, p. 666. See also *Bennett* v. *Commissioner of Police for the Metropolis* (1997) 10 Admin LR 245.

[178] *Takaro Properties Ltd* v. *Rowling* [1986] 1 NZLR 22. The minister had refused consent for the sale of the company's shares to a Japanese firm on the ground that its undertaking (a high-class tourist lodge) ought not to pass into foreign ownership. This ground was held to be irrelevant to the minister's statutory power: [1975] 2 NZLR 62. See also *Lonrho plc* v. *Tebbit* [1992] 4 All ER 280 (claim based on minister's negligence in failing to release company from statutory undertaking held to be arguable and fit for trial).

[179] *Rowling* v. *Takaro Properties Ltd* [1988] AC 473. See similarly *Knop* v. *Johannesburg City Council* 1995 (2) SA 1 (negligent planning decision—no duty of care).

[180] Citing Craig, *Administrative Law*, 1st edn, 534–8.   [181] See below, p. 660.

[182] *Strable* v. *Dartford BC* [1984] JPL 329; and see *Ryeford Homes Ltd* v. *Sevenoaks DC* 46 BLR 34. Contrast the New Zealand planning cases cited above, p. 649. See also *Jones* v. *Department of Employment* [1989] QB

So far the English courts have progressed no further than suggesting that an action may succeed if a licence or permission is refused maliciously, i.e. if it is a case of misfeasance.[183] Legislative functions probably impose no duty of care at all, being essentially 'policy'.[184]

Combat immunity, viz. the principle that 'no duty of care in tort is owed by one soldier to another when engaging the enemy in battle conditions',[185] clearly exists in law but, the Supreme Court has held, it must be narrowly construed.[186] Thus the court did not strike out actions for negligence brought by the relatives of British soldiers killed in a 'friendly fire' incident involving tanks in Iraq. The actions alleged negligence, not in the actual battle, but in failure to provide proper equipment and training that would have avoided the incident. Lord Hope said[187] that combat immunity should not be extended to 'the planning of and preparation for the operations in which injury was sustained'; it was 'an exception to the principle... that the executive cannot simply rely on the interests of the state as a justification for the commission of wrongs.... the scope of the immunity should be construed narrowly'.

The immunity which operates in the case of judicial functions is explained later.[188]

NON-EXERCISE OF POWERS

It used to be a familiar proposition that mere failure to exercise a power was not actionable. A sharp contrast was thus made between exercising a power negligently and not exercising it at all, however negligent the latter course might in fact be. There was a corresponding contrast between failure to exercise a power and failure to perform a duty. The former by itself was not actionable, but the latter might be.[189] But the decisions discussed in the preceding section show that these contrasts are no longer so sharp. Failure to exercise a discretionary power, if sufficiently negligent, may involve breach of a duty of care and consequent liability. The House of Lords has categorically rejected the notion of 'an absolute distinction in the law between statutory duty and statutory power—the former giving rise to possible liability, the latter not, or at least not doing so unless the exercise of the power involves some positive act creating some fresh or additional damage'.[190]

Accidents in ill-lit streets formerly provided many illustrations of the 'absolute distinction' which used to be made. If the local authority had a statutory duty to provide lighting, and failed to do so negligently, an injured wayfarer might obtain damages.[191] But if it had a mere power, there was no remedy. Thus the injured plaintiff failed in a case where the Act said merely that the local authority 'may provide' such lighting 'as they may think

---

1 (no liability for negligent decision of social security adjudication officer). In *Revesz* v. *Commonwealth of Australia* (1951) 51 SR (NSW) 63 an importer was held to have no remedy for the negligent loss and delay of an import licence which should have been issued to him by the customs department, with the result that he later had to pay higher rates of import duty. For the duty to deal with applications fairly and in a reasonable time, see above, p. 464.

[183] See below, p. 664.

[184] *Wellbridge Holdings Ltd* v. *Greater Winnipeg* [1970] 22 DLR (3d) 470 (city not liable in negligence for procedural mistakes invalidating planning byelaw in reliance on which builder expended money and suffered loss).

[185] *Mulcahy* v. *Ministry of Defence* [1996] EWCA Civ 1323, para. 27 (not using the phrase 'combat immunity').   [186] *Smith and ors v The Ministry of Defence* [2013] UKSC 41, para. 92 (Lord Hope).

[187] Giving an account and approving the approach of Elias J in *Bici* v. *Ministry of Defence* [2004] EWHC 786 (QB), para. 90.   [188] Below, p. 669.

[189] See below, p. 658.

[190] *Anns* v. *Merton LBC*, above (Lord Wilberforce). Although this case has been overruled (above, p. 649) this dictum is believed to remain correct. But see *Gorringe* v. *Calderdale Metropolitan Borough Council* [2004] UKHL 15, paras. 38–44.   [191] *Carpenter* v. *Finsbury Borough Council* [1920] 2 KB 195.

necessary', even though the authority was in fact in the habit of providing lighting at the dangerous place during certain hours.[192] But permissive words such as 'may' were not an infallible guide, since what appeared to be a mere power might be held to involve duty, as explained elsewhere.[193]

The House of Lords has reassessed one of its decisions which turned upon the former distinction between power and duty.[194] A river catchment board had taken an excessive time to repair a sea-wall, so that land which need only have been flooded for fourteen days remained flooded for 178 days. The board had merely a power to repair sea-walls, so that had they done nothing they could not (under the former law) have been held liable. The House of Lords held that the true cause of the loss was the flood, and that the board were not liable for their slowness because this was mere inaction. But Lord Atkin, dissenting, held that, once the board had undertaken the repair, they were under the ordinary duty of care which a man owes to his neighbour, and that their breach of this duty was the cause of the damage. The House of Lords has since made it clear that it approves Lord Atkin's analysis and that, in any case, there is no longer an absolute immunity for failure to exercise a power.[195] That plaintiffs will not easily succeed, however, is shown by a highway case where a motor cyclist was injured at a road junction which was known to be dangerous because visibility was restricted by a bank of earth. Difficulties and delays had prevented action by the local council. A divided House of Lords held that since the council had a discretionary power to carry out road improvements, which would amount to a duty only if it would have been irrational not to have exercised it, and since there was no indication that the statute contemplated remedies for injured individuals, the claim must fail.[196] Negligent failure to perform a statutory duty, on the other hand, may sometimes support a successful action for damages, as is illustrated below.

NONFEASANCE AND MISFEASANCE IN HIGHWAY CASES

There used to be an illogical distinction between misfeasance and nonfeasance which expressed the liability of the local authorities to which responsibility for highways was transferred by statute.[197] If they merely neglected the highway (nonfeasance), an injured traveller had no remedy.[198] But if they opened a manhole or dug a trench and left it inadequately protected (misfeasance), they were liable for any injury.[199] This distinction would have been correct if the highway authority had merely a power; but in fact it was a case of duty. The courts confined the immunity for nonfeasance to the narrowest possible area,[200] and rejected arguments for extending it into other areas so as to create a general

---

[192] *Sheppard* v. *Glossop Cpn* [1921] 3 KB 132.   [193] Above, p. 194.

[194] *East Suffolk Rivers Catchment Board* v. *Kent* [1941] AC 74.

[195] *Anns* v. *Merton LBC* [1978] AC 728. Lord Wilberforce thought that the full effect of *Donoghue* v. *Stevenson* [1932] AC 562 had not then been fully recognised. Lord Salmon expressed his agreement with Lord Atkin. See also *Parramatta City Council* v. *Lutz* (1988) 12 NSWLR 293 (council liable for failure to execute demolition order causing plaintiff's house to be destroyed by fire). Cf. *Gorringe*, para. 41.

[196] *Stovin* v. *Wise* [1996] AC 923. Lords Slynn and Nicholls, dissenting, held that the conditions for liability were fulfilled. A large number of academic and other authorities are cited in Lord Nicholls's speech. For the suggested doctrine of 'general reliance', derived from Australian decisions, see Lord Hoffmann's speech at 415. *Stovin* v. *Wise* has been followed by the High Court of Australia: *Pyrenees Shire Council* v. *Day* (1998) 151 ALR 147.

[197] The Highways Act 1959 finally abolished the duty of the inhabitants at large to repair and imposed on highway authorities a duty to maintain public highways. Duties had been imposed from the Highway Act 1835 onwards.   [198] *Cowley* v. *Newmarket Local Board* [1892] AC 345.

[199] *Newsome* v. *Darton UDC* [1938] 3 All ER 93.

[200] See e.g. *Skilton* v. *Epsom & Ewell UDC* [1937] 1 KB 112; *A-G* v. *St Ives RDC* [1961] 1 QB 366.

defence of inactivity.[201] The immunity for nonfeasance was abolished in 1961, since when highway authorities have been made equally liable for the exercise or non-exercise of their powers, and for neglect of their duties, subject to a statutory defence of showing that they have used reasonable care in all the circumstances.[202] Although their duty to maintain the highway is absolute[203] (as in the case with statutory duties generally),[204] the statutory defence makes it in effect a liability for negligence only; and in any case there is no breach of the duty if the highway authority could not, in a difficult situation, be blamed for non-performance.[205] Even if a breach of duty is shown, the authority's liability is limited to personal injury or damage to property resulting from the dangerous condition of the road, thus excluding loss of profit to a business.[206]

STRICT LIABILITY—*RYLANDS V. FLETCHER*

Even in the absence of negligence the law of tort imposes liability on those who create situations of special danger. This strict liability is imposed by the rule in *Rylands* v. *Fletcher*[207] on 'the person who for his own purposes brings on his lands and collects and keeps there anything likely to do mischief if it escapes', if the operation involves abnormal risk; and this rule has been held to cover many situations where damage has been done by such things as chemicals, fire and electricity.[208] Considering how many dangerous operations are undertaken by public authorities, it is curious that few cases under this rubric have been reported. Statute has made special provision in a number of cases, as in the Gas Act 1965,[209] the Nuclear Installations Act 1965[210] and the Deposit of Poisonous Waste Act 1972.[211]

The Court of Appeal has held that a public authority, since it acts for the public benefit, does not act 'for its own purposes' within the meaning of the above rule, and is therefore not liable in the absence of negligence.[212] This is an unfortunate example of literal verbal interpretation, treating the rule like a clause in an Act of Parliament rather than

---

[201] *Pride of Derby and Derbyshire Angling Association Ltd* v. *British Celanese Ltd* [1953] Ch 149.

[202] Highways (Miscellaneous Provisions) Act 1961, s. 1. See now Highways Act 1980, s. 58.

[203] *Griffiths* v. *Liverpool Cpn* [1967] 1 QB 374.   [204] Below, p. 662.

[205] *Haydon* v. *Kent CC* [1978] QB 343, where the statutory defence was not pleaded. The majority of the Court of Appeal held that 'maintain' went further than 'repair', so as to impose liability for failure to remove snow and ice; but Lord Denning MR held that the Act of 1961 removed the former immunity for non-repair only, so that there was no liability in damages for non-maintenance in other respects. No culpable breach of duty was proved, and a claim for injury from a fall on an icy footpath failed. So for the same reason did a claim by the widow of a driver killed on icy roads which the defendant's workers, being on strike, refused to grit: *Bartlett* v. *Department of Transport* (1984) 83 LGR 579. Contrast *Goodes* v. *East Sussex CC* [1999] RTR 210 (council liable for failure to de-ice road). See also *Cross* v. *Kirklees MBC* [1998] 1 All ER 564 (council not liable for failure to grit footpath). Contrast too *Valentine* v. *Transport for London and anor* [2010] EWCA Civ 1358 (strike-out refused).   [206] *Wentworth* v. *Wiltshire CC* [1993] QB 654.

[207] (1868) LR 3 HL 330. See now *Cambridge Water Co* v. *Eastern Counties Leather plc* [1994] 2 AC 264.

[208] See *Salmond and Heuston on Torts*, 21st edn, ch. 13.

[209] s. 14 (underground storage of gas).

[210] s. 12, as amended by Nuclear Installations Act 1969.   [211] s. 2.

[212] *Dunne* v. *North Western Gas Board* [1964] 2 QB 806; *Pearson* v. *North Western Gas Board* [1968] 2 All ER 669, suggesting that the House of Lords might have other views; *Lloyde* v. *West Midlands Gas Board* [1971] 2 All ER 1240. *Lowery* v. *Vickers Armstrong Ltd* [1969] 8 KIR 603 at 606 suggests the possibility of liability in nuisance without negligence but *RHM Bakeries (Scotland) Ltd* v. *Strathclyde Regional Council*, 1985 SLT 214 (HL) denies it. In the Aberfan Disaster report (1966 HC 553, para. 74) Edmund-Davies LJ treated *Rylands* v. *Fletcher* as incontestably applicable to the National Coal Board.

as a statement of principle. A leaky water main had washed away the soil supporting a gas main, which then broke and caused an explosion. It was said that the provision of services such as gas, water and electricity, being well-nigh necessities of modern life, ought not to impose liability without fault on suppliers acting under powers approved by Parliament.[213] But where the suppliers are acting for the benefit of the community, it would be altogether fairer to require them to bear liability for accidents irrespective of fault, for then the cost would be spread equitably over the users of the service instead of being charged wholly upon the unfortunate person injured. The argument that a statutory 'nuisance clause' implies no liability without fault is also unconvincing.[214] The anomaly is all the more glaring in that the Crown has, it seems, been duly made liable to the rule in *Rylands* v. *Fletcher* under the Crown Proceedings Act 1947.[215]

There are signs that Parliament is alive to this injustice. The Water Act 1981[216] makes water authorities liable without fault for damage caused by the escape of water from their mains and pipes, subject to the ordinary law about contributory negligence and limitation of actions and except where the damage is wholly the fault of the injured party. There ought to be general legislation on the same lines.

BREACH OF STATUTORY DUTY

Where a statute imposes a duty, it is sometimes to be inferred that any person injured as the result of breach of the duty shall have a remedy in damages, even in the absence of carelessness.[217] This is another form of strict liability and public authorities (or others subject to a statutory duty) will be held liable for damages even if they are not at fault at all. As will be explained, the principle is of relatively limited scope. Not every breach of a statutory duty entails a private law liability for damages. In the leading modern case[218] Lord Browne-Wilkinson explained the position in these canonical words:

> The basic proposition is that in the ordinary case a breach of statutory duty does not, by itself, give rise to any private law cause of action. However a private law cause of action will arise if it can be shown, as a matter of construction of the statute, that the statutory duty was imposed for the protection of a limited class of the public and that Parliament intended to confer on members of that class a private right of action for breach of the duty. There is no general rule by reference to which it can be decided whether a statute does create such a right of action but there are a number of indicators. If the statute provides no other remedy for its breach and the Parliamentary intention to protect a limited class is shown, that indicates that there may be a private right of action since otherwise there is no method of securing the protection the statute was intended to confer. If the statute does provide some other means of enforcing the duty that will normally indicate that the statutory right was intended to be enforceable by those means and not by private right of action: *Cutler* v. *Wandsworth Stadium Ltd.* [1949] A.C. 398; *Lonrho Ltd.* v. *Shell Petroleum*

---

[213] The Law Commission's Report No. 32 (1970), para. 15, attributes the decision to the fact that the gas board were acting under statutory duty and not mere power. But the decision probably rested upon broader grounds. The Royal Commission on Civil Liability recommended a statutory code for dangerous operations, Cmnd. 7054–1 (1978), para. 1641. See also (1980) 96 *LQR* 419 (P. P. Craig).   [214] Above, p. 644.

[215] Below, p. 694.   [216] s. 6.

[217] See Harding, *Public Duties and Public Law*, ch. 7; *Salmond & Heuston on Torts*, 21st edn, ch. 10. For valuable discussion see (1984) 100 *LQR* 204 (R. A. Buckley); [1998] *PL* 407 (Sir R. Carnwath).

[218] *X (minors)* v. *Bedfordshire CC* [1995] 2 AC 633, [1995] 3 WLR 152 (appeals against striking out orders).

Co. Ltd. (No. 2) [1982] A.C. 173. However, the mere existence of some other statutory remedy is not necessarily decisive. It is still possible to show that on the true construction of the statute the protected class was intended by Parliament to have a private remedy. Thus the specific duties imposed on employers in relation to factory premises are enforceable by an action for damages, notwithstanding the imposition by the statutes of criminal penalties for any breach: see *Groves* v. *Lord Wimborne* [1898] 2 Q.B. 402.

Everything depends upon the true intent of the statute which may be difficult to divine when it says nothing relevant.[219] But, as adumbrated by Lord Browne-Wilkinson, the court is usually sympathetic to an action for damages if the statute has no scheme of its own for penalties and enforcement: 'for, if it were not so, the statute would be but a pious aspiration'.[220] And where the statute provides penalties, there is prima facie no private law remedy, for otherwise crimes would too freely be turned into torts. Thus a bookmaker failed in an action against the proprietors of a dog-racing track for failure to provide him with facilities as required by the Betting and Lotteries Act 1934, which made this an offence punishable with fine and imprisonment.[221] As noted by Lord Browne-Wilkinson this principle is subject to exception, such as the private law liability of factory owners for breaches of safety regulations, even though such breaches are crimes.

Schemes of social welfare serving the general public interest are unlikely to create private rights of action for breach of statutory duty, particularly where judgment had to be exercised. Thus the House of Lords has held that a homeless person could not recover damages against the local council for its breach of its duty to accommodate him under Part III of the Housing Act 1985. Such 'regulatory or welfare legislation' although it does protect a class of person (in this case the homeless) is in fact passed for 'the benefit of society in general'.[222]

This House of Lords' decision along with the leading case (*X (minors)*) mentioned above confirm that

> the House has set itself firmly against damages as a remedy for breach of statutory duty in public law. In future, where Parliament fails to specify a particular remedy for breach of a public duty the presumption will be that judicial review is the normal and exclusive means of enforcement. It is difficult now to see any scope for extending the application of the tort of breach of statutory duty in the public field.[223]

In (*X (minors)*) the House of Lords disposed of a large number of child welfare cases in a consolidated proceeding.[224] Lord Browne-Wilkinson held that failure by local authorities in their statutory duties of identifying children in need or at risk of abuse or with special educational needs did not give rise to any claim for damages in private law. Legislation setting up a regulatory system or a scheme of social welfare was to be treated as intended

---

[219] Lord Denning MR called the dividing line 'so blurred and so ill-defined that you might as well toss a coin to decide it': *ex p. Island Records Ltd* [1978] Ch 122.

[220] *Cutler* v. *Wandsworth Stadium Ltd* [1949] AC 398 (Lord Simonds). See *Thornton* v. *Kirklees BC* [1979] QB 626 at 639; *Booth* v. *National Enterprise Board* [1978] 3 All ER 624; *West Wiltshire DC* v. *Garland* [1995] Ch 297 (district auditor's liability to local authority). [221] *Cutler* (above).

[222] *O'Rourke* v. *Camden LBC* [1997] UKHL 24; [1998] AC 188 at 192 citing Lord Browne-Wilkinson in *X (minors)* at 731–2.

[223] See [1988] *PL* 407 (Sir R. Carnwath), advocating more generous rules and making comparisons with relief available from the Parliamentary Commissioner and in European law.

[224] *X (minors)* v. *Bedfordshire CC* [1995] 2 AC 633 (appeals against striking out orders). See similarly *E (minor)* v. *Dorset CC* (1994) 92 LGR 484; *A-G* v. *Prince & Gardner* [1998] 1 NZLR 262; and *Phelps* v. *Hillingdon LBC* [2001] 2 AC 619 (failure to diagnose dyslexia).

for the benefit of society in general rather than for the benefit of individuals, except where the statutory duty was very limited and specific. But a claim could succeed if it were 'based on a free standing common law cause of action, whether in trespass, nuisance or breach of a common law duty of care'.[225]

Since *X (minors)* claimants have, unsurprisingly, had little success in actions for breach of statutory duty. But, as explained earlier in considering liability for negligence, there has been success in holding the local authorities liable for the negligence of their employees, the courts sometimes restricting the impact of *X (minors)* to the decision to take a child into care and not its treatment thereafter.[226]

Another possibility is that statutory duties may be held to be merely directory, so that there is no liability for disregard of them. On this ground it has been held that neither the police regulations[227] nor the prison rules[228] give any right of action for violation of them in disciplinary proceedings, and that Parliament cannot be supposed to have had any such intention in passing the legislation. Nor do the rules of mental health tribunals protecting privacy give any remedy for unauthorised publication, for the same reason.[229] There are also statutory exceptions: persons performing functions under the Mental Health Act 1983 are protected unless they act in bad faith or without reasonable care, and an action lies only with leave of the court.[230]

Other remedies for the non-performance of duties, such as a mandatory order, are discussed in Chapter 18. Since the authority will be directly liable for its breach of duty, no question of vicarious liability will generally arise. But if an employee is under a duty, his employer may be vicariously liable, unless the statute expressly or impliedly indicates otherwise, to pay damages when the employee breaches his duty.[231]

BREACH OF DUTY UNDER EUROPEAN UNION LAW

Member States of the European Union and their public authorities have many duties under the Treaties and subordinate Community legislation. These duties are to be given legal effect in the United Kingdom, and enforced by the courts, under the European Communities Act 1972.[232] In a general sense, therefore, all these duties are statutory.[233] But that does not mean that they will be governed by English law, since their operation is a matter of European Union law under principles laid down by the European Court of Justice, notably in two decisions of 1996. Previously the House of Lords held in the

---

[225] Thus the House of Lords allowed a common law claim for neglect of the interests of a child in care to go to trial, stressing the dangers of striking out claims on assumed facts which may prove to be wrong, *Barrett v. Enfield LBC* [2001] 2 AC 550 (HL). For analysis and comment see [1999] *PL* 626 (P. Craig and D. Fairgrieve); [2000] *CLJ* 85 (S. Bailey and M. Bowman).

[226] The Court of Appeal has remarked that in child care matters the *X (minors)* case 'cannot survive the Human Rights Act' (the *East Berkshire* case, above, para. 85 (Lord Phillips MR)) portending the eclipse of the common law here.   [227] *Calveley* v. *Chief Constable of Merseyside Police* [1989] AC 1228.

[228] *R* v. *Deputy Governor of Parkhurst Prison ex p Hague* [1992] AC 58. But see below, p. 733.

[229] *R* v. *Liverpool Daily Post plc* [1991] 2 AC 370.   [230] s. 139. See *Winch* v. *Jones* [1986] QB 296.

[231] *Majrowski* v. *Guy's and St. Thomas' NHS Trust* [2006] UKHL 34, [2007] 1 AC 224, para. 17 (Lord Nicholls) and para. 81. The statute in question was the Protection from Harassment Act 1997, which made express provision for vicarious liability (although this was first noticed by the law lords).

[232] s. 2(1).

[233] See (2012) 128 *LQR* 324 (Giliker) and (2004) 120 *LQR* 324 arguing, convincingly, that the label 'breach of statutory duty' should be rejected in this context to reflect the fact this law is 'created and developed' by the ECJ (at 562).

Garden Cottage Foods case[234] that the duty imposed by Article 86 (now 82) (not to abuse a dominant position) was to be categorised in English law as a statutory duty and gave a strong hint that breach of it should be remediable in damages. The Court of Appeal, however, held in the *Bourgoin* case[235] that a minister's duty under Article 30 (now 28) (not to impose restrictions on imports) was not a statutory duty under the above analysis, and that an invalid restriction imposed by the minister should be classified as 'a simple excess of power', with no remedy in damages.

The decisions of 1996 were two cases decided and reported together. In the first, a French brewery company lost its market in Germany because its beer did not meet the standards of purity required by German legislation, but those standards had earlier been held by the European Court to be unduly stringent and so an unlawful restriction on imports.[236] In the second case that Court held that restrictions imposed by the Merchant Shipping Act 1988 as to the nationality, residence and domicile of the owners of fishing vessels infringed the commercial freedom required by Community law, Spanish ship-owners having in the meantime suffered heavy losses by losing their fishing rights.[237] The question then was whether the French brewers and the Spanish ship-owners could recover damages from Germany and Britain respectively. In upholding their claims the Court of Justice laid down three conditions of liability:

1. The Community law infringed must be intended to confer rights on individuals.

2. The breach must be sufficiently serious, in that the Member State has manifestly and gravely disregarded the limits on its discretion.

3. There must be a direct causal link between the breach and the damage sustained.

It was then for the national court, obeying Community law, to decide whether these conditions were satisfied. But the Court of Justice made it clear what the decision should be and gave further directions. The reparation must be commensurate with the loss and the rules must be not less favourable than for similar domestic claims. It was immaterial that the loss resulted from legislation. There was no requirement of fault (beyond 'manifestly and gravely') such as intention or negligence. There should be reparation for loss of profit, and there might be exemplary damages. The House of Lords in due course awarded full but not exemplary damages against the government, holding that their deliberate adoption of discriminatory legislation was a manifest and grave breach of fundamental treaty obligations.[238]

The House was applying the Court of Justice's criterion, that a breach is 'sufficiently serious' if the national authority has 'manifestly and gravely disregarded the limits on the exercise of its powers'.[239] This is the same test as that for abuse of power by the EU organs

---

[234] *Garden Cottage Foods Ltd* v. *Milk Marketing Board* [1984] AC 130 (allegation of discriminatory supply of bulk butter; application for interim injunction failed since damages, if obtainable, would be an adequate remedy. Lord Wilberforce dissented, holding that the remedy might be injunction but not damages). See also *An Board Bainne* v. *Milk Marketing Board* [1984] 2 CMLR 584 (above, p. 574).

[235] *Bourgoin SA* v. *Ministry of Agriculture, Fisheries and Food* [1986] QB 716 (Ministry's order prohibiting import of French turkeys held unlawful by European Court. Plaintiff's claim to damages held to show a cause of action for misfeasance in public office if the minister knew that he had no power so to act, but not for breach of statutory duty. Oliver LJ dissented on the latter point, agreeing with Mann J at first instance). For this case see further below, p. 668.

[236] *Brasserie du Pêcheur SA* v. *Federal Republic of Germany*, C-46/93, [1996] QB 404 (ECJ).

[237] *R* v. *Secretary of State for Transport ex p Factortame Ltd (No 4)*, C-48/93, [1996] QB 404 (ECJ).

[238] *R* v. *Secretary of State for Transport ex p Factortame Ltd (No 5)* [1999] 3 WLR 1062.

[239] See *Factortame (No 3)* [1996] QB 404 at 499 (ECJ).

themselves, as explained earlier.[240] It was again enforced against the British government when on grounds of cruelty to animals it had refused licences for the export to Spain of live animals for slaughter, in violation of the treaty provision against quantitative restrictions on exports between Member States and the Court of Justice ordered reparation.[241] But the Court later exonerated Britain for failure to implement a Community directive about procurement contracts, since the directive was capable of different interpretations, even though the British interpretation was held to be wrong; the breach was therefore not 'sufficiently serious'.[242]

The decisions discussed in these pages show that English law and Community law are evolving in opposite directions.[243] The House of Lords 'has set itself firmly against damages as a remedy for breach of statutory duty in public law'.[244] Community law, on the other hand, provides a comprehensive remedy in reparation against national governments for breach of their duties, irrespective of fault and limited in effect only by the 'sufficiently serious' requirement. The obvious difficulty in the Court of Appeal's decision in the *Bourgoin* case is that, since it was a matter of Community law, it should have been decided under the positive Community rules and not the negative English rules.[245] How far these contradictory rules will be able to coexist is questionable. It seems likely that under Community pressure the English law will eventually have to conform. It has long been criticised for its grudging attitude to the remedy of damages in public law;[246] and a learned judge has recently observed with good reason:[247]

> In principle... where serious harm has been caused to individuals by illegal action by public authorities, or by failure to carry out legal duties or obligations imposed upon them for the benefit of individuals, justice demands a suitable remedy for breach. For past failures the only efficient remedy in most circumstances is monetary compensation. As the European Court of Justice has recognised, failure to afford such a remedy impairs the effectiveness of the law.

Here, therefore, is another situation where English law may be under pressure to conform.

MISFEASANCE IN PUBLIC OFFICE

Even where there is no ministerial duty as above, and even where no recognised tort such as trespass, nuisance or negligence is committed, public authorities or officers may be liable in damages for malicious, deliberate or injurious wrong-doing.[248] There is thus a

---

[240] Above, p. 171.

[241] *R* v. *Ministry of Agriculture, Fisheries and Food ex p Hedley Lomas (Ireland) Ltd* [1997] QB 139.

[242] *R* v. *HM Treasury ex p British Telecommunications plc* [1996] QB 615 (ECJ).

[243] For full discussion see (1997) 113 *LQR* 67 (P. P. Craig); C. Lewis in Forsyth and Hare (eds.), *The Golden Metwand*, 319.   [244] As quoted above, p. 661.

[245] See *Kirklees MBC* v. *Wickes Building Supplies Ltd* [1993] AC 227 at 281.

[246] See Lord Wilberforce (dissenting) in *Hoffmann–La Roche & Co* v. *Secretary of State for Trade and Industry* [1975] AC 295: 'an unwillingness to accept that a subject should be indemnified for loss sustained by invalid administrative action... the subject requires protection against action taken against him or his property under administrative orders which may turn out to be invalid'.

[247] Sir R. Carnwath (as above).

[248] See particularly R. Moules, *Actions Against Public Officials* (2009), ch. 5. See further [1964] *CLJ* 4 (A. W. Bradley); [1964] *PL* 367 (G. Ganz); (1972) 5 *NZULR* 105 (B. C. Gould); [1979] *CLJ* 323 (J. McBride); [2005] *JR* 227 (Hannett); (2002) 51 *ICLQ* 757 (Andenas and Fairgrieve); (2011) 35 Melbourne University LR 1 (Aronson). 14th Report of the Public and Administrative Law Reform Committee, New Zealand (1980). There may also be criminal liability: *R* v. *Llewellyn-Jones* [1968] 1 QB 429.

tort which has been called misfeasance in public office,[249] and which includes malicious abuse of power, deliberate maladministration and perhaps also other unlawful acts causing injury.[250] To the credit of public authorities it must be said that there are remarkably few reported English decisions on this form of malpractice.

The famous case of *Ashby* v. *White* (1703)[251] is the best known of the early English examples, arising as it did from the disputed Aylesbury election which brought the two Houses of Parliament and the courts of law into such sharp conflicts that they were resolved only by the dissolution of Parliament.[252] The plaintiff was one of the electors who was wrongfully prevented from voting and who sued the borough constables in charge of the poll for £200 damages, pleading their fraud and malicious intent. There seems to have been no breach of ministerial duty.[253] The plaintiff failed in the Court of King's Bench, Holt CJ vigorously dissenting; but the House of Lords (involved as it was in the controversy, on the plaintiff's side) reversed the judgment by a majority of fifty to sixteen. Holt CJ's opinion is a classic instance of invoking the principle *ubi jus, ibi remedium*.

But the true gist of the action for damages was later held to have been malice, and similar actions failed where malice could not be established.[254] Otherwise, it was said, 'the officer could not discharge his duty without great peril and apprehension, if, in consequence of a mistake, he became liable to an action'.[255] Actions for damages for breach of official duty at elections were abolished by statute in 1949, since when there are only criminal penalties.[256]

Ashby v. *White* misleads in so far as it suggests that misfeasance in public office is a tort actionable per se, i.e. without proof of damage. The House of Lords has held that damage must be shown in all cases. Lord Bingham remarked 'the primary role of the law of tort is to provide monetary compensation for those who have suffered material damage rather than to vindicate the rights of those who have not. If public officers behave with outrageous disregard for their legal duties, but without causing material damage, there are other and more appropriate ways of bringing them to book.'[257] Thus a prisoner whose correspondence with his legal advisers had been unlawfully and maliciously opened by prison officers failed in his action for damages for misfeasance, because no damage was shown.[258]

[249] A public office or authority exercises 'governmental powers, that is, the power to interfere with the way in which other citizens wish to conduct their affairs' *Stockwell* v. *Society of Lloyd's* [2007] EWCA Civ 930, [2008] Lloyd's Rep. IR 317, para. 25 (Buxton LJ). Thus the Society of Lloyd's which was 'concerned with the internal commercial interests of its own members' and had no power to regulate the insurance market was not a public officer. See also *R (West)* v. *Lloyd's of London* [2004] EWCA Civ 506, [2004] 3 All ER 251, paras. 38–9. A public officer exercising private law powers (local authority exercising powers of landlord) is potentially liable (*Jones* v. *Swansea CC* [1990] 1 WLR 54 (CA)).

[250] It is also a crime at common law: *R* v. *Bowden* [1996] 1 WLR 98.

[251] (1703) 2 Ld Raym 938, 3 Ld Raym 320; 1 Smith's *Leading Cases*, 13th edn, 253, with notes supplementing the defective reports.

[252] The events are summarised in 1 Smith's *Leading Cases*, 13th edn, at 281.

[253] See *Tozer* v. *Child* (below) at 382.

[254] *Cullen* v. *Morris* (1819) 2 Stark 577; *Tozer* v. *Child* (1857) 7 E & B 377; and see *Drewe* v. *Coulton* (1787) 1 East 563, note Holt CJ's opinion and other early authorities are discussed by Clarke J in the *Three Rivers* case, below.   [255] *Cullen* v. *Morris* (above) at 587.

[256] Representation of the People Act 1949, s. 50.

[257] *Watkins* v. *Home Office* [2006] UKHL 17, [2006] 2 AC 395, para. 9. Differing from the Court of Appeal ([2004] EWCA Civ 966, [2005] QB 883), their Lordships held that even where the right infringed was 'a constitutional right' (such as that of access to the courts) damage had to be shown.

[258] But 'loss of liberty is a form of special or material damage sufficient to support a claim for misfeasance in public office' *Karagozlu* v. *Commissioner of Police of the Metropolis* [2006] EWCA Civ 1691, [2007] 1 WLR

A further well-known case was that in which the Supreme Court of Canada awarded damages against the Premier of Quebec personally for directing the cancellation of a restaurant-owner's liquor licence solely because the licensee provided bail on many occasions for fellow-members of the sect of Jehovah's Witnesses, which was then unpopular with the authorities.[259] The Premier had no legal power to interfere with the liquor commission which on his directions nevertheless cancelled the licence, and the cancellation was an abuse of discretion based on irrelevant and illegal grounds. It was indeed said that an allegation of good faith would be no defence for such a flagrant abuse of power, there being in fact no power at all; but it seems right to regard the case as one of malicious abuse of power because of the deliberate intent to injure without legal justification.[260]

According to the nearest comparable English authority, such an action will succeed only on proof of malice. The Court of Appeal so held in dismissing an action by a dentist who had been struck off the register without being given a hearing but without malice.[261] And to like effect is a Privy Council decision, which decided that an action might lie for the malicious refusal of a licence for a cinema in Ceylon.[262] Likewise the House of Lords has held that an action for damages might proceed against the clerk of a local authority personally on the ground that he had procured the compulsory purchase of the plaintiff's property wrongfully and in bad faith (though in fact the bad faith was not proved).[263] The House of Lords, in dismissing a claim, has added 'or (possibly) without reasonable cause' to the requirement of bad faith,[264] but that *obiter dictum* must be doubted.[265]

A very thorough examination of this tort and of the authorities was undertaken in a case where plaintiffs who had lost money in a bank failure claimed damages from the Bank of England, which had powers of regulation over banks.[266] The claimants alleged misfeasance in public office in that the Bank of England had either wrongly granted a licence to the failed bank or else wrongly failed to revoke it. Since the Bank of England was protected both by a statutory immunity, except in case of bad faith,[267] and also by the decisions about regulators, explained earlier, negativing a duty of care,[268] the plaintiffs attempted to show misfeasance, alleging that the Bank knew that it was acting unlawfully or else that it was reckless in so acting. Preliminary issues were tried on these assumed facts. The House of Lords confirmed that there were two varieties of the tort but that the Court of Appeal had gone too far in basing the second of the two varieties on knowledge that the decision *would* cause damages to the plaintiffs.[269] The correct test was that of

---

1881, para. 45 (Sir Anthony Clarke MR) (malicious recategorisation of prisoner sufficient to support the claim: strike out refused).

[259] *Roncarelli* v. *Duplessis* (1959) 16 DLR (2d) 689 (damages of $33,123 awarded).

[260] See Rand J at 706. And liability, even were there was no malice, was imposed by the same court in *McGillivray* v. *Kimber* (1915) 26 DLR 164. ·

[261] *Partridge* v. *General Medical Council* (1890) 25 QBD 90. The plaintiff had been restored to the register by mandamus. See also *Ross* v. *Secretary of State for Scotland*, 1990 SLT 13 (injury from unauthorised vaccination not actionable unless in bad faith). Cf. *Davis* v. *Bromley Cpn* [1908] 1 KB 170 (CA) (no recovery even when there was malice; no authority cited).

[262] *David* v. *Abdul Cader* [1963] 1 WLR 834. See similarly *Ballantyne* v. *City of Glasgow Licensing Board*, 1987 SLT 745 (action for wrongful refusal of liquor licences; malice not alleged: action dismissed).

[263] *Smith* v. *East Elloe Rural District Council* [1956] AC 736; *Smith* v. *Pyewell* The Times, 29 April 1959. See also *R* v. *Secretary of State for the Environment ex p Ostler* [1977] QB 122.

[264] *Calveley* v. *Chief Constable of Merseyside Police* [1989] AC 1228.

[265] It is rejected in *Whithair* v. *A-G* [1996] 2 NZLR 45.

[266] *Three Rivers DC* v. *Bank of England* [1996] 3 All ER 558 (Clarke J), [2000] 2 WLR 15 (Hirst and Robert Walker LJJ, Auld LJ dissenting on the ground that there was an arguable case both in English and in EU law).

[267] Banking Act 1987, s. 1(4).   [268] Above, p. 655.

[269] *Three Rivers DC* v. *The Governor and Company of the Bank of England (No 3)* [2000] 2 WLR 1220 (HL).

knowledge that the decision would *probably* damage the plaintiffs.[270] This was more than a test of foreseeability of damage, which by itself was not enough. The requisite knowledge could be imputed from recklessness, in the sense of not caring whether the consequences happen or not. This state of mind is described in Lord Steyn's leading speech as 'reckless indifference' to the consequence in question. The correct test 'represents a satisfactory balance between two competing policy considerations, namely enlisting tort law to combat executive and administrative abuse of power and not allowing public officers, who must always act for the public good, to be assailed by unmeritorious actions.' These propositions are taken from the speech of Lord Steyn, supported by the speeches of the other law lords. Lord Millett added that the tort could not be committed negligently or inadvertently; that the core concepts were abuse of power, bad faith or improper purpose; and that the tort was one of misfeasance, not nonfeasance. Its two varieties, as expressed by Lord Steyn, are as follows:

> First there is the case of targeted malice by a public officer, i.e. conduct specifically intended to injure a person or persons. This type of case involves bad faith in the sense of the exercise of public power for an improper or ulterior motive. The second form is where a public officer acts knowing that he has no power to do the act complained of and the act will probably injure the plaintiff. It involves bad faith inasmuch as the public officer does not have an honest belief that his act is lawful.[271]

There have been many cases since in which claimants have sought to establish targeted[272] or untargeted malice[273] but it must be said without much success.

The *Three Rivers* case, has greatly clarified the law. The marshalling and analysis of multifarious issues in the judgments of the Court of Appeal and in the speeches in the House of Lords has done much to establish the tort of misfeasance on a solid basis. Even so, not every point is dealt with in the several detailed judgments; and subsequent litigation, although dominated by the *Three Rivers* case, has generally dealt either with points not discussed or with the application of its principles in novel situations.

As we have already seen, it is now established that misfeasance of any type is not actionable per se.[274] Another case arose from the temporary admission to the United Kingdom of a man known to the immigration authorities and the police to be a very violent criminal. While so admitted he murdered a woman whose personal representatives then sought damages for misfeasance from the Home Secretary and Commissioner of the Metropolitan Police.[275] The defendants sought to strike out the action, arguing that in

---

[270] There need be no relationship of proximity between the claimant and the defendant, but there was a 'special rule of remoteness' to the effect that 'the intent required must be directed at the harm complained of, or at least to harm of the type suffered by the plaintiffs. This results in the rule that the plaintiff must establish not only that the defendant acted in the knowledge that the act was beyond his powers but also in the knowledge that his act would probably injure the plaintiff or persons of a class of which the plaintiff was a member' (at 1235, WLR).

[271] And see Lord Hope's description of the requirements in *Three Rivers DC v. The Governors and Company of the Bank of England (No 3)* (second hearing) [2001] UKHL 16, [2003] 2 AC 1, paras. 41–6.

[272] *Masters v. Chief Constable of Sussex* [2002] EWCA Civ 1482 (malice not found when fingerprints taken while arm broken); *Weir v. Secretary of State for Transport* [2005] EWHC 2192 (no malice found to shareholders when minister put company into administration).

[273] *Carter v. Chief Constable of the Cumbria Police* [2008] EWHC 1072 (untargeted malice not found; court alert to the possibility of claimants evading the partial immunity of the police for negligence (above, pp. 653–4) by pleading misfeasance); *Luck v. Tower Hamlets LBC* [2003] EWCA Civ 52 (allegation that local government officers acted with malice when giving corporate reference asserting claimant's unsuitability as contractor: malice not found). [274] Above, p. 665 in the *Watkins* case.

[275] *Akenzua v. Home Secretary* [2002] EWCA Civ 1470, [2003] 1 WLR 741. The criminal was apparently recruited as a police informer.

untargeted malice cases liability 'cannot go wider than the members of a closely defined class'. But the Court of Appeal held that Lord Steyn's reference to 'persons of a class of which the plaintiff was a member' was but a way of describing the limits of the 'reckless indifference'. An action could be maintained 'even where the identities of the eventual victims are not known at the time when the tort is committed, so long as it is clear that there will be such victims'.[276] The strike out was refused.[277]

All indications now are that the courts will not award damages against public authorities merely because they have made some order which turns out to be ultra vires, unless there is malice or conscious abuse. Indeed, misfeasance is a tort of personal bad faith so the individual responsible must be identified; an allegation of misfeasance 'should not be a vehicle for a general inquiry into wrongdoing'.[278] Where an Australian local authority had passed resolutions restricting building on a particular site without giving notice and fair hearing to the landowner and also in conflict with the planning ordinance, the Privy Council rejected the owner's claim for damages for depreciation of his land in the interval before the resolutions were held to be invalid.[279] 'The well-established tort of misfeasance by a public officer', it was held, required as a necessary element either malice or knowledge by the council of the invalidity of its resolutions. In New Zealand, also, a company failed in a claim for damages resulting from a minister's refusal of permission for it to obtain finance from a Japanese concern.[280] The minister's refusal was quashed as ultra vires, but it was held that this alone was not a cause of action.[281] Nor does it appear that claims of this kind can be strengthened by pleading breach of statutory duty.[282]

It was for the same reasons that the Court of Appeal refused relief in the Bourgoin case, as mentioned earlier.[283] A ministerial revocation order had prohibited the import of turkey meat from France and was held unlawful by the European Court as being in breach of Article 30 (now 28) of the Treaty of Rome. French traders who had suffered losses then sued the ministry for damages. On preliminary issues it was held that they had no cause of action merely for breach of statutory duty, as already related.[284] Likewise there was no cause of action merely because the minister's order was unlawful: it could be quashed or declared unlawful on judicial review, but there was no remedy in damages for 'a simple

---

[276] Sedley LJ, para. 19. Otherwise the reckless release of a criminal known to wish to murder his wife would entail liability when he killed her, but the reckless release of a criminal known to wish to commit a terrorist bombing would entail no liability for misfeasance when he committed an outrage killing several people (para. 16).

[277] It was not contested that misfeasance would lie for personal injury, not just for economic loss.

[278] Chagos Islanders v. A-G [2003] EWHC 2222, para. 281 (Ouseley J).

[279] Dunlop v. Woollahra Municipal Council [1982] AC 158. See also R v. Knowlsley MBC ex p Maguire [1992] COD 499 (taxi licences wrongly refused, later granted: interim loss not recoverable). Claims similarly failed in Park Oh Ho v. Minister for Immigration (1989) 88 ALR 517 and Chan Yee Kin v. Minister for Immigration (1991) 103 ALR 499.

[280] Takaro Properties Ltd v. Rowling [1978] 2 NZLR 314. The Court of Appeal (NZ) later awarded damages for negligence but was reversed by the Privy Council: above, p. 656.

[281] The so-called Beaudesert principle, that there is liability in tort for 'unlawful, intentional and positive acts', laid down by the High Court of Australia in Beaudesert Shire Council v. Smith (1966) 120 CLR 145 but never applied since, was rejected by the House of Lords in Lonrho Ltd v. Shell Petroleum Co Ltd [1982] AC 173 and overruled by the High Court of Australia in Northern Territory v. Mengel (1995) 69 ALJR 527.

[282] See above, p. 660.

[283] Bourgoin SA v. Ministry of Agriculture, Fisheries and Food [1986] QB 716. Art. 28 (ex 30) prohibits quantitative restrictions on imports. See also An Bord Bainne Co-operative Ltd v. Milk Marketing Board [1988] 1 FTLR 145, where the Court of Appeal held that there was no remedy in damages for alleged failure by the minister to ensure the due observance of Community law.   [284] Above, p. 662.

excess of power'.[285] Since that decision, however, it has become clear that the rules of Community law are more generous and that, since Community law was in question, there may have been a right to damages enforceable in the British court without proof of malice.[286] According to this doctrine the government's liability for infringing Community law will be much wider than it is for acting ultra vires in domestic law, since innocent infringements are common but malicious infringements are rare.

STATEMENT OF GENERAL PRINCIPLES OF LIABILITY

The principles of liability seem now to be emerging clearly. It can be said that administrative action[287] which is not actionable merely as a breach of duty will found an action for damages in any of the following situations:

1. if it involves the commission of a recognised tort such as trespass, false imprisonment or negligence[288]

2. if it is actuated by malice, e.g. personal spite or a desire to injure for improper reasons[289]

3. if the authority knows that it does not possess the power to take the action in question or is recklessly indifferent to its existence[290]

4. if the case is governed by Community law and that law would allow reparation[291]

5. if human rights have been infringed entitling the victim to 'just satisfaction'.[292]

The decisions suggest that there is unlikely to be liability in the absence of all these elements, for example where a licensing authority cancels a licence in good faith but invalidly, perhaps in breach of natural justice or for irrelevant reasons. Since loss of livelihood by cancellation of a licence is just as serious an injury as many forms of trespass or other torts, it may seem illogical and unjust that it should not be equally actionable in damages; and in *obiter dicta* in a dissenting judgment Denning LJ once suggested that it was.[293] Some cases of this kind may involve breach of statutory duty, but that head of liability is now confined as explained above.[294] In general it seems probable that public authorities and their officers[295] will be held to be free from liability so long as they exercise their

---

[285] Parker and Nourse LJJ treated this as a self-evident proposition, without citing authority. Oliver LJ dissented. In fact the government paid £3.5m. in compensation: [1989] *PL* at 47 (J. A. Weir). The European Court had found the government to be in default: see [1986] QB at 725.   [286] See above, p. 663.

[287] Which is not necessarily ultra vires; see the discussion of the abandonment of the 'public law hurdle' above, p. 650.   [288] Above, p. 640.

[289] *Ashby* v. *White; Roncarelli* v. *Duplessis; Smith* v. *East Elloe Rural District Council; David* v. *Abdul Cader* (above); and see the review of authorities in *Takaro Properties Ltd* v. *Rowling* (above). The court will not allow misfeasance to be used to evade the requirements of malicious prosecution: *Silcott* v. *Commissioner of Police of the Metropolis* (1996) 8 Admin LR 633 overruled in part in *Parker* v. *Chief Constable of the West Midlands Police* [2001] 1 AC 435 (HL), and see *Gizzonio* v. *Chief Constable of Derbyshire* The Times, 29 April 1998 (no liability for refusal of bail).

[290] *Farrington* v. *Thomson* [1959] VR 286; the *Bourgoin* case (above); the *Three Rivers* case (above).

[291] The *Factortame* case, above, p. 663.   [292] Above, p. 637.

[293] *Abbott* v. *Sullivan* [1952] 1 KB 189 at 202; and see *Davis* v. *Carew-Pole* [1956] 1 WLR 833. Contrast *Hlookoff* v. *Vancouver City* (1968) 67 DLR (3d) 119.   [294] Above, p. 660.

[295] Misfeasance by an officer outside the course of employment will not render the authority liable: *Weldon* v. *Home Office* [1992] 1 AC 58 at 164; *Racz* v. *Home Office* [1994] 2 AC 45.

discretionary powers in good faith and with reasonable care. Losses caused by bona fide but mistaken acts of government may have to be suffered just as much when they are invalid as when they are valid.[296] This unjust doctrine is in need of reform.

A comparable, but not identical, doctrine prevails in the European Court, based upon the provision of the Treaty that 'the Community shall, in accordance with the general principles common to the laws of the Member States, make good any damage caused by its institutions or by its servants in the performance of their duties'.[297] It is held that the mere illegality of regulations made by the Council of the EC gives no cause of action to traders who have suffered loss by obeying them,[298] but that damages must be paid for loss suffered if a Community authority has 'manifestly and gravely disregarded the limits on the exercise of its powers'.[299] This test is, as mentioned earlier, the same as that applied to breaches of Community law by Member States.[300] Since it lacks the element of malice or conscious abuse which is essential in the British doctrine of misfeasance, it comes nearer to providing just reparation for unlawful but innocent executive action. The non-liability for mere illegality committed by Community organs is justified by 'the exercise of a wide discretion essential for the implementation of the common agricultural policy'—a ground reminiscent of the House of Lords' 'policy or operational' distinction in the law of negligence, where 'policy' also restricts liability.[301]

IMMUNITIES AND TIME LIMITS

JUDICIAL IMMUNITY

Judges in courts of law enjoy special immunity from actions in tort. The object is to strengthen their independence, so that their decisions may not be warped by fear of personal liability:

> It is a principle of our law that no action will lie against a judge of one of the superior courts for a judicial act though it be alleged to have been done maliciously and corruptly.[302]

The fact that the judge may have exceeded his jurisdiction is irrelevant. But a judge may be liable in damages, like any other judicial officer, if in bad faith he does what he knows he has no power to do. Lord Bridge has said:[303]

> If the Lord Chief Justice himself, on the acquittal of a defendant charged before him with a criminal offence, were to say: 'That is a perverse verdict', and thereupon proceed to pass a sentence of imprisonment, he could be sued for trespass.

---

[296] For discussion of this issue see the Law Commission report 'Administrative Redress: Public Bodies and the Citizen', above, p. 633; Cornford, *Towards a Public Law of Tort* (2008); [2009] *PL* 70 (Cornford) and 'Damages in Public Law' (1999) 9 *Otago Law Review* 489. In South Africa the Promotion of Administrative Justice Act 3 of 2000, s. 8(1)(c)(ii)(bb) provides for compensation to be awarded exceptionally if such award is 'just and equitable'.   [297] Treaty of Rome, Art. 288 (ex 215).

[298] *Bayerische HNL Vermehrungsbetriebe* v. *Council and Commission* [1978] 3 CMLR 566; *Koninklijke Scholten Honig NV* v. *Council and Commission of the European Communities* [1982] 2 CMLR 590; *Mulder* v. *Council and Commission* [1992] ECR I-3061 (with examples on both sides of the line).

[299] As in *Deutsche Getreideverwertung* v. *Council and Commission* [1979] ECR 3017.

[300] Above, p. 663.   [301] Above, p. 651.

[302] *Fray* v. *Blackburn* (1863) 3 B & S 576 at 578 (Crompton J) (unsuccessful action against Blackburn J). See also *Anderson* v. *Gorrie* [1895] 1 QB 668. A judge wrongfully refusing a writ of habeas corpus was by statute made personally liable for a penalty of £500.   [303] *Re McC.* [1985] AC 528 at 540.

In the case of judges of inferior courts, meaning courts which were subject to control by mandatory, quashing and prohibiting orders,[304] it used to be the law that they were liable if they acted maliciously and without reasonable and probable cause, even though within their jurisdiction.[305] For acts done outside their jurisdiction they had no protection at all, and were liable in damages for any injury so caused.[306] In reaffirming the latter rule, though not the former, the House of Lords explained that legislation had to some extent restricted the liability of justices of the peace and provided for them to be indemnified at public expense where they had acted reasonably and in good faith.[307] Now, however, justices of the peace are exempted by statute from liability for acting outside their jurisdiction, except only where they act in bad faith; and for acting within their jurisdiction they have full immunity.[308]

In this context 'jurisdiction' is used in a wider sense than for the purposes of the ultra vires doctrine, where errors of many kinds may destroy jurisdiction. It requires 'some gross and obvious irregularity of procedure, as for example if one justice absented himself for part of the hearing and relied on another to tell him what had happened during his absence', or a flagrant breach of the rules of natural justice, as opposed to 'some narrow technical ground' such as an error of jurisdictional fact[309] or a minor violation of natural justice.[310] Earlier examples of inferior courts exceeding jurisdiction in this sense were where the judge of the Court of the Marshalsea, having jurisdiction over members of the king's household, imprisoned someone who was not a member of it;[311] where a county court judge in Lancashire committed for contempt a party in Cambridgeshire who was outside the judge's territorial jurisdiction;[312] and where a revising barrister wrongly expelled a plaintiff from his court.[313] In all these cases the judges were held personally liable in damages for the false imprisonment and assault, even where they had acted in good faith; and officers executing their judgments were liable similarly.[314]

The rules of common law which benefit magistrates ought also to benefit statutory tribunals which operate like courts, by finding facts and applying law, as do for example social security tribunals and employment tribunals. At the other end of the scale, it seems obvious that judicial immunity will not extend to an administrative authority merely because its function is denominated judicial or quasi-judicial for the purposes of the rules of natural justice or of control by quashing order;[315] for in those cases the function is basically administrative. Thus no immunity should be enjoyed by an inspector holding a public inquiry. The same might apply to licensing agencies such as planning authorities. Such bodies have only limited opportunities for committing torts, since they possess no powers of arrest or detention. Mental health review tribunals possess such powers, but their members have statutory protection provided that they act in good faith and with

---

[304] This includes the Crown Court except in relation to trial on indictment: Senior Courts Act 1981, s. 29(3).

[305] The authorities seem to be *obiter dicta*, e.g. *Cave* v. *Mountain* (1840) 1 M & G 257 at 263.

[306] Examples concerning magistrates are *Jones* v. *Gurdon* (1842) 2 QB 600; *Clark* v. *Woods* (1848) 2 Ex 395; *R* v. *Manchester City Magistrates' Court ex p Davies* [1989] QB 631; and see *Beaurain* v. *Scott* (above, p. 405). But honest mistake of fact was a defence: *Pease* v. *Chaytor* (1861) 1 B & S 658; *London Cpn* v. *Cox* (1867) LR 2 HL 239 at 263. [307] *Re McC.* [1985] AC 528.

[308] Courts and Legal Services Act 1990, s. 108. Provision for indemnity is made by Justices of the Peace Act 1997, as amended by Access to Justice Act 1999, s. 99. [309] See *Pease* v. *Chaytor* (above).

[310] *Re McC.* (above) at 546–7. But see the *Manchester City Magistrates'* case (above) holding that failure to consider a statutory requirement was actionable. [311] *Marshalsea Case* (1613) 10 Co Rep 68b.

[312] *Houlden* v. *Smith* (1850) 14 QB 841. [313] *Willis* v. *Maclachlan* (1876) 1 Ex D 376.

[314] *Marshalsea Case* (above); *London Cpn* v. *Cox* (above).

[315] See e.g. *Cooper* v. *Wandsworth Board of Works* (1863) 14 CB (NS) 180 (above, p. 409).

reasonable care.[316] Where there is neither judicial immunity nor statutory protection, tribunals will have the same liability as other administrative authorities, as explained in the preceding sections.[317]

A principle which might prove important was propounded in the House of Lords in 1921 in a case where it was held that there could be no liability for negligence on the part of a justice of the peace or guardian in making an order for the detention of a lunatic, provided that the justice or guardian was honestly satisfied that it was a proper case for the order.[318] Lord Moulton said:[319]

> If a man is required in the discharge of a public duty to make a decision which affects, by its legal consequences, the liberty or property of others, and he performs that duty and makes that decision honestly and in good faith, it is, in my opinion, a fundamental principle of our law that he is protected.

This wide statement ought probably to be confined to decisions made within jurisdiction, since at the time it was made there was undoubtedly liability for interference with personal liberty or property where there was no jurisdiction.[320] It probably means no more than that members of a tribunal which acts within its jurisdiction and in good faith are not personally liable to actions for negligence or for acting on no evidence.[321] In this case the House of Lords were aware of the need to define judicial immunity with reference to the growing adjudicatory powers of administrative authorities, 'a fresh legal problem of far-reaching importance';[322] but they did not attempt to do it.

TIME LIMITS FOR ACTIONS IN TORT

Although in earlier years there were specially short statutory periods within which actions against public authorities (including the Crown) had to be brought,[323] these have now been abolished.[324] Actions in tort against public authorities and their servants or agents are now governed by the ordinary period of limitation for actions in tort generally, which is three years for actions based on personal injury and six years in other cases,[325] with an alternative, in the case of latent damage, of three years from its manifestation.[326] Discrimination in favour of public authorities was thus abolished, in conformity with the policy of making them subject to the ordinary law—the same policy which was embodied in the Crown Proceedings Act 1947.

For the purposes of computing the time limit where a public authority has acted in some way outside its powers, time runs from the tortious act committed, e.g. entry on land (trespass), detention of a person (false imprisonment), or seizure of goods (trespass), rather than from the time of any invalid determination or order under which the

---

[316] See above, p. 663.

[317] For the position of arbitrators and valuers see *Arenson v. Arenson* [1977] AC 405.

[318] *Everett v. Griffiths* [1921] AC 631. Compare *Welbridge Holdings Ltd v. Greater Winnipeg Cpn* (1970) 22 DLR (3d) 470 at 476.   [319] Ibid. at 695.

[320] See above, p. 670.

[321] See *Cave v. Mountain* (1840) 1 M & G 257.   [322] [1921] AC at 659 (Lord Haldane).

[323] A limitation period of 6 months was laid down by the Public Authorities Protection Act 1893 (replacing many earlier enactments) for most actions against public authorities for neglect or default in the execution of a statute. For the Act, its effects and its repeal, see M. J. Beloff QC, in Forsyth and Hare (eds.), *The Golden Metwand* at 267. See also *Bradford Corporation v. Myers* [1916] 1 AC 242; *Griffiths v. Smith* [1941] AC 170.

[324] Law Reform (Limitation of Actions, etc.) Act 1954, s. 1. See *Arnold v. Central Electricity Generating Board* [1988] AC 228 (no revival of claims previously barred).   [325] Limitation Act 1980, ss. 2, 11.

[326] Latent Damage Act 1986.

action was taken. This is because an invalid determination or order by itself inflicts no injury: the right of action necessarily accrues only when there is some injurious result which the invalid determination or order does not excuse.[327]

LIABILITY IN CONTRACT

BASIS OF ORDINARY LAW

English law, unlike that of France and other countries,[328] has no special legal regime governing contracts made by public authorities.[329] Formerly the Crown had a special legal position, and to some extent it still has; but, as explained in the following chapter, it has for most practical purposes been put into the same position as an ordinary litigant by the Crown Proceedings Act 1947. Central government departments normally make contracts in their own names but as agents of the Crown, so that the enforcement of such contracts is governed by the Act. Other governmental bodies such as local authorities are subject to the ordinary law of contract which applies to them in the same way as to private individuals and corporations (though with one important exception).[330] They are, as also are government departments, restricted in certain ways by rules of administrative law, such as the rules which prevent their contracts from fettering their discretionary powers[331] and from creating estoppels in some cases.[332] European Union law, moreover, has imposed a special regime for procurement contracts, designed to ensure fair competition and non-discrimination. This regime applies primarily, but not exclusively, to public authorities, as explained below.

The Crown is free to make contracts (though not to spend public money) without statutory authority since it enjoys the powers of a natural person.[333] Local authorities, on the other hand, are wholly statutory bodies and can bind themselves by contract only in so far as statute permits.

Contractual obligations are not enforceable by judicial review,[334] unless the question is whether the contracting authority has exceeded its powers. So much of the territory of government is now administered through contracts that this exclusionary rule may allow wide regions of administrative power to escape from judicial control, contrary to constitutional principles.[335] It does not yet seem that the courts are alive to this danger.

In practice, as opposed to law, there are many special aspects of public authorities' contracts which, though interpreted and enforced according to the ordinary law, may be regarded as the subject of a distinct body of rules.[336] Rates of profit on central government contracts are subject to review, either upwards or downwards, and either generally or for particular contracts, by the Review Board for Government Contracts. This advisory body was set up in 1969 by agreement between the Treasury (since replaced by the Department of Defence) and the Confederation of British Industries, after revelations of exorbitant

---

[327] *Polley* v. *Fordham* [1904] 2 KB 345.

[328] For the French regime, which applies to certain kinds of contracts only according to complicated rules, see Brown and Bell, *French Administrative Law*, 5th edn (1998), 202.

[329] See Mitchell, *The Contracts of Public Authorities* (1954), dealing also with the USA and France; Turpin, *Government Procurement and Contracts* (1989); Arrowsmith, *Civil Liability and Public Authorities* (1992), chs. 2–4; Arrowsmith, *The Law of Public and Utilities Procurement* (1996).

[330] See below, p. 673.   [331] Above, p. 277.   [332] See above, p. 196.

[333] See above, p. 180.   [334] See above, p. 535.

[335] See [1994] *PL* 86, [1998] *PL* 288 (M. Freedland); Murray Hunt in Taggart (ed.), *The Province of Administrative Law*, 21.   [336] See Turpin (as above), chs. 6–8.

profits made in defence and health service contracts. Common form clauses such as the 'Standard Conditions of Government Contracts for Stores Purchases'[337] and 'General Conditions of Government Contracts for Building and Civil Engineering Works'[338] are employed by government departments so as to produce a high degree of uniformity in contracts for procurement and public works. Widely drawn 'break clauses' allow the government to terminate the contract, subject to the payment of compensation to the contractor. Local authorities are subject to legislation on competitive tendering.[339] Local authorities are represented on the Joint Contracts Tribunal, an unofficial body which settles the terms of the commonly used standard form of building contract.

Contracts of service with public authorities rest on the same 'ordinary law' basis as other contracts, except in the case of the Crown, as explained earlier.[340]

GOVERNMENT BY CONTRACT

Contracts are widely used by public authorities as instruments both of policy and of administration.[341] It is by this means that the government in the past regulated tobacco advertising and sponsorship, by 'voluntary agreement' with traders' representative bodies,[342] and secures compensation for the victims of accidents caused by uninsured drivers, by agreement with the Motor Insurers' Bureau.[343] The government's contractual business is now so vast that it is easily tempted to use it for ulterior purposes, as mentioned earlier.[344] It is a source of great power, which has been called a 'new prerogative'.[345] Contracts have now come to play a large part in the mechanism of public services, for example in the National Health Service, in the social and educational services and in prison administration, under policies of decentralisation and privatisation and under the wide contracting powers described below. So pervasive is the technique of administration by contract that it has been called 'a revolution in the making' and 'the cutting edge of administrative law'.[346] Contract, it is said, 'has replaced command and control as the paradigm of administration'.[347] Such contracts will not always be designed for enforcement by legal sanctions, since in many cases administrative pressure will be the natural remedy.

Local authorities may make use of their statutory contract powers for ulterior purposes of policy. In the planning field they have wide powers to enter into agreements for 'restricting or regulating' the development or use of land.[348] They are often able to induce applicants for planning permission to agree to concessions which they would have no power to impose by way of statutory conditions. The legality of this practice has been questioned but it has been held to be legitimate.[349] Administrative collaboration between

---

[337] Form GC/Stores/1 (1979 edn).   [338] Form GC/Works/1 (1998 edn).

[339] Local Government, Planning and Land Act 1980, s. 7; Local Government Act 1988, s. 4.

[340] Above, p. 48.

[341] See Turpin, *British Government and the Constitution*, 5th edn (2002), 437; Harden, *The Contracting State*; [1994] *PL* 86, [1998] *PL* 288 (M. Freedland).   [342] See 29 HC Deb. 437 (WA) (27 Oct. 1982).

[343] See *Hardy* v. *Motor Insurers' Bureau* [1964] 2 QB 745, where the defence that a third party could not enforce the contract was deliberately not pleaded and the claimant succeeded. The current Agreement is that of 1999. See also *Sharp* v. *Pereira* [1999] 1 WLR 195.   [344] Above, p. 328.

[345] [1979] *CLP* 41 (T. C. Daintith); and see Daintith in Jowell and Oliver (eds.), *The Changing Constitution*, 3rd edn, 209; (1990) 106 *LQR* 277 (S. Arrowsmith).

[346] Harlow and Rawlings, *Law and Administration*, 2nd edn, 207, providing much further detail.

[347] Murray Hunt (as above), 21.   [348] Town and Country Planning Act 1990, s. 106.

[349] *Good* v. *Epping Forest DC* [1994] 1 WLR 376; *Tesco Stores Ltd* v. *Secretary of State for the Environment* [1995] 1 WLR 759 (HL).

local authorities and other public bodies may be arranged by contract, so that one may perform services on behalf of another under statutory powers.[350]

Government departments let many contracts by competitive tender, in accordance with a policy of testing the market wherever possible.[351] Local authorities have been compelled to do the same, so that their own works departments may be exposed to commercial competition. Services such as ground maintenance, refuse collection and vehicle maintenance are examples which have been subjected to 'compulsory competitive tendering'. Successive Local Government Acts empowered the Secretary of State to extend the list and to give directions to recalcitrant authorities which might be 'banning orders' restricting or regulating their powers.[352] This draconian regime was relaxed in 1999 in a change of policy, which imposed a duty to secure 'best value' as explained earlier.[353]

DELEGATION AND CONTRACTING OUT

The potentiality of 'government by contract' has been extended almost ad infinitum, both for central and local government, by sweeping statutory powers conferred in 1994 and 1997. Primarily these powers enable ministerial and local government functions, if authorised by ministerial order, to be exercised by any person or that person's employees, thus clearing the way for numerous official functions to be 'contracted out' into the private sector in accordance with the government's 'private finance initiative'.[354]

Under the Deregulation and Contracting Out Act 1994 any statutory function of a minister which is exercisable by an officer of his (either by statute or by rule of law)[355] may, if an order of the minister so provides, be made exercisable by any person (or employee) authorised by either the officer or the minister. There are corresponding provisions for local government, except that a ministerial order is still required and authorisation must be given by the local authority itself. Ministerial orders are subject to positive Parliamentary resolution. They cannot apply to judicial or legislative functions, or to powers affecting personal liberty or search or seizure of property (though there is a list of exemptions from those restrictions) nor can they endure for more than ten years.[356] But they may be limited, or subject to conditions, they are revocable and they do not denude the authorising body of the function in question. Any act or omission of the authorised person (or employee) is to be 'treated for all purposes' as that of the authorising body, except as regards so much of any contract as relates to the exercise of the function, or any criminal proceedings.[357] The responsibility of central and local government is thus preserved.

The Act of 1994 was supplemented, as regards local authorities, by the Local Government (Contracts) Act 1997. It is there provided that every statutory function of a local authority includes power to enter into a contract with another person for the provision of assets or

---

[350] Local Government Act 1972, s. 101.

[351] See e.g. *R v. Lord Chancellor ex p Hibbit and Saunders* [1993] COD 326 (above, p. 544). See generally Harlow and Rawlings, *Law and Administration*, 2nd edn, chs. 12–14; Arrowsmith, *The Law of Public and Utilities Procurement*, ch. 13.

[352] Local Government Planning and Land Act 1980, Pt III; Local Government Act 1988, Pts. I, II (now partly repealed). Local Government Act 1992, Pt I. See *Secretary of State for the Environment ex p Haringey LBC* (1994) 92 LGR 538 (Secretary of State's banning order upheld).

[353] Local Government Act 1999.

[354] See Harlow and Rawlings, *Law and Administration* (as above).

[355] As under the *Carltona* doctrine, above, p. 266.

[356] Extended to 40 years for certified contracts of local authorities (explained below): Local Government (Contracts) Act 1997, s. 9.

[357] s. 72.

services or both in connection with the function, and also to contract with any person financing the contractor. This is a wide power of procurement but it does not authorise delegation of functions as does the Act of 1994. The machinery of the latter Act is therefore still necessary for many purposes of contracting out.

VALIDITY OF LOCAL GOVERNMENT CONTRACTS

Since a local authority can act validly only within its statutory powers, any contract made in excess of its powers is wholly void: neither party can sue under it and money paid may be irrecoverable. In order to protect creditors the Local Government Act 1972 provided that a person lending money to a local authority should not be concerned with the legality of the borrowing and should not be prejudiced by any illegality.[358] But this provision did not cover all cases. After further disasters[359] the Local Government (Contracts) Act 1997 has provided for a system of 'certified contracts' under which contracting parties will have legal remedies even if the contract proves to be ultra vires.[360]

The contract has to be certified by the local authority itself within six weeks, and the certificate must state its purpose and its intended period of operation, which must be at least five years. Short-term contracts are therefore excluded. The statutory authority must be cited and the detailed requirements of regulations complied with. It is then provided that the contract shall have effect as if the local authority had had power to enter into it and had done so properly. If, however, the legality of those steps is disputed on judicial review, or under the audit procedure whereby expenditure can be challenged, the provision as to validity is suspended. If the court finds that the contract was ultra vires it may nevertheless validate it if it considers this to be right, having regard to the likely consequences for the financial position of the local authority and for the provision of services to the public. If the contract makes provision for 'discharge terms' in case of legal challenge, those terms remain effective even where the contract is invalid. In the absence of such terms, the contractor is entitled to whatever payments would have been due up to the date of the court's order and then to damages as for a repudiatory breach by the local authority.

In this way the Act attempts a compromise between validating unlawful contracts, which is objectionable on public policy grounds, and doing justice to contractors who are entitled to expect that local authorities will act lawfully and properly. Only where there are countervailing grounds of public policy will an unlawful contract be validated. If it is not, the contractor will still have remedies.

EU PROCUREMENT LAW

European Union law imposes an elaborate and strict regime on the procurement contracts of public authorities, if they exceed a certain value, in order that competition may be free and fair and without discrimination.[361] The limit of value is set at a point which is thought to be high enough to attract bids from other countries, and if that point is passed there are detailed rules about advertising and tendering and about the award of the

---

[358] 13th Sched., para. 20.

[359] As in *Hazell v. Hammersmith and Fulham LBC* [1992] AC 1 (unlawful rate swap transaction); *Crédit Suisse v. Allerdale BC* [1997] QB 306 (unlawful development scheme).

[360] And note too the Localism Act 2011, s. 1(1) which provides that a local authority 'has power to do anything that individuals generally may do'. But this power is subject to complicated restrictions in ss. 2–8. Under s. 5 the Secretary of State (who is granted a Henry VIII power (see below, p. 726)) may also impose or remove restrictions.   [361] See generally Arrowsmith (as above), ch. 3.

contract, which must be non-discriminatory and based on objective criteria. The value limit varies according to the public authority concerned and the type of contract, three types being distinguished: contracts for works, for supplies and for services. The values are set in euros, and for central government contracts they are €5,150,000 for works contracts and €133,000 for the others.

The rules are laid down in directives of the EU Council, and are given effect by regulations made under the European Communities Act 1972.[362] 'Public authorities' is given an extended meaning, including not only ministers, government departments and local authorities but also 'bodies governed by public law'. The scope of this definition is therefore similar to that of judicial review. The regulations specify many of the authorities affected, but the list is not exclusive. Certain utilities, even if not public authorities, are subject to the same regime, e.g. suppliers of water, electricity, gas, telecommunications and transport systems. The regulations pose many problems of definition and application, and their efficacy is uncertain.[363]

Proposals for contracts, if they fall within the regulations, must be notified to the EU authorities, who then advertise them. Bids must be considered objectively and without discrimination, and in accordance with specified criteria. Dissatisfied tenderers may apply to the High Court to have an award set aside, or for an injunction or for damages, and disputes may ultimately be referred to the ECJ. Since contractual and commercial relationships are outside the scope of judicial review procedure, disputes will be litigated in the ordinary way.[364]

LIABILITY TO MAKE RESTITUTION

PAYMENTS EXACTED UNLAWFULLY

If a public authority wrongfully demands[365] a payment, perhaps by imposing some charge or rate which is ultra vires, can a person who pays it later recover his money when the demand later turns out to have been illegal?[366] In the past this question has been treated as a matter of the ordinary law which governs private transactions,[367] in much the same way as contract. There were no special rules for public authorities,[368] and few reported

---

[362] See SI 1991 No. 2680; SI 1993 No. 3228; SI 1995 No. 201; SI 1996 No. 2911.

[363] Harlow and Rawlings (as above), 249.

[364] See e.g. *Matra Communications SAS* v. *Home Office* [1999] 1 WLR 1646; *R* v. *Tower Hamlets LBC ex p Luck* [1999] COD 294.

[365] There need not be a formal demand for payment but covers 'a situation in which payment is required of the taxpayer without lawful authority': *Test Claimants in the Franked Investment Income Group Litigation* v. *Commissioners of Inland Revenue* [2012] UKSC 19, para. 174 (Lord Sumption) and see Lord Walker (para. 79). [366] See [2006] *JR* 370 (Virgo).

[367] For this subject see *Goff and Jones, The Law of Restitution*, 8th edn (by Mitchell, Mitchell and Watterson) (2011), chs. 4, 5 and 9; Gareth Jones, *Restitution in Public and Private Law*; Burrows, *The Law of Restitution*, 2nd edn (2002), ch. 12; Law Commission Report No. 227 (1994), and Williams, *Unjust Enrichment and Public Law—A Comparative Study of France, England and the EC* (2004). Formerly claims against the Crown lay by petition of right and now they lie under the Crown Proceedings Act 1947, s. 1.

[368] *Twyford* v. *Manchester Cpn* [1946] Ch 236 at 241. Claims may also be made by a public body (not limited to central government) (*Charles Terence Estates Ltd* v. *Cornwall Council and anor* [2011] EWHC 2542, para. 97, relying on *Auckland Harbour Board* v. *R* [1924] AC 318; not overruled on this point in the Court of Appeal ([2012] EWCA Civ 1439) discussed above, p. 247. For discussion see [2010] *PL* 747 (Mitchell). But see *The Child Poverty Action Group* v. *Secretary of State for Work and Pensions* [2010] UKSC 54 (where there is a statutory remedy, the common law remedy may be excluded).

cases of much importance, strange though this seems. The explanation may be partly that public authorities are often willing to make restitution voluntarily when they have acted unlawfully, as witness the case of the television licences where the Home Office mounted an elaborate operation to repay all the surcharges which they had wrongly levied.[369] No litigation was reported after the House of Lords' decision in 1981 that a rate of over £100 m. levied by the Greater London Council was ultra vires.[370] In 1992, however, the House of Lords, in the *Woolwich Building Society* case, laid down[371] new and fairer rules for recovery of money from public authorities; and in 1998, in the *Kleinwort Benson* case,[372] the House redressed injustices to contractors by abolishing the rule that mistake of law is a bar to recovery. The background to those cases was the ordinary law of restitution (formerly called quasi-contract).

EARLIER LAW

Until 1998 the primary rule of the ordinary law was that there could be no recovery of money paid voluntarily under a mistake of law, as opposed to a mistake of fact.[373] In some situations this is a sound rule, since otherwise innumerable transactions might be reopened by parties who later discover that they might have acted more advantageously.[374] It was formerly applied in favour of public authorities in a number of cases, for example where a taxpayer established in litigation with the Inland Revenue that the tax was not due, but was unable to recover earlier payments made under similar assessments.[375] Rates overpaid to local authorities were as a rule not recoverable, but they could be set off against later demands.[376] Even where there has been no mistake of law any voluntary payment will be irrecoverable,[377] provided that there has been no mistake of fact and no duress.

Indiscriminate application of the primary rule could operate inequitably and unethically,[378] and in some jurisdictions it has been abolished.[379] In the past judges have sought escape from it by two different routes. One, always a judicial favourite, was to represent mistakes of law as mistakes of fact.[380] The other was to exploit the doctrine of 'duress'. That doctrine holds that the payment does not count as voluntary, and is therefore recoverable, if it in fact has to be made to secure the performance of some duty or service due

---

[369] See above, p. 301.   [370] Above, p. 341.

[371] *Woolwich Equitable Building Society* v. *Inland Revenue Commissioners* [1993] AC 70.

[372] *Kleinwort Benson Ltd* v. *Lincoln City Council* [1999] 2 AC 349.

[373] Goff and Jones (as above), 217.

[374] See *Rogers* v. *Ingham* (1876) 3 Ch D 351 at 357 (Mellish LJ).

[375] *William Whiteley Ltd* v. *R* (1909) 101 LT 741 (tax on male servants). See similarly *National Pari-Mutuel Association Ltd* v. *R* (1930) 47 TLR 110 (betting tax) and *Slater* v. *Burnley Cpn* (1888) 59 LT 636 (miscalculated water rate) and *Hydro Electric Commission of Nepean* v. *Ontario Hydro* (1982) 132 DLR (3d) 193 (overcharged for supply of electricity).

[376] See *R* v. *Tower Hamlets LBC ex p Chetnik Development Ltd* [1988] AC 858.

[377] See the *Woolwich* case (below), at 165 (Lord Goff).

[378] In the *Tower Hamlets* case, above, Lord Bridge observed (at 877) that 'although it is a course permitted to an ordinary litigant it is not regarded by the courts as a "high-minded thing" to do, but rather as a "shabby thing" or a "dirty trick" and hence is a course which the court will not allow one of its own officers, such as a trustee in bankruptcy, to take.'

[379] As in Canada and in parts of Australia and the United States: Goff and Jones (as above), 217.

[380] As in *Cooper* v. *Phibbs* (1867) LR 2 HL 149; *George Jacobs Enterprises Ltd* v. *City of Regina* (1964) 44 DLR (2d) 179 (mistake as to validity of byelaw held mistake of fact); Goff and Jones (as above), 251. Compare below, p. 786.

to or sought by the payer, such as the return of property[381] or the grant of a licence or permission.[382]

THE *WOOLWICH* CASE

This decision of the House of Lords[383] greatly improved the prospects of recovering money paid to public authorities under unlawful demands.[384] Essentially it was a reaction against the injustice, and also the constitutional impropriety, of enforcing the mistake of law rule in such cases—although, since the claimant had made no such mistake, it was rather the voluntary payment rule which was under attack.

The Building Society had successfully challenged transitional provisions in income tax regulations about building societies. In order to avoid adverse publicity, and also penalties in case they should be wrong, they had paid the tax demanded 'without prejudice'. After the invalidity of the regulations had finally been established the Inland Revenue repaid the tax in question with interest from the date of the High Court judgment which the House of Lords had upheld. The society, however, claimed that it had from the first been entitled to restitution, so that interest was due from the dates of its payments, not from the date of the judgment. Some £6.7 million was at stake. In a 3:2 decision the House of Lords upheld the society's claim as a matter of common law, the statutory provisions about overpaid tax being inapplicable. The gist of this revolutionary decision is that there is now a prima facie right to restitution of money paid to a public authority under an unlawful demand.

In Lord Goff's leading speech for the majority the theme of constitutional impropriety is prominent. Under the Bill of Rights 1688 taxation levied without the authority of Parliament is illegal—'one of the most fundamental principles of our law', so that 'the retention by the state of taxes unlawfully exacted is particularly obnoxious'.[385] He emphasised also the 'common justice' of the taxpayer's claim and the inequality of his position vis-à-vis the state, with its coercive and penal powers, amounting to 'implied duress', as Holmes J put it in a famous American case.[386] But ultimately this was not the decisive factor: 'In the end, logic appears to demand that the right of recovery should require neither mistake nor compulsion, and that the simple fact that the tax was exacted unlawfully should prima facie be enough to require its repayment'.[387] The task of the House was to do justice between the parties, undeterred by accusations of judicial legislation. Therefore the law must be reformulated[388] so as to allow recovery of any tax or levy wrongly exacted by a public authority either by an ultra vires demand or under some misunderstanding of the

---

[381] *Irving* v. *Wilson* (1791) 4 TR 485.

[382] *Morgan* v. *Palmer* (1824) 2 B & C 729 (liquor licence); *Brocklebank Ltd* v. *R* [1925] 1 KB 52 (licence to sell ship); *South of Scotland Electricity Board* v. *British Oxygen Co Ltd* [1959] 1 WLR 587 (electricity supply) (a 'duress' case: see Lord Merriman at 607); *Hooper* v. *Exeter Cpn* (1887) 56 LJQB 457 (unjustified harbour dues) evidently belongs to this class, since the payment was held to be involuntary. So would *A-G* v. *Wilts United Dairies Ltd* (1921) 37 TLR 884 if, as Atkin LJ said, the payments were recoverable, since it was a licensing case.

[383] *Woolwich Equitable Building Society* v. *Inland Revenue Commissioners* [1993] AC 70, discussed in [1993] *PL* 580 (P. B. H. Birks), (1993) 109 *LQR* 401 (J. Beatson). See also *Westdeutsche Landesbank Girozentrale* v. *Islington LBC* [1996] AC 669. Contrast *Morgan Guaranty Trust Co* v. *Lothian Regional Council*, 1995 SLT 299.   [384] Voluntary payment under void contracts are another matter: see above, p. 676.

[385] *Woolwich* at 172.

[386] *Atchison, Topeka & Santa Fe Railway Co* v. *O'Connor* 223 US 280 at 285 (1912).

[387] *Woolwich* at 173.

[388] Lord Goff and Lord Browne-Wilkinson regard this as a change in the law. Lord Slynn regarded the previous law as not precluding his decision.

law.[389] Under such a liberal rule the fact that the Society paid under protest becomes irrelevant. A payment made without protest will normally be recoverable, and the defences of mistake of law and voluntary payment will cease to be available. There is then a clear benefit in public policy, since the law will no longer set a trap for the citizen if he acts on the principle of 'pay now, sue later', which is plainly a becoming attitude vis-à-vis the state.

THE *KLEINWORT BENSON* CASE

The long-standing and much criticised rule against recovery for error of law was abrogated by the House of Lords in another 3:2 decision in 1998.[390] A bank had claimed restitution from a number of local authorities of monies paid to them under rate swap transactions which in an earlier decision[391] the House had declared to be beyond their powers and void. All these transactions had been fully performed according to their terms. The bank had already recovered its more recent payments,[392] as to which the six-year period of limitation had not expired, but its earlier payments could be reclaimed only with the extension of time allowed by the Limitation Act 1980, in an 'action for relief from the consequences of a mistake', until the mistake was, or could with reasonable diligence have been, discovered.[393] In this also the bank succeeded, although it was accepted that many long-dormant claims might thus be revived. The dissentient lords held that the problem of dormant claims would be better resolved by Act of Parliament. They held also that the bank had made no mistake, having acted in accordance with the law as understood at the time—and so they rejected the theory of absolute retrospectivity of judgments, as explained in an earlier chapter.[394] The majority view was that the judgment retrospectively revealed a mistake of law, and that the bank had a cause of action in mistake.

In abolishing the former rule, which neither party attempted to defend, the House of Lords established a general right to recover money paid under mistake, whether of fact or law, subject to defences recognised in the law of restitution such as estoppel, change of position and compromise. But they rejected alleged defences of 'settled understanding of the law', 'honest belief in a right to retain the money' or 'contract fully performed'.

LIABILITY TO PAY COMPENSATION WHERE THERE HAS BEEN NO TORT OR BREACH OF CONTRACT

COMPENSATION AND EXPROPRIATION

Compensation will often have to be paid by a public authority even though it has committed no tort or breach of contract, for instance where it takes land by compulsory purchase. The duty to pay is normally imposed by statute, but this is not invariably so. In 1964 the House of Lords held that the government had a duty at common law to pay compensation to an oil company for the destruction in 1942 of its installations in Burma, then about to fall to the Japanese; this was carried out on the orders of the Crown in the lawful

---

[389] The 'misunderstanding' alternative is suggested rather than decided. But since mistake of law is now a form of ultra vires (above, p. 219), the two alternatives coalesce.

[390] *Kleinwort Benson Ltd* v. *Lincoln City Council* [1999] 2 AC 349.

[391] The *Hazell* case, above, p. 676.

[392] As for total failure of consideration: *Westdeutsche Landesbank Girocentrale* v. *Islington LBC* [1996] AC 669.   [393] s. 32(1).

[394] Above, p. 247.

exercise of its prerogative power to provide for the defence of British territory.[395] It was held that there was no common law right to compensation for damage inflicted by the Crown's forces while actually fighting the enemy; but that destruction of property for the purpose of denying its use to the enemy did give rise to such a right. In other words, there was a general rule that seizure or destruction of property within the realm under prerogative powers, even in grave national emergency, could be done only on the footing that compensation was payable. This had been so with the ancient prerogative rights of purveyance and angary,[396] which respectively empowered the requisition of supplies for the royal household and of neutral property such as ships in time of war. Today prerogative powers of this kind are confined to time of war, and even then they have for the most part been replaced by statute. When provision has to be made for mobilising the whole resources of the country for wartime purposes, statutes and regulations naturally cover virtually everything.[397]

The House of Lords' decision, reached by a narrow majority, was immediately nullified by the War Damage Act 1965, which prevented the payment of compensation in that or any similar case. It provided in sweeping terms that no compensation should be payable at common law for damage or destruction of property caused by acts lawfully done by or on the authority of the Crown during or in contemplation of war, whether before or after the Act. By this unusual measure of retaliation Parliament demonstrated that it can, when it wishes, expropriate without compensation and in violation of existing legal right, in a manner not permitted in some other countries which enjoy the protection of written constitutions and bills of rights.[398] A further example was the Leasehold Reform Act 1967,[399] which gave no compensation to the expropriated owners of reversionary rights in houses let on long leases at ground rents, the tenants being empowered to purchase the property compulsorily at site value only. In this case the expropriation was claimed not to have been for public purposes, since its object was merely to enrich certain tenants at the expense of their landlords. The article in the European Convention on Human Rights, which provides that 'no one shall be deprived of his possessions except in the public interest',[400] was held by the European Court of Human Rights, nevertheless, to allow the government sufficiently wide discretion to justify the legislation.[401] The US Supreme Court, likewise, has been liberal in allowing 'public use' to extend to almost any legislative purpose. A 'public purpose' or 'public interest' limitation is so commonly included as a fundamental right in British Commonwealth constitutions that it deserves to be respected as an inviolable constitutional principle.[402] But courts will naturally be inclined to treat it as satisfied by any kind of general legislation, leaving it to Parliament to decide where the public interest lies.

---

[395] *Burmah Oil Co Ltd* v. *Lord Advocate* [1965] AC 75. On the pleadings it had to be assumed that the Crown was acting lawfully under the prerogative. Contrast *Re a Petition of Right* [1915] 3 KB 649, now no longer good law.

[396] See the *Burmah* case at 102 (Lord Reid). Purveyance was also used to obtain military supplies: see the *Saltpetre Case* (1606) 12 Co Rep 12.   [397] See *A-G* v. *De Keyser's Royal Hotel Ltd* [1920] AC 508.

[398] e.g. United States of America (5th amendment, also 14th amendment as interpreted); Federal Republic of Germany (Art. 14). Both constitutions also require that expropriation shall be for public purposes only.

[399] Extended so as to include flats as well as houses by the Housing and Urban Development Act 1993.

[400] First Protocol (1952), Art. 1.   [401] *James* v. *UK* (1986) 8 EHRR 123.

[402] For a wide survey of this aspect, with British, Commonwealth and American authorities, see Taggart, 'Expropriation and Public Purpose' in Forsyth and Hare (eds.), *The Golden Metwand*, 91.

PRESUMPTION IN FAVOUR OF COMPENSATION

Despite occasional departures of the kind just illustrated, Parliament has in the past usually respected the principle that compensation should be paid. It has accordingly become an established presumption that 'an intention to take away the property of a subject without giving him a legal right to compensation for the loss of it is not to be imputed to the Legislature unless that intention is expressed in unequivocal terms'.[403] On this ground the House of Lords invalidated a government scheme for assessing compensation on an ex gratia basis for property taken under wartime regulations, holding that there was a legal right to have compensation assessed in the ordinary way under the Lands Clauses Act 1845.[404] For the same reason the Privy Council held that an Australian statute vesting Melbourne Harbour in commissioners did not override private rights which had been acquired over part of the land.[405] Where there are no provisions for compensation, therefore, it may be presumed that existing rights are not to be infringed. The House of Lords applied this principle in a planning case where the local authority, in granting permission for the use of a caravan site, had imposed conditions which materially cut down the pre-existing rights of the owner.[406] Although the local authority were empowered to impose such conditions as they thought fit, it was presumed that Parliament could not have intended to infringe rights already existing, particularly since there were other powers under which this could be done, subject to payment of compensation.

This presumption does not, however, empower the court to award compensation for administrative acts authorised by Act of Parliament, unless the Act itself so provides. The planning legislation as a whole is in effect an extensive system of expropriation without compensation, since no compensation is payable in the great majority of cases where permission to develop land is refused, even though the land is then greatly reduced in value.[407] The most that can be done with the aid of the presumption is to place a narrower interpretation on administrative powers where no compensation is provided for interference with rights of property.

COMPENSATION ON COMPULSORY PURCHASE

The machinery for making, confirming and executing orders for the compulsory purchase of land was briefly mentioned earlier.[408] Compensation has to be assessed after the service of a 'notice to treat' and in accordance with the Land Compensation Acts 1961 and 1973. Any dispute over compensation is decided by the Lands Tribunal, from which appeal lies direct to the Court of Appeal. Compensation used to be assessed as at the date of the notice to treat, but the unfairness of this rule when there has been delay and a fall in the value of money has led the House of Lords to hold that the correct time is when the compensation is assessed or when possession is taken.[409] The measure of compensation has varied over the years. Should this be based on the existing use value, i.e. a value which took no account of possibilities of development or should it be the open market value?

---

[403] *Central Control Board* v. *Cannon Brewery Co Ltd* [1919] AC 744 (Lord Atkinson). See also *Manitoba Fisheries* v. *R* (1978) 88 DLR (3d) 462.   [404] In the *Central Control Board* case (above).

[405] *Colonial Sugar Refining Co Ltd* v. *Melbourne Harbour Trust Commissioners* [1927] AC 343.

[406] *Hartnell* v. *Minister of Housing and Local Government* [1965] AC 1134; see above, p. 345.

[407] But this is regulation rather than 'taking' of property: *Belfast Corporation* v. *OD Cars Ltd* [1960] AC 490 (a decision that planning restrictions did not conflict with s. 5 of the Government of Ireland Act 1920, prohibiting legislation for the taking of property without compensation).   [408] Above, p. 54.

[409] *West Midland Baptist Association* v. *Birmingham Cpn* [1970] AC 874; and see *Chilton* v. *Telford Development Corporation* [1987] 1 WLR 872.

But it is impossible in many cases to assess the open market value without knowing what development might be permitted by the planning authorities, so complex rules were laid down as to the assumptions to be made.

During this phase, therefore, the owner was given the benefit of the development to be carried out on the land acquired from him, but not of the rest of the scheme, e.g. the development of a new town on the surrounding land.[410] The statutory rules were consolidated in the Land Compensation Act 1961. The system remained based on open market value, but with allowance for the fact that the owner, like all other owners, might suffer from uncompensated planning restrictions.

ADDITIONAL RULES

Where land in a clearance area, i.e. an area of houses unfit for human habitation, was purchased compulsorily by a local authority for clearance under the Housing Act 1985, compensation was limited to 'cleared site value', being the value of the site cleared of buildings and available for development,[411] and disregarding any increase which might flow from the clearance of adjacent land.[412] But since this value might easily exceed the previous open market value of the land (with bad houses and protected tenants), compensation was limited also to the latter value, if it was in fact the lower.[413] The Secretary of State might require the local authority to make an additional payment if he was satisfied, after inspection, that a house within the clearance area had been well maintained.[414] The local authority must also pay compensation in respect of well-maintained houses which are required to be demolished under demolition or clearance orders or which are purchased compulsorily as unfit for human habitation.[415] In certain conditions also compensation is payable in respect of the house in any event, in order that owner-occupiers and others may not suffer undue loss.[416]

On a compulsory purchase the owner is also entitled to compensation for 'injurious affection' of his remaining land, if its value is impaired by severance or by the use made of the land taken from him.[417] If part of his land is taken for a motorway, for example, he may claim compensation for any fall in the value of his adjacent land caused by the noise and disturbance of traffic. Formerly, however, compensation under this head was limited to the proportion of the noise etc., attributable to the land actually taken from him, so that if only a small piece of his land was taken the compensation might be little or nothing.[418] This restriction was removed by the Land Compensation Act 1973, in accordance with its policy as explained below. Injurious affection of retained land is now assessed by reference to the whole of the works causing it.

---

[410] See *Myers* v. *Milton Keynes Development Cpn* [1974] 1 WLR 696, where the rules are explained by Lord Denning MR.   [411] s. 585.

[412] See *Davy* v. *Leeds Cpn* [1965] 1 WLR 445.

[413] Land Compensation Act 1961, s. 10 and 2nd Sched.   [414] Housing Act 1985, 23rd Sched.

[415] Ibid.   [416] Housing Act 1985, 24th Sched.

[417] Compulsory Purchase Act 1965, ss. 7, 10, replacing provisions of the Lands Clauses Consolidation Act 1845, as interpreted in *Buccleugh (Duke)* v. *Metropolitan Board of Works* (1872) LR 5 HL 418. The same applies on purchase by agreement: *Kirby* v. *Harrogate School Board* [1896] 1 Ch 437. The principle covers subsidiary rights such as rights of way and restrictive covenants: *Re Simeon and Isle of Wight Rural District Council* [1937] Ch 525.

[418] *Edwards* v. *Minister of Transport* [1964] 2 QB 134. It was assessed 'by some alchemy which I do not understand' (Harman LJ).

COMPENSATION FOR NUISANCE AND DISTURBANCE

It used to be the general rule that no compensation was payable to a person from whom no land was taken, however injuriously affected his property might be as a consequence of public works lawfully executed and operated, e.g. a motorway or an airport. An action for nuisance at common law is of no avail against the lawful exercise of statutory pow-ers.[419] In addition, there is the unrealistic rule that ordinary user of the highway is not a nuisance,[420] and aircraft are exempted by legislation.[421] There was therefore an artificial contrast between those from whom part of their land was taken, and who were compen-sated for the injury to the remainder, and those from whom nothing was taken but who might suffer heavy uncompensated loss. This was an inducement to many people to resist projects for roads, airports and other public works by every possible means, thus caus-ing many lengthy public inquiries into objections. Parliament made repeated attempts to secure for the community the increase of land values created by social development.[422] But the loss of land values inflicted for the benefit of the community had to be borne in a great many cases by the owners upon whom it happened to fall, 'for the greater good of the greater number'.[423] In a leading case of 1869 the House of Lords held that the owner of a house beside a new railway, from whom no land was taken, had no right to compen-sation for damage caused by vibration from the trains.[424] It was said that the common law contained the principle of sacrifice, since any landowner could dedicate a highway beside his neighbour's land, and ordinary user of the highway was not a nuisance. With this unconvincing analogy the House of Lords paved the way for technological progress at the expense of individual rights. Nor does their attitude appear to be different today.[425]

Not until a century later did Parliament take steps to remedy the injustice. Under the Land Compensation Act 1973 compensation is now payable by public authorities and other bodies where the value of an interest in land is depreciated by 'physical factors caused by the use of public works', whether highways, aerodromes, or other works on land provided or used under statutory powers.[426] The 'physical factors' in question are noise, smell, fumes, smoke, artificial lighting, and the discharge of any substance onto the land. The 'interest in land' must be that of a freeholder or of a leaseholder with at least three years of his term unexpired (both may claim simultaneously); but if the land is not a dwelling, the interest must be that of an owner-occupier and, unless agricultural, its rateable value must not exceed a prescribed sum.[427] No claim may be made until twelve

---

[419] Above, p. 641.

[420] *Hammersmith Railway Co* v. *Brand* (1869) LR 4 HL 171 at 196. But see *Gillingham BC* v. *Medway (Chatham) Dock Co Ltd* [1993] QB 343, above, p. 647, where the possibility of exceptions is suggested. Unreasonable use of the highway by noisy vehicles was held to be a nuisance in *Halsey* v. *Esso Petroleum Co Ltd* [1961] 1 WLR 683.   [421] Civil Aviation Act 1949, ss. 40, 41.

[422] See below, p. 685 (planning restrictions).

[423] *Edwards* v. *Minister of Transport* (above), at 144 (Harman LJ).

[424] *Hammersmith Rly Co* v. *Brand* (above). This fundamental question was decided by 2 votes to 1 and against the advice of the majority of the judges.

[425] See *Allen* v. *Gulf Oil Refining Ltd* [1981] AC 1001. But there is a qualification to this, viz. that 'the statu-tory powers are exercised without "negligence"—that word here being used in a special sense so as to require the undertaker, as a condition of obtaining immunity from action, to carry out the work and conduct the operation with all reasonable regard and care for the interests of other persons' (Lord Wilberforce at 1011). Thus in *Dobson and ors* v. *Thames Water Utilities Ltd (No 2)* [2011] EWHC 3253 some claimants obtained a declaration and damages in respect of odour caused by negligent (in this sense) control of statutorily author-ised sewage treatment works (*Allen* negligence did not extend to failing to apply for additional funding to carry out work to prevent odour). Nuisance and a breach of Art. 8 found.

[426] s. 1. See (1974) 90 *LQR* 361 (K. Davies).   [427] s. 2.

months after the nuisance began (this is the 'settling down' period) and then it must be made within the ensuing six years.[428] Compensation is assessed at prices current on the first day when a claim could be made and is the whole amount of the depreciation, subject to certain assumptions about planning permission[429] and to provisions about overlapping compensation and other matters.[430] No compensation is payable if the amount does not exceed £50,[431] or in respect of highway or aircraft accidents.[432] Disputed claims are adjudicated by the Lands Tribunal.

The same Act made provision, *inter alia*, for 'home loss payments',[433] 'farm loss payments' and 'disturbance payments',[434] as well as for higher compensation in some cases of compulsory purchase. It has therefore done much to shift the true social cost of public works and developments from the shoulders of individual victims onto the broader shoulders of the community at large. But there are still cases where the social cost may fall heavily on individuals, for example where a business is ruined because a through road is turned into a cul-de-sac.[435]

PLANNING RESTRICTIONS

Compensation is sometimes payable to a landowner for restrictions imposed by the Town and Country Planning Acts on his liberty to use his land as he wishes.[436] The rules are highly involved, and have been subject to sharp changes arising from Parliament's repeated attempts to find a workable method of expropriating for the benefit of the community the development rights in land held in private ownership. But apart from such remnants of the original scheme for buying out development value, there is in general no right to compensation for refusal of planning permission. To a large extent, therefore, the planning legislation is a system of expropriation without compensation, the element expropriated being the development value of the land. This principle has been maintained continuously since it was introduced by the Act of 1947, even during the period (1958–75) when compensation upon compulsory purchase was based upon open market value—nor was this contradictory, since open market value was assessed only with the benefit of such planning permission as was reasonably probable. For half a century it has been recognised that the value of land to the owner is subject to social policy, which may restrict it severely.

Nevertheless there are a few cases of particularly stringent control in which the law provides for compensation.[437] The most important instances are where a planning authority exercises its overriding powers of requiring some lawful use of land to be discontinued or some building to be removed or of revoking[438] or modifying a planning permission already given (drastic powers of interference with vested rights which are normally exercisable only with the consent of the Secretary of State).[439]

---

[428] Under the Act of 1973 this period was 2 years. After many complaints and criticism by the Parliamentary Commissioner for Administration the Local Government, Planning and Land Act 1980, s. 112, adopted the normal period for statutory claims, i.e. 6 years (Limitation Act 1980, s. 9).

[429] s. 5.   [430] ss. 4, 5, 6.   [431] s. 7.   [432] s. 1(7).

[433] An example is *Greater London Council* v. *Holmes* [1986] QB 989.

[434] An example is *Prasad* v. *Wolverhampton BC* [1983] Ch 333.

[435] As in *Jolliffe* v. *Exeter Cpn* [1967] 1 WLR 993.   [436] For this legislation see above, p. 55.

[437] Town and Country Planning Act 1990, Pt IV.

[438] See e.g. *Pennine Raceway Ltd* v. *Kirklees LBC* [1983] QB 382 (licensee entitled to claim).

[439] Town and Country Planning Act 1990, ss. 97, 102. Compensation for refusal of permission for 'existing use development' and for alteration of listed buildings was abolished by the Planning and Compensation Act 1991, s. 31.

COMPULSORY SALE TO PUBLIC AUTHORITIES

There are certain situations in which the owner of land can turn the tables on a public authority and make a compulsory sale to them. In effect this is a form of compensation for the blighting effect of planning schemes and controls, generally known as 'planning blight'. The procedure is sometimes called compulsory purchase in reverse. One such situation is where land has become 'incapable of reasonably beneficial use in its existing state' after the refusal, revocation or modification of planning permission or after an order requiring discontinuance of an existing use or the removal of a building.[440] The owner may then serve a notice calling on the local authority to purchase the land, subject to confirmation by the Secretary of State if the local authority resists. If the notice is confirmed, compulsory purchase by the local authority is deemed to be authorised, and a notice to treat is deemed to have been served.[441] The owner may then compel the local authority to complete the purchase. This procedure may also be invoked where a building listed as of special architectural or historic interest is similarly blighted by refusal, revocation or modification of permission.[442] All these provisions apply equally in the case of restrictive conditions attached to a permission, as they do in the case of refusal.

Planning blight has become the statutory name for the special kind of injury which can be inflicted by the mere existence of overall plans for some area, quite apart from questions of planning permission. If, for example, a structure plan or local plan shows the land as being intended for a new road, or a municipal car park, there is likely to be no market for it. Owners of land affected in such ways may serve a 'blight notice' on the potential acquiring authority, which will be the Department of the Environment in the case of a trunk road or motorway and the local authority in the case of the car park.[443] The owner must show that he has made reasonable endeavours to sell his interest since the blight occurred and has been unable to do so except at a substantial loss. If he satisfies the various statutory conditions, which are numerous and technical, he may then compel the appropriate authority to acquire his interest at its unblighted value. The authority may object on a number of specified grounds, which if disputed are adjudicated by the Lands Tribunal. The authority may stave off the compulsory purchase altogether by giving notice that they do not intend to acquire the land or, in a group of cases including land earmarked for governmental authorities and highways, by declaring that they do not propose to proceed within fifteen years.[444] The Land Compensation Act 1973[445] extended the scope of this system in various ways, for example by including blight inflicted by plans not yet in force and compulsory purchase orders advertised but not confirmed.

MISCARRIAGE OF JUSTICE AND CRIMINAL INJURY

Compensation has long been paid to victims of miscarriages of justice, but only as a matter of grace and without any legal entitlement. A measure of legal right was however introduced by the Criminal Justice Act 1988, so as to accord with the International Covenant on Civil and Political Rights[446] and with the European Convention on Human Rights and

---

[440] Town and Country Planning Act 1990, s. 137. See e.g. *Plymouth Cpn v. Secretary of State for the Environment* [1972] 1 WLR 1347; *Colley v. Secretary of State for the Environment* [1998] COD 491.

[441] Town and Country Planning Act, 1990, s. 143.

[442] Planning (Listed Buildings and Conservation Areas) Act 1990, ss. 32–7.

[443] Town and Country Planning Act 1990, ss. 149, 171.   [444] s. 151(4).

[445] Pt V, extended to urban development areas by the Local Government, Planning and Land Act 1980, s. 147, replaced by the Town and Country Planning Act 1990, s. 149.   [446] Art. 14.

Fundamental Freedoms.[447] The provisions of the Covenant, the Convention and the Act are in closely similar terms.

The Act applies where a conviction has been quashed or a pardon granted 'on the ground that a new or newly discovered fact shows beyond reasonable doubt that there has been a miscarriage of justice'. The Secretary of State (in practice the Home Secretary) is then required to pay compensation to the person who has suffered punishment, provided that the non-disclosure of the unknown fact was not attributable to him, and to appoint an assessor to determine the amount. Whether there is a right to compensation is to be determined by the Secretary of State. The Act sets up a mechanism whereby an Independent Assessor thereafter determines the amount payable.[448] The Act applies only to cases based on new facts, and not (for example) to a case of unfair trial.[449] For cases outside the Act the system of ex gratia compensation (which was subject to judicial review)[450] remained in operation until 19 April 2006 when it was withdrawn.[451]

The Criminal Injuries Compensation Scheme was introduced in 1964 in order to provide compensation at public expense for injuries to victims of violent crime. Originally it was an ex gratia scheme, based on no statute and no legal right and constituted merely administratively. The Home Secretary presented the scheme to Parliament and Parliament annually voted the money for it and claims were adjudicated by the Criminal Injuries Compensation Board, but all without legislation of any kind. The courts nevertheless undertook to review the Board's decisions, applying the scheme as if it were law, thus making their first breakthrough into non-legal territory, as already explained.[452] The Criminal Justice Act 1988 (s. 133) provided for the scheme to become statutory, but the Home Secretary refused to bring the Act into force, having meanwhile decided to change to a new 'tariff scheme' which would save public money by substituting fixed payments for specified injuries instead of the ordinary measure of damages and which, like the old scheme, would be operated merely administratively. When the House of Lords (as related earlier) held this course to be unlawful,[453] the government procured legitimation of the tariff scheme under the Criminal Injuries Compensation Act 1995. The Board has become the Authority and the scheme, now statutory, was approved in draft by both Houses of Parliament. The Authority's decisions, like those of the Board, are subject to judicial review.

---

[447] 7th Protocol, Art. 3.

[448] s. 133(4). Section 133(4A) (inserted by the Criminal Appeal Act 1995, s. 28) lists the matters to which the assessor shall have regard. These include the severity of the punishment wrongly imposed, the conduct of the investigation and prosecution and any other convictions of the victim. In assessing pecuniary loss the assessor may reduce the award to represent the expenditure on necessities of life (food, clothing etc.) saved through imprisonment (*O'Brien* v. *Independent Assessor* [2007] UKHL 10).

[449] For discussion of the scheme see *Re McFarland* [2004] UKHL 17, [2004] 1 WLR 1289, paras. 8–9, 22, and *R (Mullen)* v. *Secretary of State for the Home Department* [2004] UKHL 18, [2005] 1 AC 1, paras. 5–6, 25–9.

[450] See *R* v. *Home Secretary ex p Garner* (1999) 11 Admin LR 595 (Home Secretary's published policy statement reviewed and decisions refusing compensation quashed). See also *R (Raissi)* v. *Home Secretary* [2008] EWCA Civ 72, [2008] 2 All ER 1023 applying the test of the 'reasonable and literate man's understanding' of the published policy. Thus the minister's restriction of the policy to persons wrongly facing charges before the domestic courts rejected and claimant wrongly facing extradition to USA (erroneously accused of training 9/11 bombers) held within ex gratia policy. Discussed above, p. 277.

[451] Ministerial statement by the Home Secretary (Charles Clarke, MP). A challenge to the withdrawal of the scheme failed: *R (Niazi)* v. *Home Secretary* [2007] EWHC 1495 and [2008] EWCA Civ 755, discussed above, p. 460.

[452] Above, p. 539.

[453] Above, p. 334.

The scheme is lengthy and is framed in great detail. Criminal injury means personal injury directly attributable to a crime of violence or to an attempted arrest or to preventive action or to helping a constable so engaged. Under a controversial rule compensation is refused where the victim and the assailant were living in the same household as members of the same family unless the assailant has been prosecuted and the parties have ceased to live in the same household.[454] Claims to compensation are determined by claims officers and there are internal procedures for review and appeal and oral hearings may be allowed as regulations prescribe. The lengthy tariff of injuries lists more than 300 sorts with standard maximum amounts against them, to which may be added compensation for loss of earnings. In fatal cases there is provision for dependents.

A corresponding scheme (non-statutory) is operated by the Ministry of Defence for members of the armed forces injured overseas, but it excludes injury caused by warlike or military conduct.[455]

---

[454] Scheme of 1995, Art. 16. The earlier version of this rule was upheld on judicial review in R v. *Criminal Injuries Compensation Board ex p P* [1995] 1 WLR 845.

[455] See R v. *Ministry of Defence ex p Walker* [2000] 1 WLR 806 (HL).

21

CROWN PROCEEDINGS

THE CROWN IN LITIGATION

LEGAL STATUS OF THE CROWN

It is fundamental to the rule of law that the Crown, like other public authorities, should bear its fair share of legal liability and be answerable for wrongs done to its subjects. The immense expansion of governmental activity from the latter part of the nineteenth century onwards made it intolerable for the government, in the name of the Crown, to enjoy exemption from the ordinary law. For a long time the government contrived, in the manner dear to the official heart, to meet the demands of the time by administrative measures, while preserving the Crown's ancient legal immunity. But the law caught up with the practice when finally the Crown Proceedings Act was passed in 1947. In principle the Crown is now in the position of an ordinary employer and of an ordinary litigant. But the history and development of the law of Crown proceedings, together with some important surviving peculiarities, make it essential to explain this subject separately.[1]

'The Crown' means the sovereign acting in a public or official capacity. In law the sovereign has two personalities, one natural and the other corporate.[2] In its corporate capacity the Crown is a corporation sole,[3] though other suggestions have at times been made.[4] A corporation sole, as opposed to a corporation aggregate, consists of a single office-holder whose corporate capacity and property passes automatically to his successors in office. Crown property thus descends directly from sovereign to sovereign.

The Crown itself is immune from legal process, save only where statute provides otherwise.[5] But this privilege causes little difficulty in the law which governs judicial control of

---

[1] Different aspects of the Crown's constitutional position, powers and functions are discussed in Sunkin and Payne (eds.), *The Nature of the Crown.* See also Sir Stephen Sedley in Forsyth and Hare (eds.), *The Golden Metwand*, 253. [2] *Duchy of Lancaster Case* (1561) 1 Plowd 212 at 213; *Willion v. Berkley* (below).

[3] *Willion v. Berkley* (1559) 1 Plowd 223 at 242 and 250; *Case of Sutton's Hospital* (1612) 10 Co Rep 1a at 29b; Hale, *Prerogatives of the King*, Selden Soc., vol. 92, p. 84; Bl. Comm. i. 469; Hargrave's notes to Co. Litt. 15b; *A-G v. Köhler* (1861) 9 HCL 654 at 670 (Lord Cranworth); *Re Mason* [1928] Ch 385 at 401 (Romer J); Holdsworth, *History of English Law*, iv. 203; *Town Investments Ltd v. Department of the Environment* [1987] AC 359 at 384 (Lord Diplock).

[4] In the *Town Investments* case (above) at 400 Lord Simon held that the Crown was a corporation aggregate together with ministers and government departments, but for this strange proposition there is no authority. Elementary constitutional principles, explained above, p. 36, and again below, require that the Crown's personality should be separate from that of its ministers and servants. Maitland, following an argument of counsel in *Willion v. Berkley* (above), preferred to regard the Crown as incorporated together with all its subjects as 'the Commonwealth': Coll. pp. iii, 259. Statements in the Court of Appeal in *M v. Home Office* [1992] QB 270 at 300 and 313, that the Crown has no legal personality, must be regarded as aberrations: see *M v. Home Office* [1994] AC 377 at 424. In *Madras Electric Supply Cpn v. Boarland* [1955] AC 667 the House of Lords held that the Crown was a 'person' for purposes of income tax legislation.

[5] 'No suit or action can be brought against the king, even in civil matters, because no court can have jurisdiction over him': Bl. Comm. i. 242. The immunity is recognised in *M v. Home Office* (above) in terms of 'the king can do no wrong': see at 395, 408 and 412.

powers, since statutory powers are in the vast majority of cases conferred upon designated ministers or public authorities rather than upon the Crown itself[6] and the same is true of duties. Ministers and public authorities acting in their own names enjoy none of the immunities of the Crown, as many examples have already illustrated. This artificial cleavage between the Crown and its agents may be criticised as an impediment to a coherent theory of the state as a legal entity.[7] But it is deeply rooted historically and of fundamental importance in the law.[8]

Ordinary proceedings by judicial review or otherwise against ministers and other Crown servants do not here count as proceedings against the Crown,[9] nor do the exceptional cases where action under the royal prerogative has been reviewed in proceedings against a minister for a declaratory judgment.[10] Indeed, in all such cases the Crown is usually the nominal plaintiff. In the present context we must consider the Crown's position in the law of tort and contract, since Crown employees often commit torts and the Crown itself is legally the employer of the central government's officials and is legally the contracting party in many central government contracts. Consequently this chapter may be regarded as an extension of the preceding one, but dealing especially with the liability of the Crown itself, as distinct from that of its servants.[11]

Discussion of the Act of 1947 requires, as an essential prologue, some account of the traditional position of the Crown as litigant at common law.

'THE KING CAN DO NO WRONG'

English law has always clung to the theory that the king is subject to law and, accordingly, can break the law. There is no more famous statement of this ideal than Bracton's, made more than 700 years ago: 'rex non debet esse sub homine sed sub deo et sub lege, quia lex facit regem'.[12] But in practice rights depend upon remedies, and the theory broke down—as Bracton's words suggest that it would—because there was no human agency to enforce the law against the king. The courts were the king's courts, and like other feudal lords the king could not be sued in his own court. He could be plaintiff (claimant in the modern jargon)—and as plaintiff he had important prerogatives in the law of procedure[13]—but he

---

[6] See above, p. 36.   [7] See *The Nature of the Crown* (as above), ch. 3 (M. Loughlin).

[8] The distinction between ministers and the Crown they serve is a principle quite distinct from the divisibility of the Crown. This is the principle that Her Majesty, although one person, has separate and distinct personalities for each realm in which she reigns. Thus there is a Queen of the United Kingdom, a Queen of Australia, a Queen of Canada etc., and even a Queen of South Georgia and the South Sandwich Islands. In earlier times the Crown was considered indivisible but its divisibility is now uncontroversial (*R v. Secretary of State for Foreign and Commonwealth Affairs ex p Indian Association of Alberta* [1982] QB 892, 911, 916–17, 920–1, 928; and *Quark Fishing*, below, para. 9 (Lord Bingham)) although it may sometimes be difficult to determine in which personality a particular act was done (*R (Quark Fishing Ltd) v. Secretary of State for Foreign and Commonwealth Affairs* [2005] UKHL 57, [2006] 1 AC 529 (act by Foreign Secretary (a UK minister) on behalf of Her Majesty directing the Commissioner of SGSSI held an act of Her Majesty in right of the SGSSI).

[9] *Minister of Foreign Affairs, Trade and Industry v. Vehicles and Supplies Ltd* [1991] 1 WLR 550 (PC).

[10] Above, p. 487.

[11] See generally Glanville Williams, *Crown Proceedings*; Street, *Government Liability*; Hogg, *Liability of the Crown*, 3rd edn (2000).

[12] 'The king must not be under man but under God and under the law, because it is the law that makes the king': Bracton, *De legibus et consuetudinibus Angliae*, fo. 5b (S. E. Thorne's edn, p. 32); cited by Coke, *Prohibitions del Roy* (1608) 12 Co Rep 63 at 65. For later instances of this principle see Holdsworth, *History of English Law*, ii. 435; v. 348.

[13] Thus costs could not be awarded against the king and lapse of time could not prejudice his claims.

could not be defendant. No form of writ or execution would issue against him, for there was no way of compelling his submission to it. Even today, when most of the obstacles to justice have been removed, it has been found necessary to make important modifications of the law of procedure and execution in the Crown's favour.

The maxim that 'the king can do no wrong' does not in fact have much to do with this procedural immunity. Its meaning is rather that the king has no legal power to do wrong. His legal position, the powers and prerogatives which distinguish him from an ordinary subject, is given to him by the law, and the law gives him no authority to transgress. This also is implicit in Bracton's statement, and it provided the justification, such as it was, for the rule that the Crown could not be sued in tort in a representative capacity, as the employer of its servants. But the king had a personal as well as a political capacity, and in his personal capacity he was just as capable of acting illegally as was anyone else—and there were special temptations in his path. But the procedural obstacles were the same in either capacity. English law never succeeded in distinguishing effectively between the king's two capacities.[14] One of the best illustrations of this is that, despite the doctrines that the Crown is a corporation sole and that 'the king never dies', the death of the king caused great trouble even in relatively modern times: Parliament was dissolved; all litigation had to be begun again; and all offices of state (even commissions in the army) had to be regranted. Until numerous Acts of Parliament had come to the rescue the powers of government appeared wholly personal, and it could truly be said that 'on a demise of the Crown we see all the wheels of the state stopping or even running backwards'.[15]

THE PETITION OF RIGHT

Justice had somehow to be done, despite the Crown's immunity, and out of the streams of petitions which flowed in upon medieval monarchs came the procedure known as petition of right.[16] This held the field until the new system began in 1948, and many of the vagaries of its early procedure were rationalised by the Petitions of Right Act 1860, which provided a simplified form of petition and made provision for awarding costs on either side. In essence the petition of right was a petition by a subject which the Crown referred voluntarily to the decision of a court of law. The Crown's consent was signified by the Attorney-General endorsing the petition 'Let Right be Done' (fiat justitia), so that after obtaining this fiat the plaintiff could obtain the judgment of one of the regular courts. Employed originally for the recovery of land or other property, this remedy made an important stride after the Revolution of 1688, when it was agreed by the judges that it would lie to enforce a debt. This was in the *Bankers' Case* (1690–1700),[17] in which various bankers attempted to sue the Crown for payments due on loans to Charles II on which that king had defaulted. It was, in fact, by other means that the bankers finally obtained their judgment—though not their money, for the problem of enforcement was as intractable as ever. No further case of importance arose until 1874, when an inventor of a new kind of heavy artillery sued for a reward promised to him by the War Office.[18] This case finally settled the point that judgment could be given against the Crown on a petition of right for breach of contract made by the Crown's agent. Since in any normal case the

---

[14] The Crown could dispose of Crown lands by grant but not by will until permitted by the Crown Private Estates Acts 1800–1961. [15] Maitland, *Collected Papers*, iii. 253.

[16] For the form of the petition of right see below, p. 699. [17] 14 How St Tr 1.

[18] *Thomas v. The Queen* (1874) LR 10 QB 31.

Crown would grant the fiat[19] and respect the judgment, there was now a reasonably effective remedy in contract.

A claim made by petition of right was judged in accordance with the ordinary law, under which the Crown enjoyed no special advantages. A case of 1865 was at one time thought to lay down that monetary liability of the Crown in contract was contingent upon funds being voted by Parliament.[20] But the notion of contingent liability as a general rule was rejected in a strong decision of the High Court of Australia[21] and may be regarded as exploded. If Parliament refuses to vote the money for the due performance of a Crown contract, payment cannot properly be made. But there is no reason why the other contracting party should not recover damages for the breach.[22] Nor is there any sign that the Crown would wish to assert the contrary.

NO LIABILITY IN TORT

Meanwhile the judges had set their faces against any remedy in tort. This was an unfortunate by-product of the law of master and servant as it was understood in the nineteenth century. For obvious reasons it had become necessary that employers should be liable for the torts—most commonly negligence—committed by their employees in the course of their employment. But in seeking a legal basis for this, judges at first tended to say that it depended on the implied authority given by the master to the servant, or that the fault was the master's for not choosing his servants more carefully. Neither line of thought would bring liability home to the Crown, for as we have seen the theory has always been that the Crown's powers cannot be exercised wrongly. Thus 'the king can do no wrong' meant that the Crown was not liable in tort—even though a breach of contract is just as much a 'wrong' as a tort, and even though the social necessity for a remedy against the Crown as employer was just as great as, if not greater than, the need for a remedy in contract. The first important case was an unsuccessful petition of right by Viscount Canterbury in 1842.[23] He had been Speaker of the House of Commons in 1834 when some workmen in the employ of the Crown, being told to burn the piles of old tallies from the Exchequer, succeeded in burning down both Houses of Parliament and the Speaker's house in addition. But the Speaker's claim against the Crown for the value of his household goods foundered on the objection that the negligence of the workmen could not be imputed to the Crown either directly or indirectly. Similarly, where a British naval commander, suppressing the slave trade off the coast of Africa, seized and burnt an allegedly innocent ship from Liverpool, the owner's petition of right was rejected.[24] It was later recognised that employer's liability is quite independent of fault on the part of the master, and depends rather on the fact that it is for the master's benefit that the servant acts and that the master, having put the servant in a position where he can do damage, must accept the responsibility. But it was then too late to challenge the doctrine that the Crown could have no liability

[19] The fiat could not properly be refused where the claim was arguable: *Dyson* v. *A-G* [1911] 1 KB 410 at 422.

[20] *Churchward* v. *R* (1865) LR 1 QB 173, especially at 209 (Shee J). On this question see Mitchell, *The Contracts of Public Authorities*, 68.

[21] *New South Wales* v. *Bardolph* (1934) 52 CLR 455, upholding a notable judgment of Evatt J and considering inconclusive decisions of the House of Lords and Privy Council.

[22] This proposition seems clearly supported by Cockburn CJ in the *Churchward* case (above) at 200 and by Lord Haldane in *A-G* v. *Great Southern and Eastern Rly Co of Ireland* [1925] AC 754 at 771: see the *Bardolph* case (above) at 514 (Dixon J).   [23] *Canterbury (Viscount)* v. *A-G* (1842) 1 Ph 306.

[24] *Tobin* v. *The Queen* (1864) 16 CBNS 310. Similarly *Feather* v. *The Queen* (1865) 6 B & S 257.

in tort, which was an unshakeable dogma until Parliament abolished it in 1947. But for any claim which did not 'sound in tort'—such as for breach of contract, recovery of property, restitution or statutory compensation—a petition of right would lie.

PERSONAL LIABILITY OF CROWN SERVANTS

The Crown was always, as it still is, immune from legal process at common law. Against the king the law had no coercive power.[25] But this immunity never extended to the Crown's servants. It was, and still is, a constitutional principle of the first importance that ministers and officials of all kinds, high or low, are personally liable for any injury or wrongdoing for which they cannot produce legal authority.[26] The orders of the Crown are not legal authority unless it is one of the rare acts which the prerogative justifies, such as the detention of an enemy alien in time of war. Thus although in past times the Crown was not liable in tort, the injured party could always sue the particular Crown servant who did the deed, including any minister or superior officer who ordered him to do it or otherwise caused it directly.[27] In a famous eighteenth-century case, where damages of £4,000 were awarded to Wilkes against the Secretary of State, Lord Halifax, for trespass and false imprisonment, Wilmot CJ said: 'The law makes no difference between great and petty officers. Thank God they are all amenable to justice.'[28]

A superior officer cannot be liable merely as such, for it is not he but the Crown who is the employer;[29] but if he takes part in the wrongful act he is no less liable than any other participant. Superior orders can never be a defence, since neither the Crown nor its servants have power to authorise wrong.[30] The ordinary law of master and servant makes the master and the servant jointly and severally liable for torts committed in course of the employment. Before 1948, therefore, someone negligently injured by an army lorry could sue the driver of the lorry but not the commander-in-chief or the war minister or the Crown. Had the lorry been owned by a private employer, the action would have lain both against the driver and against the employer, although the damages could have been recovered only once.

Crown servants were equally liable to the remedy of injunction. The events which led to the settlement of a vexed question by the House of Lords, after much difference of judicial opinion and not without anomalies will be explained below.[31] The final decision is a landmark for the rule of law and sheds much light on the legal position of the Crown and its servants. Lord Templeman said that the proposition that the executive obeyed the law as a matter of grace and not of necessity 'would reverse the result of the Civil War'.

The personal liability of officials was not only one of the great bulwarks of the rule of law: it also provided a peg on which a remedial official practice was hung. The Crown did in fact assume the liability which could not lie upon it in law by regularly defending actions brought against its servants for torts committed by them in the course of their

[25] Maitland, *Constitutional History*, 100; *M v. Home Office* (below) (Lord Templeman).

[26] Statements by the House of Lords in *R v. Secretary of State for Transport ex p Factortame Ltd* [1990] 2 AC 85 at 145 that Crown officers were immune from suit both before and after the Crown Proceedings Act 1947 were based on erroneous argument and are corrected by *M v. Home Office* [1994] AC 377 at 418. For erroneous dicta in *Town Investments Ltd v. Department of the Environment* [1978] AC 359, see above, p. 36.

[27] See *Raleigh v. Goschen* [1898] 1 Ch 73; *Roncarelli v. Duplessis* (1959) 16 DLR (2d) 689 (above, p. 300).

[28] *Wilkes v. Wood* (1769) 19 St Tr 1406 at 1408.

[29] *Bainbridge v. Postmaster-General* [1906] 1 KB 178.

[30] The law as stated in the text is confirmed in *M v. Home Office* (above) at 407–10.

[31] Below, p. 704 (*M v. Home Office*).

duties.[32] The legal process was issued solely against the individual servant, but his defence was in practice conducted by the Crown, and if damages were awarded they were paid out of public funds. Government departments did their best to be helpful in making this practice work smoothly, and if there was any doubt as to which servant to sue they would supply the name of a suggested defendant, known as a 'nominated defendant'.[33]

BREAKDOWN OF THE FICTION: THE CROWN PROCEEDINGS ACT 1947

For many years the practice of supplying nominated defendants provided a satisfactory antidote to the shortcomings of the law. But ultimately two fatal flaws appeared. One was in a case where it was clear that some Crown servant was liable but the evidence did not show which. A representative defendant might then be nominated merely in order that the action might in substance proceed against the Crown, but this practice was condemned by the House of Lords in 1946.[34] The other difficulty was that there can be torts (such as failure to maintain a safe system of work in a factory) which render only the employer liable, so that there could be no one to nominate in, say, a government-owned factory where the occupier was in law the Crown.[35] These two cases exposed the weaknesses of the makeshift practice of suing the Crown indirectly through a nominated defendant. The time had at last come—and was, indeed, overdue—for abolishing the general immunity in tort which had been an anomaly of the Crown's legal position for more than a hundred years. This was the genesis of the Crown Proceedings Act 1947.[36]

The law as it now stands under the Act may be divided under four headings: 1. Tort; 2. Contract; 3. Remedies and procedure; 4. Statutes affecting the Crown.

LIABILITY IN TORT

GENERAL RULES

The Act subjects the Crown to the same general liability in tort which it would bear 'if it were a private person of full age and capacity'.[37] The general policy, therefore, is to put the Crown into the shoes of an ordinary defendant. Furthermore, the Act leaves untouched the personal liability of Crown servants, which was the mainstay of the old law, except in certain cases concerning the armed forces (now repealed), to be mentioned presently. The principle of the new law is that where a servant of the Crown commits a tort in the course of his employment,[38] the servant and the Crown are jointly and severally liable. This corresponds to the ordinary law of master and servant.

The Act[39] specifically makes the Crown liable for:

(a) torts committed by its servants or agents;

---

[32] See *M* v. *Home Office* [1994] AC 377 at 410.

[33] This device was adopted by statute for criminal liability for traffic offences: Road Traffic Act 1972, s. 188 (8); *Barnett* v. *French* [1981] 1 WLR 848. But it was omitted from the Road Traffic Act 1988.

[34] *Adams* v. *Naylor* [1946] AC 543.   [35] *Royster* v. *Cavey* [1947] KB 204.

[36] For a good account of the legislative history see [1992] *PL* 452 (J. M. Jacob). And see the valuable historical discussion in several speeches in *Matthews* v. *Ministry of Defence* [2003] UKHL 4, [2003] 2 WLR 435 (HL).   [37] s. 2(1). There is no liability in tort outside the Act: *Trawnik* v. *Lennox* [1985] 1 WLR 532.

[38] Misfeasance, i.e. deliberate excess of authority, by a Crown servant will normally be outside the course of his employment: *Weldon* v. *Home Office* [1992] 1 AC 58 at 164.   [39] s. 2(1).

(b) breach of duties which a person owes to his servants or agents at common law by reason of being their employer; and

(c) breach of duties attaching at common law to the ownership, occupation, possession or control of property.

Head (a) is subject to the proviso that the Crown shall not be liable unless the servant or agent would himself have been liable. This proviso gives the Crown a dispensation which a private employer does not enjoy in occasional cases where the servant has some defence but the employer is still liable as such; for the doctrine is that personal defences belonging to the servant do not extend to the employer unless he also is entitled to them personally, and they may not prevent the servant's act from being a tort even though he personally is not liable. But in other respects it seems that the three heads are comprehensive. Head (c) subjects the Crown to the normal rule of strict liability for dangerous operations (*Rylands* v. *Fletcher*), so that the position is more satisfactory than in the case of other public authorities.[40]

The Crown is also given the benefit of any statutory restriction on the liability of any government department or officer.[41] A number of statutes contain such limitations of liability, for example the Mental Health Act 1983 which protects those who detain mental patients under the Act unless they act in bad faith or without reasonable care,[42] and the Land Registration Act 1925, which frees officials of the Land Registry from liability for acts or omissions made in good faith in the exercise or supposed exercise of their functions under the Act.[43]

STATUTORY DUTIES

Statutory duties can give rise to liability in tort, as already explained. The Act therefore subjects the Crown to the same liabilities as a private person in any case where the Crown is bound by a statutory duty which is binding also upon other persons.[44] The Act makes no change in the general rule that statutes do not bind the Crown unless an intention to do so is expressed or implied,[45] so the Crown will normally be liable only where the statute in question says so. This rule might well be the other way round, so that (so to speak) the Crown would have to contract out instead of having to contract in. But many important statutes do expressly bind the Crown, such as the Road Traffic Act 1960, the Factories Act 1961 and the Occupiers' Liability Act 1957. The Act does not allow the Crown to shelter behind the fact that powers may be given (either by common law or statute) to a minister or other servant of the Crown directly, and not to the Crown itself. In such cases the Crown is made liable in tort as if the minister or servant were acting on the Crown's own instructions.[46]

These primary rules for imposing liability in tort may be said, in general, to achieve their object well. The Crown occasionally claims that public policy should entitle it to exemption in respect of its governmental functions. But this claim is now, as in the past,

---

[40] See above, p. 659. But if the same meaning as there mentioned is given to 'its own purposes', the Crown also might escape liability anomalously. [41] s. 2(4).

[42] See *R* v. *Bracknell Justices ex p Griffiths* [1976] AC 314. [43] s. 131.

[44] s. 2(2). In *Ministry of Housing and Local Government* v. *Sharp* [1970] 2 QB 233 at 268 Lord Denning MR says that the Crown is not liable for mistakes in the Land Registry by virtue of s. 23(3)(f) of the Crown Proceedings Act 1947. That provision however applies only to Pt II of the Act (Jurisdiction and Procedure) and does not exclude Crown liability under s. 2(3). But Land Registry officials acting in good faith are not liable: see above. [45] s. 40(2)(f); below, p. 706.

[46] s. 2(3).

rejected by the courts. Thus where boys escaped from an 'open Borstal' and damaged a yacht, the Home Office was held to have no defence if negligent custody could be established, despite its claims to immunity on grounds of public policy.[47]

WHO IS A CROWN SERVANT?

In broaching the question who is a servant of the Crown, it must be remembered that the Crown is liable to the same extent as a private person for torts committed by its servants *or agents*, and that 'agent' includes an independent contractor.[48] The general principle in tort is that the employer is liable for the misdeeds of his servant or agent done in the course of the employer's business but not for the misdeeds of independent contractors, who bear their own responsibility. Where the employer can control what the employee does and how he does it, the relationship is likely to be that of master and servant, so that they are liable jointly. The same is true when an agent is employed. But an agent has to be distinguished from an independent contractor, for whose tortious acts the employer is not liable at all. For example, a person who takes his car for repair to an apparently competent garage is not liable if, because of careless work by the garage, a wheel comes off and injures someone.[49] Yet there are some special cases where there is liability even for independent contractors, for example where the work is particularly dangerous. Thus a householder had to share the liability when she called in workmen to thaw out frozen pipes and by using blowlamps they set fire both to her house and her neighbour's.[50] If this had happened on Crown land, the Crown would have been equally liable under the Act because of its general liability for the torts of its agents.

In the case of *servants* the Act sets up a special criterion based on appointment and pay. It says that the Crown shall not be liable for the torts of any officer of the Crown 'unless that officer has been directly or indirectly appointed by the Crown' and was at the material time paid wholly out of monies provided by Parliament or out of certain funds (which in case of doubt may be certified by the Treasury), or would normally be so paid.[51] The final words cover the case of voluntary office-holders, such as ministers acting without salary. But the principal importance of this provision is that it prevents the Crown becoming answerable for the police. It can be said, as explained earlier,[52] that in some of their functions at least the police act as officers of the Crown. Yet since the police, both in London and in the provinces, are partly paid out of local taxes, and in the provinces are appointed by local authorities, they are all excluded by the Act.[53] This left an unsatisfactory situation until the Police Act 1964 remedied it by placing representative liability on the chief constable as explained previously.[54] Under the Official Secrets Act 1989[55] a police constable is treated as a 'Crown servant', but only for the purposes of that Act. Whether the employees of statutory corporations and authorities are 'Crown Servants' so that they may render the Crown liable for their torts must depend on careful examination of their constituent Acts as was explained earlier.[56]

---

[47] *Dorset Yacht Co Ltd* v. *Home Office* [1970] AC 1044; above, p. 650.   [48] s. 38(2).
[49] Compare *Phillips* v. *Britannia Hygienic Laundry* [1923] 2 KB 823, where the plaintiff failed to circumvent this principle by pleading breach of statutory duty.
[50] *Balfour* v. *Barty-King* [1957] 1 QB 496.   [51] s. 2(6).   [52] Above, p. 103.
[53] Above, p. 103.   [54] Above, p. 103.   [55] s. 12(1)(e).   [56] Above, p. 103.

JUDICIAL FUNCTIONS

The Crown has one general immunity in tort which is a matter of constitutional propriety. The Act provides against Crown liability in tort for any person discharging judicial functions or executing judicial process.[57] This expresses the essential separation of powers between executive and judiciary. Judges and magistrates are appointed by the Crown or by ministers. They are paid (if at all) out of public funds, and so may be said to be servants of the Crown in a broad sense[58]—a sense that was brought home to them when their salaries were reduced as 'persons in His Majesty's service' under the National Economy Act 1931.[59] But the relationship between the Crown and the judges is entirely unlike the relationship of employer and employee on which liability in tort is based. The master can tell his servant not only what to do but how to do it. The Crown has had no such authority over the judges since the days of Coke's conflicts with James I.[60] The master can terminate his servant's employment, but the superior judges are protected by legislation, dating from 1700, against dismissal except at the instance of both Houses of Parliament.[61] Their independence is sacrosanct, and if they are independent no one else can be vicariously answerable for any wrong that they may do.

It is virtually impossible for judges of the superior courts to commit torts in their official capacity, since they are clothed with absolute privilege, and this privilege has now been extended to lower judges, such as magistrates.[62] But the Act comprehensively protects the Crown in the case of anyone 'discharging or purporting to discharge' judicial functions.[63] In this context the word 'judicial' ought naturally to cover members of independent statutory tribunals, e.g. rent tribunals, even when they are whole-time employees of the Crown as are some of the Special Commissioners of Income Tax.[64] A contrasting case is that of independent authorities such as social security adjudication officers, whose functions are basically administrative.[65] Nor would the functions of inspectors holding public inquiries seem to be 'judicial' in this sense, though they are so denominated for other purposes. The same question arises here as has already been discussed in the context of personal liability. If there is no personal liability, the Crown cannot be liable in the capacity of employer.[66] But the Court Service, although an executive agency, facilitates and implements the functions of the judiciary; and the acts of court officers are thus immune as being responsibilities 'in connection with the execution of judicial process'.[67]

---

[57] s. 2(5).   [58] See above, p. 52.   [59] See (1932) 48 *LQR* 35 (W. S. Holdsworth).
[60] *Prohibitions del Roy* (1608) 12 Co Rep 63.   [61] See above, p. 53.   [62] See above, p. 670.
[63] s. 2(5).

[64] See *Slaney* v. *Kean* [1970] Ch 243. But see also above, p. 31. Note the questionable reasoning of the majority of the Judicial Committee of the Privy Council in *Ranaweera* v. *Ramachandran* [1970] AC 951, holding that for the purposes of the constitution of Ceylon members of the income tax Board of Review did not exercise judicial functions and were not servants of the Crown.

[65] *Jones* v. *Department of Employment* [1989] QB 1. Likewise administrative functions of the Crown Prosecution Service: *Welsh* v. *Chief Constable of Merseyside Police* [1993] 1 All ER 692.

[66] There would be no basis of liability at common law and in any case the proviso to s. 2(1) of the Act would exclude liability.

[67] s. 2(5). See *Quinland* v. *Governor of Swaleside Prison* [2002] EWCA Civ 174, [2002] 3 WLR 807 (CA) (prisoner served 6 weeks more than proper sentence because the Registrar of Criminal Appeals failed to place a matter before the full court in due time; dicta in the *Welsh* case (above) restricting immunity to judicial functions doubted and human rights compliance left open). In *Hinds* v. *Liverpool County Court and ors* [2008] EWHC 665, on the other hand, the judge said: 'I do not see that these provisions [of the 1998 Act] add anything to the common law [on judicial immunity]' (para. 18). And see *Branch and ors* v. *Department for Constitutional Affairs* [2005] EWHC 550.

THE ARMED FORCES

In the case of the armed forces there were provisions (now repealed) designed to prevent the taxpayer from paying twice over for accidents in the services, once by way of damages and once more by way of disability pension to the injured person or his dependants. The main provision was that, provided that pensionability was certified, neither the Crown nor the tortfeasor was liable for death or personal injury caused by one member of the armed forces,[68] while on duty as such, to another member of the armed forces who was either on duty as such or was on any land, premises, ship, aircraft or vehicle for the time being used for service purposes.[69] Similarly the Crown and its servants, as owners or occupiers of any such land etc., were exempted if a certificate of pensionability was given and the injured party was a member of the forces. Ministers were empowered to give certificates to settle the question whether any person was or was not on duty, or whether any land etc., was in use by the forces at the relevant time. This procedure has, however, been held by the House of Lords to be substantive as opposed to procedural; and thus not a breach of the claimant's right of access to a court in the determination of his civil rights and obligations under Article 6(1) of the European Convention.[70]

Although these provisions were supposed to produce equitable results, they were too restrictive and caused injustice.[71] In one case a territorial reservist was accidentally killed by the firing of a live shell, and the death was duly certified as attributable to service for pension purposes; but the award was nil, since his parents, who were his nearest surviving relatives, did not themselves qualify under the pension scheme.[72] Thus the sole result was to deprive the parents of their remedy in damages, as their son's personal representatives, for his death. Protest at this injustice has brought about the repeal of the whole provision for exemption in respect of the armed forces.[73] But the Secretary of State is empowered to revive it by statutory instrument in case of imminent national danger or great emergency or warlike operations outside the United Kingdom.

LIABILITY IN CONTRACT

GENERAL PRINCIPLES

The Crown's liability for breach of contract was, as previously explained, acknowledged in principle long before the Crown Proceedings Act 1947, but was subject to the ancient

---

[68] In *Pearce* v. *Secretary of State for Defence* [1988] AC 755, where the plaintiff claimed to have been injured by the negligence of employees of the Atomic Energy Authority while on duty on Christmas Island in connection with tests of nuclear weapons. The transfer to the Secretary of State of the AEA's liabilities, effected by statute, did not enable the Secretary of State to claim exemption. The Court of Appeal, upholding Caulfield J, declined to apply *Town Investments Ltd* v. *Department of the Environment* [1978] AC 359, criticised above, p. 36; the House of Lords affirmed, overruling the *Bell* case (below).

[69] s. 10. In *Bell* v. *Secretary of State for Defence* [1986] QB 322, where a fatally injured soldier in Germany was sent to a civilian hospital, the Court of Appeal were divided on the question where the alleged injury took place and the claim failed. It failed also in the similar case of *Derry* v. *Ministry of Defence* (1998) 11 Admin LR 1.

[70] *Mathews* v. *Minister of Defence* (below). For discussion of Art. 6(1) in this context see above, p. 377.

[71] See [1985] *PL* at 287 (G. Zellick).   [72] *Adams* v. *War Office* [1955] 1 WLR 1116.

[73] Crown Proceedings (Armed Forces) Act 1987. But this Act is not retrospective, thus claims based on injuries incurred prior to 1987 may still be met with a s. 10 defence: *Mathews* v. *Minister of Defence* [2003] UKHL 4, [2003] 2 WLR 435 (HL) (injuries allegedly caused by exposure to asbestos during service in the Royal Navy between 1955 and 1968).

procedure of petition of right. There were also a few special cases where statute had provided other remedies.

The Crown Proceedings Act 1947 modernised and simplified the procedure, without altering the general principle of Crown liability. The petition of right was abolished, together with a number of old forms of procedure. Instead, all actions against the Crown in contract are brought by suing the appropriate government department, or else the Attorney-General, under the standard procedure laid down in the Act. Proceedings both in contract and in tort are thus covered by the same set of rules, which are explained in the next section.

The principal provision of the Act is that any claim against the Crown which might have been enforced, subject to the fiat, by petition of right or under any of the statutory liabilities repealed by the Act, may now be enforced as of right and without the fiat in proceedings under the Act.[74] Thus the scope of the Act depends upon the scope of the petition of right and the other old procedures, and the old law relating to them will still be of importance if the Crown ever resists a claim on the ground that it falls outside the area of Crown liability. But apart from tort and certain cases such as actions by servants of the Crown (discussed elsewhere),[75] and the special case of salvage (now covered by the Act),[76] the scope of the old actions was probably comprehensive. The petition of right, for instance, appears to have been available for recovery of money from the Crown where an ordinary subject would have been liable in restitution, a head of liability which is not truly contractual; and, as already noted, the petition of right could be used to recover money due from the Crown under statute. The substance of these remedies is thus infused into the new statutory scheme, and there are no obvious gaps.

The Act applies to proceedings by or against the Crown, however, only in respect of the United Kingdom.[77] Except where local legislation provides otherwise, therefore, claimants attempting to enforce Crown liabilities in respect of other territories must fall back on the old pre-1947 procedures. Such claimants have even been deprived of the benefits of the Petitions of Right Act 1860, since it has been held that the repeal of that Act by the Crown Proceedings Act 1947 is total.[78] This inconvenient conclusion does not seem to be necessary, since the Act of 1947 merely provides that nothing in it shall affect proceedings against the Crown in respect of non-United Kingdom claims, and this saving should qualify the repeal of the Act of 1860 as much as any other provision of the Act of 1947.

PERSONAL LIABILITY OF THE SOVEREIGN

The Act of 1947 may have created a lacuna, though of more theoretical than practical importance, as regards actions against the sovereign personally. A petition of right used to lie, and the Petitions of Right Act 1860 provided for payments from the privy purse. But now the Crown Proceedings Act both abolishes the petition of right and provides that 'nothing in this Act shall apply to' proceedings by or against the sovereign in his private capacity, or authorise proceedings in tort against him.[79] Is the Crown then no longer

---

[74] s. 1.   [75] Above, p. 48.   [76] s. 8.

[77] s. 40(2)(b), (c). See *Trawnik v. Lennox* [1985] 1 WLR 532 (no Crown liability for nuisance created by British forces in Germany).

[78] *Franklin v. A-G* [1974] 1 QB 185 at 201, where the reasoning of Lawson J is not explained. The pre-1860 procedure was however simplified by agreement of the Crown: see at 202, where the form of petition is given. But under the pre-1860 procedure there may be difficulty as to costs: see above, p. 691. This was one of a series of claims by holders of Rhodesian stocks: see also *Franklin v. The Queen (No 2)* [1974] 1 QB 205; *Barclays Bank Ltd v. The Queen* [1974] 1 QB 823. In none of these cases was there any order as to costs.

[79] s. 40(1).

personally liable in contract? It seems possible, following the words of the Act, that the petition of right is not abolished to that extent,[80] so that it still survives for claims against the Crown in person, which remain under the old law, with or without the benefit of the Act of 1860.[81] This result would be far from ideal, but at least it would preserve the remedy in some form.

AGENTS IN CONTRACT

The Crown servant or agent who actually makes the contract—for example, an MOD official who orders boots for the army—is not in law a party to the contract, and is not liable on it personally. He is merely the Crown's agent, and the ordinary law is that where a contract is made through an authorised agent, the principal is liable but the agent is not. The agent is merely a mechanism for bringing about a contract between his principal and the other contracting party. Thus if the boots are ordered from a manufacturing company, the parties to the contract are the Crown and the company. If a minister in his official capacity takes a lease of land, the parties to the contract are the lessor and the Crown, and the Crown becomes the tenant.[82] The agents on either side are not personally liable on the contract. It has long been clear that Crown servants, acting in their official capacity, are as immune as any other agents: in 1786 it was decided that the Governor of Quebec could not be sued on promises made by him to pay for supplies for the army in Canada.[83] This immunity of the agent must be contrasted with the position in tort, where master and servant are both fully liable personally for torts committed by the servant in the course of his employment, and where the personal liability of Crown servants is an important safeguard—though not quite so important as it was in the era before the Crown itself became liable in tort.

Where a contract is made through an agent duly authorised,[84] the principal is liable but not the agent. Where the agent is unauthorised, the agent is liable but not the principal. This latter result is achieved by allowing the other party an action against the agent for breach of warranty of authority. This is a contractual remedy, for a contract is implied by law to the effect that the agent promises, in consideration of the party agreeing to deal with him, that he had the authority of his principal. Thus the law finds a means of making agents responsible for any loss which they may cause by exceeding their authority. But it is doubtful whether this remedy is available against agents of the Crown. The Court of Appeal has upheld a judgment to the effect that a Crown servant acting in his official capacity is, on grounds of public policy, not liable to actions for breach of warranty or authority. 'No action lies against a public servant upon any contract which he makes in that capacity, and an action will only lie on an express personal contract'.[85] There seem to be two distinct strands of argument, one that public policy requires Crown agents to be

---

[80] The petition of right is listed in the 1st Schedule among 'Proceedings abolished by this Act'; but the Act itself contains no other provision for abolition: it merely substitutes the new procedure under s. 1. Where that does not apply, therefore, the petition of right may survive.

[81] See the comment on the *Franklin* case, above.

[82] *Town Investments Ltd* v. *Department of the Environment* [1978] AC 359, where the House of Lords held that a special principle of public law equates the government, i.e. ministers and officials, with the Crown. But this rule must be confined to similar property transactions: see above, p. 36.

[83] *Macbeath* v. *Haldimand* (1786) 1 TR 172.

[84] Actual or ostensible authority is determined according to the ordinary law of agency (subject to doubts created by the *Town Investments* case): *Verrault* v. *A-G for Quebec* (1975) 57 DLR (3d) 403: *Meates* v. *A-G* [1979] 1 NZLR 415 (Prime Minister held not authorised to contract on behalf of the Crown).

[85] *Dunn* v. *Macdonald* [1897] 1 QB 401, 555.

able to contract free of personal liability, and the other that in such cases the implied contract of warranty is unjustified on the facts. Public policy should weigh less heavily now that the Crown Proceedings Act has gone so far towards assimilating the Crown's prerogatives with the ordinary law of the land. The other argument is also of dubious validity. Since the case was one arising out of a contract of employment, where (as explained elsewhere)[86] the principles underlying the case law are confused, it is sometimes regarded as a less formidable obstacle than it appears at first sight. There were also other alternative grounds for the decision in the Court of Appeal. Nevertheless, while this authority stands, Crown agents appear to have a privileged position and to enjoy an anomalous personal immunity in making contracts on behalf of the Crown. If they exceed their authority, therefore, neither the Crown nor its agent is liable, and the law fails to provide the remedy which justice demands.

Difficulty also arises over subjecting the Crown to the normal rule that the principal may be liable for an unauthorised contract made by the agent if the principal has given the agent ostensible authority, as by putting him in a position where the other contracting party might reasonably assume that the agent was duly authorised. This rule in effect rests on the principle of estoppel; and as has been explained previously there are problems in applying this principle to governmental powers exercised in the public interest, so that officers of the Crown cannot be safely assumed to have the powers which they purport to exercise.[87] Consequently the fact that a customs officer would appear to have authority to sell unclaimed goods from a customs warehouse will not give a good title to the buyer if in fact the sale was outside his statutory powers.[88] This does not mean that the Crown cannot be made liable in contract by way of an estoppel. In one case a supplier of ships' stores made an oral contract with an Admiralty officer and next day wrote to the Admiralty confirming the agreed terms as he understood them. When the Admiralty later disputed the terms, the supplier succeeded in enforcing them because the Admiralty had not replied to his letter and had consequently induced him to believe that his version was correct, thereby estopping the Crown from maintaining otherwise.[89] This ruling, however, did not turn on any question of agency.

REMEDIES AND PROCEDURE

THE STATUTORY PROCEDURE

The Crown Proceedings Act 1947 has much to say about procedure. The general policy is that the ordinary procedure in civil actions shall apply so far as possible to actions by and against the Crown, both in the High Court and in the county court. But inevitably there must be modifications in detail. The Crown is not nominally a party to proceedings under the Act: where the Crown is suing, the plaintiff is a government department or the Attorney-General; where the Crown is being sued, it is represented similarly.[90] The Treasury is required to issue a list of the departments which can sue and be sued under the Act, and if there is no suitable department or if there is doubt in any particular case the Attorney-General will fill the gap.[91] It is a departure from ordinary legal notions that

---

[86] Above, p. 48.   [87] Above, p. 281.

[88] *A-G for Ceylon* v. *AD Silva* [1953] AC 461, quoted above, p. 284. See [1957] *PL* at 337 (G. H. Treitel).

[89] *Orient Steam Navigation Co Ltd* v. *The Crown* (1952) 21 Ll LR 301 (successful petition of right); see Turpin, *Government Procurement and Contracts*, 96.   [90] s. 17.

[91] s. 17.

departments which are not juristic persons (for some departments are not incorporated) should be able to be parties to actions, but all things are possible by Act of Parliament.[92]

The Act also exempts the Crown from the compulsory machinery of law enforcement. This is not in order to enable the Crown to flout the law, but because it would be unseemly if, for example, a sheriff's execution could be issued against a government department which failed to satisfy a judgment. For the purposes of the Act the Crown must be treated as an honest man, and the ordinary laws must have their teeth drawn. Therefore the Act provides that no execution or attachment or process shall issue for enforcing payment by the Crown.[93] Nor can the Crown be made the object of any injunction or order for specific performance or order for the delivery up of property. Instead of these remedies the court merely makes a declaratory order so that the plaintiff's rights are recognised but not enforced.[94]

A special provision prohibits any injunction or order against an officer of the Crown where the effect would be to grant relief against the Crown which could not be obtained in proceedings against the Crown.[95] As explained below,[96] this formula was for many years misunderstood until the House of Lords made it clear that it is only where the power is conferred upon the Crown itself, as opposed to some minister or official, that the prohibition applies, thus protecting the Crown's immunity from being indirectly infringed. Ministers as such are subject to the ordinary law, and can therefore be subjected to compulsory orders such as injunctions and mandatory orders and they can be liable for contempt of court.[97]

The remedy most often desired is the payment of money. Here the court's order will state the amount payable, whether by way of damages, or costs, or otherwise, and the Act provides that the appropriate government department shall pay that amount to the person entitled.[98] It is also provided that payments made under the Act shall be defrayed out of moneys provided by Parliament.[99] A successful plaintiff against the Crown must thus be content with a declaration of his rights or with a mandatory order for payment. The statutory duty to pay, being cast upon the department rather than the Crown, should be enforceable, if necessary, by mandatory order.[100]

The Act in no way affects the prerogative remedies, e.g. quashing and mandatory orders, which are outside its definition of 'civil proceedings'[101] and which in any case do not lie against the Crown.[102]

In his or her private capacity the sovereign stands wholly outside the Act and under the older law.[103] Nor does the Act apply in respect of matters arising outside the government of the United Kingdom.[104]

---

[92] An example in common law is the case of the prerogative remedies, where the respondent is often a tribunal.   [93] s. 25(4).

[94] s. 21(1). For the problem of interim injunctive orders see below, p. 709.   [95] s. 21(2).

[96] Below, p. 703.

[97] M v. Home Office [1994] AC 377. Lord Woolf's speech contains an illuminating commentary on Crown proceedings both before and after the Act.   [98] s. 25(3).   [99] s. 37.

[100] As suggested by Lord Donaldson MR in M v. Home Office [1992] QB 270 at 301. Section 21(2) is inapplicable owing to the definition of 'civil proceedings' (below). When a Malaysian State government refused to pay a contractual award with 'no excuse whatsoever' mandamus was issued against the responsible minister (Minister of Finance, Government of Sabah v. Petrojasa Sdn Bhd [2008] 5 CLJ (Malaysia) 321 (Federal Court).

[101] s. 38(2).   [102] See above, p. 520.   [103] s. 41; see above, p. 689.

[104] s. 40(2). Thus in jurisdictions previously subject to British Sovereignty, if there is no remedial local legislation, the successor sovereigns may continue to enjoy the immunities of the British Crown. See 'The Spectre of Crown Immunity after the End of Empire in Hong Kong and India' (2013) 21 Asia Pacific Law Review 77 (Forsyth and Upadhyaya). And see Intraline Resources Sdn Bhd v. The Owners of the Ship or Vessel

The ordinary legal rules as to indemnity and contribution, and also the rules as to third party proceedings,[105] apply in Crown proceedings.[106] The rule most likely to come into play is that which allows an employer, who has to pay damages for his servant's wrongful act, to recover the amount from the servant. This illustrates the general principle that where there are joint tortfeasors—and master and servant are in law joint tortfeasors—the tortfeasor who is innocent may claim contribution from the tortfeasor who is to blame. Thus if a government driver knocks down and injures someone negligently, and the injured man sues the Crown and obtains damages, the Crown has a legal right as employer to make the driver indemnify it.[107]

The Act now provides one uniform procedure for all actions against the Crown, including interlocutory matters such as discovery of documents and interrogatories.[108] The Act has therefore abolished the petition of right and various other antiquated forms of procedure.[109] But, as already noticed, a petition of right may still have to be used in cases not covered by the Act, such as proceedings in respect of overseas territories.[110]

PROBLEMS OF INJUNCTIVE RELIEF

The Crown itself (as opposed to its servants) is immune from legal process except as authorised by statute. The Crown Proceedings Act 1947 expressly forbids the grant of an injunction in the proceedings which it authorises but provides that in lieu of an injunction the court may make 'an order declaratory of the rights of the parties'. It has been held, however, that the Act authorises only a definitive order, corresponding to a final injunction, and not a provisional order, corresponding to an interim injunction,[111] apparently because of the reference to 'the rights of the parties', which is assumed to mean final as opposed to interim rights. There seems to be no necessity for this narrow interpretation of the Act, which is contrary to its policy of putting the Crown, so far as practicable, on the same footing as a private litigant. The Law Commission made a recommendation[112] for statutory reform of this 'triumph of logic over justice'.[113] Nevertheless a majority of the House of Lords positively approved the restriction, though Lord Diplock and a unanimous Court of Appeal deplored it.[114] It seems unlikely to survive after M v. Home Office rejected narrow interpretations in this area.[115] Indeed, CPR 25.1(1)(b) now provides that the court may make an 'interim declaration' and may do so whether or not a declaration has been sought as final relief or not. Although an interim declaration in circumstances in which an injunction is not available has not yet been made, this is the likely role of this remedy.

Servants of the Crown, as opposed to the Crown itself, ought to be liable to injunctions as much as to other legal remedies, on the principle already explained. But this question was bedevilled for many years by misunderstanding of the Act's provision that no

---

'Hua Tian Long' [2010] HKCFI 361, HCAJ000059/2008 where Stone J concluded that the People's Republic of China 'must enjoy the like crown immunity hitherto accorded to the British Crown'.

[105] See St Martin's Property Investments Ltd v. Philips Electronics (UK) Ltd [1995] Ch 73.
[106] s. 4.   [107] See Lister v. Romford Ice and Cold Storage Co Ltd [1957] AC 555.   [108] s. 28.
[109] s. 23 and 1st Sched. For an example of a 'latin information' see A-G v. Valle-Jones [1935] 2 KB 209.
[110] Above, p. 698.
[111] International General Electric Co v. Customs & Excise Commissioners [1962] Ch 784; Underhill v. Ministry of Food [1950] 1 All ER 591.   [112] Cmnd 6407 (1976), para. 52.
[113] Working Paper No. 40 (1971), para. 48. In fact the logic seems no better than the justice.
[114] R v. Inland Revenue Commissioners ex p Rossminster Ltd [1980] AC 952. Lords Wilberforce, Dilhorne and Scarman approved. Lord Diplock considered it 'a serious procedural defect in the English system of administrative law'.   [115] See below.

injunction or order should issue against an officer of the Crown if the effect would be to give a remedy against the Crown which could not have been obtained in proceedings against the Crown.[116] This was held to bar any relief by injunction against ministers or other officers of the Crown. But, correctly understood, it applies only to protect the Crown's own immunity, and does not alter the personal liability of a minister or official who commits a wrong or who misuses a power conferred upon him in his own name. For example, take the provision of the European Communities Act 1972[117] that 'Her Majesty may by Order in Council, and any designated minister or department may by regulations, make provision' for implementing Community obligations, subject to the restriction (among others) that no tax may thereby be imposed. If an Order in Council attempted to impose a tax, no injunction could be granted either against the Crown or against a tax-collecting official since to restrain the latter would stultify the immunity of the former. But if a designated minister made regulations to the same effect, he or his officials could be restrained by injunction since that would not be to give relief against the Crown. This is the vital distinction, already emphasised,[118] between the Crown, which is immune, and ministers and Crown servants, who are not.

The misunderstanding derived from a case of 1955 where it was held that this provision of the Crown Proceedings Act prevented the grant of an injunction against the Minister of Agriculture, even though the minister's power was conferred upon him in his own name rather than upon the Crown.[119] That decision, though criticised,[120] was expressly approved by the House of Lords in 1989,[121] but finally disapproved in 1993.[122] The House has now made it clear that injunctions, both final and interim, have always been and are today still available against ministers and officials of the Crown,[123] and that in judicial review proceedings the Senior Courts Act 1981 confirms this position.[124] A long period of

---

[116] s. 21(2).   [117] s. 2(2) and Sched. 2.   [118] Above, p. 693.

[119] *Merricks* v. *Heathcoat-Amory* [1955] Ch 567 (unsuccessful application for injunction requiring minister to withdraw marketing scheme). This decision did not affect applications for prerogative remedies, which were outside the Crown Proceedings Act, and the correct remedy might have been prohibition.

[120] In the 6th edition of this book, p. 589, cited in *R* v. *Home Secretary ex p Herbage* [1987] QB 872.

[121] *R* v. *Secretary of State for Transport ex p Factortame Ltd* [1990] 2 AC 85.

[122] *M* v. *Home Office* [1994] 1 AC 377.

[123] As in *Rankin* v. *Huskisson* (1830) 4 Sim 13; *Ellis* v. *Earl Grey* (1833) 6 Sim 214 (interim injunction against the prime minister); *Tamaki* v. *Baker* [1901] AC 561; *A-G of New South Wales* v. *Trethowan* [1932] AC 526; *Conseil des Ports Nationaux* v. *Langlier* [1969] SC 60 (Can.).

[124] See *M* v. *Home Office* (above) at 420–2. There is a narrower ground for the decision in *M*. Section 21(2) of the 1947 Act precludes an injunction being made 'in any civil proceedings' against an officer of the Crown, if the effect thereof is to give relief against the Crown that could not be obtained directly against the Crown. But by s. 38(2) 'civil proceedings' does not include 'proceedings on the Crown side of the [Queen's] Bench Division', i.e. in the modern jargon the application for judicial review. Thus, whatever its precise meaning, s. 21(2) does not apply to injunctions made (under s. 31 of the Senior Courts Act 1981) in judicial review proceedings (such as the injunction made in *M*.). In Scotland the phrase 'civil proceedings' in s. 21(2) is read as not including 'proceedings invoking the supervisory jurisdiction of the Court of Session', i.e. judicial review proceedings (*Davidson* v. *Scottish Ministers* [2005] UKHL 74, para. 33 (Lord Nicholls) (prisoner held in allegedly non-Convention compliant conditions, seeking interim coercive relief)). This narrow approach does not preclude the broader and more principled approach advocated here that even an application for judicial review under s. 21(2) precludes an injunction against a minister, even if prior to the 1947 Act an injunction would have been available. And this was the view of Lord Woolf in *M*. who said that s. 21(2) 'is restricted…to situations where the effect of the grant of an injunction…against an officer of the Crown will be to give any relief against the Crown which could not have been obtained against the Crown prior to the [1947] Act' (at 412D–E). But Lord Woolf's view was doubted by Lord Rodger in *Davidson* (para. 93) and Lord Mance (para. 102) shared some of these doubts but nonetheless recognised that not all coercive relief against ministers outside judicial review would be precluded by s. 21(2) (for instance to prevent a threatened tort or a breach of duty imposed upon the officer of the Crown personally). On the narrower ground ministers would obey the law purely as a matter of grace were it not that injunctive relief was (following the

judicial aberration is now ended, and the constitutional principle that Crown officers do not partake of the Crown's immunity is reinstated.

The decision of 1993 concerned an unsuccessful application for asylum by a citizen of Zaïre who was ordered to be deported and sought judicial review. The Home Office deported him while his case was before the High Court, contrary to the expressed wishes of the judge and to an undertaking by the Home Office which the judge thought had been given to him. When the deportee reached Zaïre there was still an opportunity to secure his return, and the judge made an order that this should be done; but the Home Secretary personally decided to take no action, being advised that the judge's order was made without jurisdiction, the law then being misunderstood as explained above. But since an order of the High Court, however wrong, cannot be without jurisdiction,[125] the Home Secretary was adjudged to be in contempt of court, though no penalty was imposed.[126] Since contempt of court is the sanction for disobedience of injunctions, the contempt jurisdiction is of great importance. But in the last analysis the House of Lords' judgment contains an inconsistency about enforcement. According to Lord Templeman, 'the courts are armed with coercive powers' against ministers and officials.[127] According to Lord Woolf, 'the Crown's relationship with the courts does not depend on coercion' and 'the object of the exercise is not so much to punish an individual as to vindicate the rule of law by a finding of contempt', leaving it to Parliament to determine the consequences.[128] Yet he recognises that 'in cases not involving a government department or a minister the ability to punish for contempt may be necessary'. As the Zaïrean case shows, ministers do not invariably respect orders of the court, and just how coercive such orders really are in various situations may be in issue on future occasions. Ultimately it is the executive power which has to enforce court orders, whose efficacy against the government thus depends upon the government's willingness to police itself.[129] When the Scottish Ministers were found to be in contempt[130] the First Division[131] ordered the attendance before it of two senior civil servants, one as a representative of the Scottish Ministers the other for his own failings in the events leading up to the contempt. The House of Lords held it would have been proper to make such orders (and even to order a minister to appear) had they been given proper notice and the reasons for the order and an opportunity to be heard.[132] But when civil servants in the Home Office deliberately failed to comply with an undertaking to release a detainee, the court simply made a finding of contempt against the Home Office[133] and remarked that 'apart from a finding of contempt there [is] . . . no other sanction potentially

procedural reforms of 1977 (see above, p. 549)) available in applications for judicial review. This leaves the rule of law under threat were those reforms to be reversed or were coercive relief against a minister needed outside judicial review. The rule of law should not rest on such a contingent and narrow basis. The broader reasoning in M., viz., that coercive relief against ministers is not relief against the Crown (and so s. 21(2) is not engaged) is thus far preferable.

[125] See above, p. 255.

[126] For a case of contempt by revenue officers, purged after full apology, see *R v. Inland Revenue Commissioners ex p Kingston Smith* [1996] STC 1210.

[127] See the quotation above, p. 693. Examples concerning ministers are *Bhatnager v. Minister of Employment and Immigration* (1990) 71 DLR (4th) 84; *State of Victoria v. Australian Building Federation* (1982) 152 CLR 25.   [128] *M v. Home Office* (above) at 425.

[129] As observed by Nolan LJ, [1992] QB at 314.

[130] Prison authorities had interfered with prisoner's correspondence with legal representatives and the courts after undertaking not to do so.   [131] Of the Inner House of the Court of Session.

[132] *Beggs v. Scottish Ministers* [2007] UKHL 3.

[133] *R (Lamari) v. Home Secretary* [2012] EWHC 1895.

open to the court'.[134] No consideration was given, it seems, to ordering the erring civil servants to attend court to account for their failings.

STATUTES AFFECTING THE CROWN

PRESUMPTION AGAINST CROWN LIABILITY

An Act of Parliament is presumed not to bind the Crown in the absence of express provision or necessary implication.[135] This is a long-standing rule of interpretation,[136] which has nothing to do with the royal prerogative.[137] 'The Crown' in this case includes the Crown's ministers and servants, since it is necessarily by their agency that the Crown's immunity is enjoyed. The Crown Proceedings Act 1947 expressly refrains from altering the position.[138] In this respect, contrary to its general policy, the Act does not impose on the Crown the same liability as lies upon other people.

In fact it is frequently necessary that statutes should bind the Crown, and in such cases each statute makes the necessary provision. Thus the speed limits now in force under the Road Traffic Act 1960 are expressly made applicable to the Crown by the Act itself, which makes detailed provision for these and other traffic rules to apply to vehicles and persons in the public service of the Crown.[139] Sometimes the Act will provide for its partial application to the Crown: thus the Crown is bound by the Equal Pay Act 1970[140] and the Sex Discrimination Act 1975[141] in respect of the civil service but not in respect of the armed forces. Formerly the Crown was not bound by the National Health Service Act 1977 and associated legislation, but this immunity was removed in 1990.[142]

Other statutes which have been held not to bind the Crown, because of the absence of any provision, are the Town and Country Planning Act 1947 (now 1990) and the Contracts of Employment Act 1972. Accordingly the Crown does not need planning permission for developing Crown land,[143] and a Crown employee is not entitled to a written statement of the terms of his employment.[144] The House of Lords reversed a Scots decision which

---

[134] Para. 37. *Beggs* not referred to; exemplary damages and costs were for later consideration.

[135] Examples are *Province of Bombay* v. *Municipal Corporation of Bombay* [1947] AC 58; *A-G for Ceylon* v. *AD Silva* [1953] AC 461; *Madras Electric Supply Co Ltd* v. *Boarland* [1955] AC 667; *China Ocean Shipping Co* v. *South Australia* (1979) 27 ALR 1. But note the more liberal approach favoured by the High Court of Australia in *Bropho* v. *Western Australia* [1990] HCA 24, (1990) 171 CLR 1 (no presumption that Crown not bound; matter of construction). Note also the Canadian Supreme Court in *Friends of the Oldman River Society* v. *Canada (Minister of Transport)* [1992] 1 SCR 3 (test was whether purpose of statute would be 'wholly frustrated' if Crown not bound). For the rule generally see Hogg, *Liability of the Crown*, 2nd edn, 201.

[136] In earlier times the Crown was more readily held bound, it being said that it was bound by statutes passed for the public good, the relief of the poor, the advancement of learning, religion and justice, and the prevention of fraud, injury and wrong: *Willion* v. *Berkeley* (1561) 1 Plowd 223; *Magdalen College Case* (1615) 11 Co Rep 66b; *R* v. *Archbishop of Armagh* (1711) 1 Str 516; Chitty, *Prerogatives of the Crown*, 382. But these exceptions are no longer admitted: see the *Province of Bombay* case (above).

[137] *Madras Electric Supply Corporation Ltd* v. *Boarland* [1955] AC 667 at 684–5. But 'prerogative' is sometimes used in a loose sense (see above, p. 182) in connection with this rule: *Coomber* v. *Berkshire Justices* (1883) 9 App Cas 61 at 66, 71, 77; and see the *Madras* case (above) at 687. [138] s. 40(2)(f).

[139] s. 250. Other examples are the Social Security Act 1975, ss. 127, 128; Social Security Contributions and Benefits Act 1992, s. 115; Race Relations Act 1976, s. 75, applying the procedure of Crown Proceedings Act 1947.

[140] s. 1(8). [141] s. 85.

[142] National Health Service and Community Care Act 1990, s. 60 (health service bodies no longer to be regarded as Crown servants). [143] *Ministry of Agriculture* v. *Jenkins* [1963] 2 QB 317.

[144] *Wood* v. *Leeds Area Health Authority* [1974] 2 ICR 535.

attempted to confine the doctrine to cases where the statute encroached upon the Crown's own rights or interests, and so held the Ministry of Defence liable under highway and planning legislation when it fenced off part of a main road in which the Crown claimed no proprietary or other right.[145] In allowing the Crown's appeal the House reinstated the established rule without qualification.[146]

Whether the Crown can commit a criminal offence under a statute made binding upon it was discussed in one case by the High Court of Australia.[147]

CROWN MAY CLAIM BENEFIT OF STATUTES

It has been maintained consistently for centuries that the Crown, although not bound by the obligations of a statute, might take the benefit of it in the same way as other persons.[148] Accordingly the Crown was able to claim the benefit of statutes of limitation which prevented actions being brought after a fixed time.[149] Although the historical justification for this one-sided arrangement has been treated as an open question,[150] there can be little doubt that it represents the law. There is no reason why the Crown's exemption from the burden of a statute should prevent its taking the benefit, since the exemption was originally a limited rule for the protection of the Crown's executive powers and prerogatives rather than a rule that statutes did not concern the Crown. On the other hand, the Crown cannot pick out the parts of a statute which benefit it without taking account of qualifications: if it claims some statutory right, it must take that right subject to its own statutory limitations, whether imposed by the original Act or otherwise.[151]

The Crown's common law rights are confirmed by the Crown Proceedings Act 1947, which provides that the Act shall not prejudice 'the right of the Crown to take advantage of the provisions of an Act of Parliament although not named therein', and that in any civil proceedings against the Crown the Crown may rely upon any defence which would be available if the proceedings were between subjects.[152]

---

[145] *Lord Advocate* v. *Strathclyde Regional Council* [1990] 2 AC 580.

[146] The High Court of Australia rejects an inflexible rule and seeks the legislative intention by the ordinary canons of interpretation: *Bropho* v. *State of Western Australia* (1990) 171 CLR 1 (Act safeguarding aboriginal heritage held to bind government departments).

[147] *Cain* v. *Doyle* (1946) 72 CLR 409. The question was raised on the prosecution of a Commonwealth munition factory manager for aiding and abetting an offence by the Crown in wrongfully dismissing an ex-serviceman. The majority opinion was that an offence could be committed, but the accused was acquitted.

[148] *Case of the King's Fine* (1605) 7 Co Rep 32a; *Magdalen College Case* (1615) 11 Co Rep 66b at 68b; *R* v. *Cruise* (1852) 2 Ir Ch Rep 65; Bl. Comm. i. 262; Chitty, *Prerogatives of the Crown*, 382; Hogg, *Liability of the Crown*, 2nd edn, 215. See also *Town Investments Ltd* v. *Department of the Environment* [1978] AC 359, criticised above, p. 36.

[149] *A-G* v. *Tomline* (1880) 15 Ch D 150; *Cayzer Irvine & Co Ltd* v. *Board of Trade* [1927] 1 KB 269 at 274 (Rowlatt J). [150] By Scrutton LJ in the *Cayzer Irvine* case (above) at 294.

[151] *R and Buckberd's Case* (1594) 1 Leon 149; *Crooke's Case* (1691) 1 Show KB 208; *Nisbet Shipping Co* v. *The Queen* [1955] 1 WLR 1031; *Housing Commission of New South Wales* v. *Panayides* (1963) 63 SR (NSW) 1; Hogg (as above), 216.

[152] s. 31(1). It may be that 'therein' refers to 'provisions' rather than to 'Act', so that mention of the Crown elsewhere in the Act is immaterial.

LIMITATIONS OF STATE LIABILITY

POLITICAL ACTION: TORT

A line has to be drawn between governmental acts which can give rise to legal liability because they are analogous to the acts of ordinary persons, and acts which give rise to no such liability because the analogy breaks down. There is a certain sphere of activity where the state is outside the law, and where actions against the Crown and its servants will not lie. The rule of law demands that this sphere should be as narrow as possible. In English law the only available examples relate in one way or another to foreign affairs.

In tort the Crown and its servants can sometimes plead the defence of act of state.[153] But this plea is only available for acts performed abroad. It would subvert the rights of the citizen entirely if it would justify acts done within the jurisdiction, for it would be the same as the defence of state necessity, which has always been rejected. But acts of force committed by the Crown in foreign countries are no concern of the English courts. In the time of the naval campaign against the slave trade, for example, a Spanish slave trader failed in an action for damages against a British naval commander who destroyed one of his establishments in West Africa.[154] It is by this fundamental rule that acts of violence in foreign affairs, including acts of war, if committed abroad, cannot be questioned in English courts.[155] It also casts a complete immunity over all acts of the Crown done in the course of annexing or administering foreign territory.

A British protectorate was in principle considered to be a foreign territory, so that a person arrested by the government's orders had no remedy.[156] But where, as used to happen in practice, a protectorate was in fact completely 'under the subjection of the Crown' and was ruled as if it were a colony, the courts asserted their jurisdiction and the Crown was required to act according to law.[157] The boundaries of the area within which the rule of law is upheld may thus sometimes be difficult to draw. But it is clear that within that area the Crown cannot extend its limited legal power by plea of act of state. In another naval case, where the British and French governments had made an arrangement by which no new lobster factory was to be established in Newfoundland without joint consent, a factory was in fact established by the plaintiff, contrary to the terms of the inter-governmental agreement, and the defendant, a naval captain acting under Admiralty orders, seized it. The plaintiff was a British subject and his factory was within British territory. The Crown's attempt to justify the seizure as an act of state therefore failed, and the plaintiff was awarded damages against the responsible Crown officer.[158] Today, under the Crown Proceedings Act, the Crown would also be liable directly. The enforcement of treaties, so far as it affects the rights of persons within the jurisdiction, must be authorised by Act of Parliament. The Crown has no paramount powers.

It is often said that act of state cannot be pleaded against a British subject. No such rule was laid down in the lobster-fishing case; but the case was treated as an illustration of

---

[153] See 'British Acts of State in English Courts' (2008) *BYBIL* 176 (Perreau-Saussine) for a comprehensive review. See also [2006] *JR* 94 (Sales). See further Appendix 6.

[154] *Buron* v. *Denman* (1848) 2 Ex 167.

[155] Previous 3 sentences followed by Pill LJ in *R* v. *Secretary of State for Defence ex p Thring* (CA, 20 July 2000; unreported but available on <http://www.icrc.org>) (applicant sought to quash decision to authorise RAF action over Iraq on ground *inter alia* that it was in breach of international law).

[156] *R* v. *Crewe (Earl) ex p Sekgome* [1910] 2 KB 576.

[157] *Ex p. Mwenya* [1960] 1 QB 241 (Northern Rhodesia, now Zambia).

[158] *Walker* v. *Baird* [1892] AC 491.

some such rule in a number of *obiter dicta* in a later case in the House of Lords.[159] This is weighty authority, but even so there are grounds for thinking that the proposition may be too wide. All the cases in question were cases where the acts took place within the jurisdiction—and within the jurisdiction the rights of an alien (not being an enemy alien) are similar to those of a subject. If in British territory an alien has his property taken, or is detained, in any way not justified by law, he has full legal protection[160]—not because of his nationality, but because he is within the area where the government must show legal warrant for its acts. Conversely, if a British subject chooses to live outside the jurisdiction, it is hard to believe that he can thereby fetter the Crown's freedom of action in foreign affairs. If the house of a British subject living in Egypt had been damaged by British bombs in the operations against the Suez Canal in 1956, would its owner really have been able to recover damages in an English court?

An affirmative answer indeed appears to be given by Lord Reid in a later case where a British subject claimed compensation from the Crown for injury done to his hotel in Cyprus (a foreign country) when it was in the occupation of a 'truce force' of British troops.[161] But the other Lords of Appeal left this question open, holding that there was in fact no act of state. In any case, the gist of the action allowed was for use and occupation of the land and for breach of contract, and act of state is no defence to contractual or quasi-contractual claims as opposed to claims in tort. A different answer is suggested by another case in which British subjects lost valuable concessions granted by the paramount chief of Pondoland when that territory was annexed by the Crown. The Crown refused to recognise the concessions and pleaded act of state successfully.[162]

The latter case perhaps gives the right lead. Generalities about the immunity of British subjects ought probably to be confined to (a) acts done within the realm, and (b) acts against British subjects abroad which are not in themselves acts of international policy, such as the above-mentioned injury to the hotel in Cyprus. A logical basis for 'act of state' then emerges. It is not so much a matter of nationality as of geography—that is to say, the Crown enjoys no dispensation for acts done within the jurisdiction, whether the plaintiff be British or foreign; but foreign parts are beyond the pale (in Kipling's words, 'without the law'), and there the Crown has a free hand, whether the plaintiff be foreign or British.

To the extent that the Human Rights Act 1998 applies extra-territorially[163] the protection of the Act may trump the defence of act of state.

---

[159] *Johnstone* v. *Pedlar* [1921] 2 AC 262 (successful action by American citizen resident in Ireland for recovery of money taken from him by the police: plea of act of state rejected by the House of Lords). See Appendix 6.

[160] *Johnstone* v. *Pedlar* (above); *Kuchenmeister* v. *Home Office* [1958] 1 QB 496; *R* v. *Home Secretary ex p Khawaja* [1984] AC 74 at 111.

[161] *Nissan* v. *A-G* [1970] AC 179. The fact that the 'truce force' was for some time part of a United Nations peace-keeping force was held to make no difference to the Crown's responsibility. On the questions raised by this case see [1968] *CLJ* 102 (J. C. Collier). Act of state was not pleaded in *Bici* v. *Ministry of Defence* [2004] EWHC 786 and damages were recovered for injury and death negligently caused by British troops part of a Nato force maintaining order (not in combat). 'The Queen's uniform is not a licence to commit wrongdoing' (para. 113, Elias J). Defence that the UK forces conduct was attributable to the U N since at the time they were authorised under a Security Council Resolution was rejected in *Al-Jedda*, below.

[162] *Cook* v. *Sprigg* [1899] QC 572; and see *Winfat Enterprise (HK) Co Ltd* v. *A-G of Hong Kong* [1985] AC 733.

[163] Above, p. 149. But the protection may be illusory when another international obligation overrides that of the Convention. See *R (Al-Jedda)* v. *Secretary of State for Defence* [2007] UKHL 58 (detention without trial of Iraqi-British national (a prima facie breach of Art. 5) upheld since a state's obligations under the UN Charter prevail over those under other Conventions (s. 103 of the Charter) and the UK was authorised under Security Council Resolutions to detain without trial in the interests of public safety).

POLITICAL ACTION: CONTRACT

In contract there are also cases where ordinary business must be distinguished from political acts. It has been laid down that 'it is not competent for the Government to fetter its future executive action, which must necessarily be determined by the needs of the community when the question arises'.[164] But this was an isolated decision, and its scope is by no means clear. It concerned a Swedish ship which was detained in England in 1918 after its owners had been given an assurance through the British Legation in Stockholm, on behalf of the British government, that the ship would be given clearance if she brought (as she did) an approved cargo. The owners sued the Crown by petition of right for damages for breach of contract. The court held that this was not a contract at all—so far from being a commercial transaction, it was merely a statement by the government that it intended to act in a particular way in a certain event. Up to this point there is no difficulty, for plainly a boundary must be drawn between legal contracts and mere administrative assurances which may or may not create rights.[165] But the judge went on to say that the Crown not only *had* not made such a contract but *could* not make such a contract, because it could not hamper its freedom of action in matters which concerned the welfare of the state; and he argued a fortiori from the doctrine that Crown servants are always dismissible at will, which is discussed elsewhere.[166]

The rule thus laid down is very dubious; it rests on no authority, and it has been criticised judicially.[167] Very many contracts made by the Crown must fetter its future executive action to some extent. If the Admiralty makes a contract for the sale of a surplus warship, that fetters the Crown's future executive action in that the ship will have to be surrendered or damages will have to be paid. Yet there ought to be a remedy against the Crown for breach of contract in that case as much as in any other.[168] The only concession that need be made to public policy is that the remedy should be in damages rather than by way of specific performance or injunction. But that is achieved by the Crown Proceedings Act 1947, and in any case the court would use its discretion.

Another case which falls outside the ordinary law of contract is that of treaties. No English court will enforce a treaty, that is to say an agreement made between states rather than between individuals. 'The transactions of independent states between each other are governed by other laws than those which municipal courts administer'.[169] In the days when much of India was governed by the East India Company this principle was often invoked by English courts in order to disclaim jurisdiction over transactions between the Company, acting in effect as a sovereign power, and the native rulers of India. For the same reason the Company was given the benefit of the doctrine of act of state, so that it could commit acts of force with no legal responsibility.[170] Its commercial and its governmental activities had to be separated, so that while liable for the one it was not liable for the other. Similarly, where money is paid to the Crown under a treaty as compensation for injury inflicted on British subjects, those subjects cannot sue the Crown to recover the money, for the transaction is on the plane of international affairs out of which no

---

[164] *Rederiaktiebolaget 'Amphitrite' v. The King* [1921] 3 KB 500. See Mitchell, *The Contracts of Public Authorities*, 27; Turpin, *Government Procurement and Contracts*, 86. [165] See above, p. 318.

[166] Above, p. 48.

[167] In *Robertson* v. *Minister of Pensions* [1949] 1 KB 227 and *Howell* v. *Falmouth Boat Co* [1951] AC 837, for which see above, p. 282.

[168] Compare the problems of contracts which fetter statutory powers: above, p. 277.

[169] *Secretary of State for India* v. *Kamachee Boye Sahaba* (1859) 13 Moo PC 22.

[170] *Salaman* v. *Secretary of State for India* [1906] 1 KB 613.

justiciable rights arise.[171] The ordinary principles of trust or agency are no more suitable to the case than the law of contract is suitable for the enforcement of treaties.

SUPPRESSION OF EVIDENCE IN THE PUBLIC INTEREST

'CROWN PRIVILEGE'

A dilemma arises in cases where it would be injurious to the public interest to disclose evidence which a litigant wishes to use. The public interest requires that justice should be done, but it may also require that the necessary evidence should be suppressed. In many cases the Crown has successfully intervened to prevent evidence being revealed, both in cases where it was a party and in cases where it was not. To hear the evidence in camera is no solution, since to reveal it to the parties and their advisers may be as dangerous as to reveal it to the public generally. The Crown's object must therefore be to suppress it altogether, even at the cost of depriving the litigant of his rights.

It was for long supposed that only the Crown could make application to the court for this purpose, and its right to do so was known as 'Crown privilege'.[172] But in 1972 the House of Lords disapproved this expression, and held that anyone may make such an application. The turning-point in the history of the subject had come in 1968, when in Conway v. Rimmer[173] the House held that the court should investigate the Crown's claims and disallow them if on balance the need for secrecy was less than the need to do justice to the litigant. This was the culmination of a classic story of undue indulgence by the courts to executive discretion, followed by executive abuse, leading ultimately to a radical reform achieved by the courts and, later, by government concessions. Since the struggle was one between the Crown and litigants, it belongs properly to this chapter, even though the House of Lords has now thrown open the door to all comers.

The Crown's claims had caused so much discontent that important administrative concessions were made in 1956 and again in 1996. Judicial rebellion began in the Court of Appeal in 1964. The initial wrong turning had been made in 1942, when the House of Lords, departing from the current of earlier authority, declared in wide terms that a ministerial claim of privilege must be accepted without question by the court. This meant that the court was obliged to refuse to receive any evidence if a minister swore an affidavit stating that he objected to the production of the evidence since in his opinion its disclosure would be contrary to the public interest. The power thus given to the Crown was dangerous since, unlike other governmental powers, it was exempt from judicial control. The law must of course protect genuine secrets of state. But 'Crown privilege' was also used for suppressing whole classes of relatively innocuous documents, thereby sometimes depriving litigants of the ability to enforce their legal rights. This was, in effect, expropriation without compensation. It revealed the truth of the United States Supreme Court's statement in the same context, that 'a complete abandonment of judicial control would lead to intolerable abuses'.[174]

---

[171] Rustomjee v. The Queen (1876) 2 QBD 69; Civilian War Claimants Association v. The King [1932] AC 14. The principle is not changed by the Foreign Compensation Acts 1950–69.

[172] For the history of Crown privilege and of its conversion into public interest immunity see [1993] PL 121 (J. M. Jacob). For historical synopsis and a critical account of the law as it stood in 1994 see [1994] PL 579 (Simon Brown LJ). See also Sunkin and Payne (eds.), The Nature of the Crown, 191 (A. Tomkins).

[173] [1968] AC 910; below, p. 714.   [174] US v. Reynolds 345 US 1 (1953).

The Crown Proceedings Act 1947 made no attempt to resolve the difficulty. It applied to Crown proceedings the ordinary procedure for obtaining discovery of documents and answers to interrogatories.[175] The Crown may therefore be required to authorise the disclosure of official information, which would otherwise be an offence under the Official Secrets Act 1911. But the Crown Proceedings Act also provides that this shall not prejudice any rule of law which authorises or requires the withholding of any document or the refusal to answer any question on the ground that disclosure would be injurious to the public interest.[176]

THE MISGUIDED '*THETIS*' DOCTRINE

The case of 1942[177] was for long a source of trouble because the House of Lords laid down the law in terms far wider than were required by the question before them. In 1939 the submarine *Thetis* sank during her trials with the loss of ninety-nine men. Many of their dependants brought actions for negligence against the contractors who had built the submarine, and this was a test case. The plaintiffs called on the contractors to produce certain important papers, including the contract with the Admiralty for the hull and machinery and salvage reports made after the accident. But the First Lord of the Admiralty swore an affidavit that disclosure would be against the public interest. The House of Lords held that this affidavit could not be questioned, so that the plaintiffs inevitably lost their case. After the war it was divulged that the *Thetis* class of submarines had a new type of torpedo tube which in 1942 was still secret. The case is a good example of the most genuine type, where it seems plain that the interests of litigants must be sacrificed in order to preserve secrets of state. Diplomatic secrets and methods for the detection of crime might demand similar protection.

But the House of Lords unanimously laid down a sweeping rule that the court could not question a claim of Crown privilege made in proper form, regardless of the nature of the document. Thus the Crown was given legal power to override the rights of litigants not only in cases of genuine necessity but in any cases where a government department thought fit. This had not been the law previously. In several English cases judges had called for and inspected documents for which privilege was claimed in order to satisfy themselves that the claim was justified. In 1931 the Privy Council held that the court could examine such a claim, and remitted a case to Australia with directions to examine the documents and strong hints that the claim of privilege should be disallowed.[178] An English court had actually disallowed a claim of privilege in one case, and the document (quite innocuous) may be seen in the report.[179]

The principal danger of the *Thetis* doctrine was that it enabled privilege to be claimed merely on the ground that documents belonged to a class which the public interest required to be withheld from production, i.e. not because the particular documents were themselves secret but merely because it was thought that all documents of that kind should be confidential. A favourite argument—and one to which courts of law have given approval[180]—was that official reports of many kinds would not be made fearlessly and candidly if there was any possibility that they might later be made public. Once this unsound argument gained currency, free rein was given to the tendency to secrecy which

---

[175] s. 28.   [176] s. 28.   [177] *Duncan v. Cammell, Laird & Co Ltd* [1942] AC 624.
[178] *Robinson v. South Australia (No 2)* [1931] AC 704.
[179] *Spiegelman v. Hocker* (1933) 50 TLR 87 (statement to police after accident).
[180] *Smith v. East India Co* (1841) 1 Ph 50; *Hennessy v. Wright* (1888) 21 QBD 509.

is inherent in the public service. It is not surprising that the Crown, having been given a blank cheque, yielded to the temptation to overdraw.

OFFICIAL CONCESSIONS

In 1956 the government made important concessions administratively. The Lord Chancellor announced that privilege would no longer be claimed for reports of witnesses of accidents on the road, or on government premises, or involving government employees; for ordinary medical reports on the health of civilian employees; for medical reports (including those of prison doctors) where the Crown or the doctor was sued for negligence; for papers needed for defence against a criminal charge; for witnesses' ordinary statements to the police; and for reports on matters of fact (as distinct from comment or advice) relating to liability in contract.[181] These heads, which were defined in more detail in the statement, were said to comprise the majority of cases which came before the courts. Privilege would still be claimed in cases of inspectors' reports into accidents not involving the Crown (such as factory inspectors' reports), though the inspector would not be prevented from giving evidence; for medical reports and records in the fighting services and in prisons in cases not involving negligence; and for departmental minutes and memoranda. These were said to be the cases where freedom and candour of communication with and within the public service would be imperilled if there were to be the slightest risk of disclosure at a later date. Supplementary announcements were made in 1962 and 1964.[182] The concessions of 1996 are noted later.

After these concessions it became all the harder to accept the argument about 'freedom and candour of communication with and within the public service'. Lord Radcliffe said in the House of Lords: 'I should myself have supposed Crown servants to be made of sterner stuff', and he criticised the insidious tendency to suppress 'everything however commonplace that has passed between one civil servant and another behind the departmental screen'.[183] Lord Keith likewise said scornfully:[184]

> The notion that any competent or conscientious public servant would be inhibited at all in the candour of his writings by consideration of the off-chance that they might have to be produced in litigation is in my opinion grotesque. To represent that the possibility of it might significantly impair the public service is even more so…the candour argument is an utterly insubstantial ground for denying [the citizen] access to relevant documents.

When this favourite argument was later deployed by the Home Office to justify withholding top-level departmental documents about prison policy McNeill J rejected it out of hand.[185]

THE JUDICIAL REBELLION

The government's concessions helped legal opinion to mobilise for the overthrow of the extreme doctrine of the *Thetis* case and the unrestricted use of 'class' privilege. In 1956

[181] 197 HL Deb. col. 741 (6 June 1956).
[182] 237 HL Deb. 1191 (8 March 1962), referring to this book (proceedings against police and statements made to police); 261 HL Deb. 423 (12 November 1964) (claims based on national security).
[183] *Glasgow Cpn* v. *Central Land Board* 1956 SC 1 at 20, 19.
[184] *Burmah Oil Co Ltd* v. *Bank of England* [1980] AC 1090.
[185] *Williams* v. *Home Office* [1981] 1 All ER 1151.

the House of Lords held that in Scotland the court had power to disallow a claim by the Crown, and that in the *Thetis* case the House had failed to consider a long line of authority.[186] In 1964 the Court of Appeal, noting the superior law of Scotland, Canada, Australia, New Zealand and the United States,[187] held that the same was true of England and asserted (though without exercising) its own power to inspect the documents in a 'class' case and order their production.[188] But the Court of Appeal changed its mind in 1967 and relapsed into the unqualified *Thetis* doctrine.[189]

Finally in 1968 the House of Lords was given the opportunity to lay down more acceptable law. In *Conway* v. *Rimmer*[190] the House unanimously reversed what it unanimously stated in 1942, it shattered the basis of the unrestricted 'class' privilege, and it successfully ordered the production of documents against the objections of the Crown. These documents were reports by his superiors on a probationer police constable who was prosecuted by the police for theft of an electric torch and decisively acquitted. He sued the prosecutor for damages for malicious prosecution, and applied for discovery of five reports about himself which were in the police records and which were important as evidence on the question of malice. Both parties wished this evidence to be produced, but the Home Secretary interposed with a wide claim of 'class' privilege, asserting that confidential reports on the conduct of police officers were a class of documents the production of which would be injurious to the public interest.

The House of Lords heaped withering criticism on the overworked argument that whole classes of official documents should be withheld, at whatever cost to the interests of litigants, for the sake of 'freedom and candour of communications with and within the public service'. On the other hand they made it clear that the court would seldom dispute a claim based upon the specific contents of a document concerning, for example, decisions of the cabinet,[191] criminal investigations, national defence or foreign affairs. But in every case the court had the power and the duty to weigh the public interest of justice to litigants against the public interest asserted by the government. In many cases this could be done only by inspecting the documents, which could properly be shown to the court, but not to the parties, before the court decided whether to order production.

At a later date the House itself inspected the five documents in question, held that their disclosure would not prejudice the public interest, and ordered them to be produced to the plaintiff.[192]

Thus did the House of Lords bring back a dangerous executive power into legal custody. Some of the earlier decisions, and the official concessions in administrative practice, may remain of importance. The legal foundation of excessive 'class' claims had been destroyed, but it was to take nearly thirty years for that abuse to be given decent burial.

---

[186] *Glasgow Cpn* case (above). For a case of a claim disallowed see *Whitehall* v. *Whitehall* 1957 SC 30.

[187] As in *R* v. *Snider* (1953) 2 DLR (2d) 9; *Corbett* v. *Social Security Commission* [1962] NZLR 878; *Bruce* v. *Waldron* [1963] VR 3. Later cases rejecting claims of privilege are *US* v. *Nixon* 418 US 683 (1974); *Konia* v. *Morley* (1976) 1 NZLR 455; *Sankey* v. *Whitlam* (1978) 21 ALR 505.

[188] *Re Grosvenor Hotel (No 2)* [1965] Ch 1210.

[189] *Conway* v. *Rimmer* [1967] 1 WLR 1031, Lord Denning MR strongly dissenting.

[190] [1968] AC 910. Little mention was made of the precedents in the Court of Appeal and in other countries of the Commonwealth which prepared the way for this reform. Lord Denning MR in *Air Canada* v. *Secretary of State for Trade* [1983] 2 AC 394 at 408 gave a spirited and dramatised account of the deeds of the 'Three Musketeers' who shot down earlier claims, of how he was 'taken prisoner' by a different Court of Appeal, and how 'from over the hill there came, most unexpectedly, a relief force. It was the House of Lords themselves.'   [191] As to cabinet decisions and papers see below, p. 716.

[192] See [1968] AC 996.

'CROWN PRIVILEGE' REPLACED BY 'PUBLIC INTEREST IMMUNITY'

The House of Lords once again put the law onto a fresh basis in a case where a would-be gaming club proprietor took proceedings for criminal libel against a police officer who had supplied the Gaming Board with unfavourable information about him.[193] The Home Secretary asked the court to quash orders requiring the police and the board to produce the correspondence, and the board itself applied similarly. Lord Reid said:[194]

> The ground put forward has been said to be Crown privilege. I think that that expression is wrong and may be misleading. There is no question of any privilege in any ordinary sense of the word. The real question is whether the public interest requires that the letter shall not be produced and whether that public interest is so strong as to override the ordinary right and interest of a litigant that he shall be able to lay before a court of justice all relevant evidence. A Minister of the Crown is always an appropriate and often the most appropriate person to assert this public interest, and the evidence or advice which he gives the court is always valuable and may sometimes be indispensable. But, in my view, it must always be open to any person interested to raise the question and there may be cases where the trial judge should himself raise the question if no-one else has done so.

The House of Lords then allowed not only the Home Secretary's claim but also the claim made independently by the board. It was held that the board would be seriously hampered in its statutory duty of making stringent inquiries into the character of applicants if information obtained from the police or from sources 'of dubious character' was liable to be disclosed; and that in weighing the opposing claims in the balance the risk of a gaming club getting into the wrong hands should outweigh the risk of a licence being denied to a respectable applicant.[195] The social evils which had attended gaming clubs before the Gaming Act 1968, and the obvious necessity for the board to be able to make confidential inquiries in order to fulfil its duties, tilted the balance against disclosure.

Public interest immunity may now be claimed by any party or witness in any proceedings[196] without using ministerial certificates, affidavits or special formalities. As with the old 'Crown privilege' there could be 'class' cases in which whole classes of documents were to be protected in the public interest, but the 'class' examples which follow are now out of date, as explained below. The doctrine extends beyond the sphere of central government and, indeed, beyond the sphere of government altogether.

Where, after immunity has been successfully claimed, later events make the documents of crucial importance in a criminal case, they may be disclosed without leave of the court, provided that the implications for the public interest are properly considered, with more weight being given to the interests of the defence than to those of the prosecution.[197] The special problems of criminal cases are discussed at the end of this chapter.

---

[193] R v. Lewes Justices ex p Home Secretary [1973] AC 388.

[194] Ibid. at 400. Lords Pearson, Simon and Salmon also criticised the expression 'Crown privilege'. Lord Salmon said (at 412) that in such cases as cabinet minutes, dealings between heads of government departments, despatches from ambassadors and police sources of information the law had long recognised their immunity from disclosure and that 'the affidavit or certificate of a Minister is hardly necessary'. In Buttes Gas & Oil Co v. Hammer (No 3) [1981] QB 223 the Court of Appeal recognised a public interest in non-disclosure of certain kinds of information relating to foreign states, but the interest is that of this country, not that of foreign states.   [195] See ibid. at 412 (Lord Salmon).

[196] Including habeas corpus and criminal proceedings: R v. Brixton Prison Governor ex p Osman [1991] 1 WLR 281.

[197] R v. Horseferry Road Magistrates Court ex p Bennett (No 2) [1994] 1 All ER 289. The later event was the decision of the House of Lords in ex p Bennett (No 1) [1994] 1 AC 42.

WEIGHING THE PUBLIC INTEREST

The operation of balancing the public interest against the interests of a litigant may or may not require the inspection of the documents. There will be no need for inspection where the preponderance is clear one way or the other. In a case where a company sued the Bank of England for the recovery of a large holding of securities, and the Attorney-General intervened to resist disclosure of papers about government policy and confidential matters, a majority of the House of Lords decided that inspection was necessary. But, having inspected, the House upheld the claim of immunity, largely on the ground that the evidential value of the papers was insufficient to outweigh the objections to disclosure.[198] The relevance and cogency of the evidence may thus be weighed in the balance along with other matters.

In confirming this last proposition the House has since held that the court should not inspect documents unless satisfied that they are likely to give substantial support to the applicant's case, and that he is not merely undertaking a 'fishing expedition'.[199] The House for this reason declined to authorise inspection of ministerial papers about decisions of policy, and also correspondence between senior civil servants, of which a group of airlines sought disclosure in attempting to show that the government had unlawfully compelled the British Airports Authority to make a large increase in their charges. Since it was not contended that the government had other motives than those published in their White Paper, there was nothing to outweigh the consideration that, as the law then stood, high-level documents about policy should not normally be disclosed.

As regards cabinet documents Lord Fraser said:

> I do not think that even Cabinet minutes are completely immune from disclosure in a case where, for example, the issue in a litigation involves serious misconduct by a Cabinet minister.

He cited such cases in Australia[200] and the United States[201] where claims of immunity had been disallowed. But he made it clear that cabinet documents were entitled to 'a high degree of protection against disclosure'. In previous cases dicta in the House of Lords have been conflicting, some favouring absolute immunity and others not.[202]

The weight to be given to the private rights of citizens is shown by a decision that the customs and excise authorities may not, in the absence of a strong public interest, withhold information which is vital to the enforcement of a person's rights.[203] The owners of a patent for a chemical compound found that it was being infringed by unknown importers and they applied for orders to make the customs authorities disclose the importers' names, in accordance with the duty of persons possessing information about legal wrongs

[198] *Burmah Oil Co Ltd* v. *Bank of England* [1980] AC 1090.

[199] *Air Canada* v. *Secretary of State for Trade* [1983] 2 AC 394. Contrast *Fowler & Roderique Ltd* v. *A-G* [1981] 2 NZLR 728 (correspondence between minister and official advisers about grant of licences inspected and ordered to be disclosed). Disclosure was also ordered in *Brightwell* v. *Accident Compensation Commission* [1985] 1 NZLR 132. See (1985) 101 *LQR* 200 (T. R. S. Allan).

[200] *Sankey* v. *Whitlam* (1978) 21 ALR 505.   [201] *United States* v. *Nixon* 418 US 683 (1974).

[202] See the *Lewes Justices* and *Burmah Oil* cases (above). See also *A-G* v. *Jonathan Cape Ltd* [1976] QB 752 (Attorney-General's application for injunction against publication of the Crossman Diaries refused since the cabinet materials contained in them were about 10 years old and no longer required protection in the public interest); *Lanyon Pty Ltd* v. *Commonwealth of Australia* (1974) 3 ALR 58 (discovery of cabinet and cabinet committee papers refused); *Environment Defence Society Inc* v. *South Pacific Aluminium Ltd (No 3)* [1981] 1 NZLR 153 (cabinet papers inspected but production not ordered); [1980] *PL* 263 (I. G. Eagles).

[203] *Norwich Pharmacal Co* v. *Customs and Excise Commissioners* [1974] AC 133. The same principle was applied in *British Steel Cpn* v. *Granada Television Ltd* [1981] AC 1096.

to make it available to the party wronged. This duty was held by the House of Lords to prevail over the Crown's objection that disclosure of the information might cause importers to use false names and so hamper the customs administration; and the 'candour' argument was once again rejected.[204] There was in fact no head of public policy to set against the rights of the owners of the patent.

CONFIDENTIAL INFORMATION

Information is not protected from disclosure merely because it has been supplied in confidence. The House of Lords made this clear in another case in which they accepted a Crown claim to withhold documents on the ground that disclosure would be harmful to the efficient working of an Act of Parliament.[205] The customs and excise authorities objected to disclosing details which they had obtained in confidence from traders about dealings in amusement machines supplied by a manufacturer whose liability to purchase tax was in dispute. It was held that, much as traders might resent disclosure of such details, 'confidentiality' was not a separate head of immunity, though it might be very material in the balancing of the public interest against the interest of justice to the litigant.[206] Lord Cross also said:[207]

In a case where the considerations for and against disclosure appear to be fairly evenly balanced the courts should I think uphold a claim to privilege on the grounds of public interest and trust to the head of the department concerned to do whatever he can to mitigate the effects of non-disclosure.

Although the case against disclosure was apparently not very strong, and although some of the documents were of a routine character, the House of Lords decided on this basis that the confidential character of these particular inquiries should be protected. But since the taxpayers' liability was to be decided by arbitration, and the documents withheld would not be available for use by either side, the case for disclosure was also not strong. By contrast, a plea by the Home Office to protect top-level departmental documents about prison policy did not avail when a prisoner brought an action against them, and after inspection several were ordered to be disclosed.[208] Where a local authority pleaded confidentiality in resisting a claim for preliminary discovery of their records about a violent schoolboy who had severely injured a teacher, the Court of Appeal ordered discovery after inspecting the documents.[209] But records of child care investigations may in a suitable case be protected.[210]

The House of Lords have also held that the anonymity of informers should be protected where the public interest so demands.[211] This applies both to police informers[212] and also

---

[204] See ibid. at 190 (Lord Dilhorne). It was rejected also in *Barrett* v. *Ministry of Defence*, The Times, 24 January 1990 (evidence at naval board of inquiry).

[205] *Alfred Crompton Amusement Machines Ltd* v. *Customs and Excise Commissioners (No 2)* [1974] AC 405. The Court of Appeal had inspected the documents (see at 426). See also *Science Research Council* v. *Nassé* [1980] AC 1028; *British Steel Cpn* v. *Granada Television Ltd* [1981] AC 1096.

[206] Or, where there is no public interest, in deciding whether discovery is really necessary for disposing fairly of the proceedings: *Science Research Council* v. *Nassé* (above).   [207] [1974] AC 405 at 434.

[208] *Williams* v. *Home Office* [1981] 1 All ER 1151, taking into account that documents so disclosed may not be used for other purposes.

[209] *Campbell* v. *Tameside MBC* [1982] QB 1065 (the teacher was the prospective plaintiff, applying under the Administration of Justice Act 1970, s. 31).   [210] *Re M.* (1989) 88 LGR 841.

[211] *D* v. *National Society for the Prevention of Cruelty to Children* [1978] AC 171. And see *R* v. *Cheltenham Justices ex p Secretary of State for Trade* [1977] 1 WLR 95; *Buckley* v. *The Law Society (No 2)* [1984] 1 WLR 1101.

[212] As in *Friel, Petitioner*, 1981 SLT 113. See also *R* v. *Rankine* [1986] QB 861 (police not required to disclose location of observation post).

to those who report maltreatment of children to a local authority or protection society. The Court of Appeal has refused to order production of a local authority's records of children in their care, holding that confidentiality was essential for the proper functioning of the child care service and this public interest outweighed that of facilitating an action for negligence by a former child in care.[213] Where, on the other hand, a police investigation concerned a violent death, and a possible charge of serious crime, the public interest in clearing up the matter outweighed the claim to secrecy.[214]

Amid a welter of conflicting authorities the House of Lords refused to give class immunity to documents generated by complaints against the police under the statutory complaints procedure, although 'contents' claims might be allowable on their merits.[215] In overruling four earlier decisions the House rejected a proposition which had been taken (probably wrongly) to lay down that a litigant holding documents prima facie entitled to 'class' immunity should refuse to disclose them as a matter of duty since the ultimate judge of where the balance of public interest lay was not him but the court.[216] That would have led to what Lord Templeman called 'a rubber stamp approach to public interest immunity' which could not be acceptable. No minister ought to claim immunity unless he is himself convinced that the public interest demands it specifically.

The strong criticisms made in the Scott Report (see below) of ministerial claims to immunity and of class claims in general led the government to announce in 1996 the abandonment of class claims altogether.[217] Future claims would be made only on a 'contents' basis and only where ministers believed that disclosure would cause real harm to the public interest. The certificate would explain the nature of the harm and how disclosure could cause it, unless this would itself cause the harm in question.[218] These concessions give a well-deserved quietus to class claims, for example for internal policy advice and matters of national security. The duty of explanation should help to meet the criticisms of the European Court of Human Rights, which has held that claims of immunity in matters of national security ought not to be accepted without positive judicial investigation, perhaps with a hearing in camera.[219] The Human Rights Act 1998 now gives domestic legal force to this ruling.

The concessions apply only to the central government, but their lead will doubtless be followed generally. Yet another chapter of this tangled story should now have been closed.

CRIMINAL PROSECUTIONS

Before the House of Lords' last-mentioned decision the supposed proposition which they rejected had played a highly unsuitable part in criminal prosecutions in the *Matrix*

---

[213] *Gaskin* v. *Liverpool CC* [1980] 1 WLR 1549.

[214] *Peach* v. *Commissioner of Metropolitan Police* [1986] QB 1064 (action for damages by mother and administratrix of man killed during disturbance: discovery ordered); and see *Ex p. Coventry Evening Newspapers Ltd* [1993] QB 278 (Police Complaints Authority documents allowed to be disclosed to defendants in libel actions).

[215] *R* v. *Chief Constable of West Midlands Police ex p Wiley* [1995] 1 AC 274.

[216] Propounded in *Makanjuola* v. *Commissioner of Metropolitan Police* [1992] 3 All ER 617 at 623 (Bingham LJ) and criticised in [1997] *CLJ* 51 (Forsyth). The practice of submitting all such documents to the scrutiny of the judge in criminal cases may have caused misunderstanding.

[217] See 287 HC Deb. 949–58, 576 HL Deb. 1507–17 (18 December 1996); *The Times*, 19 December 1996.

[218] As was done in *Balfour* v. *Foreign and Commonwealth Office* [1994] 1 WLR 681 and in the *Chahal* case, below.

[219] *Chahal* v. *United Kingdom* (1997) 23 EHRR 413; *Rowe and Davis* v. *UK*, The Times, 1 March 2000. Compare the similar attitude to conclusive evidence certificates, above, p. 618.

Churchill case, which led to no reported judgment but to the massive report by Sir Richard Scott V-C.[220] Arms manufacturers were prosecuted for illegally exporting military equipment to Iraq, and for their defence they sought the disclosure of official documents from several government departments. Ministers claimed public interest immunity for many documents in order to protect intelligence operations and sources in Iraq. A number of these claims were rejected by the trial judge, who ordered disclosure to the defence. That disclosure led to revelations that the equipment had been exported with ministerial encouragement, whereupon the trial collapsed and Sir Richard Scott's inquiry was commissioned. He was concerned particularly with suspicions that ministers had tried to use public interest immunity to cover up a change of policy which had not been made public, even at the risk of the conviction of innocent defendants.

The ministers who made the claims to public interest immunity, with marked reluctance in one case, were persuaded to do so by the Attorney-General, who advised that this was their legal duty, and that the question whether the claims should be allowed should be left to the trial judge.[221] The Attorney-General's failure to disclose the ministerial reluctance to the trial court was criticised in the Scott report, where it was also argued that criminal prosecutions were entirely different from the civil cases in which public interest immunity had mostly been claimed.[222] In a prosecution the accused is in danger of fine or imprisonment, and no public interest, however genuine, can justify the withholding of documents which he may need to prove his innocence. 'Even the name of an informer may be revealed if it is necessary to establish a prisoner's innocence'.[223] Therefore the choice before the authorities is simple: either disclose the documents or drop the prosecution.[224]

This may, however, be too stark a dilemma in some cases, for example where sensitive documents will plainly be of no help to the defence so that a weighing exercise is legitimate.[225] Otherwise an undeserving defendant could abuse the rules for the purpose of aborting the prosecution. As long ago as 1956, long before the battle against Crown privilege was won, the government conceded that privilege would not be claimed for documents needed for defence against a criminal charge.[226] Citing long-standing legal authority, Sir Richard Scott cogently confirmed his conclusions in a published lecture.[227] Although they are not yet affirmed by judgment or statute, they are bound to carry great authority.

---

[220] *Report of the Inquiry into the Export of Defence Equipment and Dual Use Goods to Iraq and Related Prosecutions*, 1995–6, HC 115 (February, 1996). The events took place in 1992. For discussion see [1996] *PL* 357–527 (various authors).

[221] Scott Report, G13.100 (Attorney-General's advice), G13.103 (Mr Heseltine's doubts).

[222] Ibid., G13.125 and K6.

[223] *Makanjuola* v. *Commissioner of Metropolitan Police* [1992] 3 All ER 617 at 623 (Bingham LJ), citing *Marks* v. *Beyfus* (1890) 25 QBD at 498, where Lord Esher MR explains the rule. Despite the demise of *Makanjuola* Bingham LJ's statement should still be authoritative. A police informer may reveal his own identity if that will not prejudice police operations: *Savage* v. *Chief Constable of Hampshire* [1997] 1 WLR 1061.

[224] As recommended by Sir Richard Scott, [1996] *PL* 427 at 435. It may be that there should be some safeguard against the Crown Prosecution Service, when put to this dilemma, disclosing sensitive documents too readily. See *R* v. *Horseferry Road Magistrates ex p Bennett (No 2)* [1994] 1 All ER 289 at 297 and [1997] *CLJ* 51 at 56 (Forsyth).

[225] As in *R* v. *Keane* [1994] 1 WLR 746, where the correct course is explained by Lord Taylor CJ. See also *R* v. *Governor of Brixton Prison ex p Osman* [1991] 1 WLR 281 (government claims to immunity allowed on grounds of irrelevance in habeas corpus proceedings of a criminal nature). The dilemma in habeas corpus cases is similar to that in criminal prosecutions.   [226] See above, p. 713.

[227] See [1996] *PL* 427.

The European Court of Human Rights has recognised in the context of a criminal trial that the accused's right to disclosure of evidence is not absolute.[228] But only such limitations on full disclosure as are strictly necessary are permitted and these must be counterbalanced by procedures adopted by the judge to secure fairness to the accused.[229] Thus in exceptional circumstances a public interest immunity application might be made ex parte (without notice to the defence). And where no other course would secure fairness to the accused special counsel might be appointed to ensure that the case for the accused was properly heard in deciding whether to restrict disclosure.[230] However, procedural fairness in deciding whether to suppress evidence cannot resolve the central dilemma: if the jury might properly conclude that the disputed evidence raised a doubt as to the guilt of the accused, the evidence cannot be suppressed without tainting the fairness of the trial.

[228] *Rowe* v. *UK* (2000) 30 EHRR 1, para. 61, national security, the protection of witnesses and police methods being the recognised competing interests. And see *Botmeh and Alami* v. *UK* [2007] ECtHR 456 (summaries of the documents subject to public interest immunity certificates disclosed to accused: no violation of Art. 6 found). [229] Ibid.

[230] *R* v. *H and ors* [2004] UKHL 3, [2004] 2 WLR 335 (HL) (adoption of such procedures held premature in the particular circumstances). See the discussion of the 'special advocates' procedure, above p. 433.

PART VIII

ADMINISTRATIVE LEGISLATION AND ADJUDICATION

22

DELEGATED LEGISLATION

NECESSITY OF DELEGATED LEGISLATION

ADMINISTRATIVE LEGISLATION

There is no more characteristic administrative activity than legislation.[1] Measured merely by volume, more legislation is produced by the executive government than by the legislature. All the orders, rules and regulations made by ministers, departments and other bodies owe their legal force to Acts of Parliament, except in the few cases where the Crown retains original prerogative power.[2] Parliament is obliged to delegate very extensive law-making power over matters of detail, and to content itself with providing a framework of more or less permanent statutes. Law-making power is also vested in local authorities,[3] utility regulators and like bodies,[4] which have power to make byelaws. Outside the sphere of government it is also conferred upon professional bodies such as the Law Society, and various other bodies authorised by Parliament to make statutes or regulations for their own government.[5]

Administrative legislation is traditionally looked upon as a necessary evil, an unfortunate but inevitable infringement of the separation of powers. But in reality it is no more difficult to justify it in theory than it is possible to do without it in practice. There is only a hazy borderline between legislation and administration, and the assumption that they are two fundamentally different forms of power is misleading. There are some obvious general differences. But the idea that a clean division can be made (as it can be more readily in the case of the judicial power) is a legacy from an older era of political theory. It is easy to see that legislative power is the power to lay down the law for people in general, whereas administrative power is the power to lay down the law for them, or apply the law to them, in some particular situation. In the case of the scheme for centralising the electricity supply undertakings in London, which has been instanced already as a matter of administrative power,[6] it might be said that the power was just as much legislative. The same might be said of ministerial orders establishing new towns or airports[7] or approving county councils' structure plans, which are specific in character but lay down the law for large numbers of people. Are these various orders legislative or administrative? Probably the only correct answer is that they are both, and that there is an infinite series

---

[1] Classic works on this subject are Allen, *Law and Orders*, 3rd edn; Carr, *Delegated Legislation* and *Concerning English Administrative Law*, ch. 2; *Report of the Committee on Ministers' Powers*, Cmd 4060 (1932). See also Pearce, *Delegated Legislation in Australia and New Zealand* and Page, *Governing by Numbers: Delegated Legislation and Everyday Policy-Making* (Oxford, 2001).   [2] Above, p. 179.
[3] Local Government Act 1972, s. 235; above, p. 99.   [4] See above, pp. 123 and 124.
[5] e.g. Oxford and Cambridge Universities under the Universities of Oxford and Cambridge Act 1923, s. 7, subject to approval by the Privy Council.   [6] Above, p. 513.
[7] The development order for Stansted Airport was judicially described as 'purely administrative or legislative': see above, p. 473.

of gradations, with a large area of overlap, between what is plainly legislation and what is plainly administration. Nevertheless a distinction must be maintained to some extent. For one thing, it is a general principle that legislative acts should be public; for another, the distinction may sometimes affect legal rights.[8]

For the most part, however, administrative legislation is governed by the same legal principles that govern administrative action generally. For the purposes of judicial review, statutory interpretation and the doctrine of ultra vires there is common ground throughout both subjects. Both involve the grant of wide discretionary powers to the government. Much that has already been said about the legal control of powers can be taken for granted in this chapter, which is concerned primarily with the special features of the administrative power to legislate.

A new dimension has been added to the subject by European Community law, which prevails over delegated legislation of all kinds just as it does over Acts of Parliament. Illustrations of its overriding effect will be found below; and note must be taken of the arrangements for parliamentary scrutiny of Community legislation.

With the advent of devolution a new class of delegated legislation has been created— Acts of the Scottish Parliament and Measures (and now Acts) of the Welsh Assembly. As explained elsewhere[9] the Scotland Act 1998 sets limits to the competence of the Scottish Parliament and sets up a special procedure for testing whether a particular Act falls within its competence.[10] And there are similar provisions for the Welsh Assembly under the Government of Wales Act 2006.[11]

THE GROWTH OF A PROBLEM

Uneasiness at the extent of delegated legislation began to be evident towards the end of the nineteenth century. It was not a new device, but the scale on which it began to be used in what Dicey called 'The Period of Collectivism'[12] was a symptom of a new era. One of the most striking pieces of delegation ever effected by Parliament was the Statute of Proclamations 1539 (repealed in 1547), by which Henry VIII was given wide power to legislate by proclamation. In 1531 the Statute of Sewers delegated legislative powers to the Commissioners of Sewers, who were empowered to make drainage schemes and levy rates on landowners. These were early examples of a technique which Parliament has always felt able to use. But the flow of these powers was no more than a trickle until the age of reform arrived in the nineteenth century. Then very sweeping powers began to be conferred. The Poor Law Act 1834 gave to the Poor Law Commissioners, who had no responsibility to Parliament, power to make rules and orders for 'the management of the poor'. This power, which lasted for over a century (though responsibility to Parliament was established in 1847), remained a leading example of delegation which put not merely the detailed execution but also the formulation of policy into executive hands.[13]

---

[8] e.g. the right to a fair hearing (above, p. 473). For discussion of the distinction see *Yates (Arthur) & Co Pty Ltd* v. *Vegetable Seeds Committee* (1945) 72 CLR 37; *A-G of Canada* v. *Inuit Tapirisat of Canada* (1980) 115 DLR (3d) 1 at 19; *Fedsure Life Assurance Ltd* v. *Greater Johannesburg Metropolitan Council* 1999 (1) SA 374 where the Constitutional Court of South Africa held that the levying of rates by a local authority, since it was legislative action, was outside the constitutional right to 'procedurally fair administrative action'.

[9] Above, pp. 104 and 106.   [10] Act of 1998, s. 33. Above, p. 109.

[11] As explained above, p. 110.   [12] *Law and Opinion in England*, 64.

[13] See Report of the Committee on Ministers' Powers, Cmd 4060 (1932), p. 31. For the development of delegated legislation see the Report, p. 21; Holdsworth, *History of English Law*, xiv. 100.

But this was part of a particular experiment in bureaucratic government. As a thing in itself, delegated legislation did not begin to provoke criticism until later in the century. The publication of all delegated legislation in a uniform series under the title of *Statutory Rules and Orders* (since 1947, *Statutory Instruments*) began in 1890, and in 1893 the Rules Publication Act made provision (as will be explained) for systematic printing, publication and numbering, and for advance publicity. These measures brought the proportions of the problem to public notice. In 1891, for instance, the *Statutory Rules and Orders* were more than twice as extensive as the statutes enacted by Parliament. Notwithstanding regularly expressed concern, the growth of delegated legislation, fuelled by two World Wars and the welfare state, has continued unabated. In 2008 the published Statutory Instruments were more than six times as extensive as the Acts of Parliament. The establishment of the Delegated Powers and Regulatory Reform Committee in the House of Lords with the task of reporting 'whether the provisions of any Bill inappropriately delegate legislative power'[14] has led to many useful reports on important pieces of legislation.[15] The government provides a memorandum explaining and justifying the degree of delegation in a Bill.[16] The Committee reports on all Public Bills except supply bills and consolidating bills. It also reports on Regulatory Reform Orders under the Legislative and Regulatory Reform Act 2006.[17]

The government has established the Better Regulation Executive (which is part of the Department of Business, Innovation and Skills). The BRE has published its principles of good regulation, viz., transparency, proportionality, targeting, consistency and accountability, and seeks to see that they are followed.[18]

SCOPE OF ADMINISTRATIVE LEGISLATION

WIDE GENERAL POWERS

A standard argument for delegated legislation is that it is necessary for cases where Parliament cannot attend to small matters of detail. But, quite apart from emergency powers (considered below), Parliament sometimes delegates law-making power that is quite general. Some of the regulatory powers are very wide, for instance the power in the National Health Service Act 2006 (replacing earlier legislation) for the Secretary of State to control the medical services to be provided, to secure that adequate personal care and attendance is given, and so on.

Some of the most indefinite powers ever conferred are those of the European Communities Act 1972, under which Orders in Council and departmental regulations can alter the law in any way that may be needed for the purpose of implementing Community obligations or giving effect to Community rights, or matters related thereto, subject only to the exceptions mentioned below.[19]

---

[14] Set up following the 4th Report from the Committee on the Procedure of the House, HL Paper 92 (1992–4) (predecessor committee). See [1995] *PL* 34–6 (C. M. G. Himsworth).

[15] The Committee's reports will be found at <http://www.parliament.uk/hldprrcpublications>.

[16] Himsworth (as above), 35. Guidance for Departments in drawing up the memorandum is given by the Committee at <http://www.parliament.uk/documents/DPRR/Guidance%20for%20Departments%20 Nov%2009.pdf>. [17] See below, p. 727.

[18] A list of the most recent proposals is available at <http://www.gov.uk/government/policies/ reducing-the-impact-of-regulation-on-business/activity>. [19] Below, p. 727.

TAXATION

Even the tender subject of taxation, so jealously guarded by the House of Commons, has been invaded to a considerable extent. Under the European Communities Act 1972[20] the Treasury is authorised to specify the classes of goods chargeable and the rates of import duty, subject to Community obligations. The rate of value added tax is variable within limits by Treasury order under the Finance Act 1972, but again subject to an affirmative vote of the House of Commons if the tax is increased. Many Acts give power to prescribe charges for services rendered—which are not, of course, taxes—for example by the Post Office or under the National Health Service.[21]

POWER TO VARY ACTS OF PARLIAMENT

It is quite possible for Parliament to delegate a power to amend its own Acts. This used to be regarded as incongruous, and the clause by which it was done was nicknamed 'the Henry VIII clause'—because, said the Committee of 1932, 'that King is regarded popularly as the impersonation of executive autocracy'. The usual object was to assist in bringing a new Act into effect, particularly where previous legislation had been complicated, or where there might be local Acts of Parliament which some centralised scheme had to be made to fit. Such clauses were not uncommon, and sometimes they gave power to amend other Acts as well; but the Committee of 1932 criticised them as constituting a temptation to slipshod work in the preparation of Bills.[22]

In reality, as the intricacy of legislation grows steadily more formidable, some power to adjust or reconcile statutory provisions has to be tolerated. If there is to be delegated legislation at all, it is inevitable that it should affect statute law as well as common law. Although such clauses may no longer be cast in such striking terms, substantially similar devices have been even more in vogue since the Report than before it. One need look no further than the Statutory Instruments Act 1946 itself to find an example: the King in Council may direct that certain provisions about laying statutory instruments before Parliament shall not apply to instruments made under pre-existing Acts if those provisions are deemed inexpedient. However, most Henry VIII clauses, today and in the past, are of limited scope granting power only to amend particular earlier Acts and for a limited period of time. The power is granted in order to enable the making of changes incidental or consequential upon the original enactment.[23]

Several modern clauses empowering the amendment or alteration of primary legislation by subordinate legislation are, however, of very much wider scope. They empower the amendment of any Act, sometimes for an ill-defined purpose. And, in particular, they empower ministers to amend Acts of Parliament enacted after the enactment containing the Henry VIII clause.[24] These prospective clauses have often been criticised, yet, as will be seen, mechanisms of this type are implied by the UK's constitutional arrangements with the EU and, ironically, by the method chosen to protect fundamental rights in the Human Rights Act 1998. Abuse of these powers must be prevented by proper judicial

---

[20] s. 5.

[21] Widely phrased charging powers will be narrowly construed so as not to amount to a taxing power: *Daymond* v. *Plymouth City Council* [1976] AC 609 (power to impose sewerage charges 'as thought fit' did not extend to charges upon properties not served by sewers).   [22] Cmd 4060 (1932), 61.

[23] For many examples and general discussion of 'incidental and consequential' clauses see the Third Report of the House of Lords Delegated Powers and Regulatory Reform Committee (HL 21 (2002–3)).

[24] For discussion see [2003] *PL* 112 (Barber and Young); [2004] *JR* 17 (Forsyth and Kong).

control and how this is being achieved is discussed below.[25] Three remarkable prospective Henry VIII clauses may be noted.

First, the provision of the European Communities Act 1972, which gives power to make Orders in Council and regulations for giving effect to Community law which are to prevail over all Acts of Parliament, whether past or future, subject only to safeguards against increased taxation, retrospective operation, delegated legislation and excessive penalties.[26] Wide though these powers are, the duty of the UK to give effect in domestic law to EU directives, requires some mechanism of this kind.[27] The leading case on the prospective operation of these powers is discussed below.[28]

Second, section 1 of the Legislative and Regulatory Reform Act 2006[29] provides that a Minister of the Crown may amend any legislation (including Acts of Parliament)[30] for the purpose of reducing 'any burden'.[31] This power is now hedged with restrictions. The Act spells out that this power can only be exercised to ensure that 'regulatory functions'[32] are carried out in a 'transparent, accountable, proportionate and consistent' way; and are 'targeted only at cases in which action is needed'.[33] Moreover, the minister cannot make provision under the Act unless satisfied that '(a) the policy objective intended to be secured by the provision could not be satisfactorily secured by non-legislative means; (b) the effect of the provision is proportionate to the policy objective; (c) the provision, taken as a whole, strikes a fair balance between the public interest and the interests of any person adversely affected by it; (d) the provision does not remove any necessary protection; (e) the provision does not prevent any person from continuing to exercise any right or freedom which that person might reasonably expect to continue to exercise; (f) the provision is not of constitutional significance.'[34] As originally proposed, the Bill contained none of these safeguards and was consequently very controversial. If passed as proposed it would have allowed a minister to 'curtail or abolish jury trial; permit the Home Secretary to place citizens under house-arrest; allow the Prime Minister to sack judges; rewrite the law on nationality and immigration; [and] "reform" Magna Carta (or what remains of it).'[35] After intense public debate the government capitulated and the Act took its current form.[36]

There are further restrictions on the delegation of legislative functions, taxation, providing for forcible entry and criminal sanctions.[37] No amendment under the 2006 Act may be made to the relevant part of the Act itself or the Human Rights Act 1998.[38]

---

[25] Below, p. 729.

[26] s. 2(2), (4), and 2nd Sched. See above, p. 194. Section 2(2)(b) provides for the making of regulations to deal 'with matters arising out of or related to any such [Community] obligation or rights'. But these words do not justify a minister using this power to create rights in domestic law beyond those provided for by EU law. See *Oakley Inc.* v. *Animal Ltd* [2005] EWCA Civ 1191. See further *ITV Broadcasting* v. *TV Catchup* [2011] EWHC 1874 esp. at para. 66.   [27] Above, p. 158.

[28] Below, p. 728.

[29] Replacing the Regulatory Reform Act 2001.   [30] Passed at any time (Act of 2006, s. 1(6)(a)).

[31] s. 1(2). 'Burden' is widely defined and includes financial cost, administrative inconvenience, obstacles to efficiency and sanctions (s. 1(3)).   [32] Curiously this phrase is not defined in the Act.

[33] s. 2(2) and (3).

[34] s. 3(2). For discussion of the 'constitutional significance' limitation in the 2006 Act and other statutes see Khaitan, 'Constitution as a Statutory Term' (2013) 129 *LQR* 589.

[35] From the letter in *The Times* newspaper of 16 February 2006, written by 6 Cambridge law professors, that sparked the public debate on the Bill.

[36] For an account see Davis, 'The Significance of Parliamentary Procedures in Control of the Executive: A Case Study: The Passage of Part 1 of the Legislative and Regulatory Reform Act 2006' [2007] *PL* 677.

[37] s. 4(2) (delegating legislative functions), s. 5 (taxation), s. 6 (criminal penalties) and s. 7 (forcible entry).

[38] s. 8.

There has to be widespread consultation before a draft Order is made and laid before Parliament.[39] A draft Legislative Reform Order once laid before Parliament may be subject to the negative resolution procedure,[40] the affirmative resolution procedure[41] or the super-affirmative resolution procedure.[42] This latter procedure, unlike the first two mentioned, requires the minister to have regard to any presentations made to him about the draft Order and, in particular, 'any resolution of either House of Parliament, and (c) any recommendations of a committee of either House of Parliament charged with reporting on the draft order'. A mechanism is laid down (with Parliament having the last word in determining which procedure is adopted).[43] If either the Delegated Powers and Regulatory Reform Committee (in the House of Lords) or the Regulatory Reform Committee (in the Commons), charged with scrutinising the draft, recommend that the minister not make the Order in the form proposed, the minster cannot make that Order unless the relevant House resolves to reject the recommendation of its Committee.[44]

This Act is now so set about with restrictions that its impact will probably be limited to its proper field, regulatory reform. The Act, like its predecessors, may not be proving effective. In November 2013 some nineteen 19 Orders had been made under section 1 of the 2006 Act and 3 Orders made under section 2.[45]

Third, where 'a declaration of incompatibility' has been made under section 4 of the Human Rights Act 1998[46] declaring a statutory provision ('primary legislation') to be incompatible with a Convention right, a minister may by order ('remedial order') make the necessary amendments to primary legislation—including legislation that has not been declared incompatible.[47] Such orders may be retrospective.[48] Remedial orders may not be made unless draft orders have been approved by both Houses of Parliament.[49] It may be noted that remedial orders are made by executive authorities whereas the protection of Convention rights might be considered a judicial task. Moreover, this mechanism itself may breach Convention rights, for instance, in the case where the Crown has an interest in the litigation that led to the declaration. The minister's decision whether to make a remedial order (and whether to make it retrospective) determines the 'rights and obligations' of the parties. Since the minister cannot be considered impartial is this not contrary to Article 6(1)?[50] Alternatively, the minister may decide not to make an order thus leaving the victim of the breach without an effective remedy contrary to Article 13.[51] Some such mechanism was necessary to reconcile parliamentary supremacy with the protection of Convention rights; and was implied by the scheme of the Act of 1998.[52]

---

[39] s. 13. An explanatory memorandum also has to be provided.

[40] s. 16 (Order can be made after an appropriate period unless draft disapproved by resolution). For the detail and the time limits, see the statute.

[41] s. 17 (Order can only be made if draft approved by resolution in both Houses). For the detail and the time limits, see the statute.   [42] s. 18.

[43] s. 15 (The minister recommends the procedure but either House may override his recommendation by resolution).

[44] This applies to all three procedures. See ss. 16(5), 17(4) and 18(5) except that there are strict time limits for the recommendation in the first two procedures, but a recommendation at any time prior to approval will call a halt to the procedure in the case of the super-affirmative procedure.

[45] The most recent Order made under s. 1 is the Legislative Reform (Annual Review of Local Authorities) Order (SI 2012/1879).   [46] Described above, p. 134.

[47] 2nd Sched., para. 1(2).   [48] 2nd Sched., para. 1(1)(b).

[49] 2nd Sched., para. 2(a). Urgent orders may be made immediately (para. 2(b)) but cease to have effect after 120 days unless approved by Parliament.   [50] See above, p. 137, for this and other problems.

[51] Art. 13 is not given effect by the Act of 1998 (see 1st Sched.) but a victim may still petition the Strasbourg court.

[52] For criticism see *Constitutional Reform in the UK: Practice and Principles* (1998, Centre for Public Law), 66–7; [1998] *EHRLR* 520 (Wade).

JUDICIAL REVIEW OF THE POWER TO VARY ACTS OF PARLIAMENT

Powers to vary Acts of Parliament, particularly those that go beyond incidental and consequential changes, place exceptional power in the hands of ministers and also raise constitutional issues over the supremacy of Parliament.[53] The courts in reviewing the exercise of these powers have naturally responded to this context. They insist upon 'a narrow and strict construction and any doubts [about the clause's] scope [are] resolved by a restrictive approach'.[54] They also require that any modification of an Act must be expressly stated in the statutory instrument and not merely inferred from its content.[55] And the power to modify an Act cannot overcome express terms restricting modification.[56]

The implications of prospective Henry VIII clauses were explored for the first time in the 'Metric Martyrs' case.[57] The defendants were convicted of selling loose goods from bulk using only imperial measurements of weight, contrary to the Weights and Measures Act 1985 as amended in 1994 under powers conferred by s. 2(2) and (4) of the European Communities Act 1972. As enacted, the 1985 Act allowed the use of imperial measures but after the 1994 amendment it did not. The appellants contented that the Henry VIII power in the 1972 Act had been impliedly repealed by the 1985 Act. Thus the 1994 amendments were beyond the minister's powers under the 1972 Act. Laws LJ, however, reasoned that the doctrine of implied repeal, under which the later statute always prevails over the earlier, was not engaged unless there was conflict of subject matter between the statutes.[58] Thus a general earlier statute would always prevail over a specific later one. Thus the judge concluded: 'Generally, there is no inconsistency between a provision conferring a Henry VIII power to amend future legislation and the terms of any such future legislation.'[59]

The alternative ground for Laws LJ's dismissal of the appeals was his development of the common law concept of a 'constitutional statute'. These either condition the legal relationship between citizen and state or touch fundamental rights.[60] A constitutional statute, the

---

[53] Discussed above, p. 19.

[54] *R* v. *Secretary of State for the Environment ex p Spath Holme Ltd* [2001] 2 AC 349 (para. 35). Thus clauses that authorise the varying of 'any enactment' are not prospective and will only apply to past Acts: Barber and Young, below, at 119. For an example see *R (ToTel Ltd)* v. *First-tier Tribunal* [2012] EWCA Civ 1401 (statutory wording—'to make provision in connection with appeals' (Finance Act 2008, s. 124)—not sufficiently clear to remove right of appeal in the circumstances).

[55] *McKiernon* v. *Secretary of State for Social Security* (1990) Admin LR 133 at 137 (approved in *R* v. *Secretary of State for Social Security ex p Britnell* [1991] 1 WLR 198 (HL)); *Bairstow* v. *Queens Moat Houses plc* [1998] 1 All ER 343 at 352–3. And see *R (Orange Personal Communications Ltd)* v. *Secretary of State for Trade and Industry* [2001] 3 CMLR 781 (existing statutory provisions to modify (as required by EU directive) telecommunication licences should be utilised rather than making an order under s. 2(2) of the European Communities Act 1972; s. 2(2) could not be considered as impliedly repealing the statutory provisions). See also *Brown (formerly Bajinya)* v. *HMP Belmarsh* [2007] EWHC 498. Exercise of the Home Secretary's power under s. 194(4) of the Extradition Act 2003 to 'modify' the Act in a particular case (where there were no extradition arrangements in respect of the territory in question) was upheld. Modification (which was not required to be laid before Parliament) to time limits upheld.

[56] *Bairstow* v. *Queens Moat Houses plc* (above) (power to amend 'any statutory provision relating to practice and procedure of the Senior Courts' (Senior Courts Act 1981, s. 87(3)) did not extend to rendering provisions of the Civil Evidence Act 1995 retrospective when that Act itself provided against such retrospective operation).

[57] *Thoburn* v. *Sunderland City Council* [2002] EWHC 195, [2003] QB 151. For commentary see (2003) 54 *NILQ* 25 (Elliott); [2003] *PL* 112 (Barber and Young).

[58] Adopting the language of Barber and Young at 115.

[59] *Thoburn* at para. 50. See (2002) 118 *LQR* (Marshall) setting out how the general assumption had been that Henry VIII clauses did not operate prospectively.

[60] Ibid. at para. 62. See D. Feldman, 'The Nature and Significance of "Constitutional" Legislation' (2013) 129 *LQR* 343 for the argument that a fundamental rights approach to this question is inadequate.

judge held, such as the European Communities Act 1972, could only be repealed expressly. Since the 1985 Act did not expressly repeal in any way the 1972 Act, the section 2(2) and (4) powers were unlimited and provided the vires for the 1994 amendments.

While this latter ground is not without difficulty,[61] it allows a distinction to be drawn between prospective Henry VIII clauses which are necessary or implied by our constitutional arrangements and those that are not. Section 10 of the Human Rights Act 1998 and section 2(2) and (4) of the European Communities Act 1972 may thus only be able to be expressly repealed. But section 1 of the Legislative and Regulatory Reform Act 2006 may yet be open to implied repeal by later statutes.

ADMINISTRATIVE REPEAL

It is common for statutes to come into operation on a date to be fixed by ministerial order. Cases have occurred where the commencement order deliberately omitted some provision of the Act, thereby in effect repealing it administratively.[62]

EMERGENCY POWERS

The common law contains a doctrine of last resort under which, if war or insurrection should prevent the ordinary courts from operating, the actions of the military authority in restoring order are legally unchallengeable. When the courts are thus reduced to silence, martial law (truly said to be 'no law at all') prevails. This principle has had to be called into play in Ireland as late as 1921, but it lies outside our subject.[63] All other emergency legislative powers derive from Parliament by delegation.[64]

The standing provision for dealing with emergencies is now Part 2 of the Civil Contingencies Act 2004. The 2004 Act is of much wider scope than the Emergency Powers Act 1920, which it replaces. The 1920 Act's purpose was primarily to protect the public from the effects of serious strikes, but the definition of an emergency in the 2004 Act is very wide. It comprises 'serious threats' to the welfare of any part of the population, the environment, the political, administrative or economic stability or, the security of the United Kingdom.[65] There is no requirement that an emergency be declared, but Her Majesty may by Order in Council make emergency regulations for the purpose of preventing, controlling or mitigating an aspect or effect of the emergency if satisfied that an emergency is occurring or about to occur, that the regulations are necessary and the need is urgent.[66] Practically anything may be required to be done, or prohibited, by the regulations; and it may be made a criminal offence to breach the regulations or to fail to comply with a direction given under the regulations or obstruct someone performing a

Constitutional provisions should instead be identified by reference to their propensity to (a) define the institutions of the state and (b) regulate the relationships between those institutions.

[61] Necessary implication may suffice to displace a constitutional right: *R v. Secretary of State for the Home Department ex p Pierson* [1998] AC 539 at 575. And see Marshall, above, at 496 pointing to the absence of any parliamentary warrant for the distinction between 'first and second class statutes'.

[62] See *R v. Home Secretary ex p Anosike* [1971] 1 WLR 1136 (right of appeal under Immigration Appeals Act 1969 not brought into force).

[63] See Bradley and Ewing, *Constitutional and Administrative Law*, 15th edn, 586–8.

[64] Executive action may be taken by the government under the royal prerogative in order to keep the peace or to deal with emergency: *R v. Home Secretary ex p Northumbria Police Authority* [1989] QB 26 (maintenance by Home Secretary of a stock of baton rounds and CS gas for supply to the police in times of emergency held authorised both by statute and by prerogative).

[65] See the extensive definition in s. 19 and also s. 1.   [66] ss. 20 and 21.

function under the regulations.[67] Where a 'senior minister' considers that there would be 'serious delay' in involving Her Majesty either in declaring the emergency or making the regulations, he may act in her stead.[68] The full plenary powers of Parliament have been given to the maker of the regulations for they 'may make provision of any kind that could be made by Act of Parliament' including disapplying or modifying an Act.[69]

They may not require military or industrial service, prohibit a strike, create offences punishable by more than three months in prison or a fine in excess of level 5 on the standard scale.[70] The proclamation of the emergency (and the regulations) lapse after thirty days although fresh proclamations and regulations may be made.[71] The regulations must 'as soon as reasonably practical' be laid before Parliament (which shall be recalled if necessary). If not approved by both Houses within seven days after being laid, the regulations lapse.[72]

LEGAL FORMS AND CHARACTERISTICS

REGULATIONS, RULES, ORDERS ETC.

Parliament follows no particular policy in choosing the forms of delegated legislation, and there is a wide range of varieties and nomenclature. An Act may empower an authority to make regulations, rules or byelaws, to make orders, or to give directions. Acts often empower the Crown to make Orders in Council, and particularly where the subject-matter falls within the province of no designated minister.[73] Such orders must be distinguished from Orders in Council made in the exercise of the royal prerogative:[74] the former are valid only in so far as they conform to the power conferred by Parliament; the latter are valid only in so far as they fall within the Crown's remaining prerogative powers at common law.

The Committee on Ministers' Powers recommended that the expressions 'regulation', 'rule' and 'order' should not be used indiscriminately, but that 'rule' should be confined to provisions about procedure and that 'order' should be used only for executive acts and legal decisions.[75] But the nomenclature in practice honours these distinctions nearly as much in the breach as in the observance. Untidy though the language is, it makes no legal difference. 'Byelaws', for example, are subject to no special rules merely because they are given this title.

'Directions' are also used for general legislation. They may be given for example under the Town and Country Planning Act 1990, the National Health Service Act 2006, the Social Security Contributions and Benefits Act 1992 and under Acts providing for ministerial powers over denationalised industries.[76] Other Acts empower a minister to give 'guidance', the observance of which may or may not be mandatory, according as the Act intends.[77] The use of directions and guidance is now a common technique of government.

---

[67] See s. 22(2) and (3). Regulations may reorganise the administrative machine, set up special tribunals for trials, confiscate or destroy property etc.   [68] s. 20(2).

[69] s. 22(3)(j). The regulations remain subordinate legislation (even though they may amend primary legislation) and do not override the Human Rights Act 1998 or the safeguards within Pt 2 of the 2004 Act (ss. 23(5) and 30(2)). See also s. 20(5)(b)(iv) (maker of emergency regulations to be satisfied that they are consistent with 1998 Act).

[70] s. 23(4).   [71] s. 26.   [72] s. 27.   [73] Above, p. 40.

[74] Above, p. 179.   [75] Cmd 4060 (1932), 64.

[76] See e.g. the Railways Act 1993, ss. 84, 95, 98 and 106.

[77] See R v. Islington LBC ex p Rixon [1997] ELR 66, holding that 'guidance' giving effect to statutory policy was mandatory in the case of educational facilities for the disabled.

They allow ministers to change the rules rapidly to suit changing circumstances. On the other hand, directions and guidance are seldom required to be laid before Parliament and the benefits of such scrutiny are lost.[78] The way in which guidance to be taken into account is sometimes explicitly specified in the relevant Act.[79]

There is scarcely a limit to the varieties of legislative provisions which may exist under different names. The statutory 'code of practice' is now in constant use, and since this has, or may have, legal effects in certain circumstances it ranks as legislation of a kind.[80] Under the Trade Union and Labour Relations (Consolidation) Act 1992 (replacing earlier legislation in force since 1975) the Advisory Conciliation and Arbitration Service issues a code of practice, giving guidance for the purpose of promoting good industrial relations.[81] Its legal effect is that it is admissible in evidence before the employment tribunals which adjudicate employment cases, and is to be taken into account on any question to which the tribunal thinks it relevant.[82] The ministerial code of guidance to which local authorities must 'have regard' in administering the Housing Act 1996 is statutory but not absolutely binding since 'have regard' does not mean 'comply'.[83] By contrast, the code of practice which the Secretary of State has published explaining the arrangements for the 'examination in public' of structure plans is not statutory in any way: it is merely a statement of administrative policy. Under the Mental Health Act 1983, the Secretary of State is obliged to prepare a code of practice 'for the guidance' of those involved in the management of mental hospitals and nursing homes.[84] The House of Lords has held that 'the Code...should be given great weight...[It is] much more than mere advice which an addressee is free to follow or not as it chooses...[A mental hospital]...should depart [from the Code] only if it has cogent reasons for doing so.'[85] But a decision-maker who is obliged to 'take into consideration any recommendation' need not attach special weight to it but has a wide discretion.[86]

Codes of practice, guidance and so forth have proliferated into a jungle of quasi-legislation of this kind, some codes having legal effect and others not and some, though only a minority, being subject to parliamentary approval. In a debate twenty years

---

[78] Directions and guidance will, of course, be struck down if ultra vires: *Laker Airways Ltd* v. *Department of Trade* [1977] QB 643 (guidance ultra vires); *R* v. *Secretary of State for Social Services ex p Stitt*, The Times, 5 July 1990 (directions upheld but recognised that they could be ultra vires).

[79] The Equality Act 2010, Sched. 1, para. 12, for instance, provides 'In determining whether a person is a disabled person, an adjudicating body must take account of such guidance as it thinks is relevant.'

[80] See Ganz, *Quasi-legislation*, discussing many examples from the Highway Code of 1930 onwards. The great majority of these codes are recent. See also [1986] *PL* 239 (R. Baldwin and J. Houghton) for a detailed survey and comment. The Equality Act 2006, s. 14 empowers the Equality and Human Rights Commission to issue codes of practice on a variety of subjects.

[81] The Secretary of State may do the same (with overriding effect) under the 1992 Act, ss. 203–6.

[82] Act of 1992, ss. 207 and 207A replacing earlier legislation in force since 1974. Section 207A empowers an Employment Tribunal to increase damages by 25% for an employer's unreasonable failure to observe the codes of conduct.

[83] *De Falco* v. *Crawley BC* [1980] QB 460. See similarly *R* v. *Police Complaints Board ex p Madden* [1983] 1 WLR 447. For another example of 'have regard to' guidance, see the School Standards and Framework Act 1998, ss. 84 and 85.

[84] s. 118(1). The Secretary of State must consult with others concerned (sub-s. (3)) in preparing the code which is laid before Parliament (which may require withdrawal or amendment) (sub-s. (4) and (5)).

[85] *R (Munjaz)* v. *Mersey Care NHS Trust* [2005] UKHL 58, [2006] 2 AC 148, para. 21 (Lord Bingham (for the majority)). In the event the hospital's policy to depart from code (regarding seclusion of patients) upheld; followed in *R (X)* v. *Tower Hamlets LBC* [2013] EWCA Civ 904 (local authority failed to demonstrate cogent reasons for departing from its guidance on equal treatment of related and unrelated foster carers).

[86] *The Staff Side of the Police Negotiating Board* v. *Home Secretary* [2008] EWHC 1173, paras. 40–4 (recommendation in regard to police pay not followed by Home Secretary: decision upheld).

ago upon them[87] the House of Lords deplored the general confusion, the lack of parliamentary control, the lack of rules for publication and numbering and other deficiencies; and a code of practice on codes of practice was suggested.[88] There has been little change since. Informal codes offer a way of escape from the rules governing statutory instruments and this is being freely exploited.

ADMINISTRATIVE RULES

Mere administrative rules, for example as to the allocation of business within the civil service, or for extra-statutory concessions to taxpayers,[89] are not legislation of any kind. The same applies to statements of policy and of practice and to many other pronouncements of government departments, whether published or otherwise. But the clear line which ought to divide legislative from administrative rules is blurred by ambiguous categories. Statutory rules which are undoubtedly legislation may be held to be merely regulatory and not legally enforceable. This is the case with the prison rules, made under the Prison Act 1952, which have sometimes been held to be regulatory directions only and not enforceable at the suit of prisoners, but at other times are held to be mandatory in law and fully enforceable.[90] On the other hand non-statutory rules may be treated as if they were statutory. As explained elsewhere, the High Court assumed jurisdiction to quash decisions of the (former) Criminal Injuries Compensation Board, the Civil Service Appeal Board and the Panel on Takeovers and Mergers[91] if they do not accord with their published rules, even though the rules rest upon no statutory authority. The last of these cases is especially striking, since the rules of the Panel are not made by a minister or other agency of government, and thus have no constitutional or democratic basis. Yet rules which the court will enforce must be admitted to be genuine legislation, anomalous though this is in the absence of any statutory warrant.

Another dubious case is that of the immigration rules,[92] which are made by the Home Secretary under the Immigration Act 1971, subject to parliamentary disapproval, and which explain how his wide discretionary powers over visitors from overseas and immigrants are to be exercised.[93] These rules have repeatedly been held to be rules of administrative practice merely, not rules of law and not delegated legislation,[94] and the House of Lords has held that they have 'no statutory force'.[95] Breach of them by an immigrant does not therefore make him an illegal immigrant under the Act,[96] though breach of them by an immigration officer may show that he had no authority to grant

---

[87] 469 HL Deb. 1075 (15 January 1986).   [88] Col. 1086 (Lord Renton).

[89] For these see above, p. 349.   [90] See above, p. 57.

[91] For these cases see above, pp. 540 and 541.

[92] The Immigration Rules are discussed above, p. 61 where the following two decisions of the Supreme Court and one decision of the Court of Appeal are considered: *R (Alvi) v. Home Secretary* [2012] UKSC 33; *R (Munir) v. Home Secretary* [2012] UKSC 32; and *Home Secretary v. Pankina* [2010] EWCA Civ 719. See Elliott (2012) 71 *CLJ* 468. The result of these decisions is that regardless of the label used where a 'policy/guidance' document is rigid and prescriptive it will qualify as an 'immigration rule', and will therefore attract the parliamentary scrutiny procedure under s. 3(2) of the 1971 Act (*Alvi*) but where the guidance is flexible it will not do so (*Munir*).

[93] See above, p. 60. The rules are published as House of Commons papers, not as statutory instruments. The current rules are HC 395 (1994) as amended from time to time. For the up to date version see at <http://www.ukba.homeoffice.gov.uk/policyandlaw/immigrationlaw/immigrationrules/>.

[94] *R v. Home Secretary ex p Hosenball* [1977] 1 WLR 766 and cases cited below.

[95] *R v. Home Secretary ex p Zamir* [1980] AC 930; *R v. Entry Clearance Officer, Bombay ex p Amin* [1983] 2 AC 818.   [96] *R v. Home Secretary ex p Mangoo Khan* [1980] 1 WLR 569.

admission, thus making the immigrant illegal.[97] The rules undoubtedly have statutory force to some extent, in that an immigrant's appeal must be allowed if the adjudicator considers that the immigration officer's decision was not in accordance with them.[98] Furthermore, the courts have several times quashed immigration decisions for misconstruction or misapplication of the rules, for example where admission was wrongly refused to a boy coming to this country for education,[99] or where a rule was invalid for unreasonableness.[100] The courts did not explain whether they were treating the rules as having statutory force, or whether they were enforcing non-statutory rules as in the case of the Criminal Injuries Compensation Board. It is not surprising that the rules have been called 'very difficult to categorise or classify', being 'a curious amalgam of information and description of executive procedures'.[101] Earlier statements that the rules 'quite unlike ordinary delegated legislation', that they 'do not purport to enact a precise code having statutory force', and that they are 'discursive in style and, on their face, frequently offer no more than broad guidance as to how discretion is to be exercised'[102] are no longer applicable to the current rules. As Lord Hope has remarked in the Supreme Court the 'introduction of the points-based system has created an entirely different means of immigration control. The emphasis now is on certainty in place of discretion, on detail rather than broad guidance. There is much in this change of approach that is to be commended.'[103]

In the United States the assimilation of different categories has been carried further,[104] and the courts have enforced administrative rules and practices merely because they have been followed in fact rather than because they have statutory backing.[105] 'He that takes the procedural sword shall perish with that sword', said Mr Justice Frankfurter.[106] English judges have confined themselves to cases where formal rules have been promulgated, as in the case of the Criminal Injuries Compensation Board and other cases mentioned earlier,[107] and to cases where an established practice creates a legitimate expectation of a fair hearing.[108] So they also have made a breach in the legal barrier, and this may be exploited further.

---

[97] *R* v. *Home Secretary ex p Choudhary* [1978] 1 WLR 1177.

[98] Immigration Act 1971, s. 19. For discussion of the status of the immigration rules, see above, p. 60. Note, in particular, *R (Alvi)* v. *Home Secretary* [2012] UKSC 33, para. 39 where Lord Hope observes that s. 86(3)(a) Nationality, Immigration and Asylum Act 2002 includes the Immigration Rules within its definition of 'law' for the purpose of determining immigration appeals.

[99] *R* v. *Gatwick Airport Immigration Officer ex p Kharrazi* [1980] 1 WLR 1396, holding that the immigration officer had erred in 'law' and so acted ultra vires under the doctrine of the *Racal* case (above, p. 255). See similarly *R* v. *Immigration Appeal Tribunal ex p Shaikh* [1981] 1 WLR 1107, quashing the tribunal's decision for misapplication of the rules; *R* v. *Immigration Appeal Tribunal ex p Swaran Singh* [1987] 1 WLR 1394 (similar). And see (*R (BAPIO Action Ltd)* v. *Home Secretary* [2007] EWCA Civ 1139 (Rules may be subject to judicial review on the usual public law grounds (para. 32)).

[100] *R* v. *Immigration Appeal Tribunal ex p Begum Manshoora* [1986] Imm. AR 385. For discussion of challenges to the immigration rules see *R (Chapti and ors)* v. *Home Secretary* [2011] EWHC 3370, paras. 56–60 (Beatson J).   [101] Lane and Cumming-Bruce LJJ respectively in the *Hosenball* case, above.

[102] *R* v. *Immigration Appeal Tribunal ex p Bakhtaur Singh* [1986] 1 WLR 910.

[103] *Munir*, para. 42.

[104] The definition of 'rule' in the federal Administrative Procedure Act of 1946 includes statements of policy, organisation, procedure or practice made by government agencies.

[105] Schwartz and Wade, *Legal Control of Government*, 92. But this practice may discourage public authorities from publicising their procedures.   [106] In *Vitarelli* v. *Seaton* 359 US 535 (1959) at 547.

[107] Above, p. 539.   [108] Above, p. 450.

CIRCULARS

Departmental circulars are a common form of administrative document by which instructions are disseminated, e.g. from a department in Whitehall to its local offices or to local authorities over which it exercises control. Many such circulars are identified by serial numbers and published, and many of them contain general statements of policy, for instance as to the Secretary of State's practices in dealing with planning appeals. They are therefore of great importance to the public, giving much guidance about governmental organisation and the exercise of discretionary powers. In themselves they have no legal effect whatever, having no statutory authority.[109] But they may be used as a vehicle for conveying instructions to which some statute gives legal force, such as directions to local planning authorities under the Town and Country Planning Act 1990.[110] They may also contain legal advice of which the courts will take notice.[111]

Much confusion has been caused by the failure to distinguish between the legal and the non-legal elements in circulars. A leading example is *Blackpool Corporation v. Locker*.[112] Under wartime regulations, continued in force, the Minister of Health was empowered to take possession of land for any purpose and to delegate that power, subject to such restrictions as he thought proper. He delegated the power to local authorities by a series of circulars sent out from his department, which contained numerous instructions. Two of these instructions were that there should be no requisitioning of furniture, or of any house which the owner himself wished to occupy. Both these were disregarded in an attempted requisition of the plaintiff's house. The question then was, were the instructions in the circulars legal conditions restricting the delegated power, or were they merely administrative directions as to how that power, delegated in all its plenitude, should in practice be exercised? On this vital point the circulars were entirely ambiguous. The Court of Appeal held that the instructions were legal restrictions limiting the delegated power and that the requisition was therefore invalid. But the local authority and the ministry had acted on the opposite view: they had refused to disclose the terms of the circulars, and had even at first resisted disclosing them to the court on grounds of privilege.[113] Thus they had 'radically misunderstood their own legal rights and duties', and had refused to let the plaintiff see the very legislation by which his rights were determined. A judgment notable for its forceful language, as well as for its awareness of the wide constitutional implications, was delivered by Scott LJ who had formerly been chairman of the Committee on Ministers' Powers and was inclined to deplore the failure to implement its report. He described some of the events as 'an example of the very worst kind of bureaucracy'. But the root of the trouble may well have been the difficulty of telling where legislation began and ended.

In a case of the same kind, where the requisition was held invalid for non-observance of the condition in the circular requiring notice to be given to the owner, Streatfield J said:[114]

---

[109] See e.g. *Colman (JJ) Ltd v. Commissioners of Customs and Excise* [1968] 1 WLR 1286 at 1291 (Commissioners' 'notices' cannot alter law).   [110] Above, p. 55.

[111] As in the *Gillick* case, below. In *R (Enstone Uplands and District Conservation Trust) v. West Oxfordshire DC* [2009] EWCA Civ 1555 Sullivan LJ (para. 36) said that: 'Whether the advice in the circular has or has not been followed may very well be a good indicator as to whether a condition is or is not lawful; but failure to follow the advice does not necessarily result in unlawfulness.' Thus the authority's failure to follow central government circular did not render its planning decision unlawful.

[112] [1948] 1 KB 349. See similarly *Patchett v. Leathem* (1949) 65 TLR 69; *Acton Borough Council v. Morris* [1953] 1 WLR 1228. Scott LJ's legal analysis was criticised in *Lewisham BC v. Roberts* [1949] 2 KB 608.

[113] For privilege see above, p. 711.   [114] *Patchett v. Leathem* (above) at 70.

Whereas ordinary legislation, by passing through both Houses of Parliament or, at least, lying on the table of both Houses, is thus twice blessed, this type of so-called legislation is at least four times cursed. First, it has seen neither House of Parliament; secondly, it is unpublished and is inaccessible even to those whose valuable rights of property may be affected; thirdly, it is a jumble of provisions, legislative, administrative, or directive in character, and sometimes difficult to disentangle one from the other; and, fourthly, it is expressed not in the precise language of an Act of Parliament or an Order in Council but in the more colloquial language of correspondence, which is not always susceptible of the ordinary canons of construction.

Contradictory opinions as to the legal status of a circular were expressed in the House of Lords in a case where a departmental 'memorandum of guidance', issued to local health authorities, was alleged to contain erroneous legal advice as to the counselling of young girls about contraception.[115] Lords Fraser and Scarman held that the error would be ultra vires, thus treating the circular as having legal effect. Lords Bridge and Templeman held that it could have no legal effect but was subject to judicial review. Lord Brandon expressed no opinion. The source of this confusion was the National Health Service Act 1977, which gave the Secretary of State a duty 'to meet all reasonable requirements' for providing contraceptive advice, so that the question whether the circular was issued under specific statutory authority was arguable either way. In another case the court reviewed a government circular about taxation without considering whether it could have legal force.[116] The curiosity of these decisions was noted in the context of remedies.[117] It has been accepted in Scotland that a circular delegating a function from a chief constable to an assistant chief constable could have legal effect, against the terms of the relevant regulation.[118]

It is now the practice to publish circulars which are of any importance to the public and for a long time there has been no judicial criticism of the use made of them.

AMENDMENT, REVOCATION, DISPENSATION

In addition to providing that statutory powers and duties may be exercised and performed from time to time as occasion requires,[119] the Interpretation Act 1978 also lays down that a statutory power to make 'rules, regulations or byelaws' or statutory instruments shall be construed as including a power to revoke, amend or re-enact them, subject to the same conditions as applied to the making of them.[120] This is to be done, of course, only in so far as no contrary intention appears in the empowering Act.

---

[115] *Gillick v. West Norfolk and Wisbech Area Health Authority* [1986] AC 112. For comment see (1986) 102 LQR 173 (Wade).

[116] *R v. Secretary of State for the Environment ex p Greenwich LBC* [1989] COD 530. Similarly declarations were made by the Court of Appeal in *R v. Deputy Governor of Parkhurst Prison ex p Hague* [1992] 1 AC 58, holding that a Prisons Department circular was contrary to the Prison Rules 1964. And see *R v. Secretary of State ex p Pfizer Ltd* [1999] 3 CMLR 875, where a Department of Health circular advised doctors not to prescribe the drug Viagra save in exceptional circumstances. It was said to be 'for guidance only' but prevented GPs from fulfilling their statutory duty to exercise their clinical judgment in each case. It was held to be unlawful, as well as contrary to the EU law forbidding quantitative restrictions on imports.

[117] Above, p. 481.

[118] *Rooney v. Chief Constable, Strathclyde Police*, 1997 SLT 1261 (assistant chief constable's acceptance of constable's resignation upheld although jurisdiction under statutory regulations to accept resignation vesting in chief constable). [119] s. 12; above, p. 191.

[120] s. 14. But note the need for consistency: above, p. 318. In addition a person making subordinate legislation is empowered to require a review of the effectiveness of the legislation and to impose a 'sunset clause' (a date on which the legislation ceases to take effect) (Interpretation Act 1978, s. 14A inserted by Enterprise and Regulatory Reform Act 2013, s. 59).

When an Act is repealed, any rules or regulations made under it cease to have effect,[121] despite the statutory saving clause for things done while the Act was in force.[122] But where an Act is repealed and replaced, with or without modification, rules etc. made under it are treated as if made under the new Act in so far as that Act gives power to make them.[123] Rules also continue in force notwithstanding any change in the person or body constituting the rule-making authority.[124]

So long as its rules stand, a public authority has no power to grant dispensation from them, either generally or in particular cases.[125] Whether there may be an exception to this rule in the case of formal or procedural irregularities is controversial. This has already been discussed in the context of waiver.[126]

JUDICIAL REVIEW

CONTROL BY THE COURTS

In Britain the executive has no inherent legislative power.[127] It cannot, as can the French government, resort to a constitutional *pouvoir réglementaire* when it is necessary to make regulations for purposes of public order or in emergencies. Statutory authority is indispensable, and it follows that rules and regulations not duly made under Act of Parliament are legally ineffective. Exceptions have been made, it is true, in the case of a number of non-statutory bodies.[128] But they do not alter the fact that the courts must determine the validity of delegated legislation by applying the test of ultra vires, just as they do in other contexts. It is axiomatic that delegated legislation in no way partakes of the immunity which Acts of Parliament enjoy from challenge in the courts, for there is a fundamental difference between a sovereign and a subordinate law-making power. Even where, as is often the case, a regulation is required to be approved by resolutions of both Houses of Parliament, it still falls on the 'subordinate' side of the line, so that the court may determine its validity.[129]

The court has to look for the true intent of the empowering Act in the usual way. A local authority's power to make byelaws, for example, will not extend to allow it to modify Acts of Parliament. A county council's byelaw was accordingly void when it forbade betting in public places altogether whereas the applicable Act of Parliament allowed it under certain conditions.[130] A straightforward example of the ultra vires principle was where the House of Lords invalidated an order of the Minister of Labour which would have imposed industrial training levy on clubs which were not within the Industrial Training

---

[121] *Watson* v. *Winch* [1916] 1 KB 688.   [122] Interpretation Act 1978, s. 16.

[123] s. 17. Even where s. 17 is not applicable, the byelaws made under a repealed Act may be saved: *DPP* v. *Jackson* (1990) 88 LGR 876 (strained interpretation, 'not...intended by draftsman', of s. 272 of the Local Government Act 1972 adopted to preserve byelaws made under the repealed Local Government Act 1933); see also *Aitken* v. *South Hams DC* [1995] 1 AC 262; *B* v. *B* [1995] 1 WLR 440 and *DPP* v. *Inegbu* [2008] EWHC 3242 (presumption that s. 17 will save subordinate legislation unless the repealing Act displays a contrary intention (paras. 20–2)).   [124] *Wiseman* v. *Canterbury Bye-Products Co Ltd* [1983] 2 AC 685.

[125] *Yabbicom* v. *King* [1899] 1 QB 444; *Bean (William) & Sons* v. *Flaxton Rural District Council* [1929] 1 KB 450; above, p. 201.   [126] Above, pp. 198–200.

[127] Except where the law breaks down and martial law is in force (above, p. 730). The Crown's prerogative power to legislate for colonies acquired by cession or conquest is also an exception, but it has been superseded by the British Settlement Acts 1887–1945 and the Foreign Jurisdiction Acts 1890–1913.

[128] For the judicial enforcement of the rules of such bodies see above, p. 532.

[129] See above, pp. 19, 323; below, p. 745.   [130] *Powell* v. *May* [1946] 1 KB 330.

Act 1964.[131] Another was where the Inland Revenue made regulations taxing dividends and interest paid by building societies on which tax had already been paid.[132] Where the statute permitted the Secretary of State to make regulations to distribute air traffic between airports he could not make regulations that prohibited the traffic altogether.[133] And where the statute permitted the minister to limit the number of aircraft landing at an aerodrome in order to mitigate noise, he could not make a scheme that limited the amount of noise rather than the number of aircraft.[134] A provision of the Prison Rules was ultra vires because it authorised excessive interference with prisoners' correspondence.[135] In holding a social security regulation to be ultra vires Laws J said:

> I do not consider there to be much room for purposive constructions of subordinate leg-islation; where the executive has been allowed by the legislative to make law, it must abide strictly by the terms of its delegated authority.[136]

Despite their strict standards, the courts will lean in favour of upholding a regulation which forms part of a statutory scheme and which has long been relied upon in property transactions.[137] It is probably not necessary to the validity of an order or regulation that it should specify the source of the power exercised.[138]

CONSTITUTIONAL PRINCIPLES

It is axiomatic that primary constitutional statutes such as the Bill of Rights 1688, Act of Settlement 1700 and, now, the Human Rights Act 1998 are just as subject to repeal or amendment as any others, since constitutional guarantees are inconsistent with the sov-ereignty of Parliament. Safeguards like those provided in the constitution of the United States, or in 'entrenched provisions' in many Commonwealth countries, are unknown in this country. Faced with an Act of Parliament, the court can do no more than make certain presumptions, for example that property will not be taken without compensa-tion.[139] There is also a common law presumption that any ambiguity in a statute should be resolved in favour of the interpretation that was consistent with the European Convention on Human Rights.[140] The Human Rights Act 1998 has now greatly strengthened this pro-tection. Henceforth delegated legislation must be read and given effect, so far as possible, in a way which is compatible with the Convention rights.[141]

---

[131] *Hotel & Catering Industry Training Board* v. *Automobile Pty Ltd* [1969] 1 WLR 697.

[132] *R* v. *Inland Revenue Commissioners ex p Woolwich Equitable Building Society* [1990] 1 WLR 1400 (the society recovered £57 m.).

[133] *Air 2000 Ltd* v. *Secretary of State for Transport*, 1989 SLT 698; *Air 2000 Ltd* v. *Secretary of State for Transport*, 1990 SLT 335 (regulations compelling flights to land at Prestwick invalid).

[134] *R* v. *Secretary of State for Transport ex p Richmond LBC* [1994] 1 WLR 74 (scheme allowing operators to fix the number of landings within specified noise quota invalid).

[135] *R* v. *Home Secretary ex p Leech* [1994] QB 198.

[136] *R* v. *Secretary of State for Social Security ex p Sutherland* [1997] COD 222.

[137] As in *Ministry of Housing and Local Government* v. *Sharp* [1970] 2 QB 223.

[138] See *Milk Board* v. *Grisnich* (1995) 126 DLR (4th) 191 (Supreme Court of Canada); *Harris* v. *Great Barrier Reef Marine Park Authority* (1999) 162 ALR 651 (Federal Court of Australia).

[139] Above, p. 682.   [140] *R* v. *Miah* [1974] 1 WLR 683 at 694 (Lord Reid).

[141] Act of 1998, s. 3(1). See above, p. 142, for the provisions about interpretation and incompatibility. Since it is 'unlawful' for public authorities to act incompatibly with Convention rights (s. 6(1)), subordinate legislation that breaches the Convention is itself unlawful to that extent. For the technical difficulties in challenging subordinate legislation made before the 1998 Act came into force see [2000] EHRLR 116 (D. Squires).

But even before the 1998 Act the judges often treated fundamental rights as exempt from infringement unless Parliament expressed itself with unmistakable clarity. An example occurred in 1921 under the Defence of the Realm Regulations, which gave the Food Controller power to make regulations for controlling the sale, purchase, consumption, transport etc. of food, and to control prices. The Controller gave a dairy company a licence to deal in milk, but on condition that they paid a charge of two pence per gallon, as part of a scheme for regulating prices and controlling distribution. The company expressly agreed to accept this condition, but later refused to pay the charge. It was held by the House of Lords that the condition infringed the famous provision of the Bill of Rights 1688, that no money may be levied to the use of the Crown without consent of Parliament; and that even the company's own written consent could not legalise what the statute made illegal.[142] The argument that the general power to impose controls impliedly included the power to tax was rejected. Atkin LJ said:

> The circumstances would be remarkable indeed which would induce the courts to believe that the Legislature had sacrificed all the well-known checks and precautions, and, not in express words, but merely by implication, had entrusted a Minister of the Crown with undefined and unlimited powers of imposing charges upon the subject for purposes connected with his department.

In the Second World War the statute itself silenced all such arguments by supplementing its general provision with a battery of specific powers.[143] But in a case from the earlier war a regulation was held invalid because it purported to authorise requisitioning of property without fair compensation at market value, and without any right to dispute the value in a court of law.[144]

In the absence of clear parliamentary sanction delegated legislation will not be able to have retrospective operation—at any rate where a criminal penalty is imposed. In the past there was scant authority for this. But now the European Convention on Human Rights has been incorporated into domestic law.[145] The Convention outlaws retrospective criminal offences (including the imposition of a heavier penalty than that which existed at the time of the offence).[146] And the Human Rights Act 1998 requires that, if possible, subordinate legislation be read and given effect in a way that is compatible with the Convention.[147] Where the legislation does not create an offence retrospective delegated legislation may be valid even if there are no words expressly sanctioning it. However, since Parliament uses its power to legislate retrospectively only sparingly, it seems unlikely to confer such a power impliedly.[148]

The right of access to the courts is a matter that the courts themselves guard strictly,[149] and has led to the overthrow of both wartime and peacetime regulations. In 1920 a

---

[142] *A-G v. Wilts. United Dairies Ltd* (1921) 39 TLR 781, (1922) 127 LT 822. But contrast *Institute of Patent Agents v. Lockwood* [1894] AC 347.　　　　　　　　　　　　　　　　　　　　　　　　　[143] Above, p. 357.

[144] *Newcastle Breweries v. The King* [1920] 1 KB 854.

[145] By the Human Rights Act 1998. See above, p. 134.

[146] Art. 7. See *R v. Oliver* [1944] KB 68 for an example of the imposition of a heavier penalty.

[147] Act of 1998, s. 3(1).

[148] Cf. *Blyth v. Blyth* [1966] AC 643, 666 (presumption against retrospectivity has no effect in procedural and evidential matters).

[149] Note the right of access must be effective: *R (Medical Justice) v. Home Secretary* [2010] EWHC 1925, affirmed [2011] EWCA Civ 1710 (successful challenge to Home Secretary's policy which permitted removal of some unsuccessful immigration applicants within 72 hours of notification). Cf. *R (ToTel Ltd) v. First-tier Tribunal* [2012] EWCA Civ 1401 (right to appeal from First-tier Tribunal to Upper Tribunal not a 'fundamental right'). Note also the classic case: the courts resisting attempts to oust their jurisdiction: above, p. 608.

Defence of the Realm Regulation was held ultra vires because, in order to prevent disturbance of munition workers, it provided that no one might sue for possession of a munition worker's house without the permission of the minister.[150] So extreme a disability, it was held, could only be imposed by express enactment; and it could not really be said to be relevant to the public safety or the defence of the realm. In 1937 a byelaw made by the Wheat Commission, which had power to make byelaws for the settlement by arbitration of disputes under the Wheat Act 1932, was invalidated in the House of Lords because it purported to exclude the Arbitration Act 1889 from applying to any such arbitration, and thus it purported to exclude the right to carry a point of law to the High Court.[151] In 1997 the Lord Chancellor, who had statutory power to fix court fees, purported to repeal the regulation that exempted persons in receipt of income support from the payment of fees and in other cases allowed the Lord Chancellor to waive the fees. It was held that the right of access to the courts was a common law constitutional right which could only be abrogated by express statutory authority. The Lord Chancellor's repealing order was declared unlawful.[152] There are many similar examples.[153]

A particularly robust judicial defence of fundamental rights purportedly removed by delegated legislation is found in a decision on regulations which excluded asylum seekers (who did not claim asylum on arrival in the UK) from any social security benefit payments.[154] The regulations deprived asylum seekers of basic subsistence while their claims to asylum were determined. This constituted a 'serious impediment' to their exercise of their rights under the Asylum and Immigration Appeals Act 1993. Simon Brown LJ said that the regulations were:[155]

> so uncompromisingly draconian in effect that they must indeed be held ultra vires.... Parliament cannot have intended a significant number of genuine asylum seekers to be impaled on the horns of so intolerable a dilemma: the need either to abandon their claim to refugee status or alternatively to maintain them...in a state of utter destitution. Primary legislation alone could achieve that sorry state of affairs.

[150] *Chester* v. *Bateson* [1920] 1 KB 829; and see *Raymond* v. *Honey* [1983] 1 AC 1.

[151] *R&W Paul Ltd* v. *The Wheat Commission* [1937] AC 139; and see *Commissioners of Customs and Excise* v. *Cure and Deeley Ltd* [1962] 1 QB 340 (below, p. 744).

[152] *R* v. *Lord Chancellor ex p Witham* [1998] QB 575 (Laws J). For comment see (1997) *CLJ* 474 (Elliott). But access to the statutory bankruptcy scheme was not so protected; this was a 'benign administrative system' to deal with a debtor who could not pay his debts not a matter of constitutional right: *R* v. *Lord Chancellor ex p Lightfoot* [1999] 2 WLR 1126 (Laws J), [2000] 2 WLR 318 (CA). For comment see (1998) *JR* 217 (Elliott). In *R* v. *Home Secretary ex p Pierson* [1998] AC 539 at 575 it was doubted (Lord Browne-Wilkinson) whether *ex p Witham* was correct in requiring express words—necessary implication would suffice.

[153] For instance, *R* v. *Home Secretary ex p Leech* [1994] QB 198 (interference with prisoner's correspondence with solicitor infringed right of access to courts) and *FP (Iran)* v. *Home Secretary* [2007] EWCA Civ 13, paras. 49–50 (Asylum and Immigration Tribunal (Procedure) Rules 2005 unlawful because, inter alia, they interfered with the constitutional right to access a court). In *Ahmed* v. *HM Treasury* [2010] UKSC 2—where Orders made under the United Nations Act 1946, s. 1 froze the assets of certain terrorist suspects—one of the grounds on which the second order was found unlawful was its denial of access to the courts. The question is discussed in detail above, p. 358.

[154] *R* v. *Secretary of State for Social Security ex p Joint Council for the Welfare of Immigrants* [1997] 1 WLR 275 (CA).

[155] Ibid. at 293. But Parliament in fact enacted the substance of the impugned regulations in primary legislation with retrospective effect shortly thereafter (Asylum and Immigration Act 1996, s. 11). Asylum seekers are now entitled to special benefits largely given in kind. See above, p. 61.

And he quoted from a judgment of Lord Ellenborough CJ holding that 'the law of humanity, which is anterior to all positive laws, obliges us to afford them ['poor foreigners'] relief, to save them from starving'.[156]

Judicial intervention in all these cases has been justified in terms of classic constitutional principle: Parliament could never have intended to authorise such infractions of fundamental rights and principles. Thus the offending regulation was ultra vires and void. Parliament has now, by the enactment of the Human Rights Act 1998, strengthened the judicial role in ensuring that delegated legislation does not intrude upon Convention rights. But once more this is in accord with constitutional principle: subject to the paramountcy of European Community law, Parliament remains supreme. And the judges, however bold and creative, must operate within that framework.

CONFLICT WITH EUROPEAN UNION LAW

The paramountcy of European Union law requires that delegated legislation, along with domestic law generally, should give way to EU law which is 'directly applicable', i.e. which takes effect without the aid of domestic legislation; and that domestic courts should give effect to this principle. An example was where a Northern Ireland sex discrimination order made a certificate of the Secretary of State conclusive evidence of the ground of dismissal of a woman police officer, thus violating an EC Council directive requiring an effective judicial remedy in such matters; since the directive was directly applicable, the dismissed officer could enforce it in a domestic court.[157] Other examples of regulations and orders held void for similar reasons are to be found in cases already discussed.[158] Relevant delegated legislation must also comply with the the European Charter of Fundamental Rights.[159]

UNCERTAINTY

A regulation or byelaw whose meaning cannot be ascertained with reasonable certainty is ultra vires and void.[160] Thus a local authority byelaw which ordained that 'no person shall wilfully annoy passengers in the streets' was struck down.[161] And a byelaw forbidding the flying of hang-gliders over a pleasure ground without specifying the height below which the offence was committed was also invalid.[162]

The decided cases reveal two approaches to determining whether a byelaw is sufficiently uncertain to render it invalid. Is it necessary that the byelaw must contain 'adequate information as to the duties of those who are to obey'[163] or is a byelaw invalid only if 'it can be given no meaning or no sensible or ascertainable meaning'?[164] The Court of

---

[156] R v. Inhabitants of Eastbourne (1803) 4 East 103 at 107.

[157] Johnston v. Chief Constable of the Royal Irish Constabulary [1987] QB 129 (ECJ). For a comparable case under the Human Rights Convention see Tinnelly & Sons Ltd v. UK (1999) 27 EHRR 249.

[158] In R v. Secretary of State for Transport ex p Factortame Ltd (No 2) [1990] 1 AC 603 (above, pp. 21, 163) regulations as well as an Act were required to be disapplied. In Bourgoin SA v. Ministry of Agriculture, Fisheries and Food [1986] QB 716 (above, p. 663) a ministerial order was unlawful on account of conflict with the EC Treaty.

[159] Conceded by Secretary of State in R (NS) v. Home Secretary [2010] EWCA Civ 990, para. 7. Discussed above, p. 172.   [160] McEldowney v. Forde [1971] AC 632 at 665 (Lord Diplock).

[161] Nash v. Findlay (1901) 85 LT 682.

[162] Staden v. Tarjanyi (1980) 78 LGR 614. It had already been held that it was permissible to fly at a height at which no one could be inconvenienced: Lord Bernstein of Leigh v. Skyviews and General Ltd [1978] QB 479.

[163] Kruse v. Johnson [1898] 2 QB 91 at 108 (Mathew J).

[164] Fawcett Properties Ltd v. Buckingham CC [1961] AC 636 at 677–8 (Lord Denning).

Appeal prefers the latter approach; and has upheld byelaws notwithstanding that the plan outlining the lands by way of a thickly drawn line to which they applied 'could have been better and clearer'. This was because 'however narrow and precise the line on a map, there will always be...a borderline of uncertainty'.[165] The Court of Appeal cited a speech of Lord Denning in the House of Lords, where he said:[166]

> But if the uncertainty stems only from the fact that the words of the byelaw are ambiguous, it is well settled that it must, if possible, be given such a meaning as to make it reasonable and valid, rather than unreasonable and invalid...It is the daily task of the courts to resolve ambiguities of language and to choose between them; and to construe words so as to avoid absurdities or to put up with them.

Adequate guidance to those who must obey the byelaws is important.[167] But absolute certainty may be impossible to achieve and the existence of some ambiguity is often inevitable. Where the byelaw creates an offence ambiguous words will be construed so as to avoid a penalty: 'A man is not to be put in peril upon an ambiguity'.[168]

CORRECTION OF OBVIOUS DRAFTING ERRORS

Where 'Homer, in the person of the draftsman [of an Act of Parliament], nodded' and omitted words from a statute necessary to secure its purpose, those words may, in appropriate circumstances, be read into the statute.[169] The rule is the same for delegated legislation.[170] Before exercising this power the intended purpose of the legislation in question must be clear, but through the inadvertence of the draftsman effect has not been given to that purpose. In addition the substance of what the legislator would have done, if aware of the error, must be obvious.[171] In assessing these matters the court may have regard to extraneous materials such as explanatory notes and decision letters.[172] Thus an Order made by the Secretary of State authorising the levying of tolls on traffic crossing the Humber Bridge, which inadvertently omitted to levy a toll on large buses, was construed, after reference to extraneous materials, as containing that provision.[173] There are several examples of this principle at work.[174]

---

[165] *Percy* v. *Hall* [1996] 4 All ER 522 at 532 (Simon Brown LJ) upholding the byelaws, the Forest Moor and Menwith Hill Station Byelaws 1996, previously held uncertain in *Bugg* v. *DPP* [1993] QB 473. The plaintiffs had entered the Menwith Hill Station on many occasions (in breach of the byelaws) and had been arrested and removed. [166] Ibid.

[167] But what does 'adequate' mean in this context? See *Percy* v. *Hall* at 534. And see *Tabernacle* v. *Secretary of State for Defence* [2008] EWHC 416 (discussion of uncertainty and Strasbourg requirement of 'prescribed by law').

[168] *London and North Eastern Rly Co* v. *Berriman* [1946] AC 278 at 313–14 (Viscount Simonds). See to like effect *Fawcett Properties* at 662 (Lord Cohen) and *Percy* v. *Hall* at 534.

[169] *Inco Europe Ltd* v. *First Choice Distribution* [2000] 1 WLR 586 (HL) at 589 (Lord Nicholls). The principle is not limited to the insertion of necessary words. Words may be substituted or omitted as required (at 592).

[170] *R (Confederation of Passenger Transport UK)* v. *Humber Bridge Board* [2003] EWCA 842, [2004] 2 WLR 98 (CA), paras. 34–8. [171] Ibid.

[172] Ibid., paras. 48–52. [173] Ibid.

[174] See *Gibson* v. *Secretary of State for Justice* [2008] EWCA Civ 177 (Court of Appeal corrected a drafting error in a Criminal Justice Act Commencement Order) and *Davies t/a All Star Nurseries* v. *Scottish Commission for the Regulation of Care* [2013] UKSC 12 (Supreme Court corrected a drafting error in transitional provisions which transferred responsibilities from the Scottish Commission for the Regulation of Care to 'Social Work and Social Care Scotland'.

UNREASONABLENESS

Just as with other kinds of administrative action, the courts must sometimes condemn rules or regulations for unreasonableness.[175] In interpreting statutes it is natural to make the assumption that Parliament could not have intended powers of delegated legislation to be exercised unreasonably, so that the legality of the regulations becomes dependent upon their content. Only an indistinct line, however, can be drawn between the examples which now follow and the examples of constitutional limits already given.

This assumption has often been called into play in the case of local authorities' byelaws, which they are empowered to make for the good rule and government of their area and for the suppression of nuisances.[176] In the leading case, where in fact the court upheld a byelaw against singing within fifty yards of a dwelling-house, it was said:[177]

> If, for instance [byelaws] were found to be partial and unequal in their operation as between different classes; if they were manifestly unjust; if they disclosed bad faith; if they involved such oppressive or gratuitous interference with the rights of those subject to them as could find no justification in the minds of reasonable men, the Court might well say, 'Parliament never intended to give authority to make such rules; they are unreasonable and ultra vires.' But . . . a byelaw is not unreasonable merely because particular judges may think that it goes further than is prudent or necessary or convenient.

But a byelaw which forbade playing music, singing or preaching in any street, except under express licence from the mayor, was held void as being plainly arbitrary and unreasonable.[178] The same fate befell a byelaw which prohibited selling cockles on the beach at Bournemouth without the agreement of the Corporation[179] and a byelaw which restricted sales by auction in a public market.[180] The Supreme Court of Canada upholds 'the rule of administrative law that the power to make byelaws does not include a power to enact discriminatory provisions'.[181] This is 'a principle of fundamental freedom'. Similarly, the UK Supreme Court has said: 'A measure may respond to a real problem but nevertheless be irrational or disproportionate by reason of its being discriminatory in some respect that is incapable of objective justification.'[182]

Byelaws have often failed to pass the test of reasonableness, which in some respects is strict in relation to the wide words of the statutory power. Clear examples of unreasonable byelaws were where landlords of lodging-houses were required to clean them annually

---

[175] Above, p. 350. See (1973) 36 *MLR* 611 (A. Wharam).

[176] Local Government Act 1972, s. 235. The doctrine was developed originally for the byelaws or regulations made by chartered corporations and other institutions under common law powers: *Slattery* v. *Naylor* (1888) 13 App Cas 446 at 452. The Localism Act 2011, s. 1(1) which empowers local authorities 'to do anything that individuals generally may do' should not prevent challenges on this ground: *The Manydown Company Ltd* v. *Basingstoke and Deane Borough Council* [2012] EWHC 977, para. 154. The effect of this new power on rationality review is yet to be explored. In *Manydown Co Ltd* v. *Basingstoke and Deane BC* Lindblom J at [145] held (*obiter*): 'In my judgment it would not be right for this new power [i.e. s. 1 Localism Act 2011] to be relied upon to justify an authority's use or management of land inconsistently with the statutory purpose for which that land was acquired.' Lindblom J did not consider the effect of s. 1 on the court's power to review byelaws on rationality grounds.   [177] *Kruse* v. *Johnson* [1898] 2 QB 91 (Lord Russell CJ).

[178] *Munro* v. *Watson* (1887) 57 LT 366.

[179] *Parker* v. *Bournemouth Cpn* (1902) 66 JP 440; and see *Moorman* v. *Tordoff* (1908) 98 LT 416.

[180] *Nicholls* v. *Tavistock UDC* [1923] 2 Ch 18.

[181] *Re City of Montreal and Arcade Amusements Inc.* (1985) 18 DLR (4th) 161, holding invalid a byelaw prohibiting minors from entering amusement halls or using amusement machines. Challenge to the validity of byelaws is particularly common in Canada.

[182] *Bank Mellat* v. *HM Treasury* [2013] UKSC 39, para. 25 (Lord Sumption).

under penalty, yet would in many cases have no right of access against their lodgers;[183] and where a building byelaw required an open space to be left at the rear of every new building, so that in many cases it became impossible to build new extensions to existing buildings.[184] But the court normally construes byelaws benevolently and upholds them if possible, as already explained.[185]

The same doctrine applies to rules and regulations as well as to byelaws.[186] It is true that where the power is granted to a minister responsible to Parliament, the court is less willing to suppose that Parliament intended his discretion to be limited; and this attitude is further reinforced if the regulations themselves must be laid before Parliament. On these grounds the Ministry of Transport's regulations for pedestrian crossings were upheld in 1943, despite the argument that to give the right of way to pedestrians was unreasonable during the nightly wartime blackout.[187] But in a later case a purchase tax regulation made by the Commissioners of Customs and Excise, and duly laid before Parliament, was held invalid.[188] The Commissioners had power to make regulations 'for any matter for which provision appears to them to be necessary' for the purpose of collecting purchase tax. Their regulation provided that where a proper return was not made they might themselves determine the tax due and that the amount so determined should be deemed to be the proper tax payable. This was held ultra vires as an attempt to take arbitrary power to determine a tax liability which was properly to be determined according to the Act with a right of appeal to the court, and as an attempt to oust the court's jurisdiction. The court regarded the regulation as an arbitrary and unreasonable exercise of the power conferred. This case well shows how even the widest power will admit judicial review.[189]

One of the Home Secretary's immigration rules, which restricted the admission of dependent relatives to those 'having a standard of living substantially below that of their own country', was 'manifestly unjust and unreasonable' and also 'partial and unequal in its operation as between different classes', and therefore invalid.[190] The rules had been laid before Parliament. So too, an asylum appeal procedure rule that 'deemed [a notice of a right of appeal to the Immigration Appeal Tribunal] to have been received...on the second day after which it was sent regardless of when or whether it was received' was held unreasonable and of no effect. The rule was 'not necessary to achieve the timely and effective disposal of appeals and may deny an asylum seeker just disposal of her appeal'.[191] In one exceptional case, also, regulations were quashed for unfair procedure in the consultation of one business specially affected.[192] The

---

[183] *Arlidge* v. *Mayor etc of Islington* [1909] 2 KB 127.

[184] *Repton School Governors* v. *Repton RDC* [1918] 2 KB 133. See also *A-G* v. *Denby* [1925] 1 Ch 596 (building byelaw uncertain and unreasonable); *London Passenger Transport Board* v. *Sumner* (1935) 154 LT 108 (byelaw penalising non-payment of fare unreasonable); *Cassidy* v. *Minister for Industry and Commerce* [1978] IR 297 (unreasonable price control order).

[185] Above, p. 741; *Kruse* v. *Johnson* (above); *Townsend (Builders) Ltd* v. *Cinema News and Property Management Ltd* [1959] 1 WLR 119; *Cinnamond* v. *British Airports Authority* [1980] 1 WLR 582; and *Southern Inshore Fisheries and Conservation Authority* v. *Carlin Boat Charter Ltd* [2012] EWHC 1359.

[186] The doctrine does not apply or applies only in a very attenuated form to the Acts of the devolved legislatures: *AXA General Insurance Ltd* v. *Lord Advocate* [2011] UKSC 46, para. 52 (Lord Hope); cf. Lord Mance, para. 97 and Lord Reed, para. 143.   [187] *Sparks* v. *Edward Ash Ltd* [1943] KB 223.

[188] *Commissioners of Customs and Excise* v. *Cure and Deeley Ltd* [1962] 1 QB 340 (Sachs J); above, p. 360. The Crown did not appeal.

[189] See also *R* v. *Customs and Excise Commissioners ex p Hedges and Butler Ltd* [1986] 2 All ER 164.

[190] *R* v. *Immigration Appeal Tribunal ex p Begum Manshoora* [1986] Imm. AR 385 (tribunal's decision quashed). The phrases quoted are from *Kruse* v. *Johnson*, above.

[191] *R* v. *Home Secretary ex p Saleem* [2001] 1 WLR 443 (CA) (notice sent to old address). The rules were also discriminatory: notice to the appellate authority deemed received when 'in fact received'.

[192] This was the *United States Tobacco* case, below, p. 756.

Supreme Court has held in a leading case[193] that an Order adopted by the Treasury restricting a particular Iranian bank's ability to access UK financial markets (but did not similarly restrict other Iranian banks) was unlawful. Lord Sumption said: 'the distinction between Bank Mellat and other Iranian banks which was at the heart of the case put to Parliament by ministers was an arbitrary and irrational distinction and that the measure as a whole was disproportionate'.

As these cases show, judicial review is not normally inhibited by the fact that rules or regulations have been laid before Parliament and approved,[194] though account must be taken of the House of Lords' decisions which raise the threshold of unreasonableness in cases dominated by questions of political judgment.[195] The Court of Appeal has emphasised that in the case of subordinate legislation such as an Order in Council approved in draft by both Houses, 'the courts would without doubt be competent to consider whether or not the Order was properly made in the sense of being intra vires'.[196]

SUBJECTIVE LANGUAGE

The purchase tax case also illustrates the court's refusal to be disarmed by language which appears to make the legislating authority the sole judge of the extent of its power or of the purposes for which it may be used. Even where the Act says that the minister may make regulations 'if he is satisfied' that they are required, the court can enquire whether he could reasonably have been satisfied in the circumstances. A number of instances of the application of this principle to subordinate legislation have been given in an earlier chapter[197] and need not be repeated here.

WRONG PURPOSES AND BAD FAITH

An Act of Parliament is immune from challenge on the ground of improper motives or bad faith, even in the case of a private Act allegedly obtained by fraud.[198] But subordinate legislation is necessarily subject to the principle of ultra vires. Since delegated powers of legislation are nearly always given for specific purposes, their use for other purposes will be unlawful.[199] One clear case of legislation being condemned for improper purposes was the Western Australian decision that regulations prescribing bus routes were invalid since their object was to protect the state-owned trains from competition.[200] In Canada municipal byelaws have been set aside where they were made with the object of restricting or penalising some individual owner of property rather than for the general benefit.[201] The Privy Council has clearly approved

---

[193] *Bank Mellat* v. *HM Treasury* [2013] UKSC 39, para. 27.

[194] The Order quashed in *Bank Mellat* v. *HM Treasury* [2013] UKSC 39 had been laid before Parliament; there are many similar cases. [195] See above, p. 323.

[196] *R* v. *HM Treasury ex p Smedley* [1985] QB 657 (unsuccessful challenge to proposal to pay British contribution to the European Communities without specific statutory authority). See also *R* v. *Secretary of State for the Environment ex p Greater London Council* (QBD, 3 April 1985) discussed in 1985 SLT at 373 (C. M. G. Himsworth). Confirmed in *R (Javed)* v. *Home Secretary* [2001] EWCA Civ 789, [2002] QB 129 at 147.

[197] Above, pp. 359 and 364. [198] *Pickin* v. *British Railways Board* [1974] AC 765.

[199] *Yates (Arthur) & Co Pty Ltd* v. *Vegetable Seeds Committee* (1945) 72 CLR 37 contains a valuable discussion by Dixon J of the law applicable to legislative and administrative acts, holding that regulations restricting dealings in seeds would be invalid if intended to promote the Committee's own trade rather than to ensure the supply of seeds in the market.

[200] *Bailey* v. *Conole* (1931) 34 WALR 18, above, p. 338.

[201] *Boyd Builders Ltd* v. *City of Ottawa* (1964) 45 DLR (2d) 211; *Re Burns and Township of Haldimand* (1965) 52 DLR (2d) 101.

the same principle,[202] and hints to the same effect have been dropped in the House of Lords.[203] Many Colonial and Commonwealth legislatures have power 'to make laws for the peace, order and good government of the relevant territory'. When the legislative authority of the British Indian Ocean Territory (a Commissioner appointed by the Crown) made—for reasons of military security—an ordinance for the compulsory removal of the entire population of the BIOT, the Divisional Court in a bold decision condemned this as 'an abject legal failure'. The legislation could not be said 'reasonably . . . to touch the peace, order and good government of BIOT'.[204] But this approach has since been disapproved in the House of Lords.[205] After all, the words 'peace, order and good government' 'connote . . . the widest law-making powers appropriate to a sovereign'.[206]

NATURAL JUSTICE

One context in which legislative and administrative functions must be distinguished is that of natural justice.[207] This was made clear in a case arising out of the abolition of the scale fees formerly charged by solicitors in conveyancing business. Under the Solicitors Act 1957[208] solicitors' charges were regulated by a statutory committee, which had to submit its orders in draft to the Law Society and allow them a month for comment. This procedure was followed in the case of the draft order of 1972 abolishing scale fees. But a member of another association of solicitors, which was not consulted, sought a declaration and injunction in order to postpone the making of the order and to allow wider consultation. Refusing these remedies Megarry J said:[209]

> Let me accept that in the sphere of the so-called quasi-judicial the rules of natural justice run, and that in the administrative or executive field there is a general duty of fairness. Nevertheless, these considerations do not seem to me to affect the process of legislation, whether primary or delegated. Many of those affected by delegated legislation, and affected very substantially, are never consulted in the process of enacting that legislation; and yet they have no remedy. . . . I do not know of any implied right to be consulted or make objections, or any principle upon which the courts may enjoin the legislative process at the suit of those who contend that insufficient time for consultation and consideration has been given.

Since it was plain that the proposed order was legislative rather than executive, there was no room for the principle that persons affected must be given a fair hearing.

---

[202] *A-G for Canada* v. *Hallett & Carey Ltd* [1952] AC 427 at 444; above, p. 357.

[203] *Scott* v. *Glasgow Cpn* [1899] AC 470 at 492; and see *Baird (Robert) Ltd* v. *Glasgow Cpn* [1936] AC 32 at 42.

[204] *R (Bancoult)* v. *Secretary of State for the Foreign and Commonwealth Office* [2001] QB 1067 (Laws LJ) (decision also based on *Wednesbury* alone and intrusion upon fundamental rights without specific provision). Discussed in detail [2001] *PL* 571 (A. Tomkins).　　　　　[205] Ibid., para. 51 (Lord Hoffmann).

[206] *Ibralebbe* v. *The Queen* [1964] AC 900, 923. Such powers extend to extra-territorial legislation where that legislation has a 'sufficiently substantial relationship' with the peace, order and good government of the territory in question (*Jersey Fishermen's Association Ltd* v. *States of Guernsey* [2007] UKPC 30, para. 32).

[207] Above, p. 473, citing additional cases.　　　　[208] Since replaced by the Solicitors Act 1974.

[209] *Bates* v. *Lord Hailsham* [1972] 1 WLR 1373 at 1378. For comment on the first sentence see above, p. 416. See also *Fedsure Life Assurance Ltd* v. *Greater Johannesburg Metropolitan Council* 1999 (1) SA 374 (South African Constitutional Court). Cf. *R (BAPIO Action Ltd)* v. *Home Secretary* [2007] EWCA Civ 1139, paras. 33 and 34 (Sedley LJ doubting *Bates* but in the event not finding a duty to consult over changes to the Immigration Rules). Principle affirmed by Beatson J in *R (Chapti)* v. *Secretary of State for the Home Department* [2011] EWHC 3370, para. 145.

Difficult problems may therefore lie ahead in the wide area in which legislative and administrative functions overlap. But although the law gives no general right to be consulted, a duty of consultation is widely acknowledged in practice and sometimes also by statute, as was the duty to consult the Law Society in the above case. And special circumstances may give rise to exceptions, as mentioned below.[210] So that the decision-maker fully understands the issues consultation may sometimes be required to comply with the Public Sector Equality Duty.[211]

With reference to the other principle of natural justice, that no man may be judge in his own cause, it has been held that a regulation empowering an insurance commission to decide claims against its own insurance fund is not for this reason invalid, at any rate where the power delegated is wide.[212]

The right to reasoned decisions under the Tribunals and Inquiries Act 1992 is expressly excluded in the case of rules, orders or schemes 'of a legislative and not an executive character'.[213]

PROCEDURAL ERRORS

Innumerable statutes empower delegated legislation by various procedures, some requiring the laying of drafts before Parliament or the laying of orders before Parliament when made, others prescribing consultation with advisory bodies or with persons affected. There is thus ample scope for false steps in procedure. Errors of this kind will invalidate the legislation if the statutory procedure is mandatory, but not if it is merely directory. Once again, the principle is the same as in the case of other administrative action.[214]

A statutory duty to consult is a matter of importance and so normally mandatory. In one case a minister was required, before making an industrial training order, to consult associations appearing to him to be representative of those concerned. He invited numerous organisations to consult with him about an order for the agricultural industries, but in one case the letter miscarried so that the mushroom growers' association was not consulted. Members of the association, it was held, were not bound by the order, since a mandatory requirement had not been observed.[215] And in another case the legislation provided that draft regulations were to be referred to an advisory committee unless the committee agreed otherwise. Where the committee was misled into agreeing, the subsequent regulations were invalid.[216]

How far the validity of regulations may be affected by failure to follow the prescribed procedure for publishing them is separately dealt with below.[217]

SUB-DELEGATION

The general rule against sub-delegation of statutory powers, encountered once already, turns upon statutory construction.[218] If Parliament confers power upon A, the evident

---

[210] Below, p. 756 (the *United States Tobacco* case).   [211] Above, p. 325.

[212] *Low* v. *Earthquake and War Damage Commission* [1959] NZLR 1198.   [213] s. 10(5)(b).

[214] Above, p. 183.

[215] *Agricultural etc Training Board* v. *Aylesbury Mushrooms Ltd* [1972] 1 WLR 190.

[216] *Howker* v. *Secretary of State for Work and Pensions* [2002] EWCA Civ 1623, [2003] ICR 405. The committee was misled by the Secretary of State's officials. For another example see *Simcoe* v. *Jacuzzi UK Group Ltd* [2012] EWCA Civ 137.   [217] Below, p. 753.

[218] Above, p. 259.

intention is that it shall be exercised by A and not by B. But where power is conferred upon a minister, it is (as we have seen)[219] taken for granted that his officials may exercise it in his name, since that is the normal way in which government business is done. This is as true of legislative as of administrative powers.[220] Many ministerial regulations, though made in the minister's name, are validly signed by officials, with or without the minister's official seal.[221]

Delegation to some different authority is another matter. In accordance with general principle, and with the few available authorities,[222] it seems safe to presume that unless Parliament expresses or implies a dispensation, legislative power must be exercised by those to whom it is given, and not by further delegates. But this presumption is subject to circumstances, and may be greatly weakened in time of emergency. Power to make regulations was freely delegated in the First World War, although the Defence of the Realm Act did not authorise it expressly. No case came before the courts to show whether delegation was lawful. But in the Second World War the Supreme Court of Canada held that the Governor-General's emergency powers entitled him without express authorisation to delegate the power to make regulations.[223] In Britain the Emergency Powers (Defence) Act 1939 itself gave express powers to delegate, so that an elaborate pyramid of regulations was constructed, delegated, sub-delegated, sub-sub-delegated and so on.

PARTIAL INVALIDITY

As several cases already cited illustrate, it is possible for delegated legislation to be partially good and partially bad.[224] In the mushroom growers' case, where the minister was required to consult certain representative associations, it was held that the industrial training order was valid as regards the organisations consulted and invalid as to those not consulted.[225] In the case of water authorities' sewerage charges the House of Lords held that the statutory instrument fixing the charges for services was valid as regards properties served by a public sewer and invalid as to others.[226] Since legislation by definition consists of general rules affecting large numbers of people, it is easy for such situations to arise, and there is no necessary reason for condemning what is good along with what is bad. On this principle an order prohibiting herring fishery, which purported to extend slightly beyond the waters covered by the Act, was held ultra vires as to the excess only, and enforceable in respect of the remainder.[227] In contrast, the House of Lords totally

---

[219] Above, p. 266.   [220] See *Lewisham BC* v. *Roberts* (above, p. 266).

[221] *R* v. *Skinner* [1968] 2 QB 700.

[222] There is a clear line of New Zealand authorities from *Geraghty* v. *Porter* [1917] NZLR 554 to *Hawke's Bay Raw Milk Products Co-operative Ltd* v. *New Zealand Milk Board* [1961] NZLR 218; and see *King-Emperor* v. *Benoari Lal Sarma* [1945] AC 14 at 24.

[223] *Re Chemicals Regulations* [1943] SCR 1.

[224] See above, p. 241, which should be read together with this section. For a further example, see *Ahmed* v. *HM Treasury* [2010] UKSC 2. Only Art. 3(1)(b) of the Al-Qaida and Taliban (United Nations Measures) Order 2006/2952 was quashed. Discussed above, p. 358.

[225] *Agricultural Horticultural and Forestry Industrial Training Board* v. *Aylesbury Mushrooms Ltd* [1972] 1 WLR 190.

[226] *Daymond* v. *Plymouth City Council* [1976] AC 609; above, p. 726, n. 21. See also *Malloch* v. *Aberdeen Cpn (No 2)*, 1974 SLT 5 (regulations requiring registration of teachers void as regards teachers already employed); *Cassidy* v. *Minister for Industry and Commerce* [1978] IR 297 (order unreasonable for some purposes, but not others); *Burke* v. *Minister for Labour* [1979] IR 354 (similar); *Transport Ministry* v. *Alexander* [1978] 1 NZLR 306 (regulation partially invalid for uncertainty).

[227] *Dunkley* v. *Evans* [1981] 1 WLR 1522, rejecting the so-called 'blue pencil' test under which amendment may be made only by textual deletion.

invalidated a byelaw which prohibited unauthorised access to Greenham Common air force base. The empowering Act provided that no such byelaw should affect the rights of commoners and there were sixty-two registered commoners with rights thus protected.[228] The striking result of this case was that anti-nuclear protesters, who were not commoners, escaped conviction for trespassing by pleading the invalidity of the byelaw. The House of Lords held that a byelaw drawn so as to permit access by commoners and their animals would be totally different in character and quite incapable of serving the purposes of security at the air base. No solution by severance was therefore feasible. The House did not accept the possibility, suggested by previous decisions, that the byelaw was valid against all except the commoners, who were not in fact asserting their rights.[229]

Where, as in the above cases, the valid and invalid elements are inseparably contained in the same words, there can be no possibility of effecting textual severance by merely striking out the offending words (the so-called 'blue pencil test') as is sometimes allowed where they stand apart.[230] According to the Greenham Common decision, where the words are inseparable the court 'must modify the text in order to achieve severance' and will do so only where this 'substantial severance' will effect no change in the substantial purpose and effect of the impugned provisions. Lord Bridge, with the agreement of the majority of the House, held that rigid insistence on textual severability might operate unreasonably by defeating subordinate legislation which was substantially intra vires. Lord Lowry held that it was only where the regulation first cleared the hurdle of textual severability that it could face the further hurdle of substantial severability: a more liberal doctrine would 'encourage the law-maker to enact what he pleases' and would be 'anarchic, not progressive'.[231] Thus the House of Lords turned against the concept of relative invalidity which seemed to be emerging in the previous decisions and which, depending upon a different principle, requires no severance and no textual modification of the partially invalid law.[232]

---

[228] *Director of Public Prosecutions* v. *Hutchinson* [1990] 2 AC 783.

[229] For a decision similar in principle see *Owners of SS Kalibia* v. *Wilson* (1910) 11 CLR 689, discussed by Lord Bridge [1990] 2 AC at 807. The dissenting opinion of Higgins J well expresses the relative invalidity doctrine. See also the analogous cases discussed above, p. 748.

[230] As in *R* v. *Immigration Appeal Tribunal ex p Begum Manshoora* [1986] Imm. AR 385 (provision of immigration rules, void for unreasonableness, severed from the rest without affecting their validity). Contrast *R* v. *Inland Revenue Commissioners ex p Woolwich Equitable Building Society* [1990] 1 WLR 1400 (textual severance possible but alteration of substance too great). The 'blue pencil' test was applied in *A* v. *HM Treasury* [2008] EWCA Civ 1187 (the words 'or may be' were deleted from the phrase 'have reasonable grounds for suspecting that the person is or may be...a person who commits,...or facilitates the commission of acts of terrorism'. The Order in Council in question froze the assets of terrorist suspects and was made under s. 1 of the United Nations Act 1946 which granted powers to Her Majesty to do what is 'necessary or expedient for enabling [Security Council] measures to be effectively applied. But the Supreme Court in *Ahmed* v. *HM Treasury* [2010] UKSC 2 found the Orders invalid and did not apply the 'blue pencil' test (para. 231). For discussion of 'necessary or expedient' powers and *Ahmed* in the Supreme Court see above, p. 358.

[231] And see *R (National Association of Health Stores)* v. *Department of Health* [2005] EWCA Civ 154, para. 20, extending the principle of *Hutchinson* from improper inclusions to 'improper omissions' (in this case the omission of goods in transit from an Order) 'if so far the omission appears to have done no harm, I see no good reason why, instead of permitting the rule-maker to insert the missing brick, the entire structure should be pulled down' (Sedley LJ). For a further example of the application of the test see *R (Public and Commercial Services Union)* v. *Minister for the Civil Service* [2010] EWHC 1463, paras. 23–8 (Sales J).

[232] This explains why the issue of severance was not raised in the *Daymond* and *Aylesbury Mushrooms* cases (above). Lord Bridge (at 810) suggests a doubt on the latter case and (ibid.) remarks that in the former the possibility of severance was taken for granted; and see likewise Lord Lowry (at 819). It appears that the *Daymond* and *Hutchinson* decisions are in principle in conflict.

REMEDIES

The commonest method of resisting an invalid regulation or byelaw is to plead its invalidity in defence to a prosecution or enforcement proceedings.[233] Parliament may, of course, restrict such defensive, or collateral, challenges and require the validity of byelaws to be tested by way of applications for judicial review.[234] But judicial review, being discretionary, is no substitute for the right to raise the invalidity of a byelaw as a defence.[235] Such restriction is only to be implied where the challenge precluded was to an administrative act—such as an enforcement notice—specifically directed at those challenging it and where there was an adequate alternative avenue for challenge.[236]

The court in suitable circumstances may also grant an injunction, for example where a local authority is threatening demolition of a building;[237] and if unjustified demolition were carried out, an action for damages would lie.

In several cases also the courts have granted declarations to the effect that some general order or byelaw was invalid.[238] The rule that the declaration is a discretionary remedy is a sufficient protection against plaintiffs who are not genuinely concerned.

Quashing and prohibiting orders apply to 'judicial' rather than legislative action, but the dividing line is far from distinct.[239] A mandatory order, which has no such limitations, has been used to compel the making of a byelaw.[240]

STATUTORY RESTRICTION OF JUDICIAL REVIEW

Just as with administrative powers,[241] Parliament may make delegated legislation virtually judge-proof. Normally this is done by granting very wide powers rather than by clauses restricting the jurisdiction of the courts. 'Modern drafting technique is to use words which do not exclude jurisdiction in terms but positively repose arbitrary power in a named authority'.[242] But, as already emphasised, it is almost impossible to find language wide enough to exclude judicial control entirely, when the courts are determined to preserve it.[243] All subordinate power must have legal limits somewhere.

In the past Parliament has experimented with protective clauses of varying degrees of severity. It has, for instance, been enacted that regulations purporting to be made under the Act shall be deemed to be within the powers of the Act, and shall have effect as if enacted by the Act.[244] In 1894 a majority of the House of Lords, preferring literal verbal construction to legal principle, declared that 'as if enacted in this Act' clauses made the regulations as unquestionable by a court of law as if they were actually incorporated in the Act.[245] But in 1931 the House found a more reasonable solution in a case under the Housing Act 1925, where the Minister of Health had power to confirm a housing scheme

---

[233] See *Boddington* v. *British Transport Police* [1998] AC, discussed above, p. 238; and see [1998] *PL* 364 (Forsyth); [1998] *JR* 144 (Elliott); (1998) 114 *LQR* 535 (Craig). The holding in *Bugg* v. *DPP* [1993] QB 473 that only substantive invalidity could be raised as a defence was rightly rejected.

[234] Or other procedure (such as a statutory appeal) as may be available. See *R* v. *Wicks* [1997] 2 WLR 576.

[235] See Lord Steyn in *Boddington* (above) at 663–4.   [236] See Lord Irvine in *Boddington* at 652.

[237] As in the *Repton* case, above, p. 744.

[238] This was done in both the cases of partial invalidity mentioned above.

[239] See above, p. 491.   [240] See *R* v. *Manchester Cpn* [1911] 1 KB 560.

[241] Above, p. 608.

[242] *Customs and Excise Commissioners* v. *Cure & Deeley Ltd* [1962] 1 QB 340 at 364 (Sachs J).

[243] Above, p. 614.   [244] e.g. Foreign Marriage Act 1892, s. 21(2).

[245] *Institute of Patent Agents* v. *Lockwood* [1894] AC 347, followed in *Insurance Committee for Glasgow* v. *Scottish Insurance Commissioners* 1915 SC 504.

and the Act said that his order when made 'shall have effect as if enacted in this Act'. The minister, it was held, was empowered to confirm only schemes which conformed to the Act; if the scheme itself conflicted with the Act, the order was not an order within the meaning of the Act, and was not saved by the clause.[246] Lord Dunedin said:[247]

> It is evident that it is inconceivable that the protection should extend without limit. If the Minister went out of his province altogether... it is repugnant to common sense that the order would be protected, although, if there were an Act of Parliament to that effect, it could not be touched.

Although in fact the House upheld the order on its merits, they drew the teeth of the 'as if enacted' clause—which, as the Ministers' Powers Committee recommended,[248] has now fallen into disuse.

These decisions exhibit the same dilemma that has already been pointed out in relation to statutes which take away judicial remedies. Such provisions must either be held to make lawful action which ought to be unlawful, or else they must be virtually meaningless. The long-established policy of the courts is to resist all attempts to confer unlimited executive power, and to uphold the ultra vires principle at all costs. This has been amply illustrated elsewhere.

What has happened in practice is that government draftsmen have preferred to put their faith in clauses which confer the widest possible discretionary power rather than in clauses which attempt to exclude the jurisdiction of the court.

Finally it must be added that all restrictions on the reviewing powers of the courts are now likely to be challengeable as infringements of the right to a judicial determination under the Human Rights Act 1998[249] and sometimes also under European Union law.[250]

PUBLICATION

ARRANGEMENTS FOR PUBLICATION

> The maxim that ignorance of the law does not excuse any subject represents the working hypothesis on which the rule of law rests in British democracy.... But the very justification for that basic maxim is that the whole of our law, written or unwritten, is accessible to the public—in the sense, of course, that, at any rate, its legal advisers have access to it, at any moment, as of right.

The theory so stated in *Blackpool Corporation* v. *Locker*[251] is of the greatest importance, but as that case itself showed, it may break down occasionally. It was long ago realised that the first remedial measure demanded by the growing stream of delegated legislation was a systematic scheme for publication and reference. The first statute was the Rules Publication Act 1893, which regulated the publication of *Statutory Rules and Orders*, begun in 1890. The statute now in force is the Statutory Instruments Act 1946, under which the title of the series has been changed to Statutory Instruments.

---

[246] *Minister of Health* v. *R ex p Yaffé* [1931] AC 494. The minister modified the scheme so as to make it conform to the Act. See likewise *McEwen's Trustees* v. *Church of Scotland General Trustees*, 1940 SLT 357. Other cases involving clauses of this kind are *R* v. *Electricity Commissioners ex p London Electricity Joint Committee Co* [1924] 1 KB 171; *R* v. *Minister of Health ex p Davis* [1929] 1 KB 619; *London Parochial Charities Trustees* v. *A-G* [1955] 1 WLR 42; *Foster* v. *Aloni* [1951] VLR 481.   [247] Ibid. at 501.

[248] Above, p. 611.   [249] See above, p. 135.   [250] See above, p. 618.   [251] Above, p. 735.

Under the Act of 1893 all statutory rules (whether or not to be laid before Parliament) were to be published after they were made, by requiring them to be sent to the Queen's printer to be numbered, printed and sold. Statutory rules were comprehensively defined as including rules made under any Act of Parliament, by Order in Council, or by any minister or government department. The Treasury were given power to alter the effect of the definition by regulations, and a number of exceptions were so made for special cases, and the definition was confined to cases 'of a legislative and not an executive character'.[252] The great bulk of delegated legislation became subject to an orderly system of publication, and this was a great gain. Eventually a new Act was needed, and this appeared in 1946, in time to deal with the flood tide of rules and regulations which arrived with the welfare state.

THE ACT OF 1946

The Statutory Instruments Act of 1946 came into force in 1948, repealing and replacing the Act of 1893. Its definition of 'statutory instrument' covers three categories of 'subordinate legislation' made (or confirmed or approved) under the authority of some statute:[253]

(i) Orders in Council

(ii) Ministerial powers stated in the statute to be exercisable by statutory instrument

(iii) future rules made under past statutes to which the Act of 1893 applied.

As regards (iii), regulations under the Act continue the requirement that such rules shall be 'of a legislative and not an executive character'.[254] But as regards (ii), though it applies only to 'legislation', the real test is that it will only apply where Parliament provides, as it now normally does in each statute, that 'regulations made under this Act shall be made by statutory instrument'. Parliament has abandoned the attempt to define subordinate legislation by its substance, since this could never achieve precision. It now relies on itself to prescribe on each occasion that the provisions for publication etc., shall apply. For statutes made after 1947, therefore, there is a clear-cut but mechanical definition. For statutes made before 1948, the older, vaguer, but more ambitious definition continues. The Act again gives power to control the scope of the old definition by Treasury regulations.[255] And Treasury regulations may exempt any classes of statutory instruments from the requirements of being printed and sold. Exemption has been given to local instruments,[256] and also to instruments regularly printed in some other series. Subject to this, all statutory instruments must be sent to the Queen's printer as soon as made, and must be numbered, printed and sold.[257]

Reference to statutory instruments and other delegated legislation on any subject is facilitated by an official index, the Index to Government Orders in Force, published biennially. Most statutory instruments made since 1987 are available on the internet.[258]

---

[252] SR & O 1894 No. 734.

[253] s. 1. Orders, rules, regulations and other subordinate legislation made by Welsh Ministers is included (s. 1(1A)).   [254] SI 1947 No. 1.

[255] s. 8.

[256] This exemption renders inaccessible many orders, for example those made in the Clay Cross case, mentioned in *Asher* v. *Secretary of State for the Environment* [1974] Ch 208.   [257] s. 2.

[258] See <http://www.legislation.gov.uk/uksi>.

EFFECT OF NON-PUBLICATION ON VALIDITY

Another question is whether the validity of rules and regulations is affected by failure to obey the statutory requirements for publication. It may be that these requirements are merely directory—that is to say, that they embody Parliament's directions, but without imposing any penalty for disobedience.[259] In one case a minister was empowered by statute to control the use of explosives in mines by order, 'of which notice shall be given in such manner as he may direct', and though he failed to give any notice, his order was upheld on the ground that the condition was directory only.[260] It would seem a fortiori that neglect of a general statute requiring publication would be less serious. It was, indeed, held in 1918 that an order made by the Food Controller did not take effect until it was published: A had sold 1,000 bags of beans to B on 16 May 1917, and on that same day an order was made requisitioning all such beans, but it was not published until the following day; B tried to recover his money from A but failed, since the order was held to take effect only when it was made known.[261] But the true explanation is probably that the order, as construed by the court, was intended to take effect only at that time.

This hypothesis is impliedly supported by a provision of the Statutory Instruments Act 1946. It requires the Stationery Office to publish lists showing the dates on which they issue statutory instruments, and in any proceedings against any person for offending under such statutory instruments

> it shall be a defence to prove that the instrument had not been issued by His Majesty's Stationery Office at the date of the alleged contravention unless it is proved that at that date reasonable steps had been taken for the purpose of bringing the purport of the instrument to the notice of the public, or of persons likely to be affected by it, or of the person charged.[262]

It seems to be assumed that non-publication would not by itself be a sufficient defence, and since the provision deals only with criminal liability, it suggests that non-publication would not affect the validity of a statutory instrument altering civil rights. This was the construction adopted in a case of 1954, where a company was prosecuted for infringing an Iron and Steel Prices Order. The order had been printed, but not the schedules for it, which were extensive and bulky. The judge decided that non-publication of the schedules did not invalidate the order, because the Act made an obvious distinction between the making of the instrument and the issue of it, and the provisions for printing and publication were merely procedural.[263] The making of the instrument was complete, in his opinion, when it was made by the minister and (if so required by the empowering statute) laid before Parliament. Since the prosecution were able to prove that reasonable steps had been taken for notification by other channels, a conviction followed. The judge's suggestion that validity might depend upon laying before Parliament is in conflict with at least two previous judicial opinions;[264] and it may be held that even that requirement, important though it is, would be held to be directory merely, as being essentially a form

---

[259] See above, p. 183. For discussion and criticism see (1974) 37 *MLR* 510 (D. J. Lanham); [1982] *PL* 569 (A. I. L. Campbell); [1983] *PL* 385 (D. J. Lanham).

[260] *Jones* v. *Robson* [1901] 1 QB 673; and see *Duncan* v. *Knill* (1907) 96 LT 911 (order valid although statutory notice not given). But see the views expressed by the High Court of Australia in *Watson* v. *Lee* (1979) 26 ALR 461.   [261] *Johnson* v. *Sargant & Sons* [1918] 1 KB 101.

[262] s. 3(2).

[263] *The Queen* v. *Sheer Metalcraft Ltd* [1954] 1 QB 586. See also *Smith* v. *Hingston* [2000] GWD 2–62 (s. 3(2) shows unpublished instrument not necessarily a nullity).

[264] *Bailey* v. *Williamson* (1873) LR 8 QB 118; *Starey* v. *Graham* [1899] 1 QB 406 at 412. But much depends upon the precise statutory language.

of supervision *ex post facto*. As we have seen, Acts of Indemnity have been used to prevent the question arising.[265]

RULES REQUIRED TO BE LAID BEFORE PARLIAMENT

The Rules Publication Act 1893 also provided for advance publication of regulations which had to be laid before Parliament. Laying before Parliament is commonly required by the statute under which the regulations are made, as explained below. The Statutory Instruments Act 1946 has the same objective as the Act of 1893, but prescribes a different procedure. It requires the laying to take place before the instrument comes into operation.[266] If, however, it is essential that it should come into operation before it can be laid, it may do so; but a reasoned notification must be sent to both Houses. There will obviously be occasions, especially when Parliament is not sitting, when orders may have to be brought into force urgently.[267]

The Laying of Documents (Interpretation) Act 1948 allowed each House to give its own meaning to 'laying' for the purposes of the Act;[268] the Houses then made standing orders to the effect that delivery of copies to their offices should count as 'laying' at any time when a Parliament was legally in being, even though it was prorogued or adjourned at the time. The safeguards designed in 1893 were thus progressively whittled down as the weight of delegated legislation grew greater and greater.

The timetable for 'laying' has also been made more uniform by the Statutory Instruments Act 1946 in two classes of cases:

(i)   instruments which are subject to annulment on an adverse resolution of either House

(ii) instruments which must be laid before Parliament in draft, but which may later be made if no hostile resolution is carried.

The first class is much more common than the second. In order to escape from the provisions of numerous Acts which had laid down different timetables, and in order to provide one timetable for the future, it is now provided that instruments of class (i) shall be duly laid and shall be subject to annulment for forty days, and that instruments of class (ii) shall not be made within forty days of being laid. In counting the forty days, no account is taken of periods when Parliament is dissolved or prorogued, or adjourned for more than four days. It will be observed that no provision is made for regulations which expire within a time-limit unless expressly confirmed by Parliament (of which we have already met examples)[269] or for regulations which do not take effect at all unless so confirmed. In those cases the timetable is usually of intrinsic importance to the subject-matter, and is best left as it is.

---

[265] Above, p. 747.   [266] s. 4.

[267] Cf. The House of Lords' Constitution Select Committee Fifteenth Report (2008–9), 'Fast-track Legislation: Constitutional Implications and Safeguards' (HL 116-I), ch. 5, para. 139, urged restraint in the use of 'fast-track parliamentary procedure of draft affirmative instruments'. The Report is at <http://www.publications.parliament.uk/pa/ld200809/ldselect/ldconst/116/116.pdf>.

[268] 'Laying' has no technical meaning: see *R v. Immigration Tribunal ex p Joyles* [1972] 1 WLR 1390 (unsuccessful challenge to validity of the immigration rules of 1970 on the ground that they were presented to Parliament but not 'laid').   [269] Above, p. 731.

PRELIMINARY CONSULTATION

HEARING OF OBJECTIONS

In the case of rules and orders which are clearly legislative as opposed to administrative, there is normally no room for the principle of natural justice which entitles persons affected to a fair hearing in advance.[270] But where regulations, though general in form, bear particularly hardly on one person or group, an exception may be made.[271] Orders for such things as housing and planning schemes, although they may affect numerous people, are for this purpose treated by Parliament, and also by the courts, as matters of administration and not of legislation. They are subject to the procedure of preliminary public inquiry under various Acts, and also to the principles of natural justice, as we have seen.[272] The right to reasoned decisions given by the Tribunals and Inquiries Act 1992 is expressly excluded in the case of rules, orders or schemes 'of a legislative and not an executive character'.[273] But it may be presumed that the right extends to all orders and schemes of the kind just mentioned.

The US Federal Administrative Procedure Act of 1946[274] gives a right to 'interested persons' to 'participate in the rule-making through submission of written data, views or arguments', and in some cases Congress has prescribed a formal hearing. Hearings preliminary to rule-making have thus become an important part of the administrative process in the United States.[275] But there is often no right to an oral hearing and there is a wide exception where the authority finds 'for good cause' 'that notice and public procedure thereon are impracticable, unnecessary or contrary to the public interest'.

In Britain the practice counts for more than the law. Consultation with interests and organisations likely to be affected by rules and regulations is a firmly established convention,[276] so much so that it is unusual to hear complaint although they are not unknown.[277] Whether or not consultation is a legal requirement, once 'embarked upon it must be carried out properly'.[278] This requires consultation while the proposals are still in a formative stage, adequate reasons for the proposals to be given so that those consulted may give an 'intelligent response', adequate time to do so and proper consideration of those responses.[279] It may be that consultation which is not subject to statutory procedure is

---

[270] Above, p. 473.

[271] See *Bank Mellat* v. *HM Treasury* [2013] UKSC 39 at paras. 44–9 (especially 47). Lord Sumption held that the usual rule does not apply to a measure 'targeted against "designated persons"'. Thus measures taken without consultation by the Treasury under the Counter-Terrorism Act 2008 to deny Bank Mellat (an Iranian Bank) access to UK financial markets were found invalid. The requirement of fairness (and thus consultation) was implied into the statute. See Lord Sumption, paras. 44–9. Cf. the dissent of Lord Reed and Lord Hope, esp. paras. 152–3. For other aspects of the *Bank Mellat* case see above, pp. 423–4. For another example of this principle see the *United States Tobacco* case, below, p. 756.   [272] Above, p. 411.

[273] s. 10(5)(b).   [274] s. 4. See Schwartz and Wade, *Legal Control of Government*, 87.

[275] For comparative discussion, see (1983) 3 *OJLS* 253 (M. Asimow).

[276] See [1964] *PL* 105 (J. F. Garner); [1978] *PL* 290 (A. D. Jergesen).

[277] A rare exception was *Bates* v. *Lord Hailsham* [1972] 1 WLR 1373; above, p. 746.

[278] *R* v. *North and East Devon HA ex p Coughlan* [2001] QB 213, para. 108 (non-legislative context).

[279] But consultees do not need to have circulated to them the submissions of other consultees: *R (Murray & Co)* v. *Lord Chancellor* [2011] EWHC 1528 (consultation re closure of a magistrates' court). But enough must be revealed of the proposals to enable those consulated to give intelligent consideration and an intelligent response, and the product of the consultation has to be conscientiously taken into account when the ultimate decision is taken. *R (Save our Surgery Limited)* v. *Joint Committee of Primary Care Trusts* [2013] EWHC 439 (consultation on closure of paediatric cardiac surgery centres).

more effective than formal hearing, which may produce legalism and artificiality.[280] The Cabinet Office has published a code of practice on consultation[281] which will apply to most government initiatives, including delegated legislation. It has no formal legal force[282] but urges timely, thorough and focused consultation.[283]

STATUTORY CONSULTATION AND ADVISORY BODIES

Particular Acts often require affected interests to be consulted by the responsible minister. Some statutes provide for schemes of control to be formulated by the persons affected themselves. Another device which is often used is that of an advisory committee or council, which is set up under the Act and which must be consulted. The council will usually be constituted so as to represent various interests, and so as to be independent of ministerial control. And, in its turn, it may often consult other persons. In these cases there is no statutory procedure for consulting other interests such as there is with the Social Security Advisory Committee. But these councils may consult other people and hear evidence if they wish, and frequently they do so.

A statutory duty to consult requires that the person or body consulted should be given a reasonably ample and sufficient opportunity to state their views[284] 'before the mind of the executive becomes unduly fixed'.[285] It is not satisfied if it is treated as a mere opportunity to make ineffective representations.[286] Moreover, where there is a history of dealing between consultor and consultee and the impact of the proposed regulations on the consultee's business would be profound, fairness requires disclosure of the reports of independent experts on which the consultor seeks to rely.[287] To this extent the principles of natural justice can apply to delegated legislation.[288] There is no general duty, however, to disclose the representations to any other person.[289]

Failure to consult will normally render the order void, as for neglect of a mandatory requirement.[290]

---

[280] There are arguments that favour pre-legislative consultation (even before primary legislation) as a form of democratic representation. See Forsyth and Hare (eds.), *The Golden Metwand*, 39–64 (P. Cane).

[281] It is consulting on a new code of practice but the proposals have been criticised as being insufficiently robust by the House of Lords Secondary Legislation Scrutiny Committee, Seventeenth Report (2013–14) (HL 75): <http://www.publications.parliament.uk/pa/ld201314/ldselect/ldsecleg/75/75.pdf>.

[282] But may give rise to a legitimate expectation of consultation. See above, p. 450.

[283] <http://www.gov.uk/government/uploads/system/uploads/attachment_data/file/255180/Consultation-Principles-Oct-2013.pdf>.

[284] *Port Louis Corporation* v. *Attorney-General of Mauritius* [1965] AC 1111. See also *Rollo* v. *Minister of Town and Country Planning* [1948] 1 All ER 13; *Re Union of Benefices of Whippingham and East Cowes, St James* [1954] AC 245.   [285] *Sinfield* v. *London Transport Executive* [1970] Ch 550 at 558.

[286] Ibid. Compare the question of 'blowing off steam' below, p. 800. For an example, see *Devon CC* v. *Secretary of State for Communities and Local Government* [2010] EWHC 1456 (Secretary of State changed the basis of his proposal to create 2 unitary authorities but failed to give consultees an opportunity to respond to this change; orders quashed).

[287] *R* v. *Secretary of State for Health ex p United States Tobacco International Inc.* [1992] QB 353 at 369–72 (restriction of trade in oral snuff, only one company severely affected, regulations quashed).

[288] Above, p. 473.

[289] *R* v. *Secretary of State for Social Security ex p United States Tobacco International Inc.* Court of Appeal (Civil Division) 634/1988 unreported but see [1992] QB 353 at 370.   [290] Above, p. 183.

PARLIAMENTARY SUPERVISION

THE TREND OF THE TIMES

One prominent feature of the twentieth century has been a shift of the constitutional centre of gravity, away from Parliament and towards the executive. Mr Lloyd George once said: 'Parliament has really no control over the Executive; it is a pure fiction'.[291] Party discipline gives the government a tight control over Parliament in all but the last resort; and the current electoral system, tending as it does to eliminate minority parties, normally gives the government a solid basis for its power. But, in addition, the sheer volume of legislation and other government work is so great that the parliamentary machine is unequal to it. This is itself one of the principal reasons for delegated legislation. It is also the reason why it is difficult for Parliament to supervise it effectively. To treat the subject of parliamentary control in any detail would take us beyond administrative law. But mention may be made of a few matters of general interest.[292]

LAYING BEFORE PARLIAMENT

An Act of Parliament will normally require that rules or regulations made under the Act shall be laid before both Houses of Parliament. Parliament can then keep its eye upon them and provide opportunities for criticism. Rules or regulations laid before Parliament may be attacked on any ground. The object of the system is to keep them under general political control, so that criticism in Parliament is frequently on grounds of policy. The legislation concerning 'laying' has already been explained.[293]

Laying before Parliament is done in a number of different ways.[294] The regulations may merely have to be laid; or they may be subject to negative resolution within forty days; or they may expire unless confirmed by affirmative resolution; or they may have to be laid in draft. Occasionally they do not have to be laid at all, because Parliament has omitted to make any provision.[295]

There are two clear categories into which the majority of cases fall. Either the regulations will be of no effect unless confirmed by resolution of each House (or, if financial, of the House of Commons only);[296] or else they will take effect without further formality in Parliament, but subject to annulment in pursuance of a resolution of either House

---

[291] Quoted by Sir Carleton Allen, *Law and Orders*, 3rd edn, 161.

[292] For a useful discussion including proposals for reform see [1988] *PL* 547 (J. D. Hayhurst and P. Wallington); [1998] 19 Stat. LR 155 (T. StJ. N. Bates); Kersell, *Parliamentary Supervision of Delegated Legislation* (1960). The Royal Commission on the Reform of the House of Lords (Cm. 4534, January 2000), describes the existing scrutiny procedure and makes proposals for reform. See also the House of Lords Delegated Powers and Regulation Committee's Third Report (2012–13) HL 19 'Strengthened Statutory Procedures for the Scrutiny of Delegated Powers' at <http://www.publications.parliament.uk/pa/ld201213/ldselect/lddelreg/19/1902.htm>. The Report's main recommendation is that 'in proposing a strengthened scrutiny procedure in any future Bill the Government should normally use an existing model rather than creating a new variation'. [293] Above, p. 754.

[294] Documents referred to in the regulations but not forming part of them do not have to be laid: *R v. Secretary of State for Social Services ex p Camden LBC* [1987] 1 WLR 819 confirmed in *R (Alvi) v. Home Secretary* [2012] UKSC 33, para. 40 and *Pankina v. Home Secretary* [2010] EWCA Civ 719, paras. 24–6 (outside source must be 'extant and accessible').

[295] e.g. regulations for Rent Tribunals under the Furnished Houses (Rent Control) Act 1946, s. 8. The omission is inexplicable.

[296] If the Act says 'Parliament' in such a case, this may mean the House of Commons only: *R v. Secretary of State for the Environment ex p Leicester CC*, The Times, 1 February 1985.

(with some exceptions). These are known as the 'affirmative' and 'negative' procedures respectively. The affirmative procedure is normal for regulations which increase taxes or charges.[297] The negative procedure is normal in the great majority of other cases. Sometimes an Act will employ both procedures[298] and it may even allow a choice between them.[299] But whatever course is adopted, the regulations are either approved or disapproved. Parliament cannot itself amend them.

OPPORTUNITIES FOR CHALLENGE

Where regulations have merely to be laid, there is no special opportunity for control, and the laying does no more than advertise the regulations to members, who may then put questions to ministers.[300] At the other extreme, where an affirmative resolution is necessary, the government must find time for a motion and debate, so that there is full scope for criticism. In the intermediate and commonest case, where the regulations are subject to annulment, the procedure of the House of Commons allows them to be challenged by any member at the end of the day's business. He must move a 'prayer', because the method of annulment is by Order in Council (as provided by the Statutory Instruments Act 1946),[301] and the motion is for a humble prayer to the Crown that the regulations be annulled. Provided that the necessary quorum of forty can be kept in the House, the annulment procedure ensures an opportunity for debate at the instance of any member. Every member may therefore 'watch and pray'.[302] But the House could not possibly debate all the annullable regulations laid before it.

Scrutiny of the merits of statutory instruments by the House of Lords is generally more effective. There is a House of Lords Secondary Legislation Scrutiny Committee (previously named the Select Committee on the Merits of Statutory Instruments) which regularly reports to the House of Lords on the merits of the instruments laid before Parliament.[303] The House of Lords retains the right to veto any instrument except for financial instruments (which are reserved to the Commons).[304] There is no similar Select Committee in the Commons but there is the General Committee (previously Standing Committee) on Delegated Legislation in the Commons which debates the measures referred to it.[305]

THE JOINT COMMITTEE ON STATUTORY INSTRUMENTS

In 1973, following the Report of a joint committee of Lords and Commons,[306] the two Houses formed the Joint Committee on Statutory Instruments.[307] The Joint Committee

---

[297] e.g. under Customs and Excise Duties (General Reliefs) Act 1979, s. 17(4); Taxation (International and Other Provisions) Act 2010, ss. 2 and 5.   [298] e.g. Census Act 1920, s. 1(2).

[299] As does the European Communities Act 1972, 2nd Sched., para. 2(2).

[300] The Royal Commission (above, para. 7.7) states that more than half of all statutory instruments are subject to 'no Parliamentary procedure', i.e. are simply 'laid'.   [301] s. 5.

[302] Allen (as above), 123.

[303] These are available at <http://www.parliament.uk/business/committees/committees-a-z/lords-select/secondary-legislation-scrutiny-committee/publications/previous-sessions/session-2012-13/>.

[304] Bradley and Ewing (p. 631) give an account of the role of the House of Lords in scrutinising legislation. For the reports of the 'Merits Committee' (above note).

[305] Records of the debates can be accessed at <http://www.parliament.uk/business/publications/hansard/commons/gc-debates/delegated-legislation-committee/>.

[306] Bradley and Ewing, above.

[307] See 850 HC Deb. col. 1217 (13 February 1973). This took the place of the Commons' Scrutiny Committee which had operated since 1944, and the Lords' Special Orders Committee in existence since 1924.

has seven members from each House. The Commons' members sit by themselves as a select committee in the case of financial instruments which are laid before the House of Commons only.

The Joint Committee is not concerned with policy but with the manner, form and technique of the exercise of rule-making powers. Consequently it can do its work without party strife, with the single object of keeping statutory instruments up to a satisfactory administrative standard. Its chairman is normally a member of the Opposition in the House of Commons, thus signifying that it exists in order to criticise.

The Joint Committee is required to consider every statutory instrument, rule, order or scheme laid or laid in draft before each House if proceedings may be taken upon it in either House under any statute.[308] The Committee has to decide whether to bring it to the attention of the House on any of the following grounds:[309]

(i)   that it imposes a charge on the public revenues, or imposes or prescribes charges for any licence, consent, or service from any public authority

(ii)   that it is made under a statute which precludes challenge in the courts

(iii)   that it purports to have retrospective effect, without statutory authorisation

(iv)   that publication or laying before Parliament appears to have been unjustifiably delayed

(v)   that notification to the Speaker appears to have been unjustifiably delayed, in cases where the Statutory Instruments Act 1946 requires it[310]

(vi)   that there is doubt whether it is intra vires or that it appears to make 'some unusual or unexpected use' of the powers conferred

(vii)   'that for any special reason its form or purport calls for elucidation'

(viii) 'that its drafting appears to be defective'.

But the Committee may also act 'on any other ground which does not impinge on its merits or on the policy behind it'. They therefore have a free rein for non-political comment.

One case of 'unexpected use of the powers' was where the power to prescribe forms was used to enforce metric measurement of the height of stallions instead of the traditional measurement by hands and inches.[311] Another was where rules made for the Employment Appeal Tribunal allowed the tribunal to depart from the rules at its own discretion.[312] The need for elucidation is illustrated by an order under the Sex Discrimination Act 1975 which was not clear and whose explanatory note was misleading.[313] Defective drafting was found in an order designating bodies able to grant permits for the use of minibuses.[314] Defective drafting was also found in a regulation that permitted the tax representatives

---

[308] Remedial Orders under the Human Rights Act 1998, s. 10 are excluded (being considered by the Joint Select Committee on Human Rights (above, p. 138) as are Regulatory Reform Orders made under the Legislative and Regulatory Reform Act 2006 (also considered elsewhere (above, p. 728). The Standing Orders mentioned in the next note make effective the exclusion of these instruments from the remit of the Joint Select Committee.

[309] Standing Order 151 (Commons) and Standing Order 74 (House of Lords).

[310] Above, p. 754.

[311] HC 55—iii (1975–6) criticising Horse Breeding (Amendment) Rules 1975 (SI 1975 No. 1777).

[312] HC 54—xxi (1975–6) criticising Employment Appeal Tribunal Rules 1976 (SI 1976 No. 322).

[313] HC 54—iv (1975–6) criticising Sex Discrimination (Designated Educational Establishments) Order 1975 (SI 1975 No. 1902).

[314] HC 33—xv (1978–9), criticising Minibus (Designated Bodies) (Amendment) Order (SI 1978 No. 1930).

of overseas insurers to remain in office while they were not qualified to do so.[315] These are examples taken at random from a large number of reports. Much the commonest reasons for reporting an order are that it requires elucidation, or makes an unexpected use of the powers conferred or is marred by defective drafting.[316] During 2007 the Committee considered 1,473 statutory instruments and drew the special attention of each House to some seventy instruments.[317]

The Committee also makes general reports. It has criticised lax departmental practices such as the laying of instruments before Parliament 'in a scruffy form with manuscript amendments, and the omission of necessary details so as to confer wide discretion on ministers and thus bypass Parliament'.[318]

Probably the most important result of the Committee's vigilance is not that it brings regulations to debate in Parliament (though there have been some notable, if rare, examples of this happening), but that it gives government departments a lively consciousness that critical eyes are kept upon them. Relatively few of the instruments scrutinised are reported to the House, but this is in part a measure of the Committee's success in establishing a standard. Its work is another example of the value of a standing body as opposed to periodical inquests by ad hoc committees.

In particular, the successive committees have been able to secure more satisfactory explanatory notes, which now accompany statutory instruments as a matter of course and are particularly useful when the instrument is complicated. Obscurities have often been criticised, and also the practices of legislating by reference, sub-delegation on dubious authority and (occasionally) retrospective operation. The terms of reference expressly allow a point of ultra vires to be raised, as is done from time to time. A few regulations escape scrutiny, since statutes sometimes omit to provide for them to be laid. But the system extends to much the greater part of delegated legislation which is of national as opposed to local effect. It may be said to be the one successful result of the efforts of reformers to impose discipline on all this legislative activity.

The Joint Committee reports on every instrument within its terms of reference, even if only to say that it has no comment to make. The fruits of its labours are not to be counted in motions carried against the government, but in the improvements in departmental practice which its vigilance has secured. In this respect its work may be compared with that of the Parliamentary Commissioner for Administration—another example of the value of non-political scrutiny of administrative action. The impartial character of the Committee's reports means that they do not have to face the steamroller of the ruling majority.

LEGISLATION OF THE EUROPEAN COMMUNITIES

New problems of parliamentary supervision of regulations arose when the United Kingdom became a member of the European Communities and the European Communities Act 1972 gave the force of law to Community legislation. Under this Act Parliament has renounced its power to legislate contrary to the law of the Communities, as laid down in

---

[315] HC 456—i (1998–9) criticising the Overseas Insurers (Tax Representatives) Regulations 1999 (SI 1999 No. 881).

[316] Approximately 5 per cent of the instruments considered are reported. For these and other statistics see Hayhurst and Wallington (as above) at 562; 62 per cent of instruments reported are reported on the ground of defective drafting (see report cited in following note).

[317] Joint Committee's Second Special Report in 2007–8 Session (see at <http://www.publications.parliament.uk/pa/jt200708/jtselect/jtstatin/jtstatin.htm>).   [318] HC 169 (1977–8).

the case of the European Community by the Council and the Commission in accordance with the Treaty of Rome.[319] So long as this self-denying ordinance is observed, Parliament has no control over Community legislation, even though it automatically becomes part of the law of this country.

Most Community legislation is made by the Council on proposals from the Commission. Each House of Parliament has established a select committee to scrutinise these proposals. Although the Houses have no direct powers, they can call ministers to account for what they do as members of the Council, and a House of Commons resolution (the 'scrutiny reserve resolution') restrains ministers from assenting in the Council to any resolution which is still subject to parliamentary scrutiny. The object of the two select committees is to keep Parliament informed of Community legislation due to come before the Council, so that pressure can be brought to bear on ministers before they consider it in the Council; and the government undertakes to arrange debates for this purpose.[320] Both Committees make regular reports to their Houses.[321] The Commons Committee scrutinises more than a thousand EU documents per year, mostly legislative proposals, but also pre- legislative documents such as Green and White papers. For each document the Government provides an Explanatory Memorandum setting out its policy. The committee works speedily, reporting weekly. It 'clears' most documents but recommends a small number (two or three p.a.) for debate by the full House, and several dozen for debate in the European Standing Committee. The Committee focuses on the legal and political importance of the proposals.

The House of Lords' Committee is called the European Union Select Committee; it has six sub-committees dealing with different areas of policy. It operates under a similar 'scrutiny reserve resolution' but its focus lies on the merits of the proposal.[322] The House of Commons' Committee is called the European Scrutiny Committee. Community legislation must of course be distinguished from orders and regulations made under the European Communities Act 1972 for enforcing Community law, which are subject to affirmative resolution or annulment in Parliament in accordance with that Act.[323]

[319] European Communities Act 1972, s. 2(4). See above, p. 20.

[320] See Erskine May, *Parliamentary Practice*, 22nd edn, 829.

[321] Note particularly the Thirtieth Report of the European Scrutiny Committee on the operation of the Committee: <www.publications.parliament.uk/pa/cm200102/cmselect/cmeuleg/152-xxx/15202.htm>. The report deprecates the delays caused by failure of EU documents or explanatory memoranda to reach it in time, as well as a tendency to override the scrutiny reserve resolution. Delays in correspondence, the late availability of explanatory memoranda and frequent scrutiny 'overrides' continue to concern the Committee. See Annual Report 2007, HL 181 (1 November 2007).

[322] Note the Committee's 1st Report, 2002–3 HL Paper 15, reviewing its scrutiny of EU legislation and making many proposals for improvement. There is a useful guide to the select committee's work at <http://www.parliament.uk/business/committees/committees-a-z/lords-select/eu-select-committee-/role/>.

[323] s. 2 and 2nd Sched. See above, p. 158.

23

STATUTORY TRIBUNALS

THE TRIBUNAL SYSTEM: AN INTRODUCTION

SPECIAL TRIBUNALS

A prominent feature of the governmental scene is the multitude of special tribunals[1] created by Act of Parliament.[2] Each of these is designed to be part of some scheme of administration, and collectively they are sometimes called administrative tribunals,[3] although they are more properly known as 'statutory tribunals' or just tribunals.

A host of these tribunals has arisen under the welfare state, such as the local tribunals which decide disputed claims to benefit under the social security legislation, and employment tribunals which decide many disputes involving employers and employees and often involving the state also. Other tribunals deal with taxation, property rights, immigration, mental health, allocation of pupils to schools and much else.[4] A vast range of controversies is committed to the jurisdiction of these bodies, which is by no means confined to claims against public authorities. Can B claim jobseeker's allowance or a pension or a redundancy payment? Should C, an alien or Commonwealth citizen, be refused admission to the country? Should E be forbidden to conduct an independent school? These are samples of the many questions which may come before statutory tribunals. The ordinary law-abiding citizen is more likely to find himself concerned with them than with the regular courts of law.

---

[1] For tribunals see Report of the Committee of Administrative Tribunals and Enquiries (the Franks Report), Cmnd 218 (1957); Wraith and Hutchesson, *Administrative Tribunals* (1973); Farmer, *Tribunals and Government*; Bell, *Tribunals in the Social Services*; Van Dyk, *Tribunals and Inquiries*; Jackson, *The Machinery of Justice in England*, 8th edn (by J. R. Spencer), pt 3; Bowers, *Tribunals, Practice and Procedure*. The Annual Reports of the Council on Tribunals are an important source. Leggatt Report, 'Tribunals for Users—One System One Service' (16 August 2001) (<http://www.tribunals-review.org.uk>) is another source of useful information (but of the unreformed system). Post-Leggatt accounts include: Coppel and Hanif, *Tribunal Practice* (2012),Thomas, *Administrative Justice and Asylum Appeals* (2011) and Le Sueur, 'Administrative Justice and the Resolution of Disputes' in Jowell and Oliver (eds.), *The Changing Constitution*, 7th edn (2011). Quarterly statistics on the use of Tribunals in England and Wales, and non-devolved Tribunals in Scotland are published by the Ministry of Justice. In 2012–13 there were 874,000 claims and 741,000 disposals: <http://www.gov.uk/government/uploads/system/uploads/attachment_data/file/207857/tribunal-stats-q4-2013.pdf>.

[2] In *R (Cart)* v. *Upper Tribunal* [2011] UKSC 28, Baroness Hale described the 'proliferation of statutory tribunals' as '[o]ne of the most important and controversial features of the development of the legal system in the 20th century' (para. 11).

[3] Tribunals have to find facts and then apply legal rules to them impartially; this is a judicial not an administrative task. They are also independent (like a judge); no minister can be held responsible for any tribunal's decision.

[4] A specialised planning tribunal has been proposed. See 'Judicial Review: Proposals for Further Reform', Cm. 8703 (discussed above, p. 567), paras. 34–52.

Tribunals are conspicuous in administrative law because they have limited jurisdictions and their errors are in principle subject to judicial review in the High Court. In this chapter we are concerned rather with the organisation and normal operation of the tribunal system. This aspect of the machinery of administrative justice is important, for the more satisfactory tribunals are, the less judicial review will be required. Legal technicalities therefore play a relatively small part in this chapter: the problems which arise are mainly of legal policy and organisation. Tribunals exist in order to provide simpler, speedier, cheaper, and more accessible justice than do the ordinary courts. The question which runs through the subject is how far the standards set by the courts can be reconciled with the needs of administration. It may be taken for granted that the principles of natural justice must be observed, as illustrated in earlier chapters.[5] These supply the essential minimum of fairness in administration and adjudication alike. But should there be rights of appeal to other tribunals? Or to the courts? Ought reasons always to be given for decisions? Should legal representation always be allowed? And are there too many different tribunals? There is no shortage of questions of this kind.

Tribunals have attracted the attention of the legislature on several occasions most recently with the Tribunals, Courts and Enforcement Act 2007. As will be explained below this measure implements far reaching and fundamental reforms seeking to impose system and order on the maze of specialised tribunals.[6] Prior to the 2007 Act the Tribunals and Inquiries Act 1958 was the most important reform. The substantial implementation of the Report of the Committee on Administrative Tribunals and Enquiries (the Franks Committee)[7] in the 1958 Act was an early sign of the renaissance of administrative law. The present law is contained in the Tribunals and Inquiries Act 1992[8] (replacing the 1958 Act and earlier consolidating statutes). There now follows a short account of the system prior to its reform by the 2007 Act.

HISTORICAL ANTECEDENTS

Tribunals are mainly a twentieth-century phenomenon, for it was long part of the conception of the rule of law that the determination of questions of law—that is to say, questions which require the finding of facts and the application of definite legal rules or principles—belonged to the courts exclusively. The first breaches of this principle were made for the purpose of efficient collection of revenue. The Commissioners of Customs and Excise were given judicial powers by statutes dating from 1660,[9] but though these were criticised by Blackstone[10] and execrated in the definition of 'excise' in Johnson's Dictionary,[11] they were the forerunners of many such powers, such as the General Commissioners of Income Tax, a tribunal established in 1799 which still exists.

The type of tribunal so familiar today, and so prominent in the administration of the welfare state, arrived on the scene with the Old Age Pensions Act of 1908 and the National Insurance Act 1911. The Act of 1908 established local pensions committees to decide disputes, with a right of appeal to the Local Government Board. The Act of 1911, which in

---

[5] Tribunals figure in many of the cases cited in Chs. 13 and 14.

[6] The 2007 Act was preceded by the Leggatt Report (above) (discussed [2002] PL 200 (Bradley)) and a White Paper 'Transforming Public Services: Complaints, Redress and Tribunals' July 2004 (Cm. 6243).

[7] Cmnd 218 (1957).   [8] Itself in part repealed by the 2007 Act.

[9] 12 Charles II, c. 23, s. 31, giving a right of appeal to justices of the peace.

[10] Bl. Comm. iv. 281. See Report of the Committee on Ministers' Powers, Cmd 4060 (1932), 11.

[11] 'A hateful tax levied upon commodities, and adjudged not by the common judges of property, but wretches hired by those to whom excise is paid.'

important ways was the prototype of modern social legislation, provided for appeals concerning unemployment insurance (now jobseeker's allowance) to go to a court of referees with a further right of appeal to an umpire.

Although several different methods of settling disputes were tried during the early years of the century, it was soon found that the unemployment insurance system was the most successful. It has served as the model for tribunals in other fields. But later developments have modified it in one important respect. It made no provision for reference to the courts of any questions of any kind. The normal rule today is that there is a right of appeal from a tribunal to the High Court on a question of law.

HISTORICAL ANTECEDENTS: THE FRANKS COMMITTEE AND THE TRIBUNALS AND INQUIRIES ACT 1958

The intensive social legislation which followed the Second World War not only put great trust in tribunals: it was based on an attitude of positive hostility to the courts of law. This was the era when a minister could speak of 'judicial sabotage of socialist legislation'.[12] The policy was to administer social services in the greatest possible detachment from the ordinary legal system, and to dispense with the refined techniques which the courts had developed over the centuries. The result was a mass of procedural anomalies. Some tribunals sat in public, others sat in private. Some allowed unrestricted legal representation, others allowed none. Some followed the legal rules of evidence, others disregarded them. Some allowed full examination and cross-examination of witnesses; others allowed witnesses to be questioned only through the chairman. Some took evidence on oath, others did not. Some gave reasoned decisions, others did not.

During the following decade a swelling chorus of complaint forced a reappraisal of the philosophy of the tribunal system. Steps had to be taken to bring the tribunals back into touch with the regular courts, to improve the standard of justice meted out by them and to impose order and discipline generally. The spadework was done by the Committee on Administrative Tribunals and Enquiries (the Franks Committee). The necessary reforms were made by the Tribunals and Inquiries Act 1958 and by administrative changes prompted by it.

The Committee, presided over by Sir Oliver Franks (as he then was), was commissioned by the Lord Chancellor in 1955 as an immediate, though illogical, result of the Crichel Down case of 1954.[13]

The Committee had to make a fundamental choice between two conflicting attitudes, the legal and the administrative. In their Report the Committee came down firmly on the legal side. They said:[14]

> Much of the official evidence, including that of the Joint Permanent Secretary to the Treasury, appeared to reflect the view that tribunals should properly be regarded as part of the machinery of administration, for which the government must retain a close and continuing responsibility. Thus, for example, tribunals in the social service field would be regarded as adjuncts to the administration of the services themselves. We do not accept this view. We consider that tribunals should properly be regarded as machinery provided by Parliament for adjudication rather than as part of the machinery of administration.

---

[12] 425 HC Deb. 1983 (27 July 1946, Mr A. Bevan).

[13] Report of the Inquiry by Sir Andrew Clarke QC, Cmnd 9176 (1954). This was a case of maladministration for which the correct remedy was the ombudsman, but the time for him was not yet ripe.

[14] Cmnd 218 (1957), para. 40.

The essential point is that in all these cases Parliament has deliberately provided for a decision independent of the Department concerned...and the intention of Parliament to provide for the independence of tribunals is clear and unmistakable.

To make tribunals conform to the standard which Parliament thus had in mind, three fundamental objectives were proclaimed: openness, fairness and impartiality.

> In the field of tribunals openness appears to us to require the publicity of proceedings and knowledge of the essential reasoning underlying the decisions; fairness to require the adoption of a clear procedure which enables parties to know their rights, to present their case fully and to know the case which they have to meet; and impartiality to require the freedom of tribunals from the influence, real or apparent, of Departments concerned with the subject-matter of their decisions.

The Committee's central proposal was that there should be a permanent Council on Tribunals in order to provide some standing machinery for the general supervision of tribunal organisation and procedure. It was to consist of both legal and lay members, with lay members in the majority—thus manifesting the spirit which ran all through the Report, that tribunal reform was to be based on general public opinion, and was not a kind of lawyers' counter-revolution against modern methods of government and the welfare state. Such a body would provide the focal point which had previously been lacking. After establishment by the 1958 Act the Council emerged as a purely advisory body, without the function of appointing tribunal members, but with general oversight over tribunals and inquiries. It was designed to bark but not to bite.[15] It must be consulted before any new procedural rules for them are made.[16] There were many other reforms contained in the 1958 Act and in the administrative reforms prompted by the Franks Committee.[17]

ADVANTAGES AND DISADVANTAGES OF TRIBUNALS

The social legislation of the twentieth century demanded tribunals for purely administrative reasons: they could offer speedier, cheaper and more accessible justice, essential for the administration of welfare schemes involving large numbers of small claims. The process of the courts of law is elaborate, slow and costly. Its defects are those of its merits, for the object is to provide the highest standard of justice; generally speaking, the public wants the best possible article, and is prepared to pay for it. But in administering social services the aim is different. The object is not the best article at any price but the best article that is consistent with efficient administration. Disputes must be disposed of quickly and cheaply, for the benefit of the public purse as well as for that of the claimant.[18] Thus when in 1946 workmen's compensation claims were removed from the courts and brought within the tribunal system much unproductive and expensive litigation, particularly on whether an accident occurred in the course of employment, came to an end. The whole system is based on compromise, and it is from the dilemma of weighing quality against convenience that many of its problems arise.

---

[15] Lord Woolf considers that this remark underestimates the Council's positive role in maintaining the standard of justice: Council on Tribunals, *Annual Report*, 1991–2, 83.   [16] Act of 1992, ss. 5, 8.

[17] For the detail see the 9th edn of this book, pp. 922–4.

[18] Baroness Hale in *Cart* gives a lengthy account at para. 13 of the advantages and disadvantages of tribunals.

An accompanying advantage is that of expertise.[19] Qualified surveyors sit on the Lands Tribunal (now the Upper Tribunal (Lands Chamber))[20] and experts in tax law sit as Special Commissioners of Income Tax (now the First-tier Tribunal (Tax)).[21] Specialised tribunals can deal both more expertly and more rapidly with special classes of cases, whereas in the High Court counsel may take a day or more to explain to the judge how some statutory scheme is designed to operate. Even without technical expertise, a specialised tribunal quickly builds up expertise in its own field. Where there is a continuous flow of claims of a particular class, there is every advantage in a specialised jurisdiction.

But on the other hand, tribunals are subject to a law of evolution which fosters diversity of species. Each one is devised for the purposes of some particular statute and is therefore, so to speak, tailor-made. When any new scheme of social welfare or regulation is introduced the line of least resistance is usually to set up new ad hoc tribunals rather than reorganise those already existing. Uncontrolled growth has produced over fifty different types of tribunal falling within the Tribunals and Inquiries Act 1992. They range from extremely busy tribunals such as those dealing with social security, employment, valuation appeals and rent assessment to tribunals which have no business at all and have therefore never been appointed, such as the mines and quarries tribunals. It is a bewildering kaleidoscope that cries out for the imposition of some systematic reform.

The responsibilities of tribunals are in general no less important than those of courts of law. Large awards of money may be made by tribunals, for example, employment tribunals or in cases of industrial injuries. Mental health review tribunals[22] determine whether a patient ought to be compulsorily detained, and so lose his personal liberty, whereas the administration of his property is a matter for the courts of law.

INDEPENDENCE

An essential feature of tribunals, as mentioned already, is that they make their own decisions independently and are free from political influence. In the abnormal cases where appeal lies only to a minister it is true that the minister's policy may influence the tribunal through the minister's appellate decisions; but then this is what Parliament intended. In all other cases tribunals are completely free from political control, since Parliament has put the power of decision into the hands of the tribunal and of no one else. A decision taken under any sort of external influence would be invalid.[23]

In order to make this independence a reality, it is fundamental that members of tribunals shall be independent persons, not civil servants.[24] Tribunals have more the character of people's courts than of bureaucratic boards. The Lord Chancellor or the relevant minister will appoint the chairmen and members, but people outside the government service will be chosen. Various devices are employed for insulating tribunals from any possibility of influence by ministers. Often there will be a panel system by which the names on the panel are approved by the Lord Chancellor or the minister, but the selection for any one

---

[19] For a discussion of the value of expertise in tribunal members see *Gillies* v. *Secretary of State for Work and Pensions* [2006] UKHL 2, [2006] 1 WLR 781 (speech of Baroness Hale).   [20] Below, p. 788.

[21] Below, p. 788.

[22] The tribunals have power to direct the discharge of the patient. Formerly in criminal cases they could only give advice to the Home Secretary, but this restriction was held to violate Art. 5 of the European Convention on Human Rights (ECHR), which requires access to a court for persons deprived of liberty: *X* v. *UK*, ECtHR Series A, No. 46 (5 November 1981). The restriction was removed by Mental Health (Amendment) Act 1982, s. 28(4), since replaced by Mental Health Act 1983, s. 79.

[23] See above, p. 266.   [24] For two exceptional cases see below, p. 766.

sitting is made by the chairman. The Lord Chancellor is usually made responsible where legal qualifications are required, but he is also sometimes responsible for non-legal members.[25] Rent assessment committees are made up from panels of names supplied both by the Lord Chancellor and by the Secretary of State for the Environment; the chairman must be a 'Lord Chancellor's man', and the other members may or may not be.[26]

The public by no means always gives tribunals credit for their impartiality, often because of minor factors which arouse suspicion. A typical tribunal will have a civil servant as its clerk, who will tell the appellant how to proceed and require him to fill in forms. Where a large number of more or less routine decisions have to be given in rapid succession, it can sometimes appear that the tribunal and the clerk are working hand in glove and in favour of the ministry.

MEMBERSHIP

The personnel of tribunals varies greatly in accordance with the character of their business. A form frequently adopted is the 'balanced tribunal', consisting of an independent chairman, usually legally qualified and appointed by the Lord Chancellor, and two members representing opposed interests. These two members may be chosen from two different panels of persons willing to serve, not themselves in the employment of the ministry but appointed by the minister as representatives of, for example, employers' organisations on one panel and trade unions on the other. Thus an employment tribunal will usually[27] consist of a chairman from a Lord Chancellor's panel, and one member from each of the Secretary of State's panels.[28] Experience has shown that members selected in this way seldom show bias in favour of the interest they are supposed to represent. The principal purpose of the system is to assure every party before the tribunal that at least one member will understand his interests. In tribunals of this kind the chairman will usually be paid, but the members will sometimes be unpaid, giving their time as a public service in the same way as magistrates.

In other cases expert qualifications are indispensable. The law which tribunals have to apply is often of great complexity, sometimes to a degree which perplexes the courts themselves,[29] and tribunals such as social security tribunals, employment tribunals, the Lands Tribunal and taxation tribunals may be confronted with formidable legal problems.

[25] The Qualifications for Appointment of Members to the First-tier Tribunal and Upper Tribunal Order 2008 (SI 2008/2692), Art. 2 empowers the Lord Chancellor to appoint medical practitioners, nurses, surveyors, accountants etc. to the First-tier and Upper Tribunals.

[26] Rent Act 1977, 10th Sched. (now applicable only in Wales). The powers of the rent assessment committees have been transferred to the First-tier Tribunal: Transfer of Tribunal Functions Order 2013 (SI 2013/1036).

[27] With the consent of the parties the chairman and one other member may comprise the tribunal (Employment Tribunals Act 1996, s. 4(1)); and on some, primarily legal, questions the chairman alone comprises the tribunal (s. 4(2), (3), (5) and (6)).

[28] In *Smith* v. *Secretary of State for Trade and Industry* [2000] IRLR 6, 69, the question was raised whether employment tribunals were 'independent and impartial' as required by Art. 6(1) of the ECHR (above, p. 377), especially when hearing claims made against the Secretary of State. The court remitted the case so that this question could be argued. See, however, *Ilangaratne* v. *British Medical Association* (CA, 23 November 2000) holding Employment Appeal Tribunals Art. 6(1) compliant.

[29] See e.g. *R* v. *Industrial Injuries Commissioner ex p Cable* [1968] 1 QB 729 (difficulties of the 'paired organ' regulations in industrial injury cases); *R* v. *National Insurance Commissioner ex p Hudson* [1972] AC 944.

Many tribunals are organised on a presidential system, the president being the chief adjudicator and also having general responsibility for the working of the tribunals (including the production of annual reports).[30] Tribunals' clerks have an important function and can much assist parties by explaining procedure and other matters. In most cases they are civil servants supplied by the ministry under which the tribunal falls. In some areas the administration of the tribunal system has been transferred to an executive agency.[31]

THE 2007 REFORMS

The 2007 Act was preceded by the Leggatt Report[32] and a White Paper[33] that accepted many of its recommendations. The Act may be seen as the culmination and full implementation of the much delayed legal view adopted by the Franks Committee (described above). It recognises unequivocally that tribunals do not form part of the administration; they form part of the machinery of adjudication. Thus all formal links with the 'sponsoring department' (the department that generated the disputes that the tribunal had to decide) are severed. And tribunals emerge as a fully fledged part of the judicial system. The reforms have been described by Lord Justice Sedley as a 'complete reordering of administrative justice'.[34]

INDEPENDENCE AND IMPARTIALITY

Thus the 'guarantee of continued judicial independence' contained in section 3 of the Constitutional Reform Act 2005[35] is extended to most tribunal members.[36] Furthermore, the White Paper accepted that 'in a modern democratic society it is no longer acceptable for judicial appointments to be entirely in the hands of a government minister. Therefore we intend to build upon the principles behind the establishment of a Judicial Appointments Commission and to place under the remit of the Commission the responsibility for recommending candidates for appointment to all tribunal panels.'[37] Members of the new tribunals created by the 2007 Act are appointed by the Senior President of Tribunals [38] or by Her Majesty (Upper Tribunal) (on the recommendation of the Lord

---

[30] Which are collated into Senior President of Tribunals Report. Recent Reports are available at <http://www.judiciary.gov.uk/publications-and-reports/reports/Tribunals/?WBCMODE=PresentationUnpu.rss>

[31] *Annual Report*, 1997–8, 4, criticising the proposed Appeals Agency in the social security field.

[32] The Report was commissioned by the Lord Chancellor *inter alia* to review whether 'fair, timely, proportionate and effective arrangements' were in place for handling tribunal disputes and whether they encouraged 'the systematic development of the area of law concerned' forming 'a coherent structure...for the delivery of administrative justice'. Sir Andrew Leggatt was also asked to review whether the arrangements 'meet the requirements of the European Convention on Human Rights for independence and impartiality'. The Report is available on-line (see <http://www.tribunals-review.org.uk/>).

[33] *Transforming Public Services: Complaints, Redress and Tribunals* (Cm. 6243 (2004)). As its name indicates, the White Paper was directed at the whole administrative justice system and indeed had as a goal 'moving out of courts and tribunals disputes that could be resolved elsewhere' with encouraging words for alternative dispute resolution, mediation and ombudsmen etc.). Here we focus on reforms to tribunals. There was also a Consultation Paper by the Ministry of Justice on the implementation of the 2007 Act (*Transforming Tribunals* (see <http://www.justice.gov.uk/news/cp3007.htm>)).

[34] *R (Cart)* v. *Upper Tribunal* [2010] EWCA Civ 859, para. 29.   [35] Discussed above, p. 515.

[36] Act of 2007, s. 1.   [37] para. 6.48.

[38] Act of 2007, Sched. 2 as amended by the Crime and Courts Act 2013, Sched. 13, Pt IV, para. 45. Under the unamended legislation this task was that of the Lord Chancellor.

Chancellor).[39] And, transitional provisions aside, appointments to these offices will be only after the Judicial Appointments Commission has made its recommendations. There is thus no remnant of appointment by a minister from the 'sponsoring department'. And it is now commonplace, in the statute book and elsewhere, for legally qualified tribunal members to be referred to as 'judges'. Tribunal members must take the oath of allegiance and the judicial oath.[40]

But, as described above, perceptions of independence were undermined when tribunals sat within the department and were serviced by clerks drawn from the department that was the respondent in many of the matters on which the tribunal adjudicated. The 2007 Act imposes upon the Lord Chancellor the duty of providing an 'efficient and effective system of support' for tribunals.[41] This extends to engaging staff to carry out the administrative tasks of tribunals and the acquisition of property in which tribunal hearings can be held. Her Majesty's Courts and Tribunals Service has been established as an executive agency in the Ministry of Justice.[42] Once more any link with the department which generates the disputes upon which a tribunal adjudicates is severed.[43]

Furthermore, the office of Senior President of Tribunals is created. This is a senior judicial office[44] held by a judge who may 'lay before Parliament' representations on matters concerning tribunal members and the 'administration of justice by tribunals'.[45] He is also now responsible for the appointment of First-tier Tribunal members.[46]

He is responsible 'for representing the views of tribunal members to Parliament, to the Lord Chancellor and to Ministers of the Crown generally'.[47] He reports annually to the Lord Chancellor.[48] The Senior President presides over both the First-tier Tribunal and the Upper Tribunal[49] and he assigns the members of these tribunals to the chambers in which they will serve.[50] He has the power to issue practice directions.[51] He is responsible 'within the resources made available by the Lord Chancellor for making arrangements for the training, and welfare of judges and other members of the First-tier Tribunal'.[52] He is obliged in carrying out his functions to 'have regard to' the need for tribunals to

---

[39] Act of 2007, Sched. 3.

[40] Act of 2007, Sched. 2, para. 9. The oaths are administered by the Senior President or his delegate.

[41] Act of 2007, s. 39.   [42] For executive agencies, see above, p. 37.

[43] A concern of the Leggatt Report was that breaking the channels of communication between the department and the tribunals would be to the detriment of decision-making in the department (Richardson and Genn, as below, 124; Leggatt Report, ch. 9).

[44] The Senior President is appointed by Her Majesty on the recommendation of the Lord Chancellor. There are two routes to appointment. Where there is agreement between the Lord Chancellor, the Lord Chief Justice of England and Wales, the Lord President of the Court of Session, the Lord Chief Justice of Northern Ireland on an eligible person for appointment that appointment 'must' be made (see Act of 2007, Sched. 1, Pt 1). The alternative route is for the Lord Chancellor to seek a recommendation from the Judicial Appointments Committee (who set up an eminent panel for the purpose) (Act of 2007, s. 2 and Sched. 1 (adding s. 75A–G to the Constitutional Reform Act 2005)).

[45] Act of 2007, Sched. 1, para. 13. The Reports are available here: <http://www.judiciary.gov.uk/publications-and-reports/reports/Tribunals/?WBCMODE=PresentationUnpu.rss>.

[46] Act of 2007, Sched. 2, para. 1 as amended by the Crime and Courts Act 2013.

[47] Act of 2007, Sched. 1, para. 14.

[48] Act of 2007, s. 43. The report covers 'in relation to relevant tribunal cases' matters which the Lord Chancellor has requested should be included and matters on which the Senior President wishes to report. The Lord Chancellor must publish the report.   [49] Act of 2007, s. 3(4).

[50] Act of 2007, Sched. 4, Pt 2.

[51] Act of 2007, s. 23 (but only with the approval of the Lord Chancellor).

[52] Act of 2007, Sched. 2, para. 8. His training obligations extend beyond the First-tier Tribunal to the Upper Tribunal, the Employment Tribunal and the Employment Appeal Tribunal (Act of 2007, Sched. 3, para. 9).

be accessible, for tribunal proceedings to be fair, quick and efficient and for the members of tribunals to have appropriate expertise.[53] He also has to have regard to 'innovative methods of resolving disputes that … may be brought before tribunals'.[54] The first Senior President of Tribunals is Lord Justice Carnwath and his successor is Lord Justice Sullivan.

Thus the tribunals system emerges de jure and de facto as independent from the administration and in particular from the 'sponsoring department' of the tribunal. At their apex, tribunals now have a powerful officer with the ability to make the voice of tribunals heard to Parliament and elsewhere unmediated by the view of the administration.

THE FIRST-TIER TRIBUNAL AND THE UPPER TRIBUNAL (THE '2007 ACT TRIBUNALS')

But the Act is concerned with much more than the independence and impartiality of tribunals; it seeks to impose a 'system' on the maze of diverse tribunals. The first such step is the creation of the First-tier Tribunal and the Upper Tribunal.[55] Each of these tribunals may be organised into several chambers, each with the Chamber President who presides over that chamber.[56]

The Lord Chancellor may by Order transfer to either the First-tier Tribunal or the Upper Tribunal the functions of any 'scheduled tribunal' (these are specified in schedule 6 and include most tribunals concerned with disputes arising out of central government departments).[57] The Lord Chancellor or the Senior President may with the concurrence of the other then allocate the functions of the First-tier Tribunal and the Upper Tribunal between chambers.[58]

The First-tier Tribunal is divided into seven chambers.[59] These are: (a) social entitlement (e.g. social security benefits, criminal injuries compensation, asylum support); (b) general regulatory (e.g. regulation of gambling, charities, claims management services, estate agents, information, transport etc.); (c) war pensions and armed forces compensation; (d) health, education and social care (e.g. mental health, special educational needs, care standards); (e) taxation (e.g. VAT and direct taxes); (f) property (e.g. leasehold valuation tribunals, land registration appeals); and (g) Immigration and Asylum. There are plans for a specialist planning tribunal.[60]

The Upper Tribunal chambers are:[61] (i) administrative appeals (appeals on law from first-tier chambers (a), (b), (c) and (d)); (ii) tax and chancery (appeals from first-tier tax chamber, and first-instance jurisdiction in complex tax cases; appeals from financial regulators); (iii) lands (compensation for compulsory acquisition, land valuation, land

---

[53] Act of 2007, s. 2(3).   [54] Ibid.

[55] The two 2007 Act tribunals came into existence on 3 November 2008.

[56] The organisation into chambers is effected by the Lord Chancellor with the concurrence of the Senior President (s. 7(1)). Chamber Presidents are appointed by the Lord Chancellor after consultation (s. 7(7) and Sched. 4) or they may be appointed after the Judicial Appointments Commission has made a recommendation (Sched. 8, para. 66). There is also provision for Deputy Chamber Presidents.   [57] s. 30(1).

[58] s. 7(9).

[59] See First Tier Tribunal and Upper Tribunal (Chambers) Order 2010 (SI 2010/2655), Art. 2. See also Sir Robert Carnwath, 'Tribunal Justice—Judicial Review by Another Route' in Forsyth, Elliott, Jhaveri, Ramsden and Scully Hill (eds.), Effective Judicial Review: A Cornerstone of Good Governance (2009) (hereinafter Carnwath), especially notes to para. 11. Also published as 'Tribunal Justice—A New Start' [2009] PL 48. Later reports of the Senior President (with more detail) are at <http://www.judiciary.gov.uk/publications-and-reports/reports/Tribunals/?WBCMODE=presentationun>.   [60] Above, p. 567.

[61] See First Tier Tribunal and Upper Tribunal (Chambers) Order 2010 (SI 2010/2655), Arts. 9–13, setting out the names and functions of the different Chambers.

registration); and (iv) immigration and asylum chamber (appeals from the immigration and asylum chamber of the first-tier tribunal).[62]

One important group of tribunals currently remains outside the new system. They are the Employment Tribunals, and the Employment Appeal Tribunal. These will, however, be served by the HM Courts and Tribunals Service and fall under the leadership of the Senior President of Tribunals (who has responsibility for their training).

RIGHTS OF APPEAL AND 'INTERNAL REVIEW'

Under the law as unreformed by the 2007 Act there were numerous different avenues of appeal from tribunals. No right of appeal exists unless conferred by statute,[63] but Parliament, though it has created many appellate procedures, had followed no consistent pattern. Appeal might lie from one tribunal to another; from a tribunal to a minister; from a tribunal to a court of law; from a minister to a court of law; from a minister to a tribunal; or no appeal may lie at all. An appeal may be on questions of law or fact or both. Lord Woolf aptly castigated the various avenues as a 'hotch-potch'[64] and the Leggatt Report recommended simplification.[65]

This simplification has now been largely delivered by the 2007 Act. In general[66] there is a right to appeal on 'any point of law' from a decision of the First-tier Tribunal to the Upper Tribunal, but only with the permission of either the First-tier Tribunal or the Upper Tribunal.[67] From the Upper Tribunal there is a further appeal to the Court of Appeal on 'any point of law' but only with the permission of the Upper Tribunal or the Court of Appeal.[68] The meaning of 'any point of law' is discussed elsewhere.[69]

An important innovation in the 2007 Act is the formal institution of the 'internal review'. Once a tribunal has announced its decision it has, as a general rule, no power to reconsider it or to reopen the case. However, both the First-tier Tribunal[70] and the Upper Tribunal[71] are given the power to review a decision either on their own motion or on application of a person who has a right of appeal against the decision. On this review the tribunal may correct accidental errors, amend the reasons given or set the decision aside. It may then make the decision again.[72] The statute does not specify the grounds on which the tribunal may set the decision aside[73] but the decided cases make it clear that the statute's purpose is to 'allow the First-tier Tribunal to avoid the need for an appeal to the Upper Tribunal in the case of clear errors'.[74] This innovation provides a swift and cheap alternative to an appeal in the case of such errors but the finality of judicial decisions

---

[62] See Transfer of Functions of the Asylum and Immigration Tribunal Order 2010 (2010/21).

[63] *A-G* v. *Sillem* (1864) 10 HLC 704; *R* v. *Special Commissioners of Income Tax* (1888) 21 QBD 313 at 319.

[64] (1988) *Civil Justice Quarterly* 44–52.   [65] Paras. 6.9–6.10.

[66] See Appeals (Excluded Decisions) Order 2009 (SI 2009/275), Art. 3, for a list of decisions from which there is no right to appeal from the First-tier Tribunal to the Upper Tribunal.

[67] Act of 2007, s. 11.   [68] Act of 2007, s. 13.   [69] Below, p. 786.   [70] Act of 2007, s. 9.

[71] Act of 2007, s. 10.

[72] The First-tier Tribunal may alternatively refer the matter to the Upper Tribunal for decision.

[73] But the Tribunal Procedure (Upper Tribunal) Rules 2008 (SI 2008 No. 2698) provide (r. 43) that a decision may be set aside where it is in the interests of justice and there has been a procedural irregularity.

[74] See *JS* v. *Secretary of State for Work and Pensions* [2013] UKUT 100, para. 28. A balance must be struck 'between the efficiency of a review power and the proper role of an appeal to the Upper Tribunal' (para. 29). Similarly *R (RB)* v. *First-tier Tribunal* [2010] UKUT 160 and *Scriven* v. *Calthorpe Estates* [2013] UKUT 469. But even in clear cases of simple error the 'error may be a common one and, for that or other reasons, it may be helpful to have an authoritative decision of the Upper Tribunal on the point' *R (RB)* v. *First-tier Tribunal*, para. 27.

(subject only to any appeal) is an important policy that must not be lost sight of. It is not surprising that these rights to 'internal review' are limited to one 'review' and the Tribunal Procedure Committee (described below) may exclude categories of case from 'internal review'.[75]

JUDICIAL REVIEW AND THE 2007 ACT TRIBUNALS

The Upper Tribunal's judicial status is further underlined by its establishment as 'a superior court of record'.[76] But this does not mean that its decisions are not subject to judicial review.[77] Generally speaking though the only remedy available to a litigant dissatisfied with a decision of the Upper Tribunal will be by way of the appeal to the Court of Appeal just described. This is because the Supreme Court has made it clear that judicial review of decision of the Upper Tribunal is only available exceptionally. Although in principle available for any error of law, the only clear example is where the Upper Tribunal has refused leave to appeal.[78] This is a matter on which there is no appeal to the Court of Appeal, so the only remedy available is an application for judicial review of the Upper Tribunal's refusal of permission. The Supreme Court laid down that judicial review would be available provided the so-called 'second-tier appeal criteria' were satisfied, i.e. the criteria that would apply to an appeal to the Court of Appeal from the Upper Tribunal. The criteria were whether judicial review 'would raise an important point of principle or practice; or...there is some other compelling reason for the Court of Appeal to hear it'.[79] If this test was not satisfied permission to apply for judicial review would not be granted.[80]

However, the Upper Tribunal has its own power to grant judicial review. It is given by the 2007 Act the power to award the prerogative and other remedies available in an application for judicial review;[81] and those remedies are to be granted on judicial review principles and are enforceable as if they were made in judicial review proceedings.[82] Before hearing such an application, the tribunal must first grant permission. The Upper Tribunal may only exercise these powers if certain conditions are met and where those conditions are not met the tribunal must transfer the application to the High Court.[83] The conditions are mostly formal: the relief sought must fall within the powers of the tribunal, it must not call into question anything done in the Crown Court and the judge hearing the matter must be a High Court judge.[84] The substantive (third) condition is that the application must fall into a class of application specified by the Lord Chief Justice (or his agreed nominee).[85] Significantly, when an application is made in the High Court for judicial

---

[75] s. 9(10) and s. 9 (3).   [76] Act of 2007, s. 3(5).

[77] See above, p. 255. And see *Cart*, below, paras. 30–1 and 86–7.

[78] *R (Cart)* v. *Upper Tribunal* [2011] UKSC 28, paras. 30–1 and 86–7.

[79] Access to Justice Act 1999, s. 55.   [80] Such *Cart* judicial reviews discussed above, p. 222.

[81] Act of 2007, s. 15(1). This relates to prerogative relief as well as injunctions and declarations (see above, p. 550). In addition, the Upper Tribunal may grant damages, restitution or a sum due if the High Court in a judicial review application has such power (s. 16(6)). The tribunal also has a power similar to that of the judicial review court to make a substitutionary order (s. 17). For discussion of such orders, see above, p. 555. See *LS* v. *London Borough of Lambeth* [2010] UKUT 461, where the UT recognised that its judicial review jurisdiction was 'far more limited' than its appellate jurisdiction over the FTT (para. 82).

[82] Act of 2007, s. 15(4) and (5).   [83] Act of 2007, s. 18(3).

[84] Act of 2007, s. 18(4), (5) and (8) (the Chief Justices and the Senior President may agree on alternatives).

[85] Act of 2007, s. 18(6) subjecting the giving of directions pursuant to the process set out in the Constitutional Reform Act 2005, Sched. 2, Pt 1. The Practice Direction (Upper Tribunal: Judicial Review Jurisdiction) [2009] 1 WLR 327 specifies the following types of application: (a) any decision of the First-tier Tribunal on an appeal made in the exercise of a right conferred by the Criminal Injuries Compensation Scheme; (b) any decision of the First-tier Tribunal made under Tribunal Procedure Rules

review then, if certain conditions are met, the High Court must transfer the application to the Upper Tribunal.[86] If all the conditions are met save that the application is not in a class specified by the Lord Chief Justice (condition 3), the High Court may, if it considers it 'just and convenient', order the transfer to the tribunal.[87] The upshot is that the 2007 Act fashions for the Upper Tribunal a relatively exclusive judicial review jurisdiction.[88]

One effect of these somewhat convoluted provisions will be to preclude judicial review before the Administrative Court of decisions of the First-tier Tribunal.[89] But more significant will be the emergence of the Upper Tribunal as a powerful and expert tribunal with a jurisdiction to match that of the Administrative Court. It will give guidance not only on questions of law but also on a wide range of matters touching the administration of administrative justice.[90] The 2007 Act has brought system and order into the structure of administrative justice; the Upper Tribunal may achieve a similar systematisation of the principles of administrative justice.

THE ADMINISTRATIVE JUSTICE AND TRIBUNALS COUNCIL

The Council on Tribunals, as described above, is, after fifty years of service, abolished;[91] and in its stead the Administrative Justice and Tribunals Council is established.[92] But the new council lasted barely six years before it too was abolished in a 'bonfire of the quangoes'.[93] There is no replacement body. The old council did much good work (as recognised by the Leggatt Report)[94] but it was handicapped by its weak political position and its scanty resources. The new council, which had new and wider responsibilities, was intended to emerge, as the Leggatt Report envisaged, 'as the hub of the wheel of administrative justice' championing the cause of users of tribunals.[95] But many of the weaknesses of the old council remained; the AJTC proved too weak to avoid abolition notwithstanding the good work that it did in its short life.[96]

---

or s. 9 of the 2007 Act where there is no right of appeal to the Upper Tribunal and that decision is not an excluded decision within paragraph (b), (c) or (f) of s. 11(5) of the 2007 Act. See also Practice Direction (Upper Tribunal: Judicial Review Jurisdiction) (No. 2) [2012] 1 WLR 16, which specifies the following type of application: 'applications calling into question a decision of the Secretary of State not to treat submissions as an asylum claim or a human rights claim within the meaning of Pt 5 of the Nationality, Immigration and Asylum Act 2002 wholly or partly on the basis that they are not significantly different from material that has previously been considered'.

[86] Act of 2007, s. 19 inserting a new s. 31A into the Senior Courts Act 1981.

[87] Act of 1981, s. 31A(3). See R (Independent Schools Council) v. Charity Commission for England and Wales [2010] EWHC 2604, para. 8 for the exercise of this power.

[88] The Upper Tribunal has no power to make a declaration of incompatibility under the Human Rights Act 1998 (s. 4(5)).

[89] The availability of the alternative remedy of an appeal to the Upper Tribunal would, save where fairness requires otherwise, usually preclude judicial review. Above, p. 600. The Leggatt Report recommended that judicial review should be excluded by an ouster clause (para. 6.34).

[90] See Carnwath 2008, generally, but especially at paras. 48–53.   [91] Act of 2007, s. 45.

[92] Act of 2007, s. 44 and Sched. 7.

[93] See the Public Bodies (Abolition of the Administrative Justice Tribunals Council) Order 2013 (SI 2013/2042).   [94] Paras. 7.45–7.51.

[95] Paras. 7.45–7.51.

[96] The Justice Select Committee (see Eighth Report 2012–13 HC 965) (available at <http://www.publications.parliament.uk/pa/cm201213/cmselect/cmjust/965/965.pdf>) and the Public Administration Committee (see 21st Report 2010–12) (available at <http://www.publications.parliament.uk/pa/cm201012/cmselect/cmpubadm/1621/1621.pdf>) both criticised the abolition of the AJTC.

TRIBUNAL PROCEDURE COMMITTEE

The 2007 Act makes provision for tribunal procedure rules for both the First-tier Tribunal and the Upper Tribunal.[97] These are to be made by the Tribunal Procedure Committee and allowed by the Lord Chancellor.[98] The Committee is made up of some nine members appointed or nominated by the Senior President (who may serve himself), the Lord Chancellor, the Lord President of the Court of Session and the Lord Chief Justice.[99] The Committee must make the rules with a view to ensuring that proceedings before the tribunals is 'accessible and fair' and 'handled quickly and efficiently'. The rules have to be 'both simple and simply expressed' and must allocate responsibility to the members for ensuring that 'proceedings before the tribunal are handled quickly and efficiently'.[100]

The following points about the Upper Tribunal Rules may be noted. Their 'overriding objective' is to enable the tribunal 'to deal with cases fairly and justly'. This means that the rules must deal with a case in ways that 'are proportionate to the importance of the case, the complexity of the issues, the anticipated costs and the resources of the parties'. Also that matters should be dealt with flexibly and without 'unnecessary formality' and that delay should be avoided 'so far as compatible with proper consideration of the issues'.[101] These worthy goals probably mean that the Tribunal will be expected to manage the proceedings more effectively. The judge will not be passive but will intervene to secure efficient decisions. A less adversarial and more inquisitorial procedure is implied.[102] Consistent with this more efficient approach decisions may be made without an oral hearing.[103]

MEDIATION

As will be recalled, the White Paper gave encouragement to alternative forms of dispute resolution including mediation.[104] And, moreover, the Senior President of Tribunals in exercising his functions (including the making of practice directions) was to have regard to 'innovative methods' of resolving disputes.[105] Unsurprisingly, therefore, the 2007 Act envisages that practice directions and procedural rules might be made that make provision for mediation in both the First-tier and the Upper Tribunal.[106] It is envisaged that the member of the Tribunal may act as mediator.[107] But mediation may only take place with the consent of the parties and the failure of mediation is to have no effect on the outcome of the proceedings.[108] The Senior President of Tribunals reports (in 2013) that although judicial mediation is a popular method of dispute resolution in the employment tribunals, it has been less successful in the First-tier Tribunals generally.[109]

---

[97] Act of 2007, s. 22 and Sched. 5.   [98] Act of 2007, Sched.5, para. 28.

[99] The detail will be found in Sched.5, Pt 2.   [100] Act of 2007, s. 22(4).

[101] r. 2(1). The overriding objective also requires that parties should be able to participate in the proceedings and that the special expertise of the tribunal should be used.

[102] But note that Sir Robert Carnwath (Carnwath 2008, as above, para. 21) considers that the 2007 Act is 'neutral' on the question whether procedure should be inquisitorial or adversarial.

[103] r. 34. But the Tribunal must consider (the written) views of any party on this issue. For discussion of oral tribunal hearings, see [2007] PL 116 (Richardson and Genn). For discussion of when fairness requires an oral hearing, see above, p. 436. The Upper Tribunal may not dispense with a hearing in immigration judicial review cases (r. 34(3)).   [104] Above, p. 768.

[105] Above, p. 770.

[106] Act of 2007, s. 24. See now Tribunal Procedure (Upper Tribunal) Rules 2008 (SI 2008/2698), r. 3 (UT should, where appropriate, seek 'to bring to the attention of the parties the availability of any appropriate alternative procedure for the resolution of the dispute' and to 'facilitate' that procedure).

[107] s. 24(5).   [108] s. 24(1).

[109] The Senior President of Tribunals 2013 Annual Report will be found at <http://www.judiciary.gov.uk/Resources/JCO/Documents/Reports/SPT%20Annual%20Report_2013.pdf>. See p. 30 (mediation has failed

PROCEDURE OF TRIBUNALS

The Tribunal Procedure Committee has since its establishment made rules for the tribunals within the several chambers of the First-tier and the Upper-tier Tribunals.[110] Obviously the rules will form the primary source of guidance for the procedure to be adopted by tribunals. But issues of general principle still arise and are dealt with in this section referring to past decisions and procedural rules as appropriate.

ARTICLE 6(1) OF THE HUMAN RIGHTS CONVENTION

Since tribunals often determine 'civil rights and obligations',[111] Article 6(1) requiring 'a fair and public hearing' before 'an independent and impartial tribunal' will generally be applicable. Since the coming into force of the Human Rights Act 1998 it is necessary to ensure that there is compliance with Article 6(1). Compliance with Article 6(1), including the curative effect of access to a court of 'full jurisdiction' is discussed elsewhere.[112]

ADVERSARIAL OR INQUISITORIAL PROCEDURE

Procedure before a tribunal in the past has generally been considered adversarial and not inquisitorial.[113] As Sir Andrew Leggatt stated in his Report it 'is certainly possible for tribunal proceedings to be conducted in [an inquisitorial] manner, and we have seen examples in Australia.[114] But none of those we have observed in this country can be described as inquisitorial.'[115]

On the other hand Baroness Hale has said that 'the process of benefits adjudication is inquisitorial rather than adversarial'[116] pointing out that there is no *lis inter partes* between claimant and the officer who makes the initial decision. This is significant support for an inquisitorial procedure before some tribunals but will doubtless not extend to tribunals which do resolve disputes between individuals (for instance, employment tribunals).[117] But even where the department and the claimant should cooperate in

to take hold in Social Entitlement Chamber because DWP has no power to settle disputes) and p. 55 (judicial mediation 'continues to be a popular facility offered by the Employment Tribunal'). The use of mediation is being actively promoted by the Health, Education and Social Care Chamber: see p. 45 of the 2011 Annual Report: <http://www.judiciary.gov.uk/Resources/JCO/Documents/Reports/spt-annual-report-2011.pdf>.

[110] Up-to-date versions of the Rules are available at <http://www.justice.gov.uk/tribunals/rules>. The Upper Tribunal has a harmonised body of Rules for all Chambers except the Lands Chamber.

[111] Above, pp. 449 and 451 noting inconsistencies in the application of Art. 61 to social security payments.

[112] Above, p. 452. The Leggatt Report (para. 2.17) recommends that no distinction be drawn between tribunals to which Art. 6(1) applies and those to which it does not. Given its status as a court of record, access to the Upper Tier Tribunals will presumably often serve as access to a court of 'full jurisdiction'.

[113] This was recognised in the Leggatt Report, paras. 7.3–7.5. And see the 9th edn of this book, p. 928.

[114] For discussion of the Australian procedures see Carnwath 2008, as above, para. 20.

[115] Ibid.

[116] *Kerr* v. *Department for Social Development (Northern Ireland)* [2004] UKHL 23, [2004] 1 WLR 1372, para. 61 relying on Diplock LJ's judgment in *R* v. *Medical Appeal Tribunal (North Midland Region) ex p Hubble* [1958] 2 QB 228. If such an approach is adopted, said Baroness Hale, 'it will rarely be necessary to resort to concepts taken from adversarial litigation such as the burden of proof' (para. 63). In *Amos* v. *Home Secretary* [2011] EWCA Civ 552, para. 42 Stanley Burton LJ restricted this approach to social security cases. Similarly *Novitskaya* v. *London Borough of Brent* [2009] EWCA Civ 1260, para. 25 (Arden LJ).

[117] See *HM (Iraq)* v. *Home Secretary* [2012] UKUT 409, para. 22: individual asylum and immigration appeals are an 'adversarial process'; when it is deciding a Country Guidance issue 'the Tribunal must be sure so far as possible that it has considered all relevant material. Thus it must have an inquisitorial role.'

determining the claimant's eligibility, does it follow that tribunal proceedings in which the department's decision is challenged are inquisitorial? And once it is recognised that a dispute has arisen then, in the common law tradition, a relatively adversarial procedure is implied.

This is consistent with the integration of tribunals into the judicial system as ordained by the 2007 Act. A tribunal should have both sides of the case presented to it and should judge between them, without itself having to conduct an inquiry of its own motion, enter into the controversy, and call evidence for or against either party. If the tribunal allows itself to become involved in the investigation and argument, parties may lose confidence in its impartiality, however fair-minded it may be.

Naturally this does not mean that the tribunal should not tactfully assist an applicant to develop his case, particularly when he has no representative to speak for him,[118] just as a judge will do with an unrepresented litigant. And this may require a more inquisitorial role.[119] Moreover, as noted above, the 2007 Act reforms also imply a less passive tribunal to ensure that all cases are dealt with justly and fairly; and a shift toward a less adversarial procedure may be anticipated. But '[a] balance has to be struck as to what an inquisitorial Tribunal should, and should not, do in order to guide an unrepresented claimant'.[120]

Finally, tribunals concerned with financial business are often given investigatory functions. Two examples are the Financial Services and Markets Tribunal (now part of the First-tier Tribunal),[121] and the Insolvency Practitioners Tribunal.[122]

PROCEDURAL RULES

Tribunal procedures ought to be simple and not legalistic, but this ideal is difficult to attain when the statutes and regulations to be applied are complex, as they are most conspicuously in the field of social security.[123] The Council on Tribunals' 'Model Rules of Procedure for Tribunals' which have been much admired will doubtless continue to exert a beneficial influence.[124]

---

[118] Legal aid is seldom available for proceedings before tribunals and the unrepresented applicant is common.

[119] See *Mongan* v. *Department for Social Development* [2005] NICA 16, para. 18 ('A poorly represented party should not be placed at any greater disadvantage than an unrepresented party' per Kerr LCJ).

[120] *R (Nicholas)* v. *Upper Tribunal* [2012] EWHC 2724, para. 46 (confirmed on appeal: [2013] EWCA Civ 799). The High Court refused to interfere with the Tribunal's decision not to adjourn a case (with an unrepresented claimant) on its own motion in order to obtain further information. Cf. *OR* v. *London Borough of Ealing* [2012] UKUT 211 where is was said that a First-tier Tribunal has in such cases (special educational needs) 'a duty to act inquisitorially when the occasion arises by making sure they have the basic information to decide the appeal before them' (para. 38).

[121] Financial Services and Markets Act 2000, s. 132. See the Transfer of Tribunal Functions Order 2010 (SI 2010/22), Art. 2(2).

[122] Insolvency Act 1986, s. 396, Sched. 7, criticised by the Council on Tribunals. *Annual Report* 1985–6, para. 4.19. Another example, for which there are special reasons, is the tribunal established by the Regulation of Investigatory Powers Act 2000, s. 65 (with which the Council on Tribunals is not concerned).

[123] See the Tribunal Procedure (First-tier Tribunal) (Social Entitlement Chamber) Rules 2008 (SI 2008/2685), for a taste of the complexity and technicality.

[124] Cm. 1434 (1991). The Model Rules are more than mere rules; the notes on each rule contain much useful discussion of the law applicable and the pitfalls that may attend the application of the rule. The Council has been advised that 'with limited exceptions' the Model Rules are compatible with the Human Rights Convention.

HEARINGS— EVIDENCE—PRECEDENT

The great majority of tribunals give oral hearings, and may have a legal duty to do so.[125] But there are some exceptions and under the 2007 Act paper 'hearings' are likely to grow in numbers. Procedural rules will frequently empower a tribunal 'to make a decision without a hearing'.[126] Statutory rules of procedure also commonly provide for the right to call, examine and cross-examine witnesses.

A statutory tribunal is not normally bound by the legal rules of evidence. It may therefore receive hearsay evidence (and the procedural rules often so provide),[127] provided always that the party affected is given a fair opportunity to contest it, as natural justice requires.[128] Thus in an industrial injury case the commissioner was entitled to receive evidence at the hearing about previous medical reports which technically would have been inadmissible as hearsay.[129] Even a court of law, when acting in an administrative capacity in hearing licensing appeals, is not bound by the legal rules;[130] for otherwise it might have to decide on different evidence from that which was before the licensing officer. Nor need a tribunal's decision be based exclusively on the evidence given before it: it may rely on its own general knowledge and experience, since one of the reasons for specialised tribunals is that they may be able to do so.[131] But this does not entitle it to make use of its members' specialised knowledge,[132] or an independent expert's report,[133] without disclosing it so that the parties can comment. An appeal tribunal may refuse to receive evidence not given in the proceedings at first instance.[134] But the Upper Tribunal Procedure Rules make

[125] See R v. Immigration Tribunal ex p Mehmet [1977] 1 WLR 795. But see Jussila v. Finland (2007) 45 EHRR 39 where the ECtHR said that 'the obligation to hold a hearing is not absolute. There may be proceedings in which an oral hearing may not be required: for example where there are no issues of credibility or contested facts which necessitate a hearing and the courts may fairly and reasonably decide the case on the basis of the parties' submissions and other written materials' (para. 41). See the discussion of oral hearings in Ch. 14 above, p. 436.

[126] Tribunal Procedure (Upper Tribunal) Rules 2008 (SI 2008/2698), r. 34.

[127] See Tribunal Procedure (Upper Tribunal) Rules 2008 (SI 2008/2698), r. 15(2) (Upper Tribunal may admit evidence 'whether or not the evidence would be admissible in a civil trial in the United Kingdom').

[128] R v. Hull Prison Visitors ex p St Germain (No 2) [1979] 1 WLR 1401 (prisoners' punishments quashed for failure to allow them to call witnesses to contravene hearsay evidence). Where hearsay is properly before the decision-maker, the court, on an application for judicial review or habeas corpus, may consider the same evidence after making appropriate allowance: R v. Home Secretary ex p Rahman [1998] QB 136 (CA). '[N]o inherent objection to a Tribunal accepting hearsay evidence': JP v. South London and Maudsley NHS Foundation Trust [2012] UKUT 486, para. 38. FTT decision made in reliance on hearsay not set aside).

[129] R v. Deputy Industrial Injuries Commissioner ex p Moore [1965] 1 QB 456.

[130] Kavanagh v. Chief Constable of Devon and Cornwall [1974] QB 624 (licensing of firearms); R v. Aylesbury Crown Court ex p Farrer, The Times, 9 March 1988 (similar); R v. Licensing Justices of East Gwent ex p Chief Constable of Gwent [1999] 164 JP 339 (public house).

[131] R v. City of Westminster Assessment Committee ex p Grosvenor House (Park Lane) Ltd [1941] 1 KB 53; R v. Brighton and Area Rent Tribunal ex p Marine Parade Estates (1936) Ltd [1950] 2 KB 410; Crofton Investment Trust Ltd v. Greater London Investment Committee [1967] 1 QB 955; Metropolitan Properties Ltd v. Lannon [1969] 1 QB 577. See [1975] PL 65 (J. A. Smillie). Dugdale v. Kraft Foods (below) and Queensway Housing Association Ltd v. Chiltern, Thames and Eastern Rent Assessment Committee (1998) 31 HLR 945.

[132] Hammington v. Berker Sportcraft Ltd [1980] ICR 248; Dagg v. Lovett [1980] Est. Gaz. Dig. 27; Dugdale v. Kraft Foods Ltd [1976] 1 WLR 1288. See now Bristol CC v. Alford Two LLP [2011] UKUT 130.

[133] R v. City of Westminster Assessment Committee (above); R v. Deputy Industrial Injuries Commissioner ex p Jones (below, n. 158); and see above, p. 430.

[134] National Graphical Association v. Howard [1985] ICR 97. An immigration adjudicator has no power to take account of facts occurring after the Secretary of State's initial decision: R v. Immigration Appeal

provision for the admission of evidence 'whether or not that evidence was available to a previous decision-maker'.[135]

Tribunals are now generally equipped with compulsory powers to summon witnesses and to order production of documents.[136] In the case of employment tribunals disobedience is a punishable offence[137] and in the case of the Lands Tribunal it may be penalised in costs.[138] In other cases a party may be able to use a High Court subpoena, as explained below.

A statutory tribunal has inherent power to control its own procedure.[139] It has power to require evidence to be given on oath,[140] but most tribunal proceedings are conducted informally without requiring witnesses to be sworn.[141]

Pre-hearing assessments or reviews are provided for in the rules of some tribunals, so that the nature of the case can be assessed in advance and time saved at the hearing itself.[142]

In the use of its own precedents a tribunal is, as explained earlier,[143] in a radically different position from a court of law. Its duty is to reach the right decision in the circumstances of the moment, any discretion must be genuinely exercised, and there must be no blind following of its previous decisions. This does not mean that discretion cannot be exercised according to some reasonable and consistent principle. Nor does it mean that no regard may be had to previous decisions. It is most desirable that the principles followed by tribunals should be known to the public, and for this purpose selected decisions of the more important tribunals are published.[144]

Tribunal ex p Weerasuriya [1983] 1 All ER 195; nor may he or the appeal tribunal take account of facts existing but unknown at the time of that decision: *R v. Immigration Appeal Tribunal ex p Nashouki*, The Times, 17 October 1985. See also *Brady* v. *Group Lotus Car plc* [1987] 2 All ER 674 (tax case remitted to special commissioners; new evidence not admissible).

[135] Tribunal Procedure (Upper Tribunal) Rules 2008 (SI 2008/2698), r. 15(2); see also r. 15(2A) (notification procedure in immigration or asylum cases of intention to use evidence that was not made available to the FTT).

[136] Tribunal Procedure (Upper Tribunal) Rules 2008 (SI 2008/2698), r. 16. An employment tribunal had no power to order interrogatories or the production of a Schedule of facts where there was no documentation on which to base the Schedule: *Carrington* v. *Helix Lighting Ltd* [1990] ICR 125.

[137] Employment Tribunals Act 1996, s. 7(3), (4).   [138] SI 1996 No. 1022, reg. 46.

[139] The Tribunal Procedure (Upper Tribunal) Rules 2008 (SI 2008/2698), r. 5(1) provides 'Subject to the provisions of the 2007 Act and any other enactment, the Tribunal may regulate its own procedure.' See also *R (V)* v. *Asylum and Immigration Tribunal* [2009] EWHC 1902: tribunal possesses all those 'powers that can properly be implied into the statutory scheme on the usual principles of statutory interpretation' (para. 28).

[140] The Evidence Act 1851, s. 16, confers this power on every person authorised by law or by consent of parties to receive evidence. See *General Medical Council* v. *Spackman* [1943] AC 627 at 638 (Lord Atkin), correcting *Board of Education* v. *Rice* (above, p. 479). The Act was also overlooked in *R v. Fulham etc Rent Tribunal ex p Zerek* [1951] 2 KB 1 at 7.

[141] See the Franks Report, Cmnd 218 (1957), para. 91. Tribunal Procedure (Upper Tribunal) Rules 2008 (SI 2008/2698), r. 15(3) provides that the UT 'may consent to a witness giving, or require any witness to give, evidence on oath'. NB SI 1983/942 has been repealed.

[142] Employment Tribunals (Constitution and Procedure) Regulations 2013/1237, rr. 53–4 (power to order preliminary hearing) and Tribunal Procedure (Upper Tribunal) (Lands Chamber) Rules 2010/2600, r. 5(3)(f) (power to hold a hearing concerning any matter).

[143] Above, p. 272. Approved in the Leggatt Report, para. 6.17.

[144] Mostly now in electronic form, including on BAILII.

SITTINGS—PUBLICITY—MEMBERSHIP

Tribunals being part of the machinery of justice, they ought in principle to sit in public.[145] But where tribunals have to inquire into intimate personal circumstances, private sittings are naturally preferred by most applicants and tribunal rules provide accordingly.[146] Tribunals which sit in private are the General and Special Commissioners of Income Tax (now absorbed into the First-tier Tribunal and Upper Tribunal structure),[147] Betting Levy Appeal Tribunals,[148] Mental Health Review Tribunals (now transferred to the First-tier Tribunal),[149] Service Committees of Health Authorities in the National Health Service, and social security adjudicating authorities where the claimant so requests or where, in a hearing by a Commissioner, intimate personal circumstances or public security are involved.[150] On an appeal to the High Court the right of privacy is lost, as may be seen from the details of tax cases and supplementary benefit cases in the law reports.

Many applications, particularly if of a preliminary or subsidiary character, may be disposed of without any sitting at all: the papers may be circulated to the members, who may express their opinions in writing to the chairman.[151] The majority of social security cases, including appeals to a Commissioner, are in practice disposed of in this way.[152]

Where a tribunal consists of a fixed number of members it is necessary that all should participate;[153] but if timely objection is not made it may be held to have been waived.[154] In one case of ambiguity the statute was construed as creating, in effect, a panel, so that a lesser number sufficed.[155] The same members who heard the evidence must give the decision.[156] Where a tribunal has power to use an assessor, and does so at an oral hearing, the assessor must sit with the tribunal throughout that part of the hearing in which the evidence is given on which his assistance is required.[157] Legal directions to an assessor should be given in open court and the assessor's findings (if in the nature of expert evidence) should be disclosed to the parties.[158]

Administrative or investigatory functions are another matter: all the members of a board or committee need not then participate.[159]

---

[145] Tribunal Procedure (Upper Tribunal) Rules 2008 (SI 2008/2698), r. 37. The starting point is that all hearings must be held in public (r. 37(1)) but the UT has a discretion to hold hearings in private (r. 37(2)). For exceptions in the FTT see Tribunal Procedure (First-tier Tribunal) (Health, Education and Social Care Chamber) Rules 2008 (SI 2008/2699), r. 26(2) (SEN and disability discrimination) and Tribunal Procedure (First-tier Tribunal) (Social Entitlement Chamber) Rules 2008 (SI 2008/2685) r. 26(2) (criminal injuries compensation).

[146] Art. 6(1) does not insist on public hearings where 'the interests of morals, public order or national security,...the interests of juveniles...the protection of the private lives of the parties [or] the interests of justice' require otherwise. See above, p. 408.

[147] Though the Taxes Management Act 1970, s. 50, so provides only by implication.

[148] Unless the appellant requests otherwise: SI 1963 No. 748, r. 7.

[149] SI 1983 No. 942, r. 21 (the tribunal may direct otherwise). See *R (Mersey Care NHS Trust)* v. *Mental Health Review Tribunal* [2004] EWHC 1749, [2005] 1 WLR 2469 (now extant only in Wales).

[150] SI 1999 No. 1495, reg. 24(5) hearing in public in absence of 'special reasons'. Commissioner's functions now transferred to the UT: Transfer of Tribunal Functions Order 2008 (SI 2008/2833), Art. 3 and Sched. 1.

[151] See *Howard* v. *Borneman (No 2)* [1975] Ch 201 (determination of prima facie case of tax avoidance) (upheld on appeal [1976] AC 301). [152] Above, p. 776.

[153] *R* v. *Race Relations Board ex p Selvarajan* [1975] 1 WLR 1686 at 1695.

[154] *Turner* v. *Allison* [1971] NZLR 833.

[155] *Howard* v. *Borneman* (above). As to non-members see above, p. 259.

[156] *Irish Land Commission* v. *Hession* [1978] ICR 297.

[157] *R* v. *Deputy Industrial Injuries Commissioner ex p Jones* [1962] 2 QB 677.

[158] *Ahmed* v. *University of Oxford* [2002] EWCA Civ 1907, para. 33.

[159] *R* v. *Race Relations Board ex p Selvarajan* (above).

A tribunal may itself make an inspection, e.g. of a site or building, though it should do so with the knowledge of the parties[160] and preferably in their presence.[161] It must always be careful not to take evidence without disclosing it to all of them,[162] and it must remember that to make an inspection is to take evidence.[163] These matters are now generally governed by procedure rules.[164]

CONTEMPT OF COURT—SUBPOENA

The High Court will sometimes use its own inherent powers in order to aid and protect inferior courts which do not themselves possess the power to punish for contempt of court. The High Court's powers at common law, however, did not extend to the protection of tribunals.[165] Thus the House of Lords has held that a local valuation court (a tribunal subject to the supervision of the Council on Tribunals), although acting judicially, discharged administrative functions and was not a court of law.[166] The House, therefore, refused to intervene where it was claimed that a religious sect's application for exemption from rates before the local valuation court would be prejudiced by a television programme about the sect. Only where a tribunal is expressly given the status of a court, like the Transport Tribunal, the Employment Appeal Tribunal, the Iron and Steel Arbitration Tribunal,[167] and now the Upper Tribunal, which is established as 'a superior court of record',[168] or where it has a distinct legal status,[169] will it qualify for the protection of the High Court at common law.[170] In other cases a tribunal will have no such protection. If its proceedings are disrupted by misconduct, that is a matter for the criminal law.[171] If they are subjected to prejudicial comment, that is within the right of free speech.[172] Procedure rules provide for the exclusion from the hearing of disruptive persons.[173]

The Contempt of Court Act 1981, however, provides that for the purposes of the Act 'court' 'includes any tribunal or body exercising the judicial power of the State'.[174] The

---

[160] *Hickmott* v. *Dorset CC* (1977) 35 P & CR 195.

[161] See *Salsbury* v. *Woodland* [1970] 1 QB 324. Rent Assessment Committees may make inspections at any stage of the proceedings but must allow the parties to attend: SI 1971 No. 1065, reg. 7.

[162] See above, p. 428, also *Wilcox* v. *HGS* [1976] ICR 306.

[163] *Gould* v. *Evans & Co* [1951] 2 TLR 1189 applied *R (Broxbourne BC)* v. *North and East Hertfordshire Magistrates Court* [2009] EWHC 965, paras. 60–5.

[164] See e.g. the Tribunal Procedure (First-tier Tribunal) (Property Chamber) Rules 2013, r. 21 (express power) and Tribunal Procedure (First-tier Tribunal) (Health, Education and Social Care Chamber) Rules 2008 (SI 2008/2699), r. 7(3)(f) (implied).

[165] There is likewise no protection for commissions or committees of inquiry: *Badry* v. *Director of Public Prosecutions* [1983] 2 AC 297.

[166] *A-G* v. *British Broadcasting Corporation* [1981] AC 303 at 339–40 (Lord Dilhorne). Lord Salmon reserved the question whether the High Court might protect such tribunals in case of obstruction of their proceedings. But the majority held that protection was not available at all. For comment see [1982] PL 418 (N. V. Lowe and H. F. Rawlings) and D. Eady and A. T. H. Smith, *Arlidge, Eady and Smith on Contempt*, 2nd edn (1999), 818–27. [167] Made courts of record by their constituent statutes.

[168] Above, p. 255. Act of 2007, s. 25 (UT may exercise all the privileges of the High Court in relation to (a) the attendance and examination of witnesses, (b) the production and inspection of documents and (c) all other matters incidental to its functions.

[169] As the Lands Tribunal used (somewhat questionably) to have, until incorporated into the First-tier Tribunal structure. [170] See the *BBC* case at 338 (Lord Dilhorne).

[171] Ibid. at 362 (Lord Scarman). [172] Ibid. at 342 (Lord Salmon).

[173] The Tribunal Procedure (First-tier Tribunal) (Health, Education and Social Care Chamber) Rules 2008 (SI 2008/2699), r. 26(4) and Tribunal Procedure (Upper Tribunal) Rules 2008 (SI 2008/2698), r. 37(4).

[174] s. 19. Other statutes sometimes make provisions for a particular tribunal (Data Protection Act 1998, Sched. 6, para. 8 (Information Tribunal)).

Act expressly confers limited contempt powers upon magistrates but none upon tribunals.[175] Nonetheless, the House of Lords has held that a Mental Health Review Tribunal was a 'court' and protected by the law of contempt.[176] But this was because these tribunals have power to order the release of patients;[177] and deciding on the liberty of the subject must be the task of a court. An employment tribunal has also been held to be a court.[178] Whether the same result will be reached when the tribunal determines less important rights remains to be seen.[179]

The High Court's powers are available to tribunals on a more generous basis for the purpose of enforcing the attendance of witnesses and the production of documents by subpoena. High Court subpoenas are obtainable without restriction by parties appearing before tribunals, so that they have the same facilities for this purpose as before courts of law.[180] In principle subpoenas are available in aid of any tribunal discharging judicial or quasi-judicial functions, for example a police disciplinary hearing.[181] The recipient of a subpoena may apply to the court for it to be set aside and he has a right of appeal to the court.

IMMUNITY AND PRIVILEGE

Whether members of tribunals, and parties and witnesses who appear before them, are entitled to the same personal immunities as apply in courts of law is a doubtful question.[182] The problem of the liability of members will rarely arise; the only tribunals with power to affect personal liberty are immigration tribunals and mental health review tribunals (both now absorbed into the First-tier Tribunal), and members of the latter are given statutory protection while acting in good faith and with reasonable care.[183] It has been held in New Zealand that a witness at a tribunal may claim the usual privilege against self-incrimination, provided that it does not stultify the statutory scheme.[184] But where a professional body's rules exclude the privilege, it is waived on joining.[185]

Witnesses before tribunals appear to enjoy absolute privilege, so that they cannot be made personally liable if their evidence is defamatory. This follows a fortiori from the House of Lords' decision that witnesses at inquiries enjoy this protection.[186]

---

[175] s. 12.

[176] *Pickering* v. *Liverpool Daily Post and Echo Newspapers plc* [1991] 2 AC 370, overruling *A-G* v. *Associated Newspaper Group plc* [1989] 1 WLR 322. An additional ground for the decision was that s. 12(1)(b) of the Administration of Justice Act 1960 implied that it was contempt to publish information concerning the Mental Health Review Tribunal's proceedings.

[177] Prior to the Mental Health Act 1983 the tribunals could only recommend release.

[178] *Peach Grey & Co* v. *Sommers* [1995] 2 All ER 513. *South London & Maudsley NHS Trust* v. *Dathi* [2008] IRLR 350 (EAT), para. 21. And *Vidler* v. *Unison* 1999 ICR 746.

[179] The Professional Conduct Committee of the General Medical Council, although statutory, does not exercise 'the judicial power of the state': *General Medical Council* v. *BBC* [1998] 1 WLR 1573. Similarly, *Subramanian* v. *GMC* [2002] UKPC 64, paras. 11–12. The reasoning in the *Peach Grey* case (above), however, was that since the employment tribunal 'sat in public, was established by Parliament, allowed legal representation, administered oaths, compelled attendance, gave reasons and awarded costs', it was a court, is potentially applicable to many tribunals. In *Re Ewing* [2002] All ER (D) 350 the Information Tribunal, however, was found to be a court for the purpose of the Senior Courts Act 1981, s. 42 (vexatious litigants).

[180] *Soul* v. *Inland Revenue Commissioners* [1963] 1 WLR 112.

[181] *Currie* v. *Chief Constable of Surrey* [1982] 1 WLR 215. Contrast *Re Sterritt* [1980] N. Ireland Bulletin No. 11 (police complaint investigation: subpoenas set aside).　　　　[182] For which see above, p. 671.

[183] Mental Health Act 1983, s. 139. Actions may be brought only with leave of the High Court. See *Winch* v. *Jones* [1986] QB 296.　　　　[184] *Taylor* v. *New Zealand Poultry Board* [1984] 1 NZLR 394.

[185] *R* v. *Institute of Chartered Accountants ex p Nawaz* [1997] COD 111.　　　　[186] See below, p. 811.

LEGAL REPRESENTATION—LEGAL AID—COSTS—FEES

As a general rule, any party before a tribunal may be represented by a lawyer or by anyone else. Whether this is a legal right is not at all clear. It is not certain that it is covered by the principles of natural justice.[187] In practice the position is that representation is freely permitted except in rare cases where it is restricted by regulation. The procedural rules of many tribunals give an unrestricted right of representation. Rule 11 of the Rules of the Upper Tribunal provide that a party may appoint a representative (who may be a legal representative) in the proceedings. Representation by an experienced trade union representative or social worker may often be the most effective, and this is very common before social security tribunals and comparable bodies.[188]

Representation is restricted before service committees of family health services authorities in the National Health Service, in order that patients making complaints against their doctors are not confronted with a professional lawyer defending the doctor. But a barrister or solicitor, if unpaid, may assist a party in the capacity of a friend.[189]

In courts of law there is a legal right for a party appearing in person to have the assistance of someone to give advice and take notes,[190] and this right presumably applies equally before tribunals, at any rate when they sit in public.

With legal aid (representation as opposed to advice and assistance) the starting point is that legal aid is not available.[191] But there are exceptions to this principle and the prominent ones may be listed:[192] FTT proceedings under the Mental Health Act 1983, FTT proceedings under Schedule 2 (detention) to the Immigration Act 1971, FTT proceedings under sections 4 or 4A Children Act 1999, UT proceedings under any of the provisions excepted with regard to FTT proceedings, Judicial review proceedings in the UT brought under section 15 of the Tribunals, Courts and Enforcement Act 2007 and Employment Appeal Tribunal proceedings under the Equality Act 2010.

In practice the proceedings in many tribunals are inexpensive and informal, so that legal representation is often not a necessity. But difficult problems of law and fact are always prone to occur, particularly under complicated regulations. It has often been recommended that legal aid should be provided for those appearing before tribunals,[193] but the thrust of the reforms is to create a 'user friendly' system in which parties can manage without representation.[194] There is little prospect of any extension of legal aid.[195]

---

[187] Above, p. 439.

[188] See [1972] PL 278 (J. E. Alder).   [189] SI 1992 No. 664 (now only in Wales).

[190] McKenzie v. McKenzie [1971] P 33. The right to a 'McKenzie friend' is simply a consequence of the public's right of access to public proceedings; thus where the proceedings are not public (e.g. before a board of prison visitors) the tribunal has a discretion whether to allow the adviser access: R v. Home Secretary ex p Tarrant [1985] QB 251 and R v. Bow County Court ex p Pelling [1999] 1 WLR 1807 (no right of access by 'McKenzie friend' to chambers proceedings but 'normally allowed'). Even where the proceedings are public the courts (and presumably also tribunals) can restrict or exclude the adviser if it is apparent that his assistance is unreasonable or not bona fide or inimical to the proper administration of justice: R v. Leicester City Justices ex p Barrow [1991] 2 QB 260. See [1992] PL 208 (P. A. Thomas). See also Izzo v. Philip Ross & Co, The Times, 9 August 2001 and Djina v. Home Secretary (11 July 2013 IAC), <https://tribunalsdecisions.service. gov.uk/utiac/decisions/aa-00037-2011>(full description of role).

[191] Legal Aid, Sentencing and Punishment of Offenders Act 2012, Sched. 1, Pt 3, para. 1.

[192] Act of 2012, Sched. 1, Pt 3, paras. 9–20.

[193] Council on Tribunals, Annual Report, 1976–7, 6; Legal Aid Advisory Committee's Report, HC 160 (1979–80), 97 (mental health review tribunals); and Royal Commission on Legal Services, Cmnd 7640 (1979), 172. But the Leggatt Report only recommended the 'encouragement' of pro bono representation and that, 'exceptionally', the remit of the Community Legal Service might be extended to 'specific cases or classes of case' (para. 4.22).   [194] See, for instance, the Leggatt Report, para. 7.1.

[195] Note the criticism of the Administrative Justice and Tribunals Council 'Securing Fairness and Redress: Administrative Justice at Risk?' (October 2011)). Available at <http://ajtc.justice.gov.uk/docs/ AJTC_at_risk_(10.11)_web.pdf>.

Parties usually bear their own costs in cases involving expense.[196] The First-tier Tribunal (Property Chamber)[197] has a limited power to make costs orders and usually only makes awards where one party has acted unreasonably.[198] Similarly an employment tribunal will not normally award costs, but may do so against a party who acts unreasonably.[199] And the First-tier Tribunal (Tax Chamber) has similar powers.[200] Under the Litigants in Person (Costs and Expenses) Act 1975 the Lord Chancellor has power[201] to extend the Act to specified tribunals, but this has never been done. If the Act did apply, the costs of litigants in person of preparing the litigation would be recoverable.

Tribunals normally have no power to award interest on delayed payments of compensation.[202] Judges presiding over the Employment Appeal Tribunal have called this a blot on the administration of justice in cases where, for example, redundancy payments have been long delayed.[203] But European law may override and require interest to be paid to secure full compensation.[204]

Many tribunals charge a small fee for the use of their services. But the imposition of large fees undermines that cheapness and accessibility long recognised as important advantages of tribunals over courts.[205] Thus the Council was critical of the decision to impose full cost fees upon the users of leasehold valuation tribunals, and after opposition in Parliament the government agreed to an upper limit of £500.[206] The imposition of full cost fees is particularly objectionable in matters—such as leasehold valuation—which would otherwise fall within the jurisdiction of the county court and be eligible for legal aid.

DECISIONS

The general rule is that a tribunal, like a court of law, may decide by a majority of its members and need not be unanimous.[207] In addition its rules of procedure may provide for majority decisions; but even where they do not, the general rule will apply in the absence of contrary intent in the statute. It has been held that a rent assessment committee may decide by majority in accordance with the general rule.[208] It does not appear to make any

---

[196] No change was recommended by the Leggatt Report, para. 4.20. The Tribunal Procedure (Upper Tribunal) Rules 2008 (SI 2008/2698), r. 10 provides that the UT may not make a costs order, subject to a number of exceptions (such as on appeals from the Tax Chamber of the FTT).

[197] The Lands Tribunal, the Property Chamber's predecessor, had power to award costs in the same way as a court of law: Lands Tribunal Act 1949, s. 3(5).

[198] Tribunal Procedure (First-tier Tribunal) (Property Chamber) Rules 2013 (SI 2013/1169), r. 13.

[199] Employment Tribunals (Constitution and Procedure) Rules 2013 (SI 2013/1237), Sched. 1, para. 76.

[200] Tribunal Procedure (First-tier Tribunal) (Tax Chamber) Rules 2009 (SI 2009/273), r. 10. The power of the VAT Tribunals to award costs was somewhat wider. [201] s. 1.

[202] *Marshall* v. *Southampton Health Authority (No 2)* [1991] ICR 136.

[203] See *Caledonian Mining Co* v. *Bassett* [1987] ICR 425.

[204] *Marshall* v. *Southampton Health Authority* [1994] QB 126 (ECJ), [1994] AC 530 (HL).

[205] The Employment Tribunal and the Employment Appeal Tribunal Fees Order 2013 (SI 2013/1893) has controversially significantly increased the fees in Employment Tribunals (the fee for a single claimant under the new regime will range from £410 to £1,180 if the case proceeds to a full hearing (see Table 3, para. 1, Sched. 2 to the Order)). [206] Housing Act 1996, ss. 83, 86; *Annual Report*, 1995–6, 4–5.

[207] *Picea Holdings Ltd* v. *London Rent Assessment Panel* [1971] 2 QB 216. For the principle see *Grindley* v. *Barker* (1798) 1 B & P 229. If a member dies, the others can still give a majority decision: *R* v. *Greater Manchester Valuation Panel ex p Shell Chemicals Ltd* [1982] QB 255 (local valuation court). If there is no clear majority decision the tribunal may refer the case to a differently constituted tribunal, where that is possible: *R* v. *Industrial Tribunal ex p Cotswold Collotype Ltd* [1979] ICR 190. Similarly, distinguishing *Shell Chemicals*: *R* v. *Dept of Health ex p Bhangeerutty*, The Times, 1 May 1998.

[208] Same case, approving *Atkinson* v. *Brown* [1963] NZLR 755 and referring to *Grindley* v. *Barker* (1798) 1 B & P 229. This is now confirmed by procedural regulations: SI 1980 No. 1700, reg. 8.

difference that the tribunal may be composed of members chosen from panels representative of opposed interests; or that two lay members overrule a legal chairman on a question of law.[209] In two earlier cases it had been held that the decisions of pensions appeal tribunals must be unanimous,[210] but these were treated as special cases and their correctness must be doubted.

As noted above once a tribunal has announced its decision it has, as a general rule, no power to reconsider it or to reopen the case,[211] unless of course its decision is quashed by the High Court.[212] This applies equally where one of the parties later discovers fresh evidence which might well alter the decision, and in such a case the court has no power to assist by quashing.[213] But there may be exceptional power to reopen the case where the tribunal's decision is given in ignorance that something has gone wrong, e.g. that a notice sent to one of the parties has miscarried.[214] But this power must be exercised sparingly and only where the party prejudiced by the mistake has a reasonable excuse.[215] There are also important statutory exceptions. As we have seen the 2007 Act introduces a general power of 'internal review' that will enable the First-tier Tribunal and the Upper Tribunal to set aside earlier decisions in the circumstances specified.[216]

A binding decision by a tribunal is res judicata and cannot be relitigated by the same parties.[217]

REASONS FOR DECISIONS

Perhaps the most important of all the Franks Committee's achievements in the sphere of tribunal procedure is the rule which gives a right to a reasoned decision. Reasoned decisions are not only vital for the purpose of showing the citizen that he is receiving justice: they are also a valuable discipline for the tribunal itself.

The Tribunals and Inquiries Act 1992, replacing similar provisions in the earlier Acts, requires the tribunals listed in the Act

---

[209] As in *President of the Methodist Conference* v. *Parfitt* [1984] ICR 176; but the Court of Appeal reversed them: [1984] QB 368.

[210] *Brain* v. *Minister of Pensions* [1947] KB 625; *Minister of Pensions* v. *Horsey* [1949] 2 KB 526. See also *R (T)* v. *Central and North West London NHS Trust* [2003] EWCA Civ 330 (mental health review tribunal had to reach its decision unanimously).

[211] *Akewushola* v. *Home Secretary* [2000] 1 WLR 2295, followed several times since (e.g. *R (Home Secretary)* v. *Immigration Appeal Tribunal* [2001] QB 1224). An oral decision of an employment tribunal, communicated to the parties but not recorded in a document signed by the chairman (as required by the procedural rules), is a decision of the tribunal and cannot be reopened: *Spring Grove Services Group plc* v. *Hickinbottom* [1990] ICR 111; and see *Guinness (Arthur) Son & Co (Great Britain) Ltd* v. *Green* [1989] ICR 241. Even though an interlocutory order, such as a striking out order, is not a 'decision' by the tribunal in terms of its procedural rules, the chairman of the tribunal has no power to reconsider that order: *Casella London Ltd* v. *Banai* [1990] ICR 215. Cf. *Re Darley's Application* [1997] NI 384. Above, p. 192.

[212] The Administrative Court on judicial review may 'stay' a decision of a tribunal, even after it has been implemented: *R (H)* v. *Ashworth Special Hospital* [2002] EWCA Civ 923, [2003] 1 WLR 127 (CA).

[213] Above, p. 232. See also *Jones* v. *Douglas Ltd* [1979] ICR 278 (new point requiring evidence not entertained by Employment Appeal Tribunal).

[214] But in *R (B)* v. *The Nursing and Midwifery Council* [2012] EWHC 1264 Lang J said that there was at most 'limited power "to correct accidental errors which do not substantially affect the rights of the parties or the decision arrived at" (per Sedley LJ in *Akewushola*)' (para. 35).

[215] *R* v. *Kensington & Chelsea Rent Tribunal ex p MacFarlane* [1974] 1 WLR 1486; and see *Charman* v. *Palmers Ltd* [1979] ICR 335 (power to order rehearing); *Hanks* v. *Ace High Productions Ltd* [1978] ICR 1155.

[216] Above, p. 771.   [217] Above, p. 201.

to furnish a statement, either written or oral, of the reasons for the decision if requested, on or before the giving or notification of the decision, to state the reasons.[218]

A request therefore has to be made before the right to a reasoned decision arises. It has been held that the word 'on' is capable of 'an elastic meaning' in such a context,[219] so that a reasonably prompt request made after receipt of a tribunal's decision ought to satisfy the Act. In fact the policy of the Council on Tribunals was to require that procedural rules for particular tribunals should incorporate an unqualified duty to give reasoned decisions, and this has been done in many cases and will doubtless continue.[220]

One important feature of the Act is the provision that reasons, when given, 'shall be taken to form part of the decision and accordingly to be incorporated in the record'.[221] This is a warrant of parliamentary approval for the court's jurisdiction to quash decisions of tribunals for error on the face of the record. It must, apparently, apply even where the reasons are stated orally, despite the incongruity of an oral 'record'.[222]

The Act contains a number of exceptions from the duty to give reasons. It does not apply to decisions in connection with a scheme or order 'of a legislative and not an executive character'. Reasons may also be withheld or restricted on grounds of national security; and they may be withheld from a person not primarily concerned where to furnish them would be contrary to the interests of any person primarily concerned. Nor does the Act apply where any other Act or regulation governs the giving of reasons. Thus under the Mental Health Act 1959 reasons need not necessarily be given by Mental Health Review Tribunals,[223] for in some cases this may be contrary to the interests of the patient.

In some cases formal and exiguous reasons may be held adequate, as where an immigration officer stated simply that 'I am not satisfied that you are genuinely seeking entry only for this limited period'.[224] But the Master of the Rolls indicated that the court would intervene if it appeared that such a formula was used merely as a 'ritual incantation'. A case of that kind was where the court allowed an appeal from a mental health review tribunal which had merely recited the statutory words which empowered it to refuse to discharge a patient.[225]

The duty to state reasons is now so generally accepted that the Industrial Relations Court held that it applied to an employment tribunal in the same way as it applied to that court itself, since otherwise parties would be deprived of their right of appeal on questions of law.[226] No mention was made of the Tribunals and Inquiries Act or of any need for a request.

---

[218] s. 10. See (1970) 33 *MLR* 154 (M. Akehurst). See *R (Burke)* v. *Broomhead* [2009] EWHC 1855 (s. 10 considered but reasons adequate and intelligible).

[219] *Scott* v. *Scott* [1921] P 107. See also *R* v. *Special Commissioners of Income Tax* (1888) 21 QBD 313.

[220] Under r. 40(3) the Upper Tribunal must give reasons for its decisions. The Procedural Rules of the various Chambers of the FTT now require the Tribunals to provide written reasons. See e.g. Tribunal Procedure (First-tier Tribunal) (Health, Education and Social Care Chamber) Rules 2008 (SI 2008/2699), r. 30(2).

[221] s. 10(6). For this see above, p. 272. Applied *Shared Housing Management Ltd* v. *Lands Tribunal for Scotland*, 2009 SC 109.   [222] See above, p. 272, for this question.

[223] Mental Health Act 1983, s. 78(2)(i) which now applies only in Wales; for England the functions of the Mental Health Review Tribunals have now been transferred to the FTT (Transfer of Tribunal Functions Order 2008 (SI 2008/2833), Sched. 1).

[224] *R* v. *Home Secretary ex p Swati* [1986] 1 WLR 477; *R* v. *Home Secretary ex p Cheblak* [1991] 1 WLR 890.

[225] *Bone* v. *Mental Health Review Tribunal* [1985] 3 All ER 330; and see *R* v. *Mental Health Review Tribunal ex p Clatworthy* [1985] 3 All ER 699; applied *FC* v. *Suffolk CC* [2010] UKUT 368 (AAC) and *RH* v. *South London and Maudsley NHS Trust* [2010] UKUT 32 (AAC).

[226] *Norton Tool Co Ltd* v. *Tewson* [1973] 1 WLR 45. See also *Alexander Machinery (Dudley) Ltd* v. *Crabtree* [1974] ICR 120; *Beardmore* v. *Westinghouse Brake Co* [1976] ICR 49; *Green* v. *Waterhouse* [1977] ICR 759; *Albyn Properties Ltd* v. *Knox* 1977 SC 108; *Cairns (RW) Ltd* v. *Busby Session*, 1985 SLT 493.

The Court of Appeal has emphasised that the statutory duty to give reasons 'is a responsible one and cannot be discharged by the use of vague general words'.[227] It requires, as the High Court has held, 'proper, adequate reasons', being 'reasons which will not only be intelligible but which deal with the substantial points which have been raised'. In the same case the court treated inadequacy of reasons as error on the face of the record, so that an inadequately reasoned decision could be quashed, even if the duty to give reasons was not mandatory.[228]

Sir John Donaldson has said that 'in the absence of reasons it is impossible to determine whether or not there has been an error of law. Failure to give reasons therefore amounts to a denial of justice and is itself an error of law'.[229] Lord Lane CJ, while not wishing to go so far, has held that a statement of reasons must show that the tribunal has considered the point at issue between the parties and must indicate the evidence for its conclusion.[230] Where there is a conflict of evidence, the tribunal ought to state its findings.[231]

As explained earlier, the duty to state reasons is normally held to be mandatory, so that a decision not supported by adequate reasons will be quashed or remitted to the deciding authority.[232]

APPEALS ON QUESTIONS OF LAW AND DISCRETION

APPEAL ON A POINT OF LAW

Where statute gives a right of appeal from a tribunal to a court of law, it is usually confined to a right of appeal on a point of law. The wide extension of this right as part of the reform of the tribunal system has already been noted.[233] It is of great importance that it should be generally available, so that the courts may give guidance on the proper interpretation of the law and so that there may not be inconsistent rulings by tribunals in different localities.[234] It is through appeals that the courts and the tribunals are kept in touch, so that the tribunals are integrated into the machinery of justice. Difficult questions of law can if necessary be carried to the appellate courts, and thus they may reach the House of Lords.[235]

As we have seen[236] there is a right to appeal on 'any point of law' from a decision of the First-tier Tribunal to the Upper Tribunal and from the Upper Tribunal to the Court of Appeal on the same ground. The Tribunals and Inquiries Act 1992[237] gives a right of appeal to a party 'dissatisfied in point of law' with a decision of one of the tribunals specified, and

---

[227] Elliott v. Southwark LBC [1976] 1 WLR 499. See similarly Dagg v. Lovett [1980] Est Gaz Dig 27. The duty was described in detail in R (W) v. National Care Standards Commission [2003] EWHC 621, para. 36.

[228] Re Poyser and Mills' Arbitration [1964] 2 QB 467 (vague reasoning concerning dilapidations not remedied: decision quashed). See likewise R v. Industrial Injuries Commissioner ex p Howarth (1968) 4 KIR 621 (ambiguous reasons: decision quashed); Elliott v. University Computing Co [1977] ICR 147 (adequate findings required). [229] In the Alexander Machinery case (above) at 122.

[230] R v. Immigration Appeal Tribunal ex p Khan (Mahmud) [1983] QB 790. It is sufficient if the adjudicator's reasons tell the applicant 'why he lost on the particular issue': R (Bahrami) v. Immigration Appeal Tribunal [2003] EWHC 1453. [231] Levy v. Marrable & Co Ltd [1984] ICR 583.

[232] Above, p. 188. [233] Above, p. 769.

[234] See Pearlman v. Harrow School Governors [1979] QB 56. And see (2012) 71 CLJ 298 (Elliott and Thomas) on proportionate dispute resolution balancing administrative convenience and the rule of law.

[235] Supplementary benefit appeals reached the House of Lords in Supplementary Benefits Commission v. Jull [1981] AC 1025. [236] Above, p. 771.

[237] s. 11. See Esso Petroleum Co Ltd v. Ministry of Labour [1969] 1 QB 98 at 110 for a suggested but questionable restriction on raising new points of appeal.

the party may appeal to the High Court, or require a case to be stated to the High Court, as rules of court may provide. In fact the rules of court provide for both procedures.[238]

Since appellate courts are concerned almost exclusively with questions of law, there should be little difference in practice between an unrestricted right of appeal and a right of appeal on a point of law only. But the definition of 'law' for this purpose is liable to be narrowed artificially, so that many questions of legal interpretation which appellate courts can suitably resolve are not regarded as questions of law and are therefore not appealable. As explained above,[239] the breadth of a right of appeal may bear on whether there is compliance with Article 6(1) of the Human Rights Convention.

WHAT IS 'LAW'?

Questions of law must be distinguished from questions of fact, but this has always been one of the situations where the rules have taken different forms under judicial manipulation.[240] The House of Lords has made determined efforts to clarify them, but two rival doctrines are still contending for supremacy. Much of the tension may be resolved with the emerging doctrine that to make a material error of fact may be to make an error of law.[241] Thus an appeal on a point of law will include an appeal on the ground that the decision-maker unfairly made an error of fact.

The simpler and more logical doctrine has been recognised in many judgments.[242] This is that matters of fact are the primary facts of the particular case which have to be established before the law can be applied, the 'facts which are observed by the witnesses and proved by testimony',[243] to which should be added any facts of common knowledge of which the court will take notice without proof. Whether these facts, once established, satisfy some legal definition or requirement must be a question of law, for the question then is how to interpret and apply the law to those established facts.[244] If the question is whether some building is a 'house' within the meaning of the Housing Acts, its location, condition, purpose of use, and so forth are questions of fact. But once these facts are established, the question whether it counts as a house within the meaning of the Act is a question of law.[245] The facts themselves not being in dispute, the conclusion is a matter of legal inference.

It follows that such questions as 'is the building a house?', or 'did the defendant cause the accident?' cannot be characterised as questions of fact or questions of law without knowing what is in issue. If the question is whether the defendant's act was part of the chain of events, that is a question of fact. But if the question is whether it was sufficiently proximate to amount in law to the real cause, that is a question of law.[246] Where both

---

[238] CPR 52.19. See *Hoser v. Minister of Town and Country Planning* [1963] Ch 428.

[239] Above, p. 382.

[240] See Emery and Smythe, *Judicial Review*, chs. 2, 3; (1982) 98 *LQR* 587 (E. Mureinik); (1984) 4 *OJLS* 22 (J. Beatson); (1987) 104 *LQR* 264 (C. T. Emery); (1984) 100 *LQR* 612 (C. T. Emery and B. Smythe); (1998) 114 *LQR* 292 (T. Endicott).   [241] Above, p. 230.

[242] One of the earliest and clearest is *Johnstone v. Sutton* (1785) 1 TR 510 at 545 (Lords Mansfield and Loughborough): 'The question of probable cause is a mixed proposition of law and fact. Whether the circumstances alleged to show it probable, or not probable, are true and existed, is a matter of fact; but whether, supposing them true, they amount to a probable cause, is a question of law'. Other examples are cited below.

[243] *Bracegirdle v. Oxley* [1947] KB 349 (Denning J).   [244] See below, p. 790.

[245] *Re Butler* [1939] 1 KB 570; *Quiltotex Co Ltd v. Minister of Housing and Local Government* [1966] 1 QB 704; *Lake v. Bennett* [1970] 1 QB 663; *Tandon v. Trustees of Spurgeon's Homes* [1982] AC 755; *R v. Camden LBC ex p Rowton Ltd* (1983) 82 LGR 614.

[246] On causation see *Hoveringham Gravels Ltd v. Secretary of State for the Environment* [1975] QB 754.

questions are in dispute the question is sometimes called a mixed question of law and fact, or a question of mixed law and fact. The former expression is the more accurate, since law and fact are two different things which ought not to be mixed. As Sir John Donaldson MR has said, 'the appeal tribunal has no jurisdiction to consider any question of mixed fact and law until it has purified or distilled the mixture and extracted a question of pure law'.[247]

According to this analysis, an appeal on a point of law should be available on every question of legal interpretation arising after the primary facts have been established. It ought to cover all legal inferences of the kind mentioned above. But although judges have frequently acted upon this principle, and still do so, the reigning rule today is more sophisticated and less logical. It is designed to give greater latitude to tribunals where there is room for difference of opinion.

The orthodox rule is, in effect, that the application of a legal definition or principle to ascertained facts is erroneous in point of law only if the conclusion reached by the tribunal is unreasonable. If it is within the range of interpretations within which different persons might reasonably reach different conclusions, the court will hold that there is no error of law. In his above-quoted judgment the Master of the Rolls thus explained the limited function of the appellate court or tribunal:

> Unpalatable though it may be on occasion, it must loyally accept the conclusions of fact with which it is presented and, accepting those conclusions, it must be satisfied that there *must* have been a misdirection on a question of law before it can intervene. Unless the direction of law has been expressed it can only be so satisfied if, in its opinion, no reasonable tribunal, properly directing itself on the relevant questions of law, could have reached the conclusions under appeal. This is a heavy burden on the appellant.

An alternative but substantially similar doctrine is that 'the meaning of an ordinary word in the English language is not a question of law', unless the tribunal's interpretation is unreasonable; but that where the word is used 'in an unusual sense' the appellate court will determine the meaning.[248]

Moreover, the emergence of specialised (and more independent) tribunals has increased the latitude allowed to them. The House of Lords has said that the decision of 'an expert tribunal charged with administering a complex area of law in challenging circumstances...should be respected unless it is quite clear that they have misdirected themselves in law'. These remarks have a 'wider significance' in that they adumbrate the development of 'a flexible approach to the dividing line between fact and law' in the jurisprudence of specialist tribunals as now discussed.[249]

The malleability of the distinction between law and fact has recently come to the fore with a decision of the Supreme Court discussed elsewhere.[250] In this case the Supreme

---

[247] *O'Kelly* v. *Trusthouse Forte plc* [1984] QB 90. In fact the Court of Appeal followed *Edwards* v. *Bairstow* (below), holding that the Employment Appeal Tribunal was not entitled to interfere with an employment tribunal's reasonable findings on whether applicants were 'employees' under a 'contract of employment'. *O'Kelly* was applied in *MT, RB and U (Algeria)* v. *Home Secretary* [2007] EWCA Civ 808, paras. 96 and 109 (question of whether there was a 'sufficient risk' of torture was an 'undifferentiated finding of fact, for the fact-finding tribunal to determine').

[248] *Cozens* v. *Brutus* [1973] AC 854 at 861 (Lord Reid), not followed in *ACT Construction Ltd* v. *Customs & Excise Cmrs* [1979] 1 WLR 870, affirmed [1981] 1 WLR 1542. Compare *Inland Revenue Commissioners* v. *Lysaght* [1928] AC 235 at 246 and 247.

[249] *AA (Uganda)* v. *Home Secretary* [2008] EWCA Civ 579, Carnwath LJ at para. 47 relying on *Moyna* v. *Secretary of State* [2003] UKHL 44, para. 20, *Beynon* v. *Customs & Excise* [2004] UKHL 53, para. 27 and *Serco* v. *Lawson* [2006] UKHL 3.

[250] *R (Jones)* v. *First-tier Tribunal* [2013] UKSC 19; discussed above, p. 216.

Court considered whether the First-tier Tribunal had erred in law when deciding that a particular road accident did not amount to a 'crime of violence' under the Criminal Injuries Compensation Scheme 2001; the Supreme Court upheld the tribunal adopting, consistent with the earlier discussion, a deferential attitude to the decision of the First-tier Tribunal, Lord Hope, for instance, remarking 'that judicial restraint should be exercised when the reasons that a tribunal gives for its decision are being examined. The appellate court should not assume too readily that the tribunal misdirected itself just because not every step in its reasoning is fully set out in it.'[251] But Lord Carnwath remarked in words quoted earlier that it was for the tribunals to develop a 'pragmatic approach...to the dividing line between law and fact, so that the expertise of tribunals at the first tier and that of the Upper Tribunal can be used to best effect. An appeal court should not venture too readily into this area by classifying issues as issues of law which are really best left for determination by the specialist appellate tribunals.'[252]

This pragmatic approach has its attractions and may prove to be influential. It is not unprecedented and it enables the expertise of the tribunals to be given full effect. But it has nothing to do with what is law and what is fact.

The truth is that in the past there has hardly been a subject on which the courts have acted with such total lack of consistency as the difference between fact and law. The House of Lords has indeed laid down the rule explained in the following paragraphs, but it is commonplace to find courts proceeding in complete disregard of it. It may be that judges instinctively agree with an American comment:[253]

> No two terms of legal science have rendered better service than 'law' and 'fact'... They are the creations of centuries. What judge has not found refuge in them? The man who could succeed in defining them would be a public enemy.

EARLIER LEADING CASES ON 'LAW'

The House of Lords has expounded the law in two tax cases, where appeal lay from the inland revenue commissioners to the High Court only on a point of law.[254] But these cases must be read subject to the Supreme Court decision just discussed. The question was whether

---

[251] Para. 25.

[252] Paras. 16 and 47, relying on *Moyna* and *Serco*, above. See also Carnwath, 'Tribunal Justice—A New Start' [2009] *PL* 48, 63–4.

[253] Leon Green, *Judge and Jury*, 270. And see Lord Hoffmann in *Serco Ltd* v. *Lawson* [2006] UKHL 3, para. 34; 'Whether one characterizes this as a question of fact depends...upon whether as a matter of policy one thinks that it is a decision which an appellate body with jurisdiction limited to errors of law should be able to review.'

[254] There is another more recent House of Lords decision in which the question was whether a disabled person was entitled to an element of disability living allowance on the ground that she 'cannot prepare a cooked main meal for [herself] if [she] has the ingredients' (Social Security Contributions and Benefits Act 1992, s. 72). The appeal tribunal decided that the disabled person did not satisfy this test. Did it thereby make an error of law justifying further appeal? Lord Hoffmann said: 'There is a good deal of high authority for saying that the question of whether the facts as found or admitted fall one side or the other of some conceptual line drawn by the law is a question of fact: see, for example, *Edwards* v. *Bairstow* [1956] AC 14 and *O'Kelly* v. *Trusthouse Forte plc* [1984] QB 90. What this means in practice is that an appellate court with jurisdiction to entertain appeals only on questions of law will not hear an appeal against such a decision unless it falls outside the bounds of reasonable judgment'(*Moyna* v. *Secretary of State for Work and Pensions* [2003] UKHL 44, [2003] 1 WLR 1929, para. 25).

transactions amounted to 'trade' for tax purposes. In the first case[255] there had been a pur-chase and sale of machinery as an isolated transaction, and the facts themselves were not in dispute. All the lower courts nevertheless held that the question whether this amounted legally to 'trade' was 'purely a question of fact'. The House of Lords held that it was a question of law, since on the particular facts no reasonable person could fail to conclude that the transaction was 'trade' within the meaning of the Act. Lord Radcliffe said:

> If the Case contains anything ex facie which is bad law and which bears on the determi-nation, it is, obviously, erroneous in point of law. But without any such misconception appearing ex facie, it may be that the facts found are such that no person acting judicially and properly instructed as to the relevant law could have come to the determination under appeal. In these circumstances, too, the court must intervene. It has no option but to assume that there has been some misconception of the law, and that this has been respon-sible for the determination. So there too, there has been an error in point of law. I do not think it much matters whether this state of affairs is described as one in which there is no evidence to support the determination, or as one in which the evidence is inconsist-ent with, and contradictory of, the determination, or as one in which the true and only reasonable conclusion contradicts the determination. Rightly understood, each phrase propounds the same test. For my part, I prefer the last of the three.

Lord Radcliffe emphasised, however, that there were many combinations of circum-stances in which it could not be said to be wrong to arrive at a conclusion one way or the other on the same facts. And he added:

> All these cases in which the facts warrant a determination either way can be described as questions of degree and, therefore, as questions of fact.

This last statement is the basis of the expression 'questions of fact and degree'[256] which is often applied to conclusions which fall within the permitted range of reasonableness and which the court holds to be ineligible for appeal on a point of law.

In the second case,[257] where the House of Lords held that on the facts it could not rea-sonably be concluded that there was 'trade', Lord Wilberforce similarly said:

> Sometimes the question whether an activity is to be found to be a trade becomes a matter of degree, of frequency, of organisation, even of intention, and in such cases it is for the fact-finding body to decide on the evidence whether a line is passed. The present is not such a case: it involves the question as one of recognition whether the characteristics of trade are sufficiently present.

Lord Simon also explained how the facts may fall into three categories: if they plainly amount to trade, or plainly do not, the court must reverse any decision to the contrary as erroneous in law; but between these extremes is the third category which depends on the evaluation of the facts, and is suitably called one of 'fact and degree'.

---

[255] *Edwards* v. *Bairstow* [1956] AC 14 applied *Shaw (Inspector of Taxes)* v. *Vicky Construction Ltd*, The Times, 27 December 2002; approved *AA (Uganda)* v. *Home Secretary* [2008] EWCA Civ 579, para. 52 (Carnwath LJ). See (1946) 62 *LQR* 248, (1955) 71 *LQR* 467 (A. Farnsworth).

[256] See e.g. *Birmingham Cpn* v. *Habib Ullah* [1964] 1 QB 178; *Marriott* v. *Oxford & District Co-operative Society Ltd* [1969] 1 WLR 254; *Global Plant Ltd* v. *Secretary of State for Health and Social Security* [1972] 1 QB 139. Earlier decisions equating questions of degree with questions of fact are *Currie* v. *IRC* [1921] 2 KB 332; *Inland Revenue Commissioners* v. *Lysaght* [1928] AC 234.

[257] *Ransom* v. *Higgs* [1974] 1 WLR 1594. See also *Taylor* v. *Good* [1974] 1 WLR 556; *Central Electricity Generating Board* v. *Clwyd County Council* [1976] 1 WLR 151; *Furniss* v. *Dawson* [1984] AC 474.

LOGIC VERSUS LEGAL POLICY

The House of Lords' third or intermediate category, as defined above, may be vulnerable to logical analysis in that, once the facts of the case are established, the application to them of some legal definition or test is in its nature a matter of law. Law and fact are two different things, and a question of law should not become one of fact merely because it is one on which opinions may reasonably differ. Questions of degree are not 'therefore' questions of fact. In one case, where the question was whether there had been a 'transfer' of a business, two industrial tribunals (now employment tribunals) came to different con-clusions on the same established facts: one of them must therefore have erred in law, and the court naturally entertained an appeal on 'law'.[258] Citing this in a similar case, Lord Denning MR held that if a tribunal drew a wrong conclusion from the primary facts, thus misinterpreting the statute, they went wrong in law.[259] The House of Lords' doctrine that the error must be one which a reasonable tribunal could not make is frequently disre-garded,[260] and judges willingly revert to the simpler and more logical doctrine as stated in a typical income tax case of 1915 by Lord Parker:[261]

> My Lords, it may not always be easy to distinguish between questions of fact and ques-tions of law...The views from time to time expressed in this House have been far from unanimous, but in my humble judgment where all the material facts are fully found, and the only question is whether the facts are such as to bring the case within the provisions properly construed of some statutory enactment, the question is one of law only.

The House of Lords' 'fact and degree' doctrine, on the other hand, provides a more toler-ant and flexible rule for appeals than would exist under a rigid dichotomy where the court was obliged to substitute its own opinion in every borderline case of legal interpreta-tion. Courts are in any case reluctant to reverse the conclusions of expert tribunals on matters falling peculiarly within their province,[262] for example where an employment tribunal has to apply the complicated classification of industrial operations.[263] The prin-ciple expounded by Lord Radcliffe, as quoted above, has obvious affinities both with the doctrine of reasonableness[264] and with the doctrine of review for 'no evidence'.[265] Here, as elsewhere, the courts have been working towards a broad power to review unjustifiable decisions while always leaving to the administrative authority or tribunal a reasonable margin of error. American administrative law has taken a similar direction in evolving the substantial evidence rule for testing the reasonableness of findings of fact and the 'rea-sonable basis' rule for testing determinations of law.[266] The Upper Tribunal has said that an 'appeal court should be slow to interfere with a multi-factorial assessment based on

---

[258] *Huggins* v. *Gordon (AJ) Ltd* (1971) 6 ITR 164.

[259] *Woodhouse* v. *Brotherhood Ltd* [1972] 2 QB 520 at 536, rejecting the 'fact and degree' category; see similarly *British Railways Board* v. *Customs and Excise Commissioners* [1971] 1 WLR 588.

[260] In the *Huggins* case (above) both decisions might have been reasonable.

[261] *Farmer* v. *Cotton's Trustees* [1915] AC 922 at 932. See similarly *R* v. *Port of London Authority* [1920] AC 1 at 31; *Great Western Rly* v. *Bater* [1922] AC 1 at 22.

[262] But a specialist appellate tribunal may be less reluctant to overrule a specialist first-tier tribu-nal: *HMRC* v. *Arkeley Ltd* [2013] UKUT 393, para. 29.

[263] As in *Maurice (C) & Co Ltd* v. *Ministry of Labour* [1969] 2 AC 346; *Esso Petroleum Co Ltd* v. *Ministry of Labour* [1969] 1 QB 98. Compare *Libman* v. *General Medical Council* [1972] AC 217 disapproved in *Selvanathan* v. *GMC*, The Times, 26 October 2000 (PC).

[264] Above, p. 293. See *Griffiths* v. *JP Harrison (Watford) Ltd* [1963] AC 1 at 15–16.

[265] Above, p. 227.   [266] See Schwartz and Wade, *Legal Control of Government*, 228.

a number of primary facts, or a value judgment'.[267] But specialist tribunals may venture into the 'grey area' between fact and law in order to make best use of their expertise.[268]

The courts ought, however, to guard against any artificial narrowing of the right of appeal on a point of law, which is clearly intended to be a wide and beneficial remedy.[269] Very difficult questions of law have to be determined by many tribunals and for the sake of consistency and fairness it is important that the guidance of the courts should be available. On an appeal from an employment tribunal in a redundancy payment case, where the question was whether a certain term could be implied in the claimants' contracts of employment, the Queen's Bench Divisional Court held that this was a question of fact, so that the appeal was incompetent; but the Court of Appeal reversed them, holding that it was clearly a question of law, and allowed the appeal.[270] In another case, where it was held that an official referee had exercised his discretion wrongly in striking out a claim for want of prosecution, Lord Denning MR said:[271]

> There are many tribunals from which an appeal lies only on a 'point of law': and we always interpret the provision widely and liberally.

The extension in recent years of the right of appeal on questions of law has, as already noted, done much to assist the integration of the tribunal system with the general machinery of justice. Judicial policy ought to reinforce this beneficial trend.

APPEALS AGAINST DISCRETIONARY DECISIONS

Where appeal lies only on a point of law, an appeal against an exercise of discretion by a tribunal should succeed, in theory at least, only where the decision is vitiated by unreasonableness, self-misdirection, irrelevant considerations or some other legal error. For otherwise no point of law arises.[272] But in fact the court may allow such an appeal if it appears that the tribunal's decision produces 'manifest injustice'[273] or is 'plainly wrong'.[274] In any case, unreasonableness, self-misdirection, and so forth are grounds which are 'so many and so various that it virtually means that an erroneous exercise of discretion is nearly always due to an error in point of law'.[275]

It is where the right of appeal is unrestricted that judges are inclined to restrict it. It has many times been said in the House of Lords that the appellate court ought to interfere with an exercise of discretion by a lower court or tribunal only where there has been disregard of some legal principle and not merely where it would itself exercise the discretion differently.[276] In addition, an appellate court is naturally disinclined to intervene where

---

[267] *Ramsey* v. *HMRC* [2013] UKUT 226 at para. 48(7).

[268] Para. 49 relying on *Jones* v. *First-tier Tribunal and Criminal Injuries Compensation Authority* [2013] UKSC 19, above, p. 216.

[269] See the discussion on material error of fact being 'a point of law', above, p. 230. And see Carnwath, 'Tribunal Justice—A New Start' [2009] *PL* 48 at 58.

[270] *O'Brien* v. *Associated Fire Alarms Ltd* [1969] 1 WLR 1916.

[271] *Instrumatic Ltd* v. *Supabrase Ltd* [1969] 1 WLR 519.

[272] *Nelsovil Ltd* v. *Minister of Housing and Local Government* [1962] 1 WLR 404.

[273] *Wootton* v. *Central Land Board* [1957] 1 WLR 424 at 432.

[274] *Instrumatic Ltd* v. *Supabrase Ltd* (above).

[275] *Re DJMS* [1977] 3 All ER 582 at 589 (Lord Denning MR). See e.g. *Priddle* v. *Fisher & Sons* [1968] 1 WLR 1478; *Hadmor Productions Ltd* v. *Hamilton* [1983] 1 AC 191.

[276] *Zacharia* v. *Republic of Cyprus* [1963] AC 634 at 661; *Shiloh Spinners Ltd* v. *Harding* [1973] AC 691 at 727; *Duport Steels Ltd* v. *Sirs* [1980] 1 WLR 142 at 171; *Customs and Excise Cmrs* v. *JH Corbitt (Numismatics) Ltd* [1981] AC 22 at 52.

the tribunal's decision is based on its own observance of witnesses and its assessment of oral evidence.[277] Where, on the other hand, the evidence is entirely documentary the appellate court is in an equally good position to exercise the discretion.[278] The same may be true of interlocutory orders made before any evidence has been heard.[279] Although there are different nuances in the judicial statements, which mostly concern appeals from courts of law, the correct position is probably as explained by Lord Atkin:[280]

> I conceive it to be a mistake to hold...that the jurisdiction of the Court of Appeal on appeal from such an order is limited so that...the Court of Appeal have no power to interfere with [the judge's] exercise of discretion unless we think that he acted upon some wrong principle of law. Appellate jurisdiction is always statutory: there is in the statute no restriction on the jurisdiction of the Court of Appeal; and while the appellate court in the exercise of its appellate power is no doubt entirely justified in saying that normally it will not interfere with the exercise of the judge's discretion except on grounds of law, yet if it sees that on other grounds the decision will result in injustice being done it has both the power and the duty to remedy it.

Appellate courts therefore keep their options open, and in practice they are likely to allow an appeal when they think that a substantial mistake has been made. Much may depend upon the legal context.[281] In appeals against refusal of leave to apply for judicial review,[282] for example, the Court of Appeal uses its own discretion freely.

UNAPPEALABLE DISCRETION

Where a right of appeal is subject to leave from a court or tribunal, there is no right of appeal from a refusal of leave[283] or from a refusal to extend the time for appeal,[284] unless it is expressly conferred in those cases. Otherwise appeals would be multiplied in situations where it is thought necessary to restrict them.[285]

---

[277] *Blunt* v. *Blunt* [1943] AC 517 at 526–7.

[278] *Osenton (Charles)* v. *Johnston* [1942] AC 130; *Blunt* v. *Blunt* (above).

[279] *British Library* v. *Palyza* [1984] ICR 504 (industrial tribunal's order for discovery of documents held fully reviewable on appeal).

[280] *Evans* v. *Bartlam* [1937] AC 473 at 480. See similarly Lord Wright's speech. See also *Tsai* v. *Woodworth*, The Times, 30 November 1983, holding that the right of appeal would be nugatory unless Lord Atkin's principle was accepted.

[281] See *Oxfam* v. *HMRC* [2009] EWHC 3078 (*JH Corbitt*, above, held to depend on statutory context) (Sales J, paras. 73–4). [282] Above, p. 552.

[283] *Re Poh* [1983] 1 WLR 2 (immigration appeal). But significant doubt has been cast on this case. *R (Burkett)* v. *Hammersmith LBC* [2002] 1 WLR 1593 (HL), paras. 10–14. And see above, p. 552.

[284] *White* v. *Chief Adjudication Officer* [1983] 1 WLR 262 (social security pension appeal).

[285] See authorities cited in *Bland* v. *Supplementary Benefit Officer* [1983] 1 WLR 262.

24

STATUTORY AND OTHER INQUIRIES

THE SYSTEM OF INQUIRIES

Inquiries come in many forms and it will be well to start by setting out the different forms clearly. On the one hand, by far the most common is the statutory inquiry which is the standard technique for giving a fair hearing to objectors before the final decision is made on some question of government policy affecting citizens' rights or interests.[1] Many statutes provide for such inquiries in the fields of planning, compulsory purchase and others. The subject matter of the inquiry may be rather mundane (although of vital importance to those involved) such as a planning inquiry following a refusal of a householder's application to extend his home; or it might be of national importance such as an inquiry into where a new nuclear power station should be sited. What is characteristic of these inquiries is that they assist in the proper formation of policy in the decision-making process. They generally take place in public.

On the other hand, there is the inquiry which essentially finds facts and may attribute responsibility once something has gone wrong. Into this category falls the accident inquiry or the inquest into an unnatural death. The law generally requires such inquiries to be held once certain events have occurred. But the law does not always require an inquiry and then such inquiries are discretionary. Whether they are held at all may depend upon the strength of the political pressure calling for an inquiry. Specific statutory provision exists for such inquiries, but such inquiries may also be set upon in a non-statutory basis.

What all these forms of inquiry have in common is the independence of the person (or persons) who conducts the inquiry and writes the report. Very different forms of procedure may be adopted. The inquiry may sit in public or private. But in every case the person conducting the inquiry must act free from external influence and report accordingly. The first class of inquiry, the statutory inquiry, although less likely to appear in the headlines, does raise more important questions of administrative law; and it is considered first.

---

[1] For a detailed treatment of public inquiries and their problems see Wraith and Lamb, *Public Inquiries as an Instrument of Government*. See also Ganz, *Administrative Procedures*, 39 and [1996] *PL* 359–527 (discussion by several authors of the *Report of the Scott Inquiry* (below, p. 820)). See also [2004] *PL* 738 (Steele). See also, 'What Went Wrong on Bloody Sunday: A Critique of the Saville Inquiry' [2010] *PL* 61 (Blom Cooper); Beer, Dingemans and Lissack, *Public Inquiries* (2011) and the Centre for Effective Dispute Resolution's (CERD) Consultation Paper, 'Public Inquiries—Proposals for a Rethink' (December 2012), <http://www.cedr.com/docslib/Public_Inquiries_-Proposals_for_a_Design_Rethink_-_December_2012.pdf>.

THE STATUTORY INQUIRY PROPER

Any project such as the compulsory acquisition of land, the siting of a power station or an airport, or the building of a motorway will provide for a public inquiry as a preliminary to the decision; and the same applies to some very common procedures such as planning appeals. People who wish to object have important procedural rights, derived partly from statute and partly from the principles of natural justice and regulated in some respects by the Tribunals and Inquiries Act 1992.

The distinction between tribunals and inquiries—that tribunals are concerned with finding facts and applying legal rules to those facts, while inquiries, although also concerned with fact-finding are directed towards making recommendations on questions of policy[2]—is based on the difference between judicial and administrative power. Statutory inquiries are part of the procedure for ensuring that administrative power is fairly and reasonably exercised, so that they have the same purpose as the legal principles of natural justice. Many statutes themselves provide for inquiries or hearings and lay down a mandatory procedure for dealing with objections. But the statutory procedure is usually only a framework, within which the principles of natural justice operate to fill in details and ensure that fair procedures are followed.[3]

Although an object of these inquiries is to assuage the feelings of the citizen, and to give his objections the fairest possible consideration, they have given rise to many complaints. They are a hybrid legal-and-administrative process, and for the very reason that they have been made to look as much as possible like judicial proceedings, people grumble at the fact that they fall short of it.

Statutory inquiries are now so common that it is unusual to find a statute concerned with planning control or with the acquisition of land, or indeed with any important scheme of administrative control, which does not provide this machinery for one or more purposes. Acts concerned with housing, town and country planning, roads, agriculture, health, transport, police, local government as well as the compulsory acquisition of land all utilise this technique. Moreover, the Parliamentary Private Bill procedure as a means of obtaining authorisation for railway, tramway and other transport works has been replaced by a system of Ministerial Orders preceded where appropriate by a public local inquiry.[4]

Planning inquiries are the most numerous class, since they are held not only before the adoption of planning schemes of a general character but also in many cases of individual appeals against refusal of planning permission or against conditions imposed by a local planning authority. The Planning Inspectorate[5] which arranges inquiries concerning local authorities and some central departments, as well as housing and planning cases has in England a corps of over 334 inspectors responsible for about 19,466 inquiries of all types a year. The Planning Inspectorate has, since April 1992, been established as an

---

[2] Above, p. 762.   [3] Above, p. 423.

[4] Transport and Works Act 1992, ss. 1–3, 6–7. Where the proposed scheme is, in the Secretary of State's opinion, of national significance, approval (by resolution) of both Houses of Parliament is required. This approval will precede the public local inquiry (Council on Tribunals, *Annual Report*, 1991–2, para. 2.105).

[5] The Inspectorate publishes Annual Reports and Statistical Reports available at <http://www.gov.uk/government/publications?departments%5B%5D=planning-inspectorate> (Annual Reports) and <http://www.planningportal.gov.uk/planning/planninginspectorate/statistics> (Statistical Reports). The figures given are drawn from the 2012–13 Statistical Report (for England alone). See also, D. Hanchet, (2001) *Journal of Planning Law* (Supp.) 24 for discussion of the operation of the Inspectorate.

executive agency.[6] The Council on Tribunals (now abolished) accepted that this poses no danger to the independence and adjudicative standards of the inspectorate.[7]

RELATION OF LAW AND POLICY

In the vast majority of cases in which statutory inquiry procedures are employed the ultimate decision is one of policy. It is essentially for such decisions that the technique of inquiries has been developed. Should the minister confirm a scheme for the motorway? Should he allow an appeal against refusal of planning permission by the local authority? The answers will depend on what he decides is expedient in the public interest.[8] They cannot be found by applying rules of law.

The inquiries which matter most in administrative law are those which are required by statute before the minister may lawfully make some order. If some part of the statutory procedure has not been properly followed, or there has been a breach of natural justice, there will have been no valid inquiry and any order made in consequence, if challenged within any statutory time limit, can be quashed by the court.[9] Legal irregularity here has a clear legal result.

But inquiries are set up by ministers in many other situations where they have no effect on the validity of any particular act or order which may be made thereafter. An Act will often give power for the minister to hold an inquiry, if he thinks fit, into any matter connected with his functions under the Act. There are many other cases where the Act makes the holding of the inquiry discretionary. And it would be rash to say that irregularity in an inquiry of this class could never affect the validity of a ministerial order, even though the minister could have dispensed with the inquiry altogether had he wished.

EVOLUTION OF THE INQUIRY SYSTEM

The statutory inquiries which are the subject of this chapter came into prominence along with the expansion of central and local government powers in the nineteenth century.[10] When it became impossible to provide for all the details of government by Act of Parliament, inquiries were adopted as a kind of substitute, in the administrative sphere, for the parliamentary process which accompanied legislation.

At first the statutory authority would be given power, after holding a public inquiry and considering objections, to make a provisional order. This would not take effect until confirmed by Act of Parliament. A further simplification was made by the Statutory Orders (Special Procedure) Act 1945 which, for matters within its scope, substituted a procedure whereby the provisional order took effect if not annulled by either House of Parliament. In due course, Parliament's role was reduced still further with the minister being given power to confirm the provisional order. This familiar combination of public inquiry followed by ministerial order, made without reference to Parliament, is the standard pattern today.

---

[6] See above, p. 37, for discussion of executive agencies. Previously the Inspectorate fell under the Department of the Environment; it is now under the office of the Deputy Prime Minister.

[7] *Annual Report*, 1991–2, para. 1.67.

[8] Exceptionally a minister may be required to decide a question of fact or law (above, p. 762).

[9] For examples see above, p. 430.

[10] But Wraith and Lamb, *Public Inquiries as an Instrument of Government*, 17, point out that the Domesday surveys may be considered the first public inquiries.

SPECIMEN PROCEDURE

The procedure of statutory inquiries has now become standardised. No single statute lays down the procedure, but the numerous modern statutes which prescribe inquiries follow a common pattern, with only a few significant variations. The compulsory purchase for slum clearance procedure[11] under the Housing Acts provides a typical example.

The first step is for the local authority to pass a resolution defining the clearance area, which it are obliged to do if satisfied as to certain facts. The resolution is only a preliminary step to prepare the way for either a compulsory purchase order or else a purchase by agreement. A compulsory purchase order requires the consent of the Secretary of State before it can become effective, and the time for making objections is between the making of the order and the Secretary of State's decision upon it. Before the local authority may submit a clearance order to the Secretary of State it must make it available for inspection and advertise it in the local press. It must also notify owners, occupiers and mortgagees of the land, and inform them of their opportunities for making objections. If no objection is made, the Secretary of State may confirm the order with or without modification. But the important provision is to the following effect:[12]

> If any objection duly made is not withdrawn, the Secretary of State shall, before confirming the order, either cause a public local inquiry to be held or afford to any person by whom an objection has been duly made and not withdrawn an opportunity of appearing before and being heard by a person appointed for the purpose, and, after considering any objection not withdrawn and the report of the person who held the inquiry or was so appointed, may confirm the order with or without modification. Where every objector consents a 'written representations procedure' can be adopted instead of a public inquiry.

It has been held that the penultimate sentence of the above passage empowers the Secretary of State to modify an invalid order so as to make it a valid one, at least in cases where the flaw is not of a fundamental character;[13] and that an order of this two-stage type is legally 'made' when it is confirmed by the Secretary of State, since before then it has no operative force in law.[14] Human rights challenges to the procedure outlined have generally failed.[15]

If the order is confirmed, the local authority must again advertise it and inform objectors. A period of six weeks is then allowed within which anyone who wishes to challenge the order on legal grounds (e.g. ultra vires) must apply to the High Court. Subject to any legal dispute, the order becomes operative at the end of the six weeks, and thereafter 'shall not be questioned in any legal proceedings whatsoever'.[16] The significance of this drastic clause is explained elsewhere.[17] Standardised provisions of the same kind are found in

---

[11] See Housing Act 1985, Pt IX read with the relevant parts of the Acquisition of Land Act 1981.

[12] Acquisition of Land Act 1981, s. 13(2), slightly paraphrased as amended by Planning and Compulsory Purchase Act 2004 with the addition of s. 13A.

[13] *Minister of Health* v. *The King ex p Yaffé* [1931] AC 494. See also *Re Bowman* [1932] 2 KB 621; *Legg* v. *Inner London Education Authority* [1972] 1 WLR 1245 (Secretary of State's power to approve with 'modifications' exceeded). But see *R (Collis)* v. *Secretary of State for Communities and Local Government* [2007] EWHC 2625 (para. 16) (curative effect of confirmatory power doubted).

[14] *Iveagh (Earl)* v. *Minister of Housing and Local Government* [1964] 1 QB 395 (historic building preservation order).

[15] *R (Maley)* v. *Secretary of State for Communities and Local Government* [2008] EWHC 2652 (challenge based on Art. 8 and Art. 1 Protocol 1 to clearance order inquiry process; inspector had no duty to consider specific human rights issues (paras. 38–9)). See also *Smith* v. *Secretary of State for Trade and Industry* [2007] EWHC 1013 (Art. 8).   [16] Acquisition of Land Act 1981, s. 25.

[17] Above, p. 620.

many other Acts governing the compulsory purchase of land such as the Water Resources Act 1991 and the Forestry Act 1967.[18]

HEARING, REPORT AND DECISION

Where there is opposition to the order, the usual sequence of events is that objection is formally lodged and a public local inquiry is held unless all the objectors consent and a 'written representations procedure' is held.[19] In fact the statutory formula allows the Secretary of State to hold either a public local inquiry or a hearing, which suggests that a hearing need not be public.[20] But other statutes speak merely of a 'local inquiry',[21] and it is not clear how this is intended to differ from a hearing, although the words seem to indicate an investigation going beyond a hearing of those who have lodged formal objections.[22] It may be that the word 'public' is omitted in order to prevent the validity of the inquiry being questioned if the public, or members of it, are excluded, for instance where they try to disrupt the inquiry by misbehaviour. The regular practice, in any case, is to hold public inquiries rather than hearings,[23] thus giving the public an opportunity to participate and giving the minister the benefit of all points of view. The Tribunals and Inquiries Act 1992 will apply in either case,[24] but in other statutes there may be differences.[25]

The person appointed by the Secretary of State to hold the inquiry or hearing is in most cases an inspector from the Planning Inspectorate. The 'case' is thus 'heard' before an official who is not from the department concerned. The local authority[26] and the objectors may be legally represented,[27] and an important inquiry will have some of the atmosphere of a trial. The inspector may conduct the inquiry as he wishes, subject in some cases to procedural regulations.[28] The objectors will call witnesses and examine them, and the local authority's representatives may cross-examine them. The authority will also frequently call witnesses of its own.[29] The inspector, like a judge, will often take very little part in the argument; his task is to hear the objections and the arguments and then give

---

[18] See above, p. 54.

[19] Act of 1981, ss. 13A and 13B. And see Compulsory Purchase of Land (Written Representations Procedure) (Ministers) Regulations 2004 (SI 2004/2594).

[20] Cf. [2001] *JPL* 1109 (Freer) suggesting that in a 'hearing' there was an inquisitional burden on the inspector which was absent in a public inquiry.

[21] e.g. Town and Country Planning Act 1990, s. 320; Local Government Act 1972, s. 250; Highways Act 1980, 1st Sched., para. 7. 'Public local inquiries' are required in compulsory purchase cases under the Acquisition of Land Act 1981, s. 13 and 1st Sched., para. 4 and the Housing and Regeneration Act 2008, Sched. 3, para. 10, uses 'public local inquiry' (power to hold public local inquiry before extinguishing a public right of way).

[22] See below, pp. 800–1. Where there are statutory rules of procedure (below, p. 809) they normally apply to both inquiries and hearings.

[23] A hearing rather than an inquiry is now exceptional: Parliamentary Commissioner for Administration, *Annual Report for 1974* (HC 1974–5, No. 126), 7. See also Wraith and Lamb, *Public Inquiries as an Instrument of Government*, 159. But note the growth in the use of the 'written representation' procedures where the objectors consent. The policy of the Secretary of State is to write to the parties if he considers the written representation procedure is appropriate. See the Department for Communities and Local Government's guidance document, 'Compulsory Purchase and Compensation' (October 2004), para. 39, available at <http://www.gov.uk/government/uploads/system/uploads/attachment_data/file/11487/147639.pdf>.

[24] Below, p. 800.   [25] As in the matter of costs: below, p. 812.   [26] 2007 Rules, r. 12(1).

[27] 2007 Rules, r. 14(1).

[28] 2007 Rules, r. 16 setting out basic principles; and note r. 16(1): 'Except as otherwise provided in these Rules, the inspector shall determine the procedure at the inquiry.'

[29] 2007 Rules, r. 12(1)(b) obliges the acquiring authority to make available a representative to give evidence.

advice to the minister. Despite the implications of 'inquiry', the procedure is basically adversarial, i.e. between opposing parties, and not inquisitorial.[30]

In due course the inquiry is closed, and the inspector makes his report. Until 1958 the normal practice was to refuse disclosure of this report to the objectors: it was treated like any other confidential report from a civil servant to his department.[31] Eventually the minister's decision would be given; but usually it would be unaccompanied by reasons. The failure to disclose the report and to state reasons was the source of much of the dissatisfaction with inquiries before the reforms of 1958. Although the controversies which raged round these questions have now passed into history, they provide a classic illustration of the clash between the legal and administrative points of view.

STATUTORY INQUIRIES AND NATURAL JUSTICE

A statutory inquiry is a formalised version of the fair hearing which is required by the common law according to the principles of natural justice. It does not displace natural justice:[32] it should be regarded rather as a framework within which natural justice can operate and supply missing details. The common law's presumption that Parliament intends power to be exercised fairly is all the stronger where Parliament itself has provided for a hearing.

COMPLAINTS AND REFORMS

LAWYERS' CRITICISMS

Lord Hewart spoke for many lawyers when he made his attack on the then prevailing procedures in his book *The New Despotism*, published in 1929 when he was Lord Chief Justice. He wrote of inquiries:[33]

It is sometimes enacted that, before the Minister comes to a decision, he shall hold a public inquiry, at which interested parties are entitled to adduce evidence and be heard. But that provision is no real safeguard, because the person who has the power of deciding is in no way bound by the report or the recommendations of the person who holds the inquiry, and may entirely ignore the evidence which the inquiry brought to light. He can, and in practice sometimes does, give a decision wholly inconsistent with the report, the recommendations, and the evidence, which are not published or disclosed to interested individuals. In any case, as the official who decides has not seen or heard the witnesses, he is as a rule quite incapable of estimating the value of their evidence... the requirement of a public inquiry is in practice nugatory.... It seems absurd that one official should hold a public inquiry into the merits of a proposal, and that another official should be entitled, disregarding the report of the first, to give a decision on the merits.

---

[30] For the argument that fairness in inquiries should not be viewed 'through the prism of adversarialism' see [1996] *PL* 508 (M. C. Harris). [31] Above, p. 411.
[32] In *Bushell* v. *Secretary of State for the Environment* [1981] AC 75 at 95 Lord Diplock preferred the terminology of 'fairness', which had come into vogue since the earlier decisions. But in *Cummings* v. *Weymouth & Portland BC* [2007] EWHC 1601 Hickinbottom J said that 'the holder of the inquiry is required to conduct a fair hearing, and act in accordance with the rules of natural justice' (para. 49). Article 6(1) will generally be applicable (above, p. 378 and *Pascoe* v. *First Secretary of State* [2006] EWHC 2356, para. 92) but Art. 6 and the right to fair trial at common law were 'coterminous' (*Cummings*, para. 49). [33] p. 45.

THE ESSENTIAL COMPROMISE

The fact that these criticisms failed to face was that where the decision is one of policy there is no reason why the final decision should be based exclusively on evidence given at the inquiry—and often it will not be. Suppose, to take the case of the new town at Stevenage,[34] that the local residents oppose the scheme for a new town on the grounds that there will be serious difficulties of water supply and sewage disposal. The objections are merely one factor which must be weighed by the minister and his advisers against the demands of national policy. It may be that these objections apply to all the other eligible sites for the new town. It may be, also, that the need to develop new towns is so great that the expense of overcoming serious physical obstacles will justify itself. It may be, again, that the other advantages of the site outweigh the objections. These are eminently the sort of matters upon which the final decision will turn. But it is impossible to bring them all to a head at a public inquiry in the same way in which a legal issue can be brought to a head in a court of law.[35]

A minister's decision on a planning scheme or a clearance scheme is a different kind of mental exercise, for there is the whole exterior world of political motive.[36] It is fundamental that political decisions should be taken by a minister responsible to Parliament, and that the political responsibility should rest entirely upon him and not upon his officials or advisers. Furthermore, the place where policy should be explained is Parliament, where the responsibility lies. Nothing, therefore, can prevent the ultimate responsibility lying outside the forum of an inquiry, whereas it must lie inside the forum of a court of law.[37]

Nevertheless there are exceptional cases. Courts of law may appear to take decisions of policy and ministers may decide particular cases into which policy does not seem to enter. For reasons of convenience inspectors hearing planning appeals have been empowered to decide a great many of the cases themselves.[38] This does not alter the fact that legal decisions and political decisions are different things and require different procedures.

'BLOWING OFF STEAM'

These realities often leave objectors with a sense of frustration, feeling that they are fighting a phantom opponent, and that they have no assurance of coming to grips with the real issues which are going to decide the case. That 'the sole use of the liberty to make objections was that the objectors ... might "blow off steam" and so rally public opinion to which alone the Minister might bow.'[39]

---

[34] Above, p. 403.

[35] The minister may naturally use knowledge acquired elsewhere: *Price* v. *Minister of Health* (1947) 116 LJR 291. This is subject to the limits indicated below.

[36] See *Johnson (B.) & Co Ltd* v. *Minister of Health* [1947] 2 All ER 395 at 399 (Lord Greene MR).

[37] Note the Compulsory Purchase (Inquiries Procedure) Rules 2007 (SI 2007/3617), rr. 12(2), 13(4) and 18(4) providing that questions may not be asked of government departments or acquiring authority representatives 'directed at the merits of government policy'.

[38] SI 1997 No. 420. With the consent of the parties most of these are dealt with by way of written representations without any hearing (SI 2000 No. 1628). For the relevant procedural rules, see Town and Country Planning (Appeals) (Written Representations Procedure) (England) Regulations 2009 (SI 2009/452.

[39] From the first-instance judge in the Stevenage case (*Franklin* v. *Minister of Town and Country Planning* [1947] 1 All ER 396 at 398) giving an account of the Attorney-General's argument. See for further discussion of 'blowing off steam': *Nicholson* v. *Secretary of State for Energy* [1978] 76 LGR 693 at 700 and *Aston* v. *Secretary of State Communities and Local Government* [2013] EWHC 1936 paras. 87–9.

But as is obvious, and as the appellate courts held,[40] the minister's decision cannot be dictated to him by the inspector's conclusions from the inquiry.

To conclude from this that the inquiry is merely an opportunity to blow off steam is cynical and unrealistic. The important thing is not that the decision should be dictated by the report but that the objectors' case should be fairly heard and should be fairly taken into account. The law can ensure that their case is heard, but it cannot ensure that any particular weight is given to it.[41] That, after all, is precisely the basis on which the judges have developed the principles of natural justice. The real risk is not that the minister will perversely disregard the evidence but that he will be tempted to act before he has discovered that there is another side to the case. The statutory inquiry has proved to be an essential piece of mechanism and the committees who have reported upon it have been unable to suggest anything better.

THE FRANKS COMMITTEE (1957)

The Committee on Tribunals and Inquiries (the Franks Committee) surveyed the whole ground in its report of 1957.[42] This was an extensive, factual and practical report, and it caught a favouring tide of public opinion. The Committee made many proposals for improving the existing system, which have greatly reduced the volume of public complaint. Of outstanding importance were the recommendations (accepted) that inspectors' reports should be published and that objectors should be able to know as early as possible what case they had to meet.

Just as in the case of tribunals,[43] the Committee contrasted 'two strongly opposed views': the 'administrative' and the 'judicial' views.[44] The administrative view, which had been dominant previously, stressed that the minister was responsible to Parliament and to Parliament only for his decision, and that it could not in any way be governed by rules. The judicial view held that an inquiry was something like a trial before a judge and that the decision should be based wholly and directly on the evidence. Both these extremes were rejected—and this involved rejecting the established philosophy that was supposed to justify non-disclosure of the government's case and non-disclosure of the inspector's report. The Committee said:[45]

> If the administrative view is dominant the public enquiry cannot play its full part in the total process, and there is a danger that the rights and interests of the individual citizens affected will not be sufficiently protected. In these cases it is idle to argue that Parliament can be relied upon to protect the citizen, save exceptionally. . . . If the judicial view is dominant there is a danger that people will regard the person before whom they state their case as a kind of judge provisionally deciding the matter, subject to an appeal to the Minister. This view overlooks the true nature of the proceedings, the form of which is necessitated

---

[40] Above, p. 403.

[41] Subject to the rules as to judicial review for unreasonableness etc.: above, p. 353. See also *R (Powell)* v. *Secretary of State for Communities and Local Government* [2007] EWHC 2051 (inspector's failure to make an essential finding of fact—not a matter of disputed judgment—may form the basis of a challenge (para. 8, Sullivan J)).

[42] Cmnd 218 (1957). This ground was first surveyed in the Report of the Ministers' Powers Committee, Cmnd 4060 (1932). Although that report recommended that reasons should be given for decisions and that inspectors' reports should be published, nothing was done. [43] Above, p. 764.

[44] Para. 262.   [45] Paras. 273–4.

by the fact that the Minister himself, who is responsible to Parliament for the ultimate decision, cannot conduct the enquiry in person.

The Committee rejected the notion that objectors could not expect the same standard of justice when the scheme was initiated by the same minister who had ultimately to decide its fate rather than by some other authority.[46]

THE PLAN OF REFORM

Two primary recommendations were that there should be a permanent and independent body, the Council on Tribunals, and that the Council should formulate rules of procedure for inquiries which would have statutory force. But neither was ever fully implemented. The Council on Tribunals was constituted by the Tribunals and Inquiries Act 1958 as a purely advisory body. But now it (and its replacement, the Administrative Justice and Tribunals Council) has been abolished.[47] As regards inquiries, the Council had to consider and report on such matters as may be referred to it by the Lord Chancellor, or as it may itself determine to be of special importance, concerning 'administrative procedures involving, or which may involve, the holding by or on behalf of a Minister of a statutory inquiry'.[48] A statutory inquiry is defined as 'an inquiry or hearing held or to be held in pursuance of a duty imposed by any statutory provision'—that is to say, an inquiry which the minister is obliged to hold—with the addition of such other inquiries or hearings as may be designated by order.[49]

Power to make procedural rules for inquiries was given by an Act of 1959.[50] The power is conferred on the Lord Chancellor, acting by statutory instrument and after consultation with the Council on Tribunals. Rules have been made for a number of the commoner types of inquiries, as explained below.[51] In Scottish affairs the Secretary of State for Scotland acts in place of the Lord Chancellor.[52] The Report made a great many further recommendations for improvement in the fairness of inquiry procedures.[53]

The great majority of these recommendations were accepted and put into effect.[54] The necessary changes were effected more by administrative directions than by alteration of the law. The Act of 1958 (and its successors) also provided for reasons to be given for decisions. The statutory rules of procedure which have now been made for some inquiries also give legal force to some of the other improvements. These various matters are explained below. But the chief instrument of reform has been the ministerial circular, a document which has no legal operation but which 'invites' local authorities and other bodies to make arrangements suggested by the minister, or else explains the minister's own departmental practice. Many important reforms, such as the publication of inspectors' reports and the giving of reasoned decisions, could be made merely by changes of practice and without any alteration of the law. These changes were therefore explained in circulars, which were published documents freely available to all concerned.

---

[46] Para. 267.
[47] See the Public Bodies (Abolition of Administrative Justice and Tribunals Council) Order 2013 (SI 2013/2042).   [48] s. 1(1)(c) of the Act of 1992.
[49] Tribunals and Inquiries Act 1992, s. 16(1).
[50] That power is now vouchsafed by the Tribunals and Inquiries Act 1992, s. 9.
[51] Below, p. 810.   [52] Act of 1992, s. 9(4); SI 1999 No. 678.
[53] For the list of these see the 9th edn of this book, pp. 971–2.   [54] See below, p. 806.

LAW AND PRACTICE TODAY IN STATUTORY INQUIRIES

THE RIGHT TO KNOW THE OPPOSING CASE

One important requirement of natural justice is that the objector should have the opportunity to know and meet the case against him.[55] 'The case against him', in the context of an inquiry, will be some scheme or order proposed by some public authority, such as a compulsory purchase order, or some adverse decision such as the refusal of planning permission.

In accordance with a recommendation of the Franks Committee, ministerial instructions ask local authorities to prepare written statements setting out the reasons for their proposals and to make these available to objectors in good time before the inquiry. This has now become standard practice. In the cases where the rules of procedure now apply, they require the authority to serve on the objector, usually at least twenty-eight days before the inquiry, a written statement (known as the 'policy statement') of their reasons for seeking confirmation of their order or else a written statement of the submissions which they will make at the inquiry. If directions or opinions of other government departments are to be relied upon, they must be disclosed in advance. Facilities must be given for inspection and copying of relevant documents and plans. Where the minister is himself the originating authority, he will act similarly.

Although the government rejected the recommendation that the deciding minister, as opposed to the initiating authority, should provide a statement of policy before the inquiry, there has been an improvement in the issue of explanatory material, particularly from the Department of the Environment.

INSPECTORS' REPORTS

None of the reforms achieved by the Franks Committee was of greater importance than the successful conclusion of the long struggle to secure publication of inspectors' reports. Before the Committee there was strong official opposition to the proposal. Much of this opposition was based on the well-worn objections of the secretive civil servant. To reveal the report would be administratively inconvenient; it would embarrass the minister; it would reduce the candour with which the report was written; and would not be understood by the objectors. Even though the official case was not so weak as might be thought from some of these arguments used to defend it, the overriding fact was that it was impossible to persuade people that they had received justice if they were not allowed to see the document which conveyed their objections to the minister.

Since 1958 it has been the standard practice for a copy of the report to accompany the minister's letter of decision. Where statutory rules apply, they require this specifically. Where they do not, there is no legal right to disclosure of the report, but in practice it is supplied. None of the evils that were feared seem to have resulted. Inspectors gained in public respect, since it could be seen how fairly they handled cases. At the same time it is easier for objectors to tell whether legal remedies may be open to them. The public's sense of grievance has been assuaged. Good administration and the principles of justice have once again proved to be friends, not enemies. The departments that were most tenacious of secrecy have found that it has done them good to abandon it.

[55] Above, p. 428.

The minister is in no way bound to follow the recommendations of the report: his duty is to decide according to his own independent view,[56] taking account of all relevant information.[57] It is not necessary that the inspector should always make recommendations[58] or that he should make findings on all the issues raised.[59]

REASONS FOR DECISIONS

The Tribunals and Inquiries Act 1992[60] provides, as did the Acts of 1958 and 1971, for the giving of reasons for decisions. This is a matter of great importance. It enables the citizen to understand the connection between the inspector's report and the minister's decision. It also enables the court to quash the decision if the reasons are not adequately given,[61] thus making a notable extension of judicial control over inquiry procedures.

As regards inquiries the Act provides that where

> any Minister notifies any decision taken by him after a statutory inquiry has been held by him or on his behalf, or in a case in which a person concerned could (whether by objecting or otherwise) have required the holding as aforesaid of a statutory inquiry, it shall be the duty...of the Minister to furnish a statement of the reasons for the decision.[62]

The meaning of 'statutory inquiry' is explained below.[63] The second limb of the provision covers cases where a party may waive his right to a formal hearing, as is common in planning appeals.[64]

The terms and qualifications of the Act were explained in the chapter on tribunals, where it is noted that the reasons may be written or oral, and that the statutory duty applies only where reasons are requested. But in practice a reasoned decision letter is now sent out as a matter of course. Where procedural rules have been made (as explained below), they impose an unqualified duty to give reasons, so that there is no need to make any request.

It has been held that reasons given under the rules must be as full and as adequate as reasons given under the Act, though if they are clear and adequate they may be briefly stated.[65] Where a bad decision letter leaves real and substantial doubts as to the minister's reasons,[66] or fails to deal with a substantial objection,[67] or does not explain a departure from the development plan[68] or the minister's published policy[69] or is misleading,[70] the

---

[56] *Nelsovil Ltd* v. *Minister of Housing and Local Government* [1962] 1 WLR 404.

[57] See *Prest* v. *Secretary of State for Wales* (1982) 81 LGR 193, allowing the use of evidence which was not available at the inquiry.

[58] *R* v. *Secretary of State for Transport ex p Gwent CC* [1988] QB 429. Although he must give reasons if he does not make recommendations: the Compulsory Purchase (Inquiries Procedure) Rules 2007 (SI 2007/3617), r. 18(1).　　　[59] *London & Clydeside Estates Ltd* v. *Aberdeen DC*, 1984 SLT 50.

[60] s. 10.　　[61] See above, p. 783.　　[62] s. 10(1)(b).　　[63] p. 812.

[64] See below, p. 814.

[65] *Westminster City Council* v. *Great Portland Estates plc* [1985] AC 661. As to structure plans see below, p. 806.

[66] *Givaudan & Co Ltd* v. *Minister of Housing and Local Government* [1967] 1 WLR 250 (obscurely worded decision quashed under Town and Country Planning Act 1962, s. 179, applying the reasoning of *Re Poyser and Mills' Arbitration* [1964] 2 QB 467, above, p. 786). See similarly *French Kier Developments Ltd* v. *Secretary of State for the Environment* [1977] 1 All ER 296; *Niarchos* v. *Secretary of State for the Environment* [1977] 76 LGR 480; *Strathclyde Passenger Executive* v. *McGill Bus Service*, 1984 SLT 377. And see *Cummings* v. *Weymouth & Portland BC* [2007] EWHC 1601 (Admin), para. 57 for general description of duty to give reasons in this context.

[67] *Barnham* v. *Secretary of State for the Environment* (1986) 52 P & CR 10 (structure plan).

[68] *Reading BC* v. *Secretary of State for the Environment* (1986) 52 P & CR 385.

[69] See the *Barnham* case (above).

[70] *London Residuary Body* v. *Secretary of State for the Environment*, The Times, 30 March 1988.

decision may be quashed on the same grounds as apply in the case of tribunals. In another case[71] Lord Denning MR said:

> Section 12(1) of the Tribunals and Inquiries Act 1958 says that the minister must give his reasons, and that his reasons are to form part of the record. The whole purpose of that enactment is to enable the parties and the courts to see what matters he has taken into consideration and what view he has reached on the points of fact and law which arise. If he does not deal with the points that arise, he fails in his duty, and the court can order him to make good the omission.

However, the pendulum has begun to swing in the other direction. The House of Lords has held that decision letters should be read 'with a measure of benevolence' and that the duty to give reasons does not require the decision-maker 'to dot every i and cross every t'.[72] 'Excessively legalistic textual criticism of planning decision letters', the House of Lords has said, 'is something the court should strongly discourage'.[73]

The Act has been made applicable also to inspectors who decide planning appeals themselves.[74] But otherwise it has no application where the inquiry is held by or on behalf of someone other than a minister or a board presided over by a minister.[75]

THE RIGHT TO PARTICIPATE

A 'public local inquiry', and likewise a 'local inquiry', implies that there will be a right of audience for all persons in the locality who are genuinely concerned for good reasons, and not merely for those who have legal rights at stake.[76]

These members of the public are allowed to give evidence and cross-examine opposing witnesses, but the inspector has a wide discretion to curb irrelevance and repetition, and to control the proceedings generally.[77]

But the statutory procedural rules which have been made for certain classes of inquiries confer the right of appearance and participation only upon parties who have legal rights which are in some way in issue, and allow other members of the public to appear only in the inspector's discretion. In so far as these restrictions conflict with the judicial statement just quoted, their validity may be open to question, since the power to make procedural rules can hardly avail to cut down rights of participation granted by Act of Parliament. But the question has not yet arisen before a court, since in practice public inquiries and local inquiries, including planning appeals, are open freely to all comers.[78]

---

[71] *Iveagh (Earl)* v. *Minister of Housing and Local Government* [1964] 1 QB 395. And see *R* v. *Secretary of State for Transport ex p Cumbria CC* [1983] RTR 129 (reasons particularly important when minister differs from inspector).

[72] *Save Britain's Heritage* v. *No 1 Poultry Ltd* [1991] 1 WLR 153 at 164. Thus deficiencies in the Secretary of State's reasoning could be remedied by an exemplary inspector's report, where the Secretary of State had impliedly adopted the inspector's reasoning by using the same words as the inspector.

[73] *South Lakeland DC* v. *Secretary of State for the Environment* [1992] 2 AC 141 at 148. But the limits of the benevolent approach to reasons were reached in *Proudfoot Properties* v. *Secretary of State for Communities and Local Government* [2012] EWHC 2043 (failure of inspector to record in his reasons his finding on a crucial issue; decision quashed).   [74] Town and Country Planning Act 1990, 6th Sched., para. 8.

[75] Tribunals and Inquiries Act 1992, s. 16(1).

[76] *Local Government Board* v. *Arlidge* [1915] AC 120 at 147; above, p. 487. And see *Wednesbury Corporation* v. *Ministry of Housing and Local Government (No 2)* [1966] 2 QB 275 at 302 (Diplock LJ).

[77] *Wednesbury Corporation* case (ibid.). And *Cummings* v. *Weymouth & Portland BC* [2007] EWHC 1601, para. 51(ii): 'The discretion in an inspector as to what evidence to admit is wide' (Hickinbottom J).

[78] On the position of third parties see Wraith and Lamb, *Public Inquiries as an Instrument of Government*, 253.

This is good administration, since neighbours, amenity societies and other third parties may often be able to make important contributions, and the object is to enable the best decision to be made in the public interest. This does not mean that third parties have in practice all the advantages of those whose legal rights are affected. They may some-times be unable to challenge the validity of the proceedings as 'persons aggrieved'[79] and they have a number of disadvantages in cases covered by procedural rules, as explained below.[80]

SCOPE OF INQUIRIES: THE PROBLEM OF POLICY

The parties who participate in an inquiry, whether as of right or otherwise, are entitled to a fair hearing of their cases or objections. But these rights cannot be used to carry the inquiry beyond its proper scope. Even where the Act says that the minister 'shall consider all objections' he need not consider objections which do not fairly and reasonably relate to the true purpose of the inquiry or which merely repeat objections made more suitably at an earlier inquiry.[81]

The central difficulty is to know how far matters of general policy should be open to question. The place for debating general policy is Parliament, and at an inquiry there should be no 'useless discussion of policy in the wrong forum'.[82] The purpose of a local inquiry is to provide the minister with information about local objections so that he can weigh the harm to local interests and private persons against the public benefit to be achieved by the scheme.[83] The policy behind the scheme, as opposed to its local impact, should therefore be taken for granted. Thus, following a recommendation of the Franks Committee, statutory rules of procedure normally provide that the inspector shall disal-low questions directed to the merits of government policy.[84]

But the line between general policy and its local application may not be easy to draw,[85] and it is often the underlying policy which objectors wish to attack. In practice inspectors tend to be indulgent, allowing objectors to criticise policy and reporting such objections to the minister. Where this is done the inquiry is likely to be fairer to all concerned, since it is unrealistic to suppose that objectors have any effective voice to criticise policy in Parliament. The latitude allowed to them may vary according to the subject matter, and they may more reasonably claim to attack the policy underlying a development plan (for example) than that underlying the need for a power station or an airport.

This issue came to a head before the House of Lords in a case where objectors wished to dispute the need for a motorway. In advance of the inquiry into the schemes for two sec-tions of the motorway the minister announced that the government's policy to build the motorways would not be open to debate at the inquiry, but that objectors could contest the lines proposed. The inspector in fact allowed the objectors to call evidence questioning the

---

[79] Above, p. 626.   [80] Below, p. 810.

[81] *Lovelock v. Minister of Transport* (1980) 40 P & CR 336 (objection disputing need for motorway held out of order).   [82] Franks Report, Cmnd 218 (1957), para. 288.

[83] *Bushell* v. *Secretary of State for the Environment* [1981] AC 75 at 94 (Lord Diplock). See also *Lovelock* v. *Vespra Township* (1981) 123 DLR (3d) 530 (right to cross-examine on policy statement upheld by Supreme Court of Canada).

[84] e.g. Compulsory Purchase (Inquiries Procedure) Rules 2007 (SI 2007/3617), r. 12(2) (Inspector may not require acquiring authority representative to answer questions about the merits of policy).

[85] See Sullivan J in *R (Powell)* v. *Secretary of State for Communities and Local Government* [2007] EWHC 2051 commenting on the difficulties of disentangling 'straightforward findings of fact from matters of judgment or opinion and thus one very often sees findings of fact and conclusions and opinions mixed up' (para. 8).

need for the motorway as a whole, but he refused to allow cross-examination of departmental witnesses about the methods used for predicting traffic flow for roads generally, which the objectors maintained were faulty. Upholding this refusal as fair in the circumstances, the House of Lords held that traffic prediction technique was a part of general policy and beyond the true scope of a local inquiry.[86] In admitting evidence about need the inspector had made a concession beyond what was required by law, and it was for him to say where the concession should stop. Lord Diplock observed that it would be a rash inspector who felt able to make recommendations on such a matter merely on evidence from one particular inquiry and that it would be an unwise minister who acted on it. Lord Lane also pointed out that it would be no help to the minister to receive differing recommendations about need from a series of local inquiries dealing with separate sections of the route.

The problem of distinguishing between general policy and its local application will appear again in connection with extrinsic evidence, discussed below.

There are strong practical reasons for not allowing local inquiries to be carried too far beyond their proper range. It is not unusual for a major inquiry to take a hundred days or more. The Sizewell B nuclear power station inquiry of 1985–7, for instance, held 340 sittings and produced a 3,000-page report. In the weighing of conflicting public and private interests some account must be taken of expenditure of time and money.

SCOPE OF INQUIRIES: STATUTORY RESTRICTION

The scope of some inquiries is restricted. The normal enactment requires the minister to hold an inquiry and to consider the inspector's report. But some Acts say that the inquiry shall be merely an inquiry into the objection. Thus the formula in the Police Act 1996 provides that the minister proposing a change in police areas should 'consider the objections [duly made to the proposal], and (b) give to [the objector] a further notice stating whether he accepts the objections and, if he does not, giving his reasons'.[87] Its intention is to prevent discussion of the merits of the scheme as opposed to the merits of the objection.

An inquiry 'into the objection' merely is fundamentally inadequate, for as the Franks Committee observed, 'an objection cannot reasonably be considered as a thing in itself, in isolation from what is objected to'.[88] The restriction is a crude and imperfect attempt to make the distinction between general policy and its local application explained above. In fact it is questionable whether an inquiry 'into the objection' is really restricted in any significant way, since it is easy to frame an objection so as to put in issue the whole policy behind the scheme.

A more effective restriction is the power which some statutes give to the minister to disregard objections of certain kinds. For example, under the Acquisition of Land Act 1981[89] the minister may call upon the objector to a compulsory purchase order to state his grounds of objection, and he may disregard the objection if he is satisfied that it can be

---

[86] Bushell v. Secretary of State for the Environment (above) followed in Barbone v. Secretary of State for Transport [2009] EWHC 463. Cf. Carnwath LJ in R (Hillingdon LBC) v. Secretary of State for Transport [2010] EWHC 626 at para. 61: 'I do not accept that Bushell can be read as laying down any general rule that government "policy" is automatically outside the scope of debate at a local planning inquiry.'

[87] Police Act 1996, s. 33.

[88] Cmnd 218 (1957), para. 271. This paragraph erroneously assumes that the standard form of inquiry is into objections only. [89] s. 13 and 1st Sched., para. 4.

dealt with in the assessment of compensation. For other examples of such restrictions see the Highways Act 1980[90] and the Town and Country Planning Act 1990.[91]

EXTRINSIC EVIDENCE: THE PROBLEM

Acute difficulty can arise where the minister bases his decision on facts which he obtains otherwise than through the inquiry. This is another case where the mixture of semi-legal procedure and political decision readily causes misunderstanding. If the objector finds that the minister has taken account of facts which there was no opportunity of contesting at the inquiry, he may feel that the inquiry is a waste of time and money. But, as has been emphasised already, it is inherent in most inquiry procedures that in the end the minister takes a decision of policy, and that the inquiry provides him with only part of the material for his decision. *Ex hypothesi* he may take account of other material. But of what sort of other material?

In its special report to the Lord Chancellor on the Essex chalkpit case[92]—where the minister had rejected the inspector's recommendation in reliance upon expert evidence from the Ministry of Agriculture which was not put before the inspector and which the objectors had no opportunity to controvert—the Council on Tribunals criticised the rejection by the minister of his inspector's recommendation in cases where (i) the rejection was based on ministerial policy which could and should have been made clear at the inquiry or (ii) the minister took advice after the inquiry from persons who neither heard the evidence nor saw the site, but yet controverted the inspector's findings as to the facts of the local situation. These final words contain the heart of the matter. The minister's policy may be formed on the basis of all kinds of fact, reports and advice which have nothing to do with the local situation which is the subject of the inquiry, and which therefore need not necessarily be known to the objectors or investigated at the inquiry. But the facts of the local situation are in a different category, and there is bound to be complaint if due respect is not paid to the inspector's findings. In the chalkpit case the government's explanations were not clear on this vital question: was the advice given by the Ministry of Agriculture general advice, to the effect that a certain mode of chalk-working was incapable of creating excessive dust; or was it really advice about the local situation, to the effect that chalk-working in that particular pit would be innocuous? It was the possibility that the advice was of the latter character that justified the complaint.

EXTRINSIC EVIDENCE: THE SOLUTION

The Council on Tribunals recommended that there should be a rule for future cases providing that the minister, if differing from the inspector's recommendation on a finding or a fact or on account of fresh evidence (including expert opinion) or a fresh issue (not being a matter of government policy), should first notify the parties and allow them to comment in writing; and that they should be entitled to have the inquiry reopened if fresh evidence or a fresh issue emerged. This proposed rule was accepted and has since been followed in practice. It is also embodied in the statutory rules of procedure which have been made for

---

[90] 1st Sched., paras. 7, 14.   [91] s. 245(1).
[92] Above, p. 627 (the *Buxton* case).

various classes of inquiries including planning appeals.[93] Failure to observe it has led to the quashing or remitting of a number of decisions.[94]

In some situations it may be difficult to tell what is a finding of fact and what is a matter of opinion.[95] The rule was held not to apply where the minister rejected his inspector's finding that a house in a particular place would be unobjectionable, since the minister was held not to be differing from the inspector on the facts but forming a different opinion of them on the 'planning merits' and enforcing a general policy of not permitting building outside the village boundaries.[96]

It is fully established that the principles of natural justice do not permit the minister, any more than the inspector, to receive evidence as to the local situation from one of the parties concerned in the inquiry, without disclosing it to the others and allowing them to comment. To take evidence from one party behind the backs of the others vitiates the whole inquiry and renders the minister's order liable to be quashed.[97] To take evidence or advice from other sources raises cognate but different questions which the courts have not yet fully explored. It is clear that the inspector must not himself obtain local evidence without disclosing it to the parties,[98] and in principle the minister should be subject to the same restriction. In one case Lord Denning LJ said:[99]

> The minister on his part must also act judicially. He must only consider the report and the material properly before him. He must not act on extrinsic information which the house-owner has had no opportunity of contradicting. Thus far have the courts gone.

But this 'extrinsic information' should be limited to information about the local situation in the particular case. It can hardly extend to information relating only to general policy, which the minister should always be able to obtain and use with complete freedom.[100]

---

[93] See next section. For planning appeals see SI 2000 No. 1624, r. 17(5). A technical defect is that the rule does not apply where the inspector makes no recommendation: see *Westminster Bank Ltd* v. *Beverley Borough Council* [1971] AC 508. A further defect is that it 'only bites where the Secretary of State is disposed to disagree with the Inspector' (Council on Tribunals, *Annual Report*, 1987–8, para. 2.82). Parties opposed to the inspector's recommendation may be prejudiced by being unable to controvert fresh evidence supporting the recommendation. See also *Hamilton* v. *Roxburgh County Council* 1971 SC 2. The Parliamentary Commissioner for Administration is willing to investigate complaints of breach of the rule, despite the obvious legal remedy: see his *Annual Report for 1969* (HC 138, 1969–70) at 169 (Case C.54/L). See *R (Hughes)* v. *Deputy Prime Minister* [2006] EWCA Civ 838 (r. 17(5) did not apply to matters of law that were or were deemed to be public knowledge (para. 13)).

[94] *French Kier Developments Ltd* v. *Secretary of State for the Environment* [1977] 1 All ER 296; *Penwith DC* v. *Secretary of State for the Environment* (1977) 34 P & CR 269 (erroneously citing the Tribunals and Inquiries Act instead of the inquiry rules); *Pyrford Properties Ltd* v. *Secretary of State for the Environment* (1977) 36 P & CR 28; *Pollock* v. *Secretary of State for the Environment* (1979) 40 P & CR 94.

[95] See *R (Hughes)* v. *Deputy Prime Minister* [2006] EWCA Civ 838 for the drawing of a distinction between (a) a finding of fact and (b) an attribution of weight to the finding of fact (paras. 13–19).

[96] *Luke (Lord)* v. *Minister of Housing and Local Government* [1968] 1 QB 172; *Vale Estates Ltd* v. *Secretary of State for the Environment* (1970) 69 LGR 543; *Murphy & Sons Ltd* v. *Secretary of State for the Environment* [1973] 1 WLR 560; *Brown* v. *Secretary of State for the Environment* (1980) 40 P & CR 285. See similarly *Darlassis* v. *Minister of Education* (1954) 52 LGR 304 (minister at liberty to consult another minister on matter of policy) and *Summers* v. *Minister of Health* [1947] 1 All ER 184; *Lithgow* v. *Secretary of State for Scotland*, 1973 SLT 81. Contrast *Burwoods (Caterers) Ltd* v. *Secretary of State for the Environment* (1972) Est. Gaz. Dig. 1007 (local information used: decision quashed); *De Mulder* v. *First Secretary of State* [2005] EWHC 2640 (minister entitled to disagree with inspector without notifying parties).

[97] As in the cases cited above, p. 430.

[98] As in *Hibernian Property Co Ltd* v. *Secretary of State for the Environment* (1973) 27 P & CR 197 and *Fairmount Investments Ltd* v. *Secretary of State for the Environment* [1976] 1 WLR 1255 (above, p. 430). *Hibernian* applied in *Bancon Developments Ltd* v. *Scottish Ministers* [2011] CSOH 137.

[99] *Steele* v. *Minister of Housing and Local Government* (1956) 6 P & CR 386 at 392.

[100] See *Bushell* v. *Secretary of State for the Environment* [1981] AC 75, discussed above, p. 806.

PROCEDURAL RULES

The Tribunals and Inquiries Act 1992[101] empowers the Lord Chancellor to make rules of procedure for statutory inquiries, or classes of inquiries, held by or on behalf of ministers. The rules may provide for preliminary matters; they must be made by statutory instrument.[102] Among the more important provisions of the Lord Chancellor's rules are those dealing with:

1. the timetable for the various steps and formalities[103]

2. the written statement of its case by the initiating or opposing authority,[104] usually to be supplied at least forty-two days before the inquiry

3. the persons entitled to appear at the inquiry

4. the right of representation

5. evidence of government departments concerned with the proposal; the right to call evidence and cross-examine departmental representatives and witnesses (though not to ask questions directed to the merits of government policy)

6. procedure for site inspections

7. evidence obtained after the inquiry[105]

8. notification of the decision, with reasons[106]

9. the right to obtain a copy of the inspector's report[107]

10. the holding of pre-inquiry meetings (at which the timetable for the inquiry will be set).[108]

The persons entitled to appear as of right under the rules are those who have some statutory standing in the matter. In compulsory purchase cases this means any owner, lessee or occupier of the land who is entitled to have notice of the compulsory purchase order and has made formal objections, and also the acquiring authority.[109] In planning appeals it means the appellant, the local planning authority, certain other local authorities in some cases, certain other persons with legal rights in the land affected, persons who have made formal objection in cases where advertisement of the application is required, and any person on whom the Secretary of State has required notice of it to be served.[110] The rules then provide that any other person may appear at the inspector's discretion, and in practice appearances by neighbours, amenity societies and others are freely allowed.[111]

---

[101] s. 9. Similar provisions have been in force since 1959.

[102] Previously the Lord Chancellor was obliged to consult the Administrative Justice and Tribunals Council but that body has now been abolished. See Public Bodies (Abolition of Administrative Justice and Tribunals Council) Order 2013 (SI 2013/2042).

[103] The practice of the Lord Chancellor (e.g. in the Planning (Inquiries Procedure) Rules (SI 2000 No. 1624)) has been to calculate the times allowed from the date of the Secretary of State's notification to the parties that an inquiry would be held, rather than backwards from the date of the inquiry. Generally the inquiry has to be held within 22 weeks of the date of notification (r. 10(1)); 28 days' notice of the date of the inquiry must be given to all entitled to appear (r. 10(3)). In *Ostreicher v. Secretary of State for the Environment* [1978] 1 WLR 810 a complaint that the objector could not attend on the specified date for religious reasons was disallowed.   [104] Above, p. 801.

[105] Above, p. 807.   [106] Above, p. 803.

[107] Above, p. 803.   [108] SI 2000 Nos. 1624 and 1625, r. 5 and r. 7 respectively.

[109] Compulsory Purchase (Inquiry Procedure) Rules 2007 (SI 2007/3617). See now r. 14(3): 'The inspector may permit any other person to appear at the inquiry, and such permission shall not be unreasonably withheld.'   [110] SI 2000 No. 1625, r. 6.

[111] The Code of Practice for Major Inquiries (Circular 10/88 (Department of the Environment)) provides for more equal treatment of those with direct interests in the land and others such as neighbours and amenity societies. All those interested in participating may register with the Inspector and are given

The question whether there is really any legal power to exclude them has been mentioned above.[112] At any rate, they do not under the statutory rules enjoy the full rights of a party. They are not entitled to be sent the statement of the initiating or opposing authority's case; and they are not entitled to the benefit of the rule, discussed above, about disclosure of evidence from sources other than the inquiry. The Council on Tribunals was unsuccessful in asking for an assurance that the benefit of the latter rule should in practice be extended to them.[113] Their only protection is that they will usually have similar interests to one of the statutory parties, who will be officially encouraged to keep them informed.[114] Any person who so requests must be afforded a reasonable opportunity to inspect and take copies of relevant documents.[115]

This difficulty illustrates the paradox which underlies many inquiries where an issue which in law lies between particular parties is in practice thrown open to the public at large. The principal legal advantage that has so far been won by third party objectors is that an objector who under the rules has been given leave to appear at the inquiry thereby acquires the character of a 'person aggrieved' for the purpose of challenging the legality of the decision under statutory procedure.[116] This improvement in his position is held to flow from the existence of the rules, though they do not in fact alter the previous practice in this respect. He may also benefit from the progressive relaxation of the rules about the standing of third party objectors, of which examples have been given earlier.[117]

An objector's right of representation is unrestricted, so that he may appear by a lawyer or by any other person, as well as by himself.

PUBLIC OR PRIVATE HEARINGS

The rules contain no requirement that the proceedings should be held in public. Although public hearings have always been the rule, the inspector was able (as in a court of law) to exclude the public and even other parties where the evidence to be given was confidential, for example a secret commercial process. In such cases there is an irreconcilable conflict between the objectors' rights to know the case against them and to cross-examine witnesses and, on the other hand, the need for secrecy in genuine cases. Since 1972 the policy has been that inspectors should not hear evidence in private at planning inquiries;[118] and in 1982 this rule was made statutory, subject only to exceptions where the national interest required secrecy in order to protect national security or to safeguard measures taken for the security of premises or property.[119]

Where the rules are silent there is no presumption that the inquiry will take place in public and Article 10 of the European Convention on Human Rights (ECHR) (freedom of expression) is not engaged.[120] Whether to hold an inquiry at all and whether it should sit in public

---

an opportunity to put their case to him. The 2007 Rules, above, now provide (r. 14(3)): 'The inspector may permit any other person to appear at the inquiry, and such permission shall not be unreasonably withheld.'

[112] Above, p. 804.

[113] *Annual Report*, 1962, para. 37. The Council on Tribunals' further attempt also failed: *Annual Report*, 1987–8, para. 2.82.   [114] Same report, para. 39.

[115] SI 2000/1625, r. 6(13) and SI 2007/3617, r. 15(5).   [116] See above, p. 629.

[117] Above, pp. 590 and 593.   [118] 836 HC Deb., written answers, col. 199 (4 May 1972).

[119] Town and Country Planning Act 1990, s. 321, replacing Planning Inquiries (Attendance of Public) Act 1982. See the Planning (National Security Directions and Appointed Representatives) (England) Rules 2006 (SI 2006/1284).

[120] *R (Persey)* v. *Secretary of State for the Environment, Food and Rural Affairs* [2002] EWHC 371 (Admin), [2003] QB 794 (Minister's decision that 'Lessons Learnt' Inquiry (non-statutory) into outbreak of Foot and Mouth Disease should sit in private upheld) and *R (Howard)* v. *Secretary of State for Health* [2002] EWHC

were 'pre-eminently…political decision[s]'.[121] But sometimes the ECHR will require the inquiry to be held in public.[122]

PROCEDURE, EVIDENCE, COSTS

The inspector is master of the procedure at an inquiry, always provided that the principles of natural justice and the statutory rules, if any, are properly observed.[123] He may adjourn it if this is reasonable,[124] and he may exclude anyone who disrupts the proceedings.[125] The legal rules of evidence do not apply, so that hearsay may be admitted, if relevant, without vitiating the proceedings, whether or not the evidence is taken on oath.[126] Cross-examination is allowed by procedural rules[127] and evidently also by the rules of natural justice,[128] if it is within the proper scope of the inquiry. The House of Lords has decided that witnesses enjoy absolute privilege against actions for defamation.[129]

Powers to take evidence on oath[130] or affirmation, and also to require persons to attend and produce documents, are conferred on the inspector in many classes of inquiries, including planning and compulsory purchase inquiries.[131]

Legal representation is always allowed in practice, as well as under procedural rules, and is probably a matter of natural justice. Legal advice and assistance, but not legal aid,[132] are available in connection with statutory inquiries on the same basis as in the case of tribunals.[133]

Ministers have power in numerous cases, again including planning and compulsory purchase, to make orders for the recovery of costs incurred in connection with inquiries either by the department or by local authorities or by other parties.[134] Following a special

396, [2003] QB 830. But a decision by the minister setting up an inquiry that it will not sit in public was in the circumstances quashed as irrational (*R (Wagstaff)* v. *Secretary of State for Health* [2001] 1 WLR 292) discussed below, p. 818.   [121] Simon Brown LJ in *Persey*, para. 66.

[122] *R (D)* v. *Home Secretary* [2006] EWCA Civ 143 (closed inquiry into prisoner's attempted suicide would violate Art. 2).

[123] See *Miller (TA) Ltd* v. *Minister of Housing and Local Government* [1968] 1 WLR 992; *Winchester City Council* v. *Secretary of State for the Environment* (1979) 39 P & CR 1 (inspector rightly refused to hear expert witness); and *Eley* v. *Secretary of State for Communities and Local Government* [2009] EWHC 660 (inspector's discretion to consider information (even outside procedural timetable) was wide and challengeable only if unreasonable or irrational: para. 67).

[124] *Ostreicher* v. *Secretary of State for the Environment* [1978] 1 WLR 810; *Greycoat Commercial Estates Ltd* v. *Radmore*, The Times, 14 July 1981 (3 months adjournment upheld).

[125] *Lovelock* v. *Secretary of State for Transport* (1979) 39 P & CR 468 (disrupters removed by police; disrupter excluded from the inquiry cannot complain of breach of natural justice). The inspector in planning appeals is given power to exclude disrupters from the pre-inquiry meeting as well as from the inquiry proper (SI 2000 Nos. 1624 and 955, r. 5(8) and r. 7(3) respectively). Previously inspectors lacked an explicit power to exclude from the pre-inquiry meeting (Council on Tribunals, *Annual Report*, 1987–8, para. 2.80). See also the Compulsory Purchase (Inquiries Procedure) Rules, SI 2007/3617, r. 16(7).

[126] *Marriott* v. *Minister of Health* (1935) 154 LT 47; *Miller (TA) Ltd* v. *MHLC* (above).

[127] Above, p. 810.   [128] Above, p. 428.

[129] *Trapp* v. *Mackie* [1979] 1 WLR 377 (Secretary of State's inquiry into reasons for dismissal of headmaster), holding that it is not necessary for the inspector to have the power of decision. See [1982] *PL* at 432 (N. V. Lowe and H. F. Rawlings).

[130] This power exists in any case: Evidence Act 1851, s. 16; above, p. 777.

[131] e.g. Acquisition of Land Act 1981, s. 5(2); Town and Country Planning Act 1990, s. 320; both applying (as is usual) the powers of Local Government Act 1972, s. 250 (as it now is).

[132] See *Pascoe* v. *First Secretary of State* [2006] EWHC 2356 (although Art. 6 applicable, it did not require legal aid in the inquisitorial inquiry (in any event no application made to minister for assistance)).

[133] Above, p. 781 and below p. 817 (Tribunals of Inquiry).   [134] As in *Pascoe*, above n. 134.

report by the Council on Tribunals,[135] this power has been exercised more freely. Costs are usually awarded against any party who behaves unreasonably and vexatiously, including a public authority. Costs are usually awarded to successful objectors in compulsory purchase and similar cases; and inspectors usually make recommendations as to costs in their reports.[136] After a long interval legislation has extended the power to award costs to hearings in addition to inquiries and also to planning appeals decided on written representations.[137] Inspectors have also been empowered to award costs on the same basis as the Secretary of State.[138] That basis is now very wide, since it may extend to 'the entire administrative cost of the inquiry' including staff costs and overheads.[139] Since these costs can only be computed by the department, and in any case the department acts as judge in its own cause when costs are awarded in its favour, the arrangements seem far from satisfactory in principle.

DISCRETIONARY INQUIRIES

The Tribunals and Inquiries Act 1992 defines a 'statutory inquiry' as an inquiry or hearing held under a statutory duty.[140] The other provisions of the Act therefore apply where an Act provides that the minister *shall* hold an inquiry, but do not apply where the provision is merely that the minister *may* hold an inquiry. There are many discretionary inquiries of the latter class, and it is no less important that they should be brought within the Act. Examples of discretionary inquiries are those held under the Local Government Act 1972, where departments have a general power to hold inquiries in connection with their functions under the Act,[141] inquiries into objections to compulsory purchase orders for defence purposes,[142] and inquiries held under the Health and Safety at Work Act 1974[143] and the Highways Act 1980.[144]

The Tribunals and Inquiries Act 1966 dealt with this problem by giving power to the Lord Chancellor to make orders designating particular classes of inquiries as subject to the relevant parts of the Tribunals and Inquiries Act 1958 relating to supervision by the Council on Tribunals and the making of procedural rules.[145] The duty to give reasons for decisions could also be made applicable, but this required express direction in the order.[146] The current order, made in 1975, has extended the list to more than eighty classes where reasons must be given, and has added thirty-five additional classes where reasons need not be given.[147] In this latter group are, amongst others, certain accident inquiries,[148]

---

[135] Cmnd 2471 (1964).

[136] The details are set out in the Department for Communities and Local Government circular on costs in planning appeals (Circular 03/2009), available at <http://www.gov.uk/government/uploads/system/uploads/attachment_data/file/7680/circularcostsawards.pdf>. The Town and Country Planning Act 1990, s. 320(3) and Acquisition of Land Act 1981, s. 5(4) (as inserted by the Growth and Infrastructure Act 2013, ss. 2–3) empower the inspector in planning and compulsory purchase inquiries to award a proportion of a participant's costs (i.e. it is no longer necessary to award 'all or nothing').

[137] Town and Country Planning Act 1990, s. 322 and 6th Sched., para. 6.

[138] Act of 1990, 6th Sched., para. 6(5).

[139] Housing and Planning Act 1986, s. 42. This applies even where the inquiry does not take place.

[140] Above, p. 801.   [141] s. 250.

[142] See Council on Tribunals, *Annual Report*, 1961, para. 79.

[143] s. 14 (power to investigate accident with a view to introducing new health and safety regulations).

[144] s. 302.

[145] See now Tribunals and Inquiries Act 1992, s. 16(2), making the designated inquiries subject to the Act generally, except as regards reasons for decisions.   [146] Tribunals and Inquiries Act 1992, s. 10(4).

[147] SI 1975 No. 1379, as amended most recently by SI 1992 No. 2171.   [148] Below, p. 824.

certain cases where inquiries may be held into any matter arising under an Act,[149] and also decisions on 'Secretary of State's questions' in social security matters.[150]

INFORMAL PROCEDURES

Since any inquiry into anything may always be held informally, ministers sometimes prefer to avoid statutory procedures altogether and to hold non-statutory inquiries. In such cases objectors have no procedural rights (apart from the principles of natural justice) and the safeguards intended by the Act of 1966 cannot operate. The Council on Tribunals publicly criticised this practice.[151]

An informal inquiry procedure, which proved so useful that it was made statutory in 1986, was that by which appellants in planning appeals were invited by the department to agree to have their appeals decided on written representations only, without an inquiry or hearing.[152] The attraction of this voluntary alternative was that it saved time and expense and was frequently satisfactory—so much so that the great majority of all planning appeals came to be decided by inspectors after an exchange of written representations and a site visit.[153] The inspector's report and the Secretary of State's decision (if any) are now made available and there is the usual right to a reasoned decision on request. But this procedure makes limited provision for the views of third party objectors such as neighbours and amenity societies.[154]

MAJOR INQUIRIES

Big projects for such things as major airports and power stations often raise difficult questions about alternative sites and other problems of more than local character which cannot well be handled at an ordinary local inquiry.[155] Sometimes they are of gigantic proportions, such as the inquiries concerned with the Greater London Development Plan (1970), which sat on 240 days, the Sizewell B nuclear power station (1983–5), which sat on 340 days and the Heathrow Terminal 5 Inquiry, which sat on 524 days.

There have been several attempts by Parliament to set up new procedures to deal more effectively with major projects. Given the delays just set out, the public interest in more effective procedures for such projects can scarcely be denied. But several of these were still-born, discarded before they were implemented. The current arrangements as established under the Planning Act 2008 (as amended by the Localism Act 2011) seem more effective. The current arrangements contain elements of the earlier attempts—in

---

[149] e.g. Land Compensation Act 1961, s. 39 (power to hold inquiry into exercise of any of the Secretary of State's powers under the Act).

[150] Under Social Security Administration Act 1992, s. 17. For these questions see above, p. 767.

[151] *Annual Report*, 1967, p. 27; 1968, p. 14.

[152] Council on Tribunals, *Annual Report*, 1964, para. 76; 1966, para. 89. The written representations procedure has been extended to compulsory purchase appeals by the Planning and Compulsory Purchase Act 2004 (amending Acquisition of Land Act 1981, ss. 13–13B).

[153] In 2012–13 it took an average of 7 weeks to decide an appeal under the written representations procedure for 'householders'. For non-'householder' cases the average time was 21 weeks (Planning Inspectorate, *Annual Statistical Report 2012–13*, p. 12).

[154] The Compulsory Purchase of Land (Written Representations Procedure) (Ministers) Regulations 2004 (SI 2004/2594), reg. 6 empowers an authorising authority to permit written representations to be made by third parties.

[155] For discussion of government proposals for reform see (2002) *JPL* 137 (Popham and Purdue). See above, p. 806.

particular the consultation requirement is 'front-loaded'; it precedes the application for consent itself. But the final decision is taken by a minister. The idea of entrusting the decision to an unelected Commission has been discarded.

The Act of 2008 applies to 'nationally significant infrastructure projects', which are listed by type in section 14 and include the construction of generating stations, airport-related development, railways, highways and facilities for electricity and gas distribution. The applicant must apply for 'development consent' to the Secretary of State.[156] Consultation is a pre-application obligation.[157] The statutory consultees do not include the public in general but do include relevant local authorities, prescribed persons, those with an interest in the land, those with a relevant claim for compensation if the development goes ahead and those living in the vicinity of the land to be developed.[158]

Once the application is made, the Secretary of State appoints either a single person or a panel[159] to (a) examine the application and (b) produce a report for the Secretary of State.[160] Subject to the rules laid down in the 2008 Act, the examining authority must decide how to examine the application.[161] Chapter 4 of Part 6 of the 2008 Act sets out various rules which apply to different types of examination (e.g. written representations, oral hearings etc.). The decision whether to grant development consent falls to the Secretary of State.[162] And in doing so he is to 'have regard' to national policy statements.[163] A decision to grant or refuse consent may be challenged only by an application for judicial review brought within six weeks of the day on which the order refusing or granting consent is published or, if later, the day on which the statement of reasons for making the order is published'.[164]

As of October 2013 some twelve applications had been dealt with through the new system but this included the grant of consent for the Hinkley Point C nuclear generator within one year (following three years of pre-application consultation).[165]

DECISIONS BY INSPECTORS

The large number of planning appeals, now in the order of 15,500 a year,[166] inevitably led to severe delays. In order to reduce the time-lag the Secretary of State was empowered in 1968 to prescribe classes of appeals to be decided by the inspector himself without reference to the Department, subject to the Secretary of State's option to require any particular case to be referred.[167] The prescribed classes have now been extended to cover the great majority of planning appeals.[168] The Tribunals and Inquiries Act 1992 applies in all respects,[169] and rules of procedure of the usual kind have been made.[170] Furthermore, there is provision for the parties to waive their right to an oral hearing, so that in these

---

[156] s. 37.   [157] ss. 41–50.

[158] ss. 42, 44, 47. Consultation is also subject to a timetable: s. 45.   [159] s. 61.   [160] s. 74.

[161] s. 87.

[162] s. 103. The 2008 Act introduced an (unelected) Infrastructure Planning Commission which would decide applications for consent. The Commission's power was returned to the Secretary of State by amendments introduced by the Localism Act 2011.

[163] s. 104. National Policy Statements are made under a procedure set out in s. 29.   [164] s. 118.

[165] See 'Post Legislative Scrutiny Planning Act 2008', Cm. 8716, p. 11. For the Hinkley Point C nuclear generator decision see p. 11, <http://www.official-documents.gov.uk/document/cm87/8716/8716.pdf>.

[166] *Planning Inspectorate Statistical Report 2012–13*, <http://www.planningportal.gov.uk/uploads/pins/statistics_eng/annual_2012_13.pdf>.   [167] Town and Country Planning Act 1990, Sched. 6.

[168] SI 1997 No. 420.   [169] 6th Sched. (as above), para. 8(1).   [170] SI 2000 No. 1625.

cases also the procedure for determining appeals on written representations only has acquired a statutory basis and is subject to the general law governing inquiries.[171]

This procedure has in general worked well, despite the abnormal expedient of putting final decisions on matters of policy into the hands of officials not responsible to Parliament. However, it has not solved the problem of delay. Severe delays were experienced in the late 1980s. These have been significantly reduced since the planning inspectorate was established as an executive agency, and now generally meet the targets set by ministers.[172]

The Secretary of State has experimented with 'informal hearings' which he may offer in selected 'inspector's decision' cases where the appellant and the local planning authority agree. The timetable is accelerated[173] and the hearing takes the form of a discussion led by the inspector, sitting with the parties and their advisers round the same table. Evidence is circulated in advance and is not read out at the hearing, and cross-examination is by informal questioning. The inspector gives his decision in writing soon after the hearing and the formal decision letter follows later. These are statutory hearings and the normal rules of procedure apply with minor adjustments, and with the aid of a code of practice. They have proved to be a popular and efficient alternative to a formal local inquiry.[174]

INSPECTORS GENERALLY

All the evidence before the Franks Committee of 1955–7 was to the effect that the inspectors were competent, patient and open to very little criticism[175] as to the manner in which they controlled the proceedings. Their reputation was strengthened still further by the practice of publishing their reports.

As explained above, all the inspectors have now been organised into an executive agency, the Planning Inspectorate.[176] Although the agency continues to operate within the government planning policy, agency status enhances the perceived independence of the inspectors; and the quality of adjudication by inspectors is not threatened by this development.[177]

In the past the status of departmental inspectors has been controversial, especially when the department initiated the proposal under enquiry. But the establishment of the Planning Inspectorate has weakened links with the department and the use of such inspectors has ceased to be controversial. There is a danger, if the inspector is too independent of the department that is the engine of planning policy, that objectors will be misled as to the nature of the inquiry and believe that the decision will be based entirely on evidence led at the inquiry.

---

[171] 6th Sched. (as above), para. 2(3).

[172] In 2012–13 average time to decide appeals under written representations procedure: 7 weeks ('householder' cases); 21 weeks (non-'householder' cases); average time to decide appeals by way of hearing: 22 weeks; average time to decide appeals by way of inquiry: 30 weeks (Planning Inspectorate, *Statistical Report 2012–13*, p.12), <http://www.planningportal.gov.uk/uploads/pins/statistics_eng/annual_2012_13.pdf>.

[173] In 1991–2 the median overall time was 28 weeks.

[174] 7% of planning appeals were decided by way of informal 'hearing in 2012–13 (Planning Inspectorate, *Statistical Report 2012–13*, p. 14).

[175] In 2012–13 99.5% of inspectors' decisions were found (by the Planning Inspectorate) to be free from justified complaint (Planning Inspectorate, *Statistical Report 2012–13*, p. 11).

[176] For executive agencies see p. 37.   [177] *Annual Report*, 1991–2, paras. 1.64–1.69.

OTHER INQUIRY PROCEDURES

'Other inquiries', i.e. inquiries that find facts and may attribute responsibility once something has gone wrong, take many different forms.[178] Most of these inquiries are discretionary in that they are not required to be held by law. But there are some such inquiries which the law requires to be held once an unexplained death or an accident has occurred. Accident inquiries are relatively uncontroversial and take place under many different statutes about which there is little that can be said generally. But judicial review of coroners' courts have become prominent both because Article 2 of the Convention (the right to life) has been held to require an adequate and effective investigation into a violent death[179] and because the practice of returning the bodies of fallen soldiers to the United Kingdom, so they fall within the jurisdiction of the coroner, has brought within judicial scrutiny the failings of the kit and equipment supplied to troops in the Iraq war when these failings have contributed to the death of a soldier. Similarly, Article 3—prohibition on torture and 'inhuman or degrading treatment or punishment'—may require an inquiry to be held.[180]

Discretionary inquiries are particularly various in form.[181] On the one hand there is the inquiry set up by a minister on an ad hoc basis under no statute and with no legal powers, of which one prominent example in recent times is the Hutton Inquiry into the death of Dr David Kelly and another is the Chilcot Inquiry into the Iraq war (which is yet to report).

Also without legal powers are the private inquiries established by universities or other bodies to inquire into matters of concern (e.g. alleged scientific misconduct). Being private these inquiries are not subject to judicial review and so do not have proper standards of impartiality and fairness (taking evidence from all sides etc.) imposed upon them by public law. This is unfortunate when the matter inquired into is of public importance.[182]

On the other hand, is the inquiry clothed with the legal powers of the High Court to call and compel witnesses. Such inquiries, when held, were previously held either under subject-specific legislation or under the Tribunals of Inquiry (Evidence) Act 1921.[183] They are now generally held under the Inquiries Act 2005 (which repealed the 1921 Act). Inquiries of this kind have no particular or necessary connection with administrative powers or with administrative law; for though they have often been used to investigate allegations of administrative misdeeds by ministers of the Crown, civil servants, local authorities or the police, it is not confined to such matters.[184] An inquiry of this kind is often a procedure of last resort, to be used when nothing else will serve to allay public disquiet, usually based on sensational allegations, rumours or disasters. Inquiries

---

[178] See Beer, *Public Inquiries* (2011) for a comprehensive account.

[179] *Jordan* v. *UK* (2001) 37 EHRR 70 at para. 135; *McCann* v. *UK* (1995) 21 EHRR 97. And note particularly *R (Mousa)* v. *Secretary of State Defence (No 2)* [2013] EWHC 2941 (very specific guidance given to the Secretary of State as to the inquiry in relation to civilian deaths in Iraq).

[180] *R (AM)* v. *Home Secretary* [2009] EWCA Civ 219 (government obliged to investigate a disturbance at an immigration detention centre which caused some inmates to experience degrading situations).

[181] There is a useful discussion of the various forms of inquiry in Parry, 'Investigatory inquiries and the Inquiries Act 2005' (Parliament and Constitution Centre, 2008). For discussion of the Hutton Inquiry see [2004] *PL* 472 (Blom-Cooper and Munro).

[182] For discussion see Montford, *The Climategate Inquiries* available at <http://www.thegwpf.org/the-climategate-inquries/>.   [183] For a general account see Keeton, *Trial by Tribunal*.

[184] In *Haughey* v. *Moriarty* 103/98 (28 July 1998) the Irish Supreme Court, considering the very similar Irish legislation, held that a tribunal of inquiry was properly established into the tax affairs of a former Taoiseach; tribunals were not limited to inquiries that might aid legislation. But the court stressed that tribunals of inquiry should not be used for local or minor matters. See [1999] *PL* 175 (L. Blom-Cooper).

are generally subject to judicial review and are under a general duty of fairness, so the principles of administrative law are engaged in this way. The courts will intervene where there is 'very good reason'.[185] Even so the courts have several times intervened securing fairness in inquiry procedures,[186] finding that the particular form of inquiry chosen by the Secretary of State was irrational[187] and challenging the findings of the inquiry.[188] But it should be noted that the 2005 Act provides that any application for judicial review of an inquiry must be brought within '14 days after the day on which the applicant became aware of the decision'.[189] The decision of a minister not to hold an inquiry has also frequently been challenged but not often with success.[190]

The 2005 Act arose from concern that inquiries were sometimes unnecessarily 'protracted and costly' and steps should be taken to ensure that they were more economical and that their recommendations were more speedily reached.[191] These concerns were prompted in the main by the second 'Bloody Sunday' Inquiry which reported in June 2010 (having been established in 1998) and has been estimated to have cost over

---

[185] *R v. Lord Saville of Newdigate ex p B*, The Times, 15 April 1999 (CA) (quashing tribunal's decision to disclose identity of witnesses since the tribunal misunderstood assurances given (by first tribunal of inquiry into same matter) that anonymity was guaranteed because of threats to witnesses' lives and security). This was the second inquiry held under the 1921 Act into the events of 'Bloody Sunday' (30 January 1972). The tribunal's subsequent decision not to grant anonymity notwithstanding the assurances was also quashed for failure to have sufficient regard to the witnesses' fundamental rights, especially the right to life (*R v. The Same* [2000] 1 WLR 1855 (CA)). See [1999] PL 663 (B. Hadfield) and [2000] PL 1 (Blom-Cooper). There has also been litigation on where the soldiers should give evidence: *R (A) v. Lord Saville of Newdigate* [2002] 1 WLR 1249 (CA) (tribunal of inquiry directed that soldiers' evidence should not be taken in Londonderry). While 'good reason' to intervene seems to have been readily found in the Bloody Sunday cases, it proved more difficult to find in *Mount Murray Country Club Ltd v. Macleod* [2003] UKPC 53, [2003] STC 1525. The Privy Council said that judicial review should not restrict the work of the inquiry unless it was 'being unreasonable'. See [2003] PL 578 (Blom-Cooper). For a further example, see *Peters v. Davison* [1999] 2 NZLR 164 (CA), intervention justified on ground of error of law on face of record. For further discussion of the Saville Inquiry see [2010] PL 61 (Blom-Cooper). Identifying witnesses is a frequent theme of challenges to inquiry procedures with challenges seldom succeeding: *R (Associated Newspapers Ltd) v. Leveson* [2012] EWHC 57 (Admin) (Chairman's decision to extend anonymity to journalists who feared for their jobs or professional reputation upheld); *R (E) v. Chairman of the Inquiry into the Death of Azelle Rodney* [2012] EWHC 563 (decision not to permit witnesses to give evidence behind a screen upheld) and *Re Officer L* [2007] UKHL 36 (police officer's request for anonymity properly refused by the chairman).

[186] See the several reviews of the procedures of the Second Bloody Sunday Inquiry referred to in the previous note.

[187] *R (Wagstaff) v. Secretary of State for Health* [2001] 1 WLR 292 (minister's decision that inquiry under National Health Service Act 1977, s. 2 into Shipman case (GP who murdered many of his patients) should sit in private, held irrational). This decision led to the stopping of the s. 2 inquiry and a full public inquiry under the 1921 Act chaired by Dame Janet Smith.

[188] As in *Mahon v. Air New Zealand* [1984] AC 808. Cf. [2007] PL 529 (Quane). But see Beer, *Public Inquiries* (2011), paras. 11.07–9.

[189] 2005 Act, s. 38(1). The normal period is 6 weeks (see above, p. 624). But the short time period does not apply to judicial review of the report itself or of matters that were only apparent from the report (s. 38(3)). The court may extend time (s. 38(1)).

[190] *Keyu v. Secretary of State for Foreign and Commonwealth Affairs* [2012] EWHC 2445, para. 105 (no common law right to inquiry into a death (*Re McKerr* [2004] UKHL 12 followed) thus no further inquiry into the deaths of civilians killed by British troops in Malaya in 1948); *Kennedy v. Lord Advocate* [2008] CSOH 21, 2008 SLT 195 (Lord Advocate not obliged to order inquiry into hepatitis C deaths caused by infected blood products). Success rates are higher where Art. 2 is engaged (e.g. *Smith v. Ministry of Defence* [2013] UKSC 41). But not every death will require an inquiry: *Judicial Review of the Lord Advocate's Refusal to hold a Fatal Accident Inquiry* [2007] CSOH 184 (non-suspicious death in hospital; no inquiry required).

[191] See 'Modern Public Inquiries' (2008) (Giffin) an ALBA paper available at <http://www.adminlaw.org.uk/docs/Nigel%20Giffin%20QC%20-%2018%20June%202008.doc>.

£195 million.[192] There was also concern that non-statutory inquiries might in the absence of legal power be ineffective although there are no obvious examples of this.[193]

The 2005 Act significantly alters the way in which inquiries will operate in the future. Under the 1921 Act both Houses of Parliament needed to resolve that a tribunal shall investigate some matter described as being 'of urgent public importance'. The tribunal was then appointed by the Crown or Secretary of State in a document reciting that the Act was to apply. But under the 2005 Act a minister 'may cause an inquiry to be held' under the Act when it appears to him that 'public concern' has been caused or may be caused by particular events.[194] The minister must inform Parliament (or the appropriate devolved legislature) of the setting up of the inquiry including details of the members of the inquiry panel etc.[195] But the minister determines the membership of the inquiry panel and the terms of reference without reference to the legislature.[196] In accordance with past practice the law now lays down that the inquiry has 'no power' to determine any person's civil or criminal liability.[197] The chairman of the inquiry has power to require the production of evidence by any person and this includes the making of a written statement to presenting themselves for examination.[198] It is an offence to fail to comply with such a requirement.[199] Where the failure to comply with such a requirement is certified by the chairman to the High Court the court may then after hearing representations enforce the requirement as if the matter had arisen in proceedings before it.[200]

Judges may be appointed to the inquiry panel after consultation with a senior member of the judiciary.[201] The appointment of such judicial commissions of inquiry is problematical since judges who chair inquiries are easily drawn into matters of acute political dispute. A judicial chairman of an inquiry may be (and some have been) criticised unfairly by those dissatisfied with the inquiry's findings of fact or recommendations. 'When a judge enters the market place of public affairs outside his court and throws coconuts he is likely to have the coconuts thrown back at him.'[202] The dangers to perceptions of independence are obvious. A persuasive study concludes that '[j]udges should only be used to conduct inquiries where there is a vital public interest in them doing so'.[203] It has also been pointed out that judges, amongst other perceived failings, are 'not immediately practised…[in] negotiating and controlling the processes of social policymaking or of implementation of organisational or societal reforms'.[204]

---

[192] See the estimate by Justice at <http://www.justice.gov.uk/downloads/publications/moj/2010/Post-Legislative-Assessment-Inquiries-Act.pdf> (p. 24).

[193] See the Lord Chancellor's introduction to the 'Effective Inquiries' Consultation Paper (which preceded the 2005 Act) available at <http://webarchive.nationalarchives.gov.uk/+/http:/www.dca.gov.uk/consult/inquiries/inquiries.pdf>.

[194] Act of 2005, s. 1(1). The 'Minister' includes ministers in the devolved administrations.

[195] s. 6.

[196] ss. 3, 4 and 5. There are statutory duties on the minister to secure 'balance', 'expertise' and 'impartiality' in the panel (ss. 8 and 9) which might be thought to be so obvious as to be unnecessary.

[197] s. 2. But note s. 2(2). The inquiry should not be 'inhibited in the discharge of its functions' by considerations of any liability that may result from a finding of fact or a recommendation that it makes.

[198] s. 21. But privilege may be claimed in the same way as in a court (including public interest immunity) (s. 22).　　　　　　　　　　　　　　　　　　　　　　　　　　[199] s. 35.

[200] s. 36. In Scotland certification is to the Court of Session (s. 36(3)).

[201] s. 10. The senior judge consulted (who has no veto) varies with jurisdiction.

[202] Lord Morris of Aberavon QC, 648 HL Deb. Col 883 (21 May 2003), cited in Beatson, as below, p. 48.

[203] See Sir Jack Beatson, 'Should Judges conduct public inquiries?', p. 48, the 51st Lionel Cohen Lecture which can be found at <http://www.dca.gov.uk/judicial/speeches/jb070704.pdf> and (2005) 121 LQR 221.

[204] Centre for Effective Dispute Resolution's 'Inquiry into Inquiries' project consultation paper, above, para. 14.4.

In its post-enactment review of the operation of the 2005 Act, the Ministry of Justice[205] identified several issues including the implications for judicial independence of ministers' statutory powers to interfere with inquiries as outlined above.[206] A House of Lords Select Committee on the Inquiries Act 2005 was appointed in May 2013 'to consider and report on the law and practice relating to inquiries into matters of public concern, in particular the Inquiries Act 2005'. The Committee is due to report by 28 February 2014.[207]

THE FAIRNESS OF INQUIRY PROCEDURES

An inquiry is generally inquisitorial in character, and often takes place in a blaze of publicity. Very damaging allegations may be made against persons who may have little opportunity of defending themselves and against whom no legal charge is preferred.

A royal commission (chaired by Salmon LJ) reviewed the whole procedure in 1966 and made fifty recommendations.[208]

In order to minimise the risk of injustice to individuals the Commission identified six 'cardinal principles' that all tribunals established under the 1921 Act should observe. In summary these are: (1) that the tribunal should be satisfied that each witness called was really involved; (2) that every witness should be informed of any allegations, and the substance of the evidence, against him; (3) that he should have an adequate opportunity of preparing his case and of being assisted by legal advisers (normally to be paid for out of public funds); (4) that he should have the opportunity of being examined by his own solicitor or counsel; (5) that all material witnesses a witness wishes to be called should, if reasonably practical, be called; and (6) every witness should have the opportunity of testing any evidence which might affect him by cross-examination conducted by his own solicitor or counsel. But the 'Salmon principles' were never implemented in full and are now more honoured in the breach.[209] The Scott Inquiry into the Export of Defence Equipment and Dual-Use Goods to Iraq[210] did not follow the Salmon principles. Only counsel for the inquiry cross-examined witnesses. Witnesses were not always informed of the allegations against them since nothing might be alleged against them; the tribunal was simply trying to find out what happened. It gave witnesses notice of the matters about which they would be asked questions. Witnesses were not represented by counsel before the inquiry but they were given an opportunity to correct errors in their evidence. In adopting these procedures Sir Richard Scott was guided not only by fairness to the individuals concerned but also by considerations of cost and efficiency. The inquisitorial nature of his inquiry was, he felt, at odds with the adversarial values immanent in the

---

[205] 'Memorandum to the Justice Select Committee: Post-Legislative Assessment of the Inquiries Act 2005', Cm. 7943 (October 2010), <http://www.justice.gov.uk/downloads/publications/moj/2010/Post-Legislative-Assessment-Inquiries-Act.pdf>. [206] Para. 54.

[207] Any developments will be found in Appendix 3. The Select Committee has already published evidence. See <http://www.parliament.uk/documents/lords-committees/Inquiries-Act-2005/IA_Written_Oral_evidencevol.pdf>. [208] Cmnd 3121 (1966).

[209] Even before the Scott Report the Salmon principles were more honoured in the breach. See Appendix to the *Croom-Johnson Report into the Operations of the Crown Agents*, HC 364 (1982); *Crampton* v. *Secretary of State for Health* (CA, 9 July 1993)) (inquiry may be satisfactorily conducted without observing 'the letter' of the 6 cardinal principles (Sir Thomas Bingham MR)). In *R (Hoffmann)* v. *Commissioner of Inquiry* [2012] UKPC 17 at para. 38 Lord Phillips said: 'the Salmon principles cannot be inflexibly applied'.

[210] HC 115 (1995–6). This inquiry was not held under the 1921 Act. All aspects of the inquiry are discussed by several authors in [1996] *PL* 359–527. Lord Phillips' Inquiry into Bovine Spongiform Encephalopathy was also not conducted under statutory authority and was simply a 'report to Ministers' although announced in Parliament (see <http://webarchive.nationalarchives.gov.uk/20090505194948/http://www.bseinquiry.gov.uk/>).

Salmon principles;[211] and he made detailed recommendations about inquiry procedures stressing that the nature of the inquiry should determine the procedures adopted subject to an overriding duty of fairness.[212]

The conduct of the Scott Inquiry has been severely criticised by Lord Howe of Aberavon because of its denial of legal representation before the inquiry and because in these circumstances the inquisitorial nature of the proceedings impaired the impartiality of the tribunal.[213] He considers that the Salmon principles should be strictly applied. However, the Council on Tribunals, when asked by the Lord Chancellor to consider Sir Richard's views, came to the conclusion that it was 'wholly impractical' to devise a set of model rules that would serve for every inquiry.[214] All that could be done was to set out the key objectives which were effectiveness, fairness, speed and economy and the practical considerations that would determine the procedure actually adopted. The government has accepted the advice of the Council as a response to Sir Richard's recommendations.[215] The Salmon principles, it seems, will no longer be followed slavishly (if at all).

The 2005 Act contains provision for the Lord Chancellor to make rules on 'matters of evidence and procedure in relation to inquiries'[216] and the Inquiry Rules 2006 have been made.[217] The chairman is in charge of the procedure of the inquiry but 'must act with fairness and with regard also to the need to avoid any unnecesary cost (whether to public funds or to witnesses or others)'.[218] The Ministry of Justice has recognised the criticism made by many consultees that the 2006 Rules 'lack an appreciation of the practical realities of inquiry proceedings, are too prescriptive and can inhibit the chairman's flexibility... to direct the procedure and conduct of the inquiry'.[219]

The rules provide that the chairman may, with consent, designate as 'core participants' those who played or may have played a 'direct and significant' part in the events that led to the inquiry or have 'a significant interest' in the matters to which the inquiry relates or who may be explictly criticised by the inquiry in its report.[220] 'Core participants' may through their legal representatives (or by themselves otherwise) make opening and closing statements to the inquiry.[221] A 'core participant' may appoint a legal representative who will be a 'recognised legal representative'[222] although there are powers to direct joint representation where, for instance, they have the same interest in the proceedings.[223] Provision is made in the Act (supplemented by a complicated procedure in the Rules) for the chairman to make awards to cover compensation (for loss of time) and expenses, and in suitable cases legal representation before the tribunal.[224]

All witnesses must make written statements[225] and should they give oral evidence they will only be questioned by counsel to the inquiry and the inquiry panel itself save in a

---

[211] In (1995) 111 *LQR* 596 Sir Richard describes and defends the conduct of his inquiry.

[212] Para. B2.29 of the *Report*.

[213] [1996] *PL* 445.   [214] *Annual Report*, 1995–6, 6–8 and Appendix A.

[215] *Annual Report*, 1996–7, 46.

[216] s. 41. For the devolved administrations an appropriate minister in that administration is the rule-making authority.   [217] SI 2006 No. 1838.

[218] s. 17(3). The chairman has power to administer oaths to those giving evidence (s. 17(2)).

[219] 'Memorandum to the Justice Select Committee: Post-Legislative Assessment of the Inquiries Act 2005', Cm. 7943 (October 2010), at para. 66. Available at <http://www.justice.gov.uk/downloads/publications/moj/2010/Post-Legislative-Assessment-Inquiries-Act.pdf>.   [220] r. 5.

[221] r. 11.   [222] r. 6.   [223] r. 7.

[224] s. 40 read with rr. 19–34. An award is subject to an upper limit and various conditions related to the hourly rate of pay of the representative employed and the maximum numbers of hours are set. There is a process of assessment by the solicitor to the inquiry.   [225] r. 9.

range of specified circumstances.[226] Where a witness is questioned by the legal representative of another the questions that may be asked are restricted by the chairman.[227]

The Rules formalise the practice of the 'Salmon letter', a confidential warning letter sent to a person criticised in evidence before the tribunal or likely to be criticised in the Report.[228] That person can not thereafter be criticised unless afforded a 'reasonable opportunity' of responding.[229]

The minster setting up the inquiry has many controversial powers over the inquiry. He may place restrictions on public access to the inquiry and its evidence or documents by issuing a 'restriction notice' to the chairman.[230] But he may only do so if he considers that such restriction is 'conducive to the inquiry fulfilling its terms of reference or to be necessary in the public interest'.[231] He may, for instance, if he consults the chairman and gives his reasons and informs Parliament, terminate the inquiry.[232] Less controversially the minister also has the power to suspend the inquiry, for instance, to allow the completion of another investigation or of civil or criminal proceedings.[233] He also has power to terminate the appointment of members of the inquiry but this power is subject to considerable restriction.[234] Even so, since the inquiry will often be investigating the conduct of the minister's officials or the minister himself these provisions have been criticised as undermining the independence of the inquiry process.

The 2005 Act does not expressly provide that ministers should not set up ad hoc non-statutory inquiries.[235] But the 2005 Act procedure will doubtless emerge as the standard with its tight control over the direction and costs of the discretionary inquiry.[236]

INVESTIGATIONS BY THE SERIOUS FRAUD OFFICE AND DEPARTMENT OF TRADE INSPECTORS

Parliament has on several occasions, out of concern for the integrity and honesty of commercial life, granted to officials extensive powers of investigation backed by the coercion of the criminal law. The most prominent examples of such powers are those of

---

[226] r. 10(1). The legal representative of a 'core participant' may apply to question a witness but the right so to apply is restricted in the case of other witnesses to where that witness' evidence 'directly relates to the evidence of another witness' (r. 10(3). Where a core participant has been questioned by counsel to the inquiry or the inquiry itself he may be questioned by his legal representative (r. 10(2)).

[227] r. 10(5). Generally new matters will not be able to be raised.

[228] r. 13 (the 'statutory successor' to the Salmon letter ([2014] *PL* 2 at 4 (Sir Louis Blom-Cooper). The author argues (at 2–3) that r. 13 is ultra vires the 2005 Act (unwarranted restriction on chairman's freedom to express opinion). Rule 15 specifies the contents of the letter, the nature of the criticism and the evidence upon which the criticism rests.   [229] r. 13(3).

[230] Act of 2005, s. 19. The chairman has similar powers to make a 'restriction order'.

[231] s. 19(3). In forming his opinion the minister (or chairman) is to have regard to the matters specified in s. 19(4). These relate primarily to whether the restriction 'might inhibit the allaying of public concern' and whether the restriction would reduce 'any risk of harm or damage'. Any additional costs is also a matter to be considered.

[232] s. 14. See *Re An Application by David Wright for Judicial Review* [2007] NICA 24 (power to terminate does not compromise the independence of the inquiry; the possibility of termination 'may affect…usefulness [of inquiry] in that it halts the investigation on which the inquiry is embarked but it does not alter the autonomy of the inquiry while it is taking place' (para. 29)).   [233] s. 13.

[234] s. 12.

[235] Evidence has been sought by the Select Committee on the Inquiries Act 2005 on non-statutory inquiries: <http://www.parliament.uk/documents/lords-committees/Inquiries-Act-2005/IA_Written_Oral_evidencevol.pdf> (generally).

[236] But a wide range of statutory provisions that make provision for inquiries are repealed (Sched. 3) including of course the 1921 Act, leaving the 2005 Act procedure as the only route to a statutory inquiry.

inspectors appointed by the Secretary of State for Trade and Industry under Part XIV of the Companies Act 1985 'to investigate the affairs of a company' and those of the Director of the Serious Fraud Office to 'investigate...serious or complex fraud'.[237]

The Director of the Serious Fraud Office, for instance, can, while carrying out an investigation, require 'any person', whether under investigation or not, whom he has reason to believe has relevant information about a matter under investigation, to answer any questions or otherwise furnish relevant information.[238] He may also require such a person to produce any documents which the director believes relate to the matter under investigation.[239]

There are some safeguards for the person under investigation. A statement made in response to the exercise of the Director's powers is not admissible as evidence against him;[240] and legal professional privilege prevails over the requirement to disclose information or produce documents to the Director.[241] But the position of the person under investigation is unenviable: not only has the privilege against self-incrimination and the right to silence been significantly abrogated but the Serious Fraud Office is not required while investigating to disclose documents and information in their possession,[242] and the investigation by the Serious Fraud Office can continue even after the person under investigation has been charged.[243] It is not surprising that the powers of the Director have been criticised.[244] But an investigation under the Companies Act 1985 was held by the ECtHR not to breach Article 6(1) of the European Convention.[245] The inspectors' functions were investigative, not adjudicative, and the procedures adopted did not exceed the national authorities' margin of appreciation.

---

[237] Criminal Justice Act 1987, s. 1. There are other occasions on which such powers are granted. For instance, provisional liquidators of companies who have obtained orders under s. 236(3) of the Insolvency Act 1986 have similar powers (see *Bishopsgate Investment Management Ltd* v. *Maxwell and anor* [1993] Ch 1).

[238] Criminal Justice Act 1987, s. 2(2). It is a criminal offence not to comply with such an order from the director of the SFO (s. 2(13)—failing to comply without reasonable excuse—and s. 2(14)—knowingly or recklessly making a false statement). The obstruction of Department of Trade inspectors, for example, by not answering the inspectors' questions or refusing to produce documents, is treated as contempt of court (Companies Act 1985, s. 436).

[239] s. 2(3). Furthermore, this power is buttressed by provisions that allow a search warrant to be issued (by a justice of the peace) to search for such documents (s. 2(4), (5), (6)).

[240] Criminal Justice Act 1987, s. 2(8). There are special circumstances in which the statement is admissible: where the maker is prosecuted for knowingly or recklessly making a false statement (s. 2(8)(a)), or where the maker in giving evidence on prosecution for some other offence makes another statement inconsistent with his earlier statement (s. 2(8)(b)). A statement made to Department of Trade inspectors is no longer admissible against its maker in any subsequent proceedings (Companies Act 1985, s. 434(5), (5A) (as amended by the Youth Justice and Criminal Evidence Act 1999, s. 59, Sched. 3, paras. 4, 5)). The admissibility of such evidence was held a breach of Art. 6(1) in *Saunders* v. *UK* (1997) 23 EHRR 313.

[241] s. 2(9).

[242] *R* v. *Director of the Serious Fraud Office ex p Maxwell*, The Times, 9 October 1992. Neither do Department of Trade inspectors need to disclose such matters (*Re Pergamon Press* [1971] Ch 388).

[243] *R* v. *Director of the Serious Fraud Office ex p Smith* [1993] AC 1.

[244] See D. Pannick, 'The SFO May be Going Too Far', *The Times*, 22 June 1993. Cf. G. Staple, 'Serious and Complex Fraud: A New Perspective' (1993) 56 *MLR* 127.

[245] *Fayed* v. *UK* (1994) 18 EHRR 393. For discussion of Art. 6(1) see above, p. 449.

ACCIDENT INQUIRIES

Railway accidents, shipwrecks, air crashes, factory accidents, and so forth often have to be inquired into, and in general the familiar form of the public inquiry is followed.[246] But under the various statutes providing for such inquiries the practice varies a good deal. It is obviously of great importance that it should be satisfactory, since the reputation and livelihood of drivers, pilots and others—not to mention the safety of their passengers—will often depend upon the findings.

[246] On accident inquiries see Wraith and Lamb, *Public Inquiries as an Instrument of Government*, 146.

APPENDIX 1

LORD DIPLOCK'S FORMAL STATEMENT ON JUDICIAL REVIEW

There are many references in this book to Lord Diplock's exposition of the principles of judicial review in *Council of Civil Service Unions* v. *Minister for the Civil Service*.[1] This statement was described by high authority as 'classical but certainly not exhaustive';[2] and Lord Hoffmann has said in a lecture: 'the principles of judicial review... cannot be captured even by Lord Diplock in three or four bullet points with single word headings elucidated by a single sentence of explanation'.[3] Subject to these caveats, the following extract from Lord Diplock's speech is appended in order that his propositions may be read in their context. Lord Diplock said:

> Judicial review, now regulated by RSC, Ord. 53, provides the means by which judicial control of administrative action is exercised. The subject matter of every judicial review is a decision made by some person (or body of persons) whom I will call the 'decision-maker' or else a refusal by him to make a decision.

To qualify as a subject for judicial review the decision must have consequences which affect some person (or body of persons) other than the decision-maker, although it may affect him too. It must affect such other person either:

(a) by altering rights or obligations of that person which are enforceable by or against him in private law; or

(b) by depriving him of some benefit or advantage which either (i) he had in the past been permitted by the decision-maker to enjoy and which he can legitimately expect to be permitted to continue to do until there has been communicated to him some rational grounds for withdrawing it on which he has been given an opportunity to comment; or (ii) he has received assurance from the decision-maker will not be withdrawn without giving him first an opportunity of advancing reasons for contending that they should not be withdrawn. (I prefer to continue to call the kind of expectation that qualifies a decision for inclusion in class (b) a 'legitimate expectation' rather than a 'reasonable expectation', in order thereby to indicate that it has consequences to which effect will be given in public law, whereas an expectation or hope that some benefit or advantage would continue to be enjoyed, although it might well be entertained by a 'reasonable' man, would not necessarily have such consequences. The recent decision of this House in *In re Findlay* [1985] AC 318 presents an example of the latter kind of expectation. 'Reasonable' furthermore bears different meanings according to whether the context in which it is being used is that of private law or of public law. To eliminate confusion it is best avoided in the latter.)

---

[1] [1985] AC 374 at 408.
[2] *R* v. *Secretary of State for the Environment ex p Nottinghamshire CC* [1986] AC 240 at 249 (Lord Scarman).   [3] (1997) 32 Ir Jur 49 at 53.

For a decision to be susceptible to judicial review the decision-maker must be empowered by public law (and not merely, as in arbitration, by agreement between private parties) to make decisions that, if validly made, will lead to administrative action or abstention from action by an authority endowed by law with executive powers, which have one or other of the consequences mentioned in the preceding paragraph. The ultimate source of the decision-making power is nearly always nowadays a statute or subordinate legislation made under the statute; but in the absence of any statute regulating the subject matter of the decision the source of the decision-making power may still be the common law itself, i.e. that part of the common law that is given by lawyers the label of 'the prerogative'. Where this is the source of decision-making power, the power is confined to executive officers of central as distinct from local government and in constitutional practice is generally exercised by those holding ministerial rank.

It was the prerogative that was relied on as the source of the power of the Minister for the Civil Service in reaching her decision of 22 December 1983 that membership of national trade unions should in future be barred to all members of the home civil service employed at GCHQ.

My Lords, I intended no discourtesy to counsel when I say that, intellectual interest apart, in answering the question of law raised in this appeal, I have derived little practical assistance from learned and esoteric analyses of the precise legal nature, boundaries and historical origin of 'the prerogative', or what powers exercisable by executive officers acting on behalf of central government that are not shared by private citizens qualify for inclusion under this particular label. It does not, for instance, seem to me to matter whether today the right of the executive government that happens to be in power to dismiss without notice any member of the home civil service upon which perforce it must rely for the administration of its policies, and the correlative disability of the executive government that is in power to agree with a civil servant that his service should be on terms that did not make him subject to instant dismissal, should be ascribed to 'the prerogative' or merely to a consequence of the survival, for entirely different reasons, of a rule of constitutional law whose origin is to be found in the theory that those by whom the administration of the realm is carried on do so as personal servants of the monarch who can dismiss them at will, because the King can do no wrong.[4]

Nevertheless, whatever label may be attached to them there have unquestionably survived into the present day a residue of miscellaneous fields of law in which the executive government retains decision-making powers that are not dependent upon any statutory authority but nevertheless have consequences on the private rights or legitimate expectations of other persons which would render the decision subject to judicial review if the power of the decision-maker to make them were statutory in origin. From matters so relatively minor as the grant of pardons to condemned criminals, of honours to the good and great, of corporate personality to deserving bodies of persons, and of bounty from monies made available to the executive government by Parliament, they extend to matters so vital to the survival and welfare of the nation as the conduct of relations with foreign states and—what lies at the heart of the present case—the defence of the realm against potential enemies. Adopting the phraseology used in the European Convention on Human Rights 1953[5] (Convention for the Protection of Human Rights and Fundamental Freedoms (1953) (Cmd. 8969)) to which the United Kingdom is a party it has now become usual in statutes to refer to the latter as 'national security'.

---

[4] *Note by the senior author*: In a conversation with Lord Diplock at the time when judgment in this case was pending I expressed (I am afraid impertinently) the fear that it would contain much nonsense about the royal prerogative. 'It will,' he replied, 'but not from me.' I have always attributed this paragraph to that conversation.

[5] The date of the Convention was 1950.

My Lords, I see no reason why simply because a decision-making power is derived from a common law and not a statutory source, it should *for that reason only* be immune from judicial review. Judicial review has I think developed to a stage today when without reiterating any analysis of the steps by which the development has come about, one can conveniently classify under three heads the grounds upon which administrative action is subject to control by judicial review. The first ground I would call 'illegality', the second 'irrationality' and the third 'procedural impropriety'. That is not to say that further development on a case-by-case basis may not in course of time add further groups. I have in mind particularly the possible adoption in the future of the principle of 'proportionality' which is recognized in the administrative law of several of our fellow members of the European EconomicCommunity; but to dispose of the instant case the three already well-established heads that I have mentioned will suffice.

By 'illegality' as a ground for judicial review I mean that the decision-maker must understand correctly the law that regulates his decision-making power and must give effect to it. Whether he has or not is *par excellence* a justiciable question to be decided in the event of dispute, by those persons, the judges, by whom the judicial power of the state is exercisable.

By 'irrationality' I mean what can by now be succinctly referred to as '*Wednesbury* unreasonableness' (*Associated Provincial Picture Houses Ltd.* v. *Wednesbury Corporation* [1948] 1 KB 223). It applies to a decision which is so outrageous in its defiance of logic or of accepted moral standards that no sensible person who had applied his mind to the question to be decided could have arrived at it. Whether a decision falls within this category is a question that judges by their training and experience should be well equipped to answer, or else there would be something badly wrong with our judicial system. To justify the court's exercise of this role, resort I think is today no longer needed to Viscount Radcliffe's ingenious explanation in *Edwards* v. *Bairstow* [1956] AC 14 of irrationality as a ground for a court's reversal of a decision by ascribing it to an inferred unidentifiable mistake of law by the decision-maker. 'Irrationality' by now can stand upon its own feet as an accepted ground on which a decision may be attacked by judicial review.

I have described the third head as 'procedural impropriety' rather than failure to observe basic rules of natural justice or failure to act with procedural fairness towards the person who will be affected by the decision. This is because susceptibility to judicial review under this head covers also failure by an administrative tribunal to observe procedural rules that are expressly laid down in the legislative instrument by which its jurisdiction is conferred, even where such failure does not involve any denial of natural justice. But the instant case is not concerned with the proceedings of an administrative tribunal at all.

APPENDIX 2

CATALOGUE OF EUROPEAN HUMAN RIGHTS

Articles 1–14 of the European Convention and Articles 1–3 of its First Protocol, and also its Sixth Protocol, are set out below (these articles are reproduced verbatim, with the exception of Articles 1 and 13, in the first schedule to the Human Rights Act 1998).

Article 1

Obligation to respect human rights
The High Contracting Parties shall secure to everyone within their jurisdiction the rights and freedoms defined in Section 1 of this Convention.

Article 2

Right to life
1. Everyone's right to life shall be protected by law. No one shall be deprived of his life intentionally save in the execution of a sentence of a court following his conviction of a crime for which this penalty is provided by law.
2. Deprivation of life shall not be regarded as inflicted in contravention of this Article when it results from the use of force which is no more than absolutely necessary:
   (a) in defence of any person from unlawful violence;
   (b) in order to effect a lawful arrest or to prevent the escape of a person lawfully detained;
   (c) in action lawfully taken for the purpose of quelling a riot or insurrection.

Article 3

Prohibition of torture
No one shall be subjected to torture or to inhuman or degrading treatment or punishment.

Article 4

Prohibition of slavery and forced labour
1. No one shall be held in slavery or servitude.
2. No one shall be required to perform forced or compulsory labour.
3. For the purposes of this Article the term 'forced or compulsory labour' shall not include:
   (a) any work required to be done in the ordinary course of detention imposed according to the provisions of Article 5 of this Convention or during conditional release from such detention;
   (b) any service of a military character or, in the case of conscientious objectors in countries where they are recognised, service exacted instead of compulsory military service;
   (c) any service exacted in case of an emergency or calamity threatening the life or well-being of the community;
   (d) any work or service which forms part of normal civic obligations.

Article 5

Right to liberty and security

1. Everyone has the right to liberty and security of the person. No one shall be deprived of his liberty save in the following cases and in accordance with a procedure prescribed by law:
   (a) the lawful detention of a person after conviction by a competent court;
   (b) the lawful arrest or detention of a person for non-compliance with the lawful order of a court or in order to secure the fulfilment of any obligation prescribed by law;
   (c) the lawful arrest or detention of a person effected for the purpose of bringing him before the competent legal authority on reasonable suspicion of having committed an offence or when it is reasonably considered necessary to prevent his committing an offence or fleeing after having done so;
   (d) the detention of a minor by lawful order for the purpose of educational supervision or his lawful detention for the purpose of bringing him before the competent legal authority;
   (e) the lawful detention of persons for the prevention of the spreading of infectious diseases, of persons of unsound mind, alcoholics or drug addicts or vagrants;
   (f) the lawful arrest or detention of a person to prevent his effecting an unauthorised entry into the country or of a person against whom action is being taken with a view to deportation or extradition.
2. Everyone who is arrested shall be informed promptly, in a language which he understands, of the reasons for his arrest and of any charge against him.
3. Everyone arrested or detained in accordance with the provisions of paragraph (1)(c) of this Article shall be brought promptly before a judge or other officer authorised by law to exercise judicial power and shall be entitled to trial within a reasonable time or to release pending trial. Release may be conditioned by guarantees to appear for trial.
4. Everyone who is deprived of his liberty by arrest or detention shall be entitled to take proceedings by which the lawfulness of his detention shall be decided speedily by a court and his release ordered if the detention is not lawful.
5. Everyone who has been the victim of arrest or detention in contravention of the provisions of this Article shall have an enforceable right to compensation.

Article 6

Right to a fair trial

1. In the determination of his civil rights and obligations or of any criminal charge against him, everyone is entitled to a fair and public hearing within a reasonable time by an independent and impartial tribunal established by law. Judgment shall be pronounced publicly but the press and public may be excluded from all or part of the trial in the interests of morals, public order or national security in a democratic society, where the interests of juveniles or the protection of the private life of the parties so require, or to the extent strictly necessary in the opinion of the court in special circumstances where publicity would prejudice the interests of justice.
2. Everyone charged with a criminal offence shall be presumed innocent until proved guilty according to law.
3. Everyone charged with a criminal offence has the following minimum rights:
   (a) to be informed promptly, in a language which he understands and in detail, of the nature and cause of the accusation against him;
   (b) to have adequate time and facilities for the preparation of his defence;

(c) to defend himself in person or through legal assistance of his own choosing or, if he has
     not sufficient means to pay for legal assistance, to be given it free when the interests of
     justice so require;

(d) to examine or have examined witnesses against him and to obtain the attendance and
     examination of witnesses on his behalf under the same conditions as witnesses against
     him;

(e) to have the free assistance of an interpreter if he cannot understand or speak the lan-
     guage used in court.

Article 7

No punishment without law

1. No one shall be held guilty of any criminal offence on account of any act or omission which
   did not constitute a criminal offence under national or international law at the time when it
   was committed. Nor shall a heavier penalty be imposed than the one that was applicable at
   the time the criminal offence was committed.

2. This Article shall not prejudice the trial and punishment of any person for any act or omission which, at the time when it was committed, was criminal according to the general principles of law recognised by civilised nations.

Article 8

Right to respect for private and family life

1. Everyone has the right to respect for his private and family life, his home and his
   correspondence.

2. There shall be no interference by a public authority with the exercise of this right except
   such as is in accordance with the law and is necessary in a democratic society in the interests
   of national security, public safety or the economic well-being of the country, for the prevention of disorder or crime, for the protection of health or morals, or for the protection of the
   rights and freedoms of others.

Article 9

Freedom of thought, conscience and religion

1. Everyone has the right to freedom of thought, conscience and religion; this right includes
   freedom to change his religion or belief and freedom, either alone or in community with
   others and in public or private, to manifest his religion or belief, in worship, teaching, practice and observance.

2. Freedom to manifest one's religion or beliefs shall be subject only to such limitations as are
   prescribed by law and are necessary in a democratic society in the interests of public safety,
   for the protection of public order, health or morals, or for the protection of the rights and
   freedoms of others.

Article 10

Freedom of expression

1. Everyone has the right to freedom of expression. This right shall include freedom to hold
   opinions and to receive and impart information and ideas without interference by public
   authority and regardless of frontiers. This Article shall not prevent States from requiring the
   licensing of broadcasting, television or cinema enterprises.

2. The exercise of these freedoms, since it carries with it duties and responsibilities, may be subject to such formalities, conditions, restrictions or penalties as are prescribed by law and are necessary in a democratic society, in the interests of national security, territorial integrity or public safety, for the prevention of disorder or crime, for the protection of health or morals, for the protection of the reputation or rights of others, for preventing the disclosure of information received in confidence, or for maintaining the authority and impartiality of the judiciary.

Article 11

Freedom of assembly and association

1. Everyone has the right to freedom of peaceful assembly and to freedom of association with others, including the right to form and to join trade unions for the protection of his interests.
2. No restrictions shall be placed on the exercise of these rights other than such as are prescribed by law and are necessary in a democratic society in the interests of national security or public safety, for the protection of health or morals or for the protection of the rights and freedoms of others. This Article shall not prevent the imposition of lawful restrictions on the exercise of these rights by members of the armed forces, of the police or of the administration of the State.

Article 12

Right to marry

Men and women of marriageable age have the right to marry and to found a family, according to the national laws governing the exercise of this right.

Article 13

Right to an effective remedy

Everyone whose rights and freedoms as set forth in this Convention are violated shall have an effective remedy before a national authority notwithstanding that the violation has been committed by persons acting in an official capacity.

Article 14

Prohibition of discrimination

The enjoyment of the rights and freedoms set forth in this Convention shall be secured without discrimination on any ground such as sex, race, colour, language, religion, political or other opinion, national or social origin, association with a national minority, property, birth or other status.

FIRST PROTOCOL

Article 1

Protection of property

Every natural or legal person is entitled to the peaceful enjoyment of his possessions. No one shall be deprived of his possessions except in the public interest and subject to the conditions provided for by law and by the general principles of international law.

The preceding provisions shall not, however, in any way impair the right of a State to enforce such laws as it deems necessary to control the use of property in accordance with the general interest or to secure the payment of taxes or other contributions or penalties.

Article 2

Right to education
No person shall be denied the right to education. In the exercise of any functions which it assumes in relation to education and to teaching, the State shall respect the right of parents to ensure such education and teaching in conformity with their own religious and philosophical convictions.

Article 3

Right to free elections
The High Contracting Parties undertake to hold free elections at reasonable intervals by secret ballot, under conditions which will ensure the free expression of the opinion of the people in the choice of the legislature.

SIXTH PROTOCOL

Article 1

Abolition of the death penalty
The death penalty shall be abolished. No one shall be condemned to such penalty or executed.

Article 2

Death penalty in time of war
A State may make provision in its law for the death penalty in respect of acts committed in time of war; such penalty shall be applied only in the instances laid down in the law and in accordance with its provisions. The State shall communicate to the Secretary General of the Council of Europe the relevant provisions of that law.

APPENDIX 3

MATTERS THAT AROSE OR CAME TO LIGHT
WHILE THIS BOOK WAS IN PRESS

Page 21. Note the discussion (at p. 336) of *R (HS2 Action Alliance Ltd) v Secretary of State for Transport* [2014] UKSC 3. The dictum cited there has potential consequences for the supremacy of EU law.

Page 53. Section 63 of the Constitutional Reform Act 2005 (which directs the JAC to makes it recommendations on 'merit') is amended by the Crime and Courts Act 2013, Sched. 13, clause 10 to permit the JAC 'where two persons . . . of equal merit' are under consideration for appointment to prefer 'one of them over the other for the purpose of increasing diversity'.

Page 232. See, 'Substantive Grounds of Review: Mistake of Fact', Hanna Wilberg available at: <http://papers.ssrn.com/sol3/papers.cfm?abstract_id=1875072> for an interesting discussion of mistake of fact and *E*.

Page 299. In the substantive judgment in the *Plantagenet Alliance* case, *R (Plantagenet Alliance Ltd) v Secretary of State for Justice* [2014] EWHC 1662, it was confirmed by the court that 'there is "no such thing as an unfettered discretion". The Secretary of State has a duty when granting such licences [to rebury human remains] to act rationally and in accordance with the general public law principles governing the exercise of a statutory discretion. Lord Neuberger [in *Rudewicz*] did not intend to contradict those basic principles . . . ' (para 105).

Page 307. *Miranda v Secretary of State for the Home Department* [2014] EWHC 255 concerned judicial review of the lawfulness of the detention and questioning of a journalist's assistant (in fact spouse) and the seizure of encrypted intelligence material he was carrying through Heathrow airport. Amongst other things the court had to decide whether the exercise of the power to stop under the Terrorism Act 2000, Sched. 7 was disproportionate to any legitimate aim. In applying the proportionality test the court confirmed the 'fair balance' element (whether a 'fair balance' has been struck between the rights of the individual and the community) of the test derived from *Huang* and recently confirmed in *Bank Mellat* but Laws LJ went on to say (para. 40):

> I think [the 'fair balance' element] needs to be approached with some care. It appears to require the court, in a case where the impugned measure passes muster on points (i)–(iii), to decide whether the measure, though it has a justified purpose and is no more intrusive than necessary, is nevertheless offensive because it fails to strike the right balance between private right and public interest; and the court is the judge of where the balance should lie. I think there is real difficulty in distinguishing this from a political question to be decided by the elected arm of government. If it is properly within the judicial sphere, it must be on the footing that there is a plain case.

This is a recognition of the need for deference to the balance struck by the democratic process consistent with the views expressed in the text.

Page 317. In *R (Rotherham MBC) v Secretary of State for Business, Innovation & Skills* [2014] EWHC 232 Stewart J said that the use of the proportionality test was apt where 'there is a specific legal standard and a decision by a public body which derogates from that standard. The court then has to address the question as to whether there is a legally justifiable basis for so derogating' (para. 61). But in the context of the allocation of EU structural funds to regions by the executive a wide margin of discretion is justified because decision concerned with 'political policy and macroeconomic judgment'. Irrationality test applied. This is consistent with the approach taken in the text.

But a different note was struck by Lord Mance in *Kennedy v The Charity Commission* [2014] UKSC 20 (paras. 54–5) where he said:

> . . . both reasonableness review and proportionality involve considerations of weight and balance, with the intensity of the scrutiny and the weight to be given to any primary decision maker's view depending on the context. The advantage of the terminology of proportionality is that it introduces an element of structure into the exercise, by directing attention to factors such as suitability or appropriateness, necessity and the balance or imbalance of benefits and disadvantages. There seems no reason why such factors should not be relevant in judicial review even outside the scope of Convention and EU law. Whatever the context, the court deploying them must be aware that they overlap potentially and that the intensity with which they are applied is heavily dependent on the context . . .

This dictum suggests a conglomeration of the two concepts but does not address the conceptual differences between them and adds to legal uncertainty. Lord Carnwath, on the other hand, thought (in dissent) that it was 'at best uncertain to what extent the proportionality test . . . has become part of domestic public law' (para. 246).

Clearly the last word on the relationship between *Wednesbury* and proportionality has not been said. See also 'The Nature of Reasonableness' (2013) 66 CLP 131 (Craig).

Page 318. See p. 456 for discussion of the principle of consistency in *DM v Secretary of State for the Home Department* [2014] ScotCS CSIH 29.

Page 326. For an up-to-date account of the case law on the PSED see *Hamnett v Essex County Council* [2014] EWHC 246, paras. 42–50 (Singh J).

It was confirmed in *R (Core Issues Trust) v Secretary of State for Culture, Media and Sport and Minister for Women and Equalities* [2014] EWCA Civ 34 that a 'public authority is not precluded by section 149 [of the Equality Act 2010] from deciding that equality implications are outweighed by countervailing considerations . . . . Although there is an obvious connection between the considerations stated in section 149(1) and the prohibited conduct provisions contained in other parts of the [2010 Act], they are not the same. Thus, failure to promote equality of opportunity or to foster good relations between, for example, members of different racial groups, is not the same as race discrimination prohibited by [other parts of the 2010 Act]'.

Page 336. The common law protection of fundamental rights has recently become prominent in the jurisprudence of the Supreme Court (perhaps in anticipation of a change in the statutory regime of human rights protection (see p. 156). This has already been noted in the context of *Osborn v Parole Board* [2013] UKSC 61 (reliance upon common law to determine when oral hearing needs to be held, see p. 436).

Now in three more recent decisions, *Kennedy v The Charity Commission* [2014] UKSC 20 (discussed above), *R (HS2 Action Alliance Ltd) v Secretary of State for Transport* [2014] UKSC 3 and *A v BBC* [2014] UKSC 25 common law protection of fundamental rights or principles has been prominent.

HS2 deserves special mention. *HS2* concerned the development of a high-speed rail link between London and the north of England. Planning consent for this development was to be obtained by the enactment by Parliament of two 'hybrid bills'. One of the questions to be resolved was whether that procedure was compliant with procedural requirements of an EU directive (EU Directive 2011/92/EU). Determining that question might have required the court to intrude into parliamentary privilege. In the event the court found that the procedure was compliant without needing to trespass on parliamentary privilege but Lords Neuberger and Mance (with Lady Hale, Lord Kerr, Lord Sumption, Lord Reed and Lord Carnwath concurring) said this:

> The common law itself also recognises certain principles as fundamental to the rule of law. It is, putting the point at its lowest, certainly arguable (and it is for United Kingdom law and courts to determine) that there may be fundamental principles, whether contained in other constitutional instruments or recognised at common law, of which Parliament when it enacted the European Communities Act 1972 did not either contemplate or authorise the abrogation (para. 207).

This is a startling suggestion: that fundamental common law principles might trump the supremacy of EU. Interesting times lie ahead.

Page 408. See *Okeke v Nursing & Midwifery Council* [2013] EWHC 714 (unexplained delay in disciplinary proceedings of four-and-one-half years a breach of article 6).

Page 421. Note in the general context of the flexible application of the principles of natural justice the following important passage from the judgment of Beatson LJ in *R (L) v West London Mental Health NHS Trust* [2014] EWCA Civ 47, (paras. 67–74):

> My starting point in ascertaining what fairness requires in a case such as this is to consider the commonplace orthodoxy in the modern law that what procedure is required by the common-law principles of natural justice or fairness is acutely sensitive to context . . . The post-*Ridge v Baldwin* cases . . . all contain statements about the need for flexibility. The question is what this means. In the way the term 'fairness' was used in *Re HK* and *Benaim and Khaida*, it was a signal that, although the reach of the principles of natural justice had been expanded to new situations, the procedures required in those situations might be less onerous and less formal. Within those new areas the content of procedural protection was diluted precisely because the nature of the activity in question did not fall within the classical categories of 'judicial' or 'quasi-judicial' functions.
>
> Some commentators, notably Professor Loughlin and Professor Cane (respectively in 1978 UTLJ 215 and *Administrative Law*, 5th edn., 2011, at 73–5) have been critical of the courts' approach to flexibility of procedural fairness:
>
> > . . . It is, however, in my judgment, insufficient to react to the danger of over-formalisation and 'judicialisation' simply by emphasising flexibility and context-sensitivity. There are dangers in concentrating on a flexible notion of overarching fairness. One is that it may lead to an inappropriate drawing together of the concepts of procedural and substantive fairness. . . . This can, however, lead to the view . . . that, if the procedural protection that has not been given would have 'made no difference', there is no unfairness. . . . A second danger of emphasising flexibility and saying no more is that to do so may lead to a modern version of Sir William Wade's nightmare of a Tennysonian 'wilderness of single instances' in which all the contextual factors will be relevant in considering what the requirements of procedural fairness are in a given situation without any factor or group of factors having decisive weight in shaping what is in practice required. The consequence may either risk obscuring the overarching principle or stating it at a level of generality which is not of use as a practical tool to decision making. The result could be undue uncertainty and unpredictability. There is a need for principled guidance which is practical and does not constitute either a procedural straitjacket, a 'safe harbour' for longstanding ways of doing things in a particular context, or operate with centripetal force towards an adversarial adjudicative process.

Thus the approach of the first instance judge to the question of the procedure to be adopted by a mental health trust in deciding upon the transfer of a detainee to high-security conditions was set aside. The judge had enumerated twelve factors that had to be adhered to and which had not been (in particular no 'gist' had been disclosed to the detainee). The judge held that this approach was 'inappropriately at the adversarial end of the spectrum of adjudicative methods of decision-making and, in so doing, went beyond what fairness requires in this context' (para. 8).

Page 456. In *DM (Algeria) v Secretary of State for the Home Department* [2014] ScotCS CSIH 29 the Inner House of the Court of Session (per Lord Drummond Young, Lord Wheatley and Lady Paton concurring) said 'we are of opinion that it is also essential that any person who seeks to rely on the promise [to found a legitimate expectation] must have knowledge of the promise' (para 12).

The Court of Session went on 'we are of opinion that what was decided in *Rashid* was rather that the Home Secretary must apply his or her policy consistently; any serious failure to do so will be an abuse of power. That is the interpretation placed on the decision in Wade and Forsyth, *Administrative Law* . . .' (para. 19).

The Court of Session also approved (para.18) the following words from the text at p. 456 of this edition:

> [T]o bring . . . 'no expectation' cases under the rubric 'legitimate expectation that' is to deprive that concept of clear meaning. The phrase 'protection of legitimate expectations' is not an imprecise alternative for securing fairness or avoiding abuse of power. Legitimate expectations bear, it is submitted, on the narrow issue of whether trust has been reposed in the official. Thus if no trust has been reposed, the concept has nothing to add to an inquiry into what fairness requires in the circumstances or whether the power concerned has been abused.

Page 557. Note further the collapse of the *Al-Sweady* litigation amongst allegations that the Iraqi witnesses consistently lied to the inquiry in a conspiracy to obtain compensation. See <http://www.theguardian.com/uk-news/2014/apr/16/iraqis-lied-al-sweady-inquiry-soldiers>.

Page 567. See, for criticism of the Lord Chancellor's plans, the Report of the Joint Committee on Human Rights. 'The implications for access to justice of the Government's Proposals to reform judicial review'(HL 174 HC 868 2013–14) available at: <http://www.publications.parliament. uk/pa/jt201314/jtselect/jtrights/174/174.pdf>.

The report is particularly critical of the 'politically partisan' way in which the Lord Chancellor sought to justify the reforms. This was difficult 'to reconcile with the Lord Chancellor's statutory duties in relation to the rule of law' (para 21).

Mention should be made here of the proposal in cl. 52 of the Criminal Justice and Courts Bill 2014 that would require the court both in considering applications for permission and in granting relief not to grant permission or any relief if it appears to the court 'to be highly likely that the outcome for the applicant would not have been substantially different if the conduct complained of had not occurred'.

Unsurprisingly this proposal is much criticised (by the Committee and many others) on the ground that it requires the court to 'ignore unlawful conduct by public authorities' (para. 43). But the Committee does recognise that there might be some similar restriction at the permission stage (if it were 'inevitable' not 'highly likely' that there would be 'no difference'). It points out that this change will turn the permission stages into a 'dress rehearsal' for the substantive hearing (paras. 45–6). Moreover, the senior judiciary in their response to the consultation pointed out that 'the decision whether a procedural flaw made a difference to the outcome cannot be taken without a full understanding of the facts' (usually only available at the substantive hearing) (cited in para. 47).

After representations by the higher judiciary the plans for a Planning Chamber in the Upper Tribunal have been replaced with the creation of a Planning Court in the High Court. See 'Judicial Review—proposals for further reform: the Government response' available at: <https://www.gov.uk/government/uploads/system/uploads/attachment_data/file/281330/8811.pdf>, paras 13, 92.

Page 583. In *O'Dea v Hillingdon LBC* [2013] EWHC 4407 (QB), *Trim v North Dorset DC* [2010] EWCA Civ 1446 was followed: private law proceedings apparently commenced to avoid the three-month time limit; transfer into Part 54 refused.

Page 593. In *R (Plantagenet Alliance Ltd) v Secretary of State for Justice* [2014] EWHC 1662 – the case concerning the reburial of the remains of Richard III – it was said that the claimant - a not-for-profit entity (set up by remote collateral descendants of the king) and incorporated to pursue the challenge to the reburial (and perhaps to shield those descendants from personal liability for costs) – did not have 'personal standing' but 'the points raised have a broader public interest sufficient for the Claimant to have standing in this case as a public interest litigant' (para 82). The court reached this conclusion notwithstanding that Ministry of Justice had contested the claimant's standing.

Page 597. In 'Judicial Review—proposals for further reform: the Government response' available at: <https://www.gov.uk/government/uploads/system/uploads/attachment_data/file/281330/8811.pdf> the government accepted that '[the other] changes [planned for judicial review] are a more effective means of reducing the number of unmeritorious judicial reviews that are either brought or persisted with than changing the test for standing' (para. 14).

Page 619. A statutory review (under the Road Traffic Regulation Act 1984) of two experimental traffic regulation orders was not a 'claim for judicial review' (in terms of s. 113 of the Equality Act 2010). Thus the Administrative Court had no jurisdiction to entertain a challenge based upon a breach of s. 29 of the Act; the challenge had to be brought in the county court: *Hamnett v Essex CC* [2014] EWHC 246.

INDEX